D1040113

Greece

Northern Greece (p228)

Central Greece (p186)

Ionian Islands (p632)

Evia & the Sporades (p606)

Northeastern Aegean Islands (p546)

Athens & Around (p56)

Peloponnese (p128)

Saronic Gulf Islands (p294)

Cyclades (p314)

Dodecanese (p470)

Crete (p414)

THIS EDITION WRITTEN AND RESEARCHED BY

Korina Miller,

Kate Armstrong, Alexis Averbuck, Carolyn Bain, Michael Stamatios
Clark, Anita Isalska, Anna Kaminski, Greg Ward, Richard Waters

Contents

PLAN YOUR TRIP

ON THE ROAD

SPILI P442

NISYROS VOLCANO P511

TEMPLE OF APOLLO, NAXOS P353

VIKOS GORGE P284

PHILARTPHACE / GETTY IMAGES ©

GKISAKIS / GETTY IMAGES ©

TUUL / GETTY IMAGES ©

WALTER BIBIKOW / GETTY IMAGES ©

Contents

UNDERSTAND

SURVIVAL GUIDE

SPECIAL FEATURES

Welcome to Greece

Endless miles of aquamarine coastline, sun-bleached ancient ruins, strong feta and stronger ouzo – the Greek landscape thrills, and the Greek people are passionate about politics, coffee, art and gossiping.

Naturally Inviting

It's easy to understand how so many myths of gods and giants originated in this vast and varied landscape, with wide open skies and a sea speckled with islands, where days melt from one to the next while you relish the white-sand and palm-fringed beaches. Greece is a magnet for anyone who enjoys the great outdoors. Wander along cobbled, Byzantine footpaths, hike into volcanoes, watch for dolphins and sea turtles, and cycle through lush forests. Discover world-class kitesurfing, diving and rock-climbing locations or simply hop on a boat and set sail into the glittering blue beyond.

Culturally Rich

Step into the ring where Olympic athletes competed. Gaze at Meteora's monasteries, perched atop towering rock pinnacles. Contemplate the oracle's insights from the grandeur of Delphi or take in a starlit drama at an ancient outdoor theatre. In the most unexpected places, you'll encounter thought-provoking modern art, the melancholic throb of *rembetika* (blues songs) and collections of ancient marble sculptures dredged up from beneath the Aegean. Greece balances its past, present and future in a way managed by few other countries. The result is a nation with endless cultural pursuits.

Sumptuous Feasting

Greeks pride themselves on their cuisine and will go out of their way to ensure you are well fed. The tang of homemade tzatziki and the aroma of souvlaki grilling are just the beginning. Taste test your way through regional cheeses – from crumbling feta to honeyed soft cheeses and sharp, hard rounds. Dig into rich layers of *mousakas* and sip crisp wine from grapes ripened under the hot Mediterranean sun. The Italian legacy of pasta is paired with Greek specialities like lobster, while Turkish spices find their way into delicate sweets. Mussels are steamed in ouzo, bread is baked with olives and fish is cooked straight from the sea.

Socially Spirited

Greeks are truly social beings. Their families are extended and they are quick to welcome in newcomers, whether for a coffee, a shot of ouzo, a chorus on the bouzouki or a heated debate. Greeks are passionate, if nothing else, and this passion continues to drive society forward despite the current economic turmoil. Life is lived to the fullest, even at the most difficult of times, and herein lies the secret of how a country, seemingly riddled with challenges, is full of people who remain so in love with life.

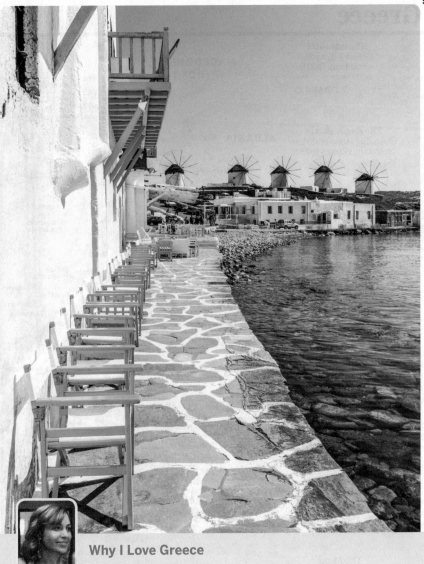

Why I Love Greece

By Korina Miller, Author

I first visited Greece as an 18-year-old, sleeping on the decks of slow-moving ferries, living on olives and feta, and constantly salt-crusted from swimming in the deep blue Aegean. But it was a starlit performance at the 3rd-century-BC Theatre of Epidavros that sealed my love of the country. Watching the ancient Greek drama unfold before me as I sat on stone seats worn smooth by thousands of years of use, I felt caught in a moment that seemed to sidestep time. I love Greece because magical moments like that one aren't so hard to find here.

For more about our authors, see page 752

Above: Little Venice (p334), Hora (Mykonos)

Greece

Thessaloniki
Greece's dynamic
second city (p231)

The Zagorohoria
Charming stone and slate
mountain villages (p283)

Corfu Town
Stunning multicultural
seaside architecture (p637)

Meteora
Soaring rock pinnacles topped
with monasteries (p221)

Ancient Delphi
Where mythology
and history meet (p189)

Acropolis
The most iconic monument
of ancient Greece (p63)

The Mani
Steeped in Maniot culture
and perfect for hiking (p157)

Samaria Gorge
Carved between unending
towering cliffs (p454)

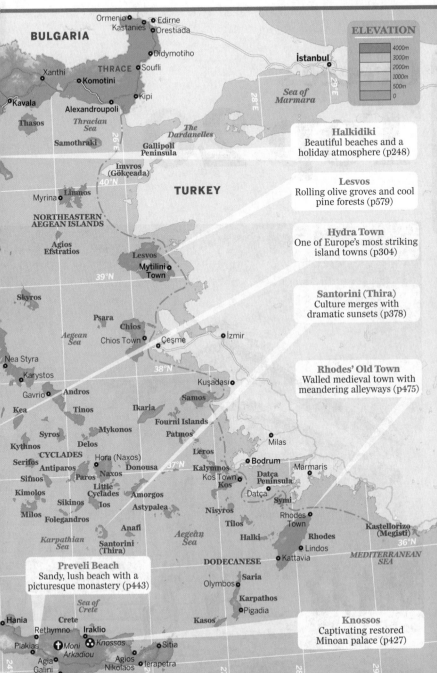

ELEVATION

4000m
3000m
2000m
1000m
500m
0

Halkidiki
Beautiful beaches and a
holiday atmosphere (p248)

Lesvos
Rolling olive groves and cool
pine forests (p579)

Hydra Town
One of Europe's most striking
island towns (p304)

Santorini (Thira)
Culture merges with
dramatic sunsets (p378)

Rhodes' Old Town
Walled medieval town with
meandering alleyways (p475)

Preveli Beach
Sandy, lush beach with a
picturesque monastery (p443)

Knossos
Captivating restored
Minoan palace (p427)

0 ——— 100km
0 ——— 50miles

BULGARIA

Ormenio
Edirne
Kastanies
Orestiada
Didymotiho
Xanthi
THRACE Soufli
Komotini
İstanbul
Kavala
Kipi
Alexandroupoli
Sea of
Marmara
Thasos
Thracian
Sea
Samothraki
The
Dardanelles
Gallipoli
Peninsula
TURKEY
Imvros
(Gökçeada)
NORTHEASTERN
AEGEAN ISLANDS
Limnos
Myrina
Agios
Efstratios
Skyros
Lesvos
Mytilini
Town
Psara
Chios
Aegean
Sea
Chios Town
Çeşme
İzmir
Nea Styra
Karystos
Gavrio
Andros
Kea
Tinos
Ikaria
Samos
Kuşadası
Syros
Mykonos
Fourni Islands
Patmos
Kythnos
Delos
Milas
Serifos
CYCLADES
Hora (Naxos)
Leros
Antiparos
Donousa
Kalymnos
Bodrum
Marmaris
Sifnos
Paros
Naxos
Kos Town
Datça
Peninsula
Kimolos
Little
Cyclades
Amorgos
Kos
Datça
Milos
Sikinos
Ios
Astypalea
Symi
Folegandros
Nisyros
Rhodes
Town
Anafi
Tilos
Rhodes
Kastellorizo
(Megisti)
Karpathian
Sea
Santorini
(Thira)
Aegean
Sea
Halki
Lindos
MEDITERRANEAN
SEA
DODECANESE
Kattavia
Saria
Olymbos
Karpathos
Sea of
Crete
Pigadia
Hania
Crete
Iraklio
Kasos
Rethymno
Moni
Arkadiou
Knossos
Sitia
Plakias
Agia
Galini
Agios
Nikolaos
Ierapetra
Gavdos
Matala

Greece's
Top 20

Experiencing the Acropolis

1 There's a reason the Acropolis (p63) remains the quintessential landmark of Western civilisation – it is spectacular. Whether experienced during an early-morning stroll or from a dinnertime terrace with the Parthenon lit up and glorious, the Acropolis embodies a power and beauty that speak to all generations. Look beyond the Parthenon and you will find more intimate spots like the exquisite Temple of Athena Nike, while the Acropolis Museum cleverly showcases the Acropolis' surviving treasures.

Meteora

2 You're not likely to forget the first moment the magnificent Meteora (p221) comes into view – soaring pillars of rock that jut heavenward, and a handful of monasteries at the summit (some dating from the 14th century). The rope ladders that once enabled the monks to reach the top have long been replaced by steps carved into the rock. Today these spectacular stone towers beckon rock climbers from around the world. Below: Moni Agias Varvaras Rousanou (p223) in the foreground, with Moni Agiou Nikolaou (p222) behind.

ED NORTON / GETTY IMAGES ©

DIMITRIOS TILIS / GETTY IMAGES ©

MICHELE FALZONE / GETTY IMAGES ©

PETER ADAMS / GETTY IMAGES ©

Ancient Delphi

3 Arrive early to catch the magic of the sun's rays pouring over the Sanctuary of Athena Pronea at Delphi (pictured; p187), the centre of the ancient Greek world. Only three columns remain of the magnificent sanctuary, but that's enough to let your imagination soar. Nearby, the Sacred Way (p189) meanders past the Temple of Apollo where prophecies were uttered that sent armies to battle and made lovers swoon.

Cutting-Edge Capital

4 Life in Athens (p58) is a magnificent mash-up of the ancient and the contemporary. Beneath the majestic facades of venerable landmarks, the city teems with life and creativity. And Athenians love to get out and enjoy it all. Galleries and clubs hold the exhibitions, performances and installations of the city's booming arts scene. Trendy restaurants and humble tavernas rustle up fine, fine fare. Ubiquitous cafes fill with stylin' locals and moods run from punk rock to haute couture. Discos and bars abound...and swing deep into the night.

Santorini Sunsets

5 There's more to Santorini (Thira; p378) than sunsets, but this remarkable island, shaped by the fire of prehistoric eruptions, has made the celebratory sunset its own. On summer evenings the cliff-top towns of Fira (p381) and Oia (pictured; p386) are packed with visitors awed by the vast blood red canvas of the cliff face as the sun struts its stuff. You can catch the sunset without the crowds from almost anywhere along the cliff edge. And if you miss sundown, you can always face east at first light for some fairly stunning sunrises too...

LARS RUECKER / GETTY IMAGES ©

5

MARTIN CHILD / GETTY IMAGES ©

6

Rhodes' Old Town

6 Getting lost in Rhodes' Old Town (p475) is a must. Away from the crowds, you 'll find yourself meandering down cobbled alleyways with archways above and squares opening up ahead. In these hidden corners your imagination will take off with flights of medieval fancy. Explore the ancient Knights' Quarter, the old Jewish neighbourhood or the Turkish Quarter. Hear traditional live music in tiny tavernas or dine on fresh seafood at atmospheric outdoor restaurants. Wander along the top of the city's walls, with the sea on one side and a bird's-eye view into this living museum.

Cretan Cuisine

7 Waistlines be damned: Crete (p414) is the perfect place to indulge your appetite. The island's Mediterranean diet is known for its health benefits but it's the farm-fresh produce, aromatic herbs, straight-from-the-ocean seafood, soft, tangy cheese and some of the world's best virgin olive oil that make it legendary. Whether it's a bowl of snails, fresh artichokes, mussels or figs, the essence of this rustic cuisine is a balance of flavours. It's hard to beat traditional hand-spun filo, *horta* (wild greens) picked from a backyard garden and red mullet just hauled in.

Island Hopping in the Cyclades

8 From the spirited nightlife and celebrity hideaways of Mykonos and Ios to the isolated sandy coasts of tiny, far-flung specks like Anafi, hopping through the Cyclades (p314) is a Greek experience not to be missed. Peppered with ancient ruins (try Delos; pictured; p341), mystical castles (head to Naxos; p351), lush scenery and dramatic coastlines (visit Milos; p397), the islands are spread like Greek jewels across the sea. Speed over the Aegean on catamarans and sway on old-fashioned ferry boats. You won't regret a single saltwater-splashed second of it.

Easter Festivities on Patmos

9 While the Greek calendar is chock-full of festivals and holidays, by far the biggest event of the Greek Orthodox church is Easter. And the best place to experience it is on Patmos (p535) in the Dodecanese. The island comes to life with fireworks, dancing in the streets, huge outdoor lamb roasts and plenty of ouzo shots. Begin by witnessing the moving, candlelit processions of flower-filled biers through the capital, marking the start of the celebration on Good Friday. By Saturday night you'll be shouting *Hristos Anesti* (Christ is Risen) and cracking vibrant red-dyed eggs.

Samaria Gorge

10 The gaping gorge of Samaria (p454), starting at Omalos and running down through an ancient riverbed to the Libyan Sea, is the most-trod canyon in Crete – and with good reason. The magnificent gorge is home to varied wildlife, soaring birds of prey and a dazzling array of wildflowers in spring. It's a full-day's walk (about six hours down), and you'll have to start early, but it certainly builds character. To get more solitude, try lesser-known gorges such as Imbros Gorge, which runs roughly parallel to Samaria.

Colourful Thessaloniki

11 Thessaloniki (p231) remains northern Greece's liveliest town, thanks to its universities, cultural scene, arts and nightlife. Explore the old quarter, full of colourful, winding streets marked by white-plastered houses, lazy cats and Byzantine churches. Taste your way through the city's *zaharoplasteia* (patisseries) for Ottoman-inspired sweets. Drink with throngs of students at stylish bars and clubs. Tour the galleries of one of Greece's most artistically fertile locations and save time for first-rate museums. Thessaloniki has it all going on.

10

11

Hydra

12 Everyone approaches Hydra (p303) by sea. There is no airport, there are no cars. As you sail in, you find, simply, a stunningly preserved stone village with white-gold houses filling a natural cove and hugging the edges of surrounding mountains. Then you join the ballet of port life. Sailboats, caïques and mega-yachts fill Hydra's quays and a people-watching potpourri fills the ubiquitous harbourside cafes. Here, a mere hour and a half from Athens, you'll find a great cappuccino, rich naval and architectural history, and the raw sea coast beckoning you for a swim.

Preveli Beach

13 Crete's Preveli Beach (p443) is one of Greece's most instantly recognisable stretches of sand. Bisected by a freshwater river and flanked by cliffs concealing sea caves, Preveli is lapped by the Libyan Sea, with clear pools of water along its palm-lined river bank that are perfect for cool dips. The beach lies under the sacred gaze of a magnificent monastery perched high above. Once the centre of anti-Ottoman resistance and later a shelter for Allied soldiers, this tranquil building offers magnificent views.

KONSTANTINOS_K / GETTY IMAGES ©

CHRIS CHRISTO / GETTY IMAGES ©

Knossos

14 Rub shoulders with the ghosts of the Minoans, a Bronze Age people that attained an astonishingly high level of civilisation and ruled large parts of the Aegean from their capital in Knossos (p427) 4000 years ago. Until the site's excavation in the early 20th century, an extraordinary wealth of frescoes, sculptures, jewellery, seals and other remnants lay buried under the Cretan soil. Despite a controversial partial reconstruction, Knossos remains one of the most important archaeological sites in the Mediterranean.

The Zagorohoria

15 After passing through a seemingly endless array of tunnels, the Egnatia Odos highway brings you into rugged Epiros, home of the Pindos Mountains and the Zagorohoria (p283) – an immaculately preserved region of traditional villages spread along the ridges of Europe's deepest canyon, the Vikos Gorge. Here, the air is clear, fresh and cool, and the views astounding. You can explore the region by hiking or mountain biking, or simply get cosy by the fire in one of the many rustic B&Bs dotting the region.

Corfu

16 The story of Corfu (p634) is written across the handsome facades of its main town's buildings. This is a place that crams a remarkable mix of architecture into its small compass. Stroll past Byzantine fortresses, neoclassical British buildings of the 19th century, Parisian-style arcades, Orthodox church towers, and the narrow, sun-dappled streets of the Venetian Old Town. Beyond town, Corfu is lush green mountains, rolling countryside and dramatic coastlines. And if the architecture and scenery aren't enough, come for the Italian-influenced food.

DIMITRIOS TILIS / GETTY IMAGES ©

PAUL BIRIS / GETTY IMAGES ©

Halkidiki & Mt Athos

17 The Halkidiki Peninsula (p248) combines great beaches, nightlife, camping spots and some serious history. Kassandra buzzes in summer with open-air discos and fleshed-out beaches, while Sithonia is quieter and reserved for escapists on its sandy shores. Ouranoupoli, on Athos, offers family-friendly beaches. This is also home to the heavily forested Mt Athos (p252) with its monastic community, which has preserved its Byzantine rituals for over 1000 years. Top: Moni Xenofondos (p255)

Hiking the Mani

18 Although it can no longer be described as 'remote', the Mani (p157) holds a magic unlike anywhere else in Greece. For centuries, the feuding families here were literally a law unto themselves, and this has contributed to the unique Maniot culture. The Mani's footpaths and landscape beckon hikers from around the world. With everything from rugged rocky highlands and hidden lush green oases to small fishing tavernas and severe rock-solid tower houses, this pocket of the Peloponnese is well worth exploring. Above: Vathia (p161)

GUIZIOU FRANCK / HEMIS.FR / GETTY IMAGES ©

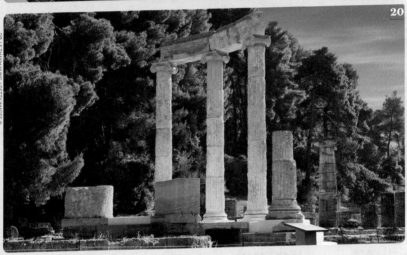

DR LE THANH HUNG / GETTY IMAGES ©

Lesvos (Mytilini)

19 Imposing Lesvos (p579) does its size justice with tremendously varied landscapes. Olive groves and cool pine forests stretch into grassy plains, with one of the world's few petrified forests. The coast is lined with beaches, many hardly touched by tourism. Mytilini Town (p581) has a large student population and a busy cafe and bar scene aided by fine local ouzo and wine. Island exploration will reveal a medieval castle town and two exquisite Byzantine churches. The only thing you may find yourself short of on Lesvos is time. Top: Plomari (p590)

Ancient Olympia

20 The atmosphere at the site (p173) of the first Olympics is almost magical. Feel the watchful eye of Zeus as you tour the ruins of the stadium, gymnasium and temples, imagining the thousands of men that gathered to compete with hands full of offerings. The games were held here for at least 100 years and the nearby museums offer a glimpse into the world of the long ago athletes. The historical significance of this site is both humbling and inspiring. You may even be motivated to run a lap or two.

Need to Know

For more information, see Survival Guide (p715)

Currency
Euro (€)

Language
Greek

Visas
Generally not required for stays of up to 90 days; however, travellers from some nations may require a visa, so double-check with the Greek embassy.

Money
ATMs widely available. Credit cards accepted in larger establishments and destinations. Cash necessary in villages and on smaller islands.

Mobile Phones
Local SIM cards can be used in European and Australian phones. Most other phones can be set to roaming. US and Canadian phones need to have a dual- or tri-band system.

Time
East European Time (GMT/UTC plus two hours)

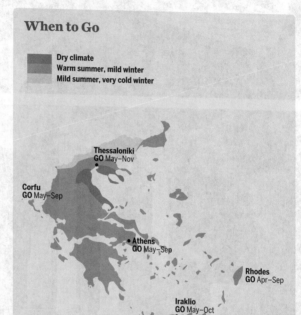

When to Go

- Dry climate
- Warm summer, mild winter
- Mild summer, very cold winter

Thessaloniki
GO May–Nov

Corfu
GO May–Sep

Athens
GO May–Sep

Rhodes
GO Apr–Sep

Iraklio
GO May–Oct

High Season
(Easter & May–Aug)

➡ Everything is in full swing and transport is plentiful.

➡ Accommodation sometimes costs twice as much.

➡ Crowds and temperatures soar.

Shoulder
(Apr, Sep & Oct)

➡ Accommodation prices can drop by 20%.

➡ Temperatures are milder.

➡ Internal flights and ferries have reduced schedules.

➡ Few crowds.

Low Season
(Nov–Mar)

➡ Many hotels, sights and restaurants shut, especially on islands.

➡ Accommodation costs up to 50% less than in high season.

➡ Ferry schedules are skeletal.

➡ Temperatures drop; Athens and Crete can see snow.

Useful Websites

EOT (Greek National Tourist Organisation; www.gnto.gr) Concise tourist information.

Greek Travel Pages (www.gtp.gr) Access to ferry schedules and accommodation.

Lonely Planet (www.lonelyplanet.com/greece) Destination information, hotel bookings and traveller forum.

Ministry of Culture (www.culture.gr) For cultural events and sights.

Important Numbers

In Greece, the area code must be dialled, meaning you always dial the full 10-digit telephone number.

Country code	☎ 30
International access code	☎ 00
Ambulance	☎ 166
Highway rescue (ELPA)	☎ 104
Police	☎ 100
Tourist police	☎ 171

Exchange Rates

Australia	A$1	€0.68
Canada	C$1	€0.72
Japan	¥100	€0.72
New Zealand	NZ$1	€0.60
UK	£1	€1.4
US	US$1	€0.89

For current exchange rates see www.xe.com.

Daily Costs

Budget:
Less than €60

➡ Dorm bed €10–20, domatio (Greek B&B) from €25

➡ Meal at markets and street stalls: under €10

Midrange:
€60–100

➡ Double room in midrange hotel: €35–60

➡ Hearty meal at a local taverna: around €15

➡ Majority of sights have entrance fees under €15

Top End:
More than €150

➡ Double room in top hotel: from €90

➡ Excellent dining, some accompanied by Michelin stars: around €60

➡ Activities like diving (certification around €400), sailing

➡ Cocktails: around €10

Opening Hours

Opening hours vary throughout the year. We've provided high-season opening hours; hours decrease significantly in the shoulder and low seasons, when many places shut completely.

Banks 8.30am–2.30pm Monday–Thursday, 8am–2pm Friday

Bars 8pm–late

Cafes 10am–midnight

Clubs 10pm–4am

Post Offices 7.30am–2pm Monday–Friday (rural); 7.30am–8pm Monday–Friday, 7.30am–2pm Saturday (urban)

Restaurants 11am–noon, 7pm–1am

Shops 8am–3pm Monday, Wednesday and Saturday; 8am–2.30pm and 5–8pm Tuesday, Thursday and Friday

Arriving in Greece

Eleftherios Venizelos International Airport (Athens; p724) Express buses operate 24 hours between the airport, city centre and Piraeus. Half-hourly metro trains run between the city centre and the airport from 5.30am to 11.30pm. Taxis to the city centre cost €30 and take an hour.

Nikos Kazantzakis International Airport (Iraklio, Crete; p724) Bus 1 runs every 10 minutes between the airport and the city centre from 6.15am to 10.45pm. Taxis to the city centre cost €10.

Getting Around

Car Rentals are reasonably priced and found on all but the tiniest islands. They give you the freedom to explore the islands, but you'll need a good dose of bravery and road smarts.

Boat Ferries link the islands to each other and the mainland, and include catamarans, well-equipped modern ferries and overnight boats with cabins. Schedules can be unreliable. In the high season it's smart to book ahead.

Aeroplane Domestic flights are abundant and significantly cut down travel time. In the high season flights fill up fast so book ahead.

Bus Generally air-conditioned and frequent, buses are a good way to travel between major cities.

Low season All public transport is significantly reduced in the low seasons with some flight and ferry routes cancelled entirely.

PLAN YOUR TRIP NEED TO KNOW

For much more on **getting around**, see p726

First Time Greece

For more information, see Survival Guide (p715)

Checklist

➡ Check the validity of your passport

➡ Make any necessary bookings for accommodation and travel

➡ Check airline baggage restrictions, including for regional flights

➡ Inform credit-/debit-card company of your travel plans

➡ Organise travel insurance

➡ Check if you'll be able to use your mobile (cell) phone

What to Pack

➡ Waterproof money belt

➡ Credit and debit cards

➡ Driver's licence

➡ Phrasebook

➡ Diving qualifications

➡ Phone charger

➡ Power adaptor

➡ Lock/padlock

➡ Lightweight raincoat

➡ Seasickness remedies

➡ Mosquito repellent

➡ Swimwear, snorkel and fins

➡ Clothes pegs and laundry line

➡ Earplugs

Top Tips for Your Trip

➡ If at all possible, visit in the shoulder seasons – late spring or early autumn. The weather is softer and the crowds are slim.

➡ Be sure to visit a few out-of-the-way villages where you can still find full-on, unselfconscious traditional culture. The best way to do this is to rent a car and explore. Stop for lunch, check out the local shops and test out your Greek.

➡ Visit at least one local coffee shop, one seafood taverna next to a port and one traditional live-music venue. This is where you'll experience Greek culture at its most potent.

What to Wear

Athenians are well-groomed and the younger crowd is trendy, so keep your smart clothes for the city. Nevertheless, in Athens and other big cities such as Rhodes and Iraklio, you'll get away with shorts or jeans and casual tops. Bars or fashionable restaurants require more effort – the scene is stylish rather than dressy. Think tops and trousers rather than T-shirts and cut-offs. In out-of-the-way places you can wear casual clothing; in summer, the heat will make you want to run naked so bring things like quick-drying tank tops and cool dresses. Sturdy walking shoes are a must for the cobbled roads.

Sleeping

Reserving your accommodation out of season is important, as in some locations many hotels close for months on end. In high season it's equally essential as hotels can be fully booked well in advance.

➡ **Hotels** Classed from A through E, with A being five-star resort-style hotels and E having shared bathrooms and unreliable hot water.

➡ **Domatia** The Greek equivalent of the British B&B, minus breakfast. Nowadays, many are purpose-built with fully equipped kitchens.

➡ **Camping grounds** Found in the majority of regions and islands and often include hot showers, communal kitchen, restaurants and swimming pools.

Money

In cities and large hotels, restaurants and shops, you can usually use debit and credit cards. Visa and MasterCard are widely accepted in Greece. American Express and Diners Club are accepted in larger tourist areas but unheard of elsewhere. In smaller, family-run places, particularly in out-of-the-way locations, cards won't be accepted and you'll need to have cash. Most towns have ATMs but they can often be out of order for days at a time. It's therefore wise (and necessary) to carry extra cash in a safe place like a money belt. (Note: card companies often put an automatic block on cards after the first withdrawal abroad as an antifraud mechanism. To avoid this happening, inform your bank of your travel plans.)

For more information, see p720.

Bargaining

Bargaining is acceptable in flea markets and markets, but elsewhere you are expected to pay the stated price.

Tipping

➡ **Restaurants** If a service charge is included, a small tip is appreciated. If there's no service charge, leave 10% to 20%.

➡ **Taxis** Round up the fare by a couple of euros. There's a small fee for handling bags; this is an official charge, not a tip.

➡ **Bellhops** Bellhops in hotels or stewards on ferries expect a small gratuity of €1 to €3.

Language

Tourism is big business in Greece, and being good business people, many Greeks have learned the tools of the trade – English. In cities and popular towns, you can get by with less than a smattering of Greek; in smaller villages or out-of-the-way islands and destinations, a few phrases in Greek will go a long way. Wherever you are, Greeks will hugely appreciate your efforts to speak their language.

Etiquette

➡ **Eating and dining** Meals are commonly laid in the middle of the table and shared. Always accept an offer of a drink as it's a show of goodwill. Don't insist on paying if invited out; it insults your hosts. In restaurants, the pace of service might feel slow; dining is a drawn-out experience in Greece and it's impolite to rush waitstaff.

➡ **Photography** In churches, avoid using a flash or photographing the main altar, which is considered taboo. At archaeological sites, you'll be stopped from using a tripod, which marks you as a professional and thereby requires special permissions.

➡ **Places of worship** If you plan to visit churches, carry a shawl or long sleeves and a long skirt or trousers to cover up in a show of respect. Some places will deny admission if you're showing too much skin.

➡ **Body language** If you feel you're not getting a straight answer, you might need literacy in Greek body language. 'Yes' is a swing of the head and 'no' is a curt raising of the head or eyebrows, often accompanied by a 'ts' click-of-the-tongue sound.

Eating

Like much of Europe, the Greeks dine late and many restaurants don't open their doors for dinner until after 7pm. You will only need reservations in the most popular restaurants and these can usually be made a day in advance.

➡ **Taverna** Informal and often specialising in seafood, chargrilled meat or traditional homestyle baked dishes.

➡ **Estiatorio** More formal restaurant serving similar fare to tavernas or international cuisine.

➡ **Mezedhopoleio** Serves mezedhes (small plates); an *ouzerie* is similar but serves a round of ouzo with a round of mezedhes.

➡ **Kafeneio** One of Greece's oldest traditions, serving coffee, spirits and little else.

If You Like...

Art

For the oldest artistic expressions, countless archaeological museums contain ancient sculptures and bronze statues, often dredged up from the Aegean.

Byzantine iconography This art is thriving in galleries around the country where artists create exquisite, gold-hued creations; check out galleries at Ouranoupoli near Mt Athos, on Patmos and in Rhodes' Old Town. (p701)

National Museum of Contemporary Art Start with this excellent museum, then get out and see the capital's flourishing modern-art scene at numerous events and galleries. (p75)

Art Space This atmospheric gallery is housed in the wine caverns of one of Santorini's oldest vineyards; showing some of the country's top current artists, it's one of Greece's largest art galleries. (p388)

National Art Gallery Home to a rich collection spanning Greece's creative history, this gallery in Athens is currently being expanded by over 11,000 sq metres and is due to reopen by 2016. While it's closed, visit the gallery's offshoots including the National Sculpture Gallery. (p90)

Walking

Stroll along the ancient promenade in Athens, hike a windswept donkey trail or wander an ancient footpath beneath olive and cypress trees.

Crete's gorges Hikers flock to the spectacular Samaria Gorge, but its nearby cousins, the slender Imbros Gorge and lush Agia Irini Gorge, are equally breathtaking. (p454)

Mt Olympus Follow trails from ancient times up thickly forested slopes towards the cloud-covered peak, once the lair of the ancient Greek pantheon. (p256)

Pelion Peninsula Follow donkey trails that zigzag over rolling hills to quiet, sandy coves and quaint villages. (p209)

Homer's Ithaki Step into the setting of Odysseus, hiking through dramatic island scenery and past archaeological sites. (p662)

Museums

While it can't be denied that many Greek museums are dusty affairs, there are some modern and well-maintained gems to thoroughly impress you.

Acropolis Museum Treasures unearthed from the neighbouring Acropolis are on display in these state-of-the-art exhibition halls. (p73)

Benaki Museum A private museum filled to the gills with Bronze Age finds from Mycenae and Thessaly, works by El Greco and stunning collections of Greek regional costumes. (p86)

Heraklion Archaeological Museum A collection spanning 5500 years, but most famous for its Minoan collection, including the gob-smacking frescoes from Knossos. (p421)

Museum of Marble Crafts Creatively explains quarrying and sculpting techniques with top examples and fascinating exhibits. (p325)

Regional Cuisine

From rich *mousakas* to grilled souvlaki and honey-laced baklava, Greek cuisine has a homemade authenticity.

Ottoman influence The Turkish influence is felt strongly in the kitchens of Thessaloniki and northern Greece, from *yiaourtlou* kebab (grilled beef on pitta bread with Greek yoghurt) to patisseries piled high with *loukoumi* (Turkish delight). (p241)

Italian influence The Italians left behind pastas that the Greeks have added to their

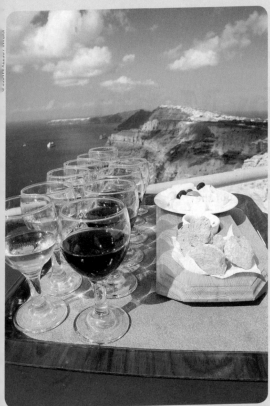

own dishes; try *makarounes* (homemade pasta cooked with cheese and onions) and visit Corfu Town where some of the finest homemade pasta is rolled out. (p640)

Seafood Harbourside kitchens land everything from mackerel to cuttlefish, squid and sea urchins; have yours grilled, fried, baked or stuffed with cheese and herbs. Fill yourself to the gills at 1500bc (p385) on Santorini and Nireas (p483) on Rhodes.

Wine The islands have a vibrant wine industry with crisp whites made from indigenous grapes, rich dessert wines and heady reds. Visit the Iraklio Wine Country (p434) on Crete or Santorini's Argyros Canava (p388), one of the islands' oldest wineries.

Live Music

Clubs throughout the country host traditional *rembetika* bands, playing evocative Greek blues. Live music is often accompanied by dining or ouzo.

Thessaloniki From traditional *bouzoukia* to major international acts, plus music in the strangest places, from jazz trios in bookshops to punk bands in anarchist dive bars. (p242)

Cafe Chantant At this atmospheric club in Rhodes' Old Town musicians whip up energetic tunes and locals sway and shoot ouzo from long wooden tables. (p484)

Rockwave Festival Big-name bands and massive crowds gather outside in an Athens park. It's every rocker's dream. (p95)

Corfu Philharmonic Society Since 1840, this forward-thinking society has been keeping the island melodic with free concerts. (p639)

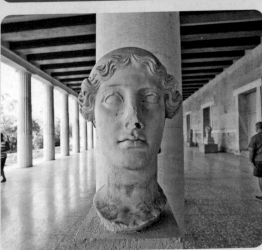

Top: Food and wine tasting on Santorini (Thira; p378)
Bottom: Bust at Athens' Ancient Agora (p76)

Month by Month

January

Most of the islands are snoozing during the winter months. However, the capital and surrounding mainland is awake and welcomes visitors with festivals that aren't really aimed at tourists. Expect local insight and warmth from hospitality (rather than the sun).

Feast of Agios Vasilios (St Basil)

The first day of January sees a busy church ceremony followed by gifts, singing, dancing and feasting. The *vasilopita* (golden glazed cake for New Year's Eve) is cut; if you're fortunate enough to get the slice containing a coin, you'll supposedly have a lucky year.

Epiphany (Blessing of the Waters)

The day of Christ's baptism by St John is celebrated throughout Greece on 6 January. Seas, lakes and rivers are all blessed, with the largest ceremony held at Piraeus.

Gynaikokratia

The villages of the prefectures of Rodopi, Kilkis and Seres in northern Greece hold a day of role reversal on 8 January. Women spend the day in *kafeneia* (coffee houses) while the men stay at home to do the housework.

February

Carnival Season

Carnival season kicks off three weeks prior to the fasting of Lent, from mid-January to late February or early March. A host of minor events leads up to a wild weekend of costume parades, colourful floats, feasting and traditional dancing. Celebrations see distinct regional variations; the Patra Carnival is the largest, while the most bizarre is on Skyros.

Clean Monday (Shrove Monday)

On the first day of Lent (a day which is referred to as Kathara Deftera), people take to the hills throughout Greece to enjoy picnicking and kite-flying.

March

Independence Day

The anniversary of the hoisting of the Greek flag by independence supporters at Moni Agias Lavras is celebrated with parades and dancing on 25 March. This act of revolt marked the start of the War of Independence.

April

The biggest day of the year is Easter when Greece, particularly the islands, shakes off its winter slumber. The holiday weekend is busy; be sure to reserve well in advance.

Orthodox Easter

Communities joyously celebrate Jesus' resurrection beginning with candlelit processions on Good Friday. One of the most impressive of these processions climbs

Lykavittos Hill in Athens. The Lenten fast ends after 40 days on Easter Sunday with the cracking of red-dyed Easter eggs, firecrackers, feasting and dancing. The Monastery of St John the Theologian on Patmos is a great place to witness it.

✴ Festival of Agios Georgios

The feast day of Agios Georgios (St George), the country's patron saint and the patron saint of shepherds, falls on 23 April or the first Tuesday following Easter. It's celebrated with particular exuberance in Arahova, near Delphi. Expect dancing, feasting and a general party atmosphere.

May

If you're planning to head out on hiking trails, May is a great time to visit. Temperatures are still relatively mild and wildflowers create a huge splash of colour. Local greens, vegies and produce fill Greek kitchens.

🏃 May Day

The first of May is marked by a mass exodus from towns for picnics in the country. Wildflowers are gathered and made into wreaths to decorate houses. As a day associated with workers' rights, recent years have also seen mass walk-outs and strikes on this day.

June

For festivalgoers looking for contemporary acts rather than traditional village parties, June is hopping

Top: *Tsoureki* (p43), the traditional Greek Easter bread
Bottom: Lighting candles during Easter celebrations

on the mainland. Top national and international performers fill atmospheric stages with dance, music and drama.

☆ Navy Week

Celebrating their long relationship with the sea, fishing villages and ports throughout the country host historical re-enactments and parties in early June.

☆ Classical Music Festival

Featuring Greek and international performers, this festival (www.nafplion festival.gr) in the Peloponnese uses the Palamidi fortress as one of its atmospheric concert venues.

🎇 Feast of St John the Baptist

The country is ablaze with bonfires on 24 June as Greeks light up the wreaths they made on May Day.

☆ Rockwave Festival

Rockwave has major international artists and massive crowds. It's held in late June on a huge parkland at the edge of Athens. (p95)

☆ Hellenic Festival

The most prominent Greek summer festival features local and international music, dance and drama staged at the ancient Odeon of Herodes Atticus on the slopes of the Acropolis in Athens and at the world-famous Theatre of Epidavros, near Nafplio. Events run from June through August. (p94)

🎇 Miaoulia Festival

Held approximately the third weekend of June, Hydra ignites in celebration of Admiral Miaoulis and the Hydriot contribution to the War of Independence. Witness a spectacular boat burning, fireworks, boat racing and folk dancing.

July

Temperatures soar and life buzzes on the islands' beaches, while outdoor cinemas and giant beach clubs continue to draw visitors to Athens' nightlife. If you're staying anywhere near the water, fill your belly with seafood that's hauled in daily.

☆ Delphi Cultural Festival

Every July, the European Cultural Centre of Delphi hosts a 10-day cultural festival with fine arts, a sculpture park and drama performances at its own open-air theatre.

August

Respect the heat of August; expect to do just a little bit less, move a little more slowly and relax just a little more fully. If you're planning to travel mid-month, reserve well ahead as Greeks take to the roads and boats in large numbers.

☆ Wine & Cultural Festival

Held at Evia's coastal town of Karystos, this festival includes theatre, traditional dancing, music and visual-art exhibits as well as a sampling of every local wine imaginable. (p612)

☆ August Moon Festival

Under the brightest moon of the year, historical venues in Athens open with free moonlit performances. Watch theatre, dance and music at venues such as the Acropolis or Roman Agora. The festival is also celebrated at other towns and sites around the country; check locally for details.

October

While the islands quieten down, the sunny weather often holds in October. City life continues apace.

🎇 Ohi Day

A simple 'no' (*ohi* in Greek) was Prime Minister Metaxas' famous response when Mussolini demanded free passage through Greece for his troops on 28 October 1940. The date is now a major national holiday with remembrance services, parades, feasting and dance.

November

Autumn sees temperatures drop. Olive-picking is in full swing in places like Crete and feta production picks up, giving you the opportunity to taste some seriously fresh cheese.

🎇 Thessaloniki International Film Festival

Around 150 films are crammed into 10 days of screenings in mid-November. The focus is on independent film-makers and the festival (www.filmfestival.gr) is gaining increasing notoriety.

Itineraries

 The Grand Tour

First trip to Greece? Take in the country's biggest sights, best beaches and cultural highs, complemented with contemporary cities and laid-back island life.

Begin in **Athens**, visiting grand ancient sites and museums. Take in the markets, contemporary-art scene and award-winning restaurants. Catch a ferry to chic **Mykonos**, with its crowd-pleasing bars and beaches. Day-trip to the sacred island of **Delos** to explore ancient ruins. Hop a ferry to spectacular **Santorini** to watch the sun sink from the dramatic cliffs of its volcanic caldera.

It's not far from here to Crete. Rent a car and head south to stunning **Elafonisi** beach. Journey north to **Hania**, with its charming harbour and labyrinth of backstreets, then on to the capital **Iraklio** and nearby magnificent Minoan ruins of **Knossos**.

Hop a flight to cultured **Thessaloniki** for architecture, Ottoman-inspired cuisine and the vivacious arts scene. Scale the slopes of **Mt Olympus** (2918m), Greece's highest peak and first national park. Visit the monasteries of **Meteora**, perched high on narrow pinnacles of rock. Your last stop is atmospheric **Ancient Delphi**, former home of the mysterious Delphic oracle.

3 WEEKS

Ionians & the Peloponnese

If you've a hankering for island life along with beautiful medieval towns, ancient historic sights and dramatic scenery, a tour of the Ionian Islands and the neighbouring Peloponnesian peninsula will more than satisfy you. This is doubly true if you're keen to toss some outdoor activities into your trip.

Begin in **Corfu**, spending a couple of days wandering through the amazing blend of Italian, French and British architecture in Corfu's Old Town, indulging in gourmet cuisine, exploring picturesque coastal villages and lounging on sandy beaches. Corfu is also great for windsurfing, or biking in the mountainous interior. From Corfu, hop on a ferry to **Kefallonia** to visit the picturesque village of Fiskardo, kayak to isolated beaches and sample the island's local wine.

From Kefallonia, it's a short ferry ride to **Kyllini** on the Peloponnesian peninsula. Visit the sanctuary of **Ancient Olympia**, and stand in the stadium that hosted the first Olympic Games. Stay overnight in the town and take in some of the excellent museums. Head south to the captivating, World Heritage–listed ruins of **Mystras**. This massive ancient fortress town was the last stronghold of the Byzantine Empire.

Continue south to the rugged and remote **Mani**, to encounter villages filled with fascinating architecture and the remnants of the unique Maniot culture. This region is a haven for hikers with the dramatic Taÿgetos Mountains and tiny, isolated coves. It's also home to one of mainland Europe's most southerly points at **Cape Tenaro**, made famous in Homer's 'Iliad'. Follow the coast east to spectacular **Monemvasia** and spend at least a day exploring the medieval cobbled alleyways and a night staying in atmospheric lodgings within the walls of its medieval town.

Next head north to graceful **Nafplio** with its mansions, museums and lively port. From here, it's easy to do day trips to the impressive acropolis at **Tiryns** and the citadel of **Mycenae**. East of here is the ancient theatre of **Epidavros**, where it's well worth taking in some star-lit classical performances. Then hop on ferry from nearby **Methana** to end your journey in **Athens**.

Crete & the Dodecanese

Once considered out of the way, Crete's eastern half has some fantastic sights and excellent towns that are making it an increasingly magnetic region. From here it's a short hop to the neighbouring Dodecanese, with their wealth of diversity and speedy catamaran services that make island hopping a joy.

Begin in **Iraklio**, taking in the excellent archaeological museum and making a day trip to the impressive Minoan ruins of **Knossos**. En route take in the surrounding **Peza** wine region, which is nestled amid a landscape of shapely hills, sun-baked slopes and lush valleys. From Iraklio head east along the northern coast to the relaxed resort town of **Agios Nikolaos**, which dishes out charm and hip ambience in equal portions. This makes a great base for exploring the surrounding region. Check out the massive fortress on **Spinalonga Island**, a fascinating spot that's just a short ferry ride across the Gulf of Mirabello. Visit the surrounding Minoan ruins, such as **Malia**, a palace still filled with mysteries, and rent a bike to explore the tranquil villages of the fertile **Lasithi Plateau**, lying snugly between mountain ranges and home to Zeus' birthplace.

Continue on to **Sitia**, from where you can head for the clear water and white sand of **Vaï**, Europe's only natural palm-forest beach. You can also head south from here to **Kato Zakros** to hike through the dramatic, cave-honeycombed Valley of the Dead and the red jaws of the Zakros Gorge.

From Sitia, get settled on a 10-hour ferry ride to **Rhodes**. Spend a couple of days exploring Rhodes' walled medieval Old Town and checking out its burgeoning nightlife. Visit some of the surrounding beaches and stunning Byzantine chapels. Catch a catamaran to lush **Nisyros** to explore atop the alarmingly thin crust of its caldera and then carry on to **Patmos** to experience its artistic and religious vibe and to visit the cave where St John wrote the Book of Revelations. There are also some laid-back beaches here and excellent restaurants. Backtrack to **Kos** to spend a final couple of days on gorgeous, sandy **Kefalos Bay** and to sip coffee and cocktails in Kos Town's lively squares. From Kos Town you can catch onward flights to **Athens**.

Plan Your Trip
Island Hopping

In Greece, getting there really is half the adventure and island hopping remains an essential part of the Greek experience. Whether you're sailing into a colourful harbour, listening to the pounding surf on a sun-drenched deck, or flying low over azure waters in a propeller-driven twin-engine plane, you will undoubtedly be filled with a sense of adventure.

Island Highlights

Best for Culture

Delos A stunning archaeological site.

Karpathos Experience Olymbos' Dorian-based culture.

Patmos See the cave where St John wrote the Book of Revelations.

Rhodes Roam around the medieval Old Town.

Crete Explore the Minoan palace of Knossos.

Best for Activities

Ios Dive, windsurf and waterski.

Crete Hike Europe's longest gorge.

Karpathos Try world-class kitesurfing.

Best for Low Season

Santorini Watch gorgeous sunsets.

Hydra Escape from Athens.

Crete Medieval cities and mountain villages.

Lesvos Unwind on this isolated island.

Best for Drinking & Dining

Santorini Taste test at local wineries.

Crete Sample the flavor-rich Mediterranean diet.

Ikaria Have your fill of fresh lobster.

Corfu Dine on braised meat, risottos and pasta.

Planning Essentials

While the local laissez-faire attitude is worth emulating while island hopping, a little bit of planning can also take you a long way. Deciding where and when you want to go and getting your head around routes and schedules before you go will take the work out of your holiday.

Travelling in Greece is that much more enjoyable when you have room to be somewhat flexible and to go with the flow. Transport information is always vulnerable to change, and nowhere is this truer than in Greece. Everything from windy weather to striking workers mean planes and boats are regularly subject to delays and cancellations at short notice. Ferry and airline timetables change from year to year and season to season, with ferry companies often 'winning' contracts to operate different routes annually. When island hopping, it's important to remember that no timetable is watertight.

When to Go

High Season

➡ Lots of ferries and transport links but book ahead.

➡ Water temperature is warm enough for swimming.

➡ The *meltemi* (dry northerly wind) blows south across the Aegean, sometimes playing havoc with ferry schedules.

Shoulder Season

➡ Transport is slightly limited but connects most destinations.

➡ Water temperature can still be very chilly.

➡ The best sea-life watching begins in May and runs through to September.

Low Season

➡ Planning ahead is essential as boats and planes are limited.

➡ Swimming in the sea is only for those immune to cold water.

➡ Most businesses offering water sports are closed for the winter.

Travelling by Sea

With a network covering every inhabited island, the Greek ferry system is vast and varied. The slow rust buckets that used to ply the seas are nearly a thing of the past. You'll still find slow boats, but high-speed ferries are more common and cover most of the popular routes. Local ferries, excursion boats and tiny, private fishing boats called caïques often connect neighbouring islands and islets. You'll also find water taxis that will take you to isolated beaches and coves. At the other end of the spectrum, hydrofoils and catamarans can cut down travel time drastically. Hydrofoils have seen their heyday but continue to link some of the more remote islands and island groups. Catamarans have taken to the sea in a big way, offering more comfort and coping better with poor weather conditions.

For long-haul ferry travel, it is still possible to board one of the slow boats chugging between the islands and to curl up on deck in your sleeping bag to save a night's accommodation. Nevertheless, Greece's domestic-ferry scene has undergone a radical transformation in the past decade and these days you can also travel in serious comfort and at a decent speed. Of course, the trade off is that long-haul sea travel can be quite expensive. A bed for the night in a cabin from Piraeus to Rhodes can be more expensive than a discounted airline ticket.

Ticketing & Fares

As ferries are prone to delays and cancellations, for short trips it's often best not to purchase a ticket until it has been confirmed that the ferry is leaving. In high season, or if you need to reserve a car space, you should book in advance. High-speed boats like catamarans tend to sell out long before slow chuggers. For overnight ferries it's always best to book in advance, particularly if you want a cabin or particular type of accommodation. If a service is cancelled you can usually transfer your ticket to the next available service with that company.

Many ferry companies have online booking services or you can purchase tickets from their local offices and most travel agents in Greece. Agencies selling tickets line the waterfront of most ports, but rarely is there one that sells tickets for every boat, and often an agency is reluctant to give you information about a boat they do not sell tickets for. Most have timetables displayed outside; check these for the next departing boat or ask the *limenarhio* (port police).

Ferry prices are fixed by the government, and are determined by the distance of the destination from the port of origin. The small differences in price you find at ticket agencies are the results of some agencies

---

GETTING YOUR SEA LEGS

Even those with the sturdiest stomachs can feel seasick when a boat hits rough weather. Here are a few tips to calm your tummy:

➡ Gaze at the horizon, not the sea. Don't read or stare at objects that your mind will assume are stable.

➡ Drink plenty and eat lightly. Many people claim ginger biscuits and ginger tea settle the stomach.

➡ Don't use binoculars.

➡ If possible stay in the fresh air – don't go below deck and avoid hydrofoils where you are trapped indoors.

➡ Try to keep your mind occupied.

➡ If you're prone to seasickness, consider investing in acupressure wrist bands.

sacrificing part of their designated commission to qualify as a 'discount service'. (The discount is seldom more than €0.50.)

High-speed ferries and hydrofoils cost about 20% more than the traditional ferries, while catamarans are often 30% to 100% more expensive than their slower counterparts. Caïques and water taxis are usually very reasonable, while excursion boats can be pricey but very useful if you're

ISLAND FINDER

ISLAND	FOOD	FAMILY FRIENDLY	OFF THE BEATEN TRACK	NIGHTLIFE	BEACH	CULTURE	ACTIVITIES	EASY ACCESS
Aegina						x		x
Alonnisos						x	x	
Amorgos			x			x	x	
Andros			x			x	x	x
Chios	x	x			x	x	x	x
Corfu	x	x				x		
Crete	x	x			x	x	x	x
Evia	x				x	x	x	x
Fourni Islands			x		x	x		
Hydra		x		x		x	x	x
Ios	x			x	x		x	x
Kalymnos		x		x		x	x	x
Karpathos			x			x	x	
Kefallonia	x	x				x	x	
Kos		x			x		x	x
Lefkada		x		x	x	x	x	x
Leros					x	x	x	x
Lesvos		x	x					
Little Cyclades			x		x	x		x
Milos		x			x	x	x	x
Mykonos				x	x	x		x
Naxos	x	x		x	x	x	x	x
Paros	x	x		x	x	x		x
Patmos	x	x			x	x		x
Paxi			x			x	x	x
Rhodes	x	x		x	x	x	x	x
Samos	x	x				x		x
Samothraki			x		x	x	x	
Santorini	x			x	x	x	x	x
Sifnos			x		x	x	x	
Skiathos				x	x		x	x
Skyros			x			x	x	x
Symi					x	x	x	x
Thasos		x				x		x
Zakynthos					x	x	x	x

trying to reach out-of-the-way islands. Children under five years of age travel for free while those aged between five and 10 are usually given half-price tickets.

Classes

On smaller boats, hydrofoils and catamarans, there is only one type of ticket available and these days, even on larger vessels, classes are largely a thing of the past. The public spaces on the more modern ferries are generally open to all. What does differ is the level of accommodation that you can purchase for overnight boats. A 'deck class' ticket typically gives you access to the deck and interior, but no overnight accommodation. Next up, aeroplane-type seats give you a reserved, reclining seat in which you will hope to sleep. Then come various shades of cabin accommodation: four-berth, three-berth or two-berth interior cabins are cheaper than their equivalent outside cabins with a porthole. On most boats, cabins are very comfortable, resembling a small hotel room with a private bathroom.

Unless you state otherwise, you will automatically be given deck class when purchasing a ticket. Prices quoted are for deck-class tickets, unless otherwise indicated.

Taking a Car

While almost all islands are served by car ferries, they are expensive and, to ensure boarding, you'll generally need to secure tickets in advance. It's more flexible to board as a foot passenger and hire a car on each island; it's relatively cheap and possible on virtually all islands.

Resources

The comprehensive weekly list of departures from Piraeus put out by the EOT (known abroad as the GNTO, the Greek National Tourist Organisation) in Athens is as accurate as possible. While on the islands, the people to go to for the most up-to-date ferry information are the local *limenarhio* (port police), whose offices are usually on or near the quayside.

You'll find lots of information about ferry services on the internet and many of the larger ferry companies also have their own websites. Always check with online schedules, operators or travel agencies for up-to-the-minute information.

Danae Travel (www.danae.gr) A good site for booking boat tickets.

greekferries (www.greekferries.gr) Allows you to search schedules from countless providers, including accommodation options and multileg journeys.

Greek Travel Pages (www.gtp.gr) Has a useful search program and links for ferries.

Open Seas (www.openseas.gr) A reliable search engine for ferry routes and schedules.

Travelling by Air

A flight can save you hours at sea and offers views across the island groups. Flights between the islands tend to be short and aeroplanes small, often making for a bumpy ride. The vast majority of domestic flights are handled by the merged Olympic Air and Aegean Airlines, offering regular domestic services and competitive rates. In addition to these national airlines, there are a number of smaller outfits running seaplanes or complementing the most popular routes.

Ticketing & Fares

The easiest way to book tickets is online, via the carriers themselves. You can also purchase flight tickets at most travel agencies in Greece. Olympic Air has offices in the towns that flights depart from, as well as in other major towns. There are discounts for return tickets when travelling midweek (Monday to Thursday), and bigger discounts for trips that include a Saturday night away. You'll find full details and information on timetables on the airlines' websites.

Resources

Up-to-date information on flight timetables is best found online. Airlines often have local offices on the islands.

Aegean Airlines (www.aegeanair.com) For domestic flights.

Astra Airlines (www.astra-airlines.gr) Thessaloniki-based carrier with domestic flights.

Greek Travel Pages (www.gtp.gr) Ferry timetables and online booking.

Olympic Air (www.olympicair.com) Aegean's subsidiary with further domestic flights.

Sky Express (www.skyexpress.gr) Domestic flights based out of Crete.

Island-Hopping Itinerary

For intrepid travellers without a tight time schedule, Greece's eastern periphery offers languid coasts, lush scenery and divine beaches, as well as some amazing historic sights. Scheduled ferries are regular but not always very frequent – thankfully you won't be in any hurry to leave and many island hoppers would happily extend their exploration from a few weeks to a couple of months.

From **Athens**, hop a ferry for **Tinos** to visit the sacred Church of Panagia and explore marble-ornamented villages dotted across the terraced hillsides and misty mountain tops. Head east to **Ikaria** for isolated stretches of soft sand and lobster-rich menus. Join in the island culture of dancing, drinking and feasting during summertime *panigyria* (all-night celebrations held on saints' days across the island). Afterwards take a short hop to the serene **Fourni Islands**, a former pirates' lair with surreal sunsets.

Ferry north to **Samos** where you can hike through lush forests to secluded waterfalls and laze on idyllic beaches. From Samos, head to **Chios** and get lost in the labyrinth of stone alleyways in the southern village of Mesta before venturing into the interior to hike through citrus groves under the shade of towering mountain peaks.

The next stop is **Lesvos** (Mytilini), birthplace of the poet Sappho and producer of some of Greece's finest olive oil and ouzo. Not surprisingly, it's also home to hopping nightlife. Visit the island's fantastic modern-art gallery and the hill-top Byzantine monastery of Moni Ypsilou with its glittering ancient manuscripts. Lesvos' landscape, with salt marshes, gushing hot springs, dense forests and soft beaches, is as diverse as its cultural offerings.

From Lesvos, hop to **Limnos** to dine on the day's catch at Myrina's waterside seafood restaurants. Carry on to secluded **Agios Efstratios** to stretch out on volcanic sand beaches before jumping on an overnight boat to Athens.

Plan Your Trip
Cruising

With more than 1400 islands scattered across it, Greece's gorgeous azure water practically begs to be navigated. Not surprisingly, cruising is an increasingly popular way of seeing the country. Not only does it remove the stress of sorting out your own interisland itinerary, it also gets you out on the sea with the breeze at your back and another island always on the horizon.

Choosing a Cruise

Cruises aren't what they used to be and certainly no longer the domain of blue-rinses and slot machines. Catering to a discerning, ever-growing clientele, cruises are often geared to specific interests and niches. Greater competition also means better facilities, more varied excursions, worthwhile on-board diversions and increased dining options. Whether you're in the 30-something crowd, travelling with kids, after a little luxury or just want a no-frills adventure, if the idea of boarding a cruise ship appeals to you, chances are there's a perfect liner out there waiting.

Ship Size

Forget what you've heard, size does matter – at least when you're choosing a cruise ship. A ship's size says a lot about the experience it's offering: megaships can seem more like floating resorts, with a few thousand people on board, while tiny liners cater to fewer than 50 passengers.

Large or Megaships

➡ Accommodate 1000-plus people.

➡ Nonstop activities and complete amenities.

➡ Casinos, restaurants, spas, theatres, children's clubs, discos, bars, cafes and shops.

Great Cruise Lines For...

Culture
Silversea Cruises (www.silverseacruises.com) runs exclusive tours that include language and cooking classes, guest lectures and entertainment from local ports.

Freedom
Azamara (www.azamaraclubcruises.com) offers cruises with top service and few organised activities.

Luxury
Seadream Yacht Club (www.seadream.com) offers ultra-pampering with nearly as many crew as guests.

Small & Personalised Trips
Variety Cruises (www.varietycruises.com) has a maximum of 50 guests and the sea as its swimming pool.

Unconventional Trips
Star Clippers (www.starclipperscruises.com) runs cruises on the world's largest fully rigged tall ships.

➡ Often unable to squeeze into some of the smaller islands' harbours and so visit the largest, most popular ports.

➡ Can seem to dwarf an island with its passengers more than doubling the destination's population.

Medium or Midsized Ships

➡ Cater for 400 to 1000 passengers.

➡ Usually more focused on the destination, with more port stops, more excursions and fewer on-board activities.

➡ Spa, pool, restaurants and bars.

➡ More often able to dock in small island harbours.

Small

➡ Itineraries are often more varied as they can stop at small, out-of-the-way ports.

➡ Often concentrate on a particular cruise niche, such as luxury or activity-based adventure.

➡ Don't expect a pool, spa, large cabin or plethora of dining options.

Local Cruise Lines

International cruises tend to visit Greece in combination with ports from other countries – usually Italy, Turkey and Croatia, often beginning at one port and ending at another. Greece-based cruises usually focus solely on ports within Greece and offer round trips. These cruises are often much more destination focused, with one or two stops each day. The crew are usually Greek, adding to the feel of authenticity, and cuisine and entertainment is more locally based with a bit of international flavour thrown in.

Some Greek-based cruise lines worth checking out include the following:

Golden Star (www.golden-star-cruises.com) Midsized, short cruises taking in the Greek Islands, Turkey and Italy.

Variety Cruises (www.varietycruises.com) Small, luxury cruises taking in some of the smallest Greek Islands.

Windstar Cruises (www.windstarcruises.com) Yacht-style small ships cruising the Aegean to the Black Sea.

Excursions

Excursions are often what make cruises worthwhile and are designed to help you make the most of your sometimes brief visits ashore. They are generally most valuable when sights are not near the port or if a cultural expert is leading the tour. Where all of the sights are near the harbour, it's often just as worthwhile and more relaxing to go exploring on your own. If you plan to explore alone, it's worth double-checking before you book; some larger cruise boats dock at distant ports and it's difficult to reach the island's sights or main towns independently.

Excursions are usually booked before you depart or else when you first board the ship. They are offered on a first-come, first-

---

CRUISING INDEPENDENTLY

Yachting is an amazing way to sail the seas, offering the freedom to visit remote and uninhabited islands. If you can't afford to buy a yacht, there are several other options. You can hire a bare boat (a yacht without a crew), if two crew members have sailing certificates. Prices start at €1700 per week; check out **Set Sail Holidays** (www.setsail.co.uk). If you'd rather have someone else do the sailing for you, **Tasemaro** (www.tasemarosailing.eu) takes up to four passengers, allowing you to be as involved as you like in the sailing. Prices start from €1050/1800 per single/double per week.

Hellenic Yachting Server (www.yachting.gr) has general information on sailing around the islands and lots of links, including information on chartering yachts.

The sailing season is from April to October, although July to September is most popular. Unfortunately, it also happens to be when the *meltemi* (dry northerly wind) is at its strongest. This isn't an issue in the Ionian Sea, where the main summer wind is the *maïstros*, a light to moderate northwesterly that rises in the afternoon and usually dies away at sunset.

CRUISE COMPANIES

COMPANY	CONTACT	SHIP SIZE	CRUISE LENGTH	DESTINATIONS	BUDGET
Azamara	www.azamaraclubcruises.com	medium	7-10 days	Greece, Turkey, Italy	$$$
Celebrity Cruises	www.celebrity.com	mega	10-13 days	Greece, Italy, Turkey, Croatia, France	$
Celestyal Cruises	www.celestyalcruises.com	medium & large	3-7 days	Greece, Turkey, Cyprus	$$
Costa Cruise Lines	www.costacruises.com	large	7-9 days	Greece, Italy, Turkey, Croatia, Israel	$
Crystal Cruises	www.crystalcruises.com	large	7-12 days	Greece, Italy, Turkey, Spain, Portugal	$$
Cunard Line	www.cunard.com	large	7-21 days	Greece, Italy, Croatia, Turkey, France, Spain	$
Golden Star	www.golden-star-cruises.com	medium	3-7 days	Greece, Turkey	$
Holland America Line	www.hollandamerica.com	large	6-12 days	Greece, Italy, Spain, Croatia	$
MSC	www.msccruises.com	large	7-10 days	Greece, Turkey, Croatia, Italy, Egypt	$
Oceania Cruises	www.oceaniacruises.com	medium	10-12 days	Greece, Turkey, France, Italy, Spain	$$$
Princess Cruises	www.princess.com	medium & large	6-24 days	Greece, Italy, Turkey	$
Regent Seven Sea Cruises	www.rssc.com	medium	10-20 days	Greece, Italy, Turkey, France	$$$
Seadream Yacht Club	www.seadream.com	small	6-13 days	Greece, Turkey, Italy, Croatia	$$$
Silversea Cruises	www.silverseacruises.in	small & medium	7-12 days	Greece, Spain, Turkey, Italy	$$$
Star Clippers	www.starclipperscruises.com	small	7-14 days	Greece, Turkey, Italy	$$$

served basis and are generally very popular, so if you're choosing your cruise based on the excursions on offer, it's important to book them as soon as possible. Tours generally range from €35 to €60 for a half-day or €70 to €110 for a full day. Activity-based tours such as mountain biking or kayaking tend to be more, with a half-day around €100. Ensure that you factor in the cost of any excursions from the get-go.

Budgeting

Cruise prices vary greatly depending on the time of year. Booking during the low season will get you good deals but it means you will probably only have the opportunity to visit the largest and busiest ports as smaller islands virtually close out of season.

Budget cruises can be anywhere from €100 to €175 per day, midrange from €175 to €380, and luxury liners begin at €380 and go up to as much as €630 per day. Prices on cruises include meals, on-board activities, entertainment, port fees and portage but there are sometimes additional fuel charges. You also need to budget for airfare, tips, alcohol, pre- and postcruise accommodation and excursions. Deals to look out for include two-for-one offers, prices including airfare or hotels and early-bird rates.

Booking

If you know what you want from your cruise, booking online can be a straightforward option, and certainly worth it for the virtual tours and reviews. But a knowledgable travel agent can help you through the plethora of options available and advise you on extra excursion charges and surcharges that you may miss when booking online.

There are often great rates for booking early and this allows you more choice in choosing cabins, excursions, dining options and so forth. While you can get great last-minute deals, you need to be willing and able to be flexible about dates and options. Booking your airfare through the cruise line may also mean you're collected at the airport and taken to the ship and if your flight or luggage is delayed, they will wait or transport you to the first port.

Choosing a Cabin

Standard cabins are akin to very small hotel rooms, with fully equipped en suites, a double bed and somewhere to unpack. The cheapest option is an 'inside cabin' (ie no window). If you get claustrophobic, you can pay significantly more for an 'outside cabin' where you get either a window or porthole. Prices tend to climb with each floor on the ship but so does the ship's movement. If you suffer from seasickness, choose a lower deck where it's less rocky.

Cabin pricing is for double occupancy; if you're travelling solo you pay a surcharge and if you're travelling as a group of three or four and willing to share a cabin, you can receive substantial discounts. Bunks are referred to as upper and lower berths, otherwise there is a double bed or twin beds that can be pushed together to make a double. Family rooms are sometimes available by having connecting cabins.

Things to check are how close your cabin is located to the disco and, if you're paying extra for a window, whether or not your view is likely to be blocked by a lifeboat.

Life on Board

Embarking: What to Expect

➡ A check-in time that's two or three hours before sailing.

➡ Your passport to be taken for immigration processing.

➡ The first day's program and a deck map, to be found in your cabin.

➡ The offer of a tour of the ship.

➡ A safety drill – legally required on all ships.

➡ The opportunity to set up an on-board credit account.

➡ Your dining-room table assignment.

Meals

Set mealtimes and seating assignments are still the norm on most ships and you will be able to choose your preferred dinner time and table size when you book. Many ships continue to have formal dining evenings with dress codes. Some smaller ships have an all-casual policy, while others have alternative dining options for those not interested in attending the formal evenings.

Tipping

Firstly, don't tip the captain or officers; it would be akin to tipping your dentist or airline pilot. On the final day of your cruise, you'll likely find tipping guidelines in your cabin, usually around €8 per person per day. Tipping is not required but makes up a huge part of the service staffs' wage and is expected.

Plan Your Trip

Eat & Drink Like a Local

Greeks love eating out, sharing impossibly big meals with family and friends in a drawn out, convivial fashion. Whether you are eating seafood at a seaside table or trying modern Greek fare under the floodlit Acropolis, dining out in Greece is never just about what you eat, but the whole sensory experience.

Food Experiences

Take a cue from the locals and go straight to the source, heading to seaside fishing hamlets for fresh fish or mountain villages for local meat. Seek out tavernas that produce their own vegetables, wine and oil, where the fried potatoes are hand-cut, or the fish caught by the owner (or his cousin etc), though these places are becoming rare.

Meals of a Lifetime

➡ **Varoulko** Stellar seafood by one of Greece's star chefs and with Acropolis views. (p120)

➡ **Koukoumavlos** Modern Aegean cuisine in a spectacular caldera-edge Santorini setting. (p385)

➡ **Thalassino Ageri** From the superb setting just outside Hania, peruse the changing Cretan menu, starring the day's catch. (p450)

➡ **Rambagas** Celebrity chef pays homage to Sifnos' culinary heritage. (p405)

➡ **Katogi** Tantalising and inventive mezedhes (small plates) in lively and delightful garden surrounds on Ios. (p377)

➡ **Klimataria** Stellar example of fresh, simple food from the humble taverna, in Corfu's fishing village of Benitses. (p644)

➡ **Thalassaki** Artful use of local produce and outstanding seafood in a charming seaside setting on Tinos. (p325)

When to Go

Food Seasons

Many olive-oil producers, wineries, agricultural cooperatives and cheese makers are visitor friendly year-round. Olive harvest reaches its peak in the winter. Spring sees artichokes and other fresh vegetables while cheese making kicks into high gear. In summer, fresh figs, watermelon, cherries and other fruit jam-pack markets. And in the autumn, nuts are harvested and *raki* (Cretan firewater) is distilled.

Food Festivals

Annual festivals celebrate local specialities and harvest seasons. Fisher's festivals (August to October) include the sardine festival on Lesvos and Ithaki's *maridha* (whitebait) festival. In the Peloponnese, Leonidio's Aubergine Festival is held in August. Aegina's pistachio industry celebrates Fistiki Fest mid-September. And *raki* or *tsikoudia* festivals are held in Voukolies and other Cretan villages in November, when olive oil is produced.

Best Markets

Year-round, visit Athens' Central Market, Thessaloniki's Modiano Market and Hania's historic Agora, or find rotating weekly farmers markets.

➡ **Hotzas Taverna** Exquisite traditional and fusion dishes in a classic stone taverna in Chios. (p571)

➡ **Marco Polo Cafe** Idyllic garden courtyard with an ever changing menu of delicious Greek and Italian-influenced dishes in Rhodes. (p483)

➡ **Doltso** Macedonian cuisine at its finest in an old-town tavern in Kastoria. (p264)

Cheap Treats

➡ **Souvlaki** Greece's favourite fast food, both the *gyros* (meat slivers cooked on a vertical rotisserie)and skewered-meat versions wrapped in pitta bread, with tomato, onion and lashings of tzatziki.

➡ **Pies** Bakeries make endless variations of *tyropita* (cheese pie) and *spanakopita* (spinach pie), plus other pies.

➡ **Street food** Includes *koulouria* (fresh pretzel-style bread) and seasonal snacks such as roasted chestnuts or corn.

Cooking Courses

Well-known Greece-based cooking writers and chefs run cooking workshops on several islands and in Athens, mostly during spring and autumn.

➡ **Glorious Greek Kitchen Cooking School** (www.dianekochilas.com) Diane Kochilas runs weeklong courses on her ancestral island, Ikaria, in July and August, as well as classes and culinary tours in Athens, Crete and the Cyclades.

➡ **Kea Artisanal** (www.keartisanal.com) Aglaia Kremezi and her friends open their kitchens and gardens on the island of Kea for cooking workshops.

➡ **Crete's Culinary Sanctuaries** (www.cookingincrete.com) Nikki Rose combines cooking classes, organic farm tours and cultural excursions around Crete.

➡ **Museum of Greek Gastronomy** (p84) Every Wednesday the museum's chef helps you whip up a five-course meal to enjoy alongside wine tasting in the courtyard.

Cook It at Home

Leave room in your baggage for local treats (customs and quarantine rules permitting) such as olives and extra virgin olive oil from small, organic producers; aromatic Greek thyme honey; dried oregano, mountain tea and camomile flowers; or a jar of spoon sweets (fruit preserves).

The Greek Kitchen

The essence of traditional Greek cuisine lies in seasonal home-grown produce. Dishes are simply seasoned. Lemon juice, garlic, pungent Greek oregano and extra virgin olive oil are the quintessential flavours, along with tomato, parsley, dill, cinnamon and cloves.

➡ **Mayiferta** Homestyle, one-pot, baked or casserole dishes. Prepared early, they are left to cool to enhance the flavours. Well-known *mayiferta* include *mousakas* (eggplant, minced meat, potatoes and cheese), *yemista* (vegetables stuffed with rice and herbs), *lemonato* (meat with lemon and oregano) and *stifadho* (sweet stewed meat with tomato and onion).

➡ **Grills** Greeks are masterful with grilled and spit-roasted meats. *Souvlaki* – arguably the national dish – comes in many forms, from cubes of grilled meat on a skewer to pita-wrapped snacks with pork or chicken *gyros*. *Paidakia* (lamb cutlets) and *brizoles* (pork chops) are also popular.

➡ **Fish and seafood** Fish is often grilled whole and drizzled with *ladholemono* (lemon and oil dressing). Smaller fish like *barbounia* (red mullet) or *maridha* (whitebait) are lightly fried. Octopus is grilled, marinated or stewed in wine sauce. Popular seafood dishes include *soupies* (cuttlefish), calamari stuffed with cheese and herbs, and *psarosoupa* (fish soup). The best way to avoid imports is to seek out tavernas run by local fishing families.

➡ **Mezedhes** These small dishes (or appetisers) are often shared. Classics include *tzatziki*

Top: Grilled octopus

Bottom: Traditional coffee

(yoghurt, cucumber and garlic), *melitzanosalata* (aubergine), *taramasalata* (fish roe), *fava* (split-pea purée with lemon juice) and *saganaki* (fried cheese). Also watch for *keftedhes* (meatballs), *loukaniko* (pork sausage), grilled *gavros* (white anchovies) and dolmadhes (rice wrapped in marinated vine leaves).

➡ **Greek salad** This ubiquitous salad (*horiatiki* or 'village salad') is made of tomatoes, cucumber, onions, feta and olives; however, it's often garnished with local greens (*horta*), peppers, capers or nuts. Feta is sometimes replaced by a local cheese. Beetroot salad is also popular, often served with walnuts and cheese.

➡ **Cheese** Greece's regions produce many different types of cheeses, most using goat's and sheep's milk, with infinite variations in taste. Apart from feta, local cheeses include *graviera* (a nutty, mild gruyère-like sheep's-milk cheese), *kaseri* (similar to provolone), *myzithra* (ricotta-like whey cheese), and *manouri* (creamy soft cheese) from the north.

Local Specialities

From cheese and olive oil to the raw ingredients on your plate, you will find many regional variations and specialities on your travels. Crete is a popular foodie destination, with distinct culinary traditions, but the islands and mainland offer their own culinary treats. Be sure to ask about local dishes, cheese and produce.

➡ **Northern Greece** Influenced by eastern flavours, there's less olive oil and more peppers and spices along with a strong mezes culture and Ottoman sweets.

➡ **Peloponnese** Known for its herb-rich, one-pot dishes and *ladhera* (vegetarian, peasant-style dishes).

➡ **Cyclades** A traditional reliance on beans and pulses led to popularity of *fava* (split-pea purée) and *revythadha* (chickpea stew); you'll also find

FETA

Greece's national cheese has been produced for about 6000 years from sheep and goat milk. Only feta made in Greece can be called feta, an EU ruling giving it the same protected status as Parma ham and Champagne.

spaghetti with lobster and a mean sausage tradition.

➡ **Ionian Islands** The Venetian influence is found in spicy braised beef, rooster *pastitsada* (red sauce pasta) and *sofrito* (braised veal with garlic and wine sauce).

➡ **Crete** Herb-rich dishes include *anthoi* (stuffed zucchini flowers), *soupies* (cuttlefish with wild fennel) and *hohlioi bourbouristoi* (snails with vinegar and rosemary).

What to Drink

While there is coffee strong enough to stand a spoon in and ouzo that will knock you flat, thankfully Greece also has plenty of tamer options for quenching your thirst.

Coffee

The ubiquitous *kafeneia* (coffee house) is a time-honored tradition, with older Greeks stationed over a cup of coffee, intensely debating local politics, football or gossip. Often small and unchanged for generations, it's well worth visiting at least one. The trendy cafes serving iced coffees are the modern answer to the *kafeneia* and are usually packed with a younger crowd.

Greek coffee is traditionally brewed in a *briki* (narrow-top pot), on a hot-sand apparatus called a *hovoli,* and served in a small cup. Order a *metrio* (medium, with one sugar) and sip slowly until you reach the mudlike grounds (don't drink them).

Ouzo

Ouzo – Greece's famous liquor – has come to embody a way of eating and socialising, enjoyed with mezedhes during lazy, extended summer afternoons. Sipped slowly and ritually to cleanse the palate between dishes, ouzo is usually served in small bottles or *karafakia* (carafes) with a bowl of ice cubes to dilute it (turning it a cloudy white).

Ouzo is made from distilled grapes with residuals from fruit, grains and potatoes and flavoured with spices, primarily aniseed, giving it that liquorice flavour. The best ouzo is produced in Lesvos (Mytilini).

Greek Wine

The Greek wine renaissance has been gaining international attention and awards, with first-class wines being produced from age-old indigenous varietals with unique character. The latest generation of internationally trained winemakers are producing great wines from Greece's premiere wine regions, including Nemea in the Peloponnese, the vineyards of Santorini, the Iraklioi Wine Country on Crete, and Naoussa in the Cyclades.

Greek white varieties include *moschofilero, assyrtiko, athiri, roditis, robola* and *savatiano*; the popular reds include *xynomavro, agiorgitiko* and *kotsifali*.

House or barrel wine varies dramatically in quality (white is the safer bet), and is ordered by the kilo/carafe. Few places serve wine by the glass.

Greek dessert wines include excellent muscats from Samos, Limnos and Rhodes, Santorini's Vinsanto, Mavrodafne wine (often used in cooking) and Monemvasia's Malmsey sweet wine.

Retsina, white wine flavoured with the resin of pine trees, became popular in the 1960s and retains a largely folkloric significance with foreigners. It does go well with strongly flavoured food (especially seafood) and some winemakers make a modern version.

How to Eat & Drink

Greece's relaxed and hospitable dining culture makes it easy to get into the local spirit.

When to Eat

Greece doesn't have a big breakfast tradition, unless you count coffee and a cigarette, and maybe a *koulouri* or *tyropita* eaten on the run. You'll find Western-style breakfasts in hotels and tourist areas.

While changes in working hours are affecting traditional meal patterns, lunch is still usually the big meal of the day, starting after 2pm.

Greeks eat dinner late, rarely sitting down before sunset in summer. This coincides with shop closing hours, so restaurants often don't fill until after 10pm. Get in by 9pm to avoid the crowds. Given the long summers and mild winters, alfresco dining is central to the dining experience. Most tavernas open all day, but some upmarket restaurants open for dinner only.

> **EATING PRICE RANGES**
>
> The following price ranges refer to the average cost of a main course (not including service charges):
>
> **€** less than €10
>
> **€€** €10–20
>
> **€€€** more than €20

Vegetarian Friendly

While vegetarians are an oddity in Greece, they are well catered for, since vegetables feature prominently in Greek cooking – a legacy of lean times and the Orthodox faith's fasting traditions.

Look for popular vegetable dishes such as *fasolakia yiahni* (braised green beans), *bamies* (okra), *briam* (oven-baked vegetable casserole) and vine-leaf dolmadhes. Of the nutritious *horta* (wild greens), *vlita* (amaranth) are the sweetest, but other common varieties include wild radish, dandelion, stinging nettle and sorrel.

Festive Food

Greece's religious and cultural celebrations inevitably involve a feast and many have their own culinary traditions.

The 40-day Lenten fast spawned *nistisima*, food without meat or dairy (or oil if you're strict). Lenten sweets include *halva*, both the Macedonian-style version (sold in delis) made from tahini and the semolina dessert often served after a meal.

Red-dyed boiled Easter eggs decorate the *tsoureki*, a brioche-style bread flavoured with *mahlepi* (mahaleb cherry kernels) and mastic. Saturday night's post-Resurrection Mass supper includes *mayiritsa* (offal soup), while Easter Sunday sees whole lambs cooking on spits all over the countryside.

A *vasilopita* (golden-glazed cake) is cut at midnight on New Year's Eve, giving good fortune to whoever gets the lucky coin inside.

Where to Eat

Steer away from tourist restaurants and go where locals eat. As a general rule, avoid places on the main tourist drags, especially those with touts outside and big signs with photos of food. Be wary of hotel recommendations, as some have deals with particular restaurants.

ETIQUETTE & TABLE MANNERS

➡ Greek tavernas can be disarmingly and refreshingly laid-back. The dress code is generally casual, but in upmarket places locals dress to impress.

➡ Service can be slow (and patchy) by Western standards, but there's no rushing you out of there either.

➡ Tables generally aren't cleared until you ask for the bill, which in traditional places arrives with complimentary fruit or sweets or a shot of liquor. Receipts may be placed on the table at the start of the meal in case tax inspectors visit.

➡ Greeks drink with meals (the drinking age is 16), but public drunkenness is uncommon and frowned upon.

➡ Book for upmarket restaurants, but reservations are unnecessary in most tavernas.

➡ Service charges are included in the bill, but most people leave a small tip or round up the bill; 10% to 15% is acceptable. If you want to split the bill, it's best you work it out among your group – Greeks are more likely to argue over whose turn it is to pick up the tab.

➡ Greeks are generous and proud hosts. Don't refuse a coffee or drink – it's a gesture of hospitality and goodwill. If you're invited out, the host normally pays. If you are invited to someone's home, it is polite to take a small gift (flowers or sweets), and remember to pace yourself, as you will be expected to eat everything on your plate.

➡ Smoking is banned in enclosed public spaces, including restaurants and cafes, but this rule is largely ignored, especially on distant islands.

Tavernas are casual, good-value, often family-run (and child-friendly) places, where the waiter arrives with a paper tablecloth and plonks a basket of bread and cutlery on the table.

Don't judge a place by its decor (or view). Go for places with a smaller selection (where food is more likely to be freshly cooked) rather than those with impossibly extensive menus.

Restaurant Guide

➡ **Tavernas** The classic Greek taverna has a few specialist variations: the *psarotaverna* (serving fish and seafood), and *hasapotaverna* or *psistaria* (for chargrilled or spit-roasted meat).

➡ **Mayirio** (cookhouse) Specialises in traditional one-pot stews and *mayirefta*.

➡ **Estiatorio** Serves upmarket international cuisine or Greek classics in a more formal setting.

➡ **Mezedhopoleio** Offers lots of mezedhes.

➡ **Ouzerie** In a similar vein to the *mezedhopoleio*, the *ouzerie* serves mezedhes (traditionally arriving with each round of ouzo). Regional variations focusing on the local firewater include the *rakadhiko* (serving *raki*) in

Crete and the *tsipouradhiko* (serving *tsipouro*) in the mainland north.

Menu Advice

➡ Menus with prices must be displayed outside restaurants. English menus are fairly standard but off the beaten track you may encounter Greek-only menus. Many places display big trays of the day's *mayirefta* or encourage you to see what's cooking in the kitchen.

➡ Bread and occasionally small dips or nibbles are served on arrival (you're not given a choice, and they are added to the bill).

➡ Don't stick to the three-course paradigm – locals often share a range of starters and mains (or starters can be the whole meal). Dishes may arrive in no particular order.

➡ Frozen ingredients, especially seafood, are usually flagged on the menu (an asterisk or 'kat' on Greek menu).

➡ Fish is usually sold per kilogram rather than per portion, and is generally cooked whole rather than filleted. It's customary to go into the kitchen to select your fish (go for firm flesh and glistening eyes). Check the weight (raw) so there are no surprises on the bill.

Plan Your Trip
Outdoor Activities

Greece is graced with blue water and warm winds, a profusion of undersea life, dramatic cliff faces, flourishing forests and strings of ancient walkways – but it's only recently that visitors have looked up from their sun loungers to notice. Whether you're a novice kite-surfer or an avid cyclist, you want to hike deep gorges or ski from lofty heights, opportunities abound.

Water Activities

Diving & Snorkelling

Snorkelling can be enjoyed just about anywhere along the coast and equipment is cheaply available. Especially good spots are Monastiri on Paros; Paleokastritsa on Corfu; Xirokambos Bay on Leros; and anywhere off the coast of Kastellorizo (Megisti). Many dive schools also use their boats to take groups of snorkellers to prime spots.

Greek law insists that diving be done under the supervision of a diving school in order to protect the many antiquities in the Mediterranean and Aegean Seas. Until recently dive sites were severely restricted, but more have been opened up and diving schools have flourished. You'll find schools on the islands of Corfu, Evia, Leros, Milos, Mykonos, Paros, Rhodes, Santorini and Skiathos; in Agios Nikolaos and Rethymno in Crete; in Glyfada near Athens; and in Parga and Halkidiki in northern Greece.

The **Professional Association of Diving Instructors** (PADI; www.padi.com) has lots of useful information, including a list of PADI-approved dive centres in Greece.

Windsurfing

Hrysi Akti on Paros, and Vasiliki on Lefkada vie for the position of the best windsurfing beach. There are numerous other prime

Best Outdoors

Best Hiking

Samaria Gorge Trek among towering cliffs and wildflowers.

Andros Follow well-worn footpaths across hills to deep valleys.

Nisyros Hike through lush foliage and down into the caldera.

Samos Wander through woods and swim under waterfalls.

Best for Experts

Santorini Offers a pathway of canyons and swim-through sand caverns for divers.

Naxos Hike to the Cave of Zeus.

Paros Shangri-la for kitesurfing.

Best for Novices

Vasiliki Learn how to windsurf.

Ios Dive schools catering to first-timers.

Poros Waterskiing beginners.

Paxi Walks through ancient olive groves.

Kos Cycle on the flat.

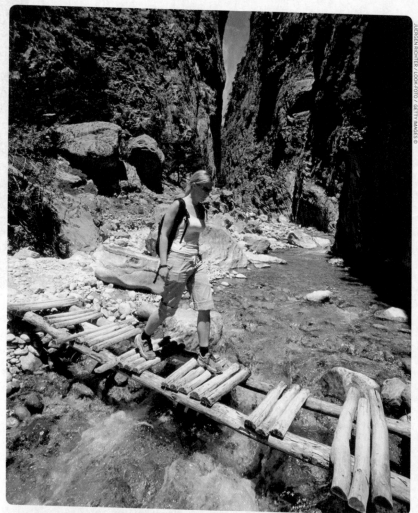

JUERGEN RICHTER / LOOK-FOTO / GETTY IMAGES ©

PAULE SEUX / GETTY IMAGES ©

Top: Hiking in Samaria Gorge (p454)

Bottom: Swimming off the Ionian Islands (p632)

locations around the islands and many outlets rent equipment. Check out Kalafatis Beach on Mykonos; Agios Georgios on Naxos; Mylopotas Beach on Ios; Cape Prasonisi in southern Rhodes; around Tingaki on Kos; and Kokkari on Samos.

You'll find sailboards for hire almost everywhere; charges range from €10 to €25, depending on the gear and location. Most places that rent equipment also give lessons. Sailboards can be imported into Greece freely (one per passenger) provided they'll be taken out on departure, but always check customs regulations for your country.

Kitesurfing & Surfing

With near-constant wind and ideal conditions, Paros' Pounda beach is a magnet for top kitesurfing talent, attracting the Professional Kiteboard Riders Association and the Kiteboard Pro World Tour. This is also a great place to learn the art of surfing. Mikri

Vigla on Naxos is also an excellent spot, with courses off the white-sand beach.

Waterskiing

Given the relatively calm and flat waters of most island locations and the generally warm waters of the Mediterranean, waterskiing can be a very pleasant activity. August can be a tricky month, when the *meltemi* (dry northerly wind) can make conditions difficult in the central Aegean. Poros is a particularly well-organised locale, with **Passage** (☑22980 42540; www.passage.gr; Neorion Bay) hosting a popular school and slalom centre.

White-Water Rafting

The popularity of white-water rafting and other river adventure sports has grown rapidly in recent years as more and more urban Greeks, particularly Athenians, head off in search of a wilderness experience.

PLAN YOUR TRIP OUTDOOR ACTIVITIES

TOP ISLAND HIKES

DESTINATION, ISLAND GROUP	SKILL LEVEL	DESCRIPTION
Samaria Gorge, Crete	easy to medium	One of Europe's most popular hikes with 500m vertical walls, countless wildflowers and endangered wildlife (impassable mid-October to mid-April)
Zakros & Kato Zakros, Crete	easy to medium	Passing through the mysterious Valley of the Dead, this trail leads to a remote Minoan palace site
Tragaea, Naxos, Cyclades	easy to medium	A broad central plain of olive groves, unspoiled villages and plenty of trails
Sifnos, Cyclades	easy to medium	Monasteries, beaches and sprawling views abound on this freshly updated network of trails, covering 200km of island terrain
Tilos, Dodecanese	easy to medium	Countless traditional trails along dramatic cliff tops and down to isolated beaches; a bird-lover's paradise
Nisyros, Dodecanese	medium to difficult	A fertile volcanic island with hikes that lead down steep cliffs to reach steaming craters
Evia, Dimosari Gorge	easy to medium	A 10km trek through a spectacular gorge of shady streams and cobbled paths ending at a small bay
Steni, Evia	medium to difficult	Day hikes and more serious trekking opportunities up Mt Dirfys, Evia's highest mountain
Paxi, Ionian Islands	easy	Paths along ancient olive groves and snaking dry-stone walls; perfect for escaping the crowds
Ithaki, Ionian Islands	easy to medium	Mythology fans can hike between sites linked to the Trojan War hero Odysseus
Samos, northeastern Aegean Islands	easy to medium	Explore the quiet interior of this Aegean Island with its mountain villages and the forested northern slopes of Mt Ambelos
Hydra, Saronic Gulf Islands	easy	A vehicle-free island with a well-maintained network of paths to beaches and monasteries
Alonnisos, Sporades	easy	A network of established trails that lead to pristine beaches

Eco Action (✆210 331 7866; www.eco action.gr; Agion Anargyron, Psyrri) offers rafting and kayaking on several rivers including the Ladonas and Arahthos. Compass Adventures (p285), based in northern Greece, guides rafting excursions from the Zagorohoria village of Aristi down the frothing Voidomatis River.

Land Activities

Hiking

Greece is in many ways a hikers' paradise. Popular routes are well maintained; however, the **EOS** (Greek Alpine Club; ✆210 321 2429) is underfunded and consequently many lesser-known paths are overgrown and inadequately marked. You'll find EOS branches in Ioannina in Epiros, Litohoro by Mt Olympus, Crete (Greek Mountaineering Association) and Evia (Halkida Alpine Club).

Northern Greece has plenty of rugged hiking terrain, especially around the Zagorohoria in the Pindos Mountains and the hill trails around Prespa Lakes. The Lousios Gorge and the Mani, both in the Peloponnese, are two of the best places in Greece to explore on foot. With the launch of the 75km Menalon Trail, hikers can embark on newly certified short walks or a five-day trek along the Lousios Gorge, Mt Menalon's western slopes and scenic villages. Crete's Samaria Gorge is rightly a global favourite, but western Crete boasts many gorges suitable for hikers of different levels.

On small islands you will encounter a variety of paths, including *kalderimia,* which are cobbled or flagstone paths that have linked settlements since Byzantine times. Other paths include *monopatia* (shepherd's or monk's trails) that link settlements with sheepfolds or link remote settlements via rough unmarked trails. Shepherd or animal trails can be very steep and difficult to navigate.

If you're venturing off the beaten track, a good map is essential. Most tourist maps are inadequate; the best hiking maps for the islands are produced by **Anavasi** (www. anavasi.gr) and **Terrain** (www.terrainmaps. gr), both Greece-based companies. Be realistic about your abilities. Always tell your planned route to your guesthouse or local hiking association before setting out.

Spring (April to June) is the best time for hiking; the countryside is green from the winter rains, and carpeted with wildflow-

ers. Autumn (September to October) is another good time, but July and August, when temperatures rise to around 40°C, are not much fun. Come equipped with a good pair of walking boots to handle the rough, rocky terrain, a wide-brimmed hat, a water bottle and a high UV-factor sunscreen.

A number of companies run organised hikes. The biggest is **Trekking Hellas** (www. trekking.gr), which offers a variety of hikes ranging from a four-hour stroll through the Lousios Valley to a week-long hike around Mt Olympus and Meteora. The company also runs hikes in Crete and the Cyclades.

Cycling

Greece is gaining popularity as a cycling destination both for mountain bikers and novices. Bicycles can usually be taken on trains for free, though you may need a ticket. On ferries, mention your bike when booking tickets.

Much of Greece is very remote; be sure to carry puncture-repair and first-aid kits. Motorists are notoriously fast and not always in the expected lane; caution on corners and narrow roads is warranted. In summer most cyclists break between noon and 4pm to avoid sunstroke and dehydration.

Bike Greece (www.bikegreece.com) Specialises in mountain biking, with weeklong tours for beginners and the experienced.

Cycle Greece (www.cyclegreece.gr) Runs road- and mountain-bike tours across most of Greece for various skill levels.

Hooked on Cycling (www.hookedoncycling. co.uk/greece) Offers boat and bike trips through the islands and tours of the mainland.

Skiing & Snowboarding

Greece's main skiing areas are Mt Parnassos (1600m to 2250m), 195km northwest of Athens, and Mt Vermio (1420m to 2005m), 110km west of Thessaloniki. In the north, Metsovo, Konitsa or the Zagori villages all are possible bases for snow sports around Vasilitsa in the Pindos Mountains. If you want to combine city and snow, ski Vigla-Pisoderi as a day trip from Florina or head to Mt Vermio from Veria.

The season depends on snow conditions but runs approximately from January to the end of April. Get info from the **Hellenic Skiing Federation** (✆210 323 0182; www.eox.gr; 28 Oktovriou 71, Athens) and check conditions and ski centres at **Snow Report** (www.snowreport.gr).

Plan Your Trip
Travel with Children

While Greece doesn't cater to kids in the way that some countries do (you won't find endless theme parks and children's menus here), children will be welcomed and included wherever you go. Greeks will generally make a fuss over your kids, who may find themselves receiving many small gifts and treats. Teach them a few Greek words and they will be made to feel even more appreciated.

Greece for Kids

Sights & Activities

While even the most modern Greek museums are often filled to the gills with relics and objects that not all children are going to appreciate, the settings (ancient palace-like buildings) are often intriguing for kids to wander through. The stories behind the objects can also captivate their imaginations – ancient statues hauled up from the depth of the sea or helmets worn by gladiators. Generally more popular than the museums are the many ancient sights where kids enjoy climbing and exploring.

The beach is one of the best sources of entertainment for children in Greece. In summer many of the larger, popular beaches have boogie boards, surfboards, snorkelling gear and windsurfing equipment for rent. Many also offer lessons or trips on boats or giant, rubber, air-filled bananas. While some beaches have steep drop-offs or strong currents, there is generally a calmer side to each island or a shallow, protected bay that locals can direct you to.

Most towns will have at least a small playground, while larger cities often have

Best Regions for Kids

Athens

With ruins to clamber over, plus museums and child-geared sights to explore, Athens is great for kids. You'll also find big parks and gardens, a variety of cuisines and family-friendly hotels.

Crete

The island's beaches are long and sandy, Knossos ignites kids' imaginations, and you can explore from a single base, sidestepping the need to pack up and move around.

Dodecanese

The magical forts and castles, glorious beaches, laid-back islands, and speedy catamarans linking the Dodecanese daily make it ideal for families. And the Italian influence means an abundance of kid-friendly pasta dishes.

Northern Greece

Offers slightly lower summertime temperatures, Ottoman patisseries and Halkidiki's beaches. Laid-back Ioannina makes a great base and Parga is popular with families. Sithonia is less crowded but also less family friendly than the rest of Halkidiki.

fantastic, modern play parks. In many cases, you can admire children's innate ability to overcome language barriers through play while you enjoy a coffee and pastry at the park's attached cafe. Some of the larger and more popular locations (such as Rhodes, Crete and Athens) also have water parks.

Dining Out

Greek cuisine is all about sharing; ordering lots of mezedhes (small dishes) lets your children try the local cuisine and find their favourites. You'll also find lots of kid-friendly options like pizza and pasta, omelettes, chips, bread, savoury pies and yoghurt.

The fast service in most restaurants is good news when it comes to feeding hungry kids. Tavernas are very family-friendly affairs and the owners will generally be more than willing to cater to your children's tastes. Ingredients like nuts and dairy find their way into lots of dishes so if your children suffer from any severe allergies, it's best to ask someone to write this down for you clearly in plain Greek to show restaurant staff.

Accommodation

Many hotels let small children stay for free and will squeeze an extra bed in the room. In all but the smallest hotels, travel cots can often be found, but it's always best to check this in advance. In larger hotels, cities and resorts, there are often package deals for families and these places are generally set up to cater to kids with childcare options, adjoining rooms, paddling pools, cots and high chairs.

Safety

Greece is a safe and easy place to travel with children. Greek children are given a huge amount of freedom and can often be seen playing in squares and playgrounds late into the night. Nevertheless, it's wise to be extra vigilant with children when travelling, and to ensure they always know where to go and who to approach for help. This is especially true on beaches or playgrounds where it's easy for children to become disoriented. It's also prudent not to have your children use bags, clothing, towels etc with their name or personal information (such as national flag) stitched onto them; this kind of information could be used by potential predators to pretend to know you or the child.

Dangers children are far more likely to encounter are heat stroke, water-borne bugs and illness, mosquito bites, and cuts and scrapes from climbing around on ancient ruins and crumbling castles. Most islands have a clinic of some sort, although hours may be irregular so it's handy to carry a first-aid kid with basic medicine and bandages.

Children's Highlights

Keep Busy

➡ **Boat trips** Whether it's zipping over the sea in a catamaran, bobbing up and down in a fishing boat or sailing on a day trip to a secluded bay.

➡ **Kayaking** Paddle alongside dolphins and visit pirate coves off Kefallonia.

➡ **Beach time** Jump waves, build sandcastles and snorkel. Always ask locally for kid-friendly beaches; Patmos is a great place to start.

WHAT TO PACK

➡ Travel high chair (either a deflatable booster seat or a cloth one that attaches to the back of a chair; these are light and easy to pack away)

➡ Lightweight pop-up cot for babies (if travelling to remote locations)

➡ Car seats (rental agencies don't always offer these)

➡ Plastic cups and cutlery for little ones

➡ Medicine, inhalers etc along with prescriptions

➡ Motion sickness medicine and mosquito repellent

➡ Hats, waterproof sunscreen, sunglasses and water bottles

→ **Cycling** Use pedal power along the flat, bike-friendly roads of Kos.

→ **Playgrounds** Every city has one and they are most often well maintained and shady.

Explore

→ **Acropolis** The home of the Greek gods is perfect for exploring early in the day. (p63)

→ **Rhodes' medieval castles** The island of Rhodes is packed with crumbling castles perched on cliffs above the sea – perfect for climbing and make-believe. (p475)

→ **Knossos** Young imaginations go into overdrive when let loose in this labyrinth. (p427)

→ **Nisyros' volcano** See it hiss and hear it bubble. (p511)

Eat Up

→ **Yemista** Vegies (usually tomatoes) stuffed with rice.

→ **Pastitsio** Buttery macaroni baked with minced lamb.

→ **Tzatziki** A sauce or dip made from cucumber, yoghurt and garlic.

→ **Loukoumadhes** Ball-shaped doughnuts served with honey and cinnamon.

→ **Galaktoboureko** Custard-filled pastry.

→ **Politiko pagoto** Constantinople-style (slightly chewy) ice cream made with mastic.

Cool Culture

→ **Carnival season** Fancy dress, parades and traditional dancing will keep even the oldest kids enthralled. (p24)

→ **Football** Snag tickets for a game to catch some national spirit. Athens and Thessaloniki stadiums draw the biggest crowds.

→ **Hellenic Children's Museum** Build, bake and investigate alongside Athenian kids. (p89)

Planning

The shoulder seasons (April and May and September and October) are great times to travel with children because the weather is milder and the crowds thinner.

An excellent way to prepare your kids for their holiday and to encourage an active interest in the destination is by introducing them to some books or DVDs ahead of time. Lots of younger children enjoy stories of Greek gods and Greek myths while slightly older kids will enjoy movies like *Mamma Mia* or *Lara Croft: Tomb Raider* for their Greek settings. You can also find children's books about life in Greece that include a few easy phrases that your kids can try out.

If your kids aren't old enough to walk on their own for long, consider a sturdy carrying backpack; pushchairs (strollers) are a struggle in towns and villages with slippery cobblestones and high pavements. Nevertheless, if the pushchair is a sturdy, off-road style, with a bit of an extra push you should be OK.

Travel on ferries, buses and trains is free for children under four. For those up to the age of 10 (ferries) or 12 (buses and trains) the fare is half. Full fares apply otherwise. On domestic flights, you'll pay 10% of the adult fare to have a child under two sitting on your knee. Kids aged two to 12 travel with half-fare. If you plan to hire a car, it's wise to bring your own car seat or booster seat as rental agencies are not always reliable for these, particularly on small islands or with local agencies.

Fresh milk is available in large towns and tourist areas, but harder to find on smaller islands. Supermarkets are the best place to look. Formula is available almost everywhere, as is condensed and heat-treated milk. Disposable nappies are also available everywhere, although it's wise to take extra supplies of all of these things to out-of-the-way islands in case of local shortages.

Online Resources

My Little Nomads (www.mylittlenomads.com/greece-with-kids) For plenty of recommendations and hearty discussion on visiting Greece with kids, visit David Hogg's site.

Travel Guide to Greece (www.greektravel.com) Matt Barrett's website has lots of useful tips for parents

Greece 4 Kids (www.greece4kids.com) Matt Barrett's daughter Amarandi has put together some tips of her own.

Regions at a Glance

Athens & Around

Ancient Ruins
Nightlife
Museums

The Acropolis

Roam the ruins of the Acropolis and watch traditional Greek drama unfold at the Odeon of Herodes Atticus. The capital and surrounding region are littered with ruins to explore, from the central Agorato to the Temple of Poseidon on Cape Sounion.

Bars & Clubs

This city refuses to snooze, with glamorous beachside clubs where thousands dance to international DJs, intimate *rembetika* clubs where you can soak up Greek blues and ouzo, and everything in between.

Ancient Treasures

Step into the Benaki mansion, filled with Bronze Age finds, works by El Greco and regional costumes. Explore the expansive collection at the Byzantine Museum and the floors of antiquities at the National Archaeological Museum. And don't miss the ultramodern Acropolis Museum housing long-lost treasures.

p56

Peloponnese

Ancient Ruins
Architecture
Activities

Citadels

The Peloponnese is packed with inspiring ancient sites. Visit the sanctuary of Ancient Olympia, explore the citadels of Mycenae and Tiryns, or take in a show at the theatre of Epidavros.

Fortresses

From Byzantine cities to Venetian fortresses, this region is peppered with architectural gems. Cross the causeway to magical Monemvasia castle or explore tower houses from the 17th century.

Hiking Trails

The Mani, the peninsula's rugged and remote southern region, is a popular place to amble, with mountains tumbling down to gorgeous coastal views. Northwest of here, hike through the Lousios Gorge to find charming village monasteries.

p128

Central Greece

Ancient Sites
Activities
Beaches

Delphi & Meteora

Two of Greece's most atmospheric architectural sites: the sanctuary of Delphi rests on the slopes of Mt Parnassos with views of the sea, and nearby Meteora's monasteries sit atop towering pinnacles of rock.

Trails & Waterways

Follow cobblestone trails past villages and through forests on the Pelion Peninsula; raft over rapids or kayak on the Aheloos River; and follow in Hercules' footsteps, exploring the green depths of Iti National Park.

Beaches

Central Greece keeps its beautiful beaches a secret. Low-key resorts dot the Gulf of Corinth and the Pelion Peninsula where hidden, sandy coves and long stretches of sand await.

p186

Northern Greece

Food & Wine
Activities
Beaches

Eastern Spice

The strong mezedhes culture brings a spiciness from the Anatolian Peninsula in Turkey. You'll encounter mussel pilaf, crayfish, lots of cheese and Macedonian wine. Sample Ottoman sweets in Thessaloniki.

Mountain Hikes

The story of Zeus takes you hiking into the clouds atop Mt Olympus, Greece's highest peak. In Zagorohoria, hike between 46 preserved hamlets in the Pindos Mountains.

Resorts

With sandy beaches, island getaways and towns with strong Italian-village influences, Parga typifies the region's resorts – popular yet relaxed, good for families yet also great for nightlife. Alternatively, head for the remote sandy coves of Halkidiki.

Saronic Gulf Islands

Activities
Architecture
Museums

Diving & Hiking

Diving is magical in these waters. Dolphin safaris, sunken pirate ships and underwater caves are just the start. When dry land beckons, Poros, Hydra and Spetses have forests to explore and hill tops to climb.

Monasteries & Mansions

Tiers of traditional buildings sweep down to Hydra's pretty harbour, and serene, ancient monasteries dot nearby hill tops. Next door on Spetses, see traditional boat building and impressive, deep-rooted mansions.

Seacraft

Hydra's museums include a restored hill-top mansion and naval collections. At Spetses, see a traditional seafarer's home, and at Baltiza, a museum of sea craft, from caïques to yachts.

Cyclades

Ancient Ruins
Cuisine
Nightlife

Delos & Akrotiki

One of the country's most important archaeological sites, the sacred relics of Delos are protected on their own private island. The Minoan city of Akrotiki on Santorini is equally atmospheric.

Trad Meals

Sample smoked eel and ham, Mykonian prosciutto, handmade cheeses and local wild mushrooms. Kitchens are filled with creative culinary flair and modern takes on traditional foods.

Glamour Clubs

The legendary Mykonos nightlife is glamorous and entertaining. Ios is less swanky but very full-on, with wall-to-wall clubs and nonstop beach parties. Quieter Santorini has cocktail bars over the caldera with unparalleled sunset views.

Crete

Ancient Ruins
Activities
Beaches

Minoan Palaces

The ruins of the Minoan civilisation grace this island, including the spectacular restored palace of Knossos and the labyrinth referred to in Greek mythology. At remote sites, there's a lingering sense of mystery.

Gorge Hikes

The Samaria is Europe's longest gorge, and one of Crete's most popular draws. The island boasts other quieter, equally dramatic gorges for hiking and rock climbing, and a mountainous interior with hermit caves and woodland to explore.

Sun Worship

Crete's beaches are palm-fringed stretches of powder-soft sand. Some are packed with sun worshippers, while others are isolated oases – but all are worth sinking your toes into.

Dodecanese

Architecture
Activities
Cuisine

Byzantine & Medieval

Architectural eye candy is everywhere. See fairy-tale, hilltop castles, frescoed Byzantine churches and Rhodes' medieval Old Town. Visit mountain villages, the ruins of ancient temples and Italian-inspired harbour towns.

Adventures

Some of the world's top rock climbing, kitesurfing, beachcombing, diving and walking is packed into the Dodecanese. Ancient footpaths, endangered bird life, a bubbling volcano and surfing too.

Culinary Mix

Mix Greek cuisine with long-term Italian influences for scrumptious results: pizzas, pastas, stews, local cheeses, honey, wild greens and herbs, seafood and grilled meats.

p470

Northeastern Aegean Islands

Activities
Cuisine
Beaches

Great Outdoors

The clear water lapping these islands is perfect for diving into. You'll be beckoned to hike to wooded waterfalls, wade through rivers and explore old-growth forests on foot or bicycle.

Seafood & Wine

Dining daily on fresh seafood is a way of life. Venus clams, sea urchins, crayfish, grilled cod and lobster are all washed down with plenty of ouzo and Samos' sweet local wine.

Aqua Aegean

From the remote, white-pebbled coast on Ikaria to hidden coves on the Fourni Islands, pristine sandy stretches on Chios and seaside resorts on Samos, you're never far from a beach on the aquamarine Aegean.

p546

Evia & the Sporades

Activities
Cuisine
Nightlife

Water Sports

Soak in thermal waters at beaches or spas, watch for dolphins in the waters of a marine park, and hike through olive groves. The region's also renowned for its diving.

Sweet & Fresh

Don't miss the local honey, especially the *elatos* (fir) and *pefko* (pine) varieties. Select amazingly fresh fish directly from the nets and served on the dock. Locally pressed olive oil produces home cooking like *yiayia* (grandma) makes.

Wine Bars

Nightlife isn't always about clubbing. Here it's about listening to some of the country's top bouzouki players and watching the sun sink over the horizon from low-key wine bars.

p606

Ionian Islands

Architecture
Activities
Cuisine

Mansions

Corfu Town is a symphony of pastel-hued Venetian mansions, French arcades and British neoclassical architecture. Corfu is dotted with other historic mansions and neighbouring islands have white-washed villages and ancient windmills.

Kayak & Ramble

Kayak remote coves, windsurf the blue Aegean, wander ancient olive groves and hike the mountains. Continuous stretches of gorgeous coastline and quiet interiors lure the adventurous.

Italian Inspired

Braised meat, plenty of garlic, homemade bread, seafood risottos and hand-rolled pasta allude to an Italian influence in the kitchen. Without a history of Turkish rule, Corfiot cuisine is distinctive and delicious.

p632

On the
Road

Northern Greece (p228)

Central Greece (p186)

Ionian Islands (p632)

Evia & the Sporades (p606)

Northeastern Aegean Islands (p546)

Athens & Around (p56)

Peloponnese (p128)

Saronic Gulf Islands (p294)

Cyclades (p314)

Dodecanese (p470)

Crete (p414)

Athens & Around

Best Places to Eat

➡ Funky Gourmet (p102)
➡ Aleria (p102)
➡ Akordeon (p103)
➡ Café Avyssinia (p101)
➡ Mani Mani (p99)

Best Places to Stay

➡ Electra Palace (p98)
➡ NEW Hotel (p98)
➡ Hotel Grande Bretagne (p98)
➡ Herodion (p96)
➡ Hera Hotel (p96)

Why Go?

Ancient and modern, with equal measures of grunge and grace, bustling Athens is a heady mix of history and edginess. Iconic monuments mingle with first-rate museums, lively cafes and al fresco dining – and it's downright fun.

The historic centre is an open-air museum, yet the city's cultural and social life takes place amid these ancient landmarks, merging past and present. The magnificent Acropolis rises above the sprawling metropolis and has stood witness to the city's many transformations.

Post-Olympics Athens, even in the face of current financial issues, is conspicuously more sophisticated and cosmopolitan than ever before. Stylish restaurants, shops and hip hotels, and artsy-industrial neighbourhoods and entertainment quarters such as Gazi, show Athens' modern face.

The surrounding region of Attiki holds some spectacular antiquities as well – such as the Temple of Poseidon at Sounion – and lovely beaches, like those near historic Marathon.

When to Go
Athens

May Soak up the city's ancient history before jumping out to the islands to soak up the sun.

Jun–Aug The Hellenic Festival lights up venues throughout the city with drama and music.

Sep–Oct Weather cools and the social scene heats up as residents return from the islands.

Athens Highlights

1 Climbing to the awe-inspiring **Acropolis** (p63).

2 Enjoying the majesty of the Parthenon sculptures in the **Acropolis Museum** (p73).

3 Promenading around the ancient sights and ruins of **Athens' historic centre** (p62).

4 Discovering Athens' hot **nightlife** in lively cafe-bars like Tailor Made (p105).

5 Marvelling at antiquities in the **National Archaeological Museum** (p84).

6 Catching a show at the **Odeon of Herodes Atticus** (p73).

7 Shopping in the **Monastiraki Flea Market** (p111).

8 Dining out with views of the floodlit Acropolis, at restaurants like **Strofi** (p100).

9 Reveling in ancient feats of strength at the **Panathenaic Stadium** (p90).

ATHENS AΘHNA

POP 3.1 MILLION

History

Early History

The early history of Athens is inextricably interwoven with mythology, making it impossible to disentangle fact from fiction. What is known is that the hill-top site of the Acropolis, with two abundant springs, drew some of Greece's earliest Neolithic settlers. When a peaceful agricultural existence gave way to war-oriented city states, the Acropolis provided an ideal defensive position.

By 1400 BC the Acropolis had become a powerful Mycenaean city. It survived a Dorian assault in 1200 BC but didn't escape the dark age that enveloped Greece for the next 400 years. Then, in the 8th century BC, during a period of peace, Athens became the artistic centre of Greece, excelling in ceramics.

By the 6th century BC, Athens was ruled by aristocrats and generals. Labourers and peasants had no rights until Solon, the harbinger of Athenian democracy, became *arhon* (chief magistrate) in 594 BC and improved the lot of the poor, with reforms such as the annulment of debts and the implementation of trial by jury. Continuing unrest over the reforms created the pretext for the tyrant Peisistratos, formerly head of the military, to seize power in 560 BC.

Peisistratos built a formidable navy and extended the boundaries of Athenian influence. A patron of the arts, he inaugurated the Festival of the Great Dionysia, the precursor of Attic drama, and commissioned many splendid works, most of which were destroyed by the Persians.

Peisistratos was succeeded by his son, Hippias, in 528 BC; Athens rid itself of this oppressor in 510 BC with the help of Sparta.

Athens' Golden Age

After Athens finally repulsed the Persian Empire at the battles of Salamis (480 BC) and Plataea (479 BC) – again, with the help of Sparta – its power knew no bounds.

In 477 BC Athens established a confederacy on the sacred island of Delos and demanded tributes from the surrounding islands to protect them from the Persians. The treasury was moved to Athens in 461 BC and Pericles, ruler from 461 BC to 429 BC, used the money to transform the city. This period has become known as Athens' golden age – the pinnacle of the classical era.

Most of the monuments on the Acropolis today date from this period. Drama and literature flourished due to such luminaries as Aeschylus, Sophocles and Euripides. The sculptors Pheidias and Myron and the historians Herodotus, Thucydides and Xenophon also lived during this time.

ATHENS IN...

Two Days

Start by climbing Plaka's early-morning streets to the glorious **Acropolis**, then wind down through the **Ancient Agora**. Explore **Plaka** and the **Monastiraki Flea Market**, taking a break at an Adrianou cafe. Head to the **Acropolis Museum** for the Parthenon masterpieces. Amble around the **grand promenade**, then up to **Filopappou Hill** and the cafes of **Thisio** before dinner at a restaurant with Acropolis views.

On day two, watch the **changing of the guard** at Plateia Syntagma before heading through the gardens to the **Panathenaic Stadium** and the **Temple of Olympian Zeus**. Take a trolleybus to the **National Archaeological Museum**, then catch an evening show at the historic **Odeon of Herodes Atticus**, or head to **Gazi** or the area around Plateia Agia Irini in **Monastiraki** for dinner and nightlife.

Four Days

With a couple more days, visit the **Benaki Museum**, the **Museum of Cycladic Art** and the **Byzantine & Christian Museum** before lunch and shopping in **Kolonaki**. Take the *teleferik* (funicular railway) or climb **Lykavittos Hill** for panoramic views. Catch a movie by moonlight at one of Athens' **outdoor cinemas**, or hit up a **rembetika club** in winter. On day four explore the dynamic **central market** and the **Keramikos** site. Trip along the coast to Cape Sounion's **Temple of Poseidon**, or else save your energy for summer nightlife at Glyfada's **beach bars**.

CONTEST FOR ATHENS

As the myth goes, Athena won the honour of being Athens' namesake and patron deity in a battle with Poseidon. After Kekrops, a Phoenician, founded a city on a huge rock near the sea, the gods of Olympus proclaimed that it should be named after the deity who could provide the most valuable legacy for mortals. Athena (goddess of wisdom, among other things) produced an olive tree, symbol of peace and prosperity. Poseidon (god of the sea) struck a rock with his trident and a saltwater spring emerged. The gods judged that Athena's gift would better serve the citizens of Athens with food, oil and wood. To this day she dominates Athens' mythology and the city's great monuments are dedicated to her.

Rivalry with Sparta

Sparta did not let Athens revel in its new-found glory. Their jockeying for power led to the Peloponnesian Wars in 431 BC, which dragged on until 404 BC, when Sparta gained the upper hand. Athens was never to return to its former glory. The 4th century BC did, however, produce three of the West's greatest orators and philosophers: Socrates, Plato and Aristotle.

In 338 BC Athens, along with the other city states of Greece, was conquered by Philip II of Macedon. After Philip's assassination, his son Alexander the Great favoured Athens over other city states. After Alexander's untimely death, Athens passed in quick succession through the hands of his generals.

Roman & Byzantine Rule

The Romans defeated the Macedonians, and in 186 BC attacked Athens after it sided against them in a botched rebellion in Asia Minor. They destroyed the city walls and took precious sculptures to Rome. During three centuries of peace under Roman rule, known as the 'Pax Romana', Athens continued to be a major seat of learning. The Romans adopted Hellenistic culture: many wealthy young Romans attended Athens' schools, and anybody who was anybody in Rome spoke Greek. The Roman emperors, particularly Hadrian, graced Athens with many grand buildings. Christianity became the official religion of Athens and worship of the 'pagan' Greek gods was outlawed.

After the subdivision of the Roman Empire into east and west, Athens remained an important cultural and intellectual centre until Emperor Justinian closed its schools of philosophy in AD 529. Athens declined and, between 1200 and 1450, was continually invaded – by the Franks, Catalans, Florentines and Venetians, all preoccupied with grabbing principalities from the crumbling Byzantine Empire.

Ottoman Rule & Independence

Athens was captured by the Turks in 1456, and nearly 400 years of Ottoman rule followed. The Acropolis became the home of the Turkish governor, the Parthenon was converted into a mosque and the Erechtheion became a harem.

On 25 March 1821 the Greeks launched the War of Independence, declaring independence in 1822. Fierce fighting broke out in the streets of Athens, which changed hands several times. Britain, France and Russia eventually stepped in and destroyed the Turkish–Egyptian fleet in the famous Battle of Navarino in October 1827.

Initially the city of Nafplio was named Greece's capital. After elected president Ioannis Kapodistrias was assassinated in 1831, Britain, France and Russia again intervened, declaring Greece a monarchy. The throne was given to 17-year-old Prince Otto of Bavaria, who transferred his court to Athens. It became the Greek capital in 1834, though was little more than a sleepy town of about 6000, with many residents having fled after the 1827 siege. Bavarian architects created imposing neoclassical buildings, tree-lined boulevards and squares. The best surviving examples are on Leoforos Vasilissis Sofias and Panepistimiou.

Otto was overthrown in 1862 after a period of power struggles, including the British and French occupation of Piraeus, aimed at quashing the 'Great Idea' – Greece's doomed expansionist goal. The imposed sovereign was Danish Prince William, crowned as Prince George in 1863.

The 20th Century

Athens grew steadily throughout the latter half of the 19th and early 20th centuries. In 1923, with the Treaty of Lausanne, nearly one million Greek refugees from Turkey descended on Athens.

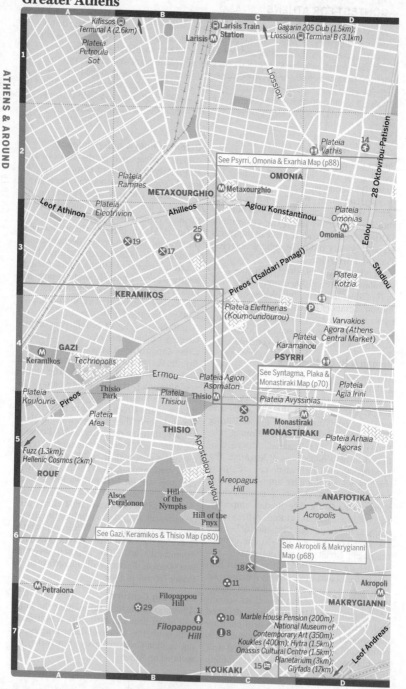

Kifissos
Terminal A (2.6km)

Plateia
Petroula
Sot

Larisis Train
Station

Larisis

Gagarin 205 Club (1.5km);
Liossion Terminal B (3.1km)

Liossion

28 Oktovriou-Patision

Plateia
Vathis

14

See Psyrri, Omonia & Exarhia Map (p88)

OMONIA

Plateia
Rammes

METAXOURGHIO

Metaxourghio

Leof Athinon

Plateia
Eleotrivion

Ahilleos

Agiou Konstantinou

Plateia
Omonias

Omonia

Eolou

Stadiou

19

17

25

Pireos (Tsaldari Panagi)

Plateia
Kotzia

KERAMIKOS

Plateia Eleftherias
(Koumoundourou)

Plateia
Karamanou

Varvakios
Agora (Athens
Central Market)

GAZI

Keramikos

Technopolis

Ermou

PSYRRI

Plateia
Koulouris

Pireos

Thisio
Park

Plateia Agion
Asomaton

Plateia
Thisiou

Thisio

See Syntagma, Plaka &
Monastiraki Map (p70)

Plateia
Agia Irini

Plateia
Afea

THISIO

20

Plateia Avyssinias

Monastiraki

MONASTIRAKI

Plateia Arhaia
Agoras

Fuzz (1.3km);
Hellenic Cosmos (2km)

ROUF

Apostolou Pavlou

Areopagus
Hill

ANAFIOTIKA

Alsos
Petralonon

Hill
of the
Nymphs

Hill of the
Pnyx

Acropolis

See Gazi, Keramikos & Thisio Map (p80)

See Akropoli & Makrygianni
Map (p68)

Petralona

5

18

Akropoli

11

Akropoli

Filopappou
Hill

29

Filopappou
Hill

1

10

MAKRYGIANNI

8

Marble House Pension (200m);
National Museum of
Contemporary Art (350m);
Koukles (400m); Hytra (1.5km);
Onassis Cultural Centre (1.5km);
Planetarium (3km);
Glyfada (17km)

Leof Andreas

KOUKAKI

15

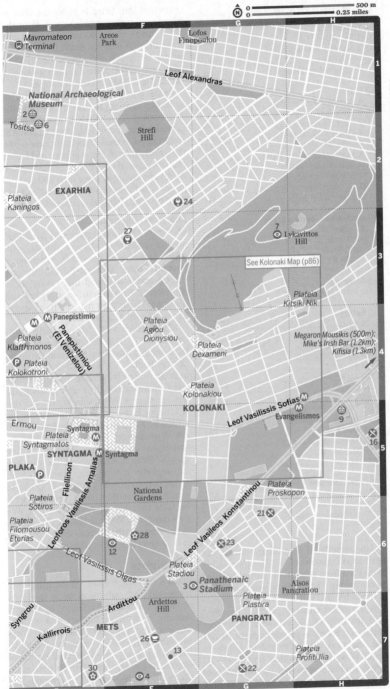

0   500 m
0   0.25 miles

Mavromateon Terminal

Areos Park

Lofos Finopoulou

Leof Alexandras

National Archaeological Museum

2

Tosita   6

Strefi Hill

EXARHIA

Plateia Kaningos

24

27

7   Lykavittos Hill

See Kolonaki Map (p86)

Panepistimio

Plateia Klafthmonos

Panepistimiou (El Venizelou)

Plateia Kolokotroni

Plateia Agiou Dionysiou

Plateia Dexameni

Plateia Kitsiki Nik

Megaron Mousikis (500m);
Mike's Irish Bar (1.2km);
Kifisia (1.3km)

Plateia Kolonakiou

KOLONAKI

Leof Vasilissis Sofias   Evangelismos

9

16

Ermou

Syntagma

Plateia Syntagmatos

SYNTAGMA   Syntagma

PLAKA

Filellinon

Plateia Sotiros

Plateia Filomousou Eterias

Leoforos Vasilissis Amalias

Leof Vasilissis Olgas

National Gardens

Leof Vasileos Konstantinou

Plateia Proskopon

21

23

12   28

Plateia Stadiou

3   **Panathenaic Stadium**

Plateia Plastira

Alsos Pangratiou

PANGRATI

Syngrou

Kallirrois

Ardittou

Ardettos Hill

METS

26

13

Plateia Profiti Ilia

30

4   22

Greater Athens

Athens suffered appallingly during the German occupation of WWII – more Athenians died from starvation than were killed by the enemy. The suffering would continue in the bitter civil war that followed.

A '50s industrialisation program, launched with the help of US aid, brought another population boom, as people from the islands and mainland villages moved to Athens in search of work. The colonels' junta (1967–74) tore down many of the old Turkish houses of Plaka and the neoclassical buildings of King Otto's time, but failed to tackle the chronic infrastructure problems resulting from the rapid growth of the 1950s. The elected governments that followed didn't do much better, and by the end of the 1980s the city had a reputation as one of the most traffic-clogged, polluted and dysfunctional in Europe.

In the 1990s authorities embarked on an ambitious program to drag the city into the 21st century. The 2004 Olympics deadline fast-tracked projects such as the expansion of road and underground metro networks and the construction of a new airport, and forced changes across the public and private sectors. As Athens absorbed more than 600,000 migrants – both documented and otherwise – the city's social fabric also changed.

The New Millennium

The 2004 Olympics legacy was a cleaner, greener and more efficient capital, with a new-found pride buoyed by a decade of booming economic growth. But the optimism and fiscal good times were to be short-lived: financial crisis and widespread disenchantment with the country's governance darkened Athens' mood.

With Greece's debt crisis, repeated bailouts (sponsored by the European Commission, International Monetary Fund and European Central Bank – the so-called troika) began in 2010. Athens is regularly beset by strikes and demonstrations in protest to strict austerity measures. With pension cuts and one of Europe's highest unemployment rates, life is hard for many. In early 2015, when the ECB cut off emergency aid, banks closed briefly and capital controls were imposed, causing lines to form at ATMs across the city. The anti-austerity government, headed by the Syriza party (elected in 2015), has sought to stanch the depression, but at the time of writing talks with the troika were still underway for a third loan. Nevertheless, small businesses persist and Athens' creative life continues to flourish in the face of adversity.

◉ Sights

Plateia Syntagmatos (Syntagma Sq; translated as Constitution Sq) is the heart of modern Athens – dominated by the Parliament; most major sights are in walking distance. South of Syntagma, the old Turkish quarter in **Plaka** is virtually all that existed when Athens was declared capital of Greece. Its paved, narrow streets nestle into the northeastern slope of the Acropolis and encompass many of Athens' ancient sites.

Touristy in the extreme, Plaka is still the most character-filled part of Athens.

Centred on busy **Plateia Monastirakiou** (Monastiraki Sq), the area just west of Syntagma is the city's grungier but very atmospheric market district, home to some of the city's hottest nightlife, with new restaurants, cafes and bars opening frequently. **Psyrri** (psee-*ree*), just north of Monastiraki, has a zippy bar-and-restaurant quarter, though other streets can be deserted at night. **Thisio** neighbourhood's Apostolou Pavlou is a lovely green pedestrian promenade with a host of cafes and youth-filled bars; most of the neighbourhood feels pleasantly residential. The red, neon-lit chimney stacks at the renovated gasworks in **Gazi** illuminate one of the city's densest nightlife districts; it's one of the burgeoning gay-friendly neighbourhoods.

Kolonaki, tucked beneath **Lykavittos Hill** east of Syntagma, is undeniably chic, with classy boutiques, art galleries, cafes and trendy restaurants. To the east of the Acropolis, **Pangrati** is an unpretentious residential neighbourhood. The quiet neighbourhoods of **Makrygianni** and **Koukaki**, south of the Acropolis, are refreshingly untouristy as well.

The commercial district around **Omonia** was once one of the city's smarter areas, but despite ongoing efforts to clean it up, it can still be quite seedy, especially at night; exercise caution. **Exarhia**, the bohemian, graffiti-covered neighbourhood between the Polytechnio (university) and Strefi Hill, is a lively spot popular with students, artists and left-wing intellectuals. The swanky suburbs of **Kifisia** (inland) and **Glyfada** (seaside) have their own shopping, cafe and nightlife scenes.

The Athens basin is surrounded by mountains, bounded to the north by **Mt Parnitha**, the northeast by **Mt Pendeli**, the west by **Mt Egaleo** and the east by **Mt Ymittos**. Downtown Athens is dominated by its much smaller hills.

Athens boasts many fine neoclassical buildings dating from the period after Independence. Foremost are the celebrated neoclassical trilogy on Panepistimiou, halfway between Omonia and Syntagma: the **National Library** (Map p88; ☎210 338 2541; www.nlg.gr; Panepistimiou 32, Syntagma; ☺9am-8pm Mon-Thu, to 2pm Fri & Sat; ℳPanepistimio) **FREE**, **Athens University** (Map p88; ☺closed to public; ℳPanepistimio), and **Athens Academy**.

At the time of research the **National Art Gallery** (Map p60; ☎210 723 5937; www.national gallery.gr; Leoforos Vasileos Konstantinou 50, Kolo-

naki; ℳEvangelismos) was closed for renovation. The **Greek Folk Art Museum** (Map p70; ☎210 322 9031; www.melt.gr; Adrianou & Areos, Plaka; ℳSyntagma) was closed as it relocated to a new building.

◎ Acropolis

★**Acropolis**   HISTORIC SITE
(Map p70; ☎210 321 0219, disabled access 210 321 4172; http://odysseus.culture.gr; adult/child/concession €12/free/6; ☺8am-8pm Apr-Oct, to 5pm Nov-Mar, last entry 30min before closing; ℳAkropoli) This is the most important ancient site in the Western world. Crowned by the Parthenon, it stands sentinel over Athens, visible from almost everywhere within the city. Its monuments and sanctuaries of Pentelic marble gleam white in the midday sun and gradually take on a honey hue as the sun sinks, while at night they stand brilliantly illuminated above the city. A glimpse of this magnificent sight cannot fail to exalt your spirit.

Inspiring as these monuments are, they are faded remnants of the city of Pericles, who spared no expense – only the best materials, architects and sculptors were good enough for a city dedicated to the cult of Athena. It was a showcase of lavishly coloured

> ### ℹ ENTERING THE ACROPOLIS
>
> There are several entry points to the Acropolis. From the south, walk along Dionysiou Areopagitou to the stairs just beyond the Odeon of Herodes Atticus to reach the **main entrance**, or go through the **Theatre of Dionysos entrance** near the Akropoli metro station, and wend your way up from there. Anyone carrying a backpack or large bag (including camera bags) must use the main entrance and leave bags at the cloakroom. The main approach from Plaka is along the path that's a continuation of Dioskouron.
>
> ➡ People in wheelchairs can access the site via a cage lift rising vertically up the rock face on the northern side. It's best to call ahead (☎210 321 4172) to arrange. When you go, go to the main entrance.
>
> ➡ Arrive as early as possible, or go late in the afternoon – it gets incredibly crowded. Wear shoes with rubber soles, as the paths around the site are uneven and slippery.

The Acropolis

Cast your imagination back in time, two and a half millennia ago, and envision the majesty of the Acropolis. Its famed and hallowed monument, the Parthenon, dedicated to the goddess Athena, stood proudly over a small city, dwarfing the population with its graceful grandeur. In the Acropolis' heyday in the 5th century BC, pilgrims and priests worshipped at the temples illustrated here (most of which still stand in varying states of restoration). Many were painted brilliant colours and were abundantly adorned with sculptural masterpieces crafted from ivory, gold and semiprecious stones.

As you enter the site today, elevated on the right, perches one of the Acropolis' best-restored buildings: the diminutive **Temple of Athena Nike** ❶. Follow the Panathenaic Way through the Propylaia and up the slope toward the Parthenon – icon of the Western world. Its **majestic columns** ❷ sweep up to some of what were the finest carvings of their time: wraparound **pediments, metopes and a frieze** ❸. Stroll around the temple's exterior and take in the spectacular views over Athens and Piraeus below.

As you circle back to the centre of the site, you will encounter those renowned lovely ladies, the **Caryatids** ❹ of the Erechtheion. On the Erechtheion's northern face, the oft-forgotten **Temple of Poseidon** ❺ sits alongside ingenious **Themistocles' Wall** ❻. Wander to the Erechtheion's western side to find Athena's gift to the city: **the olive tree** ❼.

Sanctuary of Pandion

Themistocles' Wall
Crafty general Themistocles (524–459 BC) hastened to build a protective wall around the Acropolis and in so doing incorporated elements from archaic temples on the site. Look for the column drums built into the wall.

Sanctuary of Zeus Polieus

Erechtheion

Temple of Poseidon
Though he didn't win patronage of the city, Poseidon was worshipped on the northern side of the Erechtheion which still bears the mark of his trident-strike. Imagine the finely decorated coffered porch painted in rich colours, as it was before.

TOP TIP

» **The Acropolis** is a must-see for every visitor to Athens. Avoid the crowds by arriving first thing in the morning or late in the day.

Porch of the Caryatids

Perhaps the most recognisable sculptural elements at the Acropolis are the majestic Caryatids (circa 415 BC). Modelled on women from Karyai (modern-day Karyes, in Lakonia) the maidens are thought to have held a libation bowl in one hand, and to be drawing up their dresses with the other.

Parthenon Pediments, Metopes & Frieze

The Parthenon's pediments (the triangular elements topping the east and west facades) were filled with elaborately carved three-dimensional sculptures. The west side depicted Athena and Poseidon in their contest for the city's patronage, the east Athena's birth from Zeus' head. The metopes are square carved panels set between channelled triglyphs. They depicted battle scenes, including the sacking of Troy and the clash between the Lapiths and the Centaurs. The cella was topped by the Ionic frieze, a continuous sculptured band depicting the Panathenaic Procession.

Parthenon

Chalkotheke

Sanctuary of Artemis Brauronia

Panathenaic Way

Statue of Athena Promachos

Arrephorion

Propylaia

Pinakothiki

Entrance

Spring of Klepsydra

Athena's Olive Tree

The flourishing olive tree next to the Erechtheion is meant to be the sacred tree that Athena produced to seize victory in the contest for Athens.

Parthenon Columns

The Parthenon's fluted Doric columns achieve perfect form. Their lines were ingeniously curved to create an optical illusion: the foundations (like all the 'horizontal' surfaces of the temple) are slightly concave and the columns are slightly convex making both appear straight.

Temple of Athena Nike

Recently restored, this precious tiny Pentelic marble temple was designed by Kallicrates and built around 425 BC. The cella housed a wooden statue of Athena as Victory (Nike) and the exterior friezes illustrated Athenian battle triumphs.

colossal buildings and of gargantuan statues, some of bronze, others of marble plated with gold and encrusted with precious stones.

The Acropolis was first inhabited in Neolithic times (4000–3000 BC). The first temples were built during the Mycenaean era, in homage to the goddess Athena. People lived on the Acropolis until the late 6th century BC, but in 510 BC the Delphic oracle declared that it should be the province of the gods.

After all the buildings on the Acropolis were reduced to ashes by the Persians on the eve of the Battle of Salamis (480 BC), Pericles set about his ambitious rebuilding program. He transformed the Acropolis into a city of temples, which has come to be regarded as the zenith of classical Greek achievement.

Ravages inflicted during the years of foreign occupation, pilfering by foreign archaeologists, inept renovations following Independence, visitors' footsteps, earthquakes and, more recently, acid rain and pollution have all taken their toll on the surviving monuments. The worst blow was in 1687, when the Venetians attacked the Turks, opening fire on the Acropolis and causing an explosion in the Parthenon – where the Turks had been storing gunpowder – and damaging all the buildings.

Major restoration programs are continuing and many of the original sculptures have been moved to the Acropolis Museum (p73) and replaced with casts. The Acropolis became a World Heritage–listed site in 1987.

There' free admission on the first Sunday of the month from November to March.

➡ Beulé Gate

As you walk through the main entrance of the Acropolis site, a little way along the path on your left you will see the Beulé Gate, named after the French archaeologist Ernest Beulé, who uncovered it in 1852. The 8m-high pedestal on the left, halfway up the zigzagging ramp leading to the Propylaia, was once topped by the Monument of Agrippa, a bronze statue of the Roman general riding a chariot, erected in 27 BC to commemorate victory in the Panathenaic Games.

➡ Propylaia

The Propylaia formed the monumental entrance to the Acropolis. Built by Mnesicles between 437 BC and 432 BC, its architectural brilliance ranks with that of the Parthenon. It consists of a central hall with two wings on either side; each section had a gate, and in ancient times these five gates were the only entrances to the 'upper city'. The middle gate, the largest, opened onto the **Panathenaic Way**, the route for the great Panathenaic Procession (p77).

Acropolis

The imposing **western portico** of the Propylaia consisted of six double columns, Doric on the outside and Ionic on the inside. The fourth column along has been restored. The ceiling of the **central hall** was painted with gold stars on a dark blue background. The **northern wing** was used as a *pinakothiki* (art gallery) and the **southern wing** was the antechamber to the Temple of Athena Nike.

The Propylaia is aligned with the Parthenon – the earliest example of a building designed in relation to another. It remained intact until the 13th century, when various occupiers started adding to it. It was badly damaged in the 17th century when a lightning strike set off an explosion in a Turkish gunpowder store. Archaeologist Heinrich Schliemann paid for the removal of one of its appendages – a Frankish tower – in the 19th century. Reconstruction took place between 1909 and 1917, and again after WWII.

➡ Temple of Athena Nike

The small but exquisitely proportioned Temple of Athena Nike stands on a platform perched atop the steep southwest edge of the Acropolis, to the right of the Propylaia. Designed by Kallicrates, the temple was built of Pentelic marble between 427 BC and 424 BC. The building is almost square, with four graceful Ionic columns at either end. Only fragments remain of the frieze, which had scenes from mythology, the Battle of Plataea (479 BC) and Athenians fighting Boeotians and Persians.

Parts of the frieze are in the Acropolis Museum, as are some relief sculptures, including the beautiful depiction of Athena Nike fastening her sandal. The temple housed a wooden statue of Athena.

The Turks took it apart in 1686 and put a huge cannon on the platform; it was carefully reconstructed between 1836 and 1842, but was taken apart again 60 years later because the platform was crumbling. The temple was once again dismantled, piece by piece, in 2003 in a controversial move to restore it off site; it now stands resplendent after a painstaking reassembly.

➡ Statue of Athena Promachos & Pedestals

As you walk beyond the Propylaia into the Acropolis site, along the Panathenaic Way, you will see to your left the foundations of pedestals for the statues that once lined the path, including one that held Pheidias' 9m-high statue of Athena Promachos

---

ⓘ ACROPOLIS PASS & ENTRY HOURS

➡ The Acropolis admission includes entry to Athens' main ancient sites: the Theatre of Dionysos, Ancient Agora, Roman Agora, Hadrian's Library, Keramikos and the Temple of Olympian Zeus. The ticket is valid for four days; otherwise individual site fees apply.

➡ With the changes in government budgets, be sure to double-check hours as they fluctuate from year to year, with closing sometimes as early as 3pm.

➡ Box offices close 15 minutes to half an hour before the sites. Check www. culture.gr for free-admission holidays.

(*promachos* means 'champion'). Symbolising Athenian invincibility against the Persians, the helmeted goddess held a shield in her left hand and a spear in her right.

The statue was carted off to Constantinople by Emperor Theodosius in AD 426. By 1204 it had lost its spear, so the hand appeared to be gesturing. This led the inhabitants to believe the statue had beckoned the Crusaders to the city, so they smashed it to pieces.

➡ Parthenon

More than any other monument, the Parthenon epitomises the glory of Ancient Greece. Meaning 'virgin's apartment', it's dedicated to Athena Parthenos, the goddess embodying the power and prestige of the city. The largest Doric temple ever completed in Greece, and the only one built completely of Pentelic marble (apart from the wood in its roof), it took 15 years to complete. It was designed by Iktinos and Kallicrates and completed in time for the Great Panathenaic Festival (p77) of 438 BC.

Designed to be the pre-eminent monument of the Acropolis and built on its highest ground, the Parthenon had a dual purpose – to house the great statue of Athena commissioned by Pericles, and to serve as the new treasury. It was built on the site of at least four earlier temples dedicated to Athena.

The temple consisted of eight fluted Doric **columns** at either end and 17 on each side. To achieve perfect form, its lines were ingeniously curved to create an optical illusion – the foundations are slightly concave and the columns are slightly convex to make both look straight. Supervised by Pheidias, the sculptors

Akropoli & Makrygianni

Agoracritos and Alcamenes worked on the architectural sculptures of the Parthenon, including the pediments, frieze and metopes, which were brightly coloured and gilded.

The **metopes** on the eastern side depicted the Olympian gods fighting the giants; on the western side they showed Theseus lead-

ANCIENT PROMENADE

The once-traffic-choked streets around Athens' historic centre were transformed into a spectacular 3km-long pedestrian promenade for the 2004 Olympics and connect the city's most significant ancient sites. Locals and tourists alike come out in force for an evening *volta* (walk) along the interesting heritage trail – one of Europe's longest pedestrian precincts – under the floodlit Acropolis.

The **grand promenade** starts at Dionysiou Areopagitou, opposite the Temple of Olympian Zeus, and continues along the southern foothills of the Acropolis, all the way to the Ancient Agora, branching off from Thisio to Keramikos and Gazi, and north along Adrianou to Monastiraki and Plaka.

ing the Athenian youths into battle against the Amazons. The southern metopes illustrated the contest of the Lapiths and Centaurs at a marriage feast, while the northern ones depicted the sacking of Troy.

Much of the **frieze** depicting the Panathenaic Procession was either damaged in the Turkish gunpowder explosion of 1687 or later defaced by the Christians, but the greatest existing part (over 75m long) consists of the controversial Parthenon Marbles, taken by Lord Elgin and now in the British Museum in London. The British government continues to ignore campaigns for their return.

The **ceiling** of the Parthenon, like that of the Propylaia, was painted blue and gilded with stars. At the eastern end was the holy **cella** (inner room of a temple), into which only a few privileged initiates could enter. Here stood the statue for which the temple was built – the **Athena Polias** (Athena of the City), considered one of the wonders of the ancient world. Designed by Pheidias and completed in 432 BC, it was gold-plated over an inner wooden frame and stood almost 12m high on its pedestal. The face, hands and feet were made of ivory, and the eyes were fashioned from jewels. Clad in a long gold dress with the head of Medusa carved in ivory on her breast, the goddess held a

Akropoli & Makrygianni

ATHENS & AROUND ATHENS

statuette of Nike (the goddess of victory) in her right hand; in her left, a spear with a serpent at its base. On top of her helmet was a sphinx, with griffins in relief at either side.

In AD 426 the statue was taken to Constantinople, where it disappeared. There's a Roman copy (the Athena Varvakeion) in the National Archaeological Museum.

➡ Erechtheion

Although the Parthenon was the most impressive monument of the Acropolis, it was more a showpiece than a working sanctuary. That role fell to the Erechtheion, built on the part of the Acropolis held most sacred. It was here that Poseidon struck the ground with his trident and where Athena produced the olive tree. Named after Erechtheus, a mythical king of Athens, the temple housed the cults of Athena, Poseidon and Erechtheus. Six larger-than-life maiden columns, the **Caryatids**, support its southern portico.

The Caryatids got their name because they were modelled on women from Karyai – modern-day Karyes, in Lakonia. Those you see are plaster casts. The originals (except for one removed by Lord Elgin, now in the British Museum) are in the Acropolis Museum.

The Erechtheion was part of Pericles' plan, but the project was postponed after the outbreak of the Peloponnesian Wars. Work did not start until 421 BC, eight years after his death, and was completed around 406 BC.

Architecturally it is the most unusual monument of the Acropolis, a supreme example of Ionic architecture ingeniously built on several levels to counteract the uneven bedrock. The main temple is divided into two cellae – one dedicated to Athena, the other to Poseidon – representing a reconciliation of the two deities after their contest. In **Athena's cella** stood an olive-wood statue of Athena Polias holding a shield adorned with a gorgon's head. It was this statue on which the sacred *peplos* (shawl) was placed at the culmination of the Great Panathenaic Festival (p77).

The **northern porch** consists of six Ionic columns; on the floor are the fissures supposedly left by either the thunderbolt sent by Zeus to kill Erechtheus, or by Poseidon's trident in his contest with Athena. To the south of here was the Cecropion – King Cecrops' burial place.

Except for a small temple of Rome and Augustus, which is no longer in existence, the Erechtheion was the last public building erected on the Acropolis in antiquity.

◉ South Slope of the Acropolis & Makrygianni

⭐ **Theatre of Dionysos**   THEATRE
(Map p70; ☎210 322 4625; Dionysiou Areopagitou; adult/child €2/free, with Acropolis pass free; ☉8am-8pm, reduced hours low season; Ⓜ Akropoli) The tyrant Peisistratos introduced the annual Festival of the Great Dionysia during the 6th century BC, and held it in the world's first theatre, on the south slope of the Acropolis. The original theatre on this

Syntagma, Plaka & Monastiraki

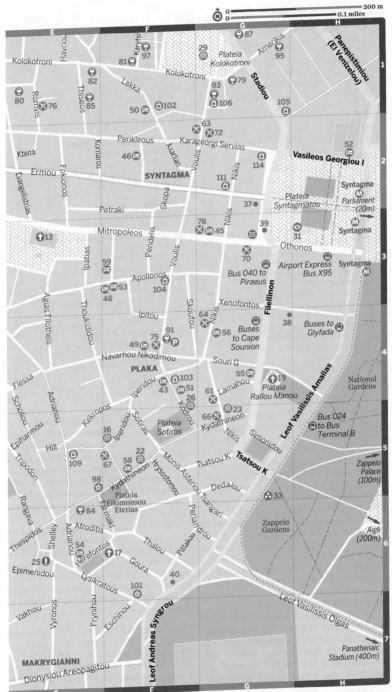

Syntagma, Plaka & Monastiraki

◉ Top Sights

◎ Sights

✪ Activities, Courses & Tours

▣ Sleeping

site was a timber structure, and masses of people attended the contests, where men clad in goatskins sang and danced, followed by feasting and revelry. Drama as we know it dates back to these contests. At one of the contests, Thespis left the ensemble and took centre stage for a solo performance, an act considered to be the first true dramatic performance – hence the term 'thespian'.

During the golden age in the 5th century BC, the annual festival was one of the state's major events. Politicians sponsored dramas by writers such as Aeschylus, Sophocles and Euripides, with some light relief provided by the bawdy comedies of Aristophanes. People came from all over Attica, with their expenses met by the state.

The theatre was reconstructed in stone and marble by Lycurgus between 342 BC and 326 BC, with a seating capacity of 17,000 spread over 64 tiers, of which about 20 survive. Apart from the front row, the seats were built of Piraeus limestone and occupied by ordinary citizens, with women confined to the back rows. The front row's 67 Pentelic marble thrones were reserved for festival officials and important priests. The grandest one – in the centre, with lion-paw armrests – was reserved for the Priest of Dionysos, who sat shaded from the sun under a canopy.

In Roman times the theatre was used for state events and performances.

The 2nd-century-BC reliefs at the rear of the stage depict the exploits of Dionysos. The two hefty men (who still have their heads) are selini, worshippers of the mythical Selinos, the debauched father of the satyrs, whose favourite pastime was charging up mountains with his oversized phallus in lecherous pursuit of nymphs.

Panagia Hrysospiliotissa   HISTORIC SITE

(Map p70) Above the Theatre of Dionysos, an indistinct rock-strewn path leads to a grotto in the cliff face. In 320 BC Thrasyllos turned the grotto into a temple dedicated to Dionysos. The tiny Panagia Hrysospiliotissa

(Chapel of Our Lady of the Cavern) is now a poignant little place, with old pictures and icons on the walls. Above the chapel are two Ionic columns, the remains of Thrasyllos' temple. It is closed to visitors except on its name day, 15 August.

Asclepion & Stoa of Eumenes   RUIN
(Map p68) Directly above the Theatre of Dionysos, steps lead to the Asclepion, a temple that was built around a sacred spring. The worship of Asclepius, the physician son of Apollo, began in Epidavros and was introduced to Athens in 429 BC, when plague was sweeping the city – people sought cures here.

Beneath the Asclepion is the Stoa of Eumenes, a colonnade built by Eumenes II, king of Pergamum (197–159 BC), as a shelter and promenade for theatre audiences.

★ Odeon of Herodes Atticus   THEATRE
(Map p70; ☑ 210 324 1807; Ⓜ Akropoli) The path continues west from the Asclepion to the Odeon of Herodes Atticus, built in AD 161 by wealthy Roman Herodes Atticus in memory of his wife, Regilla. It was excavated in 1857–58 and completely restored between 1950 and 1961. Performances of drama, music and dance are held here during the Athens Festival (p94).

★ Acropolis Museum   MUSEUM
(Map p68; ☑ 210 900 0901; www.theacropolismuseum.gr; Dionysiou Areopagitou 15, Makrygianni; adult/child €5/free; ⊙ 8am-4pm Mon, to 8pm Tue-Sun, to 10pm Fri Apr-Oct, 9am-5pm Mon-Thu, to 10pm Fri, 9am-8pm Sat & Sun Nov-Mar; Ⓜ Akropoli) This dazzling modernist museum at the foot of the Acropolis' southern slope showcases its surviving treasures still in Greek possession. While the collection covers the Archaic and Roman periods, the emphasis is on the Acropolis of the 5th century BC, considered the apotheosis of Greece's artistic achievement. The museum cleverly reveals layers of history, floating over ruins with the Acropolis visible above, showing the masterpieces in context. The surprisingly good-value

restaurant has superb views; there's also a fine museum shop.

Designed by US-based architect Bernard Tschumi with Greek architect Michael Photiadis, the €130-million museum includes items formerly held in other museums or in storage, as well as pieces returned from foreign museums.

As you enter the museum grounds, look through the plexiglass floor to see the ruins of an ancient Athenian neighbourhood, which were artfully incorporated into the museum design after being uncovered during excavations.

Finds from the slopes of the Acropolis are on display in the foyer gallery, which has an ascending glass floor emulating the climb up to the sacred hill, while allowing glimpses of the ruins below. Exhibits include painted vases and votive offerings from the sanctuaries where gods were worshipped, and more recent objects found in excavations of the settlement, including two clay statues of Nike at the entrance.

Bathed in natural light, the 1st-floor Archaic Gallery is a veritable forest of statues, mostly votive offerings to Athena. These include stunning examples of 6th-century *kore* (maidens) – statues of young women in draped clothing and elaborate braids, usually carrying a pomegranate, wreath or bird. Most were recovered from a pit on the Acropolis, where the Athenians buried them after the Battle of Salamis. The 570 BC statue of a youth bearing a calf is one of the rare male statues found. There are also bronze figurines and artefacts from temples predating the Parthenon (destroyed by the Persians), including wonderful pedimental sculptures such as Hercules slaying the Lernaian Hydra and a lioness devouring a bull. Also on this floor are five Caryatids, the maiden columns that held up the Erechtheion (the sixth is in the British Museum), and a giant floral *akrotirion* (a decorative element capping a gable) that once crowned the southern ridge of the Parthenon pediment.

The museum's crowning glory is the top-floor Parthenon Gallery, a glass atrium built in alignment with the temple, and a virtual replica of the cella of the Parthenon, which can be seen from the gallery. It showcases the temple's sculptures, metopes and 160m-long frieze, which for the first time in over 200 years is shown in sequence as one narrative about the Panathenaic Procession. The Procession starts at the southwest corner of the temple, with two groups splitting off and meeting on the east side for the delivery of the *peplos* to Athena. Interspersed between the golden-hued originals are stark-white plaster replicas of the missing pieces – the controversial Parthenon Marbles hacked off by Lord Elgin in 1801 and later sold to the British Museum (more than half the frieze is in London) – making a compelling case for their reunification. Don't miss the movie describing the history of the Acropolis.

★ Filopappou Hill   PARK
(Map p60; Ⓜ Akropoli) Also called the Hill of the Muses, Filopappou Hill – along with the Hills of the Pnyx and Nymphs – was, according to Plutarch, where Theseus and the Amazons did battle. Inhabited from prehistoric times to the post-Byzantine era, today the pine-clad slopes are a relaxing place for a stroll. They offer excellent views of Attica and the Saronic Gulf, well-signed ruins and some of the very best vantage points for photographing the Acropolis.

The hill, to the southwest of the Acropolis, is identifiable by the Monument of Filo-

---

FREE MUSEUMS

Museum of Greek Popular Instruments (Map p70; ☏ 210 325 4119; www.instruments-museum.gr; Diogenous 1-3, Plaka; ⊘ 8am-3pm Tue-Sun; Ⓜ Monastiraki) FREE Features displays and recordings of a wide selection of traditional instruments and costumes, including those of the great masters of Greek music. Concerts are held in the courtyard on weeknights in summer. Its restored *hammam* is one of the few surviving private Turkish baths in Athens.

Epigraphical Museum (Map p60; ☏ 210 821 7637; http://odysseus.culture.gr; Tositsa 1, Exarhia; ⊘ 8.30am-3pm Tue-Sun; Ⓜ Viktoria) FREE The most significant collection of Greek inscriptions on a veritable library of stone tablets; next to the National Archaeological Museum.

Centre of Folk Art & Tradition (Map p70; ☏ 210 324 3987; www.cityofathens.gr; Hatzimihali Angelikis 6, Plaka; ⊘ 9am-1pm & 5-9pm Tue-Fri, 9am-1pm Sat & Sun; Ⓜ Syntagma) FREE Stunning Plaka mansion with interesting periodic exhibitions.

pappos (Map p60) crowning its summit; it was built between AD 114 and 116 in honour of Julius Antiochus Filopappos, a prominent Roman consul and administrator. The paved path to the top starts near the *periptero* (kiosk) on Dionysiou Areopagitou. After 250m, it passes the excellent **Church of Agios Dimitrios Loumbardiaris** (Map p60), which contains fine frescoes, and continues past **Socrates' prison** (Map p60), the **Shrine of the Muses** (Map p60) and on up to the top.

In the 4th and 5th centuries BC, defensive **fortifications** – such as the Themistoclean wall and the Diateichisma – extended over the hill. You see their extensive remains today.

Areopagus Hill   PARK
(Map p70; M Monastiraki) This rocky outcrop below the Acropolis has great views over the Ancient Agora. According to mythology, it was here that Ares was tried by the council of the gods for the murder of Halirrhothios, son of Poseidon. The council accepted his defence of justifiable deicide on the grounds that he was protecting his daughter, Alcippe, from unwanted advances.

The hill became the place where murder, treason and corruption trials were heard before the Council of the Areopagus. In AD 51, St Paul delivered his famous 'Sermon to an Unknown God' from this hill and gained his first Athenian convert, Dionysos, who became patron saint of the city.

Hill of the Pnyx   PARK
(Map p80; M Thisio) North of Filopappou Hill, this rocky hill was the meeting place of the Democratic Assembly in the 5th century BC, where the great orators Aristides, Demosthenes, Pericles and Themistocles addressed assemblies. This less-visited site offers great views over Athens and a peaceful walk.

Hill of the Nymphs   PARK
(Map p80; M Thisio) Northwest of Hill of the Pnyx, this hill is home to the **old Athens observatory**, built in 1842.

★ **Temple of Olympian Zeus**   TEMPLE
(Olympieio; Map p68; ☏ 210 922 6330; http://odysseus.culture.gr; cnr Leoforos Vasilissis Olgas & Leoforos Vasilissis Amalias, Syntagma; adult/child €2/free, with Acropolis pass free; ⊙ 8am-8pm Apr-Oct, 8.30am-3pm Nov-Mar; M Akropoli, Syntagma) You can't miss this striking marvel smack in the centre of Athens. It is the largest temple in Greece; begun in the 6th century BC by Peisistratos, it was abandoned for lack of funds. Various other leaders had stabs at

completing it, but it was left to Hadrian to complete the work in AD 131 – taking more than 700 years in total to build.

The temple is impressive for the sheer size of its 104 Corinthian columns (17m high with a base diameter of 1.7m), of which 15 remain – the fallen column was blown down in a gale in 1852. Hadrian put a colossal statue of Zeus in the cella – and in typically immodest fashion, placed an equally large one of himself next to it.

★ **Hadrian's Arch**   MONUMENT
(Map p68; cnr Leoforos Vasilissis Olgas & Leoforos Vasilissis Amalias, Syntagma; M Akropoli, Syntagma) **FREE** The Roman emperor Hadrian had a great affection for Athens. Although he did his fair share of spiriting its classical artwork to Rome, he also embellished the city with many monuments influenced by classical architecture. His arch is a lofty monument of Pentelic marble that stands where busy Leoforos Vasilissis Olgas and Leoforos Vasilissis Amalias meet. Hadrian erected it in AD 132, probably to commemorate the consecration of the Temple of Olympian Zeus.

The inscriptions show that it was also intended as a dividing point between the ancient and Roman city. The northwest frieze reads, 'This is Athens, the Ancient city of Theseus', while the southeast frieze states, 'This is the city of Hadrian, and not of Theseus'.

★ **National Museum of
Contemporary Art**   MUSEUM
(☏ 210 924 2111; www.emst.gr; Kallirrois & Frantzi, Koukaki-Syngrou; adult/child €3/free; ⊙ 11am-7pm Tue, Wed & Fri-Sun, to 10pm Thu; M Syngrou-Fix) In 2015 this museum inaugurated spectacularly renovated quarters at the former Fix Brewery on Leoforos Syngrou. It shows top-notch rotating exhibitions of Greek and international contemporary art. Its permanent exhibitions include paintings, installations, photography, video and new media, as well as experimental architecture.

⊙ Syntagma, Plaka & Monastiraki

★ **Ancient Agora**   HISTORIC SITE
(Map p70; ☏ 210 321 0185; http://odysseus.culture.gr; Adrianou; adult/child €4/free, with Acropolis pass free; ⊙ 8am-8pm daily, reduced hours in low season; M Monastiraki) The heart of ancient Athens was the Agora, the lively, crowded focal point of administrative, commercial, political and social activity. Socrates expounded

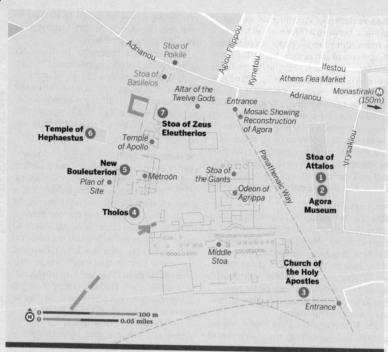

Stoa of
Poikile

Adrianou

Agiou Filippou

Kynetou

Ifestou
Athens Flea Market

Stoa of
Basileios

Adrianou

Monastiraki Ⓜ
(150m)

Altar of the
Twelve Gods

Entrance

Mosaic Showing
Reconstruction
of Agora

**Stoa of Zeus
Eleutherios** ❼

**Temple of
Hephaestus** ❻

Temple
of Apollo

**Stoa of
Attalos**

Vrysakiou

**New
Bouleuterion** ❺

Metroön

Stoa of
the Giants

Panathenaic Way

❶

❷

Plan of
Site

**Agora
Museum**

Odeon of
Agrippa

Tholos ❹

**Church of
the Holy
Apostles**

Middle
Stoa

❸

Entrance

Ⓝ 0 ┣━━━━━━┫ 100 m
0 ┣━━━━━━┫ 0.05 miles

Site Tour
Ancient Agora

LENGTH TWO HOURS

As you enter the Agora, make your way to the magnificent ❶ **Stoa of Attalos**. This two-storied stoa (covered walkway or portico), built by King Attalos II of Pergamum (159–138 BC), served as the first-ever shopping arcade. It has 45 Doric columns on the ground floor and Ionic columns on the upper. Originally, its facade was painted red and blue. People gathered here every four years to watch the Panathenaic Procession.

The excellent ❷ **Agora Museum**, inside the stoa, is a good place to make sense of the site. It holds a model of the Agora and many outstanding finds, and is surrounded by ancient statues of the gods.

Continue to the southern end of the site to the charming ❸ **Church of the Holy Apostles**, built in the early 10th century to commemorate St Paul's teaching in the Agora. Between 1954 and 1957 it was stripped of its 19th-century additions and restored to its original form. It contains fine Byzantine frescoes.

Heading northwest across the site, you'll pass the circular ❹ **Tholos**, where the heads of government met, and what was the ❺ **New Bouleuterion** (Council House), where the Senate met.

Go to the western edge of the Agora for the striking ❻ **Temple of Hephaestus**, the best-preserved Doric temple in Greece. Dedicated to Hephaestus, god of the forge, it was surrounded by foundries and metalwork shops. The temple, one of the first of Pericles' projects, was built in 449 BC by Iktinos, one of the Parthenon's architects. It has 34 columns and a frieze on the eastern side depicting nine of the Twelve Labours of Hercules. In AD 1300 it was converted into the Church of Agios Georgios. The last service held there was in 1834, in honour of King Otto's arrival in Athens.

To the northeast of the temple, you'll pass the foundation of the ❼ **Stoa of Zeus Eleutherios**, one of the places where Socrates expounded his philosophy.

his philosophy here, and in AD 49 St Paul came here to win converts to Christianity. The site today is a lush, refreshing respite, with beautiful monuments and temples and a fascinating **museum** (Map p70).

First developed as a public site in the 6th century BC, the Agora was devastated by the Persians in 480 BC, but a new one was built in its place almost immediately. It was flourishing by Pericles' time and continued to do so until AD 267, when it was destroyed by the Herulians, a Gothic tribe from Scandinavia. The Turks built a residential quarter on the site, but this was demolished by archaeologists after Independence and later excavated to classical and, in parts, Neolithic levels.

★ Roman Agora & Tower of the Winds   HISTORIC SITE

(Map p70; ☑210 324 5220; cnr Pelopida & Eolou, Monastiraki; adult/child €2/free, with Acropolis pass free; ☺8am-3pm; ⓜMonastiraki) The entrance to the Roman Agora is through the well-preserved **Gate of Athena Archegetis**, flanked by four Doric columns. It was financed by Julius Caesar and erected sometime during the 1st century AD. The well-preserved, extraordinary **Tower of the Winds** was built in the 1st century BC by Syrian astronomer Andronicus. The octagonal monument of Pentelic marble is an ingenious construction that functioned as a sundial, weathervane, water clock and compass.

Each side of the tower represents a point of the compass, with a relief of a floating figure representing the wind associated with each point. Beneath each of the reliefs are faint sundial markings. The weathervane, which disappeared long ago, was a bronze Triton that revolved on top of the tower. The Turks allowed dervishes to use the tower.

The rest of the ruins are quite bare. To the right of the entrance are foundations of a 1st-century public latrine. In the southeast area are foundations of a *propylon* (fortified tower) and a row of shops.

Hadrian's Library   RUIN

(Map p70; ☑210 324 9350; Areos 3, Monastiraki; adult/child €2/free, with Acropolis pass free; ☺8am-3pm, reduced hours in low season; ⓜMonastiraki) To the north of the Roman Agora is this vast 2nd-century-AD library, the largest structure erected by Hadrian. It included a cloistered courtyard bordered by 100 columns, and a pool in the centre. As well as books, the building housed music and lecture rooms and a theatre.

Athens Cathedral   CHURCH

(Map p70; ☑210 322 1308; Plateia Mitropoleos, Monastiraki; ☺7am-7pm, Mass Sun 6.30am; ⓜMonastiraki) The ornate 1862 Athens Cathedral on Plateia Mitropoleos (Mitropoleos Sq) is the seat of the archbishop of the Greek Orthodox Church of Athens. However, far more significant, both historically and architecturally, is the small, 12th-century, cruciform-style marble church next to the cathedral, known as the **Little Metropolis**, officially dedicated to two saints as the Church of Panagia Gorgeopikoos (Virgin Swift to Hear) and Agios Eleftherios. It was built on the ruins of an ancient temple using reliefs and pieces of ancient and early-Christian monuments.

Church of Kapnikarea   CHURCH

(Map p70; Ermou, Monastiraki; ☺8am-2pm Tue, Thu & Fri; ⓜMonastiraki, Syntagma) This small 11th-century structure stands smack in the middle of the Ermou shopping strip. It was saved from the bulldozers and restored by Athens University. Its dome is supported by four large Roman columns.

PANATHENAIC FESTIVAL & PROCESSION

The biggest event in ancient Athens was the Panathenaic Procession, the climax of the Panathenaic Festival held to venerate the goddess Athena. Colourful scenes of the Procession are depicted in the 160m-long Parthenon frieze in the Acropolis Museum.

There were actually two festivals. The Lesser Panathenaic Festival took place annually on Athena's birthday, but the Great Panathenaic Festival, which was held on every fourth anniversary of the goddess' birth, began with dancing, followed by athletic, dramatic and musical contests. On the final day, the Panathenaic Procession began at Keramikos, led by men carrying animals sacrificed to Athena, followed by maidens carrying *rhytons* (horn-shaped drinking vessels) and musicians playing a fanfare for the girls of noble birth who held the sacred *peplos* (a glorious saffron-coloured shawl). The Panathenaic Way, which cuts across the middle of the Acropolis, was the route taken by the procession. The *peplos* was placed on the statue of Athena Polias in the Erechtheion in the festival's grand finale.

1. Ceiling mosaics, Moni Dafniou 2. Frescoes, Moni Kaisarianis
3. Church of the Holy Apostles 4. Little Metropolis

Byzantine Athens

Under Byzantine rule, Christianity became the official religion of Athens; worship of 'pagan' Greek gods was outlawed. Notable Byzantine religious buildings can be found around Athens today; don't miss the outstanding Byzantine & Christian Museum.

Moni Dafniou

The area's most important Byzantine building is the World Heritage–listed 11th-century **Moni Dafniou** (210 581 1558; http://whc.unesco.org/en/list/537; 9am-2pm Tue & Fri) at Dafni, 10km northwest of Athens. It's a top example of Byzantine religious architecture, with a complex octagonal structure richly embellished with marble carvings. Part of a 6th-century wall from an earlier church (itself built atop an ancient temple) remains, as do elaborate mosaics.

Moni Kaisarianis

Nestled on the slopes of Mt Hymettos, 5km east of Athens, beautiful 11th-century **Moni Kaisarianis** (Monastery of Kaisariani; 210 723 6619; Mt Hymettos; adult/child €2/free; 8.30am-2.45pm Tue-Sun, grounds 8.30am-sunset Tue-Sun) is a peaceful walled sanctuary. The domed *katholikon* (main church), supported by four columns from an ancient temple, has well-preserved frescoes.

Church of the Holy Apostles

The charming Church of the Holy Apostles (p76), which stands near the Ancient Agora's southern entrance, was built in the early 10th century to commemorate St Paul's teaching in the Agora. It's one of the oldest in Athens.

Little Metropolis (Church of Agios Eleftherios)

This 12th-century cruciform-style church (p77), constructed partly of Pentelic marble and decorated with an external frieze of symbolic beasts, is considered one of Athens' finest. Built on the ruins of an ancient temple, it incorporates pieces of ancient and early Christian monuments and was once Athens' cathedral.

Gazi, Keramikos & Thisio

200 m
0.1 miles

PSYRRI

Museum of Islamic Art

KERAMIKOS

Archaeological Museum of Keramikos

Keramikos

Sacred & Dipylon Gates

Grand Promenade

Agios Athanasios Church

THISIO

Technopolis

Thisio Park

GAZI

VOTANIKOS

ROUF

Votanikos Kipos

Plateia Eleftherias (Koumoundourou)

Agion Asomaton

Plateia Agion Asomaton

Thisio

Plateia Thisiou

Areopagus Hill

Flammarion

Leof Konstantinoupoleos

Bath House of the Winds   MUSEUM

(Map p70; ☎210 324 4340; www.melt.gr; Kyrristou 8, Monastiraki; adult/child €2/free, Sun Nov-Mar free; ⊗8am-3pm Wed-Mon; MMonastiraki) This beautifully refurbished 17th-century *hammam* (Turkish bath) is the only surviving public bathhouse in Athens and one of the few remnants of Ottoman times. A helpful free audio tour takes you back to its glory days.

Kanellopoulos Museum   MUSEUM

(Map p70; ☎210 321 2313; http://odysseus.culture. gr; Theorias 12, cnr Panos, Plaka; admission €2; ⊗8am-3pm Tue-Sun, reduced hours low season; MMonastiraki) This excellent museum, in a 19th-century mansion on the northern slope of the Acropolis, houses the Kanellopoulos family's extensive collection, donated to the state in 1976. It includes jewellery, clay and stone vases and figurines, weapons, Byzantine icons, bronzes and objets d'art.

Agios Nikolaos Rangavas   CHURCH

(Map p70; ☎210 322 8193; Prytaniou 1, cnr Epiharmou, Plaka; ⊗8am-noon & 5-8pm; MAkropoli, Monastiraki) This lovely 11th-century church was part of the palace of the Rangavas family, who included Michael I, emperor of Byzantium. The church bell was the first installed in Athens after liberation from the Turks (who banned them), and was the first to ring in 1833 to announce the freedom of Athens.

Jewish Museum   MUSEUM

(Map p70; ☎210 322 5582; www.jewishmuseum.gr; Nikis 39, Plaka; adult/child €6/free; ⊗9am-2.30pm Mon-Fri, 10am-2pm Sun; MSyntagma) This museum traces the history of the Jewish community in Greece – back to the 3rd century BC – through an impressive collection of documents and religious and folk art. It includes a small reconstruction of a synagogue.

Church of Sotira Lykodimou   CHURCH

(Map p70; Fillelinon, Plateia Rallou Manou, Plaka; MSyntagma) Now the Russian Orthodox Cathedral, this unique 11th-century church, with an imposing dome, is the only octagonal Byzantine church.

Lysikrates Monument   MONUMENT

(Map p70; cnr Sellei & Lysikratous, Plaka; MAkropoli, Syntagma) The only surviving example of a choregic monument, Lysikrates Monument was built in 334 BC to commemorate the eponymous Lysikrates' sponsorship of a chorus that won in the dramatic contests of the Dionysia. It's the earliest-known monument using Corinthian capitals externally. The reliefs depict the battle between Dionysos and

Gazi, Keramikos & Thisio

the Tyrrhenian pirates, whom the god had transformed into dolphins.

It stands in what was once part of the Street of Tripods (Modern Tripodon), where winners of ancient dramatic and choral contests dedicated their tripod trophies to Dionysos. In the 18th century the monument was incorporated into the library of a French Capuchin convent, at which Lord Byron stayed in 1810–11 and wrote *Childe Harold*. The convent was destroyed by fire in 1890.

Plateia Syntagmatos
SQUARE
(Syntagma Sq; Map p70; MSyntagma) Athens' central square, Constitution Sq is named for the constitution granted, after uprisings, by King Otto on 3 September 1843. Today, the square serves as a major transport hub, the location of parliament (on the eastern, uphill side) and also, therefore, the epicentre of demonstrations and strikes.

Surrounded by high-end hotels and businesses, the square itself has a marble fountain, a metro entrance and two cafes, which are prime spots for people-watching. The western side of the square marks the beginning of one of Athens' main commercial districts, along pedestrianised Ermou.

★Parliament & Changing of the Guard
BUILDING
(Map p86; Plateia Syntagmatos; MSyntagma) FREE In front of the parliament building on Plateia Syntagmatos, the traditionally cos-

tumed *evzones* (guards) of the Tomb of the Unknown Soldier change every hour on the hour. On Sunday at 11am, a whole platoon marches down Vasilissis Sofias, accompanied by a band. The presidential guards' uniform of short kilts and pom-pom shoes is based on the attire worn by the *klephts* (mountain fighters of the War of Independence).

★National Gardens
GARDENS
(Map p86; cnr Leoforos Vasilissis Sofias & Leoforos Vasilissis Amalias, Syntagma; ⊙7am-dusk; MSyntagma) FREE A delightful, shady refuge during summer, the National Gardens were formerly the royal gardens, designed by Queen Amalia. There's a large children's **playground**, a duck pond and a shady cafe.

Zappeio Gardens
GARDENS
(Map p60; entrances on Leoforos Vasilissis Amalias & Leoforos Vasilissis Olgas, Syntagma; MSyntagma) These gardens sit between the National Gardens and the Panathenaic Stadium and are laid out in a network of wide walkways around the grand **Zappeio Palace**. The palace was built in the 1870s and hosts conferences and exhibitions. A pleasant cafe, restaurant and the open-air Aigli cinema (p111) are alongside the palace.

Roman Baths
RUIN
(Map p70; Leoforos Vasilissis Amalias, Syntagma; MSyntagma) FREE Excavation work to create a ventilation shaft for the metro uncovered the well-preserved ruins of a large Roman

bath complex. The baths, which extend into the National Gardens, were established near the Ilissos river after the Herulian raids in the 3rd century AD; they were destroyed and repaired again in the 5th or 6th century.

National Historical Museum MUSEUM
(Map p70; 210 323 7617; www.nhmuseum.gr; Stadiou 13, Syntagma; adult/child €3/free, Sun free; 9am-2pm Tue-Sun; Syntagma) Specialising in memorabilia from the War of Independence, this museum houses Byron's helmet and sword, a series of paintings depicting events leading up to the war and a collection of photographs and royal portraits. The museum is housed in the old parliament building, on the steps of which Prime Minister Theodoros Deligiannis was assassinated in 1905.

Church of Agii Theodori CHURCH
(Map p88; cnr Dragatsaniou & Agion Theodoron, Syntagma; Panepistimio) This 11th-century church behind Plateia Klafthmonos has a tiled dome and walls decorated with a pretty terracotta frieze of animals and plants.

Gazi, Keramikos & Thisio

Keramikos HISTORIC SITE
(Map p80; 210 346 3552; http://odysseus.culture.gr; Ermou 148, Keramikos; adult/child incl museum €2/free, with Acropolis pass free; 8am-8pm, reduced hours in low season; Thisio) A cemetery from the 3000 BC to the 6th century AD (Roman times), Keramikos was originally a settlement for potters who were attracted by the clay on the banks of the River Iridanos. Because of frequent flooding, the area was ultimately converted to a cemetery. Rediscovered in 1861 during the construction of Pireos street, Keramikos is now a lush, tranquil site with a small but excellent **museum** containing remarkable *stelae* (stone slabs) and sculptures, a good collection of vases and terracotta figurines.

Once inside, head for the small knoll ahead to the right, where you'll find a **plan of the site**. A path leads down to the right from the knoll to the remains of the **city wall** built by Themistocles in 479 BC, and rebuilt by Konon in 394 BC. The wall is broken by the foundations of two gates; tiny signs mark each one.

The first, the **Sacred Gate**, spanned the Sacred Way and was the one by which pilgrims from Eleusis entered the city during the annual Eleusian procession. To the northeast is the **Dipylon Gate** – the city's main entrance and where the Panathenaic

Procession (p77) began. It was also where the city's prostitutes gathered to offer their services to travellers. From a platform outside the Dipylon Gate, Pericles gave his famous speech extolling the virtues of Athens and honouring those who died in the first year of the Peloponnesian Wars.

Between the Sacred and Dipylon Gates are the foundations of the **Pompeion**, used as a dressing room for participants in the Panathenaic Procession.

Leading off the Sacred Way to the left as you head away from the city is the **Street of Tombs**. This avenue was reserved for the tombs of Athens' most prominent citizens. The surviving *stelae* are now in the National Archaeological Museum, so what you see are mostly replicas. The astonishing array of funerary monuments and their bas reliefs warrant close examination. Ordinary citizens were buried in the areas bordering the Street of Tombs. One well-preserved *stela* (up the stone steps on the northern side) shows a little girl with her pet dog. The site's largest *stela* is that of sisters Demetria and Pamphile.

Benaki Museum Pireos Annexe MUSEUM
(Map p80; 210 345 3111; www.benaki.gr; Pireos 138, cnr Andronikou, Rouf; admission €4-6; 10am-6pm Thu & Sun, to 10pm Fri & Sat, closed Aug; Keramikos) This massive Pireos annex of the fine Benaki Museum (p86) is housed in a former industrial building and hosts contemporary visual arts, cultural and historical exhibitions, major international shows, and musical performances in the courtyard. It has an airy cafe and excellent gift shop.

Herakleidon Museum MUSEUM
(Map p80; 210 346 1981; www.herakleidon-art.gr; Herakleidon 16, Thisio; adult/child €6/free; 10am-6pm Sun Jun, Jul, Sep & Oct; Thisio) This superb private museum showcases the interrelation of art, mathematics and philosophy. The permanent collection includes one of the world's biggest collections of MC Escher, as well as works from Victor Vasarely, in a beautifully restored neoclassical mansion. Extensive educational programs include excellent two-hour guided tour-seminars in English, available with advance booking (€25, minimum of 10 participants required).

Psyrri, Omonia & Exarhia

The jam-packed and thrilling streets around the Varvakios Agora (p103; Athens Central Market) are a must for any foodie – or lover of chaotic, aromatic capitalism.

★ **National Archaeological Museum** MUSEUM

(Map p60; ☏213 214 4800; www.namuseum.gr; 28 Oktovriou-Patision 44, Exarhia; adult/child €7/free; ☺8am-8pm Apr-Oct, reduced hours Nov-Mar; Ⓜ Viktoria, ☒2, 4, 5, 9 or 11 to Polytechnio) One of the world's most important museums, the National Archaeological Museum houses the world's finest collection of Greek antiquities. Treasures offering a view of Greek art and history – dating from the Neolithic era to classical periods – include exquisite sculptures, pottery, jewellery, frescoes and artefacts found throughout Greece. The beautifully presented exhibits are displayed mainly thematically. Allow plenty of time to view the vast and spectacular collections (over 11,000 items) housed in this enormous (8000-sq-metre) 19th-century neoclassical building.

It could take several visits to appreciate the museum's vast holdings, but it's possible to see the highlights in a half-day. The museum also hosts world-class temporary exhibitions.

In addition to the highlights, the museum has a superb pottery collection on its upper floor, which traces the development of pottery from the Bronze Age through Attic red-figured pottery (late 5th to early 4th centuries BC). Among the treasures are six Panathenaic amphorae presented to the winners of the Panathenaic Games. They contained oil from the sacred olive trees of Athens and victors might have received up to 140 of them.

A joint ticket with the Byzantine & Christian Museum (p87) and others costs €12. The museum is a 10-minute walk from Viktoria metro station, or catch trolleybus 2, 4, 5, 9 or 11 from outside St Denis Cathedral on Panepistimiou and get off at the Polytechnio stop.

★ **Museum of Islamic Art** MUSEUM

(Map p80; ☏210 325 1311; www.benaki.gr; Agion Asomaton 22 & Dipylou 12, Keramikos; adult/child €7/free, Thu free; ☺9am-5pm Thu-Sun; Ⓜ Thisio) This museum showcases one of the world's most significant collections of Islamic art. Housed in two restored neoclassical mansions near Keramikos, it exhibits more than 8000 items from the 12th to 19th centuries, including weavings, carvings, prayer rugs, tiles and ceramics. On the 3rd floor is a 17th-century reception room with an inlaid marble floor from a Cairo mansion. You can see part of the Themistoklean wall in the basement.

Museum of Greek Gastronomy MUSEUM

(Map p88; ☏210 321 1311; www.gastronomymuseum.gr; Agiou Dimitriou 13, Psyrri; ☺11am-6pm Tue,

---

🏃 Museum Tour
National Archaeological Museum

··

LENGTH TWO HOURS

··

Ahead of you as you enter the museum is the ❶ **Prehistoric collection**, showcasing some of the most important pieces of Mycenaean, Neolithic and Cycladic art, many in solid gold. The fabulous collection of ❷ **Mycenaean antiquities** (gallery 4) is the museum's tour de force. The first cabinet holds the celebrated gold ❸ **Mask of Agamemnon**, unearthed at Mycenae, and bronze daggers with intricate representations of the hunt. The exquisite ❹ **Vaphio gold cups**, with scenes of men taming wild bulls, are regarded as among the finest surviving examples of Mycenaean art.

The ❺ **Cycladic collection** (gallery 6) includes superb figurines of the 3rd and 2nd millennia BC, which inspired modern artists such as Picasso.

The galleries to the left of the entrance house the oldest, most significant pieces of the sculpture collection. The colossal, Naxian marble ❻ **Sounion Kouros** (room 8), carved in 600 BC, stood before Poseidon's temple in Sounion. Gallery 15 is dominated by the incredible 460 BC bronze ❼ **statue of Zeus or Poseidon**, found in the sea off Evia. It depicts one of the gods (no one really knows which) with his arms outstretched.

The 200 BC ❽ **statue of Athena Varvakeion** (gallery 20) is the most famous copy – much reduced in size – of the colossal statue of Athena Polias by Pheidias that once stood in the Parthenon.

In gallery 21 the striking ❾ **statue of horse and young rider** (2nd century BC), recovered from a shipwreck off Cape Artemision in Evia, stands opposite exquisite works such as the ❿ **statue of Aphrodite**.

Upstairs, the spectacular ⓫ **Minoan frescoes** from Santorini (Thira) were uncovered in the prehistoric settlement of Akrotiri, which was buried by a volcanic eruption in the late 16th century BC.

NATIONAL ARCHAEOLOGICAL MUSEUM

Cypriot Collection

Pottery Collection

Pottery Collection

Panathenaic Amphorae

Lift

Thira Gallery

Minoan Frescoes 11

First Floor

Stathatos Collection

Egyptian Gallery

Lift

Statue of Horse & Young Rider

Statue of Zeus or Poseidon 7

9

10 **Statue of Aphrodite**

4 **Vaphio Gold Cups**

Lift

Prehistoric Collection 1

8

Statue of Athena Varvakeion

2 **Mycenaean Antiquities**

Mask of Agamemnon 3

5 **Cycladic Collection**

Sounion Kouros 6

Ground Floor

Entrance

Lift

Cafe

Toilets

Museum Shop

Basement

Kolonaki

0 200 m
0 0.1 miles

to midnight Wed-Sun, restaurant 5pm-midnight Wed-Sun; MMonastiraki, Thisio) FREE This new museum and culinary centre creates specialised displays highlighting one aspect of Greece's rich culinary history (say, organic monastery food, or the traditions of Macedonia). The cafe-restaurant then serves up creative dishes (€7 to €15) tied to the exhibition, and the shop sells goods from each theme, whether it's Macedonian honey or monastery-made jam. It also has occasional cooking classes, film screenings and parties.

◎ Kolonaki & Around

★ Benaki Museum   MUSEUM
(Map p86; ☑210 367 1000; www.benaki.gr; Koumbari 1, cnr Leoforos Vasilissis Sofias, Kolonaki; adult/child €7/free, Thu free; ◎9am-5pm Wed & Fri, to midnight Thu & Sat, to 3pm Sun; MSyntagma, Evangelismos) Greece's finest private museum contains the vast collection of Antonis Benakis, accu-

mulated during 35 years of avid collecting in Europe and Asia. The collection includes Bronze Age finds from Mycenae and Thessaly; works by El Greco; ecclesiastical furniture brought from Asia Minor; pottery, copper, silver and woodwork from Egypt, Asia Minor and Mesopotamia; and a stunning collection of Greek regional costumes.

The museum has expanded into several branches, including the Pireos Annexe (p83), to house its vast and diverse collections and is a major player in the city's arts scene. It hosts a full schedule of rotating exhibitions.

★ Museum of Cycladic Art   MUSEUM
(Map p86; ☑210 722 8321; www.cycladic.gr; Neofytou Douka 4, cnr Leoforos Vasilissis Sofias, Kolonaki; adult/child €7/free, Mon half-price; ◎10am-5pm Mon, Wed, Fri & Sat, to 8pm Thu, 11am-5pm Sun; MEvangelismos) This exceptional private museum boasts the largest independent collection of distinctive Cycladic art and holds excellent periodic exhibitions. The 1st-floor

Kolonaki

Cycladic collection, dating from 3000 BC to 2000 BC, includes the marble figurines that inspired many 20th-century artists, such as Picasso and Modigliani, with their simplicity and purity of form. The rest of the museum features Greek and Cypriot art from 2000 BC to the 4th century AD. The 4th-floor exhibition, *Scenes from Daily Life in Antiquity,* includes artefacts and films depicting life in Ancient Greece. There's also a mod cafe.

★ **Byzantine & Christian Museum**   MUSEUM
(Map p86; ☎213 213 9500; www.byzantinemuseum.gr; Leoforos Vasilissis Sofias 22, Kolonaki; adult/child €4/free; �9am-8pm Apr-Oct, reduced hours Nov-Mar; MEvangelismos) This outstanding museum – on the grounds of former Villa Ilissia, an urban oasis – presents a priceless collection of Christian art from the 3rd to 20th centuries. Thematic snapshots of the Byzantine and post-Byzantine world are exceptionally presented in expansive, well-lit, multilevel galleries, clearly arranged chronologically with English translations. The collection includes icons, frescoes, sculptures, textiles, manuscripts, vestments and mosaics.

The villa grounds, which sit next to Aristotle's Lyceum (p87), include ancient ruins such as the Peisistratos aqueduct.

Aristotle's Lyceum   RUIN
(Map p86; cnr Rigillis & Leof Vasilissis Sofias; �9am-8pm Mon-Fri; MEvangelismos) FREE The Lyceum where Aristotle founded his school in 335 BC has opened to the public after years of archaeological work; admission to the site is free. The Lyceum, which used to lie outside the city walls, was a *gymnasium* where Aristotle taught rhetoric and philosophy. It was also known as a Peripatetic School, because teacher and pupils would walk as they talked.

Lykavittos Hill   LANDMARK
(Map p60; MEvangelismos) The name Lykavittos ('Hill of Wolves') derives from ancient times, when the hill was surrounded by countryside and its pine-covered slopes were inhabited by wolves. A path leads to the summit from the top of Loukianou for the finest panoramas of the city and the Attic basin – the *nefos* (pollution haze) permitting. Alternatively, take the **funicular railway** (teleferik; ☎210 721 0701; return €6; �9am-3am, runs every 30min) from the top of Ploutarhou in Kolonaki. Perched on the summit is the little **Chapel of Agios Giorgios**, floodlit like a beacon over the city at night.

Open-air **Lykavittos Theatre**, northeast of the summit, hosts concerts in summer.

Psyrri, Omonia & Exarhia

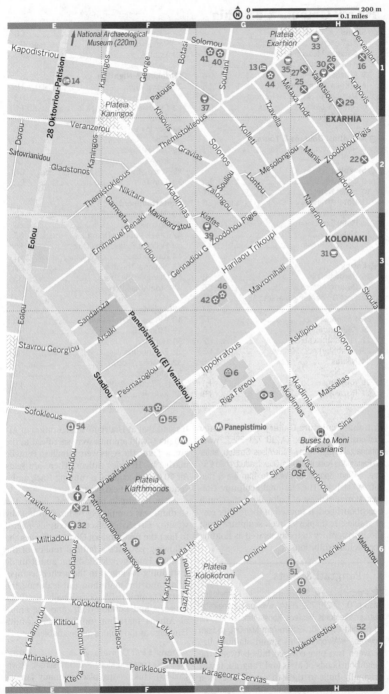

Psyrri, Omonia & Exarhia

National Sculpture Gallery MUSEUM
(National Glyptotheque; ☏210 723 5857; www.nationalgallery.gr; Army Park/Alsos Stratou, enter via Panagiotis Kanellopoulos, Goudi; adult/child €5/free; ⊙9am-8pm Mon & Wed, to 4pm Tue & Thu-Sat; M Katehaki) The National Sculpture Gallery, 4km northeast of Kolonaki in the Goudi neighbourhood, is housed in the former royal stables. It displays Greek sculpture from the 19th century to today, as well as holding occasional exhibitions.

◉ Pangrati & Mets

★ **Panathenaic Stadium** HISTORIC SITE
(Map p60; ☏210 752 2984; www.panathenaicstadium.gr; Leoforos Vasileos Konstantinou, Pangrati; adult/child €5/2.50; ⊙8am-7pm Mar-Oct, to 5pm Nov-Feb; M Akropoli) This grand stadium lies between two pine-covered hills between the neighbourhoods of Mets and Pangrati. It was originally built in the 4th century BC as a venue for the Panathenaic athletic contests.

It's said that at Hadrian's inauguration in AD 120, 1000 wild animals were sacrificed in the arena. Later, the seats were rebuilt in Pentelic marble by Herodes Atticus. There are seats for 70,000 spectators, a running track and a central area for field events.

After hundreds of years of disuse, the stadium was completely restored in 1895 by wealthy Greek benefactor Georgios Averof to host the first modern Olympic Games the following year. It's a faithful replica of the original Panathenaic Stadium, and it made a stunning backdrop to the archery competition and the marathon finish during the 2004 Olympics. It's occasionally used for concerts and public events, and the annual Athens marathon finishes here. Multi-language audio guides are available.

Athens' First Cemetery CEMETERY
(Map p60; Longinou, Mets; ⊙7.30am-sunset; M Syngrou-Fix) This resting place of many famous Greeks and philhellenes is a peaceful spot to

explore. Famous names include the archaeologist Heinrich Schliemann (1822–90), whose mausoleum is decorated with scenes from the Trojan War. Most of the tombstones and mausoleums are lavish in the extreme. Works of art include Halepas' *Sleeping Maiden* sculpture, set on the tomb of a young girl.

Activities

Planet Blue Dive Centre   DIVING
(☑ 210 418 0174; www.planetblue.gr; Velpex Factory, Lavrio; PADI certification from €300, dives €35-80) Popular with seasoned divers, but caters to all levels at sites around Cape Sounion.

ARTS EXPLOSION

Recent years have brought a burgeoning of the arts scene in Athens. Even as the city struggles with other aspects of political or social life, Greece's musicians, performing artists and visual artists remain hard at work and a new breed of multi-use gallery has sprung up to host all of the disciplines. Some feel like museums, others more like nightclubs – and for others it just depends on the time of day. One of the most anticipated sites, the **Stavros Niarchos Foundation Cultural Center** (www.snfcc.org), designed by Renzo Piano, is being erected 4.5km south of the city centre and will also hold the National Library and the National Opera, and have a large park.

Theocharakis Foundation for the Fine Arts & Music (Map p86; ☑ 210 361 1206; www.thf.gr; Leoforos Vasilissis Sofias 9, Kolonaki; adult/child €6/free; ⊙ 10am-6pm Mon-Wed & Fri-Sun, to 8pm Thu, closed Aug; M Syntagma) This excellent centre has three levels of exhibition space featuring local and international 20th- and 21st-century artists, a theatre, an art shop and a pleasant cafe. Music performances are held between September and May.

Taf (The Art Foundation; Map p70; ☑ 210 323 8757; www.theartfoundation.gr; Normanou 5, Monastiraki; ⊙ noon-9pm Mon-Sat, to 7pm Sun; M Monastiraki) The central courtyard cafe at Taf, surrounded by crumbling 1870s brick buildings, fills with an eclectic young crowd. The rest functions as an art, music and theatre space where performances and screenings are often free.

Onassis Cultural Centre (☑ 210 900 5800; www.sgt.gr; Leoforos Syngrou 107-109, Neos Kosmos; M Syngrou-Fix) The multi-million-euro visual and performing-arts centre hosts big-name productions and installations. It's 1.5km southwest of the Syngrou-Fix metro station.

Six DOGS (Map p70; ☑ 210 321 0510; www.sixdogs.gr; Avramiotou 6, Monastiraki; ⊙ 10am-late; M Monastiraki) Six degrees of separation, indeed. The rustic rear-garden courtyard here is the place for quiet chats with coffee and drinks, while the bar jams the lane to the front at night. Has theatre and art too.

Bios (Map p80; ☑ 210 342 5335; www.bios.gr; Pireos 84, Gazi; ⊙ 11am-late; M Thisio) In an industrial Bauhaus building near Gazi, this avant-garde multilevel warren has a bar, live performances, art and new-media exhibitions, a basement club, a tiny art-house cinema and a roof garden.

Technopolis (Map p80; ☑ 210 346 7322; www.technopolis-athens.com; Pireos 100, Gazi; M Keramikos) The superbly converted Athens gasworks complex presents multimedia exhibitions, concerts and special events.

Art Events

Art-Athina (www.art-athina.gr) Athens' annual three-day, international contemporary-art fair at the massive Hellexpo centre in May showcases a broad spectrum of art from Greek and international galleries, including sculpture and installations. Satellite exhibitions are also held in other venues.

Athens Biennale (☑ 210 523 2222; www.athensbiennial.org) Every two years from June to October, the Athens Biennial showcases top local and international artists.

ReMap (www.remapkm.com) This festival runs parallel to the Athens Bienniale, exhibiting more alternative shows around town.

Documenta 14 (www.documenta.de) The 2017 presentation of Documenta 14 will take place in both Kassel, Germany (as usual) as well as in Athens. It features elaborate, site-specific pieces for 100 days.

Solebike   BICYCLE RENTAL

(Map p68; ☑ 210 921 5620; www.solebike.eu; Lembesi 11, Makrygianni; 10hr from €20; ⊙ 9am-3pm Mon-Sat, also 6-8.30pm Tue, Thu & Fri; Ⓜ Akropoli) Solebike hires out electric bikes, and offers tours (from €36).

Funky Rides   BICYCLE RENTAL

(Map p68; ☑ 211 710 9366; www.funkyride.gr; Dimitrakopoulou 1, Koukaki; 3hr/day €7/15; Ⓜ Akropoli) Funky Rides rents bikes near the Acropolis.

🐟 Courses

Athens Centre   LANGUAGE

(Map p60; ☑ 210 701 2268; www.athenscentre.gr; Arhimidous 48, Mets; Ⓜ Akropoli) Top-notch modern Greek language classes (€350 to €650) and summer workshops (two weeks €1280).

Hellenic American Union   LANGUAGE

(Map p86; ☑ 210 368 0900; www.hau.gr; Massalias 22, Kolonaki; Ⓜ Panepistimio) Modern Greek and conversational courses are offered during the academic year (€1300) or in month-long intensive summer courses (€460).

Hellenic Culture Centre   LANGUAGE

(Map p88; ☑ 210 523 8149; www.hcc.edu.gr; Halkokondyli 50, Omonia; Ⓜ Omonia) Private (per hour €30) or group (per hour €22 to €30) Greek lessons and online courses. Also has a branch in Santorini.

☞ Tours

Three main companies run almost identical air-conditioned city coach tours, as well as excursions to nearby sights: **CHAT** (Map p70; ☑ 210 323 0827; www.chatours.gr; Xenofontos 9, Syntagma; Ⓜ Syntagma), **GO Tours** (Map p68; ☑ 210 921 9555; www.gotours.com.gr; Kallirrois 12, Makrygianni; Ⓜ Akropoli) and **Hop In Sightseeing** (Map p70; ☑ 210 428 5500; www.hopin.com; Leoforos Vasilissis Amalias 44, Makrygianni; ⊙ 6.30am-10pm; Ⓜ Akropoli).

Tours include a half-day sightseeing tour of Athens (from €68), usually doing little more than pointing out all the major sights and stopping at the Acropolis. There are also half-day trips to Ancient Corinth (€58) and Cape Sounion (€43); day tours to Delphi (€86), the Corinth Canal, Mycenae, Nafplio and Epidavros (€86); and cruises to Aegina, Poros and Hydra (including lunch €99). Hotels act as booking agents and often offer discounts.

CitySightseeing Athens   BUS TOUR

(Map p70; ☑ 210 921 4174; www.city-sightseeing.com; Plateia Syntagmatos, Syntagma; adult/child €18/8; ⊙ every 30min 9am-9pm Apr-Oct,

🚶 Walking Tour
Central Athens

START SYNTAGMA
END MONASTIRAKI FLEA MARKET
LENGTH 3.5KM; TWO HOURS

Start in ❶ **Plateia Syntagmatos** (p82). The square has been a favourite place for protests ever since the rally that led to the granting of a constitution on 3 September 1843, as declared by King Otto from the balcony of the royal palace (now Parliament). In 1944 the first round of the civil war began here after police opened fire on a communist rally, while in 1954 it was the location of the first demonstration demanding the *enosis* (union) of Cyprus with Greece.

The historic Hotel Grande Bretagne, the most illustrious of Athens' hotels, was built in 1862. The Nazis made it their headquarters during WWII, and in 1944 the hotel was the scene of an attempt to blow up Winston Churchill.

Left of the metro entrance is a section of the ❷ **Peisistratos aqueduct**, which was unearthed during excavations.

In front of ❸ **Parliament** (p82), the *evzones* (the presidential guards) stand sentinel at the Tomb of the Unknown Soldier. The changing of the guard takes place every hour on the hour.

Walk through the lush ❹ **National Gardens** (p82) and exit to the Zappeio Palace, which was used as the Olympic village in 2004. Pass the playground and go left until you see the crossing to the ❺ **Panathenaic Stadium** (p90), where the first modern Olympic Games were held in 1896.

Walk back along the gardens to the striking ❻ **Temple of Olympian Zeus** (p75), the largest temple ever built. Teetering on the edge of the traffic alongside the temple is ❼ **Hadrian's Arch** (p75), the ornate gateway erected to mark the boundary of Hadrian's Athens.

Cross Leoforos Vasilissis Amalias and head right towards Lysikratous, where you turn left into Plaka. Ahead on your right are the ruins of a Roman monument in the forecourt of the ❽ **Church of Agia Ekaterini**.

Continue to the **9 Lysikrates Monument** (p81). Built in 334 BC to commemorate a win in a choral festival, it's the earliest-known monument using Corinthian capitals externally.

Facing the monument, turn left and then right into Epimenidou. At the top of the steps, turn right into Stratonos, which skirts the Acropolis. Just ahead you'll see the **10 Church of St George of the Rock**, which marks the entry to the **11 Anafiotika quarter**. The picturesque maze of little whitewashed houses is the legacy of stonemasons from the small Cycladic island of Anafi, who were brought in to build the king's palace after Independence. It's a peaceful spot, with brightly painted olive-oil cans brimming with flowers in the tiny gardens in summer.

Continue past the tiny **12 Church of Agios Simeon**. It looks like a dead end but persevere and you'll emerge at the Acropolis road. Turn right and then left into Prytaniou, veering right after 50m into Tholou. The yellow-ochre building at Tholou 5 is the **13 old Athens University**, built by the Venetians; the Turks used it as public offices and it housed Athens University from 1837 to 1841.

Continue down to the ruins of the **14 Roman Agora** (p77). To the right of the Tower of the Winds on Kyrristou is the **15 Bath House of the Winds** (p81). Meanwhile, the **16 Museum of Greek Popular Instruments** (p74), on Diogenous, has one of Athens' only remaining private *hammams* in its gift shop. Turning onto Pelopida, you'll see the gate of the Muslim Seminary, built in 1721 and destroyed in a fire in 1911, and the **17 Fethiye Mosque**, on the site of the Agora.

Follow the road around the Agora to the ruins of **18 Hadrian's Library** (p77). Next to them is the **19 Museum of Traditional Greek Ceramics**, housed in the 1759 Mosque of Tzistarakis; after Independence it lost its minaret and was used as a prison.

You're now in Monastiraki, the colourful, chaotic square teeming with street vendors. To the left is **20 Monastiraki Flea Market** (p111).

to 6.30pm Nov-Mar; Ⓜ Syntagma) Open-top double-decker buses cruise around town on a 90-minute circuit starting at Syntagma. A 70-minute circuit goes to Piraeus (adult/child €22/9). You can get on and off at 15 stops on a 48-hour ticket.

Trekking Hellas
OUTDOORS

(☎210 331 0323; www.trekking.gr; Gounari 96, Marousi) Array of activities tours range from Athens walking tours (€50) to caving, cycling, or trekking in the Peloponnese and the islands.

Athens: Adventures
GUIDED TOUR

(Map p68; ☎210 922 4044; www.athensadventures.gr) Based at Athens Backpackers (p95); offers a €6 Athens walking tour and day trips to Nafplio, Delphi and Sounio.

This Is My Athens
GUIDED TOUR

(http://myathens.thisisathens.org) This volunteer program pairs you with a local to show you around for two hours. You must book online 72 hours ahead.

Alternative Athens
GUIDED TOUR

(☎6948405242; www.alternative-athens.com) Runs experience-based tours and workshops

to get you off the beaten path – from food to street art and bar-hopping.

Athens Segway Tours
GUIDED TOUR

(Map p68; ☎210 322 2500; www.athenssegway-tours.com; Eschinou 9, Plaka; 2hr tour €59; Ⓜ Akropoli) Zip through town on a Segway.

Athens Happy Train
TOUR

(Map p70; ☎213 039 0888; www.athenshappy-train.com; Plateia Syntagmatos, Syntagma; adult/child €6/4; ⊙every 30min 9am-11pm Jun-Sep, to 9pm Oct-May; Ⓜ Syntagma) Stops include the Acropolis, Monastiraki and the Panathenaic Stadium. Tours take one hour if you don't get off, or else you can get on and off over five hours. Trains leave from the top of Ermou every 30 minutes.

🎎 Festivals & Events

★ Hellenic Festival
PERFORMING ARTS

(Athens & Epidavros Festival; www.greekfestival.gr; ⊙Jun-Aug) The ancient theatre at Epidavros and Athens' Odeon of Herodes Atticus are the headline venues of Greece's annual cultural festival featuring a top line-up of local and international music, dance and theatre.

ART GALLERIES

Get a list of galleries and art spaces at www.athensartmap.net; alternatively, pick up an Athens Contemporary Art Map at galleries and cafes around town.

AD Gallery (Map p88; ☎210 322 8785; www.adgallery.gr; Pallados 3, Psyrri; ⊙noon-9pm Tue-Fri, to 4pm Sat, closed Aug; Ⓜ Monastiraki) Contemporary Greek artists in the heart of the city.

CAN (Map p86; ☎210 339 0833; www.can-gallery.com; Anagnostopoulou 42, Kolonaki; ⊙11am-3pm & 5-8pm Tue-Fri, to 4pm Sat, closed Aug; Ⓜ Syntagma) The brainchild of Christina Androulidaki, this recent entry on the Kolonaki gallery scene is building a stable of emerging contemporary Greek artists.

Bernier/Eliades (Map p80; ☎210 341 3935; www.bernier-eliades.gr; Eptachalkou 11, Thisio; ⊙10.30am-6.30pm Tue-Fri, noon-4pm Sat; Ⓜ Thisio) This well-established gallery showcases prominent Greek artists and an impressive list of international artists, from abstract American impressionists to British pop.

Qbox Gallery (Map p88; ☎211 119 9991; www.qbox.gr; Armodiou 10, Monastiraki; ⊙noon-6pm Tue-Fri, to 4pm Sat; Ⓜ Omonia, Monastiraki) Myrtia Nikolakopoulou directs this gallery, which promotes young, emerging local and visiting artists on the international scene. Great for a taste of Greece's cutting edge.

Andreas Melas & Helena Papadopoulos Gallery (Map p88; ☎210 325 1881; www.melaspapadopoulos.com; Epikourou 26, cnr Korinis, Psyrri; ⊙noon-6pm Tue-Fri, to 4pm Sat; Ⓜ Omonia, Monastiraki) Formerly the AMP Gallery, this new venture merges the efforts of two of Athens' contemporary-art powerhouses, and promotes emerging local and international artists.

Medusa Art Gallery (Map p86; ☎210 724 4552; www.medusaartgallery.com; Xenokratous 7, Kolonaki; ⊙11am-2.30pm & 6.30-9.30pm Tue-Fri, closed Aug; Ⓜ Evangelismos) For over 30 years this Kolonaki stalwart has shown excellent Greek contemporary painting, sculpture, installations and photography.

Major shows in its **Athens Festival** take place at the superb Odeon of Herodes Atticus (p73), one of the world's prime historic venues, with the floodlit Acropolis as a backdrop. Events are also held in modern venues around town. Its **Epidavros Festival** presents local and international productions of Ancient Greek drama at the famous ancient Theatre of Epidavros (p144) in the Peloponnese, two hours west of Athens, on Friday and Saturday nights in July and August. Check the festival website for special KTEL buses to Epidavros. Book tickets online, by phone, at the **Hellenic Festival box office** (Map p88; ☑ 210 327 2000; Arcade, Panepistimou 39, Syntagma; ⊙ 9am-5pm Mon-Fri, to 3pm Sat), or at Public and Papasotiriou stores. Though available at theatre box offices, queues at performances can be very long or may be sold out. Half-price student discounts (with ID) are available for most performances.

Athens Technopolis Jazz Festival　MUSIC
(www.technopolisjazzfestival.com; ⊙ late May-early Jun) Jazz festival at the converted gasworks in Gazi.

Rockwave Festival　MUSIC
(☑210 882 0426; www.rockwavefestival.gr; ⊙ late May-Jul) Annual international rock show at Terra Vibe, a parkland venue on the outskirts of Athens in Malakassa. Special buses from town. Cheap camping sometimes offered.

August Moon Festival　PERFORMING ARTS
(⊙Aug) Every August on the night of the full moon, musical performances are held at key historic venues, including the Acropolis, the Roman Agora and other sites around Greece.

Athens International Film Festival　FILM
(☑ 210 606 1413; www.aiff.gr; ⊙ Sep) Features retrospectives, premieres and international art films and documentaries.

🛌 Sleeping

Athens has a full range of options, though service may not always be up to expectations. Plaka is most popular with travellers. High-end hotels cluster around Syntagma. Some excellent smaller hotels dot the quiet neighbourhoods of Makrygianni and Koukaki. Around Omonia some hotels have been upgraded, but there is still a seediness (think drugs and prostitution), especially at night.

Book ahead in July and August. Prices quoted are for high season; you'll find considerable discounts in low season, for longer stays and online. Nonsmoking rules are often laxly enforced, if at all.

You can also book ahead for a superbly renovated, spacious apartment – or a whole house – through **Boutique Athens** (☑6985083556; www.boutiqueathens.com; 1-/2-/4-bedroom apt from €80/140/430, min 2-night stay; ✲🛜), with locations all over town.

The *Camping in Greece* booklet, produced by the EOT (Greek National Tourist Organisation), and www.travelling.gr list sites in the Attica region. Most camping grounds near Athens offer basic facilities and are not generally up to European standards. If you must, try the closest, **Athens Camping** (☑ 210 581 4114; www.campingathens.com.gr; Leoforos Athinon 198, Haidari; camp sites per adult/tent/car €8.50/5/4; ⊙ year-round; 🛜), 7km west of the city centre on the road to Corinth. Better camping options are further afield, at Shinias and Cape Sounion.

🛌 Akropoli, Makrygianni & Koukaki

★**Athens Backpackers**　HOSTEL €
(Map p68; ☑ 210 922 4044; www.backpackers.gr; Makri 12, Makrygianni; dm incl breakfast €24-29, 2-/4-/6-person apt from €100/130/160; ✲@🛜; Ⓜ Akropoli) The popular rooftop bar with cheap drinks and Acropolis views is a major drawcard for this modern and friendly Australian-run backpacker favourite. There's a barbecue in the courtyard, a well-stocked kitchen and a busy social scene. Spotless dorms with private bathrooms and lockers have bedding, but towel use costs €2. Management also runs well-priced Athens Studios (p96), with modern apartments nearby.

Art Gallery Hotel　PENSION €
(Map p68; ☑ 210 923 8376; www.artgalleryhotel.gr; Erehthiou 5, Koukaki; s/d/tr/q from €50/60/70/80; ✲🛜; Ⓜ Syngrou-Fix) Staying in this quaint, family-run place feels like staying in a home. Original furniture from the 1960s decorates the communal areas. Some rooms are a little small, but the upstairs balcony has a bit of an Acropolis view. A few cheaper rooms have shared bathrooms.

Marble House Pension　PENSION €
(☑ 210 923 4058; www.marblehouse.gr; Zini 35a, Koukaki; s/d/tr €35/45/55, d/tr/q with shared bathroom €40/50/65; ✲@🛜; Ⓜ Syngrou-Fix) Tucked into a quiet cul-de-sac is one of Athens' best-value budget hotels. Rooms have been artfully updated, with wrought-iron beds, and bathrooms are sleek marble. All rooms have a fridge and ceiling fans, and

some have air-con (€9 extra). It's a fair walk from the tourist drag, but close to the metro.

★Herodion
HOTEL €€

(Map p68; ☎210 923 6832; www.herodion.com; Rovertou Galli 4, Makrygianni; d incl breakfast from €144; ✳@🐾; ⓂAkropoli) This smart four-star hotel is geared towards the well-heeled and business travellers. Rooms are small but have all the trimmings and have super-comfortable beds. The rooftop spa and lounge have unbeatable Acropolis and museum views.

★Hera Hotel
BOUTIQUE HOTEL €€

(Map p68; ☎210 923 6682; www.herahotel.gr; Falirou 9, Makrygianni; d incl breakfast €130-145, ste €250; ✳@🐾; ⓂAkropoli) This elegant boutique hotel, a short walk from the Acropolis and Plaka, was totally rebuilt – but the formal interior design is in keeping with the lovely neoclassical facade. There's lots of brass and timber, and stylish classic furnishings. The rooftop garden, restaurant and bar have spectacular views.

Philippos Hotel
HOTEL €€

(Map p68; ☎210 922 3611; www.philipposhotel.com; Mitseon 3, Makrygianni; d incl breakfast from €105; ✳@🐾; ⓂAkropoli) A popular favourite, Philippos offers small, well-appointed rooms near the Acropolis. The double on the roof has a private terrace.

Hotel Tony
STUDIOS €€

(Map p60; ☎210 923 0561; www.hoteltony.gr; Zaharitsa 26, Koukaki; studios €70-115; ✳@🐾; ⓂSyngrou-Fix) After a total renovation in 2015, Hotel Tony now offers spacious, clean and modern studios, all with a kitchenette. The family rooms are particularly well configured: the 'superior family room' has three balconies. Great bathrooms boast walk-in showers and sleek tile all around. It's about 1km southwest of the Acropolis.

Athens Studios
APARTMENT €€

(Map p68; ☎210 923 5811; www.athensstudios.gr; Veikou 3a, Makrygianni; apt incl breakfast €80-120; @🐾; ⓂAkropoli) Run by the folk from Athens Backpackers (p95), these relaxed apartments are spacious, with kitchenettes, colourful bathrooms and a lounge area with shared balcony. The bedroom has either two beds or four bunks, making it a well-priced alternative to dormitory living.

Athens Gate
BUSINESS HOTEL €€€

(Map p68; ☎210 923 8302; www.athensgate.gr; Leoforos Syngrou Andrea 10, Makrygianni; d incl breakfast €160-185; ✳@🐾; ⓂAkropoli) With

stunning views over the Temple of Olympian Zeus from the spacious front rooms, and a central (if busy) location, this totally refurbished hotel is a great find. The chic, stylish rooms are immaculate and have all the mod cons; staff are friendly and breakfast is served on the superb rooftop terrace with 360-degree Athens views.

Athens Was
BOUTIQUE HOTEL €€€

(Map p68; ☎210 924 9954; www.athenswas.gr; Dionysiou Areopagitou 31-39; d €180-220, ste €320; ✳@🐾; ⓂAkropoli) The location at the foot of the Acropolis couldn't be better at this new hotel with boutique airs. Simple, small rooms with dark, modern decor mean it's much less luxe than you'd expect for its price, but it's clean and easy, with welcoming staff. Suites on the 5th and 6th floor have Acropolis views.

🛏 Syntagma, Plaka & Monastiraki

Hotel Phaedra
HOTEL €

(Map p70; ☎210 323 8461; www.hotelphaedra.com; Herefontos 16, Plaka; s/d/tr from €60/70/95; ✳@🐾; ⓂAkropoli) Many rooms at this small, family-run hotel have balconies overlooking a church or the Acropolis. The hotel is tastefully furnished, though rooms vary from small to snug. Some rooms have private bathrooms across the hall (double/triple €65/75). A great rooftop terrace, friendly staff and a good location make this one of the better deals in Plaka.

Hotel Cecil
HOTEL €

(Map p88; ☎210 321 7079; www.cecilhotel.gr; Athinas 39, Monastiraki; s/d/tr/q incl breakfast from €60/75/120/155; ✳@🐾; ⓂMonastiraki) This charming old hotel on busy Athinas has beautiful high, moulded ceilings, polished timber floors and an original cage-style lift. The simple rooms are tastefully furnished, but don't have fridges. Two connecting rooms with a shared bathroom are ideal for families.

Tempi Hotel
HOTEL €

(Map p70; ☎210 321 3175; www.tempihotel.gr; Eolou 29, Monastiraki; d/tr €57/67, s/d with shared bathroom €38/50; ✳🐾; ⓂMonastiraki) Location and affordability are the strengths of this older, family-run place on pedestrian Eolou. Front balconies overlook Plateia Agia Irini, the scene of some of Athens' best nightlife; side views get the Acropolis. Basic rooms have satellite TV, but bathrooms are primitive. Top-floor rooms are small and quite a hike. There is a communal kitchen.

Arethusa Hotel
HOTEL €

(Map p70; ☑ 210 322 9431; www.arethusahotel.gr; Mitropoleos 6, cnr Nikis, Syntagma; s/d incl breakfast €50/68; ☀; Ⓜ Syntagma) Arethusa is a basic, central choice.

Student & Travellers' Inn
HOSTEL €

(Map p70; ☑ 210 324 4808; www.studenttravellers inn.com; Kydathineon 16, Plaka; dm €20-25, s/d/ tr €57/73/90, without bathroom from €47/52/79; ☀@☀; Ⓜ Syntagma) Its location in the heart of Plaka makes this long-established hostel popular with visitors of all ages. There's a mix of very basic dorms and rooms, some with private bathroom and air-conditioning, though shared bathrooms are run down and complaints about cleanliness are common. It's got a pleasant, shady courtyard and a helpful travel service.

Sweet Home Hotel
BOUTIQUE HOTEL €€

(Map p70; ☑ 210 322 9029; www.thesweethome-hotel.com; Patroou 5, Plaka; d from €140; ☀@☀; Ⓜ Syntagma) This small, boutique hotel is just a stone's throw from all the major Athens sights, and offers 15 cosy, well-decorated rooms, flat-screen TVs, modern bathrooms and organic bath products.

Central Hotel
BUSINESS HOTEL €€

(Map p70; ☑ 210 323 4357; www.centralhotel. gr; Apollonos 21, Plaka; d/tr incl breakfast from €125/150; ☀@☀; Ⓜ Syntagma) This stylish hotel has been tastefully decorated in light, contemporary tones. It has comfortable rooms with all the mod cons and good bathrooms. There is a lovely roof terrace with Acropolis views, a small spa and sun lounges. As its name suggests, Central Hotel is in a great location between Syntagma and Plaka.

A for Athens
HOTEL €€

(Map p70; ☑ 210 324 4244; www.aforathens.com; Miaouli 2, Monastiraki; d from €150; ☀☀; Ⓜ Monastiraki) Modern but simple, this makes a good central base above Monastiraki's central square. The rooftop cafe-bar is grand, with sweeping 360-degree views that take in the Acropolis (as do some of the rooms).

Hotel Adonis
HOTEL €€

(Map p70; ☑ 210 324 9737; www.hotel-adonis.gr; 3 Kodrou St, Plaka; s/d/tr incl breakfast €70/88/105; ☀@☀; Ⓜ Syntagma) This comfortable pension on a quiet pedestrian street in Plaka has basic, clean rooms with TVs. Bathrooms are small but have been excellently renovated. Take in great Acropolis views from 4th-floor rooms and the rooftop terrace (where breakfast is served). No credit cards.

Hotel Hermes
HOTEL €€

(Map p70; ☑ 210 323 5514; www.hermeshotel.gr; Apollonos 19, Plaka; d/q incl breakfast €130/205; ☀@☀; Ⓜ Syntagma) Hermes offers modern amenities with snug but comfortable rooms, including two interconnecting rooms for families.

Plaka Hotel
HOTEL €€

(Map p70; ☑ 210 322 2096; www.plakahotel.gr; Kapnikareas 7, cnr Mitropoleos, Monastiraki; d incl breakfast €145-200; ☀☀; Ⓜ Monastiraki) It's hard to beat the Acropolis views from the rooftop garden, as well as those from top-floor rooms. Tidy rooms have light timber floors and furniture, and satellite TV, though bathrooms are on the small side. Though called the Plaka Hotel, it's actually closer to Monastiraki.

Adrian Hotel
HOTEL €€

(Map p70; ☑ 210 322 1553; www.douros-hotels. com; Adrianou 74, Plaka; s/d/tr incl breakfast from €95/120/140; ☀@☀; Ⓜ Monastiraki) This tiny hotel right in the heart of Plaka serves breakfast on a lovely shady terrace with Acropolis views. The well-equipped rooms are pleasant, if a bit worn. Third-floor rooms are the best, with large balconies overlooking the square.

Niki Hotel
HOTEL €€

(Map p70; ☑ 210 322 0913; www.nikihotel.gr; Nikis 27, Syntagma; d incl breakfast from €87; ☀@☀; Ⓜ Syntagma) This small hotel bordering Plaka has contemporary design and furnishings. The rooms are well appointed and there's a two-level suite for families (€180), with balconies offering Acropolis views.

Athens Cypria Hotel
HOTEL €€

(Map p70; ☑ 210 323 8034; www.athenscypria. com; Diomias 5, Syntagma; s/d incl breakfast €81/98; ☀@☀; Ⓜ Syntagma) Tucked in a side street off Ermou, this small, family-friendly hotel is a little characterless, but it is modern and comfortable, with good facilities and a very handy location. Some rooms have balconies but no great view. There are family rooms too (from €170).

Acropolis House Pension
PENSION €€

(Map p70; ☑ 210 322 2344; www.acropolishouse. gr; Kodrou 6-8, Plaka; d/tr/q incl breakfast from €83/119/149; ☀☀; Ⓜ Syntagma) This atmospheric, family-run pension is in a beautifully preserved, 19th-century house, which retains many original features and has lovely painted walls. There are discounts for stays of three days or more. Some rooms have private bathrooms across the hall.

ℹ AIRPORT HOTELS

If you need to catch an early flight, there are only two hotels near the airport: the **Sofitel** (📞210 354 4000; www.sofitel. com; Airport; d from €168; ❄🌐), at the terminal, and the **Holiday Inn** (📞210 668 9000; www.hiathens.com; Peania, near Airport; d from €112; ❄🌐), a 15-minute free shuttle ride away.

Hotel Achilleas   BUSINESS HOTEL €€
(Map p70; 📞210 323 3197; www.achilleashotel .gr; Leka 21, Syntagma; s/d/q incl breakfast €95/105/150; ❄@🌐; MSyntagma) This conveniently located, business-style hotel has a sleek lobby with marble chequerboard floors and well-appointed, slightly dark rooms, some of which open onto garden balconies.

★ Electra Palace   HOTEL €€€
(Map p70; 📞210 337 0000; www.electrahotels.gr; Navarhou Nikodimou 18, Plaka; d/ste incl breakfast from €230/350; P❄🌐❄; MSyntagma) Plaka's smartest hotel is one for the romantics – have breakfast under the Acropolis on your balcony (in higher-end rooms) and dinner in the chic rooftop restaurant. Completely refurbished with classic elegance, the well-appointed rooms are buffered from the sounds of the city streets. There's a gym and an indoor swimming pool, as well as a rooftop pool with Acropolis views.

★ NEW Hotel   BOUTIQUE HOTEL €€€
(Map p70; 📞210 628 4565; www.yeshotels.gr; Filellinon 16, Plaka; d from €179; P❄🌐; MSyntagma) Whether you dig the groovy, top-designer Campana Brothers furniture or the sleeping-pillow menu (tell 'em how you like it!), you'll find some sort of decadent treat here to tickle your fancy. Part of a renowned local design-hotel group, NEW Hotel is the latest entry on the high-end Athens scene.

★ Hotel Grande Bretagne   HOTEL €€€
(Map p70; 📞210 333 0000; www.grandebretagne. gr; Vasileos Georgiou 1, Syntagma; r/ste from €355/460; P❄@🌐❄; MSyntagma) If you aspire to the best, *the* place to stay in Athens is (and always has been) the Grande Bretagne, right on Plateia Syntagma. Built in 1862 to accommodate visiting heads of state, it ranks among the grandest hotels in the world. Renovated some years ago, it still retains its old-world grandeur. There is a divine spa, and the Acropolis-view rooftop restaurant and bar are worth a visit, even if you aren't a guest.

360 Degrees   HOTEL €€€
(Map p70; 📞210 324 0034; Plateia Monastirakiou, Monastiraki; d incl breakfast €160-180; ❄🌐; MMonastiraki) Smack on Plateia Monastiraki, these modern rooms are topped by a super roof restaurant serving up those eponymous 360-degree views. For the quietest rooms, book on an upper floor, facing away from the square.

🛏 Thisio

Phidias Hotel   HOTEL €€
(Map p80; 📞210 345 9511; www.phidias.gr; Apostolou Pavlou 39, Thisio; s/d/tr incl breakfast from €67/80/97; ❄🌐; MThisio) Smack-dab midway along Thisio's grand pedestrianised promenade, this hotel and its friendly management offer straight-up, no-frills rooms in a great location. Prices vary widely online.

🛏 Psyrri, Omonia & Exarhia

AthenStyle   HOSTEL €
(Map p70; 📞210 322 5010; www.athenstyle.com; Agias Theklas 10, Psyrri; dm €18-26, s/d €50/75, apt from €84; ❄@🌐; MMonastiraki) Bright, arty place with friendly staff, well-equipped studio apartments and hostel beds within walking distance of the Monastiraki metro, major sights and nightlife. Each dorm has lockers; some balconies have Acropolis views. The cool basement lounge, with pool table, home cinema and internet corner, holds art exhibitions. The small Acropolis-view rooftop bar hosts evening happy hours.

City Circus   HOSTEL €
(Map p88; 📞213 023 7244; www.citycircus.gr; Sarri 16, Psyrri; dm incl breakfast €25-30, d €65-110, q €120; ❄🌐; MThisio, Monastiraki) Athens' newest hostel promises good things and delivers. Bright, well-designed rooms with modern bathrooms are configured as dorms or private rooms, some with kitchens. The attitude is jaunty and helpful.

Hotel Exarchion   HOTEL €
(Map p88; 📞210 380 0731; www.exarchion.com; Themistokleous 55, Exarhia; d/q incl breakfast from €50/84; ❄@🌐; MOmonia) In the heart of bohemian Exarhia, this straightforward but comfortable 1960s high-rise offers clean, updated, well-equipped rooms, some with balconies. There's a rooftop cafe-bar and dining and entertainment options at your doorstep.

Melia   BUSINESS HOTEL €€
(Map p88; 📞210 332 0100; www.melia.com; Halkokondyli 14, cnr 28 Oktovriou-Patision, Omo-

nia; d/ste from €98/160; ❄🛜🏊; Ⓜ Omonia) Professional staff, sleek rooms and a rooftop Acropolis view with bar/pool/spa make Melia a great hideout. It's midway between Omonia and Exarhia.

Fresh Hotel   BOUTIQUE HOTEL €€

(Map p88; 🖉 210 524 8511; www.freshhotel.gr; Sofokleous 26, cnr Klisthenous, Omonia; s/d/ste incl breakfast from €110/130/250; ❄🛜; Ⓜ Omonia) The first of the hip hotels to open in the gritty Omonia area, this is a cool place so long as you're happy to ignore the working girls in the streets outside. Expect chic design and brightly coloured rooms plus a fantastic Acropolis-view rooftop, with pool, bar and restaurant.

Hotel Attalos   HOTEL €€

(Map p88; 🖉 210 321 2801; www.attaloshotel.com; Athinas 29, Psyrri; s/d/tr/q from €75/86/107/144; ❄@🛜; Ⓜ Monastiraki) Though decor has never been its strong point, this nonetheless comfortable hotel is very central. Its best feature remains the rooftop bar with wonderful views of the Acropolis. Rooms at the back have balconies with Acropolis views.

Ochre & Brown   BOUTIQUE HOTEL €€€

(Map p88; 🖉 210 331 2940; www.oandbhotel.com; Leokoriou 7, Psyrri; d €115-300, ste €200-580; ❄🛜; Ⓜ Thisio) At Psyrri's main trendy hotel, step outside to the city's liveliest shopping district in nearby Monastiraki or retreat into luxurious solitude. Has good deals online.

🛏 Kolonaki

Periscope   BOUTIQUE HOTEL €€

(Map p86; 🖉 210 729 7200; www.periscope.gr; Haritos 22, Kolonaki; d from €125; ❄🛜; Ⓜ Evangelismos) Right in chic Kolonaki overlooking Lykavittos, Periscope is a design hotel with industrial decor. Clever gadgets are sprinkled throughout, including the lobby slide show and aerial shots of the city on the ceilings. Korres organic toiletries and the trendy Pbox restaurant add to the vibe. The penthouse's private rooftop spa has sensational views.

St George Lycabettus   BOUTIQUE HOTEL €€€

(Map p86; 🖉 210 741 6000; www.sglycabettus.gr; Kleomenous 2, Kolonaki; s from €130, d €165-240; ❄@🛜; Ⓜ Evangelismos, Syntagma) Kolonaki's venerable luxury hotel on the hill, St George Lycabettus attracts a high-end clientele for its wonderful city and Acropolis views; a posh, if a bit staid, interior; and a full-service feel.

🍴 Eating

Athens' vibrant restaurant scene is marked by a delightful culture of casual, convivial alfresco dining – getting together to eat, drink and talk is the main source of entertainment for Greeks. A new generation of chefs draws inspiration from Greece's regional cuisine and local produce; this results in an interesting blend of culinary sophistication and grandma's home-style cooking. Trendy nouveau-Greek restaurants compete alongside traditional tavernas, *ouzeries* (places that serve ouzo and light snacks) and quaint old-style *mayiria* (cookhouses).

It's hard to avoid eating in Plaka if you are staying there, but the food is generally overpriced and ho-hum. Monastiraki, Psyrri and Gazi have many modern tavernas that are convenient for lining your belly before a night out in nearby clubs. Also in Monastiraki, the end of Mitropoleos is a souvlaki hub, with musicians adding to the area's bustling atmosphere. *Mezedhopoleia* (restaurants specialising in mezedhes, which are small dishes, like tapas) and more-upmarket restaurants can be found around Adrianou. Exarhia's popular eateries cater largely to locals, while chic Kolonaki has some of the best fine-dining options. At high-end restaurants, reservations are essential.

🍴 Akropoli, Makrygianni & Koukaki

Fresko Yogurt Bar   YOGHURT €

(Map p68; 🖉 210 923 3760; www.freskoyogurtbar. gr; Dionysiou Areopagitou 3, Makrygianni; yoghurt from €2.20; ⏱ 9am-9pm; Ⓜ Akropoli) Delicious fresh Greek yoghurt is the base of all things here. Either fresh or in smoothie form, it can be paired with any number of toppings, from chocolatey to black-cherry spoon sweets. A perfect cool-off after seeing the Acropolis.

Lotte Cafe-Bistrot   CAFE €

(Map p68; 🖉 211 407 8639; Tsami Karatsou 2, Makrygianni; snacks €2.50-7; ⏱ 9am-9pm; Ⓜ Akropoli) This small, charming cafe is decked out with vintage books and tea sets, and has bistro tables lining the footpath. Food tends towards cakes and light snacks.

⭐ Mani Mani   REGIONAL GREEK €€

(Map p68; 🖉 210 921 8180; www.manimani.com. gr; Falirou 10, Makrygianni; mains €9-15; ⏱ 2-11pm, closed Jul & Aug; Ⓜ Akropoli) Head upstairs to the relaxing, cheerful dining rooms of this delightful modern restaurant, which specialises in regional cuisine from Mani in the Peloponnese. Standouts include the ravioli with Swiss chard, chervil and cheese, and the tangy Mani sausage with orange. Almost all dishes can be ordered as half portions (at half-price), allowing you to sample widely.

Strofi
GREEK €€

(Map p68; ☑210 921 4130; www.strofi.gr; Rovertou Galli 25, Makrygianni; mains €11-15; ⊘noon-1am; Ⓜ Akropoli) Book ahead for a Parthenon view from the rooftop of this exquisitely renovated townhouse. Food is simple Greek, but the setting, with elegant linen and sweet service, elevates the experience to romantic levels.

Aglio, Olio & Peperoncino
ITALIAN €€

(Map p68; ☑210 921 1801; Porinou 13, Makrygianni; mains €15-25; ⊘8pm-12.45am Tue-Sat, 2-6.45pm Sun; Ⓜ Akropoli) Hardly the most obvious place for a restaurant, but this hidden gem on a side street near the Acropolis metro stop is a great choice for no-frills classic Italian pastas and a cosy, trattoria ambience.

Hytra
MEDITERRANEAN €€€

(☑210 331 6767, 217 707 1118; www.hytra.gr; Syngrou 107-109, Onassis Cultural Centre; mains €27-32; ⊘8pm-midnight Mon, Tue & Sun, to 1am Fri & Sat; Ⓜ Syngrou-Fix) Head to Hytra at the Onassis Cultural Centre for exquisitely presented Greek food with a modern twist, and amazing views. Though portions are small, flavours are large, which is how it earned its Michelin star. In summer there's also a branch at the **Westin Athens Astir Palace Beach Resort** (www.westinathens.com) in coastal Vouliagmeni.

Dionysos
MEDITERRANEAN €€€

(Map p60; ☑210 923 1936; www.dionysoszonars. gr; Rovertou Galli 43, Makrygianni; mains €19-36; ⊘restaurant noon-1am, cafe 8am-1am; Ⓜ Akropoli) Location, location, location. Eat here for the fantastic sweep of plate glass looking out onto the unblemished south slope of the Acropolis. Food is pricey but service is attentive... Date night?

✖ Syntagma, Plaka & Monastiraki

★ Tzitzikas & Mermingas
MEZEDHES €

(Map p70; ☑210 324 7607; www.tzitzikasmermigas .gr; Mitropoleos 12-14, Syntagma; mezedhes €6-12; ⊘noon-11pm; Ⓜ Syntagma) Greek merchandise lines the walls of this cheery, modern *mezedhopoleio* that sits smack in the middle of central Athens. It serves a tasty range of delicious and creative mezedhes (like the honey-drizzled, bacon-wrapped Naxos cheese) to a bustling crowd of locals.

★ Kalnterimi
TAVERNA €

(Map p88; ☑210 331 0049; www.kalnterimi.gr; Plateia Agion Theodoron, cnr Skouleniou, Monastiraki; mains €5-8; ⊘noon-11pm Mon-Sat; 🎅; Ⓜ Panepistimio) Find your way behind the Church of Agii Theodori to this hidden, open-air taverna offering Greek food at its most authentic. Everything is fresh-cooked and delicious: you can't go wrong. Hand-painted tables spill onto the footpath along a pedestrian street and give a feeling of peace in one of the busiest parts of the city.

★ Avocado
VEGETARIAN €

(Map p70; ☑210 323 7878; www.avocadoathens. com; Nikis 30, Plaka; mains €6-12; ⊘11am-10pm Mon-Sat, to 7pm Sun; 🎅🍴; Ⓜ Syntagma) This excellent, popular cafe offers a full array of vegan, gluten-free and organic treats – a rarity in Greece. Next to an organic market, and with a tiny front patio, you can enjoy everything from sandwiches to quinoa with eggplant or mixed-veg coconut curry. Fresh juices and mango lassis are made on the spot.

Mama Roux
INTERNATIONAL €

(Map p70; ☑213 004 8382; Eolou 48-50, Monastiraki; mains €5-13; ⊘9am-midnight Tue-Sat, to 6pm Mon, noon-5pm Sun; 🎅; Ⓜ Monastiraki) One of downtown's most popular cheap-eats restaurant fills up with locals digging into a fresh, delicious mix of food, from real burritos and

---

STREET FOOD

From vendors selling *koulouria* (fresh pretzel-style bread) and grilled corn or chestnuts to the raft of fast-food offerings, there's no shortage of snacks on the run in Athens. You can't go wrong with *tiropites* (cheese pies) at **Ariston** (Map p70; ☑210 322 7626; Voulis 10, Syntagma; pies €1.40-2; ⊘10am-4pm Mon-Fri; Ⓜ Syntagma), which has been around since 1910. Greece's favourite savoury snack is souvlaki, packing more punch for €2.50 than anything else. We list purveyors in most neighbourhoods. One of the best is tiny **Kostas** (Map p70; ☑210 323 2971; Plateia Agia Irini 2, Monastiraki; souvlakia €2; ⊘9am-5pm; Ⓜ Monastiraki), with its signature spicy tomato sauce, in the pleasant square opposite Agia Irini church.

Cajun specials to whopping American-style burgers. Reserve ahead for this popular hang-out, with Santorini's Yellow Donkey beer on tap and Sunday jazz brunches.

Melilotos
GREEK €

(Map p70; ☑ 210 322 2458; www.melilotos.gr; Kalamiotou 19, Monastiraki; mains €6-10; ☺ noon-1am Tue-Sat, 2-10pm Sun; Ⓜ Monastiraki) Great, affordable Greek food with a dash of sophistication and a dram of wine makes a fun start to a night out in the area's bar quarter. Specials rotate daily.

Pure Bliss
CAFE €

(Map p70; ☑ 210 325 0360; www.purebliss.gr; Romvis 24a, Syntagma; snacks €3-9; ☺ 10.30am-1am Mon-Sat, 5-9pm Sun; 🛜 🖋; Ⓜ Syntagma) 🖋 Enjoy the laid-back vibe at one of the few places in Athens where you can get organic fair-trade coffee, exotic teas and soy products. There's a range of healthy salads, sandwiches, smoothies and mostly organic food, wine and cocktails.

Kallipateira
MEZEDHES €

(Map p88; ☑ 210 321 4152; www.kallipateira.gr; Astingos 8, Monastirkai; dishes €4-10; ☺ lunch & dinner; Ⓜ Monastiraki) In a neoclassical building overlooking an archaeological dig, young Athenians gather for long sessions over mezedhes and carafes of ouzo – and *rembetika* (Greek blues music) Friday to Sunday.

Glykis
MEZEDHES €

(Map p70; ☑ 210 322 3925; Angelou Geronta 2, Plaka; mezedhes €6-8; ☺ 10.30am-1.30am; Ⓜ Akropoli) In a quiet corner of Plaka, this low-key *mezedhopoleio* with a shady courtyard is mostly frequented by students and locals. It has a tasty selection of mezedhes, including traditional dishes such as *briam* (oven-baked vegetable casserole) and cuttlefish in wine.

Thanasis
KEBAB €

(Map p70; ☑ 210 324 4705; Mitropoleos 69, Monastiraki; gyros €2.50; ☺ 8.30am-2.30am; Ⓜ Monastiraki) In the heart of Athens' souvlaki hub, at the end of Mitropoleos, Thanasis is known for its kebabs on pitta with grilled tomato and onions.

Ouzou Melathron
MEZEDHES €

(Map p70; ☑ 210 324 0716; Agiou Filipou 10, cnr Astingos, Monastiraki; mezedhes €5-7; ☺ noon-late; Ⓜ Monastiraki) The famous *ouzerie* chain from Thessaloniki has been a hit since it opened in the middle of the Monastiraki marketplace. It's a buzzing, unpretentious spot serving tasty mezedhes from a whimsical menu.

Cremino
ICE CREAM €

(Map p70; Nikis 50a, Plaka; scoops €1.50; ☺ 9am-midnight Jun-Aug, reduced hours Sep-May; Ⓜ Syntagma, Akropoli) The lovely proprietress at Cremino makes all the ice cream from scratch, using cow and buffalo milk and popular Greek recipes.

Metropolis
SANDWICHES €

(Map p70; ☑ 210 322 2122; Voulis 9-11, Syntagma; sandwiches €3.50-6; ☺ 8am-9pm; Ⓜ Syntagma) Delicious gourmet sandwiches made with fresh, local products are the order of the day. The open-faced house-marinated salmon sandwich and the fresh-squeezed juice are tops. Decor is sophisticated. Some complain the sandwiches aren't large enough.

Meatropoleos 3
SOUVLAKI €

(Map p70; ☑ 210 324 1805; www.meatropoleos3.com; Mitropoloeos 3, Syntagma; mains €6-12, souvlaki €1.50; ☺ noon-midnight; Ⓜ Syntagma) Lay into grilled meats before a night on the town.

★ Café Avyssinia
MEZEDHES €€

(Map p70; ☑ 210 321 7047; Kynetou 7, Monastiraki; mains €10-16; ☺ 11am-1am Tue-Sat, to 7pm Sun; Ⓜ Monastiraki) Hidden away on colourful Plateia Avyssinias, in the middle of the flea market, this bohemian *mezedhopoleio* gets top marks for atmosphere, food and service. It specialises in regional Greek cuisine, from warm *fava* (split-pea purée with lemon juice) to eggplants baked with tomato and cheese, and has a great selection of ouzo, *raki* (Cretan firewater) and *tsipouro* (a distilled spirit similar to ouzo but usually stronger). There is acoustic live Greek music on weekends. Snag fantastic Acropolis views upstairs.

★ 2 Mazi
FUSION €€

(Map p70; ☑ 210 322 2839; www.2mazi.gr; Nikis 48, Plaka; mains €17-22; ☺ 1pm-midnight; Ⓜ Syntagma, Akropoli) Inside a neoclassical mansion, this elegant dining room with white linen and proper crystal is the venue for inventive creations by two young chefs. They incorporate fresh local products like mountain greens, Greek cheeses and fresh-caught seafood to make interesting and beautifully presented dishes spanning the cuisines of Asia, France and the Greek islands.

Kuzina
MODERN GREEK €€

(Map p60; ☑ 210 324 0133; www.kuzina.gr; Adrianou 9, Monastiraki; mains €12-25; ☺ 11am-late; Ⓜ Thisio) Light streams through plate-glass windows, warming the crowded tables in winter. Or eat outside on pedestrianised Adrianou in summer. Expect inventive Greek fusion, such as Cretan pappardelle or chicken with figs and sesame.

Paradosiako
TAVERNA €€

(Map p70; ☑210 321 4121; Voulis 44a, Plaka; mains €5-12; ☺lunch & dinner; ☎; Ⓜ Syntagma) For great traditional fare, you can't beat this inconspicuous, no-frills taverna on the periphery of Plaka, with a few tables on the footpath. There's a basic menu but it's best to choose from the daily specials, which include fresh seafood such as prawn *saganaki*.

Palia Taverna tou Psara
TAVERNA €€

(Map p70; ☑210 321 8733; www.psaras-taverna. gr; Erechtheos 16, Plaka; mains €12-24; ☺11am-12.30am Wed-Mon; Ⓜ Akropoli) Away from the main hustle of Plaka, this taverna is a cut above the rest and fills tables cascading across the street. It's known as the best seafood taverna in Plaka (fish €65 per kilogram).

✗ Gazi, Keramikos & Thisio

Kanella
TAVERNA €

(Map p80; ☑210 347 6320; www.kanellagazi.gr; Leoforos Konstantinoupoleos 70, Gazi; dishes €7-11; ☺1.30pm-late; Ⓜ Keramikos) Homemade village-style bread, mismatched retro crockery and brown-paper tablecloths set the tone for this trendy, modern taverna serving regional Greek cuisine. Friendly staff serve daily specials such as lemon lamb with potatoes, and an excellent zucchini and avocado salad.

To Steki tou Ilia
TAVERNA €

(Map p80; ☑210 345 8052; Eptahalkou 5, Thisio; chops per portion/kg €9/30; ☺8pm-late; Ⓜ Thisio) You'll often see people waiting for a table at this *psistaria* (restaurant serving grilled food), famous for its tasty grilled lamb and pork chops. With tables under the trees on the quiet pedestrian strip opposite the church, it's a no-frills place with barrel wine and simple dips, chips and salads.

Gevomai Kai Magevomai
TAVERNA €

(Map p80; ☑210 345 2802; Nileos 11, Thisio; mains €6-11; ☺lunch & dinner; ☎; Ⓜ Thisio) Stroll off the pedestrian way to find this small corner taverna with marble-topped tables. Neighbourhood denizens know it as one of the best for home-cooked, simple food with the freshest ingredients. Menu changes constantly.

Oina Perdamata
TAVERNA €

(Map p80; ☑210 341 1461; www.oinomperdemata .gr; Vasiliou tou Megalou 10, Gazi; mains €5-10; ☺lunch & dinner; ☎; Ⓜ Keramikos) Unpretentious, fresh daily specials are the hallmark of

this simple spot off busy Pireos. Try staples such as fried cod with garlic dip and roast vegetables, or pork stew, rabbit and rooster.

★ Aleria
MEDITERRANEAN €€

(Map p60; ☑210 522 2633; www.aleria.gr; Megalou Alexandrou 57, Metaxourghio; mains €12-20; ☺8pm-midnight Mon-Sat, closed late Aug; Ⓜ Metaxourghio) Fine, fine dining is the order of the day at this contemporary, elegant restaurant in a restored mansion. A bit out of the way in the Metaxourghio neighbourhood, it's worth the trek for beautifully prepared local ingredients drawing on inspiration from around the Mediterranean.

★ Athiri
MODERN GREEK €€

(Map p80; ☑210 346 2983; www.athirirestaurant. gr; Plateon 15, Keramikos; mains €12-19; ☺8pm-1am Tue-Sat, 6pm-midnight Sun; Ⓜ Thisio) Athiri's lovely garden courtyard is a verdant surprise in this pocket of Keramikos. The small but innovative menu plays on Greek regional classics. Try Santorini fava and the hearty beef stew with *myzithra* (sheep's-milk cheese) and handmade pasta from Karpathos.

Sardelles
SEAFOOD €€

(Map p80; ☑210 347 8050; Persefonis 15, Gazi; fish dishes €10-17; ☺lunch & dinner; Ⓜ Keramikos) Dig into simply cooked seafood mezedhes at tables outside, opposite the illuminated gasworks. Nice touches include fishmonger paper tablecloths and souvenir pots of basil. Meat eaters can venture next door to its counterpart, **Butcher Shop** (Map p80; ☑210 341 3440; Persefonis 19, Gazi; ☺7-11.30pm; Ⓜ Keramikos).

Filistron
MEZEDHES €€

(Map p80; ☑210 346 7554; Apostolou Pavlou 23, Thisio; mezedhes €8-14; ☺6pm-midnight Tue-Sun; Ⓜ Thisio) It's wise to book a prized table on the rooftop terrace of this *mezedhopoleio* that enjoys breathtaking Acropolis and Lykavittos views. It has a large range of decent mezedhes and an extensive Greek wine list, though service sometimes suffers.

★ Funky Gourmet
MEDITERRANEAN €€€

(Map p60; ☑210 524 2727; www.funkygourmet.com; Paramithias 3, cnr Salaminas, Keramikos; set menu from €80; ☺7.30pm-1am Tue-Sat, last order 10.30pm; Ⓜ Metaxourghio) Nouveau gastronomy meets fresh Mediterranean ingredients at this two-Michelin-star restaurant. Elegant lighting, refinement and sheer joy in food make this a worthwhile stop for any foodie. Degustation menus can be paired with wines. Book ahead.

Psyrri, Omonia & Exarhia

In the evening or on weekends in Psyrri, an excellent array of mezedhes joints and tavernas spill onto the street and fill with chatting, chowing locals. Start around Plateia Agion Anargyron and Plateia Iroön to find the best of the scene.

★ **Akordeon**   MEZEDHES €

(Map p70; ☑ 210 325 3703; Hristokopidou 7, Psyrri; dishes €5-12; ☺ lunch & dinner; Ⓜ Monastiraki, Thisio) Slide into this charming butter yellow house across from a church in a quiet Psyrri sidestreet for a warm welcome by musician-chefs Pepi and Achilleas (and their spouses), who run this excellent new entry on the local music and mezes scene. They'll help you order authentic Greek fare, then (at night and on weekends) surround you with their soulful songs. Wear dancing shoes – you'll probably be moved to join in.

★ **Varvakios Agora**   MARKET €

(Athens Central Market; Map p88; Athinas, btwn Sofokleous & Evripidou, Omonia; ☺ 7am-3pm Mon-Sat; Ⓜ Monastiraki, Panepistimio, Omonia) The streets around the colourful, bustling Varvakios Agora are a sensory delight. The **meat and fish market** (Map p88) fills the historic building on the eastern side, and the **fruit and vegetable market** (Map p88) is across the road. The meat market might sound like a strange place to go for a meal, but its tavernas are an Athenian institution. Clients range from hungry market workers to elegant couples emerging from nightclubs in search of a bowl of hangover-busting *patsas* (tripe soup).

★ **Diporto Agoras**   TAVERNA €

(Map p88; ☑ 210 321 1463; cnr Theatrou & Sokratous; plates €5-6; ☺ 7am-7pm Mon-Sat, closed 1-20 Aug; Ⓜ Omonia, Monastiraki) This quirky old taverna is one of the dining gems of Athens. There's no signage, only two doors leading to a rustic cellar where there's no menu, just a few dishes that haven't changed in years. The house speciality is *revythia* (chickpeas), usually followed by grilled fish and washed down with wine from one of the giant barrels lining the wall. The often-erratic service is part of the appeal.

Nikitas   TAVERNA €

(Map p88; ☑ 210 325 2591; Agion Anargyron 19, Psyrri; mains €6-8; ☺ noon-6pm; Ⓜ Monastiraki) Locals swear by this tried-and-true taverna that has been serving reasonably priced, refreshingly simple and tasty traditional food since well before Psyrri became trendy. It's the only place busy on weekdays.

Kimatothrafstis   TAVERNA €

(Map p88; ☑ 213 030 8274; Harilaou Trikoupi 49, Exarhia; small/large plate €3.80/6.80; ☺ 8am-11pm, closed dinner Sun; ☎; Ⓜ Omonia) This great-value, bright and casual modern cafe with communal tables dishes out a range of homestyle Greek cooking and alternative fare. Choose from the buffet of the day's offerings. Plates come in two sizes.

Rakoumel   CRETAN €

(Map p88; ☑ 210 380 0506; www.rakoumel.gr; Emmanuel Benaki 71, Exarhia; dishes €5-9; ☺ 1pm-3am Mon-Sat; ☎; Ⓜ Omonia) Crowd into this slender restaurant packed with tables to sup on home-cooked Cretan fare. Sip Cretan *rakomelo* (honey-infused *raki* liquor) while sampling small plates featuring mountain herbs and slow-cooked meats.

Barbagiannis   TAVERNA €

(Map p88; ☑ 210 330 0185; Emmanuel Benaki 94, Exarhia; mains €5-8; ☺ lunch & dinner; Ⓜ Omonia) An Exarhia institution, this low-key *mayirio* is popular with students and those wanting good-value, homestyle Greek food.

Ivis   MEZEDHES €

(Map p88; ☑ 210 323 2554; Navarhou Apostoli 19, Psyrri; mezedhes €4-10; Ⓜ Thisio) This cosy, corner *mezedhopoleio*, with its bright, arty decor, has a small but delicious range of simple, freshly cooked mezedhes. Ask for the daily specials as there's only a rough, hand-written menu in Greek. A good ouzo selection lights things up.

Rozalia   TAVERNA €

(Map p88; ☑ 210 330 2933; www.rozalia.gr; Valtetsiou 58, Exarhia; mains €5-11; Ⓜ Omonia) An Exarhia favourite on a lively pedestrian strip, this family-run taverna serves grills and homestyle fare.

Taverna tou Psyrri   TAVERNA €

(Map p88; ☑ 210 321 4923; Eshylou 12, Psyrri; mains €6-9; ☺ lunch & dinner, closed 2 weeks Aug; Ⓜ Monastiraki) This cheerful taverna just off Plateia Iroön turns out decent, no-frills, traditional food.

Oxo Nou   CRETAN €

(Map p88; ☑ 210 380 1778; Emmanuel Benaki 63-65, Exarhia; mains €8-11; ☺ 3pm-late; ☎; Ⓜ Omonia) This was one of the trailblazers for supercasual and superdelicious Cretan food; in the heart of Athens.

★ Yiantes
TAVERNA €€

(Map p88; ☎ 210 330 1369; Valtetsiou 44, Exarhia; mains €9-12; ☺1pm-midnight; ; Ⓜ Omonia) This modern eatery, with its white linen and fresh-cut flowers set in a lovely garden courtyard, is upmarket for Exarhia, but the food is superb and made with largely organic produce. Try interesting greens such as *almirikia,* the perfectly grilled fish, or delicious mussels and calamari with saffron.

Kolonaki

★ Oikeio
MEDITERRANEAN €

(Map p86; ☎ 210 725 9216; Ploutarhou 15, Kolonaki; mains €7-14; ☺1pm-2.30am Mon-Sat; Ⓜ Evangelismos) With excellent homestyle cooking, this modern taverna lives up to its name (meaning 'homey'). It's decorated like a cosy bistro on the inside, and tables on the footpath allow people-watching without the normal Kolonaki bill. Pastas, salads and international fare are tasty, but try the *mayirefta* (ready-cooked meals) specials, such as the excellent stuffed zucchini. Book ahead.

Filippou
TAVERNA €

(Map p86; ☎ 210 721 6390; Xenokratous 19, Kolonaki; mains €8-12; ☺1-5pm & 7-11pm Mon-Fri, 1-5pm Sat; Ⓜ Evangelismos) Why mess with what works? Filippou has been dishing out yummy Greek dishes since 1923. A chance for a little soul cooking, with white linen, in the heart of Kolonaki.

Kalamaki Kolonaki
SOUVLAKI €

(Map p86; ☎ 210 721 8800; Ploutarhou 32, Kolonaki; mains €7; ☺1pm-midnight; Ⓜ Evangelismos) Order by the *kalamaki* (skewer; €1.70), add on some salad and pittas, and you've got great quick eats with all the requisite people-watching at Kolonaki's standout souvlaki joint.

Nice N' Easy
CAFE €

(Map p86; ☎ 210 361 7201; www.niceneasy.gr; Omirou 60, Kolonaki; sandwiches €5-10; ☺9am-1.30am; ; Ⓜ Panepistimio) 🖉 Dig into organic, fresh sandwiches, salads and brunch treats such as huevos rancheros beneath images of Louis Armstrong and Marilyn Monroe at this casual cafe.

Loukoumelo
DESSERTS €

(Map p86; ☎ 211 012 5330; www.loukoumelo.gr; Skoufa 37, Kolonaki; sweets €2.70-3.80; ☺8.30am-11pm Mon-Fri, 9.30am-midnight Sat & Sun; Ⓜ Syntagma) This friendly storefront specializes in *loukoumades,* a Greek style of doughnut,

served warm and with all sort of flavours. Pair with ice cream to get really decadent.

Alatsi
CRETAN €€

(Map p60; ☎ 210 721 0501; www.alatsi.gr; Vrasida 13, Ilissia; mains €12-18; ☺1pm-1am Mon-Sat; Ⓜ Evangelismos) Alatsi represents the new breed of trendy upscale restaurants, serving traditional Cretan cuisine, such as *gamopilafo* (wedding pilaf) with lamb or rare *stamnagathi* (wild greens), to fashionable Athenians. The excellent menu changes seasonally. Book ahead. You'll find it near the Hilton.

Capanna
ITALIAN €€

(Map p86; ☎ 210 724 1777; Ploutarhou 38 & Haritos 42, Kolonaki; mains €10-17; ☺1pm-1am Tue-Sun; 🖥; Ⓜ Evangelismos) Capanna hugs a Kolonaki corner, with tables wrapping around the footpath in summer. Cuisine is fresh Italian, from enormous pizzas to gnocchi with gorgonzola. Enjoy hearty eating with attentive service and a goblet of wine; prices are a tad high.

Café Boheme
CAFE €€

(Map p86; ☎ 210 360 8018; www.cafeboheme.gr; Omirou 36, Kolonaki; mains €6.50-15; ☺10.30am-late Mon-Fri, from noon Sat & Sun; Ⓜ Panepistimiou) A jazzy, brasserie-like spot with a great wine selection; serves everything from sandwiches and salads to rib-eye steak (€19.50).

Il Postino
ITALIAN €€

(Map p86; ☎ 210 364 1414; Grivaion 3, Kolonaki; pasta €8-12; ☺1pm-11.30pm; Ⓜ Panepistimio) In the mood for a plate of homemade gnocchi with pesto before a night out clubbing? Sneak into this little side street and sup under old photos of Roma.

Pangrati & Mets

★ Mavro Provato
MEZEDHES €

(Map p60; ☎ 210 722 3466; www.tomauroprovato.gr; Arrianou 31-33, Pangrati; dishes €4-12; ☺lunch & dinner; Ⓜ Evangelismos) Book ahead for this wildly popular modern *mezedhopoleio* in Pangrati, where tables line the footpath and delicious small plates are paired with *raki* or *tsipouro.*

Trapezaria
MODERN GREEK €€

(Map p60; ☎ 210 921 3500; www.trapezaria.gr; Efforionos 13, Pangrati; mains €8-15; ☺7pm-midnight Tue-Sat, 1-6pm Sun; Ⓜ Evangelismos, Akropoli) In an unassuming spot, this stylish contemporary Greek restaurant packs in locals in search of good, affordable eats, served with style. The wine list is remarkable.

★**Spondi** MEDITERRANEAN €€€

(Map p60; ☑210 756 4021; www.spondi.gr; Pyrronos 5, Pangrati; mains €38-50, set menus from €69; ☺8pm-late) Two-Michelin-starred Spondi is frequently voted Athens' best restaurant, and the accolades are deserved. It offers Mediterranean haute cuisine, with heavy French influences, in a relaxed, chic setting in a charming old house. Choose from the menu or a range of set dinner and wine *prix fixes*. The restaurant has a lovely, bougainvillea-draped garden. Book ahead, and take a cab – it's hard to reach on public transport.

🍷 Drinking & Nightlife

One local favoured pastime is going for coffee. Athens' ubiquitous, packed cafes have some of Europe's most expensive coffee (between €3 and €5) – you're essentially hiring the chair and can linger for hours. Many daytime cafes and restaurants turn into bars and clubs at night.

🍷 Akropoli, Makrygianni & Koukaki

Sfika CAFE, BAR

(Map p68; ☑210 922 1341; Stratigou Kontouli 15, Makrygianni; ☺9am-late; Ⓜ Akropoli) You don't get much more local than Sfika (which translates to 'wasp'), a small neighbourhood cafe-restaurant-bar with an alternative/student vibe and occasional live music.

Duende BAR

(Map p68; Tzireon 2, Makrygianni; ☺8pm-3am; Ⓜ Akropoli) This intimate pub feels almost like a Parisian brasserie and is tucked away on a quiet side street. It's best for wine and whiskey, not cocktails or food.

Tiki Athens BAR

(Map p68; ☑210 923 6908; www.tikiathens.com; Falirou 15, Makrygianni; ☺4.30pm-late; Ⓜ Akropoli) Funky '50s decor, varied music, an Asian-inspired menu and an alternative young crowd make this a fun place for a drink.

🍷 Syntagma, Plaka & Monastiraki

The city's hottest scene masses around Kolokotroni street north of Plateia Syntagma, and around Plateia Agia Irini in Monastiraki. A cafe-thick area in Monastiraki is Adrianou, along the Ancient Agora, where people fill shady tables. Multi-use spaces Taf

ℹ️ **TOP NIGHTLIFE TIPS**

➡ Expect bars to begin filling after 11pm and stay open till late.

➡ Right now, the areas around Plateia Karytsi (north of Syntagma) and Plateia Agia Irini (Monastiraki) have the most action. Psyrri has seen a recent resurgence, while Kolonaki steadfastly attracts the trendier set, and Gazi remains tried-and-true.

➡ With the current financially strapped climate in Athens, watch your back wherever you go.

➡ For the best dancing in summer, cab it to beach clubs (p107) along the coast near Glyfada – city locations close earlier.

(p91) and Six DOGS (p91) morph from gallery to cafe to overflowing bar. Some hotel bars, like Hotel Grande Bretagne (p98) and A for Athens (p97), have super Acropolis views.

★**Tailor Made** CAFE, BAR

(Map p70; ☑213 004 9645; www.tailormade. gr; Plateia Agia Irini 2, Monastiraki; ☺8am-2am; Ⓜ Monastiraki) This popular new microroastery offers its array of coffee blends as well as hand-pressed teas. Find the full gamut from peaberry coffee to rooibos tea, and homemade desserts (€5) and sandwiches (€6) too. Cheerful Athenians spill from the mod-art-festooned interior to the tables alongside the flower market. At night it turns into a happening cocktail and wine bar.

★**Clumsies** BAR

(Map p88; ☑210 323 2682; www.theclumsies.gr; Praxitelous 30, Syntagma; ☺9am-late; Ⓜ Syntagma) Warm, welcoming decor with a retro feel and a packed, babbling crowd of happy sippers (from coffee to creative cocktail) makes this new all-day bar a go-to hang-out for locals and visitors alike.

Drunk Sinatra COCKTAIL BAR

(Map p70; ☑210 331 3733; Thiseos 16, Syntagma; ☺10am-late; Ⓜ Syntagma) Athens' newest hipster hang-out also serves a mean cocktail.

Baba Au Rum COCKTAIL BAR

(Map p70; ☑211 710 9140; www.babaaurum. com; Klitiou 6, Monastiraki; ☺5pm-3am Mon-Thu, noon-4am Fri & Sat, 1pm-2am Sun; Ⓜ Syntagma, Monastiraki) Fab cocktail mixologists concoct the tipples of your dreams.

Melina
CAFE
(Map p70; Lyssiou 22, Plaka; ☺9am-midnight; Ⓜ Akropoli, Monastiraki) An ode to the great Merkouri, Melina offers charm and intimacy out of the hectic centre.

Seven Jokers
BAR
(Map p70; ☎210 321 9225; Voulis 7, Syntagma; ☺1pm-late; Ⓜ Syntagma) Lively and central; it anchors a party block, also shared by spacious 42 (Map p70; Kolokotroni 3, Syntagma; ☺9am-2am; Ⓜ Syntagma), around the corner, which serves cocktails in wood-panelled splendour.

Barley Cargo
BAR
(Map p70; ☎210 323 0445; Kolokotroni 6, Syntagma; ☺11am-3am; Ⓜ Syntagma) This fantastic beer bar offers over 150 different versions of the sweet elixir, many of them from Greek microbreweries. Or sip a Trappist brew at one of the wooden-barrel tables.

Brettos
BAR
(Map p70; ☎210 323 2110; www.brettosplaka.com; Kydathineon 41, Plaka; ☺10am-3am; Ⓜ Akropoli) You won't find any happening bars in Plaka, but Brettos is a delightful old bar and distillery with a wall of colourful bottles and huge barrels. Sample its home brands of wine, ouzo, brandy and other spirits.

Booze Cooperativa
CAFE, BAR
(Map p70; ☎211 405 3733; www.boozecooperativa .com; Kolokotroni 57, Monastiraki; ☺11am-late; ☎; Ⓜ Monastiraki) By day, this laid-back, arty hang-out is full of young Athenians playing chess and backgammon and working on their Macs; later it transforms into a happening bar that rocks till late. The basement hosts art exhibitions and there's a theatre upstairs.

Loukoumi
CAFE
(Map p70; www.loukoumibar.gr; Plateia Avyssinias 3, Monastiraki; ☺11am-2am; Ⓜ Monastiraki) Daytime coffee and snacks, and a night scene with DJs and live music, overlooking Plateia Avyssinias.

Galaxy Bar
BAR
(Map p70; ☎210 322 7733; Stadiou 10, Syntagma; ☺1pm-late Mon-Sat; Ⓜ Syntagma) Not to be confused with the Hilton's sky bar, this sweet little wood-panelled place has a homey saloon feel and a venerable history.

Faust
BAR
(Map p70; ☎210 323 4095; www.faust.gr; Kalamiotou 11 & Athinaidos 12, Monastiraki; ☺Sep-May; Ⓜ Monastiraki) The popular bar Faust – just a tiny hole in the wall – also hosts live music, cabarets and art shows.

Bartesera
BAR
(Map p70; ☎210 322 9805; Kolokotroni 25, Syntagma; ☺10am-late; Ⓜ Syntagma) This casual bar-cafe with great music hides out at the end of a narrow arcade.

Gin Joint
COCKTAIL BAR
(Map p88; ☎210 321 8646; Christou Lada 1, Syntagma; ☺noon-2am; Ⓜ Syntagma) They call it Gin Joint for a reason: sample 60 gins or other fancy beverages, some with historical notes on their origin.

Sixx
CLUB
(Map p70; ☎6979470638; Amerikis 6, Syntagma; ☺11pm-7am Fri-Sat; Ⓜ Syntagma) If you just can't call it a night... DJs party till dawn.

Oinoscent
WINE BAR
(Map p70; ☎210 322 9374; www.oinoscent.gr; Voulis 45-47, Plaka; ☺11am-1am; Ⓜ Syntagma) Drop in for a vast array of Greek and international wines, or pick up a bottle for the road.

Toy Cafe
COCKTAIL BAR
(Map p70; ☎210 331 1555; Plateia Karytsi 10, Syntagma; ☺noon-4am; Ⓜ Syntagma) Thirtysomethings gather at this old favourite for coffee by day and glam cocktails by night.

James Joyce
PUB
(Map p88; ☎210 323 5055; www.jjoyceirishpub athens.com; Astingos 12, Monastiraki; ☺10am-1am Sun-Thu, to 3am Fri & Sat; Ⓜ Monastiraki) The Guinness is free-flowing at this Irish pub, with decent food (mains €9 to €12), live music and loads of travellers and expats.

🍸 Gazi, Keramikos & Thisio

Get off the metro at Keramikos and you'll be smack in the middle of the thriving Gazi scene. In Thisio, cafes along the pedestrian promenade Apostolou Pavlou have great Acropolis views; those along pedestrianised Iraklidon pack 'em in at night.

★ Gazarte
BAR,
(Map p80; ☎210 346 0347; www.gazarte.gr; Voutadon 32-34, Gazi; Ⓜ Keramikos) Upstairs you'll find a cinema-sized screen playing videos, amazing city views taking in the Acropolis, mainstream music and a trendy 30-something crowd. There's occasional live music and a restaurant to boot.

Gazaki
BAR
(Map p80; ☎6940629755; Triptolemou 31, Gazi; ☺7pm-late; Ⓜ Keramikos) This Gazi trailblazer opened before the neighbourhood became *the* place to be. Friendly locals crowd the great rooftop bar.

Root Artspace
CAFE, LIVE MUSIC

(Map p80; ☑ 210 345 0003; www.rootartspace.gr; Iraklidon 10, Thisio; ☺ 9am-1am; Ⓜ Thisio) Cafe meets bar meets live-music and art venue in a renovated 19th-century stone stable, Root Artspace makes for a good hang-out in the shadow of the Acropolis. Check online for art and entertainment line-up.

Hoxton
BAR

(Map p80; ☑ 210 341 3395; Voutadon 42, Gazi; ☺ 1pm-late; Ⓜ Keramikos) Join the hip, artsy crowd for shoulder-to-shoulder hobnobbing amid original art, iron beams and leather sofas.

MoMix
COCKTAIL BAR

(Map p80; ☑ 6974350179; www.momix.gr; Keleou 1, Gazi; ☺ 7pm-late; Ⓜ Keramikos) Athens' first molecular mixology bar. There's also a branch in Glyfada (p122).

A Liar Man
BAR

(Map p80; ☑ 210 342 6322; www.aliarman.gr; Sofroniou 2, Gazi; ☺ mid-Sep–mid-Jun; Ⓜ Keramikos) A tiny hideout with a more hushed vibe. It closes during summer.

Pixi
CLUB

(Map p80; ☑ 210 342 3751; www.pixi.gr; Evmolpidon 11, Gazi; Ⓜ Keramikos) Good DJs and flashing lights for the younger set; it throws summer parties at beach clubs on the Apollo Coast (p122).

45 Moires
BAR

(Map p80; ☑ 210 347 2729; www.45moires.gr; Iakhou 18, cnr Voutadon, Gazi; Ⓜ Keramikos) Go deep into hard rock and enjoy terrace views of Gazi's neon-lit chimneys and the Acropolis.

Sin Athina
CAFE

(Map p80; ☑ 210 345 5550; www.sinathina.gr; Iraklidon 2, Thisio; ☺ 8am-late; Ⓜ Thisio) Location, location, location! This little cafe-bar sits at the junction of the two pedestrianised cafe strips, and has a sweeping view up to the Acropolis.

Nixon Bar
BAR

(Map p80; www.nixon.gr; Agisilaou 61b, Keramikos; ☺ 7pm-late; Ⓜ Thisio) More chic than most, Nixon Bar serves up food and cocktails.

Peonia Herbs
TEAHOUSE

(Map p80; ☑ 210 341 0260; www.peonia.gr; Amfiktyonos 12, Thisio; ☺ 10am-4pm Mon-Fri, to 3pm Sat; Ⓜ Thisio) There's an instantly calming, smoke-free aura to this herb shop and tearoom.

Psyrri, Omonia & Exarhia

Exarhia is a good bet for youthful, lively bars on Plateia Exarhion. The cheap bar precinct on nearby Mesolongiou is popular with students and anarchists. Omonia at night is especially dangerous these days.

Floral
CAFE

(Map p88; ☑ 210 380 0070; www.floralcafe.gr; Themistokleous 80, Exarhia; ☺ 9am-late; 🛜; Ⓜ Omonia) Floral is sleekly modern, with grey-toned images of retro life and, you guessed it, flowers on the walls. Locals come to buy books, chat and people-watch.

SUMMER BEACH CLUBS

In summer much of the city's serious nightlife moves to glamorous, enormous seafront clubs radiating out from Glyfada (p122). Many sit on the tram route, which runs to 2.30am on Friday and Saturday. If you book for dinner you don't pay cover; otherwise admission ranges from €10 to €20 and includes one drink. Glam up to get in.

Akrotiri (☑ 210 985 9147; www.akrotirilounge.gr; Vasileos Georgiou B5, Agios Kosmas, Alimos; 🚃 Elliniko) This massive, top beach club holds 3000 people in bars, a restaurant and lounges over different levels. Jamming party nights bring top resident and visiting DJs. Pool parties rock during the day.

Balux (☑ 210 894 1620; www.baluxcafe.com; Leoforos Poseidonos 58, Glyfada; 🛜; 🚃 T5 to Asteria) This glamorous club-restaurant-lounge right on the beach must be seen to be believed, with poolside chaises and four-poster beds with flowing nets.

Akanthus (☑ 210 968 0800; www.akanthus.gr; Leoforos Poseidonos, Alimos; 🚃 Zephyros) A night-time line-up of top DJs spin at Akanthus, near Akti Tou Iliou beach.

Island (☑ 210 965 3563; www.islandclubrestaurant.gr; Km 27, Athens–Sounion Rd, Varkiza; 🚃 A2/E2 to Glyfada, 🚌 117 or 122 to Camping Varkizas stop) Dreamy, classic summer club-restaurant on the seaside, with superb island decor.

Alexandrino
COCKTAIL BAR

(Map p88; ☑ 210 382 7780; Emmanuel Benaki 69, Exarhia; ⊙ 7pm-late; Ⓜ Omonia) This bar feels like a cute tiny French bistro, with excellent wines and cocktails.

Tralala
BAR

(Map p60; ☑ 210 362 8066; Asklipiou 45, Exarhia; ⊙ 11pm-3am; Ⓜ Panepistimio, Omonia) Actors frequent cool Tralala, with its original artwork, lively owners and gregarious atmosphere.

Blue Fox
BAR

(Map p60; ☑ 6942487225; Asklipiou 91, Exarhia; ⊙ 10pm-2am; Ⓜ Omonia) You might not expect this in Athens, but Blue Fox is great for '50s-era swing and rockabilly, complete with Vespas and poodle skirts.

Ginger Ale
CAFE, BAR

(Map p88; ☑ 210 330 1246; Themistokleous 74, Exarhia; ⊙ 8am-late; Ⓜ Omonia) Dip back in time to a '50s veneered coffee shop–cum–rocking nightspot. Sip espresso by day and catch a rotating line-up of live acts by night.

Revolt
BAR

(Map p88; ☑ 210 380 0016; Kolleti 29, Exarhia; ⊙ 11am-2am; Ⓜ Omonia) This small, simple bar with tables spilling out onto a pedestrianised square anchors a few solid blocks of good nightlife. The vibrant murals out front are super. Start here and explore.

Circus
CAFE, COCKTAIL BAR

(Map p88; ☑ 210 361 5255; www.circusbar.gr; Navarinou 11, Exarhia; 10am-late; 🛜; Ⓜ Panepistimiou) Presided over by a Ganesh-style wire elephant, Circus has relaxed coffees by day and cocktails by night.

Tsin Tsin
COCKTAIL BAR

(Map p88; ☑ 210 384 1460; Kiafas 6, Exarhia; ⊙ 7pm-late; Ⓜ Omonia) Teeny, tiny and out of the way, but the bartender is a true mixologist, and the loungey feel is relaxing.

Tranzistor
BAR

(Map p88; ☑ 210 322 8658; Protogenous 10, Psyrri; ⊙ 9am-midnight; Ⓜ Monastiraki) Sidle up to the backlit bar or relax at tables outside at this teeny, cool spot.

🍷 Kolonaki

Kolonaki has two main strips of bars: the top end of Skoufa, and among the crowds squeezing into tiny bars on Haritos.

★ Rock'n'Roll
BAR

(Map p86; ☑ 210 722 0649; Plateia Kolonakiou, Kolonaki; ⊙ Sep-Jun; Ⓜ Evangelismos) A Kolonaki classic, this upscale crowd-pleaser lives up to its name at night, when dance parties get wild. Popular with the trendy Kolonaki crowd, it has a good vibe, but 'face control' can be strict. During the day it's a busy, but more relaxed cafe lining Kolonaki's main square.

Da Capo
CAFE

(Map p86; ☑ 210 360 2497; Tsakalof 1, Kolonaki; ⊙ 8am-7pm; Ⓜ Syntagma) Da Capo anchors the cafes on Kolonaki's main square and is *the* place to be seen. It's self-serve (if you can find a table).

Mai Tai
BAR

(Map p86; ☑ 210 722 5846; Ploutarhou 18, Kolonaki; ⊙ noon-late; Ⓜ Evangelismos) Join Kolonaki's best-dressed as they pack into this narrow bar and spill out into the street beyond. It's a place to see and be seen.

Filion
CAFE

(Map p86; ☑ 210 361 2850; Skoufa 34, Kolonaki; ⊙ 8am-midnight; 🛜; Ⓜ Syntagma) Despite its unassuming decor, Filion consistently attracts the intellectual set: artists, writers and film-makers.

Petite Fleur
CAFE

(Map p86; www.petite-fleur.gr; Omirou 44, Kolonaki; ⊙ 8am-11pm; Ⓜ Panepistimio) Petite Fleur serves up large mugs of hot chocolate and speciality cappuccinos in a quiet, almost-Parisian ambience.

Rosebud
BAR,

(Map p86; ☑ 210 339 2370; www.rosebud.gr; Omirou 60, cnr Skoufa, Kolonaki; ⊙ 9.30am-1.30am; 🛜; Ⓜ Panepistimiou) Kolonaki professionals and chicsters cram this cocktail bar, which also offers vegetarian food.

To Tsai
TEAHOUSE

(Map p86; ☑ 210 338 8941; www.tea.gr; Alexandrou Soutsou 19, Kolonaki; ⊙ 6am-9pm Mon-Sat, daily in winter; Ⓜ Syntagma) Get a Zen vibe as you sip tea at natural-wood tables; on a lively day, a bit of Dixieland jazz will be tinkling in the background. Light meals (€6 to €9) include soup and grilled chicken.

🍷 Pangrati & Mets

Odeon Cafe
CAFE

(Map p60; ☑ 210 922 3414; Markou Mousourou 19, Mets; ⊙ 8.30am-late; Ⓜ Akropoli) This delightful slice of local life is a simple corner coffee shop where quietly chatting friends sit beneath ivy winding over the footpath. Occasional live music.

☆ Entertainment

English-language entertainment information appears daily in the *Kathimerini* supplement in the *International Herald Tribune; Athens Plus* also has listings. Athens' thriving multi-use spaces (p91) host all manner of goings-on. For comprehensive events listings, with links to online ticket sales points, try the following:

This is Athens (www.breathtakingathens.gr) Athens tourism site.

elculture (www.elculture.gr) Arts and culture.

tickethour (www.tickethour.com) Also has sports matches.

Tickethouse (www.tickethouse.gr) Rockwave and other festivals.

Ticket Services (www.ticketservices.gr) Range of events.

☆ Greek Music

Athens has some of the best *rembetika* (Greek blues) in intimate, evocative venues. Performances usually include both *rembetika* and *laïka* (urban popular music), start at around 11.30pm and do not have a cover charge, though drinks can be expensive. Most close May to September, so in summer try live-music tavernas around Plaka and Psyrri. There's also live music most weekends at Café Avyssinia (p101) and Akordeon (p103).

Stoa Athanaton TRADITIONAL MUSIC
(Map p88; ☎ 210 321 4362; Sofokleous 19, Central Market, Omonia; ⊙3-6pm & midnight-6am Mon-Sat, closed Jun-Sep; Ⓜ Monastiraki, Panepistimio, Omonia) This legendary club occupies a hall

GAY & LESBIAN ATHENS

For the most part, Athens' gay and lesbian scene is relatively low-key, though the **Athens Pride** (www.athenspride.eu) march, held in June, has been an annual event since 2005. Check out www.athensinfoguide.com or a copy of the *Greek Gay Guide* booklet at *periptera* (newspaper kiosks). For nightlife, Gazi has become Athens' gay and lesbian hub, with a gay triangle emerging near the railway line on Leoforos Konstantinoupoleos and Megalou Alexandrou. Gay and gay-friendly clubs around town are also in Makrygianni, Psyrri, Metaxourghio and Exarhia.

Limanakia The rocky coves below the bus stop at Limanakia B (near Varkiza on the Apollo Coast) are a popular gay, nudist hang-out. Take the tram or A2/E2 express bus to Glyfada, then bus 117 or 122 to the Limnakia B stop.

Rooster (Map p70; www.roostercafe.gr; Plateia Agia Irini 4, Monastiraki; ⊙9am-3am; Ⓜ Monastiraki) This wonderfully packed gay cafe is straight-friendly too, and so fills with chatting locals on lively Plateia Agia Irini.

Magaze (Map p70; ☎ 210 324 3740; Eolou 33, Monastiraki; ⊙noon-late; Ⓜ Monastiraki) Gay-friendly Magaze has Acropolis views from footpath tables.

S-Cape (Map p80; www.s-capeclub.gr; Iakhou 32, Gazi; Ⓜ Keramikos) Stays packed with the younger gay, lesbian and transgender crowd. Check theme nights online.

Sodade (Map p80; ☎ 210 346 8657; Triptolemou 10, Gazi; ⊙11pm-6am; Ⓜ Keramikos) In Gazi, tiny, sleek Sodade is superfun for dancing.

Noiz Club (Map p80; ☎ 210 346 7850; www.facebook.com/noizclubgaz; Konstantinoupoleos 78, Gazi; Ⓜ Keramikos) Athens' main lesbian club has retro dance nights.

Myrovolos (Map p60; ☎ 210 522 8806; Giatrakou 12, Metaxourghio; Ⓜ Metaxourghio) Popular lesbian cafe-bar-restaurant.

BIG (Map p80; ☎ 6946282845; www.barbig.gr; Falesias 12, Gazi; ⊙10pm-4am Tue-Sun; Ⓜ Keramikos) Hub of Athens' lively bear scene.

Moe Club (Map p80; www.moeclub-gazi.blogspot.com; Keleou 5, Gazi; ⊙1am-6am; Ⓜ Keramikos) After-hours hang-out with occasional special parties.

Lamda Club (Map p68; ☎ 210 942 4202; Lembesi 15, Makrygianni; Ⓜ Akropoli) Busy, three-level Lamda Club is not for the faint of heart. Look for the λ symbol on the sign.

Koukles (☎ 694 755 7443; Zan Moreas 32, Koukaki; ⊙midnight-4am; Ⓜ Syngrou-Fix) The glam drag show here rocks.

above the central meat market. Popular for classic *rembetika* and *laïka* from a respected band of musicians, it often starts from midafternoon. Access is by a lift in the arcade. Food is not the attraction.

Perivoli tou Ouranou TRADITIONAL MUSIC
(Map p70; ☑ 210 323 5517; www.perivolitouranou.gr; Lysikratous 19, Plaka; ⊙ 9pm-late Thu-Sun, closed Jul-Sep; Ⓜ Akropoli) A favourite rustic, old-style Plaka music haunt with dinner (mains €18 to €29).

Kavouras TRADITIONAL MUSIC
(Map p88; ☑ 210 381 0202; Themistokleous 64, Exarhia; ⊙ 11pm-late Thu-Sat, closed Jul & Aug; Ⓜ Omonia) Above Exarhia's popular souvlaki joint, this lively club usually plays until dawn for a student crowd.

**Palea Plakiotiki Taverna
Stamatopoulos** TRADITIONAL MUSIC
(Map p70; ☑ 210 322 8722; www.stamatopoulos tavern.gr; Lyssiou 26, Plaka; ⊙ 7pm-2am Mon-Sat, 11am-2am Sun; Ⓜ Monastiraki) This Plaka restaurant is an institution, with live music nightly. It fills up late with locals – arrive early for a table.

Mostrou TRADITIONAL MUSIC
(Map p70; ☑ 210 322 5558; www.mostrou.gr; Mnisikleous 22, cnr Lyssiou, Plaka; ⊙ 6pm-2am Thu-Sun; Ⓜ Monastiraki) There's a popular full-sized stage and dance floor at this restaurant; in summer there's more sedate live music on the terrace.

Boemissa TRADITIONAL MUSIC
(Map p88; ☑ 210 383 8803; www.boemissa.gr; Solomou 13-15, Exarhia; ⊙ 10pm-late Thu-Sat; Ⓜ Omonia) *Rembetika*, *laïka* and decent grub are on offer at this divey joint.

☆ Rock & Jazz Music

Athens has a healthy rock-music scene and many European tours stop here. In summer check Rockwave and other festival schedules.

★**Half Note Jazz Club** JAZZ
(Map p60; ☑ 210 921 3310; www.halfnote.gr; Trivonianou 17, Mets; Ⓜ Akropoli) Athens' stylish, principal and most serious jazz venue hosts an array of international musicians.

Gagarin 205 Club LIVE MUSIC
(☑ 213 024 8358; www.gagarin205.gr; Liossion 205, Thymarakia; Ⓜ Agios Nikolaos) Friday- and Saturday-night gigs feature leading rock and underground bands

AN Club LIVE MUSIC
(Map p88; ☑ 210 330 5056; www.anclub.gr; Solomou 13-15, Exarhia; Ⓜ Omonia) A small spot for lesser-known international and local rock bands.

Mike's Irish Bar LIVE MUSIC
(☑ 210 777 6797; www.mikesirishbar.com; Sinopis 6, Ambelokipi; Ⓜ Ambelokipi) A long-time favourite of the expatriate community, with live music or karaoke most nights.

Fuzz LIVE MUSIC
(☑ 210 345 0817; www.fuzzclub.gr; Pireos 209, Tavros; Ⓜ Petraluna) Fuzz jams with international acts such as the Wailers and Gypsy punk band Gogol Bordello.

☆ Theatre & Performing Arts

In summer the main cultural happening is the Hellenic Festival (p94).

Megaron Mousikis PERFORMING ARTS
(Athens Concert Hall; ☑ 210 728 2333; www.me garon.gr; Kokkali 1, cnr Leoforos Vasilissis Sofias, Ilissia; ⊙ box office 10am-6pm Mon-Fri, to 2pm Sat, later on performance days; Ⓜ Megaro Mousikis) The city's state-of-the-art concert hall presents a rich winter program of operas and concerts featuring world-class international and Greek performers.

Dora Stratou Dance Theatre DANCE
(Map p60; ☑ 210 324 4395; www.grdance.org; Filopappou Hill; adult/child €15/5; ⊙ performances 9.30pm Wed-Fri, 8.15pm Sat & Sun Jun-Sep; Ⓜ Pe-

---

BOUZOUKIA

Greek *bouzoukia*, or *skyladika* (literally 'dog houses', a mocking term for second-rate places with crooning singers), is a one-of-a-kind thing. Athens' grandest incarnation is a decadent circus for adults. These glitzy cabaret-style venues host famous headliners, exotic dancers, costumes, aerialists, glitter – the works! Women dancing the sinewy *tsifteteli* (belly dance) are showered with expensive trays of carnations while revellers party till sunrise. Check local listings or try glam **Athinon Arena** (Map p80; ☑ 210 347 1111; www.athens pantheon.com; Pireos 166, Rouf; ⊙ Fri & Sat; Ⓜ Petraluna) if you have a bankroll (buy table tickets in advance and pricey bottles once you're there) and an appetite for adventure.

DON'T MISS

SUMMER CINEMA

One of the delights of hot summer nights in Athens is the enduring tradition of open-air cinema, where you can watch the latest Hollywood or art-house flick under moonlight. Many original outdoor cinemas have been refurbished and are still operating in gardens and on rooftops around Athens, with modern sound systems.

The most historic outdoor cinema is **Aigli** (Map p60; ☎ 210 336 9369; www.aeglizappiou. gr; Zappeio Gardens, Syntagma; Ⓜ Syntagma), in the verdant Zappeio Gardens, where you can watch a movie in style with a glass of wine.

Kolonaki's **Dexameni** (Map p86; ☎ 210 362 3942; www.cinedexameni.gr; Plateia Dexameni, Kolonaki; Ⓜ Evangelismos) is in a peaceful square.

Try to nab a seat with Acropolis views on the rooftop of Plaka's **Cine Paris** (Map p70; ☎ 210 322 0721; www.cineparis.gr; Kydathineon 22, Plaka; Ⓜ Syntagma), or meander around the foothills of the Acropolis to **Thission** (Map p80; ☎ 210 342 0864; www.cine-thisio.gr; Apostolou Pavlou 7, Thisio; Ⓜ Thisio).

tralona, Akropoli) Every summer this company performs its repertoire of Greek folk dances at its open-air theatre on the western side of Filopappou Hill. It also runs folk-dancing workshops in summer.

Greek National Opera OPERA
(Ethniki Lyriki Skini; Map p88; ☎ 210 366 2100; www.nationalopera.gr) The season runs from November to June. Performances are usually held at the **Olympia Theatre** (Map p88; ☎ 210 361 2461; Akadimias 59, Exarhia; Ⓜ Panepistimio) or the Odeon of Herodes Atticus (p73) in summer.

National Theatre THEATRE
(Map p88; ☎ 210 528 8100; www.n-t.gr; Agiou Konstantinou 22-24, Omonia; Ⓜ Omonia) Performances of contemporary plays and ancient theatre in one of the city's finest neoclassical buildings, as well as in venues around town and, in summer, in ancient theatres across Greece.

☆ Sport

Athens' most popular sports are basketball (www.basket.gr) and football. Greece's top football teams are Athens-based **Panathinaikos** (www.pao.gr) and **AEK** (www.aekfc.gr), and Piraeus-based **Olympiakos** (www.olympiacos. org), all three of which are in the European Champions League. Check club websites, English-language press or www.tickethour.gr.

🔒 Shopping

Central Athens is one big, bustling shopping hub, with an eclectic mix of stores and speciality shopping strips. The central shopping street is Ermou, the pedestrian street lined with mainstream fashion stores running from Syntagma to Monastiraki.

Top-brand international designers and jewellers surround Syntagma, from the **Attica department store** (Map p88; ☎ 211 180 2500; www.atticadps.gr; Panepistimiou 9, Syntagma; ⊘ 10am-9pm Mon-Fri, to 7pm Sat; Ⓜ Syntagma) past pedestrian Voukourestiou to the fashion boutiques of Kolonaki. Plaka and Monastiraki are rife with souvenir stores and streetwear; the main streets are Kydathineon and Adrianou. Department stores dot Stadiou from Syntagma to Omonia. Kifisia and Glyfada also have excellent high-end shopping.

Find a delectable array of food and spices at the colourful central market (p103) and along Evripidou, and all manner of housewares in the surrounding streets.

August to September and January to February are the big sales months, especially on clothes.

★ Monastiraki Flea Market MARKET
(Map p70; btwn Adrianou, Ifestou & Ermou, Monastiraki; ⊘ daily; Ⓜ Monastiraki) This traditional market has a festive atmosphere, combined with an onslaught of more modern souvenir stalls. Permanent antique and collectables shops are open all week, while the streets around the station and Adrianou fill with vendors selling jewellery, handicrafts and bric-a-brac.

★ Forget Me Not GIFTS
(Map p70; ☎ 210 325 3740; www.forgetmenot athens.gr; Adrianou 100, Plaka; ⊘ 10am-10pm May-Sep, to 8pm Oct-Apr; Ⓜ Syntagma, Monastiraki) This impeccable small store stocks supercool design gear, from fashion to housewares and gifts, all by contemporary Greek designers. Souvenirs and gifts have never had it so good:

from cheerful 'evil eye' coasters to Hermes rubber beach sandals.

Mastiha Shop
FOOD, BEAUTY

(Map p88; ☑ 210 363 2750; www.mastihashop.com; Panepistimiou 6, Syntagma; ⊙ 9am-9pm; Ⓜ Syntagma) Mastic, the medicinal resin from rare mastic trees produced only on the island of Chios, is the key ingredient in everything in this store, from natural skin products to a liqueur that's divine when served chilled. There's also an airport branch.

Mompso
CRAFTS

(Map p88; ☑ 210 323 0670; www.mompso.com; Athinas 33, Psyrri; ⊙ 10am-6pm Mon-Sat; Ⓜ Monastiraki) Find all manner of equestrian supplies and traditional accessories for donkeys (beaded headdresses), shepherds (bronze bells) and country folk (walking sticks).

To Pantopoleion
FOOD & DRINK

(Map p88; ☑ 210 323 4612; www.atenco.gr; Sofokleous 1, Omonia; ⊙ 8am-7pm; Ⓜ Panepistimio) Expansive store selling traditional food products from all over Greece, from Santorini capers and boutique olive oils to Cretan rusks, jars of goodies for edible souvenirs and Greek wines and spirits.

Gusto di Grecia
FOOD & DRINK

(Map p86; ☑ 210 362 6809; Pindarou 16-20, Kolonaki; ⊙ 8am-10pm Mon-Sat; Ⓜ Syntagma) Shop for the best treats from all over Greece, from cheese to local honeys, cold cuts, olive oil and wine.

Bahar
FOOD

(Map p88; ☑ 210 321 7225; www.bahar.gr; Evripidou 31, Omonia; ⊙ 7am-3pm Mon-Thu & Sat, to 6pm Fri; Ⓜ Omonia, Monastiraki) Drop into this vibrant spice shop to browse fresh saffron, rose hips and all manner of aromatic goodness.

Aristokratikon
FOOD

(Map p70; ☑ 210 323 4373; www.aristokratikon. com; Voulis 7, Syntagma; ⊙ 8am-9pm Mon-Fri, to 6pm Sat; Ⓜ Syntagma) Chocaholics will be thrilled by the dazzling array of handmade chocolates at this tiny store, past of a cluster of nut and sweet shops around Karageorgi Servias street.

Xylouris
MUSIC

(Map p88; ☑ 210 322 2711; www.xilouris.gr; Stoa Pesmatzoglou, Panepistimiou 39, Panepistimio; ⊙ 9am-4pm Mon, Wed & Sat, to 8pm Tue, Thu & Fri; Ⓜ Syntagma) This music treasure trove is run by the family of Cretan musical legend Nikos Xylouris. They can guide you through the comprehensive range of Greek music, including select and rare recordings. Also has a branch at the Museum of Greek Popular Instruments (p74).

John Samuelin
MUSIC

(Map p70; ☑ 210 321 2433; www.musicshop.gr; Ifestou 36, Monastiraki; ⊙ 9am-7pm; Ⓜ Monastiraki) This central spot is jam-packed with Greek and other musical instruments.

Amorgos
HANDICRAFTS

(Map p70; ☑ 210 324 3836; www.amorgosart.gr; Kodrou 3, Plaka; ⊙ 11am-8pm Mon-Fri, to 7pm Sat; Ⓜ Syntagma) Charming store crammed with Greek folk art, trinkets, ceramics, embroidery and carved wooden furniture made by the owner.

Centre of Hellenic Tradition
HANDICRAFTS

(Map p70; ☑ 210 321 3023; www.kelp.gr; Pandrosou 36, Monastiraki; ⊙ 9am-8pm Apr-Nov, to 6pm Oct-Mar; Ⓜ Monastiraki) Traditional ceramics, sculpture and handicrafts from all parts of Greece.

Graffito
GIFTS,

(Map p86; ☑ 210 360 8936; www.graffito.gr; Solonos 34, Kolonaki; ⊙ 8am-9pm; Ⓜ Panepistimio, Syntagma) A new entry on the Athens shopping scene, Graffito combines homewares, fashion and other high-design items with a welcoming cafe.

Apivita
BEAUTY

(Map p86; ☑ 210 364 0560; www.apivita.com; Solonos 6, Kolonaki; ⊙ 10am-9pm Tue, Thu & Fri, to 5pm Mon, Wed & Sat, spa closed Mon & Sun; Ⓜ Syntagma) Apivita's flagship store has the full range of its excellent natural beauty products and an express spa downstairs for pampering on the run. There's also a branch at the airport.

Korres
BEAUTY

(Map p70; ☑ 210 321 0054; www.korres.com; Ermou 4, Syntagma; ⊙ 9am-9pm Mon-Fri, to 8pm Sat; Ⓜ Syntagma) You can get the full range from this natural beauty-product guru at the company's original homeopathic pharmacy – at a fraction of the price you'll pay in London or New York. There's also a branch at the airport, and one near the Panathenaic Stadium.

Ioanna Kourbela
FASHION

(Map p70; ☑ 210 322 4591; www.ioannakourbela. com; Adrianou 109, Plaka; ⊙ 10am-9pm Mon-Sat, from 11am Sun; Ⓜ Syntagma) Classic, cool fashion by a young Greek designer. Think elegantly draped cottons and silks in natural, warm tones, and slouchy casual wear for the street. Her men's collection and couture boutiques are just around the corner.

Parthenis
FASHION

(Map p86; ☑ 210 363 3158; www.orsalia-parthenis. gr; Dimokritou 20, cnr Tsakalof, Kolonaki; ☺10am-3pm Mon & Wed, to 8.30pm Tue, Thu & Fri, to 4pm Sat; M Syntagma) Totally Greek and totally natural, these women's clothes designed by a father-and-daughter team emphasize high-quality, classic silhouettes in natural fibres.

Fanourakis
JEWELLERY

(Map p86; ☑ 210 721 1762; www.fanourakis.gr; Patriarhou Ioakeim 23, Kolonaki; ☺10am-5pm Mon, Wed & Sat, to 9pm Tue, Thu & Fri; M Syntagma) One of the most creative, exciting Greek jewellers, Fanourakis designs delicate pieces of folded gold, encrusted rings, bows and other unique creations. The distinctive forms are sheer art, a factor that is also reflected in the prices (though it now has a more inexpensive line as well).

Apriati
JEWELLERY

(Map p70; ☑ 210 322 9183; www.apriati.com; Stadiou 3, Syntagma; ☺10am-4.30pm Mon, Wed & Sat, to 8.30pm Tue, Thu & Fri; M Syntagma) This tiny, delightful store has a tempting selection of fun and original contemporary designs from Athena Axioti, Themis Bobolas and other local designers. There are additional shops in Kolonaki and on Ermou.

Elena Votsi
JEWELLERY

(Map p86; ☑ 210 360 0936; www.elenavotsi.com; Xanthou 7, Kolonaki; ☺10am-8pm Tue-Sat; M Evangelismos) Votsi is renowned for her original, big and bold designs using exquisite semiprecious stones. Her work also sells in New York and London, and her profile got a big boost when she was chosen to design the new Olympic Games medal.

El.Marneri Galerie
JEWELLERY, ART

(Map p68; ☑ 210 861 9488; www.elenimarneri. com; Lembesi 5-7, Makrygianni; ☺10am-8pm Tue, Thu & Fri, to 6pm Wed & Sat; M Akropoli) Sample rotating exhibitions of local modern art and some of the best jewellery in the city. Handmade, unusual, and totally eye-catching.

Actipis
JEWELLERY

(Map p70; ☑ 210 323 6907; www.actipis.com; Lekka 20, Syntagma; ☺11.30am-8pm Mon-Fri, to 5pm

Sat Nov-Apr; M Syntagma) Elegant jewellery based around smooth pebbles and gleaming silver or raw leather help this art jeweller stand out from the crowd. In summers Spiros Actipis has a shop in Mykonos.

Olgianna Melissinos
SHOES, ACCESSORIES

(Map p70; ☑ 210 331 1925; www.melissinos-sandals.gr; Normanou 7, Monastiraki; ☺10am-6pm Mon, Wed, Sat & Sun, to 8pm Tue, Thu & Fri; M Monastiraki) Olgianna Melissinos designs and crafts a wide range of excellent leather goods, from sandals to backpacks. Her father, Stavros, was a famous poet/sandal-maker whose customers included the Beatles, Sophia Loren and Jackie Onassis. She can make things to order.

Melissinos Art
SHOES

(Map p70; ☑ 210 321 9247; www.melissinos-art. com; Agias Theklas 2, Psyrri; ☺10am-8pm, to 6pm winter; M Monastiraki) Pantelis Melissinos continues the sandal-making tradition of his famous poet/sandal-maker father Stavros.

Spiliopoulos
SHOES, ACCESSORIES

(Map p70; ☑ 210 322 7590; Ermou 63, Monastiraki; ☺10am-4.30pm Mon, Wed & Sat, to 8.30pm Tue, Thu & Fri; M Monastiraki) Chaos reigns but you may find a bargain among the overcrowded racks of imported designer seconds and old-season shoes and bags. It also stocks leather jackets. There's a branch on Adrianou.

Anavasi
MAPS, BOOKS

(Map p70; ☑ 210 321 8104; www.anavasi.gr; Voulis 32, cnr Apollonos, Syntagma; ☺9.30am-5.30pm Mon & Wed, to 8.30pm Tue, Thu & Fri, 10am-4.30pm Sat; M Syntagma) Great travel bookshop with an extensive range of Greece maps and walking and activity guides.

Public
BOOKS, ELECTRONICS

(Map p70; ☑ 210 324 6210; www.public.gr; Plateia Syntagmatos, Syntagma; ☺9am-9pm Mon-Fri, to 8pm Sat; 🛜; M Syntagma) This multimedia behemoth includes computers, stationery and English-language books (3rd floor).

Eleftheroudakis
BOOKS

(Map p88; ☑ 210 325 8440; Panepistimiou 15, Syntagma; ☺9am-9pm Mon-Fri, 10am-4pm Sat; M Syntagma) A large bookshop chain with a wide selection of books from and about Greece, plus English-language books, including maps and travel guides.

ℹ Information

DANGERS & ANNOYANCES

Crime has risen in Athens with the onset of the financial crisis. Though violent street crime remains relatively rare, travellers should be alert when out and about, especially at night, and beware the traps listed here.

Streets surrounding Omonia have become markedly seedier, with an increase in prostitutes and junkies; avoid the area, especially at night.

Strikes & Demonstrations

Strikes and demonstrations can disrupt public transport and whether sights or shops open, but they are often announed in advance. They usually proceed to Syntagma Square; steer clear. Check www.livingingreece.gr/strikes/ for the latest.

Pickpockets

Favoured hunting grounds are the metro, particularly the Piraeus–Kifisia line, and crowded streets around Omonia, Athinas and the Monastiraki Flea Market.

Taxi Scams

➡ Most (but not all) rip-offs involve taxis hired from ranks at the airport, train stations, bus terminals and particularly the port of Piraeus. At Piraeus, avoid the drivers at the port exit asking if you need a taxi; hail one off the street.

➡ Some drivers don't turn on the meter and demand whatever they think they can get away with; others claim you gave them a smaller bill than you did and short-change you. Only negotiate a set fare if you have some idea of the cost.

➡ Some drivers may try to persuade you that the hotel you want to go to is full, even if you have a booking.

Bar Scams

➡ Scammers target tourists in central Athens, particularly around Syntagma. One scam goes like this: friendly Greek approaches solo male traveller; friendly Greek reveals that he, too, is from out of town (or else he 'has a cousin' in the traveller's home country) and suggests they go to a bar for a drink. Soon some women appear, more drinks are ordered and the conman disappears, leaving the traveller to pay an exorbitant bill. Smiles disappear and the atmosphere turns threatening.

➡ Some bars lure intoxicated males with talk of sex and present them with outrageous bills.

➡ Some bars and clubs serve what are locally known as *bombes*, adulterated drinks diluted with cheap illegal imports or methanol-based spirit substitutes. They leave you feeling decidedly low the next day.

EMERGENCY

Police (⏧100)

Police station Central (⏧210 770 5711; Leoforos Alexandras 173, Ambelokipi; Ⓜ Ambelokipi); Syntagma (⏧210 725 7000; Mimnermou 6-8; Ⓜ Syntagma).

Tourist Police (⏧210 920 0724, 24hr 171; Veïkou 43-45, Koukaki; ⊘8am-10pm; Ⓜ Syngrou-Fix, Akropoli)

Visitor Emergency Assistance (⏧112) Toll-free 24-hour service in English.

INTERNET ACCESS

Most hotels have internet access and wi-fi. Free wireless hot spots are at Syntagma, Thisio, Gazi and the port of Piraeus. Buy prepaid internet cards for your laptop at OTE (Greece's main telecommunications carrier) shops or Germanos stores.

LEFT LUGGAGE

Most hotels store luggage free for guests, although many simply pile bags in a hallway. Storage facilities are also at the airport and at Omonia, Monastiraki and Piraeus metro stations.

MEDIA

Athens Plus Weekly English news and entertainment newspaper; published Fridays by *Kathimerini* and online.

Kathimerini (www.ekathimerini.com) English edition of *Kathimerini*, published daily (except Sunday) with the *International Herald Tribune*, with news, arts, cinema listings and daily ferry schedules.

Press Project (www.thepressproject.gr) Online news project with an English version.

MEDICAL SERVICES

Ambulance/First-Aid Advice (⏧166)

Pharmacies (⏧in Greek 1434) Check pharmacy windows for details of the nearest duty pharmacy. There's a 24-hour pharmacy at the airport.

SOS Doctors (⏧1016, 210 821 1888; ⊘24hr) Pay service with English-speaking doctors.

MONEY

Major banks have branches around Syntagma. ATMs blanket the city.

Eurochange Monastiraki (⏧210 322 2657; Areos 1, Monastiraki; ⊘9am-9pm; Ⓜ Monastiraki); Syntagma (⏧210 331 2462; www.euro change.gr; Karageorgi Servias 2, Syntagma; ⊘9am-9pm; Ⓜ Syntagma) Exchanges travellers cheques and arranges money transfers.

National Bank of Greece (⏧210 334 0500; cnr Karageorgi Servias & Stadiou, Syntagma; Ⓜ Syntagma) Has a 24-hour automated exchange machine.

POST

Syntagma post office (Map p70; Plateia Syntagmatos, Syntagma; ⊙7.30am-8pm Mon-Fri, to 2pm Sat; Ⓜ Syntagma)

TELEPHONE

Public phones allow international calls. Purchase phonecards at kiosks, and reasonably priced local SIM cards at mobile shops.

TOURIST INFORMATION

EOT (Greek National Tourist Organisation; Map p68; ☑ 210 331 0716, 210 331 0347; www. visitgreece.gr; Dionysiou Areopagitou 18-20, Makrygianni; ⊙8am-8pm Mon-Fri, 10am-4pm Sat & Sun May-Sep, 9am-7pm Mon-Fri Oct-Apr; Ⓜ Akropoli) Free Athens map, transport information and *Athens & Attica* booklet. There's also a desk at Athens Airport (⊙9am-5pm Mon-Fri, 10am-4pm Sat).

Athens Airport Information Desk (⊙24hr) This 24-hour desk has Athens info, booklets and the Athens Spotlighted discount card for goods and services.

Athens City Information Kiosks (www.breathtakingathens.com) Acropolis (Map p68; ☑210 321 7116; Dionysiou Areopagitou & Leoforos Syngrou; ⊙9am-9pm May-Sep; Ⓜ Akropoli); Airport (☑210 353 0390; ⊙8am-8pm; Ⓜ Airport) Maps, transport information and all Athens info.

USEFUL WEBSITES

Several Greek-language sites are useful if you have a webpage translator: **Athinorama** (www. athinorama.gr), **Athens Voice** (www.athens voice.gr), and **Lifo** (www.lifo.gr). They have print editions in Greek as well.

Athens Living (www.athensliving.net) Short video clips of Athens life.

elculture (www.elculture.gr) Bilingual; has theatre, music and cinema listings.

Ministry of Culture (www.culture.gr) Museums, archaeological sites and cultural events.

This is Athens (www.breathtakingathens.gr) Athens tourism site, with what's-on listings.

❶ Getting There & Away

AIR

Modern Eleftherios Venizelos International Airport (p724), at Spata, 27km east of Athens, has all the modern conveniences, including 24-hour luggage storage in the arrivals hall and a children's playroom – even a small archaeological museum above the check-in hall for passing time.

It's served by many major and budget airlines as well as high-season charters.

Average domestic one-way fares range from €56 to €140, but vary dramatically depending on season. Aegean Airlines and Olympic Air

(which have merged, but still run seprate routes) have flights to all islands with airports.

Aegean Airlines (☑210 626 1000, 801 112 0000; www.aegeanair.com)

Astra Airlines (A2; ☑2310 489 392; www. astra-airlines.gr) Thessaloniki-based airline.

Olympic Air (☑801 801 0101, 210 355 0500; www.olympicair.com)

Sky Express (☑281 022 3500; www.skyexpress.gr) Cretan airline with flights around Greece. Beware harsh baggage restrictions.

BOAT

Most ferry, hydrofoil and high-speed catamaran services to the islands leave from Athens' massive port at Piraeus.

Some services for Evia and the Cyclades also depart from smaller ports at Rafina and Lavrio.

Purchase tickets at booths on the quay next to each ferry, over the phone or online; travel agencies selling tickets also surround each port. See port listings for more details.

BUS

Athens has two main intercity (IC) **KTEL** (☑14505; www.ktel.org) bus stations, 5km and 7km to the north of Omonia. Pick up timetables at the tourist office, or look online.

Kifissos Terminal A (☑210 512 4910; Leoforos Kifisou 100, Peristeri; Ⓜ Agios Antonios) has buses to Thessaloniki, the Peloponnese, Ionian Islands and destinations in western Greece such as Igoumenitsa, Ioannina, Kastoria and Edessa, among other places. Local bus 051 goes to central Athens (junction of Zinonos and Menandrou, near Omonia) every 15 minutes from 5am to midnight. Local bus X93 goes to/from the airport. Local bus 420 goes to/from Piraeus (junction of Akti Kondili and Thermopilon).

Taxis to Syntagma cost about €9.

Liossion Terminal B (☑210 831 7153; Liossion 260, Thymarakia; Ⓜ Agios Nikolaos, Attiki) has buses to central and northern Greece, such as Trikala (for Meteora), Delphi, Larissa, Thiva and Volos. To get here take bus 024 from the main gate of the National Gardens on Amalias and ask to get off at Praktoria KTEL. Or take the metro to Attiki and catch any local bus north towards the station. Get off the bus at Liossion 260, turn right onto Gousiou and you'll see the terminal.

There are no buses to the centre from 11.40pm to 5am; taxis to Syntagma cost about €9. Local bus X93 connects Kiffisos Terminal A, Liossion Terminal B and the Athens Airport.

Buses for destinations in southern Attica leave from **Mavromateon terminal** (Map p60; ☑210 880 8080, 210 822 5148, 210 880 8000; www. ktelattikis.gr; cnr Leoforos Alexandras & 28 Oktovriou-Patision, Pedion Areos; Ⓜ Viktoria), about 250m north of the National Archaeological Museum. Buses to Rafina, Lavrio and Marathon leave from the northern section of the Mavromateon terminal (just 150m to the north).

Key Buses from Kifissos Terminal A

DESTINATION	TIME	FARE	FREQUENCY
Alexandroupoli	11hr	€71	5 daily
Corfu*	9½hr	€56	3 daily
Epidavros	2½hr	€12.50	2 daily
Igoumenitsa	7½hr	€47	3 daily
Ioannina	7hr	€39	6 daily
Ithaki*	7½hr	€50	3 weekly
Kalavryta	3hr	€18	1 daily
Kefallonia*	7hr	€55	4 daily
Lefkada	5½hr	€36	5 daily
Monemvasia	6hr	€29.60	3 daily
Nafplio	2½hr	€13.50	hourly
Olympia	5½hr	€31	2 daily
Patra	3hr	€22	half-hourly
Thessaloniki	7hr	€42	12 daily
Zakynthos*	6hr	€34	3 daily

*includes ferry ticket

Key Buses from Liossion Terminal B

DESTINATION	TIME	FARE	FREQUENCY
Agios Konstantinos	2½hr	€15	8 daily
Delphi	2½hr	€17	5 daily
Halkida	1¼hr	€7	half-hourly
Karpenisi	4½hr	€25	2 daily
Paralia Kymis	4½hr	€23	1 daily
Trikala (for transfer to Meteora)	4½hr	€28	7 daily
Volos	4½hr	€28	10 daily

Key Buses from Mavromateon Terminal

DESTINATION	TIME	FARE	FREQUENCY
Cape Sounion (coastal road)	2hr	€7.50	hourly
Lavrio port	1½hr	€5.20	half-hourly
Marathon	1½hr	€4.50	half-hourly
Rafina port	1hr	€2.40	half-hourly

CAR & MOTORCYCLE

Attiki Odos (Attiki Rd), Ethniki Odos (National Rd) and various ring roads facilitate getting in and out of Athens.

The airport has all major car-hire companies, and the top end of Leoforos Syngrou, near the Temple of Olympian Zeus, is dotted with firms. Local companies tend to offer better deals than the multinationals. Expect to pay €45 per day, less for three or more days.

Budget (210 922 4200; www.budget-athens .gr; Leoforos Syngrou 23, Makrygianni; 8.30am-8.30pm; Akropoli)

Europcar (210 921 1444; www.europcar -greece.gr; Leoforos Syngrou 25, Makrygianni; 8.30am-9pm; Akropoli)

Hertz (210 922 0102; www.hertz.gr; Leoforos Syngrou 12, Makrygianni; 8am-9pm; Akropoli)

Kosmos (210 923 4696; www.kosmos-car rental.com; Leoforos Syngrou 5, Makrygianni; 8am-8.30pm; Akropoli)

Motorent (210 923 4939; www.motorent.gr; Kavalloti 4, Makrygianni; 9am-6pm Mon-Fri, 9.30am-4pm Sat; Akropoli) From 50cc to 250cc (from €19 per day); must have motorcycle licence (and nerves of steel).

TRAIN

Intercity (IC) trains to central and northern Greece depart from the central **Larisis train station** (Stathmos Larisis; 210 529 8837, 14511; www.trainose.gr; Larisis), about 1km northwest of Plateia Omonias.

For the Peloponnese, take the **suburban rail** (1110; www.trainose.gr) to Kiato and change for a bus there. At time of research, the Patra train line was closed for repairs, so OSE buses replace its services. It's easier to just take a bus from Athens' Kifissos Terminal A to your ultimate destination.

At the time of research, Greece's train system was in a state of flux due to the financial crisis. Domestic schedules/fares should be confirmed online or at **OSE** (210 362 4402/6, 1110; www. trainose.gr; Sina 6, Syntagma; 8am-3.30pm Mon-Fri; Panepistimio). Tickets can be bought online.

Consult www.seat61.com for great tips on international trains to/from Greece; you will need to go via Thessaloniki.

DESTINATION	TIME	FARE	FREQUENCY
Alexandroupoli	12¼hr	€40	1 daily (via Thessaloniki)
Alexandroupoli (IC)	11hr	€65	1 daily (via Thessaloniki)
Corinth (suburban rail)	1hr 20min	€8	13 daily
Kiato (suburban rail)	1hr 40min	€8	13 daily
Thessaloniki	6hr	€25	1 daily
Thessaloniki (IC)	5hr	€45	6 daily
Volos (IC)	5hr	€30	6 daily (via Larisa)

ℹ Getting Around

TO/FROM THE AIRPORT

The metro and suburban rail provide quick connections to central Athens. The bus is cheapest, though it takes longer. The suburban rail also goes to Piraeus and Larisis Train Station.

Bus

Express buses operate 24 hours between the airport and the city centre, Piraeus and KTEL bus terminals. At the airport, buy tickets (€5; not valid for other forms of public transport) at the booth near the stops.

Plateia Syntagmatos Bus X95, one to 1½ hours, every 30 minutes, 24 hours. The Syntagma stop is on Othonos St.

Kifissos Terminal A bus station Bus X93, one hour, every 30 minutes (60 minutes at night), 24 hours

Metro line 3 at Ethniki Amyna station Bus X94, 25 minutes, every 10 minutes, 7.30am to 11.30pm

Piraeus Bus X96, 1½ hours, every 20 minutes, 24 hours. To Plateia Karaïskaki.

Kifisia Bus X92, about 45 minutes, every 45 minutes, 24 hours

Metro line 2 at Dafni station Bus X97, one hour, every 30 minutes, 24 hours

Metro

Metro line 3 goes to the airport. Some trains terminate early at Doukissis Plakentias; disembark and wait for airport train (displayed on the train and platform screen). Trains run every 30 minutes, leaving Monastiraki between 5.50am and midnight, and the airport between 5.30am and 11.30pm.

Airport tickets costs €8 per adult or €14 return (return valid 48 hours). The fare for two or more passengers is €7 each, so purchase tickets together (same with suburban rail). Tickets are valid for all forms of public transport for 90 minutes (revalidate your ticket on final mode of transport).

Suburban Rail

Take the suburban rail (one hour) from central Athens (Larisis station) then change trains for the airport at Ano Liosia, or Nerantziotissa (on metro line 1); it's the same price as the metro but the return ticket is valid for a month. The metro also connects with the suburban rail at Doukissis Plakentias (line 3). Trains to the airport run from 6am to midnight; trains from the airport to Athens run from 5.10am to 11.30pm; trains run every 15 minutes from Nerantziotissa.

Suburban rail also goes from the airport to Piraeus (change trains at Nerantziotissa) and Kiato in the Peloponnese (via Corinth).

Taxi

Fixed fares are posted. Expect day/night (midnight to 5am) €35/50 to the city centre, and €47/72 to Piraeus. Both trips often take at least an hour, longer with heavy traffic. Check www.athensairporttaxi.com for more info.

BICYCLE

Even experienced cyclists might find Athens' roads a challenge, with no cycle lanes and often reckless drivers. A new 27km bike lane between Kifisia in the north and Faliro in the south should have opened in Athens by the time you read this. A few outfits offer bicycle hire (p92).

CAR & MOTORCYCLE

Athens' notorious traffic congestion, confusing signage, impatient/erratic drivers and one-way streets make for occasionally nightmarish driving.

Contrary to what you see, parking is actually illegal alongside kerbs marked with yellow lines, on footpaths and in pedestrian malls. Paid parking areas require tickets available from kiosks.

PUBLIC TRANSPORT

Athens has an extensive and inexpensive integrated public-transport network of buses, metro, trolleybuses and trams. Get maps at tourist offices or online: **Athens Urban Transport Organisation** (OASA; ☏185; www.oasa.gr).

Athens tramway and additional metro extensions to the port of Piraeus are underway, and scheduled to be completed by 2017.

Tickets

Tickets good for 70 minutes (€1.20) and a 24-hour/five-day travel pass (€4/10) are valid for all forms of public transport except for airport services; the three-day tourist ticket (€20) includes one round-trip airport ride. Bus/trolleybus-only tickets (€1.20) cannot be used on the metro. Children under six travel free; people under 18 and over 65 pay half-fare.

Buy tickets in metro stations or transport kiosks or most *periptera* (newspaper kiosks). Validate the ticket in the machine as you board your transport of choice.

Bus & Trolleybus

Local express buses, regular buses and electric trolleybuses operate every 15 minutes from 5am to midnight. The free OASA map shows most routes.

Piraeus buses operate 24 hours (every 20 minutes from 6am to midnight, then hourly):

From Syntagma (bus 040) At the corner of Syntagma and Filellinon to Akti Xaveriou.

From Omonia (bus 049) At the Omonia end of Athinas to Plateia Themistokleous.

Metro

The metro works well and posted maps are self-explanatory (with icons and English translations). Trains operate from 5am to midnight (every four minutes during peak periods and every 10 minutes off-peak); on Friday and Saturday, lines 2 and 3 run till 2am. Get information at www.stasy.gr and www.ametro.gr. All stations have wheelchair access.

Line 1 (Green) The old Kifisia–Piraeus line, known as the Ilektriko, travels slower than the others and above ground. Transfer at Omonia and Attiki for line 2, Monastiraki for line 3 and Nerantziotissa for suburban rail. The hourly all-night bus service (bus 500, Piraeus–Kifisia) follows this route, with bus stops located outside the train stations.

Line 2 (Red) Runs from Agios Antonios in the northwest to Agios Dimitrios in the southeast. Attiki and Omonia connect with line 1; Syntagma connects with line 3.

Line 3 (Blue) Runs northeast from Egaleo to Doukissis Plakentias, with airport trains continuing on from there. Transfer for line 1 at Monastiraki; for line 2 at Syntagma.

Train

Fast suburban rail (p116) links Athens with the airport, Piraeus, the outer regions and the northern Peloponnese. It connects to the metro at Larisis, Doukissis Plakentias and Nerantziotissa stations, and goes from the airport to Kiato (€14, 1¾ hours).

Tram

Athens' **tram** (www.stasy.gr) offers a slow, scenic coastal journey to Faliro and Voula, via Glyfada.

Trams run from Syntagma to Faliro (45 minutes), Syntagma to Voula (one hour) and Faliro to Voula from 5.30am to 1am Sunday to Thursday (every 10 minutes), and from 5.30am to 2.30am on Friday and Saturday (every 40 minutes).

The Syntagma terminus is on Leoforos Vasilissis Amalias, opposite the National Gardens, with ticket vending machines on platforms.

TAXI

Despite the many yellow taxis, it can be tricky getting one, especially during rush hour. Thrust your arm out vigorously...and still you may have to shout your destination to the driver to see if he or she is interested. Make sure the meter is on. The smartphone app **Uber** (www.uber.com) is usable in Athens.

If a taxi picks you up while already carrying passengers, the fare is not shared: each person pays the fare on the meter minus any diversions to drop others (note what it's at when you get in). Short trips around central Athens cost about €5; there are surcharges for pick-ups at the airport

and transport hubs, as well as holiday and night tariffs. Taxi services include **Athina 1** (🖉 210 921 7942), **Enotita** (🖉 210 645 9000, 18388; www. athensradiotaxienotita.gr), **Taxibeat** (www. taxibeat.gr) and **Parthenon** (🖉 210 581 4711).

ATHENS PORTS

Piraeus   Πειραιάς

POP 163,700

The highlights of Greece's main port and ferry hub, Piraeus, are the other-worldly rows of ferries, ships and hydrofoils filling its seemingly endless quays. Piraeus, 10km southwest of central Athens, is the biggest port in the Mediterranean (with more than 20 million passengers passing through annually), the hub of the Aegean ferry network, the centre of Greece's maritime trade and the base for its large merchant navy. While technically a separate city, these days Piraeus virtually melds into the urban sprawl of Athens.

Central Piraeus is not a place where visitors choose to linger because it's congested with traffic. Beyond its shipping offices, banks and public buildings are a jumble of pedestrian precincts, shopping strips and rather grungy areas. The most attractive quarter lies to the east around **Zea Marina** and touristy **Mikrolimano** harbour, which is lined with cafes, restaurants and bars.

Piraeus has been the port of Athens since classical times, when Themistocles transferred his Athenian fleet from the exposed port of Phaleron (modern Faliro) to the security of Piraeus in the 5th century BC. It was eventually overtaken by other ports, and during medieval and Turkish times, it diminished into a tiny fishing village. Its resurgence began in 1834 when Athens became the capital of independent Greece. To kill time, visit the **Piraeus Archaeological Museum** (🖉 210 452 1598; http://odysseus. culture.gr; Harilaou Trikoupi 31; adult/child €3/ free; ⊙8am-3pm Tue-Sun) with its magnificent statue of Apollo, or the **Hellenic Maritime Museum** (🖉 210 451 6264; http://odysseus. culture.gr; Akti Themistokleous, Plateia Freatidas, Zea Marina; admission €4; ⊙9am-2pm Tue-Sun).

🛏 Sleeping

If you're catching an early ferry you can stay in Piraeus instead of central Athens,

Piraeus

Piraeus

⊙ Sights
1 Piraeus Archaeological Museum D4

🛏 Sleeping
2 Hotel Triton D2
3 Piraeus Theoxenia D2
4 Pireaus Dream City Hotel D3

🍴 Eating
5 General Market D2
6 Mandragoras D2
7 Marinopoulos–Carrefour D2
8 Rakadiko D2
9 Yperokeanio A4

ⓘ Transport
10 Bus 040 to Syntagma D2

11 Bus X96 to Airport C2
12 Gate E1 (for the Dodecanese) A2
13 Gate E2 (for Crete & Northeastern
   Aegean Islands) B2
14 Gate E4 (for Crete) B1
15 Gate E7 (for the Western &
   Central Cyclades) C1
16 Gate E7 (for the Western &
   Central Cyclades) C1
17 Gate E8 (for the Cyclades) C2
18 Gate E8 (for the Saronic Gulf
   Islands) C2
19 Gate E9 (for the Cyclades) D2
20 Gate E9 (for the Cyclades, Samos,
   Ikaria) C3
21 Shuttle Bus to Gates E1 to E3 .... C1

but many of the hotels around Megas Limani (Great Harbour) are shabby and are aimed at sailors and clandestine liaisons. Don't sleep outside: Piraeus is probably one of the most dangerous places in Greece to do so.

Pireaus Dream City Hotel
HOTEL €

(☏ 210 411 0555; www.pireausdream.gr; Filonos 79-81; d/tr incl breakfast from €60/97; ✳@🛜; Ⓜ Piraeus) This renovated hotel is about 500m from the metro; quiet rooms start on the 4th floor. It has a rooftop restaurant.

Hotel Triton
HOTEL €

(☏ 210 417 3457; www.htriton.gr; Tsamadou 8; d/tr incl breakfast from €60/90; ✳@🛜; Ⓜ Piraeus) This simple, conveniently located hotel with helpful staff is a treat compared to the usual rundown joints in Piraeus. Some rooms overlook the bustling market square. There's one family suite (€100).

Piraeus Theoxenia
HOTEL €€

(☏ 210 411 2550; www.theoxeniapalace.com; Karaoli Dimitriou 23; d/tr incl breakfast from €90/125, 2-bedroom ste incl breakfast €248; ✳@🛜; Ⓜ Piraeus) Piraeus' swanky, central hotel, with plump bathrobes and satellite TV. Get the best deals online.

🍴 Eating & Drinking

The Great Harbour is backed by lots of gritty cafes and fast-food joints; better food and ambience hide away in the backstreets – or further afield around Mikrolimano harbour, Zea Marina and along the waterfront promenade at Freatida.

Yperokeanio
MEZEDHES €

(☏ 210 418 0030; Marias Chatzikiriakou 48; dishes €6-12; ☉noon-11.30pm) Grab a cab to hit this fantastic seafood *mezedhopoleio*, where you can tuck into small plates tapas-style, from grilled sardines to steamed mussels. Save room for the special *kaimaki* ice cream – made from a traditional Greek recipe using mastic and *sahlep* (a flour made from orchid tubers). Book ahead, if possible; it's often packed.

Rakadiko
TAVERNA €

(☏ 210 417 8470; www.rakadiko.gr; Karaoli Dimitriou 5, Stoa Kouvelou; mains €6-15; ☉lunch & dinner Tue-Sat; Ⓜ Piraeus) Dine quietly under grapevines on mezedhes or classic dishes from all over Greece. Live *rembetika* on weekends.

Margaro
SEAFOOD €€

(☏ 210 451 4226; Marias Chatzikiriakou 126; mains €6-21; ☉noon-midnight Sep-Jul; 🚌904) It's worth a taxi ride to this long-time local favourite known for its fresh crayfish, eaten in a giant pile. Indulge in whatever's fresh at this off-the-beaten-path, casual gem.

★ Varoulko
SEAFOOD €€€

(☏ 210 522 8400; www.varoulko.gr; Akti Koumoundourou 52, Mikrolimano, Piraeus; mains €45-65; ☉1pm-1am) For a heady Greek dining experience, try the Michelin-starred combination of waterfront views and Lefteris Lazarou's delicious seafood. Sip on top wines as sailboats bob in the harbour at Mikrolimano.

Self-Catering

★ Mandragoras
DELI €

(☏ 210 417 2961; Gounari 14; ☉7.45am-4pm Mon, Wed & Sat, to 8pm Tue, Thu & Fri; Ⓜ Piraeus) This superb delicatessen offers a fine selection of gourmet cheeses, ready-made mezedhes, spices, olive oils and preserved foods.

General Market
MARKET €

(Dimosthenous; ☉6am-4pm Mon-Fri; Ⓜ Piraeus) Broad range of food and bric-a-brac.

Marinopoulos–Carrefour
SUPERMARKET €

(☏ 210 417 5764; Makras Stoas 1; ☉8am-8pm Mon-Fri, to 4pm Sat; Ⓜ Piraeus) Convenient for provisioning for longer trips.

ℹ️ Information

There are luggage lockers at the metro station (€3 for 24 hours), and free wifi around the port.

ATMs and money changers line the Great Harbour.

Alpha Bank (Makras Stoas 15; ☉8am-2pm Mon-Fri)

National Bank of Greece (cnr Antistaseos & Tsamadou; ☉8am-2pm Mon-Fri)

ℹ️ Getting There & Away

The metro and suburban rail lines from Athens terminate at the northeastern corner of the Great Harbour on Akti Kalimassioti. Most ferry departure points are a short walk over the footbridge from here. A left turn out of the metro station leads 250m to Plateia Karaïskaki, the terminus for airport buses.

Athens tramway and an additional metro extension to the port of Piraeus are underway, and scheduled to be completed by 2017.

BOAT

Piraeus is the busiest port in Greece, with a bewildering array of departures, including daily service to most island groups. The exceptions are the Ionians, with boats only to Kythira (for the other islands, sail from Patra and Igoumenitsa) and the Sporades, plus Kea (Tzia) and Andros in the Cyclades (which sail from Rafina and Lavrio). Piraeus ferries also serve the Peloponnese (Methana, Ermioni, Porto Heli, Monemvasia and Gythio).

Always check departure docks with the ticketing agent.

Note that there are two departure points for Crete at Piraeus port: ferries for Iraklio leave from the western end of Akti Kondyli, but ferries for other Cretan ports occasionally dock there as well, or in other places.

Schedules & Tickets

All ferry companies have online timetables and booths on the quays. Ferry schedules are reduced in April, May and October, and are radically cut in winter, especially to smaller islands. Find schedules and buy tickets online (www.greekferries.gr, www.openseas.gr, www.ferries.gr or company websites) or at travel agents, or phone companies directly. In this book, we list ferry schedules in the relevant island/destination chapters. **Piraeus Port Authority** (☏14541; www.olp.gr) also has schedule information.

BUS

The X96 Piraeus–Athens Airport Express (tickets €5) leaves from the southwestern corner of Plateia Karaïskaki and also stops on Kalimassioti. Bus 040 goes from Leoforeos Vasileos Georgiou to Athens.

METRO

The fastest and most convenient link between the Great Harbour and Athens is the metro (€1.40, 30 minutes, every 10 minutes, 5am to midnight), near the ferries at the northern end of Akti Kalimassioti. Take extra care as the section between Piraeus and Monastiraki is notorious for pickpockets.

TRAIN

Piraeus is also connected to the suburban rail, the terminus of which is located opposite the metro station. To get to the airport or to Kiato in the Peloponnese, you need to change trains at Nerantziotissa.

❶ Getting Around

The port is massive, so a free shuttle bus runs regularly along the quay nearest the metro station (see signposted maps).

The city of Piraeus has its own network of buses. The services likely to interest travellers are buses 904 and 905 between Zea Marina and the metro station.

Athens tramway and metro extensions are underway (completion is scheduled for 2017) and have made the port area a zoo of blocked streets and redirected traffic.

Rafina   Ραφήνα

Rafina, on Attica's east coast, is Athens' main fishing port and the second-most important port for passenger ferries. It is far smaller than Piraeus and less confusing – and fares are about 20% cheaper – but the trip does take an hour on the bus.

BOAT SERVICES FROM RAFINA

DESTINATION	COMPANY	TIME	FARE	FREQUENCY
Andros	Fast Ferries, Golden Star	2½hr	€17	4-6 daily
Evia (Marmari)	J/V Rafinas - Marmariou	1hr	€8	3-6 daily
Ios	Blue Star	7¼ hr	€35	6 weekly
Ios*	Hellenic Seaways, Blue Star, Sea Jets	4hr	€55	5 weekly
Mykonos	Golden Star, Blue Star, Fast Ferries	4½hr	€27	2-3 daily
Mykonos*	Hellenic Seaways, Sea Jets	2hr 10min	€49	2 daily
Naxos	Blue Star	6hr	€32	6 weekly
Naxos*	Hellenic Seaways, Sea Jets	4hr	€52	1 daily
Paros	Blue Star	5hr	€30	6 weekly
Paros*	Hellenic Seaways	3hr	€50	1 daily
Santorini (Thira)*	Hellenic Seaways, Sea Jets	5½hr	€22-69	1 daily
Tinos	Golden Star, Fast Ferries	4hr	€24	4 daily
Tinos*	Hellenic Seaways, Sea Jets	2hr	€49-54.50	2-4 daily

*high-speed services

ⓘ Getting There & Away

BUS

Frequent **KTEL** (☏ 210 880 8000, 210 880 8080, Rafina 22940 23440; www.ktelattikis. gr) buses run from Athens to Rafina (€2.40, one hour) between 5.45am and 10.30pm, departing Athens' Mavromateon terminal. Buses from Athens Airport (€3, 45 minutes) leave from in front of the arrivals hall, near the Sofitel. Both stop on the Rafina quay.

BOAT

Rafina Port Authority (☏ 22940 28888; www. rafinaport.gr) and www.openseas.gr have information on ferries.

Lavrio   Λαύριο

Lavrio, an industrial town on the coast 60km southeast of Athens, is the port for ferries to Kea and Kythnos and high-season catamarans to the western Cyclades. In antiquity it was an important mining town. The silver mines here funded the great classical-building boom in Athens and helped build the fleet that defeated the Persians – some of the underground shafts and mining galleries are still visible. Lavrio has also become a windsurfing spot.

Lavrio has many fish tavernas and *ouzeries,* as well as a great fish market.

⦿ Sights

Mineralogical Museum   MUSEUM
(☏ 22920 26270; http://odysseus.culture.gr; Iroön Polytehniou; adult/child €2/free; ⊙ 9am-3pm Mon-Sat) Fabulous crystals and metals mined from the area are the highlights of Lavrio's tiny Mineralogical Museum, which also traces the region's rich mining history. It's in the town's old steam-powered ore-washing facility.

Archaeological Museum   MUSEUM
(☏ 22920 22817; http://odysseus.culture.gr; cnr M Mitropoulou & Perikleous, Sepieri; adult/child €2/free; ⊙ 8am-3pm Tue-Sun) Lavrio's small ar-

ⓘ SHORTCUTS

Because of Lavrio's, and especially Rafina's, close proximity to Athens' airport, if you are going to the northern Cyclades it is often fastest to go straight from the airport to the port, bypassing Athens and Piraeus completely.

chaeological museum holds finds from the area, some dating to 5000 BC.

ⓘ Getting There & Away

BUS

KTEL buses to Lavrio (€5.20, two hours, every 30 minutes) run from the Mavromateon terminal in Athens. Airport buses (€5, one hour) leave from the front of the arrivals hall near the Sofitel; you must change buses at Markopoulo. Both stop on the Lavrio quay.

BOAT

Lavrio Port Authority (☏ 22920 25249) and www.openseas.gr have ferry information.

TAXI

Lavrio taxis (☏ 22920 25871, 6981040085) can run you to the airport (€40, 30 minutes), central Athens (€50, one hour) and Piraeus (€60, 1½ hours).

AROUND ATHENS

Until the 7th century, Attica was home to a number of smaller kingdoms, such as those at Eleusis (Elefsina), Ramnous and Brauron (Vravrona). The remains of these cities continue to be among the region's attractions, although they pale alongside the superb Temple of Poseidon at Cape Sounion.

An agricultural and wine-growing region with several large population centres, Attica has some fine beaches, particularly along the Apollo Coast and at Shinias, near Marathon. Area vintners have created an excellent clearing house of information on local wineries (see www.winesofathens.com), including a downloadable map.

Many of these places can be reached (often with some difficulty, as schedules can be infrequent) by regular city buses or KTEL services from the Mavromateon terminal. It's easiest to go with your own wheels.

The Apollo Coast

Glyfada, about 17km southeast of Athens, marks the beginning of a 48km stretch of coastline known as the Apollo Coast (sometines referred to as the Athenian Riviera), which is fringed by a string of fine beaches and upmarket resorts running south to Cape Sounion. Much of the summer nightlife (p107) takes place here, and it can be a refreshing getaway from Athens if you don't have time to hit the islands.

Continuing south from busy Glyfada, which functions as an upscale suburb to Athens, the coast road (Leoforos Poseidonos, often just called *paraliaki*) leads to **Voula**, **Kavouri**, and then bustling and popular **Vouliagmeni** and ritzy Astir Beach, on a small peninsula. Continuing on you come to Vouliagmeni's magical mineral lake (Limni Vouliagmenis) and its cluster of resorts. As the road curves around a small point, the nudist and gay beach rocky coves of Limanakia (p109) give way to laid-back **Varkiza**, **Agia Marina** and beyond. The further you go beyond Vouliagemeni, the more unspoilt the coastline.

There is also good (free) swimming northeast and east of Athens, at Shinias, Marathon and Vravrona, though these take much longer to get to and are best reached by car – the Apollo Coast is the easiest bet for a dip.

Sights & Activities

Most of the Apollo Coast beaches are privately run and charge admission (€5 to €15 per adult). They're usually open between 8am and dusk, May to October (later during heatwaves), and have sunbeds and umbrellas (additional charge in some places), changing rooms, children's playgrounds and cafes. Many morph into summertime nightclubs (p107) as well.

Akti tou Iliou   BEACH
(☑210 985 5169; www.aktitouiliou.gr; Alimos; adult/child Mon-Fri €5/3, Sat & Sun €6/3 ; ☒T5 to Zefyros) Relatively laid-back, with a slew of sun loungers and some reed-roofed beach bars, it's one of the closer beaches to Athens (just 7.5km south).

Asteras Beach   BEACH
(☑210 894 1620; www.asterascomplex.com; Glyfada; adult/child Mon-Fri €6/3, Sat & Sun €7/3; ☒790 from Syntagma, ☒T5 to Asteria) Swish Asteras is convenient to Glyfada, with waterfront bars, see-and-be-seen Balux (p107) restaurant-bar and a pool (if the beach isn't enough for you).

Astir Beach   BEACH
(☑210 890 1621; www.astir-beach.com; adult/child Mon-Fri €15/8, Sat & Sun mid-Jun–mid-Sep €25/13, reduced prices rest of year; ☒114 from Glyfada or Voula tram stops) The flashiest and

most exclusive summer beach playground is Astir Beach, with water sports, shops and restaurants. You can even book online. It's 19.5km south of Athens, 7.5km south of Glyfada.

Limni Vouliagmenis   SWIMMING
(☑210 896 2239; www.limnivouliagmenis.gr; Leoforos Vouliagmenis; adult/child Mon-Fri €9/6, Sat & Sun €10/6; ⊙7am-8pm; ☒; ☒114, 115 or 149, ☒A2 or E2) You can swim year-round at Limni Vouliagmenis, a part-saltwater/part-springwater lake whose temperature never falls below 21°C. It's also known for its therapeutic mineral qualities. Set dramatically against a huge cliff 19.5km south of Athens, its regular clientele of elderly citizens dressed in bathing caps and towelling gowns gives it a quaint, old-world atmosphere. There are sunbeds, a playground, showers and a cafe. Family packages available from €19.

Take the A2 bus (or E2 express in summer) to Plateia Glyfada (aka Plateia Katraki Vasos), then take bus 114, 115 or 149.

Yabanaki   BEACH
(☑210 897 2414; www.yabanaki.gr; Varkiza; adult/child Mon-Fri €5/3.50, Sat & Sun €6/3.50; ⊙8am-7pm Jun-Aug, 9am-5pm May; ☒122) Less flash than the beach clubs near Glyfada, Yabanaki (21km south of Syntagma) has a full complement of entertainment options, from a restaurant to beach volleyball.

Attica

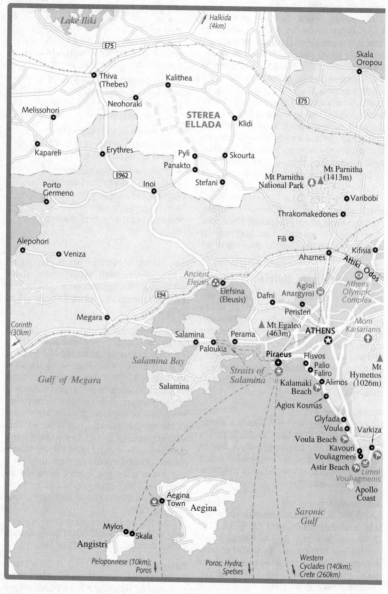

🛏 Sleeping

Villa Orion   HOTEL €

(☎210 895 8000; www.villaorionhotel.gr; I Metaxa 4, Voula; s/d incl breakfast from €35/50; 🖳122, 171, X96) This simple hotel has been dressed up with some creative interior paint, but its real attraction is its great value. It's a few blocks inland, yes, but convenient to all the beaches.

✖ Eating & Drinking

The beach clubs all have cafes and restaurants. Much of the Apollo Coast is a see-and-be-seen scene, so expect high prices and trendy hang-outs that change frequently.

Trigono
TAVERNA €

(☑ 22990 48540; Athinon 36, Kalyvia; mains €6-12; ⊙ lunch & dinner) This beloved taverna, about 8km inland near Agios Dimitrios, attracts folks from all over the Athens area for its perfectly grilled carnivores' delights.

Moouu Quality Meats
STEAK €€

(☑ 211 409 6295; Foivis 17, Glyfada; mains €10-25; ⊙ 12.30pm-2am; ⊞ 5) Sup on grilled meats at this steakhouse du jour in the heart of Glyfada's restaurant and cafe district.

Matsuhisa
SUSHI €€€

(☑ 210 896 0510; www.matsuhisaathens.com; Apollonos 40, Vouliagmeni; sushi rolls €5-15; ⊙ 7.30pm-1am; ⊞ 122) Come to Greece to eat sushi? Well why not, if you're in the mood to hang with chic Athenians at this popular waterfront restaurant that's run by world-famous restaurateur Nobu Matsuhisa. Views are exquisite – to match the people and the pricetag. Book ahead.

Malabar
LOUNGE

(☑ 210 892 9160; www.themargi.gr; Litous 11, Margi Hotel, Vouliagmeni; ⊙ 11am-2am; ⊞ 122) The cushy pool bar and restaurant at the **Margi Hotel** (doubles from €215) is popular for its comfy lounges and trendy atmosphere. The hotel also has a high-concept Greek restaurant called Baku.

Cape Sounion
Ακρωτήριο Σούνιο

★ Temple of Poseidon
RUIN

(☑ 22920 39363; http://odysseus.culture.gr; Cape Sounion; adult/child €4/free; ⊙ 8am-sunset, from 9.30am winter) The Ancient Greeks certainly knew how to choose a site for a temple. Nowhere is this more evident than at Cape Sounion, 70km south of Athens, where the Temple of Poseidon stands on a craggy spur that plunges 65m down to the sea. Built in 444 BC (at the same time as the Parthenon), it is constructed of local marble from Agrilesa; its slender columns, of which 16 remain, are Doric.

It is thought that the temple was built by Iktinos, the architect of the Temple of Hephaestus in Athens' Ancient Agora.

Hotel Vouliagmeni Suites
HOTEL €€

(☑ 210 896 4901; www.vouliagmenisuites.com; Panos 8, Vouliagmeni; s/d incl breakfast from €130/140; ⊞ 122) This posh pad a bit back from the beach has quirkily decorated luxe rooms, some with sea views.

It looks gleaming white when viewed from the sea, which gave great comfort to sailors in ancient times: they knew they were nearly home when they saw the first glimpse of white, far off in the distance. The views from the temple are equally impressive: on a clear day you can see Kea, Kythnos and Serifos to the southeast, and Aegina and the Peloponnese to the west. The site also contains scant remains of a **propylaeum**, a fortified **tower** and, to the northeast, a 6th-century **temple to Athena**.

Visit early in the morning before the tourist buses arrive, or head there for sunset to enact Byron's lines from *Don Juan*: 'Place me on Sunium's marbled steep / Where nothing save the waves and I / May hear our mutual murmurs sweep.'

Byron was so impressed by Sounion that he carved his name on one of the columns (sadly, many other not-so-famous travellers followed suit).

There are a couple of tavernas just below the site – perfect for lunch and a swim.

Mt Parnitha   Πάρνηθα

◉ Sights & Activities

Mt Parnitha National Park   NATIONAL PARK
(☑ 21024 34061; www.parnitha-np.gr) The densely forested Mt Parnitha National Park, about 25km north of Athens, is the highest mountain range surrounding the city. More than 4200 hectares of century-old fir and pine forest were razed in devastating fires in 2007; the state has since tripled the area designated as national park and launched a reforestation program. Criss-crossed by walking trails, the park is also popular for mountain biking and has two hikers' shelters. Buy the Road Editions hiking map of the area.

Mt Parnitha comprises a number of smaller peaks, the highest of which is **Karavola** (1413m), tall enough to get snow in winter. There are many caves and much wildlife, including red deer.

Dasoktima Tatoiou is the area of the former royal palace (closed); it has forested grounds and is great for hiking and biking as well.

✖ Eating

Agios Merkourios II   TAVERNA €€
(☑ 210 816 9617; Varibobi; mains €6-15; ⊙ lunch & dinner) Weekends, this busy taverna is packed with Athenians making the country pilgrimage for top meat. Lamb, kid and veal are the order of the day. Find it in Varimbombi at the foot of Mt Parnitha.

Marathon & Around
Μαραθώνας

The plain surrounding this small, unremarkable town, 42km northeast of Athens, is the site of one of the most celebrated battles in world history. In 490 BC an army of 9000 Greeks and 1000 Plataeans defeated the 25,000-strong Persian army, proving that the Persians were not invincible. The Greeks were indebted to the ingenious tactics of Miltiades, who altered the conventional battle formation so that there were fewer soldiers in the centre, but more in the wings. The Persians, thinking that the Greeks would be easily beat, broke through in the centre, only to be ambushed by the soldiers in the wings. At day's end, 6000 Persians but just 192 Greeks lay dead. Legend has it that after the battle, Pheidippides ran to Athens to announce the victory; after shouting '*Enikesame*!' ('We won!') he collapsed and died – thus the origin of today's marathon endurance races. The Marathon battlefield is where the **Athens Marathon** (www.athensauthenticmarathon.gr) begins.

◉ Sights & Activities

Marathon Battlefield & Tomb   MONUMENT
(☑ 22940 55462; http://odysseus.culture.gr; site & archaeological museum adult/child €3/free; ⊙ 8am-8pm Mon-Fri, to 3pm Sat & Sun, reduced hours Oct-May) Four kilometres outside the town of Marathon, 350m from the Athens–Marathon road, sits this 10m-high tumulus, (burial mound). In Ancient Greece, bodies of those killed in battle were returned to their families for private burial, but as a sign of honour the 192 men who fell at Marathon were cremated and buried in this collective tomb. The site has a model of the battle and historical information.

Marathon Archaeological Museum   MUSEUM
(☑ 22940 55155; http://odysseus.culture.gr; museum & Marathon Tomb site adult/child €3/free; ⊙ 8am-8pm Mon-Fri, to 3pm Sat & Sun, reduced hours Oct-May) Near the town of Marathon, this excellent museum displays local discoveries from various periods, including neolithic pottery from the Cave of Pan and finds from the Tomb of the Athenians. New finds

include several larger-than-life statues from an **Egyptian sanctuary** in nearby **Brexiza**. Next to the museum is one of the area's **prehistoric grave circle sites**, which has been preserved under a hangarlike shelter, with raised platforms and walkways. Another hangar nearby contains an early Helladic **cemetery site**.

Ramnous RUIN
(☑22940 63477; http://odysseus.culture.gr; adult/child €2/free; ☉8.30am-3pm Tue-Sun) The evocative, overgrown and secluded ruins of the ancient port of Ramnous, about 10km northeast of Marathon, stand on a picturesque plateau overlooking the sea. Among the ruins are the remains of the Doric **Temple of Nemesis** (435 BC). Another section of the site leads 1km down a track to a cliff-top with the relatively well-preserved town **fortress** and the remains of the city, a temple, a gymnasium and a theatre. There is no public transport to the site.

Nemesis was the goddess of divine retribution, and mother of Helen of Troy. There are also ruins of a smaller 6th-century temple dedicated to Themis, goddess of justice.

Shinias BEACH
The long, sandy, pine-fringed beach at Shinias, southeast of Marathon, is the best in this part of Attica. It's very popular at weekends.

🛏 Sleeping & Eating

Ramnous Camping CAMPGROUND €
(☑22940 55855; www.ramnous.gr; Leoforos Poseidonos 174, Shinias; camp sites per adult/car/tent €7.50/3.50/7; ☉Apr-Oct) Ramnous Camping, about 1km from Shinias Beach, is the most pleasant camping ground in Attica, with sites nestled among shrubberies and trees. There's a minimarket, bar-restaurant, playground and laundry, as well as tents for hire.

Galazia Akti BEACH CLUB €€
(☑22940 55800; www.galaziaakti.com; Leoforos Poseidonos 206, Shinias; mains €6-15; ☉Easter-Oct) Renovated in 2014, this waterfront beach club at Shinias beach, near Marathon, makes a welcome respite from the heat. Grab a bite to eat and take a cool dip.

Vravrona Βραυρώνα

Sanctuary of Artemis RUIN
(Brauron; ☑22990 27020; adult/child €4/free; ☉8am-2.45pm Tue-Sun) This site, originally a neolithic settlement, came to be revered by worshippers of Artemis, the goddess of the hunt and protector of women in childbirth and newborns. The current remains of the temple date from approximately 420 BC, though the remains of other structures predate that. The **museum** houses exceptional finds from the sanctuary and excavations in the area.

From Athens, take metro line 3 to Nomismatikopio, then bus 304 to Artemis (Vravrona). It's a 10-minute taxi ride from there, with a nice stretch of beach on the way.

Peania Παιανία

Once Peania's biggest claim to fame was as the birthplace of Greek statesman Demosthenes (384-322 BC). Today the area is known primarily for remarkable **Koutouki Cave** (Σπήλαιο Κουτούκι Παιανίας; ☑210 664 2910; http://odysseus.culture.gr; Peania; adult/child €5/free; ☉9am-3pm Mon-Fri, 9.30am-2.30pm Sat & Sun), which is 4.5 km outside Peania and best reached by car, and a fine art and culture museum, the **Vorres Museum** (☑210 664 2520; www.vorresmuseum.gr; Parodos Diadohou Konstantinou 4, Peania; adult/child €5/free; ☉10am-2pm Sat & Sun; ☐125 or 308 to Koropi-Peania; Ⓜ Nomismatikopio).

Elefsina Ελευσίνα

The **Ancient Eleusis** (☑210 554 6019; adult/child €3/free; ☉8.30am-3pm Tue-Sun; ☐A16 or B16 from Plateia Eleftherias/Koumoundourou) ruins lie beside the industrial town of Elefsina, 22km west of Athens. In ancient times it nestled on the slopes of a low hill close to the shore of the Saronic Gulf, built around the Sanctuary of Demeter. The site dates to Mycenaean times, when the cult of Demeter began. By classical times it was celebrated with a huge annual festival. In the 4th century AD, Roman emperor Theodosius closed it.

Peloponnese

Best Places to Eat

➡ 3Sixty° (p142)

➡ Voula's Yesterday & Today (p162)

➡ Chrisovoulo (p156)

➡ Teloneio (p160)

➡ Elies (p164)

Best Places to Stay

➡ Antares (p159)

➡ Traditional Guesthouse Mazaraki (p154)

➡ Nafplion 1841 (p141)

➡ Tainaron Blue (p159)

➡ Mpelleiko (p146)

Why Go?

The Peloponnese (pe-lo-*po*-nih-sos; Πελοπόννησος) is the stuff of legends. Literally. It is here that Hercules fought the Nemean lion and gods walked the earth, meddling in mortal affairs; it's from here that Paris of Troy eloped with Helen and the Argonauts set sail in search of the Golden Fleece. Celestial and mythological charms aside, this region bears tangible traces of the many civilisations that once called it home, witnessed in its classical temples, Mycenaean palaces, Byzantine cities, and Ottoman, Frankish and Venetian fortresses.

The very topography that kept invaders at bay for centuries – lofty, snowcapped mountains, vast gorges, sandy beaches and azure waters – now draws visitors of a very different kind. *Filoxenia* (hospitality) is as strong here as anywhere in the country; the food is among Greece's best; and the region's vineyards are contributing to Greece's wine renaissance. Locals claim to have the best of everything to give. And that's no myth.

When to Go
Nafplio

| °C/°F Temp | | Rainfall inches/mm |

Apr–Jun Perfect hiking and beach weather, without the summer crowds.

Sep Take part in the gruelling Spartathlon...if you think you're tough enough.

Easter The pomp and ceremony of religious festivities during Orthodox Easter week are unforgettable.

History

Since ancient times the Peloponnese (named after the mythical Pelops) has played a major role in Greek history. When the Minoan civilisation declined after 1450 BC, the focus of power in the ancient Aegean world moved from Crete to the hill-fortress palaces of Mycenae and Tiryns in the Peloponnese. As elsewhere in Greece, the 400 years following the Dorian conquests in the 12th century BC are known as the Dark Ages. When the region emerged from darkness in the 7th century BC, Athens' arch rival, Sparta, had surpassed Mycenae as the most powerful city in the Peloponnese, sparking the Peloponnesian Wars (431–04 BC).

A period of peace and prosperity ensued under Roman rule (146 BC to around AD 250) but was shattered by a series of invasions by Goths, Avars and Slavs.

The Byzantines were slow to make inroads into the Peloponnese, only becoming firmly established during the 9th century AD. In 1204, after the fall of Constantinople to the Crusaders, the Frankish Crusader chiefs William de Champlitte and Geoffrey de Villehardouin divided the region into 12 fiefs, which they parcelled out to various barons of France, Flanders and Burgundy. These fiefs were overseen by de Villehardouin, the self-appointed prince of the Morea, as the region was called in medieval times.

The Byzantines gradually won back the Morea and although the empire as a whole was now in decline, a glorious renaissance took place in the area, centred on Mystras, the region's seat of government.

The Morea fell to the Turks in 1460, and hundreds of years of power struggles between the Turks and Venetians followed. The Venetians had long coveted the Morea and succeeded in establishing profitable trading ports at Methoni, Pylos, Koroni and Monemvasia.

The Greek War of Independence supposedly began in the Peloponnese, when Bishop Germanos of Patra raised the flag of revolt near Kalavryta on 25 March 1821. The Egyptian army, under the leadership of Ibrahim Pasha, brutally restored Turkish rule in 1825.

In 1827 the Triple Alliance of Great Britain, France and Russia – moved by Greek suffering and by the activities of philhellenes (the death of Lord Byron in 1824 was particularly influential) – came to the rescue of the Greeks by destroying the Turkish–Egyptian fleet at the Battle of Navarino, ending Turkish domination of the area.

The Peloponnese became part of the independent state of Greece, and Nafplio became the first national capital. Ioannis Kapodistrias, Greece's first president, was assassinated on the steps of Nafplio's Church of St Spyridon in October 1831, and the new king, Otto, moved the capital to Athens in 1834.

Like the rest of Greece, the Peloponnese suffered badly during WWII and the civil war (1944–49) that followed. During the 1950s many villagers migrated to Athens, and further abroad to Australia, Canada, South Africa and the USA.

ℹ Information

Due to the Greek financial crisis, the hours of museums and sites in the Peloponnese are particularly vulnerable to change. Check in advance.

ℹ Getting There & Around

BUSES

Be aware of the difference between Corinth Isthmus (the canal) and Corinth (the city). Located on a main road on the Peloponnese side of the Corinth Canal, the **Corinth Isthmus (Peloponnese) KTEL bus station** (☑ 27410 75410, in Athens 210 512 4919) is the spot to change for buses south to the rest of the Peloponnese. No formal timetables are available; most buses from Athens heading to the Peloponnese stop here.

The **KTEL Korinthos bus station** (☑ 27410 75425; www.ktel-korinthias.gr; Dimocratias 4) in Corinth (city) is the departure point for buses to Ancient Corinth (€1.60, 20 minutes, seven daily Monday to Saturday), Nemea (€4.50, one hour, four to five daily, one Sunday) and Loutraki (for Corinth Isthmus; €1.70, 10 minutes, half-hourly).

Weekend bus services range from infrequent to nonexistent.

CAR

If driving the winding, scenic minor roads across the peninsula, always allow yourself plenty of time. When going around sharp bends, watch out for oncoming drivers who can tend to cut across your lane without sounding their horn.

At research time, the E65, the coastal motorway that connects Athens to Patra, was in the process of being turned into a four-lane highway; however, work has been suspended in the past due to lack of funding. The barrier in the middle of the road means travelling in heavy traffic at the speed of the slowest vehicle, with few opportunities for overtaking.

TRAINS

At research time the OSE train services in the Peloponnese were suspended. Only one line – Athens to Patra – was operating, with a replacement bus service between Kiato and Patra.

Peloponnese Highlights

1 Soaking up the past and present of **Nafplio** (p138) and **Monemvasia** (p154).

2 Marvelling at the sanctuary of **Ancient Olympia** (p173), birthplace of the Olympic Games.

3 Hiking the remote and rugged **Mani** (p157) and staying in traditional Maniot tower houses.

4 Hiking the **Menalon Trail** (p146) through the **Lousios Gorge** and discovering the delights of charming mountain villages **Stemnitsa** and **Dimitsana**.

5 Meandering through the magical **Mystras** (p152), a World Heritage–listed Byzantine site.

6 Exploring the historic sites of **Ancient Mycenae** (p135), **Ancient Nemea** (p133) and **Epidavros** (p143).

7 Tackling the dramatic **Vouraïkos Gorge** (p184) via the unique rack-and-pinion train or on foot from the historic village of Kalavryta.

The *proastiako*, Athens' suburban rail service, runs between Kiato, Corinth (city) train station and Athens international airport (around €12, 1½ hours, around eight daily). A handy bus shuttles between Corinth city's Plateia Kentriki (€1.50, 20 minutes) and the train station.

A small local train runs between Pyrgos and Olympia (for Ancient Olympia) and a rack-and-pinion railway connects Diakofto with Kalavryta.

CORINTHIA   ΚΟΡΙΝΘΙΑ

Corinthia has had a rich and tumultuous history, owing largely to its strategic position adjoining the Corinth Isthmus. Throughout time several empires have wrestled here for dominance over the Peloponnese: the Romans constructed a vast wall across the isthmus; many centuries later the Turks overran it; and pretty much everyone else has attempted to carve a canal across it.

Once dominated by the mighty ancient city of Corinth, Corinthia is now the keeper of its remains.

In the pretty hinterland west of Corinth you can take part in the resurrected Nemean Games, or travel the Nemea region's wine route in search of Greece's best vintages.

Ancient Corinth & Acrocorinth
Αρχαία Κόρινθος & Ακροκόρινθος

Ancient Corinth was an affluent and powerful city during its first golden age. Earthquakes and centuries of pillage, however, have left only the remnants of once-grand buildings, 7km southwest of the modern city, surrounded by the village of Ancient Corinth and overlooked by the Acrocorinth fortress.

History

During the 6th century BC Corinth was one of Ancient Greece's richest cities, thanks to its strategic position on the Corinth Isthmus. Its twin ports, one on the Aegean Sea (Kenchreai, near Kechries) and one on the Ionian side (Lecheon), enabled it to trade throughout the Mediterranean. It survived the Peloponnesian Wars and flourished under Macedonian rule, but it was sacked by the Roman consul Mummius in 146 BC for rebelling against Roman rule. In 44 BC Julius Caesar began rebuilding the city and it again became a prosperous port.

☉ Sights

★ Ancient Corinth   ARCHAEOLOGICAL SITE
(🖉 27410 31207; admission €6; ☉ 8.30am-8pm)
In the centre of a modern village loom the extensive yet compact ruins of this ancient (mostly Roman) city. Home to the legendary Jason of the Argonauts, stealer of the Golden Fleece, the streets of Ancient Corinth were once trodden by the likes of Roman traveller Pausanias and St Paul, who taught the gospel of Christ in vain here. You can follow in their footsteps by visiting the Temple of Apollo, the Peribolos of Apollo, the ancient theatre and other site highlights. The on-site museum puts everything into context.

An exception to the Roman ruins is the prominent 5th-century-BC Doric **Temple of Apollo**. To the south of this temple is a huge **agora** (market) bounded on its southern side by the foundations of a **stoa** (long colonnaded building). This was built to accommodate the bigwigs summoned here in 337 BC by Philip II to sign oaths of allegiance to Macedon. In the middle of the central row of shops is a **bema**, a marble podium from which Roman officials addressed the people.

At the eastern end of the *agora* are the remains of the Julian basilica. To the north is the **Lower Peirene fountain** – the Upper Peirene fountain is on Acrocorinth. According to mythology, Peirene wept so much when her son Kenchrias was killed by Artemis that the gods, rather than let all the precious water go to waste, turned her into a fountain.

West of the fountain, steps lead to the Lecheon road, once the main thoroughfare to the port of Lecheon. On the east side of the road is the **Peribolos of Apollo**, a courtyard flanked by Ionic columns, some of which have been restored. Nearby is a public latrine, where some seats remain.

South of the museum are the columns of **Temple E** (Pausanias describes it as being dedicated to Octavia, sister of Augustus).

The site's excellent **museum** has three main rooms: the first two exhibit fine Greek and Roman statues, mosaics, figurines, reliefs and friezes. The third room houses the finds of excavations at the nearby Sanctuary of Asklepios (500 BC). Highlights include grave markers, votive genitalia from the 4th century BC and an ancient 'keep off the grass' sign.

Opposite the site entrance is the **ancient theatre**, built in the 5th century BC for up to 15,000 spectators, and the Roman **odeion** (indoor theatre), from the 1st century AD.

Acrocorinth

FORTRESS

(☉8am-8pm) FREE High up above Ancient Corinth, crowning the sheer bulk of limestone known as Acrocorinth, are the ruins of one of the finest natural fortifications in Ancient Greece. Cast your eyes upwards and you'll give an involuntary gasp. Commanding wonderful views over the surrounding region, the fortress is a stiff but utterly worthwhile 4km uphill hike (or taxi ride) if you don't have your own wheels.

The original fortress has been modified many times over the centuries by a string of invaders. Passing through the three gates (Turkish, Frankish and Byzantine), you can explore the medley of imposing Roman, Byzantine, Frankish, Venetian and Turkish ramparts, harbouring remains of Byzantine chapels, Turkish houses and mosques.

From the main path, the right fork leads to the remains of a 14th-century **Frankish keep**. The central path leads you to the **Fountain of Peirene**, the favourite watering hole of Pegasus the winged horse. Accessible by the left-hand path, on the higher of Acrocorinth's two summits are the remains of the **Temple of Aphrodite**, where sacred courtesans catered to the desires of the insatiable Corinthians.

Wear stout shoes and take plenty of water.

Ancient Nemea
Αρχαία Νεμέα

Situated 31km southwest of Corinth, on the northeastern edge of modern Nemea, **Ancient Nemea** (☏27460 22739; site, museum & stadium adult/concession €4/2, site & museum adult/concession €3/2; ☉museum 8am-3pm) was once the venue for the biennial Nemean Games, held in honour of Zeus. Three original columns of the imposing 4th-century-BC Doric Temple of Zeus survive, and the on-site museum displays rich finds from the area. The stadium where the Games were held is nearby; once connected to the sanctuary by a sacred road, it plays host to the resurrected Games once again, the next in 2016.

Like Ancient Olympia, Nemea was not a city but a **sanctuary of Zeus**. The Nemean Games were hosted by the nearby city of Kleonai and became one of the great Panhellenic festivals. There's a mythological side to Nemea as well: it was around here that Hercules carried out the first of his labours – the slaying of the lion that had been sent by Hera to destroy Nemea. After Hercules had killed the lion by lifting it off the ground and choking it to death, using his prodigious strength, the lion became the constellation

CORINTH CANAL

ΤΗΣ ΚΟΡΙΝΘΟΥ

The Corinth Canal is an engineering marvel. A project that spanned many centuries, it was conceived by a ruler of Ancient Corinth, begun by Roman emperor Nero and completed in the 19th century by the French. Cut through solid rock, the canal is more than 6km long and 23m wide, its vertical sides rising 90m above the water. The canal did much to elevate Piraeus' status as a major Mediterranean port and is particularly impressive when a ship is passing through.

The concept of cutting a canal through the Corinth Isthmus to link the Ionian and Aegean Seas was first proposed by Periander, tyrant of Ancient Corinth at the end of the 7th century BC. The magnitude of the task defeated him, so he opted instead to build a *diolkos* (paved slipway), across which sailors dragged small ships on rollers, a method used until the 13th century.

In the intervening years many leaders, including Alexander the Great and Caligula, toyed with the canal idea, but it was Nero who struck the first blow himself, using a golden pickaxe in AD 67 before leaving it to 6000 Jewish slaves to do the hard work. The project was soon halted by invasions by the Gauls. Ironically, it was a French engineering company that finally completed the canal in 1893.

If you're adventurous, **Zulu Bungy Jump** (☏693 270 2535; www.zulubungy.com; €60; ☉10am-6pm Wed-Sun Jun-Sep) offers the chance to see the canal walls from a unique angle.

If you have your own transport, head to nearby **Isthmia** to the submersible bridge, one of two bridges crossing the canal. The nearby banks are great vantage points if you're lucky enough to be there when a ship passes over the submerged bridge.

All buses from Athens pass over the bridge and stop at the Corinth Isthmus KTEL bus station (p129), 200m from the canal.

NEMEA'S WINE ROUTE

In the rolling hills southwest of Corinth, the Nemea region is one of Greece's premier wine-producing areas, famous for its full-bodied reds, many produced from the local *agioritiko* grape. Look out also for wine made from *roditis*, a local variety of white grape.

Nemea has been known for its fine wines since Mycenaean times, when nearby Phlius supplied the wine for the royal court at Mycenae. Half a dozen or so wineries provide tastings for visitors (many free, some by appointment). The best spots for a tipple include the following:

Lafkiotis Winery (☎ 27460 31000; www.lafkiotis.gr; Ancient Kleonai; ⊗11am-4pm) The Lafkiotis family has been specialising in wines made from local grape varieties since 1963. Besides the *agiorgitiko*, *agionymo*, Nemea and *rodamos* reds, you can also sample the fruity *moschofilero* white.

Skouras (☎ 27510 23688; www.skouraswines.com; ⊗by appointment) George Skouras has two wineries, one near Argos and the other in the AOC region of Nemea, and has been producing wines from local and international grape varieties since 1986.

Domaine Spiropoulos (☎ 27960 61400; www.domainspiropoulos.com; Corinthos-Tripoli National Rd; ⊗by appointment) With two vineyards that have been in the family since 1860 – one near Nemea and the other one on the Martinia plateau in the heart of the Peloponnese – Apostolos Spiropoulos is a pioneering figure in organic viticulture and produces *moschofilero*, *agiorgitiko*, merlot, cabernet sauvignon, cabernet franc, chardonnay, sauvignon blanc and syrah wines.

Ktima Palivou (☎ 27460 24190; www.palivos.gr; Ancient Nemea; ⊗by appointment) Third-generation winemaker George Palivos specialises in *agiorgitiko* wines.

Gaia Wines (☎ 21080 55642; www.gaia-wines.gr; Koutsi; wine tastings €4-8; ⊗by appointment) North of Nemea in pretty hill country, Gaia Wines produces unfiltered wines, including *appellation d'origine controlée* (AOC) varieties. Its signature wine is the dry white *thalassitis*, made from the *asyrtiko* grape.

Leo (each of Hercules' 12 labours is related to a sign of the zodiac).

It's worth visiting the site's **museum** before seeing the remains of the temple. It has two models of the ancient site – the first shows what it would have looked like in 573 BC, the second in AD 500 – as well as ancient paraphernalia from the Games and treasures from the area's Mycenaean tombs. The jewel of the collection, quite literally, is the Gold of Aidonia, an exquisite assortment of gold rings, seals and beads from the site of Aidonia, near Nemea. Don't miss the video that explains the extraordinarily advanced race-starting mechanism (English subtitles).

At the temple site, the three original columns of the 4th-century-BC **Temple of Zeus** have been joined by six more, reassembled by an American team; reconstruction is in progress. Other ruins include a bathhouse, probably used by athletes to oil up precompetition, and a hostelry.

The **stadium** is 500m back along the road. There's a fantastic view of it in all its restored glory from the the path that skirts it through the pine trees. Alternatively, enter it the way the athletes would have done, through the tunnel hidden behind the columns by the site entrance. The athletes' starting line is still in place, together with the distance markers. Look out for ancient 'graffiti' in the tunnel. Resurrected in 1996, the two-day **Modern Nemean Games** (www.nemeangames.org) take place over two days each Olympic year in June.

ⓘ Getting There & Away

Buses to/from Corinth Isthmus (€4.50, one hour, four to five Monday to Saturday, one Sunday) stop on request outside the site on the way to modern Nemea, about 4km northwest.

ARGOLIS   ΑΡΓΟΛΙΔΑ

The Argolis peninsula, which separates the Saronic and Argolic Gulfs, is steeped in legend and history. The town of Argos, from which the region takes its name, is thought to be the longest continually inhabited town in Greece. Argolis was the seat of power of the Mycenaean empire that ruled Greece from 1600 to 1100 BC. Traces of this mighty civilisation lie scattered across the region in the shape of *tholos* tombs, citadels and ancient theatres. The Venetian seafront town of Nafplio makes a handy base for ventures into the surrounding countryside.

Argos   Αργος

POP 22,200

The ancient town of Argos stretches back an astonishing 6000 years, though today most vestiges of its past glory lie buried beneath the bustling modern town. Overshadowed by its neighbour, Nafplio (12km away), Argos is worth a detour for its archaeological museum, as well as the nearby ruins and fortress.

◉ Sights

Archaeological Museum of Argos   MUSEUM
(☎27510 68819; Plateia Agiou Petrou; adult/concession €2/1; ⊗8am-3pm Tue-Sun) Just off the central square, the archaeological museum includes some outstanding and complete Roman mosaics and sculptures in its collection, as well as bronze objects from Mycenaean tombs. Highlights include the statuette of a goddess, a mosaic of the four seasons in the courtyard, a suit of bronze armour from the 8th century BC and some fine Neolithic, Mycenaean and Geometric Age pottery, including some Argive grey and brown vases dating to before 1600 BC. Note the museum was under renovation and closed at research time, with no set reopening date.

Larissa Castle   CASTLE
FREE Looming over Argos, Larissa Castle is a crumbling conglomeration of purple-flower-studded towers, bastions and wall sections – contributed by Roman, Frankish, Venetian and Ottoman Turk conquerors – that stands on the foundations of the city's principal ancient citadel. Much of the citadel is undergoing restoration, but the all-encompassing views from the top are well worth the ascent. Take Tsokri street west from the centre and follow the signposts to the narrow road that winds around the back of the ruined keep.

Roman Ruins   RUIN
(⊗8am-3pm) FREE Impressive Roman ruins straddle both sides of the Tripolis road. The star attraction is the half-crumbled **theatre**, which originally seated 20,000 people. Dating from Classical times, it was greatly modified by the Romans. Nearby are the remains of a 1st-century-AD **odeion** (a smaller theatre) and **Roman baths**. Opposite is the **Ancient Agora**. Signs provide diagrams and contextualise the setting. From central Argos, head south along Danaou for about 500m and then turn right onto Theatrou.

ⓘ Getting There & Away

Just south of the central square, **KTEL Argolis** (☎27510 67324; www.ktel-argolidas.gr; Kapodistriou 8) has bus services to Nafplio (€1.60, 30 minutes, hourly) and Mycenae (€1.60, 30 minutes, two daily except Sunday).

There are also bus services to Athens (€11.90, two hours, 12 to 15 daily) via Corinth Isthmus (€5.20, 50 minutes), and to Tripoli (€6.70, one hour, two daily).

Ancient Mycenae
Αρχαία Μυκήνες

In the barren foothills of Mt Agios Ilias (750m) and Mt Zara (600m) stand the sombre and mighty ruins of **Ancient Mycenae** (☎27510 76585; adult/concession €8/4; ⊗8am-8pm Apr-Oct, to 3pm Nov-Mar), home of the mythical Agamemnon. For 400 years (1600–1200 BC) this kingdom was the most powerful in Greece, holding sway over the Argolid and influencing other Mycenaean kingdoms.

History

World Heritage–listed Mycenae is synonymous with the names Homer and Schliemann. In the 9th century BC Homer told in his epic poems, the *Iliad* and the *Odyssey,* of 'well-built Mycenae, rich in gold'. These poems were, until the 19th century, regarded as no more than gripping and beautiful legends. But in the 1870s the amateur archaeologist Heinrich Schliemann (1822–90), despite derision from professional archaeologists, struck gold, first at Troy then at Mycenae.

In Mycenae, myth and history are inextricably linked. According to Homer, Mycenae was founded by Perseus, the son of Danae and Zeus. Perseus' greatest heroic deed was the killing of the hideous snake-haired Medusa, whose gaze literally petrified the beholder. Eventually, the dynasty of Perseus was overthrown by Pelops, a son of Tantalus. The Mycenaean Royal House of Atreus was probably descended from Pelops, and by Agamemnon's time the Royal House of Atreus was the most powerful of the Achaeans (Homer's name for the Greeks). It eventually came to a sticky end, fulfilling the curse that had been cast because of Pelops' misdeeds.

Site Tour
Citadel of Mycenae

START LION GATE
END THOLOS TOMBS
LENGTH 2.5KM; TWO HOURS

Enter Agamemnon's Palace through the dramatic ① **Lion Gate**, a solid construction of massive stone blocks over which rear two large lionesses. The lion motif is believed to have been the insignia of the Royal House of Atreus.

Inside the citadel, ② **Grave Circle A** is on the right. Five shafts of this royal cemetery were excavated by Heinrich Schliemann between 1874 and 1876, uncovering a rich archaeological haul, including a well-preserved gold death mask. Schliemann sent a telegram to the Greek king stating, 'I have gazed upon the face of Agamemnon,' though the mask turned out to belong to an unknown king.

South of Grave Circle A is a group of ruined ③ **houses**. The famous Warrior Vase, unearthed here, was regarded by Schliemann as one of his greatest discoveries because it offered a glimpse of what Mycenae's legendary warriors looked like.

Follow the main path up to ④ **Agamemnon's Palace**, centred on the Great Court. The rooms to the north were private royal apartments where it is thought that Agamemnon was murdered. On the palace's southeastern side is the ⑤ **megaron** (reception hall where the great hearth would have been), with the column bases remaining and, beyond this, the ⑥ **artisans' quarters**.

At the northeast extension you'll find the entrance to the ⑦ **secret cistern** in the corner. You'll need a torch to descend the 100 or so steps into the subterranean gloom.

Follow the main path anticlockwise; on the northern boundary of the citadel is the ⑧ **Postern Gate**, through which, it is said, Orestes escaped after murdering his mother.

Until the late 15th century BC the Mycenaeans interred their royal dead in shaft graves; later they used a new form of burial – the beehive-shaped *tholos* tomb. Back outside the Lion Gate, head down to the **tholos tombs** of Aegisthus, with its collapsed roof, and Clytemnestra's tomb, with its dramatic entrance and restored dome roof.

The historical facts are that Mycenae was first settled by Neolithic people in the 6th millennium BC. Between 2100 and 1900 BC, during the Bronze Age, Greece was invaded by people of Indo-European heritage who had crossed Anatolia via Troy to Greece. The newcomers brought an advanced culture to then-primitive Mycenae and other mainland settlements. This new civilisation is now referred to as the Mycenaean, named after its most powerful kingdom. The other kingdoms included Pylos, Tiryns, Corinth and Argos, all in the Peloponnese.

Mycenae consisted of a fortified citadel and surrounding settlement. Due to the sheer size of the citadel walls (13m high and 7m thick), formed by stone blocks weighing 6 tonnes in places, the Ancient Greeks believed they must have been built by a Cyclops, one of the giants described in the *Odyssey*.

Archaeological evidence indicates that the palaces of the Mycenaean kingdoms declined some time around 1200 BC and the palace itself was set ablaze around 1100 BC. Whether the destruction was the work of outsiders or due to internal division between the various Mycenaean kingdoms remains unresolved.

As to whether the Agamemnon of legend ever existed, if Homer's *Odyssey* is to be believed he took part in the siege of Troy around 1100 BC, whereas the tombs attributed to him and his wife date back to around 1300 BC.

⦿ Sights

★ Treasury of Atreus (Agamemnon's Tomb)
ARCHAEOLOGICAL SITE

(adult/concession incl Ancient Mycenae site & museum €8/4; ⊙8am-6pm) Dating back to around 1300 BC, this is the finest existing example of a domed *tholos* tomb, made by filing down the layers of breccia blocks to create the smooth interior. It's wonderfully misnamed, since it has little to do with the mythical Atreus, or with his equally mythical son, Agamemnon, but the interior is truly awe-inspiring, with a 40m-long passage leading to the vast beehive-shaped chamber. Spot the original bronze nails that once held the door in place.

Ancient Mycenae Museum
MUSEUM

(adult/concession incl Ancient Mycenae site & Agamemnon's Tomb €8/4; ⊙8am-6pm) Part of the Ancient Mycenae complex, this museum is well worth visiting before seeing the rest of the site. It initiates you into the mysteries of Mycenae's construction, its various incarnations and its excavation from 1841 onwards. The displays run the gamut from fine stirrup jars and fresco fragments to ritual objects, jewellery and bronze weaponry. Replicas of archaeologist Heinrich Schliemann's most spectacular Mycenae finds are also displayed; the originals are in Athens' National Archaeological Museum.

PELOPONNESE ANCIENT MYCENAE

AGAMEMNON, KING OF MYCENAE

Agamemnon, son of Atreus, is one of the principal characters in Homer's epic poem *The Iliad* and crops up regularly in Greek legend. The king of Mycenae, he led the Greeks during the Trojan War.

Agamemnon and his brother Menelaus married the daughters of the King of Sparta, Clytemnestra and Helen, respectively. According to legend, Helen then eloped with Paris, the son of the Trojan king, taking all of her (rather valuable) possessions with her. This was the catalyst for the Trojan War (her face 'had launched a thousand ships'), as Agamemnon called on the Greek princes to unite in a war of revenge. Artemis, the goddess of hunting, however, stalled the departing warships with adverse winds because Agamemnon had angered her by claiming he was the better hunter. To make peace with Artemis, Agamemnon was forced to sacrifice his daughter, Iphigenia. Artemis set the seas right again, and the Greek ships sailed for Troy, where a 10-year siege ensued. In the war's final year, Agamemnon had a jealous quarrel with Achilles over the attentions of a captive female, which could have cost the Greeks the war.

Finally, though, Agamemnon returned home victorious with his war spoils, which included the Trojan princess Cassandra. His victory was short-lived: his wife Clytemnestra was justifiably upset about her sacrificed daughter and murdered Agamemnon with the help of her lover, Aegisthus. In classic dysfunctional-family Greek-legend style, Agamemnon's daughter, Electra, and her brother, Orestes, avenged their father's death by then murdering Aegisthus and Clytemnestra.

ⓘ Getting There & Away

Two daily buses (excluding Sundays) head to Mycenae from Nafplio (€2.60, one hour) and Argos (€1.60, 30 minutes). Buses stop both in the village and at the ancient site.

Nafplio   Ναύπλιο

POP 14,200

Nafplio, 12km southeast of Argos on the Argolic Gulf, occupies a knockout location on a small port beneath the towering Palamidi fortress. It is graced with attractive narrow streets, elegant Venetian houses, neoclassical mansions and interesting museums. It's also full of quayside cafes, posh boutiques and many comfortable hotels and guesthouses, but it does get seriously overcrowded in high season and holidays.

Nafplio was the first capital of Greece after Independence (between 1833 and 1834) and has been a major port since the Bronze Age. So strategic was its position that it had three fortresses: the massive principal fortress of Palamidi, the smaller Akronafplia and the diminutive Bourtzi on an islet west of the old town.

◎ Sights & Activities

★ Palamidi Fortress   FORTRESS

(☑ 27520 28036; adult/concession €4/free; ☺ 8am-6.45pm) This vast, spectacular citadel, reachable either by steep ascent on foot or a short drive, stands on a 216m-high outcrop of rock that gives all-encompassing views of Nafplio and the Argolic Gulf. It was built by the Venetians between 1711 and 1714, and is regarded as a masterpiece of military architecture in spite of being successfully stormed in one night by Greek troops in 1822, causing the Turkish garrison within to surrender without a fight.

Within its walls stands a series of independent, strategically located bastions. The most important, and best preserved, is the western **Agios Andreas Bastion**, which stands at the top of the steps from town. The former home of the garrison commander, it is named after the tiny church in the courtyard.

The **Miltiades Bastion**, to the northeast, is the largest of the bastions. It was used as a prison for condemned criminals from 1840 to 1920. War of Independence hero Theodoros Kolokotronis spent several years here after being condemned for treason.

There are two main approaches to the fortress. You can go via the road (taxis cost about €10 one way) or tackle the steps that

begin southeast of the bus station. It's 576 steps to the outer gate and 901 steps to the entrance to the castle (we've counted!). Climb early and take water.

★ Archaeological Museum   MUSEUM

(☑ 27520 27502; Plateia Syntagmatos; adult/child €3/free; ☺ 8.30am-3pm Tue-Sun) Inside a splendid Venetian building, this museum traces the social development of Argolis, from the hunter-gatherers of the Fragthi cave to the sophisticated Mycenaean-era civilisations, through beautifully presented archaeological finds from the surrounding area. Exhibits range from Paleolithic fire middens, dating from 32,000 BC, to elaborately painted amphorae (c 520 BC). You may also spot the only existing bronze armour from near Mycenae (3500 years old and complete with boar-tusk helmet), a wealth of funereal offerings and ceremonial clay masks.

Peloponnese Folklore Foundation Museum   MUSEUM

(☑ 27520 28947; www.pli.gr; Vasileos Alexandrou 1; admission €2; ☺ 9am-2pm Wed-Mon) Established by its philanthropic owner, Nafplio's award-winning museum is a beautifully arranged collection of folk costumes and household items from Nafplio's 19th- and early 20th-century history. Be wowed by the intricate embroidery of traditional costumes and the heavy silver adornments; admire the turn-of-the-century couture and see if you can spot a horse-tricycle. The gift shop sells high-quality local crafts.

Bourtzi   FORTRESS

The island fortress of Bourtzi (1473), which lies about 600m west of the town's port, has served variously as a pirate deterrent, a home for executioners to protect them from vengeance and a hotel. Note that the battlements are identical in design to Moscow's Kremlin; both it and Bourtzi were built by 15th-century Venetians. Boats to the island (return €4) leave from the northeastern end of Akti Miaouli.

Komboloi Museum   MUSEUM

(☑ 27520 21618; www.komboloi.gr; Staïkopoulou 25; adult/concession €2/free; ☺ 9.30am-6.30pm, hours vary seasonally) Whether or not you wish to buy Nafplio's most popular souvenir item – *komboloï* (worry beads) – at the shop below, it's well worth popping into the incense-scented museum upstairs to learn what distinguishes the *komboloï* from prayer beads and why the amber-mastic mix is so special. You may spot tiny wooden skulls, black coral inlaid with mother-of-pearl and carved ivory among the adjacent collection of prayer beads belonging to assorted religions.

National Gallery – Alexandros Soutzos Museum
GALLERY

(www.nationalgallery.gr; Sidiras Merarhias 23; adult/concession €3/2, Mon free; ⊙10am-3pm Mon, Thu & Sat, 10am-3pm & 5-8pm Wed & Fri, to 2pm Sun) This arm of the Athens National Gallery is housed in a stunningly restored neoclassical building. It features numerous seascapes and different thematic takes on the 1821 Greek War of Independence, including paintings by Theodoros Vryzakis and Dionysios Tsokos, who are considered the most important Greek artists of the postwar years.

Church of Agios Spyridon
CHURCH

This 18th-century church was the site of an assassination of great political significance to the Greeks. On 9 October 1831 Ioannis Kapodistrias, elected the first president of an independent Greece in 1828, was stabbed and shot near the door of the church by Konstantinos and Georgios Mavromichalis, brother and son of the leader of the Maniots. They had had a bitter disagreement with Kapodistrias over the spoils of victory.

Cruise to Saronic Gulf Islands
BOAT TOUR

(☑27250 59430; www.pegasus-cruises.gr; adult/child €34/17; ⊙late Apr-late Sep) Pegasus Cruises offers popular full-day trips to the islands of Hydra and Spetses from Tolo, 10km southeast of Nafplio. The tour stops for a couple of hours in each place. You can get to/from

Tolo by taxi (around €12) or bus, depending on the schedule. There are at least two weekly departures (more in July and August).

Tickets are available at travel agencies.

Nafplio Bike
BICYCLE RENTAL

(www.nafplio-bike.gr; Kipou 2; per day €15; ⊙9am-9pm Mon-Sat) This is the place to hire city and trekking bikes. Hourly rates available.

🏖 Beaches

Arvanitia Beach
BEACH

This small pebble beach is just five minutes' walk south of town, tucked beside the Akronafplia fortress, past the Land Gate. For a scenic stroll, take the blustery, cactus-adorned path that skirts the headland from the bottom of the promenade.

Karathona Beach
BEACH

A gorgeous pine-tree-lined 3km path runs from the car park next to Arvanitia Beach to the long, sandy Karathona Beach. It's a flat, easy walk, though the beach could be cleaner. Don't feel like walking? Take 25 Martiou east of town to the end of the road.

🎉 Festivals & Events

Nafplio is a good base for visits to Epidavros in July and August for performances at the famous ancient theatre (p144) during the Epidavros Festival, part of the larger cultural Hellenic Festival (p94).

Classical Music Festival
MUSIC

(www.nafplionfestival.gr; ⊙late May-Jul) Nafplio hosts a classical-music festival, featuring Greek and international performers.

NAFPLIO'S BOUTIQUE SLEEPS

Nafplio's streets burst with boutique hotels. These renovated former mansions vary in style, though most have four to eight (rather compact) rooms with contemporary, period or kitsch furnishings. Prices include cable TV. Note: all have steep internal stairs. We love the following places:

Aetoma (☑27520 27373; www.nafplionhotel.com; Plateia Agios Spiridonos 2; d incl breakfast €75-120; ✲🛜) Intimate and comfortable, the Aetoma has dark, heavy and stylish furnishings, and hospitable owners who go out of their way to be helpful. Generous traditional breakfast included.

Adiandi (☑27520 22073; www.hotel-adiandi.com; Othonos 31; d incl breakfast €75-110, s/ste incl breakfast €65/130; ✲🛜) Rooms in this fun place are individually decorated with bright colours, artistic door bedheads and marble sinks. A funky cafe-cum-breakfast-room is downstairs.

Amymone (☑27520 99477; www.amymone.gr; Othonos 39; d incl breakfast €75-105, s/ste incl breakfast €65/130; ✲@🛜) Amymone is all about stencilled art, faux graffiti and Blaxploitation silhouettes on funky door bedsteads. Will appeal to pop art fans. Mod cons and an excellent breakfast included.

Nafplio

🛏 Sleeping

⭐ Nafplion 1841 PENSION €

(☏27520 24622; www.nafplion1841.gr; Kapo-distriou 9; s/d incl breakfast €40/45; ❋�351) Not only does this delightful pension occupy a 19th-century mansion, but its five bright rooms offer contemporary creature comforts without diminishing the building's character. Expect Cocomat mattresses, superior bed linens, climate control, hydro-massage showers and plasma-screen TVs. The hostess is a delight and so is the breakfast.

Pension Eleni PENSION €

(☏27520 27036; www.pensioneleni.gr; Zygomala 5; d/tr/ste incl breakfast €45/50/75; P❋�351) This friendly pension, tucked away down a quiet street, is run by a Greek grandma who will fuss over you, her hospitality transcending the language barrier. The en suite rooms share a warm colour scheme and sea views; the 'superior' rooms come with thimble-sized balconies. Park in the nearby square.

Klymeni Traditional Homes APARTMENT €€

(☏27520 96194; www.klymeni.gr; studio/apt incl breakfast €85/105; P�351) On a hillside overlooking the peaceful countryside, these traditional stone houses offer comfort (luxurious beds, vast living areas, Jacuzzi-style bathtubs) and respite from town traffic while remaining within easy reach of Nafplio. Helpful owner Alexander provides breakfast goodies. Take 25 Martiou out of town for 2.5km towards the Palamidi Fortress.

Pension Marianna HOTEL €€

(☏27520 24256; www.pensionmarianna.gr; Potamianou 9; s/d/tr/q incl breakfast €50/75/95/105; P❋�351) For value and hospitality, it doesn't get better than this. The welcoming owner-hosts, the warm Zotos brothers, epitomise Greek *filoxenia* (hospitality) and serve up conviviality, travel advice and delicious breakfasts (comprising homemade produce where possible). The squeaky-clean rooms open onto terraces where you can feast on the killer view from your hilltop position. Rates are €5 less per person without breakfast.

Grand Sarai BOUTIQUE HOTEL €€

(☏27520 22563; www.grandsarainafplio.com; Foto-mara & Potamianou 3; s incl breakfast €70-145, d incl breakfast €80-150; �351) A beautifully renovated pink mansion that's sleek and modern on the inside. Stylish rooms are decorated in neutral tones; most boast views, some have jacuzzis. Extensive breakfasts using local produce are served in an intimate setting downstairs.

3Sixty° Hotel & Suites BOUTIQUE HOTEL €€€

(☏27525 00501; www.3sixtyhotel.gr; cnr Koletti & Papanikolau 26; ste incl breakfast €200-250; ❋�351) Ascend the spiral staircase beneath the enormous glittering chandelier and you're faced with a handful of sumptuous suites. Each is individually decorated in classic creams, charcoals and browns but features welcome crimson, yellow and even pop-art accents. Oversized beds and bathrooms are top-notch, and breakfast is extensive – hot dishes cooked to order.

PELOPONNESE NAFPLIO

✕ Eating

Antica Gelateria di Roma
GELATERIA €

(☑ 27520 23520; www.anticagelateria.gr; cnr Far-makopoulou & Komninou; ice cream from €2.50; ☺10am-11pm) The only 'true' gelato shop in Nafplio is still holding back the competition. Italian gelati maestros Marcello, Claudia and Monica Raffo greet you with: '*Bongior-no* – this is an *Italian* gelati shop!' Only natural and local ingredients are used and it's all made on the premises.

Mezedopoleio O Noulis
GREEK €

(☑ 27520 25541; Moutzouridou 22; mezedhes €5-11; ☺lunch & dinner; ⌨) Popular with locals and decked out with prints of ye olde Naf-plio, this family-run restaurant does seafood (grilled calamari, battered whitebait) and vegetarian mezedhes particularly well.

Ta Fanaria
GREEK €

(☑ 27520 27141; www.fanaria.gr; Staikopoulou 14; mains €7-15; ☺lunch & dinner; ⌨) This intimate taverna wins points not just for the attentive service but also for its superior selection of vegetarian dishes (think spinach and feta pie, okra stew, oven-baked veggies) along-side the dolmadhes and other Greek classics.

MitaTo
KEBAB €

(Staikopoulou 14; mains €3-12; ☺lunch & dinner) A worthy contender for Nafplio's best souvla-kia and *gyros* (meat slivers cooked on a ver-tical rotisserie, eaten with pitta bread), this grilled meat joint has whimsical decor and a meaty menu extensive enough to satisfy most carnivorously inclined clients.

Fougaro
CAFE €

(www.fougaro.gr; Asklipiou 98; mains €8-12; ☺6pm-midnight Wed-Sun) Lovely cafe-restaurant and cultural space 3km from Nafplio in a con-verted canning factory, on the road to Epida-vros. Good coffee, light bites for lunch and a smarter dinner menu; particularly good dur-ing events. Look for the *fougaro* (chimney).

Carrefour Express
SUPERMARKET €

(cnr Sygrou & Flessa; ☺8am-9pm Mon-Sat) Cen-tral, reasonably well stocked supermarket.

Faro Taverna
SEAFOOD €

(☑ 27520 27704; Mili; mains €8-15; ☺noon-11pm) Locally famous and well worth the 10-minute drive from Nafplio, this taverna, run by the grandson of the original owner, sits right on Mili Beach. You can't go wrong with the catch of the day, be it freshly grilled squid, red mul-let, fresh sardines or anchovies.

To Omorfo Tavernaki
GREEK €

(☑ 27520 25944; Vasilissis Olgas 1; mains €8-15; ☺lunch & dinner; ⌨) Ample servings of homemade delights in a convivial restau-rant adorned with antique oddments. The mezedhes plates (zucchini balls, feta with honey, tzatziki etc...) are particularly good.

★ 3Sixty°
INTERNATIONAL €€

(☑ 27525 00501; www.3sixtycafe.gr; Papanikolaou 26 & Koletti; mains €10-19; ☺breakfast, lunch & dinner; ⌨⌨) Nafplio punches above its culi-nary weight at the most imaginative restau-rant in town. Sophisticated fare includes the likes of smoky aubergine *imam* with veal, wild mushroom risotto with truffle oil, and lamb stuffed with goat Gruyère. Salads are equally creative. The sultry bar serves potent signature cocktails (we're fans of Legendary Star) and numerous Greek wines.

🍷 Drinking & Nightlife

Es Aei
WINE BAR

(☑ 27520 22884; Staikopoulou 8; glass of wine €4.50; ☺3pm-late) Mismatched furniture, bare light bulbs and posters on the walls conjure up a grungy, student hangout image, but the jazz and candlelight transform this joint into something mellower. Sample from an exten-sive list of Greek wines, accompanied by a succinct selection of excellent tapas.

O Mavros Gatos
BAR

(Sofroni 1; ☺8.30am-late) A chilled-out cafe by day, buzzy bar by night, with DJs some nights. There are comfy seats outside and an interior decorated with vintage adverts.

🛍 Shopping

Glykos Peirasmos
FOOD

(Plapouta 10; ☺10am-9pm) *The* place for deli-cious chocolate, baklava, *loukoumi* (Turkish delight) and honey-sodden walnut cake.

Karonis
WINE

(☑ 27520 24446; www.karoniswineshop.gr; Amalias 5; ☺8.30am-2.30pm & 6-9.30pm Mon-Sat) Wine enthusiasts can find a fine selection of wines from all over the country, especially Nemean reds and spirits. Wine tastings offered.

ℹ Information

Hospital (☑ 27523 61100; Kountouriotou 1)

National Bank of Greece (Plateia Syntagma-tos) Has ATMs.

Post office (cnr Sygrou & Sidiras Merarhias; ☺7.30am-2pm Mon-Fri)

Staikos Tours (27520 27950; Bouboulinas 50; 8.30am-2.30pm & 5.30-9pm) Helpful outfit offers Avis rental cars and full travel services.

Tourist police (27520 98728; Eleftherias 2)

❶ Getting There & Away

The **KTEL Argolis bus station** (27520 27423; www.ktel-argolidas.gr; Syngrou) has buses to Athens (€13.10, 2½ hours, 11 to 13 daily) via Corinth Isthmus (Peloponnese) KTEL bus station (€6.50, 1½ hours). Other services include the following:

Argos (€1.60, 30 minutes, hourly)

Epidavros (€2.90, 45 minutes, six Monday to Friday, four Saturday, one Sunday)

Galatas (€8.20, two hours, two daily except weekends)

Kranidi (€7.70, two hours, four Monday to Friday, three Saturday, one Sunday)

Mycenae (€2.90, one hour, three Monday to Friday, two Saturday)

Tolo (€1.60, 15 minutes, nine to 12 daily)

Tripoli (€6.70, 1½ hours, two daily)

❶ Getting Around

Call a **taxi** (27520 29096) or head to the rank on Sygrou. Car-hire agencies include the following:

Avis (27520 24160; www.avis.gr; Bouboulinas 51)

Bounos Rent a Car (27520 24390; www.bounos-carrental.com; Sygrou 14)

Hermes Car Rental (27520 25308; www.hermestravel.gr; Sygrou 18)

Tiryns   Τίρυνθα

The Mycenaean acropolis of **Tiryns** (27520 22657; adult/concession €3/2; 8am-7pm), 4km north of Nafplio, is the apogee of Mycenaean architectural achievement. Legend has it that its massive walls, 7m thick in parts, were built by a Cyclops. You can stroll around the immense stonework and explore the Upper and Lower Citadels, but the vaulted passageways, the secret stairway and the impressive gallery are off-limits. Any Nafplio–Argos bus can drop you outside the site.

Built in the 13th century BC, this World Heritage site in its heyday was second only to Mycenae in terms of regional importance. The layout of some of the ruins is easy to make out, and there are few crowds. The site has little in the way of signs or descriptions, so it's worth buying *Tiryns* (by Dr Alkestis Papademetriou; €8) at the ticket office.

Epidavros   Επ

In its day **Epidavros** (27530 22 concession €6/3; 8am-7pm), 30k Nafplio, was famed as far away a a place of miraculous healing. Visitors came great distances to this Sanctuary of Asclepius (god of medicine), set amid pine-clad hills, to seek a cure for their ailments. Today visitors are drawn more to this World Heritage site's remarkably well-preserved theatre, which remains a venue during the Hellenic Festival (p94) for Classical Greek theatre, first performed here up to 2000 years ago.

History

Legend has it that Asclepius was the son of Apollo and Coronis. While giving birth to Asclepius, Coronis was killed by the jealous Apollo, who'd found out that she'd been unfaithful to him. Apollo took his son to Mt Pelion, where the physician centaur Chiron instructed the boy in the healing arts. Asclepius became a healer of such great renown that he brought a man back from the dead, which angered Hades, the god of the underworld, who asked Zeus to strike Asclepius down. Zeus did so, provoking, in turn, the wrath of Apollo, and Asclepius was eventually deified.

Apollo was worshipped at Epidavros in Mycenaean and Archaic times, but by the 4th century BC he had been superseded by his son. Epidavros became acknowledged as the birthplace of Asclepius. Although the afflicted worshipped Asclepius at sanctuaries throughout Greece, the two most important sites were at Epidavros and on the island of Kos. The fame of the Epidavros sanctuary spread, and when a plague raged in Rome, Livy and Ovid came to Epidavros to seek help.

> ### ❶ VISITING EPIDAVROS
>
> If visiting Epidavros on your own by car, follow the signs to Ancient Theatre of Epidavros, and not to P Epidavros (Paleia Epidavros) or A Epidavros (Archaia Epidavros) – the two latter are both signs to the seaside village of Ancient Epidavros. Incidentally, Archaia Epidavros (formerly Paleia Epidavros) is home to the so-called 'small theatre', also used for some Hellenic Festival (p144) performances; the 'large theatre' referred to on festival programs is at the main Epidavros site.

PEREGRINATIONS OF PAUSANIAS

Lonely Planet and its alternatives were beaten to the publishing of guidebooks by nearly 20 centuries. The traveller and geographer Pausanias wrote what is believed to be the first – and most definitive – 'guidebook' for tourists in the 2nd century AD. His work, *Description of Greece* (sometimes known as *Tour* or *Itinerary of Greece*), is a series of 10 volumes in which he describes most of Greece as seen at the time (between AD 143 and 161), covering the regions of Attica, Boeotia, Phocis and Ozolian Locris, plus the regions that make up much of the Peloponnese: Corinthia, Lakonia, Messinia, Elia, Achaïa and Arkadia. Classical Greek scholars, historians and archaeologists regard it as an extremely important historical work for its insight into places, people, monuments and sites, as well as associated facts and legends. Pausanias is believed to be from Lydia in Asia Minor and travelled extensively throughout Greece, Macedonia, Italy and parts of Asia and Africa.

It is believed that licks from snakes were one of the curative practices at the sanctuary. Asclepius is normally shown with a serpent, which – by renewing its skin – symbolises rejuvenation. Other treatments provided at the sanctuary involved diet instruction, herbal medicines and occasionally even surgery. The sanctuary also served as an entertainment venue; and every four years, during the Festival of Asclepieia, Epidavros hosted dramas and athletic competitions.

◉ Sights

★ Theatre of Epidavros   HISTORIC SITE

(site adult/concession €6/3; ⊙8am-7pm) One of the best-preserved Classical Greek structures in existence, now used for performances of Ancient Greek drama during the annual Hellenic Festival, the 3rd-century BC theatre is the undisputed highlight of Epidavros. It's renowned for its amazing acoustics; a coin dropped in the theatre's centre can be heard from the highest seat. Built of limestone, the theatre seats up to 14,000 people. Its entrance is flanked by restored **Corinthian pilasters** and the foundations of the ancient stage are beyond the circle.

Sanctuary of Asclepius   RUIN

(site adult/concession €6/3; ⊙8am-7pm) A short walk from the Theatre of Epidavros, and dotted with pine trees, lie the ruins of the Sanctuary of Asclepius, dedicated to the god of healing. The ruins include the huge **katagogeion**, a hostelry for pilgrims and patients, the large **banquet hall** in which the Romans built an **odeum** (a room for musical performances), and the **stadium** – the venue for the Festival of Asclepieia's athletic competitions. Just beyond is the remarkable **tholos** building, the **Temple of Asclepius** and the **abaton**. You first reach the large, square

katagogeion, beyond which is the former gymnasium-cum-banquet-hall in which the Romans built an odeum. It was here that the Festival of Asclepieia took place.

The path meanders past the remains of the **stadium** on your left. Ahead is the circular **tholos** (built 360–320 BC and under heavy reconstruction at research time), originally surrounded by two circles of columns: Doric and Corinthian. In the centre there used to be a small labyrinth and one of the theories is that patients were put in there for a 'healing encounter' with snakes.

To the northeast are the foundations of the **Temple of Asclepius** and next to them is the **abaton**. The therapies practised here seemed to have depended on the influence of the mind upon the body. It is believed that patients were given a pep talk by a priest on the powers of Asclepius, then put to sleep in the abaton to dream of a visitation by the god. The dream would hold the key to the healing process.

East is the **Sanctuary of Egyptian Gods**, which indicates that the cult of Asclepius was an adaptation of the cult of Imhotep, worshipped in Egypt for his healing powers.

Museum   MUSEUM

(adult/concession incl site entry €6/3; ⊙8am-7pm) Between the Sanctuary of Asclepius and the Theatre of Epidavros, this museum houses statuary (mostly copies) that once adorned the Temple of Asclepius, stone inscriptions recording miraculous cures, some alarming-looking surgical instruments, votive offerings and fragments of intricately carved reliefs from the ceiling of the sanctuary's *tholos*.

✱ Festivals & Events

Athens & Epidavros Festival   THEATRE

(☑ 210 928 2900, 27530 22026; www.greekfestival.gr/en; ⊙Jul & Aug) The Theatre of Epidavros (p144) stages both modern theatre and Ancient Greek dramas during the annual Athens and Epidavros Festival, part of the larger cultural Hellenic Festival (p94). Tickets can be bought in Epidavros at the theatre box office, online or from Athens' box office (p95). There are special bus services available from Athens (around €25, two hours) and Nafplio (around €10, 45 minutes).

ⓘ Getting There & Away

There are buses from Nafplio to Epidavros (€2.90, 45 minutes, six Monday to Friday, four Saturday, one Sunday).

Southwest Argolis

Very few travellers take the time to venture to the southwestern heel of the Argolis peninsula, yet the zigzagging drive (or bike ride) along the east coast, past the pretty coastal town of **Galatas** and a scattering of picturesque houses across the narrow bay that is **Poros**, is absolutely spectacular.

The western part of the peninsula, centred on the agricultural town of **Kranidi**, features the small resorts of **Porto Heli**, 4km south of Kranidi, and **Ermioni**, 4km east of Kranidi. Both offer convenient connections to the Saronic Gulf islands of Hydra and Spetses. Additional Hydra services fly across the water from **Metochi**, essentially a waterfront car park, around 10km east of Ermioni.

Off the main road between Kranidi and Epidavros, 1km west of the village of Didyma, don't miss the **Didyma Caves** FREE, two extraordinary sinkholes. The caves collapsed thousands of years ago, leaving large crater-like holes. One hides a tiny Byzantine church, constructed under a crevice.

ⓘ Getting There & Away

Regular boat services run to Piraeus via Hydra and Spetses. There are **bus services** (☑27540 21237; www.ktel-argolidas.gr) between Kranidi and Nafplio (€7.70, two hours, four on weekdays, three on Saturday, one on Sunday), and local buses from Kranidi to Ermioni (€1.85, 10 minutes, one or two daily) and Porto Heli (€1.85, 10 minutes, one to two daily).

ARKADIA   ΑΡΚΑΔΙΑ

The picturesque rural prefecture of Arkadia occupies much of the central Peloponnese. Its name evokes images of grassy meadows, forested mountains, gurgling streams and shady grottoes. According to mythology, it was a favourite haunt of Pan, the flute-playing, cloven-hooved god of nature.

Almost encircled by mountain ranges, Arkadia was remote enough in ancient times to remain largely untouched by the battles and intrigues of the rest of Greece, and was the only region of the Peloponnese not conquered by the Dorians. The region is dotted with crumbling medieval villages, remote monasteries and Frankish castles, and is popular among fresh-air fiends.

ⓘ Getting There & Away

KTEL Arkadia (☑27102 22560; www.ktelark adias.gr; Plateia Kolokotroni) in Tripoli is the departure point for buses to Stemnitsa (€5, one hour, one daily Monday to Friday), Dimitsana (€6.50, 1½ hours, one daily) and Andritsena (€8.60, 1½ hours, one daily).

This office also handles buses to Athens (via Corinth Isthmus, €15, up to 14 daily), Olympia (€12.40, one daily), Pyrgos (€14, one daily),

BOAT SERVICES FROM ARGOLIS

Regular **Hellenic Seaways** (☑27540 32408; www.hellenicseaways.gr) high-speed boats depart from Porto Heli to Piraeus via Spetses and Hydra, and from Ermioni to Piraeus via Hydra. The cheapest and most frequent boats to Hydra from Argolis are **Hydra Lines** (☑22980 52961; www. hydralines.gr; one way/return €6.50/13) from Metochi; park for free by the waterfront or leave your car in a secure, shaded car park (€5). Caïques shuttle between Galatas and Poros (€1, five minutes; €1.50 between midnight and 5am). From Poros there are four daily fast boats to Piraeus (€6.50, 1¼ hours).

DESTINATION	PORT	TIME	FARE	FREQUENCY
Hydra	Ermioni	20-40min	€7.50	3 daily
Hydra	Poros	30min	€12.50	4 daily
Hydra	Metochi	20min	€6.50	6-7 daily
Spetses	Porto Heli	10min	€5.50	3 daily
Spetses	Ermioni	25min	€7.50	2 daily

Nafplio (€6.70, two daily) and Patra (€16.20, one to two daily).

The **bus stop** (☎ 27102 42086; www.ktelark-adias.gr; Lagopati, Tripoli) handles departures to Sparta (€5.40, nine daily) and Kalamata (€8.10, two daily on weekdays).

Central Arkadia

To the west of Tripoli is a tangle of precipitous ravines and narrow roads that wind their way through the medieval-village-speckled valleys of the Menalon Mountains. This is the heart of Arkadia, where you'll find some of the most breathtaking mountainous scenery in the Peloponnese, along with some excellent hiking opportunities (and skiing in winter). Having your own wheels is a real boon here, as public transport to the main villages is limited to one or two buses per day.

Stemnitsa   Στεμνίτσα

POP 200

Stemnitsa (stem-*nee*-tsah), 26km northwest of Tripoli, is a striking village of stone houses and Byzantine churches, known for its silver and gold craftsmanship. If you want to peek in any churches, ask around for the keys.

The starting (or finishing) point for the Menalon Trail (p146), Stemnitsa is a good base for hikers.

🛌 Sleeping & Eating

⭐ **Mpelleiko**   B&B €€

(☎6976607967, 27950 81286; www.mpelleiko.gr; s/d/tr incl breakfast €65/75/85; 🛜) The ultrahospitable and knowledgeable English-speaking owner, Nena, has converted her family home (dating from 1650) into a stylish, contempo-

---

THE MENALON TRAIL

The well-signposted, 72.5km **Menalon Trail** (www.menalontrail.eu) stretches from Stemnitsa to Lagkadia, passing through the dramatic scenery of the Lousios Gorge, the western slopes of Mt Menalon, the Mylaon River valley and the Gortynian Mountains. Completed in May 2015 by a group of volunteers, the trail is divided into eight sections of varying difficulty, the Stemnitsa–Dimitsana leg being the most popular.

The eight trail sections are as follows:

Stemnitsa–Dimitsana (12.5km, 4½ hours) A picturesque descent into the Lousios Gorge past Prodromos Monastery, followed by an ascent to the Old and New Philosophou Monasteries. The trail then follows the course of the river before leading up to the Open Air Water Power Museum. From the Prodromos Monastery there's a worthwhile detour south to Ancient Gortys.

Dimitsana–Zygovisti (4.2km, 1½ hours) A gentle ascent past St Apostoli Monastery, and along footpaths and dirt roads through fields.

Zygovisti–Elati (15km, five hours) This section ascends to the Bilali Pass over the Western Menalon massif, with some steep sections and an optional detour to Pliovouni Peak (1643m).

Elati–Vytina (8.5km, 2¼ hours) Partially paved, wooded trail that passes by some ancient ruins and abandoned windmills.

Vytina–Nymphasia (5.6km, 1½ hours) The trail descends to a short gorge before ascending gently through a rock-and-shrub landscape.

Nymphasia–Magouliana (9km, 3½ hours) Through oak and spruce forests, the trail descends to Kernitsas Monastery and passes by Sfyrida Hermitage and Gavros Spring.

Magouliana–Valtesiniko (7.5km, two hours) The path descends past an old sanitorium and follows a riverbed.

Valtesiniko–Lagkadia (13.9km, five hours) The path ascends past a Byzantine fortress, then passes through open country and traverses valleys before ending at a war memorial.

You can download the excellent digital app **Menalon Trail topoGuide** for detailed offline maps and numerous points of interest. If you're not digitally inclined, the Anavasi Topo25 *Lousios 8.51; 1:22,000* map is very handy for the Lousios Gorge section and the surrounding villages.

Of the villages, Stemnitsa, Dimitsana, Valtesiniko and Lagkadia all have places to stay and eat, and you can pick up provisions at Vytina, Nymphasia and Magouliana.

rary guesthouse perched above the village. You can even sleep in the former 'donkey basement'. Breakfast includes homemade organic produce and is served in a beautiful room with an open fireplace.

Xenonas Tsarbou   BOUTIQUE HOTEL €€

(☑ 27950 81406; www.xenonas-tsarbou.gr; d incl breakfast from €60; P ⸫) This delightful guesthouse is a happy merging of a converted historic stone building with contemporary decor, its compact rooms trimmed with gold and velvet. There's a cosy bar with fireplace for post-hike relaxation, and hospitable hostess Christina prepares an extensive breakfast spread.

Gerousia   GREEK €

(mains €7-12; ⸰ breakfast, lunch & dinner) A dining establishment since 1870, this appealing cafe on the square is a good place to linger over a coffee, glass of wine or an assortment of traditional Greek dishes.

ⓘ Getting There & Away

There is one bus in each direction on weekdays between Tripoli and Dimitsana via Stemnitsa (€4.10, one hour). A taxi to Dimitsana costs around €10, to Prodromos Monastery €15, to Ancient Gortys €25 and to the Philosophou Monasteries €20.

Dimitsana   Δημητσάνα

POP 340

Built amphitheatrically on two hills at the beginning of the Lousios Gorge, Dimitsana, 11km north of Stemnitsa, is a delightful medieval village. This small place played a significant role in the country's struggle for self-determination. Its Greek school, founded in 1764, was an important spawning ground for the ideas leading to the uprisings against the Turks. Its students included Bishop Germanos of Patra and Patriarch Gregory V, who was hanged by the Turks in retaliation for the massacre in Tripoli. The village also had a number of gunpowder factories and a branch of the secret Filiki Eteria (Friendly Society), where Greeks met to discuss the revolution. Today, this sleepy village is hiker central in summer and full of skiing weekenders in winter.

⦿ Sights & Activities

Open Air Water Power Museum   MUSEUM

(☑ 27950 31630; www.piop.gr; adult/concession €3/1.50; ⸰ 10am-6pm Wed-Mon) This excellent little museum is an entertaining romp through the region's pre-industrial past. It occupies the old Agios Yiannis mill complex, 1.6km south of town (signposted), where a spring-fed stream once supplied power for a succession of mills spread down the hillside. The lush grounds are criss-crossed with channels alive with rushing water that power the fully operational fulling mill, flour mill and gunpowder mill, the last having provided ammunition during the Greek War of Independence.

Trekking Hellas   OUTDOORS

(☑ 27910 25978, 6974459753; www.trekkinghellas. gr) Trekking Hellas offers various activities, including white-water rafting (€50 to €80) on the Lousios River and half-day guided treks along the Lousios Gorge (€20 to €50). Contact them in advance.

🛏 Sleeping

Kazakou Guesthouse   B&B €

(☑ 27950 31660; www.xenonaskazakou.gr; d/tr incl breakfast €51/60; ⸫) This rambling stone house above central Dimitsana features spacious rooms with wooden floors, a vast breakfast served in the vaulted lounge and friendly owners. Wi-fi only works in the lounge and the location is either a boon or a bane, depending on whether you enjoy the sound of church bells.

★ Amanites   BOUTIQUE HOTEL €€

(☑ 27950 31090; www.amanites.gr; d/studio incl breakfast €65/80; P ⸫) This lovely place, a converted historic home, has seven elegant rooms with heavy drapes and tasteful fabrics. Four rooms have front-facing balconies overlooking the gorge; others have kitchenettes. Delightful English-speaking owner Panos goes out of his way to be helpful.

Enastron Guesthouse   B&B €€

(☑ 27950 31684; www.xenonasenastron.gr; d incl breakfast €65; ⸫) This appealing guesthouse is distinguished not just by the friendliness of and helpfulness of its owners, but also by the meticulous attention to detail. The spacious wooden-beamed rooms come with contemporary fittings and excellent bathrooms, and the extensive breakfast buffet comprises fresh local produce.

🍴 Eating & Drinking

Most of the village tavernas serve typical mountain fare, such as game casseroles or roasts, rooster in red wine and *fasoladha* (bean soup).

WORTH A TRIP

SUSTAINABLE FOOD SOJOURN

Zerzova (🖉27950 31753, 6932847358; Panaghia; mains €7-15; ☺lunch & dinner Fri-Mon Sep-May; 🖉), a tiny eatery 14km southwest of Dimitsana in the village of Panaghia, ticks all the right boxes. Sustainable practices? Tick – the husband-and-wife team collect all wild herbs and cultivate their own produce. Home cooking? Tick – even Greek grandmothers are happy to come here. Traditional? Tick again – it's in a lovely old building with a cellar below.

Me Meraki
PIZZA €
(🖉27950 31113; pizza from €7; ☺lunch & dinner; 🖉) Affable Chicago transplant Maria has returned to her mother's home village and opened a pizza parlour. Come here for satisfying homemade pizza and the lowdown on Dimitsana.

To Kapilio Ton Athonaton
STEAK €€
(mains €5-18; ☺lunch & dinner Thu-Tues) The summer terrace overlooking the gorge, this place is sought out by discerning carnivores for its meaty specials – roast lamb, pork chops, locally made sausage...

Kato Apo To Roloi
WINE BAR
(glass of wine €3; ☺lunch & dinner; 🖘) The 'Under the Clock' cafe is *the* spot to unwind after a day's hiking. Look down at the gorge with a large glass of wine or an expertly mixed cocktail (€7.50) in hand.

ℹ️ Getting There & Around

There is one daily bus in each direction on weekdays between Tripoli and Dimitsana (€5, 1½ hours). A taxi to Stemnitsa costs around €10, to Monastery of Philosophou €15 and to Ancient Gortys €25.

Kynouria
Κυνουρία

Kynouria is the coastal region of Arkadia. It covers a narrow strip of territory that stretches south from the tiny village of Kiveri, 41km east of Tripoli, to Kosmas, perched high in the Parnonas Mountains. Much of the land is incredibly rugged, with a narrow coastal plain and very little fertile ground.

In ancient times the region was contested by Argos and Sparta – the Argives held sway in the north and the Spartans in the south.

Leonidio to Geraki

The drive (or bike ride) from **Leonidio**, 76km south of Argos, over the Parnonas Mountains to the village of Geraki in Lakonia, 48km away, is one of the most scenic in the Peloponnese. An archetypal white-washed village, Leonidio is dramatically situated at the mouth of the **Badron Gorge**, with sheer red cliffs looming above it.

For the first 12km, the road snakes west up the Badron Gorge, climbing slowly away from the river until at times the water is no more than a silver ribbon far below. The road then leaves the Badron and climbs rapidly towards Kosmas on dramatic hairpin bends.

Just before the top of the climb, there's a road to the left leading to **Moni Panagias Elonis**, a monastery perched precariously on the mountainside.

It's another 14km up from the monastery to the peaceful mountain village of **Kosmas**. It makes an ideal rest stop: you can admire the stone cathedral or try the town speciality (goat) at one of the tavernas beneath the huge plane trees. After Kosmas the road gently descends to the village of **Geraki**, where you can check out the appealing churches before heading 40km west to Sparta, or continuing south to Monemvasia.

Note to cyclists: this route is even more dramatic (and easier on the muscles) if done in reverse order.

LAKONIA
ΛΑΚΩΝΙΑ

The region of Lakonia occupies almost identical boundaries to the powerful mountain-skirted kingdom ruled by King Menelaus in Mycenaean times. It is home to legends, including the city of Sparta and the spectacular ruins of Mystras, the Byzantine Empire's last stronghold. Dominating the landscape are two massive mountain ranges, the Taÿgetos Mountains in the west and the Parnonas Mountains in the east. These taper away to create the central and eastern fingers of the Peloponnese.

English speakers can thank the Lakonians for the word 'laconic'.

Sparta
Σπάρτη

POP 16,200

Sparta, fearing no one, was without city walls or fortification, which is probably why so few traces are left of a remarkable people.

At the height of their power, Greece's toughest, incorruptible, legendary warriors triumphed over Athens and the rest of Greece in the Peloponnesian Wars (431–404 BC). However, the decisive defeat by the Thebans in the Battle of Leuctra in 371 BC was the beginning of the end for Sparta, which was followed by successive subjugation by the Macedonians, Romans, Goths and Slavs.

The town was refounded in AD 1834 on the orders of King Otto. Mindful of history, Otto and his court felt that since Athens was to be rebuilt to reflect its former glory, so too should Sparta. He didn't succeed, though a few ruins attest to its ancient pre-eminence. Most visitors pass through on their way to and from the Byzantine glories of Mystras.

◎ Sights

★ Museum of the Olive & Greek Olive Oil
·MUSEUM

(✆ 27310 89315; www.piop.gr; Othonos Amalias 129; adult/concession €3/1.50; ⊙10am-6pm Wed-Mon) This beautifully designed museum initiates you into the mysteries of the olive from its initial appearance in the Mediterranean in 60,000 BC to the present day. Learn about its immense importance in millennia of Greek life. Immerse yourself in olive oil's many uses (cooking, fuel, ritual, perfume-making). Check out the magnificent reconstructions of olive presses in the courtyard, ranging from prehistoric to Byzantine. Finally, marvel at the minute working models (press the button!) that demonstrate changes in pressing technology.

Ancient Sparta
RUIN

Few buildings dating back to the height of Sparta's greatness have been left standing. Still it's worthwhile to wander to the north end of town to see the ruined theatre and the **Sanctuary of Athena Halkioitou** against the backdrop of the snowcapped Taÿgetos Mountains, as well as the **Sanctuary of Artemis Orthia** on the northern outskirts of Sparta. To get here, head to the **King Leonidas statue** that belligerently hefts its sword and shield at the northern end of Paleologou. When the Persians attacked Sparta and told them to lay down their weapons, the Spartans' response, immortalised beneath Leonidas' feet, was *'Molon labe'* (Come and get them). West of here, signs point the way to the acropolis.

GROWING UP SPARTAN

Maybe you saw the gory but brilliant film *300*, imaginatively based on the battle of Thermopylae in 480 BC, one of the most talked about battles in history. Three hundred elite Spartan soldiers held an entire Persian army (whose force numbered several thousand) at bay at the pass ('hot gates') of Thermopylae (near today's Lamia). For three days, wave upon wave of Persian soldiers fell upon their deadly spears and unbridgeable tortoise-shell formation. What kind of soldiers could display such bravery? Ones raised in Sparta, where warfare was held to be the only occupation worthy of its men and where warriors embodied ferocious, self-sacrificing martial supremacy, living (and very often dying) by the motto 'return with your shield or on it'.

If you were born male and deemed too weak and feeble to make it to adulthood, you would be left on the slopes of the Taÿgetos Mountains to die. Passed the first round? Then at the age of seven, you'd be plucked from the bosom of your family and sent to live in barracks with other boys, to undergo the military education system known as *agoge*, designed to build physical and emotional toughness. You'd be habitually underfed to encourage you to survive by living off the land and by stealing, but punished harshly if caught. You'd undergo brutal institutionalised beatings, which you'd be expected to bear without showing pain. At the age of 12, you'd form a sexual bond with an older mentor, who'd be responsible for your training. Upon turning 18, you'd become a member of the army until the age of 30, when you'd finally be granted Spartan citizenship, if you had proved yourself worthy.

Born a girl? Then you'd be better off than anywhere else in Greece at the time. You would eat the same food as your brothers, participate in sport and exercise nude. You'd be well educated and literate, and forbidden to marry until in your early 20s, which would spare you from teenage pregnancies and miscarriages. Then when you finally did marry, your husband-to-be would 'abduct' you, and you'd have your head shaved and be dressed in men's clothing before the marriage could be consummated. (That'd be to make your husband comfortable, since he wouldn't have spent much time around women.)

From the main cobbled road, a footpath runs left (west) through olive groves to the 2nd- or 3rd-century-BC **ancient theatre**, a few steps and seats of which are still visible along the overgrown half-circle.

The main road leads north to the fenced-off acropolis, passing the Byzantine **Church of Christ the Saviour** on the way to the 6000 BC Sanctuary of Athena Halkioitou on a small hillock. Some of the most important finds in the town's archaeological museum were unearthed here.

If you follow the Tripoli-bound road north of town, a signposted path leads downhill to the remains of the **Sanctuary of Artemis Orthia**; this is where Spartan boys were flogged, the bravest awarded bronze sickles that they dedicated to the goddess.

Archaeological Museum   MUSEUM
(☑ 27310 28575; cnr Lykourgou & Agiou Nikonos; adult €2; ☺ 8am-3pm Tue-Sun) Sparta's old-style archaeological museum hosts artefacts from Sparta's illustrious past, many unlabelled and most without any protective covering. You may spot a votive sickle of the kind that Spartan boys dedicated to Artemis Orthia, reliefs featuring Helen and Menelaus (and Helen with Paris), bronze and lead votive figurines, heads and torsos of various deities, a statue thought to be King Leonidas, votive terracotta masks and grave stelae. Fine mosaics from Hellenistic and Roman Sparta are also on show.

🏃 Activities

Spartathlon   SPORTS
(www.spartathlon.gr; ☺ Sep) This gruelling annual foot race takes place over the 246km between Athens and Sparta. It follows in the footsteps of Pheidippides, the messenger who ran from Athens to Sparta in one day in 490 BC, to ask for the Spartans' assistance in the battle of Marathon against the Persians. The record currently stands at 20 hours and 25 minutes.

Sparta

🛏 Sleeping & Eating

The closest campgrounds are 2km from central Sparta, near Mystras village.

Hotel Lakonia
HOTEL €

(☑ 27310 28951; www.lakoniahotel.gr; Palaeologou 89; s/d incl breakfast €40/55; ✳️ 🛜) The rooms at the Lakonia are not hugely memorable, but far from spartan nonetheless. Boons include a supercental location and double-glazed windows that cut out street noise, and the service is friendly and helpful.

Hotel Maniatis
HOTEL €

(☑ 27310 22665; www.maniatishotel.gr; Paleologou 72-76; s/d incl breakfast €44/60; ✳️ 🛜) Light and pleasant rooms with firm beds and more designer shapes than an NYC contemporary-design exhibition. The service is efficient and the upmarket **Zeys** restaurant (mains €8 to €17) is attached.

Kápari
MEDITERRANEAN €€

(☑ 27313 00520; www.kaparirestaurant.gr; Gortsoglou 77; mains €8-15; ⊘noon-11pm) This homey, friendly restaurant is a cut above Sparta's largely uninspiring taverna scene. Greek standards are present and correct, but there are also lovely salads, pastas and an extensive seafood menu; shrimp *saganaki* (prawns in a savoury tomato sauce with cheese) stands out.

Dionysos Garden
GREEK €€

(☑ 27310 25050; mains €7-18; ⊘lunch daily, dinner Tue-Sat; 🅿) Around 1.2km on the road to Mystras, this tranquil restaurant is appropriately festooned with greenery. There may be a shortage of frolicking nymphs and satyrs, but you will find a large selection of well-executed Greek standards.

ℹ Information

National Bank of Greece (cnr Paleologou & Dioskouron)

Police (☑27310 89580; Episkopou Vresthenis 18)

Post office (Archidamou 10; ⊘7.30am-2pm Mon-Fri)

Revanche Internet Cafe (Gortsologou 51; per hr €2; ⊘9am-late)

Sparta Tourism (☑ 27310 28166; www.sparti.gr; Evangelistrias 83-91; ⊘8am-3pm Mon-Fri)

ℹ Getting There & Away

Sparta's **KTEL Lakonia bus station** (☑ 27310 26441; www.ktel-lakonias.gr; cnr Lykourgou & Thivronos) has buses to Athens (€19.50, 3¼ hours, seven to nine daily) via Corinth (two hours), and buses to Gythio (€4.30, one hour, six daily), Neapoli (€14.20, three hours, three daily), Tripoli (€5.40, one hour, nine daily) and Monemvasia (€10, two hours, four daily).

Buses run to Mystras (€1.60, 15 minutes, three daily) from the stop next to the OTE building on Lykourgou; a taxi costs around €10.

Travelling to Kalamata (€3.20, one hour, one to two daily) involves changing buses at Artemisia (€3.20, 40 minutes) on the Messinian side of the Langada Pass.

Departures to the Mani peninsula include buses to Gerolimenas (€10.30, 2¼ hours, three daily), Areopoli (€6.90, two hours, three daily) and a 9am service to the Diros Caves (€8); the return times change.

Mystras
Μυστράς

The captivating ruins of churches, libraries, strongholds and palaces in the fortress town of Mystras (miss-*trahss*), a World Heritage–listed site, spill from a spur of the Taÿgetos Mountains 7km west of Sparta. It's among the most important historical sites in the Peloponnese. This is where the Byzantine Empire's richly artistic and intellectual culture made its last stand before an invading Ottoman army, almost 1000 years after its foundation.

Traveller facilities are split between Mystras village, 1km or so below the main gate of ancient Mystras, and Pikoulianika village, 800m from Mystras' fortress gate.

History

The Frankish leader Guillaume de Villehardouin built the fortress in 1249. When the Byzantines won back the Morea from the Franks, Emperor Michael VIII Palaeologos made Mystras its capital and seat of government. Settlers from the surrounding plains began to move here, seeking refuge from the invading Slavs. From this time until Dimitrios surrendered to the Turks in 1460, a despot of Morea (usually a son or brother of the ruling Byzantine emperor) lived and reigned at Mystras.

While the empire plunged into decline elsewhere, Mystras enjoyed a renaissance. Gemistos Plethon (1355–1452) founded a school of humanistic philosophy here and his enlightened ideas, including the revival of the teachings of Plato and Pythagoras, attracted intellectuals from all corners of Byzantium. Art and architecture also flourished, as seen in the town's splendid buildings and frescoes.

Mystras declined under Ottoman rule, but thrived again after the Venetians captured it in 1687 and developed a flourishing silk industry. The population swelled to 40,000. The Turks recaptured the town in 1715 and from then it was downhill all the way; the Russians burnt it in 1770, as did the Albanians in 1780, and Ibrahim Pasha torched what was left in 1825. By the time of Independence it was a largely abandoned ruin. Much restoration has taken place since the 1950s (and continues to this day) and in 1989 it was declared a Unesco World Heritage site.

◉ Sights

★ Mystras
RUIN

(☎ 23315 25363; adult/concession €5/3; ⊙ 8am-8pm) Spread over a steep, verdant mountainside of the Taÿgetos ranges, this former capital of the Byzantine Empire is the single most compelling set of medieval ruins in Greece. A classic fortified city, Mystras is surrounded by verdant olive and orange trees.

Treading the cobblestones, worn smooth by centuries of footsteps, you can walk with the ghosts, ducking into the ruins of palaces, monasteries and churches, most dating from between 1271 and 1460.

From the **upper-entrance** ticket office, the right-hand path (signposted 'Castle') leads up to the fortress; it's a 10-minute ascent. The fortress was built by the Franks and extended by the Turks; the views of the Lakonia plain, spread out below, are nothing short of fantastic. The left-hand path descends from the ticket office to **Agia Sofia**, which served as the palace church and burial ground for several emperors' wives; some frescoes survive in a side chapel. Steps descend from here to a T-junction.

A left turn leads to the **Nafplio Gate**. Near the gate is the huge **Palace of Despots**, largely restored but closed to the public at the time of writing. The complex was started by the Franks and finished by the Byzantines; various buildings were con-

Mystras

structed between 1250 and 1450 and the main palace between 1350 and 1400.

The right fork leads down to the **Monemvasia Gate**, the entrance to the lower town. Through the gate, turn right to reach the 14th-century **Convent of Pantanassa**. This features a beautifully ornate stone-carved facade and is still maintained by nuns, Mystras' only inhabitants besides the motley crew of stray cats. The convent is an elaborate, perfectly proportioned building that's never overstated. The exquisite, richly coloured 15th-century frescoes here are among the finest examples of late-Byzantine art. Look out for the tiny stamped silver and gold votive offerings beneath the large icon of the Virgin. You'll find images of eyes, ears, legs, arms, breasts, babies, husbands and wives stamped onto these small tablets, depending on the problems (health or personal life) for which the faithful are hoping for supernatural help. The nuns ask that, before entering, you cover bare legs with the cloths provided.

The path continues down to the **Monastery of Perivleptos**, which is built into a rock and tucked away in a pine grove. Inside, the 14th-century frescoes, preserved virtually intact, equal those of Pantanassa. The church has a very high dome and in the centre you'll find the Pantokrator (the Byzantine depiction of Christ as the universal, all-powerful ruler) surrounded by the Apostles, and the Virgin flanked by two angels.

Continue down towards the Mitropolis and you'll pass **Agios Georgios**, one of Mystras' many private chapels. Further down, and above the path on the left, is the **Laskaris Mansion**, a typical Byzantine house.

The **Mitropolis (Cathedral of Agios Dimitrios)** is a complex of buildings enclosed by a high wall. The original church was built in the 1200s, but was greatly altered in the 15th century. The church stands in an attractive courtyard surrounded by stoae and balconies. Its impressive ecclesiastical ornaments and furniture include a marble iconostasis, an intricately carved wooden throne, and a marble slab in the floor featuring a two-headed eagle (the symbol of Byzantium) located on the exact site where Emperor Constantine XI was crowned. The church also has some fine frescoes. Exhibits at the small but modern museum upstairs include fragments of ancient cloth, buttons, jewellery and other everyday items of Mystras' inhabitants.

Beyond the Mitropolis is the **Vrontokhion Monastery**. This was once the wealth-

> ### ⓘ TACKLING MYSTRAS
>
> At least three hours are needed to do justice to the ruins of Mystras. Start early in the morning to beat the tour groups; wear sensible shoes; and bring water (you can refill at the monastery). The site is divided into two interconnected sections – the *kastro* (the fortress on the summit) and the *hora* (upper town), accessible from the fortress gate; and the *kato hora* (lower town), accesible via the main gate.
>
> If you don't have your own wheels, it makes sense to catch a taxi to the fortress gate and walk down. If you do have a car, it's best to cover the lower town first (as it has the lion's share of attractions) from the main gate and then head up to the fortress gate to visit the fortress and the upper town ruins. You can use the same ticket to re-enter at either entrance.

iest monastery of Mystras, the focus of cultural activities and the burial place of the despots. Of its two churches, **Agios Theodoros** and **Aphentiko**, the latter is the more impressive, with striking frescoes.

🍴 Sleeping & Eating

There are some upmarket guesthouses around the village of Mystras and further out. Pikoulianika is an equally good village at which to base yourself, and it has better eating options than Mystras.

Mystras Castle Town   APARTMENT €
(☑ 27310 20047; www.mystras-castle-town.com; d/tr/q €45/50/55; 🅿 🛜) Run by a friendly Russian-Greek couple, these compact, fully equipped apartments are excellent value and just a stone's throw from Mystras' main square. Balconies look out onto the Mystras ruins, and the owners can provide a full breakfast (€4 per person). Wi-fi comes and goes like a stray cat.

Castle View   CAMPGROUND €
(☑ 27310 83303; www.castleview.gr; camp sites per adult/tent/car €6/4/4, 2-person bungalow €25; ⊘ Apr-Oct; 🛜 🏊) This recently renovated campground, set amoung olive trees, features a restaurant, pool and hot showers. Owners are happy to give tips on hiking in the Taÿgetos Mountains. It's about 1km before Nea Mystras village.

WORTH A TRIP

LANGADA PASS   ΟΡΕΙΝΗ ΔΙΑΒΑΣΗ ΛΑΓΚΑΔΑ

If you have time and your own wheels, the 59km Sparta–Kalamata road is one of the most stunning, if time consuming and winding, routes in Greece. The road crosses the Taÿgetos Mountains by way of the Langada Pass.

The climb begins in earnest at the village of **Trypi**, 9km west of Sparta, where the road enters the dramatic **Langada Gorge**. To the north of this gorge is the site where the ancient Spartans left to die those babies too weak or deformed to become good soldiers.

The road then follows the course of the Langada River before climbing sharply through a series of hairpin bends, fringed with plane trees and pines, to emerge in a sheltered valley. This is a good spot to stop for a stroll among the plane trees along the riverbank. The road then climbs steeply once more, to the high point of 1524m, crossing the boundary from Lakonia into Messinia on the way. The descent to Kalamata is equally dramatic.

★ **Traditional Guesthouse Mazaraki**   GUESTHOUSE €€

(☑ 27310 20414; www.xenonasmazaraki.gr; Poukoulianika; d/ste incl breakfast €95/125; P ☎) 🚲
By far the most original accommodation for miles around, Mazaraki consists of three beautiful houses divided into individually decorated studios and apartments. Breakfast arrives on your doorstep in a basket, with produce from the owners' organic farm. The welcoming owners are happy to advise about hiking and biking in the area (and to lend you mountain bikes).

Taverna Pikoulianika   GREEK €

(☑ 27310 82403; Poukoulianika; mains €5-9; ☉ lunch & dinner) The convivial owner welcomes you on the terrace with delicious, homemade meatballs, garlicky aubergine 'caviar', rabbit stew and other classic dishes. You may get a hefty slice of drizzle cake on the house even if you don't order dessert.

ℹ Getting There & Away

From Sparta, buses run to Mystras (€1.60, 15 minutes) daily at 7am, noon and 4pm; return trips depart around 7.15am, 12.15pm and 4.15pm. A taxi between Sparta and Mystras costs around €10.

Monemvasia   Μονεμβασιά

Surrounded by the teal waters of the Aegean Sea, vast, imposing Monemvasia (moh-nem-vah-sia) is an iceberg-like slab of rock, with sheer cliffs rising hundreds of metres from the sea, linked to the mainland by a single, highly defendable causeway.

These days Monemvasia incorporates both the rock, with its medieval village enclosed within the walls of its *kastro* (fort), and the modern mainland village of Gefyra, just across the causeway. 'You can find everything you want in this city – except water', observed an 18th-century Turkish traveller. Remarkably – given that for most of its existence Monemvasia's only source of drinking water came from the sky – Monemvasia has remained inhabited to this day, unlike its Byzantine contemporary, Mystras. Only 12 people live in the *kastro* permanently, however; the rest go home to Gefyra after a day's work. In spite of Monemvasia's immense popularity, the extraordinary visual impact of the medieval village – and the delights of exploring it – override the effects of mass tourism in summer.

Cross the causeway and follow the curving road that skirts the cliff to the official entrance, a narrow tunnel in a massive fortifying wall. The tunnel is L-shaped, so the magical town is concealed until you emerge on the other side.

History

The rock island of Monemvasia was part of the mainland until it was cut off by an earthquake in AD 375. Its name means 'single entry' (*moni* – single, *emvasia* – entry), as there is only one way into the town.

During the 6th century, barbarian incursions forced inhabitants of the surrounding area to retreat to this natural rock fortress, where they founded the upper town that eventually spread downwards. By the 13th century, if Mystras was the spiritual centre of the Byzantine Empire, then Monemvasia was one of its biggest trade centres. It was famous throughout Europe for its highly praised *malvasia*-grape Malmsey wine; George, Duke of Clarence, in Shakespeare's *Richard III,* drowned in a barrel of the stuff.

Monemvasia changed hands several times as the Franks, Venetians and Ottoman Turks all invaded in the following centuries, each adding their own elements to the architectural melange. During the War of Independence its Turkish inhabitants were massacred after their surrender, following a three-month siege; the fortress remained impregnable to the end, its only weakness being the food supply.

Falling into obscurity by the 18th century, Monemvasia was revived as a luxury destination in the 1970s.

◉ Sights

★ **Kastro – Medieval Town**   HISTORIC SITE

Almost wholly surrounded by ocean, Monemvasia's fortified medieval village is divided into the **lower town**, bisected by a main cobbled street lined with souvenir shops and tavernas that leads to the main square, and the **upper town**, with its ruins and **fortress**. The greatest pleasure of visiting the *kastro* comes from wandering the labyrinth: exploring the tiny alleyways and winding stairways that weave between a complex network of stone houses, and ducking into atmospheric nooks and crannies.

In the lower town, the central square is dominated by the **Cathedral of Christos Elkomenos**, dating from the 13th century. Head up through the stone archway opposite the bell tower and you come across the handsome 17th-century **Church of Myrtidiotissa**. Down near the waterfront fortifications is the whitewashed 16th-century **Church of Panagia Chrysafitissa**.

The path to the fortress and the upper town is signposted off the main street in several locations. A walking path skirts the edge of the upper-town ruins all the way to just above the main gate, affording great views of Monemvasia's cluster of rooftops against a cliff backdrop. The upper town's extensive ruins were undergoing intensive restoration at the time of research but its paths should reopen in 2016. Don't miss the **Church of Agia Sofia**, which perches on the edge of a sheer cliff, and mind you don't fall down the overgrown cisterns.

Monemvasia Archaeological Collection   MUSEUM

(☑27320 61403; adult/concession €2/1; ☉8.30am-3pm Tue-Sun) This small museum housed in a former temple displays finds unearthed in the course of old town excavations, such as pottery from Asia Minor, cementing Monemvasia's status as an important trading post. The star turn is the **templon** (chancel screen) from an 11th-century church. Other objects of note include a marble door frame from the Church of Agia Sofia, coats of arms (the trend introduced by Frankish invaders) and well-heads of ancient cisterns.

🛌 Sleeping

There's no budget accommodation in the *kastro* itself; accommodation is cheaper in Gefyra. Prices fluctuate drastically depending on supply and demand. In November and February Monemvasia pretty much shuts down. A torch (flashlight) is a good idea for those staying in the cobbled, dimly lit *kastro*.

Flower of Monemvasia   HOTEL €

(☑27320 61395; www.flower-hotel.gr; Gefyra; d €42-55, tr €54-70, ste €84, all incl breakfast; P ✳ 🛜) Located in mainland Gefyra, opposite Monemvasia's *kastro*, this clean, modern spot is a far cry from the region's more traditional offerings. Nearly all 20 rooms have sea views and some have kitchenettes. Staff are very helpful.

Hotel Filoxenia   HOTEL €

(☑27320 61716; www.filoxenia-monemvasia.gr; d/tr €53/66; P ✳ 🛜) Spotless cheapie off Gefyra's main street, with views of the Monemvasia rock from its balconies. Breakfast €5.

Hotel Byzantino   HOTEL €€

(☑27320 61351; www.hotelbyzantino.com; Monemvasia; d €55-110, tr €90-115, q €125; ✳ 🛜) This range of atmospheric rooms offers a great experience of the traditional *kastro*; rooms occupy around five different buildings and come in varying shapes, sizes and prices (from cheaper rooms with no views to smarter digs with sea-facing balconies and vaulted stone ceilings); most are decked out in antiques. Extensive Greek breakfast costs €6. Wi-fi in lounge only.

Malvasia Traditional Hotel   HOTEL €€

(☑27320 61160; www.malvasiahotel-traditional. gr; d/tr/q incl breakfast from €65/120/160; ✳ 🛜) One of Monemvasia's oldest and most established hotels makes the most of traditional architecture. Its renovated rooms feature heavy wooden beams, light, bright colour schemes and contemporary art; some are cosy, cave-like nooks with vaulted stone ceilings. The pricier rooms come with sea views; some have balconies overlooking the water. Wi-fi in lobby only.

★ Moni Emvasis Luxury Suites   BOUTIQUE HOTEL €€€

(☑27320 62022; www.moniemvasis.gr; ste incl breakfast €240-340; ✳ 🛜) Consisting of just three individually conceived suites, Moni Emvasis doesn't hold back with luxurious touches, from rainshowers and jacuzzis to oversized, sumptuous beds. The sea views from the balconies of the Junior and the Deluxe suites are the best, but the Moni Emvasis suite has a decadent, medieval ambience with its vaulted ceilings and marble fireplace. Extensive breakfast showcases local produce.

🍴 Eating & Drinking

Self-caterers will find most things at the Lefkakis supermarket, just past the post office in Gefyra. Tavernas on Monemvasia's main street all serve similar fare.

Matoula   TAVERNA €
(☑27320 61660; mains €8-13) Of all the tavernas on the main street, Matoula is the oldest, has the best sea views from its vine-trellis-shaded terrace, and serves a reliable selection of classic dishes including dolmadhes, grilled calamari and courgette fritters. All but the veggie dishes are a big hit with the local cats, too.

★ Chrisovoulo   INTERNATIONAL €€€
(☑27320 62022; www.chrisovoulo.gr; mains €14-30; 🍽) Monemvasia's most imaginative restaurant by far, Chrisovoulo conjures up the likes of quinoa salad, veal with morel sauce and risotto with *siglino* pork from the Mani, all with equal ease and flair. The service is professional, the sea views fantastic and there's a serious local wine list to boot. The three-course dinner menu is a steal at €25.

WORTH A TRIP

THE CAVE OF KASTANIA
ΣΠΗΛΑΙΟ ΚΑΣΤΑΝΙΑ

The extraordinary **Kastania Cave** (☑27343 60100; www.monemvasia.gr; adult/concession €7/3; 🕙10am-4pm Sat & Sun, additional seasonal dates), located at the end of a spectacularly winding 17km route northeast of Neapoli, contains some of the best examples of rare stalactites and stalagmites in Europe, estimated to be around 3 million years old. Guided tours in English depart hourly; as you walk around a raised and lit 3km circuit, guides are quick to point out octopi, exotic plants and otherworldly creatures cast in stone. Call ahead to double-check opening times.

★ Wine Tasting Kamara   WINE BAR
(☑6972319434, 27320 61704; glass of wine €3; 🕙noon-late) During your perambulations, you may stumble across this enchanting 11th-century wine cellar. The home of Byron and Vivienne, its walls are decorated with eclectica from a lifetime's travels. Get talking to the gregarious retired owners over a glass or two of Greek wine, and you may not want to leave. Follow the 'wine tasting' signs towards the waterfront.

ℹ Information

ATMs, the **post office** (🕙7.30am-2pm Mon-Fri), **police** (☑27320 61210; Spartis 137) and the supermarket are all located in Gefyra. **Malvasia Travel** (☑27320 61752; 🕙7.30am-2.30pm & 5.15-8pm Mon-Sat) in Gefyra sells tickets for ferries.

ℹ Getting There & Away

Buses leave from outside Malvasia Travel (p156) just over the causeway in Gefyra. There are buses to Athens (€30, six hours, at least four daily) via Sparta (€10, 2½ hours), Tripoli (€15.50, 3½ hours) and Corinth Isthmus (€23, 4½ hours).

ℹ Getting Around

The medieval *kastro* of Monemvasia is pedestrian only, but cars and motorcycles can cross the causeway. Parking is available on the left-hand side of the narrow road skirting the rock. Alternatively, park in the waterfront car park in Gefyra.

A **shuttle bus** (€1; 🕙8am-midnight) ferries visitors between Gefyra and the *kastro* every 30 minutes.

Neapoli   Νεάπολη
POP 2730

Neapoli (neh-ah-po-lih), close to the southern tip of the eastern prong of the Peloponnese, is the departure point for the Ionian Island of Kythira, clearly visible across the bay. You also pass through Neapoli to see the Kastania Cave.

From March to December, a daily ferry runs between Neapoli and Diakofti on Kythira (€11/44 per person/car, 1¼ hours). Tickets are sold at **Vatika Bay Shipping Agency** (☑27340 24004; www.vatikabay.gr; 🕙9am-9pm summer, 2 hours before departure rest of year), 350m before the small bridge. Leave plenty of time to find the place and buy the ticket.

KTEL (☑27340 23222; www.ktel-lakonias.gr) has buses from Neapoli to Athens (€33.70, three daily) via Sparta (€14.20, three hours) and Molai (€7, 1¼ hours). Change in Molai for Monemvasia.

Nearby, the small island of **Elafonisi** is renowned for its white beaches and visiting loggerhead turtles. Regular ferries make the 10-minute trip (up to 15 daily) from Pounda, 8km west of Neapoli.

Gythio   Γύθειο

POP 4700

Once the port of ancient Sparta, Gythio (*yee-thih-o*) is the gateway to the Lakonian Mani. This pretty fishing town makes a pleasant but not terribly thrilling stopover if you're travelling between the Mani and Sparta or Monemvasia or if you're taking a ferry to Kythira. You can count Gythio's attractions on two fingers: the long stretch of **Mavrovouni beach**, 2km south of Gythio, and pine-shaded **Marathonisi Islet**, alleged to be ancient Cranae, where Paris of Troy and Helen consummated the affair that sparked the Trojan War.

You can bed down at **Saga Pension** (☑ 27330 23220; www.sagapension.gr; Kranais; s/d/tr €40/50/55; ❄ �), a tranquil French-run place overlooking the islet, or seek out **Camping Meltemi** (☑ 27330 23260; www.campingmeltemi.gr; camp sites per tent/adult €5.50/6, bungalows €30-60; ☉ Apr-Oct; �), the pick of Mavrovouni's campgrounds, with excellent facilities.

As you can imagine, fresh fish features rather prominently on the menus of tavernas that cluster along the seafront between the pier and the causeway to Marathonisi Islet; family-run **O Potis** (☑ 27330 23245; mains €8-15; ☉ noon-11pm) is our favourite.

❶ Getting There & Away

BOAT

LANE Lines (www.lane.gr; per person/car €23/70) has one weekly ferry to Crete via Kythira and Antikythira. Check the schedule with **Rozakis Travel** (☑ 27330 22207; rosakigy@otenet.gr; Pavlou 5), on the waterfront.

BUS

The **KTEL Lakonia bus station** (☑ 27330 22228; www.ktel-lakonias.gr; cnr Vasileos Georgios & Evrikleos) is northwest along the waterfront, near Jande Café. Services run north to Athens (€23.80, 4½ hours, six daily) or via Sparta (€4.30, one hour) and Tripoli (€9.70); and south to Areopoli (€2.60, 30 minutes, four daily), Gerolimenas (€6, 1¼ hours, three daily), the Diros Caves (€3.70, one hour, one daily) and Vathia (€6.80, 1½ hours, Monday, Wednesday and Friday).

To make the 6.15am Kalamata connection at Itilo, take the 5am bus (€3.80, 45 minutes, daily except Sunday) or go via Sparta. For Monemvasia, change at Sparta.

THE MANI   Η ΜΑΝΗ

Covering the central peninsula in the south of the Peloponnese, the Mani is a wild, rugged region. Greeks from elsewhere will tell you: so are its people, who regard themselves as direct descendants of the Spartans. After the decline of Sparta, citizens loyal to the principles of Lycurgus (founder of Sparta's constitution) chose to withdraw to the mountains rather than serve under foreign masters. Later, refugees from occupying powers joined these people, who became known as Maniots, from the Greek word 'mania'. For centuries the Maniots were a law unto themselves, renowned for their fierce independence, resentment of attempts to govern them and for their bitter, spectacularly murderous internal feuds.

The Ottoman Turks failed to subdue the Maniots and largely left them alone, yet Mani became the cradle of rebellion that grew into the War of Independence. Post-Greek victory, though there had been a fatal falling out with the first president of independent Greece over the spoils of victory bypassing the Maniots, they nevertheless reluctantly became part of the new kingdom in 1834.

From the steep foothills of the snow-tipped Taÿgetos Mountains to the pristine coastal coves; from the tiny villages nestling amid olive groves, connected by threads of walking trails, to the arid scenery in the south of peninsula, speckled with abandoned stone towers; the Mani has some of the most dramatic and varied scenery in the Peloponnese, much of it still wonderfully underexplored.

The Mani is generally divided into the **Messinian Mani** (or outer Mani) and the **Lakonian Mani** (or inner Mani). The Messinian Mani starts southeast of Kalamata and runs south between the coast and the Taÿgetos Mountains, while the Lakonian Mani covers the rest of the peninsula south of Itilo.

Lakonian Mani

Grey rock, mottled with defiant clumps of green scrub, characterises the steep, forbidding mountains of inner Mani. Cultivatable land is at a premium here, and supports little more than a few stunted olives and figs.

ⓘ ITILO BUS INTERCHANGE

To travel between Lakonian and Messinian Mani, you must change buses at Itilo. **Itilo** (*eet*-ih-lo), 11km north of Areopoli, was once the medieval capital of the Mani and was traditionally regarded as the border between outer and inner Mani. There are buses to Areopoli (€1.60, 20 minutes, two daily except Sunday) and Kalamata (€4, 2¼ hours, daily). Areopoli–Itilo buses travel via Limeni.

The indented coast's sheer cliffs plunge into the sea, and rocky outcrops shelter pebbled beaches. This wild and barren landscape is broken only by imposing **stone towers**, which still stand sentinel over the region.

Long known to locals as Kakavoulia, or 'Land of evil counsel', this tough, mesmerising land makes for a fantastic road trip if you have your own wheels. You can follow the loop that runs south along the west coast from the main town, Areopoli, detouring along narrow lanes into semi-deserted villages. Stop to peek into family chapels (there are almost as many churches and chapels as there are towers, as you wouldn't worship with the enemy), and walk to Mani's southernmost tip before returning via the east coast (or vice versa). For detailed exploration, arm yourself with a copy of the Anavasi Topo 25 map, *Mani 8.4; 1:30,000*.

Areopoli   Αρεόπολη
POP 800

Areopoli (ah-reh-*o*-po-lih), capital of the Mani, is aptly named after Ares, the god of war. Dominating the main square, Plateia Athanaton, is a statue of Petrobey Mavromihalis, who proclaimed the Maniot insurrection against the Ottoman Empire in 1821. His brother and son, Konstantinos and Georgios Mavromichalis, were responsible for the assassination of Ioannis Kapodistrias (p139), the first president of independent Greece, in 1831. The town retains many other reminders of its rumbustious past.

◉ Sights

There are some fine examples of Maniot architecture in the narrow, cobbled alleyways surrounding Plateia 17 Martiou, with most of the fortified towers built by the Mavromichalis clan.

Church of Taxiarhes   CHURCH
(Plateia 17 Martiou) On the southern side of Plateia 17 Martiou is this 18th-century church. Its four-storey bell tower marks it as the most important of Areopoli's many churches. The extremely well-preserved relief carvings above the main door look as if they belong to a much earlier era than the 18th century.

Church of Agios Ioannis   CHURCH
Built by the Mavromichalis family on a tiny square west of the main square, this church contains a series of well-preserved frescoes relating the life of Jesus.

Pikoulakis Tower House Museum   MUSEUM
(admission €2; ⊙ 8.30am-3pm Tue-Sun) Housed in a restored tower, this museum displays exquisite Byzantine pieces from Mani churches. These include a 12th-century marble templon from the Church of Agios Ioannis in Mina, near Pyrgos Dirou. Upstairs is a clutch of well-preserved icons spanning five centuries. Take the westbound road from the southwest corner of the main square.

Mavromichalis Tower   RUIN
(Tzani Tzanaki) The Mavromichalis Tower, in a little square southwest of Plateia 17 Martiou, was once the mightiest tower in town, but now it stands sadly derelict.

🏃 Activities

There is some rewarding walking in the area, though the trails are not as straightforward to follow as their colour-coded counterparts in Kardamyli. A number of local guesthouse owners, including that of Antares (p159), are involved in trail maintenance and are happy to give walking tips.

🛏 Sleeping

Hotel Kouris   HOTEL €
(☏ 27330 51340; www.hotelkouris.gr; Plateia Athanaton; s/d/tr €30/50/60; P 🛜) Right on the main square, this concrete cheapie may lack ambience, but it's clean, central and has reliable wi-fi.

★ Londas Guesthouse   B&B €€
(☏ 27330 51360; www.londas.com; near Church of Taxiarhes; s/d/tr incl breakfast €70/80/110, s/d incl breakfast & without bathroom €60/70; 🛜) This 200-year-old tower is the undisputed king of the castle: stylish whitewashed rooms tastefully decorated in an antique and modern fusion; a gorgeous rooftop terrace; a bright, vaulted guest lounge; and extensive break-

fasts that use fresh local produce. It's just north of the Church of Taxiarhes and has a minimum two-night stay. The owners can help organise walks in the mountains.

Hotel Trapela
BOUTIQUE HOTEL €€

(☑27330 52690; www.trapela.gr; s/d/tr €60/80/90; ❄☎) The rough-hewn stone and lack of balconies at this 12-room boutique hotel are a nod to traditional Maniot architecture. The rooms, each named after a Maniot settlement, sport explosed stone, muted colours and wooden beams, coupled with supremely comfortable furnishings.

✖ Eating & Drinking

Areopoli has half a dozen tavernas and several cafes and bars clustered along its main street. For self-caterers, there's a small Koilakos supermarket near Plateia Athanaton.

Barba Petros
TAVERNA €

(☑27330 51205; mains €6.50-14; ☉noon-11pm) This long-standing taverna has been in the family since 1917. The current grandchild/owner and his daughter run the show. This is the place to pig out in every sense – the owner breeds his own pigs, and other meats are sourced locally. Local specialities include

---

TOWER HOUSES

Dotted around the Mani, particularly around Kakavoulia (or inner Mani), scores of stone towers rise eerily from the landscape. Some are solitary; some stand in clusters. Some are intact and fortress-like; others are crumbling. From the 17th century until well into the 19th century, the Mani was ruled by clans with chieftains, with bloody feuds constantly fought over what little fertile land there was. These towers were family fortresses. Feuds between warring clans were fought according to strict rules of engagement, the objective being the destruction of the rival's tower and the deaths of the male members of the rival's family. Male children were known as 'guns' (what else would they be useful for?) and women were exempt from the feuds; after all, someone had to till the fields and bury the dead.

Today, a growing number of towers are being restored beyond their former glory and turned into unique places to stay. Here are our favourite retreats:

Antares (☑27330 51700; www.antareshotel.gr; Omales; d/ste incl breakfast €90/170; P☎) Run by the knowledgeable Mina, this beautiful tower house, 1.5km south of Areopoli, seamlessly blends the historic (centuries-old vaulted ceilings, exposed stone walls) with the contemporary (superb beds, powerful showers). Rooms look out over the lovingly tended herb garden and breakfast ingredients are hand-picked from local suppliers. The tranquillity and care that guests experience here inspire many to linger or return.

Citta dei Nicliani (www.cittadeinicliani.com; d/ste incl breakfast from €100/140; P☎) The former stronghold of the namesake Mani clan is split between this luxurious hotel and the tower house in nearby Stavri. Expect individual engravings on stone walls, exquisite beds and heavy wooden beams (the split-level Timeless room is our favourite). The extensive breakfast makes great use of fresh local produce, and guests can engage in hiking and wine tasting.

Sventoura Hotel (☑6975798180, 27330 53006; www.sventourahotel.com; r incl breakfast €60-120; P☎) Tucked away en route from Pyrgos Dirou to the Diros Caves, this handsome tower, run by a wonderfully welcoming family, has just five unique, characterful rooms. Vaulted ceilings, an antler chandelier, antique chests, wrought-iron bedsteads and bathroom sinks, hewn artfully out of stone, all conspire to give the lodgings that potent Maniot vibe.

Tainaron Blue (☑27333 00461; www.tainatonblue.com; d/ste incl breakfast €150/200; P ❄☎❄) This lonely stone tower en route from Gerolimenas to Porto Kagio is truly a retreat: there's nothing for miles around, except for breathtaking coastline views...which you can enjoy from the clifftop infinity pool. The three luxurious rooms are all unadorned stone and vaulted ceilings, combined with sumptuous beds. The Maniot cuisine is top-notch.

Pirgos Mavromichali Hotel (☑27330 51042; www.pirgosmavromichali.gr; d incl breakfast €130, ste €300; ☉closed Jan & Feb; ❄☎) The owner has beautifully converted his family's 300-year-old tower house in Limeni into 13 chic rooms with rain showers and Cocomat beds. Delightful touches abound, from the vaulted lounge and little private beach to the luxurious split-level suite.

LIMENI ΛΙΜΕΝΙ

The tiny village of Limeni, 3km north of Areopoli on the southern flank of aquamarine Limeni Bay, is well worth a stop for two culinary heavyweights.

Teloneio (☑ 27330 52702; www. teloneio-limeni.gr; mains €9-18; ⊘ lunch & dinner; 🛜☑) This colourful seafront restaurant and bar serves imaginative fare, such as roasted *kritharaki* (rice-shaped pasta) with crayfish, stuffed zucchini flowers, and grilled *talagani* cheese with prickly-pear marmalade. The presentation is on par with the flavours.

Takis (☑ 27330 51327; fish per kg €50-65; ⊘ lunch & dinner Apr-Oct) In a beautiful seafront location, Takis lures in diners with simply yet beautifully prepared fresh fish. The results are consistently good, according to modest Takis, 'because I love what I do'.

vegetable stew, piglet with plum sauce and aubergines baked with potatoes.

Bukka Home Bar COCKTAIL BAR
A creeper-clad cafe by day, come evening this joint morphs into a sultry cocktail bar. Slip into the vaulted cavern and sip on a smoky margarita or a pornstar martini.

🛍 Shopping

Invincible Mani BOOKS
(☑ 27330 53670; Plateia Athanaton) Has an excellent selection of hiking maps and books on the region.

ℹ Information

The town is split into two parts: the new upper town, around Plateia Athanaton, and the old lower town, around Plateia 17 Martiou. The two are linked by a 'main' lane.

National Bank of Greece (Petrobey Mavromihali) The only bank in town; has an ATM. In the upper town.

Post office (Petrobey Mavromihali; ⊘ 7.30am-2pm Mon-Fri) At the northern edge of the upper town.

ℹ Getting There & Away

The **bus station** (☑ 27330 51229; Plateia Athanaton) is situated in the middle of a vast car park at the town's northern end.

Buses to Gythio (€2.60, 30 minutes, four daily) proceed to Athens (€27).

Buses to Itilo (€1.60, 20 minutes, two daily except Sunday) run via Limeni. Other destinations include Gerolimenas (€3.40, 45 minutes, three daily), the Diros Caves (€1.60, 15 minutes, departs 10.15am and returns 12.45pm), Lagia (€3.70, 40 minutes, one daily) and Vathia (€4.20, one hour, daily in summer).

Diros Caves Σπήλαιο Διρού

The extraordinary **Diros caves** (☑ 27330 52222; www.diroscave.gr; adult/concession €12/7; ⊘ 8.30am-5.30pm), inhabited for thousands of years from Neolithic times and systematically explored from 1949, lie 11km south of Areopoli, and are signposted near the village of Pyrgos Dirou.

The entrance to the caves is on the beach. Guides speak Greek, so if you're with non-Greeks you'll be treated to a half-hour's silent, eerie glide by boat through the cave's many passages, giving you time to admire the beautiful stalagmites and stalactites, many of the latter as fine as gossamer threads. You then walk the remaining 300m on foot.

Abandoned as human habitation in 4 BC after an earthquake, the caves weren't rediscovered until around 1895. Then in 1949 the local husband and wife speleology team of Yiannis and Anna Petrocheilou began to systematically explore the caves, now estimated to be around 14km long. Underwater exploration continues to this day.

Pyrgos Dirou to Gerolimenas Πύργος Διρού προς Γερολιμένας

Journeying south down Mani's west coast from Pyrgos Dirou to Gerolimenas, the barren mountain landscape is broken only by semi-deserted settlements with mighty towers. A left turn-off 3km south of Pyrgos Dirou heads up through the picturesque villages of **Drialos**, **Vamvaka**, **Briki** and **Mina**, which have fine examples of Maniot stonework, before depositing you back on the main road, 3km north of Kita. A right turn 9km south of Pyrgos Dirou leads down to the **Bay of Mezapos**, sheltered to the east by the frying-pan-shaped Tigani peninsula. The ruins on the peninsula are those of the **Castle of Maina**, built by the Frankish leader Guillaume de Villehardouin in 1248 and subsequently adapted by the Byzantines.

Kita, 13km south of Pyrgos Dirou, has the lion's share of the west coast's war towers and fortified houses. It was the setting for the last great interfamily feud recorded in the Mani, which erupted in 1870 and required the intervention of the army, complete with artillery, to force a truce. Just west of Kita, Nomia also bristles with some superb tower remains.

Gerolimenas   Γερολιμένας

POP 60

Gerolimenas (yeh-ro-lih-*meh*-nahss) is a tranquil fishing village built around a small, sheltered bay at the southwestern tip of the Mani peninsula. Its pebble beach overlooks teal waters and it's a popular weekend getaway for well-heeled Athenians.

🛌 Sleeping & Eating

There is a small supermarket on the promenade, and several cafes and tavernas.

Kyrimi B&B   B&B €€
(📞27330 53078; www.kyrimi.com; r incl breakfast €90-120; P❄🛜) Consisting of just four luxurious rooms, this intimate B&B inside a traditional stone house is run by a friendly family. Your hosts are happy to explain the history of the area and will feed you an ample breakfast that includes delicious homemade pies. Each room has a patio overlooking the sea – perfect for sunbathing.

Hotel Kirimai   LUXURY HOTEL €€€
(📞27330 54288; www.kyrimai.gr; d incl breakfast €110-200, ste incl breakfast €260-300; P❄🛜❄) Kirimai is a luxurious converted historic building in an idyllic setting at the far southern end of the harbour. Opt for the stone-floored, timber-beamed suites if you can, as the cheaper doubles are cramped and dark in typical Maniot style. The breakfast is substantial; the international restaurant is open to nonguests, but staff could use some training in professionalism.

ℹ️ Getting There & Away

There are three buses daily from Gerolimenas to Areopoli (€5, 45 minutes), which head on to Athens (€30, five hours), Gythio (€10, 1¼ hours) and Sparta (€17, 2¼ hours). The bus stop is outside Hotel Akrotenaritis.

Gerolimenas to Porto Kagio
Γερολιμένας προς Πόρτο Καγιο

South of Gerolimenas, the road continues 4km to the small village of Alika, where it divides. One road leads across the mountains to the east coast, and the other goes south to Vathia and Porto Kagio. The southern road follows the coast, passing pebbly beaches. It then climbs steeply inland to Vathia, the most photographed of the traditional Mani villages, comprising a cluster of closely packed tower houses perched on a rocky spur.

If you have nerves of steel and wish to see an equally impressive traditional village with practically no visitors, take the road into the mountains from Alika and then the turn-off to Mountanistika. The road is very narrow, with a drop to one side and few places for passing, so pray for a lack of oncoming vehicles.

A turn-off to the right 3km south of Vathia splits in two. The right-hand road also splits in two: the right branch leads to Marmari, with its two sandy beaches, while the main road heads as far south as you can go for 3km, to Kokinogia, where there's a taverna and little else.

The left-hand road from the turn-off south of Vathia cuts across the peninsula to the tiny east-coast fishing village of Porto Kagio, set on a perfect horseshoe bay popular with the international yachting set. It's a tranquil place to spend the night. The waterfront tavernas there have similar menus (mains €7 to €17, fish per kilogram €40 to €70) featuring seafood and local specialities, such as wild greens pie.

OFF THE BEATEN TRACK

CAPE TENARO

From the car park below the taverna at Kokinogia, at the south of the Mani peninsula, it's a beautiful 30-minute walk along an uneven rocky path to one of Europe's southernmost points, Cape Tenaro (or Cape Matapan), where a restored lighthouse stands. The cape has been an important location for millennia and was first mentioned in Homer's *Iliad*.

At the beginning of the path are the ruins of ancient Tainaron, once a thriving Roman city (look out for the stunning wave-patterned, circular mosaic), while another short path leads to the ruined church built on the foundations of Poseidon's Temple. Nearby is a cave rumoured to be the entrance to Hades.

🛏 Sleeping

Hotel Psamathous   HOTEL €

(☑ 27330 55221; www.portokayio.com; Porto Kagio; d/tr incl breakfast €55/80; P❄🅿) This Flintstones-style modern Maniot place is set back from the waterfront and has stone-platform beds, mezzanines, heavy wooden beam ceilings and iron bedsteads.

Porto Kale   GUESTHOUSE €

(☑ 6980755528, 27330 54202; Porto Kagio; d/q €55/80; P🅿) A good option in Porto Kagio – simple, snug rooms with stone walls and sun terraces.

East Coast

The east coast of the Mani peninsula is even more rugged and barren than the west. The main town is the formidable-looking **Lagia**, 12km northeast of the Alika turn-off. Perched some 400m above sea level, it was once the chief town of the southeastern Mani, and some of its towers stand derelict.

From Lagia, the road winds down with spectacular views of the little fishing harbour of **Agios Kyprianos** – a short diversion from the main road. The next village is **Kokala**, a busy place with two pebbled beaches. The best beach is further north at **Nyfi**, where a turn-off to the right leads to sheltered **Alipa Beach**. Continuing north, a turn-off beyond tower-studded **Flomochori** descends east to **Kotronas**, while the main road cuts west across the peninsula to Areopoli.

Messinian Mani

The Messinian Mani, or outer Mani, lies to the north of its Lakonian counterpart, sandwiched between the Taÿgetos Mountains and the west coast of the Mani peninsula. The rugged coast is scattered with small coves and beaches, and backed by mountains that remain snowcapped until late May. Kardamyli features the region's best-organised hiking opportunities, and there are some good options around Stoupa, too.

Stoupa   Στούπα

POP 630

The former fishing village of Stoupa, 10km south of Kardamyli, is a resort village popular with British and German package tourists, and is at its most pleasant during the shoulder seasons. It has excellent beaches with wonderfully clean, cold water, courte-sy of underground springs, and there's good hiking in the hills above the village.

Celebrated author Nikos Kazantzakis lived here for a while and based the protagonist of *Zorba the Greek* on Alexis Zorbas, a coal-mine supervisor in Pastrova, near Stoupa.

🏖 Beaches

Stoupa has two main beaches: the large, main crescent of golden sand, sheltered from waves and popular with families, and the smaller **Kalogria**, with deeper waters, just beyond the headland to the north of the main beach. From Kalogria it's a 10-minute walk to the peaceful **Delfini Cove**.

🛏 Sleeping & Eating

Stoupa's many pensions and custom-built domatia are often block-booked by package-tour operators in summer; book ahead.

With one notable exception, Stoupa's underwhelming restaurants all cater to the package-holiday crowd; you're better off with the taverns in Kardamyli or Exochori.

Hotel Lefktron   HOTEL €€

(☑ 27210 77322; www.lefktron-hotel.gr; s/d/tr incl breakfast from €72/82/113; ⊗Apr-Oct; ❄🅿🏊) A five-minute walk from the main beach, family-run Lefktron is well appointed and has rooms overlooking the pool. A good Greek breakfast is included and the staff is happy to give tips on local walks.

Hotel Stoupa   HOTEL €€

(☑ 27210 77308; www.hotel-stoupa.gr; s/d incl breakfast €75/85; P❄🅿) This 20-room hotel is simple but clean and comfortable, and it's Stoupa's only hotel open in winter. It's a couple of blocks behind the beach.

★ Voula's Yesterday & Today   MEDITERRANEAN €€

(☑ 27210 77535; www.voula-yesterdayandtoday.gr; mains €7-12.50; ⊗6.30pm-late May-Oct; 🅿) Indomitable Voula, in her words, 'cooks from her heart'. She serves up traditional foods from a bygone era with a personal, contemporary take. Treats include smoked pork dishes (€12.50), superb homemade pies and *trachana* (homemade pasta). She hosts exhibits on the Mani and has a recipe book – the culmination of clients asking for her secrets.

ℹ Information

Stoupa is 1km west of the main Areopoli–Kalamata road, connected by roads both north and south of town. Both roads lead to the larger of Stoupa's main beaches.

Katerina's Supermarket (☑ 27210 77777)
Well-stocked supermarket that doubles as the post office.

Thomeas Travel (☑ 27210 77689; www.thomeastravel.gr; ⊙ 9am-1pm & 5-9pm Mon-Sat) Changes money and organises car hire, excursions to sites, and ferry and air tickets. Also has a good book exchange and up-to-date bus timetables.

ⓘ Getting There & Away

Buses stop at the junctions of the northern and southern approach roads but don't enter the town. One bus (two in summer) heads daily to Itilo (50 minutes) at 2.10pm, and four head to Kalamata (€4.40, 1½ hours) at 7.30am, 10.55am, 3.50pm and 8.40pm, via Kardamyli. Get to the bus stop early, as buses sometimes pass ahead of schedule.

Kardamyli   Καρδαμύλη

POP 300

It's easy to see why Kardamyli (kahr-dah-*mee*-lih) was one of the seven cities offered to Achilles by Agamemnon. This tiny village has one of the prettiest settings in the Peloponnese, nestled between the blue waters of the Messinian Gulf and the Taÿgetos Mountains. The **Vyros Gorge**, which emerges just north of town, runs to the foot of **Mt Profitis Ilias** (2407m), the highest peak of the Taÿgetos. Today the gorge and surrounding areas are very popular with hikers, with numerous trails passing through tiny, timeless villages.

Several scenes from the movie *Before Midnight,* featuring Ethan Hawke and Julie Delpy (released in 2013), were shot around Kardamyli. The area has also long been a place of pilgrimage for devotees of the legendary writer Patrick Leigh Fermor, who lived in nearby Kalamitsi Bay for several decades until his death in 2011. Fermor fought in the Greek Resistance in WWII and wrote *Mani,* which is considered by many to be the definitive book on the region.

🕴 Activities

Hiking is easily Kardamyli's biggest drawcard. The hills behind the village are criss-crossed by an extensive network of well-marked hiking trails that consist of old stone paths, minor roads, dirt footpaths and a dry riverbed. A number of villages above Kardamyli and Stoupa are connected by winding, narrow paved roads, which make for fairly strenuous, scenic cycling.

Several walking trails pass through the mountain village of **Exohorio,** perched on the edge of the Vyros Gorge at an altitude of 450m, where author Patrick Leigh Fermor scattered fellow travel writer Bruce Chatwin's ashes. The turn-off to Exohorio is 3km south of Kardamyli.

Our favourite hiking route around Kardamyli include **Kardamyli–Aghia Sofia–Petrovouni–Kardamyli,** a gorgeous two-hour loop from Kardamyli's old town up to the Aghia Sofia Church, then a descent through an enchanted forest to Petrovouni and back to Kardamyli.

Chora–Likaki Monastery–Kardamyli is a four-hour descent through the picturesquely ramshackle Chora village, a downhill ramble through olive groves and a tramp through the striking canyon along a rock-strewn riverbed with a detour to see the Likaki Monastery frescoes.

Chora–Saidona–Prastio is a 2¼-hour downhill walk from Chora through the village of Nikovo, passing through olive groves and lush greenery en route to Saidona. There are fantastic coastal views along the Saidona–Prastio descent.

2407 Mountain Activities   OUTDOORS
(☑ 27210 73752; www.2407m.com) 🏃 This professional outfit offers a range of outdoor adventures, from half-day hikes (from €50 per person; minimum four people) to full-day assaults on Taÿgetos peak (€200), rock climbing (on an 80m-high rock; €40), occasional mountain-bike trips (and advice

---

ⓘ HIKING AROUND KARDAMYLI & STOUPA

To make sense of Kardamyli's colour-coded trails and to navigate your hike above Stoupa, invest in the excellent Anavasi Topo25 map: *Mani: Kardamyli–Stoupa–Aghios Nikolaos 8.12/13; 1:25,000,* available from village supermarkets. To avoid retracing your steps, you can get a taxi to drop you off in the village of your choice (book in advance via your lodgings) and walk back to Kardamyli or Stoupa.

Carry more drinking water than you think you'll need, a sun hat, a torch (flashlight) and strong footwear to support your ankles on the uneven ground. Watch out for the odd scorpion and snake (most snakes are harmless).

PELOPONNESE MESSINIAN MANI

for independent mountain bikers) and even cooking courses. They don't enter villages en masse, and prefer to stick to secret locations. The office is halfway along the main street.

🛏 Sleeping

There are plenty of domatia signs along the main road. Prices are considerably lower outside high season.

Olympia Koumounakou Rooms   PENSION €
(🖉 27210 73623; s/d €35/40; ﹡🔊) Olympia loves her budget travellers (as they do her) and offers five clean rooms with bathrooms in the centre of the village. It's a stone's throw from the water, and has an appealing garden to boot.

Y Volvere Studios (Stratis Bravakos Rooms)   APARTMENT €
(🖉 27210 73326; www.yvolvere.gr; d/tr €40/55) Y Volvere is great value for compact, spotless studio apartments with kitchenettes. It's at the south end of the village, along a street leading towards the water.

★ Hotel Vardia   HOTEL €€
(🖉 27210 73777; www.vardia-hotel.gr; studio €80, apt €115-165; ⊘ Mar-Nov; 🅿@🔊) This relaxing and stylish stone hotel (near a former sentry tower and situated high behind the village beyond Old Kardamyli) sits amid lush grounds, and has very helpful owners. The 18 spacious studio-style rooms have exceptional views of the Messinian Gulf and there are lounge chairs overlooking the gorge for sunset-watching. Vardia is signposted from the southern end of town.

Maison Viros   APARTMENT €€
(🖉 6972098289; www.maison-viros.com; studio/apt €140/180; 🅿﹡🔊🏊) Just across the bridge from central Kardamyli, these spacious split-level apartments and studios are found inside delightful stone houses arranged around a pool, surrounded by attractively landscaped grounds. The apartments sleep up to six people, the studios four, and owner Nikos goes out of his way to be helpful.

Kalamitsi Hotel   HOTEL €€
(🖉 27210 73131; www.kalamitsi-hotel.gr; d/ste incl breakfast €110/160; 🅿🔊) Situated 1km south of town, the Kalamitsi is a lovely, modern stone-built hotel with serene, well-appointed rooms. Family bungalows are also available for €220. Within its shady grounds are paths leading to a secluded pebbly beach. Home-cooked dinners and fresh buffet breakfasts are available to guests.

🍴 Eating

The inland villages of Saidona, Mileu and Exochori also have some excellent tavernas.

There are two well-stocked supermarkets at the northern edge of the village.

O Perivolis   TAVERNA €
(🖉 27210 73713; mains €8-12; ⊘ dinner Tue-Sun, closed Dec; 🖋) In the heart of the village, this excellent taverna with a large garden usually has a selection of vegetarian dishes of the day (spinach and ricotta cannelloni, baked aubergine) alongside Greek classics such as lamb *kleftiko,* all of which incorporate local ingredients where possible.

Taverna Kiki   TAVERNA €
(🖉 27210 73148; mains €6.50-9; ⊘ lunch & dinner) The kindly owners at this appealing taverna, tucked away off the main street, tell you the day's dishes on arrival. These tend to be more imaginative than usual; expect the likes of veal stew with shallots and cloves, and cauliflower baked with tomatoes.

Lola Frozen Yogurt   ICE CREAM €
(medium yoghurt €2.50; ⊘ 9.30am-late; 🔊🖋) A cool, sweet balm for sweaty hikers on hot days, right on the main street. Go for regular or guest flavours, such as cherry or mango.

★ Elies   TAVERNA €€
(🖉 27210 73140; mains €8-14; ⊘ lunch Apr-Oct, dinner mid-Jun–mid-Sep; 🔊🖋) Right by Ritsa beach, 1km north of town, and nestled in olive groves, Kardamyli's most popular lunch venue has the atmosphere of a provincial Mediterranean private garden. It presents the best selection of top-notch Greek and Mani fare to boot, including numerous veggie dishes.

ℹ Information

Kardamyli is on the main Areopoli–Kalamata road. The central square, Plateia 25 Martiou 1821, lies at the northern end of the main thoroughfare.

Kardamyli's main pebble-and-stone beach is off the road to Kalamata; turn left beyond the bridge on the northern edge of town. The road up to Old (or Upper) Kardamyli is on the right before the bridge.

The **post office** (⊘ 7.30am-2pm Mon-Fri) is on the main strip.

A useful website is www.kardamili-greece.com.

❶ Getting There & Around

Kardamyli is on the bus route between Kalamata (around €4, one hour, four daily) and Stoupa (€1.50, 15 minutes); one bus daily continues south to Itilo. The bus stops at the central square at the northern end of the main thoroughfare, and at the bookshop at the southern end.

Buses to the villages in the hills above Kardamyli are too infrequent and sporadic to be useful. A taxi to Exochorio costs around €20.

MESSINIA   ΜΕΣΣΗΝΙΑ

The southwestern corner of the Peloponnese has many boons, from the peninsula's loveliest beaches to old Venetian towns, impressive castles and even an underwater park in the making.

Messinia's boundaries were established in 371 BC following the defeat of Sparta by the Thebans at the Battle of Leuctra. The defeat ended almost 350 years of Spartan domination of the Peloponnese – during which time Messinian exiles founded the city of Messinia in Sicily – and meant the Messinians were left free to develop their kingdom in the region stretching west from the Taÿgetos Mountains. Their capital was Ancient Messini, about 25km northwest of Kalamata on the slopes of Mt Ithomi.

Kalamata   Καλαμάτα

Kalamata is the capital of Messinia and the second-largest city in the Peloponnese. Most travellers just pass through it, only pausing to partake of its facilities and its decent restaurants.

Built on the site of ancient Pharai, the city takes its modern name from a miracle-working icon of the Virgin Mary known as *kalo mata* (good eye). It was discovered in the stables of the Ottoman *aga* (governor), who converted to Christianity as a result of the miracles it was believed to have performed. The icon now resides inside the city's oversized cathedral, the Church of Ypapantis.

Below the *kastro* is the small but attractive old town, which was almost totally destroyed by the Turks during the War of Independence, rebuilt by French engineers in the 1830s, then levelled again by an earthquake in 1986. A lively Saturday food market just to the west of the old town sells Kalamata olives and other local produce.

◉ Sights

Archaeological Museum of Messenia   MUSEUM
(☑ 27210 83485; www.archmusmes.gr; Benaki & Agiou Ioannou; admission €3; ⊙ 1.30-8pm Mon & 8am-8pm Tue-Sun) This partially interactive, child-friendly museum focuses on treasures found in four regions – Kalamata, Pylia, Messini and Trifylia. A trail snakes through the maze of exhibits, revealing everything from sculpture, pottery and funereal objects found in Mycenaean *tholos* tombs, to Roman mosaics, gold jewellery and votive offerings.

Kastro   FORT
(Vilardouinou; €2; ⊙ 8am-5pm Tue-Sun) Looming over the town is the 13th-century *kastro*. Remarkably, it survived the powerful 1986 earthquake that levelled the city. The entry gate is its most impressive feature. Inside, the *kastro* is a lush haven of tranquillity and there are good views from the battlements.

✵ Festivals & Events

Kalamata International Dance Festival   MUSIC, DANCE
(www.kalamatadancefestival.gr; ⊙ Jul) This annual festival draws crowds to its quality performances of traditional music and dance. Venues include the amphitheatre of the *kastro*. See the website for dates and prices.

KALAMATA OLIVES

Kalamata gives its name to the prized Kalamata olive, a plump, purple-black variety found in delicatessens around the world. The region's reliable winter rains and hot summers make for perfect olive-growing conditions.

The Kalamata tree is distinguished from the common olive (grown for oil) by the size of its leaves. Like its fruit, the leaves of the Kalamata are twice the size of other varieties and a darker shade of green.

Unlike other varieties, Kalamata olives can't be picked green. They ripen in late November and must be hand-picked to avoid bruising. You can buy and sample these famous olives at the markets in Kalamata.

Kalamata

🍴 Sleeping & Eating

The majority of lodgings are located along the waterfront. The marina is lined with restaurants and tavernas; good options are also found in the old town.

Hotel Rex
HOTEL €€

(☎ 27210 22334; www.rexhotel.gr; Aristomenous 26; d/ste incl breakfast from €99/199; ❄ 🛜) The Rex has a superb central location and will appeal if you like unapologetically retro decor, a Fawlty Towers–esque attitude from some staff and a touch of faded grandeur. The rooms are reasonably modern but the air-con struggles in the summer heat. The corner room 403 has good rooftop views.

Hotel Haikos
HOTEL €€

(☎ 27210 88902; www.haikos.gr; Navarino 115; s/d €57/75; 🅿 🛜) One of the best choices along the beachfront is this business-like, modern hotel, with funky wallpaper, balconies and beachfront parking. Rooms at the front catch the sea breeze (and street noise). Breakfast €5.

Street Pasta
ITALIAN €

(☎ 27214 01328; Amfias 20; mains €6-11; ⏱ 2-11pm Tue-Sun; 🥗) Hip, tiny eatery specialising in oodles of pasta, with imaginative sauces alongside good ol' bolognese and pesto. Elbow your way in and be prepared for leisurely service if the place is full.

Burgery
BURGERS €

(www.theburgery.gr; Navarinou 93; mains €5-8; ⏱ 1pm-midnight; 🛜) One of the very, very few places along the marina that doesn't do seafood, the Burgery grills up huge, freshly made burgers, generously stacked with toppings that slither out the sides and ooze all over your fingers as you try to take a bite.

ℹ Information

National Bank of Greece (Aristomenous, Central Sq, cnr Akrita & Navarinou)

Post office (cnr Olgas & Navarinou; ⊙7.30am-2pm Mon-Fri)

Tourist police (☑ 27210 24680; Iroon Polytechniou; ⊙8am-9pm Mon-Fri)

Tourist support office (☑ 27210 90413; Benaki; ⊙9am-2pm & 6-9pm Mon-Fri, 9am-2pm Sat & Sun) This helpful tourist office, in the same building as the Archaeological Museum, has a plethora of brochures on Messinia's attractions.

ℹ Getting There & Away

AIR

Kalamata International Airport is served by various airlines from Nuremburg, Amsterdam and London Gatwick in summer. **Aegean Airlines** (www.aegeanair.com) operates daily flights between Kalamata and Athens and Thessaloniki from June through September.

BOAT

Between mid-June and September, a weekly ferry service operated by **LANE Ferries** (www.lane.gr) runs on Sundays from Kalamata to Kissamos, Crete (€32/84 per person/car, 9¾ hours) via Kythira (€21.50/56 per person/car, 5½ hours). Contact **SMAN Travel/Maniatis** (☑ 27210 20704; cnr Likourgou & Psaron 148), by the port, for the schedule.

BUS

KTEL Messinia bus station (☑ 27210 28581; www.ktelmessinias.gr; Artemidos) has buses to Athens (€22.20, 4½ hours, 12 daily) via Corinth Isthmus (€15.80, 2½ hours). It also has buses to Tripoli (€8.10, 1¼ hours, five daily), Kyparissia (€7, 1¼ hours, four weekdays) and Patra (€22.80, four hours, two daily) via Pyrgos (€14, two hours).

Heading west, buses go to Koroni (€5, 1½ hours, three to six daily), Methoni (€6.10, 1½ hours, five daily) and Pylos (€5, 1¼ hours, five daily).

Heading east across the Langada Pass, buses run to Sparta (€5, 1¾ hours, daily at 9.15am) with a change at Artemisia. Four daily buses head to Kardamyli (€4, one hour) and Stoupa (€4.40, 1¼ hours), with one continuing to Itilo (€7.40, 2¼ hours). There are also direct buses to Thessaloniki (€65, three weekly, 11 hours).

ℹ Getting Around

TO/FROM THE AIRPORT

Kalamata's airport is 10.5km west of the city, near Messini. A taxi costs around €20.

BUS

Local buses leave from the KTEL Messinia bus station. The most useful service is bus 1, which goes south to the seafront and then east along Navarinou as far as the Filoxenia Hotel. Buy tickets (€1.20) from kiosks or the driver.

CAR

Recommended car rental options:

Avis (☑ 27210 20352; www.avis.gr; Kesari 2)

Verga Rent a Car (☑ 27210 95190; www.car-rental-kalamata.gr; Faron 202)

Ancient Messini
Αρχαία Μεσσήνη

POP 350

The extensive ruins of Ancient Messini lie scattered across a small valley below the pretty village of Mavromati, 25km northwest of Kalamata, signposted from the modern town of Messini. The village takes its name from the fountain in the central square; the water gushes from a hole in the rock that looks like a black eye (*mavro mati*, in Greek). The name Ancient Messini is used to refer to both the historic site and the village itself.

History

Ancient Messini was founded in 371 BC after the Theban general Epaminondas defeated Sparta at the Battle of Leuctra, freeing the Messinians from almost 350 years of Spartan rule. Built on the site of an earlier stronghold, the new Messinian capital was one of a string of defensive positions designed to keep watch over Sparta. Epaminondas himself helped to plan the fortifications, which were based on a massive wall that stretched 9km around the surrounding ridges and completely enclosed the town.

Apart from its defensive potential, Ancient Messini was also favoured by the gods. According to local myth, Zeus was born here – not Crete – and raised by the nymphs Neda and Ithomi, who bathed him in the same spring that gives the modern village its name.

◎ Sights

★ **Ancient Messini** HISTORIC SITE
(☑ 27240 51201; www.ancientmessene.gr; adult/concession €4/2, museum & site €5/3; ⊙8am-8pm) The remains of this vast ancient city are at least as extensive as those of Olympia and Epidavros, yet Ancient Messini receives only a fraction of their visitors. Picturesquely situated on a hillside below the village of Mavromati and still undergoing excavation, the site comprises a large theatre, an *agora*, a vast Sanctuary of Asclepius and the most

UNDERWATER WORLDS

Messinia's rich historical heritage also lies underwater. The latest ambitious government project is to create an underwater park in two locations, one near Pylos and the other around Sapienza Islet, just south of Methoni, to allow divers to explore a wealth of shipwrecks from through the ages.

Sapienza once lay on an important maritime route between Italy and the Middle East, and the wrecks around the islet yield treasures such as granite columns from King Herod of Palestine, Roman stone sarcophagi and amphorae.

The Bay of Navarino near Pylos hosted the immense naval Battle of Navarino in 1827 and the sea floor is littered with ship remains, the most impressive being the three Ottoman warships. There's also an immense recent shipwreck of the *Irene Serenade* tanker.

The project is still in the making; for updates, contact **Ionian Divers** (☑ 27630 61551; www.ioniandivecenter.gr).

intact and impressive of all ancient Greek stadiums.

Take the downhill turn-off near the museum, about 300m northwest of the square. The first construction you come across is the large **amphitheatre**, reconstructed for contemporary use. The path leads past the **Fountain of Arsinoe** building, which supplied the ancient city with water. The extensive columned remains next to it are the **agora** (marketplace) with the **treasury** in its southwest corner. The Greek general Philopoemen was held prisoner by the Messinians here in 183 BC and dispatched to the other world with poison.

Beyond is the **Sanctuary of Asclepius**, the spiritual centre that lay at the heart of the ancient city, consisting of a rectangular courtyard fringed with Corinthian columns. This extensive complex was centred on a Doric temple that once housed a golden statue of Ithomi. The modern awning west of the temple protects the **artemision**, where fragments of an enormous statue of Artemis Orthia were found. The structures to the east of the asclepion include the **ekklesiasterion**, which looks like a small amphitheatre but once acted as an assembly hall. Nearby are the remains of a **Roman villa**, the steel roof protecting the mosaic remains.

Head downhill to the large **stadium**, which is surrounded by a forest of columns. You can see where the Romans closed off part of the athletics track, turning it into a gladiator arena. On the left-hand side, near the arena, are the **VIP seats** – the ones with backs and with lion paws for legs. On the right-hand side, near the intact gate of the enormous gymnasium, are round holes in stone slabs – ingenious **Roman public toilets** positioned over a now dry stream.

The cube-like building near the toilets is a **grave memorial** to an important Messinian family, and the Doric temple at the far end of the stadium is a **mausoleum** of the Saithidae, a prominent Roman family.

Museum MUSEUM
(adult/concession €2/1, museum & site €5/3; ☽ 8.30am-8pm) The compact museum, by the turn-off for the site, houses some wonderful statuary from Ancient Messini. They include the fine specimen of manhood that is Hermes, fierce Artemis, an ugly Roman emperor statue carved from a female Greek statue, and also Machaon and Podaleiros, the sons of Asclepius. The latter are thought to be the work of Damophon, who specialised in oversized statues of gods and heroes and who was responsible for many of the statues that once adorned Ancient Messini.

Arcadian Gate ARCHAEOLOGICAL SITE
It's worth heading 800m along the road from Mavromati village, past the museum at the turn-off to the site, to the celebrated Arcadian Gate. This unusual stone portal with a circular courtyard between the double gates and an immense, half-collapsed gate post guarded the ancient route to Megalopoli – now the road north to Meligalas and Zerbisia – which runs through the gate. Running uphill from the gate is the finest surviving section of the mighty defensive wall built by Epaminondas.

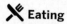 Eating

Taverna Ithomi TAVERNA €
(☑ 27240 51298; www.ithomi.gr; mains €5.50-11; ☽ noon-11pm) The pick of a handful of local *kafeneia* (coffee houses) and tavernas, this one offers traditional cuisine with a view over the ruins. Friendly owner Nikos is the local 'man in the know', and besides grilled

meats, he makes a mean *briam* (oven-baked vegetable casserole).

ℹ Getting There & Away

There are two buses between Ancient Messini/Mavromati and Kalamata (€3, one hour, daily except Sundays), one in the early morning, the other in the afternoon, on a changing schedule. Check at Taverna Ithomi.

Koroni   Κορώνη

POP 1700

Koroni (ko-*ro*-nih) is a lovely Venetian port town on Messinia Bay, 43km southwest of Kalamata. Medieval mansions and churches line the town's quaint, narrow and winding streets. These lead to a promontory, on which perches an extensive castle and monastery.

◉ Sights & Activities

Castle   CASTLE
The castle crowns a bluff overlooking the town. Much of it is occupied by the **Timios Prodromos Convent**, so a strict dress code applies. You can enter via the castle's impressive Gothic entrance. The small promontory beyond the castle is a tranquil place for a stroll, with lovely views over the Messinian Gulf to the Taÿgetos Mountains.

Zaga Beach   BEACH
Koroni's main attraction is Zaga Beach, a 2km sweep of golden sand just south of town. It takes about 20 minutes to walk to here – you can cut through the castle or go via the road. Koroni also sees loggerhead turtles, which lay their eggs near Zaga.

🛏 Sleeping & Eating

The harbourfront street is lined with restaurants.

Hotel Diana   HOTEL €
(☎/fax 27250 22312; www.dianahotel-koroni.gr; d €45; ❋ 🛜) This place is blessed (or otherwise) with Byzantine gold-plated bar stools, icons and the like. Rooms are not quite as glossy – they are simple but adequate. It's off the central square, almost on the seafront. Breakfast costs €5.

Camping Koroni   CAMPGROUND €
(☎27250 22119; www.koronicamping.com; camp sites per adult/child/tent €8/4/5; 🅿 🛜 ⛱) Located only 200m from Koroni, near the beach. On-site restaurant, washing machines and supermarket; popular with families.

Parthenon   GREEK €
(☎27250 22146; mains €7-12; ⊙lunch & dinner) On the waterfront, a block from the main square, this family-run seafront taverna specialises in seafood, along with a supporting cast of classic Greek dishes.

Peroulia Restaurant   GREEK €€
(☎27250 41777; www.peroulia.gr; mains €7-15; ⊙breakfast, lunch & dinner) Overlooking the teal waters of the gorgeous Peroulia Beach, 6km north of Koroni, this waterfront restaurant has earned a loyal local following for its traditional Greek cuisine and fresh seafood. It does have occasional off-days, but the beach alone is worth the trip. In the grounds of the Colonides Hotel.

ℹ Getting There & Away

Buses will drop you in the central square outside the Church of Agios Dimitrios, one block back from the harbour. There are services to Kalamata (€5, 1½ hours, five daily), Athens (€27.20, four hours, daily) and Pylos (€3.50, 1½ hours, five daily).

Methoni   Μεθώνη

POP 1170

Methoni (meh-*tho*-nih), 12km south of Pylos, was one of the seven cities offered to Achilles by Agamemnon. Homer described it as 'rich in vines'. Today it's a pretty seaside town with a popular beach, next to which looms the most impressive example of a 15th-century Venetian fortress in the Peloponnese.

◉ Sights

Kastro   FORTRESS
(⊙8am-3pm) **FREE** This vast, crumbling *kastro*, a great example of 15th-century Venetian military architecture, is built on a promontory south of Methoni. It's surrounded on three sides by the sea and separated from the mainland by a dry moat. Enter the inner keep through the mighty gateway to discover a Turkish bath, a cathedral, a house, a cistern and underground passages. A short causeway leads from the fortress to the diminutive octagonal Bourtzi fortress on an adjacent islet.

The medieval port town, which was located within the fortress walls, was the Venetians' first, and their longest-held, possession in the Peloponnese. It was also a stopover for pilgrims en route to the Holy Land.

🛏 Sleeping & Eating

Hotel Aris
HOTEL €

(☑ 27230 31125; s/d/tr €35/40/50; P ☀ 🤶)
Two blocks from the sea and overlooking a
tree-lined square, this immaculately clean
cheapie is run by kind, helpful owners who
don't speak much English.

Hotel Achilles
HOTEL €€

(☑ 27230 31819; www.achilles-hotel.com; Plateia
Eleftherias; s/d €60/75; P ☀ 🤶) The smartest of
a range of small family hotels in town, Achilles has 13 comfortable, modern rooms and a
pleasant outdoor terrace. There's a light, airy
dining area, too. Breakfast costs €6.

Taverna Alector
TAVERNA €

(☑ 27230 31838; mains €7-11; ☺ lunch & dinner)
Traditional Greek dishes are served with ap-
plomb by the friendly and accommodating
multilingual husband-and-wife team at this
central taverna. Live music on Thursdays;
linger with a beer or carafe of house wine.

Taverna Klimataria
TAVERNA €

(☑ 27230 31544; Miaouli; mains €7-11; ☺ noon-11pm
May-Oct) Locals are in agreement: this is the
place to head to for traditional dishes. It's in
an old home, with seating on the front porch
and in the courtyard. Typical choices include
onion pie and stuffed zucchini flowers.

ℹ Information

The road from Pylos forks on the edge of town to
create Methoni's two main streets, which then run
parallel through town to the fortress. As you come
from Pylos, the fork to the right is the main street,
where there's a National Bank of Greece (and ATE
Bank ATM) and a supermarket. The left fork leads
directly to the fortress car park, passing the **post
office** (☺ 7.30am-2pm Mon-Fri) on the way.

ℹ Getting There & Away

Buses depart from Methoni from the fork at the
Pylos end of town where the two main streets
meet. Buses travel to Pylos (€1.60, 15 minutes,
three to six daily) and on to Kalamata (€6, 1½
hours). Services also run to Finikounda (€2.60,
15 minutes, one to two daily except Sundays);
change there for Koroni, though connections
may not match up. The bus to Kalamata stops at
Harakopio, 4.5km from Koroni. For bus information call ☑ 27230 22230.

Pylos
Πύλος

POP 2760

Coastal Pylos (pee-loss), 51km southwest of
Kalamata, presides over the southern end of
an immense bay. With its huge natural harbour that's almost enclosed by the Sfaktiria
Islet, its castle and surrounding pine-covered
hills, Pylos is not just picturesque but also
one of the most historically significant towns
in the Peloponnese.

'Sandy Pylos', the Mycenaean kingdom
mentioned by Homer, lay a short distance
from here, near Gialova Lagoon, and was
one of the few places where the Spartans
suffered an ignoble defeat at the hands of
the Athenians. Also, from this very bay on
20 October 1827, the British, French and
Russian fleets, under the command of Admiral Codrington, fired at point-blank range
on Ibrahim Pasha's combined Turkish, Egyptian and Tunisian fleet, sinking 53 ships and
killing 6000 men, with negligible losses on
the Allies' side. The attack was known as
the Battle of Navarino (Navarino being the
town's former name) and was a decisive moment in the War of Independence.

⊙ Sights & Activities

Neo Kastro
CASTLE

(☑ 27230 22955; adult/concession €3/2;
☺ 8.30am-3pm Tue-Sun) The more intact and
accessible of two castles that lie on either
side of Navarino Bay, this was built by the
Turks in 1573 on the hilltop at the southern
edge of town, off the road to Methoni. Within
its formidable walls is an excellent little **museum** with exhibits on underwater archaeology, a citadel, a mosque converted into a
church (under renovation) and a courtyard
surrounded by dungeons (used as a prison
to contain warring Maniots until the 1900s).

The well-presented museum focuses on
the remains of several shipwrecks: the marble columns and stone sarcophagi that were
found off the island of Sapienza, near Methoni; and the remains of the *Mentor,* the
ship that carried the Parthenon Marbles that
then had to be retrieved from the deep.

René Puaux Exhibition
MUSEUM

(admission €2; ☺ 8.30am-3pm Tue-Sun) Housed
in a red mansion on the seafront, this collection of pictures depicts the War of Independence with a focus on the Battle of Navarino.
It was donated by René Puaux (1878-1937),
who bequeathed porcelain, engravings and
lithographs on condition that they be exhibited at Pylos, near the battle's location.

Club Boats
BOAT TOUR

(☑ 6972263565, 27230 23155; www.pyloscruises
.gr; kiosk on the quay; ☺ Jun-Sep) Runs boat
tours around the Bay of Navarino and to
Sfaktiria Islet, where silt-covered wrecks of

sunken Turkish ships are discernible in the clear waters. The price depends on the number of passengers, but reckon on about €15 per person (minimum numbers apply).

Sleeping & Eating

There is a much better selection of restaurants clustered along the pedestrianised waterfront in nearby Gialova, 8km north along Navarino Bay.

★ Tina's House   B&B €

(☏27230 23653; www.pylosrooms.com; d incl breakfast €50; ❄🛜) A handful of stylish rooms in a bluff-top location, unbeatable views of the bay, a wonderfully friendly hostess and an excellent breakfast make this a superb, homey choice. Bring your own wheels or be prepared for a stiff uphill 15-minute walk from town.

Karalís Beach Hotel   HOTEL €€

(☏27230 23021; www.karalisbeach.gr; Paralia; d/tr/f €75/85/160; ❄🛜) Pylos' clear winner in the hotel stakes is this intimate little place with 14 compact, stylish rooms, all with wood floors and decorated in tranquil creams. Front rooms have balconies. You'll like this place for the setting alone – under the castle walls, clinging to a cliff over the water.

Koukos   TAVERNA €

(☏27230 22950; mains €7.50-11; ⏲lunch & dinner) A plain, unpretentious, good old-fashioned taverna with a loyal local clientele, serving hearty portions of grills and oven-baked dishes on a changing menu. It's a short walk up the hill above the port – ask for directions in the plaza.

ℹ Getting There & Away

The **KTEL Messinia bus station** (☏27230 22230; www.ktelmessinias.gr) is on the inland side of the central square. From the bus station, there are services to Kalamata (€5, 1¾ hours, four to seven daily); Kyparissia (€6.10, 1¼ hours, two to four daily) via Nestor's Palace (€2, 30 minutes) and Chora (€2, 35 minutes); Methoni (€1.60, 20 minutes, three to four daily); and Athens (€28, five hours, two daily). There's one connection a day for Patra departing Kyparissia.

Gialova   Γιάλοβα

POP 280

The village of Gialova lies 8km north of Pylos on the northeastern edge of Navarino Bay. There's a fine sandy beach and safe swimming in the sheltered waters of the bay. The Gialova Lagoon is a prime birdwatching site in winter.

Sleeping & Eating

Camping Erodios   CAMPGROUND €

(☏27230 23269; www.erodioss.gr; camp sites per adult/tent/car €7/5/4, 2-/4-bed cabins €65/75; 🛜) Neat as a pin, this campground has a good stretch of beach on Navarino Bay and great facilities. It's northwest of the village on the road leading out to the Gialova Lagoon and Paleokastro.

Zoe Resort   HOTEL €€

(☏27230 22025; www.zoeresort.com; r incl breakfast from €70, apt from €90; 🅿❄🛜🏊) This once-small family-run place on the seafront near the pier has morphed into an appealing

---

BIRDWATCHING & THE GIALOVA LAGOON

The best, and most accessible, birdwatching site in the Peloponnese is the Gialova Lagoon. Between September and March the lagoon is home to up to 20,000 assorted waterbirds, while many others pause on their spring migration between Africa and Eastern Europe.

The Hellenic Ornithological Society has recorded here 265 of around 400 species found in Greece, including 79 protected species, 10 species of duck and eight types of heron. Waders descend in their thousands, along with flamingos and glossy ibises. Birds of prey include the internationally threatened imperial eagle, plus ospreys, peregrine falcons and harriers. Birds aside, 28 types of mammal and 26 species of reptile also call the lagoon's environs home.

The lagoon and associated wetlands cover 700 hectares at the northern end of Navarino Bay, separated from the bay by a narrow spit of land leading out to Koryphasion Hill. They are fed by two freshwater streams that flow into the reed beds on the northern and eastern flanks of the lagoon and empty into Navarino Bay, below Koryphasion Hill.

The wetlands and surrounding coastal habitats were declared a protected area in 1997. The old pump house has been converted into an information centre staffed by volunteers in summer and is the starting point for a walking trail that guides visitors through a range of habitats.

resort. We like the older hotel rooms with the small front balconies, although they're potentially noisy if Zoe's outdoor taverna rocks on. The resort section is modern, but the service can be a little chaotic.

★ **Elia** MEDITERRANEAN €
(☑ 27230 23503; www.elia-gialova.gr; mains €6-15; ☺ Feb-Oct; ☎ ☑) Gourmet Greek meets contemporary Mediterranean eatery. The outstanding smoked pork and orzo pasta with seafood is matched by the ambience, trendy designer lights and flower boxes.

★ **La Cucina Italiana** ITALIAN €€
(☑ 27230 23301; mains €7-17; ☺ 6.30pm-late) From the seasonal *spaghetti vongole* (with clams) and chicken sautéed with oranges and honey, to the ample servings of *pizza piccante*, this Italian restaurant really delivers. The sea views from the upstairs terrace are complemented by friendly service, and a free glass of sparkling wine comes accompanies the noteworthy desserts.

ⓘ Getting There & Away

There are four buses a day south to Pylos (€2, 15 minutes) and up to six daily north to Kyparissia via Nestor's Palace and Chora. A taxi between Gialova and Pylos costs around €15.

Around Gialova

★ **Paleokastro** RUIN
The ruins of this ancient castle, built by the Franks in the 13th century on the site of the acropolis of Ancient Pylos, lie 5km west of Gialova on rugged Koryphasion Hill, a formidable natural defensive position overlooking the northern entrance to Navarino Bay.

The castle (officially closed) can be explored with care; avoid falling down cisterns hidden by overgrowth. The views from the top are magnificent. The road out to the castle is signposted on the northern edge of the village.

Follow signs to Paleokastro, where the road ends in a little car park. From there you'll find two ways of reaching the castle: the left-hand path (20 minutes) skirts Koryphasion Hill and gradually leads up to the entrance. The other route (40 minutes) is signposted 'Nestor's Cave'; the path skirts the lagoon before leading towards Voidokilia Beach through the sand dunes; a fork in the path leads up towards the cave where Hermes hid Apollo's cattle, according to the legend. From the cave, it's a tough scramble

up to the castle's crumbling battlements, rewarded by views of the perfect crescent of the beach below.

Voidokilia Beach BEACH
This perfect, sandy crescent with clear waters is presumed to be Homer's 'sandy Pylos', where Telemachus was warmly welcomed when he came to ask wise old King Nestor the whereabouts of his long-lost father, Odysseus, King of Ithaca.

Follow the signs to Paleokastro and walk the lagoonside track labelled 'Nestor's Cave' from the Paleokastro car park (20 minutes) or approach by road from the village of Petrohori, 6km north of Gialova off the road to Chora.

Nestor's Palace RUIN
(☑ 27630 31437) The best preserved of all Mycenaean palaces lies 17km north of modern Pylos. It is described in Homer's *Odyssey* as the court of the mythical hero Nestor, who took part in the voyage of the Argonauts and sent 90 ships to fight in the Trojan War. Originally a two-storey building, the palace's walls stand 1m high, giving a good idea of the layout of a Mycenaean palace complex.

At the time of writing, renovations of the palace were ongoing.

The main palace, in the middle, was a building of many rooms. The largest room, the throne room, was where the king dealt with state business. In its centre was a large, circular hearth surrounded by four ornate columns that supported a 1st-floor balcony. Surrounding the throne is the sentry box, pantry, waiting room, a vestibule and, most fascinating, a bathroom with a terracotta tub still in place where, according to legend, Polycaste, Nestor's youngest daughter, bathed the hero Telemachus.

Some of the palace frescoes and some of the Linear B script tablets – the first to be discovered on the mainland – are housed in the museum in the nearby village of Chora.

Chora Archaeological Museum MUSEUM
(☑ 27632 31358; adult €2; ☺ 8.30am-3pm Tue-Sun) This little museum, 4km northeast of Nestor's Palace in the village of Chora, houses finds from the palace site and other Mycenaean weaponry, jewellery and pottery from tombs around Messinia. The prize pieces are the incomplete frescoes from the throne rooms at Nestor's Palace and the Linear B tablets (the latter are copies).

Buses from Pylos to Kyparissia stop at Chora. If driving, follow signs for Kalamata.

OLYMPIA ΟΛΥΜΠΙΑ

Most people come to Olympia for one reason: to visit the historically important and impressive site of Ancient Olympia, birthplace of the Olympic Games. Otherwise the surrounding region of Elia (Ελιά) is largely agricultural.

Ancient Elia took its name from the mythical King Helios. Its capital was the city of Elis, now a forgotten ruin on the road from Gastouni to Lake Pinios. When the Franks arrived, they made Andravida the capital of their principate of Morea. Pyrgos is the underwhelming modern capital.

ⓘ Getting There & Around

From the **KTEL bus terminal** (☑ 26210 20600; www.ktelileias.gr) in Pyrgos, there are services to Athens (€27.70, four hours, up to 10 daily), Patra (€9, two hours, up to 10 daily), Andritsena (€6.20, two hours, two daily except Friday and Sunday), Kalamata (€13.10, two hours, two daily) and Olympia (€2.20, 30 minutes, eight to 13 daily).

There's also a small train that runs on the branch line from Pyrgos to Olympia.

Olympia Ολυμπία

POP 1000

The compact modern village of Olympia (o-lim-bee-ah), lined with souvenir shops and eateries, caters to the coach-loads of tourists who pass through on their way to the most famous sight in the Peloponnese: Ancient Olympia. This is where myth and fact merge: it's where Zeus allegedly held the first Olympic Games to celebrate beating his father Cronos at wrestling. This is also birthplace of the ideal that still brings states together and makes them put aside their differences for the sake of friendly atheletic competition, just as it did more than 4000 years ago.

Just 500m south of the village, across the Kladeos River, the remains of Ancient Olympia rest amid luxurious greenery. As you walk around, or stand at the starting line of the ancient stadium, you may contemplate the influence of this site through millennia. This is where they still light the Olympic Flame every four years. This is where the Games began.

◉ Sights

A handy website to the area is www.ancient olympiahotels.gr.

★ **Ancient Olympia** HISTORIC SITE
(☑ 26240 22517; adult/concession €6/3, site & museum €9/5; ⊙ 8am-8pm) The Olympic Games took place here for at least 1000 years, held every four years until their abolition by Emperor Theodosius I in AD 393. Today, the Olympic flame continues to be lit here for the modern Games. Thanks to the destruction ordered by Theodosius II and various subsequent earthquakes, little remains of the magnificent temples and athletic facilities, but enough exists to give you a hint of this World Heritage–listed sanctuary's former glory. The ancient site is a signposted five-minute walk from the modern village.

Wandering amid the tree-shaded ruins, you can almost picture the blood and smoke of oxen sacrificed to Zeus and Hera; the sweaty, oiled-up athletes waiting inside the original stadium; the jostling crowds; and the women and slaves watching the proceedings from a nearby hill. It's worth remembering that some buildings precede others by centuries; a visit to the archaeological museum beforehand will provide context and help with visualising the ancient buildings.

The first ruin encountered is the **gymnasium**, which dates from the 2nd century BC. South of here are the columns of the partly restored **palaestra** (wrestling school), where contestants practised and trained. The next building was the **theokoleon** (priests' house). Behind it is **Pheidias' workshop**, where the gargantuan ivory-and-gold Statue of Zeus, one of the Seven Wonders of the Ancient World, was sculpted. The workshop was identified by archaeologists after the discovery of tools and moulds. Beyond the theokoleon is the **leonidaion**, an elaborate structure that accommodated dignitaries.

The Altis, or **Sacred Precinct of Zeus**, lies east of the path. Its most important building was the immense 5th-century Doric **Temple of Zeus**, which enshrined Pheidias' statue, later removed to Constantinople by Theodosius II (where it was destroyed by fire in AD 475). One column of the temple has been restored and re-erected, and helps put into perspective the sheer size of the structure.

South of the Temple of Zeus is the **bouleuterion** (council house), which contains the **altar of oaths**, where competitors swore to abide by the rules decreed by the Olympic Senate and not to commit foul play.

The Olympic Games

The Olympic Games were undoubtedly the ancient world's biggest sporting event and remain for most athletes today the biggest of dreams. Then, as now, the Games made warring states temporarily halt their squabbles, and victorious competitors won great fame and considerable fortune.

Origins of the Games

Some Ancient Greek texts attribute the founding of the Games to the hero Pelops; others name Hercules as the founder who made Zeus the patron god of the Olympic sanctuary. The first official quadrennial Olympic Games were declared in 776 BC by King Iphitos of Elis, took place around the first full moon in August, reaching the height of their prestige in 576 BC.

During the ancient Games, writers, poets and historians read their works to large audiences; traders clinched business deals; and city-state leaders attempted to resolve differences through diplomacy.

Olympic Qualifications

In Ancient Greece only free-born Greek males were allowed to compete in the Games; the Romans changed the rules to include Roman citizens. Slaves and women were not allowed to enter the Olympic sanctuary even as spectators; women trying to sneak in were thrown from Mt Typaion. Today's Summer Olympics includes athletes from 204 countries, with 88 countries competing in the Winter Olympics.

Demise & Rebirth

During Roman times the Games declined. Held for the last time in AD 393, they were banned by Emperor Theodosius I as part of a purge of pagan festivals.

1. Wall mural depicting athletes
2. Lighting the flame in Ancient Olympia in preparation for the 2014 Sochi Winter Olympic Games
3. Helliniko Olympic complex, part of the Athens 2004 Olympic Games site

The modern Olympic Games were instituted in 1896 and, except during WWI and WWII, have been held every four years around the world ever since. The Olympic flame is lit at the ancient site and carried by runners to the city where the Games are held.

Scandal & Controversies

Throughout history the Olympics has been marred by scandals. These range from the farcical – Emperor Nero entering the chariot race in AD 67 with 10 horses, ordering that other competitors could only have four, falling off and still being declared winner – to the serious, including Israeli athletes being murdered by Palestinian group Black September in 1972, and Hitler refusing to award gold medals to African American sprinter Jesse Owens in 1936.

ANCIENT OLYMPICS VS MODERN OLYMPICS

➡ Contemporary opening ceremonies may involve such displays as James Bond parachuting in. In Ancient Greece, it was all about sacrificing oxen to Zeus.

➡ Ancient Greek events included wrestling, chariot and horse racing, the pentathlon (three foot races, the long jump and the discus), javelin, boxing and pankration (few-holds-barred fighting). Today's Summer Olympics have been joined by the Winter Olympics; a total of 56 events across both games include modified sprinting, equestrian, boxing and wrestling.

➡ Victorious ancient Olympians were crowned with sacred olive branches and enjoyed tax exemption and other privileges. Modern Olympians receive medals, TV fame and sponsorship fortune.

Ancient Olympia

Ancient Olympia

East of the temple is the **echo portico**, with a Doric colonnade leading towards the stadium. Its remarkable acoustics meant that a sound uttered within was repeated seven times. Just east of the portico are the remains of a lavish **villa** used by Emperor Nero during his participation in the Games in AD 67; it replaced the original Sanctuary of Hestia.

The **stadium** lies to the east of the Altis and is entered through a stone archway. It's rectangular, unlike today's stadiums, and the stone start and finish lines of the 120m sprint track and the judges' seats still survive. The stadium could seat at least 45,000 spectators. Slaves and women spectators, however, had to be content to watch from outside on the Hill of Kronos.

To the north of the Temple of Zeus was the **pelopion**, a small, wooded hillock with an altar to Pelops, the first hero of the Olympic Games. It was surrounded by a wall containing the remains of its Doric portico. Many artefacts now displayed in the museum were found on the hillock.

Further north is the 6th-century Doric **Temple of Hera**, the site's most intact structure. Hera was worshipped along with Rea until the two were superseded by Zeus. The Hermes statue was found here.

To the east of this temple is the **nymphaeum** (AD 156–60), erected by the wealthy Roman banker Herodes Atticus. Typical of buildings financed by Roman benefactors, it was grandiose, consisting of a semicircular building with Doric columns flanked at each side by a circular temple. The building contained statues of Herodes Atticus and his family, though Zeus took centre stage. Despite its elaborate appearance, the nymphaeum had a practical purpose; it was a fountain house supplying Olympia with fresh spring water.

Just in front of the nymphaeum is the spot where the altar of Hestia would have maintained a continuous **fire** during the Games, symbolising the fire stolen from the gods by Prometheus; fires were also lit in the temples of Zeus and Hera. Today, the **Olympic Flame** is lit where the Temple of Hestia once stood.

Beyond the nymphaeum and up a flight of stone steps, a row of 12 **treasuries** stretched to the stadium, each erected by a city-state for use as a storehouse for offerings to the gods; these were mainly used to advertise the city-state's prestige and wealth.

At the bottom of these steps are the scant remains of the 5th-century-BC **metroön**, a temple dedicated to Rea, the mother of the gods. Apparently the ancients worshipped Rea in this temple with orgies.

The foundations of the **philippeion**, west of the Temple of Hera, are the remains of a circular construction with Ionic columns built by Philip of Macedon to commemorate the Battle of Chaironeia (338 BC), where he defeated a combined army of Athenians and Thebans. The building contained gold-and-ivory-covered statues of Philip and his family, including his son, Alexander the Great.

North of the philippeion was the **prytaneum**, the magistrate's residence. Here, winning athletes were entertained and feasted.

★**Archaeological Museum**   MUSEUM
(adult/concession €6/3; ⊙8am-8pm) This superb museum at Ancient Olympia features finds from the archaeological site. Visiting it before touring the ruins helps to put the ancient site and its buildings into perspective. The museum's exhibits span the Olympic sanctuary's history, from the prehistoric to the Roman periods. Artefacts include increasingly sophisticated ceramics, votive offerings to Zeus and Hera, sacrificial cauldron adornments and statuary from the Temple of Hera. The main hall dramatically displays the biggest highlight: reassembled pediments and metopes from the Temple of Zeus.

Among the museum's treasures, you may spot a tiny helmet (a votive offering), a bronze arm protector decorated with the face of the Gorgon Medusa, a tiny bronze figure of Silenus (tutor to Dionysis, the god of wine) featuring optimistically proportioned genitalia, and a 4th-century Parian marble statue of Hermes of Praxiteles, a masterpiece of classical sculpture from the Temple of Hera.

The pediments and metopes from the Temple of Zeus deserve some extra attention. The **eastern pediment** depicts the chariot race between Pelops and Oinomaos, while the **western pediment** shows the fight between the centaurs and Lapiths at the wedding feast of Pirithous (the centaurs got drunk and tried to abduct the women). The **metopes** depict the Twelve Labours of Hercules; half the fun is trying to work out which is which from the remains alone.

Museum of the History of the Olympic Games in Antiquity   MUSEUM
(adult/concession €2/1; ⊙10am-5pm Mon, 8am-3pm Tue-Fri) Beautifully presented displays depict the history of the world's most prestigious sporting competition. Learn about its core original events (foot racing, wrestling, boxing and chariot racing); why it's associated with Hercules (or Pelops); and what fate befell women who tried to watch the Games despite prohibitions. The sculptures, mosaics, pottery art and votive offerings all pay tribute to athletes and athleticism. Other Games – Heraean, Nemean, Panathenaic, Pythian and Isthmian – also get a mention.

☞ Tours

To really make the site come alive, it's well worth considering hiring a guide, especially if there are a few of you. Tours usually include both the site and the Archaeological Museum, but any preference will be catered for. Recommended guides include **Niki Vlachou** (✆6972426085; www.olympictours. gr; 4½hr tour incl museum from €40 per person), who speaks English and French; **Agelos Koutras** (✆26240 22602); and **Marieta Kolotourou** (✆26250 23596), who speaks English and Spanish.

🛏 Sleeping

Hotel Pelops   HOTEL €
(✆26240 22543; www.hotelpelops.gr; Varela 2; s/d/tr incl breakfast €40/50/70; ※@⊛) Opposite the church, this is among the town's best contenders, with comfortable rooms. The delightful Greek–Australian owners, the Spiliopoulos family, provide friendly, knowledgeable service and a decent breakfast. And, hurrah, there are tea and coffee facilities in each room.

Hotel Kronio   HOTEL €
(✆26240 22188; www.hotelkronio.gr; Tsoureka 1; s/d/tr incl breakfast €40/53/70; ※@⊛) The helpful, multilingual owner, Panagiotis, is a bonus at this pleasant spot that has excellent-value bright and airy rooms.

Best Western Europa   HOTEL €€
(✆26240 22650; www.hoteleuropa.gr; Drouva 1; s/d/tr incl breakfast €70/90/100; P※@⊛⊛) This family-run franchise is popular with groups and families. Rooms have blond wood and mod cons; larger rooms with balcony vistas are more luxurious. A bar, swimming pool, a decent poolside taverna under the olive trees, and excellent service seal the deal.

Arty Grand Hotel HOTEL €€

(☑ 26240 26000; www.artygrandhotel.gr; d/tr/ste €90/105/128; P ✴ ☎ ☒) Though its hilltop location, 800m from the ruins, means that the hotel is somewhat isolated, its spacious rooms are comfortable, the service is pleasant and the pool and spa are nice luxury touches. The restaurant is nothing special, though. Popular with tour groups.

✗ Eating

Olympia's many tavernas cater largely to the lunchtime coach crowds and, as such, most lack incentive to strive for excellence.

Self-caterers will find a good supermarket near the ELIN petrol station.

★ **Taverna Bacchus** TAVERNA €

(☑ 26240 22298; www.bacchustavern.gr; Ancient Pissa; mains €7-13; ⊙ lunch & dinner; P ✴ ☎ ✐) Bacchus, the god of wine, has extended his portfolio to include delectable delights with fresh ingredients in this smart stone taverna in nearby Ancient Pissa. Standout dishes include meatballs with rice; if you accept a complimentary carafe of house wine from the owner, you may also wish to book one of Bacchus' luxurious rooms (double/triple €60/70) with pool access.

Aegean GREEK €

(☑ 26240 22540; G Doyma 4; mains €7-12; ⊙ lunch & dinner; ✐) One of a cluster of tavernas on the main square, Aegean distinguishes itself by its extensive array of vegetarian dishes served alongside Greek favourites.

★ **Garden Taverna** GREEK €€

(☑ 26240 22650; Best Western Hotel Europa International; mains €9.50-15; ⊙ lunch & dinner May-Sep; ☎) Under olive trees in a tranquil garden overlooking the valley below, this restaurant is the most original in Olympia. Alongside the excellent grilled meats you'll find the likes of pasta in vodka cream sauce with smoked salmon and dill. The service is prompt and attentive. Lunch is light bites only.

ℹ Information

National Bank of Greece (cnr Praxitelous Kondyli & Stefanopoulou)
Post office (Pierre Coubertin 3)

ℹ Getting There & Away

BUS

Buses depart from in front of the train station. There are services to Pyrgos (€2.30, 30 min-

utes, eight to 13 daily), with four or five handy Athens connections, and to Tripoli (€14.30, three hours). Note: for tickets to Tripoli, reserve your seat with KTEL Pyrgos (p173) one day prior to travel; hotels will call on your behalf.

TRAIN

Olympia train services head to/from Pyrgos only – there are five departures daily (€2, 30 minutes).

Andritsena Ανδρίτσαινα

POP 580

Once the home of Panayotis Anagastopoulos, one of the leaders in the War of Independence, Andritsena sits on a hillside overlooking the valley of the Alfios River, 65km southeast of Pyrgos. Crumbling stone houses flank the village's narrow cobbled streets and a stream bubbles its way through the central square, Plateia Agnostopoulou. Andritsena is a handy springboard for visiting the magnificent Temple of Epicurean Apollo at Vasses.

◎ Sights

★ **Temple of Epicurean
Apollo at Vasses** HISTORIC SITE

(☑ 26260 22275; adult/concession €3/2; ⊙ 8am-8pm) Situated 14km southwest of Andritsena, on a wild, isolated spot overlooking rugged mountains and hills, the World Heritage–listed Vasses and its Temple of Epicurean Apollo is one of Greece's most atmospheric archaeological sites. The striking, well-preserved temple is robbed of some of its splendour and immediate visual impact by the giant steel-girded tent that's been protecting it from the elements since 1987 for restoration purposes, but it's magnificent all the same.

The temple was built in 420 BC by the people of nearby Figalia, who dedicated it to Apollo Epicurus (the Helper) for delivering them from the plague. Designed by Iktinos, the architect of the Parthenon, the temple combines Doric and Ionic columns and a single Corinthian column – the earliest example of this order.

The temple's most prominent decoration – a marble frieze depicting battles between Greeks and Amazons, and between Lapiths and Centaurs – was spirited away in 1814 by 'archaeologists' who procured it from Greece's Ottoman rulers and sold it to the British Museum, where it is currently displayed.

No public buses run to Vasses. A return taxi from Andritsena, including waiting time, costs around €40.

Nikolopoulos Andritsena Library   LIBRARY, MUSEUM
(☑26260 22242; ⊙8.30am-2.30pm Tue-Sat) FREE
In 1838 Konstantinos Nikopoulos, a composer, archaeologist and member of the Greek Resistance looking to liberate Greece from the Turks, donated 4000 rare books to his father's home town to establish a school. It was one of Europe's largest private book collections at the time. Displayed along with manuscripts from Greece's 1821 Independence movement is a cast of a frieze from the Temple of Epicurean Apollo at Vasses. Explanatory English video. It's behind Hotel Theoxenia.

🛏 Sleeping & Eating

For somewhere to eat, try any of the casual tavernas and grill places spread along the main street.

Archontico Hotel   HOTEL €€
(☑26260 22401; www.archontiko-andritsenas.gr; d €60; 🅿🛜) Complete with terraces and artfully scattered amphorae, this fine historic building at the western end of the village offers snug rooms with exposed stone walls and mod cons.

❶ Getting There & Away

Buses run to Athens (€24, two hours, one or two daily) via Megalopoli, Tripoli and Corinth Isthmus.

Kyllini   Κυλλήνη

The port of Kyllini (kih-*lee*-nih), 78km southwest of Patra, is the jumping-off point for ferries to Kefallonia and Zakynthos. Most people arrive on buses from Patra to board the ferries.

Ionian Ferries (www.ionianferries.gr) runs to Zakynthos (€7.50/28.50 per adult/car, 1¼ hours, four daily in summer) and to Poros (€8.80/37.90 per person/car, 1½ hours, one to two daily in summer) on Kefallonia.

Two daily buses run to Kyllini from Pyrgos (€6, one hour), and three to four buses daily run from the KTEL Zakynthos bus station in Patra (€8, 1¼ hours). Some connect with ferries to Zakynthos (bus and ferry €15.90). Note, however, when doing the reverse trip there are no buses from Kyllini to Patra. A taxi to Patra costs around €60.

WINERY STOPOVER

Mercouri Estate (☑26210 41601; www.mercouri.gr; tastings €10; ⊙9am-3pm Mon-Sat), 1km north of Korakohori village and about 15km from Pyrgos, is a worthwhile winery for a stop-off. This handsome estate produces a dry white *foloi*, and a prize-winning rich red, its flagship Domaine Mercouri. It also runs tours of the grounds (reservations required).

ACHAÏA   ΑΧΑΪΑ

The northern region of Achaïa comprises some high and skiable mountain country (reached via a historic rack-and-pinion railway), surprisingly little in the way of beaches, and a bustling port, Patra.

Achaïa owes its name to the Achaeans, an Indo-European branch of migrants who settled on mainland Greece and established the mighty Mycenaean civilisation. When the Dorians arrived, the Achaeans were pushed into this northwestern corner of the Peloponnese, displacing the original Ionians.

Legend has it that the Achaeans founded 12 cities, which later developed into the powerful Achaean Federation that survived until Roman times. Principal among these cities were the ports of Patra and Egio (on the coast of the Gulf of Corinth).

Patra (Patras)   Πάτρα

POP 168,000

Let's face it: Patra is unlikely to be your final destination or a place you'll linger long. Most travellers pass straight through, boarding or disembarking from boats that sail between here, Italy and some Ionian Islands.

The largest city in the Peloponnese, Patra is named after King Patreas who ruled Achaïa around 1100 BC. Little is evident of this busy port's 3000 years of history, during which it was an important trade centre under the Mycenaeans and the Romans. There's a darker side to Patra: the derelict buildings, groups of unemployed men hanging out by the docks and beggars contrast sharply with the attractive squares and lively pedestrian streets, and the bars and restaurants filled with the young and the trendy.

Before you escape by boat or via the Rio–Andirio suspension bridge, an engineering feat that links the city with western continental Greece, it's worth making the most of Patra's saving grace: the most diverse eating and nightlife scene in the Peloponnese, helped by the presence of Patra's 20,000 university students.

⊙ Sights & Activities

★ Archaeological Museum of Patras
MUSEUM

(☑2610 420 645; www.patrasmuseum.gr; Patras-Athens National Rd 38-40; admission €4; ☉8.30am-3pm Tue-Sun) This space-age museum, the country's second largest, displays a thorough collection of regional objects from prehistoric to Roman times across three vast themed halls: Private Life, Public Life and Cemeteries. You may spot some extraordinary mosaics, barnacle-encrusted amphorae, duck-shaped *askos* vessels, coin hoards, a gold ring decorated with a tiny phallus, oil lamps featuring erotic scenes, elaborate marble sarcophagi, Mycenaean bronze swords from warrior burials and four skulls with funereal wreaths intact.

The museum is several kilometres north of the centre.

Kastro
CASTLE

(☉8.30am-3pm Tue-Sun) FREE The *kastro* stands on the site of the acropolis of ancient Patrai. The Romans were the first to build a fort here around AD 550, but the present structure is of Frankish origin, remodelled many times over the centuries by the Byzantines, Venetians and Turks. Set in an attractive pencil-pine park, it is reached by climbing the 190-plus steps at the southeastern end of Agio Nikolaou. Great views of Zakynthos and Kefallonia are the reward.

Church of Agios Andreas
CHURCH

(Agiou Andreou) Seating 5500 people, this church is one of the largest in the Balkans. It houses religious icons and paintings, plus St Andreas' skull, along with part of the cross on which he was crucified.

✯✯ Festivals & Events

Patras Carnival
CARNIVAL

(www.carnivalpatras.gr) Patra's citizens party hard during the annual Patras Carnival. The program begins in mid-January, and features a host of minor events leading up to a wild weekend of costume parades, colourful floats and celebrations in late February or early March.

🛏 Sleeping

Prices double at Carnival time; book well in advance.

Pension Nicos
HOTEL €

(☑2610 623 757; cnr Patreos 3 & Agiou Andreou 121; s/d/tr €30/40/55, s/d without bathroom €25/35; ✳☎) This 1960s-style budget option on a busy street has flaking shutters on the outside, but inside Nicos runs a tight ship with clean rooms on several floors and a roof terrace.

★ City Loft Boutique Hotel
APARTMENT €€

(☑2610 223 552; www.cityloft.gr; Valtetsiou 6; 1-/2-/3-person apt €75/110/130; ℗✳☎) Sleek and stylish apartments in white or black on a quiet side street several blocks north of the main square. Perks include high-quality bed linens, king-sized beds with orthopaedic mattresses, balconies and a small, attractive garden.

Maison Grecque
BOUTIQUE HOTEL €€

(☑2610 241 212; www.mghotels.gr; 25 Martiou 116; s/d/ste incl breakfast €65/85/180; ✳☎) This smart boutique spot has a touch of 'sleek Greek' pretension. Each room is decked out uniquely (with an original ceiling fresco or two thrown in) – think dark hues with metallic touches. A couple of the rooms have very small windows. The rest, however, are sophisticated and smart. It's a five-minute walk from the pedestrianised centre.

Hotel Byzantino
HOTEL €€

(☑2610 243 000; www.byzantino-hotel.gr; Riga Fereou 106; s/d/tr incl breakfast €75/85/100; ✳☎) In a restored neoclassical building on the lively main pedestrian street, this small hotel features appealing rooms with fancy bedsteads, wooden floors and period furniture. There's a popular cafe downstairs.

✗ Eating & Drinking

Trendy cafes, bars and restaurants line the pedestrianised Riga Fereou (Michalakopoulou), the surrounding side streets and Agiou Nikolaou. Cheap student eateries are along Gerokostopoulou.

Labyrinthos
GREEK €

(☑26102 26436; Poukevil 44; mains €6.50-12; ☉noon-5.30pm & 8.30pm-1am Mon-Sat; ☎✎) Inside the rough stone walls of this 80-year-old family restaurant, you can expect classics such as *briam*, dolmadhes and beef casserole, as well as roasted lamb sweetbreads and intestines for the adventurous epicurean.

Patra

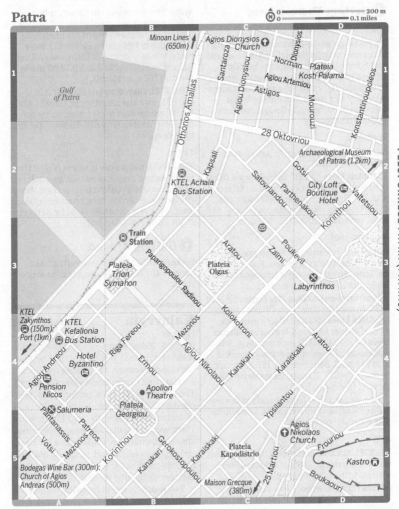

★ **Salumeria**   FUSION €€

(Pantanassis 27; mains €11-13; ⊙lunch & dinner; 🛜🍴) On a pedestrian street, this chichi bistro with exposed stone walls offers a departure from Greek cuisine with the likes of smoked salmon with black lentils and seared calamari with sweet potato and wilted greens. In the evenings it's a popular wine bar.

Bodegas Wine Bar   WINE BAR

(📞2610 221 113; Riga Feraiou 147; ⊙lunch & dinner) Whether you're nursing a margarita or a glass of wine from the extensive list of Greek vintages, this stylish bar is a spot worth lin-

gering. Salads come in an enormous bowl the size of Epidavros Theatre.

ℹ Information

Internet cafes are plentiful around Plateia Olgas.

First aid centre (📞2610 277 386; cnr Karolou & Agiou Dionysiou; ⊙8am-8pm)

National Bank of Greece (Plateia Trion Symahon; ⊙8am-2pm Mon-Fri) Opposite the train station.

Post office (cnr Zaïmi & Mezonos; ⊙7.30am-8pm Mon-Fri, to 2pm Sat & Sun)

Tourist police (📞2610 695 191; Gounari 52; ⊙7.30am-9pm)

ℹ Getting There & Away

BOAT

The passenger port is 1km south of town. Ferry offices are located at the port, and there are also boat agencies located along waterfront Othonos Amalias and its northern extension, Iroön Polytehniou. Ferry schedules and prices change seasonally; ring ahead. There are no ferries directly to Corfu; ferries to Corfu depart from Igoumenitsa only.

Domestic

Patra is the departure point for ferry services to Kefallonia and Ithaki.

Strintzis Lines (☑ 2610 240 000; www.strintzisferries.gr) has services to Sami, on Kefallonia, (€18.20/50 per person/car, three hours, two daily). The same service continues to Vathy, on Ithaki, once daily (€18.60/55, 3¾ hours).

International

Patra is Greece's main port for ferry services to Italy, with departures to Ancona, Bari and Venice. Some ferries may stop at Igoumenitsa and Corfu; no free stopovers permitted.

Superfast Ferries/Blue Star Ferries (☑ 2610 623 574; www.superfast.com; Othonos Amalias 12), **ANEK Lines** (☑ 21041 97400; www.anek.gr; cnr Othonos Amalias & Aratou) and **Minoan Lines** (☑ 2610 426 000; www.minoan.gr; Iroön Politehniou 50) run trips to Ancona (from €71, 21 to 24 hours), Bari (from €81, 15½ hours) and Venice (from €77, 31 hours). Some Minoan Lines services continue to Trieste.

Note: we give prices for deck seats; prices are higher for airline seats and cabins. Check up-to-date schedules on websites.

BUS

The **KTEL Achaia bus station** (☑ 2610 623 886; www.ktelachaias.gr; Othonos Amalias 4) has services to the following places:

Athens (€19, three hours, every 30 minutes) via Diakofto and Corinth Isthmus (€12.60, 1½ hours)

Ioannina (€24, 4½ hours, two daily)

Kalamata (€23, four hours, two daily)

Kalavryta (€7, two hours, at least two daily)

Pyrgos (€9, two hours, up to 10 daily)

Thessaloniki (€45, seven hours, three daily)

Buses link the KTEL Achaia bus station in Patra with Terminal A (aka Kifissos) in Athens, from where there are frequent buses to/from the international airport.

The **KTEL Kefallonia bus station** (☑ 2610 274 938; www.ktelkefalonias.gr; Othonos Amalias 58) has services to the Ionian islands of Lefkada (€16.20, three hours, twice weekly) and Kefallonia (€21.10, one daily). To continue on to Argostoli, travel by bus from Kefallonia to the port of Kyllini, from where you catch a ferry to Poros (1½ hours) and continue again by road to Argostoli (one hour). Buses also depart KTEL Kefallonia bus station to Amfissa (for Delphi; €13, three hours, two daily Monday to Friday, one on Saturday and Sunday) and to Tripoli (€18.90, one to two daily Friday and Sunday).

The **KTEL Zakynthos bus station** (☑ 2610 220 993; www.ktel-zakynthos.gr; Othonos Amalias 84) has services to Zakynthos, via the port of Kyllini (including ferry €16, 3½ hours, two to three daily).

TRAIN

There are six trains a day to Athens (€17). At the time of writing, a replacement bus goes as far as Kiato, from where you take the *proastiako*, Athens' local train service. Note: on arrival in Athens you can use your *proastiako* ticket for 1½ hours on the metro (validate it first).

ℹ Getting Around

Hertz (☑ 26102 20990; www.hertz.gr; Akti Dimaion 40) Recommended, reliable car-hire outlet.

Kalavryta   Καλάβρυτα

POP 1800

Perched 756m above sea level, Kalavryta (kah-*lah*-vrih-tah) is a delightful little town with fresh mountain air, gushing springs and a square that nestles under giant plane trees. Though in existence for centuries, the present-day town came into being on the ruins of ancient Kinaitha in the mid-19th century. The town is a popular ski-season destination among Athenians, who also come for weekend getaways year round. In spring and summer, visitors from abroad come here to hike and visit the nearby monasteries.

Two relatively recent historical events have assured Kalavryta a place in the hearts of all Greeks. First, despite plenty of evidence that fighting had already begun elsewhere, the official version of the War of Independence states that the revolt against the Turks began here on 25 March 1821, when Bishop Germanos of Patra raised the Greek flag at Moni Agias Lavras (p185), a monastery 5km from town. Second, on 13 December 1943, in one of the worst atrocities of WWII, the Nazis massacred most of the village's male inhabitants as part of their scorched-earth Operation Kalavryta, designed to punish Kalavryta partisans in particular for the deaths of German prisoners of war. The hands of the old cathedral clock stand eternally at 2.34pm, the time the German guns finally fell silent.

⊙ Sights

★ Museum of the Kalavryta Holocaust
MUSEUM

(☑26920 23646; www.dmko.gr; 1-5 Syngrou; admission €3; ⊙9am-4pm Tue-Sun) The country's only Holocaust museum, this is a powerful tribute to the residents of Kalavryta who perished in the 13 December 1943 slaughter perpetrated by the Nazis. It's a dignified, understated, yet extremely evocative account of the struggle between the occupying forces and partisan fighters in the area, and the events running up to the massacre – an atrocity reported to be partly put in motion by the partisans' execution of a group of German prisoners.

Set inside the rebuilt old schoolhouse that was set on fire with women, children and the elderly inside, the museum depicts the history of 19th- and 20th-century Kalavryta, the advent of the rack-and-pinion railway and the region's suffering during WWII through evocative photographs and personal effects.

ELAS, the Greek resistance movement, was very active in the Kalavryta region during WWII. On 17 October 1943 partisans captured a German batallion. Negotiations stalled when the Nazis launched 'Operation Kalavryta', designed to crush the resistance. The partisans killed the German prisoners and in retaliation, on 13 December 1943, the Nazis herded 468 men and boys over the age of thirteen to the nearby Kappi Ridge and gunned them down. The women and children who managed to break out of the burning schoolhouse were left with the task of gathering and burying the dead, as commemorated by the statues behind the schoolhouse.

Whatever you do, don't pass by the videos on continuous loop dotted throughout the exhibition. These are the accounts of surviving townspeople who escaped death, some of whom were children at the time. The walls covered with pictures of the dead Kalavryta villagers and the names of the dead is an especially stark memorial.

Martyrs' Monument
MONUMENT

A huge white cross on a cypress-covered hillside just east of town marks the site where the Nazis machine-gunned 486 men and boys from Kalavryta on 13 December 1943. Only 13 survived the massacre. Beneath this imposing monument is a poignant little shrine to the victims. It's signposted off Konstantinou.

ℹ️ KALAVRYTA CITYPASS

For bargain sightseeing in and around Kalavryta, the **Kalavryta CityPass** (www.trainose.gr) discount card covers a return trip on the Diakofto–Kalavryta railway and entrance to the Cave of the Lakes, the Kalavryta Holocaust Museum, and either Kalavryta Ski Centre or the Tetramythos Winery, saving you 40% overall. The card costs €24.80, is valid for a month and can be purchased at Kalavryta, Diakofto or Patra train stations.

🛏️ Sleeping

Lodges are dotted outside Kalavryta; the town itself has a few hotel options. Peak period is the ski season (from December to April), at which time reservations are essential. Weekend bookings are a good idea year-round. Prices are slashed on weekdays. If you roll into town without a reservation, look inside the shelter in front of the train station; all the accommodation options are listed, and those with vacancies are lit up green, Austrian-style. Also check www.kalavrita-hotels.gr, which has some good options. The cheapest accommodation is in the domatia on the streets behind the train station.

Hotel Filoxenia
HOTEL €

(☑26920 22422; www.hotelfiloxenia.gr; Ethnikis Andistasis 10; d/tr incl breakfast €53/65; P❄️🛜) Kind of like an old-fashioned ski lodge with its handsome stone exterior, Filoxenia has somewhat dowdy rooms with balconies (and jacuzzi tubs). Rates include either a sauna, *hammam* or hydromassage session per day.

Tsovolos Apartments
APARTMENT €

(☑26920 22292; Kosta Fassou 14; d/tr/apt incl breakfast €30/45/55; 🛜) Towards the west end of town, near the EKO petrol station, these warm, snug rooms and two-bedroom apartments are basic but offer good value. There are shared tea-making facilities but breakfast is unlikely to thrill you.

★ Archontiko Zafeiropoulou
APARTMENT €€

(☑26920 24500; www.archontiko.gr; Striftompala; d/ste incl breakfast €90/130; P🛜) These doubles and suites are essentially spacious, spotless studio apartments with kitchenettes. The real treasure here is the friendly South African–Greek owner, George, who has an outstanding knowledge of the town and surrounding

RIDING THE MOUNTAIN RAILS

One of the unmissable journeys to make in the Peloponnese is aboard the tiny train running along the vintage rack-and-pinion **Diakofto–Kalavryta Railway** (☑ 26910 43206; www.odontotos.com; one way/return €9.50/19) between Diakofto and Kalavryta. It takes travellers on a remarkably scenic ride through the dramatic Vouraïkos Gorge, its reddish cliffs seemingly closing in on the train. The line switches back and forth under a leafy canopy of plane trees, clinging to a narrow ledge overhanging the rushing rapids below, and passing through seven curving tunnels along the way.

To reach Kalavryta, the train climbs over 700m in 22.5km, using a rack-and-pinion (cog) system for traction on the steep sections, effectively clamping itself to the notched girder you can see running between the rails. Built by an Italian company between 1889 and 1895, the railway was a remarkable feat of engineering for its time, with only a handful of equivalents around the world (most notably in the Swiss Alps). The trains running the route are shiny and modern, but the original steam engines that first plied the route can still be seen outside Diakofto and Kalavryta stations.

The journey takes just over an hour, and stops en route at the picturesque hamlet of Zahlorou and two other tiny stations on demand, in case you want to be dropped off at one and walk to another. The railway makes an even more scenic hike, as you have more time to appreciate your surroundings.

Hiking the 22km down from Kalavryta to Diakofto takes around five hours; train drivers are used to hikers along the tracks and give them plenty of warning. Take a torch (flashlight) for the tunnels.

At the time of writing there were three departures on weekdays and five on weekends in each direction; confirm times at the respective train stations.

Kalavryta is linked by regular buses to Athens and Patra. To get to Diakofto, catch the only 'working' train line, Corinth–Patra, with OSE replacement buses running in place of trains along the Diakofto–Kiato section at time of writing. On leaving Diakofto, you can catch the same replacement bus service west to Patra or, to head east, take the replacement bus service to Kiato, from where you catch the *proastiako* train, either to Corinth or as far as Athens airport.

---

attractions, and handy maps at hand. The excellent breakfast includes local sheep's milk yoghurt, honey, preserves and cheeses.

Hotel Kynaitha　　　　　　HOTEL €€
(☑ 26920 22609; www.kynaitha.com; Ethnikis Andistasis 11; d/tr/ste incl breakfast €65/77/145; P ☎) Modern and comfortable with spacious and attractively furnished rooms. Think exposed stone walls, gleaming white bathrooms and posh toiletries.

✖ Eating & Drinking

There's an abundance of tavernas and cafes, mostly along 25 Martiou.

To Spitikou　　　　　　TAVERNA €
(☑ 26920 24260; Vasileos Constantinou; mains €7-12; ☺ lunch & dinner; ☎ ✿) This cosy place with a ski-lodge feel serves up great-quality traditional taverna meals. Expect the likes of veal with tomato sauce, chicken baked with vegetables, spinach and feta soufflé and quite possibly the best tzatziki in the Peloponnese.

Gri Gri Café　　　　　　SWEETS €
(25 Martiou; snacks €1.70-4; ☺ 8am-8pm) This good family-run spot is recommended for its sweet or savoury homemade snacks, such as cheese pie, baklava and tasty *crèma* (sweet, set custard).

ℹ Information

The train station is on the northern edge of town, opposite the Holocaust Museum. To the right of the museum is Syngrou/25 Martiou, a pedestrian precinct. To the left of the museum is Konstantinou.

The central square, Plateia Kalavrytou, is two blocks up from the train station.

The ticket office at the train station doubles as a tourist office.

National Bank of Greece (25 Martiou) Just before Plateia Kalavrytou.

Post office (☺ 7.30am-2pm Mon-Fri) Behind Plateia Kalavrytou.

ⓘ Getting There & Around

The rack-and-pinion train to/from Diakofto via Zahlorou runs to a changing timetable.

There are buses to Patra (€8, two hours, five daily on weekdays, two on weekends) and Athens (€17, three hours, two Monday to Saturday, one Sunday). The **bus station** (☑ 26920 22224) is 200m before the entrance to town (from the Diakofto approach road), beside the Jetoil petrol station.

Kalavryta's **taxi rank** (☑ 26920 22127) is in front of the train station.

Most of the attractions are out of town, so it's very handy to have your own transport.

Around Kalavryta

Kalavryta and its surrounding mountains feature several varied and interesting sites. While some are just outside the town, others are further afield but doable in a car.

◉ Sights & Activities

Cave of the Lakes   CAVE
(☑ 26920 31001; www.kastriacave.gr; adult/concession €9/4.50; ⊙ 9.30am-4.30pm, longer hours in summer) The remarkable Cave of the Lakes lies 16.5km south of Kalavryta near the village of Kastria. A 500m boardwalk snakes its way through the cave, through the vast entrance chamber, home to five species of bats, past spectacular cauliflower-like rock formations, and over the deep, crystal-clear subterranean pools – the 13 stone basins formed by mineral deposits over the millennia. The most impressive formations are in the final chamber, where delicate, ribboning curtains cascade down the wall.

The cave features in Greek mythology and is mentioned in the writings of the ancient traveller Pausanias, but its whereabouts remained unknown in modern times until 1964 when locals investigated, having noticed water pouring from the roof of a smaller cave. They discovered a large bat-filled cavern at the start of a 2km-long cave carved out by a subterranean river.

Access is by guided half-hour tour (in Greek) only. Foreign visitors are provided with a booklet in English; the sight at each designated stop along the boardwalk corresponds to the letter in the booklet.

A taxi from Kalavryta costs around €40 return (the taxi will wait for you). There's a good taverna right next to the cave entrance.

Moni Mega Spileo   MONASTERY
(Monastery of the Great Cavern; ☑ 26920 23130; ⊙ 8am-1pm & 2pm-sunset summer) **FREE** Moni Mega Spileo is a 3km walk up from Zahlorou. The original monastery was destroyed in 1943 when Nazis executed all the monks. The new monastery's most prized relic is the miraculous icon of the Virgin Mary, said to have been painted by St Luke. It was supposedly discovered in the nearby cavern by St Theodore and St Simeon in AD 362, but most likely dates back to around AD 1000. Popular with pilgrims; strict dress code applies.

Call ahead outside of summer.

Moni Agias Lavras   MONASTERY
(☑ 26920 22363; ⊙ 10am-1pm & 4-5pm) **FREE** The original 10th-century monastery that stood here was burnt down by the Nazis, and its monks killed. The chapel of the new monastery is where Greece's War of Independence was allegedly launched; the banner standard from the war is displayed alongside monastic memorabilia. The monastery is around 5km southwest of Kalavryta. A taxi from Kalavryta costs around €20 return.

Ski Centre   SKIING
(☑ 26920 24451; www.kalavrita-ski.gr; half-/full day €18/25; ⊙ 9am-4pm Dec-Apr) Head 14km east of Kalavryta on Mt Helmos (2355m) to the Ski Centre (elevation 1700m to 2340m), which has 12 runs and seven lifts (two chairlifts). There's no overnight accommodation but it rents skis and snowboard equipment (€20 for boots and skis or a snowboard). The season lasts from December to April, snow permitting. A taxi costs about €40 return.

Tetramythos Winery   WINERY
(☑ 26910 97500; www.tetramythoswines.com; ⊙ 9am-4pm) Located in Ano Diakofto village (not to be confused with Diakofto), 5km along the road from Diakofto to Kalavryta, this winery is run by two local brothers who take a lot of pride in their *agiorgitiko*, cabernet sauvignon, *tetramythos*, *malagousia* and other vintages. Tours and free wine-tasting sessions are very worthwhile.

Central Greece

Best Places to Eat

➡ Taverna Vakhos (p195)

➡ Georgaras Restaurant (p216)

➡ Yali Kafene (p196)

➡ Kerasia Tsipouradiko (p207)

Best Places to Stay

➡ Lost Unicorn Hotel (p215)

➡ Hotel Faros (p215)

➡ Doupiani House (p227)

➡ Alsos House (p225)

➡ Hotel Alexakis (p204)

Why Go?

Ancient Greece's 'centre' of the earth – Delphi – is these days among Greece's most visited places for its archaeological site, ancient footpaths and vistas of the Corinthian Gulf. Delphi is rivalled in popularity only by Meteora, the breathtaking outcrops of rocky towers topped by teetering monasteries (and rock climbers).

The central Greece (κεντρική Ελλάδα) region also holds many underrated surprises. Alpine meadows and valleys cover the Evritania mountain range, making it perfect for breezy summer hikes and winter skiing. And it doesn't get much better than the beautiful Pelion Peninsula, home to Jason and the Argonauts, and criss-crossed with historic cobblestone paths linking lush mountain hamlets with coves and beaches that rival the best islands.

And speaking of 'good, better, best'... The region's good-natured people serve up hospitality, superb experiences and great cuisine. There's no better place to navel gaze.

When to Go
Delphi

Apr & May Wild herbs and flowers mingle in alpine meadows.

Sep Stable, sunny weather and fewer crowds.

Orthodox Easter Villages follow traditional customs, with parades and copious food.

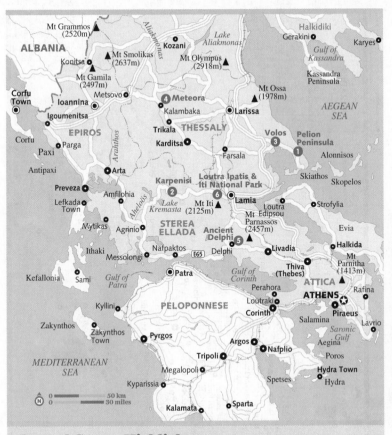

Central Greece Highlights

1 Wandering along former donkey paths to the sea on the **Pelion Peninsula** (p209).

2 Feasting on fresh trout from mountain streams near **Karpenisi** (p201).

3 Trying a *tsipouro* or three with the locals in **Volos** (p206).

4 Climbing the monastery-topped rock pinnacles at **Meteora** (p221), following ancient footpaths to hidden caves.

5 Meditating over the last light of day at the Sanctuary of Athena Pronea in **Ancient Delphi** (p189).

6 Lazing in the hot springs in **Loutra Ipatis** (p204), or hiking in nearby **Iti National Park** (p204).

DELPHI & STEREA ELLADA

Greek mythology and history seem to mingle in the rugged and scenic landscape of Sterea Ellada (Στερεά Ελλάδα). On the slopes of Mt Parnassos sits the famous site of Ancient Delphi. The land stretches east to Attica, where the legendary King Oedipus met his fate, and west to Messolongi, where British bard Lord Byron died of fever during the Greek War of Independence. The region acquired its name, meaning Mainland Greece, in 1827, as part of the newly formed Greece.

Delphi & Ancient Delphi
Δελφοί

POP 850

If the ancient Greeks hadn't chosen Delphi (from *delphis,* womb) as their navel of the earth and built the Sanctuary of Apollo here, someone else would have thought of a good

Sterea Ellada

50 km
30 miles

SPORADES

AEGEAN SEA

Skyros

Skantzoura

Peristera

Alonnisos

Skopelos

Skiathos

Pelion Peninsula

Trikeri

Pagasitikos Gulf

Volos

Larissa (20km)

Farsala

Neomonastiri

Almyros

Mt Orthys (1726m)

Stylida

Lamia

Ipati

Iti National Park

THESSALY

Trikala (20km)
Kalambaka (53km)

Karditsa

Makri

Loutra

Ipatis

Mt Iti

Mt Iti (2114m)

Pavliani

Fourna

Mt Tymfristos (2312m)

E952

Karpenisi

Tymfristos

Fidakia

Koryshades

Mikro Horio

Megalo Horio

Gavros

Krikello

Mt Kaliakouda (2098m)

Ano Hora

Moni Panagias Prousiotissas

Proussos

K Makrinou

Moni Thermo

Lake Kremasta

Lake Trihonida

ETOLO-AKARNANIA

Agrinio

Amfilohia

Vonitsa

Paleros

Mytikas

Kalamos

Meganisi

Lefkada

Astakos

Oxia

Kastos

Atokos

Ithaki

Vathy

Piso Aetos

Sami

Kefallonia

Poros

IONIAN SEA

Zakynthos

Zakynthos Town

Amaliada

Kyllini

Ioannina (18km)

E951

Arta

Preveza

Aktion

Parga (63km)

Lake Arahthos

Ambracian Gulf

EPIROS

Etoliko

Messolongi

Klisova Lagoon

Tourlida

Rio-Andirio Bridge

Rio

Andirio

Nafpaktos

Monastiraki

Trizonia

Spilia

Galaxidi

Agios Nikolaos

Itea

Kirra

Amfissa

Delphi

Ancient Delphi

Parnassos

Mt Parnassos (2457m)

Arahova

Distomo

Moni Osios Loukas

Kyriaki

Davlia

Livadia

Orhomenos

Agios Konstantinos

Theologos

Kastro

Cape Ghaidhoros

Gulf of Evia

Arkitsa

Loutra Edipsou

Evia

Halkida

Eretria

Skala Oropou

Inoi

Mt Parnitha (1413m)

ATHENS

Rafina

ATTICA

Agia Marina

Nea Styra

Marmari

Kea

Korissia

The Cyclades (10km)

Lavrio

Souni

Cape Sounion

So, Cyclades (10km)

Petalia Gulf

Gulf of Evia

Parnitha Kymis

Paralia Kymis

Patra

Egio

Kalavryta

Xylokastro

Kiato

Loutraki

Corinth

Kechries

Kechries Bay

Megara

Elefsina (Eleusis)

E962

Porto Germeno

Fortress of Aigosthena

Alkimides Gulf

Mt Kithairon

Plataea

Erythres

Thiva (Thebes)

Fortress of Elftherae

E75

Kiafa

Kirfis

Iti

Thermopylae

Glyfa

Stylida

Maliakos Gulf

Glyfada

Agios Konstantinos

Amfiklia

Aigosthena

E75

E95

Piraeus

Flisvos

Saronic Gulf

Vouliagmeni

Salamina

Aegina Town

Angistri

Aegina

Crete

PELOPONNESE

E65

E65

E55

Gulf of Corinth

Gulf of Patra

Kissova Lagoon

reason to make this eagle's-nest town a tourist attraction. Its cliffside location is spectacular and, despite its overt commercialism and the constant passage of tour buses through the modern village, it still has a special feel. Ancient Delphi (and the adjoining village of Delphi) is 178km northwest of Athens.

History

Delphi reached its height between the 6th and 4th centuries BC, when multitudes of pilgrims came to the sanctuary to consult the oracle (p193).

Delphi was protected by the Amphictyonic League, a federation of 12 tribal states (that unified most of southern Greece), which took control of the sanctuary following the First Sacred War (595–586 BC), making Delphi an autonomous state that enjoyed great prosperity from numerous benefactors, including the kings of Lydia and Egypt, and Hadrian.

The influence of the oracle had a major impact on political and intellectual life, determining – directly or otherwise through the prophecies – such decisions as the establishment of colonies and wars.

The sanctuary survived fire (548 BC) and earthquake (373 BC) and in the 3rd century BC it was conquered by the Aetolians, then by the Romans in 191 BC. Although the Roman Sulla plundered the sanctuary in 86 BC, other emperors, fascinated by its reputation, kept the rituals at Delphi alive well into the 2nd century AD, when the oracle's influence began to dwindle. The sanctuary was finally abolished by Byzantine emperor Theodosius in the late 4th century AD. By the 7th century a new village, Kastri, had appeared over the site. Much of what is known about Delphi today comes from the notes of 2nd-century-AD Athenian geographer Pausanius.

🅞 Sights

★ Ancient Delphi   ARCHAEOLOGICAL SITE

(🖉 22650 82312; www.culture.gr; site or museum adult/child €6/free, combined €9; ⏰ 8am-3pm, longer hours summer) Of all the archaeological sites in Greece, Ancient Delphi is the one with the most potent spirit of place. Built on the slopes of Mt Parnassos, overlooking the Gulf of Corinth and extending into a valley of cypress and olive trees, this World Heritage site's allure lies both in its stunning setting and its inspiring ruins.

The ancient Greeks regarded Delphi as the centre of the world – according to my-

thology, Zeus released two eagles at opposite ends of the world and they met here.

Check ahead for opening hours as these are subject to change. In summer visit the site early to avoid the crowds and the heat. Don't head into the site just before closing time; staff are already rounding visitors up by then and you won't be permitted a thorough visit.

➡ Sanctuary of Apollo

The Sanctuary of Apollo is considered the heart of the Delphic oracle. From the main entrance, the **Sacred Way** gradually winds up to the **Doric Temple of Apollo**. In ancient times the Sacred Way was lined with treasuries and statues given by grateful city-states – Athens, Sikyon, Siphnos, Knidos, Thiva (Thebes) etc – not only as thanks to Apollo, but as a kind of PR machine to show their wealth and might.

THIVA (THEBES)   ΘΗΒΑ

Thiva, the birthplace of Hercules and Dionysos, was a powerful city-state in 400 BC during Greece's golden age, occupying a strategic position between northern Greece and the Peloponnese. The tragic fate of its royal dynasty, centred on the myth of Oedipus, rivalled that of ancient Mycenae. After the Trojan War in the 12th century BC, Thiva became the dominant city of the Boeotia region. Thiva's glorious run ended in 335 BC, however, when it was sacked by Alexander the Great for siding with the Persians.

Although present-day Thiva has few vestiges of its past glory – except for exhibits in a wonderful archaeological museum that has been closed for the last few years (supposedly for renovation) – Greek-history diehards might head here for posterity; the town centre is a pleasant enough place to wander around for an hour or so.

Buses operate to Athens (€8, 1½ hours, hourly until 8pm) from Thiva's **central bus station** (🖉 22620 27512; www.ktelthivas.gr; Estias 10), 500m south of Plateia Agios Kalotinis. Trains from **Thiva station** (🖉 22620 27531; www.trainose.gr), 500m north of the museum, depart for Athens (normal/Intercity €5.80/12.90, 75/70 minutes, eight to nine daily) and Thessaloniki (Intercity €41.20, 4¼ hours, seven daily).

Ancient Delphi

The pretty, hillside-strewn ruins of Delphi were in use for over 1200 years (8th century BC to 4th century AD), but the period from the 6th to the 4th century BC was particularly active. Visitors can still walk in the footsteps of past pilgrims and, with a bit of imagination, re-create the experience of this ancient place.

The sanctuary was adorned with many buildings and dedications to Apollo erected by Greek city states. Worshippers purified themselves in the Castalian Spring (now closed to the public), paid a pelanos (tribute) and, if they hadn't brought one with them, purchased a votive offering from **The Roman Market** ❶. Then they wandered up the **Sacred Way** ❷ towards the Temple of Apollo.

En route they passed thousands of dedications, including statues, sculptures and temple-like buildings (treasuries). Treasuries, including the **Athenian Treasury** ❸, were constructed by victorious city states and filled with the spoils of war. The nearby **omphalos** ❹ (navel stone), a symbol of the centre of the earth, was left by archaeologists where it was found.

Next, visitors would pass the **Rock of the Sibyl** ❺ before arriving at the Stoa of the Athenians, behind which is an extraordinary **polygonal wall** ❻.

Finally, they arrived at the **Temple of Apollo** ❼ in the centre of the sanctuary, where consultations with the oracle took place and the Pythia's chants were interpreted by the priests of Apollo. The **theatre** ❽ behind the temple held drama, music and poetry competitions.

TOP TIPS

» Visit in the morning or late afternoon to beat the heat and crowds.

» Allow time to visit the stadium, which is located further uphill.

» Wear comfortable shoes and a hat, and bring drinking water.

» Opening hours are subject to change, so check ahead.

» Don't miss the Delphi Museum, which helps to contextualise the site.

Athenian Treasury

The impressive Athenian Treasury is one of many important treasury buildings here. Built to commemorate the Athenians' victory against the Persians at the battle of Marathon in 490 BC, it was reconstructed in the early 1900s.

RICHARD CUMMINS / GETTY IMAGES ©

Omphalos

Delphi was considered the *omphalos* (navel) of the world. After releasing two eagles, Zeus threw down a stone to mark the place they met. There was also an omphalos in the adyton (temple chamber) where the Pythia pronounced her oracles.

RICHARD CUMMINS / GETTY IMAGES ©

Siphnian Treasury

The Bouleuterion

The Sacred Way

The Sacred Way (so-named in modern times by archaeologists) leads to the Temple of Apollo. It was lined with thousands of monuments, statues and treasuries that commemorated victories (usually in war, sometimes the Games).

DEA / G. DAGLI ORTI / GETTY IMAGES ©

To Delphi Museum

Temple of Apollo

...most sacred building ...e sanctuary, this ...e third temple ...tructed on this ...4th century BC). ...ge ramp leads to ...terior, from where ...ythia delivered her ...ouncements.

Theatre

The Pythian Games, held in Delphi every four years, was not just about athletics – it also included music and drama contests (Apollo is the god of music). The original theatre was built in the 4th century BC; the current one dates fom the 1st century BC and could seat 5000 spectators.

NATALIA PAVLOVA / GETTY IMAGES ©

GEORGE TSAFOS / GETTY IMAGES ©

To Stadium ←

⑧

Acanthus Column of Dancers

⑦

Sphinx of the Naxians

⑥

⑤

②

King of Argos Monument

Votive Offering of Lacedaemon

Bull of Kerkyra

①

Stoa of the Athenians

WOLFGANG KAEHLER / GETTY IMAGES ©

Polygonal Wall

This extraordinary retaining wall comprises interlocking polygonal stones. It features around 800 inscriptions that relate to the emancipation of slaves.

To Castalian Spring and Sanctuary of Athena Pronea →

The Roman Market (Agora)

Pilgrims could buy small votives and offerings here. Wealthier and more powerful visitors, however, brought statues and valuable items from afar. The remains of many of these are in the Delphi Museum.

PETER BROWN / ALAMY ©

Rock of the Sibyl

Legend has it that this marks the spot where the first sibyl (an elderly prophetess, not to be confused with the Pythia), stood and pronounced Delphi's first oracle.

Entering the site, you pass several stone bases. The first is the pedestal that held the **statue of a bull** dedicated by the city of Corfu (Kerkyra). Just beyond it, on the right, are the remains of the **Votive Offering of Lacedaemon**, commemorating a battle victory. The next two semicircular structures on either side of the Sacred Way were erected by the Argives (people of Argos). To their right stood the **Kings of Argos Monument**.

To the north of the reconstructed Athenian Treasury are the foundations of the **bouleuterion** (council house).

The 4th-century-BC **Temple of Apollo** dominated the entire sanctuary with a statue of Apollo and a hearth where an eternal flame burned. On the temple vestibule were inscriptions from Greek philosophers, such as 'Know Thyself' and 'Nothing in Excess', known as the Delphic Commandments.

Above the temple is the well-preserved 4th-century-BC **theatre**, which was restored by the Pergamene kings in the 1st century BC, yielding magnificent views from the top row. Plays were performed here during the Pythian Festival, held, like the Olympic Games, every four years. From the theatre the path continues to the **stadium**, the best preserved in all of Greece. Check out the sprinters' etched-stone starting blocks at the eastern end. (Stadium access is currently limited because of possible rockslides).

From the Sanctuary of Apollo, the paved path towards Arahova runs parallel to the main road and leads to the **Castalian Spring** on the left, where pilgrims cleansed themselves before consulting the oracle.

➡ Gymnasium

To the south of the Sanctuary of Apollo, and west of the Sanctuary of Athena Pronea, you will find the remains of the ancient gymnasium. Two running tracks occupied an upper terrace here. On a lower terrace, boxers and wrestlers practised their art and then cooled off in the large, spring-fed circular pool, which is still visible among the ruins.

Delphi Town

Delphi Town

⊙ Sights
1 Delphi Museum D1

⊜ Sleeping
2 Arion Hotel A1
3 Fedriades Hotel B2
4 Hotel Acropole C2
5 Hotel Hermes B2
6 Hotel Leto C2
7 Hotel Sibylla C2
8 Hotel Tholos B2
9 Nidimos Hotel A1
10 Rooms Pitho B2
11 Sunview Pension A1

⊗ Eating
12 Souvlaki Pita Gyros C2
13 Taverna Gargadouas A1
14 Taverna To Patriko
  Mas A2
15 Taverna Vakhos B2

⊙ Drinking & Nightlife
16 Café Agora B2
17 Cafe Ihor A2
18 Club Katoi A2

THE DELPHIC ORACLE

The Delphic oracle was considered one of the most important religious (and political) sanctuaries in Greece. Worshippers flocked here from far and wide to consult the god Apollo on serious decisions. Apollo's instrument of communication was the Pythia (priestess), usually an older woman, who sat on a tripod in the Temple of Apollo.

During visitations and consultations, the priestess chewed laurel leaves and entered a trance after inhaling vapours from a chasm below. Archaeologists believe this could have been ethylene wafting through a crack from a fault line (carried by water running underground). Her vapour-inspired, if somewhat vague, answers were spoken in tongue then 'translated' by the priests of Apollo. In fact, the oracle's reputation for infallibility may have rested with the often ambiguous or cryptic answers. Wars were fought, marriages sealed, leaders chosen and journeys begun on the strength of the oracle's visions. After all, the prophecies were the will of a god, so the oracle's reputation remained throughout antiquity.

Legend holds that one priestess suffered for her vagueness. When Alexander the Great visited, hoping to hear a prophecy that he would soon conquer the ancient world, the priestess refused direct comment, instead asking that he return later. Enraged, he dragged her by the hair out of the chamber until she screamed, 'Let go of me; you're unbeatable'. He quickly dropped her, saying, 'I have my answer'.

➡ Sanctuary of Athena Pronea

The Sanctuary of Athena Pronea is the site of the 4th-century-BC *tholos* (rotunda). This much-photographed spot is often wrongly interpreted by tourists as the place the Pythia (priestess of Apollo) delivered her pronouncements. The graceful circular structure comprised 20 columns on a three-stepped podium; three of its columns were re-erected in the 1940s. The white portions of each column are the original marble; the darker portions are new material.

To its west, the foundations of the **Temple of Athena Pronea** are all that remain of a rectangular structure that was heavily damaged by the same rockslides and earthquake that levelled much of the *tholos*.

Delphi Museum   MUSEUM
(☑22650 82312; www.culture.gr; site or museum adult €6, adult/student combined €9/5; ⊗8am-8pm summer, to 2.45pm winter) From around the 8th century BC, Ancient Delphi managed to amass a treasure trove, much of it reflected in its magnificent museum. It's worth visiting here before your site visit. It helps construct an image of what the site must have looked like with its wealthy buildings, statues (remember, these were then painted in colour) and other valuable offerings.

On entering the museum, you'll first notice (in room 5) the **Sphinx of the Naxians**, dating from 560 BC. Also here are well-preserved parts of the **frieze from the Siphnian treasury**. It depicts the battle between the gods and the giants, and also the Judgment of Paris (far-left corner as you enter), who was called upon to decide which goddess was most beau-

tiful (he chose Aphrodite). In room 3 are two fine examples of 6th-century-BC *kouroi* (statues of young men), the 'twins of Argos'.

In the rooms to the left are fragments of **metopes** (figures within the frieze) from the Athenian treasury depicting the Labours of Hercules, the Exploits of Theseus and the Battle of the Amazons (room 7). Further on you can't miss the tall **Acanthus Column of Dancers** (room 11), with three women dancing around its top. Next to it is the **omphalos**, a sculpted cone, one of which stood at what was considered the centre of the world. In the end room is the celebrated, life-size **Bronze Charioteer**, which commemorates a victory in the Pythian Games of 478 or 474 BC.

🏃 Activities

A useful and excellent website for information on the area is www.delphi.gr. Keen walkers should download the guide *Walking on the Footsteps of History: Trekking the Delphi Pathways* in the 'Hiking' section.

Hiking

Two day hikes, both part of the E4 European long-distance path, start and end at Delphi.

The wonderful **Korykeon Cave walk** connects two ancient sites, the Temple of Apollo and Korykeon Cave, a sacred mountain cave-shrine for Pan. The cavern comprises a natural amphitheatre filled with stalactites and stalagmites. You can walk as far as 80m inside (caution: it can be slippery). Many hikers hire a taxi in Arahova as far as Kalyvia (around €25), hike to the cave (500m) and return to Delphi along a well-marked path (four hours). Along the way, there are awesome views of Delphi, the Amfissa plain and Galaxidi.

The **Delphi to Ancient Kirra hike** meanders through shady olive groves – the largest continuous olive grove in Greece – and takes three to four hours. After lunch or a swim, return by bus (around €2) to Delphi. The E4 trailhead is marked 100m east of the Hotel Acropole.

Tours

The best way to get around the Ancient Delphi site is to do a tour with a knowledgable guide. Excellent English-language tours are offered by charismatic and ultrapassionate **Penny Kolomvotsos** (📞6944644427; kpagona@hotmail.com), who also speaks German and brings the site alive; **Christina Stoli** (📞6944987411); and **Vicki Tsonis** (📞6945494583), who also speaks French.

Sleeping

Rooms Pitho   PENSION €
(📞22650 82850; www.pithohotel.gr; Vasileon Pavlou & Friderikis 40a; s/d/tr incl breakfast from €45/55/70; ❄🛜) Pitho's eight spotless, modern rooms (some on the small side), excellent service, extremely friendly owners and location – about halfway along the street above a gift shop – make it a good choice. Because it's incorporated into a home-style lodging, it's quieter than some hotels.

Hotel Sibylla   HOTEL €
(📞22650 82335; www.sibylla-hotel.gr; Vasileon Pavlou & Friderikis 9; s/d/tr €26/30/40; ❄🛜) A top budget choice, with delightful owners and seven light and tidy rooms, all with fans and several with views across to the gulf.

Sunview Pension   PENSION €
(📞22650 82349; dkal@otenet.gr; Apollonos 84; s/d/tr incl breakfast from €30/40/45; 🅿❄🛜) This basic but pleasant pension commands a stunning location in upper Delphi, with brightly painted rooms and friendly family owners who treat it like their own home, which it happens to be.

Arion Hotel   HOTEL €
(📞22650 82097; www.ariondelphihotel.com; Syngrou 29; s/d/tr/q incl breakfast €30/40/50/60; ❄@🛜) Basic with apricot-coloured decor, it offers value in a quiet, higher location at the back of town.

Hotel Tholos   HOTEL €
(📞22650 82268; www.tholoshotel.com; Apollonos 31; s/d/tr €25/30/50; ❄🛜) This budget

option is clean and minimalist in its decor, but it's central and does the job. Breakfast €5 per person.

Hotel Hermes   HOTEL €
(📞22650 82318; www.hermeshotel.com.gr; Vasileon Pavlou & Friderikis 27; s/d/tr incl breakfast €35/45/55; ❄🛜) Family-run Hermes is in the heart of Delphi. Most of the wood-shuttered rooms have balconies facing the gulf but the marble floors can mean noisy corridors. Splendid views from the breakfast lounge.

Chrissa Camping   CAMPGROUND €
(📞22650 82020; www.chrissacamping.gr; camp sites per person/tent/car €6.50/6/3.50; 🛜) About 6km west of modern Delphi.

Delphi Camping   CAMPGROUND €
(📞22650 82209; www.delphicamping.com; camp sites per person/tent/car €6.70/5/3.90; 🅿🛜) About 4.5km from Delphi towards Itea is this well-run spot in a pretty setting. Mind the killer entrance on a sharp corner.

Apollon Camping   CAMPGROUND €
(📞22650 82762; www.apolloncamping.gr; camp sites per person/tent €8.50/5; 🅿@🛜) Decent site only 2km west of modern Delphi.

Fedriades Hotel   HOTEL €€
(📞22650 82370; www.fedriades.com; Vasileon Pavlou & Friderikis 46; s/d/tr incl breakfast €45/62/75; ❄🛜) Fedriades is a reliable bet with small and neat, but bright and modern, motel-style rooms and extra-friendly staff. Enthusiastic and helpful owner Babis will help with onward routes. Breakfast includes some homemade treats. The lobby is a pleasant place to lounge after a site visit.

Hotel Leto   HOTEL €€
(📞22650 82302; www.leto-delphi.gr; Apollonos 15; s €45-50, d €65, tr €78, incl breakfast; ❄🛜) If the traditional Greek motif is getting you down, head to these compact but smartly decorated digs where the slick lighting and cream-and-orange trim make it one of the town's most contemporary choices.

Nidimos Hotel   HOTEL €€
(📞22650 82056; www.nidimoshotel.gr; D Fragou 10; s €44-51, d €55-64, tr €66-78; ❄🛜) Among Delphi's sleekest options, this recently renovated spot is for those who want modern – there are lots of contemporary taupes and whites. Let's hope the quality can be maintained with wear. The rooms at the front boast massive terraces and cost slightly more, though those at the back look out onto wall art and are much quieter.

Hotel Acropole
HOTEL €€

(☑22650 82675; www.delphi.com.gr; Filellinon 13; s/d/tr incl breakfast €55/70/89; ❄🐾) On a quieter street below the main drag, the Acropole has a ski-lodge ambience, though it hasn't changed its on-piste wear for a while. Rooms are pleasant and most have wood and wrought-iron fittings. Top-floor rooms have angled roofs and views across to the gulf.

🍴 Eating

Eating in Delphi can be a so-so experience. Try these worthy exceptions.

Taverna Gargadouas
TAVERNA €

(Vasileon Pavlou & Friderikis; mains €8-10; ⏰noon-midnight) The local favourite for grilled meats. The house summer speciality is *provatina* (slow-roasted lamb). You can tuck into a combo of pasta, souvlaki, salad and seasonal fruit for a modest €13. Generally, it's good value.

Souvlaki Pita Gyros
KEBAB €

(Apollonos; mains €2-6; ⏰8am-3pm) Run by a family who conscientiously and efficiently whip up tasty budget options, including souvlaki and great Greek salads. Eat in or take away. Opposite Hotel Leto.

⭐Taverna Vakhos
TAVERNA €€

(☑22650 83186; www.vakhos.com; Apollonos 31; mains €8-14.50; ⏰noon-midnight; 🐾) Take the steps above the National Bank to this excellent family taverna featuring traditional local fare. Ask for what's fresh that day – it gets local produce if possible and staff gather the herbs themselves. If nothing appeals, make a meal of appetisers alone, eg *formaela,* the local cheese (€6).

Taverna To Patriko Mas
TAVERNA €€

(Vasileon Pavlou & Friderikis 69; mains €8-14; ⏰noon-late) Set in a 19th-century stone building, this swanky taverna is decidedly upscale and the food keeps its end of the bargain. You'll find generous mezedhes and salads, great grills and seafood (in summer) and a fine all-Greek wine list.

🍷 Drinking & Nightlife

There are plenty of cafe-bars along Vasileon Pavlou & Friderikis, and while the rest of Delphi sleeps, one main-street club provides plenty of DJ dancing into the wee hours.

Cafe Ihor
CAFE

(☑22650 83095; Vasileon Pavlou & Friderikis 61; ⏰10am-late; 🐾) Funky, contemporary-style place with wi-fi access and great views.

Café Agora
CAFE

(☑22650 83116; www.agoracafe.gr; Vasileon Pavlou & Friderikis; breakfast & snacks €2-10; 🐾) Along with the wi-fi and the views from the verandah, this place also serves up Delphi's best pizza and crêpes.

Club Katoi
CLUB

(Vasileon Pavlou & Friderikis; admission €5-10) Delphi's only late-night spot to let your hair down.

ℹ️ Information

Almost everything you'll need in Delphi is on Vasileon Pavlou & Friderikis. Delphi's other through roads are Apollonos, which runs north of and parallel to Vasileon Pavlou & Friderikis, and Filellinon, which runs south and parallel to the main drag. Four steep stairways connect all three roads. Incredibly, there is no tourist office. Several ATMs are on Friderikis.

Amfissa Hospital (☑22650 22222) For serious medical matters, it's best to head here.

Delphi Medical Centre (Apollonos) For minor medical matters you can head here.

Post office (Vasileon Pavlou & Friderikis; ⏰7.30am-2pm Mon-Fri)

ℹ️ Getting There & Away

BUS

KTEL (☑22650 82317; www.ktel-fokidas.gr; Vasileon Pavlou & Friderikis) buses depart from the eastern end of Friderikis, opposite the old Hotel Vouza. Tickets must be purchased from The Delphi restaurant between 9am and 8pm (the bus system's closing time). If you're taking an early bus, you will need to plan ahead; buy tickets one day earlier. The same applies in high season when buses fill up quickly. Travellers to Kalambaka/Meteora should find better connections via Lamia and Trikala, rather than Larissa.

DESTINATION	TIME	FARE	FREQUENCY
Amfissa	30min	€2.10	5 daily
Arahova	20min	€1.60	4-5 daily
Athens	3hr	€15.10	4-5 daily
Galaxidi	45min	€3.50	3 daily
Itea	30min	€1.90	5 daily
Lamia	2hr	€9.10	1 daily
Larissa	3½hr	€21.70	1 daily
Livadia	55min	€4.20	4-5 daily
Nafpaktos	2½hr	€10.90	3 daily Mon-Sat
Patra	4hr	€14	1 daily
Thessaloniki	5hr	€35	1 daily
Thiva	1¼hr	€8	1-5 daily

PARNASSOS NATIONAL PARK
ΕΘΝΙΚΟΣ ΔΡΥΜΟΣ ΠΑΡΝΑΣΣΟΥ

Established in 1938, Parnassos National Park, to the north of Delphi and Arahova, has three peaks over 2300m: Parnassos (2457m), the highest; Tsarkos (2416m); and Gerondovrachos (2396m). Kouvelos (1882m) is a popular rock-climbing face. Mt Parnassos is part of the elaborate E4 European long-distance path (orivatiko monopati) from Gibraltar to Cyprus (see www.era-ewv-ferp.com for details).

The Parnassos Ski Centre, 24km from Arahova, handles ski and snowboard operations on Kelaria (1950m; 13 lifts). For accommodation, it's best to stay in Arahova. Adjacent to Kelaria are the steeper slopes of Fterolakkas (six lifts), popular with extreme skiers. For more information, see www.snow-report.gr.

There is no public transport between Arahova and the ski centre. A taxi from Delphi costs around €45.

Around Delphi

Olive groves and clear skies mark the road south from Delphi, which stretches 18km to the Gulf of Corinth before branching east to Kirra (2km). This was **Ancient Kirra**, the port of Delphi, now a quiet suburb of the market town of Itea, with a long sand-and-pebble beach, very clean sea and good beach-side camping.

Amfissa   Άμφισσα
POP 6920

The town of Amfissa (the capital of the new Municipality of Delphi) sits in the foothills 21km from Delphi on the road to Lamia. The village was sacked in 338 BC by Philip of Macedon and, more recently, it played an important role in the 1821 Greek Revolution.

◎ Sights

Amfissa Castle   CASTLE
Also known as the Castle of Salona, the Castle of Amfissa dominates the hill behind the village. Around 600m of the castle's fortified wall remains and you can wander through the castle grounds. Believed to have been constructed under the orders of Thomas I d'Autremencourt, the first Lord of Salona, after division of the Byzantine Empire after the Fourth Crusade, it was the fort for subsequent invaders, including the Romans, Catalans, Franks and Turks. All left their mark, as shown in the melange of architectural elements that survive today, especially those from Byzantine and Frankish times.

Archaeological Museum
of Amfissa   MUSEUM
(http://odysseus.culture.gr; 2 Kechagia St; adult/child €2/free; ◎9am-4pm Tue-Sun) This small but stunning museum, housed in a renovated 20th-century building (previously a bank and a police station), holds a wonderful collection of artefacts from Fokida region, dating from the Bronze Age to the early Byzantine period. Highlights include rare idols purchased by pilgrims in Ancient Kirra and taken to Delphi, miniature marionettes and a bronze helmet from 300 BC.

Moni Profiti Ilia   CONVENT
(◎8am-2pm & 4pm-sunset) Heading west from Delphi towards Amfissa, the 19th-century convent of Moni Profiti Ilia rests on a hillside with superb views of the Gulf of Corinth and Amfissa olive grove. This is where Essaeas, the bishop of Salona (Amfissa), raised the flag of revolution on 24 March 1821. The turn-off is marked with a small cross and '3km' sign. Note: it has a strict dress code. Definitely no shorts for men or women.

✖ Eating

★**Yali Kafene**   CAFE
This beautiful, traditional kafeneio (coffee house) is a must-visit. Relax over a traditional Greek coffee and have a chat with the friendly 80-something-year-old owner, who will regale you with stories of the past, especially about live-theatre performances (note the stage) and professional film shoots (given its authenticity, you'll see why). To say more would be to give the game away.

It's located in the upper square (pano platea), beside the town hall.

Arahova   Αράχωβα
POP 3240

Arahova (ah-ra-ho-vah), only 12km from Delphi, rests on a rocky spur of Mt Parnassos at an altitude of 960m. While it's easy to stick to the main drag, the stepped alleyways of the mountain town are also charming and include the historic 'clock on the rock'. As well as a side trip from Delphi, the town is primarily a fashionable winter resort for skiers.

Arahova's more touristy shops sell embroidery, hand-woven bags and *flokati* (shaggy woollen rugs) and traditional products, but it's also noted for its cheese, honey, *hilopites* (fettuccine-style pasta) and red wine.

✶✶ Festivals & Events

Festival of Agios Georgios CARNIVAL
Held in town around 23 April (if this date falls during Lent, the festival is postponed until the following Easter Tuesday). It's a joyous three-day celebration with virtually the entire village in costume. There's dancing and singing, a tug-of-war contest and, on the last day, feasting on roasted lamb, all compliments of the town.

🛏 Sleeping

Room prices in Arahova can jump about 50% (or even double) on winter weekends and holidays.

Xenonas Maria HOTEL €€
(📞22670 31803; www.mariarooms.com; d €50-70, tr €70; 🛜) Atmospheric, old-style, split-level rooms and lots of red carpets and fur-covered trim. Behind the town hall. Open all year.

Hotel Likoria HOTEL €€
(📞22670 31180; www.likoria.gr; s/d/tr incl breakfast from €60/75/95; P🅿️❄️@🛜) Off the main road, 250m northwest of Plateia Xenias, the low-key Likoria feels more like a country inn. Rooms are quite traditional, with carpeting, huge soft beds and shuttered doors opening to large balconies. The friendly English-speaking staff are a plus.

🍴 Eating

Taverna Agnantio TAVERNA €€
(www.toagnantio.gr; mains €7-12) This handsome Greek eatery, 30m east of Plateia Lakka, has a let's-dig-in-here-for-the-afternoon ambience and serves a daily selection of oven-ready dishes and grills.

To Yefira Taverna TAVERNA €€
(mains €8.50-17; ⊙noon-midnight, closed Jun) By the bridge, with a lovely view of the tower, this basic spot (which looks like it was a fabric shop, such as its array of colourful tablecloths) whips up home fare, including good *pites* (pies) and moussaka.

ℹ Information

The **post office** (Plateia Xenias) is near ATMs, and the entire village is a wi-fi hot spot.

ℹ Getting There & Away

The daily buses that run between Athens and Delphi stop at Arahova's Plateia Xenias (€15.10, 2½ hours).

Galaxidi Γαλαξίδι

POP 2010
The prettiest of the low-key resorts on the Gulf of Corinth, Galaxidi has narrow cobblestone streets, handsome stone mansions and two small harbours. It's a great alternative to staying in Delphi, should you not want bus hordes. A forested headland, opposite the waterfront, is fringed by a 1.5km walking path and pebbled coves popular with swimmers.

DON'T MISS

MONI OSIOS LOUKAS

The World Heritage–listed monastery **Moni Osios Loukas** (Μονή Οσίου Λουκά | Monastery of St Luke; 📞22670 22228; admission €3; ⊙8am-1pm summer, to 5pm winter) is 23km southeast of Arahova, between the villages of Distomo and Kyriaki. Its principal church contains some of Greece's finest Byzantine frescoes. Modest dress is required (no shorts).

The monastery is dedicated to a local hermit who was canonised for his healing and prophetic powers. The monastic complex includes two churches. The interior of the larger, **Agios Loukas**, is a glorious symphony of marble and mosaics, with icons by Michael Damaskinos, the 16th-century Cretan painter.

In the main body of the church, the light is partially blocked by the ornate marble window decorations, creating striking contrasts of light and shade. Walk around the corner to find several fine frescoes that brighten up the crypt where St Luke is buried. Nearby is the smaller 10th-century **Agia Panagia** (Church of the Virgin Mary).

To get here from Delphi, you can take the Livadia/Athens bus as far as the Distomo crossing (€2.10, 35 minutes, five daily). Taxis will get you to the monastery from Distomo (€20 return), Livadia (€30 return) or Delphi (€40 return). For an extra charge, the taxi will wait an hour at the monastery. Coming from Livadia, one daily bus heads to Moni Osios Loukas (€3.50, 30 minutes).

CENTRAL GREECE GALAXIDI

DISTOMO

Distomo is remembered throughout Greece for the massacre of 10 June 1944, when Nazi troops killed 218 villagers in a door-to-door reprisal for a guerrilla ambush in nearby Steiri. In 1966 the German government erected a dramatic white-marble war memorial, with inscriptions in both Greek and German.

The town is reasonably tranquil except during summer and holiday weekends, when its charm is tested by carloads of Athenians. Galaxidi's most prosperous period was between 1830 and 1910 when it was a major centre for building caïques (small boats).

◎ Sights

Nautical Historical Museum　MUSEUM
(☑ 22650 41795; Plateia Manousakia; adult/child €5/free; ⊙ 10.10am-1.30pm & 5.30-8.30pm Jun-Sep, 10.10am-4.15pm Oct-May) The excellent Nautical Historical Museum documents Greece's maritime history and Galaxidi's unique shipbuilding lore, and includes several splendid ship figureheads.

Church of Agios Nikolaos　CHURCH
The carved-wood iconostasis in the Church of Agios Nikolaos is one of Greece's finest. Follow the English signs for the museum and church.

Moni Metamorfosis　MONASTERY
The little 13th-century Moni Metamorfosis stands amid olive groves and cypress trees, 4km inland from Galaxidi. From this vantage point there are terrific views down to the Gulf of Corinth. To reach it, go under the flyover and take the road opposite.

🛏 Sleeping

In summer several of the waterfront cafes have rooms to let, though they're not great value.

Hotel Galaxidi　HOTEL €
(☑ 22650 41850; www.hotelgalaxidi.gr; r incl breakfast €60; 🐱) Seventies-style pine and low beds in an unfussy environment.

Galaxa Mansion　BOUTIQUE HOTEL €€
(www.galaxamansion.com; s/d/tr incl breakfast €50/65/85; 🐱🐱) Housed in a former shipowner's residence, this historic house has been refurbished. Each of the nine rooms – named after Greek characters – is charm-

ing. The downside is the squeezy bathrooms, but there are still some lovely antique-style touches as testimony to its seafaring days. There are stunning views of the old harbour from some of the rooms, plus the terrace.

Hotel Ganimede　BOUTIQUE HOTEL €€
(☑ 22650 41328, 6937154567; www.ganimede.gr; Nik Gourgouris 20; s/d/tr incl breakfast €55/75/90, studio €110; 🐱🐱) This courtyard hotel in a 19th-century captain's house offers a range of slightly dated but charming pastel-shaded rooms with wood-panelled ceilings and period furniture. What it's best known for is owner Chrisoula's gut-busting breakfasts – think homemade jams, cheeses, fresh-squeezed juices and bread from the family bakery. Also has studios with kitchenettes. A casual taverna operates in the pretty courtyard.

MiraMare Studios　ROOMS €€
(☑ 6937154567; studio s/d €55/75; 🐱) These lovely bright and airy studios, equipped with small kitchenettes and balconies, are a pebble's throw from the waterfront action.

To Spitaki　PENSION €€
(☑ 22650 41257, 6977512238; www.tospitaki.com; d €60-110, f €110-130, incl breakfast; P 🐱 @) Its name meaning 'little house' in Greek, this converted 1850s stone *ouzerie* (ouzo bar) is one of three neighbouring properties, each complete with kitchen and pretty flower garden, halfway between the port and the main square. Lovely ambience and a delightful owner, Stella.

Arhontiko Art Hotel　BOUTIQUE HOTEL €€
(☑ 22650 42292; www.archontikoarthotel.gr; s €45, d €55-75, incl breakfast; P 🐱) Tucked away behind the old harbour, this mansion has quirky themed rooms – think 'sun room' with a round bed, 'moon room' with a mirrored ceiling, and a boat-shaped bed anchored in the 'navy room'. Pretty courtyard for breakfast in warmer times makes for a pleasant stay.

🍴 Eating

You can't go wrong eating in Galaxidi. You can find excellent bites in every taverna along the waterfront, but don't be afraid to go off-piste too. Eateries are also hidden in the backstreets.

Bebelis　TAVERNA €
(mains €7-13.50; ⊙ Sep-May) Fresh flowers, lace curtains and its location – a couple of blocks from the 'new harbour' – add a touch of taverna class to Galaxidi. Proud owner Bebelis (the

owner's nickname) offers a lovely go-slow experience. Perfect for a long lunch or dinner.

Albatross   TAVERNA €
(☎ 22650 42233; Konstadinou Satha 36; mains €6-8; ⊙ lunch & dinner) We love this little place near the Church of Agios Nikolaos, run by a long-standing, elderly-if-young-at-heart couple. Prices haven't changed in years and the generous offerings of mezedhes (try the dolmadhes), along with a few oven-ready dishes, are always tasty.

Zygos   TAVERNA €
(mains €6.50-14; ⊙ 11am-late) The German beer mugs seem a little incongruous until you realise this appealing Greek tavern, on the 'new harbour', offers over 40 beers, plus a range of *tsipouro*. Although new, it manages to re-create a traditional tavern atmosphere minus the sticky-bum-on-seat factor associated with a beer-fest. The cuisine is fabulous. Don't miss the 'drunk pork hock' – it's been cooked slowly. In beer, of course.

ℹ Information

The post office and a bank are on Nikolaou Mama. All the cafes have wi-fi access.

ℹ Getting There & Away

The **bus stop** (☎ 22650 42087) is on Plateia Manousakia. There are buses to Delphi (€3.50, 45 minutes, two to three daily), Athens (€18.70, 3½ hours, two to three daily) and Patra (€10.10, 1¾ hours, one to two daily). For Delphi and Athens, you must change bus in Itea, but ticket prices cover the entire journey.

Nafpaktos   Ναύπακτος
POP 19,800

West of Galaxidi, and only 9km after the bridge crossing (Rio Andiro) from Patras that joins the Peloponnese with Sterea Ellada, is this delightful, bustling town. It spreads out from a handsome circular-walled harbour dotted with plane trees, cafes and a good **swimming beach** (Psani). Above it looms a Venetian *kastro* (castle). It's an excellent accommodation alternative to more expensive Patras (and you get to cross this amazing bridge; tolls apply), or a pleasant en-route stop to Delphi, if coming from the Peloponnese. An open market takes place every Saturday.

History

Nafpaktos was known as Lepanto in medieval times, and it was here on 7 October 1571 that the naval battle of Lepanto took place between the Ottoman Empire and the combined navies of the Vatican, Spain and Venice. The decisive victory over the Turks temporarily ended the Ottoman's naval domination of the Mediterranean.

The Spanish author Cervantes fought in the battle of Lepanto (and lost an arm). A small statue on the waterfront honours him, along with a Greek hero, Giorgos Anemogiannis (1796–1821), who, during the Greek War of Independence, tried to burn the Turkish fleet that was moored in the harbour (he failed and was killed by the Turks).

◎ Sights

Botsari Museum   MUSEUM
(☎ 26340 29779; ⊙ 9am-1.30pm Mon-Fri) FREE Battle aficionados must head to the Venetian-style Tower of Botsaris, currently a museum run by the Botsaris Foundation (the owner). It houses a collection of replicas of paintings and engravings – the originals made by the most famous artists of that era (Vasari, Tintoretto and the like) – recording the Battle of Lepanto. Ring the bell during opening hours; ring ahead for weekend visits.

Castle   CASTLE
The town's well-preserved fortress and Venetian *kastro* that overlook the town are fascinating. The *kastro* comprises a series of five terraced stone walls, built by a succession of conquerors (Doric, Roman, Byzantine, Venetian and Turk), that end at the town's waterfront. The walk and views alone are well worth checking out. (Note: if you drive, turn uphill at the Shell service station.)

Fethiye Mosque   MOSQUE
(⊙ 9am-1pm) Located on the eastern jetty (look for the domed roof) is this stunning Ottoman mosque, named Fethiye Mosque (Conquest Mosque) because it was built after the conquest of the city by Sultan Beyazid II, who ruled the Ottoman Empire between 1481 and 1512. Open only when exhibitions are on.

🛏 Sleeping & Eating

Hotel Akti   HOTEL €€
(☎ 26340 28464; www.akti.gr; Grimbovo Beach; s/d/tr/ste €45/60/75/130; ✳ 🕾) The Akti's exterior looks like a pastel colour chart with balconies. Inside this delightful surprise are beautiful rugs and antiques galore and rooms that are high, wide and comfortable. Delightful English-speaking owner Giorgos serves

BUSES FROM NAFPAKTOS

DESTINATION	STATION	TIME	FARE	FREQUENCY
Athens (via Rio–Andirio)	Nafpaktos	3hr	€21	2 daily
Delphi (via Itea)	Fokida	3hr	€11	3-4 daily
Galaxidi	Fokida	1½hr	€7.40	3-4 daily
Lamia	Nafpaktos	3½hr	€14.50	1 daily
Messolongi	Nafpaktos	50min	€5	3-4 daily
Patra	Nafpaktos	30min	€3.30	2-8 daily Mon-Sat
Thessaloniki	Nafpaktos	6hr	€44	1 daily

up a ridiculously good continental breakfast with homemade produce. Great location amid leafy surrounds and opposite the beach.

Evinos MEDITERRANEAN €
(Sismani 3, Stenopazaro; mains €6.50-9.50; ☺noon-midnight, 6pm-1am summer) A twist of gourmet hits Nafpaktos' eateries at this pleasant spot, the name of which translates as 'good wine'. Don't expect any plate smashing here – it's not traditional. Instead, it's a Mediterranean-Greek fusion – pastas and risotti – plus traditional dishes with a twist, such as haloumi *torta*. Great salads, too. A lovely setting, though not by the sea.

❶ Getting There & Away

Nafpaktos has two bus stations. The **KTEL Nafpaktos station** (☑ 26340 27224; cnr Manassi & Botsari) is behind the large Church of Agios Dimitrios. The **KTEL Fokida station** (☑ 26340 27241; cnr Kefalourisou & Asklipiou) is 400m further east.

Messolongi   Μεσολόγγι

POP 14,400

From a distance, Messolongi's flat landscape lacks the siren's irresistible draw. The town skirts the **Klisova Lagoon**, the largest natural wetland in Greece, a favourite winter stop-over for thousands of migrating birds and an important breeding ground for the endangered Dalmatian pelican – not to mention a pilgrimage site for birdwatchers and photographers, thanks to the remarkable *pelades* (stilt huts) in the water. In the town centre are pedestrian lanes around the central square lined with lively bars and tavernas. While there's not a lot to do, it's an extremely 'genuine' place, though it has been hit hard by the economic crisis.

History

During the War of Independence (1821–30), Britain's philhellenic bard, Lord Byron, arrived in Messolongi with the intention of organising the troops and supporting the Greek war effort. After months of vain attempts, Byron contracted a fever and died on 19 April 1824, his immediate aims unfulfilled.

Byron's death spurred international forces to hasten the end of the War of Independence, making him to this day a Greek national hero. Many men bear the name Byron (Vyronas in Greek) and most Greek towns have a street named after him.

In the spring of 1826, under the helm of Egyptian general Ibrahim, Messolongi was captured by the Turks. Their year-long siege drove 9000 men, women and children to escape on the night of 22 April 1826 through what is now called the Gate of Exodus. Many took refuge on nearby Mt Zygos, only to be caught or killed by an Albanian mercenary force. A smaller group remained behind to detonate explosives as the Turks approached. This tragic exodus was immortalised in Dionysios Solomos' epic poem 'I Eleftheri Poliorkimeni' (The Free Besieged).

◉ Sights

Garden of the Heroes GARDENS
(☺8am-8pm) Just beyond the Gate of Exodus is this memorial garden, which contains, among many others, a prominent statue of

---

BRIDGE TO PATRA

The striking Rio–Andirio, a suspension bridge, connects mainland Andirio and Rio in the Peloponnese, a crossing formerly only made by ferry. Despite the steep toll (€14 each way), getting to Patra and beyond couldn't be easier. If you're not in a hurry, a ferry (€6.50) also departs from under the bridge (follow the signs) every 20 minutes and you get a great view of the bridge's underbelly.

Lord Byron. It was established by the first governor of Greece following independence, Ioannis Kapodistrias.

He issued the following decree (the Greek text of which is on the marble slab to the right as you enter the garden): '...within these walls of the city of Messolongi lie the bones of those brave men, who fell bravely while defending the city...it is our duty to gather together, with reverence, the holy remains of these men and to lay them to rest in a memorial where our country may, each year, repay its debt of gratitude'.

When Byron died, the Greeks were heartbroken at the loss of a British nobleman who had given his life for their freedom. At the end of a national 21-day mourning period, Byron's embalmed body was returned to England, but his heart was kept by the Greeks and is buried beneath the statue. The English authorities at the time refused Byron's burial at Westminster Abbey.

Museum of History & Art　　　MUSEUM
(📞 26310 22134; Plateia Markou Botsari; ⊙ 9am-1.30pm & 4-6pm) **FREE** Dedicated to the revolution, this museum features a collection of Byron memorabilia and paintings. The passionate ticket seller has clocked up over 26 years in his chair.

Diexodos Museum–Picture Gallery　GALLERY
(📞26310 51260; www.diexodos.com.gr; Razikotsika 23; ⊙10.30am-1pm Wed-Sun) **FREE** A labour of love for a local lawyer, who restored the 18th-century mansion, this beautiful gallery houses a private collection of paintings and hosts temporary exhibitions and events.

🛏 Sleeping & Eating

Any of the *ouzeries* and eateries along and near Razikotsika are reliable bets. *Heli* (eel) and *avgotaraho* (egg roe of the grey mullet) are the culinary go here.

Hotel Avra　　　　　　　　　　　HOTEL €
(📞26310 22284; hotelayram@panafonet.gr; Harilaou Trikoupi 1; s/d/tr €35/40/50; ❄) The 16-room Avra is basic but tidy. Rear-facing rooms avoid the din of the adjacent central Plateia Markou Botsari.

Dimitroukas Restaurant　　　　TAVERNA €
(Razikotsika 11; mains €7-12; ⊙ noon-late Tue-Sun) Operating since 1975, this is Messolongi's longest-standing eatery. A third generation now runs this friendly spot, which serves up no-nonsense Greek cuisine of fish and roasted meats (plus five daily dishes).

> **WORTH A TRIP**
>
> ### TOURLIDA　　　　　　ΤΟΥΡΛΑΙΔΑ
> ....
> From Messolongi you can drive, walk or cycle across the surreal **Klisova Lagoon** on the 5km-long causeway to visit the sandy hamlet of Tourlida. Besides the scenery afforded from the crossing, the main reason to be here is to wile away a few hours at the **Tourlida Restaurant** (www.tourlis.gr; mains €5-12; ⊙11am-11pm), a light and airy spot with multicoloured rush-seated chairs, a 180-degree view of the water and fishing boats, and plenty of local businesspeople lapping up the atmosphere and tucking into hearty helpings of Greek and seafood delights.

ℹ Information
Messolongi is the capital of the prefecture of Etolo-Akarnania. The central square, Plateia Markou Botsari, is dominated by the gallery and mayoral office on its eastern side. Several of the surrounding cafes have free wi-fi.

ℹ Getting There & Away
The **KTEL Messolongi station** (📞 26310 22371) is outside the walled town, near the arched Gate of Exodus. There are regular buses to Athens (€24, 3½ hours, 10 daily) via Rio–Andirio, as well as buses to Patra (€6, one hour, eight daily), Nafpaktos (€5, 50 minutes, two daily) and Mytikas (€9, 1½ hours, one daily).

Karpenisi　　　Καρπενήσι
POP 8580

The underrated, attractive capital of the mountainous prefecture of Evritania lies in the well-wooded foothills of Mt Tymfristos (2312m), or Velouchi, between Lamia and Lake Kremasta. Billed as the 'Switzerland of Greece', it has an alpine-village feel, with chalet-style lodgings, churches and tavernas. Lovely walks are dotted around the area. For the less action-oriented, driving through the forest to steep villages and monasteries is equally rewarding.

🛏 Sleeping

Hotel Galini　　　　　　　　　HOTEL €
(📞22370 22914; www.galini-hotel.com; Riga Fereou 3; s/d incl breakfast €25/40) The side-street Galini is a great budget choice, with simple rooms and friendly owners. From the *plateia* (square), walk 100m down Tsitsara.

FERRIES TO IONIAN ISLANDS FROM ASTAKOS

The only reason to head to Astakos (Αστακός) is as a convenient stepping stone for access to the Ionian Islands, via the daily ferry to/from Kefallonia (Sami) in summer (per person/car €11/42, three hours). Two ferries depart Sami for Astakos on Monday and Thursday, but check ahead, as this changes seasonally. In Astakos, a few cafes, domatia and tavernas line the small waterfront so you can get your fill while waiting.

Deluxe Hotel Anesis HOTEL €€
(☑22370 80700; www.anesis.gr; Zinopoulou 50; s/d/tr incl breakfast €65/80/95; ❄️🛜) The nearest thing to a Swiss chalet without the snow, this slightly twee, warm place is nevertheless handsome, with a welcoming lobby and warm rooms.

✕ Eating & Drinking

If you have your own wheels, you can also find good tavernas dotted between Karpenisi and Megalo Horio/Gavros.

Taverna En Elladi TAVERNA €
(☑22370 22235; www.enelladi-tavern.gr; Kotsidou 4; mains €6-12.50) This place earns marks for its handy location, just above the main square. The food is reasonable, too – hearty homemade soups, along with oven-ready dishes such as veal *en elladi* (veal with potatoes and cheese, €8).

Taverna Panorama TAVERNA €
(☑22370 25976; Riga Fereou 18; mains €6-13) It's all about the food and less about the ambience in this cavernous space with a leafy outdoor terrace. The huge menu features plenty of grilled lamb and pork, plus a hearty goat soup.

Saloon Park BAR
(Karpenisi–Prousos rd; snacks €2.50-5; ☉9am-midnight) A popular, if incongruous, bar-cafe 3km south of town. The unmistakable theme is the American Old West, with a Jack Daniels–meets-ouzo ambience.

❶ Information

Several banks around the central square have ATMs.
Hospital (☑22373 50100; Pavlou Bakagianni 2)
Police (☑22370 23666; Anistastis 9)

Post office (cnr Agiou Nikolaou & Athanasiou Karpenisiotou; ☉7.30am-2pm)

❶ Getting There & Away

Karpenisi's **KTEL bus station** (☑22370 80013/4) is 1.5km southeast of town. Buses run to Athens (€25, five hours, two daily) and Lamia (€7.20, 1½ hours, three daily).

Around Karpenisi

From Karpenisi a scenic mountain road leads south for 34km towards the village of Prousos and the 12th-century **Moni Panagias Proussiotissas** (☑22370 80705). Pilgrims flock here on 23 August for the Feast of the Assumption, during which they drink holy water from the spring and step into the cave-like *katholikon* (principal church of a monastery), which claims to have a miracle-working icon of the Virgin Mary.

Just 14km south of Karpenisi are the twin villages of **Mikro Horio** (Little Village), with a couple of good tavernas, and scenic **Megalo Horio** (Big Village). This latter village boasts traditional stone houses and a charming **Folklore Museum** (Megalo Horio; admission €2; ☉10am-2pm Sat & Sun).

Megalo Horio is also the starting point for the all-day hike to **Mt Kaliakouda** (2098m) and back. If you fancy something more level, you can take a stroll along the banks of the Karpenisiotis River on a footpath that begins opposite the village bus terminal.

Back on the main road, at the foot of Megalo Horio, the riverside **Gavros** attracts Karpenisi families in search of a good meal in the countryside, or a stroll along the Karpenisiotis River.

With your own transport, you can visit the restored village of **Koryshades**, reached through a marked turn-off about 3km southwest of Karpenisi.

🛏 Sleeping & Eating

Pension Agrambeli PENSION €€
(☑22370 41148; www.agrampeli.gr; Gavros; d/tr from €50/60, ste €95, incl breakfast; @🛜❄️) This uniquely decorated mountain lodging in Gavros overlooks the river and Mt Talakondia. The seven rooms vary in size and features, some with iron beds and locally made rugs, others with kitchens and fireplaces.

Taverna To Spiti tou Psara TAVERNA €
(Fisherman's House, Gavros; mains €6.50-11; ☉lunch & dinner) At this excellent riverside taverna, a house speciality is fresh *pestrofa*

(grilled wild trout). The handmade *pites,* baked lamb and the owner's house-made wine justify the trip from Karpenisi.

ℹ Getting There & Away

BUS

Without your own transport, getting around is tricky. One municipality bus does a morning return circuit (on Monday, Wednesday and Friday) between Karpenisi and Megalo Horio, Mikro Horio and Gavros (around €2, 25 minutes). The schedule changes regularly, so first check with the municipality (☑ 22373 50000). One KTEL bus heads to Prousos each Friday (€3.40, 50 minutes); if you take the 5.45am bus, you can catch the 3pm return service.

TAXI

From Karpenisi's central *plateia* it's around €18 to Gavros, Megalo Horio or Mikro Horio. To Prousos, it's about €40. A driver will wait for you for around €10 per hour.

Lamia   Λαμία

POP 52,000

Lamia is the capital of the prefecture of Fthiotida, midway between Delphi and Meteora. Lamia rarely figures on travellers' itineraries, but it's a vibrant and lively place year-round. Life here revolves around the town's rambling squares and it's famous for its *kokoretsi* (lambs' intestines), *kourabiedes* (almond shortcake) and *xynogalo* (sour milk). It's the gateway to Iti National Park.

◉ Sights

There's a bustling street market on Riga Fereou and its side streets every Saturday morning.

Fortress   FORT

Lamia's *frourio* (fortress) is worth the hike just for the views. Within it is the **Archaeological Museum** (admission €2; ⊙ 8.30am-3pm Tue-Sun), chock-a-block with amazing finds from Neolithic to Roman times, including some classical, Hellenistic and Roman children's toys.

Gorgopotamos Railway Bridge   BRIDGE

The original Gorgopotamos Railway Bridge, 7km south of Lamia, was blown up by a coalition of British and Greek guerrilla forces on 25 November 1942, in order to delay the German advance, and is considered one of the greatest acts of sabotage of the time. The spectacular attack put the Greek underground on the map and forced the Germans to divert resources away from the Russian front. The reconstructed bridge spans a deep ravine.

Thermopylae   HISTORIC SITE

About 20km southeast of Lamia is the narrow pass of Thermopylae where, in 480 BC, Leonidas and a band of 300 brave Spartans managed to temporarily halt the invading Persian army of Xerxes. There's little here now, except for a statue of Leonidas, honouring the heroic battle site where the Spartans ultimately perished against overwhelming odds. Nearby (when open) are some hot-spring baths where you can relax in water that reaches up to 40°C.

🛏 Sleeping & Eating

The southern end of Plateia Laou is full of excellent-value *psistarias* (restaurants serving grilled meat) with whole lambs, goats and pigs adorning the windows. *Ouzeries* line a pedestrian street 50m west of here.

Hotel Athina   HOTEL €

(☑ 22310 27700; www.hotelathinalamia.gr; Rozaki Angeli 41; s/d/tr incl breakfast €40/50/70; P ❄ 🛜) The efficient, friendly and family-managed Athina has modern tile-floored rooms, large bathrooms, comfortable beds and, remarkably, its own parking. It's handy to Plateias Laou and Eleftherias.

Fitilis Restaurant   TAVERNA €

(Plateia Laou 6; mains €6-12; ⊙ lunch & dinner) On a lovely square, Fitilis serves classic *mayirefta* (ready-cooked) dishes at value-for-money prices. If you're lucky, there might be slow-cooked goat, which sizzles over an open, antique wood oven.

ℹ Information

Banks, all with ATMs, encircle Plateia Parkou.
Police station (☑ 22310 22431; Leoforos Athinon 188) Located on the southern edge of Lamia.

ℹ LOCAL VILLAGES

With your own transport, the village of Loutra Ipatis is a cheap and more tranquil alternative to staying in Lamia and perfect for a stopover on the way to/from Delphi. This, along with the nearby village of Ipati, makes a good base for exploring the region.

ℹ️ Getting There & Away

BUS

All buses depart from the **KTEL bus station** (☑22310 51345/6; www.ktelfthiotidos.gr; Taygetou), 2.5km southwest of the centre. A taxi between the centre and the bus station costs €6.

For Iti National Park, head to Ipati (€2.20, 40 minutes, five to seven daily) via Loutra Ipatis (€1.70).

DESTINATION	TIME	FARE	FREQUENCY
Agios Konstantinos	50min	€4.70	hourly
Amfissa	1½hr	€7.10	1 daily
Athens	3hr	€20.50	hourly
Delphi*	2hr	€9.20	1 daily
Karpenisi	1¾hr	€7.20	2 daily
Larissa	1½hr	€12.70	1-5 daily
Patra	3hr	€18.80	2-3 daily
Thessaloniki	4hr	€25.80	4-7 daily
Trikala**	2hr	€11.80	6 daily
Volos	2hr	€12.70	1-3 daily

* change in Amfissa
** change for Meteora and Kalambaka

TRAIN

Lamia's main train station is 6km west of the town centre at Lianokladi. Train tickets should be purchased in Lamia from the **OSE ticket office** (☑22310 44883; www.trainose.gr; Konstadinopoleos, Kon/Poleos), where an OSE shuttle bus links with the Lianokladi train station. Regular trains run to Athens (€12.50 to €24, three hours) and Thessaloniki (€29; 3½ to five hours).

Iti National Park & Around
Εθνικός Δρυμός Οίτης

Iti is one of Greece's most beautiful but least developed national parks. It's a verdant region with forests of fir and black pine, meadows and snow-melt pools fringed by marsh orchids, and is home to woodpeckers, eagles, deer and boar. According to mythology, Hercules built his own funeral pyre on Mt Iti, before joining his divine peers on Mt Olympus.

The bordering village of **Ipati**, 22km west of Lamia and 8km south of the Karpenisi–Lamia road, has the remains of a fortress and is (along with Pavliani to the south) a starting point for hikes on Mt Iti. The hub of the village is the tree-shaded central square, Plateia Ainianon, flanked by traditional *kafeneia*.

Loutra Ipatis, a sweet and sleepy little village on the approach to Ipati, is home to a summer **sulphur spa**.

👁️ Sights & Activities

Agathon Monastery MONASTERY
(⌚sunrise-sunset) Just past the village of Ipati is this lovely Byzantine monastery in a stunning setting over 550m above sea level, clinging to to the slopes of Mt Iti. A natural-history museum is here, among other relics.

Walking Trails

Trails around Iti National Park are not uniformly well marked, though a good day hike begins clearly at Ipati and climbs to a refuge (Trapeza at 1850m) near the Pyrgos summit (2152m). Other day hikes reach the villages of Kastania and Kapnohori. Check out Road Editions Map No 43, Iti, or *Anavasi* Map No 2.3, *Central Greece: Giona, Iti, Vardhousia*. Further information can be obtained through the **Hellenic Federation of Mountaineering** (☑21036 45904; www.eooa.gr).

🛏️ Sleeping & Eating

⭐**Hotel Alexakis** HOTEL €
(☑22310 59380; www.alexakis.gr; Loutra Ipatis; s/d/tr incl breakfast €35/50/60; 🅿🌀@) The immaculate, newly renovated Alexakis has contemporary rooms, a lovely terrace and broad views of Mt Iti. The delightful, friendly owners, Julia and Sofia, epitomise *filoxenia* (hospitality).

I Mouries TAVERNA €
(www.lymouries.gr; Loutra Ipatis; mains €6-10; ⌚lunch & dinner; 🍴) A cosy village spot with fabulous *mayirefta* dishes and excellent daily grills (each day, a different meat).

Agios Konstantinos
Αγιος Κωνσταντίνος
POP 3410

The pretty village of Agios Konstantinos, on the main Athens–Thessaloniki route, is one of the three mainland ports (along with Volos and Thessaloniki) that serve the islands of Skiathos, Skopelos and Alonnisos, which make up the northern Sporades.

ℹ️ Getting There & Away

Two English-speaking agencies, both on the plaza in front of the port, can help you with ferry travel: **Alkyon** (☑22350 32444, 210 383 2545; http://alkyontravel.gr) and **Bilalis Travel** (☑22350 31614; www.bta.gr; Karaiskaki 4).

BOAT

Hellenic Seaways operates the crossings to Skiathos (per person/car €30.50/75.50), Skopelos (per person/car €38/82) and Alonnisos (per person/car €38/82). In summer a boat departs daily to a changing schedule and with different companies. Between October and April, a small passenger boat ferries foot passengers only (though check ahead as this can vary year to year). See www.ferries.gr/greek-islands-ferry/ferry_agios_konstantinos.htm.

BUS

From the **KTEL bus station** (☑ 22350 32223), 200m south of the ferry landing, there are buses to Athens (€15.70, 2½ hours, eight to nine daily) and Lamia (€4.70, one hour, 12 daily). For Patra and Thessaloniki, you must change at Lamia.

METEORA & THESSALY

The region of Thessaly (Θεσσαλία) occupies much of east-central Greece between the Pindos Mountains and the Aegean Sea. The fertile and river-fed Thessalian plain supported one of the earliest Neolithic settlements on the continent. Today it boasts two of Greece's most extraordinary natural phenomena: the lofty, monastery-capped rock pinnacles of Meteora, and the lush Pelion Peninsula. The mountains and alpine meadows around Elati are destinations for outdoor enthusiasts.

Larissa Λάρισα
POP 162,600

Occupying the east bank of the ancient Pinios River, Larissa is a major transport, military and service hub for the vast agricultural plain of Thessaly. Larissa has been inhabited for nearly 10,000 years, and remnants of its layered Byzantine and Ottoman pasts are dotted about town. Despite its workaday feel, it is a vibrant university town, with bustling cafes, shops galore and numerous fountains. It's worth popping through.

⊙ Sights

You can gaze at the ongoing archaeological excavation of a well-preserved 3rd-century-BC **theatre** in the city centre, 100m north of Plateia Sarka. Nearby, the **acropolis** on Agios Ahillios hill dates from Neolithic times (6000 BC).

Municipal Art Gallery of Larissa GALLERY
(☑2410616266; www.katsigrasmuseum.gr; Pinakothiki Katsigra, cnr Papandreou & Kliou Patera; admission €3; ⊙9am-2pm & 6-9pm Mon-Fri summer, 10am-2pm & 6-9pm Tue-Fri, 9am-2pm Sat & Sun winter) Houses a superb private collection of Greek art from 1850 to 1950 (said to rival the National Art Gallery in Athens) plus temporary exhibits in a stunning contemporary building.

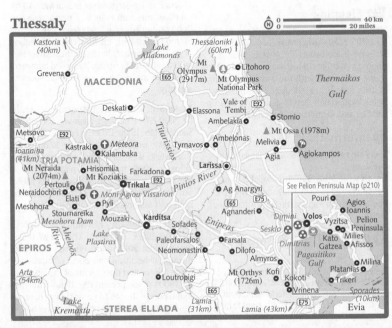

Thessaly

WORTH A TRIP

AROUND LARISSA

If you have time, it's a pleasant drive 28km northeast of Larissa to the **Vale of Tembi**, a dramatic gorge cut by the Pinios River between Mt Olympus and Mt Ossa that was sacred to Apollo in ancient times. A small bridge connects the car park with 13th-century **Agia Paraskevi** church and, 2km further on, the ruins of a **medieval fortress**.

The picturesque village of **Ambelakia**, 5km up a winding road from the village of Tembi, was a prosperous textile centre in the 18th century. A few dozen of the original 600 mansions remain, and walking the cobbled streets is a pleasure.

Diachronic Museum of Larissa   MUSEUM
(Timeless Museum; Karampilia 12) This museum was being constructed at the time of research; it should be open by the time you read this. It will display outstanding archaeological finds from the Larissa area, from the Middle Palaeolithic to the late Byzantine times, including exceptional discoveries from the Neolithic period. It's about 6km southwest of Larissa, beyond Neapoli.

🛏 Sleeping

Hotel Metropol   BUSINESS HOTEL €
(☑ 24105 37161; www.hotelmetropol.gr; Rousvelt 14; s/d/f incl breakfast €39/48/85; P ✳ @ 🐱) Should you linger in Larissa, you'll find large rooms decorated with the owner's paintings at this dated, but adequate, business-style hotel, located between Plateia Kentriki (Central Sq) and Ethnarhou Makariou.

ⓘ Information

There are several banks around Plateia Mihail Sapka.
Hospital (☑ 24102 30031; Tsakalof 1)
Police station (☑ 100; Papandreou 14)
Post office (cnr Papanastasiou & Athanasiou Diakou)

ⓘ Getting There & Away

BUS
Buses leave Larissa's **KTEL station** (☑ 24105 67600; www.ktellarisas.gr; cnr Georgiadou & Olympou) for Athens (€28, four hours, eight daily), Thessaloniki (€15, two hours, eight to nine

daily) and Volos (€5.30, one hour, half-hourly until 9pm).

From the branch **KTEL Trikalon station** (☑ 24106 10124; Iroön Polytechniou), near the junction with Gazi Anthimou, buses run hourly to/from Trikala (€6.30, one hour). For Meteora, take the Trikala bus then change for Kalambaka.

TRAIN
Trains pass daily through Larissa's **train station** (☑ 24102 36250; www.trainose.gr; cnr 28 Octovriou & Iroön Polytechniou) to/from Athens (Intercity €35, 3½ hours, six to seven daily) and Thessaloniki (express €14, 1¾ hours; Intercity €19, 1½ hours). You can buy tickets at the **OSE office** (☑ 24105 90239; Papakyriazi 35-37; ⊙9am-2pm Tue & Thu, 9am-2pm & 5-9pm Wed & Fri).

Volos   Βόλος

POP 144,000

Once called ancient Iolkos, Volos was the mythic home of Jason and his band of Argonauts. These days, Volos is a large and bustling university city on the northern shores of the Pagasitikos Gulf, and its function as the gateway to the Pelion Peninsula or the Sporades draws travellers to the city.

⊙ Sights

Archaeological Museum   MUSEUM
(☑ 24210 25285; Athanasaki 1; admission €3; ⊙ 8am-5pm Tue-Sun summer, to 3pm winter) This excellent museum is set in a pretty rose garden and houses area finds from Dimini and Sesklo, along with an impressive collection of painted grave stelae from the nearby Hellenistic site of Dimitrias. Recorded commentaries are available; leave your passport as security.

Tsalapatas Brickworks Museum   MUSEUM
(☑ 24210 29844; old town; admission €3; ⊙10am-5pm Wed-Mon 15 Mar-15 Oct, to 6pm 16 Oct-14 Mar) From 1926 until 1975, Tsalapatas Rooftile and Brickworks was part of the cultural fabric of Volos. In 2006 the restored plant opened as the handsome Tsalapatas Brickworks Museum with brick-making machinery, grinding mills and massive kilns on display.

Museum of the City of Volos   MUSEUM
(☑ 24210 29878; 15 Feron) This new museum (opened 2015) addresses recent history through a beautiful collection of black-and-white photos and documents of the city from the 1800s to the present day. Behind the museum, part of the old-town world has been reconstructed. Check ahead for opening hours;

the museum was new at the time of research and these were being determined.

🛏 Sleeping

Camping Hellas CAMPGROUND €
(📞 24230 22267; www.campinghellas.gr; camp sites per adult/tent/car €7/4/3; @ 🛜) This pleasant spot is located 17km southest of Volos and fronts a beach on the west coast of the Pelion Peninsula.

Sikia Camping CAMPGROUND €
(📞 24230 22279; www.camping-sikia.gr; camp sites per adult/tent €5.50/3.60; @ 🛜) A well-managed facility, with restaurant, mini market and beach bar. Located 17km southeast of Volos.

Hotel Jason HOTEL €
(📞 24210 26075; www.jason-hotel.gr; s/d/tr €40/50/60) One of Volos' few real budget hotels, it offers simple rooms with few frills. The upside is its close proximity to the port. Rooms at the rear are €10 less.

Hotel Philippos HOTEL €
(📞 24210 37607; www.philippos.gr; Solonos 9; d/tr incl breakfast €55/75; ❄🛜) Named after Philippos II of Macedon (382–336 BC, for those interested), this respectable spot has professional staff and a large foyer, but little else that alludes to a grand history. Rooms are basic, but neat.

Hotel Kipseli HOTEL €€
(📞 24210 24420; www.hotelkipseli.gr; Agiou Nikolaou 1; s/d/ste incl breakfast from €55/65/85; ❄🛜) This boutique lodging, with a great boardwalk location near the quay, is smart and modern, with handsome rooms. Its central location can mean noise, however. The rooftop bar has the best night views of the harbour.

Hotel Domotel Xenia Volou HOTEL €€
(www.domotel.gr/hotel/4/Xenia-Volos; s €80, d €100-120; P🛜❄) Volos' most upmarket place, this spot appeals to Greek visitors because of its sleekness. We like it more for its position on the eastern end of the harbour, in a pretty spot on the water and looking back at town. It morphs from a weekday business hotel into a more luxury option for holidaymakers. Smart rooms, half facing the sea, the other half the city, a gym and all the mod-con options make it a reliable stay. Check for internet deals.

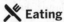 Eating

Stafylos GREEK €€
(Melounas 6; mains €8-12; ⊘ lunch & dinner) Your welcome is a small glass of *tsipouro* and some olives and a tomato dip before you've even ordered. There are lovely dishes from all over Greece, including a delicious *apaki* (Cretan cured pork), snails and much more.

THE TSIPOURADHIKA

Volos is famous throughout Greece for its *ouzeries* and *tsipouradhika*. If you have not already come across one, an *ouzerie* (strictly speaking, called a *tsipouradhiko*) is a type of small restaurant serving various plates of mezedhes and tiny bottles of *tsipouro*, a distilled spirit, like ouzo but stronger. You can dilute it with water if you prefer it weaker. When you've finished one round of mezedhes or *tsipouro*, you keep ordering until you've had your fill (or can't stand up!). The basic rule: don't expect a drink without a plate. Typical mezedhes include grilled *ohtapodi* (octopus) and fried calamari. Traditional *tsipouradhika* were open during the day only. Some of our old-time favourites in Volos:

⭐ **Kerasia Tsipouradiko** (Cherry Tree; Papakiatzi 40; drink & mezedhes €4-5; ⊘ 9am-6pm) For nearly 30 years, a husband-and-wife team have kept their heads down and clients happy at this traditional *tsipouradhiko*. Locals are known to traipse across town for their Greek coffee. Old photos on the establishment's wall attest to former times, though thankfully little has changed.

Sesklo (Papakiatzi 44; mezedhes €2-6; ⊘ 11am-6pm) A traditional *tsipouradhiko* serving up ouzo. The more you drink, the more you eat. Think sardines and grilled fish and other delicious morsels.

Kavouras Tsipouradiko (Gatziagiri 8; drink & mezedhes plate €4-5; ⊘ 11am-5pm Mon-Sat) Believed to be one of Volos' oldest *tsipouradhika*, up a tiny street between Dimitriados and Iasonos, this is a no-nonsense, no-frills, hard-drinking and eating experience. *Tsipouro* is poured from bottle to glass as per the old days. It bustles with locals and there's a heavy dose of testosterone, but all are welcome.

Ba Ca Re
GREEK €€

(www.bacare.gr; Skenderani 14; mains €8-15; ☺10am-late) A bar-cafe-restaurant all in one (as in ba-ca-re...get it?). That means it starts early for coffee, morphs into a lunchtime spot with great fish and salads, and ends up the after-sundown spot to have a tipple. Does modern takes on traditional dishes, including eggs with *horta* (wild greens), sausages and excellent *fava* (split-pea purée with lemon juice).

Plagios
MEDITERRANEAN €€

(cnr Kontaratou & Skirou; mains €9-20; ☺10.30am-1am) An alternative to Volos' traditional *tsipouradhika* (place that serves ouzo and light snacks) scene, this smart place has a low-key snob factor and touts itself as an all-day bar-restaurant. It adds a touch of contemporary gourmet to the Greek cuisine.

Drinking & Nightlife

For a night of music, drinking and dancing, head to the revitalised old industrial district known as the Palaia, the popular hangout for university students. Most of Volos seems to booze the evenings away in the city centre, especially around Koumoundourou and Kontaratou.

Poco Pico Cafe Bar
BAR

(Koumoundourou; ☺7am-late) This tiny spot – a hole-in-the-wall cafe-cum-bar – is the nearest thing you'll get to a street party. Everyone, it seems, especially university students, gathers here for an evening drink, but it's also great for early risers who need their java fix.

Kyklos Tsipouradiko
BAR

(☑24210 20872; Mikrasiaton 85; mezedhes €2-6; ☺Mon-Sat) Traditional rush chairs and small marble-topped tables lend atmosphere to this popular university bar hang-out. Try the house favourite: potatoes baked in a wood-fired oven.

1000 Chilia
CLUB

(☺11.30pm-6am) Hang an all-nighter at this club, popular among the young 'it' crowd.

Shopping

Ekonomou O Papous
FOOD

(☑24210 34606; Anthimou Gazi 135) Charming shop with only one item for sale: *loukoumi*, a traditional Greek version of Turkish delight.

ℹ Information

Parking in Volos can be tricky. Head straight for a parking lot – the one on the quay (€1.50 per hour, with price decreasing to €1 after two hours) is the most convenient. There are several ATMs on Argonafton, Iasonos and Dimitriados.

Post office (cnr Dimitriados & Agiou Nikolaou) Near Agios Nikolaos church.

Tourist police (☑24210 39057; 28 Octovriou 179) Any crime-related issues? Head here.

Volos General Hospital (☑24210 94200; Polymeri 134) Near the Archaeological Museum.

Volos Information Centre & Hotels' Association of Magnesia (☑24210 30940; www.voloinfo.gr; cnr Grigoriou Lambraki & Sekeri; ☺8am-8pm Mon-Fri, to 2pm Sat & Sun) Just opposite the KTEL bus station, this modern facility offers hotel information, town maps and bus, train and ferry schedules, along with helpful travel tips for the Pelion Peninsula.

The Web (Iasonos 137; per hr €1.90; ☺24hr) Internet shop. Many waterfront cafe-bars also have free wi-fi.

ℹ Getting There & Away

BOAT

Volos is a gateway to the northern Sporades isles of Skiathos, Skopelos and Alonnisos. Ferries arrive and depart from the far end of the dock; hydrofoils from the near end. The following are high-season schedules as at the time of research. Note: these change regularly.

DESTINATION	TIME	FARE	FREQUENCY
Alonnisos	5½hr	€27.50	2 daily
Alonnisos*	3hr	€48	1 daily
Skiathos	2hr	€23	2 daily
Skiathos*	1½hr	€37.50	2 daily
Skopelos (Skopelos Town)	4hr	€27.50	2 daily
Skopelos (Skopelos Town)*	3hr	€48	4 daily
Skopelos (Glossa)*	2hr	€40	1 daily

*high-speed service

BUS

From the **KTEL Volos bus station** (☑24210 33254; www.ktelvolou.gr; cnr Zachou & Almyrou), opposite the tourist info centre, buses depart for Athens (€28, 4½ hours, 10 daily), Larissa (€5.30, one hour, 10 to 12 daily), Thessaloniki (€19, 2½ hours, eight to nine daily), Trikala (€14, 2½ hours, four daily) and Ioannina (€24, 4½ hours, three daily). If you don't want to traipse to the station, you can buy tickets in advance at **Amugdalo Sweet Shop** (Dimitriados 84b; ⊙9am-2.30pm & 5.30-9.45pm Mon-Fri, 9am-3pm Sat) in central Volos.

TRAIN

The atmospheric Volos **train station** (📞24210 24056; www.trainose.gr; Papadiamanti) is 200m northwest of Plateia Riga Fereou. Nine trains run daily to Larissa (€3.60, one hour), which is the place to catch connections to Athens (normal/express €19/36, seven daily) and Thessaloniki (normal/express €12/22, hourly). You can also check schedules and buy tickets at the **OSE outlet** (Dimitriados 186; ⊙7.30am-2pm Wed & Fri, to 8.30pm Tue, Thu & Fri, 8am-2pm Sat, closed Sat Jun-Aug) near the university.

🛈 Getting Around

Cars can be hired from a friendly team at **Hertz** (📞24210 22544; stvolos@herz.gr), at the port next to the fish market, and **Avis** (📞24210 22880; avisvolos@otenet.gr; Argonafton 41).

Around Volos

Just west of Volos are two major archaeological sites, both dating from early Greek civilisation in Thessaly. The architecture at both sites typifies the complex agrarian communities that could sustain much larger populations than those of their Palaeolithic hunter-gatherer ancestors.

⊙ Sights

Sesklo   ARCHAEOLOGICAL SITE

(adult/child €2/1; ⊙8am-3pm Tue-Sun) Features the remains of the oldest acropolis in Greece (6000 BC). Once believed to have had a population of up to around 5000.

Dimini   ARCHAEOLOGICAL SITE

(adult/child €2/1; ⊙8am-3pm Tue-Sun) A late Neolithic site (4800–4500 BC) inhabited through to the Bronze Age, complete with traces of streets and houses and a wonderful *tholos* (Mycenaean tomb shaped like a beehive).

Pelion Peninsula
Πήλιον Όρος

The Pelion Peninsula lies to the east and south of Volos. It's formed by a dramatic mountain range, where the highest peak is Mt Pliassidi (1651m). The largely inaccessible eastern flank consists of high cliffs that plunge into the sea. The gentler western flank coils around the Pagasitikos Gulf. The interior is a green wonderland where trees heavy with fruit vie with wild olive groves and forests of horse chestnut, oak, walnut, eucalyptus and beech to reach the light of day. The villages tucked away in this profuse foliage are characterised by whitewashed, half-timbered houses with overhanging

---

WALKING IN THE PELION

The Pelion is a hiking mecca, and a centuries-old network of frequently restored *kalderimia* (cobbled mule pathways) connects most mountain and seaside villages around the region. The presence of many of the wonderful walking trails, former donkey routes, is thanks to the **Friends of the Kalderimi** (www.friendsofthekalderimi.org), which is dedicated to maintaining and restoring these historic cobblestone paths.

In the north, two relatively simple hikes begin near **Tsagarada**: from the square of Agia Paraskevi, it's two hours down to the small bay at Damouhari; and from the village of **Xourichti**, 4km south of Agia Paraskevi, a good cross-ridge path leads to the village of **Milies**, a hike of nearly three hours. A beautiful forest hike begins above the road at Fakistra beach and follows the coast to Plaka beach in about two hours.

In the south, a wonderful downhill trek is from **Promiri** to **Platanias**. Here too, **Lafkos** to **Milina** is a classic hike, where you can see both sides of the peninsula. **Argalasti** to **Kalamos** and **Lefokastro** is a popular walk.

The most useful of all resources are the websites www.pilionwalks.com, run by passionate expat walkers, with excellent circuit hikes, and http://walking-pelion.blogspot.gr by Kyriakos Stathakis, the president of Friends of the Kalderimi. It features maps, photographs and GPS points. For maps, the detailed 1:25,000 Anavasi Maps of *North, Central* and *South Pelion* are available in Volos bookshops, as is the excellent Terrain Map No 218, *Central Pelion*. Several accommodation places sell a wonderful map, *Pelion Walks* (€5 to €6), outlining seven different walks around Tsagarada.

Pelion Peninsula

balconies, grey slate roofs and old winding footpaths.

Many lodgings in the Pelion are traditional *arhontika* (stone mansions), tastefully converted into reasonably priced pensions. The peninsula has an enduring tradition of regional cooking, often flavoured with mountain herbs. Local specialities include *fasoladha* (bean soup), *kouneli stifadho* (rabbit stew), *spetzofaï* (stewed pork sausages and peppers) and *tyropsomo* (cheese bread).

For accommodation, you can expect the higher July and August rates quoted here to drop by at least 30% at other times.

History

In mythology the Pelion was inhabited by *kentavri* (centaurs) – half-man, half-horse creatures who took delight in drinking wine, deflowering virgins and generally ripping up the countryside. Not all were random reprobates, however – Chiron, considered the wisest of the group, was renowned for his skill in medicine.

The Turkish occupation did not extend into the inaccessible central and eastern parts of the Pelion and, as a result, the western coastal towns were abandoned in favour of mountain villages. In these remote settlements, culture and the economy flourished – silk and wool were exported to many places in Europe. The Orthodox Church at the time was instrumental in maintaining Kryfa Skolia (Hidden Schools). Like many remote areas in Greece, the Pelion became a spawning ground for ideas that culminated in the War of Independence.

ⓘ Getting There & Away

Buses to villages throughout the Pelion leave from the Volos bus station.

DESTINATION	TIME	FARE	FREQUENCY
Agios Ioannis	2hr	€6.60	1-2 daily
Kala Nera	50min	€1.70	15 daily
Makrinitsa (via Portaria)	45min	€1.60	6-8 daily
Milina (via Argalasti & Horto)	1½hr	€4.60	3-5 daily
Pinakates	1hr	€2.40	3 each weekday
Platanias	2hr	€6.40	2-3 daily
Pouri	1¾hr	€5	2-3 daily
Trikeri	3hr	€7.60	1-2 daily
Tsagarada	1½hr	€5.10	1-3 daily
Vyzitsa (via Milies)	1¼hr	€2.80	4-6 daily
Zagora (via Hania)	1½hr	€4.30	1-2 daily

Northwest Pelion
VOLOS TO MAKRINITSA

Taking the northeastern route from Volos to Makrinitsa (Μακρινίτσα), the road climbs 6km to the village of **Anakasia** (just after Ano Volos), home to the fascinating Theophilos Museum.

Portaria, 2km east of Makrinitsa, is 12km northeast of Volos. True to Pelion form, its *plateia* has a splendid old plane tree, and the little 13th-century **Church of Panagia of Portaria** has fine frescoes.

Sights

Theophilos Museum　　　MUSEUM
(Anakasia; ⊙8am-2.30pm Mon-Fri) FREE The only mansion in the Pelion that features intact work of Greek artist Theofilos Hatzimihail (1866–1934). Theofilos is believed to have been a 'wanderer' from Lesbos, who earned his food and keep painting the interiors of houses and cafes. In 1912 he painted the home of local miller Giannis Kontos. The rooms are a riot of beautiful figures – flowers, birds, animals and scenes of the Greek revolution. There are four gods of Olympus and topography paintings of nearby villages.

Sleeping & Eating

Midrange to upmarket places line Portaria. New ones seem to hit the market regularly.

Dryanoubaina　　　GUESTHOUSE €
(☑6979333492; www.dryanoybaina.gr; Portaria; d incl breakfast €50) Little English is spoken here, but it doesn't much matter thanks to the enthusiasm of the owner, Dina. She runs a tight ship with three rooms, communal sitting room and kitchen. There are lots of fluffy carpets and embroidered pictures (done by Dina).

Hotel Despotiko　　　BOUTIQUE HOTEL €€€
(☑24280 99046; www.despotiko.gr; Portaria; r from €125, ste €225; ⓢ☀) For an upmarket experience (with varied reviews about service), try this handsomely converted mansion. Significantly cheaper outside high season.

Kritsa Hotel Restaurant　　　TAVERNA €
(☑24280 99121; www.hotel-kritsa.gr; Portaria; mains €7.50-14; ⊙12.30pm-late) Head to the Portaria *plateia* to find this welcoming spot, set under plane trees and serving outstanding Pelion favourites such as slow-cooked 'lamb in parchment paper' and roasted wild greens with egg. It's famous for its excellent pies (think zucchini, leek, pepper, cheese; €5). A good wine list to boot. Summer cooking classes also available; contact in advance. If you want to fall into bed after sating yourself, consider staying in one of its rooms (double €50 to €60). They're a bit dated, but adequate.

MAKRINITSA　　　ΜΑΚΡΙΝΙΤΣΑ
POP 650

Clinging to a mountainside, Makrinitsa is aptly called the Balcony of Pelion. From a distance, the traditional houses give the impression that they're stacked on top of one another. Up close, the whitewashed structures are threaded with steep stairs crowded with geraniums, hydrangeas and roses. Further up, the path leads to more than 50 stone water fountains. It is one of the loveliest of the Pelion villages and, because of its proximity to Volos, also the most visited.

The village is a pedestrian zone – a bus terminus and shaded car park mark the entrance. The central square is anchored by a massive plane tree with a kid-friendly hollow, a marble fountain and the tiny chapel of **Agia Panagia**.

Sights

Museum of Folk Art　　　MUSEUM
(admission €2; ⊙10am-4.30pm Sat & Sun) This restored 1844 mansion, Arhontiko Topali, has well-displayed relics, including an old *tsipouro* still, a Victrola phonograph 'talking machine' and a hidden water fountain built into a stone wall.

CENTRAL GREECE PELION PENINSULA

WORTH A TRIP

POURI ΠΟΥΡΙ

The laid-back village of Pouri, 3km down the hill from Zagora, spills down a steep mountainside to a small bay. It's home to a few tavernas clustered beneath the church. Pouri boasts two fine swimming beaches, pebbly **Elitsa** and **Analipsi**. Enjoy a meal at the delightful **Taverna Plimari** (Analipsi beach; mains €8-13; ⊙ Easter-Oct; 🛜), where, as the owner says as he views his olive trees and water, 'If someone wants to live their dream in Greece, this is the place'.

🛏 Sleeping & Eating

Several hotels are scattered around the village. Prices listed here can increase by 50% on winter weekends. Stop at the main square for the views, but look beyond it for the best eateries.

Arhontiko Repana GUESTHOUSE €€
(☑ 24280 99067; www.repana.gr; s/d/tr incl breakfast from €45/60/70) For hospitality and value, we love this friendly, family-run converted mansion (built in 1858). Each of the five rooms is homely, comfortable and decked out with wood and red carpets (only one is a bit squeezy). Gut-busting breakfasts are worth the stay alone.

Melanthi Traditional Hotel GUESTHOUSE €€
(☑ 24280 99977; www.melanthi.gr; d/ste €70/150; 🛜) Dating from 1855, this mansion has been decorated with atmosphere in mind and a view-from-the-bed focus. Traditional Greek fittings add charm. Less appealing for some are the steep stairs and the tiniest bathrooms this side of the Aegean Sea (definitely not for larger people). Once you're on the outdoor terrace, surrounded by pot plants and looking out yonder, plumbing will be the furthest thing from your mind.

Theophilos Cafe CAFE €
(snacks from €3; ⊙ 10am-7pm summer, 11am-3pm winter) A historic *kafeneio* on the terrace behind the church. Inside is a superb fresco by wandering Greek artist Theophilos (p211).

Paschalis Cafe Art House CAFE €
(www.paschalishouse.com; ⊙ noon-9pm, closed Tue & Wed winter) A gorgeous gallery-cum-cafe with a range of cosy spaces, colourful cushions and an artistic vibe and some wonderful Greek and European artworks on display.

Taverna Leonidas TAVERNA €
(mains €7-13; ⊙ lunch & dinner daily, closed Mon-Fri in winter) Just past the square, this is a good choice for local fare (try the meatballs) and views below.

Aeriko Café-bar CAFE €
(www.aeriko-pelion.gr; snacks €3-5; ⊙ 10am-late, from 5pm Jun & Jul) Between Makrinitsa and Portaria, this place is worthy of an ice-cream stop to take in the wonderful view.

Northeast Pelion

ZAGORA ΖΑΓΟΡΑ
POP 3820

From Hania, the road zigzags down through chestnut trees to a junction leading to Zagora, the largest of the Pelion villages and a major fruit-growing centre – it's the apple capital of Greece. The town exported fine silk around the continent until blight ruined the silk industry in 1850. Two War of Independence landmarks – the museum and library – have their roots in Zagora.

◎ Sights

Library of Zagora LIBRARY
(☑ 24260 22591; www.library-zagora.gr; ⊙ Mon-Sat) **FREE** Starting with just 48 schoolbooks in 1767, the fascinating Library of Zagora is now home to one of Greece's largest collections of rare books and manuscripts, including 10th-century publications. Ask to see the exhibits.

Women's Agritourism Cooperative Zagora CULTURAL CENTRE
(www.agrosweet.gt) A women's cooperative that makes a range of delicious jams and sweet products. Knock on its door and see what might be available.

🛏 Sleeping & Eating

Arhontiko Dhrakopoulou HOSTEL €
(☑ 24260 23566; fax 24260 23460; r incl breakfast €40) The local women's cooperative manages this homey lodging, next to Plateia Agios Georgios. A local flower designates each of five simply furnished rooms.

Arhontiko Stamou GUESTHOUSE €€
(☑ 24260 23880; www.stamou-hotel.com; s €55, d €55-70, tr €80, incl breakfast; 🅿 @ 🛜) Arhontiko Stamou is a handsome and spacious villa (c 1863) that in the summer shares the courtyard with the mellow Café Anemella (Greek for silkworm), which is in the building up the steps to your left. The knowledgable

owner, George, will point you in the right direction.

Taverna Niki
TAVERNA €

(Meintani; www.meintani.gr; mains €6.50-10; ⊘noon-late) In Plateia Sotira, flower-draped Taverna Niki is excellent for *mayirefta*, grills and salads (Niki is a chef).

ℹ Information

Zagora Health Centre (☑24260 22591) For medical emergencies in the Pelion.

ZAGORA TO KISSOS

Picturesque villages adorn the road from Zagora to Tsagarada, one of the most scenically spectacular in the Pelion. The village of **Anilio** ('sunless' in Greek) rests in the shadow of a ridge of chestnut and walnut trees.

The flower-draped village of **Kissos** is built on steep terraces surrounding the 18th-century **Church of Agia Marina**, where the frescoes are considered the finest in the Pelion. It's a pleasant stop for a coffee or meal.

✕ Eating

Taverna 5F
TAVERNA €

(O Makis; Kissos; mains €5-10; ⊘lunch & dinner) Typical Greek, but appealing for the 5F in its name – this means *fili, fere filous, fae, fiye* (friends bring friends, eat and depart at leisure). Serves up a predictable array of Greek food. Not fancy, but fine.

Taverna Klimataria
TAVERNA €

(Kissos; mains €6.50-9.50) This pretty spot on the square and near the ancient church is the place to try *spetzofai* (spicy sausage dish).

HOREFTO
ΧΟΡΕΥΤΟ

Eight kilometres downhill from Zagora, Horefto is a low-key resort with palm trees and a long sandy beach. It's also the mythical home of Chiron, a roving centaur who healed the sick in the days when doctors still made house calls. The main beach is very decent, while isolated **Agioi Seranta beach** fills a beautiful cove 2km south, with a simple domatia and taverna nearby.

🛏 Sleeping & Eating

Hotel Cleopatra
HOTEL €€

(☑24260 22606; www.hotelcleopatra.gr; s/d €40/60; ⊘Apr-Oct; P ✳ 🛜) This vine-adorned hotel has spacious tile-and-wood rooms, balconies and overhead fans, making it good value. It's opposite the beach as you enter Horefto.

Hotel Aeolos
HOTEL €€

(☑24260 23260; www.aeolos.com.gr; studio/apt from €110/160; ✳🛜☳) Elegant in-town spot near the beach with studio and apartments.

Marabou Hotel
HOTEL €€

(☑24260 23710; www.marabouhotel.gr; s/d/ste €55/70/110; P✳@) Marabou Hotel is a comfortable hotel with an expansive verandah. It's perched on a green hillside 250m from the beach (a track provides a short cut). Meals available in high season. Open all year.

Taverna O Petros
TAVERNA €

(Horefto; mains €5-9; ⊘May-Oct) This reliable seaside eatery starts you out with a complimentary shot of local *tsipouro* and mezes, and serves up fine fish grills and a variety of meat and veg dishes, including local favourite *hortopita* (pie with wild greens and cheese).

Taverna Ta Delfinia
TAVERNA €

(mains €6-9; ⊘10am-late) The spot for local *mayirefta*.

AGIOS IOANNIS
ΑΓΙΟΣ ΙΩΑΝΝΗΣ
POP 660

Agios Ioannis is the busiest of the eastern coastal resorts, but there's still plenty of room. Small hotels, tavernas and pizzerias line the waterfront, and two sandy beaches are just a short walk north (Plaka) and south (Papa Nero).

🛏 Sleeping

Katerina's Apartments
APARTMENT €

(☑24260 31159, 6945762183; www.pilio-katerina. gr; d//tr/f from €45/55/85; ⊘Apr-Oct; ✳🛜) A narrow lane south of Papa Nero opens to a cosy courtyard anchored by a lemon and orange tree at this welcoming, family-run gem. Rooms are light, tidy and charming and have small kitchenettes.

Camping Papa Nero
CAMPGROUND €

(☑24260 31319; www.campingpapanero.com; camp sites per adult/tent/car €6/5/4; 🛜) Clean and shaded, 200m south of the waterfront.

★To Pelagos Studios
APARTMENT €€

(☑24260 31404; www.topelagos.gr; Papa Nero; d & tr €90; ⊘May-Oct) This stunning spot is out on its own in every league, sitting alone in front of Papa Nero beach, with standout features that include its light, breezy rooms with small kitchenettes. You need only enough energy to cover around 100m from the balcony, then down the stairs, over the green lawn, across the road and – plonk – into the water.

Hotel Kentrikon
HOTEL €€

(☑ 24260 31232; www.bungalows-kentrikon.gr; Agios Ioannis; s €80, d €100-180, ste €220, incl breakfast; P✳@☎) A reasonable choice with a strange mix of luxurious suites and some faded studio-style rooms.

Eating

Taverna Orea Ammoudia
TAVERNA €€

(Agios Ioannis; mains €8-15; ☺9am-late May-Sep; ☎) Spread out under lush foliage at the southern end of Papa Nero beach, this efficient family taverna does excellent oven-ready mains such as baked cod, chicken and potatoes, lamb grills and unusual salads such as *kritama* (tomatoes with sea herbs). An outdoor bar serves up cool drinks and ice cream in summer.

Taverna Akrogiali
SEAFOOD €€

(www.akrogialipelion.gr; mains €8.50-13, fish per 1kg €30-50; ☺noon-late May-Oct) A favourite of the Volos locals, who love its seafood dishes, including *rizi tou psara* (seafood risotto, or a Greek version of paella; €8.50). The owner says 'our food is honest' – think Greek produce (cooked by the matriarch, Elefteria, for over 40 years) and realistic prices.

Taverna Poseidonas
SEAFOOD €€

(www.poseidwnas.gr; mains €8-12, fish per 1kg €30-50; ☺noon-late) The owners are proud of their local reputation for serving only their own catch. In addition to the usual by-the-kilo offerings, you can sample oven-ready standbys.

DAMOUHARI & MOURESSI
ΝΤΑΜΟΥΧΑΡΗ & ΜΟΥΡΕΣΙ

Picturesque **Damouhari** is next to a rambling grove of olive trees bordering a pebble beach and protected cove that once shielded the hamlet from passing pirate ships. According to local lore, the village got its name from the expression *dos mou hari* (give me grace). Damouhari enjoyed brief fame from the 2008 movie *Mamma Mia!* (with Meryl Streep), which borrowed the secluded port for two weeks of filming. Damouhari is also the starting point for a beautiful 4km walk to Fakistra Beach.

Nestled off the main road, 3km north of Tsagarada, is the mellow village of Mouressi, known for its cherries, chestnuts and *mouries* (mulberries). There are great views of the Aegean from the lime-tree-shaded *plateia*.

Sights & Activities

Agios Nikolaos
CHURCH

(Damouhari) Don't miss (as it's a bit hidden) the gorgeous, but sadly crumbling, little church of Agios Nikolaos. The interiors are covered in fine frescoes by an unknown artist. See the folk at Ghermaniko or the sea-kayaking company at the entrance to the village for the key.

Sea Kayaking Damouchari
KAYAKING

(☑ 24260 49872; www.pelionsecrets.com; Damouhari; short/half-day/full-day tour €14/25/45) Since Damouhari is a small natural harbour it makes sense that this is the spot from which to launch kayaks and stand-up paddle (SUP) boards. Excellent guided trips range from short jaunts (a brief paddle in the vicinity) to half-day journeys (as far as Fakistra caves and beach). Or go the whole paddling hog to Mylopotamos, Limniounas and Lambinou.

SUP boards available for hire (hourly/half-day €10/35).

Sleeping & Eating

Old Silk Store
GUESTHOUSE €

(☑ 24260 49086, 6937156780; www.pelionet.gr; Mouressi; d from €50; ☺mid-Apr–mid-Oct) The rambling Old Silk Store is showing its age these days, but it's a 19th-century neoclassical gem with a personable owner, British transplant Jill Sleeman. There's a range of traditional-style rooms in an overgrown garden setting, with an available breakfast (€7.50) of homemade goodies. There's even a resident donkey, Boy George. Prices for singles on request.

Hotel Damouhari
HOTEL €€

(☑ 24260 49840; www.damouchari.gr; Damouhari; r from €60, apt €100; ☎✖) Hotel Damouhari is right on the beach and its range of unique stone rooms, which face a garden, are quaint, creaky and filled with quirky antiques and paraphernalia. The Kleopatra Miramar bar brims with nautical finds and is the spot for a post-beach drink.

Domatia Victoria
PENSION €€

(☑ 24260 49872; Damouhari; d/apt €60/90; ✳@) One of two very decent domatia in Damouhari (the owners are related). Has a cafe below and good views of the bay.

Taverna Karagatsi
TAVERNA €

(Damouhari; mains €7-9) Apostolis serves up fine taverna standards, plus big Greek salads and tasty mezedhes such as *taramasalata* (a thick purée of fish roe, potato, oil and lemon juice), all overlooking the tiny bay.

He'll talk about Meryl (Streep) as though she's his best client, which, judging by the faded photos on the wall, she may have been while filming at the port in the noughties.

Taverna To Tavernaki TAVERNA €
(Mouressi; mains €5.50-10) A long-standing spot, opposite the petrol station. Well regarded for *mayirefta*.

TSAGARADA ΤΣΑΓΚΑΡΑΔΑ
POP 530

Tsagarada (tsag-ah-*rah*-dah, sometimes written as Tsangarada) nestles in oak and plane forests. This rambling and spread-out village comprises the four separate communities of Agio Taxiarhes, Agios Stefanos, Agia Kyriaki and Agia Paraskevi, the largest of the group, just north of the main Volos–Milies–Tsagarada road. The plane tree in Agia Paraskevi's *plateia* is said to be one of the largest and oldest in Greece. There is an ATM next to the post office.

Hotels, domatia and tavernas dot rambling Tsagarada.

Sights

Serpentine Organic Garden GARDENS
(24260 49060; www.serpentin-garden.com; Taxiadhes; admission by donation) Serpentine Organic Garden is a one-woman labour of love, the inspiration of Doris, who, over 30 years, has created a virtual museum of all things green and flowering, including rare trees and roses, along with sustainable vegetable, berry and herb gardens. Opens to visitors by appointment only.

Sleeping & Eating

★**Lost Unicorn Hotel** HOTEL €€
(24260 49930, 6979795252; www.lostunicorn .com; Agia Paraskevi; s/d incl breakfast from €50/90; Apr-Oct; P✸@🕾) Lost Unicorn Hotel features Persian carpets, slow-swirling fans and antique-outfitted rooms in an elegant and well-appointed 19th-century mansion set in a beautiful glade. The Greek and English owners, Christos and Clare, make a breakfast worthy of the scenery, complete with singing nightingales.

In summer the patio and dining room morph into a restaurant dining room, where you can enjoy the international cuisine of Christos, a trained chef (mains €9 to €18).

Villa Ton Rodon GUESTHOUSE €€
(24260 49340; www.villatonrodon.gr; Agia Paraskevi; s/d/tr incl breakfast €35/60/65; P) This simple, unpretentious but comfortable pine-clad spot is surrounded by the friendly owners' garden. It's 50m down a small path off the main road (signed in Greek).

Aleka's House GUESTHOUSE €€
(24260 49380; www.alekas-house.gr; Tsagarada; d/tr incl breakfast €65/75; P✸🕾) Attractive Aleka's House is in a smart spot and is one of the few accommodation options in the region to open all year. It also has an upstairs cafeteria and lovely restaurant with fresh and local produce. It's worth going for the daily specials (mains €8 to €14).

Taverna To Agnanti TAVERNA €€
(Agio Taxiarches; mains €8-15) This atmospheric eatery cooks up the likes of pork leg and lamb, risotto with shrimps and spaghetti with octopus. Located in Plateia Taxiarhes, opposite the church and under the cover of the plaza's ancient plane tree.

MYLOPOTAMOS ΜΥΛΟΠΟΤΑΜΟΣ

Scenic Mylopotamos is divided by a rocky outcrop, with a natural tunnel connecting two small beautiful beaches. It's 7km along the road from Tsagarada's Agia Paraskevi.

Sleeping & Eating

★**Hotel Faros** HOTEL €€
(6946897965, 24260 49994; http://pelion.org/ faros; d €75-85; May-Oct) Faros means 'lighthouse' and this place is a shining beacon. For those who like seclusion (yet easy access by car to a coffee), this place, on a quiet spot on a cliff overlooking the Aegean Sea and surrounded by olive groves, is the spot. There are 17 simple and neat rooms, but it's all about the location. Breakfast €8.

Access is from Xourihti along a 2km sealed road and then 700m of dirt road, or via the 7km asphalted road from Tsagarada. From here you must walk for around 500m, across a bridge over a dry creek bed and then along a footpath to the hotel. Rates significantly lower outside high season.

Diakoumis Rooms GUESTHOUSE €€
(24260 49203; www.diakoumis.com; s/d/tr from €50/70/80, apt €90; P✸🕾) At Diakoumis Rooms, just 1km before the village and beach, genial owners Stathis and Athina have made the most of the dramatic cliffside setting. Light and airy stone-floored rooms

have clear views of the bay and beyond, as well as four self-catering apartments.

Taverna Angelika
TAVERNA €

(mains €8.50-13; ⊘ daily May-Oct, Sat & Sun in winter) Taverna Angelika is a regular stop for many Pelion residents who appreciate the casual atmosphere, good food (great seafood treats) and the breezy view over Mylopotamos beach.

West-Central Pelion
VOLOS TO PINAKATES, VYZITSA & MILIES

From Volos, the west-coast road heads south through the touristy villages of Agria and Ano Lehonia, where a branch road leads inland to Agios Vlasios, Pinakates, Vyzitsa and Milies, while the main road continues to neighbouring Kato Gatzea, Ano Gatzea and Kala Nera. After the tortuous and narrow roads of the eastern Pelion villages, this stretch of road is a blessing.

Museum of the Olive
MUSEUM

(www.mouseioelias.gr; Ano Gatzea; ⊘ 8am-5pm, or when train pulls in) FREE Set in an old stone mansion, this inviting little spot is dedicated to the olive. It has detailed displays of picking tools and ladders, presses and storage vessels, plus a small shop. Ano Gatzea is a stop on the To Trenaki train ride.

PINAKATES
ΠΙΝΑΚΑΤΕΣ
POP 211

An old plane tree anchors Plateia Agios Dimitrios, home to the church, two tavernas, a small fountain, ceramic shop and wood-oven bakery. Pristine Pinakates only acquired electricity in 1973 and, from the looks of it, things haven't gotten out of hand.

🛏 Sleeping & Eating

Hotel Ta Xelidonakia
HOTEL €€

(Little Swallows; ☎ 24230 86920, 6976215187; www.pinakates.com; d/tr incl breakfast €100/120; P @ 🛜 ⊠) This restored classic mansion balances history and comfort in grand fashion (read elaborate rooms). The verandah is anchored by a 3000L chestnut wine barrel.

Taverna Drosia
TAVERNA €

(mains €7-10; ⊘ noon-late) This eatery is an extension of a family house and serves Pelion favourites such as baked goat and spetzofaï, with good local wine always on hand. It's one of the few places open all year.

O Pileas
TAVERNA €

(mains €5.50-9) One of two tavernas in town, popular with locals for village fare.

VYZITSA
ΒΥΖΙΤΣΑ
POP 280

Handsome Vyzitsa's cobbled pathways wind between traditional (these days, upmarket) slate-roofed mansions. To reach its shady central square and tavernas, walk up the cobbled path beside Cafe Mpapaki (Baraki).

🛏 Sleeping & Eating

Mansion Karagiannopoulou
GUESTHOUSE €€

(☎ 24230 86717, 6945479570; www.karagiannopoulou.com; d €60-80, tr from €70, incl breakfast; 🛜) Built in 1791 with the extraordinary architecture of the region, this beautiful guesthouse ingeniously combines traditional and modern and boasts a range of stunning sitting rooms and bedrooms.

Hotel Stoikos
HOTEL €€

(☎ 24230 86406; www.hotelstoikos.gr; d/tr from €60/70; P ✳ 🛜) This well-managed place has a traditional look, especially with the beamed ceilings and stained glass of the spacious upper-floor rooms (great views).

★ Georgaras Restaurant
GREEK €

(www.georgarasvizitsa.gr; mains €8-12; ⊘ 9am-late May-Sep, 6pm-late weekends Oct-Apr) The pick of Vyzitsa's eateries, with a mountain menu featuring salads, stews and rich soups, along with stuffed pork with orange, and *kouneli stifadho*. It claims that clients say, 'If you visit Vyzitsa and you don't eat there, is as bad as visiting Athens for the first time and not seeing the Acropolis'. Big statement, but we like the experience.

🛍 Shopping

Esperides
FOOD

(⊘ 10am-2pm & 5-7pm Mon-Fri, 10am-7pm Sat & Sun) The place for edible souvenirs. It comprises a group of 13 women who handmake traditional jams, biscuits, baklava and other (very irresistible) sweet delights.

MILIES
ΜΗΛΙΕΣ
POP 640

Beautiful Milies (mih-lih-*ess*) has a ubiquitous shady square and a plethora of fountains. The village played a major role in the intellectual and cultural awakening that led to Greek independence. It was the birthplace of Anthimos Gazis (1761–1828), who organised revolutionary forces in Thessaly in 1821 and toured mountain villages of the Pelion inspiring local resistance and leadership.

Milies is also the start/end point for the Little Train. The walk down to the old station is very pretty and well worth doing (note: there are many steps).

◉ Sights

Agioi Taxiarhes
CHURCH

On the central square is Agioi Taxiarhes, a church with beautiful 18th-century frescoes. It's extraordinary for the 48 internal ceramic 'jars' that enhance acoustics, and for the unique frescoes, completed over 33 years by one monk.

Milies Museum
MUSEUM

(⊙ 10am-2.30pm & 6.30-9pm Wed-Sun 16 Jun-14 Sep, 10am-2pm Wed-Fri, 11am-3pm Sat & Sun 15 Sep-15 Jun) FREE The quaint Milies Museum houses a display of local crafts and costumes, along with the history of the area.

Library of Milies
LIBRARY

(⊙ 8am-2pm Mon-Sat) FREE The Library of Milies is home to an extraordinary display of 3000 books (of a collection of around 10,000) printed between 1498 and 1899.

🛏 Sleeping & Eating

Palios Stathmos & Restaurant
GUESTHOUSE €€

(Old Station; ☑ 24230 86425; www.paliosstathmos. com; s/d/f incl breakfast from €40/60/80) Nestled among a grove of plane trees, and built in 1903, Palios Stathmos is a comfortable pension that recalls a bygone era on the outside. Plain balconied rooms face the narrow-gauge railway station. The restaurant (mains €7 to €10) is open all day and serves up good Greek fare. It's a lovely spot to wait for the train.

Taverna Panorama
TAVERNA €

(mains €7.50-8; ⊙ lunch & dinner) This cosy grill serves up Pelion favourites such as spinach pie, pork chops in wine and *spetzofaï*. It's located about 200m north of the central square (and nearly covered in climbing roses).

Anna Na Ena Milo
CAFE €

(snacks €4-6; ⊙ 9am-late; 🤛) A cosy crêpe-and-jam cafe with a quirky interior of old posters and children's book covers (Anna Na Ena Milo is an old children's book). It's a wonderful spot to watch the world go by. Owners Nicoletta and Nicos make everything (the cheesecake is delicious).

Korbas Bakery
BAKERY €

(snacks €1.50-4) Head here for gastronomic highlights – try the scrumptious *tyropsomo* (cheese bread) and *eliopsomo* (olive bread). It's located on the main road.

South Pelion
SOUTH TO TRIKERI

The southern part of the Pelion has a wide-open feel to it, with sparsely forested hills, olive groves and lovely beaches. Before heading inland after Kala Nera, the road skirts the little coastal fishing village of Afissos, winds up to the attractive farming community of Argalasti and then forks – the left fork continues inland, the right goes to the

---

WORTH A TRIP

THE LITTLE TRAIN

Even if you have a car, it's well worth the effort to coordinate a ride on the quaint **To Trenaki** (The Little Train; ☑ 24210 39723; www.trainose.gr; 1 way adult/child €10/6, return €18/10; ⊙ daily Aug & Sep, Sat & Sun Apr-Jul & Oct). In 1895 a 13km narrow-gauge railway line was built between Volos and Ano Lehonia and, by 1903, to Milies, making the town a prosperous centre of commerce. To Trenaki, the steam train that used to chug along this route, retired formally in 1971, but was revived in 1997 as a tourist attraction.

A restored Belgian coal-burning locomotive pulled the train when the route first re-opened. But in 2000 a new diesel engine went into service after the train operators grew tired of following the smoke-belching original with a water tanker to put out the frequent grass fires started by airborne sparks. Despite the environmental upgrade, To Trenaki is still called Moudzouris, an affectionate term meaning 'the smudger'.

The popular four-carriage train leaves Ano Lehonia at 10am and returns around 3pm, leaving you time to stroll around Milies. Check schedules and departure times as these change annually.

coastal resorts of Horto and Milina. From Milina the road branches southeast towards Platanias and southwest to Trikeri.

There is an end-of-the-world feel about this part of the Pelion, as the road from Milina to Trikeri becomes more and more desolate. Residents pride themselves on their tradition as seafarers, fighters against the Turks in the War of Independence and upholders of traditional customs and dress.

HORTO & MILINA   XOPTO & MHΛINA

Milina is the larger of these two coastal villages and sees many package tourists. Both are on a quiet part of the peninsula with pristine water and a few inviting pebble beaches.

◉ Sights & Activities

Old Radio Museum   MUSEUM
(☑ 6970374922; Lafkos; ☺ daily 16 May-14 Sep, Sat & Sun 15 Sep-15 May) FREE If you're one of those people who think nostalgia isn't what it used to be, turn your dial to this spot, in the village of Lafkos, 5km east of Milina, to check out one collector's pre-digital love affair with the original wireless. Hours can be unpredictable.

🛌 Sleeping & Eating

Hotel Nicolas   GUESTHOUSE €€
(☑ English 6932689782, German & Greek 24230 65296; www.nicolaspelion.gr; Horto; d/tr €40/45; ☺ May-Oct; 🛜) Okay, so the rooms are of the no-frills variety, but once you meet friendly Nicolas himself, and look out of the window (if you're lucky enough to have a front-facing room) to the turquoise water below, you'll think you're in budget paradise. A case of coming here for the lovely hosts and the location. German spoken.

Gibraltar   TAVERNA €
(www.gibraltar-restaurant.gr; Milina; mains €8-11; ☺ lunch & dinner) Started by the owners' grandparents in the 1950s, this place continues the tradition of delivering their 'secret': 'only local fish and meat, a lot of artistry... and good wine and *tsipouro* from our vineyard'. Originally aimed at feeding the region's shipbuilders, these days visitors and locals enjoy the fine Greek *fagito* (food). It's located 1.5km south of Milina.

ⓘ Information

Milina Holidays (☑ 24230 65020; www.milina-holidays.com; ☺ 9am-2.30pm & 6-9pm May-Oct) Resourceful George Fleris of Milina Holidays, on the waterfront, can help with accommodation, as well as arranging bike hire and day cruises to nearby Palio Trikeri (adult/child €25/15).

AGIA KYRIAKI   AΓIA KYPIAKH

This is the last stop on the Pelion Peninsula, a steep 2km drive off the main road, or a quick 1km walk down a cobblestone path. This fishing village sees few tourists and the bright, orange-coloured boats are put to good use by a hard-working population of around 200.

🛌 Sleeping & Eating

Agia Kyriaki Guesthouse   GUESTHOUSE €
(☑ 6978771831, 24230 91112; http://agiakyriaki.gr; s/d incl breakfast €35/50; ☺ May-Sep) Just what you need for a quaint stay in a quaint spot, this top guesthouse has a stunning setting just behind the main strip, plus clean doubles and a friendly owner.

O Manolas   GREEK €
(mains €7-10, seafood per 1kg €45-70; ☺ 8am-late 15 Mar-28 Oct, weekends all year) Of Agia Kyriaki's three fish tavernas in a row, all facing the opposite shores of Evia, we love this one for the uber-personality, Manolas, plus the lobster and spaghetti (among other fresh-fish delicacies).

PALIO TRIKERI   ΠΑΛΙΟ TPIKEPI

If you really must go that one step further to get away from it all, then head for this little island, just off the coast, with a year-round population of 15 – it's often called I Nisos (The Island) for short. To reach I Nisos from the fishing village of **Alogoporos**, you need to take a taxi for the five-minute boat ride (around €2 per person). Several water-taxi signs are on the beach. Alternatively, telephone Nikos at **Taverna Diavlos** (☑ 6976851056) on the island. There are a couple of basic domatia at the taverna. The main activities on Palio Trikeri are explaining to locals why you're there, and then explaining to yourself why you're leaving.

PLATANIAS   ΠΛΑΤΑΝΙΑΣ

Platanias' (plah-tah-nih-*ahs*) natural harbour was used as a base by the Persians. More recently, it was a popular resort, until the hydrofoil service stopped in 2001. Since then, it's returned to its low-key roots. There's a good sand-and-pebble beach, a camping ground and a few tavernas and domatia. Pretty **Mikro Beach** is a 10-minute walk away.

🏃 Activities

Africana   BOAT TOUR
(☑6973496818, 6939848464; www.africana-cruis es.gr; adult/child €25/12.50) From roughly early June through to the end of August, this excursion boat makes runs (if there are people) between Platanias and the island of Skiathos. The 100-passenger boat departs Platanias at 9.30am and returns at 5.30pm.

🍽 Sleeping & Eating

Hotel des Roses   HOTEL €
(☑24230 71268; www.peliondesroses.gr; Platanias; d/tr inc breakfast €50/55) Platanias' first-ever hotel, and one that put the small resort on the map. This pretty hotel, the entrance of which is framed by rose bushes, offers a no-nonsense, clean experience. Appropriately, owner Nikos also makes soaps, and you can learn the art at an on-site class.

You can also head off on an eco-tour and learn about everything from herbs to the Pelion's night sky (€12 per person, minimum four).

Olive Store Cottage   GUESTHOUSE €€
(☑6945575360; www.holidaylettings.co.uk/ rentals/pelion/347420; cottage for 2 €100) To prolong the extraordinary end-of-the-earth feeling, head 4km north of Platanias for this beautiful self-catering cottage run by two enthusiastic expats and keen walkers.

Taverna Ondas   GREEK €€
(Promyri; mains €6-10; ☺lunch & dinner) Eight kilometres northeast of Platanias, in the mountain-top village of Promyri, is this quaint, family-run taverna on a square. The owners are real hunter-gatherers so the products are simple, but as fresh as can be. Forget the menu, just ask them to recommend whatever is going. You're guaranteed something hearty and tasty.

Alternatively, you can gather with the locals for an evening drink and mezedes.

Trikala   Τρίκαλα

POP 81,400
Roughly halfway between Karditsa and Kalambaka is Trikala (*tree-kah-lah*), an attractive and bustling agricultural centre. The first thing you might notice about the town are the bicycles. Many souls, young and old, pedal around on their treadlies. Trikala was once ancient Trikki, and home to Asclepius, the god of healing. A statue honouring the mythic doctor stands on a small bridge by the main square.

👁 Sights

Fortress of Trikala   FORT
It's worth a wander up to the gardens surrounding the restored Byzantine fort. An adjacent cafe-bar overlooks the town. Walk 400m up Sarafi from the central square and look for the sign pointing right.

Sanctuary of Asclepius   RUIN
Asclepius' sanctuary ruins are located before the turn to the Fortress of Trikala.

Varousi   AREA
The old Turkish quarter of Varousi, just east of the fortress, is a fascinating area of narrow streets and fine old houses with overhanging balconies. At the corner of Anagiron and Virvou, peek at the fine murals within the 16th-century church of **Agioi Anargiri**. Another 200m up the hill from Varousi is the **Chapel of Profitis Ilias**.

Koursoun Tzami   MOSQUE
(☺8am-2pm Mon-Fri) The Koursoun Tzami was built in the 16th century by Sinan Pasha, the same architect who built the Blue Mosque in İstanbul. The mosque was restored in the mid-1990s with EU funding. From the bus station head south and follow the river for 300m.

🍽 Sleeping

Hostel Meteora   HOSTEL €
(☑6975949554; www.hostelmeteora.com; Tiouson 51 & Papagou; dm €13) The jury is still out on this hostel, given that it's a recent addition, if a welcome one, to the accommodation scene. Some travellers report that it's a bit on the noisy side but, as one of the cheapest sleeps around, let's not be too harsh. The pluses are a friendly owner and central location. Can also arrange tours.

Hotel Panellinion   HOTEL €€
(www.hotelpanellinion.com; Plateia Riga Fereou; s €45-50, d €60, incl breakfast; ✴🛜) Dating from 1914, this restored and spacious neoclassical hotel is filled with traditional memorabilia, including old telephones and beautiful rugs. It's just opposite the river.

Eating

Trikala's cafe life is centred on the northern end of Asklipiou and across the river in the old Manavika district. Ypsilanti is flanked by tavernas and *tsipouradhika*.

Kebab Karthoutsos
KEBAB €

(Ioulietas Adam 5; mains €3-7; ⊙7pm-late) With over 35 years standing, this is the place for grills, including great pork kebab (served on paper), *horta*, feta and local wine, all for around €10 per head.

Taverna Katogi
GREEK €€

(Kariskaki 58 & Ypsilantou; mains €8-15; ⊙12.30pm-late) A smart place, with wooden interiors and beams, that attracts a range of clientele, from businessfolk to families. All want what this spot does best: grills. There's roast pork, chicken, lamb and *loukaniko*, a village sausage comprising leek and fat. Lots of it. Bring it on.

Drinking & Nightlife

On weekend nights, the idea in Trikala seems to be to tank up on coffee along Asklipiou until midnight, then cross the bridge to the humming Manavika district for mojitos, mezedhes and music. This three-block maze of narrow passageways and outdoor tables jumps with lamp-lit music bars, small *ouzeries* and all-night cafes.

Information

Banks with ATMs ring the squares on either side of the river. Most cafes around Plateia Riga Fereou offer free wi-fi.

Neos Kosmos Internet Cafe (Vyronos 20; ⊙8am-late; 🛜) Has wi-fi and several fast computers. All for the price of a drink or two.

Police station (📞24310 63013; cnr Yiannitson & Farmaki)

Post office (Sarafi 13) Next to Plateia Riga Fereou.

ℹ Getting There & Away

BUS

Buses depart from Trikala's **KTEL bus station** (📞24310 73130; Rizargio; ⊙6.30am-10.30pm), 4km south of town. A shuttle (€0.60) runs from the **ticket office** (cnr Othonos & Garivaldi) in town.

DESTINATION	TIME	FARE	FREQUENCY
Athens	4½hr	€28	7 daily
Elati	1hr	€3.60	1-2 daily
Ioannina	2½hr	€14.60	2 daily
Kalambaka	30min	€2.30	hourly
Lamia	2hr	€11.80	7 daily
Larissa	1hr	€6.30	hourly
Thessaloniki	3hr	€18.70	5 daily
Volos	2¼hr	€13.70	4 daily

WORTH A TRIP

CIRCUITS FROM KALAMBAKA, KASTRAKI & TRIKALA

About 18km southwest of Trikala is the village of **Pyli** ('gate' in Greek), opening to a spectacular gorge and one of Greece's more inviting wilderness areas in the southern Pindos Range. It is home to the stunning little 13th-century **Church of Porta Panagia**. To reach it, cross the bridge from Pyli and follow the signs to the left. On arrival, ask at the taverna opposite for the elderly man with the keys, if he hasn't already run out to greet you. Five kilometres from Pyli is the **Moni Agiou Vissarion**, a 16th-century monastery that stands on a slope of Mt Koziakas. Only men are permitted to enter. To get here, cross the bridge over the river, take the first turn left (annoyingly the sign, in Greek, is 20m after the left turn so don't except a clear indicator). From here, you must wind your way up the hill for another 4.2km.

From Pyli, you can do two driving routes. The first is a half-day circuit around each side of the gorge. The route goes via **Elati,** a mountain-top village and something of a hill station for Trikali. Elati was called Tierna before the Germans burned it to the ground for harbouring Greek Resistance fighters in WWII. After Elati you then head around the gorge in an anticlockwise direction. The second circuit heads from Pyli all the way to Kalambaka, a route that climbs steadily through breathtaking alpine scenery, passing Elati with an optional detour via the smaller alpine outposts of **Neraidochori** and **Pertouli** (also a ski centre). Back on the main road, continue to head north, passing several mountain villages, before coming out at Kalambaka. Allow a leisurely day.

Both routes are on snake-like roads, but make enjoyable circuits from Kalambaka, Kastraki or Trikala.

THE METEORA: GEOLOGY OF A ROCK FOREST

The jutting pinnacles and cliffs of the Meteora were once sediments of an inland sea. About 10 million years ago, vertical tectonic movements pushed the entire region out of the sea at a sloping angle. The same tectonic movements caused the flanking mountains to move closer, exerting extreme pressure on the hardened sedimentary deposits. The Meteora developed netlike fissures and cracks. The weathering and erosion that followed formed the towering outcrops of rock that now vault heavenwards. The rocks were conglomerates of many types: limestone, marble, serpentinite and metamorphic, interspersed with layers of sand and shale.

By the dawn of human civilisation, the rocks had weathered and eroded into fantastic shapes – the sandstone and shale washed away, isolating blocks of rock and cliffs. Where erosion was less extreme, caves and overhangs appeared in the rock face.

As early as the 11th century AD, these awesome natural caves had become the solitary abodes of hermit monks. Eventually, 24 monasteries were built on these pinnacles. Today, six are active religious sites, occupied by monks or nuns and visited by the faithful and curious alike.

TRAIN

From Trikala **train station** (☎24310 27529; www.trainose.gr; ⊗5am-9pm) there are trains to Kalambaka (€1.80, 15 minutes, five daily), Larissa (€5.80, one hour, two daily), Athens (Intercity €17.80, four hours, two daily) and Thessaloniki (€14.10, three hours, one daily).

Meteora   Μετέωρα

The World Heritage–listed Meteora (meh-teh-o-rah) is an extraordinary place and one of the most visited in all of Greece. The massive pinnacles of smooth rock are ancient and yet could be the setting for a futuristic science-fiction tale. The monasteries atop them add to the strange and beautiful landscape.

Each monastery is built around a central courtyard surrounded by monks' cells, chapels and a refectory. In the centre of each courtyard is the *katholikon*.

The geological heart of Meteora is considered the **Adhrakhti** (obelisk), a striking column visible from anywhere in Kastraki. Nearby, on the east-facing side of the Pixari rock face, closer to Kastraki, look for the cave chapel of **Agios Andonios**.

To the left of the chapel, in the hollows and cavities of the rock face, are the Askitaria (cave hermitages), complete with hanging ladders and nesting doves. The Askitaria were occupied until the early 20th century by solitary monks, and they remain a testament to the original spirit of Meteora.

History

The name Meteora derives from the Greek adjective *meteoros,* which means 'suspended in the air' (the word 'meteor' is from the same root).

From the 11th century, hermit monks lived in the scattered caverns of Meteora. By the 14th century, the Byzantine power of the Roman Empire was on the wane and Turkish incursions into Greece were on the rise, so monks began to seek safe havens away from the bloodshed. The inaccessibility of the rocks of Meteora made them an ideal retreat.

The earliest monasteries were reached by climbing removable ladders. Later, windlasses were used so monks could be hauled up in nets. A story goes that when curious visitors asked how frequently the ropes were replaced, the monks' stock reply was 'when the Lord lets them break'.

These days, access to the monasteries is by steps that were hewn into the rocks in the 1920s and by a convenient access road.

◉ Sights

Before setting out to the area's monasteries, decide on a route. If you start early, you can see several, if not all, *mones* (monasteries) in one day.

The main sealed road surrounding the entire Meteora complex of rocks and monasteries is about 15km in length, and with your own transport, you can visit them all should you wish.

For those without a car, a bus (€1.20, 20 minutes) departs from Kalambaka and

Kastraki at 9am and returns at 1pm (12.40pm on weekends). That's enough time to explore three monasteries – Moni Megalou Meteorou, Moni Varlaam and Moni Agias Varvaras Rousanou. Perhaps the best route is to take the bus one way to the top and then work your way down and around on foot, finishing at either Moni Agiou Nikolaou on the Kastraki side, or at Moni Agios Triados on the Kalambaka side.

Keen walkers should definitely explore the area on foot on the old and once-secret *monopatia* (monk paths).

Moni Agiou Nikolaou
MONASTERY

(Monastery of St Nikolaou Anapafsa; admission €3; ⊘9am-3.30pm Sat-Thu Nov-Mar, to 2pm Apr-Oct) Moni Agiou Nikolaou is the nearest *moni* to Kastraki, just 2km from the village square to the steep steps leading to the *moni*. Many people bypass this, but they shouldn't. The monastery was built in the 15th century and the exceptional frescoes in its *katholikon* were painted by the monk Theophanes Strelizas from Crete. Especially beautiful is the 1527 fresco *The Naming of Animals by Adam in Paradise*.

Meteora, Kastraki & Kalambaka

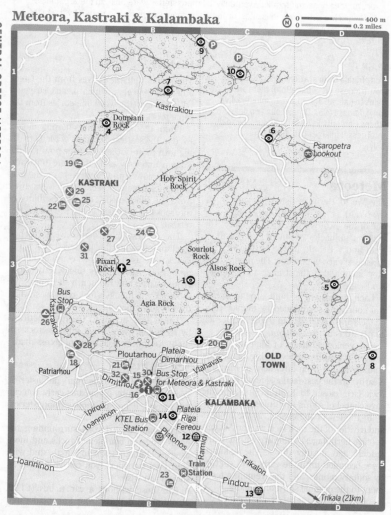

Moni Megalou Meteorou MONASTERY

(Grand Meteoron; admission €3; ⊙ 9am-5pm Wed-Mon Apr-Oct, to 4pm Thu-Mon Nov-Mar) The best known of the Meteora monasteries, Moni Megalou Meteorou is an imposing form built on the highest rock in the valley, 613m above sea level. Founded by St Athanasios in the 14th century, it became the richest and most powerful monastery thanks to the Serbian emperor Symeon Uros, who turned all his wealth over to the monastery and became a monk. Its *katholikon* has a magnificent 12-sided central dome.

Its striking series of frescoes, entitled *Martyrdom of Saints*, depicts the graphic persecution of Christians by the Romans.

Moni Varlaam MONASTERY

(admission €3; ⊙ 9am-4pm Sat-Thu Apr-Oct, 9am-3pm Sat-Wed Nov-Mar) About 700m down from Moni Megalou, Moni Varlaam has a small museum, an original rope-basket (until the 1930s, the method for hauling up provisions and monks) and fine late-Byzantine frescoes by Frangos Kastellanos. The mural *The Blessed Sisois at the Tomb of Alexander the Great* shows the great conqueror as a humble skeleton. Look just above the door, past the candles.

For a panoramic break, visit the rambling **Psaropetra lookout**, 300m east of the signposted fork northeast of Moni Varlaam.

Moni Agias Varvaras Rousanou MONASTERY

(admission €3; ⊙ 9am-6pm Thu-Tue Apr-Oct, to 2pm Nov-Mar) Access to Moni Agias Varvaras Rousanou is via a small wooden bridge. The beautiful coloured-glass-illuminated *katholikon* is the highlight here, with superb frescoes of the *Resurrection* (on your left as you enter) and *Transfiguration* (on your right). The imposing steep structure of Rousanou is itself a stunning accomplishment and is today home to an order of around 15 nuns. If you're here near closing, listen for the call to vespers.

Moni Agias Triados MONASTERY

(Holy Trinity; admission €3; ⊙ 9am-5pm Fri-Wed Apr-Oct, 9am-3pm Sat-Wed Nov-Mar) Of all the monasteries at Meteora, Moni Agias Triados has the most remote feel, plus the longest approach. It was featured in the 1981 James Bond film *For Your Eyes Only*. The views here are extraordinary, and the small 17th-century *katholikon* is beautiful, in particular the *Judgement of Pilate* and the *Hospitality of Abraham*. A well-marked 1km *monopati* (pathway) leads back to Kalambaka.

Moni Agiou Stefanou MONASTERY

(admission €3; ⊙ 9am-1.30pm & 3.30-5.30pm Tue-Sun Apr-Oct, 9.30am-1pm & 3-5pm Tue-Sun Nov-Mar) Moni Agiou Stefanou was built in 1798 and is dedicated to St Charalambos. In recent years Greek hagiographer Vlassios Tsotsonis has been repainting the *katholikon* (depicting the life of Christ) with beautiful results. Efficient nuns do a thriving trade selling religious souvenirs. The monastery is at the very end of the road, 1.5km beyond Agias Triados.

CENTRAL GREECE METEORA

Meteora, Kastraki & Kalambaka

VISITING THE MONASTERIES

Entry to each monastery is €3 and dress codes apply: no bare shoulders are allowed, men must wear trousers and women must wear skirts below the knee (wraparound skirts are generally provided at the entrances). Before planning your route, double-check days and opening hours. Between November and March a couple might be closed for two days, not one. The following is a list of closures as at the time of research.

➡ **Moni Agiou Nikolaou** Closed Friday

➡ **Moni Megalou Meteorou** Closed Tuesday

➡ **Moni Varlaam** Closed Friday

➡ **Moni Agias Varvaras Roussanou** Closed Wednesday

➡ **Moni Agias Triados** Closed Thursday

➡ **Moni Agiou Stefanou** Closed Monday

🏃 Activities

Walking

Keen walkers will be in their element exploring several days' worth of *monopatia* that thread through the region.

Lovely walks head along the path above Alsos House to the monasteries of **Agia Triada** and **Agios Stefanos**. Once at the top, from the side of **Valaam**, you can head back into Kastraki.

To head further off piste to some 'secret' locations, Visit Meteora offers some fabulous half-day walks (from €30 per person), or an adrenaline-pumping hiking and scrambling tour (€50 per person).

Good maps outline routes. An excellent booklet, *The Footpaths of Meteora* by Andonis Kalogirou (Kritiki Publishers), is available from the no-name souvenir shop at Patriachou Dimitriou 1, Kalambaka. Several maps are available, including Orama Editions' 1:8000 *Meteora*.

Rock Climbing

The area is a rock-climbers' mecca, and people from around the world head here to tackle these extraordinary peaks and towers. Beginners, too, can have a go at some of the smaller rocks, such as Doupiani Rock. Visit Meteora offers some excellent opportunities with professional guides Lazaros Botelis and Kostas Liolios.

🧭 Tours

Visit Meteora TOUR
(📞 24320 23820; www.visitmeteora.travel; Patriarchou Dimitriou 2, Kalambaka; ⏰ 9am-9pm) Most of Meteora's tours and guided activities are run through this crew. Guides are professional and experienced. Guided activities-cum-tours include walking; rock climbing, including for beginners (from €60 per person, three hours); horse riding (€50, three hours); canyoning (€110, five hours); and rafting (from €95).

The same team also offers good-value tours around Meteora (€30 per person, including pick-up from your accommodation). Its sunset tour (€35 per person) is a highlight, especially for keen photographers who want to capture the monasteries in their best light. Some activities and tours require a minimum of two people. Its website gives a clear listing with details.

ℹ️ Getting Around

BICYCLE

Hobby Shop (www.meteora-bike-rentals.gr; Patriarhou Dimitriou 28; per day bike €8, motorcycle €18-20; ⏰ 8am-9pm Mon-Sat, to 2pm Sun) Efficient service for bicycle and motorcycle hire.

BUS

Every two hours, buses for Kastraki (€1) leave from beside the Plateia Dimarhiou fountain. Four daily Meteora-bound buses (one way/return/day €1.60/3/5) depart from the KTEL station (also picking tourists up at the fountain and bus stops en route) between May and September. Ask at the KTEL office or Visit Meteora office for the schedule.

TAXI

Taxi stations are at each of the town's four squares. Taxis go to Kastraki (€4) and all the monasteries (for example, Moni Megalou Meteorou for around €10). Some drivers speak English, German or Italian, and you can arrange a taxi tour from about €20 per hour.

Kalambaka   Καλαμπακά

POP 9000

Kalambaka is the gateway to Meteora. It's almost entirely modern, having been burned to the ground by the Nazis in WWII. It takes at least a day to see all of the monasteries of Meteora, so you'll need to spend the night either in Kalambaka or the village of Kastraki (p226).

◉ Sights

As well as the rocks, Kalambaka boasts some new museums, which provide an alternative to the monasteries. A bustling **market** takes place every Friday.

Church of the Assumption of the Virgin Mary   CHURCH

(admission €2; ☺8am-1pm & 3-8.30pm) It's worth finding your way to this 7th-century Byzantine cathedral, a three-aisle basilica with superb frescoes dating to the 14th century. (Note: don't be confused with the church in the centre.) At 6.30pm you can hear the vespers.

Museum of Hellenic Culture   MUSEUM

(www.kivep.com; M Alexandros & Chatzipetrou; ☺9am-9pm) A passionate local collector has amassed a collection of over 10,000 items related to Greek education since 1830, plus historic books. This is no dull exhibit, but a delightfully colourful journey through the world of literature, from *Aesop's Fables* to a 1567 Homer text, student's writing implements to a re-creation of a minotaur's labyrinth (still being constructed at time of research).

Museum of Natural History   MUSEUM

(www.meteoramuseum.gr; Pildou 20; adult/child €5/4; ☺10am-8pm winter, to 10pm summer) To give the kids a nature-based break from the Meteora monasteries, this new educative museum with a quirky collection of stuffed animals from around the globe might appeal. If taxidermy isn't your thing, head upstairs to view the extraordinary collection of copies of all Greek mushroom species (over 350).

Theopetra Cave   CAVE

(admission €3; ☺8am-3pm Tue-Sun) For over 130,000 years humans inhabited this cave, a 500-sq-metre chamber, 7km southeast of Kalambaka. A boardwalk ensures an easy circuit around the site and clear descriptions explain the remarkable cave history. Elements of the cave indicate the evolution from Neanderthals to Homo sapiens and, later still, the transition from hunter-gatherers to farmers. Incredibly, a 23,000-year-old stone wall in front of the cave is believed to be one of the oldest-known human-made structures in the world.

You can visit on your own, or on a tour with Visit Meteora.

⌕ Sleeping

Rooms are plentiful in Kalambaka, though it's best to avoid noisy Trikalon.

★ Alsos House   PENSION €

(☏24320 24097; www.alsoshouse.gr; Kanari 5; s/d/tr incl breakfast €35/45/65, f incl breakfast €75-80, apt €80-100; P❋@☎) The well-managed Alsos House has a communal kitchen, laundry service and great views of the rocks from the massive terrace and rooms. It's 500m from the centre and a stone's throw from wonderful walking paths. Welcoming and delightful multilingual owner Yiannis Karakantas wants the best for his guests; he knows as much about Meteora as the monks do about prayers.

The new sleek apartments in the same complex are particularly appealing.

Guest House Elena   BOUTIQUE HOTEL €

(☏24320 77789, 6976562529; www.elenaguesthouse.gr; Kanari 3; s/d/tr incl breakfast from €40/50/70, ste €100; P❋☎) Period furnishings in lovely rooms with an intimate atmosphere; multilingual owner.

Hotel Meteora   PENSION €

(☏24320 22367; www.hotel-meteora.com; Ploutarhou 14; s/d/tr incl breakfast €30/40/50; P❋☎) On a quiet cul-de-sac below the rocks, this is a reliable budget option, with great breakfasts using home-grown produce. Guests have use of a swimming pool at a relative's large hotel.

Monastiri Guest House   BOUTIQUE HOTEL €€

(☏24320 23952; www.monastiri-guesthouse.gr; Agios Kostantinos Elenis; s/d/tr/ste incl breakfast €50/65/90/140; P❋☎) Behind the railway station, this converted stone mansion has colourful decorations, long poster-beds and light and airy bathrooms. The handsome wood-and-stone lobby sports a fireplace and bar.

✗ Eating

The restaurant scene won't blow your culinary mind. Most are tavernas that serve up hearty dishes of *mayirefta*.

Taverna To Paramithi TAVERNA €
(Patriarhou Dimitriou 14; mains €5.50-9; ⊙lunch & dinner Mar-Dec) Along with very good grills and fresh pasta served in a convivial environment, owner-cooks Makis and Eleni bring in fresh seafood daily and cook up good classic dishes. Local musicians often end the night here, with guitar or bouzouki in hand (and possibly a glass of the tasty house wine or some homemade *tsipouro*).

Taverna Panellinion TAVERNA €
(☑ 24320 24735; Plateia Dimarhiou; mains €6.50-11) Opposite the fountain and filled with antique bric-a-brac, the popular Panellinion serves good mezedhes, such as roasted feta, and fine versions of traditional dishes such as *pastitsio* (macaroni and meat bake) and chicken in lemon sauce. It's open all year.

Panorama GREEK €€
(www.meteoronpanorama.gr; mains €8-12; ⊙lunch & dinner) It's a large place (which is a bit overwhelming if you're eating alone), but true to its name, it offers beautiful vistas. The cuisine is excellent, especially the grills. The lamb in paper is worth trying.

ℹ Information

Banks with ATMs surround the central Plateia Riga Fereou on Trikalon. There is also a currency-exchange window next to the post office on Pindou.

Health Care Centre (☑ 24320 22222) At the western entrance to town.

Post office (Trikalon 24)

Tourist police (☑ 24320 76100; cnr Ipirou & Pindou)

Visit Meteora (☑ 24320 23820; www.visit meteora.travel; Patriarchou Dimitriou 2; ⊙9am-9pm; ☎) Run by a young crowd, this private tourist office is *the* information hub for the region. It provides maps, information on opening hours and coordinates most of the area's guided tours, transport and activities (climbing, hiking, walking).

ℹ Getting There & Away

BUS

Kalambaka's **KTEL bus station** (☑ 24320 22432; www.ktel-trikala.gr; Ikonomou) is 50m down from the main square and fountain, and is the arrival/departure point for regular Trikala bus connections. For Delphi, travellers should go via Trikala (not Larissa). The trip requires three bus changes. Take the 8am bus from Kalambaka. In Trikala change to the 9am Athens bus but alight in Lamia. From Lamia, take the 11am bus to Amfissa. From Amfissa, there are regular buses to Delphi. The thrice-weekly Trikala–Patras bus also goes near Delphi, but you may have to walk a couple of kilometres, so check first.

DESTINATION	TIME	FARE	FREQUENCY
Athens	5hr	€29	7 daily
Ioannina	2½hr	€12.50	2 daily
Lamia	2hr	€14.10	7 daily (change in Trikala)
Thessaloniki	3½hr	€20	5 daily
Trikala	30min	€2.30	hourly
Volos	2½hr	€16	4 daily (change in Trikala)

TRAIN

Trains depart from the Kalambaka **train station** (☑ 24320 22451; www.trainose.gr). For trains to Athens and Thessaloniki you may need to change at Paleofarsalos. For Volos you must change at Larissa.

DESTINATION	TIME	FARE	FREQUENCY
Athens (normal)	5½hr	€18.30	1 daily
Athens (Intercity)	5hr	€18.30	1 daily
Thessaloniki	3-4½hr	€15.20-25.10	3 daily
Volos (via Larissa)	2hr	€9.40	1 daily

Kastraki Καστράκι

POP 1600

Kastraki is less than 2km from Kalambaka, but its location right under the rocks gives it an other-worldly feel. For those after a more peaceful sleep, Kastraki is a good bet.

🛏 Sleeping

Rooms Ziogas Vasiliki PENSION €
(☑ 24320 24037; www.ziogasrooms.com; s/d/tr from €25/35/40; ▣❄☎) This friendly budget option is clean and airy and there are great views from several rooms facing the rocks. Breakfast costs €5.

Vrachos Camping
CAMPGROUND €

(☑24320 22293; www.campingmeteora.gr; camp sites per tent €8; ☺Mar-Oct; 🛜🏊) A well-shaded camping ground on the Kalamba-ka–Kastraki road with excellent facilities, including barbecue and spotless bathrooms. Also cooks up a great grill in its casual taverna (open to the public; mains €6 to €9.50).

★Doupiani House
PENSION €€

(☑24320 75326; www.doupianihouse.com; s/d/tr incl breakfast from €50/60/75; 🅿🕸@🛜) The delightful Doupiani House has the lot: spotless, tastefully decorated rooms, with balconies or garden access. Its location – just outside the village – provides a window to Meteora, boasting one of the region's best panoramic views. There's breakfast on the terrace, birdsong and attentive hosts, Toula and Thanasis.

Hotel Tsikeli
HOTEL €€

(☑24320 22438; www.tsikelihotel.gr; s €35, d €60-70, incl breakfast; 🅿🕸🛜) Tsikeli has had a makeover so has sparkling modern bathrooms to complement its otherwise pleasant and simple rooms. Large balconies and a lovely grassy front garden.

Dellas Boutique Hotel
BOUTIQUE HOTEL €€

(☑24320 78260; www.dellasboutiquehotel.com; s €55, d €65-100, tr €90-100, incl breakfast; ☺Apr-Oct) While it doesn't boast a wide-angled panoramic view, this handsome place between Kastraki and Kalambaka receives accolades for its elegant, tidy rooms and high service standards. Prices vary according to the views.

Pyrgos Adrachti
BOUTIQUE HOTEL €€

(☑24320 22275; www.hotel-adrachti.gr; d €56-78, tr €83; 🅿🕸🛜) Slick and cool sums up this place – think designer-style touches throughout the rooms, bar and common areas, and an up-close-and-personal rock experience. Plus there's a tidy garden to relax in post-activities. It's at the northern end of the village, nestled under the rocks; follow the signs.

✖ Eating

Batalogianni
TAVERNA €

(www.batalogianni.com; mains €7-12; ☺8am-late) You know the type of place you wouldn't look twice at 'cos it's slightly off the road and you don't realise it has an oasis of a garden terrace and serves up delicious 100% home-made *mayirefta*? This charming little spot is all that. Open all year.

Taverna Paradisos
TAVERNA €

(mains €6.50-9; ☺noon-4pm & 6pm-late) The traditional meals at roomy Paradisos will have you exclaiming '*nostimo!*' (delicious!) all the way through your dishes, thanks to local and high-quality ingredients and owner-chef Koula's magic touch. Excellent fried zucchini.

Taverna Meteora Vavitsas
TAVERNA €€

(mains €8.50-12; ☺lunch & dinner) Opposite Hotel Kastraki, this popular meat-and-more-meat taverna is set back in a leafy brick terrace.

❶ Information

All Time Café (per hour €2; ☺8am-midnight) Kastraki's only internet place, on the main road opposite Taverna Paradisos.

Northern Greece

Includes ➜

Why Go?

Immense northern Greece (βόρεια Ελλάδα) stretches across more cultures and terrains than any other region in the country. Mighty civilisations, including Macedonians, Thracians, Romans, Byzantines, Slavs and Turks, have left traces here. You'll find beaches to rival the islands, especially in popular Halkidiki and around Parga, along the golden Ionian coast. Ruins such as Ancient Dion and the Byzantine castles in Kavala and Platamonas fire the imagination. Discover the mountains of Epirus, ripe for hiking and winter sports, and Macedonia's serene lakes. Within this rich tapestry is Greece's second city, Thessaloniki, teeming with inventive nightlife and festivals. The terrain stretches into the plains and woodlands of Thrace, right to the Turkish border and the birdlife-rich Evros River. Border influences from Albania, the Former Yugoslav Republic of Macedonia, Bulgaria and Turkey add distinctive flair to culture and cuisine. For travellers hungry for variety, northern Greece is the place to tuck in.

Best Places to Eat

➜ Doltso (p264)
➜ Castello Restaurant (p292)
➜ Paparouna (p242)
➜ Eleas Gi (p258)
➜ Petrino (p271)

Best Places to Stay

➜ Primoula (p286)
➜ Kokkino Spiti (p258)
➜ Daios Luxury Living (p240)
➜ Porto Elea Camping (p250)
➜ Xenonas Papanikolaou (p255)

When to Go
Thessaloniki

May–Aug Sizzle on beaches in Parga and Halkidiki, or cool down in refreshing Edessa.

Sep–Nov Bask in lower coastal prices then hit Thessaloniki's music and film fests.

Dec–Apr Snuggle into a ski lodge in Zagorohoria, or combine city and snow in Florina or Veria.

Northern Greece Highlights

1 Gorging yourself on the cultural riches, dining and nightlife of **Thessaloniki** (p231).

2 Slinging a hammock or hitting mountain-biking trails on the popular **Halkidiki Peninsula** (p248).

3 Hiking the **Vikos Gorge** (p284).

4 Roaming the old quarter by the Kastro in **Ioannina** (p279) before taking a ferry to the tranquil Island (p282).

5 Pointing your binoculars at wheeling birds of prey in Thrace's **Dadia Forest Reserve** (p274).

6 Cycling, kayaking or simply sitting back and enjoying the lake at **Kastoria** (p263).

7 Being charmed by ruins, museums and a beauteous bridge in **Arta** (p289).

8 Feeling the spray of **Edessa's** thundering waterfalls (p259).

9 Contemplating Mt Olympus from the **Castle of Platamonas** (p257).

Macedonia

NORTHERN GREECE

0 ——— 50 km
0 ——— 30 miles

THRACE

Smoljan
Plovdiv (75km)
Karadere Forest
Xanthi
Elatia
Skaloti
Agora
Adriani
Hrysoupoli
Keramoti
Limenas
Skala Prinou
Thasos

See Thrace Map (p267)

Gotse Delchev
Exohi
Kato Nevrokopi
Mt Falakro (2232m)
Drama
Philippi
Kavala
Gulf of Kavala
THRACIAN SEA

BULGARIA

Mt Vrontous (1888m)
Promahonas
Laillas
Sidirokastro
Serres
Nigrita
Stavros
Egnatia Odos Hwy
Mt Symvolon
Athos Peninsula
Karyes
Mt Athos (2033m)
Dafni
Oros

See Athos Peninsula Map (p251)

Mt Kerkini (2031m)
Lake Kerkini
Kilkis
Langadas
Lake Volvi
Arnea
Vrastama
Polygyros
HALKIDIKI
Ierissos
Ammouliani
Ouranoupoli
Gulf of Agion Oros
Sarti
Sithonian Peninsula
Neos Marmaras
Kalamitsi Peninsula
Camping Kalamitsi

Strumica
Evzoni
Lake Doirani
THESSALONIKI
Hortiatis
Mt Hortiatis (1201m)
Lake Koronia
Krini
Petralona Cave
Ormos
Panagias
Metamorfosi
Nikiti
Kallithea
Kryopigi
Paradisos
Polychrono
Pefkohori
Haniotis
Paliouri
Loutra

MACEDONIA

Gevgelija
Axios
Paleokastro
Pella
Halkidona
Alexandria
Panorama
Epanomi
Agia Triada
Pyrgos
Faros Beach & Potamies Beach
Ancient Olynthos
Eleohoria
Nea Moudania
Kassandra Peninsula
Afytos
Kassandra
Nea Skioni
Possidi

Strumica
E75

Giannitsa
E86
Vergina
Veria
Naoussa
Polla Nera
Edessa
Amissa
Katerini
Litohoro
Plaka Litohoro
Castle of Platamonas
Platamonas
Thermaic Gulf

MACEDONIA (FYROM)

Prilep
Bitola
E65
Florina
NIKI
Aetos
Nymfeo
Amyntaio
Lake Vegoritis
Lake Petron
Mt Vermio (320m)
Velvendos
Ancient Dion
Mt Olympus (2918m)
Leptokarya
Skopje (90km)
Mt Voras (Kaïmaktsalan) (2524m)
Andrea
Ardea
Ptolemaida
E65
Kozani
Lake Aliakmonas
Servia
Deskati
Elassona

THESSALY

Ohrid
Prespa Lakes
Agios Germanos
Psarades
Vronero
Krystallopigi
Korce
Mt Grammos (2520m)
Pisoderi Pass
Vigla (1759m)
Mt Vernon
Mt Vitsi (2128m)
Kastoria
Nestorio
Lake Orestiada
Lake Himaditis
E90
Neapoli
Siatista
Pendalofos
Grevena
Mt Vasilitsa (2249m)

See Epiros Map (p277)

Eptahori
Mt Smolikas (2637m)
Mt Gamila (2497m)
Egnatia Odos Hwy

ALBANIA

EPIROS

MACEDONIA ΜΑΚΕΔΟΝΙΑ

For many foreigners the word Macedonia (in Greek, mah-keh-dho-*nee*-ah) conjures up ancient conqueror Alexander the Great. But Greece's biggest province has major modern attractions to rival the museums and key historical sites at Pella and Vergina. Thessaloniki, Greece's sophisticated second city, has fantastic dining and nightlife, while the Halkidiki Peninsula offers fine sandy coves and big beaches, as well as the 1000-year-old Athonite monastic community.

Macedonia's other big-ticket sights include legendary Mt Olympus, Greece's highest peak at 2918m and a great place for hiking. Just opposite, more beaches stretch down the wooded Pieria coast, punctuated by a clifftop Byzantine castle at Platamonas. Traces of this heritage meet shimmering waters again in Macedonia's far northwest, where grand basilica ruins and frescoed church grottoes meet the Prespa Lakes, and in tranquil Kastoria, where a Byzantine shrine sits above a lake.

Macedonia's kaleidoscope of landscapes – from mountains and deep forests to arid plains and wetland marshes – make it ideal for outdoor adventurers and nature buffs (particularly birdwatchers).

History

Although life in Macedonia goes back 700,000 years, it's best known for the powerful Macedonian civilisation that peaked with Alexander the Great (d 323 BC), who conquered as far as India. Deemed barbarians by cultivated Athenians, the Macedonians subjugated Greece under Alexander's father, Philip II, yet adopted Greek mores. Alexander spread the Greek culture and language widely, creating a Hellenistic society that would be absorbed by the Romans. Later, after their empire split into eastern and western halves in the 4th century AD, the Greek-speaking Byzantine Empire emerged.

Thessaloniki became Byzantium's second city, a vital commercial, cultural and strategic centre on the Balkan trade routes. However, 6th- and 7th-century-AD Slavic migrations brought new populations and challenges. The empire frequently battled with the medieval Bulgarian kingdom from the 9th century to the 11th century. In 1018 Emperor Basil II finally defeated Bulgarian Tsar Samuel, who had ruled much of the southern Balkans from Macedonia's Mikri Prespa Lake.

After Serbian rule in the 14th century, Macedonia and the Balkans were overrun by the Ottoman Turks. The Ottoman system distinguished subjects by religion, not race, causing strife in the late 19th century, when guerrilla movements arose to fight the Turks, pledging to annex Macedonia for Greece, Bulgaria or even an independent 'Macedonia for the Macedonians'; in the very early 20th century, great powers such as Britain favoured the latter.

Ottoman atrocities against Macedonia's Christian populations presaged the First Balkan War of 1912, in which Greece, Bulgaria and Serbia drove the Turks from Macedonia; however, the Bulgarians were unhappy with their share, and declared war on their former allies in 1913, starting the Second Balkan War. Bulgaria's quick defeat lost its allotted portions of eastern Macedonia and Thrace, and Greece was the big winner, taking half of geographical Macedonia, with Serbia taking 38%. Bulgaria was left with 13%. Newly created Albania received a sliver around Ohrid and the Prespa Lakes.

In 1923, with the massive Greek–Turkish population exchanges, the government resettled many Anatolian Greek refugees in Macedonia, displacing the indigenous (non-Greek) populations. A vigorous program for assimilating non-Greeks was already under way, primarily through education and the Church. In WWII Greece was occupied by the Nazis, who deported and killed most of Macedonia's significant Sephardic Jewish population. Afterwards, during the Greek Civil War (1944–49), authorities targeted 'communist supporters' – often a label for ethnic minorities – causing the expulsion of thousands of (Slavic) Macedonians, many of them children, as well as Bulgarians and others. Greek Macedonia today is thus different from how it was even 60 years ago.

Thessaloniki Θεσσαλονίκη

POP 325,200

Thessaloniki (thess-ah-lo-*nee-kee*) is fuelled by optimism, hedonism and just a dash of chaos. Greece's thriving second city has monuments and museums to thrill history-lovers, and the city is mostly walkable and has a more upbeat quality than the capital.

The centre is laced with historic sights, from the Byzantine walls threading its romantic Upper Town to the imposing Rotunda. This is a city where old and new cohabit wonderfully: the Arch of Galerius, an intricate 4th-century monument, overlooks the busy shopping drag of Egnatia, while the

Thessaloniki

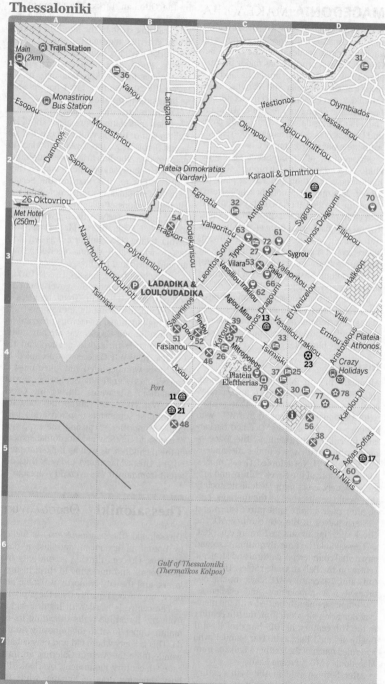

Main (2km)
Train Station
36
Vahou
Esopou
Monastiriou Bus Station
Monastiriou
Langada
Ifestionos
Olymbiados
Kassandrou
Damonos
Sapfous
Olympou
Agiou Dimitriou
26 Oktovriou
Met Hotel (250m)
Plateia Dimokratias (Vardari)
Karaoli & Dimitriou
16
70
Egnatia
Antigonidon
32
Sygrou
Ionos Dragoumi
Filippou
54
Fragkon
Valaoritou
63
61
Dodekanisou
Typou
72
27
Sygrou
Navarhou Koundourioti
Polytehniou
Leontos Sofou
Vilara 53
Pako
Valaoritou
Halkeon
Tsimiski
Vassiliou Irakliou
66
62
El Venizelou
LADADIKA & LOULOUDADIKA
Agiou Mina
Viali
Ionos Dragoumi
39
13
Ermou
Plateia Athonos
Galaminos
Pindou
Doxis
51
Katouni
75
33
Vassiliou Irakliou
Aristotelous
Fasianou
52
26
Mitropoleos
Tsimiski
23
Crazy Holidays
46
37
25
Axiou
65
79
30
77
78
Port
Plateia Eleftherias
67
41
Karolou Dil
11
21
56
i
48
38
74
17
Agias Sofias
60
Leof Nikis

Gulf of Thessaloniki
(Thermaïkos Kolpos)

0 _____ 400 m
0 _____ 0.2 miles

NORTHERN GREECE

12

Klious

14   15   Eptapyrgio

9   Akropoleos

KASTRA
(ANO POLI)

Akropoleos

24   Theotokopoulou   34
Church of   Agiou Nikolaou   Moreas   55
Agios   Sofokleous
Dimitrios 2   Agias Sofias   Olymbiados   Irodotou
Plateia   47   Kassandrou   Apostolou Pavlou   8
Dikastirion   Agiou Dimitriou   Elenis Zografou
19   64   Agiou
Agnostou Stratiotou   Olympou   Dragoumi   5
6   Olympou   Manolaki Kyriakou
29   Filippou   Arrianou   49
10   Isonidou   Armenopoulou
Kastritsiou
Egnatia   Ethnikis Amynis
Plateia   80   20   Aristotle
Agias   Mt Athos   Plateia Agiou   University
Sofias 7   Pilgrims' Bureau   Georgiou   Campus
Dimitriou   35
68   Gounari   4 Kamara
40   73   Paleon Patron Germanou   81   Konstantinou
Iktiniou   45   Svolou Gounari   Meleniko
43   Plateia   Nikiforos Fokas   Egnatia
18   Navarinou   44
Smyrnis   69   Dimitriou Gounari
82   Tsimiski   Ethnikis Amynis
Proxenou   58   Pavlou Mela   Angelaki
Koromila   57
28   71
Leof Nikis   42
50   Tsirogianni
Plateia   76   Nikolaou Germanou   P
Lefkos Pyrgos
22   Archaeological
1   Museum
3   Museum of
Byzantine Culture
Rihardos
(300m)
59
Villa Allatini (4km); Villa Mordoch (4km); Casa Bianca (4km);
Halkidiki (5km); Makedonia (12km); Halkidiki (65km)

city's most famous sight, the White Tower, anchors a waterfront packed with cocktail bars. By night, the city reverberates with music and nightlife, powered by an excitable stream of international students and backpackers.

For a port city, Thessaloniki's dearth of beaches and ferry links is confounding. But excellent bus connections make it a natural base for travel across northern Greece – if you ever tire of exploring Thessaloniki's monuments, galleries and raucous bars.

Thessaloniki

History

With the help of remarkable Thessalian horsemanship, Philip II achieved a spectacular victory over a Phocian tribe. To celebrate, he named his daughter Thessalonike (literally, 'victory of Thessalians'). Later, when Thessalonike married the Macedonian general Kassandros, her name was chosen for the city of Thessaloniki, founded in 315 BC.

In 168 BC the Romans conquered Macedon. Thessaloniki's importance was enhanced by its ideal location on the Thermaic Gulf, the east–west Via Egnatia and the Axios/Vardar River valley leading north. Under Galerius, Thessaloniki became the eastern imperial capital; with the empire's division in AD 395, it became Byzantium's second city, a flourishing Constantinople in miniature.

However, it was also frequently attacked by Goths, Slavs, Saracens and Crusaders. Still, Thessaloniki remained a cultural centre. It bore the 9th-century monks Cyril and Methodius (creators of Glagolitic, precursor to Cyrillic), who expanded Orthodox Byzantine literary culture among the Slavs. The city also nurtured great 14th-century theologian St Gregory Palamas, who also became Archbishop of Thessaloniki.

In 1430 the Ottoman Turks captured Thessaloniki; after 1492 they resettled Sephardic Jews fleeing the Inquisition to here, adding to the city's diversity.

With the 1821–27 War of Independence only a partial success, 19th-century Thessaloniki became a lurid hub for intrigue, secret societies and mutually antagonistic rebels and reformers. Along with Greek revolutionaries, these included the pro-Bulgarian Internal Macedonian Revolutionary Organisation (IMRO), and the Young Turks, who wanted Western-style reforms for the empire. Indeed, one Young Turk and Thessaloniki native, Mustafa Kemal (Atatürk), would become modern Turkey's founding father.

Thessaloniki suffered successive tragedies over the following four decades. The August 1917 fire burned two-thirds of it, and ethnic diversity shrank with the 1923 population exchanges. During the WWII Nazi occupation, Thessaloniki's Jews were deported to concentration camps and other non-Greeks were expelled following the Greek Civil War.

Recent decades have brought cultural acclaim, including the city's 1997 reign as European Capital of Culture and its hosting of sporting events during the 2004 Athens Olympics. In 2014 Thessaloniki was European Youth Capital.

◉ Sights

◉ White Tower & Waterfront

White Tower HISTORIC BUILDING
(Lefkos Pyrgos; ✆ 2310 267 832; www.lpth.gr; adult/student €3/2; ⊗ 8.30am-3pm Tue-Sun, to 8pm in summer) Thessaloniki's most famous landmark, the 34m-high White Tower has a harrowing history as a prison and torture chamber. In 1826 Ottoman sultan Mahmud II massacred rebellious janissaries (elite troops of forcibly Islamicised Christian boys) here. After the 1913 Greek reconquest, the 'bloody tower' was whitewashed to expunge this grisly past. Grab a free audio guide to help navigate the multimedia displays in the tower, then drink in views of the bay from the top.

★ **Archaeological Museum** MUSEUM
(✆ 2310 830 538; www.amth.gr; Manoli Andronikou 6; adult/student/child €6/3/free, adult/student incl Museum of Byzantine Culture €8/4; ⊗ 8am-8pm Tue-Sun, 1.30-8pm Mon Apr-Oct, 8.30am-3pm Tue-Sun, 10.30am-5pm Mon Nov-Mar) Macedonia's major prehistoric and ancient Macedonian and Hellenistic finds are housed here, bar Vergina's gold tomb finds, which are exhibited at the Vergina Royal Tombs Museum (p259). Highlights include the **Derveni Crater** (330–320 BC) a huge, ornate Hellenistic bronze-and-tin vase. Used for mixing wine and water, and later as a funerary urn, it's marked by intricate relief carvings of Dionysos, along with mythical figures, animals and ivy vines. The Derveni Treasure contains Greece's oldest surviving papyrus piece (320–250 BC).

The lower-floor exhibit, Pre-Historic Thessaloniki, boasts prehistoric implements from the **Petralona Cave** north of Halkidiki, plus neolithic and Bronze Age daggers, pottery and tools.

★ **Museum of Byzantine Culture** MUSEUM
(✆ 2313 306 400; www.mbp.gr; Leoforos Stratou 2; adult/child/student €4/free/2, adult/student incl Archaeological Museum €8/4; ⊗ 8am-8pm Apr-Oct, 9am-4pm Nov-Mar) This fascinating museum has plenty of treasures to please Byzantine buffs, plus simple explanations to introduce the empire to total beginners. More than 3000 Byzantine objects, including mosaics, intriguing tomb paintings, jewellery and glassware, are showcased with characterful asides about daily life. You'll be confidently discerning early-Christian from late-Byzantine icons in no time.

Museum of the Macedonian Struggle
MUSEUM

(☑2310 229 778; www.imma.edu.gr; Proxenou Koromila 23; admission €2; ⊘9am-2pm Tue-Fri, 10am-2pm Sat) Ground zero for Greek nationalism, this museum recounts how heroic Hellenes wrested Macedonia from both Turks and Bulgarians. Housed in Greece's former Ottoman consulate, the museum has hard-to-find maps, old firearms, photos, uniforms and more.

◉ Egnatia & Central

Three major Roman monuments of early 4th-century emperor Galerius spill across Egnatia at Plateia Navarinou: the ruined Palace of Galerius, the Arch of Galerius and the Rotunda to its north. This central Thessaloniki neighbourhood also has some of the city's most fascinating churches.

Rotunda of Galerius
HISTORIC BUILDING

(☑2310 218 720; Plateia Agiou Georgiou; ⊘9am-5pm Tue-Sun) FREE In AD 306 Roman emperor Galerius built this stocky 30m-high brick structure as his future mausoleum. But instead of being laid to rest within the 6m-thick walls of the Rotunda, he was buried in today's Serbia after succumbing to an unpleasant disease that still puzzles historians today. Later, Constantine the Great made the Rotunda Thessaloniki's first church (Agios Georgios; observe dragon-slaying St George above the door). The Ottomans made it a mosque (note the restored minaret). The Rotunda was undergoing restoration on our visit. You may have to squint through some scaffolding to discern its lovely inner frescoes.

Arch of Galerius
HISTORIC SITE

FREE The Arch of Galerius (AD 303) celebrates a victory over the Persians with carved, lunging soldiers. It's south of the Rotunda of Galerius on Egnatia.

Palace of Galerius
RUIN

(Plateia Navarinou; ⊘8.30am-3pm Tue-Sun) FREE The ruined Palace of Galerius sprawls east–west across Plateia Navarinou. You can descend into it, or just peer over the handrail. Pieces of floor mosaic, columns and a few walls survive.

Roman Agora
RUIN

(Plateia Dikastirion; ⊘8am-3pm Tue-Sun) FREE The 1st-century AD *agora* (forum) lies north of Plateia Aristotelous, on Plateia Dikastirion. In the 3rd century BC, the

🚶 City Walk
Thessaloniki

START ANO POLI
END PORT
LENGTH 8KM; FOUR HOURS (OR ALL DAY WITH CAFE AND LUNCH STOPS)

Start early; many churches close by noon. Avoid Monday, when most sites are closed. If you're starting in the centre, skip Ano Poli and pick up the route from Yeni Hammam.

Begin at Ano Poli's tower by the eastern end of the ❶ **Byzantine Walls** (p239). Follow the walls west on main road Eptapirgiou; turn left onto Akropoleos (becoming narrow walkway Agathaggelou) to the church and museum at the ❷ **Monastery of Vlatadon** (p239). This 14th-century edifice has well-preserved frescoes and a leafy setting.

Double-back to Eptapirgiou and continue west, following more ragged Byzantine walls. Turn left and follow the stairs on Sthenonos along pastel-painted walls and houses with blooming window boxes. At the bottom of the stairs, veer right along Dimitriou Poliorkitou. Look out for the easy-to-miss stairway that doubles backwards; follow it down to Unesco-listed ❸ **Church of Osios David** (p239; a sign for the church marks the stairway). This 5th-century gem is resplendent with rare frescoes.

From here, wander Ano Poli eastwards along the small streets. The most direct route follows Fotiou across Akropoleos, turning left onto Krispou. These residential streets are a soothing palette of coral and pink. The road wiggles into Eolou, and then hits Moreas. Follow Moreas to the left, then find 14th-century ❹ **Church of Nikolaos Orfanos** (p239) by turning right onto Amfitryonos. Burnished angels blaze from the walls of this intimate Byzantine church.

Returning to Moreas, go southwest to leave behind Ano Poli's steep streets. Once you cross Olymbiados and reach Kassandrou, you're well and truly back in the city.

Dodge the pedestrian bustle for a few blocks west along Kassandrou and turn south on Agiou Nikolaou. You'll see the bulging red-domed roof of ❺ **Yeni Hammam** (p238), a restored 17th-century Turkish bath, in front of you. A few steps south of Yeni Hammam is the burly brick ❻ **Church of Agios Dimitrios** (p238), occupying its own square and sheltering relics of St Dimitrios within.

Go south on Agnostou Stratiotou across Olympou and you'll soon see the ruin of the **7 Roman Agora** (p236), with a backdrop of modern tower blocks. After marvelling at the contrast of ancient and new, double-back to Agiou Dimitriou and proceed east 10 blocks to **8 Atatürk House** (p238) on your left, inside the Turkish consulate. This high-security attraction resembles a fortress more than a museum.

A block further east on Agiou Dimitriou, go right on Dimitriou Gounari; at the end is the imposing **9 Rotunda of Galerius**. This squat, rounded building has a history as a mauseoleum, temple, church and mosque. Downhill along the path is the statue-studded 3rd-century **10 Arch of Galerius**, created to commemorate Galerius' victory over the Persian army. After crossing busy Egnatia, meander down the pedestrianised street until you see excavated walls. The ruins may look scant, but they are the remnants of the once-vast **11 Palace of Galerius**.

Continue downhill. Cross Tsimiski and, at Plateia Fanarioton, arc left to see the iconic **12 White Tower** (p235). Once a notorious prison, it now harbours a multimedia museum. Next wander west for a waterside stroll on Leoforos Nikis. Some of the city's most effervescent nightlife is along this road.

Leave the water by turning right up Agias Sofias towards the **13 Church of Agia Sofia** (p238). If your energy is low after craning your neck at its mosaic-decorated inner dome, pause for a quick sugar rush at **14 Blé** (p243) before returning to Tsimiski to proceed west.

Soon you'll hit Aristotelous; **15 Plateia Aristotelous** is to the left. Follow your rumbling belly to the right; between Irakliou and Ermou you'll discover **16 Modiano Market**, full of fish on ice and trays of olives and cheese.

Nibble your way through Modiano before rejoining Ermou. You'll cross busy Venizelou. Next turn towards the sea once more by pacing down Ionos Dragoumi, through the former florists' market, the Louloudadika district, which now overflows with clothes shops, bars and restaurants. If your feet are sore, end here with a visit to the excellent **17 Jewish Museum** (p238); or quench your thirst by returning to Leoforos Nikis' waterfront bars.

Further down Ionos Dragoumi, at the Tsimiski intersection, note the **18 National Bank of Greece** building; after it, turn right onto Mitropoleos and zigzag into the **19 Ladadika district**, home to atmospheric restaurants and bars. Walk south to Kountouriotou towards the beautified **20 port**.

Macedonians made it a commercial centre and the Romans maintained this function. An English-language placard explains the site, which contains clustered shop walls and mosaic floor remnants.

★ **Church of Agios Dimitrios**   CHURCH
(☑2310 270 008; Agiou Dimitriou 97; ☺8am-10pm) This enormous 5th-century structure honours Thessaloniki's patron saint. A Roman soldier, Dimitrios was killed around AD 306 at this former Roman bath site by order of Emperor Galerius, infamous persecutor of Christians. The martyrdom site is now an underground crypt. Dimitrios' relics occupy a silver reliquary inside. The Ottomans made Agios Dimitrios a mosque, and plastered over frescoes that were again revealed after the 1913 Greek reconquest. While the city's devastating fire of 1917 was very damaging, five 8th-century mosaics survive, spanning the altar.

Church of the Panagia Achiropiitos   CHURCH
(Odos Agias Sofias 56; ☺7am-noon & 4.30-6.30pm) This basilica-style 5th-century Byzantine church has notable mosaics and frescoes. The name, meaning 'made without hands', refers to a miraculous 12th-century appearance of an icon of the Virgin. It was the first of Thessaloniki's churches to be transformed into a mosque under Ottoman rule.

Atatürk House   HISTORIC BUILDING
(☑2310 248 452; Apostolou Pavlou 75; ☺10am-5pm Tue-Sun) FREE Modern Turkey's illustrious founder, Mustafa Kemal, was born here in 1881. Bring your identity card or passport for this three-floor museum within the Turkish consulate and be prepared for security checks. Along with numerous original furnishings and memorabilia, you'll see Atatürk paraphernalia such as dapper suits, white gloves and a cane.

Church of Agia Sofia   CHURCH
(Plateia Agias Sofias; ☺7am-1pm & 6-7.30pm) Candlelight twinkles from gold chandeliers in this functioning 8th-century church, modelled on its İstanbul namesake. The dome has a striking mosaic of the Ascension of Christ. Built over a previous 3rd-century church, it's notable for the cross-basilica style associated with middle-Byzantine architecture. The narthex and south aisle were used as a burial place for dignitaries from the 10th century. Like many Thessaloniki churches, it spent a period as a mosque (1535–1912) before returning to Christian worship.

Bey Hammam   HISTORIC BUILDING
(Paradeisos Baths; ☑2313 310 400; cnr Egnatia & Plateia Dikastirion) FREE Stocky Bey Hammam was built in 1444, making it Thessaloniki's oldest Turkish bathhouse. Currently this former 'Baths of Paradise' only opens on request.

Yeni Hammam   HISTORIC BUILDING
(☑6946688588; cnr Kassandrou & Agiou Nikolaou; ☺11am-5pm) An atmospheric 16th-century structure, this former Turkish bath has great acoustics. Today it hosts occasional exhibitions and a restaurant.

◉ Ladadika & Port

Former bazaar neighbourhood Ladadika has Thessaloniki's favourite eateries and nightlife, and is bordered to its east by the former Jewish neighbourhood along Mitropoleos. Opposite, the pier area hosts two hip museums and is a favourite evening haunt for students.

Jewish Museum of Thessaloniki   MUSEUM
(☑2310 250 406; www.jmth.gr; Agiou Mina 13; ☺11am-2pm Tue, Fri & Sun, 11am-2pm & 5-8pm Wed & Thu) FREE This touching museum is housed in one of the few Jewish buildings to survive the great fire of 1917, the former office of Jewish newspaper *L'Independent*. The museum traces the city's Jewish heritage through the 15th-century Sephardic immigrations and its peak period of creativity in the 16th century, before the community was brutally annihilated during the Holocaust. The upper floor has a timeline of Jewish life in Thessaloniki. The ground floor is split between a collection of photos and Jewish gravestones on one side, and a moving hall of remembrance on the other.

Thessaloniki Museum of Photography   MUSEUM
(☑2310 566 716; www.thmphoto.gr; Warehouse A, Port; adult/student €2/1; ☺11am-7pm Tue-Sun) This 1910 port warehouse is home to thought-provoking exhibitions of historic and contemporary Greek photography. It's worth lingering for the sea views from the cafe.

Cinema Museum   MUSEUM
(☑2310 508 398; www.cinemuseum.gr; Warehouse A, Port; adult/student €2/1; ☺9am-3pm Mon-Wed, to 7pm Thu & Fri) Delve into the history of the silver screen via realism, musicals and modern Greek cinema at this passionate and well-executed small museum.

◉ Ano Poli

Punish your calf muscles in the steep streets of Ano Poli, the upper town, for magnificent ruins and lesser-visited churches. Only Ano Poli (then, the Turkish Quarter) largely survived the city-wide devastation of the 1917 fire – although the fire originated here, the wind swept the flames towards the sea.

Kastro & Byzantine Walls   HISTORIC SITE

FREE The *kastro* (castle) encloses Byzantine churches and timber-framed houses with overhanging upper storeys. Enjoy panoramic views from the tower by the eastern edge of the Byzantine Walls, built in the late 4th century BC to survive sieges. Emperor Theodosius fortified the walls; in places they were 10m high and 5m thick. They stood until the 19th century when the Ottomans demolished large stretches.

Monastery of Vlatadon   MONASTERY

(cnr Eptapyrgiou & Agathangelou; ⊘7.30am-5pm & 5.30-8pm, museum 10am-noon Sun) **FREE** Near Byzantine Walls, the salmon-coloured arches of this secluded monastery are a relaxing place for a stroll. Thought to have been founded around 1351 by the pious brothers Vlatades, this monastery was significant for Hesychasm, a controversial movement based around solitary spiritual reflection. Its foremost 14th-century proponent, St Gregory Palamas, is depicted in a fresco here.

Church of Nikolaos Orfanos   CHURCH

(Irodotou 20) This early 14th-century church has superb (though age-darkened) frescoes. The 'orphan' in the church's name remains a mystery: it may be a nod to an anonymous benefactor or be linked to a former orphanage nearby. Opening hours vary.

Church of Osios David   CHURCH

(Vlatadon 1; ⊘10am-5pm Tue-Sat) This little 5th-century church was allegedly built by the orders of Theodora, daughter of anti-Christian Galerius, who was baptised in secret. It contains well-preserved mosaics and rare 12th-century frescoes.

Eptapyrgion   HISTORIC BUILDING

(Yedi Kule) **FREE** A prison from Ottoman times until 1989, the Eptapyrgion, or Yedi Kule in Ottoman Turkish (in both languages, 'Seven Towers'), is a grim reminder of Thessaloniki's penal past, recounted in *rembetika* (old Greek blues) songs. It's in Ano Poli, behind the Byzantine Walls.

⌖ Tours

Free Walking Tours   WALKING TOUR

Well-informed free walking tours run on most days during high season. They're led by energetic local enthusiasts in multiple languages (with advance notice). Find 'Thessaloniki Free Walking Tours' on Facebook for details.

✷ Festivals & Events

Festivals in Thessaloniki are youth-focused, vibrant and often provocative. Book accommodation far in advance if your visit coincides with HelExpo or Reworks.

Thessaloniki Documentary Festival   FILM

(☑2310 378 400; www.filmfestival.gr; ⊘Mar) A rich program of documentary film events is screened at various Thessaloniki venues.

NORTHERN GREECE THESSALONIKI

JEWISH THESSALONIKI

Thessaloniki's Jewish community swelled following the arrival of exiled Sephardic Jews from Spain in the 15th century. The city enjoyed a golden age of Jewish industry and culture, including crafts such as weaving and silk dyeing, in the 16th century. The flourishing Jewish community was brutally cut down in 1943 when 43,850 Jews were deported to their deaths at Auschwitz. The history is movingly conveyed at the city's **Jewish Museum**.

In the city centre, find Thessaloniki's principal synagogue, **Monastirioton** (Sygrou 35), used as a Red Cross centre during the WWII Nazi occupation and therefore spared. Services are held at **Yad Lazikaron** (Vassiliou Irakliou 24).

Find other traces of this rich history at 19th- and 20th-century former Jewish mansions **Villa Allatini** (Olgas 198), **Casa Bianca** (Olgas 214) and **Villa Mordoch** (Olgas 162), a 15-minute bus ride along Leoforos Vasilissis Olgas. To dig deeper into Thessaloniki's Jewish heritage, buy a copy of *Jewish Sites in Thessaloniki: Brief History and Guide* by Rena Molho and Vilma Hastaoglou-Martinidi (Lycabettus Press) from bookshops or the Jewish Museum.

PicNic Urban Festival   CULTURAL
(☑2310 273 660; www.urbanpicnic.gr; ◎end Aug)
On the festival scene since 2012, Urban Picnic
reconnects the community with archaeological sites by hosting concerts and short film
screenings at Thessaloniki's Roman Agora.

Reworks International Music Festival MUSIC
(☑2310 266 648; www.reworks.gr; ◎Sep) Reworks Festival kicks off a deck-destroying
three days of DJs, electronica and international bands performing in public squares
and clubs across Thessaloniki.

**Thessaloniki International
Film Festival**   FILM
(☑2310 378 400; www.filmfestival.gr; ◎Sep-Nov)
This popular film festival unfurls alongside
a calendar of concerts, exhibitions and the-
atrical performances.

🛏 Sleeping

🛏 White Tower & Waterfront

Tourist Hotel   HOTEL €€
(☑2310 270 501; www.touristhotel.gr; Mitropoleos
21; s/d/tr incl breakfast from €52/60/90; 🕸 🛜)
Forget the name: this classic place (built
1925) is a comfortable and charming midrange choice with a somewhat nostalgic
feel. A gated lift leads to rooms with soundproofed windows and elegant decor.

City Hotel   BUSINESS HOTEL €€
(☑2310 269 421; www.cityhotel.gr; Komninon 11;
d/tr/ste incl breakfast from €70/90/110; 🕸@🛜)
This swanky four-star near Plateia Eleftherias balances elegant rooms with friendly,
cheerful service. There's a big American-style
breakfast and a spa centre with gym and
hammam (Turkish baths).

★ Daios Luxury Living   BOUTIQUE HOTEL €€€
(☑2310 250 200; www.daioshotels.com; Leoforos
Nikis 59; s/d/ste from €145/165/190; 🕸 🛜) Close
to the White Tower, this boutique hotel
wraps spacious, opulent rooms into a glorious seafront location. The suites have enormous soundproofed windows and balconies
(from some you see only water). The hotel's
waterfront cafe is just as sophisticated, with
an excellent range of cocktails. Enter on side
street Smyrnis.

Electra Palace Hotel   HOTEL €€€
(☑2310 294 000; www.electrahotels.gr; Plateia
Aristotelous 9; d incl breakfast €130-275; 🕸🛜🌊)
Even if just coming to gaze on the harbour
from the rooftop garden cafe, you can't miss

the appeal of this fabulous five-star city
landmark, standing splendidly over Plateia
Aristotelous. The renovated rooms are spacious, with ornate furnishings, and there's a
mosaic-tiled indoor pool, a rooftop outdoor
pool and a *hammam*.

🛏 Egnatia & Central

Rent Rooms Thessaloniki   HOSTEL €€
(☑2310 204 080; www.rentrooms-thessaloniki.com;
Konstantinou Melenikou 9; dm/s/d/tr/q incl breakfast €22/54/64/85/97; 🕸🛜) This excellent-
value hostel and apartment accommodation
has a charming back-garden cafe, where you
can tuck into a choice of filling breakfasts
with views of the Rotunda of Galerius. Some
dorms and rooms have mini-kitchens; all
have fridges and bathrooms. Security lockers
and luggage storage available. The friendly
staff brim with local info.

Egnatia Palace Hotel   HOTEL €€
(☑2310 222 900; www.egnatia-hotel.gr; Egnatia 61;
s/d/ste €75/120/150; 🕸🛜🌊) This four-star
hotel offers bright, individually decorated
rooms and suites. It's slightly overpriced and
some guests gripe about the wi-fi signal, but
it's well located on central Egnatia.

🛏 Valaoritou & Western Egnatia

Hotel Aegeon   HOTEL €
(☑2310 522 921; www.aegeon-hotel.gr; Egnatia
19; s/d incl breakfast €40/50; 🕸🛜) Although
rooms are simple and somewhat cramped,
the Aegeon is a budget godsend by western
Egnatia standards, surrounded as it is by
pricey chain hotels and sordid cheap digs.
The train station's a 10-minute walk, and the
popular Valaoritou bars are just behind Egnatia opposite.

Thess Hostel   HOSTEL €
(☑6937320162, 2310 554 120; http://thesshostel.
gr; Ag Panton 12; dm/apt €18/49; 🛜) This brand-
new hostel is a splash of colour tucked into
the backstreets behind the train station.
The effusive warmth of the staff, the hostel's
immaculate cleanliness and its provision of
backpacker essentials (good wi-fi, 24-hour
reception, a quirkily decorated hang-out
area) are all impressive. Thess is well situated if you have an early start at the train or
main bus station.

Colors Rooms & Apartments APARTMENTS €€
(☑2310 502 280; www.colors.com.gr; Valaoritou
21; s/d/ste €59/65/80; 🕸🛜) Valaoritou party
people: finally you have somewhere suitably

hip to crash. These 15 sparkling apartments (some self-catering) rival more expensive hotel rooms, with cool lighting and minimalist decor. At weekends they're perfect for night owls exploring the surrounding bars (but bring ear plugs if you plan to tuck up in bed early).

Ladadika & Port

Colors Central Ladadika BOUTIQUE HOTEL €€
(📞2316 007 676; www.colorscentral.gr; Oplopiou 1, cnr Katouni; s/d/ste €62/68/92; 🕸🛜) This stylish boutique hotel, sister to the Colours hotel in Valaoritou, occupies a grand heritage house with 12 uniquely decorated rooms. The modern pop-art decor and vibrant tones give it an uplifting, contemporary feel, and its location in the heart of Ladadika's restaurant quarter couldn't be better.

Le Palace Art Hotel HOTEL €€
(📞2310 257 400; www.lepalace.gr; Tsimiski 12; s/d/tr incl breakfast from €50/60/75; 🕸🛜) On busy Tsimiski, Le Palace occupies a renovated neoclassical building. Its large, modern rooms have high ceilings, and (mostly) soundproofed windows keep out street noise.

Met Hotel HOTEL €€€
(📞2310 017 000; www.themethotel.gr; 26 Oktovriou 48; s/d incl breakfast from €110/150; 🅿🕸🛜🛜) Near to the port and train stations, the Met is a posh, minimalist luxury hotel with sleek modern bathrooms, a spa centre and an outdoor pool. Amenities include designer soaps, flat-screen TVs and some seriously comfortable mattresses. There's a complimentary shuttle service to the city centre.

Ano Poli

Removed from the hubbub of Egnatia and the waterfront's tourist clamour, digs in the upper town have a more laid-back and local feel.

Little Big House HOSTEL €
(📞2313 014 323; www.littlebighouse.gr; Andokidou 24; dm/d from €17/48; 🕸🛜) This clean and friendly hostel, run by the uproarious Vicky and her brother Harry, is an ideal base for exploring the charismatic upper town. There are kitchenettes, a garden, a common room and a choice of shared dorms and private accommodation. From the train station, take bus 23 to Agios Pavlos. The hostel is north of Plateia Kallithea.

Hostel Arabas HOSTEL €
(📞6944466897; www.hostelarabas.gr; Sachtouri 28; dm/d/tr €15/40/51; 🕸🛜) Located up a hill and hard to find, with a warm welcome and a washing machine: this is hostelling as it used to be. This simple place has spartan dorms, plus private doubles and triples. There's a relaxing front garden for coffee (and sometimes barbecues) plus free luggage storage. The staff enthusiastically helps arrange tours and activities.

The hostel is a 20-minute walk northeast from the train station – see the website for detailed directions.

✗ Eating

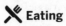 **White Tower & Waterfront**

Myrsini CRETAN €
(📞2310 220 310; Ethnikis Aminis 6; mains €8-12; ⏰lunch & dinner Sep-Jun) Down near the White Tower, Thessaloniki's original Cretan restaurant serves a delicious array of representative dishes, from *dakos* (rusks topped with tomato and olive oil) and wild *horta* (greens) to roast rabbit and *myzithropitakia* (flaky filo triangles with sweet sheep's-milk cheese). The worn wooden floors and traditional decor are enhanced by violin-driven Cretan music. Usually closed July and August.

Agioli SEAFOOD €€
(📞2310 262 888; www.agioli.gr; Leoforos Nikis 15, cnr Ploutarhou; mains €7-15; ⏰noon-1am) Just the right mix of rustic and modern, this waterfront restaurant has catch-of-the-day specials and tempting boards of fresh salads, including Florina sweet peppers and tzatziki. The bouquets of garlic hanging from the rafters and the marine murals give you something to admire while digesting squid and sausage linguine.

Dore Zythos MEDITERRANEAN €€
(📞2310 279 010; http://zithos.gr; Tsirogianni 7; mains €8-16; ⏰lunch & dinner) With their view of the White Tower, Zythos' outside tables are a scenic spot to pummel bread into smoky fava beans or feast on beautifully smoked pork.

Ergon MODERN GREEK €€
(📞2310 284 224; www.ergonproducts.gr; Kouskoura 5; mains €8-12; ⏰noon-midnight) The Ergon chain is dedicated to the best Greek produce, from Pindos mountain truffles to Alonissos tuna. While the portions can be small for the price, there's no denying that celebrity chef Dimitris Skarmoutsos, a *MasterChef*

NORTHERN GREECE THESSALONIKI

Greece TV judge who joined the team in 2011, knows his stuff. Take home some oils, jams and other regional goodies from the adjoining shop.

Egnatia & Central

I Nea Follia
GREEK €€
(☎2310 960 383; cnr Aristomenous & Haritos; mains €9-14; ⊙1.30pm-1am Sep-Jul; ☑) This is the kind of place Anthony Bourdain would like to discover. A bare-bones taverna that opened in 1966 on a nondescript north-side alley, in recent years it was commandeered by three young chefs who serve classic Greek fare with a contemporary twist. Expertly sauteed shrimp, fig-strewn salads and juicy grills are all beautifully presented.

Ladadika & Port

Athivoli
CRETAN €
(☎2310 508 509; www.athivoli.gr; Katouni 15; mezedhes €5-8; ⊙lunch & dinner) Ladadika's Cretan restaurant is enlivened by traditional music, an amiable background to platefuls of plump mussels and flaky cheese pies. Look for the neon outline of Crete.

Sempriko
GREEK €
(☎2310 557 513; Fragkon 2; mains €7-11; ⊙9am-midnight Tue-Fri, 2pm-midnight Sat & Sun) Near the western Byzantine Walls, Sempriko has been a hit since opening in 2012. It's a friendly place where gourmet flourishes belie the simple taverna-style decor. Choose between towers of Cretan cheeses, honey and vegetables, fall-off-the-bone lamb shank, and grilled octopus christened with fine olive oil.

Pizza Poselli
PIZZA €
(☎2314 019 687; Vilara 2; pizza slices €2.30; ⊙1pm-4am) Succumb to late-night pizza cravings in style. A magnet for Italians (who vouch for the crusts' quality), busy Poselli also does a roaring trade in pizza by the slice with the Valaoritou bar crowds.

Omikron
GREEK €
(☎2310 532 774; Oplopiou 3; mains €7-10; ⊙1pm-midnight) This neat and tidy local favouite does excellent fresh fish and inventive grills, but most mouth-watering are the daily specials on the chalkboard by the door. Expect masterful use of oysters, market fish and herb-strewn salads.

★Paparouna
MODERN GREEK €€
(☎2310 510 852; www.paparouna.com; Pangaiou 4, cnr Doxis; mains €10-14; ⊙11am-3am) Ever-popular Paparouna has dishes as vibrant as its interior design. Bright primary-coloured walls and a checkerboard floor set the tone for bold flavours such as thyme-infused cocktails, salads of sea fennel and spice-crumbed seafood.

Panellinion
TAVERNA €€
(☎2310 567 220; http://panellinion.gr; Doxis 1, cnr Salaminos; mains €8-12; ⊙lunch & dinner) The walls are lined with olive-oil bottles and tins of produce in this enjoyably unfussy Ladadika taverna. Choose from numerous ouzos and plenty of Greek beer to wash down the grilled meats and seafood mezedhes.

Full tou Meze
MEZEDHES €€
(☎2310 524 700; www.fullmeze.gr; Katouni 3; ⊙1pm-midnight) This packed Ladadika favourite piles plates high with towers of veal and aubergine, vast seafood risottos and inventive creations such as their magenta beetroot, yoghurt and walnut salad. In prime position on Plateia Katouni, it's an excellent spot to let the hours drift past between jugs of wine.

Kitchen Bar
INTERNATIONAL €€
(☎2310 502 241; Warehouse B, Port; mains €11-17; ⊙9am-midnight) Gaze out at the Gulf of Thessaloniki (Thermaïkos Kolpos) from this cafe-restaurant housed in a port warehouse. Seize an outdoor table (if you're quick); order a cocktail and risotto; and people-watch the style-conscious clientele. Team it with one of the port's late-opening museums for an offbeat evening out.

Ano Poli

★Taverna to Igglis
GREEK €
(Irodotou 32; mains €7; ⊙noon-2am; ☎) Slow-cooked pork shank in thyme, ever-changing daily specialities and marinated meat grills that defy science with their succulence. This local fave in Ano Poli is away from the crowds and has delicious dishes that belie its simple exterior.

Drinking & Nightlife

White Tower & Waterfront

West of the White Tower, pedestrianised Iktinou is bursting with boutique bars and charismatic cafes. Along the waterfront, most bars offer little to distinguish between them, though several have a unique style and excellent cocktails.

★ **Iktinou au Trottoir**   COCKTAIL BAR
(☑ 2310 283 133; www.iktinouautrottoir.gr; Iktinou
10; cocktails €9; ⊙ noon-late) Tucked away on
pedestrian alley Iktinou, this bar sparkles at
night with cocktails as rainbow-coloured as
the fairy lights strung around the outdoor
area. Generous free snacks accompany a
couple of cocktails, service is friendly and
the open-air seating is plush and romantic.

Thermaïkos   BAR
(☑ 2310 239 842; Leoforos Nikis 23; cocktails €7;
⊙ 10am-4am) There's a marvellously mixed
crowd at this unpretentious waterfront bar,
named after the gulf that forms the view. The
interior has vintage flourishes in a relaxing
ruby-tinged decor, while trance and techno
intoxicates as much as the cocktail menu.

Slag   BAR
(☑ 2313 040 747; Zefxidos 2; ⊙ 10am-late) Brits
may blush at the name, but this small,
quirky bar is as good for coffees as it is for
beers after sundown. Nestled into a pedestrianised alley off Iktinou, it's a superb location to nibble biscotti with a frappé (Greek-
style iced coffee). Alternatively, arrive after
11pm when the real fun begins.

Loxias   CAFE
(☑ 2310 233 925; Isavron 7; ⊙ 11am-late Mon-Sat,
8pm-late Sun) Fuel your philosophising with
ouzo and snacks at this bookstore-cafe,
where literary bar talk gets more animated
as the sun goes down. It's decorated with
wine casks, bursting with bookshelves and
full of historic photos and prints.

On the Road   BAR
(☑ 2310 271 240; Leoforos Nikis 61; ⊙ 10am-3am)
This waterfront cafe-bar is packed with nomads and locals, and its Latin music and
lack of glitz make it more interesting than
many of its Nikis neighbours.

Cafe Nikis 35   CAFE
(☑ 2310 230 449; Leoforos Nikis 35; ⊙ 10am-late;
🛜) This snug waterfront cafe sits just under

NORTHERN GREECE THESSALONIKI

SWEET INDULGENCES: THE BEST THESSALONIKI DESSERT STOPS

Thessaloniki's historic ties with the Ottoman East have bequeathed it a rich tradition of sweets. In between traditional Greek pastries, fire your taste buds with *soutzouk loukoum* (aromatic rolls of Turkish delight and pistachio), as well as halva and refreshing gelato.

Chatzis (☑ 2310 221 655; http://chatzis.gr; Mitropoleos 24; sweets €1.40-3; ⊙ 8am-late) Glistening syrup-soaked treats have been luring dessert fans into Chatzis since 1908, back when Thessaloniki was still an Ottoman city. Try the moist, sugar-rush-inducing *revani* (syrupy semolina cake), chickpea and raisin halva, or *rizogalo* (rice pudding) scented with cinnamon. There are also branches on Sofouli 73 and Venizelou 50.

Fregio (www.fregio.gr; Kouskoura 7; ⊙ 10am-midnight) This wickedly indulgent ice-cream parlour is a local favourite; its gelato-topped waffles are spoken of in rapturous whispers. We love the gourmet choc ices, hand-dipped in toasted nuts. There's another Fregio by Aristotelous.

Kokkinos Fournos (☑ 2310 206 337; www.kokkinosfournos.gr; Apostolou Pavlou 1, Rotunda) Just above the Rotunda of Galerius, this classic bakery does great breads as well as Thessaloniki's best *koulourakia vanilias* – crunchy, slightly sweet golden cookies perfect for dipping in Greek coffee.

Terkenlis (☑ 2310 271 148; www.terkenlis.gr; Aristotelous 4; ⊙ 8am-8pm) This upmarket patisserie chain has temptations including freshly baked *tzoureki* (brioche-style bread) and macarons, as well as confectionery and honey-glazed fruit salads.

Trigona Elenidis (☑ 2310 257 510; www.elenidis.gr; cnr Dimitriou Gounari & Tsimiski; trigones from €1.40; ⊙ 8am-5pm) A veritable institution since 1960, Elenidis specialises in Thessaloniki's favourite pastry, the *trigona*. This sweet, flaky triangular cone filled with tasty custard cream is legendary. Locals emerge with 2kg boxes, but you might want to save room for the Greek halva (made with semolina) or homemade ice cream.

Blé (☑ 2310 231 200; www.ble.com.gr; Agias Sofias 19, cnr Georgiou Stavrou; cakes €2-5; ⊙ 24hr) This chic patisserie (the name is French for 'wheat') has a tooth-tingling range, from traditional Cretan baked goods to dainty cupcakes. Try Monte Cristo, German-style brioche with marzipan, or chocolate gateau freshened with mango. If your taste buds are crying out for savoury, Blé's spinach-and-cheese pies are baked daily.

street level. Perfect for a Sunday-morning coffee (€1.50) or afternoon beer (€4) – get a window table and feel the dappled sunlight as it dances through the blinds.

Berlin   BAR
(Smyrnis 10; ⊙midnight-7am Mon-Fri, 10.30pm-9am Sat & Sun) Keep the party going at this after-bar to beat all after-bars. Berlin has operated since 1979, and still welcomes a crowd of bleary-eyed partiers seeking a grunge or gothic fix to see them through until morning. The music is as alternative as the clientele.

Egnatia & Central

North of Egnatia you'll have to look harder for nightlife, though some raucous and alternative spots exist.

Cantina Tropicana   BAR
(☑2310 539 727; Egnatia 31; ⊙11am-4am) Just above Egnatia, Cantina Tropicana has music (sometimes live) wafting from the western side, across an underpass where tables cluster in a secret garden and within a narrow art deco bar. Find the most tropical atmosphere over a fruit punch at an open-air table.

Mpate Skyloi   BAR
(Olympou 61; ⊙3pm-late) Ready your eardrums for an amp-busting soundtrack and punk-rock stylings. Mpate Skyloi has a gritty, dive-bar feel with a lively, open-minded crowd. Check ahead for live events across different rock genres.

Freidiriko Agapi Mou   CAFE, BAR
(☑2310 238 532; Olympou 87; ⊙10am-late) Love canines as much as cocktails? This retro corner cafe – named for the owners' dog – attracts people and pets to chill out over a coffee or mixed drink.

Valaoritou

The last decade has seen this former commercial district metamorphose into an alternative nightlife district. Graffiti and dive bars are still the main flavour but slicker drinking spots abound, too.

La Doze   BAR
(☑2310 532 986; Vilara 1; ⊙8pm-late) Skateboarding students and sports-car collectors mingle for cocktails and freestyle-DJ action at this legendary Valaoritou hang-out. Put your trust in La Doze's mixology magic: with more than 100 cocktails and rare ingredients, the bar staff delights in new creations.

Gambrinus   BAR
(☑2310 512 876; Sygrou 7; ⊙noon-late) If your love of guitar music is matched only by your devotion to beer, step into the darkness of this Czech-inspired place. Central European beers abound, with hefty carb and sausage snacks to keep you sober enough to sample another ale.

Fragile   BAR
(☑2310 547 443; Valaoritou 29; ⊙11am-late) Surrounded by the neighbourhood's dark office blocks and dive bars, this rooftop bar has views that are more Gotham City than postcard-pretty, but no matter – it's a fun spot that broadcasts an eclectic mix of pop, rock and electronica into the night. Tip: locals also call it Taratsa.

Partizan Bar   BAR
(☑6944767374; Valaoritou 29; ⊙10am-late) Bohemian Partizan is open for coffee by day, unlike most of Valaoritou's drinking haunts. But it's best by night, when revellers crowd its industrial-themed bar to gulp down one of 20 whiskys.

Coo   BAR
(☑2311 274 752; Vassiliou Irakliou 4; ⊙7pm-late) What started as a venue to promote the musical creations of a few friends has become an alternative bar. Beneath lies a cellar for experimental theatre, photo exhibits and summer concerts.

Enola   BAR
(www.enola.gr; 2nd fl, Valaoritou 19; ⊙11pm-3am) Anything from '80s to karaoke to thumping dance music awaits at Thessaloniki's liveliest gay bar. Enter from the Valaoritou side and take the elevator to the 2nd floor.

Ladadika & Port

Competition from Valaoritou inspired a comeback for Ladadika, a historic quarter of old tobacco houses and brothel buildings. Facing it, the port area increasingly swells with trendy cocktail bars and student-driven cafes.

High School   COCKTAIL BAR
(☑2310 286 161; Leoforos Nikis 9a; ⊙9am-2am) This nostalgic bar and pizzeria has the best cocktails in Thessaloniki's port area. The decor evokes school days past with pencil candle-holders, exam-room chairs and arithmetic on the walls, but the drinks are truly top of the class.

Sinatra
BAR

(☎2310 223 739; Mitropoleos 20, cnr Komninon; ⊗7am-4am) Espresso and wine, together at last. While you might not want both in a single sitting, the quality coffee and breathtaking wine selection make this a sophisticated choice. Sinatra plays jazzy numbers of which Frank himself would no doubt approve.

Froyd's Cocktail Bar
BAR

(☎6942464672; Kalapothaki 3; ⊗8pm-late) Analyse your dreams in between inventive cocktails at this bar tucked away on Kalapothaki. This cosy place constantly refreshes its drinks menu, so between seasonal mixed drinks and themed parties, you'll have plenty of ways to justify a return visit.

☆ Entertainment

City-centre cinemas include **Olympion** (☎2310 378 400; Plateia Aristotelous 10) and **Alpha Odeon** (☎2310 290 290; Tsimiski 43).

National Theatre of
Northern Greece
THEATRE

(☎info & bookings 2315 200 000; www.ntng.gr; Ethnikis Amynis 2) Offers opera, classical Greek drama and modern theatre.

🛍 Shopping

West Egnatia has bargain-basement shopping, while Tsimiski has more upscale clothing and electronics stores.

Georgiadis
HANDICRAFTS

(Egnatia 107; icons from €15; ⊗9am-2pm, 5-9pm) Ever wanted to bedeck your home in the style of a blinged-up Orthodox church? This dazzling shop is crammed with gold chandeliers and lovingly handpainted icons in ornate frames. You can commission a specific one with advance notice.

Medusa Handmade
JEWELLERY

(☎2310 270 401; Egnatia 142; ⊗9am-9pm) Opposite the Arch of Galerius, this inventive shop is stuffed with handmade jewellery and accessories, including unique pendants, vintage-inspired scarves and Mary Poppins brooches.

Beerstore
BEER

(☎2310 233 438; Kalapothaki 6; ⊗noon-2am Mon-Sat, 7pm-2am Sun) This bar and shop sells more than 200 brews, covering regions everywhere from Crete to California (with Belgium and Central Europe especially well represented). Prices are about €2 higher for consumption on the premises.

Pafyllo
CRAFTS

(☎2310 839 115; Paleon Patron Germanou 16; ⊗10am-9pm Mon-Sat) Browse an eclectic selection of jewellery, transport and nautical models, and Union Flag lunchboxes at this quirky fashion and craft shop.

Travel Bookstore Traveller
BOOKS

(☎2310 275 215; www.traveler.gr; Proxenou Koromila 41) Direct your wanderlust at this delightful bookstore that sells maps, uplifting travel souvenirs and stationery, as well as Lonely Planet and other guidebooks.

ℹ Information

INTERNET ACCESS

Free wi-fi zones abound, and many cafes and restaurants offer wi-fi for customers.

MEDICAL SERVICES

Whenever closed, Thessaloniki pharmacies must list nearby working pharmacies. If going to hospital, bring an ID card/passport and insurance information (if possible).

Farmakeio Gouva-Peraki (☎2310 205 544; Agias Sofias 110, Ano Poli) Pharmacy in Ano Poli with experienced staff.

Farmakeio Sofia Tympanidou (☎2310 522 155; Egnatia 9) Well-stocked pharmacy.

Ippokration (☎2310 837 921; Kostantinoupoleos 49) Some 2km east of the centre, this is Thessaloniki's largest public hospital.

MONEY

Except in Ano Poli, banks and ATMs are widespread. Commission-hungry exchange offices line western Egnatia.

POST

Find post-office branches on www.elta.gr. Central post offices include **Agiou Dimitriou** (☎2310 231 579; Agiou Dimitriou 98; ⊗7.30am-2.30pm Mon-Fri) and **Irakliou** (☎2310 277 434; Vassiliou Irakliou 38; ⊗7.30am-8.30pm Mon-Fri, 7.30am-2.30pm Sat, 9am-1.30pm Sun). The train station has a post window.

TOURIST INFORMATION

For local happenings and other info, visit the frequently updated www.enjoythessaloniki.com.

Mt Athos Pilgrims' Bureau (☎2310 252 575; www.agioritikiestia.gr; Egnatia 109; ⊗9am-4pm Mon-Sat) Issues permits for Mt Athos monasteries to male pilgrims.

Tourism Office (☎2310 229 070; www.visitgreece.gr; Plateia Aristotelous; ⊗10am-5pm) The tourism office on Plateia Aristotelous can assist with hotel bookings, local information, and arranging tours and excursions beyond Thessaloniki.

TRAVEL AGENCY

Remember Travel (☎ 2310 246 026; www.
remember-travel.gr; Egnatia 119) This helpful
travel agency can arrange plane tickets, car
rental and excursions.

ⓘ Getting There & Away

AIR

Besides Greece's **Aegean Airlines** (www.
aegeanair.com), many foreign carriers use Thessaloniki for domestic and international flights.
Prices and routes are fluid, so ascertain which
companies are currently flying from the Makedonia Airport (p724) website. Then visit a travel
agent or book online.

Makedonia airport (17km southeast of town) is
served by local bus 78; a taxi costs around €15
to €20. You can store luggage with Sky Bag at
the airport.

BOAT

At the time of writing, travellers were being
advised to travel to Kavala for ferry connections
to the islands. Double-check online through
Thesferry (www.thesferry.gr).

BUS
Domestic

Thessaloniki's main bus station, **KTEL Makedonia** (☎ 2310 595 400; www.ktelmacedonia.gr;
Giannitson 244), is 3km west of the centre. Each

destination has its own specific ticket counter,
signposted in Greek and English.

For Athens *only*, avoid the trip by going instead
to **Monastiriou bus station** (☎ 2310 500 111;
http://ktelthes.gr; Monastiriou 67) – an easy-
to-miss office opposite the train station – where
Athens-bound buses start before calling in at
KTEL Makedonia. Additional discounts to regular
fares apply for kids, students, special-needs
travellers, retirees and soldiers (well, Greek
ones, anyway). Travellers can leave luggage at
KTEL Makedonia (€1 to €7 for 24 hours).

Buses leave for Halkidiki from the eastern
Thessaloniki **Halkidiki bus terminal** (☎ 2310
316 555; www.ktel-chalkidikis.gr; 9km Thessaloniki–Halkidiki road). The terminal is out
towards the airport, reached via city buses 45A
or 45B. From the main bus station, buses stop
en route at the train station and Plateia Aristotelous. With waiting time and traffic, this 'express'
service to the bus terminal can take more than
an hour. Then there's the trip to Halkidiki itself.
The whole production can take three to six
hours. It's wiser to rent a car for your entire
Halkidiki trip or at least take a taxi (€10 to €15)
to Halkidiki bus terminal.

International

KTEL offers international services to Bulgaria
and Albania. Direct services reach Tirana (€30,
nine hours, twice weekly), Sofia (€20 to €23,
five hours, four daily), Plovdiv (€27, 7½ hours,

BUS SERVICES FROM THESSALONIKI'S KTEL MAKEDONIA

DESTINATION	TIME	FARE	FREQUENCY
Alexandroupoli	4hr	€29	7 daily
Arta	4½hr	€36.80	2 daily
Athens	6hr	€39	9 daily
Didymotiho	5½hr	€37.60	5 daily
Drama	2hr	€13	10 daily
Edessa	1¾hr	€8.40	14 daily
Florina	2½hr	€15.60	4 daily
Igoumenitsa	4hr	€34.30	2 daily
Ioannina	3½hr	€28	6 daily
Kastoria	2½hr	€17.60	7 daily
Kavala	2¼hr	€15	4 direct daily
Komotini	3hr	€25.30	7 daily
Litohoro	1¼hr	€8.50	12 daily
Orestiada	6½hr	€39.50	5 daily
Pella	45min	€3.30	18 daily
Serres	1½hr	€8.20	15 daily
Veria	1hr	€6.80	20 daily
Volos	2hr	€18.40	8 daily
Xanthi	2½hr	€19	9 daily

one daily, or transfer via Sofia) and Blagoevgrad (€20, four hours, four daily).

Weekly overnight buses set out to the Slovak and Czech Republics each Wednesday (€70 to €90, 19½ hours), through Bratislava, Brno and Olomouc.

Small bus companies, such as **Simeonidis Tours** (☑ 2310 540 970; www.simeonidistours. gr; 26 Oktovriou 14; ◷ 9am-9pm Mon-Fri, to 2pm Sat), opposite the courthouse, serve Turkey, Romania, Hungary, Serbia, the Czech and Slovak Republics, and Germany. **Crazy Holidays** (☑ 2310 237 696; www.crazy-holidays.gr; Aristotelous 10, 1st fl) operates daily buses to İstanbul departing at 10am and 10pm.

TRAIN

Daily international trains serve Sofia (€16.80, six hours) and Blagoevgrad (€11.60, 4½ hours) in Bulgaria, as well as Skopje (€12.20, six hours) in FYROM and Belgrade (€33.80, 14 hours) in Serbia. Check ahead at Thessaloniki **train station** (☑ 2310 599 421; www.trainose.gr; Monastiriou) or consult the OSE website (www.trainose.gr).

Trains are regular or intercity (IC or ICE). If possible, book a day ahead, as long lines are common.

Direct trains serve Athens (€55.40, 5¼ hours, seven daily), Litohoro (€9, one hour, 10 daily) and Larisa (€14 to €21, two hours, 15 daily). Several daily trains serve Veria, Edessa and Florina (mostly via Platy). Only two daily trains currently serve Xanthi, Komotini and Alexandroupoli in Thrace.

Thessaloniki's train station has ill-kept downstairs toilets, ATMs, a post office, card phones and small modern eateries, plus an Orthodox chapel. Self-serve luggage storage lockers start from €3. Additionally, a staffed luggage storage room (€3 per item per day) operates until 10pm daily – show your train ticket when depositing luggage.

❶ Getting Around

TO/FROM THE AIRPORT

Bus 78 runs half-hourly from the airport, heading west through the city to the main bus station (KTEL Makedonia) via the train station. Tickets cost €2 from the airport to the bus station; €1.10 for short journeys.

Taxis to the airport cost €15 to €20, and even more from midnight until 5am.

BUS

Dependable city buses have electronic rolling signs listing the next destination, accompanied by an audio announcement in Greek and English. Screens above most bus stops note how many minutes until the next buses.

Bus 1 connects the main bus station (KTEL Makedonia) and the train station, while buses 45A and 45B stop at both (plus Plateia Aristote-

lous and Kamara) en route to the Halkidiki bus terminal. From the train station, major points on Egnatia are constantly served by buses such as the 10 and 14.

Buy tickets at *periptera* (street kiosks) for €1, or from on-board blue ticket machines (€1.10). Validate the former in the orange machines. Machines neither give change nor accept bills; when boarding, be sure you have the right change and buy your ticket immediately. Thessaloniki's ticket police pounce at any sign of confusion. If they nab you, you'll pay €60.

CAR

If driving, avoid Ano Poli's steep and narrow streets. If you can't find free parking (a common problem in hectic Thessaloniki), try the municipal parking at the port (per hour €2).

For roadside assistance, call **ELPA** (Greek Automobile Club; ☑ 2310 426 319; Vasilissis Olgas 230).

For rental cars try the following:

Budget Rent a Car (☑ 2310 819 990; KM15 Thessaloniki–Peraia road)

Euro Rent (☑ 2310 286 327; www.eurorent cars.com; Agelaki 1)

TAXI

Thessaloniki's blue-and-white taxis carry multiple passengers, and only take you if you're going the same way. The minimum fare is €3.40. A more expensive 'night rate' takes effect from midnight until 5am. To book a cab for an airport transfer, try **Taxi Way** (☑ 2310 214 900, 2310 866 866; www.taxiway.gr).

Around Thessaloniki

Just 25km south of Thessaloniki, **Epanomi village** is close to beaches, wetlands and an excellent winery and wine museum, **Ktima Gerovassiliou** (☑ 23920 44567; www. gerovassiliou.gr; Epanomi village; ◷ 10am-4pm Mon, Tue, Thu & Fri, 1pm-7pm Wed, 11am-5pm Sun), which enjoys a spectacular setting overlooking the sea from a high bluff.

Potamos Beach, 6km south of Epanomi, has clear waters, cafes, and in summer there is beach volleyball and live music. Near the shore, well-maintained **Hotel Camping Akti Retzika** (☑ 23920 44786, 6937456551; www.retzikas.gr; Potamos Beach, Epanomi; camp sites per person/tent €6/6, r from €40; ◷ Apr-Oct) has extensive campgrounds, modern rooms, and a taverna and beach bar.

Birdwatchers will love the 5½-sq-km **Fanari protected wetlands** nearby, which host diverse flora and fauna, including migratory birds. Get more info from Ktima Gerovassiliou or Akti Retzika camping staff.

NORTHERN GREECE AROUND THESSALONIKI

Halkidiki   Χαλκιδική

The popular Halkidiki Peninsula has three tendrils stretching into the Aegean Sea. Kassandra and Sithonia draw crowds to their blissful beaches and growing adventure travel scene. Meanwhile Athos is the mysterious monks' republic.

Being closest to Thessaloniki, Kassandra is more built up with better nightlife (though it has good beaches, too). More subdued Sithonia has campgrounds, hidden coves and clear waters. Both are popular with Greek and foreign holidaymakers (most from Eastern and Central Europe). Most of the easternmost peninsula belongs to the Mt Athos monastic community. Active for well over 1000 years, it's accessible by boat and open to male pilgrims (with advance reservations).

Kassandra and Sithonia are mostly populated along the coasts, the interiors of both being rugged, with thick pine forests. The main roads, therefore, hug the coasts. Many Halkidiki beach villages were settled by refugees during the 1923 population exchanges with Turkey; the government gave the 'useless' coastal land to these newcomers, and their descendants would have the last laugh when beach tourism took off in the 1970s.

In high summer traffic can be exasperating and finding accommodation tough. For those after beach-bar parties and nightclubs, July and August are best; families and solitude-seekers will prefer September when waters are warmest and the crowds disappear.

It's always wise to plan and book ahead for summer. Outside May to October many hotels undergo refurbishment, restaurants close, and attractions limit their hours.

Kassandra Peninsula
Χερσόνησος Κασσάνδρας

Sublime beaches bring no shortage of tourists to Kassandra; its roads are clogged with Thessaloniki weekenders during the summer. These shores are as popular with Balkan families as Australian backpackers. But look beyond the built-up resorts and package tourists: its rippling forested interior is a delight for road trips; mountain-bike tours are starting to draw visitors away from the shade of their beach umbrellas; and unfussy thermal baths are an antidote to the resort gloss.

Unless you're collapsing in a single village, hire a car to explore this largely public-transport-free peninsula. Kallithea is a great base if you want nightlife. Polyhrono may be crammed with fast-food places and souvenir stands but its beaches deserve attention. Pefkohori is quieter with even more resplendent sands. You'll find the less-busy south coast has more cultural draws, such as snoozy villages and a thermal spa near Loutra.

Activities

Agia Paraskevi Thermal Baths   SPA
(☑23740 71358; Loutra, south coast; admission from €5; ☺9am-9pm summer) This bathing complex near Loutra on the south coast has a large swimming pool of thermally heated water as well as private bathing areas, a *hammam,* a sauna and other soothing amenities. The restorative properties of the mineral waters may linger as long as the sulphurous whiff in your swimsuit. Towel rental is €1 extra.

Break Free   MOUNTAIN BIKING
(☑23103 48073; www.breakfreemtb.com; ☺Apr-Oct) See a more rugged side of Halkidiki with guided mountain-biking excursions ar-

---

MYSTERIES OF ANCIENT AMPHIPOLIS

Excavation of the tombs at Amphipolis has turned into something of an ancient Greek drama. In 2012, digging at the site of ancient Amphipolis (founded 437 BC) revealed an enormous 497m-long perimeter encircling a marble and limestone tomb – the biggest ever found in Greece. While hopes of discovering Alexander the Great's final resting place here have been dashed by experts, intrigue surrounds the identities of the five skeletons pieced together so far, including one of a middle-aged woman.

Bad weather and funding issues have hampered work on the site and visits to the tombs were subject to indefinite delay when we were there. However, the Amphipolis Archaeological Museum (☑23220 32474; Thessaloniki–Kavala road, Amphipolis; adult €2/1; ☺8am-3pm Nov-Mar, to 8pm Apr-Oct) showcases treasures from the site and is open year-round; enquire about visits to the archaeological site.

Amphipolis is about an hour's drive from Thessaloniki; Zorpidis Travel (☑2310 244 400; www.zorpidis.gr) can organise excursions. Alternatively, drive 45 minutes from Kavala.

ranged through this safety-conscious outfit, based in Thessaloniki.

Grigorios Delichristos Excursions
BOAT TOUR

(🖉 6979773905; www.robinson-crusoe.biz.ly; from €100) For island camping excursions, Greg takes small groups on multiday camping trips from Thessaloniki to tiny islets between Kassandra and Sithonia. You can bliss out on the beach, swim or go spearfishing. Prices includes van and boat transport, plus all food and drinks.

🛏 Sleeping

Possidi Camping
CAMPGROUND €

(Camping Kalandra; 🖉 23740 41123; www.possidi camping.gr; Possidi; adult/tent from €6/7; ⊙ May-Sep; 🅿) This well-equipped campground is on Kassandra's south coast, five minutes' drive from Kalandra, and is a great base for water sports. There are also log cabins onsite from €30 per night.

Hotel Odysseas
HOTEL €

(🖉 23720 51923; www.odysseas.net; Polyhrono; d incl breakfast €40-60, tr incl breakfast €44-68; 🅿🍽🛜🏊) Moments from Polyhrono beach, with clean, roomy digs and a small pool.

Blue Bay Hotel
HOTEL €€

(🖉 23740 91645; www.bluebayhotel.com.gr; Afytos; d/ste from €95/125; ⊙ May-Oct; @🏊) This serene hotel, five minutes' drive north of Kallithea, has lively modern decor on the inside, and a delightful blue mosaic pool outside. With beach access, a Greek and international breakfast spread, and a lavish *hammam*, it's family-friendly and a lovely spot to unwind.

Akrogiali Boutique Hotel
BOUTIQUE HOTEL €€

(🖉 23740 51500; www.hotelakrogiali.com; Polyhrono; d €40-140; 🅿🍽) All 10 of the modern rooms at this romantic hotel, 60m from sandy Polyhrono beach, have blissful balconies.

Flegra Palace Hotel
HOTEL €€€

(🖉 23740 61702; www.flegrahotels.com; Pefkohori; d from €150; 🅿🍽🛜🏊) Spacious doubles and suites surround a refreshing pool at this family-friendly four-star hotel with breezy charm, just north of Pefkohori on Kassandra's north coast.

Flegra Beach
APARTMENT €€€

(🖉 23740 61832; Pefkohori; d/ste from €100/215) Newly renovated, opulent Flegra Beach in Pefkohori village has luxury apartments

with nautical yet modern trimmings and a dazzling beach bar and restaurant.

ⓘ Getting There & Away

Hiring a car is the best way to reach and explore Kassandra Peninsula.

Kassandra by bus from Thessaloniki can feel like a slog. Take city bus 45A or 45B to Thessaloniki's KTEL Halkidiki bus terminal (p246). Connections run to Kallithea (€8.80, 1½ hours, 10 daily), Pefkohori (€11.80, two hours, eight daily) and Polyhrono (€11, 2¼ hours, 10 daily) on the north coast, via Kryopigi and Hanioti (€10.60 and €11.50, 2½ hours). Buses also reach Agia Paraskevi spa near Loutra (€12.60, 2½ hours, three daily) and Nea Skioni (€11.90, two hours, three daily) on the south coast. Discounts apply for 15-day open-return tickets.

Return from Kassandra, check timetables with **KTEL Kallithea** (🖉 23740 23714).

Sithonian Peninsula
Χερσόνησος Σιθωνίας

Even if you usually yawn at resort-filled beach destinations, Sithonia's beauty has the power to melt cynicism. Yes, tourists flock here to laze on beaches. But allow the scenery to work its magic: pine forests crowd a wild interior, fringing cliffsides that plummet towards tranquil coves. Sunsets are remarkable; diving and water sports opportunities are excellent; and dozing on a beach might seem a little enticing after all.

Villages are widely dispersed, so hire a car if you want to beach-hop or explore the whole peninsula. Otherwise, choose your base village carefully.

From mainland Halkidiki, the road divides at Nikiti to the east and west coasts. Along the west coast you'll find Sithonia's largest resort, Neos Marmaras.

The east coast's beaches have a little more sparkle and the range of lodgings is more glamorous; Vouvourou has plenty of both. Further south the terrain gets wilder, with fantastic camp sites tucked into hidden bays.

If you don't rate total seclusion, hang your sunhat at Sarti for a 1970s vibe, an escapist feel and good nightlife. Kalamitsi, at Sithonia's southernmost tip, is also an excellent base: it's a good starting point for diving excursions and watersports and has comfortable guesthouses and campgrounds.

🏃 Activities

Along the west coast you'll find well-loved beaches including Paradisos, Kalogria and

Lagomandra. On the east coast, **Karydi** beach has ruggedly rocky views (though it's sometimes not the cleanest), and **Zografou** has stunning sands.

Sarti-based **Sithon Travel** (☑ 23750 94066, Oct-Apr 2310 425 921; www.sarti.gr; Sarti; ⊙ 10am-2pm & 6-10pm) can assist with arranging excursions and activities.

Atlantis Diving Center   DIVING
(☑ 6978165361; www.atlantis-scubadiving.com; Nikiti) Let the safety-conscious diving experts at Atlantis guide you to an underwater wonderland. The range of diving program at this PADI member outfit includes dives for absolute beginners and children. A one-day boat diving trip including transport and refreshments costs €75.

Dolphin Diving Centre   DIVING
(☑ 23750 41346; www.kalamitsi.com; Kalamitsi) Right at the tip of the Sithonian Peninsula, Dolphin offers twice-daily dives from May to mid-October. Prices start at €35 for accomplished divers with their own kit or €60 if you need gear hire. It's adjoined by **Camping Porto Kalamitsi** (☑ 23750 41565; Kalamitsi; camp sites per adult/tent €6/8).

🛏 Sleeping

★ Porto Elea Camping   CAMPGROUND €
(☑ 6984625581; www.portoelea.com; Zografou; sites per adult/child/tent €8/4/10; ⊙ May-Sep) Camping with a luxury feel, nestled in woodland shade by a glowing cove, down a dirt road 9km east from Vouvourou. Once you spy the luminous water from the beach bars or settle in at the excellent taverna, you'll see why Balkan celebs make a beeline for this camping ground. Comfortable bungalows and mobile homes are also available (from €60).

O Giorgakis   PENSION €
(☑ 23750 41013; Kalamitsi; studios €50-80; ⊙ May-Sep) Tucked away from the harbour above the eponymous seafood tavern, this great-value family-run guesthouse in Kalamitsi offers pleasant sea-facing studios. The taverna has a lavish menu, warm service and soothing views of the water.

Camping Armenistis   CAMPGROUND €
(☑ 23750 91487; www.armenistis.com.gr; Sarti; camp sites per person/tent €7.50/7.50; ⊙ May-Sep; P) Large and very popular Camping Armenistis near Sarti enjoys a fantastic setting between forest and beach. Services include a restaurant and crêperie, a cinema, sports grounds and a medical centre. Summer sees frequent concerts and DJ parties. Additionally, a 'tent hostel' sleeps eight (€15 per bed) while you can also rent a caravan or mobile home (from €60).

Thalatta Camp   CAMPGROUND €
(Camping Kalamitsi; ☑ 23750 41411; www.thalatta camp.gr; Kalamitsi; camp sites per adult/tent €5.60/5.20; ⊙ May-Sep) Surrounded by woodland and close to the beach at Kalamitsi, this great campground has decent showers and an on-site pizzeria and Greek taverna. Staff helps organise activities and watersports.

Souzana Rooms   PENSION €
(☑ 23750 41786; www.abelos-suzana.gr; Kalamitsi; apt from €50; ⊙ May-Sep) A short walk from the Kalamitsi waterfront, quiet and homely Souzana Rooms offers simple and good-value lodgings.

🍴 Eating & Drinking

Paris Restaurant   GREEK €
(☑ 23750 91312; www.parisrestaurant.gr; Vourvourou; mains €8-11; ⊙ 10am-2am May-Oct; 🛜) Be thoroughly spoiled by epic sunsets and friendly service at this waterfront taverna. There's live Greek music Friday and Saturday.

Kivotos   SEAFOOD €€
(Noah's Ark; ☑ 23750 94143; waterfront, Sarti; mains €10-12; ⊙ 10am-1am May-Oct) This gloriously situated taverna in Sarti has tables right on the sand and a menu of excellent seafood specialities. Choose from the day's catch and don't skimp on the mouthwatering mezedhes. Effusive owner Daniel is a rich source of local information.

Orange Cafe Beach Bar   CAFE
(waterfront, Sarti; ⊙ 9am-2am; 🛜) This beachfront bar has free wi-fi and relaxing couches under gauze curtains, plus loungers for a quick siesta.

Goa Beach Bar   BAR
(☑ 6977995220; ⊙ Jun-Sep) This famed long-time beach bar 4km south of Sarti pours drinks day and night. Check ahead for DJ sets and themed parties.

ⓘ Getting There & Away

Driving is by far the best way to reach and explore Sithonia. The coastal road loops around the peninsula; driving through the forested interior often takes more time than the long way around.

Budget plenty of time to account for transfers and traffic if travelling from Thessaloniki to Halkidiki by public transport. Buses to the peninsula depart from Thessaloniki's Halkidiki bus terminal (p246), reached via city bus 45A or 45B.

Buses serve Nikiti (€10.60, 1¼ hours, three daily), Neos Marmaras (€13, two hours, three daily), Sarti (€17.40, three hours, three daily) and Kalamitsi (€17.40, 3½ hours, three daily). Check at the bus station for other villages served en route. The discounted return ticket is valid for 15 days.

Crossing to Sithonia from Kassandra by bus requires changing at Nea Moudania, at Kassandra's northern foot. Halkidiki's buses do not go east to Kavala (or anywhere else); it's back to Thessaloniki for everyone.

Athos Peninsula (Secular Athos)
Χερσόνησος του Αθω

Athos offers an unforgettable, immersive experience into a 1000-year-old spiritual tradition – if you're male, that is. While main town **Ouranoupoli** is open to all, just south is a border enclosing the all-male monastic community of Mt Athos from the rest of the world.

Land entry is prohibited between secular and monastic Athos. Boats from Ouranoupoli to the 'monks' republic' are carefully guarded, with thorough checks for customs (and forbidden women).

Male visitors hoping to bunk with the monks must apply for permits well in advance, the reward being access to the peninsula's rugged terrain and dazzling religious architecture. Meanwhile, women travellers in Ouranoupoli might feel alienated or bemused by the whirl of spiritual activity. Women and mixed groups can take boat trips to get a glimpse of Athos.

OURANOUPOLI

A thriving tourist industry has sprung up around Athos' monks. Consequently the pretty seaside town of Ouranoupoli feels rather commercial: expect souvenir stands overflowing with monk-made soaps, high-end jewellery shops, and steep cafe prices. It's a dramatic contrast to the untouched terrain and ongoing spiritual activity across the border in monastic Athos. Nonetheless, it's a pleasant, friendly place with a lively centre and some excellent tavernas and guesthouses.

◉ Sights

Pyrgos Prosforeiou   HISTORIC BUILDING
(Ouranoupoli Tower) The Byzantine tower by Ouranoupoli's harbour dates from the 14th century and is the town's most distinctive landmark. Though closed during our visit, there are plans to re-open the museum within this restored tower.

NORTHERN GREECE HALKIDIKI

Athos Peninsula

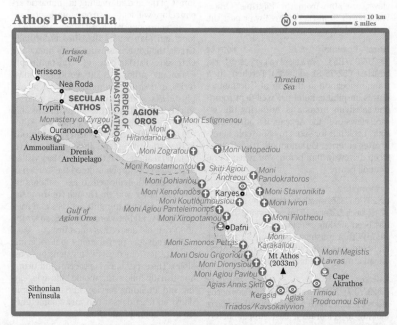

Monastery of Zyrgou
MONASTERY

The only Athos monastery visitable by both men and women, the ruins of 11th-century Zyrgou are a short drive (or hour-long hike) east of Ouranoupoli.

🛏 Sleeping & Eating

Except for high summer, simple and inexpensive domatia are easily available.

Camping Ouranoupoli
CAMPGROUND €

(✏23770 71171, Nov-Apr 23770 71165; www.camping -ouranoupoli.gr; camp sites per adult/tent €9/9; ☺late May–Oct) A solid campground on Ouranoupoli's northern beach side, with on-site supermarket and restaurant. 'Glamping' packages and bungalows are offered for nature seekers averse to pitching their own tent.

Xenios Zeus
PENSION €

(✏23770 71274; www.ouranoupoli.com/zeus; s/d/ tr €40/55/65; 🅿) Crane your neck upwards to see the sign for Xenios Zeus, a somewhat old-fashioned but very comfy family-run hotel in central Ouranoupoli. Like many other places, it will hold excess luggage for monastic pilgrims. There's a discount for members of Britain-based Friends of Mount Athos.

Lazaros Andonakis Rooms
PENSION €

(✏23770 71366; s/d €45/55; 🅿🛜) These airy, pine-furnished rooms, some with harbour views, are 50m from the Pilgrims' Office. Walk north from the White Tower past the harbourside restaurants to find them.

Hotel Filoxenia
HOTEL €€

(✏23770 71158; www.filoxenia-r.gr; s/d/t incl breakfast €52/75/81; 🅿🛜) Perched at the top of Ouranoupoli, this hospitable hotel has well-kept rooms and satisfying breakfasts. Admiring the terrace views over the Aegean, it's hard not to sigh. Look out for signs for Filoxenia shortly after entering Ouranoupoli; it's left, up a steep driveway, 1km before you reach Ouranoupoli centre.

Lemoniadis
TAVERNA €€

(✏23770 71355; www.lemoniadis.com; mains €10-14; ☺lunch & dinner) This waterside taverna has been sizzling sensational seafood since 1957. With a rousing *rembetika* soundtrack and outdoor seating with views of the Aegean, an atmospheric feast is assured.

Kritikos
SEAFOOD €€

(✏23770 71222; www.okritikos.com; Ouranoupoli; mains €12-15; ☺lunch & dinner) Whether you're looking to celebrate a 'last supper' before visiting Mt Athos or just a leisurely dinner, this bright place on a central side street offers some of Ouranoupoli's best fresh fish.

AROUND OURANOUPOLI

Just off Athos' northwestern coast, **Ammouliani** is a small island with fine beaches, pensions, camping, tavernas and 600 year-round inhabitants. Six daily ferries (€2) travel here from **Trypiti**, 7km north of Ouranoupoli; while there isn't much of a ticket office to speak of, you can enquire about timetables and tickets within the cafe at Trypiti dock.

Ammouliani's best beach, **Alykes**, is a 20-minute stroll southwest of the dock. Walking to more distant beaches and accommodation can take over an hour, and the shadeless island has no taxis, so call ahead for a free lift if staying overnight. Waterfront restaurant **Janis** (✏23770 51322; Ammouliani; fish €6-12; ☺9am-11pm May-Oct) is an excellent excuse to linger for fresh seafood and fine sunsets.

Mt Athos (Agion Oros)
Αγιον Ορος

This isolated peninsula has seen unbroken spiritual activity unfold for more than a millennium. Access is granted to male visitors only, on whom traipsing the quiet Athonite forest paths and marvelling at monastic architecture will leave a strong impression.

An enormous World Heritage site, 56km long and 8km wide, Mt Athos is formally Greek, though ecclesiastically it's under the Orthodox Patriarchate of Constantinople (İstanbul). Athos has 20 working monasteries, and *skites* (monastic dependencies), plus *kelli* (ascetic hermitages). The north is thickly forested, and the more inaccessible south is dominated by soaring Mt Athos (2033m). With neither industry nor hunting in the region, it's essentially a nature reserve.

Legend attests that the Virgin Mary visited and blessed Athos; considered the Garden of the Virgin, it's dedicated to her – there's no room for other women. Though controversial to European human-rights activists and frustrating to would-be women visitors, so far the 1000-year-old decree has stood firm.

With advance preparations, male pilgrims can visit for four days (with extensions possible). The experience is peaceful and tiring. You usually follow the monks' lifestyle, eating and attending services at 3am and 3pm daily; on feast days it can mean sometimes up to 10 hours of standing.

History

Unorganised ascetic life is thought to have begun on Athos as early as the 5th and 6th centuries. It was consolidated by Emperor Basil I's AD 885 *chrysobull* (sealed decree) and the 958 arrival of the monk Athanasios. He brought organisation to Athos' spiritual activity by framing daily life around communal food, work and prayer. In 963 the Holy Mountain was formally dedicated when Emperor Nikoforos II Fokas funded Megistis Lavras, still Athos' biggest monastery.

In response to fears that Athos' traditions were being diluted, in 1060 Constantine IX Monomahos banned women, female domestic animals, beardless persons and eunuchs. Women and female animals (except birds) are still refused access to Athos.

By the 11th century, 180 monasteries had been built on Athos, though periodic pillage and burnings by pirates necessitated ongoing investment and repair.

When the Ottomans arrived in 1430, Athonites pledged allegiance to Murad II in return for retaining semi-independent status. During the War of Independence (1821–27), Turks plundered and burned monasteries and their libraries. During the WWII Nazi occupation, Hitler agreed to place Athos under his personal protection. It survived the war unscathed.

Athos' 1927 Constitution was guaranteed in Greece's 1975 Constitution. Each of the 20 surviving monasteries has one representative on the Holy Council *(Iera Synaxis)*, which oversees Athos' 2300 monks. The Julian calendar is still followed by most monasteries.

Getting a Permit

Male visitors should book up to six months ahead for summer and Orthodox holidays. Only 10 non-Orthodox and 100 Orthodox men are admitted daily. Those under 18 must be accompanied by their father or, if with a group or guardian, need their father's written permission.

First call Thessaloniki-based Mt Athos Pilgrims' Bureau (p245) before emailing or faxing them a copy of your passport and your preferred visit dates. They will inform you when you can pick up your permit. Otherwise, if not passing through Thessaloniki, print the confirmation email or retain the fax. Clergymen need written permission from the **Ecumenical Patriarchate of Constantinople** (☑ in Turkey 90 21253 49037; İstanbul). Next, phone monasteries to reserve

specific nights; free accommodation and food is generally offered for one night.

Finally, take your written/printed confirmation to Ouranoupoli for the *diamonitirion* (final permit). Show your passport and booking confirmation at Ouranoupoli's small **Pilgrims' Office** (☑ 23770 71422; fax 23770 71450; Ouranoupoli; ⊘ 8.10am-2pm), on a side street near Jet Oil station, to get the three-night (four-day) *diamonitirion:* students pay €10, Orthodox believers €25, everyone else €30. There's a parking lot (per day €7.50) on Ouranoupoli's south side, though street parking is free.

Entering Athos

Boats leave Ouranoupoli for **Dafni** on weekdays at 8am, 9.45am and 11.45am; get tickets in advance from the **ticket office** (☑ 23770 71248; Ouranoupoli) on the waterfront. In Dafni a bus serves **Karyes**, the administrative capital (€2.60). For monasteries further down the coast, change boats at Dafni.

The *diamonitirion* can be extended in Karyes for another two days.

Exploring Athos

While monastic vehicles, buses and boats operate, walking is ideal for experiencing Athos' serenity. Paths can be overgrown and ravines steep, so watch your step and prepare as you would for any hike (wear decent boots, bring water and use a map).

Twice-daily boats from Dafni (around €2.50) serve west-coast monasteries such as Dionysiou, Simonos Petras, Agiou Pavlou and Agias Triados/Kavsokalyvion.

Dress modestly; don't take photos during church services; and if you must bathe, do it out of sight of monasteries.

◉ Sights

KARYES TO THE SOUTHEAST COAST MONASTERIES & MT ATHOS

From Karyes, walk southeast through the **Kapsala** woods to coastal **Moni Stavronikita** (☑ 23770 23255; ⊘ noon-2pm) or, just under it, **Moni Iviron** (☑ 23770 23643; fax 23770 23248; ⊘ noon-2pm). This Georgian-founded monastery contains more than 2000 manuscripts, including 100 rare Georgian-language parchments.

From Iviron, coastal paths reach hospitable **Moni Filotheou** (☑ 23770 23256; fax 23770 23674), also accessible from Karyes along a shady path with spring water (3½ hours).

ATHOS DAY TRIPS BY BOAT

Regular boat trips from Ouranoupoli skirt Athos, allowing both male and female visitors a peek at Athos' spectacular clifftop monasteries – while carefully keeping to the legal 500m distance from shore, of course.

Athos Sea Cruises (☑ 23770 71370, 23770 71071; www.athos-cruises.gr; Ouranoupoli; adult/child 7-12yr/under 7yr €20/10/free; ⊙ 10.30am Apr-Oct, 10.30am & 1.45pm mid-May–mid-Oct) runs daily three-hour excursions, passing major west-coast monasteries and giving good views of Athos' peak. There's a recorded running commentary in English, German and Greek, which explains Athos' turbulent history and the monks' unchanged lifestyle: work, prayer, sleep (and, occasionally, wine).

If you're based on Halkidiki's Sithonian Peninsula, similar tours run from Ormos Panagias – try **Ormos Travel** (☑ 23750 31522; ormostrv@otenet.gr; Ormos Panagias), whose cruises depart around 9.30am and return by 5pm. A lunch stopover in Ouranoupoli is often included.

Beyond **Moni Karakallou** (☑ 23770 23225; fax 23770 23746) the Byzantine-era path becomes a road leading (after 5½ hours) to Moni Megistis Lavras. Alternatively, buses from Karyes go there.

Magnificent **Moni Megistis Lavras** (Great Lavra; ☑ 23770 23754; fax 23770 23013) is Athos' biggest monastery and houses founder St Athanasios' tomb. From here, a small boat sometimes serves the hospitable west-coast **Agias Annis Skiti** (☑ 23770 23320).

A very tough trail leads around the peninsula's southern tip; it passes the Romanian **Timiou Prodromou Skiti** (☑ 23770 23294), then coastal **Agias Kavsokalyvion** (☑ 23770 23319).

KARYES TO THE SOUTHWEST COAST MONASTERIES

If heading southwest from Karyes you will first encounter **Moni Koutloumousiou** (☑ 23770 23226; fax 23770 23731). Further west, coastal **Moni Xiropotamou** (☑ 23770 23251; fax 23770 23733; ⊙ 12.30-2.30pm) is said to hold the largest known fragment of the True Cross. The path southward accesses Dafni; either walk the coastal path or take the boat, which leaves at 12.30pm, calling at Simonos Petras, Osiou Grigoriou, Dionysiou and Agiou Pavlou.

Spectacular **Moni Simonos Petras** (Simopetra; ☑ 23770 23254; fax 23750 94098; ⊙ 1-3pm), fronted by wooden balconies over a cliff, is Athos' most-photographed monastery. From here the coastal path branches off towards the *arsanas* (monastery port/dock) at a small shrine, accessing **Moni Osiou Grigoriou** (☑ 23770 23668; fax 23770 23671), Athos' most inhabited monastery with a community of 100 monks.

The hilly coastal path south reaches **Moni Dionysiou** (☑ 23770 23687; fax 23770 23686), another tranquil cliff-hanging monastery. Dionysiou's *katholikon* (principal church) contains a unique wax-and-mastic icon of the Virgin and Child.

After Dionysiou, the coastal path continues to the architecturally magnificent **Moni Agiou Pavlou** (☑ 23770 23741; fax 23770 23905) and Agias Annis Skiti.

KARYES TO THE NORTHERN MONASTERIES

Northwards from Karyes, the road passes sprawling **Skiti Agiou Andreou** (☑ 23770 23810). The main route continues to coastal **Moni Pandokratoros** (☑ 23770 23880; fax 23770 23685); an alternative two-hour forest path reaches coastal **Moni Vatopediou** (☑ 23770 41488; fax 23770 41462; ⊙ 9am-1pm), the only monastery to follow the modern Gregorian calendar.

From Vatopediou, a coastal path leads to **Moni Esfigmenou** (☑ 23770 23229), and further on is **Moni Hilandariou** (☑ 23770 23797; fax 23770 23494), a hospitable Serbian monastery (also accessible from Dafni by a south-coast boat, and then a connecting bus ride). The UK-based Friends of Mt Athos donated towards rebuilding structures here that were destroyed in a 2004 fire.

The humble, pretty **Moni Konstamonitou** (☑ 23770 23228) is worth visiting, as is the Bulgarian **Moni Zografou** (☑ 23770 23247) further north. Its name, meaning 'painter', comes from a miraculous icon believed not to have been painted by human hands. The northernmost west-coast monastery, **Moni Dohiariou** (☑ 23770 23245), slopes towards the sea and boasts remarkable architecture.

Next down the coastal path, venerable **Moni Xenofondos** (☏23770 23633; fax 23770 23631) was first mentioned in 998, but probably dates from the 6th century. Although loot-seeking pirates often plundered it, impressive mid-Byzantine marble and wood-carved iconostases survive in its 10th-century *katholikon*. Finally, **Moni Agiou Panteleimonos** (☏23770 23252; ⊙10am-noon), further on, is a typically grand and friendly Russian monastery.

ℹ Information

Dafni has a port authority, **police** (☏23770 23222), customs, post office, gift shops and card phones.

Karyes has an ATM, post office, **police** (☏23770 23212), OTE card phone, a **Community Clinic** (☏23770 23217), and a **Civil Administration Office** (☏23770 23314; Karyes) for permit extensions.

Greek mobile-phone networks operate.

ℹ Getting There & Away

Buses to Ouranoupoli leave Halkidiki bus terminal (p246) in Thessaloniki (€12.40, 3½ hours, seven daily), arriving in central Ouranoupoli, by the tower (Pyrgos Prosforeiou).

If you have arranged an Athos pilgrimage, either take the first bus (5.30am) from Thessaloniki on the date you'll enter Athos, or stay over the night before in Ouranoupoli, which lets you rest, buy supplies and store unnecessary luggage. Get your *diamonitirion* and ticket before the next morning's 9.45am boat.

The Athos–Ouranoupoli ferry leaves Dafni at noon, after a customs check to prevent antiquities theft. The morning boat from monasteries south of Dafni is timed to catch this ferry, which also collects passengers from the coastal monasteries north of Dafni.

The last Ouranoupoli–Thessaloniki bus leaves at 5.45pm. Unfortunately you can't continue from Ouranoupoli to eastern Macedonia or Thrace by bus.

Litohoro & Plaka Litohorou
Λιτόχωρο & Πλάκα Λιτοχώρου

POP 7260 / ELEV 293M

Dainty Litohoro (lih-*to*-ho-ro) straddles beaches, snow-kissed peaks and charismatic ruins. The town has brick bell towers and wood-balconied houses threaded by steep, winding streets. Six kilometres east, **Plaka Litohoro**'s stretch of coastal hotels and campgrounds springs to life during the summer for lazy days and sultry, cocktail-fuelled nights. The general area is known as Pieria,

and nearby beaches such as **Leptokarya** and **Skotina** are very popular with Greek and foreign tourists.

Hugging the coast 20km south of Katerini, Litohoro overlooks the Aegean to its east, with towering Mt Olympus to its west.

Both Litohoro and Plaka Litohoro are well positioned for trips to Mt Olympus, mystical Ancient Dion and Platamonas Castle. If you don't have a car, think carefully where to base yourself; public transport is scant between town and coast so you'll be reliant on taxis.

🏃 Activities

EOS   MOUNTAIN CLIMBING
(Greek Alpine Club; ☏23520 84544, 23520 82444; http://eoslitohorou.blogspot.com; ⊙9.30am-12.30pm & 6-8pm Mon-Sat Jun-Sep) Hikers and climbers should head to EOS, below the public parking lot, which distributes pamphlets with general and Olympus-specific hiking information, and runs mountain refuges. Take Ithakisiou from the square; turn left after 100m. Noticeboards detail the locations of emergency huts and general hiking conditions.

SEO   MOUNTAIN CLIMBING
(Association of Greek Climbers; ☏23520 84200; ⊙6-10pm) This place is informative for hikers and runs an Olympus refuge. Walk down Ithakisiou, turn left and then left again.

🎎 Festivals & Events

Festival Olympou   CULTURAL
(www.festivalolympou.gr; ⊙Jul-Aug) During this summer festival, concerts, plays and artistic events unfold at venues around Litohoro.

🛏 Sleeping

⭐ **Xenonas Papanikolaou**   GUESTHOUSE €
(☏23520 81236; www.xenonas-papanikolaou.gr; Nikolaou Episkopou Kitrous 1; s/d €40/45; P❄@) This romantic guesthouse in a flowery backstreet garden has spacious self-catering rooms, with uplifting views of Litohoro's terracotta rooftops. The downstairs lounge has a fireplace and couches. From the square, take 28 Oktovriou uphill and turn left on Nikolaou Episkopou Kitrous. Breakfast is an extra €4.

Olympos Beach   CAMPGROUND €
(☏23520 22111, 23520 22112; www.olympos-beach.gr; Plaka Litohorou; camp sites per adult/tent €7.50/7.50; P🛜) This leafy, well-run camping option on the Plaka Litohorou strand has a restaurant, mini-mart, well-stocked bar and some bungalows with wi-fi.

Hotel Olympus Mediterranean HOTEL €€

(☑23520 81831; www.mediterraneanhotels.gr; Dionysou 5; d/tr incl breakfast €70/90, luxury ste €100; ❄@☜) This four-star hotel occupies a neoclassical building with ornate balconies, and has 20 luxurious rooms and three suites, plus an indoor pool and sauna. Some rooms have fireplaces and spas.

Cavo Olympo Luxury
Resort & Spa RESORT €€€

(☑23520 22222; www.cavoolympo.gr; Plaka Litohorou; d/ste from €210/250; P❄@☎☜) On the seafront, this minimalist masterpiece consists of 49 rooms and suites overlooking either Olympus or the sea, some with spas or private pools. All are airy, spacious and relaxing, with big balconies. The hotel's centrepiece is an enormous infinity pool sloping towards the bluff overlooking the water.

✖ Eating & Drinking

★ Meze Meze GREEK €

(☑23520 82271; Agiou Nikolaou 40; mains €6-8; ☺6pm-10.30pm Tue-Fri, noon-3pm & 6pm-10.30pm Sat, noon-3pm Sun; ☎) Smack your lips for plump mussels on rice, grilled meats and the catch of the day at this wonderfully simple taverna near Litohoro's bus station. Rotating daily specials keep things fresh and interesting; salads are generous, and the service is attentive.

Erato MEDITERRANEAN €€

(☑23520 21100; Agiou Nikolaou; mains €8-15; ☺lunch & dinner) Tuck into seafood, baked cheeses and classic Greek grills at this chic restaurant near Agiou Nikolaou church by the main square. The mountain views are as glorious as the wine list.

Gastrodromio GREEK €€

(☑23520 21300; Agiou Nikolaou 36; mains €10-15; ☺noon-late) If Gastrodromio was around in Olympian times, Zeus and co would have dined here. Busy your fork with truffle-laced risotto, lamb stewed in rosemary and tomato, and 30 different cheese options.

Mylos Beach Bar BAR

(Plaka Litohorou; ☺9am-3am) Open in high season (from June to September), Mylos is Plaka Litohorou's most popular beach bar by day and by night.

❶ Information

Plateia Eleftheria and Ithakisiou have ATMs.
Katerini Hospital (☑23510 57200) is the near-est hospital with an accident and emergency department.

Police (☑23520 81100; cnr Ithakisiou & Agiou Nikolaou)

Tourist Information Booth (Agiou Nikolaou; ☺9am-6pm Jun-Sep) In a white building with a tiled roof, by the municipal park.

❶ Getting There & Away

From the **bus station** (☑23520 81271; Agiou Nikolaou) in Litohoro town, buses serve Katerini (€2.30, 25 minutes, 14 daily), Thessaloniki (€8.50, 1¼ hours, 13 daily) and Athens (€33, 5½ hours, two daily via Katerini). Buses from Thessaloniki to Volos and Athens drop you on the highway to catch a Katerini–Litohoro bus.

Litohoro's **train station** (☑23520 22522) is 4km north of Plaka Litohorou and serves Thessaloniki (€9, one hour, 10 daily). For Florina and Edessa, change at Platy (€6, 30 min, 10 daily).

Around Litohoro

Mt Olympus MOUNTAIN

The cloud-covered lair of the Ancient Greek pantheon, awe-inspiring Mt Olympus (Ορος Όλυμπος) fires visitors' imaginations today, just as it did for the ancients who venerated it. Greece's highest mountain, Olympus hosts more than 1700 plant species, some rare and endemic, as well as wolves, jackals, deer and more than 100 bird species. Its slopes are thickly forested and its peaks often shrouded in fog.

The first known mortals to reach **Mytikas** (2918m), Olympus' highest peak, were Litohoro local Christos Kakalos and Swiss climbers Frédéric Boissonnas and Daniel Baud-Bovy in August 1913. Olympus became Greece's first national park in 1938.

Although you can drive up Olympus, many people hike; consult the Litohoro-based hiking associations for maps and current conditions, or check with the **Management Agency of Olympus National Park** (☑23520 83000; www.olympusfd.gr), which also lists the hiking routes and the regulations for visitors. Both provide info on the mountain's 15 refuges, where hikers can sleep.

Ancient Dion HISTORIC SITE

(Δίον; ☑23510 53484; Dion Archaeological Park; adult/student €6/2 incl Archaeological Museum; ☺8am-8pm) Dion was sacred for ancient Macedonians worshipping the Olympian gods, especially Zeus. Before his epic eastern adventures, Alexander the Great made sacrifices here. A path leads through more than a dozen clearly labelled sites, including sacred springs and the ruins of a Roman theatre. This wooded area is also rich in wildlife: look out for frogs tumbling into often flooded sanctuaries and kingfishers diving with a sapphire flash.

The ruins of the 6th-century BC **Sanctuary of Demeter** are the first you'll see and are the site's oldest. Further along is the leafy **Sanctuary of Zeus Hypsistos**, which bears copies of statues and column bases (the originals are in the on-site museum). Other replicas adorn the remnants of Dion's (usually flooded) **Sanctuary to Isis**, goddess of childbirth, across a small bridge. As elsewhere in the Hellenistic world, worship of this Egyptian goddess was merged with that of Artemis and Aphrodite. Later constructions include 4th-century-AD Christian **basilica ruins** and **public baths** once paved with mosaics.

The park has a small visitors' centre with cafe. Entry includes the **Archaeological Museum of Dion** (🗗 23510 53206; Dion; adult/student incl Ancient Dion site €6/2; ☺8am-8pm), a 10-minute walk from the site. Taxis from Litohoro to Dion cost from €12.

Castle of Platamonas   CASTLE
(Κάστρο Πλαταμώνα; 🗗23250 44470; Platamonas; adult/child €2/free; ☺8am-3pm) Looming from a coastal bluff near Platamonas village, 20km south of Plaka Litohorou, this well-preserved 11th-century castle was once defended by brave Byzantines, safeguarding trade routes and scanning for pirates. Today, however, the only *stratiotes* (soldiers) you're likely to see are handymen with weed whackers and the occasional lumbering turtle. Taxis from Litohorou town cost about €22.

From the parking area, pass the (unstaffed) booth and take the hilly path 150m to the castle and ticket booth. From here, follow the walls counter-clockwise to understand the fortress' development over time. The first small tower on the right dates from the 6th-century emperor Justinian, and predates much of the existing structure. The ruined Byzantine **Church B** was rebuilt in the 17th century.

The more extensive **Church A** ruins, protected by a wooden enclosure, were built over a 2nd-century-AD Hellenistic warehouse. Squint through the gloom to see faint fresco remains. At the castle's nearby northeastern edge, drink in magnificent views of sandy **Skotina Beach** below and Mt Olympus in the distance.

Skeletal outlines of *oikous* (medieval dwellings) and shops are signposted further down the walls. The final upwards turn into the archway leads to the **acropolis**, where the castle's deep **cistern** lies under a grate. This well-protected space contains the castle's most magnificent tower, the **pyrgos**; unfortunately closed, it dates from the 14th century, and the last Byzantine (Palaeologan) dynasty. Archaeologists believe that Late Antique Herakleion was originally here. The castle hosts concerts during the Festival Olympou (p255).

Veria   Βέροια
POP 48,300

A little exploration is required to uncover the historic neighbourhoods and cultural riches of Veria. Around 75km west of Thessaloniki, this small city has colourful, crumbling old quarters, polished museums and enough excellent eateries to detain a gourmand for days. Veria is also a good spot to linger en route to Vergina's tombs or the ski areas at Mt Vermio.

⊙ Sights & Activities

Archaeological Museum   MUSEUM
(🗗23310 24972; Leoforos Anixeos 45; admission €2, combined ticket incl Byzantine Museum and Vergina €8; ☺8am-8pm) Browse an impressive haul from neolithic figurines to Vergina tomb findings at this museum, located at Anixeos' northern end. You'll find iron swords, delicate jewellery, doe-eyed portrait heads and a charming statue of Aphrodite slipping out of her sandals. A combined ticket (€80) for Veria's Archaeological and Byzantine Museums, plus the royal tombs at Vergina, saves €4.

Byzantine Museum   MUSEUM
(🗗23310 25847; Thomaidou 26; admission €2, combined ticket incl Archaeological Museum and Vergina €8; ☺8am-4pm Tue-Sun) This museum in a restored mill will turn you from novice to nerd in all things Byzantine. Splendorous Madonnas, huge 5th-century floor mosaics and ornate sarcophagi fill all three floors of the beautifully lit space. A film on the bottom floor gives the history of the mill and Veria's Barbouta quarter.

Barbouta   HISTORIC SITE
Walk from Plateia Antoniou down Vasileos Konstandinou to find Veria's atmospheric former Jewish quarter. The huge, ancient

plane tree here is where the Turks hanged Archbishop Arsenios in 1430, after taking Veria. Opposite, the decapitated minaret on the dilapidated 12th-century **cathedral** indicates Ottoman interference.

Mt Vermio   SKIING
(📞info 23310 49226) Some 22km northwest of Veria, Mt Vermio has three small ski areas with a total of 585m of vertical. It's a good spot for beginners, but check conditions in advance. Visit from December to March.

🛏 Sleeping

⭐**Kokkino Spiti**   BOUTIQUE HOTEL **€€**
(📞23310 74440; www.kokkinospiti.gr; Olganou 10, Barbouta; s/d €60/75; 🅿 ❄ 🛜) This restored 1840 mansion has six uniquely decorated bedrooms that are full of charm: wrought-iron bed frames, wood-beamed ceilings and river views. It's a boutique gem, nestled in the heart of Veria's old Jewish quarter, and as comfortable as it is elegant.

Hotel Makedonia   HOTEL **€€**
(📞23310 66902; www.makedoniahotel.gr; Kontogiorgaki 50; s/d incl breakfast €50/59; 🅿 ❄ 🛜) The reliable Makedonia has handsome, well-furnished rooms and impeccable service, all in a fine central location.

Hotel En Eari   HOTEL **€€**
(📞23310 75788; www.eneari.gr; Leoforos Anixeos 82; s/d/tr €80/89/90; 🅿 ❄ 🛜) En Eari has homely rooms and friendly service. This simple and unfussy hotel is a short walk from the nightlife on Elias, just a few paces from the Archaeological Museum and faces the new church.

🍴 Eating & Drinking

⭐**Eleas Gi**   TAVERNA **€**
(📞23310 23053; Anixeos 65, cnr Koundouriotou; mains €8-10; ⏲lunch & dinner; 🛜) Feast on home-cooked Macedonian fare in this lively taverna. Tangy pomegranate chicken is cooked to perfection; smoky cheeses demand attention among mouthwatering salads and appetisers; and there's always a tempting aroma from the grill. Service can be leisurely but the welcome is very warm.

12 Grada   MEDITERRANEAN **€€**
(📞23311 00112; Dimosthenous; mains €12-15; ⏲noon-midnight) There's no more picturesque spot to clear a plate of grilled vegetables and juicy meatballs than this riverside taverna and wine bar.

Vergiotiko   GREEK **€€**
(📞23310 74133; www.vergiotiko.gr; Thomaidou 2; mains €8-15; ⏲lunch & dinner) Loosen your belt for generous servings of oregano pork, chicken schnitzel and cheese-stuffed peppers at this grotto-like restaurant. Find it near the Byzantine Museum.

Coin Cafe-Bar   BAR
(📞23310 71727; Elias 14; ⏲7am-1am; 🛜) This cafe-bar spills onto the pavement of bubbly Elias, its decent coffees and a range of cocktails all delivering a satisfying sugar rush. The dangling lightbulbs and verandah seating give it a modern, unfussy vibe. Coffees from €2 and cocktails from €7.

ℹ Information

ATM-equipped banks line Venizelou and Mitropoleos.

Police (📞23310 22391; Mitropoleos)

Post Office (Mitropoleos 39)

ℹ Getting There & Away

BUS

Veria's two central adjoining **bus stations** (📞23310 26100, 23310 22342; Iras) serve Thessaloniki (€6.80, one hour, 14 daily), Athens (€35, 6½ hours, two daily), Edessa (€4.70, one hour, one daily) and Vergina (€1.60, 20 minutes, six daily).

TRAIN

The **train station** (📞23310 24444), 2km north of town, has trains for Thessaloniki (€5, one hour, six daily) and Florina (€9, two hours, three daily).

ℹ Getting Around

Veria is walkable and has **taxis** (📞23310 26049).

Edessa   Εδεσσα

POP 18,200

If you've spent your time sweating through hikes or wiping dust from your brow in archaeological parks, a stop in Edessa (*edh*-eh-sah) will refresh and restore you. Waterfalls, fountains and babbling brooks combine to make 'the town on the waters' the most invigorating spot in central Macedonia. The falls (the biggest in the Balkans) are the highlight, but an old quarter and pretty Byzantine bridge pile on the charm.

Until the 1977 discovery of Vergina's royal tombs, Edessa was thought to have been ancient Macedonian Aigai. With the govern-

SPLENDOURS OF ANCIENT MACEDON: VERGINA & PELLA

Northern Greece boasts two remarkable sites of the ancient Macedonia dynasty. The royal burial site at Vergina lies 11km southeast of Veria. Between Thessaloniki and Edessa lies Alexander the Great's birthplace, the former royal capital Pella.

With a car, it's possible to see both sites in a single day trip from Thessaloniki. Matching up bus connections can be a jigsaw, so if you don't have wheels consider exploring Pella and Vergina on separate days or staying overnight: hospitable **Olympia Guesthouse** (☑23310 68052; www.xenonasolympia.gr; Aristotelous, Vergina; s/d/tr 35/45/60; P 🛜) is five minutes' walk from Vergina's archaeological site.

The Sites

Archaeological Site of Pella (☑museum 23820 31160; Pella; adult/child incl museum admission €6/3; ⊗8am-8pm, closed various public holidays) Pella rose to fame when King Archelaos (413–399 BC) made it a capital of the ancient kingdom of Macedon. This atmospheric archaeological site, with re-erected columns and black-and-white geometric mosaics, fires the imagination about the city's glory days. Don't miss 300 BC Dionysus House, the largest in Pella, and the splendid stag-hunting mosaics.

Archaeological Museum of Pella (☑31160 23820; www.pella-museum.gr; Thessaloniki–Edessa national hwy; adult/child incl entrance to archaeological site €6/3; ⊗8am-8pm, closed various public holidays; P) This airy two-floor museum on Pella's western edge unravels the city's history, from Bronze Age bones in urns to well-preserved 300 BC mosaics and phallic drinking vessels. Burial treasures include helmets, swords, and the mauve garb and remarkable gold jewellery of 'The Lady of Aigai', wife of Amyntas I.

Vergina Royal Tombs Museum (☑23310 92347; www.aigai.gr; Vergina; adult/child €8/4; ⊗8am-8pm) A grass-covered *tumulus* (burial mound) has been converted into a truly spine-tingling museum where visitors can descend to the entryways of royal tombs and admire treasures unearthed at this very site. The showpiece is the 336 BC tomb of Philip II: prepared for a serious party in the afterlife, Phillip was buried with silver chalices, an ivory and gold shield, a gold-plated quiver and his full suit of armour, all on display here.

Elsewhere in the museum, Tomb I and Tomb IV boast mythic friezes, while Tomb III, the prince's tomb, is thought to be the final resting place of the son of Alexander the Great. About 400m past the Royal Tombs lie extensive palace ruins of 3rd-century-BC king Antigonos Gonatas. Closed on our visit, these ruins have a large Doric peristyle surrounded by pebble-mosaic floors.

Getting There & Away

Buses from Thessaloniki to Palia Pella (€3.30, 45 minutes, seven daily) stop by the main road, 20 minutes walk from the museum. From Thessaloniki to Vergina, take the bus to Veria (€6.80, one hour, 14 daily) and change to a bus to Vergina (€1.60, 20 minutes, six daily).

ment's Hellenisation project following the 1923 Greek–Turkish population exchanges, the town's long-existing Slavic name, Voden ('place of water') was replaced with the archaic Edessa.

⊙ Sights

Varosi, Edessa's old quarter, lies south of Waterfalls Park. Brightly coloured traditional houses and churches make it a captivating area for a stroll. Edessa's **Byzantine Bridge** offers an essential photo op; take Ir Polytechniou from central Plateia Timenidon until you reach the river fork.

Waterfalls Park   WATERFALL
(☑info 23810 20300; Edessa) **FREE** Several viewing points around Waterfalls Park allow you to gaze at Edessa's thundering star attraction. The larger of the two falls, **Karanos**, is especially impressive at 70m high; visit on a sunny day to see rainbows glint from its swirling mists. A path winds downwards to a second, smaller waterfall.

The **cave** (admission €0.50) is worth a peep for its fang-like stalactites, though the narrow grotto is sadly scarred by graffiti. Through the cave you can stand behind Karanos' curtain of falling water. A short walk away from the watery action, towards Varosi, lie family-friendly attractions including an open-air **Water Museum** (⊙11am-4pm Wed-Mon) and a small aquarium and reptile house.

Folkloric Museum
MUSEUM
(Meg Alexandrou, Varosi; adult €2; ⊙9am-4pm Tue-Sun) Written explanation is scant at this small museum in the Varosi quarter. But its three creaky floors hold enough embroidered rugs, farming implements and looms to satisfy any fan of folk history.

🛏 Sleeping

Hagiati
PENSION €
(☎23810 51501; www.hagiati.gr; Makedonomahon 40; s/d incl breakfast €50/60; P❄🛜) This colourful guesthouse in the old quarter has a wonderfully traditional feel with wooden furnishings, a rustic lounge room and a serene open courtyard.

Hotel Alfa
HOTEL €
(☎23810 22231, 23810 22221; hotel-a@otenet.gr; Egnatia 28; s/d/ste €40/55/100; P🛜) This hotel occupies two adjoining buildings by Plateia Alexandrou. Alfa does everything simply and well, thanks to its earnest and helpful staff. All 45 of its clean, spacious rooms have a balcony but the best views are from suites on the 6th floor. Special-needs rooms are available.

★ Varosi Four Seasons
BOUTIQUE HOTEL €€
(☎23810 51440; www.varosi4seasons.gr; Arhiereos Meletiou; s/d incl breakfast €70/90; P❄🛜) This boutique hotel is 50m from its related pension, Varosi Guesthouse. Six of the 10 rooms overlook the outstretched Edessa plain (as does the outdoor verandah cafe). Rooms are pristine and sumptuously decorated, and service is friendly.

Varosi Guesthouse
PENSION €€
(☎23810 21865; www.varosi.gr; Arhiereos Meletiou 45-47; s/d incl breakfast €55/70; P❄) This restful pension occupies a restored traditional wood-and-stone house in Edessa's old quarter. Rooms have double-wood doors, fine linen, colourful embroidery and antique brass beds. In winter a fireplace heats the lounge rooms, while the flower-filled balcony is superb for a relaxing coffee in summer.

🍴 Eating & Drinking

Ousies
GREEK €
(☎23815 02414; 25th Martiou 4; mains €5-8; ⊙noon-1am) Ousies serves mezedhes, such as dolmadhes and fish, and mains such as chicken wrapped in bacon and stuffed with yellow cheese and peppers. It's all accompanied by fiery *tsipouro* (distilled spirit similar to ouzo), the best being from the local grape varietal *opsimo*. The rustic decor, including historic photos and hanging instruments, is enhanced by *rembetika* music.

Irtha & Edessa
TAVERNA €€
(☎23813 00660; cnr Karaoli & Tsmiski; mains €12; ⊙lunch & dinner; 🛜🚷) This local favourite close to Edessa's waterfalls has spit-roasted lamb and grilled meat specialities to please even the hungriest carnivores. Fresh ingredients are served simply, but they sure don't skimp on the feta.

Jam
CAFE
(☎6936653868; Dimitriou Rizou 8; coffees €2; ⊙10am-3pm & 6pm-late) Wistful lyrics by the Smiths cover the frosted glass windows of this edgy cafe-bar. The Brit-fancying decor and great drinks attract a lively yet laid-back crowd. Return by evening when coffee frappés are swapped for beers and harder beats.

ℹ Information

ATM-equipped banks line Dimokratias.
Police (☎23810 23333; Iroön Polytehniou)
Post office (Pavlou Mela)
Tourist information office (☎23810 20300; www.edessacity.gr; ⊙10am-6pm) Kiosk before the waterfalls with friendly multilingual advice, and maps of Edessa and nearby attractions.

ℹ Getting There & Around

From **Edessa bus station** (KTEL Pellas; ☎23810 23511; www.ktelpellas.gr; Pavlou Mela 13) buses serve Thessaloniki (€12, two hours, hourly), Veria (€4.70, one hour, five daily) and Athens (€45.60, eight hours, three daily). The bus to Florina (€8.10, 1½ hours, two daily) departs from 30m away.

The **train station** (☎23810 23510; Leoforos Nikis) is on the Thessaloniki–Athens line and also serves Florina (€7, one hour, three daily).

Find **taxis** (☎23810 23392, 23810 22904) on the corner of Dimokratias and Monastiriou.

Florina
Φλώρινα

POP 20,000

Snug within a lush valley, at first glance Florina (*flo-rih-nah*) seems a typical student town. But lift your gaze to its mountainous backdrop and you'll soon understand why hikers and winter-sports fans find their way here. Florina is a springboard to remarkable natural spaces to its west, including cragged Mt Vigla 15km away and the wild Prespa Lakes 45km away. Florina also serves as a crossroad for further Balkan travel: south of Prespa Lakes lies Krystallopigi, the border crossing into Albania, and lively Bitola in the Former Yugoslav Republic of Macedonia (FYROM) is only 35km north of Florina.

While Florina itself doesn't overflow with attractions, a short stop will give you a taste of its distinctive local produce, including sweet red peppers and Prespa beans. There's also some effervescent nightlife, focused around pedestrianised Pavlou Mela in the centre.

Florina was the northernmost town occupied and annexed by Greek troops during the Balkan Wars of 1912–13; its location just south of the mountains kept it near the front in subsequent wars. The existence of Greece's (Slavic) Macedonian minority, denied outright by the government and Greece's latter-day fascists, has always been sensitive in the Florina, Edessa and Prespa regions, where the Macedonian language is still spoken by many Greek people. Pressure from Greek society, media and government has suppressed it, but if you have sharp ears, you'll still hear Macedonian spoken, though usually in villages and by older people.

◉ Sights & Activities

Archaeological Museum   MUSEUM
(☑ 23850 28206; Sidirodromikou Stathmou 3; admission €2; ☺ 8am-3pm Tue-Sun) This museum near the train station paints a picture of the verdant Florina region across millennia, with detailed exhibits on daily life and traditions in ancient Macedonia. Look out for stone reliefs adorned with Macedonian horsemen and haunting 1st-century-BC graves, carved with the faces of those residing within.

Vigla-Pissoderi Ski Area   SKIING, SNOW SPORTS
(☑ 23850 45010; www.vigla-ski.gr; Vigla-Pissoderi; ☺ 9am-4pm Dec-Mar) This small ski area is nestled between the Varnous and Verno mountain ranges, 19km west of Florina. With 11km of pistes and five lifts, it has enough terrain to keep snow-heads of most levels happy for a weekend. Check snow conditions before you go.

⛏ Sleeping

Hotel Hellinis   HOTEL €
(☑ 23850 22671; www.hotel-hellinis.gr; Pavlou Mela 31; s/d €35/40; ☎) This central budget option ticks all the backpacker basics with clean,

spacious rooms, free wi-fi and a location five minutes from the bus and train stations.

Pleiades   BUNGALOW €€
(☑ 23850 44070; www.pleiadesflorina.gr; Papathanasiou; s/d/tr €80/90/100; ⏫ ❄ ☎) This self-enclosed stone village of cottages and suites fuses traditional Macedonian architecture with modern amenities including a summer pool. It's 2km north of town.

Hotel Veltsi   HOTEL €€
(☑ 23850 46555; www.hotel-veltsi.gr; Km 6 Florina–Prespes Rd; d €70; ⏫ ❄ ☎ ❙) This trim boutique hotel, 6km west of Florina, has woodland views, well-furnished rooms, a pool and a playground. Veltsi is perfectly positioned for winter adventures at Vigla-Pissoderi Ski Area, 13km further west.

✗ Eating & Drinking

Sakoulevas Cafe Restaurant   CAFE €
(☑ 23850 25580; Eleftherias 68; mains €8; ☺ lunch & dinner) Feast on traditional Florina specialities at this agreeable cafe right next to the rushing River Sakoulevas. Homely favourites such as Prespa beans, grilled trout and 'grandma's meatballs' keep a bustling clientele fed at this scenic spot. Save room for the market cheeses.

Koukoutsi   GREEK €
(☑ 23850 46010; Stoa Spyraki 6; mezedhes €3-6; ☺ 11am-1am) Koukoutsi serves refreshing mezedhes, steamed mussels and famous Florina red peppers with garlic and tomato. The range of grilled meats ensures you won't leave hungry.

Prespa   TAVERNA €
(☑ 23850 23973; Tirnavou 12; mains €5-8; ☺ dinner) Tucked away from the hubbub of Pavlou Mela, this unassuming taverna has fine grills and a mouthwatering range of Greek specialities.

Duck   CAFE
(☑ 6977577322; P Mela 68; ☺ 10am-late; ☎) The swankiest spot in Pavlou Mela's stretch of cafe-bars, hip Duck unites wi-fi-seeking students and chic good-timers. Swap coffee cups for cocktail flutes at sunset.

ℹ Information

ATM-equipped banks are near the square, on Stefanoi Dragoumi.

Police (☑ 23850 22222; Saggariou 24)

Post Office (Plateia Giorgiou Modi)

GREECE'S FORGOTTEN WATERWAYS: THE PRESPA LAKES

West of Florina, the twin Prespa Lakes (collectively called Prespes by Greeks) are a breath-taking beauty spot, rich in both wildlife and history. **Megali Prespa** and **Mikri Prespa** (Great Prespa and Small Prespa) are the Balkans' highest tectonic lakes and among Europe's most ancient, at one million years old. Once a single lake, today they are separated by a narrow isthmus formed by sediment churned up over centuries. Greece shares Megali Prespa with the Former Yugoslav Republic of Macedonia (FYROM) to the north and Albania to the west, and Mikri Prespa with Albania. On all shores the inhabitants are ethnically (Slavic) Macedonian, which has meant occasional political friction in all three countries.

The wildlife is as extraordinary as Prespes' mountain-backed setting, with brown bears, wolves and wild pigs skulking around the lakes. The region is also a-flutter with more than 260 types of bird, including the world's largest colony of Dalmatian pelicans (more than 1450 breeding pairs) at Mikri Prespa, as well as great white pelicans, great white egrets and the EU's largest colony of pygmy cormorants. A clutch of sleepy villages, each with a distinct character, act as springboards to this majestic wilderness.

Driving allows you to make the most of Prespa Lakes. Once-weekly buses from Florina take a circuitous route each Wednesday at 7am (€5.20, 1½ hours), returning the same day at 2pm. Mention to the driver which village you want to get to. Taxis from Florina cost €60 to €80.

Agios Germanos

With its stone houses and well-preserved churches, Agios Germanos is the region's most visually appealing town. The highlight is 11th-century **Agios Germanos church**, an extraordinary work of ecclesiastic mid-Byzantine architecture with a domed brick structure and separate bell tower. This town makes a good base because of its homely accommodation and tavernas, and its helpful **information centre** (Prespa National Forest Management Body; ☑23850 51870; Agios Germanos; ☺9.30am-3pm) that advises on hiking, birdwatching and wildlife. For emergencies, there's a **police station** (☑23850 51202; Agios Germanos) in the village and a **health centre** (☑23850 46284; Lefkonas) further south in Lefkonas.

Agios Ahillios

The semidetached island of Agios Ahillios is Prespes' main attraction and its surrounds are excellent for birdwatching. The grand, concave outer wall of the ruined **Basilica of Agios Ahillios** stands on its eastern shore, with some half-toppled walls, columns and a stone floor. It's a legacy of the 10th-century Bulgarian tsar Samuel, who expanded his empire across much of the southern Balkans, chronically sparring with Byzantium. From Agios Germanos, cross the connecting strip between the two lakes and turn immediately left onto a 1km-long wooden bridge. A signposted path to the left hugs the east coast and leads to the basilica and other church ruins. Alternatively, turn right off the bridge for the shop and **taverna**. Agios Ahillios is sparsely inhabited, though August's Prespes Festival features a headlining concert in the amphitheatre-like basilica.

Psarades

On Lake Megali Prespa's promontory, friendly Macedonian-speaking villagers inhabit Psarades (population 144), while 1m-tall dwarf cattle meander in its surrounds. Fishers offer boat trips to Megali Prespa's isolated Byzantine *askitiria* (hermitages). These include the 13th-century **Metamorfosi**, where scant remnants survive of paintings and sections from a wood-carved *temblon* (votive screen); 15th-century **Mikri Analipsi**; and 14th-century old rock **Church of Panagia Eleousa**, tucked above a ravine, with beautiful frescoes.

Vrondero

South of Psarades and close to the Albanian border, farming village Vrondero has little to detain you other than access to excellent walking trails. **Kokkalis Cave**, used as a partisan hospital during the Greek Civil War, is a 30-minute hike from Vrondero or a short drive if you have a 4WD. For maps and info, contact the **Society for the Protection of Prespa** (☑23850 51233; www.spp.gr; Lemos) in **Lemos** village, just west of Agios Germanos.

ℹ Getting There & Away

BUS
Domestic
Florina bus station (KTEL Florinas; ☑ 23850 22430; www.ktelflorinas.gr; Makedonomahon 10) serves Athens (€50.50, nine hours, one daily) and Thessaloniki (€15.60, 2¾ hours, eight daily). Two serve Thessaloniki direct via the Egnatia Odos highway, the others go through Edessa (€8, 1½ hours, three daily).

For Prespa, buses now leave only on Wednesdays at 7am, returning at 2pm. Tell the driver your destination when you board, as they may skip some villages. For Kastoria, head to Amyntaio (€3.70, 30 minutes, eight daily) and change buses there. Amyntaio has daily buses for Kastoria (€9, 1½ hours). Twice-weekly Florina buses also reach Ioannina (€30, three hours); alternatively, take a bus to Kozani and change there.

International
The Greece–FYROM border is served by buses to Niki (€1.80, 30 minutes) twice daily during the school year and at other times once a week on Wednesdays. The Greece–Albania border crossing at Krystallopigi (€5.40, one hour) is served once-weekly by the Prespa-bound bus.

TAXI
A taxi trip to Bitola (40km) in the FYROM costs around €45 one way, or €60 return including two hours for shopping and sightseeing. Florina cabbies also drive to the Prespa Lakes villages; Agios Germanos costs around €60, Psarades €80.

TRAIN
Florina's **train station** (☑ 23850 22404) connects with Edessa (€7, 1¼ hours, three daily) and Thessaloniki (€10, 2½ hours, three daily).

Kastoria   Καστοριά
POP 17,000

Kastoria doesn't simply border the wilderness: it's practically submerged in nature. The city is nearly marooned within glassy Lake Orestiada. Enveloped by the lake, Kastoria gives the sense it might weigh anchor and drift away.

This peaceable location invigorates Kastoria's outdoor activities; 9km circuits of the lake are popular among hikers and cyclists. It's a dream scenario for wildlife lovers, who can admire preening pelicans and darting ferruginous ducks (no binoculars required). Meanwhile, Kastoria's lakeshore bars are fashionable but always laid-back.

Fur sellers are still dotted along the shore, harking back to Kastoria's enrichment through the fur trade; the city's name comes from *kástoras,* meaning beaver. Today the furs are imported. Deeper into Kastoria's steep and winding lanes you'll find a surprising wealth of post-Byzantine churches. Many could use a lick of paint and you might have to ask the tourist information kiosk to allow you in for a peep.

Most charismatic is Kastoria's historic Doltso neighbourhood. This romantically creaky quarter has several restored 18th- and 19th-century mansions housing museums and tavernas.

◎ Sights & Activities

Within the **Doltso** quarter, admire colourful and timbered *arhontika* (mansions), including the splendid **Skoutaris** and **Picheon** mansions. Signposting around the old town explains the former resident families.

For more architectural gems, walk along Chrystopoulou (parallel to the shore) for the post-Byzantine churches of **Agios Ioannis Prodramos** and **Agios Loukas**. Grand brick-built Byzantine **Agioi Anargyroi**, on the corner of Gousi and Anargyron, is perhaps the finest church in Kastoria.

Byzantine Museum   MUSEUM
(☑ 24670 26781; Plateia Dexamenis; ⊙ 8.30am-3pm Tue-Sun) FREE This museum, home to a rich collection of icons, was undergoing restoration works during our visit. Check ahead before you visit.

Kastorian Museum of Folklore   MUSEUM
(☑ 24670 28603; Kapetan Lazou; adult/child €2/free; ⊙ 10am-5pm Tue-Sat, 11am-5pm Sun) In the Nerantzis Aïvazis family's former 530-year-old mansion, this museum displays ornaments, utensils and tools.

O Podilatis   CYCLING
(☑ 24670 23834; www.yellowbike.gr; Megas Alexandrou 119; ⊙ 10am-8pm Mon-Sat, 11am-4pm Sun) This southern waterfront shop rents out mountain bikes, regular bicycles and tandem fun bikes. Staff can explain local routes and arrange guided mountain-biking trips. Bike prices are €3 for the first hour and €1 every hour after that, or €8 for 24-hour rental.

☆ Festivals & Events

Ragkountsaria Festival   DANCE, CULTURE
(⊙ 6-10 Jan) This winter festival (with likely pagan roots), features traditional dancing, costumed merrymaking, and much eating and drinking.

Nestorio River Festival
MUSIC, ARTS

(http://riverparty.org; ☉ late Jul–early Aug) This popular five-day summer festival features Greek and international musicians and DJs, as well as art, games and revelry into the early hours. Four camping areas are designed to suit different hedonism tolerance threshholds. KTEL Kastoria runs special festival buses to Nestorio.

🛏 Sleeping

Arhondiko tou Vergoula
B&B €

(☏ 24670 23415; www.vergoulas.gr; Aidistras 14; s/d/tr incl breakfast €40/50/60; 🛜) Restored but still rustic, this 150-year-old Doltso mansion comes with soothing lake views, while its traditional rooms, plus cosy breakfast/dinner salon, add homespun charm.

Anesis Hotel
HOTEL €

(☏ 24670 83908; www.anesishotelkastoria.gr; Grammou 10; s/d incl breakfast €40/50; 🅿🛜) If you're travelling car-free or have an early start at the bus station, Anesis' central location can't be beaten. The enormously helpful service, comfortable rooms and filling breakfast make it worthy of more than a quick stopover.

★ Idiston
APARTMENTS €€

(☏ 6944397909, 24670 22250; www.idiston.gr; Leoforos Megalou Alexandrou 91; s/d/tr €50/60/75) Relaxing lake views unfold from the balconies of many of these spacious suites. French- and English-speaking manager Dimitris, who has run the place for 20 years, is a wealth of local information. From the bus station Idiston is a 10-minute walk. It's above a waterfront cafe.

Esperos Palace Hotel
HOTEL €€

(☏ 24670 24670; www.esperospalacekastoria.gr; Fountoukli; s/d/tr from €59/85/115; 🅿🛜🏊) If you don't mind a short drive to the quiet northwestern coast, the Esperos spa hotel represents excellent value: spacious, gleaming rooms, a spa centre with pool and *hammam,* fine dining and more.

Katerina
APARTMENT €€

(☏ 24670 24645; www.katerinasuites.gr; Leoforos Megalou Alexandrou 127; s/d €70/80) These modern, family-friendly studios lie 15 minutes' walk from the bus station, east along the waterfront. Panoramic lake views unfurl from the balconies. The thoughtful owners can provide baby cots, a laundry service and even a boat tour on the lake.

🍴 Eating & Drinking

★ Doltso
TAVERNA €€

(☏ 24670 23377; www.ntoltso.gr; Plateia Doltso; mains €9-13; ☉ lunch & dinner) From melt-in-the-mouth pork with prunes to towers of aubergine and smoky cheese, every local speciality is cooked with panache (and served in generous portions) at Doltso. This restored 1860 manion's stone walls and wooden ceilings infuse the experience with romance, and is assisted by warm hosts and a pleasing wine list. Wild boar is available November to March.

Grada
BISTRO €€

(☏ 24670 29615; www.grada-bistrot.gr; Oresteion 37; mains €8-17; ☉ 1-5pm & 8pm-midnight Tue-Sun) This stylish northwest waterfront bistro has some of Macedonia's most inventive cuisine. Blue-cheese ravioli, and shrimp and melon risotto risk befuddling your taste buds while fast-food classics such as fish and chips also grace this menu of marvels.

Ta Kymata
TAVERNA €€

(☏ 24670 28887; Psaradika; fish €9-13; ☉ lunch & dinner) Enjoy a show of clacking pelicans from this colourful waterside fish taverna. Kymata's seafood, some from the Aegean and some sourced right from the lake, is bewitchingly succulent and well presented. Proximity to the fishmongers in the adjacent market hall carries a reassuring guarantee of freshness.

Zaza
BAR

(☏ 24670 24016; Megas Alexandrou 61; ☉ 10am-3am) Flashy tilework and rusty toy cars give you something to admire over your cappuccino at labyrinthine Zaza. Friendly service, good cocktails and an easy-going vibe draw the crowds at weekends, but it's just as amiable a stop for mid-morning coffee.

ℹ Information

Municipal tourist kiosk (☏ 24670 26777; ☉ 8am-3pm Mon-Fri) Brochures, maps and information in lakeside Park of the Olympic Flame.

Police station (☏ 24670 21551; Grammou 25) Near the bus station.

Post office (Leofos Megalou Alexandrou)

ℹ Getting There & Away

Kastoria bus station (KTEL Kastorias; ☏ 24670 83454; www.ktel-kastorias.gr; Athanasiou Diakou 14) is on the southern waterfront, facing the Park of the Olympic Flame. Buses serve Thessaloniki (€17.60, 2½ hours, six daily), Ioannina (€19.60, 3½ hours, four weekly) and Athens (€48.50, nine hours, two weekly).

Taxis (☏ 24670 21222) are available.

Kavala   Καβάλα

POP 58,800

Port city Kavala, often used as a gateway to the northeastern Aegean Islands, is hitting its stride as a destination in its own right. Cultural highlights include the aqueduct of Sultan Süleyman the Magnificent, quality museums of history and industry, and fascinating Ottoman buildings scattered through its pastel-hued old town, Panagia. Sheer relaxation can be found at nearby beaches and bustling harbourfront eateries.

Modern Kavala was once ancient Philippi's port. More infamously, Ottoman Pasha Mehmet Ali (1769–1849), eventual founder of Egypt's last royal dynasty, ruled here. This genocidal Ottoman ordered his Egyptian Muslim fleet to slaughter tens of thousands of Christian Greeks on islands such as Kassos and Psara during Greece's independence struggle. Islanders still commemorate these events annually.

⊙ Sights & Activities

A 280m-long aqueduct, **Kamares**, overlooks central Kavala at Ethnikis Dimokratias. For swimmable shores, **Rapsani Beach**, 1.5km west of town, is popular, while young people flock to **Batis Beach**, an additional 3km southwest on the coastal road. For something quieter and more family-friendly, continue for another 2km to **Tosca Beach**.

Castle   CASTLE

(☑ 25108 31388; www.castle-kavala.gr; Panagia; adult/child €2.50/1.50; ⊙ 8am-9pm May-Sep, to 8pm Apr & Oct, to 4pm Nov-Mar) Built on the ruins of a Byzantine acropolis, most of this looming fortress dates from the 15th century. Glistening panoramic views are the reward for climbing the circular tower, but claustrophobic travellers might struggle with the narrow ascent. Keep kids on a short leash; the ruins are overgrown. There's a small cafe in the grounds.

Archaeological Museum   MUSEUM

(☑ 25102 22335; Erythrou Stavrou 17; adult €2; ⊙ 8am-3pm Tue-Sun; 🅿) On Ethnikis Antistasis' western end, this museum displays sculpture, jewellery, grave stelae, terracotta figurines and vases from ancient Amfipoli in a well-lit, elegant space. Its new permanent exhibition traces the city's turbulent transition from ancient Neapolis to Byzantine Christoupolis and finally modern Kavala.

Panagia Quarter   HISTORIC SITE

Panagia's narrow, tangled streets are lined by pretty pastel houses. A walk leads up to the castle. Highlights include the restored ruby **Halil Bey Mosque** and **Mehmet Ali House** (☑ 25106 20515; adult/student €3/2; ⊙ 10am-2pm Tue-Sun), a superb example of late Ottoman architecture. Enormous 18-domed **Imaret** (1817), now a hotel, was Ottoman ruler Pasha Mehmet Ali's hostel for theology students.

Tobacco Museum   MUSEUM

(☑ 25102 23344; www.tobaccomuseum.gr; Konstantinou Palaeologou 4; adult/student €2/1; ⊙ 8am-3pm Mon-Fri, 9am-1pm Sat) This surprisingly interesting museum whirls through the history of tobacco cultivation and production in eastern Macedonia and Thrace. Bright murals, old photographs, a curious collection of pipes and a tobacco press enliven plenty of description (in Greek and English). The tang of tobacco and wood in the air adds to the ambience.

🛏 Sleeping

For a fee of €1, the tourist office can arrange accommodation for you – sometimes getting you discounts.

Batis Multiplex Camping   CAMPGROUND €

(☑ 25102 45918; www.batis-sa.gr; KM4 Kavala–Thessaloniki road; camp sites per adult/tent €6/6) This campground 4km west of the centre plants your tent in easy reach of Kavala's best beach.

Hotel Esperia   HOTEL €€

(☑ 25102 29624, 25102 29621; www.esperiakavala.gr; Erythrou Stavrou 44; s/d/ste €52/62/111; 🅿 ❋ 🛜) Esperia soars above the ranks of Kavala's midrange business hotels with exemplary service and smart but simple rooms.

Galaxy Hotel   HOTEL €€

(☑ 25102 24812; www.airotel.gr; Venizelou 27; s/d incl breakfast €59/69; ❋ 🛜) The Galaxy has pleasant, roomy digs with balconies, many boasting splendid port views. A traditional Greek breakfast is served from the 7th-floor restaurant. It's opposite the tourist office.

Oceanis Kavala Hotel   HOTEL €€

(☑ 25102 21981; www.oceaniskavala.gr; Erythrou Stavrou 32; s/d/tr incl breakfast €45/68/75; 🅿 ❋ 🛜) This business hotel behind the western waterfront has 168 comfortable, well-maintained rooms with balconies.

Imaret   BOUTIQUE HOTEL €€€

(☑ 25106 20151; www.imaret.gr; Poulidou 30-32; s/d/ste incl breakfast €200/300/550; ❋ 🛜 🏊) This luxurious hotel complex in Panagia complements the original stone architecture devised by Pasha Mehmet Ali, with modern comforts and elegant lighting. The huge rooms have some original features, vaulted ceilings and often large fireplaces. The restored Turkish *hammam,* a muscle-melting array of spa treatments and a candlelit indoor pool complete an exceedingly decadent picture.

✗ Eating & Drinking

Panos Zafira   SEAFOOD €€
(⚡25102 27978; cnr Plateia Karaoli & Dimitriou; fish €9-15; ⏰10am-1am) Since 1965 this friendly eastern waterfront taverna has been serving fresh fish dishes and good grills.

★ Wood & Rock   BAR
(⚡6931309300; Poulidou Theodorou 19; ⏰11am-4am) From chamomile teas to Campari and everything in between, this cafe-bar at the bottom of Panagia is in one of the quarter's most historic buildings. The light pop-rock soundtrack intensifies as the sun sets.

Nouvelle Vague   BAR
(⚡25102 20744; Erythrou Stavrou 18; ⏰9am-1am) The neon red sign beckons good-timers to linger over a glass of wine. This chic cafe-bar near the waterfront has outdoor seating galore, though you may have to squeeze between dallying students and hip 30-somethings to secure a space.

ℹ Information

Alkyon Travel Service (⚡25102 31096; alkyon-trv@ticketcom.gr; Eleftheriou Venizelou 37; ⏰9am-6pm) Friendly travel agency in a central upstairs office books ferry tickets to Limnos, Lesvos and Samos.

Post office (cnr Hrysostomou Kavalas & Erythrou Stavrou) Near the KTEL bus station.

Tourist office (⚡25102 31011; touristinfo@kavalagreece.gr; Plateia Eleftherias; ⏰8am-8.30pm Mon-Fri) Helpful English- and German-speaking staff provides maps, plus transport and events information and hotel bookings.

ℹ Getting There & Away

AIR

Alexander the Great Airport (⚡25910 53119) is 30km east of Kavala and 44km southwest of Xanthi. **Aegean Airlines** (⚡25102 29000; Erythrou Stavrou 1) offers two daily Athens flights (€60). Island flights go via Athens or Thessaloniki.

BOAT

Ferries serve Skala Prinos in Thasos (adult/child/car €4.70/2.40/19, 1½ hours, five daily during

summer) from the eastern waterfront. From the bus station, it's a brisk 15-minute walk along the waterfront to get here. A small building on the left sells tickets for Thasos; tickets for other islands are sold by Alkyon Travel Service, **Euro Kosmos Travel Agency** (⚡25102 21960; www.eurokosmos.gr; Erythrou Stavrou 1) and **Maritime Agency Miliadis** (⚡25102 26147; www.miliadou.gr; Karaoli-Dimitriou 36). Ferries to Limenas in Thasos (adult/child/car €3/1.50/16, 45 minutes) depart from Keramoti, 12km from Kavala airport. Ferries from Kavala to Limnos run weekly during summer.

Timetables for ferry routes and information about weather-related route suspensions are available from the **Port Authority** (⚡25102 23716; cnr Ethnikis Andistasis & Averof).

BUS

Kavala bus station (⚡25102 22294; www.ktelkavalas.gr; cnr Filikis Eterias & Hrysostomou Kavalas) serves Athens (€55, 8¾ hours, two daily), Xanthi (€5.40, one hour, 14 daily), Keramoti (€4.70, one hour, 17 daily), Serres (€9.30, two hours, four daily), Alexandroupoli (€14.90, two hours, five daily) and Thessaloniki (€15, 2¼ hours, 15 daily). The *apothiki* (storeroom) stores luggage.

ℹ Getting Around

Taxis wait near the bus station. Alkyon Travel Service rents cars from €40 per day.

THRACE   ΘΡΑΚΗ

Thrace (thr-*aaa*-kih) is among Greece's most striking but least visited areas. Once home to a powerful, non-Greek Thracian civilisation, the region has been dramatically affected by other neighbouring peoples, particularly Bulgaria and Turkey.

Thrace's agricultural traditions are attested today by tobacco crops, rolling wheat fields and vivid plains of sunflowers. Its unique Muslim minorities have roots in Ottoman times, and pockets of Thrace are indeed dotted with mosques, Turkish-style houses and traditional sweet shops.

Other Thracian attractions include unique expanses of wilderness. In the north the rolling Rhodopi Mountains demarcate the Bulgarian border, and contain pristine forests and animal life; Thrace's eastern reaches, nearer to Turkey, host significant migratory bird populations at the Dadia Forest Reserve and the Evros Delta on the Aegean. The largest town, Alexandroupoli, is also the jumping-off point for ferries to Samothraki.

Thrace

NORTHERN GREECE

MACEDONIA

BULGARIA

TURKEY

THRACIAN SEA

30 km
20 miles

See Macedonia Map (p230)

Haskovo (42km);
Stara Zagora (99km)

Plovdiv
(77km)

Kavala (29km)
Kavala (20km)

Drama (49km)

Samothraki (61km)

Haskovo (77km)

Edirne

Kardzhali

Smoljan

Mt Koula
(1827m)

Rhodopi Mountains

Thermes
Echinos
Melivia
Stavroupoli

Xanthi
Toxotes
Hrysoupoli
Mandra
Mangana
Keramoti
Limenas
Thasos

Thasos
Strait

Nestos

Egnatia Odos Hwy

Sounio
Polyantho
Egiros
Lagos
Fanari
Lake
Vistonida

Komiatos

Mt Papikio
(1460m)

Pomakohoria

Makaza

Rhodopi Mountains

Komotini

Gratini
Sapes
Polyantho
Adriani
Xilagani
Maronia

Egnatia Odos Hwy

Alexandroupoli
Demir Ali
Beach

Agia Paraskevi Beach

Evros
Delta

Loutra
Esymi
Leptokarya

Dadia
Forest
Reserve

Feres
Kipi
Tyhero

Soufli
Dadia

Mandra
Sidiro
Megalo
Derio
Goniko

Roussa

Mikro Derio

Metaxades

Didymotiho

Ladia
Mikri Doxipara
Mikri Doxipara

Erythropotamos

Evros River

Pythio

Oresтиada
Lepti
Valtos
Fylakio
Kastanies
Dikea
Plati
Pendalofos
Kypinos
Petrota
Ormenio

Ardas

Filiouri

Evros River

History

The ancient Thracians spoke a now-lost language. Greek-language sources, myth and supposition depict them as warlike sorts, devoted to mystery religions such as the Great Gods cult, which influenced Greek pagan religion, too. At the Thracians' supreme temple on Samothraki island, ancient Macedonian, Roman and Egyptian rulers were initiated. Secret rituals were associated with Orpheus, the mythical, tragic Thracian father of music.

Powerful Greek city-states vied with the Persians for Thrace's coast. Athens prevailed at the Battle of Plataea, though Philip II of Macedon took over in 346 BC. Later, with the Roman Empire's AD 395 division, Thrace's strategic positioning on the Via Egnatia trade route made it important.

Constantinople's defensive zone was the Thracian plain, though its flatness made it vulnerable to marauding Goths, Huns, Vandals, Bulgars, Pechenegs, Cumans and poorly behaved Latin Crusaders – relatively few historic structures thus remain predating the Ottomans' 14th-century invasion.

In the 19th century Thrace's turbulent past reawakened. The 1877 Russo–Turkish War, the 1912–13 Balkan Wars, WWI and, finally, Greece's failed 1922 invasion of Anatolia, saw the territory change hands frequently. A mess of treaties and tragedies resulted in its final tripartite division.

The Turks of Greek Thrace were exempt during the 1923 population exchanges. While İstanbul's Greek population was largely expelled after a 1955 pogrom, the Turks of Greek Thrace remain.

Xanthi   Ξάνθη

POP 65,100

Ambling along Xanthi's historic streets, the fragrance of traditional sweets wafting on the breeze, it's impossible not to be charmed by this ebullient Thracian city. The old quarter is justly famous for its tilting timbered Ottoman houses, most of them formerly owned by tobacco barons. Today, some of Xanthi's historic buildings have found new life as museums; others house friendly bars and tavernas.

South of Xanthi, the ports of Keramoti and Kavala have ferries to Thasos and other islands. North, the rippling Rhodopi Mountains offer forest hikes and thermal baths, and to the east the Nestos River provides kayaking and birdwatching opportunities.

◉ Sights

Old Xanthi   HISTORIC SITE

On a serene hillside above town, Old Xanthi features pastel-coloured timber-framed houses on narrow, winding lanes and grand neoclassical mansions once inhabited by tobacco barons. Though some of its structures could benefit from further restoration, this grand neighbourhood has been enlivened by a vibrant nightlife scene along Orfeas.

House of Shadow   GALLERY

(☑ 6977612726; www.vaitsis.com; Georgiou Mavromichali 3; admission €2; ☺ 10am-2pm Mon & Wed, 10am-2pm & 6-8.30pm Tue & Thu-Sun) Peer behind the blackout curtains in this tiny gallery to see original shadow installations by charismatic local artist Triandafyllos Vaitsis. His ingenious sculptures each create two different shadows, and the boutique gallery has a haunting yet beautiful feel.

Folk Museum   MUSEUM

(☑ 25410 25421; www.fex.org.gr; Antika 7; admission €2; ☺ 8.30am-2.30pm Wed-Fri, 10.30am-3pm Sat & Sun) Stroll through the former mansion of the Kougioumtzolgou brothers, made rich by the region's flourishing tobacco trade, for a nostalgic glimpse of Xanthi's past. This museum is stuffed with folk costumes and farming tools, as well as an exceptionally fancy toilet bowl. Look upwards to admire original decorated ceilings. Labels are in Greek only but helpful staff can explain the exhibits.

⚜ Festivals & Events

Winter Carnival   MUSIC, CULTURE

(www.carnivalx.gr; ☺ Feb) This nationally famous celebration in mid- to late February features colourful floats accompanied by music and masked merrymaking.

Xanthi Old Town Festival   PERFORMING ARTS, MUSIC

(☺ early Sep) Festival featuring theatre, music and art exhibitions.

⌂ Sleeping

Happy Living   HOSTEL €

(☑ 25410 73547; www.happyliving.gr; Vasilissis Sofias 1a; dm €12) This brand-new hostel is a colourful, communal affair, a backpacker's utopia in the middle of Xanthi. Bright murals and a friendly cafe contribute to the eclectic, slightly hippie vibe. Think twice if you're not the sociable type: dorms are intimate and even the private double is fairly open.

Hotel Xanthippion
HOTEL €

(☎25410 77061; www.hotelxanthippion.gr; 28 Oktovriou 212; s/d/tr incl breakfast €50/60/70; ❄️🛜) A short walk from the old town, this agreeable midrange hotel gets all the basics right: great breakfasts, ample space in its clean, well-kept rooms, good wi-fi signal and enormously helpful staff.

Hotel Dimokritos
HOTEL €

(☎25410 25111; www.hoteldimokritos.gr; 28 Oktovriou 41; s/d €40/55; ❄️@) About 100m south of Plateia Dimokratias, Dimokritos has clean, but smallish rooms.

Hotel Elisso
BOUTIQUE HOTEL €€

(☎25410 84400; www.hotelelisso.gr; Vas Sofias 9; d/ste from €86/180; P❄️@🛜) This chic hotel has pleasant suites and very comfortable double rooms, two of them equipped for people with disabilities. Decor is minimalist yet bright and cheerful, characterised by geometric patternwork and big beds.

✖️ Eating & Drinking

Glikia Gonia
SWEETS €

(☎25410 27581; 28 Oktovriou 31; sweets €3; ⊙9am-6pm) This traditional Thracian sweet shop is a treasure chest of sugary treats, all made in-house. Choose from baklava that's oozing syrup, hefty ropes of pistachio-crusted *soutzouk loukoum* (aromatic rolls of Turkish delight and pistachio) and sesame Turkish delight.

Taverna To Perasma
TAVERNA €

(☎25410 78014; Ikoniou 16; mains €5-9; ⊙lunch & dinner) Facing Meg Alexandrou park near the bus station, local secret To Perasma serves huge portions of satisfying Greek specialities. Jam a fork into cheese-slathered aubergines, zucchini balls or beef kebabs, and let the fiery *raki* (Cretan fire water) awaken you from a food coma.

Palaia Polis
TAVERNA €

(☎25410 68685; www.palaiapolis.net; Chasirtzoglou 7; mains €7-9; ⊙lunch & dinner) This wood-and-brick taverna offers inventive specialities – such as rooster in wine, hare with onions and Smyrna meatballs – in a traditional and slightly upmarket setting. While it excels at Greek fare, its vast menu overreaches a little with nods to Mexican and Asian cuisine.

Ermis
BAR

(☎25410 83514; Orfeos 37-39; ⊙10am-3am) This bar in a restored old-town mansion has a fun vibe, an old *avli* (back courtyard) with secluded tables and a colourful upstairs for winter. The owners, Theodota and Georgios, serve homemade Greek-meets-international mezedhes and thirst-quenching cocktails.

ℹ️ Information

The bus station is 700m south of Kentriki Plateia, and the train station 2km south of it. Dimokritou (later Karaoli) leads to Kentriki Plateia from the bus station.

ATM-equipped banks, restaurants and shops line 28 Oktovriou and Plateia Antiko.

Police station (☎25410 24900; 28 Oktovriou)

Post office (behind Plateia Kentriki)

ℹ️ Getting There & Away

AIR

Xanthi shares **Alexander the Great Airport** (☎25910 53119), 44km southwest near Hrysoupoli, with coastal Kavala.

BUS

Xanthi bus station (KTEL Xanthis; ☎25410 22684; www.ktelxanthis.gr; Dimokritou 6) serves Komotini (€5, one hour, eight daily), Thessaloniki (€19, 2½ hours, nine daily), Athens (€61, nine hours, one daily) and Alexandroupoli (€8, one hour, eight daily). Buses also serve northern Pomakohoria villages (€3.80, 1½ hours, two daily) and Stavroupoli to the west.

Buses (€90) leave daily at 9.30am and 5.30pm for Bulgarian destinations Svilengrad, Harmanli, Haskovo and Plovdiv (Philippopouli in Greek).

TRAIN

Xanthi's **train station** (☎25410 22581; Terma Kondyli) connects Alexandroupoli and Komotini with Thessaloniki twice daily.

ℹ️ Getting Around

Only **taxis** (☎25410 72801) serve the airport (€35) from Xanthi. Alternatively, take a Kavala-bound bus to Hrysoupoli and from there take a taxi 12km to the airport.

Around Xanthi

For a challenging road trip far from the tourist track, drive north of Xanthi to the fascinating **Pomakohoria** (Pomak villages), tucked into the forested Rhodopi Mountains near Bulgaria.

For an easier, culture-packed day trip, head to the excellent museum and archaeological site at **Abdera**, 24km south of Xanthi. Continue east to **Lake Vistonida**. As well as tranquil waters and wildlife-spotting, here you'll find two spiritual sites, **Iera Moni**

Agiou Nikolaou and Parekklisi Panagias Pantanassas. Wooden walkways lead out to this hauntingly lovely spot, seemingly afloat in the middle of the lake.

Alternatively, fire your adrenaline with kayaking and rafting on the Nestos River. Riverland Outdoor Activities (☑25410 62488; www.riverland.gr), based in Toxotes village 22km southwest of Xanthi, can organise watery adventures as well as mountain biking, ziplining and Nestos Delta birdwatching tours.

Pomakohoria Πομακοχώρια

The 25 or so Pomak villages are inhabited by Muslims speaking Greek, Bulgarian and Turkish. Spread across the borders, their ethnic identity is a subject of some uncertainty (even to themselves). In Greece, they are officially classified as 'Greek Muslims'. During the Cold War, this border area was off-limits and tourists are still rare. Be mindful when you set out that this region is conservative.

The villages, accessible via winding and sometimes steep roads, aren't rich in major sights but the views are spectacular. Echinos village, 30km north of Xanthi, has remarkable mountain views, a striking minaret that seems to glow across the valley, and a fascinating multicultural cemetery. Further north are the mineral baths of Thermes. The main bath, in a building opposite the church, charges for entry; the outdoor bath (100m to the right-hand side of the village shop, and below the entry road) is free.

Abdera Άβδηρα

Abdera is an easy, culture-packed day trip from Xanthi, 24km to the north.

⊙ Sights

Archaeological Museum of Abdera MUSEUM
(☑25410 51003; Abdera; admission €2; ⊘8.30am-3pm, to 7.30pm summer) This splendid museum paints a vivid picture of ancient Abdera, from daily life to the region's luminaries. Most interesting is the detail about Abdera's defence against incursions by the Thracians, with rich exhibits including swords, sling bullets and other weapons.

Archaeological Site of Abdera ARCHAEOLOGICAL SITE
(☑museum 25410 51003; Abdera–Nea Kessani road; ⊘8.30am-3pm) A 20-minute drive northeast of Abdera lie the ruins of the ancient town. Outdoor exhibitions display stone sarcophagi, huge urns and other imagination-spurring remnants of the town, while the foundations of temples and houses can be explored around the site. The site was accessible during our visit, though undergoing flood damage repairs; it's wise to check ahead with the Archaeological Museum in town.

Komotini Κομοτηνή
POP 60,600

Traditional sweet shops, bazaar banter and neck-craning minarets create a powerful allure in Komotini. Capital of the Rhodopi regional unit, Komotini lies 50km east of Xanthi and just south of the Nymfaia forest.

Multicultural Komotini enjoys a mix of giddy student-centred nightlife around Plateia Eirinis, some Byzantine ruins and a few interesting museums. Though the town sprawls, the neighbourhood around Yenii Cami (New Mosque) is walkable. It's here that Komotini's vibrant Turkish influences are most strongly felt: the scent of sugary *soutzouk loukoum* mingles with smoke from flamed-seared kebabs, while shopkeepers lure passers-by with bright silks and silverware.

⊙ Sights

Turkish Quarter HISTORIC SITE
Just behind Plateia Eirinis, Komotini's relaxing Turkish quarter has old houses, barber shops and teahouses. Sights include the 1884 Clock Tower (Orologio), Yeni Camii ('New Mosque' in Turkish) and Eski Camii ('Old Mosque') from 1608 and still operational.

Byzantine Fortress RUIN
Komotini's 4th-century-AD Byzantine fortress was built by Emperor Theodosius, near today's Plateia Eirinis. Remnants include one of 16 original towers.

Archaeological Museum MUSEUM
(☑25310 22411; Simeonidou 4; adult/child €2/1; ⊘8.30am-3pm) Significant archaeological finds, accompanied by English-language wall texts, detail ancient Thracian history within this elegant building. Roman coins, clay figurines, delicate gold wreaths and glazed ceramics illuminate the region's history from the neolithic to Byzantine periods.

Ecclesiastical Museum MUSEUM
(Imaret; ☑25310 34177; Xenofontos 8; admission €3; ⊘10.30am-1pm Tue, Thu, Sat & Sun, 5-8pm Wed & Fri) This museum occupies Komotini's early Ottoman *ptohokomeio* (almshouse), inside a courtyard. The structure's brickwork and de-

sign resemble a Byzantine church. It exhibits post-Byzantine icons, 500-year-old printed gospels, silver ceremonial crosses, gold embroidery and 18th-century Hebrew scrolls.

Church of the Assumption of Mary CHURCH
(☑25310 22827; Eleftheriou Venizelou) Built in 1800 on a Byzantine shrine site, the church contains 16th-century icons and carvings.

🛏 Sleeping

Orpheus Hotel HOTEL €
(☑ 25310 37180/5; www.hotelorfeas.gr; Parasiou 1; s/d/tr €35/45/55; ☀) Well positioned on the *plateia*, Orpheus occupies a characterless block but has 78 tidily furnished and comfortable rooms.

Chris & Eve Mansion BOUTIQUE HOTEL €€
(☑ 25310 33560; www.chris-eve.com; 4km Komitini–Alexandroupoli road; s/d/ste from €40/60/100; P☀🛜🏊) For a touch of quirky glamour, drive east of Komotini for the plush Chris & Eve Mansion. Away from the dust and bustle of central Komotini, its balconied rooms with bright satiny fittings overlook a pool.

Anatolia Hotel HOTEL €€
(☑ 25310 36242; www.anatoliahotels.gr; Agchialou 53; s/d €55/65; ☀🛜) The minimalist Anatolia combines simple, clean rooms with glossy decor. It's in northeastern Komotini, near Parko Agogis.

Hotel Astoria HOTEL €€
(☑ 25310 35054; www.astoriakomotini.gr; Plateia Eirinis 28; s/d €76/101; ☀@) Slightly concealed by the square's side cafes, Astoria has attractive rooms with small balconies overlooking Plateia Eirinis.

🍴 Eating & Drinking

★Petrino OUZERIE €
(☑25310 73650; Serron 25; mains €7-9; ⊙lunch & dinner) Under a creeper-strewn canopy just off pedestrianised Ermou, Petrino's dishes are as enticing as its shaded location. Try the hopelessly garlicky aubergine mezedhes and generous portions of mussels on rice.

Nedim's SWEETS €
(☑25310 22036; cnr Leoforos Orfeos & Syntagmatos Kriton 15-17; sweets €2-4) Nedim has been serving what is perhaps the best baklava this side of İstanbul since 1950. Try your teeth on *kadayif* (sweet bird's nests of pistachio and pastry), Turkish delight ranging from mint to orange and cocoa flavours, and sausage-shaped *soutzouk loukoum*.

Klimis SWEETS €
(☑25310 33177; Orfeos 8; ⊙8am-11pm) While other sweet sellers are better known, some locals swear by this unassuming little shop between the square and the mosque. The kindly owner offers myriad dried fruits and nuts.

Kouti TAVERNA €
(☑25310 25774; Orfeos 45; mains €5-9) This slightly upscale central restaurant has Greek and international fare.

Kaffeine COFFEE
(☑25310 84933; Eleftheriou Venizelou 50; 🛜) Komotini's best coffee is lovingly crafted at this student-packed cafe. Lattes are discarded for cocktails as the sun dips low.

El Clasico CAFE, BAR
(☑25310 70007; www.el-clasico.gr; Zoidi 52-54; ⊙8am-3am) Sip coffee or wine to a jazz soundtrack at this somewhat American-themed cafe-bar. El Clasico's cavernous interior contrasts wood-and-brick walls with inlaid TVs, overlooked by ventilation grates and bisected by wrap-around couches.

ⓘ Information

Hospital (☑25313 51100; Sismanogleio 45) 1km southeast of Plateia Eirinis.

ⓘ Getting There & Away
From **Komotini bus station** (KTEL Rodopis; ☑25310 22912; www.ktelrodopis.gr; Geor Mameli 15) buses serve Xanthi (€5.30, one hour, five daily) and Alexandroupoli (€4.80, one hour, eight daily). Buses also serve Thessaloniki (€25.30, 2½ hours, eight daily) and Athens (€63, 8¾ hours, one daily).

The **train station** (☑25310 22650) connects Komotini with Xanthi (€4.70, 30 minutes, twice daily) and Alexandroupoli (€6.10, 80 minutes, twice daily). The train station is 1km southwest of town parallel to Sidirochoriou.

ⓘ Getting Around
Komotini sprawls, but the centre is walkable. There are **taxis** (☑25310 37777; http://radio-taxikomotini.gr) available and **Evros Car Rental** (☑25310 32905; evroscar@gmail.com; Tountzas 1) has cars (from €45) and jeeps (€60).

Alexandroupoli
Αλεξανδρούπολη

POP 61,700

Your adventures might not equal those of Alexander the Great (yet), but arriving in his namesake town of Alexandroupoli

NORTHERN GREECE ALEXANDROUPOLI

(ah-lex-an-*dhroo*-po-lih) will elicit an intrepid thrill. For this, eastern Thrace's largest town, is an axis for travel to Turkey, Bulgaria and (in summer) Samothraki island, meaning it's lapped by different culinary and cultural influences. Alexandroupoli is also a gateway to adventures in the wildlife-rich Evros Delta and beguiling Dadia Forest Reserve.

For a leisurely pace, the taverna-lined harbour has a pretty lighthouse; the city centre has two excellent museums and sparkling nightlife; and fine beaches can be found west of the city.

◉ Sights

Drive 10km west of Alexandroupoli for sandy **Demir Ali Beach**, popular for swimming and known for the **Agios Giorgios Church**. **Agia Paraskevi Beach**, 3km further west, is even better, with beach bars and clubs.

Ethnological Museum of Thrace   MUSEUM
(☑25510 36663; www.emthrace.org; 14 Maiou 63; adult/child €2/free; ◷9am-3pm Tue-Sat, 10am-3pm Sun Oct-Feb, 9am-3pm Tue, Wed & Sat, 10am-3pm & 6-9pm Thu & Fri, 10am-3pm Sun Mar-Sep) Inside a grand sandstone mansion, this museum with backyard cafe packs its displays with colourful Thracian costumes, musical instruments, oil presses and exhibitions on traditional occupations such as beekeeping and tobacco production. There's a musty cellar full of old agrarian implements. You'll learn how many silkworms are needed to make 25g of silk and which Greek sweet is made by slamming the ingredients against a wall.

Ecclesiastical Art Museum   MUSEUM
(☑25510 82282; Plateia Agiou Nikolaou; adult/student €3/2; ◷9am-2pm Tue-Fri, to 1pm Sat) Opposite the custard-coloured Agios Nikolaos church, this excellent museum contains priceless icons, many brought by refugees in 1923, plus early printed Greek books. Look for the heart-rending realism of the lamenting Mary paintings in between embroidered priestly vestments, dragon-dispatching St Georges and delicate silverwork. English-language guide pamphlet on request.

Cathedral of Agios Nikolaos   CHURCH
(Plateia Agiou Nikolaou) This cathedral houses the miracle-working 13th-century **icon of the Panagia Trifotissa**, from Aenos (Enez in Turkish) across the Evros River. Villagers with eyes damaged by the reflected glare of the sun on the salt marshes around Aenos are said to have had their vision restored by praying before it.

🛏 Sleeping

Camping Alexandroupoli   CAMPGROUND €
(☑25510 26055, 25510 28735; www.ditea.gr; Leoforos Makris 1; camp sites per tent/car €4.20/4.70; ◷year-round; ℗🐾) This large, well-run campground has water sports and beach volleyball, plus basketball and tennis courts. It's 2km west of Alexandroupoli; take local bus 7 from Plateia Eleftherias.

Apartment Hotel Athina   HOTEL €
(☑25510 34492; Konstantinou Paleologou 53; d/tr incl breakfast €50/60; ❄🐾) Central Athina has large, clean and simple rooms with mini kitchens and balconies. First child (under four years) stays free.

★**Hotel Santa Rosa Beach**   HOTEL €€
(☑25510 33895, 25510 25551; www.santa-rosa-.gr; Km 1 Alexandroupoli–Chili road; s/d/tr incl breakfast €51/72/88; ℗❄🐾) This family-run beach hotel 3km west of the centre assures a warm welcome. The roar of the sea is audible from Santa Rosa's well-kept rooms, and a relaxing lounge overlooks the private beach.

Astir Egnatia Alexandroupolis   RESORT €€€
(☑25510 38000; www.astiregnatia.com; Egnatia Park; s/d/apt €120/140/170; ℗❄@🐾☀) Some think this 200-room shoreside resort, just west of Alexandroupoli, isn't worth its five stars. Nonetheless the behemoth of a hotel has spacious rooms, impeccably helpful staff and several pools. Check ahead out of season as some leisure facilities may not be available.

🍴 Eating

Ai Giorgis   TAVERNA €
(☑25510 71777; www.aigiorgis.com; Agios Georgios Makris; mains €7-13; ◷10am-1am) Overlooking Demir Ali Beach, Ai Giorgis sizzles up shrimp saganaki and expertly steams cockles, while guests sip ouzo and enjoy the sea breeze.

Nea Klimataria   TAVERNA €
(☑25510 26288; Plateia Polytehniou 18; mains €5-8; ◷lunch & dinner) All the classics are done well at this somewhat touristy taverna away from the harbourfront hubbub. Door-wedge-sized feta tops enormous Greek salads; oregano pork is grilled to succulence; and service is polite. It faces craft shop Myrsini.

I Love Gelato   ICE CREAM €
(☑25510 24832; cnr Megas Alexandrou & Karaiskaki; double scoop €2.50; ◷10am-midnight) This quality gelateria opposite the lighthouse has a dilemma-inducing rainbow of flavours, but we can never say no to pistachio.

Nisiotiko
SEAFOOD €€

(🖉 25510 20990; www.nisiotiko.gr; Zarifi 3; mains €8-16; ☺lunch & dinner) Starfish ornaments and nautical miscellany lead the way to this west-side fish taverna, tucked away off the waterfront. Octopus and mullet are grilled with aplomb and fresh, simple ingredients lead the menu.

🍷 Drinking

Outopia
CAFE

(Nikiforou Foka; coffee €2; ☺hours vary) Coffees brew and beers foam all day long at this park-side drinking spot. A nostalgic pop soundtrack and vintage-inspired furnishings give the cafe an uplifting air. Outdoor seating offers ample elbow room to people-watch or to flick through some poetry.

NOA
BAR

(Naftikos Omilos Alexandroupoleos; 🖉 25510 53226; port; ☺9am-2am; 🛜) All aboard for Alexandroupoli's 'yacht club' on the central ferry pier. At this classy bar, the beers are cool and the soundtrack swings. Dress smart and don't forget your shades.

SoHo Absolutely Fabulous
BAR

(🖉 25510 80134; www.sohocafe.gr; Leoforos Dimokratias 300; cocktails €7; ☺9am-late) Neon pink touches, UFO-shaped tables and an achingly cool crowd: SoHo is hardly the place for a quiet romantic drink. But squeeze in among the glamorous crowds and you can sip signature cocktails and wolf down complimentary carb-heavy snacks.

🛍 Shopping

★Myrsini
HANDICRAFTS

(🖉 25510 31205; www.silkyhouse.gr; Plateia Polytehniou; ☺10am-6pm) This treasure trove of original Soufli silks has scarves from €5 as well as flamboyant table runners, jewellery and voluminous spreads (€300). Cheerful souvenirs such as tote bags and discounted scarves crowd the entrance. Step inside to see silk being snipped and shelves that are packed with shimmering fabric.

ℹ Information

Leoforos Dimokratias has ATM-equipped banks.

Kassapidis Exchange (🖉 25510 80910; www.kasslinetravel.gr; Leoforos Dimokratias 307; ☺8am-8.30pm Mon-Sat, 10am-2pm Sun) Changes 115 currencies, including Balkan currencies, plus handles Western Union transfers.

Leon Tours (🖉 25510 27754; www.leontours.gr; 14 Maiou 51; ☺9am-3pm & 6-9.30pm Mon-Sat) Helpful Maria Karakampatzaki and the team at Leon sell plane, bus and ferry tickets, including ferries for Kavala, Samothraki and other islands. They also offer international tours including weekly trips to İstanbul, a combo trip to Cannakale and Ayvalik in Turkey, and Lesvos island.

Post office (cnr Psaron & Meg Alexandrou) Alexandroupoli's waterfront post office.

Police (🖉 25510 37440, 25510 66103; Karaïskaki 6)

ℹ Getting There & Away

AIR

Alexandroupoli's **Dimokritos Airport** (🖉 25510 89300; www.alxd.gr) is 7km east. **Aegean Airlines** (🖉 25510 89150; www.aegeanair.com), based at the airport, serves Athens (from €69). **Sky Express** (www.skyexpress.gr) serves Sitia in Crete (from €99, three flights weekly). Charter flights from Russia operate in summer.

BOAT

Ferries serve Samothraki only. There is usually one boat daily, but schedules and times can change; always check locally, at the portside SAOS kiosk, or through travel agencies such as Leon Tours (p273), and book in advance.

BUS
Domestic

From **Alexandroupoli bus station** (KTEL Evrou; 🖉 25510 26479; www.ktelevrou.gr; Eleftheriou Venizelou 36) frequent buses ply the northeastern line to Soufli (€6, 1½ hours), Didymotiho (€8.60, 1½ hours) and Orestiada (€10.60, two hours); some continue to Kastanies, for the border crossing with Turkey. Another bus terminates at Kipi, the main Turkish border crossing (€3.90, 35 minutes, five daily), east of Alexandroupoli.

Buses serve Athens (€63, 10 hours, one daily) and Thessaloniki (€29, 3¾ hours, nine daily). For Kavala (€14.90, two hours, 14 daily), buses travel via Komotini (€6.30, 70 minutes) and Xanthi (€10.60, 1¾ hours).

International

Leon Tours (p273) can assist with bus travel to Turkey.

TRAIN

The **train station** (🖉 25510 26395; www.trainose.gr) connects Alexandroupoli Port with Thessaloniki (€22.50, seven hours, two daily) and Xanthi (€9.80, 1½ hours, two daily).

ℹ Getting Around

Central Alexandroupoli is walkable but a car or taxi is helpful if you're based at the campground, beach resorts or plan to explore the Evros Delta. For the airport, take a Loutra-bound bus from

Plateia Eleftherias, or a **taxi** (☑ 25510 33500; www.alexpolistaxi.gr). Some buses plying the Alexandroupoli–Orestiada route transit the airport.

Evros Delta   Δέλτα Έβρου

Just 20km southeast of Alexandroupoli, the Evros Delta is among Europe's most important wetlands, comprising 188 sq km of coastal lakes, lagoons, interior rivers, sand dunes, swamps and reed beds. Half of the area is protected, allowing an incredible richness of wildlife to thrive. When road-tripping around the area, be wary where you point your camera lens; this is a militarised border area.

For a change of pace, dozy **Feres** village is a 20km drive northeast of the Evros visitor centre and hosts the **Church of Panagia Kosmosotira**, built in 1152.

◉ Sights & Activities

Evros Delta   NATURE RESERVE
The Evros Delta draws solitude-seekers and nature lovers to its peaceable marshlands. The western part of the delta, including the **Anthia Marshes** and **Drana Lagoon**, is readily accessible via dirt roads navigable by most (sturdy) cars. The most fascinating eastern section, near Turkey, requires a police and army permit, arranged for free by the visitor centre. Fax or email 14 days ahead with your full name, date of birth, and passport number and expiry date.

The delta is formed where the Evros River reaches the Aegean. Gushing from Bulgaria's Rila Mountains, the 530km-long Evros (Maritsa) winds through Turkey into Greece's Evros prefecture, where it forms part of the Greece–Turkey border. The delta came under threat in the 1950s due to drainage works that attempted to prepare the land for cultivation. Fortunately since 1974

half of the delta has come under Ramsar protection, allowing its fauna to flourish.

Evros Delta Visitor Centre   BIRDWATCHING
(☑ tel/fax 25510 61000; www.evros-delta.gr; Traianoupolis; ☺ 8am-4pm) Gather maps and wildlife-spotting tips at the Evros Delta's visitor centre, a 20km-drive east of Alexandroupoli. Call ahead to book into a group guided tour (€10 per person, or €30 if you're the only visitor) comprising minibus and boat excursions.

Around Alexandroupoli

Worthy of exploration are the **Dadia Forest Reserve** and the enriching silk museum in **Soufli**. Veering off the beaten track, you'll find 9th-century-BC **dolmen** (megalithic tombs) still standing just north of **Roussa**, scoured by the wind. From Alexandroupoli, drive to Mikro Derio village and follow signs to Roussa.

◉ Sights

Dadia Forest Reserve   NATURE RESERVE
Situated on one of Europe's major bird migration routes, the 73 sq km reserve at Dadia Forest is a-flutter with 203 bird species including three types of vulture. The **Ecotourist Centre** (☑ 25540 32202; www.dadia-np.gr; Dadia; ☺ 8am-4pm) has detailed bilingual wall displays and trail maps to the bird of prey observatory; it's an hour's hike following the orange trail up, and the yellow trail down. The observatory usually contains binoculars and telescopes, but dedicated birders will want to bring (or borrow) their own kit.

Visits are best in May, before migration begins, or in July, when baby vultures hop out of their nests. For even more details, seek out the itinerant World Wildlife Foundation scientist, whose office adjoins the Ecotourist Centre.

DON'T MISS

BIRDWATCHING WONDERS OF EVROS

The wildlife of the Evros Delta has the power to leave you slack-jawed. An incredible 325 bird species have been observed here, and the number is increasing.

The possibility of spotting a glossy ibis has many twitchers scrambling for their binoculars. Most impressive are the spring migrations, where thousands of wader birds pause to guzzle in the nutrient-packed waters of the delta. Three species of European swan glide through these waters, while geese forage through meadows, including endangered lesser white-fronted geese, who winter here. Meanwhile eagles (spotted, white-tailed and imperial) wheel overhead along with more common buzzards and hen harriers.

These enchanting forests deserve a couple of days. **Forest Inn** (☑ 25540 32263; www.forestinn.eu; Dadia; d from €50) 🏄 is an amiable guesthouse only a short walk from bird hides and has Dadia's nature unfolding right from the doorstep. Near sleepy Tyhero village, 22km away, friendly Sofia Xatzisavva ensures a comfortable stay in the characterful lakeside **Thrassa Guesthouse** (☑ 25540 20080; www.thrassa.gr; Tyhero; s/d/ste from €35/50/60; P✳🌀🐾).

Art of Silk Museum   MUSEUM
(☑ 25540 22371; www.artofsilkmuseum.gr; Vasilis Georgiou 199, Soufli; ⊙9am-9pm) **FREE** Located in Tsiariki House, a silk producer of 60 years, this museum beautifully illuminates the region's sericultural history. Audio guides in multiple languages (and enthusiastic staff) lead visitors through the process from voracious, wriggling worms to butter-soft silk scarves. Displays include live silkworms, hand looms and silk reeling machines, as well as elaborate traditional costumes.

The village of Soufli was once a wealthy cultural centre, fuelled largely by silk production in the 19th century. When the borders shifted in 1923, the vital mulberry orchards (silkworms' food source) were lost to Turkey and silk production declined. Today Soufli has only three functioning silk-weaving units, with only Tsiakiris processing it from start to finish.

Look out for impostor 'silk museums' around Soufli; the signs are often a ploy to lure visitors into shops. Soufli is a 66km drive north of Alexandroupoli or 30km south of Didymotiho.

Orestiada   Ορεστιάδα

POP 23,600

With wide boulevards and a tidy grid layout, Orestiada has a different feel from most other Greek cities. While other towns boast of their ancient roots, it was the 1923 Greek-Turkish population exchanges that spurred the creation of Orestiada (then Nea Orestiás).

While the border history of barely centennial Orestiada intrigues, the town doesn't brim with attractions. Visitors from countries other than Bulgaria and Turkey may be greeted with a mix of astonishment and delight by down-to-earth locals. Nonetheless, Orestiada's excellent museum, quality restaurants and animated main square make it an agreeable stopover before travelling onward to Bulgaria or Turkey – the latter

is accessible from nearby Kastanies village. Orestiada is also a convenient jumping-off point for day trips to Dadia Forest Reserve, Soufli and other parts of Evros.

⊙ Sights

Orestiada's streets are brightened by buildings such as the striking brick **Church of the Saints Theodoros**. Most of the action in this quiet town is found around Emmanouil Riga, between Konstantinopoleos and Pantazidou.

Historical & Folklore Museum   MUSEUM
(☑ 25520 28080; www.musorest.gr; Agion Theodoron 103; admission €2; ⊙10am-1pm Tue-Sun) This fascinating museum exhibits Thracian costumes, furniture and old weaponry. Most moving are graphic displays about the Greek–Turkish population exchanges, which detail the tumult experienced by displaced communities and highlight stories of their pluck and ingenuity in rebuilding their lives anew.

🛏 Sleeping & Eating

Vast Plateia Dasiou is a fine spot for an outdoor drink overlooking the square's sci-fi street lamps.

Hotel Alexandros   HOTEL €
(☑ 25520 27000; Vasileos Konstantinou 10; s/d/tr €50/60/70; P✳@) Near the train station, the Alexandros has breezy rooms with balconies.

Hotel Elektra   HOTEL €€
(☑ 25520 21110; www.hotelelectra.gr; Athanasiou Pantazidou 52; s/d incl breakfast €46/65; P✳🌀) This friendly and well-kept hotel in a restored neoclassical mansion is just off Plateia Dasiou, near the best restaurants and cafes.

★Safran   MEDITERRANEAN €
(☑ 25520 29088; http://safran.com.gr; Lochagou Diamanti 17; mains €5-12; 🍴) Longtime favourite Safran does international-style taverna cuisine. Perch at one of the outdoor tables for ouzo-marinated tenderloin, flamed saganaki cheese, or vegetarian burgers with mushroom and Florina peppers.

Sapore Cucine Italiana   ITALIAN €€
(☑ 6932385040; cnr Athanasiou Pantazidou & Emmanouil Riga; mains €8-13; ⊙10am-11pm) This Italian restaurant features a short but excellent seasonal menu. Try the tasty bruschetta, lasagne with goat's cheese or ravioli in wine sauce, accompanied by rich local wines.

DIDYMOTIHO: WHERE BYZANTINE MEETS OTTOMAN

Didymotiho, (dih-dih-*mo*-tih-ho), a military outpost north of Soufli, is a sleepy place; however, its strategic borderland nature has endowed it with intriguing historical monuments. Sadly, many are closed to visitors.

Didymotiho was thought to have been built in the 6th century to replace nearby lowland settlement Plotinopolis. In the late 8th century it was briefly seized by Bulgaria. Shortly after it served as a hinterland fort defending Constantinople. Its name derives from its once magnificent double walls (*didymo*, 'twin'; *tihos*, 'wall'). Remnants of these **Byzantine Walls** are in the upper town, near the **Church of Agios Athanasios** (Patriarchou Dionysiou).

Numerous eminent Byzantines were born in Didymotiho and in 1341 Emperor John Kantakouzenis was crowned here. However, 20 years later Turkish sultan Murad I conquered Didymotiho and it became the Ottoman capital until 1365, when the capital was relocated to Adrianoupoli (Edirne, Turkey) in 1365. The huge, now-derelict **Bayezit's Mosque** (Çelebi Sultan Mehmed Mosque; 28is Maiou) was ordained by Murad, with construction begun by his son, Bayezit. It was the first of its kind in Europe. Though boarded up on our visit, the mosque's scale is impressive and restoration works are ongoing. Another historic sight, the 16th-century **hammam** (near Erthrypotamos River) known as the 'baths of love and whispers', is also destined for renovation.

Hourly Alexandroupoli–Orestiada buses transit Didymotiho.

ℹ Information

ATM-equipped banks hug Plateia Dasiou.

Hatzigiannis Tours (☑ 25520 28333; Konstantinoupoleos 216, cnr Emmanouil Riga) Sells plane, boat and train tickets.

Police (☑ 25520 29644; Vaslieos Konstantinou 4)

Post office (☑ 25520 22435; Athanasiou Pantazidou)

ℹ Getting There & Around

From Orestiada's **bus station** (☑ 25520 22550; www.ktelevrou.gr; Andrianoupoleos 164), buses serve Didymotiho (€1.80, 20 minutes, hourly), many continuing to Alexandroupoli (€10.60, 1¼ hours, 13 daily). Other buses go northwards to Dikea (€5.70, 45 minutes, four daily) and Ormenio (€5.50, 40 minutes, two daily) for Bulgaria. The Turkish border crossing at Kastanies is also served (€1.80, 20 minutes, six daily).

The **train station** (☑ 25520 22328) connects Orestiada with Thessaloniki direct (€25.20, 8½ hours, one daily) or via Alexandroupoli (€6, two hours, two daily). **Taxis** (☑ 25520 25025) can be found near the train station.

Around Orestiada

If you want a border-skirting, way-off-the-beaten-track road trip, drive circuit around northern Evros region to access little-visited villages and untouristed sights. From Orestiada, drive west through **Valtos** for **Mikri Doxipara**, where a 1st-century-AD Roman tomb was discovered with four interred funerary carts, including horses and harnesses. From here, turn northwest towards **Kyprinos** village and its **Church of Agiou Georgiou**, which features icons and a very ancient baptistery.

Further north, stop in at **Pendalofos** village's game restaurant, **Evrothirama** (☑ 6978890861, 25560 61202; www.eurothirama.com; Pendalofos; mains €7-10; ⊙ hours vary), for boar stewed with lemon, wild rabbit and sticky traditional desserts; call ahead. Continue to **Petrota**, northwestern Evros' last village before Bulgaria, for vineyards and traditional stone houses. The border road continues eastwards through **Ormenio**, Greece's northernmost village, and **Dikea**, before looping south back to Orestiada.

Pythio Castle
CASTLE

(Kastro Pithiou; Pythio; ⊙ hours vary) FREE Guarding a tall bluff above Pythio village (Empython, in Byzantine times), this burly fortification on the border with Turkey is Thrace's only surviving example of Byzantine defensive architecture, and dates from the early 14th century. It was built by Emperor John Kantakouzenos to control the Evros plain during a turbulent period of civil wars and Turkish invasions. Reach the castle by driving 17km southeast of Orestiada on the old road following the Evros River. Like armies of old, modern visitors may find the castle difficult to penetrate: it's frequently locked. You may be able to ask the caretaker for the key.

EPIROS ΗΠΕΙΡΟΣ

Northern Greece's most dramatic terrain lies in Epiros, a place that will (literally) take your breath away, in the sprawling, impenetrable Pindos Mountains. Bisecting the Pindos is the magnificent 12km-long Vikos Gorge – among the world's deepest (900m) – a national park filled with forests, waterfalls and ice-cold mountain lakes, surrounded by the Zagorohoria's immaculate stone-and-slate villages.

South of these mountains, Ioannina is a youthful, lively city, unfolding around a placid lake. Straight west, the Ionian coast features long sandy beaches punctuated by archaeological sites. As with the Ionian Islands opposite, a Venetian legacy has flavoured the so-called 'Epirot Riviera', especially at photogenic Parga. North of Parga, Igoumenitsa's ferries access Italy.

Reaching Epiros is an event in itself. The road from Kalambaka in Thessaly winds over the Pindos Mountains; from Macedonia, the marvellous Egnatia Odos highway cuts straight through them, into massive tunnels. Note that this highway is infested with toll booths and bereft of rest stops.

Epiros

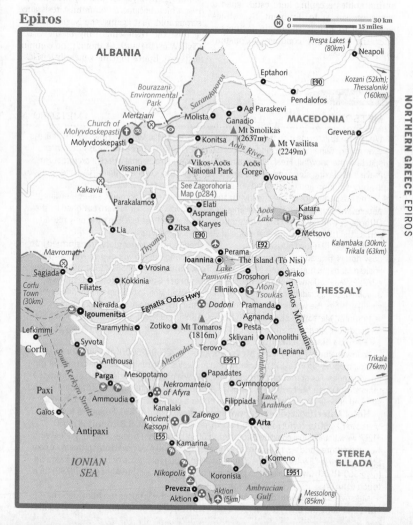

History

The Dorian invasion (1100–1000 BC) left three main Greek-speaking tribes: the Thesproti, the Chaones and the dominant Molossi. The marriage of Molossi princess Olympias to powerful Macedonian king Philip II brought conflict with emerging Rome. King Pyrrhus (319–272 BC) famously defeated the Romans at Ausculum, at a heavy cost; hence the concept of a 'Pyrrhic victory'.

After the Roman Empire split in AD 395, Epiros was ruled from Constantinople. Centuries later, it became important after the 1204 Latin sack of Constantinople; Byzantine nobles escaping here established a key successor state. Eminent Byzantines again fled to Epiros' mountain fastnesses after the Ottomans conquered Constantinople in 1453.

Infamously linked with Epiros is 18th-century Albanian despot Ali Pasha, who ransacked much of Albania and western Greece, while wheeling and dealing with Turks, Brits and even Napoleon. Ali's remorseless mass killings and torture made him infamous, while Europeans were titillated by rumours of his harem of hundreds of women. Ottoman troops finally killed him in 1822, on Ioannina's lake island. Nevertheless, Ali had aided Greek freedom fighters elsewhere by wearing down and distracting the Turks.

Epiros was divided after 1912 when newly created Albania got a northern chunk. Mussolini's 1940 invasion was repelled in Epiros, which became a communist resistance stronghold, first against the Nazis and then against the right-wing army in the Greek Civil War (1944–49). Although the communists lost, Epiros remains generally leftist.

WORTH A TRIP

METSOVO   ΜΕΤΣΟΒΟ

While some ski towns lose their lustre out of season, idyllic Metsovo (met-so-vo) charms year-round. Clinging to the Pindos Mountains at 1156m, its three ski areas lure winter sports come snowfall. Fresh alpine air, lofty views and traditional wooden architecture make it a relaxing stop – as well as a potentially gluttonous one. Bulging sausages dangle in shop windows and huge rounds of smoky cheese beg to be melted.

The hospitable locals are mostly Vlachs, descendants of a nomadic sheep-herding people who spoke the Aromanian language. Metsovo's shepherds were enriched by the Ottomans, who rewarded them for guarding the Katara Pass (1705m), the only route across the Pindos Mountains and one of Greece's highest passes.

Today, old Metsovo houses have been polished to their former glory, transformed into cosy hotels, museums or shops overflowing with hand-carved wooden souvenirs. The Tositsa Mansion houses both a fascinating **folk museum** (☑ 26560 41084; adult/student €3/2; ⊙ 9am-1.30pm & 4-6pm Fri-Wed) and the **Averoff Gallery** (☑ 26560 41210; www.averoffmuseum.gr; adult/student €3/2; ⊙ 10am-4pm Wed-Mon, to 6.30pm mid-Jul–mid-Sep), which exhibits the works of 19th- and 20th-century Greek painters and sculptors.

In winter, Metsovo's **ski centre** (☑ 26560 41095; ⊙ 9.30am-3.45pm winter) can advise on conditions, gear hire and skiing or snowboarding lessons at the three nearby ski areas, **Profitis Ilias**, **Karakoli** and **Zigos**.

Follow the bear sign to **Cafe Metsovorama** (☑ 26560 42500; Kyriakou) to enjoy a soothing après-ski vibe and panoramic Pindos views. The main square has a cluster of busy eateries. For something atmospheric, follow a creaking wooden staircase from the main street up to **Metsovitiko Saloni** (☑ 26560 42142; mains €12) for hot aubergine and smoked cheese and succulent grills from either a cosy salon or flower-draped balcony.

Hotel Asteri (☑ 26560 42222; www.asterimetsovo.com; d/tr €50/80) at the top of Metsovo has 50 cheerful rooms and warm service, while **Hotel Bitouni** (☑ 26560 41217; www.hotelbitouni.com; Tositsa; s/d/ste €30/40/60; P ⊙) brings a ski-lodge feel with wooden fixtures and a sauna. **Hotel Olympic** (☑ 26560 41337; www.olympicmetsovo.com; Stanou 3; s/d/tr €37/49/60; ⊙) is a fine, family-run budget choice or try **Hotel Egnatia** (☑ 26560 41900; www.hotelegnatia.gr; Tositsa 19; s/d/studios incl breakfast €40/70/90) for a touch of luxury.

Metsovo is a 45-minute drive from Ioannina. Alternatively, buses run from Ioannina (€10, 1½ hours, two daily) to Metsovo's **bus station** (☑ 26560 42646) by the main square.

Ioannina   Ιωάννινα

POP 80,400

Energetic Ioannina (ih-o-*ah*-nih-nah or *yah*-nih-nah) somehow harnesses Epiros' best drinking and dining, a wonderfully variegated history and lakeshore serenity into one thoroughly enjoyable city. The skyline boasts a stately fortress, jutting minarets and Byzantine arches, all backed by brooding mountains. Ioannina hugs the western shore of shimmering Lake Pamvotis, whose sleepy island has a cluster of monasteries and historic sights.

History

Byzantine emperor Justinian founded Ioannina in the 6th century, and it became an important commercial and cultural outpost. In 1204, when Latin Crusaders sacked Constantinople and dismembered Byzantium, Ioannina became a key city of Michael I Komnenos Doukas' Byzantine successor state. Ottomans conquered in 1430, a Sephardic Jewish population arrived after 1492, and despite the disarray of the early Ottoman period (including a peasant revolt in 1611) Ioannina became a leading cultural and artistic centre. Ioannina was (and still is) known for its silver craftsmanship and, through the 16th and 17th centuries, an 'Epirot School' of religious painting also blossomed.

Albanian warlord Ali Pasha (1740–1822) capitalised on Ottoman decline to vie for Ioannina. In 1789 he made it the capital of his far-ranging fiefdom. His cruelty was known to sicken poet Lord Byron, who visited Ioannina and even attended Ali's court. But Ali enforced the law and Ioannina flourished – albeit with brutal mass-drownings and torture along the way. In 1822, trapped at the Agios Panteleimon monastery on the Island (To Nisi) in Lake Pamvotis, octogenarian Ali was killed by the Ottomans, who paraded his severed head around İstanbul.

Greeks liberated Ioannina in the 1912–13 Balkan Wars. The 1923 population exchanges saw Turks replaced by Anatolian Greek refugees. In 1943 the Nazis deported the Jewish population to concentration camps.

◎ Sights

Its Kale   FORTRESS

(Kastro; ◎8am-5pm & 8-10pm Tue-Sun) FREE
Kastro's sublime citadel, including a Middle Byzantine tower, rises over a long bluff overlooking lake and mountain. The outer ramparts are cluttered with cannon balls and elegant Ottoman carvings. Within, it holds the restored **Fetiye Cami** (Victory Mosque), built in 1611 after a failed Greek uprising that saw Christians expelled from the citadel, and the **Tomb of Ali Pasha**. The decorative iron railing is a recent copy of the original, which was removed during WWII.

Byzantine Museum   MUSEUM

(📞26510 25989; Kastro; admission €3; ◎8am-3pm Tue-Sun) This museum presents early Christian and Byzantine art, pottery, coins and silverware, plus post-Byzantine icons and manuscripts, early Venetian-produced Greek books and ornate silver jewellery boxes with cloisonné enamel. Textual accompaniments detail Ioannina's history from the 4th to the 17th century. There's a separate silverware hall; buy tickets at the main counter.

Municipal Ethnographic Museum   MUSEUM

(📞26510 26356; Kastro; adult/senior/student €3/1/2; ◎8am-8pm summer, 8.30am-4.30pm winter) The erstwhile Aslan Pasha Mosque (1619) exhibits local costumes and period photographs, along with tapestries and prayer shawls from Ioannina's former synagogue (Ioustinianou 16).

Archaeological Museum   MUSEUM

(📞26510 01051; www.amio.gr; Plateia 25 Martiou 6; adult/child €2/1; ◎8.30am-3pm Tue-Sun) This top-notch museum contains more than 3000 Epirot finds, including neolithic items and antiquities from Dodoni, Vitsa and Efira.

🛏 Sleeping

Hotel Astoria   HOTEL €

(📞26510 20755; http://hotelastoria.gr; Averof & Paraskeuopoulou 2; s/d €45/60; P ❋ 🛜) Basic, clean rooms with solid wi-fi, a few paces from the laneway nightlife on Lord Byron and Stoa Liampei. Budget Hotel Astoria ticks all the boxes.

Limnopoula Camping   CAMPGROUND €

(📞26510 25265; off lot Merarchias; camp sites per tent/adult €4/8; ◎Apr-Oct) This breezy lakeside campground is 2km from the centre on Lake Pamvotis' northwestern shore. It has a kitchen, a laundry and a restaurant. Don't swim in the lake (note the algae) and do bring mosquito repellent.

Filyra & Platanos   BOUTIQUE HOTEL €€

(📞6932601240; www.hotelfilyra.gr; Andronikou Paleologou 18; d/studio €65/75; P ❋ 🛜) These flower-bedecked boutique hotels face each other on Paleologou. The spacious rooms and self-catering suites, spread across two quiet Kastro locations, are perennial favourites.

Hotel Kastro
PENSION €€

(26510 22866; www.hotelkastro.gr; Andronikou Paleologou 57; d from €55; P※) This friendly, restored Kastro mansion overlooking Its Kale citadel has great atmosphere: antique brass beds, stained-glass windows and a tranquil courtyard create a secluded feel. Follow signs for the Byzantine Museum after you enter the Kastro.

Traditional Hotel Dafni
HOTEL €€

(6932601240; Ioustinianou 12; d/q €65/90) Set discreetly inside the Kastro's enormous outer walls, Dafni offers rooms combining traditional and modern amenities. There's one grand, well-decorated family room (€90). Reception is at nearby sister establishments, Filyra & Platanos (p279).

Hotel Olympic
HOTEL €€

(26510 22233; www.hotelolymp.gr; Melanidi 2; d from €70; P※@🛜) Ioannina's fanciest hotel has fine rooms, welcoming staff and lake views from a conveniently central location.

✗ Eating

Some of Ioannina's best places only open for dinner and many more get busy from 9pm.

Mystagogia
TAVERNA €

(26510 65325; www.mystagwgia.gr; Koundouriotou 44; mains €6; ⊙dinner; 🔲) A popular *tsipouradhiko* (ouzerie) set in an old mansion, Mystagogia has nourishing mezedhes, juicy grills and an occasionally raucous ouzo-fuelled late-night ambience.

Ippotes
MEDITERRANEAN €

(6932358223; Soutsou 7; mains €7-11; ⊙8pm-2am) Great wines, Italian flair and Greek grills combine in this inventive stone-walled restaurant with a relaxing backyard.

Ioannina

Fisa Roufa
TAVERNA €

(📞26510 26262; Averof 55; mains €6; ⊗lunch & dinner; 🕸) Serious soups, roast lamb and tender rabbit are whisked to your table by the amiable staff of this cheap and cheerful taverna. Expect traditional, home-cooked fare without fuss.

Seirios
GREEK €€

(📞26510 77070; www.seirioskouzina.gr; Papandreou & Evanggelidi; mains €8-12; ⊗noon-11pm) Locally recommended Seirios has excellent and imaginative specials. Try the sausage in Greek yoghurt, stuffed pork shoulder blade or mushrooms in oil and lemon.

Stoa Louli
TAVERNA €€

(📞26510 71322; www.stoa-louli.gr; Anexartisias 78; mains €7-12) Built in 1875 Stoa Louli has been an inn, a trade centre for Jewish leather merchants and an Ottoman Bank. Fronted by grand arches, this friendly place serves Greek favourites with a contemporary twist.

🍸 Drinking & Nightlife

Popular student bars are found in Skala, opposite the Kastro's southern stretches. Off Anexartisias, check out Stoa Liampei, an arched laneway with a checkerboard pavement packed with bars, and back streets Lord Byron and Katsantoni. Southwest from here Plateia Pargis has scenic outdoor drinking spots in the shade of a lovely ochre-tiled Orthodox church.

Mpizisten
CAFE

(📞26510 27369; cnr Lord Byron & Katsantoni; ⊗10am-late) Beer bottle vases and vintage stylings give a quirky feel to this cafe in the laneways off Averof. Moreish bar snacks

such as roasted feta and miniature omelettes are a superb interlude between rounds of espresso or chilled white wine.

Blow Cafe
CAFE

(📞26510 70169; Dosiou 2; coffee €1.30; ⊗10am-late) Coffee is taken as seriously as card games in this hip, studenty cafe near Plateia Pargis.

Legacy Rock Club
BAR

(📞6947321552; Giosef Eligia 13 & Eth Antistaseos 20; ⊗9pm-late) Live acts, '80s rock tribute nights and a gritty, guitar-loving soundtrack keep Legacy Rock Club throbbing until late. Compared to some other Ioannina bars, drinks prices are lower than the growl of a '90s death-metal vocalist. Check ahead for events.

Denoar
BAR

(📞6984766894; www.denoar.de; Anexartasias 41-42; ⊗9pm-late) This bar occupies a beautifully arching 200-year-old former *agora* (market). It has friendly people, twinkling lights, strange curvy stairs and an interesting musical mix.

Fournos
BAR

(Ethnikis Antistaseos 7; ⊗9am-late) Wild about coffee and cocktails, studenty Fournos has a rotating calendar of summer parties and themed events.

Byzantine Museum Cafe
CAFE

(📞26510 64206; Its Kale; ⊗8am-5pm & 8-10pm Tue-Sun) On Its Kale, this big and busy museum cafe is the place to mull Ioannina's tumultuous history over a light meal and a coffee.

NORTHERN GREECE IOANNINA

🛍 Shopping

Centre of Traditional Handcrafts of Ioannina
HANDICRAFTS, JEWELLERY

(☑26510 27650; www.kepavi.gr; Arhiepiskopou Makariou 1; ☺9.30am-2.30pm & 5.30-8.30pm) Savour Ioannina's centuries-old silverwork tradition at this collective artisans' workshop and store. Pieces range from intricate jewellery to enormous silverware sets.

Public
BOOKS

(☑26510 70087; cnr Melanidi & Pirsinela; ☺9am-8pm) If you need maps and travel guides for an adventure into Zagorohoria or beyond, this bookstore has a decent travel section.

ℹ Information

Plateia Pyrrou and Averof have banks and ATMs.

EOS (Greek Alpine Club; ☑26510 22138; www.orivatikos.gr; Smyrnis 15; ☺hours vary)

Post office (☑26510 76880; 28 Oktovriou 9; ☺7.30am-2pm Mon-Sat) Post office branch in central Ioannina.

ℹ Getting There & Away

AIR

Aegean Airlines (☑26510 64444) serves Athens. The **airport** (☑26510 83600; Km 4 Ioannina–Kozani road) is 4km northwest of town.

BUS

Ioannina bus station (KTEL Ioanninon; ☑26510 25014; www.ktelioannina.gr; Georgiou Papandreou 45) serves Athens (€39, 6½ hours, seven daily), Konitsa (€6.20, 1¼ hours, five daily), Thessaloniki (€32, 3½ hours, six daily), Arta (€7.10, two hours, six daily) and Metsovo (€5.80, one hour, four daily). In summer buses sometimes serve Parga (€12, 1½ hours); alternatively, travel via Igoumenitsa (€9.80, 1¼ hours, seven daily) or Preveza (€10.40, two hours, eight daily). Buses also serve Dodoni (€2, 40 minutes). Zagorohoria buses are irregular, so check ahead. Buses from Ioannina serve Albanian border-post Kakavia (€6, one hour, eight daily).

ℹ Getting Around

Buses to the airport run from the **clock tower** (Plateia Dimokratis) every 20 minutes. Car rental agencies also have branches at the airport.

Avis (☑26510 46333; Dodonis 71; ☺9am-1.30pm & 6pm-8.30pm) Central car-hire outfit in Ioannina.

Budget Rent a Car (☑26510 43901; Dodonis 109) Car-hire branch in central Ioannina. Call ahead to check opening hours.

Taxi (☑26510 46777) Taxis wait near Plateia Pyrrou and the lake.

The Island
To Νησί

The Island (To Nisi) lies opposite Ioannina, amid woods and wildflowers in Lake Pamvotis. In the 17th century, refugees from Peloponnesian Mani built its portside village, where around 200 people still live. The island's secluded monasteries are significant for their unusual frescoes and book collections, while the laneways with their old, white-plastered houses lend atmosphere.

It was here that the last act in despot Ali Pasha's grand drama unfolded. After years of double-dealing and challenges the Ottomans decided to eliminate the 82-year-old 'Lion of Ioannina' in 1822. Falsely assured of a pardon, Ali withdrew with his guard to the island's Moni Panteleimon. There he was trapped and Ottoman soldiers shot him; note the fatal bullet hole in the floorboards at the Ali Pasha Museum.

👁 Sights

Information about Lake Pamvotis can be found at the stand near the Ali Pasha Museum. Just off Plateia Alieon there are souvenir stands packed with decorative weapons and jewellery.

Ali Pasha Museum
MUSEUM

(The Island; adult €1; ☺8am-10pm Jun-Sep, 10am-9pm Oct-May) This island museum commemorates Ioannina's former despot, Ali Pasha. There's a printed narrative (in English) recounting the heady events of Ali's last days, plus various personal effects and etchings of the portly pasha in full repose, sitting fat and happy with his consort, beard and hookah. To get there, walk the hill from the dock into town and turn left.

Moni Filanthropinon
MONASTERY

(Μονή Φιλανθρωπινών; ☺9am-6pm) FREE Moni Filanthropinon looks unassuming from the outside. But after entering the monastery courtyard, the caretaker will usher you through a wooden door for you to see unflinchingly macabre frescoes of the fates of the saints. No detail of amputations, skin peelings and torture by wheel is left unrendered. Just as intriguing (and easier on the eye) are the 16th-century frescoes of Greek philosophers Plato, Aristotle and Plutarch sitting alongside more suitably Christian personalities.

Built in the 13th century by the Filanthropini, a leading Constantinopolitan family who fled the Crusaders in 1204, Moni

Filanthropinon became a secret school for Christians during the Ottoman Muslim domination. Follow the right-hand path along the Island's western edge to reach this well-signposted monastery. Continue along the trail for what is the Island's oldest monastery, **Moni Diliou** (less well preserved than Filanthropinon) and **Moni Eleousis**.

✗ Eating

Small, shady square Plateia Alieon has restaurants and cafes.

Restaurant Kyra Vasiliki   TAVERNA €
(✓ 26510 81081; The Island; mains €6-8; ⊘ dinner) Watch ferries come and go from this dockside taverna that has a big menu and even bigger fish tanks.

Propodes   SEAFOOD €
(✓ 26510 81214; The Island; fish €4-6; ⊘ noon-11pm) Simple fish and grills are served at this humble island eatery.

ℹ Getting There & Away

Ioannina's ferry quay has ferries (€2, 10 minutes, every 15 minutes) from 7am to 11.30pm in high season (from June to September). Out of season, ferries run hourly from 8am to 10pm (October to May). Summer services run every 15 minutes; in winter, only hourly.

Around Ioannina

Epiros' rocky scenery lends a dramatic quality to the setting for the sights around Ioannina, from crowd-pleasing Perama Cave to sacred spots such as Dodoni. Each can be achieved in half a day if you're short on time.

Perama Cave   CAVE
(Σπήλαιο Περάματος; ✓ 26510 81521; www.spilaio-perama.gr; Perama; adult €7; ⊘ 9am-9pm summer, to 5pm winter) Stalactite-rich Perama Cave, 4km from Ioannina, is among Greece's largest and most impressive. Discovered by accident in 1940 by residents fleeing bomb attacks, 1100m of its fairy-tale passageways can be explored on hourly guided tours (45 minutes, in Greek and English). Knowledgeable guides come armed with fascinating facts about geology and unique cave fauna. The cave is several degrees colder than outside, so dress accordingly. Buses 8 and 16 from Ioannina's clock tower run regularly to Perama, 250m south of the cave.

Dodoni   RUIN
(Δωδώνη; ✓ 26510 82287; adult €2; ⊘ 8am-3pm) Flanked by mountains and wildflower meadows, the colossal 3rd-century-BC Theatre of Dodoni, 21km southwest of Ioannina, is Epiros' most imagination-firing ancient site. The north-side acropolis has wall remnants. East of the theatre are **bouleuterion** (council house) foundations and the small **Temple of Aphrodite**. Nearby, Zeus' sanctuary once stood. Dodoni is 30 minutes' drive from central Ioannina. Buses from Ioannina serve Dodoni twice daily. Taxis cost about €35 return. Dodoni was undergoing restoration on our visit, but remained open to visitors.

From around 2000 BC, the earth goddess worshipped here spoke through Greece's oldest oracle. Around 400 BC a temple to Zeus was built here, too, and oracles interpreted his messages through the rustling of an ancient oak tree's leaves and the movements of birds nesting in its branches.

Zagorohoria
Τα Ζαγοροχώρια

The Zagorohoria's 46 traditional stone-and-slate villages, tucked into the Pindos range, offer atmospheric accommodation, crisp alpine air, sublime views and myriad local legends. Once connected only by mountain paths and stone bridges, they're now connected by paved roads, some of which enjoy spectacular twists and turns.

Solitude-seekers will delight in Zagorohoria's tranquil and unpeopled villages, such as romantic **Dilofo**, which has only a handful of inhabitants; traditional **Kipi**; and barely touristed **Negades**. But most visitors head for romantic and rugged **Monodendri**, embark on outdoor adventures from **Kato Pedina**, **Ano Pedina** and **Aristi**, or navigate precipitous mountain roads to the **Papingo** villages.

Although time and emigration have depopulated many villages, boutique and environmental tourism have allowed savvy locals to prosper by converting *arhontika* (mansions) and smaller traditional homes into inviting guesthouses. Hikers also come for the immediate proximity to the Vikos Gorge and other mountain routes.

After Constantinople was conquered (first by the Crusaders in 1204, later by the Turks in 1453), noble Byzantine families

Zagorohoria

fled here, safeguarding their Greek culture and traditions. The Ottomans also gave the Zagorohorians privileges and autonomy in exchange for guarding the mountain passes. The locals thus became quite wealthy and also worldly, creating a cultured diaspora in centres of learning and commerce in early modern Europe.

◉ Sights & Activities

◎ Vikos-Aoös National Park
Εθνικός Δρυμός Βίκου-Αώου

Whether for the adrenaline rush of hiking, biking and rafting, or to seize some binoculars and admire its fauna, Vikos-Aoös National Park is a huge draw for travellers wending their way through the steep Zagorohoria. The park bursts with pristine rivers and forests, flowering meadows, and shimmering lakes that reflect jagged mountains and end-less blue sky. Almost one-third of Greece's flora (some endemic) lives here, along with native fish, foxes and chamois, rare hawks, otters and bears. The park's Tymfi Massif contains numerous ear-popping peaks including Mt Trapezitsa (2022m), Mt Astraka (2436m) and Mt Gamila (2497m). Beneath them lies 12km-long Vikos Gorge.

While hikers comprise the majority of visitors, seminomadic Vlach and Sarakatsani shepherds still take their flocks up to high grazing ground in summer, returning to the valleys in autumn.

Vikos Gorge   CANYON
The Voïdomatis River, a tributary of the Aoös, carved the 12km-long, 900m-deep Vikos Gorge over millions of years, leaving stark cliffs and yawning depths. According to Guinness, it's the world's deepest canyon in proportion to its width. It begins south of Monodendri, running north until the Papingo villages. Trail maps and signs for hikes can

be found in most major villages. Check routes and get guidance on hikes suitable for your experience level at EOS (p282) in Ioannina.

From Monodendri, you can survey the gorge from Moni Agia Paraskevi. A steep, marked path into the gorge begins a challenging four-hour walk; at canyon's end a right-hand trail leads to Mikro Papingo (2½ hours). Megalo Papingo is a further 2km west, but the track splits at the hike's base. The only water is at Klima Spring, halfway along the gorge.

Oxya Lookout, 5km beyond Monodendri on a dirt road, has fantastic gorge views, as does Beloi Lookout opposite. To get there, drive 9km along a winding road from Kapesovo to Vradeto, and hike 1.5km along a marked trail after the dirt road (it's a bumpy drive). Vradeto is set along striated limestone cliffs. For the Beloi Lookout, climb the rock stairway, Skala Vradetou, signposted outside Tsepelovo, another relaxing base for hiking northern Zagorohoria sites such as the Drakolimni (Dragon Lake).

Check the weather forecast and kit yourself out with sturdy hiking boots and drinking water. Always let someone local (such as your guesthouse) know your departure time and planned route, so they can raise the alarm if necessary.

Monodendri　　Μονοδένδρι

Around 38km north of Ioannina, Monodendri is among Zagorohoria's most-visited villages. Superb hiking trails lead from here to Papingo through Vikos Gorge (about six hours). This village of slate-roofed houses also has a cluster of great tavernas and some fascinating churches, notably the triple-bell **Church of Agios Athanasios** and charismatic 17th-century **Church of Agios Minas**.

Moni Agia Paraskevi　　MONASTERY
A short path leads from Monodendri's northeastern edge to Moni Agia Paraskevi, a monastery with spectacular views over Vikos Gorge. Agia Paraskevi has the oldest preserved church in Zagorohoria. According to legend, Michael Voevodas Therianos founded it in 1413 to thank God for healing his daughter of an incurable illness. The church's frescoes partially date to the 15th century.

Rizarios Centre　　CULTURAL CENTRE
(☎26530 71573; www.rizarios.eu; Monodendri; ☉9am-4pm) This cultural centre with an

adjoining handicrafts school is housed in a renovated manor. Rizarios shines a light on Zagorohoria history with exhibitions of photos and artworks. Coffee-table books and embroidered souvenirs are for sale here.

Kato Pedina & Ano Pedina
Κάτω Πεδινά & Ανω Πεδινά

Until the middle of the 20th century, Kato Pedina was the wheat-winnowing capital of Zagorohoria, producing the majority of the region's grain. Today it's an ideal departure point for adventure travellers to mountain bike, trek or ski the Pindos Mountains. Drive 4km east and you'll find Ano Pedina (population 170) perched at an altitude of 960m on Mt Tymfi. This village charms with 18th-century churches and exhilarating mountain views.

Moni Evaggelistria　　MONASTERY
(Ano Pedina) This wonderfully well preserved monastery, founded in the late 18th century, is blinged out with icons and frescoes spanning 200 years.

Compass Adventures　　OUTDOORS
(☎26530 71770; www.compassadventures.gr; Kato Pedina) Compass Adventures runs outdoor excursions and activities in the Zagorohoria wilds. Adventures range from one-day mountain biking tours and guided family hikes (from May to October) to multiday ski touring in the Pindos Mountains (from December to April).

Aristi　　Αρίστη

Picturesque Aristi is tucked into the Pindos Mountains at an altitude of 650m. The village has ancient roots, evidenced by Paleolithic remnants discovered nearby. Today, a clutch of guesthouses snoozes along Aristi's cobblestoned streets and adrenaline junkies descend here to raft and hike. Its most arresting sight is **Moni Panagia Spiliotissa**; this arched, frescoed spiritual site stands aside a boulder by the Voïdomatis River and dates from 1665.

If you're driving from Ioannina, Aristi is the last village before Papingo. After Aristi, prepare for white-knuckle driving as the road winds upwards. If you aren't venturing further than Aristi, take the Papingo road as far as **Voïdomatis Bridge**, a beautiful stone span over bright cerulean water.

NORTHERN GREECE ZAGOROHORIA

Papingo Πάπιγκο

The road ribboning north from Aristi to Papingo offers Zagorohoria's most breathtaking views. **Megalo Papingo** and **Mikro Papingo** – respectively, the large and the small – are two villages tucked into the Vikos-Aoös National Park at a dizzying altitude of 960m. The most distinctive element of Papingo's setting is the looming rock formations known locally as the **Towers**. The tallest is 1788m high. A 2km trail separates the two villages, along which you can find two **natural pools** fed by the Rogovo River. The pools are swimmable in summer.

Agios Vlasios CHURCH

(Megalo Papingo) The most striking of Papingo's churches is Agios Vlasios (1852) with its separate 15m-high hexagonal bell tower (1887).

🛏 Sleeping

Xenonas Dias GUESTHOUSE €

(✆26530 41257; www.diaspapigo.gr; Mikro Papingo; d incl breakfast €60) In quiet Mikro Papingo, this pension has simple, snug rooms and a restaurant that whips up regional delicacies that can be washed down with homemade *rakia*.

Archontiko Zarkada PENSION €

(✆26530 71305; www.monodendri.com; Monodendri; d incl breakfast from €45; ⓟ🤶) Gaze on the gorge from your balcony at this lovely old stone house with clean, snug rooms. Some rooms have spa baths.

★ Primoula BOUTIQUE HOTEL €€

(✆26530 71133; www.primoula.gr; Ano Pedina; d incl breakfast from €75; ⓟ) 🖋 This exceptionally friendly guesthouse in central Ano Pedina

---

ℹ NAVIGATING THE ZAGOROHORIA ZIGZAGS

Zagorohoria's vertiginious views are guaranteed to tighten your grip on the steering wheel. These challenging mountain roads are steep, often narrow, and have frequent hairpin bends. Debris from hillsides sloughs onto the road surface and even short drives are likely to be interrupted by herds of goats, dazed dogs and even lumbering tortoises. Check weather conditions before you set out; acrophobes and nervous drivers should avoid driving by night when roads are unlit.

---

has uniquely designed rooms, some glowing in warm pastel tones and others with traditional stone walls. Helpful staff assist with organising outdoor activities, and a lavish, locally sourced breakfast kickstarts each day.

Arhontiko Dilofo GUESTHOUSE €€

(✆26530 22455; www.dilofo.com; Dilofo; d incl breakfast from €60; ⓟ) One of Zagorohoria's finest guesthouses, this restored 1633 mansion in placid Dilofo village is ideal for anyone seeking peace and natural harmony. Each of its nine rooms features traditional carpets, furnishings and ornate painted window shutters. There's a charming courtyard and views over Dilofo's cluttered slate rooftops.

Zagori Suites BOUTIQUE HOTEL €€

(✆6944342739, 26530 71076; www.zagorisuites.gr; Vitsa; ste from €85; ⓟ🤶) With ornately decorated suites and chalets, this boutique hotel at the entrance to Vitsa village is one of Zagorohoria's most sumptuous choices. In summer there's a closed playground and games for children, while adults can clink glasses at the well-stocked bar.

Mikro Papigo 1700 BOUTIQUE HOTEL €€

(✆26530 41179; www.mikropapigo.gr; Mikro Papingo; d incl breakfast from €90 ; ⓟ🏊) 🖋 Fifteen handsome rooms and suites vary in styles from minimalist to rustic, while gorge views from the restaurant delight. Reward yourself for the steep uphill climb (cars aren't allowed in the village centre) by unwinding in the small sauna and steam room.

Papaevangelou GUESTHOUSE €€

(✆26530 41135; www.hotelpapaevangelou.gr; Megalo Papingo; d/studio incl breakfast from €75/120; 🤶) This popular Papingo guesthouse has four studios and 10 rooms with outstanding views and traditional trimmings galore: dark wooden floors, lace curtains and (in some spaces) fireplaces.

Arhontiko Aristis B&B €€

(✆26530 42210, 6945676261; www.arhontiko-aristis.gr; Aristi; s/d/tr from €70/80/110; ⓟ🤶) Set in an 1800 stone mansion, this Aristi guesthouse offers spectacular views and combines classic stone-and-wood decor with modern distractions such as free wi-fi, flatscreen TVs and billiards.

Porfyron B&B €€

(✆26530 71579; http://porfyron.gr; Ano Pedina; d from €65; ⓟ) This red-painted 19th-century mansion has individually decorated rooms with antique furnishings and soft-coloured walls. There are occasional workshops on cookery, liqueurs and yoga, plus excursions from rafting to fly-fishing. Half-board with tasty home cooking is available from €100.

✕ Eating

Restaurant Tsoumaniskos
TAVERNA €

(☑ 26530 41893; www.tsoumanisnikos.gr; Vikos; mains €6-9; ☺ lunch & dinner) Gorge yourself near the gorge at this iconic Vikos taverna. Excellent Greek pies and hearty local meats conspire to replace the calories lost on hikes around Vikos. There's a charming guesthouse above.

Taverna Sopotseli
TAVERNA €

(☑ 6942578095, 26530 22629; Dilofo; mains €7-10; ☺ dinner) Dilofo's little taverna lavishes salads in fine olive oil and fires the grill for a carnivore-pleasing feast. A thoughtful wine list refreshes the palate between helpings of seasonal game and fried cheese.

Konaki
GREEK €

(☑ 26530 42238; www.papigo-konaki.gr; Megalo Papigo; mains €8; ☺ lunch & dinner Mon-Sat, lunch Sun) Tuck into spit-roasted lamb, Epirot pies and lovingly simmered stews at this welcoming restaurant in the larger Papingo village. Konaki also has a five-room guesthouse in Zagorohoria's traditional stone-and-wood style.

Aris Journeys of Flavors
CAFE €€

(☑ 26530 41411; Megalo Papingo; mains €8-12; ☺ lunch & dinner) This friendly cafe-bar has a rotating selection of main dishes and plenty of homemade desserts to tempt sweet-toothed hikers.

Sta Riza
GREEK €€

(☑ 26530 71550; Elati village; mains €9-13; ☺ 12.30-10pm) It's hard to disagree with the locals – Sta Riza, overlooking rolling hills, is the place for hearty country cooking such as *manitaria fournitsa* (baked mushrooms in red wine, tomato, feta and herbs) and *arnaki vlahika* (soft baked lamb with yoghurt). Elati is in the southernmost Zagorohoria; it's a very narrow village, so park 30m before the restaurant.

❶ Information

WWF Information Centre (☑ 26530
41071; wwf-ppg@otenet.gr; Mikro Papingo; ☺ 10.30am-5.30pm Sun-Thu, 11am-6pm Fri & Sat) In Mikro Papingo's old schoolhouse, this information centre has an informative exhibition on the area's unique wildlife and fauna.

❶ Getting There & Away

To really see Zagorohoria, you should drive. Limited bus services operate from Ioannina but they are geared towards local residents rather than visitors. They tend to run only one day per week, departing very early in the morning with return journeys in the afternoon of the same day.

Buses serve Megalo Papingo and Mikro Papingo (€5.10, two hours, Tuesday), Ano Pedina and Kato Pedina (€4.30, 1½ hours, Monday) and Monodendri (€4.30, one hour, Monday) in summer.

Taxis from Ioannina to various villages cost from €20 to €55; try negotiating.

Konitsa   Κόνιτσα
POP 4630

Along the trails that flow from Konitsa (*ko-nit-sah*), only the crunch of hiking boots interrupts birdsong and rushing water. This sprawling village is carved into a hillside 60km north of Ioannina. It's where weary trekkers return to share tales of bird sightings and gorge views over a chilled Mythos beer. Greek hunters also use Konitsa as a sort of cowboy depot. Beyond Konitsa, the road arcs northeast to Kastoria. While still passable, this road can be dangerous to navigate, especially at night.

🏃 Activities

From Konitsa's southern entrance begins a 4.5km **river hike** along the Aoös River Gorge to strikingly situated monastery **Panagia Stomiou**. Begin at the elegant 20m-high, 40m-long single-arched stone **Konitsa Bridge**, dating from 1870, which straddles the river. After it, a signposted trail becomes a narrow path between the water and a steep bank, and turns upwards through thick forests.

No Limits
OUTDOORS

(☑ 26550 23777; www.nolimits.com.gr; Konitsa) This local company provides equipment and experienced guides for kayaking, horseback riding, rafting, climbing and mountain biking. Guided hikes range from four hours in Vikos Gorge to multiday adventures. You'll have more choice in spring through autumn but ask in advance for out-of-season activities.

🛏 Sleeping & Eating

To Dendro Guesthouse
PENSION €

(☑ 26550 22055; d/tr €40/55; 🅿) A moustachioed man clad in leather and answering to the name 'Johnny Dendro', Yiannis Mourehidis has been a Konitsa legend and fount of local knowledge for more than 35 years. His guesthouse offers clean and comfortable rooms, and the heartiest of welcomes. Exhausted hikers follow the scent of traditional roasted lamb to the adjoining taverna, **To Dendro Restaurant** (☑26550 22055; mains €10; ☑). Rest your feet, seize some grilled feta, and swap stories about trekking the Konitsa wilds.

Gefyri   HOTEL €

(☑26550 23780; www.gefyri.gr; Konitsa; d €50; P❋☎⚏) Right next to the stone bridge, this hospitable family-run hotel has comfortable rooms, a playground and an outdoor pool (swimmable from May to September).

Grand Hotel Dendro   HOTEL €€

(☑26550 29365; www.grandhoteldentro.gr; d/tr/ste €60/75/100; P❋☎) This luxurious place offers attic suites with hydromassage showers, spacious living rooms and a fireplace.

Konitsa Mountain Hotel   HOTEL €€

(☑26550 29390; www.konitsahotel.gr; d/tr/ste incl breakfast €70/80/105; P❋☎) This palatial hotel on the hill behind town offers spacious rooms combining smooth marble and beautifully seasoned wooden floors. The hotel has a sauna, Turkish baths and a gym. Take the road behind the centre uphill for 2km. Taxis go from the *plateia* (about €3).

ⓘ Information

Pharmacies, post office and ATM-equipped banks can be found near the main square. The bus station is a short walk downhill. There's also a small **health centre** (☑26550 23111).

ⓘ Getting There & Away

Konitsa bus station (☑26550 22214) serves Ioannina (€6.20, two hours, five daily on weekdays), but not Kastoria. Buses reach Mertziani (€1.60, 30 minutes, two daily) for Albania. **Taxis** (☑26550 22500) can be found near the main square.

Preveza   Πρέβεζα
POP 22,900

Tucked snugly into a peninsula separating the Ionian Sea and the Amvrakikos Gulf, Preveza (*preh*-veh-zah) is a fine place to drop your anchor for a day or two. Travellers here are usually about to embark on an adventure: south to the sun-kissed Ionians, north to the vast ruins of Nikopoli and the Nekromanteio of Afyra, or into the great wide ocean by yacht.

◉ Sights & Activities

A couple of blocks from the waterfront, a maze of backstreets bursts with lively tavernas. Preveza's **Venetian clock tower** (1792) and several fine churches distract from the forest of yachts lining the waterfront.

Eco Cruising   CRUISE

(☑26820 41992; www.eco-cruising.gr; Akragantos 5; dolphin cruises adult/child €40/20) On the central waterfront, Eco Cruising offers sailboat cruises on the Amvrakikos Gulf and to the islands. Tours include sunset cruises, birdwatching trips in protected wetlands, and dolphin-spotting with guaranteed sightings.

🛏 Sleeping

Hotel Urania   HOTEL €

(☑26820 89570; www.hotelurania.gr; Irinis 33; s/d/tr €40/55/65; ☎) Hospitable Hotel Urania is on busy main road Irinis, which leads towards the bus station, Nikopoli and the road to Parga. Elegant and comfortable, this hotel is well positioned for a quick stopover.

Camping Kalamitsi   CAMPGROUND €

(☑26820 22192; www.campingkalamitsi.eu; Kalamitsi; camp sites per adult/child/tent €6.50/4/4.50; P☎⚏) This large beach campground, 4km northeast of Preveza on the road to Parga, operates from May to mid-September. It has a pool and restaurant, and bungalows that sleep four people (from €65).

Hotel Avra   HOTEL €

(☑26820 21230; www.hotelavra.net; Eleftheriou Venizelou 19; s/d €36/45; P❋☎) Budget travellers will delight in the refreshing harbour views. Rooms have a light nautical touch with tiled floors and blue fittings. The hotel feels a little worn, though Avra's proximity to waterside bars and its helpful staff make up for it. There's free parking in the municipal lot opposite.

Dioni Boutique Hotel   BOUTIQUE HOTEL €€

(☑26820 27381; www.masthotels.gr/boutiquehoteldioni; cnr Kalou & Parthenagogiou; s/d/ste incl breakfast from €70/90/130; ☎) ✿ A sumptuous choice in central Preveza. The rooms are plush, service is friendly, and breakfast is served with ocean views in the rooftop cafe.

🍴 Eating

Taverna O Kaixis   SEAFOOD €

(☑6947899404; Parthenagogiou 7; fish €5-9; ☉dinner) The friendly 'mermaid' taverna on a side street near the water prepares excellent fresh fish dishes and grills.

Amvrosios
SEAFOOD €

(☑26820 27192; near Andrianoupoleos; fish €7-11; ⊙11am-2pm Tue-Sun) This well-loved taverna spills onto a flowering lane by the waterfront. A local favourite, it's pricier than some but whips up some of the town's best seafood.

ⓘ Information

Busy Leofors Irinis, two blocks up from the waterfront, has banks and ATMs. An underwater car tunnel (€3) links Preveza with Aktion; no passenger ferry exists. Cyclists and pedestrians can be transported through for free.

Karyatis Travel (☑6949225729; www.karyatis travel.gr; Salaminos 1, cnr Venizelou; ⊙9am-2pm & 5-8pm) On a southern-waterfront alley, this agency sells ferry and plane tickets. Ebullient owner Tzeni Nota speaks Greek, English, Thai and Arabic.

ⓘ Getting There & Away

AIR

Preveza airport (Aktion Airport; ☑26820 26113), 7km south of Preveza and sometimes called Lefkada or Aktio, is a European summer charter-flight hub, serving numerous destinations. **Sky Express** (☑28102 23835; www. skyexpress.gr) serves domestic destinations such as Sitia in Crete and a few Ionian islands. Taxis cost around €12.

BUS

Preveza's **bus station** (☑26820 22213; Km 2 Preveza–Parga road) is 2km north of the town centre, just off the main road; taxi drivers charge €4 or more to travel between the two. Buses serve Ioannina (€10.40, two hours, eight daily), Parga (€7.10, two hours, five daily), Igoumenitsa (€9.80, 2½ hours, one daily), Thessaloniki (€38, eight hours, two daily) and Athens (€37.30, six hours, five daily).

Nikopoli   Νικόπολη

Nikopoli was built in 31 BC by Octavian (later Emperor Augustus) to commemorate defeating Marc Antony and Cleopatra in the naval Battle of Actium (present-day Aktion). After 5th- and 6th-century barbarian raids, Emperor Justinian rebuilt it. But the 11th-century Bulgarians sacked it for good. The ruins that remain require a pinch of imagination to conjure the fabled 'City of Victory', but their scale is breathtaking.

◉ Sights

Nikopoli
RUIN

(City of Victory; ☑26820 41336; Preveza–Ioannina national road; ⊙8.30am-8pm high season) **FREE**

The ruins of Nikopoli include scant Roman walls, better-preserved Byzantine walls and churches, and a theatre, all spread across a vast site. Stairs lead to the top of the Byzantine walls in some places (such as by Church B) but ascend these crumbling steps at your own risk. Allow an hour or two to hike the site, which is 6km from Preveza. Large stretches of the walls are parallel to major roads, so beware of traffic when crossing to admire temples and towers.

Museum of Nicopolis
MUSEUM

(☑26820 89892; Preveza-Ioannina national road, E951; adult/child €3/free; ⊙8.30am-3pm Mon-Fri; ℗) This museum brims with fascinating funerary monuments and statues in an airy, naturally lit exhibition space. Abundant English-language explanations enliven the collection. Beware the eager museum staff members, who may well follow your every step. The museum is 5km from Preveza.

Arta   Άρτα

POP 27,300

In romantic Arta, there's fierce competition for the best view. First there's it's medieval stone bridge, spanning the lustrous Arahthos River. Then there are Roman ruins and Byzantine walls, spidering across the city. Add to the mix Arta's whopping great wedding cake of a church, Parigoritissa, and you won't know quite where to point your camera. One thing you won't see is crowds, as Arta remains inexplicably off the tourist trail.

Arta owes its richness of ruins to the ancient city of Ambracia, founded in 625 BC. Ambracia once vibrated with music and art as the capital of Pyrrhus' kingdom. Its population relocated to Nikopolis (now Nikopoli) in 168 BC after vicious sackings.

The centrality of Arta's ruins makes it easy – and pleasurable – to combine a historical ramble with exploring lively Plateia Antithaseos and pedestrianised Skoufa. A top-class archaeological museum, fresco-bedecked churches and satisfying restaurants are plenty to fill a weekend.

◉ Sights

Ancient sights around Arta include the remains of a **Temple of Apollo** (Pyrrhou 3) and Greece's smallest **ancient theatre** (renovated throughout 2016 but visible from outside). There's also a **cemetery** dating from the 6th to the 1st centuries BC; it has been undergoing restoration but if it's closed you can take a peep near the corner of Komenou and Garoufalia. The walls of a 13th-century **Byzantine castle** can be admired around the city; there are impressive views from Makrigianni, near the clock tower.

Old Bridge
BRIDGE

(Gefiri tis Artas; Thiakogianni) This graceful stone bridge loops 20m high over the glassy green Arahthos River. A bridge has spanned this spot since Roman times; this one is thought to be Ottoman. Folk ballads wail of a woman walled into its foundations, to banish a curse that saw the bridge crumble each time it was built – a common, if macabre, legend for many Balkan bridges. But there's nothing sinister about this photogenic structure. Take the best pics from the New Bridge opposite, a constrastingly hectic artery into the city.

Church of Parigoritissa Byzantine Museum
MUSEUM

(26810 28692; cnr Tzoumerkon & Parigoritras; adult/senior €2/1; 8am-3pm) This multistorey marvel with intricate brick domes will amaze even the most church-fatigued visitor. Craftspeople from Thessaloniki and Constantinople poured their hearts into the frescoes of this 13th-century edifice. Today it's billed as a museum of Byzantine culture – crane your neck upwards for the lavish upper floors and a gilt Christ on the top dome.

Archaeological Museum
MUSEUM

(26810 71700; www.artasmuseum.gr; Trigono; admission €3; 8am-3pm Tue-Sun; P) This wonderful museum wrapped around a central courtyard tells the story of the ancient city of Ambracia from its foundation in

---

SAILING TO ITALY: FERRIES FROM IGOUMENITSA

If you're heading to Italy by ferry, you'll have to pass through **Igoumenitsa** (ih-goo-mehnit-sah), in Epiros' far northwest, which also serves Ionian islands such as Corfu (Kerkyra) and Paxi. There's little to draw you here other than the promise of sailing to lovelier shores.

Ferries leave from three adjacent quays on the waterfront. Just show up in Igoumenitsa to buy deck-class passenger tickets to Italian ports; waterfront kiosks clearly signpost ferry destinations and departure times. Book ahead for car tickets or sleeping cabins. Be at the port two hours before departure, and check at the shipping agent's office for your boarding pass. On-board 'camping' is allowable for those with campervans (BYO oxygen).

At the time of research, passenger deck-class tickets cost around €58 to Brindisi (six to 9½ hours), €60 to Bari (8½ to 10½ hours), €72 to Ancona (15 hours), and €77 to Venice (24 hours). A passenger ticket in a four-bed cabin with shower is generally twice as expensive. Vehicle prices for Bari and Brindisi start from €57, and from €90 to €112 for Ancona and Venice. Each destination has from two to four sailings per day during summer.

Different ferry companies charge similar prices, and return tickets are sometimes cheaper than one-way; call local ferry offices or check the websites. They include **ANEK Lines** (26650 29274, 26650 29063; www.anek.gr), **Grimaldi Lines** (26650 23077, 26650 24404; www.grimaldi-lines.com), **Minoan Lines** (26650 22952, 26650 26715; www.minoan.gr), **Superfast Ferries** (26650 29200; www.superfast.com) and **Ventouris Ferries** (26650 26670, 26650 23565; www.ventourisferries.gr). The central **Milano Travel** (26650 24237; milantvl@otenet.gr; Agion Apostolon 11; 9am-7pm) also sells tickets. If you're planning ahead from Preveza, **Karyatis Travel** (p289) can find hidden discounts and cabin upgrades. In Parga, try **International Travel Services** (p293). For Corfu ferry information, call the automated **Igoumenitsa Port Authority information line** (26650 99460).

If you need to stay over, the **Angelika Pallas Hotel** (26650 26100; www.angelikapallas.gr; Agion Apostolon 63; d/tr incl breakfast from €64/96; ❄ 🐭) is Igoumenitsa's best: it's friendly, comfortable and close to the quays. Travellers sleeping in rooms with dock views endure a wake-up call of honking ferries; ask if you want a quieter room. Slightly cheaper, less attractive places line the waterfront. **Jolly Hotel** (26650 23971; jollyigm@otenet.gr; Ethnikis Antistasis 14; d incl breakfast from €40; @) feels faded but amicable staff and serviceable rooms make it a good budget choice close to the ferry terminals.

From **Igoumenitsa bus station** (KTEL Thesprotias; 26650 22309; www.ktel-thesprotias.gr; 49 Martiron), two blocks behind the Corfu ferry docks, buses serve Ioannina (€9.80, two hours, seven daily), Parga (€5.90, one hour, three daily), Athens (€44.50, eight hours, three daily), Preveza (€13, 2½ hours, one daily) and Thessaloniki (€34, eight hours, one daily). Buses are less frequent from October to May.

625 BC through its indigenous settlements right up to the foundation of Nikopolis (now Nikopoli), where Ambracia's citizens relocated. The ancient city's musical traditions and burial practices – including elaborately carved stelae – are illustrated with plenty of clear explanation in Greek and English.

Folklore Museum
MUSEUM

(☎26810 22192; Old Bridge; admission €2; ⊙10am-3pm Mon-Fri, 11am-2pm Sat & Sun) A red-painted museum by the Old Bridge with a small collection of traditional costumes and tools.

🛏 Sleeping

Hotel Cronos
HOTEL €

(☎26810 22211; www.hotelcronos.gr; Plateia Kilkis; s/d €40/55; P❄☎) Though a little faded, this comfy hotel is the best spot to snooze in central Arta. Ask for a room looking onto the *plateia* with a view of the Pyrrhus statue.

Arta Palace
HOTEL €€

(☎26810 61530; www.artapalace.gr; Km 5 Arta-Agriniou road; s/d/tr €55/60/75; P❄☎) A 10-minute drive out of town, this hotel isn't quite as grand as the name promises. Nonetheless, it's a more glamorous choice than the digs in central Arta due to its smart rooms, large balconies and zany pastel-coloured pool areas.

✗ Eating & Drinking

Synousies
TAVERNA €

(☎26810 26566; Karaiskaki 20; mains €7-10; ⊙dinner) There's a heartily old-time feel to this local favourite with a robust menu of Greek cuisine.

Fuego
EUROPEAN €€

(☎26810 74140; Matsou 7; mains €8-14; ⊙lunch & dinner; ☎) At this chic central eatery, a menu of beautifully grilled meats with mounds of rosemary-salted fries and a rich range of Italian dishes elicits stomach rumbles.

Byzantio
CAFE

(☎26810 77776; www.byzantio-cafe.gr; Plateia Antistaseos; ⊙9am-late) One of the swankier drinking spots on Plateia Antistaseos, with thirst-quenchers from coffees to cocktails.

❶ Getting There & Away

Direct buses from the main **bus station** (☎26810 26374; www.ktelartas.gr; Kristalli) connect Arta with Thessaloniki (€36.80, 4½ hours, two daily), Athens (€32.30, 5½ hours, six daily), Preveza (€5.20, one hour, four daily) and Ioannina (€7.10, 1½ hours, six daily).

Parga
Πάργα

POP 3900

With its ruined castle perched above a sandy bay, Parga has spectacular views that set it apart from other northern Greece beach towns. The fragrances of citrus trees, olive oils and sea breeze emanate through this friendly town, while the puttering of scooters provides a gentle soundtrack in the winding streets of its old quarter. This former Venetian possession is an excellent base for beaches, historic sites and excursions to Ionian islands. After the sun sets, a slew of excellent seafront tavernas and bars give Parga plenty of fizz.

During summer, sun-worshippers head for Parga's beaches and fill the waterfront bars. But even at peak season, this family-friendly destination never loses its charm. Outside May to September, Parga snoozes: expect shutdowns of some restaurants and activities if you visit during low season.

◉ Sights & Activities

The central waterfront's **Krioneri Beach** is sandy with shallow waters, opposite a small island, Panagia. A 15-minute walk over the castle hill (well signposted from the upper town) leads to the 2km-long **Valtos Beach**. Alternatively, 4km east of Parga, **Lichnos Beach** is more relaxed, with a small, shady campground and clear waters.

Several interesting churches are scattered around Parga. The **Church of the Dodeka Apostoli** (1780) seems bare at first glance, but it has lovingly painted frescoes of Christ's last supper and crucifixion. A few paces away, peer through the gloom in the **Church of Agios Dimitrios** (1850) at numerous depictions of the eponymous saint spearing a Christian-slaying gladiator from his horse. The largest is the **Church of Agios Nikolaos**, dedicated to Parga's patron saint.

Venetian Castle
CASTLE

(Kastro) FREE Centuries of turbulent history have taken their toll on Parga's castle, now a romantic ruin with remarkable sea views. Dating to the 11th century, the castle passed from Venetian to Ottoman control with numerous invasions and bouts of rebuilding in between. Pause for a drink in the cafe (open from 11am until late) to watch ferries, rather than invading pirate ships, ply the shore. The ramparts are uneven, so wear sturdy shoes and hang on to the kids.

Paragaea Olive Oil Museum
MUSEUM

(☑26840 32889; www.paragaea.gr; Tzavella 19; admission €3.50; ☉10am-11pm, by request low season) This fascinating old-town museum in an erstwhile olive-oil factory, operational from 1929 until 1974, unlocks the history of Parga's major pretourist industry. Tickets include a guided tour, which enriches the displays of original machinery and documents found during renovations. There's a sampling of bread and oils (with flavours from oregano to orange) and a museum shop with goodies from salad dressings to soaps.

Parga Tour Train
TOURIST TRAIN

(☑6944624155, 6945793049) This open-air fun train departs every morning and evening from Parga waterfront May to mid-October for a two-hour historical tour. The morning tour visits a forested former watermill (now a museum) below Anthousa village, while the evening one reaches the upper village and ruined castle of Ali Pasha. Buy tickets at the small train stop at the waterfront.

🛏 Sleeping

Enjoy Lichnos Beach Camping
CAMPGROUND €

(☑26840 31171; www.enjoy-lichnos.net; camp sites per adult/tent €6/4, d €55; P🛜) This mellow campground near Lichnos Beach is 2km away from Parga town. Relax in the shade of olive trees; hire water-sports gear; neck ouzo in the tavern; or simply idle on the shore, which is a short walk from the camp sites. Studios with wi-fi and fridges are also available.

Valtos Camping
CAMPGROUND €

(☑26840 31287; www.campingvaltos.com; Valtos Beach; camp sites per adult/tent €6.50/6; P✳) This campground set amid orange trees beside busy Valtos Beach has a restaurant, supermarket and – for the tent-averse – bungalows with kitchenette, TV and air-con. It's a steep 15-minute walk from Parga centre (or a five-minute drive).

★ Utopia
APARTMENT €€

(☑26840 31133; www.utopia.com.gr; Agiou Athanasiou 5; apt from €100; ✳🛜) With divine views overlooking Krioneri Beach, these seven spacious studio apartments couldn't be better located. The furnishings are elegant, the balconies huge, and if you don't want to make use of the kitchenette you can enjoy breakfast and a nerve-jangling coffee in the cafe below.

Hotel Acropol
HOTEL €€

(☑26840 31239; www.acropol.biz; Agion Apostolon 4; s/d €60/90; ✳🛜) Tucked in among the shady alleyways of Parga's old town, Hotel Acropol has an old-world glamour that suits its surroundings. From fine wrought-iron balconies to rooms decked out in handmade Italian furniture, its comfortable beds and kindly owner ensure a relaxing stay. Hotel Acropol is well signposted within the old quarter and it also hosts the fabulous Castello Restaurant.

Hotel Paradise
HOTEL €€

(☑26840 31229; www.paradise-palatino.com; Spyrou Livada 30; s/d €75/100; ✳@✳) The brooding maroon decor and iron trimmings give Hotel Paradise a certain faded glamour. Though slightly worn, this hospitable hotel is an excellent central choice.

🍴 Eating & Drinking

Taverna to Souli
TAVERNA €

(☑26840 31658; Anexartisias 45; mezedhes €4-6, mains €6-11; ☉noon-late) Decades of practice have gone into the fish specialities at Parga's oldest traditional Greek taverna. Plates come crowded with crayfish, spaghetti swirled with prawns, or expertly grilled catch of the day.

Motley Coffeesweet
SWEETS €

(☑26840 32115; waterfront; desserts €3-5; ☉8am-late) There's a dizzying range of sweet-toothed temptations at this late-opening cafe right by Krioneri Beach. Give in to chocolate-drizzled waffles or a rainbow of ice creams; you're sure to burn it off splashing around at the beach.

★ Castello Restaurant
GREEK €€

(☑26840 31239; www.castello-restaurant.com; Hotel Acropol, Agion Apostolon 4; mains €8-14; ☉noon-late; ✳🍴) Local favourite Castello whips up a creative menu of Mediterranean and Asian cuisine. Fish brochettes and steaks keep the grill smoking, while homemade pasta dishes burst with fresh seafood and herbs. The owners are especially proud of the well-stocked wine cellar, visible through a glass panel beneath your feet. Service is attentive, and soft music rounds off the elegant atmosphere.

★ Eden
BISTRO €€

(☑26840 31409; nastast@otenet.gr; Vassila 26; mains around €9; ☉9am-2pm) An array of Italian-inspired dishes are served with a smile at this refreshing bistro in Parga's old town. Sink your fork into a seafood risotto, zingy with fresh tomato and parsley, or grab crêpes and juices for a quick bite.

Taverna Arkoudas
SEAFOOD €€

(☑ 26840 32553; waterfront; fish €8-15; ⊙noon-1am) Let the bear logo lead you to this waterfront eatery. Arkoudas excels in all things tentacled, and charms with traditional music and sea views.

Antico
BAR

(☑26840 32713; Anexartisias 4; ⊙noon-late) The logo – a guitar swirling in a shot glass – gives you a fine idea of what to expect from Parga's rock bar, located on an old-town side street moments from Krioneri Beach. Prop up the bar and let your hair down to soft rock in this lively, unpretentious joint, or debate your favourite guitar solos with the bar staff.

Sugar Bar
BAR

(www.sugarbar.gr; waterfront; cocktails around €7; ⊙10am-late; 🛜) Fancy starting the evening with a Champagne Pick Me Up or a Devil's Kiss? You'll find a drink to suit your mood in Sugar Bar's staggering cocktail menu. If you overdo it, return the following morning for a cappuccino at adjoining Spice Cafe.

ℹ Information

The main road between Preveza and Igoumenitsa runs just north of Parga. Take the northern exit for the bus stop and central Parga (down Spyrou Livada) or the southeasterly exit for Krioneri Beach and the waterfront. Parking becomes difficult as you drive into the narrow streets, so grab a space as soon as you see one.

Parga has several ATM-equipped banks. There are pharmacies on Spyrou Livada and in the old town. The police station is near the post office.

Dr Spiros Padiotis (☑ 26840 32450, 6944162261; Baga Alexandrou 1; ⊙9am-2pm & 6-10pm) Private doctor on call 24 hours a day for medical emergencies. His office is signposted in Parga town.

International Travel Services (ITS; ☑ 26840 31833; www.parga.net; Spyrou Livada 4; ⊙9am-5pm Apr-Sep) By the bus station, long-established and very helpful ITS finds accommodation and car hire, arranges travel tickets and provides friendly information. From May to mid-October staff can help book Nekromanteio day trips, excursions to the Zagorohoria and Vikos Gorge, and trips to islands including Corfu, Paxi and Antipaxi.

Post Office (Alexandrou Baga 18)

ℹ Getting There & Away

BUS
Parga bus station (☑ 26840 31218; Spyrou Livada) serves Igoumenitsa (€5.90, 1½ hours, four daily on weekdays), Preveza (€7.10, two hours, four daily), Thessaloniki (€44, seven hours, one daily) – or travel via Preveza for more services – and Athens (€41.20, seven hours, three daily).

CAR
Hire a car at **Europcar** (☑ 26840 32777; Spyrou Livada 19; from €45 per day) or **Budget Rent a Car**; arrange through ITS travel.

WATER TAXI
During the summer, water taxis serve Valtos Beach (€2) every half hour from 9.30am to midnight and Lihnos Beach (€7) from 11am to 5pm.

Nekromanteio of Afyra

Who would have imagined the gate of Hades, god of the underworld, to be fringed by cypress glades and flower-strewn meadows? But for all its tranquil beauty today, this late 4th-century-BC site (☑ 26840 41206; adult/child €2/free; ⊙8.30am-3pm; P) near Mesopotamo, 20km from Parga, was once famed as a place to commune with the dead. The Romans burned down the site in 167 BC but an evocative ruin remains, with limestone walls enclosing the main sanctuary, labyrinth and pilgrims' purification room.

Ancient Greek pilgrims brought offerings (and substantial payment) to this site on the north bank of the Acheron River, hoping the *nekromanteio* (oracle) would channel mystical powers to help them contact long-dead ancestors. The dead were thought to hold powers of clairvoyance, so priests eagerly cashed in by selling showy rituals to dazzle and disorient. It is thought the thickness of the sanctuary walls (more than 3m) was to allow secret passageways for priests to slip through. To purify themselves ahead of rituals, pilgrims ate a diet only of beans and lupins, and made sacrifices of blood and honey (for a good price). Tiptoe down the narrow ladder to a womb-like underground chamber where dazed pilgrims would be led for a grand finale of supernatural showmanship.

By car head southeast towards Mesopotamo (20km); the Nekromanteio is on the opposite side of the village to the entrance from the main road. Park your car a few hundred metres downhill of the sanctuary; a cobbled path leads up to the ticket office. Alternatively, book a guided excursion through International Travel Services in Parga, or negotiate with a taxi driver in town – return trips, including waiting time, should cost around €40.

Saronic Gulf Islands

Best Places to Eat

➡ Sunset (p308)
➡ Akrogialia (p312)
➡ Aspros Gatos (p302)
➡ Tarsanas (p312)

Best Places to Stay

➡ Poseidonion Grand Hotel (p312)
➡ Hydra Hotel (p307)
➡ Rosy's Little Village (p300)
➡ Orloff Resort (p311)
➡ Cotommatae (p305)
➡ Hotel Miranda (p305)

Why Go?

The Saronic Gulf Islands (Νησιά του Σαρωνικού) dot the waters nearest Athens and offer a fast track to Greek island life. As with all Greek islands, each of the Saronics has a unique feel and culture, so you can hop between classical heritage, resort beaches, exquisite architecture and remote escapism.

Aegina is home to a spectacular Doric temple and ruined Byzantine village, while nearby pine-clad Angistri feels protected and peaceful outside of the booming midsummer months. Further south, Poros, with its forested hinterland, curves only a few hundred metres from the Peloponnese. The Saronic showpiece, Hydra, is a gorgeous car-free island with a port of carefully preserved stone houses rising from a chic, history-charged harbour. Deepest south of all, pine-scented Spetses also has a vibrant nautical history and pretty town architecture, plus myriad aqua coves only minutes from the Peloponnese.

When to Go
Hydra

Apr & May The islands awaken after winter; come for flower-filled Easter.

Jun Celebrate Miaoulia in Hydra with sparkling waters and warm weather.

Sep The best-kept secret: clear skies, thinning crowds and Spetses' Armata celebration.

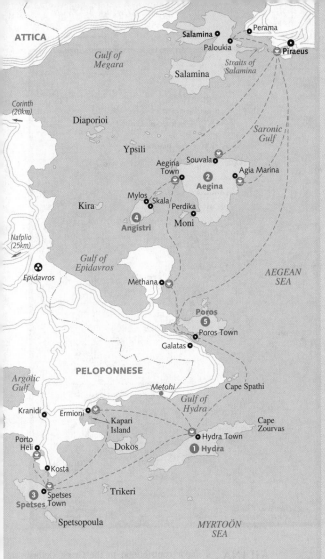

ATTICA

Gulf of
Megara

Corinth
(20km)

Diaporioi

Ypsili

Salamina

Paloukia

Perama

Piraeus

Straits of
Salamina

Salamina

Saronic
Gulf

Souvala

Aegina
Town

Agia Marina

Mylos

Skala

Aegina

Kira

Angistri

Perdika

Moni

Nafplio
(25km)

Gulf of
Epidavros

Epidavros

Methana

AEGEAN
SEA

Poros

Poros Town

Galatas

PELOPONNESE

Metohi

Cape Spathi

Gulf
of Hydra

Kranidi

Ermioni

Kapari
Island

Cape
Zourvas

Porto
Heli

Dokos

Hydra Town

Hydra

Kosta

Trikeri

Spetses
Town

Spetses

Spetsopoula

MYRTOÖN
SEA

MEDITERRANEAN

SEA

N

0   20 km
0   12 miles

Saronic Gulf Islands Highlights

❶ Bouncing between **Hydra's** (p303) gorgeous port, with its excellent museums and chic scene, and the island's deserted trails and ubiquitous swimming rocks.

❷ Delving into **Aegina's** (p296) ancient history at the beautiful Temple of Aphaia and Byzantine Paleohora.

❸ Taste testing your way through **Spetses'** (p309) top restaurants, tracing the region's history in Spetses Town's museums, or cycling the island's ring road to dip into sparkling bays.

❹ Getting away from it all in sleepy **Angistri** (p300) in the low season, when the beaches are most tranquil.

❺ Exploring the peaceful interior of **Poros** (p301).

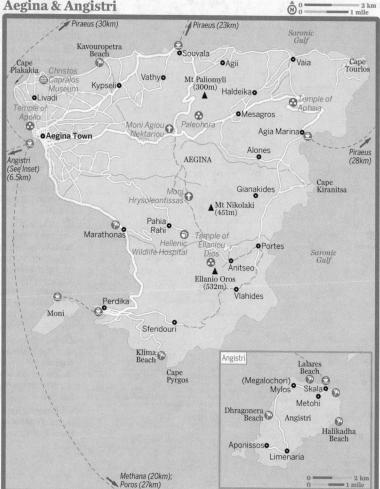

AEGINA

ΑΙΓΙΝΑ

POP 13,056

Beyond its port, Aegina (eh-yi-nah) has the easy-going character of a typical Greek island, with the added bonus of more than its fair share of prestigious ancient sites. Weekending Athenians join laid-back locals and commuters. Unique Aegina treats include a special, and delicious, pistachio nut, the splendid 5th-century Temple of Aphaia and the magical Byzantine ruins called Paleohora.

Aegina was the leading maritime power of the Saronic Gulf during the 7th century BC, when it grew wealthy through trade. It made a major contribution to the Greek victory over the Persian fleet at the Battle of Salamis in 480 BC. Despite this solidarity with the Athenian state, the latter invaded in 459 BC out of jealousy of Aegina's wealth and status and of its liaison with Sparta. Aegina never regained its glory, although in the early 19th century it played a bold part in the defeat of the Turks and was the temporary capital of a partly liberated Greece from 1827 to 1829.

ⓘ Getting There & Away

Aegina's main port, Aegina Town, has ferries (www.saronicferries.gr) operated by **Hellenic**

Seaways (☑ 22970 22945), **Nova Ferries** (☑ 22970 24200) and **Agios Nektarios** (☑ Aegina 22970 25625, Piraeus 21042 25625; www.anes.gr) and high-speed ferries operated by **Hellenic Seaways** (☑ 22970 26777; www. hsw.gr) and **Aegean Flying Dolphins** (☑ 22970 25800) to/from Piraeus and Angistri. Some ferries continue on to Methana (Peloponnese) and Poros. Ferries dock at the large outer quay, with hydrofoils at the smaller inner quay.

Alexandros (☑ Agia Marina 22970 32234, Piraeus 210 482 1006, Souvala 22970 52210; www.alexcruises.gr) serves Aegina's smaller ports, Agia Marina and Souvala, and Piraeus in high season only. Even in winter, high-speed ferries from Piraeus get fully booked for weekends.

Angistri Express (☑ 6947118863) makes several trips daily in high season to Skala and Milos on Angistri (€5.50, 20 minutes). It leaves from midway along Aegina harbour, where timetables are displayed. **Water taxis** (☑ 22970 91387, 6972229720) to Angistri cost €45 one way, regardless of the number of people.

ⓘ Getting Around

BUS

Buses from Aegina Town run several times a day on three routes across the island (departure times are displayed outside the ticket office on Plateia Ethnegersias; you must buy tickets there). Visit www.aeginagreece.com for details. Destinations include Perdika (€1.60, 15 minutes), Souvala (€1.60, 20 minutes) and Agia Marina (€1.70, 30 minutes) via Paleohora (€1.70, 15 minutes) and Temple of Aphaia (€1.70, 25 minutes).

CAR, MOTORCYCLE & BICYCLE

Hire prices start from €30 per day for cars, €15 for 50cc motorcycles and €8 for bicycles.

Karagiannis Travel (☑ 22970 28780; www. aeginatravel.gr; Pan Irioti 44, Aegina Town; ☺ 9am-2pm & 5-9pm)

Sklavenas Rent A Car (☑ Aegina Town 22970 22892, Agia Marina 22970 32871; Kazantzaki 5; ☺ 9am-2pm & 5-9pm) For cars, 4WDs, scoot-

ers, quads and bikes. In Aegina Town, located on the road towards the Temple of Apollo. Also has a branch in Agia Marina.

TAXI

Taxi (☑ Aegina Town 22970 22010, Agia Marina 22970 32107)

Aegina Town   Αίγινα

POP 8905

The sparkling harbour of Aegina Town is backed by a buzzing promenade of people, cafes and restaurants. In the narrow town streets, with kids riding bikes and laundry strung from balconies, small-town Greek life takes over again. The parallel streets backing the harbour, Irioti and Rodi, are crammed with shops of every kind and a few 19th-century neoclassical buildings intermix with whitewashed houses. Ancient Greece is represented by the impressive ruins of the Temple of Apollo, just north of the harbour.

◉ Sights

Temple of Apollo   RUIN
(☑ 22970 22637; http://odysseus.culture.gr; adult/child €3/free; ☺ 9am-5pm Tue-Sun May-Oct, reduced hours Nov-Apr) Northwest of the port, ruined walls, cisterns and broken pillars in honey-coloured stone are lorded over by a solitary surviving column. It's all that's left of a 5th-century-BC temple that was once part of an ancient acropolis (built on a prehistoric site). The informative **Sanctuary Museum** has translations in English and German.

Folklore Museum   MUSEUM
(☑ 22970 26401; S Rodi; ☺ 8.30am-2.30pm Wed-Fri, 10am-1pm Sat & Sun, also 5.30-8.30pm Fri & Sat) **FREE** Peruse historic clothing, housewares and artwork re-creating the mood of old-time island life.

BOAT SERVICES FROM AEGINA

DESTINATION	PORT	TIME	FARE	FREQUENCY
Angistri (Skala)	Aegina Town	20min	€2.50	1 daily
Angistri (Skala)*	Aegina Town	10min	€5.50	4 daily
Methana	Aegina Town	40min	€5.70	2-3 daily
Piraeus	Aegina Town	1hr 10min	€8-9.50	hourly
Piraeus*	Aegina Town	40min	€13.50	6 daily
Piraeus	Agia Marina	1hr	€9.50	3-4 daily, summer
Piraeus	Souvala	1hr 35min	€9.50	3-4 daily, summer
Poros	Aegina Town	1hr 50min	€8.50	2-3 daily

*high-speed services

ℹ️ ISLAND HOPPING

No direct ferries connect Aegina and Angistri with Hydra and Spetses; go via Piraeus or Poros. For day trips, take an Aegina–Poros–Hydra **cruise boat** (www.athensonedaycruise.com; cruise €89, with transfers €99). **Pegasus Cruises** (p139) goes from Nafplio to Spetses and Hydra.

🎎 Festivals & Events

Aegina Fistiki Fest FOOD
(www.aeginafistikifest.gr; ☺Sep) This three-day brouhaha celebrates Aegina's famous pistachio *(fistiki aeginis)* through music, art and culinary contests.

🛏️ Sleeping

Book ahead at weekends.

Aeginitiko Archontiko PENSION €
(☑22970 24968; www.aeginitikoarchontiko.gr; cnr Ag Nikolaou & Thomaiados; d incl breakfast €55-60; ❄️🛜) The rich character of this centrally located old mansion translates through period 19th-century features, a charming salon and courtyard and a splendid breakfast. Rooms are a bit cramped and worn, and bathrooms are basic. Sea views from the rooftop terrace.

Aegina Hotel HOTEL €
(☑22970 28501; www.aeginahotel.gr; Stratigou Dimitriou Petriti 23; s/d/tr from €37/48/60) This 19-room hotel sits about 500m back from the harbour and has clean, well-appointed rooms with a refrigerator and TV.

Electra Pension PENSION €
(☑22970 26715; www.aegina-electra.gr; r €45; ❄️🛜) No views from this small whitewashed pension, but rooms are impeccable and comfy in a quiet corner of the town centre. It outclasses nearby hotels by a long way.

Marianna Studios PENSION €
(☑22970 25650; www.aeginastudiosmarianna.com; Kiverniou 16-18; s/d €30/35; ❄️) Simple, very basic rooms and very friendly owners create a top-notch budget choice. Some rooms have balconies or overlook a quiet, leafy garden alongside the interior courtyard. One has a kitchen (double/triple €40/45).

Hotel Rastoni HOTEL €€
(☑22970 27039; www.rastoni.gr; Odos Stratigou Dimitri Petriti 31; d/tr/q €70/110/120; 🅿️❄️@🛜) Spacious rooms have balconies overlooking the lovely garden and the Temple of Apollo.

Generous breakfasts and friendly staff round out the experience. In a residential neighbourhood a few minutes north of the harbour.

Fistikies Holiday Apartments APARTMENT €€
(☑22970 23783; www.fistikies.gr; Logiotatidou 1; studio €90, 4-person apt €120; 🅿️❄️🛜🏊) This complex of tidy, family-friendly apartments was built in 2007 on the southern edge of town, inland from the football field. Spacious apartments have DVD players and terraces overlooking the pool.

🍴 Eating

The harbourfront restaurants make for lazy world-watching, but are not particularly outstanding, unless you hit the unvarnished *ouzeries* (places serving ouzo and light snacks). Pistachio nuts are on sale everywhere (from €6.50 for 500g, depending on quality).

⭐ Elia MEDITERRANEAN €
(☑22975 00205; Koumoundourou 4; mains €6-9; ☺lunch & dinner, reduced hours winter) Burrow into the backstreets to find this excellent eatery popular with locals. Imaginative, fresh specialities include the pistachio pesto and pittas of the day.

Gelladakis MEZEDHES €
(☑22970 27308; Pan Irioti 45; dishes €7-12; ☺lunch & dinner) Ensconced behind the noisy mid-harbour fish market, this vibrant joint is always thronged with people tucking into hell-fired octopus or sardines, plus other classic mezedhes.

Tsias TAVERNA €
(☑22970 23529; Dimokratias 47; mains €7-10; ☺lunch & dinner) Harbourside eating at its best. Try shrimps with tomatoes and feta, or one of the daily specials.

Bakalogatos MEZEDHES €€
(☑22975 00501; Pan Irioti & Neoptolemou; mains €7-13; ☺lunch & dinner Tue-Sun) Mezedhes in an elegant setting, with faux finished tables and traditional products on the walls.

🍸 Drinking & Nightlife

Remvi CAFE, BAR
(☑22970 28605; Dimokratias 51; ☺8am-late; 🛜) Popular music cafe-bar hops day and night.

International Corner BAR
(☑22970 26564; cnr I Katsa & S Rodi; ☺noon-late) Get off the main strip. The gregarious owner takes requests, from top 40 to fantastic Greek music. In a character-filled, wood-panelled bar room.

Avli BAR
(☑ 22970 26438; Pan Irioti 17; ⊙ 9am-late) This lively restaurant and bar bubbles with activity in a covered garden, and plays tunes from '60s to Greek pop.

ℹ Information

Aegina has no tourist office. Check Karagiannis Travel (p297) for car hire, tours and non-Aegina boats. Harbourfront banks have ATMs.

Hospital (☑ 22970 24489, emergency 22970 22251; Agios Dionisios Nosokomeiou 4)

Port Authority (☑ 22970 22328) At the entrance to the ferry quays.

Tourist police (☑ 22970 27777; Leonardou Lada) Up a lane opposite the hydrofoil dock.

Around Aegina Town

Aegina is wildflower laden in spring, and year-round has some of the best ancient sites in the Saronic Gulf. The interior hills and mountains add drama to the small island, but beaches are not its strongest suit. The east-coast town of **Agia Marina** is the island's main package resort. It has a shallow-water beach that is ideal for families, but it's backed by a fairly crowded main drag. A few thin, sandy beaches, such as **Marathonas**, line the roadside between Aegina Town and Perdika.

◎ Sights

★**Temple of Aphaia** TEMPLE
(☑ 22970 32398; http://odysseus.culture.gr; adult/child €4/free; ⊙ 8am-8pm daily, museum 9am-5pm Tue-Sun May-Oct, reduced hours Nov-Apr) The well-preserved remains of this impressive temple stand on a pine-covered hill with views over the Saronic Gulf. Built in 480 BC, it celebrates a local deity of pre-Hellenic times. The pediments were originally decorated with splendid Trojan War sculptures, most of which were stolen in the 19th century and now decorate Munich's Glyptothek. Panels throughout the site are also in English. Aphaia is 10km east of Aegina Town. Infrequent buses to Agia Marina stop here (20 minutes); taxis cost about €12 one way.

★**Paleohora** CHURCH, RUIN
(Παλαιοχώρα) FREE This enchanting remote hillside is dotted with the remains of a Byzantine village. More than 30 surviving **churches** punctuate the rocky heights of the original citadel, and several have been refurbished. They are linked by a network of paths, carpeted with wildflowers in spring. The ancient town of Paleohora was Aegina's capital from the 9th century through the medieval period and was only abandoned during the 1820s. Paleohora is 6.5km east of Aegina Town, near enormous modern church Moni Agiou Nektariou. Buses from Aegina Town to Agia Marina stop at the turn-off to Paleohora (10 minutes); taxis cost €8 one way.

Christos Capralos Museum MUSEUM
(☑ 22970 22001; Nikou Kazantzaki (Coast Rd), Livadi; admission €2; ⊙ 10am-2pm & 6-8pm Tue-Sun Jun-Oct, 10am-2pm Fri-Sun Nov-May) The home and studio of acclaimed sculptor Christos Capralos (1909–93), on the coast near Livadi, 1.5km north of Aegina Town, has been made into a museum displaying many of his fluid, powerful works. Monumental sculptures include the 40m-long Pindus Frieze.

Perdika & Around Πέρδικα

The quaint fishing village of Perdika lies about 9km south of Aegina Town on the southern tip of the west coast and makes for a relaxed sojourn. Its harbour is very shallow so, for the best swimming, catch one of the regular caïques (little boats, €5) to the small island of **Moni**, a few minutes offshore, with a tree-lined beach and summertime **cafe**. Tavernas line Perdika's raised harbourfront terrace, and sunset relaxation makes way for summertime buzzing nightlife when late-night music bars rev into gear.

🛏 Sleeping & Eating

Villa Rodanthos APARTMENT €
(☑ 6944250138, 22970 61400; www.villarodanthos.com; studios from €45; ❋ 🢒) A gem of a place, not least because of its charming owner. Each room has its own colourful decor and kitchen.

Angie Studios HOTEL, APARTMENT €€
(☑ 22970 61233; www.antzistudios.gr; studios €60-120; 🅿 🢒 ☀) A range of rooms and apartments overlook a central pool. Top-floor apartments in the newer building have some sea views.

O Thanasis SEAFOOD €
(☑ 22970 31348; Seafront, Portes; mains €7-8; ⊙ lunch & dinner, reduced hours winter) In Portes, 13km east of Perdika, on the east coast of the island, a charming family welcomes you to a seafront terrace festooned with flowerpots. They serve up top seafood and Greek classics.

Miltos SEAFOOD, TAVERNA €€
(☑ 22970 61051; mains €12-15; ⊙ lunch & dinner) The most popular of Perdika's seafood

ⓘ ONLINE RESOURCES

Monthly **Saronic Magazine** (www.saronicmagazine.com), available on all the main islands, has partial coverage of what's on. Island websites and holiday rental sites (www.homeaway.com, www.vrbo.com) have links to houses for rent, usually a good deal for larger groups.

Aegina www.aeginagreece.com, www.aegina.com.gr

Poros www.poros.gr

Hydra www.hydra.com.gr, www.hydradirect.com, www.hydraislandgreece.com, www.hydraview.gr

Spetses www.spetsesdirect.com, www.spetses.com.gr, www.spetses.wordpress.com/english

tavernas, known for the highest-quality seafood and no-nonsense Greek staples.

Aeginitissa   SEAFOOD €€
(☑22970 61546; www.aeginitissa.com; mains €6-15; ◷noon-late May-Sep) Plan for a sunset meal at this simple seafood taverna, 1.5km north of Perdika (6km south of Aegina Town). It's a favourite with locals for its beautiful waterfront setting. If ordering fish, have it weighed first to avoid sticker shock when you get the bill.

ANGISTRI   ΑΓΚΙΣΤΡΙ

POP 1142

Tiny Angistri lies a few kilometres off the west coast of Aegina and, out of high season, its mellow lanes and azure coves make a rewarding day trip or a worthwhile longer escape. Visit www.agistri.com.gr for island info.

The port-resort village of **Skala** is crammed with small hotels, apartments, tavernas and cafes, but life still ticks along gently. A right turn from the quay leads to the small harbour beach and then to a church on a low headland. Beyond lies the best beach on the island, but it disappears beneath sun loungers and broiling bodies in July and August. Turning left from the quay at Skala takes you south along a dirt path through the pine trees to the pebbly and clothing-optional **Halikadha Beach**. About 1km west from Skala, Angistri's other port, **Mylos** (Megalochori), has an appealing traditional character, rooms and tavernas, but no beach. **Aponissos** has turquoise waters, a small offshore island and a reliably tasty taverna. **Limenaria** has deeper green waters. The island as a whole gets super-sleepy in low season.

🛏 Sleeping & Eating

Book ahead, especially for August and summer weekends. A board on Skala's quay lists accommodation.

⭐ **Rosy's Little Village**   PENSION €€
(☑22970 91610; www.rosyslittlevillage.com; s/d/tr/q from €56/70/80/106; ❄🛜) A complex of simple Cycladic-style cubes steps gently down to the sea, a short way east of Skala's quay. Full of light and colour, with built-in couches and tiny balconies with sea views, Rosy's also offers mountain bikes, summer courses, weekly picnics and live-music evenings. Its **restaurant** (mains €6-10; ◷lunch & dinner) emphasises organics.

⭐ **Alkyoni Inn**   TAVERNA €
(☑22970 91378; www.alkyoni-agistri.com; mains €6-10; ◷breakfast, lunch & dinner Easter-Sep; ❄🛜🍴) The welcoming, family-run Alkyoni is a 10-minute stroll southeast of Skala's quay. The popular taverna dishes up well-prepared fish and meat, while the **hotel** (s/d/maisonette from €30/40/55) offers sea-facing rooms with fabulous, unobstructed views. Two-storey family maisonettes sleep up to four.

ⓘ Getting There & Away

Fast Aegean Flying Dolphins (p297) and Hellenic Seaways (p296) hydrofoils and car ferries (www.saronicferries.gr) come from Piraeus (hydrofoil/ferry €13.50/10.50, 55 minutes/1½ hours) via Aegina (hydrofoils €5.20, 10 minutes, six daily; ferry €2.50, 20 minutes, one daily). Angistri Express (p297) serves Aegina several times daily, Monday to Saturday.

Water taxis (p297) cost €45 one way between Aegina and Angistri.

ⓘ Getting Around

Several **buses** (☑6973016132, 22970 91244; Skala) a day during summer run from Skala and Mylos (Megalochori) to Limenaria and Dhragonera Beach. It's worth hiring a scooter (€15) or sturdy bike (€6) to explore the coast road.

You can also follow tracks from Metohi overland through cool pine forest to reach Dhragonera Beach. Take a compass; tracks divide often and route finding can be frustrating.

Kostas Bike Hire (☑22970 91021; Skala)

Takis Rent a Bike & Bicycles (Logothetis; ☑22970 91001; www.agistri.com.gr/logothetis; Mylos)

Taxi (☑6977618040, 22970 91455; Skala)

POROS ΠΟΡΟΣ

POP 3800

Poros is separated from the mountainous Peloponnese by a narrow sea channel, and its protected setting makes the main settlement of Poros Town seem like a cheery lakeside resort. Its pastel-hued houses stack up the hillside to a clock tower and make a vibrant first impression.

Poros is made up of two land masses connected by a tiny isthmus: **Sferia**, which is occupied mainly by the town of Poros; and the much larger and mainly forested **Kalavria**, which has the island's beaches and seasonal hotels scattered along its southern shore. Poros still maintains a sense of remoteness in its sparsely populated, forested interior.

The Peloponnesian town of **Galatas** lies on the opposite shore, making Poros a useful base from which to explore the ancient sites of the Peloponnese. For example, the exquisite ancient theatre of **Epidavros** is within reach by car or **taxi** (☑ in Galatas 22980 42888).

🛈 Getting There & Away

Daily ferries (www.saronicferries.gr) connect Piraeus to Poros in summer (reduced timetable in winter). High-speed Hellenic Seaways ferries continue south to Hydra, Spetses, Ermioni and Porto Heli. Conventional ferries connect Aegina to Poros and Methana on the mainland. Travel agents (p303) sell tickets.

Caïques shuttle constantly between Poros and Galatas (€1, five minutes). They leave from the quay opposite Plateia Iroön, the triangular plaza near the main ferry dock in Poros Town. Hydrofoils dock about 50m north of here and car ferries to Galatas (per person/car €0.90/6) leave from the dock several hundred metres north again, on the road to Kalavria.

You can also do a one-way rental between branches of **Pop's Car** (☑ in Galatas 22980 42910; www.popscar.gr) at Athens airport and Galatas (or Ermioni).

Galatas has a **bus station** (☑ 22980 42480; www.ktelargolida.gr) with connections to Nafplio and Athens.

Poros

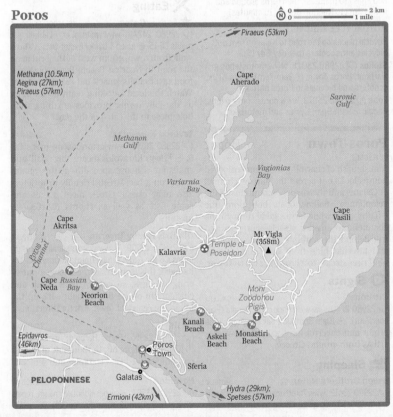

BOAT SERVICES FROM POROS

DESTI-NATION	TIME	FARE	FREQUENCY
Aegina	1¼hr	€8.30	2-3 daily
Hydra*	30min	€12.50	4 daily
Methana	30min	€4.50	2-3 daily
Piraeus	2½hr	€10.50-13	2-3 daily
Piraeus*	1hr	€22.50	4-5 daily
Spetses*	1½hr	€14.50	4 daily

*high-speed services

ⓘ Getting Around

Caïques go to beaches around the island during summer.

Taxi (Poros) (🕿 22980 23003)

BUS

A bus (€3) operates May to October every half-hour from 7am until midnight on a route that starts next to the kiosk at the eastern end of Plateia Iroön. It crosses to Kalavria and goes east along the south coast as far as Moni Zoödohou Pigis (10 minutes), then turns around and heads west to Neorion Beach (15 minutes).

MOTORCYCLE & BICYCLE

Several places on the road to Kalavria rent out bicycles and scooters (per day €4/15).

Stelios (🕿 22980 23026; www.motostelios.gr; Harbour, Poros Town; ⊙9am-7pm) Rents ATVs, scooters and bicycles in Poros harbour.

Fotis (🕿22980 25873; www.poros.com.gr/fotis; Kanali; ⊙9am-9pm) Cycles and motorbikes.

Poros Town   Πόρος

POP 3651

A mishmash of charming ice cream–coloured houses looks out across the narrow channel at Galatas and the shapely mountains of the Peloponnese. Sailing boats bob along the lengthy quay, while ferries glide through the channel and smaller vessels scurry to and fro. Behind the harbour, *plateies* (squares) and tavernas hide from view and a rocky bluff rises steeply to a crowning **clock tower**.

⊙ Sights

Citronne   GALLERY

(🕿 22980 22401; www.citronne.com; Paralia (Harbourfront); ⊙10am-3pm Mon-Sat Jun-Aug) This bright and cheerful local gallery showcases artists from around Greece.

🛏 Sleeping

Seven Brothers Hotel   HOTEL €

(🕿22980 23412; www.7brothers.gr; Poros Harbour; s/d/tr €50/55/60; ❋🛜) Close to the hydrofoil

quay, this modern hotel has bright, comfy rooms with super-duper bathrooms. Some have small balconies, some sea views.

Georgia Mellou Rooms   PENSION €

(🕿 22980 22309; http://porosnet.gr/gmellou; Plateia Georgiou; d/tr €35/40; ❋🛜) Simple, old-fashioned rooms are tucked into the heart of the old town, next to the cathedral, high above the harbour. The charming owner keeps everything shipshape. Book ahead for fantastic views from west-side rooms.

Hotel Manessi   BUSINESS HOTEL €

(🕿22980 22273; www.manessi.com; Poros Harbour; d €45-55; ❋@🛜) Well placed at the midpoint of the harbour, the Manessi is a bit worn in places, but offers clean business-style rooms.

Roloi   APARTMENT €€

(🕿 6932427267, 22980 25808; www.storoloi-poros.gr; studio/apt/house from €55/100/165; ❋) Roloi is a good source for tidy apartments around Poros Town.

🍴 Eating

★ Aspros Gatos   SEAFOOD, TAVERNA €

(🕿22980 24274; www.whitecat.gr; Labraki 49; mains €6-15; ⊙lunch & dinner Easter-Oct) A short walk from town, 400m west of the bridge on the road to Neorion Beach, Poros' best seafood taverna sits smack out over the water. Watch the local kayaking team do its thing as the jolly owner provides anything from bolognese to the catch of the day.

Taverna Karavolos   TAVERNA €

(🕿22980 26158; www.karavolos.com; mains €6-9; ⊙7-11pm) Karavolos means 'big snail' and snails are a house speciality at this quaint eatery on a backstreet. Friendly proprietors also offer classic Greek meat dishes and some fish, as well as **rooms** (d/tr€30/45) upstairs.

Dimitris Family Taverna   TAVERNA €

(🕿22980 23709; www.dimitrisfamily-poros.gr; mains €6-10; ⊙6-10pm or 11pm) Renowned for its meat, this taverna's owners have a butchering business, so cuts of pork, lamb and chicken are of the finest quality. It's up the hill in the centre of town; ask for directions.

Oasis   TAVERNA €

(🕿22980 22955; Poros Harbour; mains €6-12; ⊙10am-1am) Hang out harbourside and feast on home-cooked Greek staples and seafood.

Poseidon   SEAFOOD €€

(🕿22980 23597; www.poseidontaverna.gr; mains €6-15; ⊙9.30am-12.30am Easter-Oct) A quayside favourite for delicious seafood, friendly service and occasional Greek dancing.

❶ Information

Poros has no tourist office. Harbourfront agencies arrange accommodation, car hire, tours and cruises. Banks on Plateia Iroön have ATMs.

Askeli Travel (📌 22980 25857; www.askeli travel.com; ⊙ 8am-11pm Jun-Sep, reduced hours rest of year)

Family Tours (📌 22980 23743; www.family tours.gr; ⊙ 9am-2pm & 5-10pm) Sells conventional-ferry tickets.

Marinos Tours (📌 22980 23423; www.mari nostours.gr; ⊙ 7am-9.30pm Apr-Oct, to 7pm Nov-Mar) Across from the hydrofoil quay; sells hydrofoil tickets.

Tourist Police (📌 22980 22256; Dimosthenous 10) Behind the high school.

Around Poros

Poros' best beaches include the pebbly **Kana-li Beach**, on Kalavria islet 1km east of the bridge, and the long, sandy **Askeli Beach**, about 500m further east. **Neorion Beach**, 3km west of the bridge, has water skiing and banana-boat and air-chair rides. The best beach is at **Russian Bay**, 1.5km past Neorion.

❂ Sights

Temple of Poseidon RUIN
There's very little left of this 6th-century temple. Once a magnificent building giving sanctuary to fugitives and wrecked sailors, in the 18th century it was mostly dismantled and the materials used to build a monastery on Hydra. Still, the walk to the site gives superb views of the Saronic Gulf and the Peloponnese. From the road below Moni Zoödohou Pigis, head inland to reach the ruins. Then you can continue along the road and circle back to the bridge onto Sferia. It's about 6km in total. Or check in town – some seasons there's a mini-tram that goes to the ruins.

Moni Zoödohou Pigis MONASTERY
The 18th-century 'Monastery of the Life-giving Spring', well signposted 4km east of Poros Town, has a beautiful gilded iconostasis (a screen bearing icons) from Asia Minor.

🛏 Sleeping& Eating

Askeli beach has several good year-round seafront tavernas.

Hotel New Aegli HOTEL **€€**
(📌 22980 22372; www.newaegli.com; d €55-120; ⊙ Apr-Oct; ✳@🌐⊛) The long, sandy Askeli

Beach is one of Poros' best beaches. Hotel New Aegli, across the road from the beach, is a decent resort-style hotel and offers good, modern rooms, many with sea views.

Sirene Blue Resort RESORT **€€**
(📌 22980 22741; www.sireneblueresort.gr; Monastiri Beach; d/ste incl breakfast from €140/240; ✳🌐⊛) Offers a deluxe seaside vacation, from sparkling pool to crisp linens. Find it at Monastiri Beach, near Moni Zoödohou Pigis.

HYDRA ΥΔΡΑ

POP 1966

Hydra (*ee*-dhr-ah) is truly the gem of the Saronic Gulf and stands alone among Greek islands as the one free of wheeled vehicles. No cars. No scooters. Just tiny marble-cobbled lanes, donkeys, rocks and sea. Artists (Brice Marden, Nikos Chatzikyriakos-Ghikas, Panayiotis Tetsis), musicians (Leonard Cohen), actors and celebrities (Melina Mercouri, Sophia Loren) and travellers (you) have all been drawn to Hydra over the years. So in addition to the island's exquisitely preserved stone architecture, criss-crossing rural paths and clear, deep waters, you can find a good cappuccino along the people-watching harbour. Mules and donkeys are the main means of heavy transport and they, along with the rustic aspects of life on the island, give Hydra its two faces: chic and earthy.

History

Hydra was sparsely populated in ancient times and is only mentioned in passing by Herodotus. The most significant evidence of settlement dates from Mycenaean times. But in the 16th century, Hydra became a refuge for people fleeing skirmishes between the Venetians and the Ottomans. Many hailed from the area of modern-day Albania.

By the mid-1700s settlers began building boats and explored the thin line between maritime commerce and piracy with enthusiasm. They travelled as far as Egypt and the Black Sea and ran the British blockade during the Napoleonic Wars (1805–15). As a result of steady tax paying, they experienced only light interference under the Ottoman Empire. By the 19th century, Hydra had become a full-blown maritime power, and wealthy shipping merchants had built most of the town's grand mansions. At its height in 1821, the island's population reached 28,000. Hydra supplied 130 ships for a blockade of the Turks during the Greek War of Independence and the island bred such leaders as Admiral Andreas Miaoulis, who commanded the Greek fleet, and Georgios Koundouriotis, president of Greece's national assembly from 1822 to 1827.

❶ Getting There & Away

High-speed ferries link Hydra with Poros, Piraeus and Spetses, and Ermioni and Porto Heli on the Peloponnese. Service is greatly reduced in winter. Buy tickets from **Hydreoniki Travel** (☑ 22980 54007), up the lane to the right of the Alpha Bank in Hydra Town.

Freedom (☑ 6944242141, 6947325263; www.hydralines.gr) boats run between Hydra and Metohi (little more than a car park) on the mainland (€6.50, 10 minutes, 11 daily, schedule posted on quay and online).

DESTINATION	TIME	FARE	FREQUENCY
Ermioni*	20-40min	€7.50	3 daily
Piraeus*	1¾hr	€25.50	4-6 daily
Poros*	30min	€12.50	4 daily
Porto Heli*	1hr	€15	4 daily
Spetses*	40min	€10.50	4-5 daily

*high-speed services

❶ Getting Around

Generally, people get around Hydra by walking. In summer, caïques from Hydra Town go to the island's beaches. **Water-taxi** (☑ 22980 53690) fares are posted on the quay (Kamini costs €10, Vlyhos €15). Donkey owners clustered around the port charge €10 to €15 to transport your bags to your hotel. Quick donkey rides around the port cost about €10 per person.

Hydra Town   Υδρα
POP 1900

Life in Hydra centres around the gorgeous port. Whether you sail or ferry in, the sparkling boat-filled harbour and the bright light striking the tiers of carefully preserved stone houses make a lasting impression. The harbour in high season is an ecosystem of its own, with yachts, caïques and water taxis zipping in and out. The marble quay is a surging rhythm of donkeys, visitors, cafe denizens and boat-taxi hawkers. By night the scene becomes a promenade: grab a chair, order a drink and watch the world go by.

If you head back into the warren of portside houses, and especially if you climb the steep slopes banking away from the town centre, you get a totally different view on Hydriot life. Grandmothers chat in quiet lanes about what's for dinner, and roads peter out into dirt paths that head into the mountains, ever-changing in colour, depending on the season and the time of day.

Hydra

◉ Sights & Activities

Melina Mercouri Exhibition Hall and **Deste Foundation** (www.deste.gr) `FREE` host high-season art shows.

★ Lazaros Koundouriotis
Historical Mansion   MUSEUM
(☑22980 52421; www.nhmuseum.gr; adult/child €4/free; ⊙10am-2pm & 5.30-8.30pm Tue-Sun Mar-Oct) Hydra's star cultural attraction is this handsome ochre-coloured *arhontiko* (stone mansion) high above the harbour. It was the home of one of the major players in the Greek independence struggle and is an exquisite example of late-18th-century traditional architecture, with original furnishings, folk costumes, handicrafts and a painting exhibition.

★ Historical Archives
Museum of Hydra   MUSEUM
(☑22980 52355; www.iamy.gr; adult/child €5/3; ⊙9am-4pm & 7.30-9.30pm Jun-Aug, 9am-4pm Sep-May) This fine harbourfront museum houses an extensive collection of portraits and naval artefacts, with an emphasis on the island's role in the War of Independence. It hosts temporary exhibitions in summer, and concerts on the rooftop terrace.

★ Kimisis Tis Theotokou
Cathedral   CHURCH, MUSEUM
(Cathedral of Hydra; Metropolis) Housed in the peaceful monastery complex on the harbour, this lovely cathedral dates from the 17th century and has a Tinian marble bell tower. Its **Ecclesiastical Museum** (☑22980 54071; adult/child €2/free; ⊙10am-5pm Tue-Sun Apr-Nov) contains a collection of icons and vestments. The monastery complex is also known as Faneromeni. Dress appropriately to enter.

Harriet's Hydra Horses   HORSEBACK RIDING
(☑6980323347; www.harrietshydrahorses.com; 1½/8hr tour €20/140) Harriet, a friendly, bilingual British-Greek local, guides licensed horse-riding tours around the island, to the monasteries and to the beaches.

Vasilis Kokkos   BOATING
(☑6977649789; bkokkos@yahoo.com) Proprietor of Caprice restaurant Vasilis Kokkos rents speedboats (per day €40 to €230) and a sailing boat (by prior arrangement; one-week minimum €840). Licence required.

✦ Festivals & Events

Easter is a week-long extravaganza, including a famous parade of a flower-festooned epitaph into the harbour at Kamini.

★ Miaoulia Festival   CULTURAL
(⊙3rd weekend Jun) Celebration of Admiral Miaoulis and the Hydriot contribution to the War of Independence, with a spectacular boat burning (with fireworks) in Hydra harbour.

⊨ Sleeping

Accommodation here is of a high standard, but not cheap. Most owners will meet you at the harbour and organise luggage transfer.

Piteoussa   PENSION €
(☑22980 52810; www.piteoussa.com; Kouloura; d €50-70; ❄⑤) Jolly owners maintain beautiful rooms in two buildings on a quiet, pine tree-lined street. Rooms in the restored corner mansion drip with period character and modern amenities, while the smaller rooms in the second building were renovated in 2010 and have a mod feel.

Pension Erofili   PENSION €
(☑22980 54049; www.pensionerofili.gr; Tombazi; s/d/tr €45/50/70; ❄⑤) Tucked in the inner town, these pleasant, unassuming rooms are a good deal. Also has a studio with kitchen.

Glaros   PENSION €
(☑22980 52085, 6942523338; www.hydra.com.gr/glaros; d €55; ❄⑤) Basic, well-kept rooms in a convenient spot just back from the harbour.

★ Cotommatae   BOUTIQUE HOTEL €€
(☑22980 53873; www.cotommatae.gr; d/ste incl breakfast from €130/200) This recently renovated mansion has retained the character and some of the memorabilia of the original family while adding impeccable modern touches. Some suites have private terraces or a spa.

★ Hotel Miranda   HOTEL €€
(☑22980 52230; www.mirandahotel.gr; Miaouli; d/q/apt incl breakfast from €130/180/238; ⊙Mar-Oct; ❄⑤) Pretend you're a 19th-century sea captain in this antique-laden jewel. Public spaces are decked out in antique prints, carved woodwork and rotating exhibitions. Gaze at your inlaid ceilings or, in higher-end rooms, from your balcony. Apartments, too.

Angelica Hotel   BOUTIQUE HOTEL €€
(☑22980 53202; www.angelica.gr; Miaouli; d/tr/q incl breakfast from €120/160/220; ❄⑤) An attractive boutique hotel in a quiet location, the Angelica is popular for its comfortable, luxurious rooms and spacious, impeccable bathrooms. Superior rooms have balconies. Relax in the spa or courtyard.

SARONIC GULF ISLANDS HYDRA TOWN

Hydra Town

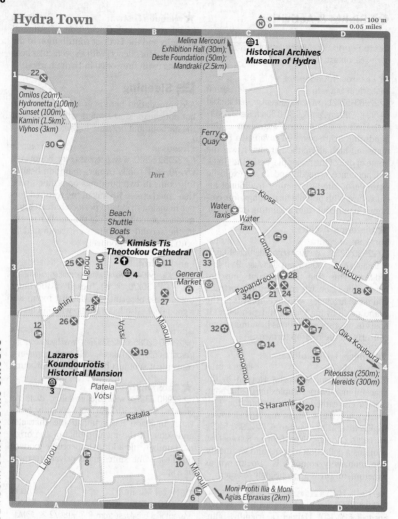

Hotel Sophia

BOUTIQUE HOTEL €€

(☑22980 52313; www.hotelsophia.gr; d incl breakfast €85-115; ☺Apr-Oct; ❋🕿) Gorgeous, small rooms sit right on the harbour. Some have balconies, some are two storeys, and each has been painstakingly outfitted with all mod cons. Bathrooms are luscious marble.

Nereids

PENSION €€

(☑22980 52875; www.nereids-hydra.com; Kouloura; d €65; ❋🕿) A carefully restored stone house with lovely rooms of exceptional value and quality. Spacious, peaceful and with beautiful decor, rooms have views to Hydra's rocky heights and top-floor rooms have sea views.

Pension Alkionides

PENSION €€

(☑22980 54055; www.alkionidespension.com; off Oikonomou; d/studio €63/80; ❋🕿) In a central, peaceful cul-de-sac, rooms are smart (some are quite small) and have tea- and coffee-making facilities and a pretty courtyard. The studio has a private terrace.

Amaryllis Hotel

HOTEL €€

(☑22980 53611; www.amarillishydra.gr; Tombazi 15; s/d €45/60; ❋🕿) Simple rooms, a friendly owner and a super location right in the hub of town make this a safe budget bet. Shared kitchen, too.

Hydra Town

★ **Hydra Hotel**   APARTMENT €€€

(☎22980 53420, 6972868161; www.hydra-hotel.gr; Petrou Voulgari 8; studio incl breakfast €150-200, maisonette €250; ❄🤖) High on the south side of the port are swishy, top-of-the-line apartments in an impeccably renovated old mansion with kitchenettes and views. Room 202 has a tiny balcony with panoramas to die for.

Hydras Chromata   APARTMENT €€€

(☎6944225576; www.hydraschromata.gr; apt €160-220; ❄🤖) Three stylishly kitted-out private apartments with terraces and all the conveniences of a home away from home.

✖ Eating

Paradosiako   TAVERNA €

(☎22980 54155; Tombazi; mains €5-14; ⏱noon-11.30pm Easter-Nov) This little streetside spot is traditional Greek personified. Sit on the corner terrace to watch the people parade as you dig into classic mezedhes such as beetroot salad with garlic dip, or meats and seafood such as fresh, filleted and grilled sardines.

Ostria   TAVERNA €

(Stathis & Tassoula; ☎22980 54077; mains €5-8; ⏱lunch & dinner) Often referred to by just the gregarious owners' names, this year-round taverna serves only what's fresh. Throw out the menu and ask: perhaps chicken cutlets, or fava, or zucchini balls. Stathis catches his own sweet and delicious calamari.

Zefyros   TAVERNA €

(☎22980 52008; Miaouli; mains €5-9; ⏱noon-10pm) Lovely Amalia and her family serve up classic Greek dishes in a low-key dining room just back from the port. Look in the glass case to see the day's specials. German expats also say it's got the best schnitzel on the island.

Psarapoula   TAVERNA €

(☎22980 52630; mains €7-12; ⏱noon-late) Look just above the quay, near the Pirate bar and main bakery, to find this reliable taverna with lovely harbour views. Visitors and locals alike dig into daily specials at the historic eatery, which was established in 1911.

Ke Kremmidi   GREEK €

(☎22980 53099; Tombazi; gyros €2.50, mains €6-9; ⏱noon-late) This friendly souvlaki joint has tables spilling out onto a busy pedestrian way and offers up good salads and grilled-meat plates as well.

Flora's   SWEETS €

(Anemoni; ☎22980 53136; Plateia Votsi; sweets from €1; ⏱9am-late) Flora's sweet shop on inland Plateia Votsi makes *galaktoboureko* (custard pie), rice pudding and ice cream from local goats' milk.

★ **Sunset**   MEDITERRANEAN €€
(☑22980 52067; mains €9-22; ☺noon-11pm Easter-Oct) Famed for its splendid panoramic spot near the cannons to the west of the harbour, Sunset also has fine, fresh cuisine. Tasty salads, inventive pastas and local fish are prepared with flair and a hint of elegance.

Barba Dimas   ITALIAN €€
(☑22980 52967; Tombazi; mains €11-20; ☺dinner) Authentic Italian food like Pietro's Neapolitan grandmother used to make. It also has a larger al fresco dining room at La Castra, 50m further inland, open for lunch as well. Menus change daily. Reserve in high season.

Bratsera   MEDITERRANEAN €€
(☑22980 52794; Tombazi; mains €9-20; ☺breakfast, lunch & dinner Apr-Oct) The in-house restaurant by the pool (no day use) of the Bratsera Hotel offers the chance to have a higher-end meal in blissful peace. The breakfast buffet (€14) is decadent.

Gitoniko   TAVERNA €€
(☑22980 53615; Haramis; mains €7-15; ☺lunch & dinner Easter-Oct) Usually referred to by its owners' names (Christina and Manolis), it offers a broad range of Greek fare, but it is particularly well known for its (pricey) fish.

Caprice   ITALIAN €€
(☑ 22980 52454; Sahtouri; mains €9-15; ☺ dinner Apr-Oct) A chance for romantic candlelit dining with a solid repertoire of Italian dishes, some using fresh-made pasta.

Veranda   MEDITERRANEAN €€
(☑22980 52259; Lignou; mains €7-15; ☺dinner Apr-Oct) Cheerful brothers run this dreamy terrace restaurant with views out across the port and mountains.

Omilos   MEDITERRANEAN €€€
(☑2298053800; www.omilos-hydra.com; mains €16-25; ☺noon-late Easter-Oct) This chic, all-white waterside restaurant is Hydra's gourmet entry. It becomes a night-time dance venue.

🍷 **Drinking & Nightlife**

Prices are high, but lively people-watching comes with your coffee or cocktail. The harbour revs up after midnight.

★ **Pirate**   CAFE, BAR
(☑ 22980 52711; www.thepiratebar.gr; harbourfront; ☺8am-late) Friendly Wendy and Takis and their kids Zara and Zeus run this daytime cafe with first-rate coffee, breakfasts and home-cooked lunches, and morph it into a raging party place at night. Music changes with the crowd and the mood.

★ **Hydronetta**   CAFE, BAR
(☑22980 54160; ☺noon-11pm Easter-Oct) You can't beat this gorgeous waterfront location on the rocks to the far west of the harbour. Brothers Andreas and Elias provide cocktails and lunch (high season only) with a smile.

Papagalos   CAFE, BAR
(☑22980 52626; harbourfront; ☺9am-late) Papagalos is just that bit away from the madding crowd, on the quieter side of the harbour. By day, it offers coffee and basic food, and by night, cocktails and a clear view of the moonrise.

Isalos   CAFE
(☑22980 53845; harbourfront; ☺7am-late) Isalos makes exceptional coffee and a solid run of sandwiches and pastas.

Amalour   COCKTAIL BAR
(☑22980 53800; Tombazi; ☺7pm-late Jun-Aug, reduced hr rest of year) A lively line in cocktails, relaxed outdoor seating and dancing inside after midnight.

☆ **Entertainment**

Cinema Club of Hydra   CINEMA, THEATRE
(☑22980 53105; http://cineclubhydras.blogspot.com; Oikonomou) In July and August the open-air cinema screens blockbusters and indie flicks. It also organises excursions to plays at the ancient theatre of Epidavros.

🔒 **Shopping**

Turquoise   FASHION, ACCESSORIES
(☑22980 54033; www.turquoise.gr; ☺10am-10pm Jun-Aug, reduced hours rest of year) Local designer Dimitris creates an annual line of women's wear and accessories using intricate block prints.

Elena Votsi   JEWELLERY
(☑22980 52637; www.elenavotsi.com; harbourfront; ☺10am-11.30pm) Hydra native Votsi is renowned for her original, bold designs using exquisite semiprecious stones; she sells in New York and London.

ℹ️ **Information**

There's no tourist office on Hydra. ATMs are at harbourfront banks.
Hospital (☑22980 53150; Votsi)
Tourist police (☑22980 52205) Shares an office with regular police.

Around Hydra

Hydra's mountainous, arid interior makes a robust but peaceful contrast to the clamour of the quayside. A useful map for walkers is Anavasi's *Hydra* map. A map is posted on the quay, and several marked trails extend across the island. Once you leave Hydra/Kamini/Vlyhos there are no services. Take plenty of water.

An unbeatable experience is the long haul up to **Moni Profiti Ilia**. The wonderful monastery complex contains beautiful icons and boasts super views. It's a solid hour or more through zigzags and pine trees to panoramic bliss on top. A smaller monastery, **Moni Agias Efpraxias**, sits just below Profiti Ilia and is run by nuns. Other paths lead to **Mt Eros** (588m), the island's highest point, and east and west along the island spine, but you need advanced route-finding skills or reliable directions from knowledgeable locals.

The coastal road turns into a simple, beautiful trail about 1.5km west of the port, after **Kamini**. Kamini has a tiny **fishing port**, several good tavernas, **swimming rocks** and a small pebble **beach**. In fact, Hydra's shortcoming – or blessing – is its lack of sandy beaches to draw the crowds. People usually swim off the rocks, but if you go as far as **Vlyhos**, 1.5km after Kamini, this last little hamlet before the mountains offers two slightly larger pebble beaches (one called Vlyhos and the other, the more pristine **Plakes**), tavernas and a restored 19th-century stone bridge.

The coastal road leads 2.5km east from the port to a pebble beach at **Mandraki**, beyond which a trampoline-and-music beach resort offers occasional watercraft rentals.

Boats run from the harbour to all of these places, but you certainly need them to reach **Bisti Bay** or **Agios Nikolaos Bay**, in the island's southwest, with their remote but umbrella-laden pebble beaches and green waters.

🛏 Sleeping & Eating

★ Christina
TAVERNA €
(📞22980 53516; Kamini; mains €6-12; ⊙lunch & dinner Thu-Tue Easter-Oct) Just inland from the port in Kamini, Mrs Christina and her kids dish out some of the island's best Greek dishes and fresh fish.

To Pefkaki
SEAFOOD, MEZEDHES €
(📞6973535709; Kamini; mains €5-10; ⊙lunch & dinner Thu-Tue Easter-Oct) Worth the short walk along the coast to Kamini for a laid-back lunch of mezedhes and fresh seafood (delicious fried anchovies).

★ Four Seasons
TAVERNA €€
(📞22980 53698; www.fourseasonshydra.gr; Plakes; mains €6-12; ⊙noon-10pm Easter-Oct; 🛜) This scrummy seaside taverna offers a different face of Hydra: the sound of the breeze and the waves instead of the portside buzz. Don't miss the *taramasalata* (fish roe dip) with bread and whatever else tickles your fancy. It also has handsome **suites** (€220, including breakfast).

Pirofani
INTERNATIONAL €€
(📞22980 53175; www.pirofani.com; Kamini; mains €12-16; ⊙7.30pm-midnight Wed-Sun late May-Sep) Gregarious Theo creates an eclectic range of dishes, from a beef fillet with rose-pepper sauce to a spicy Asian curry.

Enalion
TAVERNA €€
(📞22980 53455; www.enalion-hydra.gr; Vlyhos; mains €6-12; ⊙noon-10pm Easter-Oct) Perhaps the best seaside option at Vlyhos beach, with traditional Greek fare.

Castello
MEDITERRANEAN €€€
(📞22980 54101; www.castellohydra.gr; Kamini; snacks €7-15, mains €15-30; ⊙11am-late Jun-Sep) In a renovated 18th-century bastion and spilling onto the beach, Castello offers waterfront snacks, gourmet seaside dining or a sunset cocktail. It occasionally has an early dinner special for €24 Monday to Thursday. Amazing views.

SPETSES ΣΠΕΤΣΕΣ
POP 4027

Spetses stands just a few kilometres from mainland Peloponnese, but there's a stronger sense of carefree island Greece here than in other Saronic Gulf destinations. The lively, historic old town is the only village on the island; the rest, ringed by a simple road, is rolling hills, pine forests and crystal-clear coves. Spetses Town has great nightlife and restaurants and gorgeous, easily accessible swimming spots. With a rich naval history, it is still incredibly popular with yachties, and with its vibrant culture, it attracts artists, intellectuals and lovers of a good island party.

History

In Spetses Town there's evidence of early Helladic settlement near the Old Harbour and around the Dapia Harbour. Roman and

Spetses

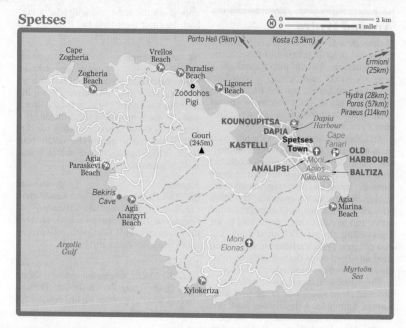

Byzantine remains have been found in the area behind Moni Agios Nikolaos, halfway between the two. From the 10th century, Spetses is thought to have been uninhabited for almost 600 years, until the arrival of Albanian refugees fleeing the fighting between Turks and Venetians in the 16th century.

Spetses, like Hydra, grew wealthy from shipbuilding. Island captains busted the British blockade during the Napoleonic Wars and refitted their ships to join the Greek fleet during the War of Independence. In the process they immortalised one local woman, albeit originally from Hydra, the formidable Laskarina Bouboulina, ship commander and fearless fighter. The island's hallmark forests of Aleppo pine, a legacy of the far-sighted philanthropist Sotirios Anargyros, have been devastated by fires several times in the past 20 years. The trees are steadily recovering.

Getting There & Away

High-speed ferries link Spetses with Hydra, Poros and Piraeus, and Ermioni and Porto Heli on the Peloponnese. In summer, caïques (€4 per person) and a car ferry (€2) go from the harbour to Kosta on the mainland. Note: only locally owned cars are allowed on Spetses. Park yours in Kosta. Get tickets at Bardakos Tours (p313). The following are all high-speed services.

DESTI-NATION	TIME	FARE	FREQUENCY
Ermioni	20-30min	€7.50	2 daily
Hydra	40min	€10.50	4 daily
Piraeus	2hr 10min	€35	5 daily
Poros	1½hr	€14.50	4 daily
Porto Heli	15min	€5.50	4 daily

Getting Around

BICYCLE

Bike Center (☎22980 72209; http://spetses bikecenter.blogspot.com; ☉10am-3.30pm & 5.30-10pm) Behind the fish market, rents out bikes (€8 per day), including baby seats.

BOAT

In summer, caïques serve the island's beaches (€11 return). **Water-taxi** (☎22980 72072; Dapia Harbour; ☉24hr) fares are displayed on a board. All leave from the quay opposite Bardakos Tours.

BUS

Two routes start over Easter and increase in frequency to three or four daily June to September. Departure times are on a board by the bus stops and around town. One goes from Plateia Agiou Mama in Spetses Town to Agia Paraskevi (€6, 40 minutes), travelling via Agia Marina and Agii Anargyri. The other leaves from in front of Poseidonion Grand Hotel, going to Vrellos (€4) via Ligoneri.

CAR & MOTORCYCLE

Only locally owned autos are allowed on Spetses, and those are not permitted in the centre of town. The transport of choice tends to be scooters. Motorbike- and quad-bike-hire shops abound (€15 to €25 per day).

Spetses Town   Σπέτσες

POP 4001

The bustling town stretches along a meandering waterfront encompassing several quays and beaches. The main Dapia Harbour, where ferries arrive, and the area around adjacent Plateia Limenarhiou and inland Plateia Orologiou (Clocktower Sq) teem with tourist shops and cafes. Further inland on the quieter lanes, or left along the harbourfront road of Sotiriou Anargyriou, past the town beach and Plateia Agiou Mama, impressive *arhontika* (old mansions) illustrate Spetses' historic (and ongoing) wealth. Passing the church of Moni Agios Nikolaos you arrive at the attractive Old Harbour (Palio Limani) and the interesting Baltiza yacht anchorage and boatbuilding area. From the north side of Dapia Harbour a promenade and road lead through the seafront Kounoupitsa area.

Sights

Spetses Museum   MUSEUM
(☑22980 72994; http://odysseus.culture.gr; adult/child €3/free; ⊗8.30am-2pm Tue-Sun) Small, fascinating collections are housed in the old mansion of Hatzigiannis Mexis (1754–1844), a shipowner who became the island's first governor. They include island artefacts, traditional costumes and portraits of the island's founding fathers.

Bouboulina's Museum   MUSEUM
(☑22980 72416; www.bouboulinamuseum-spetses .gr; adult/child €6/free; ⊗several tours daily Apr-Oct) The mansion of Spetses' famous daughter, the 19th-century seagoing commander Laskarina Bouboulina, has been converted into a museum. Entry is via 40-minute guided tours (billboards around town advertise starting times, also posted online). The museum hosts occasional concerts. There's an impressive statue of Bouboulina on the harbour, opposite the Poseidonion Grand Hotel.

Festivals & Events

★ Armata   CULTURAL
This week-long celebration culminates on 8 September in a commemoration of Spetses' victory over the Turks in a key 1822 naval battle, with re-enactments and fireworks.

Sleeping

Villa Christina Hotel   PENSION €
(☑22980 72218; www.villachristinahotel.com; s/d/ tr incl breakfast from €40/50/60; ❋⍥) About 200m uphill on the main road inland from the harbour, these well-kept rooms and lovely garden are back from the worst traffic noise.

Hotel Kamelia   PENSION €
(☑6939095513; http://hotelkamelia.gr; s/d €35/40; ⊗Easter-Oct; ❋⍥) Good-value airy rooms are tucked away from the busy seafront in the Agios Mamas area, with a bougainvillea-draped terrace.

Villa Marina   PENSION €
(☑22980 72646; www.villamarinaspetses.com; d €50-60; ❋⍥) Super-basic rooms have refrigerators and there is a well-equipped communal kitchen downstairs. Just to the right of Plateia Agiou Mama.

★ Orloff Resort   BOUTIQUE HOTEL €€
(☑22980 75444; www.orloffresort.com; d/studio/ apt incl breakfast from €125/135/255; ⊗Mar-Oct; ❋⍥⍨) On the edge of town, along the road to Agia Marina and near the old port, the pristine Orloff hides behind high white walls. Enjoy stylish rooms and a crystal-clear pool.

Economou Mansion   PENSION €€
(☑22980 73400; www.economouspetses.gr; d incl breakfast from €130; ❋⍥⍨) This beautiful pension on the ground floor of a restored captain's mansion sits right on the waterfront, about 500m north of Dapia Harbour, and offers a homey, relaxed hideaway combining antique decor and modern amenities such as swimming pool, TV, hair dryer and safe. Breakfast is bountiful.

Kastro Hotel   APARTMENT €€
(☑22980 75319; www.kastro-margarita.com; studio/4-person apt incl breakfast €120/160; ❋⍥⍨) A private, quiet complex encloses these studios and apartments close to the centre of town. Low-key decor and modern amenities combine with extensive terraces.

Klimis Hotel   HOTEL €€
(☑22980 73725; www.klimishotel.gr; Dapia Harbour; s/d incl breakfast from €65/85; ❋⍥) Serviceable

rooms, some with seafront balconies, sit above a ground-floor cafe-bar and patisserie.

★ Poseidonion Grand Hotel
LUXURY HOTEL €€€

(📞 22980 74553; www.poseidonion.com; Dapia Harbour; d incl breakfast €230-350, 4-person ste €570; ❄ 🛜 🏊) Here's your chance to live like a wealthy dame or gent in the roaring '20s. This venerable old hotel has been totally renovated and every centimetre, from the chic rooms to the gracious lobby bar and grand pool, drips with luxury. Oh, and it also has two of the island's best restaurants.

Zoe's Club
APARTMENT €€€

(📞 22980 74447; www.zoesclub.gr; studio/apt incl breakfast from €175/195; ❄ 🛜 🏊) Freestanding spacious apartments surround a decadent pool and courtyard. It's behind a high stone wall in the centre, near the Spetses Museum.

✕ Eating

The Poseidonion Grand Hotel and Nissia Hotel in Dapia have outstanding restaurants.

★ Akrogialia
SEAFOOD, TAVERNA €€

(📞 22980 74749; www.akrogialia-restaurant.gr; Kounoupitsa; mains €9-17; ⊙10.30am-midnight) This superb restaurant is on the Kounoupitsa seafront and matches delicious food with friendly service and a bright setting. Tasty options include oven-baked *melidzana rolos* (eggplant with creamy cheese and walnuts). Enjoy terrific fish risotto or settle for a choice steak. All are accompanied by a good selection of Greek wines. Book ahead weekends.

Patralis
SEAFOOD €€

(📞 22980 75380; www.patralis.gr; Kounoupitsa; mains €7-15; ⊙lunch & dinner Jan-Oct) Operating for more than 70 years and known island-wide for its outstanding seafood, Patralis sits smack on the seafront in Kounoupitsa.

To Nero tis Agapis
MEDITERRANEAN €€

(📞 22980 74009; www.nerotisagapis.gr; Kounoupitsa; mains €9-22; ⊙lunch & dinner) The sweetly named 'Water of Love' offers gourmet meat as well as fish dishes. The crayfish tagliatelle is worth every bite, as is the *zarzuela* (fish stew). There's a selection of creative salads. Book ahead for the romantic tables with the best sea views.

Orloff
MEDITERRANEAN €€

(📞 22980 75255; www.orloffrestaurant.com; Old Harbour; mains €13-21; ⊙6.30pm-1am Jun-Sep, 6.30pm-1am Fri, 12.30pm-1am Sat, 12.30-6pm Sun May & Oct) Fresh fish and super specialities such as seafood linguini or pork fillet with aubergine puree are hallmarks of the popular Orloff. The terrace sits above the water at a bend in the road just north of the Old Harbour.

★ Tarsanas
SEAFOOD €€€

(📞 22980 74490; www.tarsanas-spetses.gr; Old Harbour; mains €17-26; ⊙lunch & dinner) A hugely popular *psarotaverna* (fish taverna) on the water at the Old Harbour, this family-run place deals almost exclusively in fish dishes. It can be pricey, but the fish soup (€6) alone is a delight and other starters, such as anchovies marinated with lemon, start at €6.

🍷 Drinking & Nightlife

Head straight for the Old Harbour–Baltiza area, the epicentre of Spetses' nightlife. Bars and clubs change, but the party's always here.

Ariston
CAFE

(📞 22980 73803; Dapia Harbour; ⊙9am-late; 🛜) A touch of class on the waterfront, with coffee by day and sundowners by evening.

Roussos
CAFE

(📞 22908 72819; Dapia Harbour; ⊙9am-late) Old-time Spetsiot coffee house with pastries, on the harbour.

Bar Spetsa
BAR

(📞 22980 74131; www.barspetsa.org; Agios Mamas; ⊙8pm-late Mar-Oct) One of life's great little bars, this Spetses institution never loses its easy-going atmosphere. Find it 50m beyond Plateia Agiou Mama, on the road to the right of the kiosk.

La Luz
BAR

(📞 22980 75024; www.laluzspetses.gr; Old Harbour) La Luz often has live music and always sports super sea views in the Old Harbour area of Spetses.

Throubi
BAR

(📞 6948957398; Old Harbour) Theme nights and DJ dance parties in the Old Harbour.

Mourayo
BAR

(📞 6974335540; www.mourayospetses.gr; Old Harbour) Don't come for the food, but rather for a sunset or late-night waterfront cocktail and Greek pop.

Stavento Club
CLUB

(📞 22980 75245; www.clubstavento.com; Old Harbour; ⊙11pm-late) Dance the night away to pop and Greek hits.

ℹ Information

Banks at Dapia Harbour have ATMs.

Bardakos Tours (☑ 22980 73141; Dapia Harbour) Sells ferry tickets and assists with other arrangements.

Municipal information kiosk (www.spetses. com.gr; ⊙10am-9pm May-Sep) On the quay, seasonal staff provide answers to general questions about the island.

Port Authority (☑ 22980 72245) Just inland from the cafe terrace overlooking Dapia Harbour.

Tourist police (☑ Police 22980 73100, Tourist Police 22980 73744; ⊙ mid-May–Sep) Just inland from the cafe terrace overlooking Dapia Harbour; housed with the port authority.

Around Spetses

Spetses' gorgeous coastline undulates with pebbly coves and small, pine-shaded beaches. A 26km sealed road skirts the entire coastline, so a scooter, quad bike or bicycle are ideal for exploring. The website www. spetsesdiadromes.wordpress.com by Petros

Haritatos, a passionate local and cartographer, offers route suggestions. A detailed map is a must for inland explorers; buy the *Anavasi* map (€3.50) at news stands.

Tiny, tranquil **Xylokeriza**, on the southwest coast, has a souvlaki kiosk with yummy, freshly made salads and delicious oven potatoes.

Further along, the popular, long, pebbly **Agia Paraskevi** and the sandier **Agii Anargyri** have picturesque, albeit crowded, beaches. Both have tavernas and water sports of every description and are served by boats and buses in summer. At the north end of Anargyri, you can follow a small path to submerged, swimmable **Bekiris Cave**.

Other beautiful spots include **Vrellos** and **Zogheria** beaches.

Closer to town, **Agia Marina** is a small resort with a beach that gets packed. The beach at **Ligoneri**, about 2.5km northwest of Spetses Town, is easily reached by bus.

The small island of **Spetsopoula**, off the southern coast, is owned by the Niarchos family and not open to the public.

Cyclades

Best Places to Eat

➡ Thalassaki (p325)

➡ M-Eating (p337)

➡ O! Hamos (p399)

➡ Omega 3 (p406)

➡ Metaxi Mas (p390)

Best Places to Stay

➡ Semeli Hotel (p335)

➡ Studios Eleni II (p324)

➡ Makares (p368)

➡ Red Tractor Farm (p411)

➡ Aroma Suites (p384)

Why Go?

On a quest to find the Greek islands of your dreams? Start here, in the Cyclades (Κυκλάδες; kih-*klah*-dez). Rugged, sun-drenched outcrops of rock, anchored in azure seas and liberally peppered with snow white villages and blue-domed churches, this is Greece straight from central casting, with atmospheric archaeological sites and dozens of postcard-worthy beaches. Throw in a blossoming food scene, some renowned party destinations and a good dose of sophistication that seems to have bounced its way down from Athens, and you really do have the best of Greece's ample charms.

The biggest surprise may be the variety. You can indulge in any favourite holiday pursuit: chase hedonism on Mykonos or Ios, history on Delos, hiking trails on Andros or Amorgos. Want to woo your beloved? Try Santorini. To escape reality? Pick Donousa. You can ferry hop to your heart's content, enjoy long lazy lunches at waterside tavernas, or simply lay claim to a sunbed by a spectacular beach. You're living the dream.

When to Go
Mykonos Town

°C/°F Temp												Rainfall inches/mm
40/104 —												— 0.79/20
30/86 —												— 0.39/15
20/68 —												— 0.2/5
10/50 —												
0/32 —	J	F	M	A	M	J	J	A	S	O	N	D — 0

Apr–Jun Catch the early-season sun without overheating and boats without overcrowding.

Jul & Aug Pros: sun, sea and sand, balmy nights and lively company. Cons: peak crowds and prices.

Sep & Oct Quieter beaches, open spaces, the sweet scent of herbs and great walks on island hills.

Cyclades Highlights

1 Immersing yourself in the spellbinding archaeological sites of **Ancient Delos** (p341) and **Ancient Akrotiri** (p388).

2 Slipping away to serenity on the remote-feeling islands of the **Small Cyclades** (p363).

3 Partying until dawn on glamorous **Mykonos** (p331) and party-hard **Ios** (p374).

4 Exploring quaint villages then reclining on the white sand of **Naxos** (p351).

5 Ambling along ancient footpaths through the valleys of **Andros** (p317).

6 Marvelling in the dazzling monastery, clinging to a cliffside on **Amorgos** (p369).

7 Making a pilgrimage to **Tinos** (p321) with its famous icon and marble villages.

8 Joining the chic holiday atmosphere on idyllic **Sifnos** (p402) or **Antiparos** (p350).

9 Being mesmerised by the dramatic, volcanic coastlines of **Santorini** (Thira; p378) and **Milos** (p397).

History

The Cyclades are said to have been inhabited since at least 7000 BC. Around 3000 BC there emerged a cohesive Cycladic civilisation that was bound together by seagoing commerce and exchange. During the Early Cycladic period (3000–2000 BC) the tiny but distinctive Cycladic marble figurines, mainly stylised representations of the naked female form, were sculpted. Recent discoveries on Keros, an uninhabited island near Koufonisia in the Small Cyclades, indicate that the island was a possible pilgrimage site where figurines that had been broken up as part of rituals were deposited.

In the Middle Cycladic period (2000–1500 BC) many of the islands were occupied by the Minoans, who probably colonised from Crete. At Akrotiri, on Santorini, a Minoan town has been excavated and artefacts from the site have all the distinctive beauty of those from Crete's Minoan palaces. At the beginning of the Late Cycladic period (1500–1100 BC) the archipelago came under the influence of the Mycenaeans of the Peloponnese, who were supplanted by northern Dorians in the 8th century BC.

By the mid-5th century BC the Cyclades were part of a fully fledged Athenian empire. In the Hellenistic era (323–146 BC) they were governed by Egypt's Ptolemaic dynasties and later by the Macedonians. In 146 BC the islands became a Roman province and lucrative trade links were established with many parts of the Mediterranean.

The division of the Roman Empire in AD 395 resulted in the Cyclades being ruled from Byzantium (Constantinople), but after the fall of Byzantium in 1204 they came under a Venetian governance that doled out the islands to opportunistic aristocrats. The most powerful of these was Marco Sanudo (the self-styled Venetian Duke of Naxos), who acquired a dozen of the larger islands – including Naxos, Paros, Ios, Sifnos, Milos,

---

ⓘ PLANNER: CYCLADES ISLAND HOPPING

The Cyclades comprise 24 main islands (and a handful of uninhabited islands) dotting the Aegean Sea between the Greek mainland and Crete.

Where to Visit

It's easy to do the well-worn island hop from Mykonos to Santorini, via popular second-tier islands such as Paros, Naxos or Ios. But consider spreading your wings further and creating a combo trip (following the most obvious ferry routes where possible).

➡ When you've had your fill of partying on Mykonos, it's easy to travel north from here to Andros for superb walking and to Tinos for culture.

➡ Santorini's majestic caldera deserves the accolades, but consider contrasting this heavily touristed island with Anafi for its end-of-the-road feel, and Folegandros (photogenic local life).

➡ Naxos abounds with fab food and beaches, but a small local ferry offers easy connection to the first-class beaches of Koufonisia and the mountains and monasteries of Amorgos.

➡ The ferry schedules work well to help you plot a less-beaten path through the super-scenic western islands of Serifos, Sifnos and Milos.

How to Island Hop: Boat

The key to sculpting an itinerary through the islands is knowing which ferries go where, and when. The peak ferry services run in July and August, but in low season services are reduced or nonexistent on some routes.

Note that ferry services are in a state of flux, after the demise of NEL Lines in the summer of 2015. (NEL was a major player in interisland travel in the Cyclades, and many of the routes it served will no doubt be picked up, and possibly modified, by other operators.)

A host of companies offer connections throughout the Cyclades. They depart from the main ports of Attica: Piraeus (the largest port, with services to most islands), Rafina (particularly good for Mykonos, Andros and Tinos) and Lavrio (for Kythnos and Kea).

How to Island Hop: Air

Of the 24 Cyclades islands, six have airports – Mykonos, Syros, Paros, Naxos, Santorini and Milos – all with daily links to Athens. Some have direct links with European cities in summer

Amorgos and Folegandros – and introduced a Venetian gloss that survives to this day in island architecture.

The Cyclades came under Turkish rule in 1537, although the empire had difficulty managing, let alone protecting, such scattered dependencies. Cycladic coastal settlements suffered frequent pirate raids, a scourge that led to many villages being relocated to hidden inland sites. They survive as the 'Horas' ('capitals', also often written as Chora) that are such an attractive feature of the islands today. Ottoman neglect, piracy and shortages of food and water often led to wholesale depopulation of more remote islands, and in 1563 only five islands were still inhabited.

The Cyclades played a minimal part in the Greek War of Independence, but became havens for people fleeing from other islands where insurrections against the Turks had led to massacres and persecution. Italian forces occupied the Cyclades during WWII. After the war, the islands emerged more economically deprived than ever. Many islanders lived in deep poverty, while many more gave up the struggle and headed to the mainland, or to America and Australia, in search of work.

The tourism boom that began in the 1970s revived the fortunes of the Cyclades. The challenge remains, however, of finding alternative and sustainable economies that will not mar the beauty and appeal of these remarkable islands.

ANDROS ΑΝΔΡΟΣ
POP 9221

Andros, the second-largest of the Cyclades, has a long and proud seafaring tradition and, conversely, is a walker's paradise. Its wild mountains are cleaved by fecund valleys with bubbling streams and ancient stone mills. On this lush island, springs tend to be a feature of each village and waterfalls cascade down hillsides most of the year. It's worth renting

---

(charter flights, plus scheduled services to Mykonos and Santorini). There are rarely direct links between islands.

When to Visit

Seasons impact ferry routes, crowds, availability and prices. The travel season for the Cyclades runs from April (from Orthodox Easter) to October.

The July and August peak is hot, crowded and expensive. By all means join the party (this is when the bars and clubs are sizzling), but bear in mind that beaches are packed, tables in restaurants are hard to come by, and prices skyrocket (especially for accommodation). Ask Greeks working in tourism and they'll tell you: come in May, June and (especially) September.

High season July to early September, with 'peak peak' for six weeks from about mid-July (15 August is a big festival, and most Greeks take holidays around this time).

Shoulder season May, June and most of September.

Low season April and October. Weather may be cool, and in April the sea is cool, discouraging swimmers (water temperature in October is usually agreeable). Not all services are operating (especially on smaller islands), but hotel prices at this time are a bargain.

Winter Don't discount a winter trip. Santorini is making a concerted effort to attract and satisfy winter tourists. All the larger islands have year-round accommodation and the chance to see local life in action.

Costs

In July and August you will pay top dollar for accommodation and car hire – this is especially true on Mykonos and Santorini. Prices listed in our reviews are for the July and August peak.

Outside these months, prices drop substantially and the Cyclades can become a bargain, with accommodation reduced by 50% or more. A top-end room in Mykonos Town that costs upwards of €350 in August may sell for around €90 in April. Good-quality rooms on Ios that cost €120 in August sell for as low as €30 in late May. The exception to this is Santorini, where caldera-view rooms are invariably priced at the upper end regardless of season (although prices still peak in August). Still, beachside rooms on Santorini's east coast can drop to €25 in May.

a car to get out to the footpaths, many of them stepped and cobbled, which will lead you through majestic landscapes and among wildflowers and archaeological remnants. The handsome main town of Hora, also known as Andros, is a ship-owners' enclave packed with neoclassical mansions.

❶ Getting There & Away

Reach Andros from the mainland port of Rafina via regular ferries that continue south to Tinos and Mykonos. Direct services run to/from Syros a few times a week, from where easy onward links can be made (or you can reach Syros daily, by changing ferry in Tinos).

Buy tickets at **Ploes Travel** (☎ 22820 29220; Empirikou) in Hora or **Batsi Travel** (☎ 22820 71489) in Gavrio.

❶ Getting Around

KTEL Andros (☎ 22820 22316) has up to nine buses daily (fewer on weekends) linking Gavrio and Hora (€4, 55 minutes) via Batsi (€2, 15 minutes); schedules are posted at the bus stops in Gavrio and Hora. Low-season buses are usually timed to meet Rafina ferries.

Taxis (☎ Batsi 22820 41081, Gavrio 22820 71561, Hora 22820 22171) from Gavrio to Batsi cost about €10, and to Hora €40.

Roads can be rough and narrow, but many walking paths and sights are only accessible by car. **Escape in Andros** (☎ 22820 29120; www.escapeinandros.gr) can arrange to meet you at the port with a rental car (from about €40 per day in August, €25 in low season).

Gavrio   Γαύριο
POP 1200

Sleepy Gavrio on the west coast is the main port of Andros. The waterfront is lined with services (ATMs, ticket agencies, car hire), but the town isn't the most interesting part of the island to base yourself – there are some stretches of beach to the south (en route to Batsi) that are considerably more appealing.

Andros

0   10 km
0   5 miles

Cape Kampanos
Cape Fasa
Hartes
Zorkos Beach
Aegean Sea
▲716m
Amolohos
Vitali Beach
Vitali
Gulf of Vitali
Vori Beach
Agios Petros Beach
Gavrio
Ateni
Fellos Bay
Rafina (66km)
Golden Beach
Agios Kyprianos Beach
Batsi
Remata
Vourkoti
Andros
Cape Gria
Ahla Beach
Katakilos
Stenies
Delavoia Beach
Arni
Apikia
Gialia Beach
Anerousa Beach
Stivari
Sariza Spring
Niborio Beach
Green Beach
Mt Petalo (910m)
Mesathouri
Paraporti Beach
Hora (Andros)
Menites
Mesaria
Paleopoli Bay
Paleopoli
Sineti
Dipotamata Gorge
Pitrofos
Exo Vouni
Mesa Vouni
Kochilou
Halkolimionas
Piskopio
Zagora
Kapparia
Ormos Korthiou
Cape Orginos
Aidonia
Batsilianos
Korthi
Pera Horio
Mousionas
Piso Meria
648m
Cape Steno

Syros (39km);
Mykonos (52km);
Tinos (57km)
Tinos

BOAT SERVICES FROM ANDROS

DESTINATION	TIME	FARE	FREQUENCY
Mykonos	2½hr	€14	2-5 daily
Rafina	2hr	€17	3-5 daily
Syros	2hr 50min	€10	2 weekly
Tinos	1½hr	€11	2-5 daily

🛌 Sleeping & Eating

Standard tavernas line Gavrio's waterfront.

Andros Camping　　　　　CAMPGROUND €
(☑22820 71444; www.campingandros.gr; camp site per adult/tent/car €6.50/3.50/3; ⊙May-Sep; ❄) A rustic site set among olive trees about 400m behind the harbour. Follow the signs from the road to Batsi, turning at the Escape in Andros travel agency.

Perrakis　　　　　　　　HOTEL €€
(☑22820 71456; www.hotelperrakis.com; Chrissi Ammos; d incl breakfast from €100; ⊙year-round; ❄🐾🛜) Across the road from the sweep of Golden Beach, about 3km south of Gavrio, are super views and swell rooms – the superior rooms are lovely and have big balconies. A dive centre is based here, and there's a restaurant. Off-peak rates can drop by 50%.

Allegria Family Hotel　　　　HOTEL €€
(☑22820 72110; www.allegria-andros.com; Agios Petros Beach; d/q €75/85; ⊙Apr-Sep; ❄🛜) Geared to families and close to the beach at Agios Petros a few kilometres south of Gavrio. Studios have kitchenettes and some have bunks for kids, all set in a pretty garden.

Giannoulis　　　　　　　TAVERNA €
(☑22820 71385; Agios Petros Beach; mains €7-15; ⊙lunch & dinner Jun-Aug, lunch only Apr-May) Tuck into traditional fare at this classic taverna, going strong since 1958. It's on the waterfront at Agios Petros Beach, between Gavrio and Batsi.

Batsi　　　　　　　　Μπατσί

POP 960

Batsi lies 7km southeast of Gavrio on the overbuilt shores of a handsome bay with a long beige-sand beach. The island's main resort, it revs up through July and August.

🛌 Sleeping & Eating

Book ahead for July and August and weekends in June and September.

Cavo D'Oro　　　　　　GUESTHOUSE €
(☑22820 41776; www.andros-cavodoro.gr; d €40; ❄🛜) The handful of simple, pleasant rooms here are excellent value. It's located above a restaurant across the road from the beach.

Krinos Suites Hotel　　　BOUTIQUE HOTEL €€€
(☑22820 42038; www.krinoshotel.com; ste incl breakfast from €160; ⊙late May-Sep; ❄🛜) One of Andros' high-end entries, housing nine well-kitted-out suites and a smart 'art cafe'. Some rooms have sea-view balconies.

Stamatis Taverna　　　　　TAVERNA €€
(☑22820 41283; mains €5-15; ⊙lunch & dinner) High above the harbour, this restaurant's interior is a charming time warp and the food is renowned for its authenticity: Andros lamb and stuffed chicken are specialities, as well as fresh fish. Reserve ahead for the Wednesday night offering of slow-cooked lamb.

🛈 Information

Greek Sun Holidays (☑22820 41198; www. andros-greece.com) Helps with accommodation, car hire, ferry tickets and island walks and excursions. Has an office on the Batsi harbourfront.

Hora (Andros) Χώρα (Ανδρος)

POP 1670

Hora perches dramatically on a rocky promontory and has surprising views through the neoclassical mansions to two vibrant bays on either side: Niborio and Paraporti. The peninsula is tipped by the remains of a Venetian fortress, and the town itself owes its grand mansions and squares to both the Venetian settlement and the shipowners who came to inhabit it. Hora's cultural pedigree is burnished by its Museum of Contemporary Art, an impressive archaeological museum and several important churches.

🅞 Sights & Activities

★Museum of Contemporary Art　MUSEUM
(MOCA; ☑22820 22444; www.moca-andros.gr; admission summer/rest of year €5/3; ⊙11am-3pm

ℹ MAP RESOURCES

Every Cyclades island is now mapped by Terrain (www.terrainmaps.gr), whose maps are an invaluable (and inexpensive) resource for travellers wishing to get off the beaten track and do some exploring, on foot or on wheels. History and myths, sights, geography and walking trails are covered, and maps are regularly updated. They are available in most bookshops and souvenir stores. Look out for Terrain's English-language hiking guides too – currently available for Kythnos, and with new guides scheduled for Milos and Sifnos in 2016.

Wed-Mon plus 6-9pm Wed-Sun Jul-Sep, 10am-2pm Wed-Mon Apr-Jun & Oct, 10am-2pm Sat-Mon Nov-Mar) MOCA has earned a reputation in the international art world for its outstanding summer exhibitions of famous artists. Exhibits have included the likes of Picasso, Matisse, Toulouse-Lautrec, Miró and Man Ray. The sculpture gallery features prominent Greek artists, and a summertime sea-view cafe offers homemade sweets. It's down the steps (signposted) from Plateia Kaïri.

Andros Archaeological Museum MUSEUM
(☑ 22820 23664; Plateia Kaïri; adult/child €3/free; ⊗9am-4pm Fri & Sun Nov-Mar) At the time of research the museum had limited hours. If it's open you can peruse the exquisite 2nd-century-BC marble copy of the bronze *Hermes of Andros* by Praxiteles, and impressive finds from the 9th- to 5th-century BC settlements of Zagora and Paleopoli on Andros' west coast.

Venetian Fortress RUIN
The ruins of a Venetian fortress stand on an island linked to the tip of the headland by the worn remnants of an arched stone bridge. It's a great spot for photos.

Afanis Naftis MONUMENT
The huge bronze sailor that stands in the square at the tip of the promontory celebrates Hora's seagoing traditions. There's small nautical museum nearby (infrequently open).

🛏 Sleeping

A handful of old mansions have been converted into refined boutique hotels. Prices rise on weekends.

★ Anemomiloi Studios APARTMENT €€
(☑ 22820 24084; www.anemomiloi.gr; d/q €85/95; ❄ 🗟) This popular complex of bright, spick-and-span studios sits at the southern end of town enjoying views over green fields from all its balconies. There's friendly, helpful service from the owners, who are building more apartments nearby, set to open in 2016. Off-peak rates drop considerably.

Archontiko Eleni BOUTIQUE HOTEL €€
(☑ 22820 22270; www.archontikoeleni.gr; Empirikou 9; s/d incl breakfast €75/90; ❄ 🗟) Snuggle into comfy beds in this eight-room neoclassical mansion. The high ceilings and classy decor include original timber floors from the 1890s.

Micra Anglia BOUTIQUE HOTEL €€€
(☑ 22820 22207; www.micra-anglia.gr; Goulandri 13; d incl breakfast from €160; ⊗ May-Oct; ❄ 🗟) Hora's five-star offering has a raft of chic amenities and stylish decor. Discounts available online.

🍴 Eating

Hora's main street is lined with a dazzling array of *zaharoplasteio* (sweet shops). Stroll and sample.

I Parea TAVERNA €
(☑ 22820 23721; Plateia Kaïri; mains €6-12; ⊗lunch & dinner) Long-established and popular with locals, central Parea boasts a super terrace overlooking Paraporti Beach. Head inside to see what's been freshly cooked that day.

Ta Skalakia TAVERNA €
(☑ 22820 22822; mains €7-8; ⊗dinner Mon-Sat) Tables spill down the eponymous stairs from this buttercup yellow restaurant. Inside feels more like a bistro with quaint bric-a-brac. There's a short, tasty menu offering the likes of oregano-flavoured pork, meatballs and roasted feta.

Endochora MEDITERRANEAN €€
(☑ 22820 23207; www.endochora.com; Empirikou; mains €8-15; ⊗ lunch & dinner May–mid-Sep, weekends only rest of year) On the main drag, Endochora is a stylish hot spot offering a fresh twist on Greek classics and a great vantage point for people-watching. Salads showcase prime local produce like capers, tomatoes, figs and cheeses.

ℹ Information

The bus station is up from Plateia Goulandri (continue walking past the taxi kiosk). The pedestrianised marble main street leads downhill from here all the way to the Venetian *kastro* (fortress) and is lined with services, including numerous banks. Also check http://andros.gr/en.

Around Andros

It's well worth renting a car to explore Andros' vast mountains and sprinkling of villages and to reach its footpaths and beaches. Its mountain drives are panorama-filled.

The north of the island, with the lush watershed around **Arni**, gives way to raw windswept hills as the road zigzags to **Vourkoti** and **Agios Nikolaou** with its sweeping views.

Paleopoli, 7km south of Batsi on the coast road, is the site of **Ancient Andros** and its sunken harbour. Only rubble remains but the small **Archaeological Museum of Paleopoli** (☎22829 41985; ⊙9am-4pm Tue, Thu & Fri) FREE displays finds.

The island is cleaved by a sweeping agricultural valley, and loads of small villages with springs, often marked by marble lions' heads and the like, surround Hora. The road winds through **Sariza**, **Stenies**, **Mesathouri**, **Strapouries** and **Menites** – all fun to explore.

In the south, visit quaint agricultural villages like **Livadia**, **Kochilou**, **Piskopio**, and **Aidonia**, which has ruined tower houses. The area's charming landscape of fields and cypresses encircle **Ormos Korthiou**, an uninspiring bayside village.

◉ Sights & Activities

Beaches

Between Gavrio and Paleopoli Bay excellent beaches include Golden Beach (Hrisi Ammos), Delavoia, one half of which is naturist, Anerousa and Green Beach. Near Hora, check out lovely Gialia Beach.

Spectacular **Halkolimionas** – with tawny sand and a tiny church – sits 2km down a stone-terraced valley near the junction for Hora. A small beach bar sets up in summer.

Many of the best beaches, such as Ahla, Vori and Vitali (all in the northeast), are only reached by 4WD or boat. Boat trips can usually be arranged (or boats hired) in Batsi and Nimborio.

Walking

There are 18 wonderful waymarked trails criss-crossing Andros, which range in duration from 30 minutes to six hours, and are labelled in difficulty level from easy to average.

Your best investment is the *Andros Hiking Map* (€6) published by the marvellous **Andros Routes** (www.androsroutes.gr) project, in conjunction with Anavasi mapping company. It's available at bookshops and gift shops on the island. The Andros Routes website outlines the paths it maintains and has good advice for hiking on the island.

Locals recommend the areas north of Hora for great walks, including the villages of Stenies and Apikia. For a lovely short walk, **Pithara** is a shady glade of streams accessed from Apikia. For a longer ramble, hike up dramatic **Dipotamata Gorge**, signposted as you drive inland, after Sineti (southeast of Hora). The trail is cobbled part of the way and leads past ancient bridges and water mills and through vivid foliage, water burbling below.

Better yet, book a guided walk with **Trekking Andros** (☎22820 61368; www.trekkingandros.gr; guided walk per person from €15), a company that arranges and guides a menu of activities on the island, including hiking, mountain biking, boat trips, yoga, cooking or painting classes.

🛏 Sleeping & Eating

Onar Residence   COTTAGE €€€
(☎210 625 1052, 6932563707; www.onar-andros.gr; Ahla Beach; 3-/5-/7-person cottage €210/350/650; ⊙May-Oct; ❄🛜) 🅿 Ecofriendly, unique and luxurious secluded cottages in wetlands behind the stunning remote beach at Ahla. The resort has an organic restaurant for guests. Details on how to reach the resort are on the website (access road is for 4WD only; transfers can be arranged).

★**Tou Zozef**   TAVERNA €
(☎22820 51050; Pitrofos; mains €6-10; ⊙lunch & dinner) Gregarious Katerina Remoundou welcomes you to her sitting room or her tree-lined courtyard like she's your long-lost auntie. She chats with guests as they dine on seasonal Andriot fare like cheese-and-onion pie or stewed kid. Meals are rustic and delicious, and ingredients all sourced locally. The restaurant is in Pitrofos village, about 7km southwest of Hora; call ahead.

Gialia   TAVERNA €
(☎22820 24452; mains €7-12; ⊙lunch & dinner Apr-Oct) A few kilometres from Hora is the delightful crystal-clear blue of Gialia Beach, where this excellent restaurant serves snacks and a full menu of classics to hungry beachgoers or island explorers. Try the delicious (and ample) Andros salad.

TINOS   ΤΗΝΟΣ

POP 8640

Tinos is one of those sleeper hit islands. It's known widely for its sacred Greek Orthodox pilgrimage site: the Church of Panagia Evangelistria, in the port and main town, Hora.

But as soon as you leave the throngs in town, Tinos is a wonderland of natural beauty, dotted with more than 40 marble-ornamented villages found in hidden bays, on terraced hillsides and atop misty mountains. Also scattered across the brindled countryside are countless ornate dovecotes, a legacy of the Venetians.

There's a strong artistic tradition on Tinos, especially for marble sculpting, as in the sculptors' village of Pyrgos in the north, near the marble quarries. The food, made from local produce (cheeses, sausage, tomatoes and wild artichokes), is some of the best you'll find in Greece.

❶ Getting There & Away

Year-round ferries serve the mainland ports of Rafina and Piraeus and the islands Syros, Andros and Mykonos. Summer high-speed services include Tinos on their passage south from Rafina to major islands such as Mykonos, Paros, Naxos, Ios and Santorini. Get tickets at **Malliaris Travel** (☑ 22830 24242; www.malliaristravel.gr), on the waterfront in Hora.

Hora has two ferry-departure quays. The New (or Outer) Port is located 300m to the north of the main harbour and serves conventional and larger fast ferries. The Old (or Inner) Port, at the northern end of the town's main harbour, serves smaller fast ferries. Check which quay your ferry is leaving from.

❶ Getting Around

Between May and September, **KTEL Tinos** (☑ 22830 22440; www.kteltinou.gr) buses run from Hora to nearby Kionia (€1.60, 10 minutes, frequent), and northwest to Panormos (€4.20, one hour, several daily) via Kambos (€1.60, 15 minutes) and Pyrgos (€3.40, 50 minutes). The Hora bus station is on the harbour near the port. Buy tickets on board.

Hire motorcycles (€15 to €20 per day) and cars (€40 per weekday, €60 on weekends in high season) along the Hora waterfront. **Vidalis Rent a Car & Bike** (☑ 22830 23400; www.vidalis-rentacar.gr) has four outlets in Hora.

Phone for a **taxi** (☑ 22830 22470).

Tinos

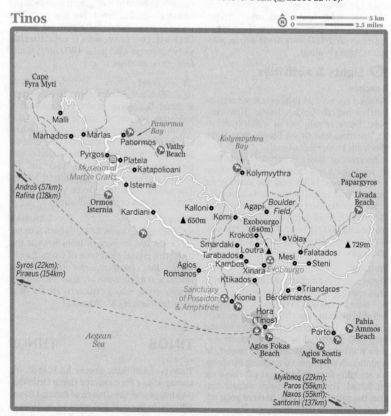

BOAT SERVICES FROM TINOS

DESTINATION	TIME	FARE	FREQUENCY
Andros	1½hr	€11	3 daily
Ios*	3hr	€38.50	1-2 daily
Mykonos	30-40min	€7	2-6 daily
Mykonos*	15min	€11.50	1-3 daily
Naxos*	2hr	€29	1-2 daily
Paros*	60-80min	€28	1-3 daily
Piraeus	4hr 40min	€31.50	3-4 weekly
Rafina	4hr	€24	2-4 daily
Rafina*	1hr 40min	€48	2-4 daily
Syros	30min	€7.50	3-4 weekly
Santorini*	3hr 40min	€40.50	1-2 daily

* high-speed services

Hora (Tinos) Χώρα (Τήνος)

POP 4762

Hora, also known as Tinos, is the island's welcoming capital and port. Though the harbourfront is lined with cafes and hotels, and the narrow backstreets are packed with restaurants, Hora's crowning glory is its Church of Panagia Evangelistria, perhaps the most important pilgrimage site for the Greek Orthodox religion.

Two main streets lead up to the church. Evangelistria is lined with shops and stalls crammed with souvenirs and religious wares, while Leoforos Megalocharis has a carpeted strip down the side, used by pilgrims crawling towards the church and pushing long candles before them. Religion certainly takes centre stage in Hora (woe betide the tourist looking for a room on one of the high holy days), but the town still hums with the vibrancy of a low-key island port.

◎ Sights

★ Church of Panagia Evangelistria   CHURCH

(Church of the Annunciation; ☑ 22830 22256; www. panagiatinou.gr; ⊙ 8am-8pm) Tinos' religious focus is this neoclassical church and its icon of the Virgin Mary. The hallowed icon was found in 1822 on land where the church now stands, after a nun in Tinos, now St Pelagia, was visited by visions from the Virgin instructing her where to find the icon. From the start, the icon was said to have healing powers, thus encouraging mass pilgrimage. Our Lady of Tinos became the patron saint of the Greek nation.

As you enter the church, the icon is on the left of the aisle, and is totally draped in jewels. The church, built of marble from the island's Panormos quarries, lies within a pleasant courtyard flanked by cool arcades. The complex has sweeping views all around and museums (with variable hours) that house collections of religious artefacts, icons and secular art. While there aren't necessarily bouncers at the door, churchgoers and priests prefer respectful garb: long pants or skirt and covered shoulders.

Cultural Foundation of Tinos   GALLERY

(☑ 22830 29070; www.itip.gr; adult/child €3/free; ⊙ 9am-3pm Mon-Thu, 10am-2pm & 5-8.30pm Fri, 10am-2pm Sat) This excellent cultural centre in a handsome neoclassical building on the southern waterfront houses a superb permanent collection of the work of famous Tinian sculptor Yannoulis Chalepas. A second gallery has rotating exhibitions. Musical events are staged in summer, and there's a gift shop and harbourfront cafe.

Archaeological Museum   MUSEUM

(☑ 22830 29063; Leoforos Megalocharis; adult/child €2/free; ⊙ 8am-3pm Tue-Sun) Just downhill from the Church of Panagia Evangelistria, this museum has a collection that includes impressive clay *pithoi* (large Minoan storage jars).

☞ Tours

KTEL Tours   BUS TOUR

(☑ 22830 22440; www.poseidontravel-tinos.com; full-day tour €12) In summer ask at the bus station about the daily tour that takes in a number of the island's villages, including

Volax, Loutra, Pyrgos, Panormos and Tarambados. It's a great way to see the sights in a day. Tours departs the bus station at 11am, returning around 5pm.

Festivals

Assumption of the Virgin Mary RELIGIOUS
(Feast of the Assumption) On 15 August the town is beyond full for the Virgin's feast day.

Sleeping

Hora is overcrowded on 25 March (Annunciation), Greek Easter, 15 August (Feast of the Assumption) and 15 November (Advent). Book months ahead or join devotees sleeping in the street.

Nikoleta PENSION €
(✆22830 25863; www.nikoletarooms.gr; Kapodistriou 11; s/d from €30/40; ❄️ 🖥️ 🛜) Little Nikoleta is a fair walk inland from the southern end of town, but it's one of the best-value options. There's a lovely garden and some rooms have kitchens.

★Studios Eleni II GUESTHOUSE €€
(✆22830 24352; www.studio-eleni.gr; Ioannou Plati 7; d/tr €80/110; ❄️ 🛜) A stone's throw from the Church of Panagia Evangelistria, pocket rocket Eleni runs this beautiful guesthouse, all whitewashed walls, pale linen and a supremely photogenic Cycladic courtyard. Rooms each have a fridge, and share a small kitchenette.

Eleni also runs Studios Eleni I, which is of an equally high standard at the southern end of town, close to Agios Fokas Beach. Port transfer is offered to both properties.

Altana Hotel BOUTIQUE HOTEL €€
(✆22830 25102; www.altanahotel.gr; s/d/ste incl breakfast from €80/90/100; ☾ May-Oct; ❄️ 🛜 🏊) Located about a 10-minute walk north of the town centre en route to Kionia Beach, this agreeable hotel has a modernist Cycladic style, with snow-white walls and cool interiors incorporating distinctive Tinian motifs.

Hotel Tinion HISTORIC HOTEL €€
(✆22830 22261; www.tinionhotel.gr; Eleftherias Sq; s/d/tr incl breakfast €55/70/85; ❄️ 🛜) This old-school central hotel dates from the 1920s, and has a broad verandah and sweeping stairs leading to comfortable high-ceilinged rooms. They are a little dated in decor but not without charm, especially for the price; try to score a balcony with sea views. Breakfast is bumper.

Eating & Drinking

Tinian food tends to be fresh and creative, using local products. Beer lovers should look for Tinos' own artisanal Nissos beer (www.nissosbeer.com).

Mesklies CAFE €
(✆22830 22151; www.mesklies.gr; snacks €3-7; ☾9am-late) This harbourfront cafe does a fine line in breakfasts, but it's the delectable sweets of the patisserie that catch most people's eyes. From homemade ice cream to traditional sweets like *liknaraki* (sweet cheese cupcakes) and almond cookies, you'll find something to like.

★Itan Ena Mikro Karavi MEDITERRANEAN €€
(✆22830 22818; www.mikrokaravi.gr; Trion Ierarchon; mains €11-20; ☾lunch & dinner) Named for the opening line of a well-known children's tale ('There was a little boat...'), this elegant indoor-outdoor eatery serves Greek fare with creative Mediterranean flair. Dishes like slow-cooked pork and rabbit ravioli are made with impeccably sourced local ingredients, and the setting and service are first-class.

To Koutouki Tis Elenis TAVERNA €€
(✆22830 24857; G Gagou 5; mains €7-20; ☾lunch & dinner) This colourful, rustic little place is on the narrow taverna-packed lane veering off the bottom of Evangelistria. The menu bursts with local flavours. Try fresh cheeses, fish soup, artichoke pie or the delicious fritters made from fennel leaf.

Tarsanas SEAFOOD €€
(✆22830 24667; mains €7-18, fish by kg; ☾lunch & dinner) The owner grills out front of this friendly, rustic spot, tucked away at the southern end of the harbour. It specialises in seafood. Try smoked-fish dip and anchovies wrapped in vine leaves, or splurge on lobster spaghetti.

Around Tinos

The countryside of Tinos is a glorious mix of broad terraced hillsides, mountain tops crowned with crags, unspoiled villages, fine beaches and fascinating architecture that includes picturesque dovecotes. Rent wheels to see it all.

Kionia, 3km northwest of Hora, has several small beaches and the scant remains of the 4th-century-BC **Sanctuary of Poseidon & Amphitrite** (admission €2; ☾8.30am-3pm Tue-Sun), a once-enormous complex that drew pilgrims.

First along the way north of town, beautiful **Ktikados** perches in a hanging valley and has a matched set of blue-topped church and campanile. **Drosia** (☎22830 21807; Ktikados; mains €7-12; ☺lunch & dinner Easter-Oct) is tops for local lunches and magnificent views.

Kambos sits on the top of a scenic hill surrounded by fields and is home to the **Costas Tsoclis Museum** (☎22830 51009; Kambos; ☺10am-1.30pm & 6-9pm Wed-Mon Jun-Sep) FREE, home to works by the renowned contemporary artist.

Don't miss **Tarabados**, a fun maze of small streets decorated with marble sculptures and leading to a breezy valley lined with dovecotes (look for the sign 'Pigeon Houses' Area'). Explore!

About 17km northwest of Hora, lovely **Kardiani** perches on a steep cliff slope enclosed by greenery. Narrow lanes wind through the village and the views towards Syros are exhilarating.

Pyrgos is a stunning, church-dotted hamlet where even the cemetery is a feast of carved marble, and the perfect village square looks like a film set. During the late 19th and early 20th centuries, Pyrgos was the centre of a remarkable sculpture enclave sustained by the supply of excellent local marble.

At the main entrance to Pyrgos, the fascinating **Museum House of Yannoulis Halepas** (adult/child €3/free; ☺11am-3pm & 5.30-7.30pm Apr–mid-Oct) preserves the sculptor's humble rooms and workshop. An adjoining gallery has splendid examples of the work of local sculptors.

Further north of Pyrgos the main road ends at **Panormos**, a popular excursion destination for its photogenic fishing harbour lined with fish tavernas.

About 12km north of Hora on the north coast is emerald **Kolymvythra Bay**, where **Tinos Surf Lessons** (www.tinossurflessons. com) takes advantage of the breaks at two excellent sandy beaches. It offers surf tuition, plus rentals of surfboards, bodyboards, kayaks and canoes.

A worthwhile detour inland takes you to **Agapi**, in a lush valley of dovecotes. Ethereal and romantic, it lives up to its name (*agapi* means 'love' in Greek).

Pass eye-catching **Krokos** with its **Evangelismou tis Panagias**, an enormous Catholic church, to reach **Volax**, about 6km directly north of Hora. This hamlet sits at the heart of an amphitheatre of low hills festooned with hundreds of enormous,

multicoloured boulders. The taverna **Volax** (☎22830 41021; mains €6-10; ☺lunch & dinner) serves reliable Tinian favourites like wild artichokes with lemon.

The ruins of the Venetian fortress of **Exobourgo** lie 2km south of Volax, on top of a mighty 640m rock outcropping.

The northeast coast beach at **Livada** is spectacular, but the ones east of Hora, like **Porto** and **Pahia Ammos**, can seem comparatively built-up.

Sleeping & Eating

Tinos Habitart COTTAGE €€€
(☎22830 41907; www.tinos-habitart.gr; Triantoros; 4-person house from €180; ☎❄) This cleverly designed complex lies in a village 6km northeast of Hora, and gives you a taste of traditional island life. Five houses incorporate local stone and marble and are fully equipped with kitchen, living spaces and outdoor areas (most with private pool). Our favourite is the dovecote irresistibly transformed into a three-bedroom villa.

★**Thalassaki** MODERN GREEK €€
(☎22830 31366; tothalassaki@gmail.com; Ormos Isternia; mains €8-16, fish by kg; ☺lunch & dinner Easter-Oct) Go to Ormos Isternia, a stony beach set among plunging hills south of Pyrgos, if only to eat here. The seafront taverna crafts local cheese, tomatoes, wild artichokes and the like into veritable works of art and has outstanding seafood prepared in deliciously creative fashion (eg octopus baked in grape molasses, mussels with wine and fennel). Book ahead in high season.

DON'T MISS

MARVELLOUS MARBLE

On the slopes above Pyrgos is the outstanding **Museum of Marble Crafts** (☎22830 31290; www.piop.gr; adult/child €3/free; ☺10am-6pm Mar–mid-Oct, to 5pm mid-Oct–Mar, closed Tue year-round), a modern, well-curated complex that creatively explains quarrying and sculpting techniques. It includes films and beautifully illustrated displays with English translations, along with top examples of artefacts and architectural features shaped from Tinian marble. The films of some of the last living quarry-men plying their trade are fascinating.

SYROS ΣΥΡΟΣ

POP 21,500

Endearing little Syros merges traditional and modern Greece. One of the smallest islands of the Cyclades and relatively rural outside of the capital, it nevertheless has the highest population since it's the legal and administrative centre of the entire archipelago. It's also the ferry hub of the northern islands and home to Ermoupoli, the grandest of all Cycladic towns, with an unusual history. As the Cyclades' capital, it pays less heed to tourism. It buzzes with life year-round, boasts great eateries, and showcases the best of everyday Greek life.

History

Excavations of an Early Cycladic fortified settlement and burial ground at Kastri in the island's northeast date from the neolithic era (2800–2300 BC). During the 17th and 18th centuries Capuchin monks and Jesuits settled on the island. Becoming overwhelmingly Catholic, Syros even called upon France for help during Turkish rule.

During the War of Independence, thousands of Orthodox refugees from islands ravaged by the Turks fled to Syros. They brought an infusion of Greek Orthodoxy and a fresh entrepreneurial drive that made Syros the commercial, naval and cultural centre of Greece during the 19th century.

Syros' position declined in the 20th century, but you still see shipyards, textile manufacturing, thriving horticulture, a sizeable administrative sector, a university campus and a continuing Catholic population.

ⓘ Getting There & Away

AIR

Olympic Air (www.olympicair.com) flies daily from Athens (€87, 35 minutes) to Syros airport, 5km south of Ermoupoli.

BOAT

Year-round ferries serve the mainland port of Piraeus. As the island group's capital, Syros theoretically has fair to good year-round ferry links with all the Cyclades islands. However, at the time of research, ferry timetables were receiving a shake-up due to the demise of NEL Lines, an important ferry operator with a base in Syros and regular connections with the further-flung Cyclades islands. Our best advice: utilise websites like www.openseas.gr to see what's feasible, or contact local travel agents.

There's a weekly **Blue Star** (www.bluestarferries.com) ferry linking Syros with each of the Small Cyclades islands and Amorgos (Aegiali port). A few times a week, Blue Star links Syros with Dodecanese islands, including Patmos, Leros, Kos and Rhodes; once a week the same company has a link between Syros and Astypalea. There are weekly **Hellenic Seaways** (www.hellenicseaways.gr) links with the northeastern Aegean islands, including Patmos, Ikaria, Samos, Lesvos and Limnos.

BOAT SERVICES FROM SYROS

DESTINATION	TIME	FARE	FREQUENCY
Anafi	6¼hr	€28	2-3 weekly
Amorgos	4½hr	€23.50	1 weekly
Astypalea	6¼hr	€25.50	1 weekly
Chios	11½hr	€45	1 weekly
Ios	4½hr	€25.50	2 weekly
Kos	5½-7½hr	€39	3 weekly
Leros	5½hr	€34	2 weekly
Lesvos	14½hr	€50	1 weekly
Mykonos	45-75min	€12-18	1-3 daily
Naxos	2hr 10min	€14.50	3 weekly
Paros	55min	€11.50	3 weekly
Patmos	4hr 5min	€32	4 weekly
Piraeus	3½-4hr	€30	1-3 daily
Rhodes	9-11hr	€46	3 weekly
Samos	6hr-8hr 20 min	€40	4 weekly
Santorini	4¾hr	€28	2-3 weekly
Tinos	30min	€7.50	3-4 weekly

Syros

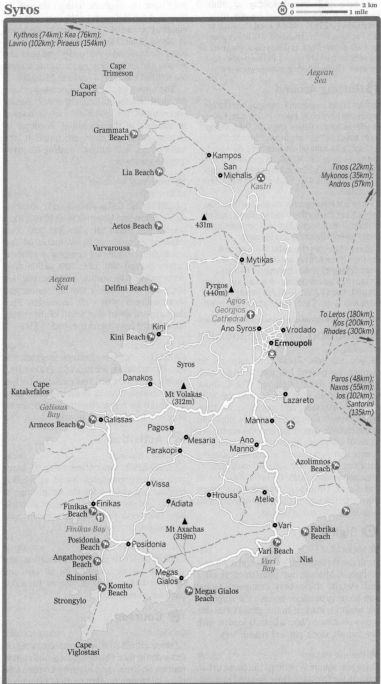

N 0 —————————— 2 km
   0 —————————— 1 mile

Kythnos (74km); Kea (76km);
Lavrio (102km); Piraeus (154km)

Cape Trimeson

Cape Diapori

Aegean Sea

Grammata Beach

Kampos
San Michalis
Kastri

Lia Beach

Aetos Beach

431m

Varvarousa

Mytikas

Aegean Sea

Delfini Beach

Pyrgos (440m)

Agios Georgios Cathedral

Tinos (22km);
Mykonos (35km);
Andros (57km)

Kini
Kini Beach

Ano Syros

Vrodado

Ermoupoli

To Leros (180km);
Kos (200km);
Rhodes (300km)

Syros

Danakos

Cape Katakefalos

Mt Volakas (312m)

Lazareto

Paros (48km);
Naxos (55km);
Ios (102km);
Santorini (135km)

Galissas Bay

Armeos Beach

Galissas

Pagos

Manna

Mesaria

Parakopi

Ano Manno

Azolimnos Beach

Vissa

Hrousa

Atelio

Finikas Beach

Finikas

Adiata

Finikas Bay

Mt Axachas (319m)

Vari

Fabrika Beach

Posidonia Beach

Posidonia

Vari Beach

Angathopes Beach

Vari Bay

Nisi

Shinonisi

Megas Gialos

Komito Beach

Strongylo

Megas Gialos Beach

Cape Viglostasi

Buy tickets at **Teamwork Holidays** (☏28810 83400; www.teamwork.gr; Akti Papagou 18) or **Vassilikos** (☏22810 84444; www.vassilikos.gr; Akti Papagou 10) in Ermoupoli. Ask where your ferry will depart from, as it may dock anywhere on the western part of the port. Both agencies have the week's ferry schedule on their websites.

❶ Getting Around

Regular buses loop from Ermoupoli bus station beside the ferry quay, taking in Galissas, Finikas, Posidonia, Megas Gialos and Vari. The full loop takes about an hour and buses run in both directions, with a maximum fare of €1.70. About five buses go to Kini (€1.60, 35 minutes) or to Ano Syros (€1.60, 15 minutes) every day except Sunday. Schedules are posted at the waterfront bus station.

A free bus traverses the harbour between the car parks at the northern and southern ends of Ermoupoli (half-hourly 7am to 10pm Monday to Friday, to 4pm Saturday and Sunday).

You can hire cars (from €40 per day) and scooters (from €15) at waterfront agencies. Avoid driving in central Ermoupoli, though, as it's mostly stairs or pedestrianised ways. From the port, **taxis** (☏22810 86222) charge around €4 to Ano Syros, €12 to Galissas and €12 to Vari.

Ermoupoli Ερμούπολη

POP 11,400

As you sail into Ermoupoli, named after Hermes, its peaked hill tops emerge, each topped by a dazzling church. The Catholic settlers built on high ground, and the 19th-century Orthodox newcomers built from below. Now buildings spread in a pink and white cascade over it all, and the centre is a maze of stairways, pedestrianised shopping streets and neoclassical mansions radiating out from the grand Plateia Miaouli with its impressive town hall. Catholic **Ano Syros** and Greek Orthodox **Vrodado** spill down from high hill tops to the north of town, with even taller hills rising behind.

◉ Sights

★ Vaporia
AREA

Stroll the Vaporia district, east and northeast of Plateia Miaouli, for palm-lined squares and elegant shipowners' mansions (some now home to boutique hotels). The shipowners' wealth is evident in the grand Orthodox **Agios Nikolaos** (Vaporia District) loaded with fine murals, icons, gilt and chandeliers.

★ Plateia Miaouli
SQUARE

This great square is perhaps the finest urban space in the Cyclades. Once situated immediately upon the seashore, today it sits well inland and is dominated by the dignified neoclassical **town hall** (Plateia Miaouli), designed by Ernst Ziller. Flanked by palm trees and lined along all sides with cafes and bars, the square and accompanying statue are named for Hydriot naval hero Andreas Miaoulis.

The town's small, unremarkable **archaeological museum** (☏22810 88487; Benaki; adult/child €2/free; ⊙8.30am-8pm) is housed in the rear of the town hall. A couple of elegant old-world cafes are found in the hall's wings, with alfresco seating for great people-watching.

★ Industrial Museum of Ermoupoli
MUSEUM

(☏22810 84762; George Papandreou 11; admission €2.50; ⊙9am-5pm Mon-Fri Oct-Mar, 10am-3.30pm Mon-Sat plus 6-8pm Sat, 10am-3pm Sun) This excellent chronicle of Syros' industrial and shipbuilding traditions occupies a restored factory packed with over 300 well-labelled items relating to sewing, printing, engines, ships and more. Ask if the Aneroussis lead shot factory is open – it's fascinating. Find the museum about 1km south of the centre, opposite the hospital on the road to Kini.

Apollo Theatre
THEATRE

(☏22810 85192; www.facebook.com/apollontheater; Plateia Vardaka; admission €2; ⊙10am-3pm) Built in the 1860s, this venerable theatre was partly modelled on La Scala in Milan. Keep an eye out for regular theatre performances, or pop in to take a look around.

🏃 Activities

Cyclades Sailing
SAILING

(☏22810 82501; www.cyclades-sailing.gr) Large yacht-charter company, based at Finikas marina. See website for the huge range of vessels and potential sailing areas. A week-long four-berth yacht in peak season costs from €1430.

Syros Windsurf School
WINDSURFING

(☏6936713547) Organises windsurfing and stand up paddle boarding for all ages and levels. Based at Finikas. See its Facebook page for more details.

🎓 Courses

Omilo
LANGUAGE COURSE

(☏Athens 210 612 2896; www.omilo.com/syros) Offers summertime Greek-language and culture courses on Syros (and Andros). Courses take place in Azolimnos, 4km south of Ermoupoli.

CYCLADES ERMOUPOLI

Ermoupoli

🛏 Sleeping

Most budget options cluster above the ferry quay, while boutique hotels in renovated mansions dot the Vaporia district. Much accommodation opens year-round, with discounts in low season.

Hermoupolis Rooms   PENSION €
(☑22810 87475; www.hermoupolis-rooms.gr; Naxou; s/d/tr from €35/40/50; 🔧🛜) There's a cheerful welcome at these well-kept, self-catering rooms, a short climb from the waterfront. Front rooms open onto tiny, bougainvillea-cloaked balconies.

★Lila Guesthouse   GUESTHOUSE €€
(☑22810 82738; www.guesthouse.gr; Kosma; s/d/tr incl breakfast €80/100/120, ste from €160; 🔧🛜) In the former French consulate, these elegantly renovated rooms and suites are kitted out with impeccable modern decor and top-notch bathrooms. Suites are spacious with dining tables and antiques. A bumper breakfast is served by the genial proprietors in the airy common area. Port pick-up available.

Ethrion   HOTEL €€
(☑22810 89066; www.ethrion.gr; Kosma 24; d/tr €70/80; 🔧🛜) Newly renovated to a high standard, the rooms and studios at family-run Ethrion are comfortable and well equipped. Upper-floor balconies sport views over the sea and town.

> **DON'T MISS**
>
> ### ANO SYROS
> ....
> The narrow lanes and whitewashed houses of Ano Syros, originally a medieval Catholic settlement, tower above Ermoupoli. From the bus terminus, head into the delightful maze and search out the finest of the Catholic churches, the 13th-century **Agios Georgios Cathedral**, with its star-fretted barrel roof and baroque capitals (still under renovation at the time of research). Continue past stunning viewpoints to reach the main street; the sweet **Our Lady of Mt Carmel**; the **Vamvakaris Museum** (admission €1; ⊙11am-2pm & 7-10pm Jul & Aug), celebrating locally born patriarch of *rembetika* (blues) Markos Vamvakaris; and the **monasteries** of the Jesuits and the Capuchins. Prepare to get lost, but try to find your way back to the view-enriched terraces of the handful of cafes and taverna along the main laneway.

Diogenis Hotel   HOTEL €€
(☑22810 86301; www.diogenishotel.gr; Plateia Papagou; s/d/tr incl breakfast €70/80/90; 🔧@🛜) Smart and stylish, with double-pane windows and modern everything, Diogenis is tops for business-class quality and super-handy for the port.

★Ploes Hotel   BOUTIQUE HOTEL €€€
(☑22810 79360; www.hotelploes.gr; Apollonos 2; d from €200; ⊙Apr-Oct; 🔧🛜) Unremitting elegance and attention to detail are hallmarks of this boutique beauty, inside a restored banker's mansion. Soaring ceilings, original artworks and designer furniture make the seven rooms here shine, and there's a private pavilion giving direct sea access to swimmers.

🍴 Eating & Drinking

Restaurants and cafe-bars fill the waterfront, especially along Akti Petrou Ralli – these fire up late, full of party people. Another great area for dining is among the bougainvillea-bedecked laneways of Emmanouil Roidi and Kyparissou.

Oneiro   MEDITERRANEAN €€
(☑22810 79416; Plateia Vardaka; mains €7-12; ⊙from 7pm) A simple menu offers good-value dishes and big local flavours: Syros sausage (made with wild fennel, one of the island's most distinctive ingredients), cheese balls, and roasted lamb from Naxos. There's a warmly lit large courtyard that turns into a thriving bar scene after hours, plus regular live music.

Mammo   INTERNATIONAL €€
(☑22810 76416; http://mammo-syros.gr; Akti Petrou Ralli 38a; mains €6-19; ⊙9am-late) The waterfront's current hot spot, Mammo is a wine and food bar that means business: stylish decor, a crowd-pleasing menu that isn't afraid of listing sushi alongside fajitas and *froutalia* (a traditional Greek omelette dish), and a big wine and cocktail list. By night, it morphs into a scene-y bar with DJ.

Kouzina   MEDITERRANEAN €€
(☑22810 89150; Androu 5; mains €10-14, steaks €26-40; ⊙lunch & dinner) In this colourfully lit, intimate dining room, fresh local ingredients are the building blocks of creative Mediterranean cuisine. Carnivores can step up a notch with top-grade Black Angus steaks.

Elia   RESTAURANT, BAR
(☑22810 76301; Hiou 32; ⊙11am-3am; 🍴) Just off Plateia Maiouli, look for a pale-green door and head up to this cosy restaurant-bar,

with timber and stonework, sofas and sunny enclosed balconies, artworks and awesome tunes. The menu offers excellent libations and well-priced, veg-friendly feeds.

Sta Vaporia CAFE, BAR

(☏22810 76486; ⊗10am-3am) Down a signposted set of stairs behind Agios Nikolaos is this perfectly positioned all-day cafe. It's a cruisy terrace with postcard panoramas and a menu of coffee, cocktails, and snacks, large and small. Down below are popular seaside swimming platforms (so bring your swimsuit).

❶ Information

Hospital (☏22810 96500; Papandreou) On western edge of city, opposite the Industrial Museum.

Around Syros

Outside of Ermoupoli, Syros comprises a series of hills and valleys folding down to small bays and beaches, most well served by buses.

The old resort town **Galissas** has seen better days, but it has an appealing beach and is still popular with French travellers (who are the main market for Syros beach holidays). **Hotel Benois** (☏22810 42833; www.benois.gr; s/d incl breakfast €85/110; ⊗Easter-Oct; ❋⊛❄), newly renovated with fresh, appealing rooms and a big pool area. Next door is a choice restaurant, **Iliovasilema** (☏22810 43325; mains €7-15; ⊗lunch & dinner Apr-Oct), with fresh seafood and a welcoming ambience.

The beaches south of Galissas all have domatia and some have hotels. It takes only about an hour to do a loop drive from Galissas around the south coast, so go exploring with your own wheels. Inland, the town of **Posidonia** (Delagrazia) was the historic shipowners' vacation spot; keep your eyes open for many grand villas.

The south-coast town of **Megas Gialos** has a couple of roadside beaches, but gorgeous **Vari Bay**, further east, is the better bet with its light grey sandy beach and hills, though the waterfront and tavernas get packed in high season. Inland and about 1.5km from Megas Gialos is peaceful **Hotel Alkyon** (☏22810 61761; www.alkyonsyros.gr; ⊗Apr-Oct), run by a charming French-Greek couple. Check the website for its range of seminars and activities, including painting and Greek gastronomy.

Kini Beach, on the west coast, has a long, thin stretch of beach and is developing into a popular resort. To stay in Kini, the new

---

WORTH A TRIP

SAN MICHALIS

If you have your own wheels, don't miss the drive to the northern village of San Michalis, along the spine of Syros, with spectacular views of unspoilt valleys and neighbouring islands on either side. Famous for its cheese, San Michalis is now a small hamlet of stone houses and vineyards.

Walk the winding rock path to the hilltop church, and get Syran food at its best at **Plakostroto** (☏6973980248; www.plakostroto.gr; mains €8-15; ⊗lunch & dinner May-Oct, Sat & Sun Nov-Apr). It serves local cheese plus rooster, lamb or rabbit grilled on the open wood fire. Views sweep down the hillside to Kea, Kythnos and beyond.

---

waterfront **Blue Harmony Hotel** (☏22810 71570; www.blueharmony.gr; d from €100; ❋☏) makes a fine choice. Tops for eats is waterfront **Allou Yialou** (☏22810 71196; mains €7-22; ⊗lunch & dinner May-Sep), with excellent seafood. It's a prime sunset spot.

MYKONOS ΜΥΚΟΝΟΣ
POP 10,100

Mykonos is the great glamour island of Greece and flaunts its sizzling St-Tropez-meets-Ibiza style and party-hard reputation.

The high-season mix of hedonistic holidaymakers, cruise-ship crowds (which can reach 15,000 a day) and posturing fashionistas throngs Mykonos Town (aka Hora), a traditional whitewashed Cycladic maze, delighting in its authentic cubist charms and its chichi cafe-bar-boutique scene.

The number of tourists (and cashed-up A-listers) visiting Mykonos is booming, and there's been a corresponding boom in construction and renovation; hip new hotels, beach bars and restaurants are mushrooming, and prices are escalating. In July and August come only if you are prepared to pay and are intent on joining the jostling street crowds, the oiled-up lounger lifestyle at the packed main beaches, and the relentless party. Out of season, devoid of gloss, glitter and preening celebrities, find more subdued local life, the occasional pelican wandering the empty streets, and beaches backed by banging clubs which have gone silent.

Mykonos

Syros (35km);
Rafina (133km);
Piraeus (174km)

5 km
2.5 miles

Dragonisi

Cape Evros

Cape Goni

Profitis Ilias
Anomeritis
(351m)

AEGEAN SEA

Lia Beach

Kalafatis Beach

Cape Kalafatis

Merchias Bay

Mersini Bay

Cape Mavros

Mersini Beach

Fokos Beach

Kalo Livadi Beach

Cape Mavrokefalas

Ano Mera

Elia

Elia Beach

Agrari Beach

Agios Sostis Beach

Panormos Beach

Panormos Bay

Ftelia Beach

Lake Marathi

Tourliani Monastery

275m

Super Paradise Beach

Paradise Beach

Excursion Boats

Marathi

Vothonas

Hora (Mykonos Town)

Psarou Platys Gialos

Platys Gialos

Paraga Beach

372m

Tourlos

Tourlos Beach

New Port

Old Port

Vrissi

Psarou Beach

Ornos

Agios Stefanos

Agios Stefanos Beach

Houlakia Beach

Cape Armenistis

Korfos

Kapari Beach

Kapari

Agios Ioannis Beach

Nea Mykonos

Cape Alogomandra

Naxos (46km); Paros (54km);
Ios (70km); Santorini (128km)

Excursion Boat

Delos

Renia

Mykonos is also the jumping-off point for the archaeological site of the nearby island of Delos.

ⓘ Getting There & Away

AIR

Mykonos Airport (www.mykonos-airport.com), 3km southeast of the town centre, has flights year-round to Athens with **Olympic Air** (www.olympicair.com) and **Aegean Airlines** (www.aegeanair.com), and to Thessaloniki with **Astra Airlines** (www.astra-airlines.gr).

From May to mid-September direct European connections are plentiful, including easyJet flights from London, Geneva, Paris, Rome and Milan, and Air Berlin flights from German and Austrian hubs.

BOAT

Year-round ferries serve mainland ports Piraeus and Rafina (the latter is usually quicker if you are coming directly from Athens airport), and nearby islands Tinos and Andros. In the high season, Mykonos is well connected with all neighbouring islands, including Paros and Santorini. Hora is loaded with ticket agents.

Mykonos has two ferry quays: the Old Port, 400m north of town, where some smaller fast ferries dock; and the New Port, 2km north of town, where the bigger fast ferries and all conventional ferries dock. When buying outgoing tickets double-check which quay your ferry leaves from.

ⓘ Getting Around

TO/FROM THE AIRPORT

Buses from the southern bus station serve Mykonos' airport (€1.60). Arrange airport transfer with your accommodation (around €7) or take a taxi to town (€10).

BOAT

Mykonos Cruises (☑ 22890 23995; www.mykonos-cruises.gr; ☉ Apr-Oct) An association of sea-taxi operators offering services to the island's best beaches. See the timetables online. The main departure point is Platys Gialos, with drop-offs and pick-ups at Ornos, Paraga, Paradise, Super Paradise, Agrari and Elia beaches (return trip costs between €5 and €7). Cruises and personalised itineraries can also be arranged.

Sea Bus (☑ 697 8830355) This water-taxi service connects the New Port with Hora (€2), running hourly from 9am to 10pm (more frequently when a cruise ship is in port).

BUS

The **KTEL Mykonos** (☑ 22890 26797, 22890 23360; www.mykonosbus.com) bus network has two main terminals plus pick-up points at the Old and New Ports. Low-season services are much reduced, but buses in high season run frequently; the fare is €1 to €2 depending on the distance travelled. Timetables are on the website. In July and August some bus services run until 2am or later from the beaches.

BOAT SERVICES TO MYKONOS

DESTINATION	TIME	FARE	FREQUENCY
Andros	2hr 20min	€14	3 daily
Ios	3hr 50min	€24.50	1 daily
Ios*	2hr	€48.50	3-4 daily
Iraklio*	4hr 35min	€79	2 daily
Naxos	2hr 20min	€18.50	1 daily
Naxos*	40min	€28.50	4-5 daily
Paros	1hr 20min	€16.50	1 daily
Paros*	40-50min	€29.50	2-3 daily
Piraeus	5½hr	€34	1-2 daily
Pireaus*	3hr	€57.50	1-2 daily
Rafina	3-4½hr	€27	2-3 daily
Rafina*	2hr 10min	€49	2-3 daily
Santorini (Thira)*	2½-3½hr	€60	5-6 daily
Syros	1¼hr	€12	1-2 daily
Syros*	45min	€18	2 weekly
Tinos	35min	€7	2-4 daily
Tinos*	15min	€11.50	2-4 daily

* high-speed services

Terminal A, the southern bus station (Fabrika Sq), known as Fabrika, serves Ornos and Agios Ioannis Beach, Platys Gialos, Paraga and Super Paradise beaches.

Terminal B, the northern bus station, sometimes called Remezzo, is behind the OTE office and has services to Agios Stefanos via Tourlos, Ano Mera, and Kalo Livadi, Kalafatis, and Elia beaches. Buses for Tourlos and Agios Stefanos stop at the Old and New Ports.

A regular bus connects the New Port with the southern bus station, and there are buses running between the southern bus station and the nearby airport. In summer there's a bus to Paradise Beach from the Old Port.

A private transfer bus operates in summer's peak every hour (11am to 11pm) from the Old Port to Paradise Beach (via Fabrika).

CAR & MOTORCYCLE

Cars start at €45 per day in high season and €30 in low season. Scooters/quads are around €20/40 in high season, and €15/30 in low season.

Avis and Sixt are among the agencies at the airport, and there are dozens of hire places all over the island, particularly near the ports and bus stations (which is where the large public car parks are found – you can't drive into Hora proper). You can rent from Mykonos Accommodation Centre (p339).

Apollon (☑22890 24136; www.apollonrenta-car.com) One of several agencies near Hora's southern bus station.

OK Rent A Car (☑22890 23761; www.ok-mykonos.com; Agios Stefanos) Near New Port.

TAXI

Taxis (☑22890 23700, 22890 22400) queue at Hora's Plateia Manto Mavrogenous (Taxi Sq), bus stations and ports, but waits can be long in high season. All have meters and the minimum fare is €3.30 (plus €0.50 per bag, €3.30 for phone booking).

Approximate fares from Hora include New Port (€5), Ornos (€9), Platys Gialos (€9), Paradise (€10), Kalafatis (€17) and Elia (€17).

Hora (Mykonos)
Χώρα (Μύκονος)

POP 8400

Hora (also known as Mykonos), the island's well-preserved port and capital, is a warren of narrow alleyways and whitewashed buildings overlooked by the town's famous windmills. In the heart of the waterfront Little Venice quarter, which is spectacular at sunset, tiny flower-bedecked churches jostle with glossy boutiques, and there's a cascade of bougainvillea around every corner. In high season

---

> ### ℹ️ NAVIGATING HORA (MYKONOS)
>
> Without question, you will soon pass the same junction twice. It's entertaining at first, but can become frustrating amid throngs of equally lost people and fast-moving locals. For quick-fix navigation, familiarise yourself with Plateia Manto Mavrogenous (Taxi Sq), and the three main streets of Matogianni, Enoplon Dynameon and Mitropoleos, which form a horseshoe behind the waterfront.

the streets are crowded with chic stores, cool galleries, jangling jewellers and bars – plus a catwalk cast of thousands.

⊙ Sights

★Panagia Paraportiani   CHURCH
(Paraportianis) Mykonos' most famous church, the rocklike Panagia Paraportiani, comprises four small chapels plus another on an upper storey reached by an exterior staircase. It's usually locked but the fabulously photogenic whitewashed exterior is the drawcard.

Archaeological Museum   MUSEUM
(☑22890 22325; Agiou Stefanou; adult/child €2/free; ☺9am-4pm Tue-Sun) Peruse pottery from Delos and grave *stelae* (pillars) and jewellery from the island of Renia (Delos' necropolis). Chief exhibits include a statue of Hercules in Parian marble.

Aegean Maritime Museum   MUSEUM
(☑22890 22700; Enoplon Dynameon 10; admission €4; ☺10.30am-1pm & 6.30-9pm Apr-Oct) Fascinating nautical paraphernalia includes detailed models of local boats and an enormous Fresnel lighthouse lantern in its sunny courtyard.

Lena's House   MUSEUM
(☑22890 22591; Enoplon Dynameon 10; ☺6-9pm May–mid-Oct) FREE This charming late-19th-century, middle-class Mykonian house (with furnishings intact) takes its name from its last owner, Lena Skrivanou. It's next door to the Aegean Maritime Museum. Its future opening was in doubt at the time of research.

Mykonos Folklore Museum   MUSEUM
(☑22890 22591; Paraportianis; ☺5.30-8.30pm Jun-Sep) FREE This folklore museum, housed in an 18th-century sea-captain's house, features a large collection of furnishings and other artefacts, including old musical instruments.

☞ Tours

Mykonos Accommodation Centre (p339) organises excursions and guided tours, and arranges private tours and charters. Tours go to Delos (adult/child €40/20), including the return boat trip, admission fee and guide, and Tinos (€59/38) to see its holy church and island sights. It also organises a walking tour of Hora and a bus tour around the island (€35/22). A full-day island cruise along the south coast (€64/35), a sunset cruise (€39/25) and a 4WD safari to isolated beaches (€59/33) are also available.

Mykonos Cruises (p333) runs sea taxis to various south-coast beaches and can arrange fishing trips and private cruises.

🛏 Sleeping

Hotel Lefteris   PENSION €
(☑22890 23128; www.lefterishotelmykonos.gr; Apollonas 9; d €150; ❄🕸) Tucked uphill and away from the crowds, a colourful entranceway leads to pristine, compact rooms and a warm welcome. A young family now runs this eight-room guesthouse (established by the owner's grandfather in the 1970s). All rooms have TV and air-con, and there's a roof terrace with views. Winter prices drop to €30.

Manto Hotel   HOTEL €
(☑ 22890 22330; www.manto-mykonos.gr; Evagelistrias 1; d incl breakfast €125-160; ☉Apr-Nov; ❄🕸) Buried in the heart of Hora, cheerful Manto is an excellent affordable option (for Mykonos), with well-kept colourful rooms, a lovely breakfast and lounge area, and a friendly father-son team running the place.

Carbonaki Hotel   BOUTIQUE HOTEL €€
(☑22890 24124; www.carbonaki.gr; 23 Panahrantou; d €180-220; ☉Apr-Oct; ❄🕸) This family-run boutique hotel is a delightful oasis with bright, comfortable rooms (of various price categories), relaxing public balconies and sunny central courtyards.

Town Suites   APARTMENT €€
(☑22890 23160; www.mykonos-accommodation. com; d/tr €220/285; ❄🕸) Owned by John, the man behind the info-rich Mykonos Accommodation Centre (MAC), this hidden complex of six bright suites and apartments makes a splendid choice. Each has well-equipped kitchen and sunny outdoor space. Gay-friendly, and in a quiet area. Check in at MAC (p339), and you'll be guided to the (unsigned) complex. Low-season rates are a marvellous €60.

Hotel Philippi   HOTEL €€
(☑22890 22294; www.philippihotel.com; Kalogera 25; s/d from €130/170; ☉Apr-Oct; ❄🕸) The street appeal of this traditional hotel is undeniable, and it lies on a strip of great eating options. Behind a bright-blue door, elegant rooms open onto a railed verandah overlooking a verdant courtyard-garden.

Fresh Hotel   BOUTIQUE HOTEL €€
(☑22890 24670; www.hotelfreshmykonos.com; Kalogera 31; s/d incl breakfast €180/190; ☉mid-May–Oct; ❄🕸) In the heart of town, with a lush and leafy garden and highly regarded on-site restaurant, Fresh is indeed fresh, with compact and stylishly minimalist rooms. Rates fall to €70/80 in the low season.

★ Semeli Hotel   HOTEL €€€
(☑22890 27466; www.semelihotel.gr; off Rohari; d incl breakfast from €385; ❄🕸🏊) Expansive grounds, a glamorous restaurant terrace and swimming pool, and stylish, contemporary rooms combine to make this one of Mykonos' loveliest (and more affordable) top-end hotels. Low-season rates make it considerably more accessible.

Belvedere Hotel   DESIGN HOTEL €€€
(☑22890 25122; www.belvederehotel.com; School of Fine Arts District; r from €585; ☉mid-Mar–mid-Nov; ❄🕸🏊) Easy access to this kind of effortlessly chic hotel is a reason to envy

---

ⓘ SLEEPING ON MYKONOS

Things to know about Mykonos accommodation:

➤ In July and August a no-frills double room with private bathroom in Hora costs about €150. Midrange options cost €150 to €300. The sky's the limit for what you want to pay in the top-end category. There are any number of luxurious hotels and villas: Mykonos is Greece's epicentre for swanky designer hotels.

➤ It's best not to arrive in July or August without a reservation, as there will be few vacancies anywhere on the island.

➤ Some places will insist on a minimum stay (from two nights or more) during peak period.

➤ Noise levels in Hora and popular resorts will be high in summer.

Hora (Mykonos)

N

0 — 100 m
0 — 0.05 miles

Old Port (350m);
Tourlos (1.5km);
New Port (2km);
Agios Stefanos (4km)

Agiou Stefanou

3

Northern
Bus Station

Aegean Sea

Port

Old
Jetty

Agia Anna

Excursion Boats
for Delos

Sea Bus

Delos Boat
Ticket Kiosk

Polikandrioti

19   21

4   Paraportianis

Plateia
Karaoli
Dimitriou

25

Plateia Manto
Mavrogenous
(Taxi Sq)

Panagia
Paraportiani

1

Akti Kambani

7

Apollonos

Inglesi

15

Drakopoulou

Agios Vlassos

Platia
Kyriakis

27

Mavrogenous

Agias Annis

22

14   23

Sotiros

Kambani

Agias Kyriakis

9

Agion Anargyron

K. Georgouli

Panteleimonos

Ag Gerasimo

26

Zouganeli

Agion Saranta

Plateia
Goumenou

LITTLE
VENICE

28

Pateraki

Kalogera

16

12

13

Litous

20

Meletopoulou

24

6   8

Malamatenias

Panahrantou

11

17

Katsoni

Plateia
Alefkandra

Mitropoleos

MAC

18   2

Eterias

Tria Pigadia
(Three Wells)

Enoplon Dynameon

Toulianis

29

Windmills

Baou

Agias Paraskevis

Legko Steno

Ipirou

5

Rohari

K Milon

Basoula

10

Mirodiou

D Koutsi

Semeli
Hotel (30m);
Belvedere
Hotel (100m)

Souheli

Aghios Efthimiou

Laka

Xenias

Artakinou

Fabrika Sq (Plateia Yialos);
Southern (80m)

A-listers. Charming service, first-class on-site restaurants (including one from Japanese marvel Nobu) and a magazine-worthy pool area seal the deal. Great low-season rates put it within reach of everyday folk too.

Eating

High prices don't necessarily reflect high quality in Mykonos. Cafe-bars line the waterfront; souvlaki shops dot the town (excellent for a cheap feed). Most places stay open late in high season. For the party-sated, get delivery from the extensive menu (available online) at **Oregano** (☑22890 27410; www.oregano -mykonos.com; mains €7-20; ⊙lunch & dinner).

Taste Diaries　　　　　　　　　CREPERIE €
(☑22890 29117; mains €5-9; ⊙24hr) Sandwiches and crêpes are served at all hours on the waterfront. Build your own from gourmet ingredients, or go with fab menu suggestions like a sweet crêpe of white praline, almond slices, caramel and kiwi.

Pepper　　　　　　　　　　　　GREEK €
(☑22890 27019; K Georgeouli 18; meals €2.50-8.50; ⊙24hr) A fresh look for a souvlaki joint: bright and cheerful, with well-priced gyros, burgers and salads.

To Maereio　　　　　　　　　GREEK €€
(☑22890 28825; Kalogera 16; mains €14-16; ⊙noon-3pm & 7pm-midnight) A busy, cosy and well-priced place favoured by locals, with a menu of Mykonian favourites. Heavy on meat – try meatballs, local ham and/or spicy sausage.

★**M-Eating**　　　　　MEDITERRANEAN €€€
(☑22890 78550; www.m-eating.gr; Kalogera 10; mains €17-30; ⊙dinner Apr-Oct) Attentive service, soft lighting and relaxed dining are the hallmarks of this creative restaurant specialising in fresh Greek products prepared with flair. Sample anything from sea-bass tartar to rib-eye veal with honey truffle. Don't miss the dessert of Mykonian honey pie.

Nautilus　　　　　　　MODERN GREEK €€€
(☑22890 27100; Kalogera 6; mains €16-27; ⊙dinner Mar-Nov) The whitewashed terrace spills out onto the street and Greek fusion dishes incorporate top ingredients.

Uno Con Carne　　　　　　　STEAK €€€
(☑22890 24020; www.unoconcarne.gr; mains €20-70; ⊙dinner Jun-Sep) Sup on prime steaks and fine wines at this chic steakhouse and oyster bar. Cocktails and DJ tunes too, on a beautifully lit terrace. It's signposted one block uphill from Panahrantou.

Avra　　　　　　　　　　　　GREEK €€€
(☑22890 22298; www.avra-mykonos.com; Kalogera 27; mains €15-30; ⊙dinner late Apr-Oct) Top Greek and fusion eats in a golden-lit, bougainvillea-draped courtyard perfect for romance.

Drinking & Nightlife

Folks come to Mykonos to party. Each major beach has at least one beach bar which gets going during the day. Night action in town starts around 11pm and warms up by 1am; in the wee hours revellers often relocate from

Hora to Cavo Paradiso (p341) on Paradise Beach. From cool sunset cocktails to sweaty trance dancing, wherever you go bring a bankroll – the high life doesn't come cheap.

Hora's Little Venice quarter puts the Aegean at your feet and is tops for rosy sunsets, windmill views and a swath of colourful bars; behind the bars (and alongside, above and underneath them) are some excellent clubs. Another prime spot is the Tria Pigadia (Three Wells) area on Enoplon Dynameon.

Galleraki
CAFE, BAR

(☑22890 27188; www.galleraki.com; Little Venice; ☺8am-late) Choose plumb waterfront seating or the upstairs balcony at this friendly cafe-bar, and order one of its ace fresh-fruit cocktails (like the signature 'katerinaki', made with melon).

Skandinavian Bar
CLUB

(☑22890 22669; www.skandinavianbar.com; Ioanni Voinovich 9; ☺8pm-6am) Supplies mainstream mayhem with ground-floor bars and an upstairs space for close-quarters moving to retro dance hits. Drinks tend to be a hair cheaper than elsewhere.

Astra
CLUB

(☑22890 24767; http://astra-mykonos.com; Enoplon Dynameon) Strict face control is exercised at glittering Astra, the haunt of local celebs and some of Athens' top DJs. It's in a hub of cool late-night bars.

★ Entertainment

★ Cine Manto
CINEMA

(☑22890 26165; www.cinemanto.gr; Meletopoulou; adult/child €8/6; ☺9pm & 11pm Jun-Sep) Need a break from the bars and clubs? Seek out this gorgeous open-air cinema, in a perfect garden setting. There's a cafe here too. Movies are shown in their original language; view the program online.

🔒 Shopping

Fashion boutiques and art galleries vie for attention. The full gamut of luxe brands have set up shop, as have many excellent Greek designers. Most stores close in the winter (November to March).

★ iMuseum Shop
ARTS

(☑22890 77370; www.i-museumshop.com; Dilou 8) An elegant and innovative boutique, selling approved, handcrafted replicas of pieces showcased in the most important museums of Greece – including classic art, jewellery, ceramics and figurines.

Parthenis
CLOTHING

(☑22890 22448; http://profile.orsalia-parthenis.gr; Plateia Alefkandra) For something special, find the work of Athens designer and longtime Mykonos resident Dimitris Parthenis and his daughter Orsalia.

GAY LIFE

Mykonos is a gay travel mecca. The many gay-centric bars and hang-outs fill with late-night crowds spilling onto the streets, and most welcome a mixed crowd too. The waterfront area, between the Old Harbour and the Church of Paraportiani, is a focus for the late-night gay scene. Check out coverage of the island's many hot spots (including beaches) on www.gayguide.gr.

Party people should visit for Xlsior (www.xlsiorfestival.com) in mid-August, a huge gay clubbing festival that draws some 30,000 partiers.

Hotel Elysium (☑22890 23952; www.elysiumhotel.com; School of Fine Arts District; d from €260; ☺Apr-Oct; ❄🐾🛋) Probably the most famous gay property on the island, this flash hotel sits high above the main town of Hora. Its high-camp sunset cabaret shows by the pool bar are an essential start to a night of partying (book a table). It's uphill from the Belvedere Hotel, in the town's southwest.

JackieO' (☑22890 77168; www.jackieomykonos.com; Old Harbour; ☺from 8pm) One of Mykonos' main gathering points for gay and straight alike. Throngs circulate from the retro-chic interior to the harbourfront, starting in early evening. There is a fab all-day outpost at Super Paradise Beach (www.jackieobeach.com) featuring restaurant, bar, pool and Jacuzzi.

Babylon (☑22890 25152; Old Harbour; ☺9pm-6am) Gay-friendly masses party pierside next to JackieO'.

Porta (☑22890 27807; Ioanni Voinovich; ☺8pm-4am) Porta's cruisey ambience fills small-scale rooms where things get crowded and close towards midnight.

Ilias Lalaounis   JEWELLERY
(☑22890 22444; www.lalaounis.gr; Polikandrioti 14) Fine pieces from the renowned Greek jewellery artist.

Mykonos Sandals   SHOES
(☑22890 22451; www.mykonos-sandals.gr; Little Venice) Come for the sunset cocktails and stay for the handmade leather sandals, from this company established in 1948.

International Press   BOOKS
(Kambani 5) International newspapers, magazines and books.

ⓘ Information

Mykonos has no tourist office; visit travel agencies instead. There is information online at www.inmykonos.com and www.mykonos.gr.

Alphabank (Matogianni)

Eurobank (Matogianni)

Hospital (☑22890 23994) About 1km along the road to Ano Mera.

Mykonos Accommodation Centre (MAC; ☑22890 23408; www.mykonos-accommodation .com; 1st fl, Enoplon Dynameon 10) Helpful for all things Mykonos (accommodation, guided tours, island info), including gay-related aspects. The website is loaded. Located next door to the Maritime Museum.

Mykonos Trauma Care (☑22890 78549; www.mykonos-orthopedics.com; ☉24hr) Private emergency-care clinic, located close to the hospital.

Police station (☑22890 22716) On the road to the airport.

Around Mykonos

Mykonos is synonomous with parties and beaches. If you want to dip into a bit of culture, rent wheels and cruise the back roads through rocky valleys and small villages. The only other village of any size is **Ano Mera**, which has the simple, peaceful **Tourliani Monastery** (Ano Mera; admission €1; ☉9.30am-1pm & 3.30-7pm) on its taverna-lined square.

◉ Sights

Mykonos' golden-sand beaches in their formerly unspoilt state were the pride of Greece. Now most are jammed with umbrellas and backed by beach bars, but they do make for a hopping scene that draws floods of beachgoers. Moods range from the simply hectic to the outright snobby, and nudity levels vary.

Without your own wheels, catch buses from Hora or caïques from Ornos and Platys Gialos to further beaches. Mykonos Cruises (p333) has a online timetable of its sea-taxi services.

The nearest beaches to Hora were overtaken by the construction of the New Port. That leaves little **Agios Stefanos** (4km north of Hora), within sight of docking cruise ships. There's a tiny strip of sand in town, **Agia Anna**.

About 5km southwest of Hora are family-oriented **Agios Ioannis** (where *Shirley Valentine* was filmed) and **Kapari**. The nearby packed and noisy **Ornos** and the package-holiday resort of **Platys Gialos** have boats for the glitzier beaches to the east. In between these two is **Psarou**, a magnet for the Greek cognoscenti.

About 1km south of Platys Gialos you'll find **Paraga Beach**, which has a small gay section. Party people should head about 1km east to famous **Paradise**, which is not a recognised gay beach but has an action-packed younger scene, a camping resort (www.paradisemykonos.com) and nightlife that doesn't quit. Down a steep access road, **Super Paradise** (aka Plintri or Super P) has a fully gay section (including the JackieO' beach club) and a huge eponymous club.

Mixed and gay-friendly **Elia** is a long, lovely stretch of sand and is the last caïque stop. A few minutes' walk west from here is the secluded **Agrari**.

Further east, **Kalafatis** is a hub for water sports (including diving and windsurfing), and **Lia** has a remote, end-of-the-road feel.

North-coast beaches can be exposed to the *meltemi* (dry northerly wind), but **Panormos** and **Agios Sostis** with their golden sand are fairly sheltered and less busy than the south-coast beaches.

For out-of-the-way beaching you'll need tough wheels to reach the likes of **Fokos** and **Mersini** on the northeast coast.

🏃 Activities

★**Yummy Pedals**   MOUNTAIN BIKING
(☑6972299282, 22890 71883; www.yummypedals .gr; 2hr tour from €35) A world away from the beach bars, multilingual Dimitra offers you guided mountain-biking tours through the back roads of Mykonos. The duration and route is personalised to fit your skill level, but may take in farms, villages and quiet beaches (with swimming and snacking stops). Tours begin and end at Dimitra's family's vineyard, with the option of food and wine. The vineyard is located outside Ano Mera. See the website for driving

directions, or arrange to be picked up from the Ano Mera bus stop.

Dive Adventures
DIVING

(☑22890 26539; www.diveadventures.gr; Paradise Beach; single dive €60, PADI certification €295, snorkelling incl gear €45; ⊘Apr-Oct) A full range of diving courses with multilingual instructors.

Windsurf Centre Mykonos
WINDSURFING

(☑22890 72345; www.pezi-huber.com; Kalafatis Beach; 1hr/1-day windsurf rental €30/80, 1hr private lesson €60; ⊘mid-May–Sep) Windsurf rental and private lessons at Kalafatis Beach.

🛏 Sleeping

Paraga Beach Hostel & Camping
CAMPGROUND, HOSTEL €

(☑22890 25915; www.mycamp.gr; Paraga Beach; camp site per adult/child/tent €10/5/10, dm €25, bungalow per person €35; ⊘May-Sep; @🛜🏊) Beachside budget digs, where options include camping (BYO tent or hire one) and dorms, or bungalows and apartments sleeping up to four (bungalows are basic; pricey apartments have bathroom, air-con and kitchen). Laundry, cooking area, party-atmosphere pool bar, cafeteria and mini-market are also here. Offers port and airport transfers.

San Giorgio Hotel
BOUTIQUE HOTEL €€€

(☑22890 27474; www.sangiorgio-mykonos.com; Paraga Beach; d incl breakfast from €270; ⊘May–mid-Oct; ❄🛜🏊) Let your biggest holiday dilemma be where to recline: by the pool at this luxe, laid-back hotel, or at Paradise Beach (seven minutes' walk) or Paraga Beach (three minutes' walk).

🍴 Eating

Tasos
TAVERNA €€

(☑22890 23002; Paraga Beach; mains €9-22; ⊘lunch & dinner Apr-Oct) Tasos is from the breed of old-school beachfront tavernas: open since 1962, this perennially popular place, bang on Paraga Beach, is relaxed and unpretentious. It serves bountiful classics with an emphasis on grilled meats and seafood.

Hippie Fish
MEDITERRANEAN €€

(☑22890 23547; www.hippiefish-mykonos.com; Agios Ioannis Beach; mains €10-25; ⊘lunch & dinner May-Oct) Part of a glossy expanding complex that now includes a hotel (www.hippiechicmykonos.com), Hippie Fish is a sprawling, all-white restaurant-bar on Agios Ioannis Beach. Linger over Greek and Mediterranean fare, fresh morsels from the sushi bar, or cocktails late into the night.

🍷 Drinking & Nightlife

Clubs are generally open June to September, but July and August is when the scene is most intense. See websites for events and ticket info.

Cavo Paradiso
CLUB

(www.cavoparadiso.gr; Paradise Beach) When dawn gleams just over the horizon, hardcore bar-hoppers move from Hora to Cavo Paradiso at Paradise Beach, the open-air cliff-top megaclub that has featured top international DJs since 1994.

Paradise Club
CLUB

(www.paradiseclubmykonos.com; Paradise Beach) Big-name international DJs headline, and white-on-white decor sets off all that bronzed skin in the island's biggest club.

DELOS
ΔΗΛΟΣ

The Cyclades fulfil their collective name (*kyklos* means circle) by encircling the sacred island of Delos (☑22890 22259; museum & site adult/child €5/free; ⊘8am-8pm Apr-Oct, to 3pm Nov-Mar). The mythical birthplace of twins Apollo and Artemis, splendid Ancient Delos was a shrine turned sacred treasury and commercial centre. This Unesco World Heritage Site is one of the most important archaeological sites in Greece. Cast your imagination wide to transform this sprawling ruin into the magnificent city it once was.

While many significant finds from Delos are in the National Archaeological Museum in Athens, the site's scruffy museum retains an interesting collection, including lions from the Terrace of the Lions (those on the terrace itself are plaster-cast replicas). These proud marble beasts (originally thought to number 16) were offerings from the people of Naxos, presented to Delos in the 7th century BC to guard the sacred area.

The island, just 5km long and 1300m wide, has no permanent population, so it offers a soothing contrast to Mykonos, from where Delos can be visited (though in peak summer, visitors throng to the island). Overnight stays are forbidden (as is swimming) and boat schedules allow a maximum of four hours at Delos. A simple cafe is located by the museum, but it pays to bring water and food. Wear a hat, sunscreen and walking shoes.

The ticket office sells detailed guidebooks, and Mykonos bookshops sell some with reconstructions which are helpful for picturing the ruins as they were in their heyday.

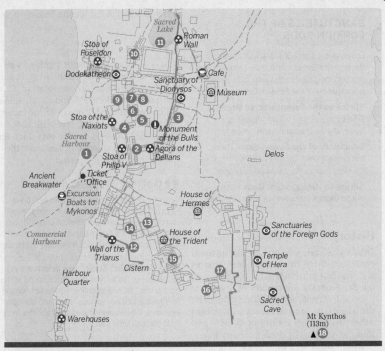

Site Tour
Ancient Delos

START & END BOAT DOCK
LENGTH THREE HOURS

Excursion boats from Mykonos dock on a bay south of the tranquil ❶ **Sacred Harbour**. The narrow spit dividing the two bays was man-made. Follow the arrowed path past the ruins of the ❷ **South Stoa**, or portico, built after the mid-3rd century BC with 28 Doric columns, and used to house shops and workshops. Continue to the ❸ **Sanctuary of Apollo**, northeast of the harbour. The Sacred Way (a wide, paved path used by ancient pilgrims) enters the complex through the ❹ **Propylaia**, to a compound of magnificent temples and treasuries. Three were dedicated to Apollo: ❺ **Temple of the Delians**, ❻ **Temple of the Athenians** and ❼ **Poros Temple**. The Sanctuary also housed the classical ❽ **treasuries** and the ❾ **Artemision**, a sanctuary of Artemis.

North of the Sanctuary is the much photographed ❿ **Terrace of the Lions**. To the northeast, the now-empty ⓫ **Sacred Lake** is where Leto gave birth to Apollo and Artemis.

Next, head south to the ⓬ **Theatre Quarter**, where Delos' wealthiest inhabitants lived in houses surrounding peristyle courtyards, with intricate, colourful mosaics. The most lavish include the ⓭ **House of Dionysos**, named after its mosaic depicting the wine god riding a panther, and the ⓮ **House of Cleopatra**.

The ⓯ **theatre** dates from 300 BC and had a large cistern which supplied much of the town's water.

The ⓰ **House of the Masks** has another mosaic of Dionysos astride a panther between two centaurs. The extraordinary mosaic at the ⓱ **House of the Dolphins** incorporates lions, griffins and dolphins.

⓲ **Mt Kynthos** (113m) rises to the southeast of the harbour. It's worth the steep climb: on clear days there are terrific views of the encircling islands. It also has monuments such as the Sanctuaries of Zeus Kynthios and Athena Kynthia and the Temple of Hera.

History

Delos won early acclaim as the mythical birthplace of the twins Apollo and Artemis and was first inhabited in the 3rd millennium BC. From the 8th century BC it became a shrine to Apollo, and the oldest temples on the island date from this era. The dominant Athenians had full control of Delos – and thus the Aegean – by the 5th century BC.

In 478 BC Athens established an alliance known as the Delian League, which maintained its treasury on Delos. A cynical decree ensured that no one could be born or die on Delos, strengthening Athens' control over the island by expelling the native population.

Delos reached the height of its power in Hellenistic times, becoming one of the three most important religious centres in Greece and a flourishing centre of commerce. Many of its inhabitants were wealthy merchants, mariners and bankers from as far away as Egypt and Syria. They built temples to their homeland gods, but Apollo remained the principal deity.

The Romans made Delos a duty-free port in 167 BC. This brought even greater prosperity, due largely to a lucrative slave market that sold up to 10,000 people a day. During the following century, as ancient religions diminished and trade routes shifted, Delos began a long decline. By the 3rd century AD there was only a small Christian settlement on the island, and in the following centuries the ancient site was a hideout for pirates who looted of many of its antiquities. It wasn't until the Renaissance that its antiquarian value was recognised.

Every now and then fresh discoveries are unearthed: in recent years a gold workshop was uncovered alongside the Terrace of the Lions.

Tours

It pays to tour the site with a guide, to give context to the various neighbourhoods and buildings. Mykonos Accommodation Centre (p339) in Hora (Mykonos) organises multilingual guided tours to Delos (adult/child €40/20) including boat, entrance fee and guide. Licensed guides may tout for business as you disembark the boat; these charge around €10 per person.

ⓘ Getting There & Away

Boats for Delos (return €18, 30 minutes) leave Hora (Mykonos) four times daily in high season starting around 9am, with the last outward boat about 5pm. Boats return between 12.15pm and 8pm. There are fewer boats November to March.

Departure/return times are posted at the **Delos Boat Ticket Kiosk** (www.delostours.gr) at the foot of the jetty at the southern end of the old harbour, as well as online. Buy tickets online or from the kiosk or various travel and transport agencies. When buying tickets, establish which boat you can return on.

PAROS   ΠΑΡΟΣ

POP 13,700

Paros rests nonchalantly in the shadows of the limelight. Long tagged as primarily a ferry hub, its stylish capital, fashionable resort towns and sweet rural villages are all the more charming for their (relative) lack of crowds or tourist kudos. For holidaymakers looking for Mykonos without the hype and the price tag, this might just be the spot. And word is spreading.

Geologically speaking, Paros has long been a Greek star; white marble drawn from the island's interior made the island prosperous from the Early Cycladic period onwards. Most famously, the *Venus de Milo* was carved from Parian marble, as was Napoleon's tomb.

The smaller island of Antiparos, 1km southwest of Paros, is easily reached by car ferry or excursion boat.

ⓘ Getting There & Away

Paros is a major ferry hub for onward travel to other islands in the Aegean. It is well served by regular ferries from Piraeus and by connections to most of the other islands of the Cyclades, and also to Thessaloniki, Crete and the Dodecanese.

There are daily flights from Athens to Paros (€98, 40 minutes) with **Olympic Air** (www.olympicair.com).

ℹ Getting Around

BOAT

Sea taxis leave from the Parikia quay for beaches around Paros. Tickets range from €8 to €15 and are available on board.

BUS

Frequent **KTEL** (🖉 22840 21395; http://ktelparou.gr) buses link Parikia and Naoussa (€1.60) directly. Buses also run from Parikia to east-coast beaches such as Piso Livadi (€2.20), Hrysi Akti (Golden Beach; €2.80) and Dryos (€2.80). Some of these services run via Naoussa, some via Lefkes (€1.60). There are frequent buses to Pounta (for Antiparos; €1.60) and Aliki (€1.60). Tickets can be purchased from machines at the bus terminals, and at kiosks and mini-markets island-wide, or from the driver at a slightly higher rate.

CAR & MOTORCYCLE

There are rental outlets along the waterfront in Parikia and all around the island. In August the minimum cost is about €45 per day for car hire and €20 for a motorbike. A good outfit is **Acropolis** (🖉 22840 21830; www.acropolisparos.com; Waterfront, Parikia).

TAXI

Taxis (🖉 22840 21500) gather beside the roundabout in Parikia. Fares include the airport (€20), Naoussa (€13), Pounta (€12), Lefkes (€14) and Piso Livadi (€22). Add €1 if going from the port. There are extra charges for booking ahead, and for luggage.

Parikia   Παροικιά

POP 6060

For its small size, Parikia packs a punch. Its labyrinthine Old Town is pristine and filled with boutiques, cafes and restaurants. You'll also find a handful of impressive

BOAT SERVICES FROM PAROS

DESTINATION	TIME	FARE	FREQUENCY
Amorgos	3hr 10min-4hr	€19	1 daily
Anafi	4hr 50min	€20.50	2 weekly
Astypalea	4hr 50min	€34.50	5 weekly
Donousa	2¼hr	€14	4 weekly
Folegandros	4½hr	€18	1 weekly
Ios	2¼hr	€16	2-4 daily
Ios*	1-1½hr	€29.50	2-3 daily
Iraklia	2hr	€16	3 weekly
Iraklio*	3¾hr	€69	1 daily
Koufonisia	3hr	€19	3 weekly
Koufonisia*	1hr 20min	€28.50	1 daily
Mykonos	1hr 20min	€16.50	1 daily
Mykonos*	40-50min	€29.50	3 daily
Naxos	45-50min	€10	4-5 daily
Naxos*	30min	€18	3 daily
Piraeus	4-5hr	€33.50	2-5 daily
Piraeus*	2¾hr	€51	1 daily
Rafina	5hr	€30	1 daily
Rafina*	3¼hr	€50	2 daily
Santorini (Thira)	3-3½hr	€20.50	1-2 daily
Santorini (Thira)*	2-2¼hr	€46.50	2-3 daily
Schinousa	2hr 20min	€13	3 weekly
Syros	1½hr	€12	3 weekly
Tinos*	1hr 20min	€28	2 daily

*high-speed services

archaeological sites, a waterfront crammed with tavernas and bars, first-class midrange accommodation, and sandy stretches of beach – particularly popular is Livadia, a short walk north of town.

◉ Sights

Panagia Ekatontapyliani   CHURCH
(www.ekatontapyliani.gr; ⊙8am-9pm) The Panagia Ekatontapyliani, which dates from AD 326, is one of the finest churches in the Cyclades. The building is three distinct church-

Paros & Antiparos

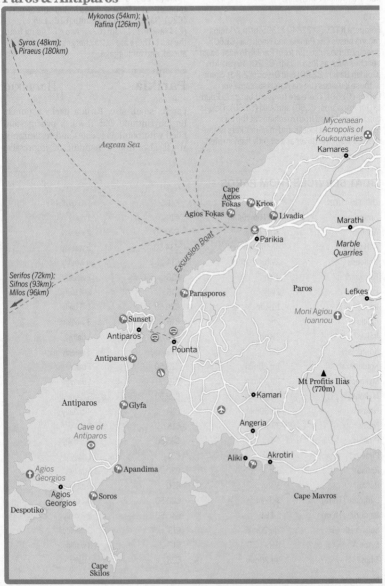

es: Agios Nikolaos, the largest, with superb columns of Parian marble and a carved iconostasis in the east of the compound; the ornate Church of Our Lady; and the ancient Baptistery. The name translates as Our Lady of the Hundred Doors, though this is a wishful rounding-up of a still-impressive

number of doorways. The **Byzantine Museum** (admission €2; ⊙ 9am-2pm & 6-8pm), within the compound, has a collection of icons and other artefacts.

★ **Archaeological Museum**　　MUSEUM
(☑ 22840 21231; admission €2; ⊙ 8am-3pm Tue-Sun) Behind the Panagia Ekatontapyliani, this museum is a cool escape into the island's past. It harbours some marvellous pieces, including a 5th-century-BC Nike on the point of alighting and a 6th-century BC Gorgon also barely in touch with the earth.

Earlier examples of splendid pottery include the bootylicious *Fat Lady of Saliagos*, while a major exhibit is a fragment slab of the 3rd-century-BC Parian Chronicle, which lists the most outstanding personalities and events of ancient Greece. It was discovered in the 17th century. (Two other slabs are in the Ashmolean Museum, in Oxford, England.)

Ancient Cemetery　　RUIN
North along the waterfront is a fenced ancient cemetery dating from the end of the 8th century BC. Excavations in 1983 discovered graves, burial pots and sarcophagi.

Frankish Kastro　　RUIN
Check out the outer walls of this fortress, built by the Venetian Duke Marco Sanudo of Naxos in AD 1260. Built with the stones from ancient buildings that once stood on this site, here you can find remnants from the archaic temples of Athena and an Ionic temple from the 5th century BC.

⏱ Tours

Travel to Paros　　BUS TOUR
(☑ 22840 24245; http://traveltoparos.gr) Opposite the bus terminal, this company books bus tours of Paros (€35), cruises around Antiparos (€50), and full-day excursions to Mykonos and Delos (€45), Santorini (€55), and the beaches of Iraklia and Koufonisia (€40).

Paros Hikes　　HIKING
(☑ 6972288821; www.paroshikes.com; guided walk from €20) Chris guides ecotours to explore the lesser-known sides of Paros and Antiparos, ranging from countryside walks to mountain hiking adventures (with cycling an option too), for 2½ to six hours. Tours can be tailor made, or you can join him for scheduled walks. Upcoming events are outlined on the website, along with route details, departure info and price.

Map labels:

0 ————— 5 km
0 ————— 2.5 miles

Naxos (30km); Ios (57km);
Amorgos (98km);
Small Cyclades (98km);
Santorini (105km);
Astypalea (130km)

Cape Korakas

Moni Agiou Ioannou
Monastiri
Plastira Bay
Kolimbythres
Naoussa

Santa Maria
Lageri
Cape Agias Marias

Ambelas

Kostos

Cape Antikefalos

Marmara　Molos
Prodromos
Moni Agiou Antonios
Marpissa
Piso Livadi
Logaras
Punda
Hrysi Akti
Dryos
Hrysi Akti (Golden Beach)

🛏 Sleeping

Koula Camping
CAMPGROUND €

(📞22840 22081; www.campingkoula.gr; Livadia Beach; camp site per adult/child/tent €8/3/4, tent rental €7; ⊙May-Oct; 🐾) With plenty of trees, and just footsteps from the sea, this is a decent (if ramshackle) place to pitch your tent. It's at the northern end of the Parikia waterfront on Livadia Beach. Free transfers to/from town are available. There's a cafe and minimarket.

★ Angie's Studios
APARTMENT €€

(📞22840 23909; www.angies-studios.gr; Makedonias; d €100; ⊙Apr-Oct; ❋🐾) Just south beyond the Old Town (a short walk to Market St), Angie's is worth seeking out. Spacious, immaculate rooms with flagstone floors and lots of local touches are set within a garden glowing with bougainvillea. Each room has a private balcony and a kitchenette and the staff are warm. Call ahead for pick-up from the dock.

★ Pension Sofia
PENSION €€

(📞22840 22085; www.sofiapension-paros.com; d/tr €100/120; ⊙Apr-Oct; ❋@🐾) A few blocks behind the waterfront, Sofia's verdant garden alone makes it worth the stay. Rooms are immaculate (the owner's artwork hangs in many) and the owners are charming and knowledgable. Breakfast is available for €8;

take it on your balcony or in the garden. Sofia is 400m east of the ferry quay (take the road next to Hotel Stella).

Hotel Argonauta
BOUTIQUE HOTEL €€

(📞22840 21440; www.argonauta.gr; Plateia Mavrogenous; s/d/tr incl breakfast €75/105/125; ⊙Apr-Oct; ❋🐾) In a chichi pocket of town, the Argonauta offers compact rooms and boutique stylings, plus some downright lovely common areas. See the website for details of studios and apartments also available nearby.

Hotel Dina
HOTEL €€

(📞22840 21325; www.hoteldina.com; Agora (Market St); s/d €75/95; ⊙May-Oct; ❋🐾) Smack-bang in the heart of the Old Town, these eight rooms are a find. With whitewashed walls and wrought-iron beds, they are spotless and comfortable. Each room has a small balcony looking over Market St, with shared courtyards and verandahs in the traditional building's centre.

La Selini
GUESTHOUSE €€

(📞22840 23106; www.laselini.com; s/d/tr €50/75/100; ⊙Apr-Oct; ❋🐾) La Selini shines under the care of its owner, North American Lou Ann. A short walk from Livadia Beach, the cheerful complex offers bright, comfy rooms and studios sleeping up to four. Try for a sea view.

Parikia

✖ Eating

Ragoussis
BAKERY €

(Plateia Mavrogenous; ⊗8am-11pm) An ode to deliciousness, this bakery-patisserie has cabinets full of baklava, cake and traditional biscuits, plus perfect beach picnic fodder like sandwiches.

Cafe Distrato
CAFE €

(☑22840 25175; G Gravari; mains €3-10; ⊗8am-midnight) This casual all-day cafe exudes wholesomeness, and is attached to a shop selling local food products. The crowd-pleasing menu lists crêpes, sandwiches, burgers, pastas and salads, plus coffee, cocktails or local wines. Dine outside under a leafy canopy.

★Levantis
MODERN GREEK €€

(☑22840 23613; www.levantisrestaurant.com; Agora (Market St); dishes €13-22; ⊗dinner May-Oct) A vine-covered courtyard and simple, whitewashed interior with splashes of modern art create a polished setting for some of the Cyclades' finest contemporary Greek cuisine. The menu makes for hungry reading – choose from inspired flavour combinations like chicken and pistachio dolmades, slow-braised honey-spiced lamb, and nut tart with aniseed ice cream.

★Ephessus
GREEK €€

(☑22840 22520; www.parosweb.com/ephessus; Livadia Beach; mains €7-15; ⊗lunch & dinner) Sit in the beachfront, lantern-filled garden, then dig into a dish of Greek or Anatolian cuisine from Ephessus' wood-fired oven, and you'll understand why this restaurant is so popular, year-round. Setting, service and food is tops. Try the *manti* (Anatolian ravioli), *peinirli* (traditional pizzas) or kebabs.

Little Green Rocket
INTERNATIONAL €€

(☑22840 27560; www.facebook.com/thelittlegreenrocket; mains €10-15; ⊗lunch & dinner) Fresh and fun waterfront restaurant-bar, with a small but varied menu grabbing influences from all over (yakitori, curry, burritos). It's a good spot for a lazy drink too.

🍷 Drinking & Nightlife

The southwestern waterfront is peppered with bars, popular with both locals and visitors.

Koukoutsi
BAR

(Plateia Mavrogenous; ⊗8am-late) On the edge of the main square, this local hang-out is a gem. Small and lively, with walls covered in posters and wooden benches filled with cushions, this is the place to nibble on mezedhes and sip juices, coffees, beer or a shot of ouzo.

Bebop
CAFE, BAR

(☑22840 28075; ⊗9am-4am) Climb steps up to this cool-cat waterfront spot with no shortage of outdoor areas, including a sunset-primed rooftop terrace. There's a long list of coffee and cocktail options, including a fine sangria. Keep an eye out for live-music events, especially jazz.

Pirate
BAR

(Agora (Market St); ⊗9am-late) Ultracool and cavelike, Pirate is an ideal refuge within the Old Town (with superb drinks, to boot).

ℹ Information

On the waterfront opposite the bus terminal, Travel to Paros (p345) sells ferry tickets, can advise on accommodation and car hire, and has luggage storage. You can also book various tours here.

CYCLADES PARIKIA

Naoussa Ναούσα

POP 3120

Heading north to Naoussa takes you through lush farmland; Naoussa itself has been transformed from a quiet fishing village into an increasingly stylish resort. Perched on the shores of the large Plastira Bay, there are good beaches nearby, excellent restaurants and an ever-expanding number of stylish beachside hotels, cafes and bars. Behind the waterfront is a maze of narrow whitewashed streets.

☉ Sights & Activities

The best beaches in the area are **Kolimbythres**, set among fabulous rock formations, and **Monastiri**, which has some good snorkelling. Low-key **Lageri** is also worth seeking out. **Santa Maria**, on the other side of the eastern headland, is ideal for windsurfing. These beaches can all be reached by road, but caïques go from Naoussa to each of them during July and August.

The town has a couple of low-key, irregularly open museums (showcasing folklore and Byzantine icons), and you can admire the crumbling remains of a 15th-century Venetian *kastro* guarding the port area.

Moraitis Winery

WINERY

(☎ 22840 51350; www.moraitiswines.gr; tastings €5; ☉ 10am-3.30pm Mon-Sat) Pressing grapes since 1910, the Moraitis family has got it down to a fine art. Wander the original stone cellars before sidling up to the bar for a taste of up to a dozen wines. Anything made with the island's indigenous grape, *monemvassia*, is particularly worth a try. The winery is an easy walk southeast of the centre.

Kokou Riding Centre

HORSE RIDING

(☎ 22840 51818; www.kokou.gr) Well-established Kokou has 2½-hour morning rides (€55), venturing into the sea, and 1½-hour evening rides (€35). Pick-up is available from Naoussa's main square for €3.

Tao's Center

MEDITATION

(☎ 22840 28882; www.taos-greece.com; Ambelas; ☉ Apr-Dec) 🌿 Tao's is a wellness retreat and meditation centre located in splendid seclusion on a hill top east of Naoussa. The centre offers courses in meditation, mindfulness, yoga, dance and creativity, as well as massage therapies, all in sympathetic surroundings. You can come for a drop-in class, a massage or a great meal at the excellent pan-Asian restaurant, or sign up for a well-priced long stay (details online). The centre is reached by turning off the main road to Ambelas and then following conspicuous signs along a mainly surfaced track.

Michael Zeppos

BOAT TOUR

(☎ 6947817125; www.mzeppos.gr; day cruise per person from €100) Sailing primarily from Naoussa (and also from Aliki), this company offers full-day sailing itineraries taking in the beaches of Paros, Antiparos and potentially calling at Naxos. There are also sunset and fishing options. See the website for details; prices depend on numbers.

🛏 Sleeping

Katerina Mare

APARTMENT €€

(☎ 22840 51642; www.katerinamare.com; d/tr incl breakfast €130/150, apt from €170; ❄ ☎) In a word: lovely. Light-filled suites are classy and pristine, each with a great view and every convenience, including kitchenette. Service is stellar. It's on a hillside southwest of the town centre, with many accommodation options as its neighbours.

Hotel Kalypso

HOTEL €€

(☎ 22840 51488; www.kalypso.gr; Agii Anargiri Beach; r from €100; ☉ Apr-Oct; ❄ @ ☎) This cheerful older complex has been given a fresh makeover. Inside there's a surprisingly chic lounge and simple, spotless rooms, studios and apartments with colourful touches. Outside is the winner: a sun-lounger-filled garden, right on the beach.

Hotel Galini

HOTEL €€

(☎ 22840 51210; www.hotelgaliniparos.com; d €70-85, tr €95; ☉ year-round; ❄ ☎) Run by a local family for three generations, this spick-and-span hotel has simple, comfortable rooms. Ask for a balcony and a sea view. It's opposite the blue-domed local church, on the main road into town from Parikia. Rooms cost €50 outside July and August.

Lilly Residence

BOUTIQUE HOTEL €€€

(☎ 22840 51377; www.lillyresidence.gr; r incl breakfast from €285; ☉ May-Oct; P ❄ ☎ ☀) Naoussa's most stylish hotel, where stone, wood and wicker combine to great effect and white is the unifying theme. The place is discreetly luxurious (eg Hermès toiletries) and grown-up (no kids under 12). Just back from the water, all 11 suites have sea views, or you can enjoy the eye-candy pool area.

🍴 Eating & Drinking

This town knows how to do waterfront dining. Tables fill every waterfront spot, creating a convivial atmosphere just inches from moored boats. Beyond the harbour, spilling out onto little pebbly 'beaches', is a row of cafes and music bars, with funky sounds and cool lounge decor worthy of Mykonos.

★ **Sousouro** CAFE, BAR €

($\boxed{2}$22840 53113; breakfast €4-6; ◷9am-3am) Occupying a small corner in the Old Town, this cafe is big on flavour. One of the islands' best breakfast menus awaits: super-food smoothies and shakes; a selection of homemade granolas with sheep's-milk yoghurt and thyme honey; and toast topped with smashed avocado or cacao hazelnut butter and banana. At night the wholesomeness makes way for killer cocktails.

Paradosiako SWEETS €

(loukoumadhes €4-5; ◷6pm-midnight) An essential stop for a serve of the doughy balls of goodness known as *loukoumadhes* (Greek doughnuts). It's a self-service operation: add honey, chocolate sauce and/or ice cream.

Glafkos MEDITERRANEAN €€

($\boxed{2}$22840 52100; mains €8-16; ◷lunch & dinner) With tables practically on top of the sea, it's not surprising that this tucked-away place specialises in seafood. Try steamed mussels and grilled calamari, or dig into shrimp *saganaki* or black risotto with cuttlefish – all great paired with local white wine.

★ **Sommaripa Consolato** CAFE, BAR

($\boxed{2}$22840 55233; ◷10am-late) The owner opened this elevated cafe-bar in the former home of his grandparents – how fortuitous that it's right in the hub of Naoussa's small port (above Mario's restaurant), making for great people-watching from the terraces. First-class drinks, snacks and service too.

To Takimi BAR

(Music Cafe; $\boxed{2}$22840 55095) Just south of the main square, this is where locals come to drink beer or ouzo and listen to live music, often played on the traditional string instruments waiting on the walls. Everything from *rembetika* (blues) to rock goes down here.

ℹ **Information**

The bus from Parikia terminates some way inland from the waterfront, where there's a large public car park (most of the Old Town area is pedestrian-only). The Old Town is east of here: to find its heart, take the pedestrian street to the left of Xamilothoris Patisserie.

Erkyna Travel ($\boxed{2}$22840 53180; www. erkynatravel.com) Sells ferry tickets and can help with accommodation, car hire, and ex-

cursions, water sports and boat trips to other islands. It's on the main road into town.

Lefkes Λεύκες

POP 490

Lovely Lefkes clings to a natural amphitheatre amid hills with summits dotted with old windmills. Siesta is taken seriously here and the village has a general air of serenity. Just 9km southeast of Parikia, it was the capital of Paros during the Middle Ages. The village's main attraction is wandering through its pristine alleyways. The **Cathedral of Agia Triada** is an impressive structure with unique bell towers. On the square in front of the cathedral is **Kafeneio tis Marigos** ($\boxed{2}$22840 44014), a delightfully retro cafe serving up mama-made meatballs and cakes.

Around Paros

Down on the southeast coast is the attractive harbour and low-key resort of **Piso Livadi**, with a handsome strip of waterfront tavernas and cafes. There's a small beach and you're within walking distance of a bigger sandy beach at **Logaras**, about 400m south.

Further south, still on the southeast coast, is Paros' top beach, **Hrysi Akti** (Golden Beach), with good sand and several tavernas and domatia. Its closest town, **Dryos**, has a growing number of quality hotels and eateries.

Paros' west coast, around **Pounta**, is the hub for top water-sports activity: a long shallow-water shoreline and perfect sideshore wind conditions make it perfect for all skill levels of kiteboarder or windsurfer.

🏃 **Activities**

Aegean Diving College DIVING

($\boxed{2}$22840 43347; www.aegeandiving.gr; shore dive from €55) At Hrysi Akti (Golden Beach), the expertly run Aegean Diving College offers a range of dives to places of archaeological and ecological interest. Dive courses are also available, plus snorkelling trips (from €40).

Force7 Surf Centre WINDSURFING

($\boxed{2}$22840 41789; www.force7paros.gr) Force7 Surf Centre is a well-run centre on Hrysi Akti (Golden Beach) offering windsurfing courses and rental (including classes for kids), plus kayaking and stand-up paddleboard rentals.

Paros Kite KITESURFING

($\boxed{2}$22840 93018; www.paroskite.gr; 2hr intro €90) At this slick, professionally run complex at

Pounta it's all about the wind: kitesurfing and windsurfing instruction and gear rental are offered, plus there's a surf shop, beach bar-cafe, massage and yoga, and (new for 2015) horse riding. Local accommodation can be arranged.

🛏 Sleeping

Golden Beach Hotel HOTEL €€
(☑22840 41366; www.goldenbeach.gr; Hrysi Akti; d/tr incl breakfast €125/40, 4-person apt €220; ☺Apr–mid-Oct; 🅿🛜) Right on Hrysi Akti (Golden Beach), offering simple, appealing rooms and apartments in pastel colours. More important is what's outside the rooms: a splendid grassy lawn down to the shore, plus restaurant, beach bar and oodles of beachy activities.

ANTIPAROS ΑΝΤΙΠΑΡΟΣ
POP 1211

Antiparos lies dreamily offshore from Paros. As soon as your ferry docks, you feel a distinct slowing down in the pace of things. The main village and port (also called Antiparos) are relaxed. There's a touristy gloss around the waterfront and main street, but the village runs deep inland to quiet squares and alleyways that give way suddenly to open fields. The rest of the island runs to the south of the main settlement through quiet countryside. There are several decent beaches, especially at Glyfa and Soros. There's also a 'secret getaway' factor to the island that puts it on the radar of those who don't like to be disturbed: Euro royalty and A-list rockstars holiday here.

◎ Sights & Activities

Antiparos Town VILLAGE
The main town is well worth a wander. Its long pedestrianised main street is lined with services and a whole lot of stylish boutiques, bars and restaurants. Follow it to the end, to the distinctive, giant plane tree of Plateia Agios Nikolaou. From here, a narrow lane leads to the intriguing remnants of the old Venetian *kastro*, entered through an archway. This old fortified settlement dates from the mid-15th century.

★Cave of Antiparos CAVE
(adult/child €5/2.50; ☺10am-6pm Jul & Aug, to 5pm Jun, to 4pm May & Sep, to 3pm Apr) About 10km south of the port, this huge and atmospheric cave remains impressive despite much looting of stalactites and stalagmites

in the past (check out the ancient graffiti from past visitors; one dates from 1776). Descending the 400-plus steps into the cave can be a dank affair – beware the climb out! To reach the cave, follow the coastal road south until you reach a signed turn-off. A bus runs here from the port (€1.60).

Blue Island Divers DIVING
(☑22840 61767; www.blueisland-divers.gr; single dive from €60, PADI certification from €230) On the northern waterfront is this operator, offering fun dives, PADI courses, and snorkelling trips around the island (€20).

🛏 Sleeping & Eating

Camping Antiparos CAMPGROUND €
(☑22840 61221; www.camping-antiparos.gr; camp site per adult/child/tent €8/4/2; ☺May-Sep) This chilled-out beachside campground is planted with bamboo 'compartments' and cedars. It's 1.5km north of the port (pick-up is available).

Artemis Hotel HOTEL €€
(☑22840 61460; www.artemisantiparos.com; d €80-90; ☺Apr–mid-Oct) The elegant, marble-lined rooms at Artemis (at the far northern end of the harbour) are compact but well priced, and have lovely private terraces (opt for a sea-view room). The common areas are stylishly appealing.

Beach House Antiparos RESORT €€€
(☑22840 64000; http://beachhouseantiparos. com; ste from €220; ☺mid-May–Sep; 🅿🛜) This is a glossy boutique resort on Apandima beach, with a 'beach house' housing nine suites (some family-sized). There's an upmarket, beachside restaurant serving brunch, lunch and dinner, a beach bar and sunbeds, all open to nonguests. From the beach, arrange a massage, charter a boat, or peek in the 'concept store'.

★Captain Pipinos TAVERNA €€
(☑22840 21823; http://captainpipinos.com; mains €6-14, fish by kg; ☺lunch & dinner) In the island's south, and with panoramas of neighbouring isle Despotiko (uninhabited), Captain Pipinos is a gloriously old-school fish taverna on the absolute waterfront. Octopus dishes are a top pick (you'll see them drying), as is anything with fresh fish.

ℹ Information

From the ferry quay go right along the waterfront. The main street, Agora, heads inland just by the Anarghyros Restaurant, and you'll find most services you need, including groceries and banks. To reach the central square turn left at the top of the main street and then right.

There are several tour and travel agencies, including **Oliaris Tours** (☑ 22840 61231; www.antiparostravel.gr) where you can ask about the local bus.

There's info online at www.antiparos.gr.

Getting There & Away

In summer, frequent small passenger boats depart for Antiparos from Parikia (€5), and numerous operators offer day cruises taking in the beaches of both islands, departing from Parikia, Pounta, Aliki and Naoussa.

There's also a regular car ferry that runs from Pounta on the west coast of Paros to Antiparos (one way €1.10, per scooter €1.40, per car €5.90, one or two services hourly, 10 minutes). The first ferry departs from Pounta at 7.15am and the last boat leaves Antiparos at 12.30am.

Getting Around

A bus service runs from the port to the cave, and another services the east-coast beaches as far as Agios Georgios; tickets cost €1.60. The schedule varies with the season; in theory buses run from April to September.

Wheels can be hired from **Aggelos** (☑ 22840 61626), the first office as you come from the ferry quay. Cars start at about €40 per day (high season), scooters €15 and bicycles €5.

NAXOS ΝΑΞΟΣ

POP 12,700

The largest of the Cyclades, Naxos packs a lot of bang for its buck. Its main city of Hora (known also as Naxos) is a web of steep cobbled alleys, filled with the hubbub of tourism and shopping. Yet you needn't travel far to find isolated beaches, atmospheric villages and ancient sites.

It was on Naxos that an ungrateful Theseus is said to have abandoned Ariadne after she helped him escape the Cretan labyrinth. She didn't pine long, and was soon entwined with Dionysos, the god of wine and ecstasy and the island's favourite deity. Naxian wine has long been considered a useful antidote to a broken heart.

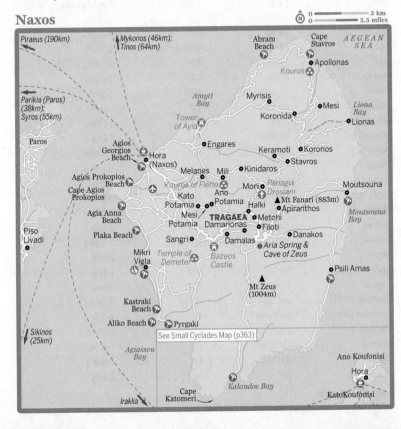

Naxos was a cultural centre of classical Greece and of Byzantium, while Venetian and Frankish influences have left their mark. It is more fertile than most of the other Cyclades islands and produces olives, grapes, figs, citrus fruit, corn and potatoes. Mt Zeus (also known as Mt Zas; 1004m) is the Cyclades' highest peak and is the central focus of the island's interior where you will find such enchanting villages as Halki and Apiranthos.

The island draws outdoor enthusiasts, with kiteboarding off the sandy southern beaches, and traditional footpaths to follow between villages, churches and other sights. Walking guides and maps are available from local bookshops – the Terrain map is excellent, outlining a dozen trails. *Walking in Naxos* by Dieter Graf covers 25 trails with GPS data.

ⓘ Getting There & Away

Like Paros, Naxos is something of a ferry hub of the Cyclades, with a similar number of conventional and fast ferries making regular calls to/from Piraeus, plus links to/from the mainland port of Rafina via the northern Cyclades.

BOAT SERVICES FROM NAXOS

DESTINATION	TIME	FARE	FREQUENCY
Amorgos	2-6hr	€11.50	2-5 daily
Amorgos*	1-1½hr	€24	2 daily
Anafi	3¾hr	€19.50	2 weekly
Astypalea	3¾hr	€34.50	5 weekly
Donousa	1-4hr	€7.50	7 weekly (note: not daily)
Folegandros	3hr 10min	€17	1 weekly
Folegandros*	2½-4hr	€49	6 weekly
Ios	1-2hr	€14.50	1-2 daily
Ios*	50min	€25	1-2 daily
Iraklia	1-1½hr	€7	1-2 daily
Iraklio*	3hr 40min	€70	1 daily
Kimolos	4hr 40min	€17	1 weekly
Koufonisia	2½hr	€8	1-2 daily
Koufonisia*	40-50min	€19	1-2 daily
Milos	6hr	€21	1 weekly
Milos*	3½-5½hr	€59.50	6 weekly
Mykonos	2½hr	€18.50	1 daily
Mykonos*	40min-1½hr	€29.50	4-5 daily
Paros	50min	€10	4-5 daily
Paros*	30min	€16	3 daily
Piraeus	5¼hr	€34.50	2-4 daily
Piraeus*	3½hr	€57.50	2 daily
Rafina	6hr	€32	1 daily
Rafina*	4hr	€52	2 daily
Santorini (Thira)	2hr	€19.50	1-2 daily
Santorini (Thira)*	1hr 35min	€38.50	4-5 daily
Schinousa	1¼-2hr	€7	1-2 daily
Sikinos	2hr 20min	€13	1 weekly
Syros	3h 10min	€15	1 weekly
Tinos*	2hr	€29	2 daily

* high-speed services
Note: journey times vary with vessel type and routing.

There are daily flights to/from Athens (€100, 45 minutes) with **Olympic Air** (www.olympicair.com).

ℹ Getting Around

TO/FROM THE AIRPORT
The airport is 3km south of Hora. There's no shuttle bus, but buses to Agios Prokopios Beach and Agia Anna pass close by. A taxi costs €10 to €15 depending on the amount of luggage you have, the time of day and if booked.

BUS
Frequent buses run to Agios Prokopios Beach (€1.60) and Agia Anna (€1.60) from Hora. Seven buses daily serve Filoti (€2.30) via Halki (€2); five serve Apiranthos (€3.10) via Filoti and Halki; and at least two serve Apollonas (€6.20), Pyrgaki (€2.30) and Melanes (€1.60). There are less frequent departures to other villages.

Buses leave from the end of the ferry quay in Hora; timetables are posted outside the **bus information office** (☑ 22850 22291; www.naxosdestinations.com; Harbour), diagonally left and across the road from the bus stop. You have to buy tickets from the office or from the machine outside (not from the bus driver).

CAR & MOTORCYCLE
August rates for hire cars range from about €45 to €65 per day, and quad bikes from €30. There are a number of rental agencies along Hora's waterfront; try **Rental Center** (☑ 22850 23395; www.rentalcenter.com.gr; Plateia Evripeou), **Auto Tour** (☑ 22850 25480; www.naxosrentacar.com) or **Fun Car** (☑ 22850 26084; www.funcarnaxos.com).

TAXI
Due to its large size, most visitors to Naxos rely on buses or their own wheels to travel around. **Taxis** (☑ 22850 22444) are an option for shorter trips (eg Hora to Agios Prokopios Beach or Agia Anna for around €10). Taxis cluster at the port, or you can call one.

Hora (Naxos) Χώρα (Νάξος)
POP 6730

Hora has the colour and bustle you'd expect of the island's port and capital. Settled on the west coast, the old town is a tangle of steep footpaths and is divided into two historic Venetian neighbourhoods: Bourgos, where the Greeks lived, and the hill-top Kastro, where the Roman Catholics lived.

Despite being fairly large, Hora can still be easily managed on foot. It's almost impossible not to get lost in the old town, however, and maps are of little use.

◉ Sights

★ Kastro   AREA
The most alluring part of Hora is the 13th-century residential neighbourhood of Kastro, which Marco Sanudo made the capital of his duchy in 1207. Located behind the waterfront, its narrow alleyways scramble up to its spectacular hilltop location. Several Venetian mansions survive in the centre of Kastro, and you can see the remnants of Sanudo's castle, the **Tower of Sanoudos**, which was once surrounded by marble balconies. Take a stroll around the chapel-dotted Kastro during siesta to experience its hushed, timeless atmosphere. If you lose your bearings (almost inevitable), remember that roads that go up eventually lead to Kastro and roads heading downwards will take you back to the sea. To see the **Bourgos** area of the old town, head into the winding backstreets behind the northern end of Paralia.

★ Temple of Apollo   ARCHAEOLOGICAL SITE
(The Portara) FREE From Naxos Town harbour, a causeway leads to the Palatia islet and the striking, unfinished Temple of Apollo (also known as the Portara, or 'Doorway'), Naxos' most famous landmark. Simply two marble columns with a crowning lintel, it makes an arresting sight, and people gather at sunset for splendid views.

Agios Georgios Beach   BEACH
Conveniently just south of the waterfront is sandy Agios Georgios, Naxos' town beach. It's backed by hotels and tavernas at the town end (where it can get crowded), but it runs for some way to the south where you can spread out a little. Its shallow waters make it great for families.

Della Rocca-Barozzi Venetian Museum   MUSEUM
(☑ 22850 22387; www.naxosfestival.com; admission €5; ◐10am-10pm) This atmospheric museum is in a handsome old tower house of the 13th century. If it feels as if someone still lives here but has just stepped out, that's because it's true; the owners (direct descendants of the original Italian aristocrat owners) continue to live here a few months each winter. Wander through their rooms to see how the original owners lived, what they wore and how they furnished their rooms. Guiding is often possible (or self-guiding). The museum is within the Kastro ramparts by the northwest gate. There are changing art exhibitions in the vaults. Concerts and other events are often staged in the museum and its grounds.

MARCO SIMONI/ROBERT HARDING / GETTY IMAGES ©

1. Ancient Delos (p340)
Statues and temple abound on the sacred island.

2. Oia (p386)
A stunning Cycladic village on the slope of the caldera in Santorini (Thira).

3. Moni Hozoviotissis (p372)
The dazzling white monastery is perched on the cliffs on Amorgos.

4. Kleftiko (p399)
Tour boats cruise the beaches and coves of southwest Milos.

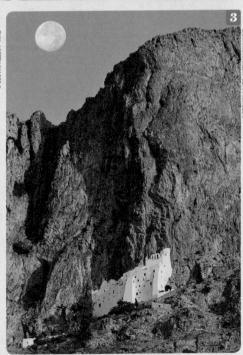

3

Hora (Naxos)

0 — 200 m
0 — 0.1 miles

Temple of
Apollo (250m)

Grotta
Beach

*Amyti
Bay*

7 ✈ Mitropoleos
5 🏛 *Plateia
Mitropolis*
Kondyli

Adriani Hotel (130m);
Hotel Grotta (200m);
Engares (8km);
Apollonas (34km)

19 ✕ 15
4 🏛 *Agiou*
23
*Plateia
Mandilara*
22
BOURGOS

Iosif

24 🏛
Apollonos

9 📇

18 ✕ 3 🏛
26 🔒

Express Scopelitis Ferry
to Small Cyclades
& Amorgos

KASTRO

Kazantzaki

6 ⊚
2 🏛

Delaroca

Neofytou

20 📇

16 ✕

21 📇

27
8 🔒
*Plateia
Pigadakia*

13 📇
Dionyssou

25 🔒
Papavasiliou

Exarhopoulou

Prantouna

Alexinoros

Halki (15km);
Filoti (19km);
Apiranthos (26km)

*AEGEAN
SEA*

P

Protopapadaki (Paralia)

P

Agios Georgios

*Plateia Evripeou
(Main Square)*

Cemetery

17 ✕

Paparrigopoulou

Town
Hall

Odos Komiakis

✉

10 🏛

Ariadnis

12 🏛

11 🏛

1 🏠

*Ippokampos
Beachfront
Hotel (50m)*

Agiou Arseniou

14 ✕

Flisvos Sport Club
(1.2km)

Folk Museum Collection   MUSEUM

(📞 22850 25561; www.naxosfolkmuseum.com; Old Market St; admission €3; ⊙10am-2pm & 7-10pm) This small but well-curated collection gives a digestible account of elements that make Naxos' history special: succinct displays cover farming, bee keeping, weaving, bread-making, winemaking and cheese production. It's a privately owned collection and well worth a stop.

Archaeological Museum   MUSEUM

(📞22850 22725; Kastro; adult/child €3/free; ⊙8.30am-3pm Tue-Sun) This museum in the Kastro is in the former Jesuit school where novelist Nikos Kazantzakis was briefly a pupil. It's slightly musty but contains fascinating finds from the Ionic and Doric eras, and some splendid Early Cycladic marble figurines.

Mitropolis Museum   MUSEUM

(📞22850 24151; Plateia Mitropolis; ⊙8.30am-3pm Tue-Sun) FREE Behind the northern end of the waterfront are several churches and chapels, as well as this museum. It features fragments of a Mycenaean city of the 13th to 11th centuries BC that was abandoned because of the threat of flooding by the sea. Glass panels underfoot reveal ancient foundations.

🏃 Activities

Flisvos Sport Club   WINDSURFING

(📞22850 24308; www.flisvos-sportclub.com; Agios Georgios Beach) Well-organised beach club offers a range of windsurfing courses (one-hour private lesson from €40), catama-ran sailing (one-hour rental from €40) and mountain-bike rental (from €10 per day). It has a cool cafe and accommodation, plus beach volleyball, a fitness centre and yoga.

★Naxos Bike   CYCLING

(📞22850 26612; www.naxosbikes.com; bike hire per day from €10) Get all of your equipment here, from trekking bikes to children's seats. Local mountain-biking expert Giannis can set you up with maps to get you out exploring, plus he leads three-hour tours (per person €30, minimum two people).

Naxos Horse Riding   HORSE RIDING

(📞6948809142; www.naxoshorseriding.com; 2/3hr ride €45/55; ⊙Mon-Sat) Organises daily morning, afternoon and evening (sunset) horse rides inland and on beaches. Staff can arrange pick-up and return to and from the stables. Beginners, young children and advanced riders are all catered for.

🕮 Tours

Naxos Tours   TOUR

(📞22850 24000; www.naxostours.net; island bus tour adult/child €30/15; ⊙8am-10pm) Call into this agency on the waterfront to find out about its array of guided tours and excursions, including an island tour by bus, guided walks and daily cruises. There are frequent excursion boats to Delos and Mykonos (adult/child €45/20), Santorini (€55/30), and Iraklia and Koufonisia (€40/20), plus sailing explorations of various parts of Naxos.

Hora (Naxos)

🛏 Sleeping

Hora has plenty of accommodation (the majority open year-round), including numerous options backing the town beach, Agios Georgios. If you settle for an offer at the port, establish with certainty the true distance of the rooms from the town centre. In high season there may be booths on the quay dispensing information about hotels and rooms. The best camping grounds are at the beaches south of Hora (Agia Anna and Plaka); minibuses meet these grounds meet the ferries.

Despina's Rooms PENSION €

(☏22850 22356; www.despinarooms.gr; Kastro; d €50; ❉🖥) Despina has been renting simple, comfy rooms for over 50 years, and they're a steal. Tucked away in the heart of the Kastro (reached with a climb), some have sea views. Rooms on the roof terrace are popular despite being smaller. There's a communal kitchen.

Hotel Grotta HOTEL €€

(☏22850 22215; www.hotelgrotta.gr; off Kontoleontos; d incl breakfast €110-125; ❉🖥) Located on high ground overlooking the Kastro and main town, this excellent hotel has immaculate rooms, great sea views from the front, spacious public areas and a cool indoor Jacuzzi area. It's made even better by the cheerful, attentive atmosphere.

Adriani Hotel HOTEL €€

(☏22850 23079; www.adriani.gr; Kontoleontos; d incl breakfast €120-160; ❉🖥) This lovely hotel on the northeastern edge of town has fresh, well-equipped rooms. The best are at the back, where it's quieter; the ground-floor rooms have delightful whitewashed patios. Rooms at the top share a spacious verandah with views of the old town. Breakfast is a stellar spread.

Hotel Galini HOTEL €€

(☏22850 22114; www.hotelgalini.com; d incl breakfast €90; ❉🖥) A nautical theme lends this super friendly place loads of character. Updated, spacious rooms have small balconies and wrought-iron beds, plus great decor creatively fashioned from seashells and driftwood. The location is first-rate – close to the old town and the beach – and breakfast is hearty.

Ippokampos Beachfront Hotel BOUTIQUE HOTEL €€

(☏22850 24648; www.ippokampos-naxos.com; Agios Georgios Beach; r incl breakfast €80-130; ☉mid-Apr–mid-Nov) Part of a stylish all-white beachfront complex that includes a restaurant-bar, this nine-room hotel offers rooms kitted out with a dash of panache. Cheaper economy rooms are smaller. All share a fab terrace.

Xenia Hotel HOTEL €€

(☏22850 25068; www.hotel-xenia.gr; Plateia Pigadakia; d incl breakfast €90-120; ❉🖥) Sleek and minimalist, this hotel (built 2012) is right in the old-town scene, close to everything. Balconies overlook the bustle of the streets but thick glass keeps the noise out when you decide to call it a night.

Hotel Glaros BOUTIQUE HOTEL €€€

(☏22850 23101; www.hotelglaros.com; Agios Georgios Beach; d €140-165; ☉Apr-Oct; ❉@🖥) Edgy yet homey, simple yet plush, this well-run and immaculate 13-room hotel has a seaside feel in its boutique fit-out. Service is thoughtful, there's an indoor Jacuzzi, the beach is only a few steps away, and it's adults only. Breakfast is €10.

Nissaki Beach Hotel HOTEL €€€

(☏22850 25710; www.nissaki-beach.com; Agios Georgios Beach; d incl breakfast from €220; ❉🖥🏊) Hard to beat on the island for luxury and locale, with a seaside restaurant and gorgeous pool area, plus elegant rooms.

🍴 Eating

Naxos town has fantastic dining. For the freshest seafood, head to the tavernas on the waterfront where the fishers hang out, and sample their catch. Naxian cheeses, sausages and potatoes are also well worth tasting.

★ Maro GREEK €

(☏22850 25113; mains €4-12; ☉lunch & dinner) There's no sea view here, or old-town romance, but the locals don't care. They're too busy tucking into mammoth portions of delicious, good-value local food (including lots of specialities from the village of Apiranthos). The zucchini balls (fritters, really) are tasty, the moussaka enormous. It's just south of Plateia Evripeou.

Anna's Garden Café CAFE €

(☏22850 26774; http://annasorganicnaxos.blogspot.com; Paparrigopoulou; dishes €5-10; ☉9am-2pm & 6-9pm May-Sep; 🍴🚻) Entirely earthy feeling and 100% organic, Anna's creates a lunchtime dish of the day, driven by local produce that's in season. Breakfasts are good: think homemade muesli and yoghurt, spelt bread or omelettes. Anna's also supplies picnic baskets if ordered a day in advance.

L'Osteria
ITALIAN €€

(☑22850 24080; www.osterianaxos.com; mains €10-14; ⊗7pm-midnight) This authentic Italian eatery is tucked away in a small alley uphill from the harbour, beneath the Kastro walls. Grab a table in the cute courtyard and prepare to be impressed: the authentic, appetising menu changes daily, but there's also an unchanging list of bruschetta, salads and delectable antipasti.

Meze 2
SEAFOOD €€

(☑22850 26401; mains €6-15; ⊗lunch & dinner) It would be easy to dismiss this waterfront restaurant at the harbour as a tourist trap, but don't. Its Cretan and Naxian menu and fantastic service make it stand out from the bunch. The seafood is superb – try squid stuffed with local cheese, grilled sardines, or mussels in ouzo and garlic. There is another Meze at Plaka Beach during July and August.

Labyrinth
GREEK €€

(☑22850 22253; mains €9-17; ⊗lunch & dinner) It's a toss-up as to which is more welcoming here: the warm interior or the private, pretty courtyard. Munch through marinated vegies with grilled *manouri* (soft cheese from the north), swordfish with herbs, or seafood risotto with ouzo sauce. The name is apt: it's signed, but easiest to find if you enter the winding alleys from the north.

O Apostolis
GREEK €€

(☑22850 26777; Old Market St; mains €8-15; ⊗lunch & dinner) Right at the heart of labyrinthine Bourgos, O Apostolis serves up tasty dishes in its pretty flagstone coutyard. The *kleftiko* (lamb in filo pastry), with sautéed vegetables and feta cheese, is delicious.

🍸 Drinking & Nightlife

There are a few large, louder clubs at the southern end of the waterfront.

520
BAR

(☑6976251135; ⊗9am-late) With a deck overlooking the harbour, this cool, comfortable bar whips up the most divine cocktails. Read a newspaper or party – it's all possible in this chic, cushioned interior.

La Vigne
WINE BAR

(☑22850 27199; www.lavignenaxos.com; ⊗7pm-1am) For a relaxed take on Naxian nightlife, head for this cheerful wine bar just behind Plateia Mandilara. It's run by two French expats who know more than a thing or two about fine wines and good conversation. Excellent fusion food too.

Naxos Cafe
BAR

(☑22850 26343; Old Market St; ⊗8pm-2am) If you want to drink but don't fancy the club scene, here's your answer. This atmospheric, traditional bar is small and candlelit and spills into the cobbled Bourgos street. Drink Naxian wine with the locals.

Citron Cafe
CAFE

(Protopapadaki; ⊗8am-late) You can begin your day here, with coffee and a harbour view, and end it with a glass of local wine or *kitron* (liqueur made from the leaves of the citron tree) from Halki's distillery. Check out the *kitron*-based cocktails (€6) for local flavour.

DaCosta
CLUB

(☑6975939104) Right behind the port police, this sleek club brings guest DJs from Athens to play dance music into the wee hours. All white and wood and chic, it has a loungey feel which gives you somewhere to relax while you contemplate the well-stocked bar.

☆ Entertainment

★ Della Rocca-Barozzi Venetian Museum
LIVE MUSIC

(☑22850 22387; www.naxosfestival.com; Kastro; event admission €15-20; ⊗8pm Apr-Oct) Special evening cultural events are held at the museum, almost nightly in summer. Posters around town advertise what's on the horizon. It may be traditional music and dance concerts, classical piano recitals, bouzouki, or jazz and blues. There may even be screenings of *Zorba the Greek*.

🛍 Shopping

Papyrus
BOOKS

(☑22850 23039) What began as a box of books left by a traveller has turned into a shockingly organised collection of over 10,000 secondhand books, covering multiple languages and genres. It's uphill from the port, behind Meze 2.

Kiriakos Tziblakis
FOOD & DRINK

(Papavasiliou) The pungent aromas will bowl you over as soon as you get through the door of this colourful wonderland, a family store dating from 1938. It's where locals come to buy bulk spices, olives, honey and cheese, and it's crammed with a photogenic jumble of local produce and goods, from pots to brushes, soaps to *raki* (Cretan firewater).

Zoom
BOOKS

(Paralia) A large, well-stocked newsagent and bookshop that has most international newspapers the day after publication and a great best collection of postcards.

ⓘ Information

There's no official tourist office on Naxos. Travel agencies can deal with most queries. Handy online resources include www.naxos.gr.

Alpha Bank (cnr Paralia & Papavasiliou) Has an ATM.

Hospital (☏ 22850 23550; Prantouna) On the eastern edge of town.

National Bank of Greece (Paralia) Has an ATM.

Naxos Tours (☏ 22850 24000; www.naxos-tours.net; Paralia; ☺ 8am-10pm) Sells ferry tickets and organises accommodation, excursions and car hire.

Police station (☏ 22850 22100; Paparrigopoulou) Southeast of Plateia Evripeou.

Zas Travel (☏ 22850 23330; www.zastravel.com; ☺ 9am-9pm) Sells ferry tickets and organises accommodation, tours and car hire. Shorter hours in winter. On the harbourfront.

Around Naxos

Southwest Beaches

Beaches south of Agios Georgios (Hora's town beach) include beautiful **Agios Prokopios**, which is sandy and shallow and lies in a sheltered bay to the south of the headland of Cape Mougkri. It merges with Agia Anna, a stretch of shining white sand, quite narrow but long enough to feel uncrowded towards its southern end. Development is fairly solid at Prokopios and the northern end of Agia Anna.

Sandy beaches continue as far as Pyrgaki, passing the beautiful turquoise waters of the long, dreamy **Plaka Beach** and gorgeous sandy bays punctuated with rocky outcrops. You'll find plenty of restaurants, rooms and bus stops along this stretch – it's an idyllic place for a chilled-out beach stay. **Maragas Beach Camping** (☏ 22850 42552; www.maragascamping.gr; Agia Anna Beach; campsites per adult/tent €9/2, d/studio from €40/€60) has a good set-up across from a long sandy strand south of Agia Anna: camping, studios and rooms, a supermarket and a taverna. There's a regular bus from Hora that stops out front.

At **Mikri Vigla** (http://mikrivigla.com), golden granite slabs and boulders divide the beach into two. This beach is becoming an increasingly big fish on the kitesurfing scene, with reliable wind conditions. **Flisvos Kite Centre** (☏ 6945457407; www.flisvos-kitescentre.com) offers kite- and windsurfing classes and rents equipment to certified surfers. You can stay next door at **Orkos Beach Hotel** (☏ 22850 75194; www.orkosbeach.gr; s/d/apt incl breakfast €75/105/166; ☺ mid-May-Sep; ✳❃✿), where rooms are clean and comfy but will hardly see you as you'll be too busy on the beach.

TRAGAEA & MT ZEUS

Naxos' lovely inland Tragaea (Τραγαία) region is a vast plain of olive groves and unspoilt villages harbouring numerous little Byzantine churches. It rests beneath the central mountains, with the Cyclades' highest peak, Mt Zeus (1004m; also known as Mt Zas), dominating.

Filoti, on the slopes of Mt Zeus, is the region's largest village. From Filoti, you can reach the **Cave of Zeus**, a large natural cavern at the foot of a cliff on the slopes of Mt Zeus. There's a junction signposted to Aria Spring and Zas Cave, about 800m south of Filoti. If travelling by bus, ask to be dropped off here.

The side road ends after 1.2km. From the road-end parking, follow a walled path past **Aria Spring**, a verdant fountain and picnic area, and on to a rough track uphill to reach the cave; it's about a 20-minute walk.

The path leads steeply from here to the **summit of Zeus**. From beyond the fountain area, it's a steep hike of about an hour, with loose rock to contend with.

An alternative (and easier option) to reach the summit – or an option for the descent if you hike up via the cave – is to walk from the little chapel of **Agia Marina**, found en route to the village of Danakos. You can walk this route – Filoti to Agia Marina to the summit – on waymarked track Number 2 in about two hours (one way). It begins next to the Platanos tavern on Filoti's square.

Either route is no mere stroll so it's essential to have good walking shoes, water and sunscreen.

Halki   Χάλκη

To visit Naxos and not visit Halki would be a crime. This historic village is a vivid reflection of historic Naxos, with the handsome facades of old villas and tower houses, a legacy of its wealthy past as the island's long-ago capital. Today it's home to a fascinating small collection of shops and galleries, drawing artists and culinary wizards. Halki lies at the heart of the Tragaea mountainous region, about 20 minutes' drive (15km) from Hora.

The main road skirts Halki, with parking areas near the entry (from Hora) and exit of town (the latter by the schoolyard). Pedestrian lanes lead off the main road to the picturesque square at the heart of Halki.

Paths radiate from Halki through peaceful olive groves and flower-filled meadows. The atmospheric 11th-century **Church of St Georgios Diasorites** lies a short distance to the north of the village. It contains some splendid frescoes.

⊙ Sights

Fish & Olive   GALLERY
(www.fish-olive-creations.com;   ⊙ May–mid-Oct) This gallery displays the exquisite work of Naxian potter Katharina Bolesch and her partner, artist and craftsman Alexander Reichardt. Each piece of work reflects ancient Mediterranean themes of fish and olives, motifs that frame the edges of shining plates, tumble down the sides of elegant jugs and bowls and dart across platters. The artists' work has been exhibited both nationally and internationally, at the UN Headquarters in New York and the Design Museum of Helsinki. The gallery also hosts exhibitions by other local and international artists. There's a boutique selling their works a few metres from the gallery.

Phos Gallery   GALLERY
(✆ 22850 31118; www.phosgallery.gr; ⊙ May-Oct) See the island through the lens of talented photographer Dimitris Gavalas. Stunning landscapes – most of Naxos – grace the walls of this gallery, along with a handful of conceptual prints.

✖ Eating

Giannis Taverna   TAVERNA €
(✆ 22850 31214; dishes €5-12; ⊙ lunch & dinner) With tables filling Halki's pretty central square, Giannis is well known for traditional fare. Try moussaka, pork souvlaki, savoury pies or village sausage.

Dolce Vita   BAKERY, CAFE €
(✆ 6981467240; snacks €3-7; ⊙ breakfast, lunch & dinner) Cool and inviting with dark wood and a gramophone daring to be wound, this is the place to lounge over homemade baking, coffees and ice creams.

Il Basilico   ITALIAN €€
(✆ 22859 31140; mains €10-25; ⊙ dinner Jun-Sep) Near the entrance to Halki coming from Hora, this lively restaurant offers an excellent changing menu and sources ingredients daily. The garden patio and colourful tiles add to the atmosphere (as do the well-sourced Italian wines).

Panagia Drosiani   Παναγία Δροσιανή

Located 2.5km north of Halki, just below Moni, the small, peaceful **Panagia Drosiani** (donations appreciated; ⊙ 10am-7pm May–mid-Oct) is among the oldest and most revered churches in Greece. Inside is a series of cave-like chapels. In the darkest chapels, monks and nuns secretly taught Greek language and religion to local children during the Turkish occupation. Several frescoes still grace the walls and date from the 7th century. Look for the depiction of Mary in the eastern chapter; the clarity and expression is incredible.

Sangri   Σαγκρί

Temple of Demeter   TEMPLE
(Dimitra's Temple; ✆ 22850 22725; ⊙ site 24hr, museum 9am-2.30pm Tue-Sun) About 1.5km south of Sangri is the impressive 6th-century-BC Temple of Demeter. The ruins and reconstructions are not large, but they are historically fascinating. There's also a good site museum with some fine reconstructions of temple features. Signs point the way from Sangri.

Bazeos Tower   TOWER
(✆ 22850 31402; www.bazeostower.gr) The handsome Bazeos Tower stands prominently in the landscape about 2km east of the village of Sangri. It was built in its original form as a monastery during the 17th century, and was later bought by the Bazeos family, whose modern descendants have refurbished the building with skill and imagination.

The castle now functions as a cultural centre and stages art exhibitions and the annual Naxos Festival in July and August, when concerts, plays and literary readings are held.

LOCAL LIQUEUR

The citron fruit (*Citrus medica*) looks like a very large, lumpy lemon and is barely edible in its raw state. Its rind is flavoursome when preserved in syrup, however, and *kitron*, a strong liqueur made from citron leaves, has been a hallmark of Naxos since the late 19th century.

Leaves are collected from October to February, dried, dampened and distilled up to three times with water and sugar. Dye is then added to mark its strength: yellow is the strongest and green is the lightest and sweetest. Clear is somewhere in the middle.

To sample all three, try Citron Cafe (p359) in Hora or visit **Vallindras Distillery** (☑ 22850 31220; ⊙ 10am-10pm Jul & Aug, to 6pm May-Jun & Sep-Oct) on Halki's main square, which has been distilling the liqueur in the same way since 1896, passing from one generation to the next. It produces up to 20,000L a year but no longer exports, making the liqueur hard to find outside Naxos. While the exact recipe is top secret, visitors can taste it and stock up on supplies.

Melanes   Μέλανες

East of Hora, the area between Melanes and Kinidaros has been the island's marble quarry since ancient times. Marble is still collected from this region and you'll see sides of the mountains sliced open and looking like huge slabs of feta.

Kouros of Flerio   MONUMENT

In the green valley of Flerio, near Mili, is an area of ancient marble-working and there remain two examples of a *kouros* (youth) – large marble statues of the 6th and 7th centuries BC. Each *kouros* measures about 5.5m and both are in a broken state (the theory being that they were damaged during transportation or were simply left unfinished by dissatisfied sculptors). Despite the area having interpretive boards, the *kouroi* are not particularly easy to find. (The one at Apollonas in the island's north is bigger and more impressive.) The first *kouros* you come to is lying on its back under a tree; its sheer size and the absurdness of it just being left there takes you by surprise. The second is on a hillside about 800m walk past the first.

Eggares Olive Press   MUSEUM

(☑ 22850 62021; www.olivemuseum.com; ⊙ 9am-7pm Apr-Sep) **FREE** From Melanes (or Hora), a worthy side trip is to this sweet set-up in the village of Engares. A guide explains the workings of this small olive press (in operation from 1850 to 1960), and there are free tastings of olive-based products. The store here sells oil, pastes, soaps and unguents, plus cake and coffee.

Apiranthos   Απείρανθος

Apiranthos seems to grow out of the stony flanks of the rugged Mt Fanari (883m), about 25km east of Hora (or 10 winding kilometres from Halki). The village's unadorned stone houses and marble-paved streets reflect a rugged individualism that is matched by the villagers themselves. Many of them are descendants of refugees who migrated from Crete, and today the village's distinctive form of the Greek language has echoes of the 'Great Island'. Apiranthos people have always been noted for their spirited politics and populism and the village has produced a remarkable number of academics. These days, the village is peppered with wonderful, quirky shops, galleries and cafes, and it's a lovely place to spend an afternoon.

If you're keen, there are signs to a handful of small local museums covering folklore, natural history, geology, archaeology and fine art, but hours are erratic at best. Better to meander and explore. Check out the **Apiranthos Women's Association**, a small shop selling handmade embroidery and traditional woven goods and run entirely by local women who sit and stitch while you browse.

✖ Eating

Taverna O Platanos   GREEK €

(☑ 22850 61192; mains €6-13; ⊙ lunch & dinner) Beneath the shade of its namesake plane tree, this lively family restaurant serves up everything from yoghurt and homemade cheese to grilled local meat. Try the hearty traditional dish of 'rosto' pork in tomato sauce. Pop in to the owner's neighbouring store, an old-world emporium of local produce.

Lefteris   GREEK €€

(☑ 22850 61333; www.stoulefteri.gr; mains €10-22; ⊙ lunch & dinner May-Oct) With a deck taking in a phenomenal view, this charming, well-regarded place has the look and feel of an old country kitchen. The short menu hones in on local cheeses and grilled meats – try lamb, steak or a burger stuffed with local cheese and tomato.

The North

Heading north from the mountains inland, the roads wind and twist like spaghetti, eventually taking you to the scrappy seaside village of **Apollonas**. In an ancient quarry on the hillside above the village is a collosal 7th-century-BC **kouros**, much larger and easier to find than the kouroi at Melanes. Follow the small signs to get here. Apollonas' beach isn't great but its seafood is. Tavernas line the waterfront and serve the freshest of fish.

A worthy side trip is to **Lionas**, where a scenic 8km drive past old emery mines leads you to a lovely stony beach and a couple of tavernas. Here, **Delfinaki** (☏ 22850 51290; www.delfinaki.gr; Lionas) is super-friendly, serving up great home cooking and farm-fresh ingredients. Vassiliki, the hostess, sells homemade jams, 'spoon sweets' and wines.

With your own transport you can return to Hora via the northwest-coast road, passing through wild and sparsely populated country with awe-inspiring sea views. En route, stop for a look at the **Tower of Ayia**, the magestic ruins of a castle with a spectacular ocean backdrop.

SMALL CYCLADES
ΜΙΚΡΕΣ ΚΥΚΛΑΔΕΣ

The tiny islands that lie between Naxos and Amorgos are like miniature outposts of calm. In the days of antiquity, all were densely populated, revealed by the large number of ancient graves that have been uncovered. During the Middle Ages, only wild goats and even wilder pirates inhabited these islands. Post-independence, intrepid souls from Naxos and Amorgos recolonised the Small Cyclades, and today four have permanent populations – Donousa, Ano Koufonisi, Iraklia and Schinousa. More recently, the islands have welcomed a growing number of independent-minded tourists.

Donousa is the northernmost of the group and the furthest from Naxos. The others are clustered near the southeast coast of Naxos. There are ATMs on all islands, though you should still bring a decent amount of ready cash with you.

Terrain produces an excellent map called *Minor Cyclades*.

❶ Getting There & Away

There are several connections a week between Piraeus and the Small Cyclades via Naxos, and daily connections to/from Naxos. Make sure you have plenty of time before committing yourself –

Small Cyclades

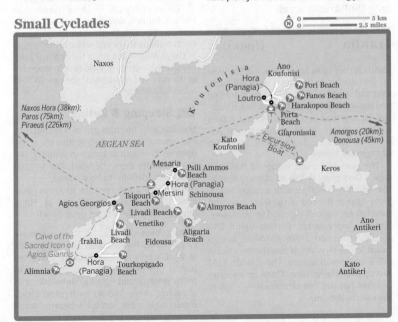

although it is technically possible, these islands are not meant for last-minute or one-night visits. For ferry schedules, visit www.openseasgr.

Blue Star Ferries (www.bluestarferries.gr) serves the Small Cyclades year-round. It has two routes, both beginning in Pireaus and calling at Paros and Naxos. From Naxos, four times a week the ferry calls at Donousa, then Amorgos (Aegiali) and terminates at Astypalea (in the Dodecanese). Three times a week, from Naxos the ferry stops at Iraklia, Schinousa and Koufonisia before terminating at Amorgos (Katapola).

The sturdy little ferry *Express Scopelitis* is the mainstay service (weather permitting in winter), except for its annual refit layoff, usually in January. The *Scopelitis* leaves from Naxos in the afternoon daily (or alternate days) Monday to Saturday, and calls at the Small Cyclades and Amorgos (usually both ports, Aegiali and Katapola). It returns to Naxos early the following morning.

Koufonisia has a growing number of visitors, and a growing number of July and August high-speed connections to plenty of Cyclades islands.

Listed under the Iraklia, Schinousa, Koufonisia and Donousa headings are peak summer services; these are significantly reduced out of season. Differences in journey durations are due to routing or vessel type.

Each of the small islands has at least one small tour boat. From June to September you may be able to negotiate one-way travel between the islands with these boats, although it will be more costly than the regular ferries.

Iraklia   Ηρακλεία

POP 140

Iraklia is only 19 sq km in area, a little Aegean gem dozing in the sun. Dump the party gear and spurn the nightlife, the sightseeing and the souvenir shops. Instead, brace yourself for a serene and quiet life and Iraklia will not disappoint. Only in July and August will you have to share the idyll with like-minded others.

The port and main village of Iraklia is **Agios Georgios**. It has an attractive cove-like harbour, complete with a sandy beach. Turn right at the end of the ferry quay and then left for the well-supplied general store, Perigiali Supermarket. Further uphill is a smaller store and *kafeneio* (coffee house) called Melissa's, which is also the ferry ticket office and postal agency. There is an ATM just up from the harbour. There are no buses or taxis, but you can hire scooters – ask at the cafe To Perasma.

◉ Sights & Activities

A surfaced road leads off to the left of the ferry quay, and after about 1km you'll reach **Livadi**, the island's best beach. A steep 2.5km further on is **Hora** (also called Panagia, and Pano Hora). From Hora, a surfaced road carries on to **Tourkopigado Beach**. Beyond the Cave of the Sacred Icon of Agios Giannis a path leads to the beach at **Alimina**, which is also served by boat from Agios Georgios in summer (offering a short cut to the cave). You can also walk to the cave from Hora in about one hour; look for the sign pointing the way from just south of the church.

During July and August, the local boat *Anemos* ferries people to island beaches and also runs day trips to nearby Schinousa. Enquire at Perigiali Supermarket.

Cave of the Sacred
Icon of Agios Giannis   CAVE
When you reach Iraklia's major 'sight', the Cave of the Sacred Icon of Agios Giannis, you'll find a large open cave on the left, and to the right, white-painted rocks surrounding the tiny entrance to the main sequence of caves. A torch is useful and the initial scramble along a low-roofed tunnel is worth it, leading as it does to caves full of stalactites and stalagmites.

The cave can be reached on foot from Agios Giorgios in about two hours (one way).

The signed path is along community trails 3, 4 and 7; details are outlined on the Terrain map, along with other island walks. Good walking shoes and water are essential.

On 28 August, the eve of the death of John the Baptist, crowds of local people assemble at the cave and crawl inside the cave to hold a candlelit service.

🛏 Sleeping & Eating

Domatia and tavernas are concentrated in and around Agios Georgios, though a few open on the beach at Livadi in summer. Domatia owners meet the boats, but in high season it's advisable to book ahead.

There are a few tavernas in Agios Georgios, and a well-regarded one in Hora. Summertime cafe-bars set up at Livadi.

Anna's Place   PENSION €
(☏ 22850 74234; www.annasplace.gr; d/q €50/80; ❄ 🐕) Located on high ground above the port is this lovely well-run complex, set in pretty gardens and with balconies taking in sweeping views. Inside, each super-clean, comfortable room has a kitchenette; some are well suited to families.

BOAT SERVICES FROM IRAKLIA

ROUTE	TIME	FARE	FREQUENCY
Amorgos	1¾-4¾hr	€8	1-2 daily
Donousa	2¼hr	€7.50	3 weekly
Koufonisia	55min	€5	1-2 daily
Naxos	1-1½hr	€7	1-2 daily
Paros	2¼hr	€12.50	3 weekly
Piraeus	8hr	€35	3 weekly
Schinousa	10min	€4	1-2 daily

Speires Hotel
BOUTIQUE HOTEL €€
(☑22850 77015; www.speireshotel.gr; d incl breakfast €125; ☺May-Oct; ❄🐱) The newest option on Iraklia is a stylish boutique offering a short walk uphill from the port, with white decor and flash bathrooms with all the mod cons. Superior double rooms can fit a family. The terrace at the elegant on-site restaurant and wine bar is a fine place to engage in a toast to holidaymaking.

Maïstrali
TAVERNA €
(☑22850 71807; www.bluehotels.gr; mains €5-15; ☺breakfast, lunch & dinner) In Agios Georgios, Maïstrali has a shady elevated terrace and has all the Greek standards covered. It also offers a range of simple, good-value rooms and apartments (from €50).

Schinousa
Σχοινούσα

POP 230

Like its neighbours, Schinousa has an easy-going pace and a rare sense of timelessness, although high season can be relatively lively. The island has a gentle landscape and the major settlement **Hora (Panagia)** has a long, narrow main street lying along the breezy crest of the island. There are several beaches scattered round the low-lying coast.

Ferries dock at the fishing harbour of **Mersini**. Hora is a hot 1km uphill. Domatia owners, with transport, meet ferries from about May onwards and will always meet booked guests. There's an ATM near Hora's main square. There are no taxis or buses, but you can hire a scooter in summer (ask at your accommodation).

⊙ Sights & Activities

Dirt tracks lead from Hora to beaches around the coast. The nearest are sandy **Tsigouri** and **Livadi**, both uncrowded outside August. Haul a little further to decent beaches at **Almyros** with its shallow water

and the small bays of **Aligaria**. Tsigouri, Livadi and Almyros have tavernas and/or beach bars.

Aeolia
BOAT TOUR
(☑6979618233; boat trip €15-35) From June to September the Aeolia tour boat runs various daily trips, including around the beaches of the island, or to Iraklia and Koufonisia. Private trips can also be arranged.

🛏 Sleeping & Eating

There are a few rooms down at Mersini and around the island, but Hora makes an ideal base.

Meltemi
PENSION €€
(☑22850 71947; www.pension-meltemi.gr; d €75; ❄🐱) Genuinely warm hospitality is the hallmark of this family-run pension and restaurant in the heart of Hora. Freshly renovated rooms are comfy and simple. All have balconies, some have kitchenette. The owners offer free beach transfer too!

Iliovasilema
HOTEL €€
(☑22850 71948; www.iliovasilemahotel.gr; Hora; d/q incl breakfast €70/85; ☺mid-May–Sep; ❄🐱) Near the village centre, with king-of-the-castle sunset views, rooms here are small, simple and spotless. The views from the balconies are fab and the service is warm.

Kafe stou Peri
CAFE €
(dishes €2-5; ☺8am-late) A colourful and friendly little cafe on the main street of Hora, Peri has crêpes, waffles, sandwiches and fresh salads, as well as breakfast options.

Mersini Taverna
SEAFOOD €€
(☑22850 71159; www.mersini.gr; mains €8-18; ☺May-Sep) Down at the port, Mersini woos diners with a stylish white fit-out, in a garden setting with great harbour views. It seals the deal with excellent seafood (especially squid).

BOAT SERVICES FROM SCHINOUSA

DESTINATION	TIME	FARE	FREQUENCY
Amorgos	1½-4½hr	€7	1-2 daily
Donousa	2hr	€7.50	3 weekly
Iraklia	10min	€4	1-2 daily
Koufonisia	30min	€5	1-2 daily
Naxos	1hr 20min	€7	1-2 daily
Paros	2hr 35min	€13	3 weekly
Piraeus	8½hr	€35	3 weekly

If you don't mind staying away from the Hora, the handful of chic all-white rooms behind the taverna are some of the nicest on the island (double €80 to €100).

Deli Restaurant & Cafe-Bar MODERN GREEK €€
(☑22850 74278; restaurant mains €15-25; ☺lunch & dinner Mar-Oct) Deli's upper floor houses the sea-view restaurant, the ground floor a cool cafe-bar. The understated name belies a gourmet menu, with dinner highlights from the Cretan owner-chef including goat cooked in cinnamon, tomato and red wine, veal meatballs, and spinach and leek pie. Ingredients are sourced as locally as possible; the wine list boasts some fine Greek vintages.

❶ Information

Grispos Travel (☑22850 71175) Grispos Travel, down at Tsigouri Beach and at an office at the far end of the village, sells all ferry tickets plus those for the *Express Scopelitis*.
Paralos Travel (☑22850 71160; Grispos Hotel) Paralos Travel is halfway along Hora's main street. It sells ferry tickets for vessels other than the *Scopelitis* and also doubles as the post office and newsagent in season.

Koufonisia   Κουφονήσια
POP 400

Koufonisia's star is on the rise, becoming a fashionable island for in-the-know visitors and referred to by locals as 'the Mykonos of the Small Cyclades'.

It's made up of three main islands (two of which are uninhabited); you'll arrive at the populated, low-lying Ano Koufonisi. It sees a flash-flood of tourism each summer season thanks to its superb beaches, good hotels and chic restaurants, and it welcomes a growing number of summer high-speed ferries from other Cycladic islands.

Still, the island retains its low-key charm, and a substantial fishing fleet sustains a thriving local community outside the fleeting summer season.

The flat profile of Kato Koufonisi is just to its south and a short caïque ride away. Kato Koufonisi has some beautiful beaches and a lovely church. East of here is the dramatic Keros, a rugged mountain of an island with dramatic cliffs. Archaeological digs on Keros have uncovered over 100 Early Cycladic figurines, including the famous harpist and flautist now on display in Athens' National Archaeological Museum.

⊙ Sights & Activities

Pick up the excellent map and village plan published annually. It's got details of roads, paths and beaches, as well as local businesses. Your accommodation will invariably have copies, or try local restaurants.

Koufonisia's only settlement spreads out behind the ferry quay. A large beach of flat, hard sand gives a great sense of space to the waterfront. Its inland edge is used as a road. The older part of town, the Hora, sprawls along a low hill above the harbour and is one long whitewashed main street lined with restaurants and cafes.

An easy 2km walk along the sandy coast road east of the port leads to Porta, Harakopou and Fanos Beaches. All tend to become swamped with grilling bodies in July and August and nudity becomes more overt the further you go. Beyond Fano a walking path leads to several rocky swimming places, including the glorious Piscina, and then continues to the great bay at Pori, where a long crescent of sand slides effortlessly into the dreamy clear sea. Pori can also be reached by an inland road from Hora.

In the other direction, a walk west from the port sees you reach Loutro, and you've hit the photogenic jackpot here, with a stony cove, small boatyard, windmill and whitewashed church.

Bike hire (📞 6989637046; per day €4-10) is available from a shop at the eastern end of the town beach. Cycling is a good transport option given the flatness of the island.

👉 Tours

Koufonissia Tours
BOAT

(📞 22850 71671; www.koufonissiatours.gr; Villa Ostria) Based at Villa Ostria, Koufonissia Tours organises caïque trips to Keros, Kato Koufonisi and other islands of the Small Cyclades. It can also help organise accommodation.

Marigo
BOAT

(📞 22850 71438, 6945042548; ⊙ Jun-Sep) Head to the marina and hop on this boat to transfer to/from various beaches, including Kato Koufonisi. It runs every two hours from 10am for about €5 return. Make enquiries at the Prasinos (p368) travel agency.

🛏 Sleeping

⭐ Anna Villas
PENSION €€

(📞 22850 71697; www.annavillas.gr; d incl breakfast €100; ❄ 🛜) In a quiet location just back from the beach, these fresh, bright studios are charming and run with warmth. All have balconies overlooking the old harbour, plus kitchenettes. It's a family-friendly spot, with a lovely reading nook and summertime cafe.

Ermis Rooms
PENSION €€

(📞 22850 71693; ermis.koufonissi@gmail.com; d €70-80; ❄ 🛜) These immaculate rooms are in a quiet location behind the post office, behind a pretty white-and-lilac exterior and a flowering garden. Try for a balcony with sea view.

Villa Ostria
HOTEL €€

(📞 22850 71671; www.ostriavilla.gr; d r/studio €75/95; ❄ 🛜) You know you're on an island here. Among several hotels on the high ground east of the beach, colourful Ostria has attractive rooms and studios with some quirky decor made from seashells and driftwood. Rooms have kitchenettes, spacious studios have kitchens. There's a fun collection of beach flotsam and jetsam in the communal outdoor space.

🍴 Eating & Drinking

Gastronautis
MEDITERRANEAN €

(📞 22850 71468; mains €5-10; ⊙ lunch & dinner May-Sep) Found on the narrow, whitewashed main street and one of a new breed of fashionable eateries. There's a beachside-chic interior and a well-priced fusion menu. Try tuna tartar, intriguing 'salty doughnuts' or pork chops in a barbecue sauce.

BOAT SERVICES FROM KOUFONISIA

DESTINATION	TIME	FARE	FREQUENCY
Amorgos	40min-3½hr	€7	1-2 daily
Amorgos*	25min	€14	1-2 daily
Donousa	1hr 10min	€6	3 weekly
Folegandros*	2¼-5½hr	€69	6 weekly
Iraklia	50min	€5	1-2 daily
Milos*	3¼-6½hr	€69	6 weekly
Mykonos*	1hr 40min	€55	3 weekly
Naxos	2-2½hr	€7.50	1-2 daily
Naxos*	40-50min	€19	1-2 daily
Paros	3hr 20min	€19	3 weekly
Paros*	1hr 25min	€30	1 daily
Piraeus	9hr	€35	3 weekly
Piraeus*	4¼-5hr	€59	1-3 daily
Santorini*	1-4hr	€50	6 weekly
Schinousa	30min	€5	1-2 daily
Serifos*	2hr	€48	1 daily
Sifnos*	1½hr	€45	1 daily

* High-speed services

★ Capetan Nikolas SEAFOOD €€

(☑ 22850 71690; Loutro; mains €5-18; ☺ dinner May-Oct) One of the best seafood places around, this cheerful restaurant overlooks the harbour at Loutro. Let the welcoming owners show you what's been freshly cooked, or help you select a fish for grilling. The lobster salad is famous and the seafood pasta delicious. Locally caught fish, such as red mullet and sea bream, are priced by the kilo. There are rooms to rent here too.

Scholio BAR

(☑ 22850 71837; Loutro; ☺ 7pm-3am; 🛜) A cosy bar and crêperie, Scholio plays to the crowd with jazz, blues or rock. It's at the western end of the main street above Loutro. The owners are accomplished photographers and often have exhibitions of their work on show.

Karnagio BAR

(Loutro; ☺ dinner Jun-Sep) Don't miss this tiny *ouzerie* at Loutro where the tables skirt the harbour. The food gets mixed reviews, as it doesn't quite live up to the magical setting.

ℹ Information

Prasinos (☑ 22850 71438) sells ferry tickets, on Hora's main street. There are a couple of supermarkets along the road that leads inland from the beach to link with the main street. The post office is signed from here, and is home to an ATM. There's information online at www.koufonisia.gr.

Donousa Δονούσα

POP 170

Donousa is the wonderfully out-on-a-limb island where you stop bothering about which day it might be. In late July and August the island can be swamped by holidaymaking Greeks and sun-seeking northern Europeans, but out of season be prepared to linger – quietly.

Stavros is Donousa's main settlement and port, a cluster of whitewashed buildings around a handsome church, overlooking a small, sandy bay. Little has changed here over the years. There's an excellent **beach**, which also serves as a thoroughfare for foot traffic to a clutch of homes, rental rooms and a taverna across the bay.

Kendros, 1.25km southeast of Stavros, best reached by a stepped track, is a sandy and secluded beach with a seasonal taverna and free camping. **Livadi**, an hour's hike further east, sees even fewer visitors. Both Kendros and Livadi are popular with naturists.

Inland there are still paths and tracks that lead into the hills to timeless little hamlets such as **Mersini**.

There are no cars or scooters for hire (and no petrol station). Walking is key, or take the *Margissa* boat to island beaches from June to August. A high-season minibus usually runs along the main road too.

🛏 Sleeping & Eating

Book ahead for stays from July to early September.

Apospiteris Rooms PENSION €

(☑ 22850 51586; www.aposperitis-rooms.com; d/tr/apt €45/60/65; ☺ mid-May–Sep; ❄🛜) Super central to the beach and village, this guesthouse has a range of simple double rooms, triple studios (with kitchen) and family-sized apartments. Decor is dated, but balconies with sea views compensate.

★ Makares APARTMENT €€

(☑ 22850 79079; www.makares-donoussa.gr; r & apt €70-115; ☺ May-Oct; ❄🛜) Loukas is an excellent host at Makares, a polished new complex of self-catering studios and apartments at the far end of Stavros bay (across the beach from the port). It's a short walk to the beach and village hub, the views are

BOAT SERVICES FROM DONOUSA

DESTINATION	TIME	FARE	FREQUENCY
Amorgos	40min-2¼hr	€8	1-2 daily
Astypalea	2hr 20min	€14	3 weekly
Iraklia	2hr	€7.50	3 weekly
Koufonisia	1hr	€5.50	3 weekly
Naxos	1hr 10min-3hr 40min	€7.50	1 daily
Paros	2hr 25min	€16	3 weekly
Piraeus	9hr 10min	€35	3 weekly
Schinousa	1hr 50min	€7.50	3 weekly

fabulous, the decor simple and elegant, and the feeling of seclusion (with all the required luxuries) is first-rate.

I Kori tou Mihali
TAVERNA €€
(☑ 22857 72322; mains €8-15; ☺ lunch & dinner) At this welcoming taverna in Mersini, Koula conjures up excellent Greek cuisine with a modern twist: wild goat from the island, pork in honey and yoghurt, smoky eggplant dip. It's worth the visit, for the food and the knockout views.

Kafeneio To Kyma
BAR
The hub of village life is by the quay, where this old-school, all-purpose general-store-cafe-bar draws locals and visitors and livens up late into the night in summer.

ℹ Information

Sigalas Travel (☑ 22850 51570) is the ticket agency for all ferries, with a main office in Stavros (behind the bakery) and a branch at the Iliovasilema restaurant complex. The main office opens every evening, plus 40 minutes before ferry arrivals.

There's an ATM next to a small shop on the harbour road (it's sometimes hidden behind a blue shutter for protection from blown sand), but be sure to bring sufficient cash in high season.

AMORGOS ΑΜΟΡΓΟΣ
POP 1970

Dramatic Amorgos lies on the distant, southeastern arc of the Cyclades, shaped like a seahorse swimming its way east towards the Dodecanese. As you approach by sea, its long ridge of mountains appears to stretch ever skyward.

Amorgos is just 30km from tip to toe but reaches over 800m at its highest point. The southeast coast is unrelentingly steep and boasts an extraordinary monastery built into the base of a soaring cliff. The opposite coast is just as spectacular, but softens a little at the narrow inlets where the main port and town of Katapola and the second port of Aegiali lie. The enchanting Hora (also known as Amorgos) lies amid a rocky landscape high above Katapola. All three towns have plenty of appeal as a base; Aegiali has the best beach.

Overall, however, Amorgos is much more about archaeology and activities than beachgoing – there's great walking, diving and a burgeoning rock-climbing scene.

ℹ Getting There & Away

Connections from Naxos are good with the small ferry, *Express Scopelitis*, running each day (or

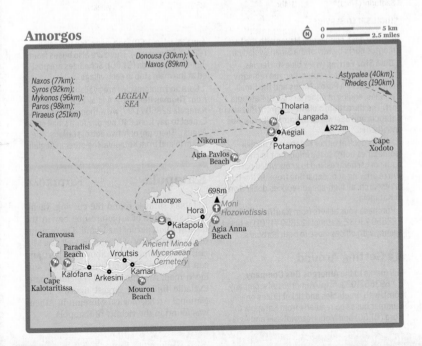
Amorgos

BOAT SERVICES FROM AMORGOS

DESTINATION	TIME	FARE	FREQUENCY
Astypalea	1½hr	€12.50	4 weekly
Donousa	2½hr	€6	1 daily
Folegandros*	2hr 35min	€69	5 weekly
Ios	5hr 20min	€12	1 weekly
Iraklia	1¾-4½hr	€8	1-2 daily
Kos	5hr	€8	1 weekly
Koufonisia	40min-3½hr	€6	1-2 daily
Koufonisia*	25min	€14	1-2 daily
Leros	3hr 10min	€2	1 weekly
Milos*	3¾hr	€69	5 weekly
Mykonos*	2¼hr	€55	3 weekly
Naxos	2-6hr	€11	1-3 daily
Naxos*	1hr 20min	€24	1-2 daily
Paros	3½-4½hr	€19	7 weekly (note: not daily)
Paros*	2hr	€29	1 daily
Patmos	2hr	€21	1 weekly
Piraeus	8-10hr	€35	7 weekly (note: not daily)
Piraeus*	5-6hr	€62	1-3 daily
Rhodes	8hr	€31	1 weekly
Schinousa	1½-4¼hr	€7	1-2 daily
Santorini (Thira)	3¼hr	€14	1 weekly
Santorini (Thira)*	1-4hr	€50	5 weekly

* HIGH-SPEED SERVICES

alternate day), connecting Naxos with the two Amorgos ports by way of the Small Cyclades.

Blue Star Ferries (www.bluestarferries. gr) has three useful routes: two run regularly from Pireaus via Paros, Naxos and the Small Cyclades, ending at either Aegiali or Katapola port. The third route sails weekly from Pireaus to Katapola and eastwards to Patmos, Leros, Kos and Rhodes.

Ferries dock at either Katapola or Aegiali (sometimes both) so it's important to check both port schedules and to know which port you're arriving at or departing from. At the time of research, all high-speed services docked only at Katapola.

Purchase your tickets from **Nautilos** (☑ Aegiali 22850 73032, Katapola 22850 71201), a ticket agency with offices close to both harbours.

ⓘ Getting Around

Full marks to the **Amorgos Bus Company** (☑ 6936671033; http://amorgosbuscompany. com), with timetables and ticket prices online. Summer buses go regularly from Katapola to Hora (€1.60) and Moni Hozoviotissis and Agia Anna Beach (€1.60), and less often to Aegiali (€2.50, 30 minutes). There are also buses from Aegiali to Langada (€1.60). Schedules are posted at the main stop in each village.

Cars and motorcycles are available for hire from **Thomas Rental** (☑ Aegiali 22850 73444, Katapola 22850 71777; www.thomas-rental.gr). Expect to pay from €40 per day for a small car in August. There are only two petrol stations: one 1.5km inland from Katapola, the other in Aegiali.

Katapola   Κατάπολα
POP 600

Katapola sprawls round the curving, yacht-filled shoreline of a picturesque bay in the most verdant part of the island. The remains of the ancient city of **Minoa**, as well as a **Mycenaean cemetery**, lie above the port and can be reached by footpath or a steep, surfaced road. Amorgos has also yielded many Cycladic finds; the largest figurine in the National Archaeological Museum in Athens was found in the vicinity of Katapola.

🛏 Sleeping

Villa Katapoliani PENSION €€
(📞22850 71664; www.villakatapoliani.gr; d €80-
85, q €120; ❄🛜) Stamatia has a high-quality
collection of rooms, studios and apartments,
handily located behind the waterfront and
ferry quay. The balconies at Villa 1 overlook a
garden filled with bougainvillea and the scattered ruins of the ancient temple of Apollo.
Or scoot upstairs to the rooftop terrace for
sea views. Apartments sleep up to four.

Pension Amorgos PENSION €€
(📞22850 71013; www.pension-amorgos.com;
€70; ❄🛜) There's a good deal of character
in this traditional guesthouse, with bright
and well-kept rooms right on the waterfront,
behind purple shutters. It has the same owner as Emprostiada in Amorgos' Hora, and a
similarly high quality.

Minoa Hotel HOTEL €€
(📞22850 74055; www.hotelminoa.gr; d/tr €90/
100; ❄🛜) This family-run place couldn't
be more convenient for early-morning ferries. Service is friendly, and the sweet, neat
rooms have revamped bathrooms and balconies overlooking a tree- and bird-filled garden. The modern lobby shares space with a
cafe and patisserie.

🍴 Eating

Honey & Cinnamon BAKERY €
(📞22850 71485; Katapola) Look for the bright
red window shutters and follow your nose.
This tiny patisserie, a block back from the
waterfront, bakes up cakes, pastries and lots
of local cookies. Try the ones made with the
local liquor, *psimeni raki,* or simply grab a
coffee or a gelato.

⭐Karamel MEDITERRANEAN €€
(📞22850 71516; dishes €4-12; ⊙lunch & dinner)
Come mealtime, pass the beach and follow
your nose to the eastern side of the harbour
to find some enticing dining options, including this colourful, French-run bistro. Sip
wine at the waterfront tables and choose between daily dishes, like chicken *à la maro-
can,* carrots *caramélisées* and juicy octopus,
which marry Greek and French flavours in a
delicious fashion.

⭐Captain Dimos MODERN GREEK €€
(📞22850 71020; mains €6-16; ⊙lunch & dinner) The captain whips up mouth-watering
dishes to serve on his convivial harbourside patio. Crowding the tempting menu
are dishes like octopus cooked in ouzo with
lemongrass and ginger, and pork cooked
with beer, apples and prunes. Creative pastas and pizza too.

ℹ Information

Boats dock right on the waterfront; the bus
station is a few minutes' walk to the left along
the water. A bank (with ATM) is mid-waterfront.
Useful websites include www.amorgos.gr, www.
amorgos.guide and www.amorgos-island-
magazine.com.

Hora (Amorgos)
Χώρα (Αμοργός)

POP 400

The old capital of Hora sparkles like a snowdrift across its rocky ridge. It's capped by a
13th-century *kastro* and guarded by windmills that stand sentinel on the surrounding
cliffs. There's a veneer of sophistication, not
least in the handful of fashionable bars and
stores that enhance Hora's appeal without
eroding its timelessness. The main activity
here is wandering, amply rewarded with
beautiful village settings around each corner.

The bus stop is on a small square at the
edge of town where there's also car parking.
There's an ATM next to a minimarket right
at the entrance to Hora and the village also
has a post office.

🛏 Sleeping & Eating

Pension Ilias PENSION €
(📞22850 71277; www.kastanisgroup.gr/pension
ilias; d/apt €60/100; ❄🛜) Tucked away amid
a jumble of traditional houses just down
from the bus stop is this friendly family-run
place with pleasant, comfortable rooms.

⭐Emprostiada GUESTHOUSE €€
(📞22850 71814; http://emprostiada.gr; d €100,
ste €130-140; ⊙Mar-Nov; ❄🛜) There's charm
in abundance at this traditional guesthouse, where private, characterful suites
are housed in an old merchant's home. It's
a postcard scene: white exterior, pale-blue
shutters, large and peaceful garden, and a
peaceful setting at the back of the village.
Choose from spacious doubles, maisonettes
and suites. Doubles are a bargain €50 outside the July and August peak.

Triporto CAFE, BAR €
(📞22850 73085; breakfast €8, snacks €3-5;
⊙9am-late) Once the village bakery, this
cafe has a strong traditional feel, plumped
up with some colourful, hip decor. Come

for breakfast to create an omelette from ingredients like olive sauce and hot paprika cream, or snack on salads, sandwiches and sweets. The friendly owner is a virtual encyclopedia of local knowledge.

Jazzmin
CAFE-BAR €

(☎22850 74017; breakfast €6-13, snacks €3-6; ⊗9am-late) Down some stairs from the main pedestrian street, Jazzmin spreads through the cosy rooms of a traditional home. Choose a magazine or book from its collection and perch in a window seat or lounge on the roof deck. Breakfast choices are particularly strong (as is the Mexican-sourced coffee) or choose a creative smoothie, juice or herbal tea. The list of cocktails hints at the impressively stocked bar, and jazz and other smooth tunes provide a chilled-out soundtrack.

Kath Odon
GREEK €

(☎22850 74148; mains €5-10; ⊗lunch & dinner) The setting is idyllic: tables under trees in a lovely little *plateia* (square) at the top end of the main street, nestled between whitewashed churches. The menu of this unpretentious bistro presents some tasty Amorgon produce, including goat, sausage, cheese and some excellent zucchini balls.

Aegiali
Αιγιάλη

POP 510

Aegiali is Amorgos' second port and sees fewer yachts and a bit more of the holidaymaker scene. A sweep of sand lines the inner edge of the bay on which the village stands, while steep slopes and impressive crags lie above.

🏃 Activities

Ask at travel agencies about boat trips around the island and to the Small Cyclades.

Amorgos Diving Center
DIVING

(☎6932249538, 22850 73611; www.amorgos-diving.com) Enthusiastic and friendly instruction can be had at this well-run centre, with a base at the camping ground and an office/store in the village (the store also stocks gear for climbing, walking and angling). Dives (with equipment) start at €50, with night dives, wreck dives and PADI courses available. It also offers a Bubblemaker class for kids, and snorkelling tours (€20).

Rock-climbing excursions can be arranged, with free diving and walking tours in the pipeline. Check the website.

👉 Tours

Special Interest Holidays
WALKING TOUR

(www.walkingingreece.com) Based at Langada, this outfit organises walking holidays (guided or self-guided) with experienced, knowledgable hosts: Paul and Henrietta Delahunt-Rimmer, an English couple who have written the excellent resource *Amorgos: A Visitor's and Walker's Guide*. See the website for full details.

🛏 Sleeping

Apollon Studios
GUESTHOUSE €

(☎22850 73297; www.apollon-amorgos.com; studio d/q €55/85; ❉🖥🛜) With a nautically themed lobby, this guesthouse in the heart of the village has studios with well-equipped kitchens and harbour-view balconies.

DON'T MISS

MONI HOZOVIOTISSIS

Nothing quite prepares you for the sight of the iconic 11th-century **Moni Hozoviotissis** (Μονή της Χοζοβιώτισσας; donations appreciated; ⊗8am-1pm & 5-7pm), a dazzling white structure seemingly embedded into the cliff-face high above the sea. This is Greek island scenery at its most dramatic. You'll even forgive the hundreds of stairs you need to climb to reach it.

Built on Amorgos' precipitous east coast below Hora, the monastery contains a miraculous icon that was found in the sea below the cliff. Enter through a green, Hobbit-sized door to discover the secrets of the monastery. With any luck, a custodian will be there to explain the significance of the monastery and its icons.

The dress code is modest and strict. No shorts, no miniskirts, no bare shoulders and no women in trousers. No exceptions (and there's no clothing available to borrow).

From about mid-May to October there's a bus service to the monastery from Katapola, Hora and Aegiali. A zigzagging walking path also reaches it from the eastern car park of Hora. While you're in this neck of the woods, head just a kilometre or so south to reach tiny Agia Anna Beach.

Rooms aren't fussy, but they're comfortable and reasonably priced. This place draws lots of repeat guests and families.

Aegiali Camping CAMPGROUND € (☑22850 73500; www.aegialicamping.gr; camp site per adult/child/tent €5.50/2/4; ☺Apr–mid-Oct) Basic facilities a block back from the beach, with tents under the vines and the majority of guests out diving with the on-site dive centre. Rent a tent for €6. On-site taverna and bar, too.

Yperia HOTEL €€ (☑22850 73084; www.yperia.com; d €100-110, f €160, all incl breakfast; ☺Apr-Oct; ❉☎☀) Yperia's modern rooms have warm, artsy touches, handmade wood and iron furnishings, big bathrooms and excellent sea views. The pool overlooks the ocean and the hotel is just a block from the beach. Staff are friendly and accommodating.

Aegialis Hotel & Spa HOTEL €€€ (☑22850 73393; www.amorgos-aegialis.com; d from €195; ❉☎☀) High on a hill and with magical views over Aegiali Bay and village, this is one of the island's smartest options. Rooms are good, but it's the facilities that make this place shine: pool and pool bar, a bliss-out day spa and indoor pool, restaurants – oh, and did we mention the view? Decent off-peak rates; book online.

🍴 Eating & Drinking

Amorgis CAFE, BAR € (☑22850 73606; www.amorgis.gr; meals €3-7; ☺9am-late) The steps leading up from the eastern end of the waterfront boast several cafe-bars open from morning until late – sunset drinks here are a fine idea. Family-friendly Amorgis is as pretty as a picture, full of pastel colours and hanging pot plants. The menu offers enticements like fresh juices, cool cocktails, baguettes and tortillas.

Falafel INTERNATIONAL € (☑6936808038; dishes €4-12) Up an alley from the waterfront, Falafel is a fresh-faced, laid-back eating and drinking venue with a menu that's a grab bag of world cuisines (spring rolls, felafels, summer salads, curries). It's an easy place to while away some time, and it's even open weekends in winter.

To Limani TAVERNA €€ (☑22850 73269; www.limani.amorgos.net; dishes €5-15; ☺breakfast, lunch & dinner) This popular restaurant carries its traditional atmosphere comfortably. Using home-grown produce,

the cooks whip up hefty portions and great local dishes: try the fish soup, *patatao* (lamb with potatoes in tomato sauce), or anything with local cheese. And save room for some homemade orange pie.

ℹ Information

Aegialis Tours (☑22850 73393; http://amorgos-aegialis.com/services), based at Aegialis Hotel & Spa, can help arrange local tours and experiences (hiking, cultural excursions, cooking classes etc).

Around Amorgos

Heading south of Hora, the road hugs the plunging east coast. The turning for **Agia Anna Beach** is the same as for Moni Hozoviotissis. The beach is popular for its starring role in the French film *Le Grand Bleu*. It's dramatic (and photogenic, with a whitewashed chapel), but it's tiny and rocky; the car park is bigger. It's a similar story with the rest of the beaches along this coast.

At the far southwestern tip of the island is the grounded ship that also featured in the film and draws French tourists in droves. A history of drugs and insurance scams is less romantic than the movie version. If you make it down this way, through the quiet, agricultural south of the island, the sandy beach at **Kalotaritissa Bay** is picturesque, and backed by a small beach cafe.

Heading northeast from Hora along the spine of the island offers arresting views back over the white village and Katapola. The lovely villages of **Langada** and **Tholaria** nestle amid the craggy slopes above Aegiali, each about 3km from the town. The two are linked to each other, and to Aegiali, by a signposted 9km circular path that takes 2½ to three hours to walk. Regular buses run between the villages and Aegiali.

Walking paths are outlined on www.amorgos.gr; check the Activities page.

🛏 Sleeping & Eating

Pagali Hotel HOTEL €€ (☑22850 73310; www.pagalihotel-amorgos.com; Langada; d €65-98; ❉☎) The highly regarded Pagali Hotel is tucked away in the lower village with superb views. Rooms and studios are comfortable and the year-round hotel offers alternative agritourism activities like grape or olive harvesting and winemaking, and/or activities including rock climbing, hiking, yoga and art workshops.

The hotel sits in a cute family-run pocket of Langada, next to the excellent Nikos Taverna and Vassalos Bakery.

IOS   ΙΟΣ

POP 2030

Ios' image has long been linked to holiday sun, sea and sex, with a reputation for non-stop booze-fuelled partying. It's partly true: there's no denying that from June to August the island is the much-loved stomping ground of youth and hedonism. But it's so much more – if you want it to be – and be assured, the partying doesn't infiltrate every village, or every beach.

Spend your days exploring the winding footpaths of the traditional hilltop old town or ensconced on a sandy beach. Discover the isolated interior and then return to town in time for the party. Or visit in the shoulder season for a quieter pace, when Ios draws families and more mature travellers.

ⓘ Getting There & Away

Ios lies conveniently on the Mykonos to Santorini ferry axis and has regular connections with Piraeus. Purchase tickets at Acteon Travel (p378) in Ormos, or its smaller branch in Hora.

ⓘ Getting Around

In summer crowded **KTEL** (☑ 22860 92015; www.ktel-ios.gr) buses run between Ormos, Hora and Mylopotas Beach (all fares €1.80) about every 20 minutes. Schedules are posted at the main village bus stops or check online. In summer, additional buses run frequently to Koubara, and less frequently to beaches at Agia Theodoti, Psathi and Manganari. For taxis call **Ios Taxi Service** (☑ 6977760570); it's €5 from the port to Hora, €5 from Hora to Mylopotas.

Summertime caïques travel from Ormos to Manganari via Mylopotas and cost about €12 per person for a return trip.

Ormos, Hora and Mylopotas Beach all have car, motorcycle and four-wheeler hire. You can book through Acteon Travel (p378).

Ios

BOAT SERVICES FROM IOS

DESTINATION	TIME	FARE	FREQUENCY
Amorgos	3hr	€12	1 weekly
Anafi	2hr 25min	€11.50	2 weekly
Folegandros	1hr 20min	€10	4 weekly
Folegandros*	25min	€44	2 weekly
Iraklio*	2hr 40min	€64	2 daily
Kimolos	2hr 50min	€16	3 weekly
Milos	3-4hr	€16	2 weekly
Milos*	1¾hr	€49.50	1 daily
Mykonos	4hr	€24.50	1 daily
Mykonos*	1hr 50min-3hr 50min	€48.50	4 daily
Naxos	1-1¾hr	€14.50	1-3 daily
Naxos*	45min	€25	1-2 daily
Paros	2hr 20min	€16	1-3 daily
Paros*	1-1½hr	€28	3 daily
Piraeus	7hr	€36	6 weekly
Piraeus*	3hr 40min-5hr	€59.50	2 daily
Rafina	7½hr	€35	1 daily
Rafina*	5-6hr	€62	2 daily
Santorini (Thira)	1-1½hr	€12	6 weekly
Santorini (Thira)*	40-50min	€29	4-7 daily
Serifos	4hr 50min	€19	1 weekly
Sifnos	4-5½hr	€18	3 weekly
Sifnos*	3hr	€54.50	1 daily
Sikinos	25min	€5	4 weekly
Syros	5hr 10min	€18	1 weekly
Tinos*	3-4½hr	€38-48	2 daily

* high-speed services

Hora, Ormos & Mylopotas
Χώρα, Ορμος & Μυλοπότας

Ios' four main centres sit nearly on top of one another on the west coast. The port, Ormos, is lined with tavernas and cafes and stretches out into sandy **Gialos Beach**, backed by beach bars. Just 2km uphill (or 1.2km up a stone staircase) sits the capital of Hora, a stunning traditional village and the nightlife hub. From here, the road winds south to the brown-sugar sand of Mylopotas Beach, with upscale and backpacker-style resorts. You'll find places to eat, sleep, drink and dance in all three settlements. Grocery stores and ATMs are also found in each; banks are in Hora.

The bus terminal in Ormos is straight ahead from the ferry quay on Plateia Emir-ou. If you don't mind stairs, it's a fairly easy walk from the port to Hora; follow the signs off the main road out of town.

In Hora there is a seasonal information kiosk at the bus stop, across the road from the big cathedral. Hora's central square is Plateia Valeta, buried deep in the old town. The road straight ahead from Hora's bus stop leads 3km to Mylopotas Beach.

◉ Sights & Activities

Hora   VILLAGE

Hora is a charming Cycladic village with a labyrinth of narrow lanes and cubist houses. Visit during the day and wander into the quiet residential quarters to get a glimpse of village life that carries on behind the tourist-hype scene. By night, the tiny central square is transformed into a noisy, open-air party.

Skarkos
ARCHAEOLOGICAL SITE

(The Snail; admission €2; ⊙8am-3pm Tue-Sun Jun-Sep) Crowning a low hill in a picturesque plain just outside Hora, this Early to Late Bronze Age settlement has restored walled terraces and low ruins of several Cycladic-style buildings for you to explore. A small visitor centre and interpretation boards in Greek and English clue you in to what you're looking at. If driving, take the signed turn-off between Ormos and Hora. To walk, follow the traditional stone footpath from the back of Hora, passing goats and farmhouses. (You will feel lost more than once but fear not.) The lovely walk takes around 15 minutes.

Archaeological Museum
MUSEUM

(☑22860 91246; Hora; admission €2; ⊙8.30am-3pm Tue-Sun) Finds from Skarkos are displayed at this thorough, if slightly dry, museum in the town hall next to the bus stop in Hora. There are also exhibits from island excavations in general.

Mylopotas Watersports & New Dive
WATER SPORTS, DIVING

(☑22860 92340; http://mylopotas-watersports. gr; Mylopotas; ⊙late May–mid-Oct) A thousand ways to fill your day: try a discover scubadiving session (€55) or more intensive PADI courses from €270. There are also wreck dives and night dives. Join a three-hour boat snorkelling trip for €35, or rent a long list of gear: windsurfing kit, kayaks, sailboats and more. Take a tube ride or do some waterskiing. Sea-taxi services too.

Meltemi Watersports & Dive Centre
WATER SPORTS, DIVING

(☑6980386990; www.meltemiwatersports.com; Mylopotas) Based at Far Out Beach Club, with a ready flow of keen customers, Meltemi has a smorgasbord of ways to get wet: try out a diving sampler (€55) or full PADI courses, then check out wreck, cave and night dives. Learn to windsurf, hire stand-up paddleboarding gear, join a canoe safari (from Mylopotas or Manganari Beach), or take a boat excursion.

Yialos Watersports
WATER SPORTS

(☑22860 92463, 6974290990; www.yialoswatersports.com; Gialos Beach) Mylopotas isn't the only beach full of activity. At Gialos Beach, this company can get you afloat with windsurfing (lessons and gear), stand-up paddleboarding, waterskiing, wakeboarding, banana rides, canoes, snorkelling gear – you name it. There are mountain bikes for the landlubbers, too, or simply sunbeds if you're worn out from the activities.

🛏 Sleeping

Ormos is considerably quieter than Hora or Mylopotas. Most accommodation offers free port transfers. Outside July and August, prices fall by 50% or more.

🛏 Ormos

★ Avra Pension
PENSION €

(☑22860 91985; www.avrapension.gr; r €60; ⊙Apr–mid-Oct; ❋🤶) Down a lane behind the marina, Katerina runs this delightful guesthouse with warmth and efficiency, and at bargain prices (outside the short summer peak, rooms fall to €30). Colourful potted plants, a restful terrace, homey common areas and fresh, appealing rooms add up to super value.

★ Petros Place Hotel
HOTEL €€

(☑22860 91421; www.petrosplace.gr; s/d €80/90, studio €130-170, all incl breakfast; ⊙May-Sep; ❋🤶🏊) Just a block up from the beach, this newly restored, 200-year-old stone building feels like the home you wish you had. Crisp, characterful rooms, wooden beamed ceilings, traditional beds and a flower-filled poolside give it the edge. The owners are attentive and the breakfast room is just like your Greek grandma's kitchen. The large pool area is shared with the owners' second property, the Yialos Beach Hotel (www.yialosbeach.gr), a more modern set-up. Off-peak rates are excellent (doubles around €50).

🛏 Hora

Francesco's
HOSTEL €€

(☑22860 91223; www.francescos.net; dm €20, dm/d/tr/q €20/70/105/140; ⊙Apr–mid-Oct; ❋@🤶) Once-upon-a-time backpackers are now sending their own 18-year-olds to Francesco's, still going strong. Rooms are spotless, views are dreamy and it's within stumbling distance of Hora's nightlife. There's a global feel and a roll-call of happy-traveller features: terrace bar, pool and cheap breakfast menu until 3pm. To find it, head towards the main square and turn left down Odos Scholarhiou for 200m. Or ask anyone.

Avanti Hotel
HOTEL €€

(☑22860 91165; www.avanti-hotelios.com; d incl breakfast €130-150; ⊙mid-Apr–mid-Oct; ❋@🤶🏊) A short stroll out of Hora, but far enough to offer a little peace, are these fresh, sparkling rooms. Private balconies and a beautiful pool and outdoor area are the icing on the cake. Rates halve outside the summer peak.

Pavezzo   GUESTHOUSE €€

(☎6977046091; www.iospavezzo.com; Hora; d €70-100) Just steps from Hora but away from the night-time noise, on a quiet side road to Kolitsani Beach. The seven rooms are a steal; they are clean and comfortable with country-style decor and private, sea-view patios. Suites have well-stocked kitchens and your hosts are welcoming and attentive.

★**Liostasi**   BOUTIQUE HOTEL €€€

(☎22860 92140; www.liostasi.gr; d/ste incl breakfast from €175/280; ⊙May-Sep; ❄@🛜🌊) Just step into the lobby of this place (halfway between Ormos and Hora) and you won't want to leave. A contemporary Scandinavian feel blends chic and comfy in just the right proportions. The on-site spa, restaurant and pool area are top quality while the rooms are crisp with splashes of colour and gorgeous sea views. Service is impeccable.

Mylopotas

Far Out Beach Club &
Beach Resort   HOSTEL, CAMPGROUND €

(☎22860 91468; www.faroutclub.com; camp sites per person €10, dm/d/q €15/90/180; 🅿@🛜🌊) Nearly on top of the beach is this backpackers party haven with poolside bars, restaurants and everything from laundry to tattooing, sushi bar, yoga and gym. There's an array of beds: pitch or hire a tent, sleep in small tent-sized affairs (aka dogboxes) or cute little roundhouses. Dorm beds are in a quad tent; en suite rooms are comparatively luxurious. What is does, this place does extremely well and that extends to the two modern, sophisticated Mylopotas hotels also in its holiday empire (doubles €130).

✗ Eating

✗ Ormos

La Randa   ITALIAN €

(☎22860 92448; www.larandaios.altervista.org; mains €7-14; 🛜) Right on the port, this place is fabulous for Italian food. The owner has carted an authentic oven over from Italy and crafts drool-worthy pizzas and pastas dripping in homemade tomato sauce.

✗ Hora

As well as Hora's raft of restaurants, there are fast-food outlets sellig *gyros*, crêpes and kebabs until the wee hours near the main square.

★**Katogi**   MEZEDHES €

(☎6983440900; dishes €4-11; ⊙dinner) This place is full of life. Stepping into it is like being welcomed into a party in someone's living room where bright, homey decor flows into a gorgeous garden, and the music selection rocks. Plus: the food is divine. Try haloumi bites with cherry tomatoes, pork bites in whisky sauce, or pasta purses filled with cheese and pear.

Thai Smile   THAI €

(☎22860 91925; mains €7-9; ⊙dinner) Ignore the international dishes and go for the authentic Thai flavours, created by the Thai owner-chef. This hole-in-the-wall place has plenty of atmosphere and serves plates overflowing with pad thai noodles, massaman curry and tom yum soup.

Nest   GREEK €€

(☎22860 91778; mains €6-18; ⊙lunch & dinner) The Nest feel authentic right down to the *rembetika* music and the tables of older men deep in discussion over rounds of *raki*. Local garlic sausage, chicken souvlaki, stuffed eggplant and lamb *keftiko* are served with bowls of tzatziki, olives and fresh bread. Wine is served by the jug and the vegies come from the owner's garden.

Lord Byron   MEDITERRANEAN €€

(☎22860 92125; www.lordbyronios.gr; dishes €7-14; ⊙dinner) An explosion of colour and quirky decor, this laid-back, lively restaurant is as pleasing to the stomach as it is to the eye. Enjoy huge portions of creative salads and mains, with dishes like cheese pies with orange and honey mustard dip, or barbecue crab. Service gets five stars.

✗ Mylopotas

Cantina del Mar   CAFE, BAR €

(☎22860 91016; http://cantinadelmar.gr; Mylopotas; sandwiches & salads €2-6; ⊙breakfast, lunch & dinner) Come here, at the entrance to the town, to chill out next to the beach over bumper brunches, sandwiches and wraps. Choose from a long, healthy-sounding list of juices and smoothies (can the hangover juice of lemon, orange and carrot really do the trick?). It has wines and cocktails for when you're feeling well again.

🍷 Drinking & Nightlife

Nightlife at the heart of Hora is full-on and radiates from the tiny main square, where it gets so crowded by midnight that you won't be able to fall down, even if you need to. Be young and carefree – but also be careful.

With everything from jazz bars to frantic backpacker bars that dole out cheap shooters, venues open and close and change in popularity regularly. Look for long-running Blue Note and highly rated Pash but follow the crowds, find a place that suits your mood and spread the love.

Fun Pub
PUB

(☑22860 92022; http://funpubios.com; ⊙5pm-late Apr-Oct) If you can't find your tribe on Hora's main square, they might be here – at the Irish-owned Fun Pub, on the main road through the town. Doing what is says on the label, it offers fun in various guises: music, dancing, food, live sports, pool tables and plenty of mingling.

Ios Club
COCKTAIL BAR

(☑6985720049; www.iosclub.gr; ⊙7pm-3am Apr-Oct) A deliciously sophisticated cocktail bar that's perfect for sunset cocktails and sweeping views on the chic terrace. It's along the pathway by Sweet Irish Dream.

Foiniki Art Cafe
BAR

(☑22860 92247; Hora; 9am-late) It's easy to settle into this funky little bar, with its friendly owners, rich colours, stacks of magazines and handcrafted beer from around Greece. Tucked behind Lord Byron, it's a great spot for a morning coffee or predinner tipple.

Free Beach Bar
CAFE, BAR

(☑22860 28357; http://freebeachbar.gr; ⊙all day May-Sep) Offering dozens of colourful, super-appealing ways to lounge and recline, this beach bar sits in the middle of Mylopotas Beach and sends a siren call via its beach cabanas and its pool, surrounded by hanging beds and cushioned pods. Aside from all-day drinks, snacks are on offer (club sandwich, pizza). There's chilling, but there's also DJ-fired action.

① Information

There's an ATM right by the kiosks at the ferry quay in Ormos. In Hora, the National Bank of Greece, behind the church, has an ATM. The post office is in Hora, a block behind the main road (signposted). There's information online at http://ios.gr.

Acteon Travel (☑22860 91343; www.acteon.gr; ⊙8am-10pm) Buy ferry tickets at Acteon Travel in Ormos, or its smaller branch in Hora.

Dr Yannis Kalathas (☑6932420200, 22860 91137; ⊙24hr) Your best contact in case of medical emergency.

Hospital (☑22863 60000) On the way to Gialos, 250m northwest of the quay.

Around Ios

It's pretty easy to escape the crowds on Ios; simply rent a car and venture into the seemingly isolated countryside with its goat farms, honey boxes and dramatic views. Head to Cape Gero Angeli, at the northernmost tip of the island and 12km from Hora, to the believed site of **Homer's Grave**. There's nothing much to see here but the panoramic sea views are fabulous.

En route to Psathi is **Paleokastro**, the remains of a Byzantine castle perched atop a seaside cliff. Follow the stone pathway from the roadside; it'll likely just be you and the goats here. Also on the road to Psathi is the island's formidable cheese dairy, called Niotiko. If it's open you can pop in for a gander and buy some of the lip-smacking wares.

Ios is well known for its beaches. Vying with Mylopotas for first place is **Manganari**, a long swath of fine white sand on the south coast, reached by bus or by caïque in summer. **Agia Theodoti** has the bluest of blue water and is favoured by Greek families in summer. Nearby **Psathi** is quieter with a popular taverna and is an ace windsurfing venue. Plenty of other fine beaches are only accessible by caïque.

SANTORINI (THIRA)
ΣΑΝΤΟΡΙΝΗ (ΘΗΡΑ)

POP 15,550

Santorini may well have conquered a corner of your imagination before you've even set eyes on it. With multicoloured cliffs soaring over 300m from a sea-drowned caldera, it rests in the middle of the indigo Aegean, looking like a giant slab of layered cake. The island spoons the vast crater left by one of the biggest volcanic eruptions in history. Smaller islands curl around the fragmented western edge of the caldera, but it is the main island of Thira that will take your breath away with its snowdrift of white Cycladic houses lining the cliff tops and, in places, spilling like icy cornices down the terraced rock. When the sun sets, the reflection on the buildings and the glow of the orange and red in the cliffs can be truly spectacular.

Santorini is no secret and draws crowds for most of the year, yet it wears its tourism well and its offerings make it worth the bustle. The island's intrigue reaches deep into the past, with the fascinating Minoan site of Akrotiri and the gorgeous traditional hilltop village of Oia. It also glides effortlessly into the future with accomplished artists, excellent wineries, a unique microbrewery, and some of the Cyclades' finest accommodation and dining experiences. The multicoloured beaches are simply the icing on the cake.

History

Minor eruptions have been the norm in Greece's earthquake-prone history, but Santorini continually bucked this trend – eruptions here were genuinely earth-shattering, and so wrenching they changed the shape of the island several times.

Dorians, Venetians and Turks occupied Santorini, but its most influential early inhabitants were Minoans. They came from Crete sometime between 2000 BC and 1600 BC, and the settlement at Akrotiri dates from the peak years of their great civilisation.

The island was circular then and was called Strongili (Round One). Thousands of years ago a colossal volcanic eruption caused the centre of Strongili to sink, leaving a caldera with towering cliffs along the

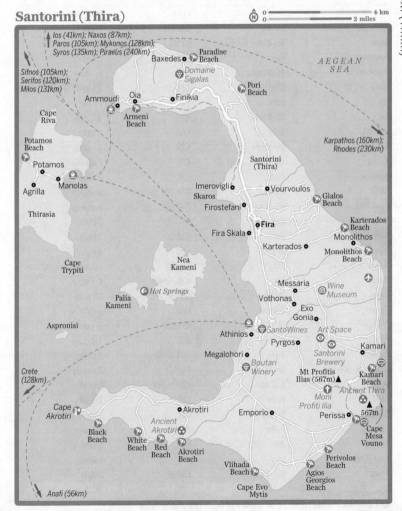

Santorini (Thira)

east side – a truly dramatic sight. The latest theory, based on carbon dating of olive-oil samples from Akrotiri, places the event 10 years either side of 1613 BC.

Santorini was recolonised during the 3rd century BC, but for the next 2000 years sporadic volcanic activity created further physical changes that included the formation of the volcanic islands of Palia Kameni and Nea Kameni at the centre of the caldera.

As recently as 1956 a major earthquake devastated Oia and Fira, yet by the 1970s the islanders had embraced tourism as tourists embraced the island, and today Santorini is a destination of truly spectacular global appeal, drawing honeymooners, backpackers, the jet set, cruise-boat passengers, Chinese bridal parties (in part due to the success of a recent film, *Beijing Love Story*, filmed partly on Santorini) and everyone else too.

For better or worse, Santorini and Mykonos have become the poster-children for the Greek islands. As well as bigger crowds, that also means considerably higher prices.

BOAT SERVICES FROM SANTORINI (THIRA)

DESTINATION	TIME	FARE	FREQUENCY
Amorgos*	1-4¼hr	€49.50	6 weekly
Anafi	1hr 10min-1hr 40min	€7.50	4 weekly
Folegandros	3hr	€12	3 weekly
Folegandros*	45-80min	€44	1-2 daily
Halki	12½-15½hr	€26	2 weekly
Ios	1-2hr	€12	1 daily
Ios*	35-45min	€29	4-6 daily
Iraklio*	1¾hr	€60	2 daily
Karpathos	8½-11½hr	€25	2 weekly
Kasos	6¾-9½hr	€25	2 weekly
Kimolos	4½hr	€16	2 weekly
Kos	4½hr	€34.50	4 weekly
Koufonisia*	1½-3½hr	€49.50	6 weekly
Milos	3½hr	€17	2 weekly
Milos*	2hr	€52.50	2 daily
Mykonos*	2-3hr	€60	5-6 daily
Naxos	2hr	€19.50	1-2 daily
Naxos*	1½hr	€38.50-42	4-5 daily
Paros	3-3½hr	€20.50	1-2 daily
Paros*	2-2¼hr	€46	3 daily
Piraeus	5½-12hr	€36-39	2-3 daily
Piraeus*	4½-6hr	€59	3-4 daily
Rafina*	5¾hr	€64-69	2 daily
Rethymno (Crete)*	2hr 20min	€65	2 weekly
Rhodes	8-17¾hr	€27-36.50	5 weekly
Serifos	6½hr	€19	1 weekly
Sifnos	5-7¼hr	€18	3 weekly
Sifnos*	3-4hr	€54.50	1-2 daily
Sikinos	2hr	€9	3 weekly
Sitia (Crete)	6hr	€26	1 weekly
Tinos*	3½-4hr	€40-60	2 daily

* high-speed services
Note: differences in durations are on account of vessel type and/or route

ⓘ Getting There & Away

AIR

Santorini Airport (☑ 22860 28400; www.santoriniairport.com) has flights year-round to/from Athens (from €64, 45 minutes) with **Olympic Air** (www.olympicair.com) and **Aegean Airlines** (www.aegeanair.com). Seasonal European connections are plentiful, including easyJet from London, Rome and Milan.

BOAT

There are plenty of ferries each day to and from Piraeus and many Cyclades islands.

Thira's main port, Athinios, stands on a cramped shelf of land at the base of sphinx-like cliffs and is a scene of marvellous chaos that always seems to work itself out when ferries arrive. Buses (and taxis) meet all ferries and then cart passengers up the towering cliffs through an ever-rising series of S-bends to Fira. Accommodation providers can usually arrange transfers (to Fira per person is around €10).

ⓘ Getting Around

TO/FROM THE AIRPORT

There are frequent bus connections between Fira's bus station and the airport, located southwest of Monolithos Beach. The first leaves Fira around 7am and the last 9pm (€1.60, 20 minutes). Most accommodation providers will arrange (paid) transfers.

BUS

KTEL Santorini Buses (☑ 22860 25404; http://ktel-santorini.gr) has a good website with schedules and prices. Tickets are purchased on the bus. In summer buses leave Fira twice hourly for Oia, with more services pre-sunset (€1.60). There are also numerous daily departures for Akrotiri (€1.80), Kamari (€1.60), Perissa and Perivolos Beach (€2.20), and a few to Monolithos (€1.60). Buses leave Fira, Perissa and Kamari for the port of Athinios (€2.20, 30 minutes) a half-dozen times per day, but it's wise to check times in advance. Buses for Fira meet all ferries, even late at night.

CAR & MOTORCYCLE

A car is the best way to explore the island during high season, when buses are intolerably overcrowded and you'll be lucky to get on one at all. Be very patient and cautious when driving – the narrow roads and heavy traffic, especially in and around Fira, can be a nightmare. Note that Oia has no petrol station, the nearest being just outside Fira.

There are representatives of all the major international car-hire outfits, plus dozens of local operators in all tourist areas. A good local hire outfit is **Damigos Rent a Car** (☑ 22860 22048; www.santorini-carhire.com). You'll pay from around €50 per day for a car, €25/30 for a scooter/four-wheeler in high season, but it pays to shop around. Note: scooter hire requires you to have a motorbike licence, while four-wheelers require just a car licence.

TAXI

Fira's **taxi stand** (☑ 22860 23951, 22860 22555) is on Dekigala just around the corner from the bus station. A taxi from the port of Athinios to Fira costs between €10 and €15 and a trip from Fira to Oia about €15. Expect to add €2 if the taxi is booked ahead or if you have luggage. A taxi to Kamari is about €15, to Perissa €18, and to Ancient Thira about €25 one way.

Santorini Transport (☑ 6984637383; www.santorinitransport.com) is a good option for arranging fixed-price transfers to/from the airport or Athinios port.

Fira   Φήρα

POP 2290

Santorini's main town of Fira is a vibrant, bustling place, its caldera edge layered with hotels, cave apartments, infinity pools and swish restaurants, all backed by narrow streets full of shops and even more bars and restaurants. A multitude of fellow admirers cannot diminish the impact of Fira's stupendous landscape. Views over the multicoloured cliffs are breathtaking, and at night the caldera edge is a frozen cascade of lights.

Fira sprawls north and merges into two more villages: **Firostefani** (about a 15-minute walk from Fira) and **Imerovigli** (the highest point of the caldera edge, about a half-hour walk from Fira). A path runs through these villages and is lined with glorious hotels, restaurants and endless photo opportunities.

⊙ Sights

Archaeological Museum   MUSEUM
(☑ 22860 22217; M Nomikou; adult/child €3/free; ☺8.30am-3pm Tue-Sun) Near the cable-car station, this museum houses impressive finds from Akrotiri and Ancient Thira, including some unbelievably detailed clay statuettes come from the latter site, including a donkey, pig, ram and birds. Check out the chariot-racing images on some of the pottery. The content is strong; however, the museum itself is in need of a little TLC.

★Museum of Prehistoric Thera   MUSEUM
(☑22860 22217; Mitropoleos; adult/child €3/free; ☺8am-3pm Tue-Sun) Opposite the bus station, this well-presented museum houses extraordinary finds excavated from Akrotiri and is

Fira

all the more impressive when you realise just how old they are. Most remarkable is the glowing gold ibex figurine, dating from the 17th century BC and in amazingly mint condition. Also look for fossilised olive tree leaves from within the caldera from 60,000 BC.

Santozeum   MUSEUM
(☑ 22860 21722; www.santozeum.com; Ypapantis; adult/child €5/3; ☉10am-6pm May-Oct) Around the corner from the archaeological museum, this modern cultural centre is home to the 'Wall Paintings of Thera' exhibition, a collection of life-size reproductions of the fin-est Akrotiri wall paintings. The short video on the work of conservators is fascinating. There's no labelling, so be sure to ask for the information sheet for context.

Megaro Gyzi Museum   MUSEUM
(☑ 22860 23077; www.megarogyzi.gr; Erythrou Stavrou; adult/child €3/free; ☉10am-4pm Mon-Sat May-Oct) Come to this quiet escape in the town's north to take in fascinating photographs of Fira before and immediately after the 1956 earthquake, along with a collection of maps, engravings, paintings and 15th-century manuscripts.

Fira

◎ Top Sights
1 Museum of Prehistoric
   Thera C5

◎ Sights
2 Archaeological Museum B1
3 Megaro Gyzi Museum B1
4 Santozeum B2

◎ Activities, Courses & Tours
5 Cable Car A1

◎ Sleeping
6 Aressana Spa Hotel &
   Suites.. B5
7 Aroma Suites B5
8 Hotel Atlantis B4
9 Pelican Hotel C3
10 Porto Fira Suites A4

11 Villa Roussa C4
12 Villa Soula D3

◎ Eating
13 1500bc A5
14 Assyrtico Wine Restaurant B4
15 Camille Stefani.. B2
16 Koukoumavlos B4
17 Mama's House C4
18 Ouzeri B4

◎ Drinking & Nightlife
19 Kira Thira B3
20 Tango B3
21 Tropical... B3

◎ Entertainment
22 Enigma B2
23 Koo Club B2

🏃 Activities

Walks in and around Fira are spectacular, particularly heading north to Firostefani and Imerovigli along the caldera-edge pathway. This is about a 30-minute walk, one way. If you want to keep walking, you can eventually reach **Oia**, but be aware that this is no small undertaking, and the trail beyond Imerovigli can be rough. It's about 9km in all, and a good three to four hours' walk one way. It's best not to undertake it in the heat of the day.

Other options include walking down to (or up from) the small port known as **Fira Skala**, from where volcanic island cruises leave (and where cruise-ship passengers come ashore). It's around 600 steps each way. You can make a more leisurely, and aromatic, upward trip by donkey (€5) – although animal-rights groups strongly urge travellers not to, due to the cruelty involved. You can also go by the **cable car** (☏22860 22977; http://scc.gr; M Nomikou; 1 way adult/child €5/2.50) that hums quickly and smoothly (every 20 minutes 6.30am to 11pm June to August) between Fira and Fira Skala. Less-frequent services operate outside the peak season; there is an additional charge to take luggage (€2.50).

From Imerovigli, a sign at Mezzo restaurant leads west to **Skaros**, a rocky headland with great views and a perfectly situated church. From Imerovigli it's about 20 minutes one way.

👉 Tours

Any tour your heart desires can be organised on Santorini – there are dozens of agencies primed and ready to help with winery visits, archaeology tours, traditional villages, sunset watching, activities etc.

The most popular option is a cruise, and the most popular itinerary takes in the caldera's volcanic islands of Nea Kameni and Palia Kameni, including a stop at the former's crater and the latter's hot springs. Some tours will also call at Thirasia, and/or a port below Oia. Sunset-watching from a boat, drink in hand, is also in demand.

Departures are from Fira Skala, below Fira. You can book with one of the agencies around town (which is wisest), or take your chances, head down to Fira Skala to see what's available, and jump on the next boat (there are short and long tours). Vessels vary, from replica schooners to sleek catamarans and yachts – therefore prices vary wildly.

The starting rate for a basic full-day excursion is around €30. Questions to ask when booking: the itinerary, inclusions (eg, lunch or drinks), how many fellow passengers?

🛏 Sleeping

Santorini Camping   HOSTEL, CAMPGROUND €
(☏22860 22944; www.santorinicamping.gr; Fira; dm/d/q €20/60/80, camp site per person €12.50; ☉Mar-Nov; P@🛜🏊) On the eastern outskirts of town, this hostel and camping ground has some shade and decent facilities. Rooms are clean but quite basic. There's a self-service restaurant, mini market, bar and pool. Free port transfer.

★ Karterados Caveland Hostel
HOSTEL €€

(☑22860 22122; www.cave-land.com; Karterados; incl breakfast dm €17-25, d with/without bathroom €70/50, apt €100; P ❋ 🛜 ☒) This fabulous, chilled-out hostel is based in an old winery complex in Karterados about 2km from central Fira (see website for directions). Accommodation is in the big old wine caves, all of them with creative, colourful decor and good facilities. The surrounding garden is relaxing, with weekly barbecues held, and there are yoga classes on offer too.

Hotel Sofia
HOTEL €€

(☑22860 22802; www.sofiahotelsantorini.com; Firostefani; d €90-100; ☺May-Oct; ❋🛜☒) Comfortable, with a touch of character, these half-dozen petite rooms at the heart of Firostefani are a great alternative to the bustle of Fira. There's no caldera view, but it's literally outside your door. The rates are a near-steal (book early) and the small, lovely pool and verandahs are a bonus. Fira's centre is about 800m south.

Villa Soula
HOTEL €€

(☑22860 23473; www.santorini-villasoula.gr; Fira; r €90; ❋🛜☒) Cheerful and spotless, this hotel is a great deal. Rooms aren't large but are freshly renovated with small, breezy balconies. Colourful public areas and a small, well-maintained undercover pool give you room to spread out a little. It's a short walk from the town centre.

Villa Roussa
HOTEL €€

(☑22860 23220; www.villaroussa.gr; Dekigala; s/d/tr from €60/85/100; P❋🛜☒) This place is all about location. Minutes from the caldera (without prices to match) and seconds from the bus station (but out of earshot), it has fresh, immaculate rooms and helpful staff.

Pelican Hotel
HOTEL €€

(☑22860 23113; www.pelicanhotel.gr; Danezi; s/d/tr €75/95/110; ❋🛜) There's no caldera view, but you're just metres from the heart of the action in this long-standing hotel with a homey feel. One of its best attributes is its restaurant next door, or the delightful garden setting.

★ Aroma Suites
BOUTIQUE HOTEL €€€

(☑22860 24112; www.aromasuites.com; Agiou Mina; d from €180; ❋@🛜) Overlooking the caldera at the quieter southern end of Fira, and more accessible than similar places, this boutique hotel has charming service and six plush, beautiful suites. Built into the side of the caldera, the traditional interiors are made all the more lovely with monochrome decor, local art, books and stereos. Balconies offer a feeling of complete seclusion.

★ Mill Houses
BOUTIQUE HOTEL €€€

(☑22860 27117; www.millhouses.gr; Firostefani; studio/ste incl breakfast from €280/325; ❋🛜☒) Built right into the side of the caldera at Firostefani, down a long flight of steps, these superb studios and suites are chic and plush. Lots of white linen and whitewashed walls fill them with light. King-sized beds, Bulgari toiletries and private patios looking out over the Aegean are just a few of the lavish touches.

Aressana Spa Hotel & Suites
BOUTIQUE HOTEL €€€

(☑22860 23900; www.aressana.gr; d from €330; P❋@🛜☒) Rooms at this rock-star joint are simple and modern, with all the niceties that give it the edge of luxury. The pool with its waterfall and private patio cabanas make the lack of a caldera view more than tolerable. The design-driven lobby, the luxe spa and the huge breakfast seal the deal.

ℹ SLEEPING ON SANTORINI

Things to know about Santorini accommodation:

➡ Few of Fira's sleeping options are cheap. For a caldera view, expect to pay a premium.

➡ The sky is the limit here (and in Oia): luxury accommodation is everywhere, with all the trimmings (private terrace is sought-after, a plunge pool is a favourite).

➡ Consider accommodation in Firostefani and Imerovigli if you don't mind a walk into Fira. There are plenty of quality hotels, restaurants and the all-important views here too.

➡ Many hotels on the caldera rim cannot be reached by vehicle and may involve several flights of steps. Many hotels have porters who can help with luggage.

➡ Some domatia touts at the port may claim that their rooms are in town, when they're actually a long way out; ask to see a map showing the exact location.

➡ Some places may offer free transfer to the port or airport; other places may charge anything from €12 upwards for a transfer.

Porto Fira Suites
BOUTIQUE HOTEL €€€

(☑ 22860 22849; www.portofira.com; Agiou Mina; 2-/4-person ste incl breakfast from €275/425; ❄ 🛜) If you're staying here, your day of luxury begins with breakfast on your balcony. Ultramodern rooms are white, crisp and cool in more ways than one, yet retain their traditional, caldera cave ambience. Grand suites sleep up to four.

Hotel Atlantis
HOTEL €€€

(☑ 22860 22232; www.atlantishotel.gr; Fira; d incl breakfast €225-345; ❄ 🛜 ⊠) The Atlantis is a regal building from 1953 that overlooks the widest section of the caldera-edge promenade. It's full of cool, pastel-coloured lounges and flower-filled terraces – you'd never know it was a tourist crush outside! The bright, airy bedrooms are quiet and well equipped; request a (pricey) front room for caldera views.

🍴 Eating

Overpriced, indifferent food geared towards tourists is still an unfortunate feature of summertime Fira; thankfully, there are many excellent exceptions. In general, there's a price hike for a caldera view. It's good to book a table in summer.

Ouzeri
TAVERNA €

(☑ 22860 21566; Fabrika Shopping Centre; mains €7-15; ⊙ lunch & dinner) Central and cheerfully dressed in red gingham, this terrace restaurant has surprisingly reasonable prices. It's a long-standing favourite with locals and tourists alike, with top traditional dishes like mussels *saganaki*, baked feta and stuffed calamari.

Mama's House
GREEK €

(☑ 22860 21577; http://mamashouse-santorini. gr; mains €7-14; ⊙ breakfast, lunch & dinner) Steps from the taxi station is this institution, famed for its mega breakfasts (€5 to €9), hearty Greek dishes and creative salads, all enjoyed on a big, bustling terrace. The mezedhes menu is vast, with items like grilled octopus with balsamic dressing and eggplant rolls stuffed with feta.

Galini Cafe
CAFE, BAR €

(☑ 22860 22095; www.galinicafesantorini.com; mains €6-14; ⊙ 8am-midnight) Just as you reach Firostefani, this breezy cafe welcomes you with brightly coloured flowerpots and a handcrafted school of fish swimming overhead. Chilled and friendly, with unparalleled caldera views, it's a great place for breakfast or a light meal and a cocktail at sunset.

Assyrtico Wine Restaurant
GREEK €€

(☑ 22860 22463; www.assyrtico-restaurant. com; Fira; mains €14-30; ⊙ lunch & dinner) Settle in on this terrace above the main drag for polished local flavours accompanied by caldera views. Start with, say, the *saganaki* wrapped in a pastry crust, and follow with the deconstructed *gyros* or the moussaka of Santorini white eggplant. Service is relaxed and friendly; the wine list is big.

Camille Stefani
GREEK €€

(☑ 22860 22762; www.camillestefani.com; mains €8-18; ⊙ lunch & dinner) Going strong since the late '70s, this old-school rooftop restaurant has views across to the east coast. Its authentic, traditional atmosphere matches its meals. Dig into countless mezedhes like *saganaki* and stuffed vine leaves or opt for moussaka, chicken souvlaki or swordfish fillet. It's as popular with locals as it is with tourists.

Mylos
MODERN GREEK €€€

(☑ 22860 25640; www.mylossantorini.com; Firostefani; mains €22-26; ⊙ lunch & dinner) Located in a converted windmill on the caldera edge in Firostefani, this uber-glam venue has upscale food that's ambitious in its techniques and beautifully presented. Try crispy fish 'covered with sea snow', or Greek black pork with *romesco* sauce. This place is getting national attention; book ahead.

Koukoumavlos
MODERN GREEK €€€

(☑ 22860 23807; www.koukoumavlos.com; mains €28-34; ⊙ dinner Apr–mid-Oct) This terrace is filled with diners partaking of fresh, modern Aegean cuisine (including a worthwhile degustation at €65). Creativity reigns and the menu is poetic, elevating dishes to new heights: 'slow-cooked shoulder of lamb with potato mousseline flavored with jasmine, fig and Greek coffee sauce'. Look for the pink building and wooden doorway. Book ahead.

1500bc
SEAFOOD €€€

(☑ 22860 21331; www.1500bc.gr; mains €22-39; ⊙ lunch & dinner) With top views south across the caldera, this elegant patio serves top-shelf food. Braised lobster, royal crab legs with green olive oil, and chateaubriand veal fillet are just a few of the quality choices. Service is impeccable – they'll debone the fish at your table and bring you a shawl if you're chilly.

🍸 Drinking & Nightlife

After midnight Erythrou Stavrou fires up as the clubbing caldera of Fira, while Marinatou is lined with fabulously chic drinking spots.

A BENT FOR CYCLADIC TRAVEL

Long before the hip lotus-eaters of the 1960s discovered their dream world in the Greek islands, a redoubtable pair of travellers had been thoroughly 'doing' the Cyclades during the late 19th century. James Theodore Bent and his wife, Mabel, travelled extensively throughout the Aegean, 'researching' the cultural life of the islands as much as their archaeology. J Theodore's 1885 island-by-island book, *The Cyclades, Or Life Among the Insular Greeks,* is a quirky masterpiece that describes the sights and cultural realities of the islands in the late 19th century – along with Bent's often eccentric reflections. Look for it online, and in bookshops on bigger islands such as Santorini.

Kira Thira
BAR

(22860 22770; Erythrou Stavrou; ⊗9pm-6am Wed-Sun) The oldest bar in Fira and one of the best. Dark wood and vaulted ceilings give it an intimate, cave-like atmosphere with smooth cocktails and smoother jazz.

Tango
BAR

(69744 98206; www.tangosantorini.gr; Marinatou; ⊗8pm-5am) Delicious cocktails, a fashionable crowd and brilliant tunes at the caldera edge. Come for sunset, stay for hours (and hours).

Tropical
BAR

(22860 23089; Marinatou) Nicely perched just before the caldera edge, Tropical draws a vibrant traveller crowd with well-made cocktails, a relaxed atmosphere and a steady mix of rock, plus unbeatable balcony views.

Enigma
CLUB

(22860 22466; Erythrou Stavrou; ⊗11pm-7am Jul & Aug) A Fira top spot with three bars and a big dance space, this is the catwalk clientele's favourite spot amid cool decor and full-on sounds from house to mainstream hits.

Koo Club
CLUB

(22860 22025; www.kooclub.gr; Erythrou Stavrou; ⊗10pm-5am Jul & Aug) Multitiered outdoor balconies with sofas to lounge on while you hang out with your new best friends, sipping cocktails to live DJs.

ℹ Information

There are public toilets near the taxi station. You may need to brace yourself (they're of squat vintage). There are numerous ATMs scattered around town.

Alpha Bank (Plateia Theotokopoulou) Has an ATM.

Central Clinic of Santorini (22860 21728; www.santorinicentralclinic.gr) Health clinic just east of the town centre. Available 24 hours for emergencies.

Dakoutros Travel (22860 22958; www.dakoutrostravel.gr; Fira; ⊗8.30am-10pm) Travel agency on the main street, just before Plateia Theotokopoulou. Ferry and air tickets sold; assitance with excursions, accommodation and transfers.

Information kiosk (⊗9am-8pm Mon-Fri May-Sep) Seasonal information kiosk with somewhat odd hours – it probably won't be open when you visit!

National Bank of Greece (Dekigala) South of Plateia Theotokopoulou, on the caldera side of the road. Has an ATM.

Police station (22860 22649; Karterados) About 2km from Fira.

Post office (Dekigala)

Oia
Οία

POP 670

Perched on the northern tip of the island, the village of Oia (ee-ah) reflects the renaissance of Santorini after the devastating earthquake of 1956. Restoration work has whipped up beauty and you will struggle to find a more stunning Cyclades village. Built on a steep slope of the caldera, many of its dwellings nestle in niches hewn into the volcanic rock.

Oia draws enormous crowds and overcrowding is the price it pays for its good looks. Try to visit in the morning or spend the night here; afternoons and evenings often bring busloads from the cruise ships moored in the bay. At sunset the town feels like a magnet for every traveller on the island.

◉ Sights & Activities

Maritime Museum
MUSEUM

(22860 71156; admission €3; ⊗10am-2pm & 5-8pm Wed-Mon) This museum is located along a narrow lane that leads off right from Nikolaou Nomikou. It's housed in an old mansion and has endearing displays on Santorini's maritime history.

★ Ammoudi
PORT

This tiny port of colourful fishing boats lies 300 steps below Oia. It's a hot haul down and up again but well worth it for the views of the blood red cliffs, the harbour and back up to Oia. Once you're down there, have lunch at one of the excellent tavernas right on the water's edge (Katina is the locals' pick). In summer, boats and tours go from Ammoudi to Thirasia daily; check with travel agencies in Fira for departure times.

🛏 Sleeping

With the closure of the hostel in Oia in 2014, there is very little budget accommodation. The town is overrun with glorious luxury villas and suites cascading down the caldera.

Maria's Place   HOTEL €€
(☏ 22860 71221; www.mariasantorini.com; d studio €120; ❄ 🗶 🕾) Excellent midrange option, inland from town on the road to Finikia, and a 10-minute walk to the caldera. Peaceful (no kids under 16), great hosts, lovely pool and very reasonable off-peak rates.

Zoe Houses   APARTMENT €€€
(☏ 22860 71466; www.zoe-aegeas.gr; studio/apt €180/240; ❄ @ 🕾) Traditional houses built into the caldera's edge with all the comforts of home. Classy decor, amazing views and unrivalled hospitality mean that this place gets a lot of happily returning guests. Book ahead. Each suite is different; some can sleep up to six.

Chelidonia Traditional Villas   APARTMENT €€€
(☏ 22860 71287; www.chelidonia.com; Nikolaou Nomikou; studio €195, villa from €225; ❄ 🕾) Traditional cliff-side dwellings that have been in the owner's family for generations and offer a grand mix of old and new. Modern niceties are balanced with traditional wooden furniture, and private patios offer uninterrupted caldera views.

🍴 Eating

Lolita's Gelato   ICE CREAM €
(☏ 22860 71279; cones €3-6) Near the bus station, Lolita's sells scoopfuls of homemade heaven, including classics like blueberry or pistachio, plus original flavours like rosewater and red pepper.

Skala   GREEK €€
(☏ 22860 71362; Nikolaou Nomikou; dishes €8-18) Watch life pass up and down to Armeni Bay from the high ground of Skala's relaxed terrace. Traditional dishes like souvlaki, baked eggplant or cheese pies fill the crowd-pleasing menu.

Karma   GREEK €€
(☏ 22860 71404; www.karma.bz; mains €11-17; ☉ dinner) With fountains, flickering candles, golden-coloured walls and wine-coloured cushions, this courtyard restaurant feels rather royal and august. The traditional nature of the food is heartwarming, and as Karma's away from the caldera, the prices are considerably more relaxed.

Ambrosia   MODERN GREEK €€€
(☏ 22860 71413; www.restaurant-ambrosia.com; mains €22-33; ☉ dinner Apr-Oct) On a stone deck overlooking the sea, Ambrosia serves tasty meals among flickering candlelight and white tablecloths. Savour modern Greek dishes like grilled shrimp with mango and sweet wine sauce or duck with wild cherry.

ℹ Information

From the bus terminal, head left and uphill to reach the rather stark central square and the beautiful marble-lined main street, Nikolaou Nomikou, which skirts the caldera.

ATMs can be found on Nikolaou Nomikou and also by the bus terminus. Travel agencies are found by the bus area.

Around Santorini

Santorini is not all about the caldera edge. The island slopes gently down to sea level on its eastern and southern sides, with dark-coloured beaches of volcanic sand at popular resorts such as **Kamari** and **Perissa**.

Inland lie charming traditional villages such as **Vourvoulos**, to the north of Fira, and **Megalohori** and **Pyrgos** to its south. Pyrgos, in particular, is worth visiting and a good alternative to Oia, with fabulous restaurants and stunning views (see www.santorinipyrgos.com). Ancient sites round out a comprehensive package.

DISAPPEARING ACT

No one knows what happened to the Minoan people of Akrotiri (p388). No human remains have been found at the site. Some believe the people fled the city following the earthquake that took place two or three weeks before the volcanic eruption and are buried elsewhere on the island, beneath tonnes of ash. Others speculate that they recognised signs of impending doom and fled by boat towards Crete.

⊙ Sights & Activities

The best beaches are on the east and south coasts. Sunbeds, beach bars and water sports operators are here to serve.

One of the main beaches is the long stretch at **Perissa**. **Perivolos** and **Agios Georgios**, further south, are long stretches of black sand, pebbles and pumice stones. While they're backed by bars, tavernas, hotels and shops, they remain fairly relaxed.

Red (Kokkini) Beach, near Ancient Akrotiri, has impressive red cliffs. It's a bit of a trek over uneven rock to reach it, or caïques from Akrotiri Beach can take you there – and further, to the neighbouring White (Aspri) and Black (Mesa Pigadia) Beaches – for about €5 return. **Vlihada**, also on the south coast, has a beach backed by weirdly eroded cliffs, tavernas plus a photogenic fishing harbour.

Kamari is 10km from Fira and is Santorini's best-developed resort. It has a long beach of black sand, with the rugged limestone cliffs of Cape Mesa Vouno framing its southern end and the site of Ancient Thira on its summit. The beachfront road is dense with restaurants and bars and things get extremely busy in high season. Boats connect it with Perissa in summer.

Note: at times, Santorini's black-sand beaches become so hot that a sun lounger or mat is essential.

★ Ancient Akrotiri   ARCHAEOLOGICAL SITE
(☎22860 81366; adult/child €5/free; ⊙8am-8pm) In 1967 excavations began at the site of Akrotiri. What they uncovered was phenomenal: an ancient Minoan city buried deep beneath volcanic ash from the catastrophic eruption of 1613 BC. Today, the site retains a strong sense of place. Housed within a cool, protective structure, wooden walkways allow you to pass through various parts of the city.

DON'T MISS

CINEKAMARI

One of the finest ways to spend a Santorini evening (well, once you've done the caldera sunset). On the road into Kamari, this tree-surrounded, open-air **cinema** (☎22860 33452; www. cinekamari.gr; Kamari; admission €8; ⊙screenings 9.30pm) screens movies in their original language throughout the summer. Pull up a deckchair, request a blanket if you're feeling chilly, and relax. Drinks and snacks available.

Peek inside three-storey buildings that survived, and see roads, drainage systems and stashes of pottery. The vibe of excitement still courses through the site, with continued excavations and discoveries.

Guided tours are available (per person €10) and help to give context to the site. There's a booth inside the gate where you should enquire.

Ancient Thira   ARCHAEOLOGICAL SITE
(adult/child €2/free; ⊙8.30am-2.30pm Tue-Sun) First settled by the Dorians in the 9th century BC, Ancient Thira consists of Hellenistic, Roman and Byzantine ruins and is an atmospheric and rewarding site to visit. The ruins include temples, houses with mosaics, an *agora* (market), a theatre and a gymnasium. There are splendid views from the site.

If you're driving, take the narrow, switch-backed road from Kamari for 3km. **Ancient Thira Tours** (☎22860 32474; www.ancient-thira.gr/ancient.html; Kamari) runs an hourly minibus (9am to 1pm) from Kamari to the site (€10 return). From Perissa, on the other side of the mountain from Kamari, a hot hike up a dusty path takes a bit over an hour to reach the site.

★ Art Space   GALLERY
(☎22860 32774; www.artspace-santorini.com; Exo Gonia; ⊙11am-sunset) **FREE** This unmissable, atmospheric gallery is just outside Kamari, in Argyros Canava, one of the oldest wineries on the island. The atmospheric old wine caverns are hung with superb artworks, while sculptures transform lost corners and niches. The collection features some of Greece's finest modern artists.

Winemaking is still in the owner's blood, and part of the complex is given over to producing some stellar vintages. Tastings (€5) enhance the experience.

⛏ Sleeping

The main concentration of rooms can be found in and around Kamari and Perissa.

⛏ Kamari

Hippocampus Hotel   HOTEL €€
(☎22860 32050; www.hippocampus-hotel.gr; Kamari; d/tr/q €130/145/165; ⊙May-Oct; ❋⚛⚛) Just steps from Kamari's beachfront, this friendly place has a freshly renovated collection of rooms and studios, with added extras like hand-painted wall murals and a commitment to ecopractices. Good family-sized studios too.

SAMPLING SANTORINI

Beyond caldera views, infinity pools and black-sand beaches, Santorini is cultivating a reputation for wine and food tourism. It's a side of the island well worth exploring.

Food

Foodwise, the island is best known in Greece for its white eggplants, capers, cherry tomatoes and *fava* (yellow split peas, not unlike lentils). Cooked and puréed, the popular *fava* dish is traditionally eaten warm, as an appetiser (or dip), or accompanying a main course of meat or fish.

Tomato Industrial Museum (☑ 22860 85141; www.tomatomuseum.gr; Vlihada; admission €3; ☺ 10am-8pm) Despite the dry-sounding name, this is a unique look inside an old tomato factory by the sea in Vlihada. It's part of the cool new **Santorini Arts Factory** (www.santoriniartsfactory.gr), which hosts exhibitions, concerts and theatre; check its program online.

Selene (☑ 22860 22249; www.selene.gr; Pyrgos) Acclaimed restaurant Selene offers a program of cooking demonstrations, wine-tasting and hands-on cooking courses, with plenty of opportunity for sampling the wares. Courses include a tour of the on-site **Cultural Village** (☑ 22860 31101; www.santorinimuseum.com), which explores culinary, agricultural and other island traditions. See the website for details.

Wine

Santorini's lauded wines are its crisp dry whites, and the amber-coloured, unfortified dessert wine known as Vinsanto. Both are made from the indigenous grape variety, *assyrtiko*.

Most local vineyards host tastings (usually for a small charge), and some offer food, with scenery and local produce combining to great effect.

It's easy to explore with your own transport, but there are plenty of companies that can take you touring: **Santorini Wine Adventure** (☑ 22860 34123; www.winetoursan torini.com; half-day tour €75) and **Santorini Wine Tour** (☑ 22860 28358; www.santorini winetour.com; ☺ half-day tour €75) are two of many operators, with knowledgable guides and tours that blend food, wine, scenery and history.

SantoWines (☑ 22860 22596; www.santowines.gr; tour €5; ☺ 10am-9pm) The best place to start your wine adventure. The island's cooperative of grape-growers, it's a large tourist-focused complex on the caldera edge near the port. It has short tours of the production process and lots of tasting options. There are also superb views, a wine bar with food, and a shop full of choice vintages as well as gourmet local products.

Domaine Sigalas (☑ 22860 71644; www.sigalas-wine.com; Oia) A polished, peaceful patch not far from Oia, with wine samples and platters among the vines.

Boutari (☑ 22860 81011; www.boutari.gr; Megalohori; ☺ 10am-6pm) A relaxed, rustic winery on the way south to Akrotiri, with a great offer: up to 34 Greek wines available to try for €1 per taste. Simple local dishes on offer too.

Wine Museum (☑ 22860 31322; www.winemuseum.gr; admission €8; ☺ 9am-7pm Apr-Oct, 9.30am-2pm Mon-Sat Nov-Mar) At the Koutsoyannopoulos Winery en route to Kamari, this heavily promoted attraction has a a pricey, slightly kitsch museum in a traditional *canava* (winery). Admission includes tastings of four wines.

Beer

Santorini Brewery Company (☑ 22860 30268; www.santorinibrewingcompany.gr; ☺ 11am-5pm Mon-Sat summer, shorter hours winter) Prefer beer to wine? Well worth a stop is the home of the island's in-demand Donkey beers (you may have see its eye-catching logo on your travels). Sample the Yellow Donkey (a blonde brew), Red Donkey (a hoppier style) and Greece's first India Pale Ale (otherwise known as Crazy Donkey). Free tastings, plus cool merchandise that makes a fun souvenir.

Narkissos Hotel HOTEL €€
(☑ 22860 34205; www.narkissoshotel.com; Kamari; r incl breakfast €70; ⊙ Apr-Nov; ❄ 🌐) A decent budget option at the southern end of town, close to the beach and with well-kept rooms. Outside the summer peak, room prices tumble (€25).

Perissa

★ **Zorzis Hotel** BOUTIQUE HOTEL €€
(☑ 22860 81104; www.santorinizorzis.com; Perissa; d incl breakfast €95; ❄ 🌐 🏊) Behind a huge bloom of geraniums on Perissa's main street, Hirohiko and Spiros (a Japanese-Greek couple) run an immaculate 10-room hotel. It's a pastel-coloured sea of calm (no kids), with delightful garden, pool and mountain backdrop.

Stelios Place HOTEL €€
(☑ 22860 81860; www.steliosplace.com; Perissa; d/tr/q €75/95/118; ❄ @ 🌐 🏊) This hotel has a great position set back from the main drag in Perissa one block from the beach. Well-equipped rooms sparkle with cleanliness, not character. Note that off-peak rates fall to a bargain €25.

Eating

Most beaches have a range of tavernas and cafes. For the best eating, head to inland villages.

Brusco CAFE €
(☑ 22860 30944; Pyrgos; platters €9-15) In Pyrgos, Brusco offers coffee, wine and local flavours in a sweet rustic cafe-deli, with plenty of outdoor space. It's well worth stopping by for the warm welcome, homemade cakes (including baklava) and platters of great Santorini produce (*fava*, tomatoes, eggplant, capers etc).

★ **Metaxi Mas** TAVERNA €€
(☑ 22860 31323; www.santorini-metaximas.gr; Exo Gonia; mains €9-19; ⊙ lunch & dinner) The *raki* flows at this convivial taverna, a favourite among locals and authenticity-seeking travellers. In the central village of Exo Gonia (between Pyrgos and Kamari), park by the large church and walk down some steps to reach it. Prebooking is a good idea. Enjoy sweeping views and a delicious menu of local and Cretan specialities.

Selene MODERN EUROPEAN €€€
(☑ 22860 22249; www.selene.gr; Pyrgos; mains €30-40; dinner) Meals here aren't just meals – they're a culinary experience. When a menu contains dishes like 'poached Aegean codfish, Santorini *fava* garlic scented, oysters', you know it's not going to be run-of-the-mill. You'll now find a museum here, along with the more moderately priced **Meze & Wine Bistro** (mains €9-18; ⊙ lunch & dinner), with a similar philosophy towards high-quality local food and great flavour. Selene also offers cooking courses.

Thirasia & Volcanic Islets
Θηρασία & Ηφαιστειακές Νησίδες

Unspoilt Thirasia (population 160) was separated from Santorini by an eruption in 236 BC. The cliff-top Hora (the main town), **Manolas**, has tavernas and domatia. It's an attractive place, noticeably more relaxed and reflective than Fira could ever be. Thirasia is a stop on a couple of ferry routes to/from Athinios a few times a week, or take one of the regular boats from Ammoudi, below Oia (€2). Ask at central travel agencies for the times of these boats.

The unpopulated islets of **Palia Kameni** and **Nea Kameni** are still volcanically active and can be visited on various boat excursions from Fira Skala and Athinios. A day's excursion taking in Nea Kameni, the **hot springs** on Palia Kameni, Thirasia and Oia starts at about €30.

ANAFI ΑΝΑΦΗ
POP 270

Anafi lies a mere 19km east of Santorini, a tiny island perched on a distant horizon somewhere with a slow-paced traditional lifestyle and striking Cycladic landscapes. There are few visitors outside high summer, which is a big part of its charm.

❶ Getting There & Away

Anafi is out on a limb and you may face challenges getting there, but in July and August the island has reasonable connections. Plan well, and consult www.openseas.gr.

Buy ferry tickets at **Roussou Travel** (☑ 22860 61220; www.anafitravel.gr) in Hora's main street or at an office on the harbourfront two hours before ferries are due.

Twice a week, **ANEK Lines** (www.anek.gr) runs from Pireaus to Anafi via Milos and Santorini. From Anafi, it sails on to Sitia in Crete and a handful of Dodecanese islands. It also operates twice a week in the opposite direction.

Also twice a week in both directions, **Blue Star Ferries** (www.bluestarferries.com) sails from Piraeus to Anafi via Syros, Paros, Naxos, Ios and Santorini.

ℹ️ Getting Around

The island's port is Agios Nikolaos. From here, the main village, Hora, is a 10-minute bus ride up a winding road, or a 1km hike up a less winding but steep walkway. In summer a bus runs regularly and usually meets boats; buses also run east to the monastery.

Summertime caïques serve various beaches and nearby islands.

In Hora, **Manos** (☑️ 22860 61430; www.rentacarmanos.com) has cars, scooters and four-wheelers for rent.

⊙ Sights & Activities

There are several lovely beaches near Agios Nikolaos. Palm-lined **Klissidi**, a 1.5km walk east of the port, is the closest and most popular. A walking trail continues along the south coast giving access to more strands, including the long, sandy **Roukounas Beach**.

Anafi's main sight is **Moni Kalamiotissas**, 9km by road from Hora or reached by a more appealing 7km walk (around 2½ to three hours one way) along the south-coast trail. The monastery lies in the east of the island, near the meagre remains of a **Sanctuary to Apollo** and below the summit of the 463m **Kalamos** (or Monastery Rock). The walk to the monastery is a rewarding expedition, but it's a fairly tough trip in places and a day's outing there and back (consider taking a bus to the monastery in summer and walking back).

The island's most celebrated trail is the rocky ascent from Moni Kalamiotissas up Kalamos to the now abandoned monastery at the top. The walk is 2.5km, about an hour each way. See trail info on the excellent Terrain map for Anafi.

🛏️ Sleeping

Many of the rooms in Hora have good views across Anafi's rolling hills to the sea and to the great summit of Kalamos. Domatia owners prefer long stays in high season, so if you're only staying one night you should take whatever you can get (and book ahead).

Margarita's Rooms   PENSION €
(☑️ 22860 61237; www.margarita-anafi.gr; d €45-55) Right by the beach and next to Margarita's cafe, these simple, beloved rooms hark back to the Greek island life of quieter times.

Apollon Village Hotel   APARTMENT €€
(☑️ 22860 28739; www.apollonvillagehotel.gr; d/studio/apt from €70/95/120; ☺ May-Sep; ❄️ 🛜) Rising in tiers above Klissidi Beach, these individual rooms, studios and apartments with glorious views are each named after a Greek god and remain outstanding value. The Blue Cafe-Bar is a cool adjunct to the hotel, with homemade sweets and pastries.

Villa Kalamiotissa   APARTMENT €€
(☑️ 22860 61415; www.villakalamiotissa.gr; d €80-110; ☺ Apr-Oct; ❄️ 🛜) A handsome, newly built complex of rooms and studios, all white and pale blue with lovely stonework. It sits on a quiet edge of Hora, with spectacular views from each verandah. Studios sleep three and have kitchen.

🍴 Eating & Drinking

There are several tavernas in Hora, all on the main street.

Margarita's   TAVERNA €
(☑️ 22860 61237; www.margarita-anafi.gr; Klissidi; mains €6-12; ☺ breakfast, lunch & dinner) A sunny little terrace overlooking the bay at Klissidi makes for an idyllic dining experience. The fresh-baked bread, handmade pasta and meatballs are staples; *fava*, goat stew and cheese pies are all full of local flavour.

Liotrivi   TAVERNA €€
(☑️ 22860 61209; mains €7-15; ☺ lunch & dinner May-Oct) A classy old-school taverna, where fresh fish is brought in from the family's boat while just about everything else, from eggs to vegetables and honey, comes from their garden.

Armenaki   TAVERNA €€
(☑️ 22860 61234; mains €7-15; ☺ lunch & dinner Jun-Sep) Tuna and swordfish are the go-to dishes at this traditional taverna, enhanced by an airy terrace and splendid views.

Glaros   BAR
In Hora, be sure to stop for a drink at this local institution. If you're lucky, you'll stumble across some live music – if not, the views won't disappoint.

ℹ️ Information

Hora's main pedestrian thoroughfare leads uphill from the first bus stop and has most of the domatia, restaurants and minimarkets. There's an ATM in a kiosk halfway along the harbourfront at Agios Nikolaos. Find more information online at www.anafi.gr.

SIKINOS ΣΙΚΙΝΟΣ

POP 273

A stone's throw from Santorini, Sikinos is really worlds away – and decidedly off the tourist radar. Quiet and remote, this is the place to come if you want to experience traditional island life at its least commercial. With a charming old town, a few low-key sights and terraced hills that sweep down to sandy beaches, Sikinos offers a true escape.

The main clusters of habitation are the port of Alopronia, and the linked inland villages of Horio and Kastro (collectively known as the Hora). Kastro has homes and businesses, Horio is purely residential. They are reached by a 3.4km road winding up from the port. There's a post office at the eastern edge of Kastro, and an ATM in Kastro's central square.

ℹ Getting There & Around

The local bus meets ferry arrivals and runs between Alopronia and Horio/Kastro (€1.60) every half-hour in August, but less frequently at other times. A timetable is posted at the terminus, just inland from the port.

There is a small agency at the port, RaC (☑ 21040 80300; www.rentacar-sikinos.gr), hiring out cars and scooters.

Ferry tickets can be bought at the port at Kountouris Travel (☑ 6981594106, 22860 51232). Out of high season, boat services are skeletal.

◎ Sights

A Venetian fortress that stood here in the 13th century gave Kastro its name. Today it is a charming, lived-in place, with winding alleyways between brilliant white houses. At its heart is the main square and the Church of Pantanassa. Check out the buildings surrounding the church, which were homes to the town's wealthy merchants; two-storey affairs with remnants of ornate stonework around the windows.

The shells of old windmills cling to the plunging cliffside on the northern side of Kastro. Also to the north, a flight of whitewashed steps leads to the once-fortified monastery of Moni Zoödohou Pigis, high above the town. Originally built as a women's monastery in 1690, this is where the villagers would hide during pirate attacks.

Just west of Kastro, above steeply terraced fields and reached by another flight of steps, is the reclusive, beautiful Horio. Still home to a dozen or so residents, it's a patchwork of derelict and well-tended houses and is definitely worth a wander.

From the saddle between Kastro and Horio, a surfaced road leads southwest to Moni Episkopis. The remains here are believed to be those of a 3rd-century-AD Roman mausoleum that was transformed into a church in the 7th century and a monastery 10 centuries later. From here you can hike south 1.4km (35 minutes; signed) to Agia Marina, via tiny Byzantine churches and ancient ruins. Other excellent trails take you to Horio (3½ hours) or to Alopronia (three hours).

En route to Episkopis, it's worth stopping at the Manalis Winery (☑ 22860 51281; www.manaliswinery.gr), where wine is produced using self-sustaining, traditional methods. You can easily spend an hour or two here nibbling on snacks and sipping wine on the view-filled patio.

The beach at Alopronia is small but sandy with some shade and a children's playground. A narrow, dramatic bay with a small sandy

BOAT SERVICES FROM SIKINOS

DESTINATION	TIME	FARE	FREQUENCY
Folegandros	45min	€7	4 weekly
Ios	25min	€5	4 weekly
Kimolos	2¼hr	€13	4 weekly
Milos	3hr 25min	€13	2 weekly
Naxos	2hr 25min	€12	1 weekly
Paros	3hr 50min	€14	1 weekly
Piraeus	7½-9½hr	€36	4 weekly
Santorini (Thira)	2hr	€9	3 weekly
Serifos	4¼hr	€18	1 weekly
Sifnos	2¾hr-5hr	€16	4 weekly
Syros	6hr	€16	1 weekly

patch, **Agios Nikolaos Beach** is a 20-minute walk through the countryside from the port. To find it, follow signs to Dialiskari. A path leads further on to **Agios Georgios**, or you can reach it by sealed road (7km).

Summertime caïques (about €6) run to beaches, including **Malta** in the north (which boasts ancient ruins on the hill above), and **Kara** in the south.

🛏 Sleeping & Eating

🛏 Alopronia

Lucas Rooms   PENSION €
(📱22860 51075; www.sikinoslucas.gr; d from €50; ❄️📶) These simple, comfy rooms and studios are lovingly decorated. Rooms in complex B are on the hillside, 600m inland from the port, while complex A is on the far side of the bay from the ferry quay. All have sea-view balconies and plenty of peace.

Porto Sikinos   HOTEL €€
(📱22860 51220; www.portosikinos.gr; s/d incl breakfast €90/105; ☉May-Oct; ❄️📶) The sweet rooms here are traditional tile-and-marble affairs with pastel-coloured accents and balconies. This central, whitewashed complex is the closest thing to a standard hotel on Sikinos and slightly pricey because of it, but it's well run and appealing, with an on-site cafe.

Veranda   CAFE, BAR €
(📱22860 51220; meals €4-11) A civilised all-day spot at Porto Sikinos hotel, with a jazzy soundtrack and a big menu of coffee, cocktails, crêpes, salads and pasta.

Lucas Taverna   TAVERNA €€
(Alopronia; dishes €7-13; ☉lunch & dinner) In the village with beachy views, this is the place to come for well-prepared Greek standards without frills including fish by the kilo.

🛏 Kastro

Rooms Kaminia   PENSION €
(📱22860 51304; d €60; ❄️📶) A whitewashed staircase next to the post office in Kastro leads up to this complex of four simple studios – large and spotless, with kitchen facilities, new bathrooms and splendid views. It's open year-round, with low-season prices a steal at €30.

Stegadi   APARTMENT €€
(📱22860 51271; www.stegadi.com; d €85; ❄️📶) Near the heart of Kastro, these traditional

Sikinos

0 ——— 5 km
0 ——— 2.5 miles

AEGEAN SEA

Moni Zoödohou Pigis
Malta Beach
Kastro
Agios Georgios Beach
Horio
Manalis Winery
▲552m
Moni Episkopis
Alopronia
Agios Nikolaos Beach
Sikinos
▲432m
Kalogeri
Kara Beach
Kardiotissa

Folegandros (19km);
Naxos (30km); Paros (30km);
Sifnos (55km); Milos (75km);
Syros (85km); Piraeus (250km)

Santorini (56km);
Ios (65km)

CYCLADES FOLEGANDROS

apartments sleep up to four and are decorated with modern furnishings and splashes of vibrant colour. The balconies are small oases with views across to the sea.

Anemelo   CAFE €
(📱22860 51216; mains €4-6; ☉breakfast, lunch & dinner) This is Kastro's most atmospheric place to grab a local tea, beer or simple crêpe-and-salad lunch. Locals yabber at the tables over chess games or lounge over coffee at the tables outside. Take the *tiny* staircase up to the terrace for ace views.

Klimataria   GREEK €€
(📱22860 51065; mains €8-13; ☉lunch & dinner May-Oct; 📶) A cute leafy laneway shades a couple of traditional eateries, including this friendly spot where you can indulge in platters heaped with mixed grills.

FOLEGANDROS
ΦΟΛΕΓΑΝΔΡΟΣ

POP 770

Folegandros lies on the southern edge of the Cyclades with the Sea of Crete sweeping away to its south. The island has a bewitching beauty that's amplified by its alluring cliff-top Hora, easily one of the most appealing villages in the Cyclades.

Folegandros is barely 12km by 4km but shoulders a somewhat dark past. The remoteness and ruggedness of the island made it a place of exile for political prisoners from Roman times to the 20th century, and as late as the military dictatorship of 1967–74. Today the seductive charm of Folegandros has left its grim history behind.

BOAT SERVICES FROM FOLEGANDROS

DESTINATION	TIME	FARE	FREQUENCY
Amorgos*	2-5½hr	€69	6 weekly
Ios	1hr 20min	€10	4 weekly
Ios*	20min	€44	2 weekly
Kimolos	1hr 20min-2hr 40min	€13	4 weekly
Koufonisia*	1hr 40min-5hr	€69	6 weekly
Milos	2½hr	€13	2 weekly
Milos*	1hr	€39.50	1-2 daily
Mykonos*	3-3½hr	€59	6 weekly
Naxos*	2hr 40min	€49	6 weekly
Piraeus	6½-9hr	€36	4 weekly
Piraeus*	3½-5hr	€59.50	1-2 daily
Santorini (Thira)	3hr	€12	3 weekly
Santorini (Thira)*	40-70min	€44	1-2 daily
Serifos	3hr 20min	€18	1 weekly
Sifnos	2-4hr	€16	4 weekly
Sifnos*	2hr	€49.50	3 weekly
Sikinos	45min	€7	5 weekly
Syros	6¾hr	€18	1 weekly

* high-speed services

Boats dock at the little harbour of Karavostasis, on the east coast. Aside from it and Hora, the only other settlement of any size is Ano Meria. There are a some good beaches, but be prepared for strenuous walking to reach some of them (or the easy option: take a boat).

ⓘ Getting There & Away

Once poorly served by ferries, Folegandros (at least in summer) has good connections with Piraeus through the western Cyclades route. It even has connections to Santorini and as far as Amorgos in the high season.

ⓘ Getting Around

The local bus meets all ferry arrivals and takes passengers to Hora (€1.60). From Hora there are buses to the port one hour before ferry departures. Buses from Hora run hourly in summer to Ano Meria (€1.60) and divert to Angali Beach (€2). The bus terminus is at the entrance to Hora from the south, behind the post office.

There is a **taxi service** (☏6944693957) on Folegandros. Fares to the port are about €7 to €10, to Ano Meria €10 and to Angali Beach €10 to €14.

You can hire cars/motorbikes from a number of outlets in high season for about €60/25 per day. Rates can drop by half outside high season.

In summer, small boats regularly ply between beaches.

Karavostasis Καραβοστάσις
POP 90

Folegandros' port is a sunny place with a pleasant pebble beach. Within a kilometre north and south lies a series of other beaches, all enjoyable and easily reached by short walks. In high season boats leave Karavostasis for beaches further afield. If beaches (or Anemi) are your allure, stay here – for our money, however, Hora is where the magic is.

🛏 Sleeping & Eating

There are a couple of tavernas at the port serving fairly standard dishes, and a couple of good beach bars. For enduring character, Evangelos is right on the beach and is the place for relaxed drinks, snacks and great conversation.

Aeolos Beach Hotel　　　　HOTEL €€
(☏22860 41205; www.aeolos-folegandros.gr; s €50, d €85-95, all incl breakfast; ☉May-Sep; ❉🕾) Settle in just behind the beach in a peaceful garden. Rooms have a sea or mountain view and are each unique with varying degrees of character; check out a few if you can. Minimum three-night stay in July and August.

★ Anemi   HOTEL €€€

(☑22860 41610; www.anemihotel.gr; d/ste incl breakfast from €275/430; ☺late May-Sep; ❋🔆🔊) Oh so modern and entirely luxurious, this is a place for pampering. Rooms are plush but sleek, brought to life by modern artwork used as headboards. The pool is a large, beckoning sheet of blue (some of the suites have private pool) and there's an enviable roll-call of extras, including family-friendly ones. It's hard to fault.

Hora (Folegandros)
Χώρα (Φολέγανδρος)

POP 425

In 2013 CNN included Folegandros in its list of seven of Europe's most beautiful villages. We can't argue with the inclusion, but we're a little sad the secret is now out. This village is probably the most charming in the Cyclades, its meandering main street winding happily from leafy square to leafy square, alfresco tables buzzing with life.

◉ Sights

Hora is a joy to wander through. The village proper starts at **Plateia Pounta**; on its north side, it stands on the edge of a formidable cliff. Just west of here is the medieval **kastro**, a small tangle of narrow alleys spanned by low archways. It dates from when Marco Sanudo ruled the island in the 13th century. The wooden balconies of the traditional houses blaze with bougainvillea and hibiscus, and a few whitewashed chapels add charm.

The extended village, outside the *kastro*, is just as attractive. From Plateia Pounta, a steep zigzag path leads up to the looming Church of the Virgin, **Panagia** (☺6-9pm), which sits perched on a dramatic cliff top above the town and acts as both a stunning photo backdrop and a mecca for sunset-watchers.

☞ Tours

Given the tough-to-access nature of many beaches, a popular excursion is the six-hour boat trip around the island (adult/child €30/15). The price includes lunch and plenty of swimming stops. The tour leaves Karavostasis at 11am, and can be booked through Diaplous Travel (p396) and Sottovento Tourism Office (p396). Private boat trips can also be arranged.

🛏 Sleeping

In July and August most domatia and hotels will be full, so book well in advance. Most accommodation offers free port transfers.

Folegandros

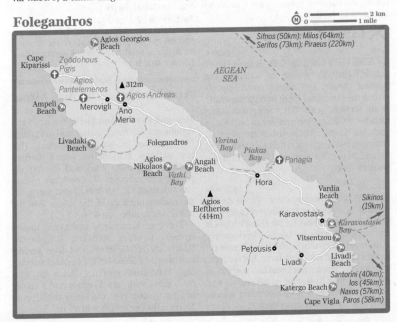

Aegeo   HOTEL €€
(☑22860 41468; www.aegeohotel.com; s/d/tr €70/95/140; ☺May-Sep; ❄@🌐) On the outskirts of town, these appealing rooms are immaculate and bright, with wooden furnishings and private balconies. Doubles in low season are excellent value at under €50.

Hotel Odysseus   HOTEL €€
(☑22860 41276; www.odysseushotel.com; s/d €75/105; ☺mid-May–Sep; ❄🌐▨) Tucked away in a quiet corner of town with some dramatic views, Odysseus has pretty, compact rooms with sweet terraces, and a lovely pool area that's shared with Aria Boutique Hotel next door. Low-season prices are ace (doubles €55) but breakfast is a steep additional €12.

Folegandros Apartments   APARTMENT €€
(☑22860 41239; www.folegandros-apartments. com; d €130-190; ☺May-Sep; ❄🌐▨) Lovely complex of studios and apartments (the largest can sleep seven) set in well-kept gardens around a pristine pool.

Anemomylos Apartments   HOTEL €€€
(☑22860 41309; www.anemomilosapartments. com; d incl breakfast from €250; ☺May-Sep; ❄🌐▨) A prime cliff-top location grants awesome views from this stylish complex and its lovely terraces. Rooms are elegant and embellished with antiques. The pool is divine, and service comes with wonderful attention to detail.

✗ Eating & Drinking

Chic   GREEK €
(☑22860 41515; mains €6.50-13; ☺dinner Easter-Oct; 🖉) Perfectly placed for watching the passing parade, but what's more impressive is the flavourful food: everything made from scratch, with the menu indicating gluten-free, dairy-free and vegan options (a rarity in Greece). Vegie dishes are plentiful (home-grown vegies and herbs); meat-lovers should plump for goat and lamb from the owners' farm.

Pounta   TAVERNA €€
(☑22860 41063; www.pounta.gr; Plateia Pounta; mains €6-12; ☺breakfast, lunch & dinner Easter–mid-Oct) A family business for 20 years, Pounta is the work of a creative Danish-Greek couple – dishes are served on Lisbet's handmade ceramics (also for sale), in a large, lush garden. The menu ranges from breakfast yoghurt to grilled octopus by way of rabbit *stifado* and baked aubergine. If it's watermelon season, definitely try the watermelon cake.

Eva's Garden   MEDITERRANEAN €€€
(☑22860 41110; mains €10-25; ☺dinner May-Sep) Eva's is a sophisticated spot that puts a gourmet spin on Greek cuisine (with portions that seem small if you've eaten at many tavernas!). Starters include octopus carpaccio or sautéed shrimps, while mains tempt with sea-bass fillet or rib-eye on the grill. Turn left after Piatsa square.

★Rakentia   CAFE, BAR
(☑22860 41581; www.rakentia.gr; ☺10.30am-3pm & 6.30pm-1am May-Sep) Head west and look for a signed laneway beside the Anemousa Hotel to find this gem, a cafe-bar with cool music and cooler views. Watch birds soar at dusk over cocktails and creative tapas dishes.

ⓘ Information

Travel agencies are good sources of information. ATMs are at the post office (as you reach town from the port) and on Plateia Dounavi. There's information (and a downloadable app) at www. infolegandros.com.

Diaplous Travel (☑22860 41158; www. diaploustravel.gr; Plateia Pounta) Helpful and efficient agency. Sells ferry tickets and arranges boat trips. There's also an office at Karavostasis.

Folegandros Travel (☑22860 41273; www. folegandros-travel.gr; Plateia Dounavi) Sells ferry tickets and exchanges money. There's also an office at the port.

Sottovento (☑22860 41444; www.folegandrosisland.com; Plateia Pounta) Sottovento doubles as the Italian consulate and is helpful on all tourism matters, including accommodation and boat trips.

Ano Meria   Ανω Μερiά

POP 240

The settlement of Ano Meria is a scattered community of small farms and dwellings that stretches for several kilometres. This is traditional Folegandros where tourism makes no intrusive mark and life happily wanders off sideways. The **folklore museum** (admission €2; ☺5-8pm Jul–mid-Sep) is on the eastern outskirts of the village. Ask the bus driver to drop you off nearby.

There are a couple of traditional, unpretentious tavernas, including **I Synantisi** (Maria's; ☑22860 41208; ☺lunch & dinner Jun-Sep) and **Mimis** (☑22860 41377; ☺lunch & dinner May-Sep). The island's specialty dish is *matsata*, fresh pasta with tomato sauce and a choice of meat (usually goat, chicken or rabbit). Ano Meria is the perfect place to try it.

Around Folegandros

For **Livadi Beach**, 1.2km southeast of Karavostasis, take the 'bypass' road just past the Anemi Hotel and follow it around the coast. There's camping (see www.folegandros.org).

Katergo Beach is on the southeastern tip of the island and is best reached by boat from Karavostasis. Boats leave regularly (weather permitting), for €8 return.

The sandy and pebbled **Angali** beach, on the central coast opposite Hora, is a popular spot. There are some rooms here and reasonable tavernas; buses run here regularly in summer from Hora. About 750m west of Angali over the hill along a footpath is **Agios Nikolaos**, a clothes-optional beach.

A number of beaches can be reached from where the road ends beyond Ano Meria: **Livadaki Beach** is a 1.5km hike from the bus stop near the church of Agios Andreas at Ano Meria. **Agios Georgios Beach** is north of Ano Meria and requires another demanding walk (about 40 minutes). Have tough footwear, sun protection and, because most beaches have no shops or tavernas, make sure you take food and water. Check out walking trails on the Terrain map of Folegandros.

Boats connect some west-coast beaches in high season: excursion boats make separate round trips from Angali to Agios Nikolaos (€5), and from Angali to Livadaki Beach (€10).

MILOS ΜΗΛΟΣ

POP 4980

Volcanic Milos arches around a central caldera and is ringed with dramatic coastal landscapes of colourful and surreal rock formations. The island's most celebrated export, the iconic *Venus de Milo*, is far away in the Louvre, but dozens of beaches (the most of any Cycladic island) and a series of picturesque villages contribute to its current, compelling, attractions.

CYCLADES AROUND FOLEGANDROS

Milos & Kimolos

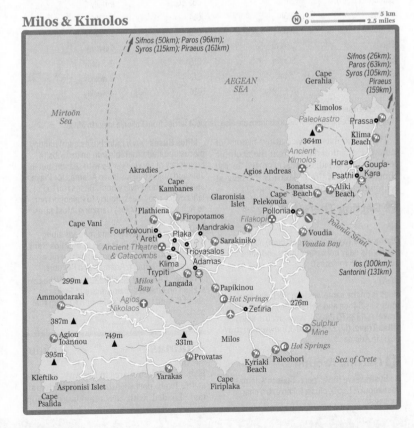

BOAT SERVICES FROM MILOS

DESTINATION	TIME	FARE	FREQUENCY
Amorgos*	4-7hr	€69	6 weekly
Anafi	6hr	€20	1 weekly
Folegandros	2½hr	€13	2 weekly
Folegandros*	55min	€39.50	1-2 daily
Ios	4hr	€16	2 weekly
Ios*	1hr 25min	€49.50	1 daily
Kimolos**	1hr	€10	6 weekly
Koufonisia*	4½-6½hr	€69	6 weekly
Kythnos	4hr 10min	€18	6 weekly
Mykonos*	5-6hr	€69	6 weekly
Naxos*	4¼-5¼hr	€59.50	6 weekly
Paros	5¼-7½hr	€16	3 weekly
Piraeus	5-7hr	€36	1-2 daily
Piraeus*	2½-4hr	€46-58	3-4 daily
Santorini (Thira)	3½-5½hr	€16	2 weekly
Santorini (Thira)*	2hr	€52.50	2 daily
Serifos	2-3hr	€14	1-2 daily
Serifos*	1½hr	€16	1-2 daily
Sifnos	1½-2hr	€13	1-3 daily
Sifnos*	50min	€15	2-3 daily
Sikinos	3½hr	€13	2 weekly
Syros	5½-9½hr	€16	4 weekly

* high-speed services
** major services from Adamas port; there are also frequent ferries from Pollonia in north Milos

The island has a fascinating history of mineral extraction dating from the neolithic period when obsidian was exported to the Minoan world of Crete. Milos is the biggest bentonite and perlite centre in the EU.

ⓘ Getting There & Away

AIR

Olympic Air (www.olympicair.com) has up to five flights daily between Athens and Milos airport (€65, 45 minutes).

BOAT

Milos is on the same western Cyclades ferry routes as Sifnos and Serifos. Buy tickets at **Riva Travel** (☑ 22870 24024; www.rivatravel.gr) or **Milos Travel** (☑ 22870 22000; www.milostravel.gr) in Adamas.

ⓘ Getting Around

No buses serve the airport. Taxis to Adamas cost about €12.50, plus a token extra charge for bags.

Milos Buses (www.milosbuses.com) handily places updated timetable info on its website. Frequency of service varies with season, but in July and August buses leave Adamas for Plaka and Trypiti about every hour. Buses run to Pollonia every two hours, hourly to Paleohori and to Achivadolimni (Milos) Camping. Most fares are €1.60.

Hire cars, motorcycles and mopeds along the waterfront, at Riva Travel , or at **Milos Rent** (☑ 22870 41473; www.milosrent.gr), which has offices at the airport, Adamas and Pollonia.

Taxis (☑ Adamas 22870 22219) from the taxi station on Adamas' main square to Plaka are about €7 and to Pollonia €14; add €1 from the port.

Adamas   Αδάμας
POP 1350

Fishers sell their wares in the early morning at the lively port of Adamas (also Adamantas). Loaded with accommodation, shops and general services, the modern village also has a diverting waterfront scene.

◎ Sights

Milos Mining Museum
MUSEUM

(☑ 22870 22481; www.milosminingmuseum.gr; adult/child €4/2; ⊙ 10am-2pm & 5.30-9.30pm Jun-Sep, shorter hours Oct-May) This excellent small museum details Milos' mining history. It's about 600m east of the ferry quay.

Ask here about the **Miloterranean Geo Experience** (www.miloterranean.gr) project, a series of maps that outline great half-day 'geo walks' through Milos. The maps detail the island's geology and volcanic origin, mining history and natural environment, and can be purchased at the museum.

Ecclesiastical Museum of Milos
MUSEUM

(☑ 22870 23956; www.ecclesiasticalmuseum.org; ⊙ 9.15am-1.15pm May-Sep) FREE Tucked in where the waterfront road turns inland, this collection in the Church of the Holy Trinity boasts fine icons and artefacts.

⌕ Tours

Tour boats line Adamas' waterfront of an evening, touting their daily cruises. These leave every morning (weather permitting) to explore the impressive coastline, bizarre rock formations, and beaches not reachable by road. The beautiful rocks and coves of **Kleftiko** in Milos' southwest is a prime destination. A number of cruises also visit Kimolos.

There are large and small boats, private charters, and speedboats, wooden-hulled boats, catamarans and sailboats. Check out what takes your fancy. It's worth asking about group sizes, itineraries, lunch arrangements and swimming time.

Prices generally start from about €30. Most travel agencies can book you on a cruise; note that in summer's peak you can usually find departures from Pollonia.

⨼ Sleeping

In summer lists of available domatia are usually kept at the quayside tourist kiosk.

Aeolis Hotel
HOTEL €€

(☑ 22870 23985; www.aeolis-hotel.com; d/tr incl breakfast €105/120; ❄ �🛜) Inland from the harbourfront, this sweet, neat, 12-room hotel is peaceful and calm, its white rooms given a pop of colour here and there. Open year-round, with prices diving in low season (double €35).

Studios Helios
APARTMENT €€

(☑ 22870 22258; www.milos-island.gr/rooms-apartments/helios; studio €90; ⊙ May-Oct; ❄ 🛜) Rising high above the port, these large self-catering studios are neat as a pin and decorated in attractive traditional style, with sea-view balconies.

Hotel Delfini
HOTEL €€

(☑ 22870 22001; www.delfinimilos.gr; d/tr €80/100; ⊙ Apr-Oct; ❄ 🛜) A comfortable, tucked away, budget-style hotel with a lovely terrace and warm ambience. It's west of the quay behind the Lagada Beach Hotel, which unfortunately blocks the view. Discounts for longer stays.

✖ Eating & Drinking

Music bars rock out just above the port during July and August.

★ O! Hamos
TAVERNA €

(☑ 22870 21672; www.ohamos-milos.gr; Papikinou Beach; dishes €5-10; ⊙ lunch & dinner Easter-Oct; 🛜 👶) In this rustic taverna across the road from the beach, sit in the garden, peruse the huge handwritten menu and choose from an array of traditional recipes (in fact, you can also pick up the recipe cards). The best picks are cheeses and grilled meats, but it's all good, and served with warmth and flair (and on cool branded ceramics).

O! Hamos is on Papikinou Beach about 2km southeast of Adamas. On the beach itself, it has a cafe area, sunbeds and play area for kids.

Barko
TAVERNA €

(☑ 22870 22660; dishes €5-13; ⊙ dinner) This classic taverna on the road to Plaka, near the outskirts of town, serves local dishes such as chickpea fritters and oven-baked lamb in a sheltered garden setting.

Flisvos
TAVERNA €€

(☑ 22870 22275; dishes €8-14; ⊙ lunch & dinner; 🛜) This place has pedigree: it's the oldest waterfront restaurant in town. Choose from grilled meats (for which it's known), fish by the kilo or traditional specialities like lamb in lemon sauce.

ℹ Information

Municipal tourist office (⊙ Jun-Sep) Helpful kiosk opposite the quay, handing out maps, directions and general info.

Plaka & Trypiti
Πλάκα & Τρυπητή

Supercharming Plaka (population 749), 5km uphill from Adamas, embodies the Cycladic ideal with its white houses and labyrinthine lanes perching along the edge of an escarpment. Plaka was built on the site of Ancient Milos, which was destroyed by the Athenians and rebuilt by the Romans. It meanders straight into the settlement to the south, Trypiti (population 540), and they both rise above several villages converging to the southwest.

Plaka's **main church courtyard** has spectacular views and gets packed out for sunset in high season.

Walks in this area are popular, especially from Plaka to Trypiti and down to Klima. Off the road to the catacombs, a dirt track leads to the spot where a farmer found the *Venus de Milo* in 1820; it's marked by a sign. A bit further along, the well-preserved **Roman theatre** hosts the Milos Festival each summer, and footpaths lead down to Klima or onto the promontory with ancient stone walls and two small churches.

Sights & Activities

Archaeology Museum
MUSEUM
(☑ 22870 28026; Plaka; adult/child €3/free; ⊙ 9am-4pm Tue-Sun) This handsome old building contains some riveting exhibits, including a plaster cast of the *Venus de Milo* – the original was likely carved from Parian marble around 100 BC, and was found on Milos by a local farmer in 1820 and now resides in the Louvre in Paris. A perky little herd of tiny bull figurines comes from the Filakopi settlement and dates from 1400 to 1100 BC.

Milos Folk & History Museum
MUSEUM
(☑ 22870 21292; Plaka; adult/child €3/free; ⊙ 11am-1pm & 7-10pm Tue-Sun) Peruse traditional costumes, woven goods and household artefacts in a series of traditionally furnished rooms, right by the main church courtyard.

Kastro
FORTRESS
Signs mark the path climbing to the hill-top fortress, built on the ancient acropolis and offering panoramic views of the island. The 13th-century church, Thalassitras, lies inside the walls.

Catacombs
MONUMENT
(☑ 22870 21625; Trypiti; admission €3; ⊙ 8.30am-1.45pm Tue-Sun) Greece's only Christian catacombs date from the 1st century and were the burial site for early believers. Get off the Trypiti bus at the T-junction with a signpost indicating the way. Once there, a guide takes you inside and explains the workings of the ancient cemetery.

Sleeping

Archondoula Studios
APARTMENT €€
(☑ 22870 23820; www.archondoula-studios.gr; Plaka; r/studio €65/95; ⊙ Mar-Nov; ❄ �) Cheerful Stavros runs sleek, white-on-white rooms and studios. Rooms are compact, while the studios give more breathing space. Take in spectacular sunset views from terraces and balconies, and enjoy the peace of Plaka after dark.

Mimallis Houses
APARTMENT €€
(☑ 22870 21094, 6972808758; www.mimallis. gr; Plaka & Klima; Plaka d €90-95, Klima d/q €200/220; ⊙ Apr-Oct; ❄ �) Rents two small houses in Plaka (eaching sleeping two), and one in precious Klima (sleeping up to five) – each different, comfortable and packed with amenities. Low-season discounts are excellent.

Studios Betty
APARTMENT €€
(☑ 22870 21538; www.studiosbetty-milos.com; Plaka; studio €100; ❄ �=) Sunset views as glorious as Santorini's from this complex of four simple studios at Plaka's cliff edge.

Windmill of Karamitsos
APARTMENT €€€
(☑ 6945568086; www.windmillmilos.gr; Trypiti; windmill €200; ⊙ Apr-Oct) Bed down in a unique converted windmill that dates from 1859 and now sleeps four in creative quarters over three levels. It's on a hill-top on the edge of Trypiti, with panoramic views.

Eating

Palaios
CAFE €
(☑ 22870 23490; Plaka) This old-world cafe is a perfect pit stop for breakfast or coffee, but it's mostly worth stopping by to try some local specialities: *karpouzopita* (watermelon cake, or pie), unique to Milos and Folegandros, and *ladenia* (not unlike a flatbread pizza).

★ Archondoula
TAVERNA €€
(☑ 22870 21384; Plaka; dishes €5-15; ⊙ lunch & dinner Easter-Nov) The whole cheerful family

is involved at this top-notch taverna in a picturesque laneway setting. Classic Greek dishes have an assured touch and range from grilled vegetables with *manouri* (soft cheese) to grilled swordfish to lamb with tomato and artichoke.

Pollonia   Πολλώνια

Pollonia, on the north coast, is a low-key fishing village with azure waters that transforms into quite a chic (albeit petite) summer resort. The town is also the jumping-off point for Kimolos; note that it's sometimes mapped as Apollonia. **Travel Me to Milos** (☑ 22870 41008; www.travelmetomilos.com) is a helpful travel agency based here, with good activities and excursions.

🛏 Sleeping & Eating

Pollonia has loads of stylish studios (especially at its northwestern arm), and excellent seafront (and seafood) dining.

Nefeli Sunset Studios   APARTMENT €€
(☑ 22870 41466; www.milos-nefelistudios.gr; studio from €130; ☉ Apr-Oct; ❄ 🞵) Whitewashed cubes combine modern design with traditional touches, in a garden-enhanced bayfront property on the northwest edge of the village.

★ Salt   BOUTIQUE HOTEL €€€
(☑ 22870 41110; www.salt-milos.com; d/ste incl breakfast from €180/230; ☉ Apr-Oct; ❄ 🞵) Sparklingly minimal, white-on-white sophistication, and with all the luxuries and views to the sea. Low-season rates fall by close to 50%.

★ Armenaki   SEAFOOD €€
(☑ 22870 41061; www.armenaki.gr; dishes €6-13, fish by kg; ☉ lunch & dinner Apr-Oct) Armenaki is revered for its fishy business – this place is all about seafood (in fact, there's little else on the menu). Seafood in all its guises is cooked to perfection, and service is first-rate (including the filleting of fish at your table). *Kakavia* (traditional fish stew) comes recommended, and there's an extensive wine list.

Gialos   SEAFOOD €€
(☑ 22870 41208; www.gialos-pollonia.gr; mains €7-18; ☉ lunch & dinner Easter-Oct) Watch port life while digging into fresh seafood and yummy pastas. Bustling Gialos has a creative menu bursting with fresh local flavour, including

---

> **DON'T MISS**
>
> ### KLIMA
>
> Tiny, photogenic Klima clings to the beachfront cliff face below Trypiti. It's the best example of Milos' *syrmata* (traditional fishers' encampments), where the downstairs, with brightly painted doors, are used for rough-weather boat storage, and the upstairs for family life.
>
> The homes, most still in use today, are incorporated into the rocks. A unique holiday experience is to rent a *syrmata* for your stay; a few of these are available on airbnb.com. You'll need your own wheels.

---

dishes like tuna *tataki*, open ravioli with shrimp, and sour-cheese patties. Save room for dessert.

Around Milos

Milos and its offshore islets are rimmed by more than 70 splendid beaches in different coloured sands and stone. Rent wheels or take a cruise to compare.

In the north, **Plathiena** is a fine sandy beach north of Plaka, and on the way you can visit fishing villages **Areti** and **Fourkovouni**. Also in this area, **Sarakiniko** is a must, with its snow white rock formations and natural terraces.

On the south coast, golden-sanded **Provatas** feels remote but has a couple of tavernas. **Kyriaki** is backed by otherworldy grey-, rose- and rust-coloured hills and has soft, grey sand. The long taupe arch of **Paleohori** is backed by banded cliffs and has beach bars, water sports and hot sand, thanks to hot springs in the area.

◉ Sights & Activities

Filakopi   HISTORIC SITE
(admission €2; ☉ 8am-3pm Tue, Thu & Sat) This ancient Minoan city in the island's northeast (close to Pollonia) was one of the earliest settlements in the Cyclades. Now it's not much more than rubble, but the seaside setting is great, with cavelike rock formations all around.

★ Sea Kayak Milos   KAYAKING
(☑ 22870 23597; www.seakayakgreece.com; ☉ Apr-Oct) A superb way to explore the coastline.

Australian Rod and his team lead highly regarded day trips (€70, including lunch); no experience required. Itineraries depend on weather conditions. Multiday kayaking and camping tours available.

Milos Diving Center   DIVING
(☑ 22870 41296; www.milosdiving.gr) Dives (from €50, including equipment) and courses, based at Pollonia.

🛏 Sleeping & Eating

Achivadolimni (Milos)

Camping   CAMPGROUND €
(☑ 22870 31410; www.miloscamping.gr; Achivadolimni; camp site for 2 people €18.50, bungalows incl breakfast €85-115; ⊘ mid-May–Sep; 🛜🐾) Beautiful oleander-filled grounds, with excellent facilities and high-standard rooms. Has a pool, minimarket, restaurant, and bar. It's 6km south of Adamas, with regular bus connections. Also does port pick-ups.

Scirocco   TAVERNA €€
(☑ 22870 31201; www.restaurantsirocco.gr; Paleohori Beach; mains €7-15; ⊘ lunch & dinner Apr-Oct) Popular eatery smack-bang on the shore, with a novel hook: 'volcanic food' (ie dishes slow-cooked underground using the sand's thermal heat). There's also a full menu of Greek favourites, and a breezy view.

KIMOLOS   ΚΙΜΩΛΟΣ

POP 910

Exquisite Kimolos, perched off the northeast tip of Milos, feels like a step back in time. Barely a trickle of visitors get the chance to take in its fantastical sienna-coloured walls hand-hewn of volcanic stones, or its sparkling bays and picturesque *syrmata*. It's an easy day trip from Milos; consider taking a car or bike on the ferry to make getting around easier.

The boat (from Pollonia in Milos' north) docks at **Psathi**, from where it's 1.5km to the pretty capital, **Hora**. Wander the maze of streets to reach Hora's central cafes and a semicrumbling medieval *kastro*. The *kastro* holds the **Church of the Nativity** (from the late 16th century) and the petite **Folk & Maritime Museum of Kimolos** (with variable hours).

Caïques from Psathi buzz out to beaches, the best of which is magnificent, white-sand **Prassa** (also reachable by car, though the unsealed road beyond Agios Minas is rough in parts). You can walk there from Hora in about two hours.

There's an ATM at the port and a petrol station.

🛏 Sleeping & Eating

Domatia, tavernas, cafes and bars pepper Hora and Psathi, and there's some development at the southern beaches of Aliki and neighbouring Bonatsa. To stay, check out **Aria Hotels** (☑ 22870 51677; www.ariahotels. gr; d from €90; ⊘ May-Sep), with five boutique properties on the island, from beach houses to beachside studios to a restored 1852 windmill.

There's a handful of appealing eateries in Hora's lovely laneways, and the beach at Psathi has good options. The taverna **To Kyma** (☑ 22870 51001; dishes €6-18; ⊘ lunch & dinner Easter-Oct) is excellent for seafood and local specialities like *ladenia*. Next door is fashionable cafe **Raventi** (☑ 22870 51212; ⊘ 9am-late), with a cabinet full of delectable sweets and a very comfy terrace.

ⓘ Getting There & Away

Some Milos long-distance ferries stop at Kimolos. **Kimolos Travel** (☑ 22870 51219; Hora) in Hora sells tickets. A small **car ferry** (☑ 6948308758; www.kimolos-link.gr; per adult/child/car €2/1/8.50) connects Pollonia, Milos with Psathi, Kimolos (30 minutes) up to eight times daily in high season, three times in low season.

ⓘ Getting Around

Buses connect Psathi and Hora in high season only; some services also visit beaches. Call for a **taxi** (☑ 6945464093).

SIFNOS   ΣΙΦΝΟΣ

POP 2630

Sifnos has a dreamlike quality. A string of three whitewashed villages, anchored by the capital Apollonia, sit like pearls along the crest of the island. The changing light kisses the landscape and as you explore the flanking slopes of the central mountains you'll discover abundant terraced olive groves, almond trees, oleander and aromatic herbs. Each of the island's bays harbours a spectrum of aqua waters, and offers breathtaking vistas.

During the Archaic period (from about the 8th century BC) Sifnos was enriched by its gold and silver deposits, but by the

5th century BC the mines were exhausted. Sifnos is now known for pottery, basket weaving and cookery. The island hibernates October to Easter (most hotels and restaurants close) and in high season it attracts the chic set (book ahead). It caters to tourists with aplomb, with good bus links and general info readily available.

ℹ Getting There & Away

Sifnos is on the Piraeus to western Cyclades ferry route with good summer connections across the Cyclades. Get tickets at Thesaurus Travel (p404) or the tourist office (p404).

ℹ Getting Around

Bus timetables are posted around the island, and frequent buses connect Kamares with Apollonia and Artemonas. Buses also link Appollonia with Kastro, Vathy, Faros and Platys Gialos. Fares are generally €1.60.

Car rental costs from €45 per day. Companies will deliver to the port or your hotel. Try **Apollo Rent a Car** (☑ 22840 33333; www.automotoapollo.gr; Apollonia) or **Moto Car**

Rental (☑ 22840 33791; www.protomotocar.gr; Kamares).

Taxis hover around the port and Apollonia's main junction. At bus stops you'll find a list of taxi numbers and indicative fares. Fares from Kamares include Apollonia €8, Platys Gialos €18 and Vathy €18.

Kamares   Καμάρες
POP 250

Scenically hemmed in by steep mountains, the port of Kamares has a holiday atmosphere with its large beach and waterfront cafes, tavernas and shops. But the real action is up near Apollonia or at more idyllic bays.

🛏 Sleeping & Eating

Domatia owners rarely meet boats; book ahead in high season.

On the northern side of the bay, Agia Marina has plenty of accommodation and some good dining options.

Camping Makis   CAMPGROUND **€**
(☑ 6945946339; www.makiscamping.gr; camp site for 2 €18, d €55, studio & apt €75-100; ☺ Apr-Nov;

BOAT SERVICES FROM SIFNOS

DESTINATION	TIME	FARE	FREQUENCY
Folegandros	2-4hr	€16	3 weekly
Folegandros*	1½-2hr	€49.50	1-2 daily
Kimolos	50min-2½hr	€10	7 weekly (note: not daily)
Kythnos	2½hr	€15	6 weekly
Ios	3-5½hr	€18	3 weekly
Ios*	2½hr	€54.50	1 daily
Milos	1¾-2¼hr	€13	1-2 daily
Milos*	30-55min	€15.50	2-4 daily
Mykonos*	5¾-7hr	€69	6 weekly
Naxos*	5hr	€59.50	6 weekly
Paros	3hr	€8	2 weekly
Paros*	5½-7hr	€69	6 weekly
Piraeus	4½-5½hr	€33	1-2 daily
Piraeus*	2-4hr	€39-48	4 daily
Santorini (Thira)	5-7hr	€18	3 weekly
Santorini (Thira)*	2½-3hr	€54.50	1-2 daily
Serifos	50min	€11	1-2 daily
Serifos*	25min	€14	2 daily
Sikinos	2½-5hr	€16	3 weekly
Syros	3hr-4½hr	€13	3 weekly

* high-speed services

✳️ 📶) Pitch your tent behind the beach in a basic lot with attractive olive trees (or hire a tent for €25). There are well-equipped studios and apartments (sleeping up to five), a cafe, barbecue, communal kitchen, minimarket and laundry.

Stavros Hotel
HOTEL €€

(☑ 22840 33383; www.sifnostravel.com; d/q €80/120; ✳️ 📶) Main street's Stavros Hotel offers good service and excellent, spacious studios with kitchenettes and sea views. A bonus: flexible room configurations work to accommodate families. The info desk downstairs can help with car hire.

Cafe Folie
CAFE, BAR €

(☑ 6936519006; mains €5-10; ⊗ 8am-late) Cafe Folie makes it far too easy to be a beach bum: it's a fun decked area right on the sea (towards Agia Marina), with sunbeds, a ladder into the water, and a menu that allows you to slip from morning coffee to a salad lunch, and then on to dinner, and finally cocktails.

Argiris
GREEK €€

(☑ 22840 32352; mains €4-14; ⊗ breakfast, lunch & dinner Apr-Oct) It's well worth the walk around the bay to Agia Marina. Sure, the view looking back to Kamares is wonderful, but it's equalled by the top-notch food. You can't go wrong with Sifnos specialities (helpfully indicated on the menu); try *revithada* (baked chickpeas), *mastelo* (lamb in wine) and caper salad.

ℹ️ Information

An ATM and information office are just a few metres from the ferry quay.

Municipal tourist office (www.sifnos.gr) Very helpful with ferry tickets, accommodation and bus timetables. Opposite the bus stop. Opening times vary with boat arrivals.

Apollonia
Απολλωνία

POP 870

Apollonia comes alive in high season with its parade of well-dressed Athenians strutting their stuff along the Steno (Odos Prokou, known as Steno because of its narrowness). Cafes, bars, clubs, shops and eateries buzz with life.

The quirky **Museum of Popular Art** (☑ 22840 31341; admission €1; ⊗ 7-11pm) at the central junction contains a fun confusion of old costumes, textiles and photographs. Hours are erratic.

🛏️ Sleeping & Eating

★ **Eleonas Apartments & Studios**
APARTMENT €€

(☑ 22840 33383; www.sifnostravel.com; d/q €100/120) An idyllic complex tucked away in an olive grove, Eleonas offers gloriously roomy apartments that sleep five, with kitchen, living space and terrace. Studios are slightly smaller, but still very spacious. It feels peaceful and rural, but it's just a few minutes' walk from the Steno.

Hotel Anthousa
HOTEL €€

(☑ 22840 31431; www.hotelanthousa-sifnos.gr; d without/with breakfast €65/80; ✳️ 📶) Behind a pretty, vine-covered facade, this year-round hotel has fresh, appealing rooms set around an inner courtyard. Sweet in decor,

---

SIFNOS' BEST ACTIVITIES

Sifnos is justifiably proud of its excellent network of **walking trails**, some 200km in all. A great investment is the €4 info pack from **Thesaurus Travel** (☑ 22840 33151; www.thesaurus.gr), on main square in Apollonia; it includes the Terrain map of Sifnos, an overview of the island's walking trails, plus the current bus and ferry timetables.

There are some wonderful short walks: Apollonia to Artemonas (15 minutes) is worthwhile, as is the loop around Kastro. Our favourite is the 40-minute walk from Faros to Chrysopigi monastery. Longer trails link major settlements via beaches, monasteries and great scenery – Apollonia to Vathy is about four hours.

Another big drawcard for travellers is Sifnos' **culinary heritage**. The island was the birthplace of Nikolaos Tselementes (1878–1958), author of the first (and best-known) Greek cookbook, published in 1910. Since then, Sifnos has enjoyed a reputation for producing excellent chefs. **Sifnos Farm Narlis** (☑ 6979778283; www.sifnos-farm-narlis.com; class €60-80) runs cooking classes where both the agricultural and culinary traditions of the island are explored and celebrated. Classes include the gathering of fresh, in-season vegetables and herbs, and plenty of eating. Book direct, or via Thesaurus Travel.

and sweet in intent: downstairs are a cafe (where breakfast is served) and a patisserie/confectioners.

Mamma Mia   ITALIAN €€
(☑ 22840 33086; mains €8-23; ☉ dinner) Sifnos has a long, proud history of local cooking, but this place is revered. Real Italians cook real Italian specialities, and the pizzas earn raves. It's on the path to Ano Petali; there's a second summertime branch on the beach at Platys Gialos.

Rambagas   MODERN GREEK €€€
(☑ 22840 32215; www.kikladonxoros.gr; restaurant mains €14-32; ☉ 9am-late) It's easy to succumb to celeb-chef hype when the setting is as beautiful as this – a huge white terrace off the Steno, with trees, lights and artworks adding stylish appeal. Well-known chef Yiannis Loucacos (a Masterchef judge in Greece) designs the dinner menu, which fuses old with new and pays homage to Sifnos' culinary traditions and first-class produce.

❶ Information

The main vehicular road cuts right through the centre of town, but park at the large free car park downhill from the village and walk up and into the warren of streets. At the central junction you'll find all the services: banks, post office, pharmacy, bookshop, taxis etc.

Ano Petali & Artemonas
Άνω Πετάλι & Αρτεμώνας

After crossing the main road from Apollonia, the string of houses continues north into Ano Petali and reaches Artemonas with its grand mansions. Walk the pedestrian-only streets to take it all in, stopping at one of the fashionable cafes.

Artemonas has a central square off the winding main road as well, with a bus stop and some appealing eateries.

⌂ Sleeping

Pension Geronti   PENSION €
(☑ 22840 31473; www.gerontisifnos.gr; d €60; ❄ ☏) Opposite Petali Village Hotel, on the walkway between Apollonia and Artemonas, is this gem of a pension, with spotless rooms, sweeping views, sweet hosts and excellent rates.

Sifnos

Serifos (24km); Kythnos (63km); Piraeus (146km); Cape Heronisos; Heronisos; Vroulidia Beach; Agios Dimos; AEGEAN SEA; 476m; Kamares Bay; Kamares; Poulati; Artemonas; Kato Petali; Ano Petali; Apollonia; Kastro; Katavati; Seralia; Milos (50km); Santorini (105km); 680m; Exambelas; Moni Profiti Ilia; Acropolis of Agios Andreas; Faros; Moni; Chrysopigi; Vathy Bay; Vathy; Platys Gialos; Chrysopigi Beach; Platys Gialos Bay; Fasolou Beach; 201m; Cape Kondou; Kitriani

Petali Village Hotel   HOTEL €€€
(☑ 22840 33024; www.petalihotel.gr; Ano Petali; d incl breakfast from €180; ☉ year-round; ❄ ☏ ☲) Suspended on a walking street between Apollonia and Artemonas, this terraced array of rooms and apartments has sweeping views to Apollonia and the sea, and an inviting pool area. Low-season discounts are decent. Port pick-up offered.

Kastro
Κάστρο

Not to be missed is the walled village of Kastro, 3km east from Apollonia. The former capital is a magical place of buttressed alleyways and whitewashed houses surrounded by valleys and sea. It has a modest **archaeological museum** (☑ 22840 31022; admission €2; ☉ 8.30am-3pm Tue-Sun), and the small port Seralia is nestled below.

⌂ Sleeping & Eating

★ Antonis Rooms   PENSION €
(☑ 22840 33708; http://sifnosholidays.gr; d €50; ❄ ☏) Brilliant value. On the road as you head to Kastro, these simple, spotless rooms beckon. There's a communal kitchen, and a terrace with splendid valley views. It's open year-round.

Aris & Maria Traditional Houses
APARTMENT €€

(22840 31161; www.arismaria-traditional.com; d/tr/q €80/95/120;) For an authentic Kastro experience, rent a traditional Sifniot house. Some have sea views.

Dolci
CAFE, BAR €

(22840 32311; snacks €3-7; 9am-late Easter-Sep) A loungey cafe making cocktails, coffee, crêpes and waffles as you enter town (close to the bus stop), and with ample outdoor space for enjoying valley vistas.

Leonidas
TAVERNA €€

(22840 31153; mains €7-15; lunch & dinner Easter-Sep) At the northern edge of the village, this popular place offers tasty local dishes, including Sifnian appetisers like chickpea croquettes and cheese patties with honey and sesame seeds.

Around Sifnos

On the southeast coast, the fishing hamlet of **Faros** has fish tavernas and a couple of nice beaches nearby, including **Fasolou**, reached up steps and over the headland from the bus stop.

Platys Gialos, 10km south of Apollonia, has a big, generous beach entirely backed by tavernas, hotels and shops. **Vathy**, on the southwest coast, is a low-key resort village on an almost circular bay of aquamarine beauty. One of the Cyclades' most upmarket five-star resorts, **Elies** (www.eliesresorts.com), is here.

Sights & Activities

Moni Chrysopigi
MONASTERY

The handsome whitewashed monastery of Chrysopigi dates back more than 600 years and perches on an islet connected to the shore by a tiny footbridge. A superb walk to Chrysopigi is from the village of Faros (about 40 minutes one way); en route you'll walk along beautiful, azure **Chrysopigi Beach**, home to two excellent tavernas.

Acropolis of Agios Andreas
MONUMENT

(22840 31488; admission €2; 8.30am-3pm Tue-Sun) At the heart of the island, about 2km south of Apollonia, this well-excavated hill-top acropolis dates from the Mycenaean period (about 13th century BC). Take in extensive views of interior valleys and neighbouring Paros from the intact defensive wall. There's a small museum. The adja-cent **Church of Agios Andreas** dates from about 1700.

Sleeping & Eating

Platys Gialos

Hotel Efrosini
HOTEL €€

(22840 71353; www.hotel-efrosini.gr; d incl breakfast €80-90; Easter-Sep;) This well-kept hotel is one of the best on the Platys Gialos strip. Small balconies overlook a leafy courtyard with the sea lapping just in front.

Verina
APARTMENT €€€

(22840 71525; www.verinahotelsifnos.com; d/apt from €180/220; May-Oct;) Effortlessly chic, Verina rents suites and villas at outposts in Platys Gialos, Vathy and above Poulati (north of Kastro). Verina Suites lies behind the beach at Platys Gialos, but try dragging yourself from the gorgeous pool and cafe-bar area...

Omega 3
SEAFOOD €€

(Platys Gialos; dishes €4-17; lunch & dinner May-Sep) The cute name (Ω3) hints at the treats on offer at this small, casual beachfront spot. There's a fresh-faced menu of fab fishy flavours, grabbing techniques from around the globe (sashimi, ceviche) but staying true to its roots too, with slow-cooked octopus or steamed mussels with red peppers and feta.

Vathy

Studios Nikos
APARTMENT €€

(22840 71512; www.sifnosrooms.com; studio €80-120; Apr-Oct;) These welcoming, well-equipped studios (with kitchenettes) sit at a sparkling corner of Vathy Bay, with a grassy lawn right next to the shore.

SERIFOS
ΣΕΡΙΦΟΣ

POP 1420

Serifos has a raw, rugged beauty with steep mountains plunging to broad ultramarine bays. Relatively deserted outside of the quaint hill-top capital of Hora or the dusty, Wild West–feeling port of Livadi down below, the island feels like it's gone beautifully feral. All that you find are the occasional remnants of past mining enterprises (rusting tracks, cranes) and the whoosh of the wind (which can be fierce). Rent wheels to

BOAT SERVICES FROM SERIFOS

DESTINATION	TIME	FARE	FREQUENCY
Folegandros	2½hr	€18	3 weekly
Ios	4-5hr	€19	2 weekly
Kimolos	1hr 40min	€14	5 weekly
Kythnos	1½hr	€15	6 weekly
Milos	3hr	€14	1-2 daily
Milos*	1½hr	€16	1-2 daily
Paros	2hr	€13	2 weekly
Piraeus	4-5hr	€28	1-2 daily
Piraeus*	2-2½hr	€43	2-3 daily
Santorini (Thira)	6½hr	€19	2 weekly
Sifnos	50min	€11	1-2 daily
Sifnos*	25min	€14	3 daily
Sikinos	3½-4½hr	€18	3 weekly
Syros	2-3¼hr	€12	3 weekly

* high-speed services

make the most of it. Serifos is one of the few islands where locals drink the water.

In Greek mythology, Serifos is where Perseus grew up and where the Cyclops were said to live. Now, there's some fine walking on Serifos; see Terrain's island map.

ⓘ Getting There & Away

Serifos is on the Piraeus to western Cyclades ferry route and has reasonable summer connections (or travel to Sifnos for more options). Buy tickets at **Kondilis** (☑ 22810 52340) on Livadi's waterfront.

ⓘ Getting Around

Buses connect Livadi and Hora (€1.60, hourly); the timetable is posted at the bus stop by the yacht quay. Other buses are infrequent.

Rent cars (per day from €45), scooters (€15) and quads (€25) at **Blue Bird** (☑ 22810 51511; www.rentacar-bluebird.gr), or **Serifos Travel** (☑ 22810 51463; www.serifostours.gr) just off the waterfront.

Taxis (☑ 6944473044, 6932431114) to Hora cost €7, Psili Ammos €7, Sykamia €20, Vagia €11 and Megalo Livadi €20.

Livadi   Λιβάδι

POP 600

The port town of Serifos is a fairly low-key place where, in spite of growing popularity, there's still a reassuring feeling that the modern world has not entirely taken over.

Just over the headland that rises from the ferry quay lies the fine, tamarisk-fringed beach at **Livadakia**.

🛏 Sleeping

Much of the accommodation clusters at Livadakia Beach. Most hoteliers can pick up at the port by arrangement.

Coralli Camping & Bungalows   CAMPGROUND, APARTMENT €
(☑ 22810 51500; www.coralli.gr; Livadakia Beach; camp site per adult/child/tent €8/4/5, bungalow d/tr/q €75/85/105; ❄ 🛜 🐾) Right behind Livadakia Beach, this well-equipped and well-run eucalyptus-shaded campground also has 'bungalows' (rooms) with mountain or sea views. The complex includes a cool pool and bar, a restaurant, minimarket, kitchen and barbecue. Nearby self-catering apartments are of an equally high standard.

★ Studios Niovi   APARTMENT €€
(☑ 22810 51900; www.studiosniovi.gr; Livadi; apt incl breakfast €80-130) On the furthest eastern curve of Livadi's bay, these immaculate apartments look at the broad expanse of the bay, bustling Livadi, towering Hora and the mountains beyond. The owner is a gem and makes a super breakfast spread. You're about a 20-minute walk from Livadi itself. Your own wheels are an advantage. Good low-season rates.

Serifos

AEGEAN SEA

Platys Gialos Bay
Moni Taxiarhon
Sykamia Beach
Galani
Kendarhos
Panagia
Pirgos
Psili Ammos Beach
582m
Agios Ioannis Beach
Avessalos
Agios Georgios
Hora
Megalo Livadi
Koutalas
502m
Livadi
Lia Beach
Ganema
Livadakia Beach
Paros (72km)
Vagia
Karavi Beach
Kalo Ambeli Beach
Kythnos (52km); Piraeus (135km)
Cape Katano
Sifnos (24km); Kimolos (41km); Milos (55km); Ios (83km); Santorini (120km)

Alexandros-Vassilia
APARTMENT €€

(📞 22810 51119; www.alexandros-vassilia.gr; Livadakia Beach; d €60-180; ⊘ Easter-Sep; ❀ ☎) Best known for its beachfront taverna in a flowering garden, this friendly Livadakia compound also has a big range of rooms and apartments. They range from decent-value economy rooms to family-sized, sea-view suites.

🍴 Eating & Drinking

Metalleio
MEDITERRANEAN €€

(📞 22810 51755; Livadi; mains €8-13; ⊘ 8.30pm-late) On the road behind the waterfront, Metalleio dishes up quality cuisine from a short menu emphasising local flavours: risotto with local goat's cheese, veal in local wine sauce, and lemon pie dessert. Come midnight, the action moves upstairs and Metalleio doubles as the island's main live-music venue and dance club (particularly in July and August).

Kali's
SEAFOOD €€

(📞 22810 52301; mains €8-15; ⊘ lunch & dinner Mar-Oct) White tables on the water's edge with gregarious waiters and delicious home cooking, much of it with with a fresh-fish focus.

Anemos Café
CAFE, BAR

Above Carrefour supermarket, Anemos' broad terrace offers top views of the marina and distant Hora. The proprietors are friendly, snacks and coffees are good and cheap, and it gets hopping around boat arrivals.

Yacht Club Serifos
BAR

(⊘ 7am-3am) This classic waterfront cafe-bar maintains a cheerful buzz. Lounge music plays by day for coffee drinkers, and mainstream rock, disco and funk late into the night.

Hora (Serifos)
Χώρα (Σέριφος)

POP 370

The Hora of Serifos cascades down the summit of a rocky hill above Livadi, putting it among the most dramatically striking (and loftiest) of all the Cycladic capitals.

Hora's bus terminus and main car park are on its upper side, near a series of windmills, as is its teeny archaeological collection (📞 22810 51138; admission €2; ⊘ 8.30am-4pm Tue & Thu-Sun), which displays fragments of mainly Hellenic and Roman sculpture excavated from the *kastro*. From there steps climb into the maze of Hora proper and lead to the charming main square, watched over by the lovely little neoclassical town hall.

From the square, narrow alleys and more steps lead ever upwards to small churches like Agios Ioannis Theologos, carved into the rock and built on the site of an ancient temple to Athena, and the remnants of the ruined 15th-century Venetian Kastro, from where the views are spectacular. As the village cascades down the slope, the alleyways lead to a blue-domed church, near which is another car park.

Note that there's a scenic 2.5km walking path (route 1A) connecting Livadi and Hora. It's one of a number of good trails signposted around the island; find good trail info on the Hiking page of http://serifos-greece.com.

🛏 Sleeping & Eating

Accommodation options are found east of upper Hora. Head down the road opposite Cuckoo cafe-bar, close to the bus terminus.

I Apanemia
PENSION €

(📞 22810 51517, 6971891106; apanemiasoula@gmail.com; s/d €35/40; ❀ ☎) This excellent-value, family-run place has decent, well-equipped rooms with front-balcony views to the distant sea and side views towards Hora. It's old-school in decor, but well cared for.

Anemoessa Studios APARTMENT €€
(☑ 22810 51132; www.serifos-anemoessa.gr; apt €80-120; ❋ ☎) Pretty, modern studios sleep four in whitewashed Cycladic splendour.

★Stou Stratou CAFE €
(☑ 22810 52566; Plateia Ag Athanasiou; dishes €4-9; ☺9am-late Easter-Oct) Sitting postcard-pretty in the main square, Stou Stratou has a menu full of art and poetry (literally), plus it serves good breakfasts and light snacks such as fennel pie or a mixed plate of cold cuts and cheese. Cocktails and coffee too.

Aloni MEDITERRANEAN €€
(☑ 22810 52603; mains €8-15; ☺dinner Jun-Oct, Sat & Sun Nov-May) Halfway up the hill between Livadi and Hora, signposted on the right, Aloni gives splendid panoramas and an upscale feel. Islanders rate it among Serifos' best, with local produce (especially roasted meat) proudly showcased.

Around Serifos

About 1.5km north of Livadi, pretty little **Psili Ammos Beach** offers the best swimming close to Livadi, and has two excellent tavernas. **Platys Gialos Beach** in the north has a good summer-only taverna of the same name.

Sykamia is one of the island's best beaches, with a dramatic approach along a steep, windy road through terrraced hills. The beach itself is grey-brown sand full of stones. **To Akrogiali** (☑ 22810 51289; mains €6-9; ☺lunch & dinner Jun-Aug), one of the only signs of development for miles, serves good food. To reach Sykamia you will pass through the quaint village of **Panagia**, or on the east coast, **Kendarhos** (also known as Kallitsos, the 'most beautiful').

Tiny **Megalo Livadi**, on the southwest coast, is a fun visit for its sparkling bay, crumbling neoclassical buildings (remnants of the mining era) and excellent seafront **Kyklopas** (☑ 22810 51009; mains €5-14; ☺lunch & dinner Easter-Sep) taverna (try the delicious wild-fennel dumplings). The cave where the Cyclops was said to dwell is near here.

The best beaches on the south coast tend to be broad and sandy, and deserted out of high season. It's a wild landscape, punctuat-ed by derelict mining machinery. Stop for a swim at exquisite bays like **Vagia**, **Ganema** and **Koutalas**.

KYTHNOS ΚΥΘΝΟΣ
POP 1460

Kythnos is a series of folding hills and sere crenellations punctuated by stone huts and ancient walls, green valleys and wonderful beaches. Port life in Merihas and village life in beautiful Hora and Dryopida remain easygoing, although the ease of access from Athens sees locals filling the island's beaches and marinas on summer weekends.

⊙ Getting There & Away

Ferries serve Piraeus and Lavrio on the mainland, Kea to the north (services are infrequent, though, so it's usually easier to travel via Lavrio), and in high season, islands to the south. Out of season it's hard to connect to the south. In

BOAT SERVICES FROM KYTHNOS

DESTINATION	TIME	FARE	FREQUENCY
Kea	1hr 40min	€8	2 weekly
Kimolos	5¼hr	€18	1 weekly
Lavrio	1hr 40min	€15	1-2 daily
Milos	4hr-4½hr	€18	6 weekly
Piraeus	3hr	€23	6 weekly
Serifos	1hr 25min	€15	6 weekly
Sifnos	2½hr	€15	4 weekly
Syros	2½hr	€12	2 weekly

Merihas buy tickets at **Anerousa Travel** (☑ 22810 32242) or Larentzakis Travel Agency.

There's a twice-weekly service with **Hellenic Seaways** (www.hellenicseaways.gr) that connects Kythnos and Syros, and continues on to central Cyclades islands including Paros, Naxos and Ios.

❶ Getting Around

In July and August buses go from Merihas to Dryopida, continuing to Kanala or Hora. Less regular services run to Loutra. There aren't any services outside these months, making the best way to see the island by car or scooter. Rentals are available at Larentzakis Travel Agency.

Taxis (☑ 69442 71609) cost about €10 to Hora and €8 to Dryopida. A **sea-taxi** (☑ 6944906568) to/from the beaches in summer costs about €10 return; this is the best option to reach Kolona.

Merihas   Μέριχας

POP 370

Tiny Merihas is home to much of the island's low-season life. Cafes and restaurants line the small harbour, and rooms for let dot its hills. The town beach is uninspiring but good beaches are within walking distance, north of the quay at **Martinakia** and **Episkopi**.

🛏 Sleeping & Eating

Domatia owners usually meet boats. Book ahead for weekends, and in July and August.

★**Kontseta**   APARTMENT €€
(☑ 22810 33024; www.kontseta.gr; d €80-100; ☺ Apr-Oct; ❊🐾) Easily the nicest option in town, these modern studio apartments are a cut above, with fresh decor and fine views. They are high above the ferry quay, with steps signed next door to the Alpha Bank.

Foinika Studios   APARTMENT €€
(☑ 22810 32203; www.foinikias-studios.gr; d/tr €90/100; ❊🐾) There are no harbour views, but you're well placed (just a few metres from the waterfront) and the studios and apartments are simple and appealing.

Kantouni   TAVERNA €
(☑ 22810 32220; mains €6-15; ☺ lunch & dinner) On the southern bend of the waterfront, Kantouni offers a menu of classic, meat-centric Greek hits in a delightful setting decked in creeping roses. There's also water-side seating.

Molos   KEBAB €
(☑ 22810 32455; gyros €2; ☺ lunch & dinner) Quick, delish souvlaki and kebabs from a sweetly unassuming spot just where the ferries dock.

Ostria   SEAFOOD €€
(☑ 22810 33017; mains €6-18; ☺ lunch & dinner) Ostria is the place for fish: fresh snapper, calamari and lobster spaghetti get the thumbs up. Funny how seafood tastes better when you're seated by moored yachts...

❶ Information

Larentzakis Travel Agency (☑ 22810 32104) Sells ferry tickets, arranges accommodation, and hires scooters/cars per day from €20/40. Located on the waterfront.

Hora (Kythnos)   Χώρα (Κύθνος)

The distinctively charming capital, Hora (also known as Kythnos or Messaria), nestles in the lap of rolling agricultural fields and perserves an inherent Greek character.

The long main street makes for a great stroll through a cute central square to a series of colourful cafes, restaurants, ceramicists and sweet shops. Traditional village lanes are tucked behind here, still populated by grannies hanging out the laundry.

Find excellent, well-priced studios and apartments with kitchens at **Filoxenia** (☑22810 31644; www.filoxenia-kythnos.gr; d €60; P❄). You'll be tripping over lovely spots for eating, drinking and people-watching – join the queue at the cool gelateria.

Around Kythnos

Low-key resort and fishing village, **Loutra**, 3km north of Hora, sits on a windy bay, its large marina full of yachts (many from Athens) and its harbourfront lined with high-standard eateries.

Loutra's claim to fame is its **hot springs**. You can access the water for free on the beachfront, where a **rockpool** marks the entry point of the hot water into the sea. You can also visit the nearby **Hydrotherapy Centre** (☑22810 31217; admission €3.50; ☺Jun-Sep) to 'take the waters'. To stay, **Porto Klaras** (☑22810 31276; www.porto-klaras.gr; d/q €90/130; ☺Apr-Oct; ❄☎) has an impeccable range of studios and apartments with kitchens, balconies and great decor.

Dryopida, a picturesque town of red-tiled roofs and winding streets clustered steeply on either side of a ravine, is connected to Hora by a footpath. It has a cluster of pretty eateries around the main church.

The island's most famous beach is the exquisite double bay of **Kolona**, a thin strip of sand like a peninsula leading to an offshore islet. In low season it's amazing and a favoured anchorage for yachts; in high season it's jammed.

It's best to reach Kolona by sea taxi (from Hora), since the road to it from **Apokrousi** (itself an excellent, easily accessible beach) is poor, and best driven in a 4WD or four-wheeler. Kolona has a high-season cafe (but no shade); Apokrousi has tavernas and a popular beach bar.

KEA (TZIA)

POP 2460

Kea (*kay*-a), though naturally beautiful with craggy cliffs, spectacular coastline and fecund hillsides, has almost been overrun by vacation homes. Being the island closest to Attica, it's just too easy to reach; but this is usually only evident on summer weekends,

and in August. Rent wheels to get off the beaten path and find the island's charms: rocky spires, verdant valleys filled with orchards, olive groves and oak trees, and excellent walking trails.

The main settlements are the port of Korissia and the attractive capital, Ioulida, about 5km inland. Local people call the island Tzia.

ⓘ Getting There & Away

Kea's only mainland service is to Lavrio; connections to other islands are few. Weekend boats are packed. There's a twice-weekly service with **Hellenic Seaways** (www.hellenicseaways.gr) that connects Kea with Kythnos (€7, one hours 20 minutes) and Syros (€12, two to four hours), and continues on to central Cyclades islands including Paros, Naxos and Ios. There are two to four daily services to Lavrio (€11.50, one hour).

Book ahead with ticket agents for **Marmari Express** (☑Kea 22880 21435, Lavrio 22920 26200), or the agent for **Makedon** (☑Kea 22880 21435, Lavrio 22920 26777). There's a ticket kiosk on the Korissia waterfront.

ⓘ Getting Around

In July and August regular buses go from Korissia to Vourkari, Otzias, Ioulida and Piosses Beach. A **taxi** (☑6932418821, 6932669493) may be a better bet; to Ioulida a taxi costs around €8, Otzias €7 and Piosses €25.

Leon Rent A Car (☑22880 21898; www.rent-acarkea.gr; scooters/cars per day from €20/45) is on the harbourfront, close to the ferry dock.

Korissia   Κορησσία

POP 710

The fairly bland port of Korissia has enough tavernas and cafes to pass the time. The north-facing beach tends to catch the wind, but you're about a 15-minute walk from small but popular **Gialiskari Beach**, backed by eucalypts.

☐ Sleeping & Eating

Domatia owners don't meet ferries. Book ahead in high season and at weekends.

★ **Red Tractor Farm**   GUESTHOUSE €€ (☑22880 21346; www.redtractorfarm.com; Korissia; d €90, studio €130-180; ❄☎) The outstanding Red Tractor Farm lies inland from Korissia harbour, just a stone's throw from the town beach, among serene vineyards and olive groves. Kostis Maroulis and Marcie Mayer operate this sustainable, creative

Kea (Tzia)

Lavrio
(30km)

Agia
Irini
Vourkari
Korissia
Gialiskari
Beach

Otzias

Moni
Panagias
Kastrianis

Spathi

Ioulida

Kythnos
(39km);
Syros (76km)

Flea

570m

Pera
Meria

Cape
Spathi

Astras

Pisses
Beach

Ellinika

Kato Meria

Koundouros

450m

Kambi

Havouna

Karthea

AEGEAN
SEA

Cape
Tamelos

agritourism farm with beautiful Cycladic buildings combining traditional and modern style and comfort. Rooms, studios and larger cottages are available.

Kostis and Marcie also produce olive oil, wine, marmalade and chutney, plus unique cookies made from the flour of locally grown acorns. During business hours, visitors can stop by the farm to make purchases. The farm is open year-round.

Aegean View
GUESTHOUSE €€

(☑22880 20046; www.roomsinkea.gr; d €60-70; ☺Mar-Dec) On the harbourfront, just metres from the ferry dock, this guesthouse has a handful of bright, modern rooms and studios with funky bathrooms. Some have small private balconies, all share a lovely communal deck.

Hotel Karthea
HOTEL €€

(☑22880 21204; www.hotelkarthea.gr; d incl breakfast €80; ☺Apr-Oct; ❄☎) This well-run central hotel on the harbour has 33 simple, tasteful rooms behind its coffee-coloured exterior. Some rooms have seafront balconies.

Odalé
CAFE €

(☑22880 29060; www.odalekea.com; breakfast €3-10, mezedhes €4-12; ☺9.30am-late Apr-Oct) Off the waterfront in a big garden (beautiful-ly lit at night), Odalé does fresh, innovative food including first-rate breakfasts (pancakes and scrambled eggs), and tempting mezedhes of an evening. Find it where the road curves inland.

Magazes
MEDITERRANEAN €€

(☑22880 21104; www.magazes.gr; mains €8-14; ☺lunch & dinner) Mid-harbourfront, Magazes is in a stylishly restored warehouse, producing high-quality local flavours. It's recommended for its fresh seafood, including lobster pasta, which comes from local fishers, and anchovies marinated in garlic and oil.

Kea Events
CAFE €

(☑22880 21841; www.keaevents.gr; ☺May-Sep) If you feel like a change from the beach, this large event complex has a big blue swimming pool open to the public free of charge, provided you buy something from the cafe menu (not hard, given it's loaded with snacks, coffees and beers). Find it 1.5km inland from Korissia (near the Eko petrol station).

Ioulida
Ιουλίδα

POP 630

Ioulida (ee-oo-*lee*-tha) is Kea's gem. Its pretty scramble of narrow alleyways and buildings drapes across two hill-tops. Once a substantial settlement of ancient Greece, it now has a distinctly cosmopolitan feel at weekends.

The bus turnaround is on a square just at the edge of town, from where an archway leads into the village. (Park in the car park below the square.) Beyond the archway, turn right and uphill along Ioulida's main street for its shops and cafes and to reach the famed Kea Lion.

◎ Sights

★Kea Lion
MONUMENT

The enigmatic Kea Lion, chiselled from slate in the 6th century BC, lies across a small valley beyond the last of Ioulida's houses. The 15-minute walk to reach it is fantastic: follow small wooden signs reading Αρχαίος Λέων from the top of the main street until the path leads you out of town. If you look closely you'll see the lion across the valley – the surrounding stones are painted white.

The footpath curves past a cemetery and the lion, with its smooth-worn haunches and Cheshire-cat smile, is reached through a gate on the left. The path continues to Otzias.

Archaeological Museum MUSEUM
(☎ 22880 22079; adult/child €2/free; ☉ 8am-3pm Fri) Find intriguing artefacts, including some superb terracotta figurines, mostly from excavations at Agia Irini. It's just before the post office on the main thoroughfare. At the time of research the opening hours had been slashed.

🛏 Sleeping & Eating

Kea Villas HOTEL €€€
(☎ 6972243330; www.keavillas.gr; r from €140; ☉ Mar–mid-Nov; ❄ 🛜 ⛱) Gorgeously situated at the highest point of Ioulida, this complex with sweeping views offers a variety of suites and villas that sleep up to six people in style. All have full kitchen and verandah.

Rolando's GREEK €
(☎ 22880 22224; mains €7-15; ☉ lunch & dinner) Ask locals where to eat and the answer is usually Rolando's. At the top of the main thoroughfare, it plates up excellent local flavours, plus Corfiot specialities like rooster *pastitsada* (red-sauce pasta). It now has a second branch, on the harbourfront at Korissia.

Around Kea

The beach road from Korissia leads past **Gialiskari Beach** for 2.5km to tiny **Vourkari**, a favourite with yachties, where the waterfront is lined with sailboats and fashionable cafes. **I Strofi tou Mimi** (☎ 22880 21480; mains €10-15; ☉ lunch & dinner, weekends only in winter), on the far side of the bay, is a picture of illuminated elegance at night and one of the best seafood tavernas on the island.

Otzias has a sandy beach and great family-friendly apartments 100m inland at **Anemousa** (☎ 22880 21335; www.anemousa. gr; studio/apt from €80/100; ☉ Apr-Oct; ❄ 🛜 ⛱). A spectacular coastal road continues 6.5km to the 18th-century **Moni Panagias Kastrianis**, high on a rock-top. If you're circling back to Ioulida, the road from here is equally gorgeous, along the crest of hills with grove-covered valleys plunging to either side.

Eight kilometres southwest of Ioulida is the unfortunately named **Pisses**, one of the island's best beaches, backed by orchards, olive groves and rugged hills. Well-kept **Camping Kea** (☎ 22880 31302; campingkea@ yahoo.gr; camp site per adult/tent/car €6.50/6/4, bungalows €50; ☉ May-Sep; 🅿 🛜), under thick eucalyptus, has a shop and cafe (tent hire available). There's also a taverna and a beach bar at Pisses.

Continuing around the coast you reach **Kondouros**, a playground for moneyed Athenians, and a number of small sandy coves. **Kambi** is an inviting swimming spot, and there's a taverna here.

Accessible only by boat or walking path (about one hour, one way) is the bay of **Poles** in the southeast, home to the ancient city of **Karthea**. It's a walk with a spectacular destination: ancient ruins by a remote beach. For route details buy a good map such as Terrain's *Tzia* map. Alternatively, **Kea Divers** (☎ 6973430860; www.keadivers. com; 1/2 dives incl equipment €50/90), based in Vourkari, can take you there by boat, and offers diving and snorkelling options.

Crete

Why Go?

Crete (Κρήτη) is the culmination of the Greek experience. Nature here is as prolific as Picasso in his prime, creating a dramatic quilt of big-shouldered mountains, stunning beaches and undulating hillsides blanketed in olive groves, vineyards and wildflowers. There are deep chiselled gorges, including one of Europe's longest, and crystal-clear lagoons and palm-tree-lined beaches that conjure up the Caribbean.

Crete's natural beauty is equalled only by the richness of a history spanning millennia. The Palace of Knossos is but one of many vestiges of the mysterious ancient Minoan civilisation. Venetian fortresses, Turkish mosques and Byzantine churches bring history alive all over Crete, but nowhere more so than in charismatic Hania and Rethymno. Crete's hospitable and spirited people uphold their unique culture, cuisine and customs. Local life and traditions remain a dynamic part of the island's soul.

Best Places to Eat

➜ To Maridaki (p449)

➜ Castelvecchio (p439)

➜ Thalassino Ageri (p450)

➜ Elia & Diosmos (p434)

➜ Avli (p439)

Best Places to Stay

➜ Casa Vitae (p438)

➜ Serenissima (p449)

➜ Eleonas Cottages (p435)

➜ Terra Minoika (p467)

➜ Enagron (p441)

When to Go
Crete (Iraklio)

| Apr A painter's palette of wildflowers blankets the island as locals prepare for Easter. | Jun Hit the beaches before they get crowded and rejoice in the bounty of local produce. | Sep–Oct Warm seas, blue skies and thinning crowds as the grape harvest gets under way. |

History

Although inhabited since neolithic times (7000–3000 BC), Crete is most famous for being the cradle of Europe's first advanced civilisation, the Minoans. Traces of this enigmatic society were only uncovered in the early 20th century, when British archaeologist Sir Arthur Evans discovered the palace at Knossos and named the civilisation after its ruler, the mythical King Minos.

Minoans migrated to Crete in the 3rd millennium BC. Their extraordinary artistic, architectural and cultural achievements culminated in the construction of huge palace complexes at Knossos, Phaestos, Malia and Zakros, which were all levelled by an earthquake around 1700 BC. Undeterred, the Minoans built bigger and better ones over the ruins, while settling more widely across Crete. Around 1450 BC, the palaces were mysteriously destroyed again, possibly by a tsunami triggered by a volcanic eruption on Santorini (Thira). Knossos, the only palace saved, finally burned down around 1400 BC.

Archaeological evidence shows that the Minoans lingered on for a few centuries in small, isolated settlements before disappearing as mysteriously as they had come. They were followed by the Mycenaeans and the Dorians (around 1100 BC). By the 5th century BC, Crete was divided into city-states but did not benefit from the cultural glories of mainland Greece; in fact, it was bypassed by Persian invaders and the Macedonian conqueror Alexander the Great.

By 67 BC Crete had become the Roman province of Cyrenaica, with Gortyna its capital. After the Roman Empire's division in AD 395, Crete fell under the jurisdiction of Greek-speaking Constantinople – the emerging Byzantine Empire. Things went more or less fine until AD 824, when Arabs appropriated the island. In AD 961, though, Byzantine general emperor Nikiforas Fokas (AD 912–69) won Crete back following a nine-month siege of Iraklio (then called El Khandak by the Arabs). Crete flourished under Byzantine rule, but with the infamous Fourth Crusade of 1204 the maritime power of Venice received Crete as part of its 'payment' for supplying the Crusaders' fleet.

Much of Crete's most impressive surviving architecture dates from the Venetian period, which lasted until 1669 when Iraklio (then called Candia) became the last domino to fall after a 21-year Ottoman siege. Turkish rule brought new administrative organisation, Islamic culture and Muslim settlers. Cretan resistance was strongest in the mountain strongholds but all revolts were put down brutally, and it was only with the Ottoman Empire's disintegration in the late 19th century that Europe's great powers expedited Crete's sovereign aspirations.

Thus, in 1898, with Russian and French consent, Crete became a British protectorate. However, the banner under which future Greek Prime Minister Eleftherios Venizelos and other Cretan rebels were fighting was *Enosis i Thanatos* (Unity or Death) – unity with Greece, not mere independence from Turkey. Yet it would take the Greek army's successes in the Balkan Wars (1912–13) to turn Crete's de facto inclusion in the country into reality, with the 1913 Treaty of Bucharest.

Crete suffered tremendously during WWII, due to being coveted by Hitler for its strategic location. On 20 May 1941 a huge flock of German parachutists quickly overwhelmed the Cretan defenders. The Battle of Crete, as it would become known, raged for 10 days between German and Allied troops from Britain, Australia, New Zealand and Greece. For two days the battle hung in the balance until the Germans captured the Maleme Airfield, near Hania. The Allied forces fought a valiant rearguard action, enabling the British Navy to evacuate 18,000 of the 32,000 Allied troops. The harsh German occupation lasted throughout WWII, with many mountain villages bombed or burnt down and their occupants executed en masse.

❶ Getting There & Away

AIR

Most travellers arrive in Crete by air, usually with a change in Athens. Iraklio's Nikos Kazantzakis Airport (p724) is Crete's busiest airport, although Hania (p450) is convenient for travellers heading to western Crete. Sitia only receives a handful of domestic flights.

Between May and October, European low-cost carriers and charter airlines such as easyJet, Germanwings, AirBerlin, Fly Thomas Cook and Jet2 operate direct flights to Crete, from all over Europe. **Aegean Airlines** (www.aegeanair.com) operates direct flights to Iraklio from many European airports, including London-Heathrow, Milan, Paris, Marseille and Rome. Travellers from North America need to connect via a European gateway city such as Paris, Amsterdam or Frankfurt and sometimes again in Athens.

To reach Crete by air from other Greek islands usually requires changing in Athens, except for certain flights operated by Aegean Airlines, **Astra Airlines** (www.astra-airlines.gr) and Crete-based airline **Sky Express** (www.skyexpress.gr), which has very strict baggage allowances.

Crete Highlights

1 Making a date with King Minos at the **Palace of Knossos** (p427).

2 Following up a pilgrimage to **Moni Preveli** with a swim on

palm-studded **Preveli Beach** (p443).

3 Exploring Minoan ruins and sampling the local tipple in **Iraklio Wine Country** (p434).

4 Embarking on awander around the evocative historic quarter of **Hania** (p445).

5 Finding out why **Moni Arkadiou** (p440) is so important to Cretans.

Cyclades ↑↑ Santorini

0 ——— 20 km
0 ——— 12 miles

Kasos;
Karpathos;
Rhodes;
Halki
→

SEA OF
CRETE

Cape
Stavros

Dia

Cape Agios
Ioannis

Spinalonga Island

Cape
Sideros

Fodele

Moni
Toplou

Vaï

Iraklio
Bay

Gournes

Hersonisos

Plaka

Elounda

Kolokytha
Peninsula

Sitia

Iraklio

Palace of
Knossos

Malia

Malia

Agios
Nikolaos

Gulf of
Mirabello

Palekastro

Tylisos

Skalani

Myrtia

Neapoli

Zakros
Palace

Arhanes

Peza

Iraklio Wine
Country

Tzermiado

Lato

Kri-Kri

Kritsa

Mohlos

Zakros

Alagni

Psyhro

Lasithi
Plateau

Istron

LASITHI

Kato
Zakros

Rouvas
Gorge

Agios Georgios

Dikteon
Cave

Mt Dikti
(2148m)

Gournia

Agia Varvara

Kalamafka

Koutsouras

Zaros

Gortyna

IRAKLIO

Ano
Viannos

Ierapetra

Koufonisi

Pyrgos

Arvi

Myrtos

Lendas

Gaïdouronisi
(Hrysi)

LIBYAN SEA

Feeling the poignant
history of the former leper
colony on **Spinalonga Island**
(p463).

Cycling among windmills
on the **Lasithi Plateau** (p468).

Revelling in isolated
Elafonisi (p459), one of
Crete's most magical beaches.

Getting lost in the
charismatic jumble of

buildings in the old town in
Rethymno (p436).

Hiking the **Samaria
Gorge** (p454), one of Europe's
longest canyons.

DOMESTIC FLIGHTS FROM CRETE

DESTINATION	AIRPORT	TIME	FREQUENCY
Alexandroupoli	Sitia	1½hr	3 weekly
Athens	Iraklio, Hania, Sitia	1hr	daily
Chios	Iraklio	1½hr	2 weekly
Ikaria	Iraklio	50min	4 weekly
Karpathos	Iraklio, Sitia	50min	2 weekly
Kos	Iraklio	45min	3 weekly
Kythira	Iraklio	1hr	3 weekly
Mytilini (Lesvos)	Iraklio	1½hr	6 weekly
Preveza	Sitia	1¾hr	3 weekly
Rhodes	Iraklio, Sitia	50min	5 weekly
Samos	Iraklio	1¾hr	2 weekly
Thessaloniki	Iraklio, Hania	1¼hr	daily
Volos	Iraklio	1½hr	2 weekly

BOAT

Crete is well served by ferry with at least one daily departure from Piraeus (near Athens) to Iraklio and Hania year-round and several per day in summer. There are also ports in Sitia in the east and Kissamos (Kastelli) in the west, which have slow-ferry routes. Services are considerably curtailed from November to April. Timetables change from season to season, and ferries are subject to delays and cancellations at short notice due to bad weather, strikes or mechanical problems.

Ferry companies operating from Crete are **Anek Lines** (www.anek.gr), **Hellenic Seaways** (www.hellenicseaways.gr), **Lane Sea Lines** (www.lane-kithira.com), **Minoan Lines** (www.minoan.gr) and **Sea Jets** (www.seajets.gr).

For current routes and timetables, consult the ferry company's website or go to www.gtp.gr, www.openseas.gr, www.ferries.gr, www.greek ferries.gr or www.greekislands.gr. The lst three websites also offer ticket bookings.

❶ Getting Around

The extensive KTEL bus network makes it relatively easy to travel around Crete, although the frequency of service changes seasonally and is often curtailed (or nonexistent) at weekends. For schedules, which change monthly, and prices, check www.bus-service-crete-ktel.com for western Crete and www.ktelherlas.gr for central and eastern Crete.

Ferries link some of the southern coast villages between Paleohora and Hora Sfakion.

Having your own wheels is a great way to explore Crete if you can brave the roads and drivers. Road rules are routinely ignored and there is barely any police presence. Cretans drivers are generally erratic. Expect to be tailgated, honked at and aggressively and illegally overtaken if you move too slowly. Overtaking on bends and ignoring double lines and stop signs is prevalent. Slower drivers are expected to straddle the narrow service lane and let the traffic pass.

Taxis are widely available except in remote villages. Large towns have taxi stands that post a list of prices, otherwise you pay what's on the meter. If a taxi has no meter, settle on a price before driving off.

CENTRAL CRETE

Central Crete comprises the Iraklio prefecture, named after the island's booming capital, and the Rethymno prefecture, named after its lovely Venetian port town. Along with its dynamic urban life and Venetian remnants, the region is home to the island's top-rated tourist attraction, the Palace of Knossos, as well as other major and minor Minoan sites. Even if the coastal stretch east of the city of Iraklio is one continuous band of hotels and resorts, just a little bit inland villages sweetly lost in time provide pleasing contrast. Taste the increasingly sophisticated tipple produced in the Iraklio Wine Country, walk in the footsteps of Nikos Kazantzakis and revel in the rustic grandeur of the mountain village of Zaros.

Rethymno is a fascinating quilt of bubbly resorts, centuries-old villages and energising towns. Away from the northern coast, you'll quickly find yourself immersed in endless tranquillity and natural beauty as you drift through such villages as Anogia, where locals cherish their timeless traditions and their music. The southern coast is a different animal altogether – a wild beauty with steep gorges and bewitching beaches in seductive isolation, along with the relaxed resort of Plakias and the old hippie cave and beach hang-out of Matala.

Iraklio   Ηράκλειο

POP 140,730

Crete's capital city, Iraklio (ee-*rah*-klee-oh, also called Heraklion), is Greece's fifth-largest city and the island's economic and administrative hub. It's a somewhat hectic place, roaring with motorbikes throttling in unison at traffic lights and aeroplanes thrusting off into the sky over a long waterfront lined with the remnants of Venetian arsenals, fortresses and shrines.

Though not pretty in a conventional way, Iraklio can grow on you if you take the time to explore its nuances and wander its backstreets. A revitalised waterfront invites strolling and the newly pedestrianised historic centre is punctuated by bustling squares rimmed by buildings from the time when Columbus set sail.

Iraklio has a certain urban sophistication, with a thriving cafe and restaurant scene, the island's best shopping and lively nightlife. Of course, don't miss its blockbuster sights either, like the amazing newly renovated archaeological museum and the nearby Palace of Knossos, both fascinating windows into Minoan culture.

FERRY ROUTES TO/FROM CRETE

ROUTE	COMPANY	FARE	TIME	FREQUENCY
Hania-Piraeus	Anek	€42	8½hr	1 daily
Iraklio-Halki	Aegeon Pelagos (Anek)	€21	11¾hr	1 weekly
Iraklio-Ios	Hellenic Seaways	€66	4hr	1 daily
Iraklio-Ios	Sea Jets	€62.70	3½hr	1 daily
Iraklio-Karpathos	Aegeon Pelagos (Anek)	€18	7½hr	1 weekly
Iraklio-Kasos	Aegeon Pelagos (Anek)	€19	5¾hr	1 weekly
Iraklio-Milos	Aegeon Pelagos (Anek)	€22	7½hr	2 weekly
Iraklio-Mykonos	Hellenic Seaways	€81	4¾hr	1 daily
Iraklio-Mykonos	Sea Jets	€82.70	5½hr	1 daily
Iraklio-Paros	Hellenic Seaways	€71	4	1 daily
Iraklio-Naxos	Sea Jets	€69.70	5hr	1 daily
Iraklio-Piraeus	Minoan	€43	6½-7½hr	1-2 daily
Iraklio-Piraeus	Anek-Superfast	€36	6½-9½hr	1-2 daily
Iraklio-Rhodes	Aegeon Pelagos (Anek)	€28	14hr	1 weekly
Iraklio-Santorini (Thira)	Anek	€15	4¼hr	2 weekly
Iraklio-Santorini (Thira)	Sea Jets	€59.70	2hr	1 daily
Iraklio-Santorini (Thira)	Hellenic Seaways	€63	2hr	1 daily
Iraklio-Sitia	Aegeon Pelagos (Anek)	€15	3hr	1 weekly
Kissamos-Antikythira	Lane	€10	2hr	4 weekly
Kissamos-Gythio	Lane	€25	5hr	4 weekly
Kissamos-Kythira	Lane	€17	4hr	4 weekly
Kissamos-Piraeus	Lane	€24	12hr	2 weekly
Sitia-Iraklio	Aegeon Pelagos (Anek)	€11	3hr	2 weekly
Sitia-Karpathos	Aegeon Pelagos (Anek)	€18	4¼hr	4 weekly
Sitia-Kassos	Aegeon Pelagos (Anek)	€11	2½hr	4 weekly
Sitia-Milos	Aegeon Pelagos (Anek)	€251	1½hr	2 weekly
Sitia-Piraeus	Aegeon Pelagos (Anek)	€41	17hr	1 weekly
Sitia-Rhodes	Aegeon Pelagos (Anek)	€27	9½hr	2 weekly
Sitia-Santorini (Thira)	Aegeon Pelagos (Anek)	€26	7½hr	2 weekly

Prices quoted are for deck seating.

Sea of Crete

Old Harbour

Sofokli Venizelou

Plateia 18 Anglon

Plateia Istorikou Mouseiou

Mitsotaki

Natural History Museum (350m); Talos Plaza (600m); Amoudara (4km)

Epimenidou

Vyronos

Koroneou

Kalimeraki

El Greco Park

Plateia Agiou Titou

Loggia

Plateia Venizelou

Station B (900m)

Kalokerinou

Agios Markos Basilica

Dikeosynis

Monis Odigitrias

Agios Minas Cathedral

Grave of Nikos Kazantzakis (900m)

Bembo Fountain (100m)

Nikos Kazantzakis Open-Air Theatre (500m)

◉ Sights

Iraklio's main sights are wedged in the historic town, hemmed in by the waterfront and the old city walls. Many of the finest buildings line up along the main thoroughfare, 25 Avgoustou, which skirts the lovely central square, Plateia Venizelou (Venizelou Sq, also called Lion Sq after its landmark Morosini Fountain). East of here, Koraï is the hub of Iraklio's cafe scene, which leads towards the sprawling Plateia Eleftherias (Eleftherias Sq) with the archaeological museum nearby.

★ Heraklion Archaeological Museum

MUSEUM

(http://odysseus.culture.gr; Xanthoudidou 2; adult/child €6/free, incl Knossos €10; ⊙8am-8pm Apr-Oct, 11am-5pm Mon, 8am-3pm Tue-Sun Nov-Mar) Reopened in 2014 after a long renovation, this museum is Crete's outstanding jewel. The two floors of the restored 1930s Bauhaus building make a gleaming showcase for the exhibits that span 5500 years, from neolithic to Roman times, and an extensive Minoan collection. The rooms are colour coded and artefacts are displayed both chronologically and thematically and are beautifully presented with descriptions in English. A visit here enhances any understanding of Crete's rich history. Don't skip it.

The museum's treasure trove includes pottery, jewellery and sarcophagi, plus famous frescoes from the sites of Knossos, Tylissos, Amnissos and Agia Triada. The pieces are grouped into comprehensive themes such as settlements, trade, death, religion and administration. Along with clear descriptions, these bring to life both the day-to-day functioning and long-term progression of societies.

➡ Ground Floor

Rooms I–III focus on the neolithic period to the middle Bronze Age (7000–1700 BC), showing life in the first settlements in Crete and around Knossos. Don't miss the **golden pendant with bees** from Malia, a sophisticated jeweller's masterpiece, and the extensive jewellery collection. The elaborately embellished set of **Kamares tableware** is possibly a royal dinner service.

Rooms IV, V and VI illustrate life in the Late Bronze period (1700–1450 BC). This is when Minoan culture reached its zenith, as reflected in the foundation of new palaces, elaborate architecture and prolific trading practices. Not surprisingly, these are among the most visited rooms and the collection is vast. Highlights include the **small clay**

Iraklio

house from **Arhanes** and a stunning **ivory-and-crystal inlaid draughts board**. Most hone in on the **Phaistos disc**, a stunning clay piece embossed with 45 signs, which has never been deciphered. Nearby, the massive **copper ingots** from Agia Triada and Zakros Palace demonstrate important units of economic exchange. Other gems include the **bull-leaping fresco** and incredible **bull-leaper sculpture** (Room VI) that show daring sporting practices of the time.

Rooms VII to **VIII** reveal the importance of Minoan religion and ideology with cult objects and figurines. Don't miss the so-called **ring of King Minos**, a signet ring rediscovered and handed to authorities in 2001. The **snake goddesses** and **stone bull head** (inlaid with seashell and crystal) are two stunning ceremonial items from Knossos.

Room IX and X are dedicated to the palace of Knossos and its emergence as a centralised state (after the administrative collapse of other palaces) along with evidence of the Mycenaens. **Linear B clay tablets** reveal the first 'Greek' script and indicate Knossos' complex administrative system and bureaucratic processes. In Room X, look for the extraordinary **boar's helmet** and **gold-handled swords**, displaying the importance of the aristocratic warrior status.

Rooms XI and **XII** highlight settlements, sanctuaries and graves of the Late Bronze Age, including fascinating visual representations of death. The extraordinary sarcophagus from **Aghia Triada** (Room XXII) is presumed to be that of a ruler, given its detailed, honorific scenes.

➡ 1st Floor

Room XIII showcases Minoan frescoes (1800-1350 BC), including Evans' famous (or infamous) re-creations. The paintings reflects the interest in art and nature at the time. All are highlights, but for your at-a-glance reference, it's home to **The Prince of the Lilies**, the **Ladies in Blue** and the **bull head**.

Rooms XV–XIX focus on the Geometric and Archaic periods (10th to 6th century BC), the transition to the Iron Age and formation of the first Greek cities. The **Apollonian Triad**, bronze statues from Deros, are the earliest known Greek hammered bronze statues and the **bronze shields of the Idaean Cave** are extravagant votive offerings.

Room XX–XXII moves to the Classical, Hellenistic and Roman periods (5th to 4th century BC) where utensils and figurines and stunning mosaic floors and amphorae set the scene for the foundation of the autonomous Greek city-states, followed by civil wars and, finally, the Roman period. The huge **Phalagari hoard of silver coins** (Room XXI) is thought to be a military state fund. The cemetery finds of these periods are especially fascinating: look out for the skull with the gold wreath (Room XXII).

Room XXIII exhibits two private collections donated to the museum.

Rooms XXVI and **XXVII** (7th to 4th century BC) exhibit the role of Crete in the development of monumental sculpture, plus Roman sculptures and the obsession with rendering (and copying) statues of heroes and gods of the preceding Classical era.

Rooms VII–VIII reveal the importance of Minoan religion and ideology with cult objects and figurines. **Room VII** houses the chieftain's cup from Agia Triada that portrays two men, one holding a staff, the other a sword. Don't miss the so-called ring of King Minos, a signet ring rediscovered and handed to authorities in 2001. The snake goddesses and stone bull's head (inlaid with seashell and crystal) are two stunning ceremonial items from Knossos.

Note: at the time of research a multimedia and conference room (those missing numbers) were still being organised, as was a cloakroom and multimedia exhibition hall.

Historical Museum of Crete

MUSEUM

(www.historical-museum.gr; Sofokli Venizelou 27; admission €5; ⊘9am-5pm Mon-Sat Apr-Oct, to 3.30pm Mon-Sat Nov-Mar) If you're wondering what Crete's been up to for the past, say, 1700 years, a spin around this highly engaging museum is in order. Exhibits hopscotch from the Byzantine to the Venetian and Turkish periods, culminating with WWII. There's excellent English labelling, multimedia and listening stations throughout. A small cafe offers post-browse drinks.

Koules Venetian Fortress

FORTRESS

(Venetian Harbour) Iraklio's main landmark is this squat and square 16th-century fortress, called Rocca al Mare under the Venetians. It helped keep the Turks out for 21 years and later became a Turkish prison for Cretan rebels. Three walls sport marble reliefs of Venice's symbol: the winged Lion of St Mark. It was closed for renovation at the time of research.

Morosini Fountain

FOUNTAIN

(Lion Fountain; Plateia Venizelou) On Plateia Venizelou, this is the most beloved among the Venetian vestiges around town. These days, unfortunately, water no longer spurts from the four lions into eight marble troughs. The centrepiece marble statue of Poseidon was destroyed under the Turks.

Municipal Art Gallery

ART GALLERY

(Agios Markos Basilica, 25 Avgoustou; ⊘10am-1pm & 6pm-8.30pm Mon-Fri, to 1pm Sat) FREE The three-aisled 13th-century Agios Markos Basilica was reconstructed many times and turned into a mosque by the Turks. Today it holds temporary exhibitions of Greek and foreign artists. It's worth swinging by to check what's on.

Church of Agios Titos

CHURCH

(Plateia Agiou Titou; ⊘7.30am-1pm & 4.30-7.30pm) This majestic church dominates the eponymous square. It has Byzantine origins from AD 961, was converted to a Catholic church by the Venetians and turned into a mosque by the Ottomans, who also rebuilt it after the devastating 1856 earthquake. It has been an Orthodox church since 1925. Since 1966 it has once again sheltered the much-prized skull relic of St Titus, returned here after being spirited to Venice for safe-keeping during the Turkish occupation.

Beaches

Ammoudara, about 4km west of Iraklio, and **Amnisos**, 2km east, are the closest beaches to town; the latter is just past the airport and gets quite a bit of noise. The strands in **Agia Pelagia**, some 20km west of town, are nicer.

🏃 Activities

Cretan Adventures

OUTDOORS

(☑28103 32772; www.cretanadventures.gr; 3rd fl, Evans 10) 🖉 This well-regarded local company run by friendly and knowledgeable English-speaking Fondas organises hiking tours, mountain biking and extreme out-

CRETE IRAKLIO

KIDS' DAY OUT

A plethora of kid-friendly activities are concentrated on the northern coast in Gournes (Γούρνες) and Hersonisos and surrounds, east of Iraklio. You can get wet and wild at water parks including **Water City** (☑28107 81317; www.watercity.gr; adult/child under 140cm/child under 90cm €25/17/free; ⊘10am-6.30pm May-Sep), **Acqua Plus** (www.acquaplus.gr; adult/child €26/17; ⊘10am-6pm May-Sept, to 7pm Jul & Aug) or **Star Beach** (www.starbeach.gr; admission free; ⊘10am-6pm Apr-May, to 7pm Jun-Sep). Get in touch with your inner Tyrannosaurus rex at **Dinosauria** (☑28103 32089; www.dinosauriapark.com; adult/child €9.50/7.50; ⊘10am-8pm May-Oct, to 5pm Nov-Apr), in Gournes, before channelling your inner mermaid at the giant aquarium, **Cretaquarium** (☑28103 37788; www.cretaquarium.gr; adult/child €9/6, audio guide €3; ⊘9.30am-9pm May-Sep, to 5pm Oct-Apr). For a hands-on reptile and aquarium experience, visit **Aqua World** (www.aquaworld-crete.com; adult/child €6/4; ⊘10am-6pm Apr-Oct, last admission 5.15pm) in Hersonisos. Horsey folk can go on the trot with **Arion Stables** (☑6973733825; www.arionstables.com; Old Hersonisos; per hr €30).

door excursions. It also coordinates fabulous self-guided tours with detailed hiking instructions, plus accommodation with breakfast and luggage transfer (from €740 for one week). Fondas' office is up on the 3rd floor and easy to miss.

Mountaineering Club of Iraklio HIKING
(28102 27609; www.eos-her.gr; Dikeosynis 53; 8.30-10.30pm Mon-Fri) The local chapter arranges hiking trips across the island most weekends (trip programs are published on its website). Anyone is welcome to join.

Sleeping

Hotel Mirabello HOTEL €
(28102 85052; www.mirabello-hotel.gr; Theotokopoulou 20; d with/without bathroom from €60/45;) This friendly and relaxed hotel is hardly of recent vintage but it's excellent value for money. Rooms are immaculate if a bit cramped and have TVs and phones. Some have a balcony, fridge and (joy of joy) coffee-and tea-making facilities. The street is mainly quiet, but the student social club next door is not, usually on Friday and Saturday evenings.

Rea Hotel HOTEL €
(28102 23638; www.hotelrea.gr; Kalimeraki 1, cnr Hortatson; d with/without bathroom €45/35, tr €55;) Renovated in 2014, the family-run Rea has an easy, friendly atmosphere. The 16 simple, neat-as-a-pin rooms are set over two floors. All have small TVs and balconies, but some bathrooms are shared. Family rooms are available. There's a book exchange and a communal fridge.

Kastro Hotel HOTEL €€
(28102 84185; www.kastro-hotel.gr; Theotokopoulou 22; s/d/tr incl breakfast €55/85/110;) The Kastro's nearly-but-not-quite-there *Home Beautiful*–style rooms feature more curves and shapes than a child's put-the-shape-in-the-cube toy. Plus funky wallpaper, marble desks and leather-padded walls-cum-bedheads. Rooms come with flat-screen TVs, small fridges and balconies. Pleasant breakfast area and the staff is extremely helpful. A good-value choice.

Atrion Hotel BUSINESS HOTEL €€
(28102 46000; www.atrion.gr; Chronaki 9; s/d/tr/f incl breakfast from €70/95/120/135;) This modern, streamlined 60-room business-style hotel has all the electronic gizmos and nondescript mainstream design you'd expect of a place that attracts business folk. Close to El Greco Park and the port, it's

also conveniently located for the traveller. A reliable, if pricier, bet.

Capsis Astoria HOTEL €€
(28103 43080; www.capsishotel.gr; Plateia Eleftherias 11; s €85-100, d €100-120, tr €115-140, all incl breakfast ;) The hulking exterior doesn't impress, but past the front door the Capsis is a class act, all the way to the rooftop pool from where you enjoy a delicious panorama of Iraklio. Rooms sport soothing neutral tones and dashing historic black-and-white photographs. Thirty of the 131 rooms are 'skylight' rooms meaning windows but no vistas. Fabulous breakfast buffet.

GDM Megaron HOTEL €€€
(28103 05300; www.gdmmegaron.gr; Doukos Beaufort 9; s/d incl breakfast from €140/170;) Don't be put off by the towering hulk of this harbour-front hotel, for inside awaits a top designer abode with comfortable rooms (all with different sizes and configurations), Jacuzzis in the VIP suites, and flat-screen TVs. Unwinding in the glass-sided pool and drinking in the sweeping views from the rooftop restaurant and bar are hardly run-of-the-mill features either.

Eating

Fyllo...Sofies CAFE €
(2810 284774; www.fillosofies.gr; Plateia Venizelou 33; snacks €3-7; 6am-late;) With tables sprawling out towards the Morosini Fountain, this is a great place for a breakfast *bougatsa* (creamy semolina pudding wrapped in a pastry envelope and sprinkled with cinnamon and sugar). The less-sweet version is made with *myzithra* (sheep's-milk cheese).

★ Peskesi CRETAN €€
(28102 88887; www.peskesicrete.gr; mains €8-16; noon-late) One of Iraklio's recent additions to the city's upmarket dining scene, and housed in a smartly converted cottage, this lovely eatery comes with a large dollop of snob value. It's best described as 'postmodern ancient Greek' (say what? we hear you ask). Think smoked pork *(apaki)* hanging off a butcher's hook with smoking herbs beneath and *kandavlos* (an ancient souvlaki).

Parasties GREEK €€
(www.parasties.gr; Historic Museum Square, Sofokli Venizelou 19; mains €7-24; noon-midnight) Parasties' owner Haris is Iraklio's answer to a city's restaurateur who is genuine about serving great-quality local produce and top Cretan wines. His passion shows in his small but

gourmet menu. Beef liver and grilled mushrooms are our top choices, while a great selection of zingy salads and superb meats will keep you munching more than you planned.

Ippokambos SEAFOOD €€

(Sofokli Venizelou 3; mains €6-13; ☺noon-midnight Mon-Sat; 🐟) Locals give this smart *ouzerie* an enthusiastic thumbs up and we are only too happy to follow suit. Fish is the thing here – it's freshly caught, simply but expertly prepared and sold at fair prices. In summer, park yourself on the covered waterfront terrace. Look for the seahorse *(ippokambos)* sign.

🍷 Drinking & Nightlife

The see-and-be-seen scene sprawls around Koraï, Perdikari and El Greco Park. West of here, Handakos, Agiostefaniton and Psaromiligkon have more alternative-flavoured hang-outs. Most places open mid-morning or at noon and close in the wee hours, changing stripes and clientele as time moves on. Clubs line Epimenidou and Beaufort near the harbour and the western waterfront near the Talos Plaza shopping mall. Cover starts at around €5; double that if there's a big international DJ at the deck. The action usually doesn't kick into high gear until 1am.

Utopia CAFE

(www.outopia.eu; Handakos 51; ☺9am-2am) This hushed and formal old-style cafe has the best hot chocolate (€5.50 to €8.50) in town, although the prices are utopian indeed. Other temptations include a decadent chocolate fondue and great ice cream and homemade cookies. Its alter ego – Beer Utopia – across the road offers over 500 beers.

★ Bar Blow-Up BAR

(http://barblowup.blogspot.de; Psaromiligkon 1; ☺10pm-late; 🐟) This cool party lair has a funky underground vibe that seems more

Berlin than Iraklio and draws an all-ages, unpretentious crowd for good music and cold beers.

Jailhouse Bar BAR

(Agiostefaniton 19a; ☺5pm-4am) This place plays punk (a fave of the owner, Yiannis) and rock tunes from Johnny Cash to Johnny Rotten. The trashy-sophisticated decor in a barrel-vaulted Venetian-era building is a bonus. Happy hour runs from 7pm to 11pm and Monday sees a two-for-one beer offering.

Mare CAFE, BAR

(www.mare-cafe.gr; Sofokli Venizelou; ☺9am-late) In an enviable location on the beautified waterfront promenade opposite the Historical Museum, contempo Mare is great for post-culture java and sunset drinks.

🛍 Shopping

Aerakis Music MUSIC

(www.aerakis.net; Koraï Sq 14) An Iraklio landmark since 1974, this little shop stocks the best range of Cretan music, from old and rare recordings to the latest releases, many on its own record label, Aerabus – Cretan Musical Workshop & Seistron.

Roadside Travel BOOKS, MAPS

(Handakos 29; ☺9am-9pm Mar-Oct, 9am-2pm & 5.30-9pm Nov-Feb, to 2.30pm Sat) One of the world's better travel specialist bookshops with a wonderful selection of guidebooks and maps plus good publications on Crete and its ancient sites.

ℹ Information

Iraklio's two hospitals are far from the centre and work alternate days – call first to find out where to go. Banks with ATMs are ubiquitous, especially along 25 Avgoustou. For online information, try www.heraklion-city.gr and http://history.heraklion.gr; in high season there is

DON'T MISS

IRAKLIO MARKET

An Iraklio institution just south of the Morosini Fountain, narrow Odos 1866 (1866 St) is part market, part bazaar and, despite being increasingly tourist-oriented, a fun place to browse and stock up on picnic supplies or souvenirs. Fruit and veg stands alternate with butchers and vendors selling local cheeses, honey, olives, herbs and mountain tea. There's also a good supply of leather goods, hats, jewellery and beach gear. Cap off a spree with lunch at **Giakoumis** (Theodosaki 5-8; mains €6-13; ☺7am-11pm) or continue north to the fish section with its own cluster of tavernas. The lane culminates at Plateia Kornarou (Kornarou Sq), where the eye-catching **Bembo Fountain** (Plateia Kornarou) was cobbled together in the 16th century from an ancient Roman sarcophagus and headless alabaster statue.

HIGH SEASON FERRY ROUTES FROM IRAKLIO

DESTINATION	COMPANY	FARE	TIME	FREQUENCY
Halki	Aegeon Pelagos (Anek)	€21	11¾hr	1 weekly
Ios	Hellenic Seaways	€66	4hr	1 daily
Ios	Sea Jets	€63	3½hr	1 daily
Karpathos	Aegeon Pelagos (Anek)	€18	7½hr	1 weekly
Kasos	Aegeon Pelagos (Anek)	€19	5¾hr	1 weekly
Mykonos	Hellenic Seaways	€81	4¾hr	1 daily
Mykonos	Sea Jets	€83	5½hr	1 daily
Naxos	Sea Jets	€70	5hr	1 daily
Paros	Hellenic Seaways	€71	4hr	1 daily
Piraeus	Minoan	€43	6½-7½hr	1-2 daily
Piraeus	Anek-Superfast	€36	6½-9½hr	1-2 daily
Rhodes	Aegeon Pelagos	€27	14hr	1 weekly
Santorini (Thira)	Sea Jets	€60	2hr	1 daily
Santorini (Thira)	Hellenic Seaways	€63	2hr	1 daily
Sitia	Aegeon Pelagos (Anek)	€15	3hr	1 weekly

sometimes a tourist office (8.30am to 2.30pm Monday to Friday) in the Aktarika building at Lion's Square.

Main Post Office (Plateia Daskalogianni; ◷7.30am-8pm Mon-Fri, to 2pm Sat)

Tourist Police (☑28103 97111; Halikarnassos; ◷7am-10pm) In the Halikarnassos suburb near the airport.

University Hospital (☑28103 92111) At Voutes, 5km south of Iraklio, this is the city's best-equipped medical facility.

Venizelio Hospital (☑28103 68000) On the road to Knossos, 4km south of Iraklio.

ⓘ Getting There & Away

AIR

About 5km east of Iraklio city centre, the Nikos Kazantzakis International Airport (p724) has a bank, an ATM, a duty-free shop and a cafe-bar.

BOAT

The ferry port is 500m to the east of the Koules Fortress and old harbour, and the bus terminal is right outside the port entrance. Iraklio is a major port for access to many of the islands, though services are greatly reduced outside high season. Tickets can be purchased through several of the town's travel agencies, including central **Paleologos** (☑28103 46185; www.greekislands. gr; 25 Avgoustou 5; ◷9am-8pm Mon-Fri, to 4pm Sat), which also sells tickets online. Daily ferries from Iraklio's port include services to Piraeus and faster catamarans to Santorini and other Cycladic Islands. Ferries sail east to Rhodes via Agios Nikolaos, Sitia, Kasos, Kapathos and Halki. See www.openseas.gr for current schedules.

BUS

Iraklio has two major bus stations. **Bus Station A** (☑2810 246530; www.ktelherlas.gr), near the waterfront, serves eastern and western Crete (including Knossos) and has a left-luggage office (per piece per day €2) that's open from 6.30am to 8pm. Local buses also stop here.

Bus Station B (☑28102 55965; www.ktelher las.gr), just west of the centre beyond Hania Gate, serves Anogia, Phaestos, Agia Galini and Matala.

For details on services to Rethymno, see www. bus-service-crete-ktel.com.

LONG-DISTANCE TAXI

For destinations around Crete, you can order a cab from **Crete Taxi Services** (☑6970021970; www.crete-taxi.gr) or **Heraklion Taxi** (www.her aklion-taxi.com). There are also long-distance cabs waiting at the airport, at Plateia Eleftherias (outside the Capsis Astoria hotel) and at Bus Station A. Sample fares for up to four people include Agios Nikolaos (€69), Elounda (€74), Malia (€39), Matala (€78) and Rethymno (€87).

ⓘ Getting Around

TO/FROM THE AIRPORT

The airport is just off the E75 motorway. In summer, Bus 1 (€1.10) connects it with the city centre every five minutes between 6.15am and midnight. Handy in-town stops are Bus Station A and Plateia Eleftherias. A taxi into town costs around €12 to €15.

CAR & MOTORCYCLE

Iraklio's streets are narrow and chaotic, so it's best to drop your vehicle in a car park (€6 per day) and explore on foot. The cheapest car park is the outdoor Marina car park, on the eastern side of town (€2 per day).

All the international car- and scooter-hire companies have branches at the airport. Outlets on 25 Avgoustou include **Caravel** (☑ 28103 00150; www.caravel.gr; 25 Avgoustou 39; car per day from €42), **Hertz** (☑ 28103 00744; www.hertz. gr; 25 Avgoustou 4) and **Motor Club** (☑ 28102 22408; www.motorclub.gr; Plateia 18 Anglon; car/scooter per day from €40/28).

TAXI
Central taxi ranks are at Bus Station A, on Plateia Eleftherias and on Plateia Kornarou, or order one by **phone** (☑ 2810 210102).

Around Iraklio

Knossos   Κνωσσός

Palace of Knossos   ARCHAEOLOGICAL SITE
(☑ 28102 31940; adult/child €6/free, incl Heraklion Archaeological Museum €10; ⊗ 8am-8pm May-Oct, to 5pm Nov-April) Crete's most famous historical attraction is the Palace of Knossos (k-nos-*os*), the grand capital of Minoan Crete, located 5km south of Iraklio. The setting is evocative and the ruins and re-creations impressive, incorporating an immense palace, courtyards, private apartments, baths, lively frescoes and more. Excavation of the site started in 1878 with Cretan archaeologist Minos Kalokeri-

nos, and continued from 1900 to 1930 with British archaeologist Sir Arthur Evans who controversially restored parts of the site.

A visit to the Heraklion Archaeological Museum in Iraklio and taking a guided tour add needed context. Guides congregate at the entrance and charge around €10 if they can join you up with others, or up to €80 for a private tour.

Knossos was the setting for the myth of the Minotaur. According to legend, King Minos of Knossos was given a magnificent white bull to sacrifice to the god Poseidon, but decided to keep it. This enraged Poseidon, who punished the king by causing his wife Pasiphae to fall in love with the animal. The result of this odd union was the Minotaur – half-man and half-bull – who was imprisoned in a labyrinth beneath the king's palace at Knossos, munching on youths and maidens, before being killed by Theseus.

Knossos' first palace (1900 BC) was destroyed by an earthquake around 1700 BC and rebuilt to a grander and more sophisticated design. It was partially destroyed again between 1500 and 1450 BC, and inhabited for another 50 years before finally burning down. Evans' reconstruction methods continue to be controversial, with many visitors and archaeologists believing that he sacrificed accuracy to his overly vivid imagination. His

CRETE AROUND IRAKLIO

Palace of Knossos

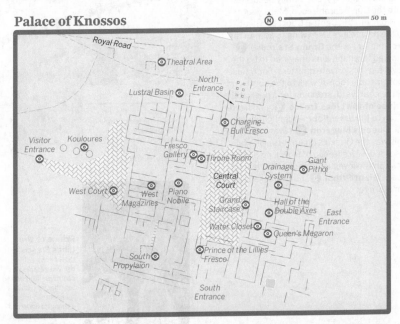

Palace of Knossos

THE HIGHLIGHTS IN TWO HOURS

The Palace of Knossos is Crete's busiest tourist attraction, and for good reason. A spin around the partially and imaginatively reconstructed complex (shown here as it was thought to be at its peak) delivers an eye-opening peek into the remarkably sophisticated society of the Minoans, who dominated southern Europe some 4000 years ago.

From the ticket booth, follow the marked trail to the **North Entrance** ❶ where the Charging Bull fresco gives you a first taste of Minoan artistry. Continue to the Central Court and join the queue waiting to glimpse the mystical **Throne Room** ❷, which probably hosted religious rituals. Turn right as you exit and follow the stairs up to the so-called Piano Nobile, where replicas of the palace's most famous artworks conveniently cluster in the **Fresco Room** ❸. Walk the length of the Piano Nobile, pausing to look at the clay storage vessels in the West Magazine. Circle back and descend to the **South Portico** ❹, beautifully decorated with the Cup Bearer fresco. Make your way back to the Central Court and head to the palace's eastern wing to admire the architecture of the **Grand Staircase** ❺ that led to what Evans imagined to be the royal family's private quarters. For a closer look at some rooms, walk to the south end of the courtyard, stopping for a peek at the **Prince of the Lilies fresco** ❻, and head down to the lower floor. A highlight here is the **Queen's Megaron** ❼ (Evans imagined this was the Queen's chambers), playfully adorned with a fresco of frolicking dolphins. Stay on the lower level and make your way to the **Giant Pithoi** ❽, huge clay jars used for storage.

South Portico
Fine frescoes, most famously the Cup Bearer, embellish this palace entrance anchored by a massive open staircase leading to the Piano Nobile. The Horns of Consecration recreated nearby once topped the entire south facade.

Fresco Room
Take in sweeping views of the palace grounds from the west wing's upper floor, the Piano Nobile, before studying copies of the palace's most famous artworks in its Fresco Room.

West Court

West Magazines

❹ **Horns of Consecration**

FOOD TIP

Save your appetite for a meal in the nearby Iraklio Wine Country, amid sunbaked slopes and lush valleys. It's just south of Knossos.

Prince of the Lilies Fresco
One of Knossos' most beloved frescoes was controversially cobbled together from various fragments and shows a young man adorned in lilies and peacock feathers.

PLANNING

To beat the crowds and avoid the heat, arrive before 10am. Budget one or two hours to explore the site thoroughly.

Throne Room

Sir Arthur Evans who began excavating the Palace of Knossos in 1900, imagined the mythical King Minos himself holding court seated on the alabaster throne of this beautifully proportioned room. However, the lustral basin and griffin frescoes suggest a religious purpose, possibly under a priestess.

North Entrance

Bulls held a special status in Minoan society as evidenced by the famous relief fresco of a charging beast gracing the columned west bastion of the north palace, which harboured workshops and storage rooms.

Grand Staircase

The royal apartments in the eastern wing were accessed via this monumental staircase sporting four flights of gypsum steps supported by columns. The lower two flights are original. It's closed to the public.

Piano Nobile

③

②

⑤

Central Court

⑥

Royal Apartments

⑧

⑦

①

Giant Pithoi

These massive clay jars are rare remnants from the Old Palace period and were used to store wine, oil and grain. The jars were transported by slinging ropes through a series of handles.

Queen's Megaron

The queen's room is among the prettiest in the residential eastern wing thanks to the playful Dolphin Fresco. The adjacent bathroom (with clay tub) and toilet are evidence of a sophisticated drainage system.

reconstructions focus on the palace's most significant parts, and over the course of 30 years of excavations, Evans unearthed the remains of a neolithic civilisation beneath the remains of the Bronze Age Minoan palace. He also discovered some 3000 clay tablets containing Linear A and Linear B script.

The first treasure to be unearthed in the flat-topped mound called Kefala was a fresco of a Minoan man, followed by the discovery of the Throne Room. The archaeological world was stunned that a civilisation of this maturity and sophistication had existed in Europe at the same time as the great pharaohs of Egypt. The Minoans' highly sophisticated society was further revealed by details like the advanced drainage system and the clever placement of rooms to passages, light wells, porches and verandahs that kept rooms cool in summer and warm in winter.

As you tour the site, keep in mind that the names and uses ascribed to the buildings do not necessarily reflect Minoan reality. The first section of the palace you come across is the West Court, which may have been a marketplace or the site of public gatherings. On your left is a trio of circular pits, called kouloures, that were used for grain storage.

Walk north along the palace's western wall to the theatral area, a series of shallow steps whose function remains unknown. It could have been a theatre where spectators watched acrobatic and dance performances, or the place where people gathered to welcome important visitors arriving by the Royal Road, which leads off to the west. Europe's first road was flanked by workshops and the houses of ordinary people. Also here, on your right, is a lustral basin where, so Evans speculated, Minoans performed a ritual water cleansing before religious ceremonies.

Near the north entrance to the palace, stop to admire the Charging Bull Fresco before continuing to the heart of the palace, the massive Central Court, which in Minoan times was hemmed in by high walls. As is typical of a Minoan palace, rooms facing the western side of the courtyard had official and religious purposes, while the residential quarters were on the opposite side.

The central court gives way to the palace's most important rooms, including the Throne Room. Peering through security glass, you can make out a simple, beautifully proportioned alabaster throne and walls decorated with frescoes of griffins: mythical beasts regarded as sacred by the Minoans. The room exudes an aura of mysticism and reverence and is thought to have been a shrine. The Minoans did not worship their deities in great temples but in small shrines, and each palace had several.

A lustral basin is in a separate room to the left of the Throne Room, but you'll get a better look at it from above in a moment. Walk past the Throne Room and up a staircase to the first floor. Inspired by Italian Renaissance palazzos, Evans called this the Piano Nobile, for this is where he believed the reception and staterooms were located. From up here you also have a great perspective on the west magazines, or storage rooms, where giant *pithoi* (clay jars) once held oil, wine and other staples.

The restored room at the northern end of the Piano Nobile looks down on the aforementioned lustral basin and also houses replicas of the most famous frescoes found at Knossos, including the Bull-Leaper, the Ladies in Blue and the Blue Bird. The originals are now in the Heraklion Archaeological Museum. At the far south end of the Piano Nobile, a staircase leads down to the South Propylaion, where you can admire the Cup Bearer Fresco.

Backtrack to the Central Court and cross it to get to the impressive grand staircase, which leads down to the royal apartments. Study their layout from above, then walk to the lower level past the Prince of the Lilies fresco on the south side of the central court.

Much of the royal apartments is inaccessible but you can still catch glimpses of the king's quarters *(megaron)* in the Hall of the Double Axes, a spacious double room; Evans proposed that the ruler both slept and carried out court duties there. The room had a light well at one end and a balcony at the other to ensure air circulation. It takes its name from the double axe marks *(labrys)* on its light well, a sacred symbol to the Minoans and the origin of our word 'labyrinth'.

A passage leads from the Hall of the Double Axes to the queen's megaron. Above the door is a copy of the Dolphin Fresco, one of the most exquisite Minoan artworks. A blue floral design decorates the portal. Next to this room is the queen's bathroom, complete with terracotta bathtub and a water closet, touted as the first ever to work on the flush principle; water was poured down by hand.

To beat the crowds and avoid the heat, get to Knossos early before tour buses arrive, or later in the afternoon when it's cooler, though budget several hours. The cafe at the site is expensive – you'd do better to bring a picnic.

Getting here is easy; all roads lead to Knossos it seems. Bus 2 leaves Bus Station A or from outside Hotel Capsis Astoria in Iraklio every 20 minutes for Knossos (€1.50).

If driving, from Iraklio or the coastal road there are signs directing you to Knossos. There is free parking across from the souvenir shops but the spaces fill quickly.

OTHER MINOAN PALACES

Besides Knossos, central Crete has a trio of other key Minoan sites that were not reconstructed and thus provide a glimpse into this ancient society without Evans' interpretations.

Phaestos

Some 63km southwest of Iraklio, near Matala, **Phaestos** (☑28920 42315; adult/child €4/free, incl Agia Triada €6/free; ⊘8am-8pm May-Oct, to 3pm Nov-Mar) was Crete's second most important Minoan palace-city and enjoys an awe-inspiring setting with panoramic views of the Mesara Plain and Mt Psiloritis. The celebrated Phaestos Disk, now in the Heraklion Archaeological Museum (p421), was found just northwest of the palace.

Like Knossos, Phaestos (fes-*tos*) was built atop a previously destroyed older palace and laid out around a central court. In contrast to its bigger cousin, though, this site had fewer frescoes as walls were apparently covered with white gypsum only.

Past the ticket booth, you'll first come across the **Upper Court**, which may have been a market square. From here, stairs lead down to the **West Court**, with the **Theatral Area** off to the right and a sweeping **Grand Stairway** to the left. This once led to the **Propylon**, the main palace entrance, of which only the pillar bases survive. Past a series of storage rooms lies the vast **Central Court** with the royal living quarters in the north wing (turn left). These include the **queen's and king's megaron** (under cover) and the **Peristyle Court**, an elegant inner courtyard.

Most **KTEL buses** (www.ktelherlas.gr) to Matala head to Phaestos from Iraklio (€6.50, 1½ hours), also stopping at Gortyna (but check first with the driver and ask for return times as these, too, can vary). There are also buses from Agia Galini (€2.10, 45 minutes) and Matala (€1.80, 30 minutes, two to three daily).

Agia Triada

In an enchanting hillside looking out to the Gulf of Messara 3km west of Phaestos, **Agia Triada** (☑27230 22448; adult/child €3/free, incl Phaestos €6/free; ⊘9.30am-4.30pm summer, 9am-4pm winter) encompasses vestiges of an L-shaped royal villa, a ramp once leading out to sea and a village with residences and stores. Built around 1550 BC, Agia Triada (ah-*yee*-ah trih-*ah*-dha) succumbed to fire around 1400 BC but was never looted. This accounts for the many Minoan masterpieces found here, most famously the **Agia Triada sarcophagus**, now a star exhibit at the Heraklion Archaeological Museum. The signposted turn-off to Agia Triada is about 500m past Phaestos on the Matala road. There's no direct public transport to the site, which is about a 5km walk from any major village.

Malia

On the northern coast, about 35km east of Iraklio, near the eponymous coastal resort, the **Palace of Malia** (☑28970 31597; adult/child €4/free; ⊘8am-5pm, closed Mon in winter) is a relatively easy site to comprehend thanks to a free map, an exhibition hall and labelling throughout.

Enter from the **West Court**, turn right and walk south along a series of **storage rooms (West Magazines)** to eight circular pits believed to have been grain silos. Continue past the silos and enter the palace's **Central Court** from the south. On your left, in the ground, is the **Kernos Stone**, a disc with 24 holes around its edge that may have had a religious function. Just beyond here are the palace's most important rooms, including the **Pillar Crypt** behind a stone-paved vestibule, the **Grand Staircase** and the elevated **Loggia**, most likely used for ceremonial purposes. Still further were the **royal apartments**, while buildings north of the central court held **workshops** and **storage rooms**.

Buses leave from Iraklio's Bus Station A several times each hour for Malia village with a stop at the palace (€3.80, one hour).

LONELY PLANET / GETTY IMAGES ©

LONELY PLANET / GETTY IMAGES ©

1. Spili (p442)
Spili's church looks out on the mountain village.

2. Rethymno (p436)
Waterfront eating in one of Crete's most enchanting towns.

3. Heraklion Archaeological Museum (p421)
This museum in Crete's capital, Iraklio, showcases exhibits spanning 5500 years in a restored Bauhaus building.

4. Spinalonga Island (p463)
Under the fortress are tunnels used to bring patients to the island when it was a leper colony.

Iraklio Wine Country

About 70% of wine produced in Crete comes from the Iraklio Wine Country, which starts south of Knossos around both Dafnes and Arhanes (which sits atop a Minoan palace, and makes an ideal base and a more laid-back alternative to Iraklio). Almost two dozen wineries are embedded in a landscape of shapely hills, sunbaked slopes and lush valleys. Winemakers cultivate indigenous Cretan grape varietals such as *kotsifali, mandilari* and *malvasia;* many estates offer tours, wine museums and tastings. Check www.winesofcrete.gr for a complete list of wineries, and pick up the excellent *Wine Roads of Heraklion* map, available at the wine estates themselves.

🏃 Activities

Boutari
WINERY

(☑28107 31617; www.boutari.gr; Skalani; ⊘9am-5pm Mon-Fri year-round, by appointment on weekends) Near Skalani, about 8km from Iraklio, Boutari is the island's biggest producer (read mass market) and it's a sleek, modern operation. Take the tour (by appointment) to learn about local grapes and winemaking or just stick around to sample the product (most of Crete's grape varieties) in the vast and modern tasting room overlooking the vineyard.

Minos-Miliarikis
WINERY

(☑28107 41213; www.minoswines.gr; Peza; ⊘9am-4pm Mon-Fri, 10.30am-3pm Sat) Right on the Peza main street, Minos is a massive winery that, in 1952, was the first to bottle wine in Crete. It makes very respectable vintages, especially under its Miliarakis label, including a full-bodied single-vineyard organic red and a fragrant Blanc de Noirs. Upon appointment, tastings are also held at the winery's **Vineyard House** (⊘11am-6pm Mon-Sat), right next to the grapes in Sambas, about 10km east of Peza towards Kastelli.

Domaine Gavalas
WINERY

(☑28940 51060; www.domainegavalas.gr; Vorias; ⊘8am-4pm Mon-Fri) Founded in 2004, this is one of the largest organic wineries in Crete. Try its award-winning Efivos reds and whites. It's in Vorias, about 20km south of Peza.

🛏 Sleeping & Eating

Eliathos
APARTMENT €€

(☑6951804929, 28107 51818; www.eliathos.gr; Arhanes; studio €110, villas €130-180; ❄ ⚹) Tucked into the hillside about half a kilometre south of Arhanes and with grand views of Mt Yiou-

htas, this cluster of six houses is a haven of peace and quiet. The owners can help you get immersed in the local culture through cooking classes, excursions, and olive oil, *raki* or winemaking workshops.

Arhontiko
APARTMENT €€

(☑28107 52985; www.arhontikoarhanes.gr; Arhanes; apt €75-95; ❄ ⚹) An air of effortless sophistication pervades these four apartments in a villa built in 1893, with incarnations as a military barracks and an elementary school. No hint of either survives in the four bilevel apartments that combine antiques and old embroideries with full kitchens, a fireplace and the gamut of mod cons.

Kritamon
CRETAN €€

(www.kritamon.gr; Vathy Petrou 4; mains €9-14; ⊘dinner daily, lunch Sat & Sun) Send your taste buds on a wild ride at this foodie outpost in a street off the main square and set attractively around a garden courtyard with walnut trees. Ancient Cretan and creative modern recipes result in soulful salads, rustic mains and to-die-for desserts. Ingredients come either from the family garden or local suppliers.

Elia & Diosmos
CRETAN €€

(☑2810 731283; www.olive-mint.gr; Skalani; mains €10-19; ⊘lunch & dinner Tue-Sun) At this foodie playground on the edge of the Iraklio Wine Country, Argiro Barda turns market-fresh ingredients into contemporary Cretan dishes that are a feast of flavours. The menu chases the seasons, but classic choices include succulent lamb chops with honey, fluffy fennel pie, and feisty pork with figs, plums and pistachios. It's only a short drive from Iraklio and about 10 minutes south of Knossos.

Zaros
Ζαρός

POP 2110

At the bottom of the mighty Rouvas Gorge in the Mt Psiloritis foothills, the rustic mountain village of Zaros is famous for its natural spring water, which is bottled and sold all over Crete. Clued-in foodies flock here for the fresh farm-raised trout, which can be enjoyed in numerous tavernas around town and on emerald-green Lake Votomos.

Zaros also lures outdoor-lovers with its easy to moderate 5km hike through the **Rouvas Gorge**. The trail starts near the Limni taverna but doesn't enter the gorge for another 1km, just past Moni Agios Nikolaos, a modern monastery that wraps around a historic church rife with icons and fresco fragments.

The path first weaves through fire-damaged forest but soon the vegetation becomes increasingly lush with oak trees, lilies, orchids, sage and other mountain flora. At the end is a little chapel of Agios Ioannis where benches and tables invite a leisurely picnic.

🛏 Sleeping & Eating

★ Eleonas Cottages   COTTAGE €€
(☏ 28940 31238, 6976670002; www.eleonas.gr; Zaros; studio/cottage incl breakfast from €90/100; P🅿✳@🛜🏊) 🕭 In an extraordinary labour of love, owner Manolis has created this paradise for guests. Cradled by olive groves, this beautiful retreat is built into a stunning terraced garden hillside. It's a '*this* is Crete' kind of place, such is the fresh air, relaxing ambience and staff *filoxenia* (hospitality). Its smartly appointed studios and apartments sport tasteful decor.

★ Vegera   CRETAN €
(☏ 28940 31730; www.vegerazaros.gr; Main St; multicourse meal €12; ⏱ 8am-late; 🍴) The vivacious Vivi has a knack for turning farm-fresh local produce into flavourful and creative dishes based on traditional recipes. Her philosophy is to 'cook the way we cook in our house'. Indeed, with the floral tablecloths, homey setting, and Vivi as your host, you could be in a welcoming Greek home.

ℹ Getting There & Away

Zaros is about 46km southwest of Iraklio. From Iraklio's Bus Station B, one daily bus stops in Zaros (€5.50, one hour) en route to Kamares; the best alternative is to take one of the hourly buses to Mires and catch a taxi (around €15) from there.

Matala   Μάταλα

POP 70

In mythology Matala (*ma*-ta-la) is the place where Zeus, in the form of a bull, swam ashore with Europa on his back before dragging her off to Gortyna and getting her pregnant with the future King Minos. In more recent times, Matala earned legacy status thanks to the scores of hippies flocking here in the late 1960s to take up rent-free residence in cliffside caves. Joni Mitchell famously immortalised the era in her song 'Carey'. In summer, the village is inundated with coachloads of day trippers. Stay overnight or visit in the off-season, though, and it's still possible to discern the Matala magic: the setting along a crescent-shaped bay flanked by headlands is simply spectacular.

⊙ Sights & Activities

Matala's sightseeing credentials are limited to the famous 'hippie' **caves** (Ancient Matala, Roman Tombs; admission €3; ⏱ 10am-7pm Apr-Sep, 8.30am-3pm Oct-Mar) that actually date back to neolithic times and were used as tombs by the Romans. To escape the main beach crowds in summer, embark on a 30-minute scramble over the rocks to clothing-optional **Red Beach** (bring snacks and water) or head to **Kommos Beach** about 2km north of Matala, home to two tavernas, and **Kalamaki Beach**, 7km north.

WORTH A TRIP

GORTYNA

The archaeological site of **Gortyna** (Γόρτυνα; ☏ 28920 31144; adult/child €4/free, incl Agia Triada €6/free; ⏱ 8am-8pm Jul & Aug, 8am-3pm Sep-Jun), 46km southwest of Iraklio, is the largest in Crete. It was once a subject town of powerful Phaestos but later became the capital of Roman Crete. Most of the ruins date from this Roman period. At its peak, as many as 100,000 people may have milled around Gortyna's streets.

There are two sections to Gortyna, with the best-preserved relics in the fenced area on the northern side of the road. These include the 6th-century Byzantine **Church of Agios Titos**, the finest early Christian church in Crete, and, even more importantly, the massive stone tablets inscribed with the 6th-century-BC **Laws of Gortyna**, the oldest law code in the Greek world. In mythology, the evergreen **plane tree** just north of here was Zeus and Europa's 'love nest'. Most of the major Roman structures are spread over a vast area south of the highway (no admission fee) and are therefore not as easy to locate. Look for road signs pointing to the **Temple of Apollo**, the main sanctuary of pre-Roman Gortyna. East of here is the 2nd-century-AD **Praetorium**, which was the Roman governor's residence, a **nymphaeum** (public bath) and an amphitheatre.

Buses between Iraklio and Phaestos or Matala can drop you off at Gortyna (€4.70).

Nearby villages worth exploring include Pitsidia, Sivas and Kamilari. They also make great alternative bases to busy Matala.

Matala and its surrounds are a popular nesting ground for *Caretta caretta* sea turtles. The Sea Turtle Protection Society has a booth near the car park.

🛏 Sleeping & Eating

Matala Valley Village
RESORT €

(☏28920 45776; www.valleyvillage.gr; s/d/bungalow €50/60/90; �May-Oct; P❄📶🏊) Near the village entrance, this sprawling garden resort is popular with families. Various room types are available, the nicest of which are the 23 whitewashed bungalows added in 2008. Each has two bedrooms, a fridge and a spacious bathroom with Jacuzzi and separate shower. Frolicking grounds for kids include a lawn, small playground and big pool.

Hotel Nikos
HOTEL €

(☏28920 45375; www.matala-nikos.com; Matala; s €25-30, d €40-45, tr €50-55, f €65-70; ❄📶) The best property on this confined hotel strip, Nikos has 17 recently renovated, pleasant and airy rooms. Rooms are over two floors along a flower-filled courtyard. Breakfast costs €7.

Gianni's
GREEK €

(mains €5.50-12; �noon-4pm & 6pm-midnight) A refreshing change from the run-of-the-mill waterfront tavernas, this been-there-forever family place just past the central square

MUSEUM OF CRETAN ETHNOLOGY

This interesting museum (☏28920 91110; www.cretanethnologymuseum. gr; Voroi Pirgiotissis, Vori; admission €3; �11am-5pm Apr-Oct, by appointment in winter) in the village of Vori, 4km east of Tymbaki, provides fascinating insights into traditional Cretan culture. The English-labelled exhibits are organised around themes such as rural life, food production, war, customs, architecture, music and food production. Most of the items are rather ordinary – hoes, olive presses, baskets, clothing, instruments etc – but they're all engagingly and intimately displayed in darkened rooms accented with spotlights. It's well signposted from the main road.

makes no-nonsense Greek food, including an excellent mixed grill with salad and potatoes.

Bunga Bunga
GREEK €

(mains €6.50-9; �10am-late) One of two tavernas at Kommos Beach, about 2km north of Matala, the Caribbean-style Bunga Bunga serves tasty, fresh, organic fare. It's named after the WWII bunker in the cliff above.

ℹ Getting There & Away

There are five buses Monday to Friday, six buses Saturday and three buses Sunday (high season only) to Iraklio (€7.80, two hours) and Phaestos (€1.70, 30 minutes). There's free roadside parking and a beach car park that charges €2.

Rethymno   Ρέθυμνο
POP 32,468

Basking between the commanding bastions of its 15th-century fortress and the glittering azure waters of the Mediterranean, Rethymno (*reth*-im-no) is one of Crete's most enchanting towns. Its Venetian-Ottoman quarter is a lyrical maze of lanes draped in floral canopies and punctuated with graceful wood-balconied houses and minarets that add an exotic flourish. Crete's third-largest town has lively nightlife with its student population, some excellent restaurants and even a worthwhile, sandy beach right in town. The busier beaches, with their requisite resorts, are all outside of town along a nearly uninterrupted stretch all the way to Panormo, some 22km away.

◉ Sights

Rethymno is fairly compact, with most sights, accommodation and tavernas wedged within the largely pedestrianised Old Quarter off the Venetian Harbour. The beach is east of the harbour.

★ Fortezza
FORTRESS

(adult/family €4/10; �8.30am-7.30pm Jun-Oct, 10am-5pm Nov-May; P) Looming over Rethymno, this Venetian fortress cuts an impressive figure with its massive walls and imposing bastions. Built in the 1570s as a reaction to pirate raids and the threat of invasion, it was still unable to stave off the Turks in 1646. Views are fabulous from up here and it's fun to poke around the ramparts, palm trees and remaining buildings, most notably the meticulously restored Sultan Bin Imbrahim Mosque.

Archaeological Museum   MUSEUM
(☑28310 54668; Argiropoulon; admission €3; ⊙8am-3pm Tue-Sun; P) In a Turkish-era building that served as a prison until the 1960s, this small museum showcases treasures from neolithic to Roman times, including bronze tools, Mycenaean figurines, Roman oil lamps and a 1st century AD sculpture of Aphrodite. You'll also find Minoan pottery and artifacts gathered from the tombs at the **Cemetery of Armeni** (admission €2; ⊙8am-3pm Tue-Sun). Other star exhibits include fine examples of blown glass and a precious coin collection.

Venetian Harbour   HISTORIC SITE
Rethymno's compact historic harbour is chock-a-block with tourist-geared fish tavernas and cafes. For a more atmospheric perspective, walk along the harbour walls, past the fishing boats to the landmark **lighthouse**, built in the 16th century by the Turks.

Agios Spyridon Church   CHAPEL
(Kefalogiannidon) Built into the cliff beneath the Venetian fortress, tiny Agios Spyridon has enough atmosphere to fill a cathedral. This Byzantine chapel is filled with richly painted icons, swinging bird candleholders and the sound of the nearby pounding surf. You'll see pairs of slippers, baby shoes and sandals in crevices in the rock wall, left as prayer offerings for the sick. Find the chapel at the top of a staircase on the western side of the fortress. Opening hours are erratic.

Neratzes Mosque   MOSQUE
(Vernardou) This beautiful, triple-domed mosque was converted from a Franciscan church in 1657 and is now used as a music conservatory and concert hall. Even if there's no show on, it's definitely worth peeking in for a look. The building's minaret, the former bell tower, was built in 1890 and is undergoing lengthy restoration.

Rimondi Fountain   FOUNTAIN
(cnr Paleologou & Petihaki Sq) Pride of place among the many vestiges of Venetian rule goes to this fountain with its spouting lion heads and Corinthian capitals, built in 1626 by city rector Alvise Rimondi. Water spouts from three lions' heads into three basins flanked by Corinthian columns. Above the central basin you can make out the Rimondi family crest.

Museum of Contemporary Art   ART GALLERY
(☑28310 52530; www.cca.gr; Himaras 5; admission €3; ⊙9am-2pm & 7-9pm Tue-Fri, 10am-3pm Sat & Sun) Near the fortress, this gallery exhibits well-known and up-and-coming local and international artists. The permanent collection showcases the oils, drawings and watercolours of local lad Lefteris Kanakakis, as well as modern Greek artists since 1950. Entrance is off Mesologiou.

Historical & Folk Art Museum   MUSEUM
(☑28310 23398; Vernardou 26-28; admission €4; ⊙9.30am-2.30pm Mon-Sat) In a lovely 17th-century mansion, this five-room exhibit documents traditional rural life with a collection spanning from clothing to baskets, weavings to farm tools. Labelling is also in English.

🏃 Activities

Dolphin Cruises   BOAT TOUR
(☑28310 57666; www.dolphin-cruises.com; Venetian Harbour; cruises €12-38; ⊙9.30am-5pm) Dolphin runs one- to four-hour boat trips, visiting pirate caves, cruising to Bali or fishing.

Paradise Dive Centre   DIVING
(☑28310 26317; www.diving-center.gr; dives from €42, open-water certification €400) Runs diving trips for all grades of divers from its base at Petres, 14km west of Rethymno. Offers cave dives, night dives and various PADI courses. Book through travel agencies or by phone.

Happy Walker   HIKING
(☑28310 52920; www.happywalker.com; Tombazi 56; day walk €32; ⊙5pm-8.30pm Mon-Fri) Runs day walks for four to 18 people through gorges, along ancient shepherd trails and to traditional villages in the lush hinterland. Add €10 for lunch and coffee en route. Book the evening before. Multiday tours also available.

World of Crete   TOUR
(☑28310 50055, 6949 791 242; www.ecoevents.gr; 30 Eleftheriou Venizelou; tour €18-70; ⊙10am-2pm & 5-9pm) These guys organise a huge array of tours, from hikes through the Samaria Gorge to boat trips and photo safaris. Its ecotours take you to traditional villages where you might see *raki* distillation or take a cooking lesson. Also sells boat and plane tickets.

Mountaineering Club of Rethymno   ROCK CLIMBING
(☑28310 57766; www.eosrethymnou.gr; Dimokratias 12; ⊙9-11pm Tue) Offers advice on local hikes along with the possibility to join excursions. It's best to contact via the website.

🛏 Sleeping

Atelier   PENSION €
(☑28310 24440; www.frosso-bora.com; Himaras 25; s €35, d €45-55; ✻🖧) Nearly next door to the

fortress, the four spotless, comfortable rooms here are attached to the **pottery studio** (www.frosso-bora.com; ⊙9am-2pm & 5-7pm) of local ceramic artist Frosso Bora. With exposed stone walls, small flat-screen TVs, new bathrooms and kitchenettes, they are the best deal in town. The upstairs rooms have small balconies while the ground floor has Venetian architectural features and a beamed ceiling.

Rethymno Youth Hostel
HOSTEL €

(☑28310 22848; www.yhrethymno.com; Tombazi 41; dm €10; ⊙reception 8am-1pm & 5-11pm; 🛜) This cheerful, well-run hostel sleeps six to eight people in clean, functional dorms. Centrally located, it has a private, sociable patio, bar and a garden to relax in. Laundry facilities, hot showers, snacks and breakfast (€2) are available, as are female-only dorm rooms.

Camping Elizabeth
CAMPGROUND €

(☑28310 28694; www.camping-elizabeth.net; 84 Ionias, Missiria; camp sites per adult/child €7.50/4, tent/car/caravan €6.50/4/6.50; ⊙year-round; @🛜) The closest campground to Rethymno is 4km east, adjacent to beautiful Missiria beach. Bamboo, palm and olive trees provide plenty of shade, and there's a taverna, snack bar and minimarket, plus a communal fridge, laundry facilities and free beach umbrellas and sun lounges. It also rents out simple bungalows and caravans from €38 and tents from €9. An Iraklio-bound bus can drop you here.

★ Casa Vitae
BOUTIQUE HOTEL €€

(☑28310 35058, 6973237897; www.casa-vitae.gr; Neophytou Patealarou 3; r €95-150; 🌸🛜) This charismatic Venetian-era hotel has eight quietly elegant rooms mixing exposed stone and wood and wrapped around a peaceful courtyard where breakfast is served beneath the vine-covered pergola. Romance rules in the larger suites with iron four-poster beds, Jacuzzi and private terrace.

Rethymno

★**Sohora** BOUTIQUE HOTEL €€
(☎2831 300913; www.sohora.gr; Plateia Iroön Politehniou; studio/d/apt €60/80/100; ❄🛜) Very comfortable and slightly quirky, the four rooms in this 200-year-old home incorporate original architectural features alongside vintage, upcycled furnishings. A solar water heater, organic bath products and homemade breakfast make staying here a guilt-free treat. Service is friendly and professional.

Casa dei Delfini BOUTIQUE HOTEL €€
(☎28310 55120, 6937254857; www.casadeidelfini.com; Nikiforou Foka 66-68; studio/maisonette €70/110; ❄🛜) The four individual rooms in this elegant guesthouse orbit a small courtyard and burst with historic character. In one you'll find a *hammam* (Turkish bath), and in another, a covered, lit, Venetian well. All have modern kitchenettes and quality linens. For extra room, book the two-storey maisonette with a large private terrace.

✗ Eating

★**Raki Baraki** GREEK €
(☎28310 26213; Arabatzoglou 17; mains €6-9; ⊙lunch & dinner; 🛜) Rustic, colourful and lively, this is a fantastic place to while away the evening over mezedhes like sardines stuffed with herbs, sausage with grilled vegetables, or mussels steamed with sage. The fried feta with carmalised figs and mint is divine. Dine to live music Thursday to Sunday.

Taverna Knossos GREEK €
(www.knosos-rethymno.com; Venetian Harbour; mains €6-12, set menu for 2 €30; ⊙lunch & dinner; 🛜📶) Nestled next to the Venetian Harbour, this taverna stands out from its neighbours for superb food and swift, gracious service. It's been run by the Stavroulaki family for half a century; look in the kitchen and you'll likely see grandma whipping up dinner. The menu is simple but authentic with excellent fish.

★**Castelvecchio** GREEK €€
(☎28310 55163; Himaras 29; mains €15-21; ⊙lunch Sep-Jun, dinner year-round) Classy yet chilled, family-run Castelvecchio is perfect for date night – especially if your date is a plate of smoked pork in wine or boneless lamb in creamy tomato and feta sauce. Be sure to save room for homemade dessert. If it's the walnut cake, you'll be pining for seconds. The terrace is hopping and the service is impeccable.

En Plo GREEK €€
(☎28310 30950; Kefalogiannidon 28; mezedhes €10-15; ⊙lunch & dinner; 🛜📶) At the water's edge, snug beneath the fortress, En Plo kicks Greek and Cretan comfort food into high gear. Mountain greens get a tangy twist with tamarind dressing, plump bacalao is paired with a feisty garlic sauce, and the creamy fish soup is hearty and satisfying. Sit in the arty interior or snag a table next to the waves.

★**Avli** CRETAN €€€
(☎28310 58250; www.avli.com; Xanthoudidou 22; mains €13-30; ⊙lunch & dinner; 🛜) This Venetian garden villa has a well-deserved reputation for serving some of the city's most creative Cretan food in a lovely patio setting. Farm-fresh fare has bold flavour pairings: kid goat meets honey and thyme, sea bass comes with lemon saffron sauce, and octopus with caramelised onions. It's all flawlessly

prepared and beautifully presented. Check the website for cooking classes.

 Drinking & Nightlife

The main bar and cafe strip is along Eleftheriou Venizelou. Another cluster is around Rimondi Fountain and on Plateia Petihaki. Wander the side streets to find quieter places.

Livingroom CAFE, BAR
(www.livingroom.gr; Eleftheriou Venizelou 5; ⊙9am-3am; 🛜) Kick back on stylish, waterfront sofas during the day or head inside in the evening to join Rethymno's young and restless amid big mirrors, velvet chairs and stylish lamps. The Livingroom has been a permanent fixture on the scene for over a decade.

Chalikouti CAFE, BAR
(☑28310 42632; Katehaki 3; ⊙9am-1am; 🛜) In the artsy quarter below the Fortezza, this cafe collective draws talkative locals who appreciate the coffee from Mexican Zapatistas, sugar from landless workers in Brazil and *raki* from a Cretan women's cooperative. The tiny interior is full of books and chess boards, and tables spill onto the cobbled street.

 Shopping

The old quarter's narrow, cobbled pedestrian streets are tightly packed with mainly tourist-geared stores. There are also some gems worth searching for. Try Mellissinou, Souliou and Arabatzoglou. The mainstream shopping strip is along Arkadiou.

ℹ **Information**

There are free public wi-fi hotspots at the town hall, Plateia Iroon (Iroon Sq), the Venetian Harbour and the Municipal Garden, all within the Old Town.

Cool Holidays (☑28310 35567; Melissinou 2; ⊙9am-2pm & 5-9pm) Helpful office that handles boat and plane tickets, hires out cars and motorcycles, and books excursions.

General Hospital of Rethymno (☑28210 27491; Triandalydou 17; ⊙24hr) Has 24-hour accident and emergency. A few blocks inland from the port, in the newer part of the city.

Post Office (Moatsou 21; ⊙7am-7pm Mon-Fri) Accepts letters and parcels.

Regional Tourist Office (☑28310 29148; www.rethymnon.gr; Sofokli Venizelou; ⊙8am-2pm Mon-Fri) Has local maps and offers regional information. Next to the water in the Commercial Harbour.

ℹ **Getting There & Away**

The **bus station** (cnr Igoumenou Gavriil & Kefalogiannidon) is on the western edge of the centre. Services are reduced at weekends and outside high season. Check KTEL (www.bus-service-crete-ktel.com) for the current schedule.

ℹ **Getting Around**

Auto Moto Sports (☑28310 24858; www.automotosport.com.gr; Sofoklis Venizelou 48; bicycle/car per day from €10/32; ⊙10am-7pm) Hires out bicycles, cars and motorbikes.

Rent-a-Bike (Paleologou 14; per day from €7; ⊙9am-2pm & 5-9pm) Rents new, durable mountain bikes, including kids' models.

Moni Arkadiou

Μονή Αρκαδίου

Moni Arkadiou (Arkadi Monastery; ☑28310 83136; www.arkadimonastery.gr; admission €2.50; ⊙9am-8pm Jun-Aug, shorter hours Sep-May), in the hills some 23km southeast of Rethymno, has deep significance for Cretans. As the

BUSES FROM RETHYMNO

DESTINATION	FARE	TIME	FREQUENCY
Agia Galini	€6.50	1½hr	up to 5 daily
Anogia	€5.50	1¼hr	2 Mon-Fri
Argyroupoli	€3.30	40min	up to 3 daily
Hania	€6.20	1hr	up to 3 daily
Hora Sfakion	€7.30	2hr	1 daily
Iraklio	€7.60	1½hr	hourly
Margarites	€3.50	30min	2 Mon-Fri
Moni Arkadiou	€2.80	40min	up to 3 daily
Omalos (Samaria Gorge)	€15	1¾hr	3 daily
Plakias	€4.50	1hr	up to 5 daily
Preveli	€4.50	1¼hr	2 daily

site where hundreds of cornered locals massacred both themselves and invading Turks, it's a stark and potent symbol of human resistance and considered a spark plug in the struggle towards freedom from Turkish occupation.

In November 1866, massive Ottoman forces arrived to crush island-wide revolts. Hundreds of Cretan men, women and children fled their villages to find shelter at Arkadiou. However, far from being a safe haven, the monastery was soon besieged by 2000 Turkish soldiers. Rather than surrender, the Cretans set fire to their kegs of gunpowder, killing everyone, Turks included, except for one small girl who lived to a ripe old age in a village nearby. A bust of this woman and one of the abbot who lit the gunpowder stand outside the monastery. Also here (next to the cafeteria – skip the food), in the monastery's old windmill, is the macabre **ossuary** with skulls and bones of some of the 1866 victims neatly arranged in a glass cabinet.

Arkadiou's most impressive structure, its Venetian **church** (1587), has a striking Renaissance facade marked by eight slender Corinthian columns and topped by an ornate triple-belled tower. Inside, its interior is hushed, ornate and filled with ancient relics.

Left of here is a cypress trunk that was scorched by the explosion and still has a bullet embedded in its bark. Beyond is the former refectory (dining room), now a small **museum** of religious objects, icons and weapons used in 1866 as well as a gift shop. At the end of the left wing is the old wine cellar where the gunpowder was stored.

When visiting, be sure to cover your shoulders out of respect. There are three buses (two on weekends) from Rethymno to the monastery (€2.80, 40 minutes).

Anogia   Ανώγεια
POP 2380

Perched aside Mt Psiloritis, 37km southwest of Iraklio, Anogia is known for its rebellious spirit and determination to express its undiluted Cretan character. During WWII, it was a centre of resistance and suffered heavily for it. The Nazis burned down the town and massacred all the men in retaliation for their role in sheltering Allied troops and aiding in the kidnapping of a Nazi general.

Anogia is also famous for its stirring music and has spawned many of Crete's best-known musicians such as Nikos Xylouris, whose home is now a small **museum** (☉9am-2pm &

WORTH A TRIP

ENAGRON

Set in the valley below Axos, **Enagron** (☎28340 61611; www.enagron.gr; studio & apt €90-150; ✴@☒) blends ecotourism and comfort flawlessly, meaning a guilt-free, cushy stay. The traditional, stone-built studios are large and comfortable, with kitchenettes and fireplaces. There's a pool overlooking the mountains and a taverna serving the estate's organic produce. Guests can participate in activities like Cretan cooking classes, botanical walks, bread- and cheese-making and *raki* distilling. Guided walks are also available. You can visit the farm and eat at the restaurant by booking ahead.

5-8pm) **FREE**. Locals cling to time-honoured traditions and it's not rare to see men gossiping in the *kafenia* (coffee houses) dressed in traditional black shirts with baggy pants tucked into boots. Elderly women, meanwhile, keep busy flogging traditional woven blankets and embroidered textiles. Though beautiful and well priced, not all are actually produced locally, so *caveat emptor*. Angonia is divided into an upper and lower village.

🛏 Sleeping & Eating

Hotel Aristea   HOTEL €
(☎28340 31459; www.hotelaristea.gr; s/d incl breakfast €35/40, apt €70-110; P�)) In the upper village, the friendly Aristea enjoys spectacular valley views and cool breezes in straightforward, clean rooms with TV, private bathrooms and big balconies. For more space and comfort, spend a little extra for one of the slightly newer apartments next door, some sleeping up to six people.

Ta Skalomata   CRETAN €
(☎28340 31316; mains €4-9; ☉lunch & dinner; �) In the upper village, Skalomata has fed locals and travellers for about 40 years, making it the oldest restaurant in town. When you peel your eyes away from the huge windows with panoramic views, check out the open kitchen and traditional decor. It does great grills, handmade sausages, homemade wine and bread, and tasty meat-free options.

Arodamos   CRETAN €
(☎28340 31100; www.arodamos.gr; mains €6-10; ☉lunch & dinner) This big restaurant in a new stone house in the upper village is held in

high regard by locals and visitors for its fresh Cretan fare and hospitality. The lamb is tops, but so is the *saganaki* (fried cheese) made with *katsohiri* (local goat's cheese). Free sweet pie with ice cream caps off every meal.

❶ Getting There & Away

There are up to three buses daily from Iraklio (€3.80, one hour) and two buses Monday to Friday from Rethymno (€5.50, 1¼ hours).

Mt Psiloritis
Ορος Ψηλορείτης

Mt Psiloritis (2456m), also known as Mt Idi, is Crete's highest mountain. At its eastern base is the **Nida Plateau** (1400m), a wide, fertile expanse reached via a paved 21km-long road from Anogia past several *mitata* (round shepherd's huts) and the turn-off to the highly regarded **Skinakas Observatory** (www.skinakas.org.gr; ☉full moon 5-11pm). At the top, a simple taverna offers refreshment and spartan rooms (€25). It gets chilly up here, even in summer, so bring a sweater or light jacket.

From the parking lot, it's a 1km uphill walk to **Ideon Cave**. A huge and fairly featureless hole in the ground, Ideon has sacred importance in mythology as the place where Zeus was reared by his mother Rhea, protected from his child-devouring father Cronos (although Dikteon Cave in Lasithi claims the same). Back on the plateau, you can make out a sprawling landscape sculpture called **Andartis – Partisan of Peace**, which looks like an angel when seen from above and commemorates Cretan WWII resistance fighters.

Spili
Σπίλι
POP 700

Spili (*spee*-lee) is a pretty mountain village and shutterbug favourite thanks to its cobbled streets, old plane trees and flower-festooned whitewashed houses. A convenient lunch stop on coast-to-coast trips, its surrounding mountains are also a haven for hikers. In town, a restored **Venetian fountain** spurts potable water from 25 stone lion heads into a long trough. Minor attractions include a folk museum and the vast modern **monastery** at the northern end of town.

🛏 Sleeping & Eating

Heracles　　　　　　　　　　　　PENSION €
(☎28320 22111, 6973667495; www.heracles-hotel.eu; s/d €30/40; ❈🖰) These five balconied rooms are quiet, spotless and simply furnished, but it's the friendly Heracles himself who makes the place memorable. A geologist by profession, he's intimately familiar with the area and can put you on the right hiking trail, birdwatching site or hidden beach. Optional homemade breakfasts start at €4. Heracles also operates the worthwhile Creta Natura shop nearby.

Stratidakis　　　　　　　　　　　CRETAN €
(specials €5-7; ☉lunch & dinner) A mother-and-son team presides over the oldest taverna in town. There's meat grilling on the spits outside and robust Cretan daily specials stewing in pots that you're free to inspect. Local honey and yoghurt is served for breakfast. The leafy garden verandah has jaw-dropping mountain views.

Panorama　　　　　　　　　　　CRETAN €€
(☎28320 22555; mains €6-13; ☉dinner daily, lunch Sun; 🖰) Pantelis Vasilakis and his wife Calliope are the masterminds behind this fine traditional taverna on the outskirts of Spili. Enjoy memorable views from the terrace while munching on homemade bread, toothsome mezedhes or such tempting mains as succulent kid goat with *horta* (wild greens). It's an accredited Concred taverna.

❶ Information

There are two ATMs and a post office on the main street. Some of the cafes near the Venetian fountain have wi-fi.

❶ Getting There & Away

Spili is on the Rethymno to Agia Galini bus route (€3.50, 40 minutes), which has up to five services daily.

Plakias
Πλακιάς
POP 200

Set beside a sweeping sandy crescent and accessed via two scenic gorges – Kotsifou and Kourtaliotiko – Plakias swarms with package tourists in summer (when it can get very windy), but otherwise remains a laid-back indie travellers' favourite. While the town itself isn't particularly peaceful, from here you can walk through olive groves, along seaside cliffs and to some sparkling hidden beaches. It's also a good base for regional excursions. There's good diving (two operators run shore and boat excursions), and in summer the owner of the **Smerna Bar** (☎28320 31940, 6936 806635; smernabar@gmail.com) runs daily boat trips to Preveli Beach.

🛌 Sleeping

A handy lodging website is www.plakias-filoxenia.gr. There's also good lodging in pretty **Myrthios** above Plakias.

Livikon Beach Hotel   HOTEL €
(📞 28320 31420; www.hotel-livikon-plakias.com; d/tr €45/50; 🅿🌀🛜) A family-run affair across the street from the beach, this hotel has 10 spotless, spacious, comfortable rooms that have had a recent lick of paint. Each has a balcony and kitchenette. Service is ace.

Plakias Youth Hostel   HOSTEL €
(📞 28320 32118; www.yhplakias.com; dm €10; ⏱ Easter-Oct; 🅿@🛜) Set around a hammock-filled lawn amid olive groves, about 500m from the waterfront, this purposefully lazy hostel fosters an atmosphere of inclusiveness and good cheer that appeals to people of all ages and nationalities. The hostel has eight-bed dorms with fans and a well-kept facilities. Inexpensive breakfast and drinks are available. Book ahead.

Plakias Suites   APARTMENT €€
(📞 28320 31680, 6975811559; www.plakiassuites. com; ste €100-150; ⏱ Apr-Oct; 🅿🌀🛜) This stylish outpost has modern yet warm aesthetics and plush touches such as large flat-screen TVs and mini hi-fis, rainforest showers and a chic kitchen. Staying here puts you within a whisker of the best stretch of local beach.

🍴 Eating & Drinking

To Xehoristo   GREEK €
(mains €3-8; ⏱ lunch & dinner) Never mind the picture menu: locals swear by the tasty souvlaki and grills. It's at the eastern end of the main road, across from the sea.

★ Tasomanolis   SEAFOOD €€
(📞 28320 31129; mains €4-16; ⏱ lunch & dinner; 🛜) Head to this friendly, nautical-themed taverna at the quiet end of town for the local catch, hauled in by Manolis and cooked by his wife Eleni. Park yourself on the colourful patio for seafood lasagna, anchovy bruschetta or the grilled daily catch paired with wild greens and wine.

Ostraco Bar   CAFE, LOUNGE BAR
(⏱ 9am-late; 🛜) With a stylish downstairs cafe, waterside tables and an upstairs bar, you could spend all day at this old favourite. In the evening, the gregarious gather for drinking and dancing. In the daytime, it's great for chilling.

FRIDAY FROLIC

Taverna Panorama (📞 28320 31450; Myrthios; mains €5-12; ⏱ 9am-late; 🛜) in pretty Myrthios, right above Plakias, bursts at the seams on Friday, when a Greek band strikes up traditional tunes and the crowd gets more raucous with each carafe of wine. It's worth the 2km uphill walk, which begins just before the Plakias Youth Hostel (or take a cab).

ℹ Information

Plakias has two ATMs on the central waterfront. The post office is on the first side street coming from the east.

ℹ Getting There & Around

Up to five daily KTEL buses link Plakias with Rethymno (€4.50, one hour); one goes to Preveli (€2.30, 30 minutes). **Cars Alianthos** (📞 28320 32033; www.alianthos-group.com; per day from €36; ⏱ 24hr) is a reliable car hire outlet.

Around Plakias

About 11km east of Plakias, the historic **Moni Preveli** (Μονή Πρεβέλης; 📞 28320 31246; www. preveli.org; admission €2.50; ⏱ 9am-6.30pm mid-Mar–May, 9am-1.30pm & 3.30-6.30pm Jun-Oct) cuts an imposing silhouette high above the Libyan Sea. Like most Cretan monasteries, it was a centre of resistance during the Turkish occupation and also played a key role in WWII when hiding trapped Allied soldiers from the Nazis until they could escape to Egypt by submarine.

On the road to the monastery, a **memorial** showing a gun-toting abbot and an Allied British soldier commemorates this heroic act, as does a **fountain** on the right as you enter the monastery. To the left is a small **museum** with some exquisite icons, richly embroidered vestments and two silver candelabra presented by grateful soldiers after the war.

Dazzling **Preveli Beach** (Παραλία Πρεβέλης; also known as Palm Beach) is located below Moni Preveli and is one of Crete's most celebrated strands. At the mouth of the Kourtaliotiko Gorge, where the river Megalopotamos empties into the Libyan Sea, the palm-lined river banks have freshwater pools good for a dip. The beach is backed by rugged cliffs and punctuated by a heart-shaped boulder at the water's edge.

A steep path leads down to the beach (10 minutes) from a car park (€2), 1km before Moni Preveli. In summer there are two daily buses from Rethymno (€4.50, 1¼ hours) and one from Plakias (€2.30, 30 minutes).

Plakias to Agia Galini

Triopetra   Τριόπετρα

Triopetra is a big beach named after three giant rocks jutting out of the sea. A headland divides the sandy strip into Little Triopetra and Big Triopetra. The former is home to **Pension & Taverna Pavlos** (28310 25189; www.triopetra.com.gr; s/d/tr €33/43/48; Apr-Oct;), which has fabulously fresh fish caught by the owner himself as well as inspired salads and vegetable sides prepared with home-grown organic produce. There are also a few simple but comfortable rooms that are often booked up by yoga workshop participants.

Because of submerged sand shelves, Little Triopetra is not ideal for swimming, so head to the 'big' beach for that. There are two more tavernas with rooms along here.

Triopetra can be reached from Agios Pavlos (about 300m is drivable dirt road) or via a 12km winding asphalt road from Akoumia village on the Rethymno–Agia Galini road.

Agios Pavlos   Αγιος Παύλος

Cradled by cliffs, Agios Pavlos is little more than a couple of small tavernas with rooms and a beach bar set around a picture-perfect crescent with dark, course sand with the distinctive silhouette of Paximadia Islands looming offshore. A steep staircase on the bay's western end leads up Cape Melissa to some intricately pleated and colourful **rock formations**.

The bay gets busy in summer when excursion boats arrive from Agia Galini, but it's possible to escape the crowds by heading to the beaches behind the headland to the west. Beware that getting there involves a scramble down (and up) a steep sand dune. Bring water and snacks.

Agios Pavlos Hotel (28320 71104; www.agiospavloshotel.gr; d €32-40, apt €45-60; Apr-Oct;) has waterfront rooms above its taverna and super-nice modern apartments up on the hill.

To get to Agios Pavlos, look for the turnoff to Saktouria on the Rethymno–Agia Galini road and follow the winding asphalt about 13km down to the sea.

Agia Galini   Αγια Γαλήνη
POP 860

An erstwhile picturesque fishing village, Agia Galini (a-ya ga-lee-nee) has had much of its original charm trampled out of it by tourism and overdevelopment. With scores of ageing hotels and apartment buildings clinging to a steep hillside and hemmed in by cliffs and a busy harbour, it has a bit of a retro resort look but can feel claustrophobic, especially in high season. It's a convenient base for visits to Phaestos, Agia Triada and the remote beaches west of here. It all but shuts down in winter.

🛏 Sleeping & Eating

Camping No Problem   CAMPGROUND €
(28320 91386; camp site per person/tent/car/caravan €6/4/2/4; year-round;) With a bright, blue pool and shady spots to pitch a tent, this well-maintained campground is about 100m from the beach and a 10-minute walk from the town centre. There's also a pleasant garden, an excellent taverna and a small supermarket.

Palazzo Greco   BOUTIQUE HOTEL €€
(28320 91187; www.palazzogreco.com; d €85-110;) A passion for design is reflected in the stylish details at this gem overlooking the sea. Match your mood to the wall colours – greens, blues and purples – in peaceful, modern rooms with view-filled decks, flat-screen TVs, fridges and fabulous showers. Breakfast on the beautiful patio above the pool. At the top of town, it's halfway between the beach and the harbour.

Faros   SEAFOOD €€
(28320 91346; Shopping St; mains €7-13, fish per kg €30-55; lunch & dinner) This no-frills family-run fish taverna is usually packed to the gills, and for good reason: the owner himself drops his nets into the Med, so you know what's on the plate that night was still swimming in the sea in the morning. Squid cooked in their own ink, lobster spaghetti and fish soup are specialities.

ℹ Information

For information visit www.agia-galini.com and www.gogalini.com.

ℹ Getting There & Away

Buses stop on the main street down near the port. In peak season there are up to six buses daily to Iraklio (€8, two hours), up to five to Rethymno (€6.20, 1½ hours) and Phaestos (€2.10, 30 minutes), and two to Matala (€3.30, 45 minutes).

NORTHWEST CRETE

Crete's northwestern coastline is anchored by the preening port city of Hania, once a jewel of a capital and full of arty boutique hotels, galleries and great eateries. Nearby, the ethereal Balos lagoon and the sweeping beach at Falasarna beckon. Hania is also the gateway to Samaria, one of Europe's grandest gorges, tucked in among steep mountains that ripple all the way down to the southern shores.

Hania   Χανιά

POP 53,910

Hania (hahn-*yah;* also spelled Chania) is Crete's most evocative city, with its pretty Venetian quarter, criss-crossed by narrow lanes, culminating at a magnificent harbour. Remnants of Venetian and Turkish architecture abound, with many old townhouses now transformed into atmospheric restaurants and boutique hotels. All this beauty means the Old Town is deluged with tourists in summer, but it's still a great place to unwind. The Venetian Harbour is super for a stroll and a coffee or cocktail. Plus it's got a university and a modern portion to the city, so in winter it retains its lively charm. Excellent local handicrafts mean there's good shopping, and with a multitude of creative restaurants you'll have some of your best meals in Greece here.

◎ Sights

Zambeliou, once Hania's main thoroughfare, is lined with craft shops, small hotels and tavernas. The Splantzia quarter is a wonderful warren of narrow streets with historic buildings, and a few shopping promenades, mostly pedestrianised. You will see one of Hania's two remaining **minarets** along Chatzimichali Daliani street and the other on nearby Plateia 1821 (Splantzia Square). The headland near the lighthouse separates the Venetian Harbour from the crowded town beach in the modern Nea Hora quarter.

★**Venetian Harbour**   HISTORIC QUARTER
A stroll around the old harbour is a must for any visitor to Hania. Pastel-coloured historic homes and businesses line the harbour, zig-zagging back into narrow lanes lined with shops. The entire area is ensconced in impressive **Venetian fortifications**, and it's worth the 1.5km walk around the sea wall to the **Venetian lighthouse**. On the eastern side of the inner harbour the prominent **Mosque of Kioutsouk Hasan** (Mosque of Janissaries) houses regular exhibitions.

★**Archaeological Museum**   MUSEUM
(☑28210 90334; Halidon 30; adult/child €3/ free; ⊘8am-8pm Mon-Fri, to 3pm Sat & Sun) The setting alone in the beautifully restored 16th-century Venetian Church of San Francisco is reason to visit this fine collection of artefacts from neolithic to Roman times. The museum's late-Minoan sarcophagi catch the eye as much as a large glass case with an entire herd of clay bulls (used to worship Poseidon). Other standouts include three Roman floor mosaics, Hellenistic gold jewellery, clay tablets with Linear A and Linear B script, and a marble sculpture of Roman emperor Hadrian.

★**Maritime Museum of Crete**   MUSEUM
(☑28210 91875; www.mar-mus-crete.gr; Akti Koundourioti; adult/child €3/2; ⊘9am-5pm Mon-Sat, 10am-6pm Sun, closed Sun Nov-Apr) Part of the hulking Venetian-built Firkas Fortress at the western port entrance, this museum celebrates Crete's nautical tradition with model ships, naval instruments, paintings, photographs, maps and memorabilia. One room is dedicated to historical sea battles while upstairs there's thorough documentation on the WWII-era Battle of Crete. The gate to the fortress itself is open from 8am to 2pm.

★**Byzantine & Post-Byzantine Collection**   MUSEUM
(☑28210 96046; Theotokopoulou 82; admission €2; ⊘8am-3pm Tue-Sun) The Byzantine museum is in the impressively restored Venetian Church of San Salvatore. It has a small but fascinating collection of artefacts, icons, jewellery and coins spanning the period from AD 62 to 1913, including a fine segment of a mosaic floor for an early-Christian basilica and a prized icon of St George slaying the dragon. The building has a mixed bag of interesting architectural features from its various occupiers. A joint ticket with the Archaeological Museum costs adult/child €3/free.

Church of Agios Nikolaos   CHURCH
(Plateia 1821; ⊘7am-noon & 2-7pm) This church is quite memorably attached to one of Hania's two remaining minarets, and a bell tower rises over its opposite end. The church's foundations were laid in 1205 by Venetians, but Franciscan monks can probably be credited with the massive structure's curving ceiling and simple stained-glass windows (1320). In 1645 the Ottomans made the church into a mosque, but the Orthodox Church recovered it in 1918. Just across the square you'll find the restored Venetian **Church of San Rocco**.

Hania

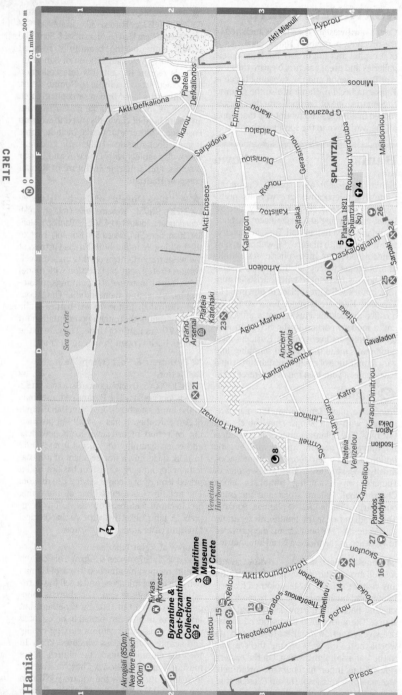

200 m
0.1 miles

Akrogiali (850m);
Nea Hora Beach
(900m)

Firkas
Fortress

Byzantine &
Post-Byzantine
Collection 2

Maritime
Museum
of Crete 3

Theotokopoulou

Ritsou

28

15

Angelou

13

Akti Koundourioti

Moschon

Theofanous

Parados

Zambeliou

Portou

Douka

14

22

Skouton

16

27

Parodos
Kondylaki

Pireos

Zambeliou

Plateia
Venizelou

Sourmeli

Lithinon

Kanevaro

Katre

Isodion

Agion
Deka

Karaoli-Dimitriou

Gavaladon

Sifaka

25

Sarpaki

24

26

Daskalogianni

10

Plateia 1821
(Splantzia
Sq) 5

SPLANTZIA

Roussou Verdouba

Melidioniou

G Pezanon

Minoos

Kyprou

Akti Miaouli

Epimenidou

Daidalou

Ikarou

Dionisiou

Gerasimou

Kalistou

Ria
nou

Kalergon

Arholeon

Agiou Markou

Ancient
Kydonia

Kantanoleontos

Akti Tombazi

21

Grand
Arsenal

Plateia
Katehaki

23

8

Venetian
Harbour

Sea of Crete

Akti Enoseos

Sarpidona

Akti Defkaliona

Plateia
Defkalionos

7

CRETE

Hania

Etz Hayyim Synagogue   SYNAGOGUE
(📞28210 86286; www.etz-hayyim-hania.org; Parodos Kondylaki; ⊙10am-6pm Mon-Thu, to 3pm Fri) Crete's only remaining synagogue (from the 15th century) was damaged in WWII and reopened in 1999. It has a *mikve* (ritual bath), tombs of rabbis and a memorial to local Jews killed by the Nazis. Today it serves a small congregation and is open to visitors. It's on a small lane accessible only from Kondylaki.

Municipal Art Gallery   GALLERY
(📞28210 92294; www.pinakothiki-chania.gr; Halidon 98; adult/child €2/free; ⊙10am-2pm Tue-Sat & 7-10pm Mon-Sat) Modern three-level art gallery hosts exhibitions of contemporary Greek art.

Beaches
The town beach 2km west of the Venetian harbour at **Nea Hora** (Akti Papanikoli) is crowded but generally clean if you need to cool off and get some rays, while that of **Koum Kapi** is less used (and less clean). For better swimming, keep heading west and you'll come to the beaches (in order) of **Agioi Apostoli**, **Hrysi Akti** and **Kalamaki** (about 3.5km). There are regular local buses heading there and all the way to **Platanias** and beyond.

🏃 Activities

Greek Mountaineering
Association   HIKING, OUTDOORS
(EOS; 📞28210 44647; www.eoshanion.gr; Tzanakaki 90, Hania; ⊙8.30am-6pm) Visit the local EOS branch or check its website to get the scoop on outdoor sports, including serious climbing in the Lefka Ori (White Mountains), mountain refuges and the E4 European Path. EOS also runs regular hiking excursions.

Blue Adventures Diving   DIVING
(📞28210 40403; www.divingchania.com; Arholeon 11; ⊙Apr-Nov) This established outfit offers a host of dive options, including PADI open water certification (€450), diving trips around Hania (two dives €90, with gear) and beginner dives. There are also snorkelling trips (€40). It also has a branch at Nea Hora beach.

🛏 Sleeping

Pension Theresa   PENSION €
(📞28210 92798; www.pensiontheresa.gr; Angelou 8; r €50-60; ❄🛜) Part of the Venetian fortifications, this creaky old house with a steep (and narrow!) spiral staircase and antique furniture delivers snug rooms with character aplenty. The location is excellent and views are stunning from the rooftop terrace with communal kitchen stocked with basic breakfast items. They have another annexe as well.

Ifigenia Rooms & Studios   APARTMENT €
(📞28210 94357; www.ifigeniastudios.gr; Gamba 23, cnr Parodos Agelou; r €50-110; ❄@🛜) This network of refurbished houses around the Venetian harbour offers anything from simple rooms to fancy suites with kitchenettes, Jacuzzis and views. There are nice touches

like elaborate stone-wrought bed frames and neat archways. Some bathrooms are very basic, though. To get a sea view in a standard room, expect to pay €15 to €30 more.

★ Elia Suites
DESIGN HOTEL €€

(☑ 28210 83778; www.eliahotels.gr; Chatzimichali Daliani 57, cnr Gavaladon; d/q €100/140; ❄ ☎) Four spacious, modern and luxurious suites fill this restored townhouse on pedestrianised Daliani, just behind the town market. Rooms were renovated in 2014 with sleek, stylish touches such as slate-coloured bedding and stone bathrooms with enormous walk-in showers. Large flat-screen TVs, firm beds and small balconies round out the offerings. No on-site reception; book ahead. It has other properties around Hania as well.

Splanzia Hotel
BOUTIQUE HOTEL €€

(☑ 28210 45313; www.splanzia.com; Daskalogianni 20; d/tr incl breakfast from €115/130; ❄ @ ☎) In the appealing Splantzia quarter, this smart recently renovated hotel in an Ottoman building has eight stylish rooms, some decorated with four-poster timber beds and drapery. The back rooms overlook a lovely courtyard with bougainvillea and features one of Hania's few remaining Turkish wells. Proprietors are friendly and down to earth.

Palazzo Duca
APARTMENT €€

(☑ 28210 70460; www.palazzoduca.gr; Douka 27-29; d/ste from €80/110; ❄ ☎) This small hotel back in the streets of Hania's old harbour is a reader favourite. It has super-comfy studios and apartments with kitchenettes, some offering port views or small balconies.

★ Serenissima
BOUTIQUE HOTEL €€€

(☑ 28210 86386; www.serenissima.gr; Skoufon 4; d/ste from €170/230; ❄ ☎) The newest entry in Hania's luxury boutique hotel game, Serenissima opened its pearlescent doors in 2015. A spacious townhouse, renovated to impeccable standards, it offers a full-service experience year-round. The minimalist restaurant-bar downstairs is painted in soft peach tones, and rooms have the latest in TV technology, high-end decor and bathroom style.

✖ Eating

Hania has some of the finest restaurants in Crete. Skip the waterfront tavernas.

★ Bougatsa tou Iordanis
CRETAN €

(☑ 28210 88855; Apokoronou 24; bougatsa €2.80; ⊙ 8am-2.30pm Mon-Sat, to noon Sun) You haven't lived until you've eaten the *bougatsa* at this little storefront dedicated to the flaky, sweet-cheesy treat. It's cooked fresh in enormous slabs and carved up in front of your eyes. Pair it with a coffee and you're set for the morning. There's nothing else on the menu!

Kouzina EPE
CRETAN €

(☑ 28210 42391; Daskalogianni 25; mains €4-8; ⊙ noon-7.30pm Mon-Sat) This cheery lunch spot gets contemporary designer flair from the cement floor, country-white tables and dangling silver origami boats. It's a local favourite away from the crowds, serving blackboard-listed *mayirefta* (ready-cooked meals) that can be inspected in the open kitchen.

Pallas
CAFE €

(Akti Tombazi 15-17; mains €8-16; ⊙ 8am-midnight; ☎) For coffee and breakfast at Hania's old harbour, head to local favourite Pallas, with a 2nd-floor dining room, superb views, and a brunch menu to match.

Mesogeiako
MEZEDHES €

(Chatzimichali Daliani 36; mezedhes €3.50-6; ⊙ 6pm-1am) Near the minaret in the Splantzia quarter, this trendy *mezedhopoleio* (restaurant specialising in small dishes) sits among a group of similarly popular eateries and serves an array of classic and more creative dishes. Try the fried zucchini flowers, aubergines, pork meatballs and its excellent *raki*.

★ To Maridaki
CRETAN €€

(☑ 28210 08880; Daskalogianni 33; dishes €7-12; ⊙ noon-midnight Mon-Sat) This modern seafood *mezedhopoleio* (restaurant specialising in mezedhes) is not to be missed. In a cheerful, bright dining room, happy visitors and locals alike tuck into impeccable local seafood and Cretan specialities. Ingredients are fresh, the fried calamari is to die for, the house white wine is crisp and delicious, and the complimentary panna cotta to finish the meal is transcendent. What's not to love?

★ Taverna Tamam
MEDITERRANEAN €€

(☑ 28210 96080; Zambeliou 49; mains €7-12; ⊙ noon-midnight; ☎ ✎) This excellent, convivial taverna in a converted Turkish bathhouse fills with chatting locals at tables spilling out onto the street. Dishes incorporate Middle Eastern spices, and include tasty soups and a superb selection of vegetarian specialities. Cretan delicacies include tender goat with *staka* (a rich goat's milk sauce).

To Karnagio
CRETAN, SEAFOOD €€

(☑ 28210 53366; Plateia Katehaki 8; mains €5-18; ⊙ noon-midnight May-Oct; ☎) Popular place with outdoor tables on a harbourside plaza next to the Great Arsenal. There's a good range of seafood and classic Cretan dishes, such as octopus *stifadho* (octopus in red tomato and wine sauce) and perfectly flaky *boureki* (stuffed pastry), plus a fine wine list.

Well of the Turk MIDDLE EASTERN €€
(Pigadi tou Tourkou; ☑28210 54547; www.wellofthe turk.com; Sarpaki 1-3; mains €8-15; ☉dinner Wed-Mon) In an age-old stone building which used to house a *hammam* (Turkish baths), and flanking a quiet square, this romantic taverna specialises in richly textured dishes inspired by North Africa, the Middle East and Turkey, yet all prepared with the finest Cretan ingredients. The cheesecake with rosewater and orange makes a great culinary coda.

⭐**Thalassino Ageri** SEAFOOD €€€
(☑28210 51136; www.thalasino-ageri.gr; Vivilaki 35; fish per kg €55; ☉from 7.30pm Apr–mid-Oct) This solitary fish taverna in a tiny port 2km east of the centre among the ruins of old tanneries is one of Crete's top eateries. Take in the sunset and peruse the menu, dictated by the day's catch. Most dishes, like the fisherman's salad, hum with creativity, or transcendent simplicity like melt-in-your-mouth calamari.

🍷 Drinking & Nightlife

The cafe-bars around the Venetian Harbour are nice places to sit, but charge top euro. For a more local vibe, head to Plateia 1821 in the Splantzia quarter, the interior streets near Potie, or alt-flavoured Sarpidona on the eastern end of the harbour.

⭐**Fagotto Jazz Bar** BAR, LIVE MUSIC
(☑28210 71877; Angelou 16; ☉7pm-2am) This Hania institution in a Venetian building offers smooth jazz, soft rock and blues (sometimes live) in a setting brimming with jazz paraphernalia, including a saxophone beer tap. The action picks up after 10pm.

Kleidi BAR
(☑28210 52974; Plateia 1821; ☉8am-late) By day locals fill the shady plaza tables and sip iced coffee, and by night the place buzzes with party life. There's no written sign, just the image of a keyhole (*kleidi* means key).

Sinagogi BAR
(☑28210 95242; Parados Kondylaki 15; ☉1pm-late Jun-Sep; 🖥) Housed in a roofless Venetian building on a small lane accessible only from Kondylaki street in the old town, this popular summer-only lounge bar is a laid-back place to relax and take it all in.

🛍 Shopping

Hania offers top shopping, especially in the back streets. Theotokopoulou is lined with souvenir and handicraft shops. Skrydlof offers a vast array of imported sandals, belts and bags. Find some of the most authentic crafts in the Splantzia quarter, along Chatzimichali Daliani and Daskalogianni. The **Agora** (Central Market; www.chaniamarket. com; Chatzimichali Giannari; ☉8am-3pm Mon-Sat) is touristy but makes a fun wander.

ℹ Information

Banks cluster around Plateia Markopoulou (Markopoulou Sq) in the new city, but there are also some ATMs in the Old Town on Halidon. Free wi-fi is widely available in public spaces, like the harbour, around the central market and at Plateia 1866, as well as at most hotels, restaurants, cafes and bars. Helpful websites include www.chaniatourism.com, www.chania-old-town-walks.com and www.west-crete.com.

Chania General Hospital St. George (☑28210 22000; www.chaniahospital.gr; Mournies) Located 4.5km south of town – take a local bus, or a taxi (€8 to €10).

Hania City Tourist Office (☑28213 41665; www.chania.gr; Milonogianni 53; ☉8.30am-2.30pm Mon-Fri) Modest selection of brochures, maps and transport timetables at the town hall. Open some Saturdays.

Post Office (☑28210 28444; Peridou 10; ☉7.30am-8pm Mon-Fri, to 2pm Sat)

Tellus Travel (☑28210 91500; www.tellus travel.gr; Halidon 108; ☉8.30am-10pm) This major agency hires cars, changes money and arranges air and boat tickets, accommodation and excursions.

Tourist Police (☑28210 25931, emergency 171; Irakleiou 24; ☉8am-2.30pm) From the central market (*agora*) square, the police station is 1.2km southeast on Apokoronou, which turns into Irakeleiou street.

ℹ Getting There & Away

AIR

Hania's **airport** (☑28210 83800; www.chania airport.com) is 14km east of town on the Akrotiri Peninsula, and is served year-round from Athens and Thessaloniki and seasonally from throughout Europe. Carriers include Aegean Airlines and Ryanair.

BOAT

Hania's port is at Souda, 7km southeast of town (and the site of a NATO base). The port is linked to town by bus (€1.50) and taxi (€9). Hania buses meet each boat, as do buses to Rethymno. The **Port Police** (☑28210 89240) provide ferry information.

Anek (📞 28210 27500; www.anek.gr; Plateia Venizelou) has a nightly overnight ferry between Piraeus and Hania (per person/car from €42/83, nine hours). Buy tickets online or at the port; reserve ahead for cars.

BUS

Hania's **KTEL bus station** (📞 info 28210 93052, tickets 28210 93306; www.bus-service-crete-ktel.com; Kydonias 73-77; 📞) has a cafeteria, mini-market, and left-luggage service (per day, per piece €2). Check the excellent website for the latest schedule; it changes month by month. Beaches are usually not served from October to April. Air-conditioned buses connect Hania regularly with towns and major beaches throughout the region, plus larger towns elsewhere in Crete. For several people, hiring a car is often more economical and convenient.

🛈 Getting Around

TO/FROM THE AIRPORT

KTEL (www.bus-service-crete-ktel.com) buses link the airport with central Hania up to 27 times daily (€2.30, 30 minutes). Taxis to/from the airport cost €20 (plus €2 per bag).

BUS

For buses to Souda, Halepa, Nea Hora and other local destinations, there is a handy central **bus stop** (📞 28210 27044; www.chaniabus.gr; tickets €1.10 or €1.50, if bought on bus €1.50 and €2) on Giannari, near the *agora* (market).

CAR

Major car hire outlets are at the airport or on Halidon. Companies at Agia Marina are competitive and deliver to Hania.

Most of the Old Town is pedestrianised. There's free parking just west of Firkas Fortress and along the waterfront towards Nea Hora beach, or by the eastern edge of the harbour off Kyprou. Avoid areas marked residents-only.

TAXI

Taxi (📞 28210 98700)

Kissamos (Kastelli)
Κίσσαμος (Καστέλλι)

POP 4236

About 40km west of Hania, the northern coast port town of Kissamos exudes an unpolished, almost gritty, air compared to other northern-coast towns. This is not a place given entirely over to tourism, and although the setting on an broad azure bay ringed by peninsulas and mountains is spectacular, the town itself is a bit rough and tumble. There are two beaches separated by a murky canal: sandy **Mavros Molos** in the west and the pebbly **Telonio beach** to the east.

The largest town and capital of Kissamos province, it is referred to interchangeably by either Kissamos or Kastelli (though the official name is the former). The port serves ferries to/from the Peloponnese or Kythira, and day boats to spectacular Balos beach (p452).

🛏 Sleeping & Eating

Thalassa STUDIO €
(📞 28220 31231; www.thalassa-apts.gr; Paralia Drapanias; studio from €40; 🅿❄@📶) This isolated complex is ideal for a quiet beach retreat 5km east of Kissamos at Drapianias beach. Immaculate studios are airy and well fitted. There's a barbecue on the lawn, and a small playground. Its helpful to have a car.

BUSES FROM HANIA

DESTINATION	FARE	TIME	FREQUENCY
Elafonisi	€10	2½hr	1 daily
Falasarna	€7.60	1½hr	3 daily
Hora Sfakion	€7.60	1hr 40min	3 daily
Iraklio	€13.80	2¾hr	half-hourly
Kissamos (Kastelli)	€4.70	1hr	13 daily
Kolymbari	€3.3	45min	half-hourly
Lakki	€2.60	1¾hr	2 daily
Moni Agias Triadas	€2.30	30min	2 daily
Omalos (for Samaria Gorge)	€6.90	1hr	3 daily
Paleohora	€7.60	1hr 50min	4 daily
Rethymno	€6.20	1hr	half-hourly
Sougia	€7.10	1hr 50min	2 daily
Stavros	€2.10	30min	3 daily

Nautilus Bay APARTMENT €€

(☑ 28220 22250; www.nautilusbay.gr; apt €75-145; P ❷ ❸ ❹) Spacious modern apartments fill this newly built complex right on the sandy beach and in the centre of town. Balconies have sweeping views and there's a restaurant and bar and large pool area.

Taverna Sunset TAVERNA €

(☑ 28220 41627; Paraliaki; mains €7-10; ⊙11am-late Apr-Oct; ❸) Locals mix with in-the-know visitors at this quintessential family taverna presided over by Giannis, who's usually behind the grill coaxing meat and fish into succulent perfection. It's right on the waterfront.

❶ Information

The main commercial drag, Iroön Polytechniou, has supermarkets, banks with ATMs, the post office and the bus stop.

❶ Getting There & Away

BOAT

From the port 3km west of town, **Lane** (☑ 27360 37055; www.lane-kithira.com) operates twice-weekly ferries to Piraeus (12 hours), and goes four times per week to Antikythira (€10, two hours), Kythira (€17, four hours) and Gythio (€25.10, five hours). It's far quicker to go to Piraeus from Hania. For tickets, try **Chalkiadaki Travel** (☑ 28220 22009; Skalidi 49). Check www.openseas.gr. In summer, a bus meets ferries; otherwise taxis into town cost around €5.

BUS

Buses leave from the **KTEL office** (☑ 28220 22035; www.e-ktel.com; Iroön Polytechniou 77) opposite the EKO petrol station. Check the website for schedules. There are as many as 14 daily buses to Hania (€4.70, one hour); change in Hania for Paleohora, Rethymno and Iraklio. There are also two to three daily buses to Falasarna (€3.50, 15 minutes) in summer only, and one daily to Elafonisi (€8.10, 1¼ hours) from May to October.

Around Kissamos

Polyrrinia   Πολυρρηνία

The wonderful mountain-top ruins of the ancient city of Polyrrinia (pol-ee-ren-*ee*-a) lie about 7km south of Kissamos, above the village of Ano Paleokastro (also called Polyrrinia). Sea, mountain and valley views from this defensible spire are stunning and the region is blanketed with wildflowers in spring.

The most impressive feature of the site is the **acropolis** built by the Byzantines and Venetians. There's also a **church** built on the foundations of a Hellenistic temple from the 4th century BC.

Gramvousa Peninsula   Χερσόνησος Γραμβούσα

Northwest of Kissamos, the wild and remote Gramvousa Peninsula cradles the lagoon-like white powdery beach of **Balos** off its western tip. This idyllic beach and looping lagoons of shallow, shimmering turquoise waters are overlooked by islets **Agria** (wild) and **Imeri** (tame), crowned by the ruins of a Venetian **fortress** built to keep pirates at (and out of the) bay.

It's a heavenly remote stretch of Crete that merits its inclusions on brochures everywhere. The beach is gorgeous, with lapping translucent waters dotted with tiny shellfish and darting fish. In summer, the crowds do come, usually by day-trip boat (May to October only), filling the beach from 11am to 4pm.

The only way to avoid the crowds is to get there by car before or after the boats arrive. The 12km of very rough dirt road (best in a 4WD) to Balos begins at the end of the main street of **Kalyviani** village and follows the eastern slope of Mt Geroskinos (762m). It ends at a car park with snack kiosk from where the steep path to the lagoon is 1.2km down the sandy cliffs. Kalyviani is the best base for the area with its good lodging and super **Gramvousa** (☑ 28220 22707; www. gramboussa-restaurant.gr; Kalyviani; mains €6-15; ⊙noon-midnight) restaurant. There is no shade and umbrellas with sunbeds cost €7.

Day boats are operated by **Gramvousa Balos Cruises** (☑ 28220 24344; www.gram vousa.com; adult/child €25/12; ⊙May-Oct) and leave from Kissamos port. Book online for discounted tickets. Reasonably priced food and drink is available on board.

Falasarna   Φαλάσαρνα

Some 16km west of Kissamos, Falasarna is little more than a long sandy beach – but what a beach! This broad sweep is considered among Crete's finest, even though views are somewhat marred by greenhouses set among the olive groves. Like Elafonisi, Falasarna has magical looking pink-cream sands and teal waters. It is known for its stunning sunsets. Along with superb water clarity, Falasarna has wonderfully big waves – long rollers coming from the open Mediterranean. Spread your towel on the **Big Beach** (Megali Paralia) at the southern end or pick a spot in one of the coves separated by rocky spits further north.

Falasarna was a 4th century BC Cretan city-state and trading centre with its own harbour. Today you can wander among the **ancient ruins**, reached via a 2km dirt road that starts where the paved road ends. The entrance is just past the 'stone throne'. Admission is free.

Falasarna has no centre as such, though there are several tavernas, bars and small supermarkets. Lodging options include **Sunset Taverna & Apartments** (☑28220 41204; www.sunset.com.gr; d/tr/apt/villa €40/45/65/160; ℙ🖵), which has a terrace with fig trees and wonderful views, its own natural spring and beach access, along with simple but comfortable rooms. **Magnolia Apartments** (☑28220 41407; www.magnolia-apartments.gr; studio/apt from €45/55; ☺year-round; ❄🖵) is just a short walk from Big Beach.

From June through August there are three buses daily from Kissamos (€3.50, 20 minutes) and Hania (€7.60, 1¼ hours). Check www.e-ktel.com for schedules.

SOUTHWEST COAST

The stark and muscular Lefka Ori (White Mountains) meet the sea along Crete's corrugated southwestern coast indented with a handful of laid-back coastal villages, some of them accessible only by boat and therefore completely untouched by mass tourism. You can walk to perfectly isolated little beaches or soak up the majestic scenery and fragrant air on a scramble through wildy romantic gorges away from the busy Samaria Gorge, which ends in Agia Roumeli.

ⓘ Getting There & Around

Anendyk (www.anendyk.gr) operates ferries between Hora Sfakion and Paleohora, also stopping in Loutro, Agia Roumeli and Sougia. There are also boats to Gavdos Island. Often boats only run as far as Agia Roumeli, where you must switch to another boat to continue

on along the coast. In low season, it is usually impossible to ferry a car between Hora Sfakion and Paleohora, as some of the boats are passenger-only.

KTEL buses travel daily to Hora Sfakion, Paleohora and Sougia from Hania; Rethymno requires a change of bus.

Frangokastello
Φραγγοκαστέλλο

POP 148

Marked by a striking 14th-century fortress, Frangokastello is a low-key resort 15km east of Hora Sfakion, with fabulous wide and sandy **Orthi Ammos Beach** that slopes gradually into shallow warm water, making it ideal for kids. There's no actual village, just a few tavernas, small markets, a petrol station, and low-rise holiday apartments and rooms scattered along the main street. The ruined **fortress** was constructed soon after the Fourth Crusade (1204) by the Venetians, who sought a stronghold against pirates and Sfakiot warriors. On 17 May 1828, 385 Cretan rebels made a last stand here in one of the bloodiest battles of the war for independence. About 800 Turks were killed along with the rebels. According to legend their ghosts – the *drosoulites* – can be seen marching past the fortress in the early dawn on the battle's anniversary.

Among the tavernas, **Oasis** (☑28250 92136; www.oasisrooms.com; mains €6-8; ☺lunch & dinner; ℙ🖵) does well-executed Cretan specials and also rents spacious self-catering apartments (€50 to €60).

Frangokastello is some 70km southwest of Hania and 30km west of Plakias. There's one daily bus to Hania (€8.40, 2½ hours).

Hora Sfakion
Χώρα Σφακίων

POP 212

The more bullet holes you see in the passing road signs, the closer you are to Hora

---

WORTH A TRIP

IMBROS GORGE   ΦΑΡΑΓΓΙ ΙΜΠΡΟΥ

Half the length of its illustrious sister at Samaria, the 8km-long **Imbros Gorge** (admission €2; ☺year-round), 57km south of Hania, is no less beautiful and a lot less busy, especially in the afternoon. Most people begin the walk in the mountain village of Imbros and then hike down to the southern coastal village of Komitades. But it's possible to park at either and taxi (€22) or bus between.

SAMARIA GORGE

Hiking the **Samaria Gorge** (Φαράγγι της Σαμαριάς; ☑28210 45570, 28210 67179; adult/child €5/free; ☉7am-sunset May-late Oct) is considered one of the must-do experiences in Crete, so you'll never be without company. In peak season, up to 3000 people per day tackle the stony 16km-long trail, and even in spring and autumn, it's rarely fewer than 1000 hikers. The vast majority arrive on organised coach excursions from the big northern resorts. You'll encounter a mix of serious trekkers as well as less experienced types attempting the trail in flip-flops.

Nevertheless, there's an undeniable raw beauty to Samaria, whose vertical walls soar up to 500m high and are just 3m apart at the narrowest point, though 150m at the broadest. The hike begins at 1230m at Xyloskalo just south of Omalos and ends in the coastal village of Agia Roumeli. It's especially scenic in April and May when wildflowers brighten the trail. Samaria is home to the *kri-kri*, a rarely seen endangered wild goat.

Hiking the Gorge

The trail begins at **Xyloskalo**, a steep and serpentine stone path that descends some 600m into the canyon to arrive at the simple cypress-framed Agios Nikolaos chapel. Beyond here the gorge is wide and open for the next 6km until you reach the abandoned settlement of **Samaria** whose inhabitants were relocated when the gorge became a national park. Just south of the village is a 14th-century **chapel** dedicated to St Maria of Egypt, after whom the gorge is named.

Further on, the gorge narrows and becomes more dramatic until, at the 11km mark, the walls are only 3.5m apart. These are the famous **Sideroportes** (Iron Gates), where a rickety wooden pathway leads hikers the 20m or so across the water.

The gorge ends at the 12.5km mark just north of the almost abandoned village of Palea (Old) Agia Roumeli. From here it's a further 2km hike to the seaside village of **Agia Roumeli**, whose fine pebble beach and sparkling water are a most welcome sight. Few people miss taking a refreshing dip or at least bathing sore and aching feet. The entire trek takes from about four hours for the sprinters to six hours for the strollers.

The Low-Down

➤ An early start (before 8am) helps to put you ahead of the crowd. Sleep over in Omalos to be first. During July and August even the early bus from Hania can be packed. Alternatively, start after noon, and plan to sleep over in Agia Roumeli.

➤ Hikers starting after about 2pm are only allowed to walk a distance of 2km from either end. There's no spending the night in the gorge — expect to be out by sunset.

➤ There's a 1200m elevation drop going north to south. Wear sturdy shoes and take sunscreen, sunglasses, some food, a hat and a water bottle, which you can refill from taps with potable water along the way. Drink plenty!

➤ There are several rest stops with toilets, water, rubbish bins and benches along the trail.

➤ Falling rocks occasionally lead to injuries but generally it's the heat that's a far bigger problem. Check ahead as park officials may close the gorge on rainy or exceptionally hot days (generally, over 40°C), and the gorge season can end early if the rains have started.

Sfakion (*ho*-ra sfa-*kee*-on), long renowned in Cretan history for its rebellious streak against foreign occupiers. But don't worry, the pint-sized fishing village is an amiable, if eccentric, place that caters well to today's foreign visitors – many of whom are Samaria Gorge hikers stumbling off the Agia Roumeli boat on their way back to Hania. Most pause only long enough to catch the next bus out, but the village, the main town in the region, and the only one with an ATM, can be a re-laxing stay for a few days and access-point to several beaches and the **Aradena Gorge**.

◎ Sights & Activities

Vrissi Beach
BEACH

Abutting the western edge of town, tiny grey-sand Vrissi beach makes for an easy dive or sunset viewing.

Sweetwater Beach
BEACH

(Glyka Nera) West of Hora Sfakion, lovely Sweetwater Beach is accessible by a small

➡ Early in the season it's sometimes necessary to wade through the stream. Later, as the flow drops, the stream-bed rocks become stepping stones.

➡ If the idea of a 16km-hike does not appeal, get a taste of Samaria by doing it 'the Easy Way', ie starting in Agia Roumeli and heading north for as long as you feel like before doubling back. The Sideroportes, for instance, can be reached in about an hour. Or consider some of the other gorges in the area, like Agia Irini (p457), Imbros (p453) or Aradena.

Sleeping & Eating

It is forbidden to camp in the gorge. Stay at Omalos on the north end, or Agia Roumeli in the south. The trailhead, Xyloskalo, near Omalos, has one restaurant and a clutch of stands selling souvenirs, snacks, bottled water and the like, when the gorge is open.

Hotel Neos Omalos (☑28210 67269; www.neos-omalos.gr; s/d/tr incl breakfast €35/45/55; P⃣🖂) A rustic mountain feel pervades this comfortable and contemporary hotel where views from your balcony will get you in the mood for hiking. The owners are a fount of information on local hikes and other outdoor activities, and can also shuttle you to the Samaria Gorge. The restaurant dishes up good, fresh food.

Paralia Taverna & Rooms (☑28250 91408; www.taverna-paralia.com; d €35-40; ❄🖂) Right on the waterfront, Paralia Taverna & Rooms offers excellent views, the best Cretan cuisine in town, cold beer and simple, clean rooms.

Agriorodo (☑28210 67237; www.omalos.com; 2-/3-bedroom villa €80/120; ☺year-round; P⃣🖂) These new and lovely individual stone cottages are the closest accommodations to the Samaria Gorge. Each sleeps four to five people and is fully kitted out with satellite TV, wi-fi, kitchens, and living rooms with fireplaces. The owners also operate the good restaurant Xyloskalo with spectacular views at the very entrance to the gorge.

Xyloskalo (☑28210 67237; www.omalos.com; dishes €5-10; ☺10am-7pm or 8pm daily Apr-Oct, Sat & Sun Nov-Mar; 🖂) Perched just over the spectacular drop of Samaria Gorge, with eagles occasionally circling outside its wrap-around windows, this cosy restaurant dishes up classic Cretan and Greek meals. And offers that last chance to use indoor plumbing and wi-fi.

Getting There & Away

Most people hike the gorge one way going north–south on an organised day trip from every sizeable town and resort in Crete. Note that prices listed usually don't include the €5 admission to the gorge or the boat ride from Agia Roumeli to Sougia or Hora Sfakion.

With some planning, it's possible to do the trek on your own. There are daily early-morning public buses to Omalos from Hania (€6.90, 45 minutes) and Rethymno (€15, 1¾ hours), as well as services from Sougia (€4.20, one hour) and Paleohora (€6.40, one hour), once or twice daily in high season. Check www.e-ktel.com for the schedule. Taxis are another option.

At the end of the trail, in Agia Roumeli, ferries (☑28250 91251; www.anendyk.gr) go to Sougia or Hora Sfakion, some of which are met by public buses to Hania, or you can continue on to Paleohora, Gavdos Island or other destinations, if you carried your pack with you the whole way (or started from Sougia or Paleohora).

daily ferry (May to October, per person €4), by taxi boat (one-way/return €20/30) or on foot via a stony and partly vertiginous one-hour coastal path starting at the first hairpin turn of the Anopoli road. A small cafe rents out umbrellas and sun chairs.

Notos Mare Diving Centre   DIVING
(☑6947270106; www.notosmare.com; 1 dive from €49) Offers dives and certifications for beginners and experienced divers, as well as snorkelling and boat excursions along the south coast.

🛏 Sleeping & Eating

The tavernas along the harbour all offer similar fare and thus vociferously compete for your business. Most also rent out rooms. Try the speciality *Sfakiani pita* (a pancake filled with sweet *myzithra* cheese and flecked with honey).

Xenia Hotel
HOTEL €

(☑28250 91490; www.sfakia-xenia-hotel.gr; d incl breakfast €55; ❋🔊) The best-value and best-located rooms in town are to be found at this refurbished hotel well positioned at the western edge overlooking the water. The 21 rooms have mod cons such as air-con, satellite TV and a fridge.

Hotel Stavris
HOTEL €

(☑28250 91220; www.hotel-stavris-sfakia-crete. com; s/d/tr from €30/35/40; ❋❋) Up the steps at the western end of the port, this long-running place owned by the Perrakis clan has clean, basic rooms – some with kitchenettes, fridges and harbour-facing balconies. Rooms vary; aim for the renovated main building.

★ Nikos
TAVERNA €

(☑28250 91111; mains €5-12; ⊙8am-midnight) Hora Sfakion's best harbour-front taverna stands out for its friendly, family-run service, special care with all of its dishes and top *Sfakiani pita,* and it's always fun to have the grilled garlic bread, which is usually thrown in free. Mains run from seafood to traditional Greek taverna fare and Cretan specialities like smoked pork or sautéed snails.

❶ Information

Hora Sfakion has two petrol stations and one ATM. The post office is on the square, opposite the police station. Get info at www.chora-sfakion.com.

The city operates a small **Tourist Kiosk** (www. chora-sfakion.com; ⊙9am-2pm & 5-7pm Easter-Sep) near the entrance to the harbour with maps and transport info in high season.

❶ Getting There & Away

Hora Sfakion is about 60km south of Hania via a winding road through the magnificent Lefka Ori (White Mountains). Gas up before you leave.

BOAT

The ferry quay is around the point on the eastern edge of the village harbour. Hora Sfakion is the western terminus for the southern-coast **Anendyk** (☑28210 95511; www.anendyk.gr) ferry route to/from Paleohora via Loutro, Agia Roumeli and Sougia, and also has boats to Gavdos Island.

Buy tickets at the **booth** (☑28250 91221) on the eastern edge of the harbour. Schedules vary seasonally; always check ahead. Often boats only run as far as Agia Roumeli, where you must change for a boat to Sougia (€14) and Paleohora (€17, three hours).

From June through August there are three daily boats from Hora Sfakion to Agia Roumeli (€11, one hour) via Loutro (€5, 15 minutes). There are four additional boats to Loutro only. There are two to three boats per week to/from Gavdos Island (€17, 1½ hours).

Boat taxis (☑6978645212) serve the coast around Hora Sfakion. Private hire to Sweetwater beach is €20; from May to September set group taxi departures cost (€4 per person).

BUS

KTEL buses leave from the square up the hill above the municipal car park. Check the schedule online. In summer there are three daily services to Hania (€7.60, two hours); to reach Rethymno change in Vryses (€7.30, one hour). The last bus tends to wait for the boat from Agia Roumeli. There are also two to three daily buses to Frangokastello (€2, 25 minutes) and one daily to Anapoli/Aradana (€2, 30 minutes) in summer.

Loutro
Λουτρό

A peaceful crescent of flower-festooned white-and-blue buildings hugging a narrow pebbly beach, this pint-sized fishing village lies between Agia Roumeli and Hora Sfakion and is only accessible by boat and on foot. It's the departure point for several coastal walks to isolated beaches, such as **Finix** (also spelled Phoenix; 1km west), **Marmara Beach** (5km west) and **Sweetwater** (p454; 3.3km east). Ask locally for directions, hire a **mini-canoe** (per hr/day €5/15) from Hotel Porto Loutro, or take a summer-only small boat. You can also explore the castle **ruins** on the point.

For overnight, try **Apartments Niki** (☑28250 91213; www.loutro-accommodation.com; studio/apartment from €50/110; ❋🔊), which has squeaky-clean rooms with sea-facing balconies, or **Hotel Porto Loutro** (☑28250 91433; www.hotelportoloutro.com; s/d/tr incl breakfast €55/65/75; ⊙Apr-Oct; ❋@🔊), with one of its buildings on the beach.

Anendyk (www.anendyk.gr) ferries serve Hora Sfakion (€5, 15 minutes), Agia Roumeli (€6, 45 minutes) and occasionally Paleohora (€16, 2½ hours) and Sougia (€13), or you can change in Agia Roumeli for reach those ports. From September to June, boats from Hora Sfakion to Gavdos Island also stop in Loutro.

High season **taxi boats** go to Sweetwater beach (ferry/private €5/25, 15 minutes) and Hora Sfakion. There is no ATM in Loutro.

Sougia
Σούγια

POP 136

Sougia (*soo*-yah), 67km south of Hania and on the Hora Sfakion–Paleohora ferry route, is one of the most laid-back and refreshingly undeveloped southern beach resorts. Cafes, bars and tavernas line a tamarisk-shaded waterfront promenade, while most lodging options enjoy a quieter inland setting.

☉ Sights & Activities

Sougia has a lovely 1km-long grey sand-and-pebble **beach**. Like most southern coast villages, it's also great hiking territory. A taxi to the Samaria Gorge trailhead is €60, but with a day or two's notice, staff at the taxi kiosk can put together a pool of hikers to share the cost. There's also a summer-only bus.

★**Agia Irini Gorge**   HIKING

(admission €1.50) Pretty Agia Irini Gorge starts some 13km north of Sougia. The 7km well-maintained trail (with a 500m elevation drop) brings you through redolent and varied verdure, plus a few caves hidden in the gorge walls. You'll emerge at excellent **Taverna Oasis** (☎28230 51121; mains €6-10; ⊙lunch & dinner Apr-Oct) from where it's another 7km walk via a quiet, paved road (or a €15 taxi ride) to Sougia. It's also possible to do the hike in reverse. To trek without a tour, take the Omalos bus from Paleohora or the Hania bus from Sougia, and get off at Agia Irini.

🛏 Sleeping

Aretousa Studios & Rooms   APARTMENT €

(☎28230 51178; s/d/studio €35/40/45; ⊙Apr-Oct; P🌸🛜) This lovely pension on the road to Hania, 200m from the sea, has bright and comfortable refurbished rooms and studios, most with kitchenettes. There's a relaxing garden and playground for kids out the back.

Santa Irene Apartments & Studios   APARTMENT €€

(☎28230 51342; www.santa-irene.gr; apt €60-80; ⊙late Mar-early Nov; P🌸🛜) This smart hotel on the beach has airy rooms with marble floors, TV and kitchenettes, while there are also two family apartments (€80 to €90) with baby cots available. Prices drop dramatically in low season.

🍽 Eating

Polyfimos   TAVERNA €

(☎28230 51343; mains €5-8; ⊙lunch & dinner; 🛜🅿) Tucked away off the Hania road behind the police station, ex-hippie Yianni makes his own oil, wine and *raki* and even makes *dolmadhes* (vine leaves stuffed with rice) from the grapevines covering the shady courtyard.

★**Omikron**   INTERNATIONAL €€

(☎28230 51492; mains €5-14; ⊙8am-late; 🛜🅿) At this elegantly rustic lair, Jean-Luc Delfosse has forged his own culinary path in a refreshing change from taverna staples. From mushroom crêpes to *Flammekuche* (Alsatian-style pizza), seafood pasta to peppersteak – it's all fresh, creative and delicious.

❶ Information

There's no ATM in Sougia. Visit www.sougia.info for info.

❶ Getting There & Away

Sougia is on the **Anendyk** (www.anendyk.gr) Paleohora–Hora Sfakion ferry route. In high season, daily boats serve Agia Roumeli (€9, 45 minutes), Loutro (€13, 1½ hours) and Hora Sfakion (€14, 1¾ hours) to the east and Paleohora (€9, 50 minutes) to the west. Twice-weekly boats from Paleohora to Gavdos Island (€18 from Sougia) pass through as well.

Captain George's Water Taxi (☎6947605802) serves the coast near Sougia.

There is no petrol station in Sougia.

In high season, two to three **KTEL buses** (www.e-ktel.com) daily connect Hania and Sougia (€7.10, one hour 50 minutes), and can stop at Agia Irini to let off gorge hikers. There are also thrice-weekly buses to Paleohora and daily buses to Omalos (for Samaria Gorge) in high season only.

Paleohora & Around
Παλαιόχωρα

POP 1675

Appealing, relaxed and full of character, Paleohora (pal-ee-*oh*-hor-a) lies on a narrow peninsula flanked by a long, curving tamarisk-shaded sandy **Pahia Ammos beach** (Sandy Beach) on one side, and a pebbly **Halikia beach** (Pebble Beach) on the other. Shallow waters and general quietude also make the town a good choice for families with small children.

The most picturesque part of Paleohora is the maze of narrow streets around the ruins of a 13th-century **Venetian castle** (FREE). Tavernas spill out onto the pavement and occasional cultural happenings, as well as Cretan and international music, inject a lively ambience.

In spring and autumn, Paleohora attracts many walkers, with great local walks to **Anydri Gorge** and **Azogires**. It's also the

CRETE PALEOHORA & AROUND

only beach town in Crete that doesn't go into total hibernation in winter.

Activities

You can hike Samaria (p454) and Agia Irini (p457) gorges from Paleohora, either with local organised tours or by using taxis or KTEL bus service to reach the trailheads, then returning by ferry from the trails' coastal endpoints (at Agia Roumeli for Samaria Gorge, and Sougia for Agia Irini).

Mid-May to September you can take a day trip to Elafonisi by boat. Tickets are sold at Selino Travel , which also offers other excursions.

Sleeping

★ Joanna's Place   APARTMENT €
(☑ 28230 41801; www.joanna-place.com; studio €45-55; ⊙ Apr-Nov; 🅿 ❄ 🛜) This charmer sits in a quiet spot across from a small stone beach at the southeastern tip of the peninsula. Spacious and spotless studios are outfitted with locally made furniture, and there's a kitchenette for preparing breakfast to enjoy on your balcony.

Homestay Anonymous   PENSION €
(☑28230 42098; www.anonymoushomestay.com; s/d/tr/2-bedroom apt €25/30/35/55; ❄🛜) This simple but good-value pension with private bathrooms and shared cooking facilities in the courtyard garden is a good bet. Friendly, well-travelled owner Manolis cultivates a welcoming atmosphere and is a mine of information on local activities. The rooms are clean and tastefully furnished, in a quaint stone building, though a bit cramped. Rooms can connect to accommodate families.

★ Corali   APARTMENT €€
(☑ 6974361868; www.corali-studios.com; d studio from €65; ❄ @ 🛜) A friendly Greek-Italian family runs these immaculate studios that are a distinct cut above standard studios for rent. A series of luxe studios with kitchenettes and waterfront balconies are kitted out with top-end modern furniture and large pristine bathrooms. Some come with computers in the room. The central location and water views are excellent.

Eating

★ To Skolio   MEZEDHES €
(☑ 28230 83001; dishes €3-7; ⊙ coffee from 9am, food noon-11pm daily Easter-Sep, Wed-Sun Oct-Easter) Whether gorge walker or hire-car driver, do not miss the chance to dine at wonderful To Skolio. 'The School' is in a converted schoolhouse, and cheerily painted tables fill a shady cliffside courtyard with grand valley views. Menus of mezedhes (small dishes) rotate with the season, incorporating the best local produce. Though prices are low, portions are huge.

Third Eye   VEGETARIAN €
(☑ 28230 41234; www.thethirdeye-paleochora.com; mains €6-7; ⊙ 8.30am-3pm & 5.30-11pm; 🛜🍴) A local institution, the Third Eye, Crete's only vegetarian restaurant, has an eclectic menu of curries, salads, pastas, and Greek and Asian dishes. There's live music weekly in summer. The restaurant is just inland from sandy Pahia Ammos.

★ Methexis   CRETAN €€
(☑28230 41431; www.methexistaverna.com; mains €6-15; ⊙12.30pm-11.30pm Tue-Sun, later Jul & Aug; 🅿🛜🍴) It's well worth the short saunter to the peninsula's southeastern tip

OFF THE BEATEN TRACK

GAVDOS ISLAND   ΝΗΣΙ ΤΗΣ ΓΑΥΔΟΥ

Gavdos is as much a state of mind as it is an island. If you want to get away from it all, there is no better place for peace and isolation. Located in the Libyan Sea, 65km from Paleohora and 45km from Hora Sfakion, Gavdos is the most southerly place in Europe, and with only a smattering of rooms and tavernas, it's a blissfully remote spot. The island attracts a loyal following of campers, nudists and free spirits happy to trade the trappings of civilisation for unspoilt beaches, long walks and rustic holidays. There are several stunning beaches, some of which are accessible only by foot or boat.

Most of the island uses generators, which are often turned off at night and in the middle of the day. The folks running the website at www.gavdos-online.com can help with reservations. **Anendyk** (☑ 28230 41222; www.anendyk.gr) ferries serve Hora Sfakion (via Agia Roumeli and Loutro) or Paleohora (via Agia Roumeli and Sougia) two to three times per week.

to sample the authentic comfort food and warm hospitality at this locally adored taverna across from a small beach. All the classics are here along with such surprises as the meat-free and superb chestnut *stifado* (stew), salt cod with garlic sauce, and other Cretan delicacies.

ℹ Information

ATMs and a petrol station are on Eleftheriou Venizelou, while the post office is at Pahia Ammos' northern end. In summer, a tourist information booth sometimes opens in the harbour.

Selino Travel (☑ 28230 42272; selino2@ otenet.gr; Kondekaki; 3hr trip €18; ⊙ 8am-1.30pm & 6-9.30pm Apr-Oct, shorter hours rest of year) has general information, boat and airline tickets and excursions, including to the gorges of Samaria and Agia Irini. From mid-May to October they offer a daily boat to Elafonisi beach on the western coast.

ℹ Getting There & Away

BOAT

Boats leave from the quay at the far southern end of Halikia pebble beach. Buy tickets for all boats at Selino Travel (p459).

Paleohora is the westernmost stop on the **Anendyk** (www.anendyk.gr) southern-coast routes. Ferries go east to Sougia (€9, 50 minutes) and Agia Roumeli (€15, 1½ hours), where you can change for a boat to Loutro (€16, 2½ hours) and Hora Sfakion (€17, three hours). Usually you cannot take a car the whole way as some of the boats carry passengers only. Three times per week in summer a ferry goes to Gavdos Island (€19, 2½ hours).

BUS

Buses from the **KTEL bus station** (☑ 28230 41914; www.e-ktel.com) go on ever-changing schedules to Hania (€7.60, 1¾ hours, three to four daily). In summer one daily service goes to Omalos (€6.40, two hours, departing 6.15am), for Samaria Gorge, and also stops at the entrance to Agia Irini Gorge (€4.50). Thrice-weekly buses also serve Sougia and Elafonisi in summer.

Elafonisi   Ελαφονήσι

Tucked into Crete's southwest corner, this symphony of fine pink-white sand, turquoise water and gentle rose dunes looks like a magical dreamscape. As the azure water swirls across the sands, prismatic rainbows shimmer across the surface. Off the long, wide strand of Elafonisi beach lies Elafonisi

Islet, occasionally connected by a thin sandy isthmus which creates a lovely double-beach but otherwise easily reached by wading through 50m of knee-deep water. The islet is marked by low dunes and a string of semi-secluded coves that attract a sprinkling of naturists. A walk to its high point offers mind-blowing views of the beaches, sea and raw mountainscape. The entire area is part of Natura 2000, the environmental protection program of the EU.

Alas, this natural gem is hardly a secret and less than idyllic in high summer when hundreds of umbrellas and lounge chairs (€7) clog the beach (dash out to the island where you can find peace). The invasion puts enormous pressure on this delicate ecosystem and on the minimal infrastructure, especially the toilets. Come early or late in the day or, better yet, stay overnight to truly sample Elafonisi's magic. And outside of high season, when there are no public transports to the beach and very few tours, you may have it all to yourself.

🛏 Sleeping & Eating

★ **Elafonisi Resort**   HOTEL, TAVERNA €
(☑ 28250 61274; www.elafonisi-resort.com; s/d €35/45; ❄ 🐾) More a small well-run hotel than a resort, these 21 spacious rooms have fridges, and there are nicely furnished cottage rooms in back among peaceful olive groves, as well as apartments with kitchens. The shared patio has sea views and there's an excellent attached restaurant (open to all) serving the catch of the day and classic Greek fare. Book well ahead.

Elafonisi Village   HOTEL €
(☑ 6942254382, 2822061548; www.elafonisi-village .gr; d/q from €55/75; ⊙ Apr-Oct) Just 250m from Elafonisi Beach, these 10 rooms string across an arid courtyard and offer refrigerator, TV and a small outdoor terrace area.

ℹ Getting There & Away

Elafonisi is 72km southwest of Hania. Selino Travel operates one daily boat daily from Paleohora to Elafonisi (€8, one hour) from mid-May through September. Those same months there is one daily **KTEL bus** (www.e-ktel.com) from Hania (€15, 2½ hours) and Kissamos (Kastelli; €8.10, 1¼ hours), which return in the afternoon. There is no public transport from October to mid-May.

EASTERN CRETE

Head east from Iraklio past the rocking package-tourist resorts of Hersonisos and Malia and you enter the island's eastern-most prefecture of Lasithi, a more relaxed Cretan world that is never short of surprises. Looking for a charming resort town with a hot-stepping after-dark vibe? There's none better than Lasithi's main tourist draw of Agios Nikolaos. Ancient sites and culture? Lasithi has Minoan and Mycenean sites aplenty. The fertile Lasithi Plateau, tucked into the Mt Dikti ranges, offers cycling opportunities through tranquil villages and the Dikteon Cave where Zeus himself was born. Outdoor types can also look forward to walking the dramatic Valley of the Dead at Kato Zakros.

Added value comes with such unique attractions as the historic monastery of Toplou and Vaï's famous palm-backed beach. Scores of smaller towns and villages, meanwhile, maintain a rich undertow of Cretan history and spirit.

Agios Nikolaos

Αγιος Νικόλαος

POP 11,421

Lasithi's capital, Agios Nikolaos (*ah*-yee-os nih-*ko*-laos) has an enviable location on hilly terrain overlooking the shores of the sensuously curving Mirabello Bay. It may feel less Cretan than other towns, partly because of its resort-style flair, tree-lined avenues and largely modern architecture. However, there's also a strong local character to Agios Nikolaos that makes it a charming and friendly place. A narrow channel separates the attractive harbour from the circular Voulismeni Lake, whose pedestrianised shore is lined with tourist cafes and restaurants. At night a decidedly chic ambience descends on the harbour as lounge-bars fill

Agios Nikolaos

with stylish young Greeks and holidaymakers from the nearby resorts.

◉ Sights & Activities

Within town, sandy **Ammos Beach** and pebbly **Kytroplatia Beach** are fairly small and can get crowded, but they are convenient for a quick dip. About 1km north and south respectively, **Ammoudi Beach** and **Almyros Beach** are also busy but much longer and with better sand. All have snack bars, cafes and umbrella and sun chairs for rent.

Archaeological Museum MUSEUM
(☑28410 24943; Paleologou Konstantinou 74) Due to the economic crisis at the time of writing, this museum was closed until 2016 for refurbishment and expansion. When open, the extensive collection is the second-most significant Minoan collection in existence, and includes clay coffins, ceramic musical instruments and gold from the island of Mohlos. The highlight is the odd-looking Goddess of Myrtos, a clay jug from 2500 BC.

🛏 Sleeping

Hotel Doxa HOTEL €
(☑28410 24214; www.doxahotel.gr; Idomeneos 7; s/d/tr incl breakfast €45/50/65; ❄️🛜) This shadowy, bijou hotel down a side street has smart but cramped rooms with chocolate brown quilts, marble floors, flat-screen TVs, and immaculate en suite bathrooms. Great breakfast. There is a lift, and Ammos beach and car parking are just a short stroll away.

Du Lac Hotel HOTEL €
(☑28410 22711; www.dulachotel.gr; 28 Oktovriou 17; s/d/studio with lake view €40/55/70; 🖲❄️🛜)

Slick and modern, this delightful central hotel is the businessman's choice with fresh studios and apartments enjoying wood-effect walls, laminate floors, and balconies with fine views over Voulismeni Lake. Studio kitchenettes are modern and well equipped, while apartments also have baths. Downstairs there's a pleasant restaurant. Expect excellent value off season.

★Villa Olga APARTMENT €€
(☑28410 25913; www.villa-olga.gr; Anapafseos 18, Ellinika; s €45, apt €80-95; ❄️🛜🏊) These delicious self-catering studios and apartments (two to six persons) enjoy serene views of the Bay of Mirabello from their rising terraces set in lush gardens scattered with urns and shaded by olive trees. The interiors are traditional chic with tiled floors and tasteful bed linen and furniture. There's a small swimming pool.

Minos Beach Art Hotel BOUTIQUE HOTEL €€€
(☑28410 22345; www.minosbeach.com; Akti Ilia Sotirchou; r incl breakfast from €280; 🅿❄️🛜🏊) In a superb location just out of town, this classy resort is a veritable art gallery, with sculptures from leading Greek and foreign artists adorning the grounds right down to the beach. The low-rise design and cool style maintain the hotel's position as one of the island's finest. Follow the waterfront road, Akti Koundourou, northeast from the centre of Agios Nikolaos for about 1km. The hotel is signposted 'Minos Beach Hotel' on the seaward side of the road.

✘ Eating

For earthier, tastier food, head around the harbour to Kitroplatia beach where the locals eat.

Sarri's GREEK €
(Kyprou 15; mains €10; ◷lunch & dinner) Shaded by the arms of a eucalyptus tree, with its check-cloth tables and sun-beaten ambience, Sarris evokes old Greece. Get stuck in to shrimp *saganaki*, souvlaki, calamari, pizza or a mezedhes platter with wine for €9. The garden terrace is ideal for breakfast, lunch or dinner. To find it reach the top of the hill and walk down 20m.

Faros GREEK €
(Kitroplatia Beach; mains €10; ◷noon-late) Right by the sea, this aromatic, family-run taverna exudes atmosphere with meat and fish aglow on the brazier out front. There's outdoor seating beneath a sheltered canopy, or

a homey interior within the restaurant. The food is no less than superb with huge salads, mouthwatering calamari, *kleftiko* (slow oven-baked lamb or goat) and *stifadho* (meat cooked with onions in a tomato puree)... maybe free baklava and *raki* too. *Filoxenia* (hospitality) in extremis!

★ **Pelagos** MEDITERRANEAN €€
(☑ 28410 25737; cnr Stratigou Koraka & Katehaki; mains €10; ⊙ lunch & dinner; ⊛) Neoclassical meets modern Greek in this breezy upscale restaurant with faux-distressed walls hung with petal glass lamps and icons, fresh orange and white tables, and a menu of salads, seafood, meat and pasta. Order the grilled prawns and try not to come back again! Exquisite. There's also a garden terrace.

🍷 Drinking & Nightlife

The chic harbour-facing lounge-bars along Akti Koundourou are busy from midmorning until the wee hours. About half-adozen dance clubs cluster on the lower end of 25 Martiou, just up from the harbour.

Bar Arudo BAR
(Akti Koundourou; ⊙ 9.30am-late) This low-lit haunt buzzes with the conversation of earnest boho locals, offering a cocktail of cool tunes, a sea-facing outside terrace and a handsome wood bar within.

Peripou Cafe CAFE
(28 Otkovriou 13; ⊙ 9.30am-2am; ⊛) This arty bar with a verandah overlooking the lagoon has a bijou bookstore, plays indie tunes, sells toasties and has a boho charm from the moment you enter its wine-coloured facade.

❶ Information

Most banks, ATMs, travel agencies and shops are on Koundourou and the parallel 28 Oktovriou.

General Hospital (☑ 28410 66000; Konstantinou Paleologou) OK for broken bones and x-rays, but for anything more serious you'll need to head to Iraklio. On the western side of town, at the top of the steep Paleologou Konstantinou.

Municipal Tourist Office (☑ 28410 22357; www.agiosnikolaos.gr; ⊙ 8am-10pm Apr-Nov) Has helpful information and maps, changes money and assists with accommodation. Opposite the northern side of the Voulismeni Lake bridge.

Post Office (28 Oktovriou 9; ⊙ 7.30am-2pm Mon-Fri)

❶ Getting There & Away

Buses leave from Agios Nikolaos' bus station for Elounda (€1.70, 20 minutes, 16 daily), Ierapetra (€3.80, one hour, seven daily), Iraklio (€7.10, 1½ hours, 18 daily), Kritsa (€1.60, 15 minutes, 10 daily), Lasithi Plateau (Dikteon Cave; €6, three hours, two daily), Vaï (€14) and Sitia (€7.60, 1½ hours, seven daily). You can catch the Elounda bus at a stop opposite the tourist centre. A local bus (every half hour) can also be boarded here for the main bus station.

❶ Getting Around

Typical **taxi** (☑ 28410 24100) charges include Elounda (€13), Plaka (€18), Kritsa (€13) and Lato (€15).

Car- and motorcycle-hire outlets, like **Club Cars** (☑ 28410 25868; www.clubcars.net; per day from €40), dot 28 Oktovriou and the northern waterfront.

Manolis Bikes (☑ 28410 24940; 25 Martiou 12; scooter/mountain bike per day from €20/12) has a huge range of scooters, motorcycles, quad bikes and mountain bikes.

Around Agios Nikolaos

Elounda Ελούντα

POP 2185

There are fine mountain and sea views along the 11km road north from Agios Nikolaos to Elounda (el-*oon*-da). This earthy little fishing village has grown in profile in recent years thanks to nearby uber-exclusive hotels enjoying an influx of A-list celebrities (think Ronaldo, Leonardo DiCaprio, U2 and Lady Gaga). The town itself lacks this style and glitz, though it seems happy enough about that. Locals will cheerfully take you fishing or to Spinalonga Island, oblivious to the odd appearance of the Hollywood deities venturing from their gated Olympian haunts. The pleasant but unremarkable town beach, to the north of the port, gets very crowded. On the southern side of Elounda an artificial causeway leads to the Kolokytha Peninsula.

🛏 Sleeping & Eating

Delfinia Apartments APARTMENT €
(☑ 28410 41641; www.pediaditis.gr; studio/apt €40/50; ❄ ⊛ ▣) These delightful sea-view rooms enjoy tasteful furnishings and well-equipped kitchenettes with sandwichmaker, fridge and microwave. So close to the waves they will lull you to sleep. The same

family also runs the nearby Milos Apartments, where there is a pool.

Corali Studios
APARTMENT €€

(☑ 28410 41712; www.coralistudios.com; Akti Poseidonos; r €45-75; P ❄ 🛜 🏊) Set amid lush lawns with a shaded patio, and overlooking the nearby town beach, Corali has stuccowalled, fresh rooms with waffle quilts, balcony, large bathroom and tasteful furniture. You'll find them a few hundred yards out of Elounda heading for Plakia. The same family runs the **Portobello Apartments** (€65-75) next door.

⭐ Arodamos
GREEK €

(☑ 28410 41122; Naksou 6; mains €4-9; ⊙ 11am-late; 🛜) This hidden jewel sits two minutes' walk behind the square occupying a century-old cube house with Cycladic blue shutters and fronted by a garden of shady olive trees and palms. The menu is trad-Greek with meat cooked on the spit before your eyes: lamb chops, local sausage and *kondosouvli* (roasted liver wrapped in intestines).

ℹ Information

The post office and ATMs are on Elounda's main square, which doubles as a car park and overlooks the harbour.

Municipal Tourist Office (☑ 28410 42464; ⊙ 8am-8pm Jun-Oct) Helps with accommodation and information, and changes money.

Olous Travel (☑ 28410 41324) Handles air and boat tickets and finds accommodation. It's overlooking the main square.

ℹ Getting There & Around

Boats cross to Spinalonga Island every half-hour (return adult/child €10/5, 10 minutes).

There are 13 buses daily from Agios Nikolaos to Elounda (€1.70, 20 minutes).

There's a **taxi booth** (☑ 28410 41151) in the main square; it costs €13 to Agios Nikolaos.

Hire cars, motorcycles and scooters at available at **Elounda Travel** (☑ 28410 41800; www. eloundatravel.gr), which has several offices including one on the main square.

Spinalonga Island
Νήσος Σπιναλόγκα

Tiny **Spinalonga Island** (admission €2; ⊙ 9am-6pm) and its fortress lie in a picturesque setting just off the northern tip of the Kolokytha Peninsula and opposite the onshore village of Plaka. With the explosion of interest in Spinalonga in the wake of Victoria Hislop's romantic novel *The Island* (in Greek *To Nisi*), about the island's time as a leper colony, you're unlikely to feel lonely on the island. There's a reconstructed section of a street from the period featured in the novel, and although tour group leaders stir up a fine old babel, you can still enjoy a very pleasant stroll round the island, passing evocative ruins of churches, turrets and other buildings.

The Venetians built the formidable **fortress** (admission €3; ⊙ 10am-6pm) in 1579 to protect the bays of Elounda and Mirabello. Spinalonga finally surrendered to Ottoman forces in 1715.

From 1903 until 1955, during the post-Ottoman era, the island was a colony where Greeks suffering from leprosy (Hansen's disease) were quarantined. The early days of the colony were allegedly squalid and miserable. However, in 1953, the arrival of the charismatic Athenian sufferer and law student, Epaminondas Remoundakis, heralded the introduction of decent living conditions and of a redemptive spirit on the island. The colony finally closed in 1973. It is this dramatic and touching story around which Hislop weaves her tale.

The island had previously featured in a short film, *Last Words,* made in 1968 by Werner Herzog.

There's a cafe and souvenir shops here. Regular excursion boats visit Spinalonga from Agios Nikolaos (from €15). Ferries also run from Elounda (€10) and Plaka (€10).

Kritsa
Κριτσά

The fine traditions of the pretty mountain village of Kritsa (krit-*sah*), 11km southwest of Agios Nikolaos, are a touch blurred by the often insistent techniques of sellers of embroidered goods. The upper village, however, beneath rugged crags, is redolent with romantic decay and the ghosts of the past. Note that tour coaches pile into Kritsa from late morning until late afternoon.

About 1km before Kritsa is the turn-off to the photogenic 13th-century **Church of Panagia Kera** (☑ 28410 51806; admission €3; ⊙ 8.30am-3pm Tue-Sun), which contains some of the finest Byzantine frescoes in Crete.

There are hourly buses here from Agios Nikolaos (€1.60, 15 minutes). A taxi costs about €13.

Lato   Λατώ

About 4km north of Kritsa, the 7th century BC Dorian city of **Ancient Lato** (Λατώ; admission €2; ☺ 8.30am-3pm Tue-Sun) is one of Crete's few non-Minoan ancient sites. Lato (lah-*to*), once a powerful city state, sprawls over two acropolises in a gorgeous mountain setting overlooking the Gulf of Mirabello. It was named after Leto, the mother of Artemis and Apollo.

There are no buses to Lato. A taxi from Agios Nikolaos costs about €18.

Gournia   Γουρνιά

The Minoan settlement of **Gournia** (admission €3; ☺ 8.30am-3pm Tue-Sun) (goor-*nyah*) lies 19km southeast of Agios Nikolaos. Comprising a small palace overlooking residential areas, it was built between 1600 and 1500 BC, destroyed in 1450 BC and re-occupied from 1375 to 1200 BC. There are streets, stairways and houses with walls up to 2m high. Domestic, trade and agricultural implements discovered here indicate that Gournia was fairly prosperous.

When exploring the site, study the overview map just past the entrance, then follow a narrow ancient road as it curves uphill to the palace ruins, skirting **workshops** and **storage rooms**, including one where a clay wine press was found. The trail ends at the palace's central courtyard with steps on your right indicating the main entrance. On the opposite (western) side of the courtyard, smaller stairs lead down to an upright slab considered a **sacred stone**. There are 10 explanatory panels scattered around the site as well as a booklet (€5) for sale at the ticket kiosk.

Sitia and Ierapetra buses from Agios Nikolaos can drop you at the site.

Mohlos   Μόχλος

POP 121

At the end of a narrow road winding past massive quarries, tranquil Mohlos (*mohlos*) is an off-the-radar gem along Crete's northern shore. In this authentic fishing village time moves as gently as the waves lapping onto the pebble-and-grey-sand beach. There's little to do but relax and soak in the peacefulness.

Mohlos was once a thriving Early Minoan community and connected to the small island that is now 200m offshore. Swimmers should be wary of strong currents.

🛏 Sleeping & Eating

Hotel Sofia   HOTEL **€**
(☑ 28430 94554; sofia-mochlos@hotmail.com; r €35-45; ✷) Right by the sea this down-to-earth taverna has small rooms upstairs with wine-coloured bedspreads, antique armoire, fridge, bathroom and some with balconies. You pay a little extra for a sea view. The owners also have spacious apartments (€40 to €55) 200m east of the harbour, where longer stays are preferred.

★ **Petra Nova Villas**   VILLA **€€**
(☑ 6984 365277, 28430 94080; www.petranovavillas.gr; Mochlou St; apt €95-125; P ✷ 🛜) These stone villas blend seamlessly into the hillside and are just a few minutes' walk up the road from the waterfront. One- or two-bedroom options have private parking, boutique-style interiors, satellite TV and balconies. Contact Elaine for more info.

★ **Ta Kochilia**   GREEK **€€**
(☑ 28430 94432; mains €7; ☺ lunch & dinner; 🛜) Famed for its sea-urchin salad, which is available only in high summer, this pretty waterfront taverna, painted Cycladic white and blue, has a menu rich with pasta and traditional Cretan dishes like spinach pies, lamb with artichokes in lemon sauce, and oven-baked feta with tomatoes, peppers, oregano and olive oil.

ℹ Getting There & Away

Buses running between Agios Nikolaos and Sitia can drop you at the turn-off for Mohlos from where you'll need to hitch or walk the steep 6km.

Sitia   Σητεία
POP 9348

Sitia (si-*tee*-ah) is an attractive seaside town with a fishing harbour hemmed by a wide promenade lined with tavernas and cafes. Its whitewashed houses cling to the hillside bisected by steep staircases. It's a friendly place where tourism is fairly low key and the farming of wine and olives are the mainstays. A long, sandy beach skirts a wide bay to the east of town.

◉ Sights

Palm-tree studded Plateia Iroön Polytechniou is Sitia's main square.

Sitia Archaeological Museum MUSEUM

(☑28430 23917; Piskokefalou; admission €2; ⊗8.30am-3pm Tue-Sun) This museum houses an important collection of local finds spanning neolithic to Roman times, with emphasis on the Minoan civilisation. One of the most significant exhibits is the *Palekastro Kouros* – a figure pieced together from elements of hippopotamus tusks and gold. Finds from Zakros Palace include a winepress, bronze saw, jars, cult objects and pots that are clearly scorched from the great fire that destroyed the palace. English and Greek labelling.

Kazarma FORT

(Neas Ionias; ⊗8.30am-3pm) **FREE** Strategically perched atop a hill above town, this structure is locally called *kazarma* (from the Venetian *casa di arma*) and was built as a garrison by the Venetians. These are the only remains of the fortifications that once protected the town. The site is now used as an open-air venue.

⊨ Sleeping

El Greco Hotel HOTEL €

(☑28430 23133; www.elgreco-sitia.gr; G Arkadiou St; r incl breakfast €40-55; ❋☎) Smart and impeccably clean rooms with tiled floors, choice furniture, TV, fridge and balcony with sea views. Buffet breakfast in an attractive wood-beamed lobby.

Sitia Bay Hotel HOTEL €€

(☑28430 24800; www.sitiabay.com; s/d €105/120; ᴘ❋☎⊠) Modern hotel with friendly service of the highest order. Most of the comfortable and tasteful one- and two-room apartments have sea views, and there's a pool, hydrospa, minigym and sauna. Breakfast is €6.

✖ Eating & Drinking

★ Zorba's Tavern TAVERNA €

(Plateia Iroon Polytehniou; mains €8; ⊗noon-late) Gregarious owner Zorba, with his sailor's roll, sea captain's cap and bushy moustache, looks as if he's stepped from a traditional Greek painting. And traditional is what this place excels in: think bouzouki music, blue tables and chairs, and the rich aromas of home-cooked food. Succulent lamb chops, zingy salads and many more. Your taste buds will be jumping!

Balcony FUSION €€

(☑28430 25084; www.balcony-restaurant.com; Foundalidou 19; mains €13-20; ⊗lunch & dinner; ☎) The most stylish dining in Sitia is on the 1st floor of a purple and cream neoclassical building where owner-chef Tonya Karandinou rules supreme with a sense of theatre. Cretan-based cuisine, with Mexican and Asian influences, ranges from grilled squid to tender goat. Fine Greek wines complement it all.

ⓘ Information

There are several banks with ATMs in the centre of town. Cash up here if you're headed further east as there is only one other ATM in Palekastro.

Post office (Dimokritou; ⊗7.30am-3pm) Heading inland, it's the first left off El Venizelou.

Tourist office (☑28430 28300; Karamanli; ⊗9.30am-2.30pm & 5-8.30pm Mon-Fri, 9.30am-2pm Sat) Winter opening hours may be uncertain. On the promenade.

Tzortzakis Travel (☑29211; www.tzortzakistravel.com; 17 M Alexandrou St; ⊗9am-9pm) This helpful travel agency books rooms, flights and boats as well as organising car hire.

ⓘ Getting There & Away

AIR

Sitia's **airport** (☑28430 24666) has an expanded international-size runway, with summer flights to Amsterdam and Lyon.

Astra Airlines (www.astra-airlines.gr) has five weekly flights to Athens (€68, one hour). **Olympic Air** (www.olympicair.com) has daily flights to Kassos (€57, 20 minutes) and then on to Karpathos (€63, one hour) and Rhodes (€63, two hours).

BOAT

Aegeon Pelagos Sea Lines (EP; ☑Hania 28210 24000) has two ferries a week from Sitia to Iraklio (€11, three hours), Milos (€25, 11½ hours), Piraeus (€41, 17 hours), Santorini (€26, 7½ hours) and Rhodes (€27, nine hours 20 minutes). There are four ferries a week to Kassos (€11, 2½ hours) and Karpathos (€18, four hours). Several of these departures are in the early hours of the morning.

BUS

From Sitia's **bus station** (☑28430 22272) there are six buses daily to Ierapetra (€8, 1½ hours), seven buses to Iraklio (€14, three hours) via Agios Nikolaos (€8, 1½ hours), four to Vaï (€3, 30 minutes), and two to Kato Zakros (€8, one hour) via Palekastro (€5, 45 minutes) and Zakros (€8, one hour). The buses to Vaï and Kato Zakros only run between May and October.

Around Sitia

Moni Toplou   Μονή Τοπλού

Perched in splendid isolation on a wind-swept bluff above the sea, **Moni Toplou** (☑ 28430 61226; admission €3; ☺ 10am-5pm Apr-Oct, Fri only Nov-Mar) is one of the most histori-cally significant monasteries in Crete, whose defences were tested by all, from pirates to crusading knights and the Turks. It is also one of the wealthiest, owning vast sweeps of land, including the beach at Vaï, and pro-ducing excellent wine and olive oil.

Its most prized possession is the stun-ningly intricate **Megas i Kyrie** (Lord Thou Art Great) icon by celebrated Cretan artist Ioannis Kornaros. Sixty-one scenes from the Old and New Testaments are depicted; see if you can find Noah's Ark, Jonah and the Whale or Moses parting the Red Sea. Other rooms hold more icons, copper engravings and a WWII memorial exhibit.

The monastery is about 18km east of Si-tia. It's a 3km walk from the Sitia–Palekastro road. Buses can drop you off at the junction. A taxi from Sitia costs about €22.

Vaï   Βάι

The beach at Vaï, 24km east of Sitia, is fa-mous for its large grove of Phoenix theo-phrastii palms. With calm, clear waters, it is one of Crete's most popular strands, whose rows of umbrellas and sunbeds (€6) often get filled by 10am in July and August. Jet skis kick into gear shortly thereafter. In oth-er words, come early or after 5pm to appre-ciate Vaï's natural beauty in tranquillity.

If you want a nice beach without the crowds (or the palms), take the 1km scram-ble east over the rocky headland; there are no facilities, so pack everything you need. The trail starts just past the gazebo lookout reached via stone steps leading up from the reasonably priced taverna.

There are five buses daily to Vaï from Sitia (€3, one hour) from May to October. Parking is €3.

Zakros & Kato Zakros
Ζάκρος & Κάτω Ζάκρος

POP 640 & 22

Zakros (*zah*-kros), 45km southeast of Sitia, is the starting point for the trail through the Zakros Gorge, known as the Valley of the Dead due to the ancient burial sites in the caves that honeycomb the canyon walls. Zakros, however, is a mere prelude to coast-al Kato Zakros, 7km down a winding road through rugged terrain. Halfway down, it loops left to reveal a vast curtain of moun-tains and the red jaws of the Zakros Gorge breaching the cliffs. Behind Kato Zakros' pebbly beach and its huddle of tavernas, the remarkable ruins of the Minoan Zakros Pal-ace are clearly defined.

◎ Sights & Activities

Zakros Palace   ARCHAEOLOGICAL SITE
(☑ 28410 22462; Kato Zakros; adult/child €3/free; ☺ 8.30am-3pm) Although Zakros Palace was the last Minoan palace to have been discov-ered (1962), the excavations proved remark-ably fruitful. The exquisite rock-crystal vase and stone bull's head, now in Heraklion Archaeological Museum, were found at Zak-ros, along with a treasure trove of Minoan antiquities. Ancient Zakros, the smallest of Crete's four palatial complexes, was a major port in Minoan times, trading with Egypt, Syria, Anatolia and Cyprus. Some parts of the palace complex are submerged.

Pelekita Cave   CAVE
In Karoumbi, 3km from Kato Zakros, this extraordinary 300m-long cave cave has magnificent views of the sea 100m below, and signs of neolithic habitation within its stalactite/stalagmite-rich interior. To explore it bring a torch and trainers.

Zakros Gorge   WALKING
This easy 8km walk starts from just below Zakros village and winds its way through a narrow and (at times) soaring canyon with a riot of vegetation and wild herbs before emerging close to Zakros Palace, 200m from the beach. For a shorter walk, pick up the trailhead about 3km down the road to Kato Zakros. A taxi back to Zakros costs about €6.

⌂ Sleeping & Eating

Head to Kato Zakros for a spectrum of ac-commodation from simple rooms to downright beautiful digs. Rooms here fill up fast in high season, so it is best to book.

Katerina Apartments
APARTMENT €

(☑ 2843026893; www.katozakros.cretefamilyhotels .com; Kato Zakros; apt €50-60) High up on the hillside overlooking Kato Zakros, with turquoise surf and an ancient ruined palace far below, the four excellent stone-built studios and maisonettes here can sleep up to four and, clearly, enjoy a superb setting.

★ Terra Minoika
VILLAS €€

(☑ 28430 23739; www.stelapts.com; Kato Zakros; villa €120; P ❋ 🛜) Set high on the hillside overlooking the surf below, these stone cube houses are breathtaking; imagine wood-beamed ceilings, widescreen views from balconies, chic rustic furniture, urns mounted on walls, and stone floors. Incurably romantic, every villa is individual and has a fully equipped kitchenette.

Akrogiali Taverna
CRETAN €

(☑ 28430 26893; Kato Zakros; mains €8; ⊙ 8am-midnight; 🛜) Decked in blue and white, this pretty seafront taverna is packed to the gills with lobster, swordfish and souvlaki. The squid portions are huge and the salads are full of vim.

❶ Getting There & Away

There are buses to Zakros from Sitia via Palekastro (€4.50, one hour, two daily). From June to August, the buses continue to Kato Zakros (€5.20, one hour 20 minutes). Buses to Kato Zakros only run between May and October.

Ierapetra   Ιεράπετρα

POP 12,355

Ierapetra (yeh-*rah*-pet-rah) is a laid-back seafront town and the commercial centre of southeastern Crete's substantial greenhouse-based agribusiness. Hot and dusty in summer, it offers a low-key, authentic Cretan experience and is also the jumping-off point to the semitropical Gaïdouronisi Island (also called Hrysi). The local grey-sand beaches are extensive and backed by tavernas and cafes where the nightlife is busy in summer.

Though little is left, Ierapetra has an impressive history with interludes as a Roman port for conquering Egypt and a Venetian stronghold based on the still-standing harbour fortress. The narrow alleyways of the Turkish quarter recall its Ottoman past.

◉ Sights & Activities

Ierapetra's main town **beach** is near the harbour, while a second beach stretches east from Patriarhou Metaxaki. Both have coarse grey sand, but the main beach has more shade.

Ierapetra Archaeological Museum
MUSEUM

(☑ 28420 28721; Adrianou 2; admission €2; ⊙ 8.30am-3pm Tue-Sun) Ierapetra's small but worthwhile archaeological collection is located in a former school of the Ottoman period. A highlight among a collection of headless classical statuary is an intact statue of the goddess Persephone that dates from the 2nd century AD. Another splendid piece is a big *larnax* (clay coffin), dated around 1300 BC, that is decorated with 12 painted panels showing hunting scenes, an octopus and a chariot procession.

Kales Fortress
FORTRESS

(⊙ 8.30am-3pm Tue-Sun) **FREE** South along the waterfront is the medieval fortress, built in the early years of Venetian rule and strengthened by Francesco Morosini in 1626. Climb to the upper walls (watch your footing) for grand views to the eastern mountains.

⌷ Sleeping

★ Cretan Villa Hotel
HOTEL €

(☑ 28420 28522; www.cretan-villa.com; Lakerda 16; d/tr €50/70; ❋ 🛜) Hidden in the centre of town behind a thick wooden door leading into a vine-shaded courtyard, this is a restful, friendly space with beautiful rooms boasting stained glass windows, fine furniture, large bathrooms, wood-beamed ceilings and satellite TV. The management are especially helpful. It's only a few minutes' walk from the bus station.

Akrolithos Apartments
APARTMENT €€

(☑ 28420 28522; www.ierapetra-apartments.net; Lakerda 16; apt €70; ❋ 🛜) These recently refurbished apartments have stunning interiors with original fireplaces, well-equipped kitchenettes, loads of space and a great central location. You may not want to leave they are so cosy.

✗ Eating & Drinking

The waterfront is lined with cafes and tavernas, many of them quite authentic and reasonably priced. Nightclubs line Kyvra.

Napoleon GREEK €

(☑28420 22410; Stratigou Samouil 26; mains €6; ⊙noon-midnight; ☏☑) This capacious traditional Cretan place has a covered area by the sea flanked by palm trees and an attractive restaurant. Expect tasty dolmadhes, snails, spinach pies, calamari and inkfish risotto.

ⓘ Information

Banks and ATMs dot Plateia Eleftherias and Lasthenous.

Ierapetra Express (☑28420 28673; express@ier.forthnet.gr; Kothri 2; ⊙9am-9pm) Central tourist office with friendly service and good information.

Post Office (Koraka 25; ⊙7.30am-2pm)

ⓘ Getting There & Away

There are nine buses per day from Ierapetra's **bus station** (☑28420 28237; www.ktelherlas.gr; Lasthenous) to Iraklio (€11, 2½ hours) via Agios Nikolaos (€3.80, one hour) and Gournia (€2.10, 40 minutes), plus seven to Sitia (€6.30, 1½ hours) and seven to Myrtos (€2.20, 30 minutes).

Taxi (☑28420 26600) fares are posted outside the town-hall rank: Iraklio (€110), Agios Nikolaos (€45), Sitia (€75) and Myrtos (€20).

Auto Tours (☑28420 22571; Plateia Plastira; per day from €25; ⊙9am-8pm) is reliable for car hire.

Myrtos Μύρτος

POP 622

Little known Myrtos (*myr*-tos), 14km west of Ierapetra, is fringed by an apron of dark sand and electric-blue water, and offers a slow boho pulse, with a few wind-battered, sun-bleached boutiques and guesthouses, plus a cluster of tavernas on its languid seafront.

🛏 Sleeping & Eating

★**Big Blue** APARTMENT €

(☑28420 51094; www.big-blue.gr; studio €30-40, apt €50-80; ℗✳☏) Modern amenities meet trad-Greece in these exquisite sea-facing studios with white walls hung with fine art. Balconies boast expansive views and awnings, and thanks to its elevation, the views are jawdropping. Apartment 'Blue Eye' has a stunning pop art display of *mati* (evil eye); in fact, every room is different. Out front there is a fragrant garden for sundowners.

Villa Mertiza APARTMENT €€

(☑6932735224, 28420 51208; www.mertiza.com; studio/apt €55/€65; ✳☏) Owned by a friendly Dutch guy, these are tastefully finished studios and apartments with self-catering facilities, Moroccan wall hangings and walls peppered with stunning photography. Rooms enjoy fresh bathrooms, flat-screen TVs and generous dimensions. There's also a book exchange. The owners also have some lovely villas (€110) a little further out, and other accommodation options.

★**Thalassa Taverna** GREEK €

(mains €8-12; ⊙10am-midnight; ✳☏) This powder-blue, hole-in-the-wall waterfront restaurant has an interior festooned with coral and shells, and a few tables outside to tuck into mussels, calamari, cuttlefish, shrimps, octopus... Enough seafood to keep a shoal of mermaids quiet.

★**Katerina** CRETAN €€

(☑6948325739; mains €5.50-19.50; ⊙lunch & dinner) Your taste buds will do somersaults at Katerina, where Yiannis is the kind of chef that puts a creative mark on even the most classic dishes. Don't overdose on the homemade bread that accompanies the free appetiser to enjoy such flavour-bombs as the aromatic lamb *kleftiko*, the ouzo-flambéed *saganaki* (fried cheese) and the gooey chocolate cake. Foodies might also be interested in Yiannis' **herb-collecting tours** and **cooking courses**.

ⓘ Getting There & Away

Seven daily buses go from Ierapetra to Myrtos (€2.20, 20 minutes).

Lasithi Plateau Οροπέδιο Λασιθίου

The tranquil Lasithi Plateau, 900m above sea level, is a vast expanse of green fields interspersed with almond trees and orchards. Hemmed in by the cloudy peaks of the rock-studded Dikti range, it is arrestingly beautiful, and offers a glimpse of secluded, rural Crete at its most authentic. Lasithi would have been a stunning sight in the 17th century when it was dotted with some 20,000 windmills with white canvas sails, which the Venetians built for irrigation purposes. The few that remain are an iconic (and much photographed) sight.

ℹ️ Getting There & Away

The Lasithi Plateau is the domain of tour buses and is poorly served by public ones. There's only one bus daily from Iraklio to Tzermiado (€6.50, two hours), Agios Georgios (€6.90, two hours) and Psyhro (€6.50, 2¼ hours). There are also buses to the villages from Agios Nikolaos.

By car, the main approach is by turning south off the coastal highway near Stalida, just past Hersonisos. The best approach from Agios Nikolaos is via Neapoli.

Tzermiado   Τζερμιάδο

The largest of Lasithi's 20 villages, Tzermiado (dzer-mee-*ah*-do) is still a bucolic place. **Taverna Kourites** (www.kourites.eu; mains €7.50-10.50; ⊙9am-10pm) does a brisk lunchtime business with coaches full of day-trippers. At other times, it's a large and peaceful spot where menu options include top-notch lamb and suckling pig roasted in a wood-fired oven. There are clean and simple rooms above the taverna and in a nearby small hotel (doubles €40).

For a more upscale rural retreat, head to **Argoulias** (☑28440 22754; www.argoulias.gr; d incl breakfast €55-80; ✼), a set of studios in stone houses built into the hillside high above the main Tzermiado village (great views!), with an excellent restaurant just across the road.

Tzermiado has two ATMs, two petrol stations and a post office.

Agios Georgios   Αγιος Γεώργιος

The quiet little village of Agios Georgios (*agh*-ios ye-*or*-gios) is a relaxing base. The intriguing **Folklore Museum** (☑28440 31462; admission €3; ⊙10am-4pm Apr-Oct) has eclectic exhibits including farming tools and WWI relics. The pleasantly quirky rooms at **Hotel Maria** (☑28440 31774; d/tr/q incl breakfast €60/80/100), on the northern side of the village, are fronted by a leafy garden. For eats, try **Taverna Rea** (mains €7-8; ⊙9am-10pm), a bright artefact-filled place on the main street. Rooms above the taverna rent for €30.

Psyhro & Dikteon Cave
Ψυχρό & Δικταίον Αντρον

Psyhro (psi-*hro*) is the closest village to **Dikteon Cave** (Cave of Psyhro; ☑28410 22462, 28440 31316; http://odysseus.culture.gr; admission €4; ⊙8am-8pm Apr-Oct, 8.30am-3pm Nov-Mar) and is often clogged with tour buses. According to legend, Rhea hid in this cave to give birth to Zeus, far from the clutches of his offspring-gobbling father Cronos. Corkscrewing up the slick, wet dark, the vertiginous staircase passes through overhanging stalactites formed over millenia. Numerous votives discovered here indicate cult worship since ancient times.

It is a steep 15-minute (800m) walk up to the cave entrance, either via a rocky but shaded natural trail or the unshaded paved path on the left of the car park. Parking is €2.

There are numerous tourist taverns in town and snack stands in the parking lot.

Dodecanese

Best Places to Eat

➜ Marco Polo Cafe (p483)
➜ Taverna Mylos (p532)
➜ To Hellenikon (p492)
➜ Tholos (p503)
➜ Pote Tin Kyriaki (p515)

Best Places to Stay

➜ Marco Polo Mansion (p481)
➜ Harry's Paradise (p529)
➜ Archontariki (p539)
➜ Hotel Fiona (p502)
➜ Nefeli Hotel (p541)

Why Go?

Ever pined for the old Greece, where timeless islands beckon modern-day adventurers just as they did Odysseus and Alexander? Enter the far-flung Dodecanese (Δωδεκάνησα; do-de-*ka*-ni-sa) archipelago, curving through the southeastern Aegean parallel to the ever-visible shoreline of Turkey. The footprints of everyone from Greeks and Romans to crusading medieval knights, Byzantine and Ottoman potentates to 20th-century Italian bureaucrats, are found here, and islands beyond better-known Rhodes and Kos beg to be explored.

Hikers and naturalists flock to Tilos, while climbers scale the limestone cliffs in Kalymnos. Aesthetes adore the neoclassical mansions of Symi, Halki and Kastellorizo, divers explore underwater caves and ancient wrecks, and kitesurfers blow in to Karpathos for its legendary winds. Archaeologists and history buffs let their imaginations loose on a bevy of ancient sites, while sybarites can worship Helios on myriad beaches, far from the package crowds.

When to Go
Rhodes

Apr & May Prices are low, few tourists are around and the sea is warming up.

Jul & Aug Peak season for accommodation and visitors – book ahead.

Sep & Oct Great time to come: low prices, warm seas and perfect hiking weather.

Dodecanese Highlights

1 Wandering beneath Byzantine arches and along the ancient cobbled alleyways of **Rhodes' Old Town** (p475).

2 Following the winding road up to the timeless mountain-top village of **Olymbos** (p495).

3 Testing your mettle diving for wrecks or climbing limestone cliffs on **Kalymnos** (p525).

4 Finding the beach of your dreams on **Lipsi** (p541).

5 Hiking or birdwatching on postcard-perfect **Tilos** (p505).

6 Entering the fabled volcano of **Nisyros** (p511).

home to an imprisoned Titan.

7 Feeling your pulse quicken as your boat pulls into the gorgeous Italianate harbour of **Symi** (p500).

8 Making a pilgrimage to **Patmos** (p535), where St John experienced his 'Revelations'.

History

The Dodecanese islands have been inhabited since pre-Minoan times. After the death of Alexander the Great in 323 BC, they were ruled by Ptolemy I of Egypt. The islanders later became the first Greeks to convert to Christianity, thanks to the tireless efforts of St Paul, who made two journeys to the archipelago during the 1st century, and St John the Divine, who was banished to Patmos, where he had his Revelation and added a chapter to the Bible.

The early Byzantine era saw the islands prosper, but by the 7th century AD they were being plundered by a string of invaders. The Knights of St John of Jerusalem (Knights Hospitaller), who arrived during the 14th century, eventually ruled almost all the Dodecanese. Their mighty fortifications have proved strong enough to withstand time, but failed to keep out the Turks in 1522.

The Turks were in turn ousted in 1912 by the Italians, who made Italian the official language and banned the Orthodox religion. Inspired by Mussolini's vision of a vast Mediterranean empire, they also constructed grandiose public buildings in the fascist style, the antithesis of archetypal Greek architecture. More beneficially, they excavated and restored many archaeological monuments.

Rhodes

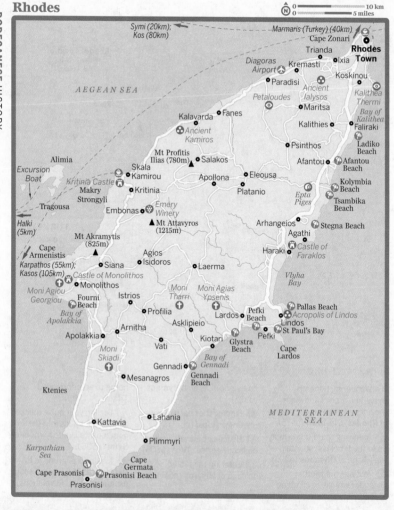

After the Italian surrender of 1943, the islands (particularly Leros) became a battleground for British and German forces, inflicting much suffering upon the population. The Dodecanese were formally returned to Greece in 1947.

RHODES ΡΟΔΟΣ

POP 115,000

By far the largest and always the most powerful of the Dodecanese islands, Rhodes (*rodos*) abounds in beaches, wooded valleys and ancient history. Whether you arrive in search of buzzing nightlife, languid sun worshipping or diving in crystal-clear waters, or embark on a culture-vulture journey through past civilisations, it's all here. The atmospheric Old Town of Rhodes is a maze of cobbled streets that will spirit you back to the days of the Byzantine Empire and beyond. Further south is the picture-perfect town of Lindos, a magical vision of sugar-cube houses spilling down to a turquoise bay.

History

The Minoans and Mycenaeans were among the first to have outposts on Rhodes, but only with the arrival of the Dorians in 1100 BC – settling in Kamiros, Ialysos and Lindos – did the island begin to make itself felt. Switching allegiances like a pendulum, Rhodes was allied to Athens when the Persians were defeated in the Battle of Marathon (490 BC), but had shifted to the Persian side by the time of the Battle of Salamis (480 BC).

After the unexpected Athenian victory at Salamis, Rhodes hastily aligned itself with Athens once more, joining the Delian League in 477 BC. Following the disastrous Sicilian Expedition (416–412 BC), Rhodes revolted against Athens and hooked up with Sparta instead, aiding it in the Peloponnesian Wars. In 408 BC the cities of Kamiros, Ialysos and Lindos consolidated their powers, cofounding the city of Rhodes. Rhodes became Athens' ally again to defeat Sparta at the Battle of Knidos (394 BC). Rhodes then joined forces with Persia to fight against Alexander the Great, only to attach itself to Alexander when he proved invincible.

In 305 BC Antigonus, a rival of Ptolemy, sent his formidable son, Demetrius Poliorketes – Besieger of Cities – to conquer Rhodes. When the city managed to repel Demetrius after a long siege, it built a 32m-high bronze statue of Helios Apollo to celebrate. Known as the Colossus of Rhodes (p475), it was later hailed as one of the Seven Wonders of the Ancient World.

Rhodes now knew no bounds. It built the biggest navy in the Aegean, and its port became a principal Mediterranean trading centre. The arts flourished. When Greece became the arena in which Roman generals fought for leadership of the empire, Rhodes allied itself with Julius Caesar. After Caesar's assassination in 44 BC, Cassius besieged the city, destroying its ships and carting its artworks off to Rome. Rhodes went into decline and became part of the Roman Empire in AD 70.

Rhodes eventually joined the Byzantine province of the Dodecanese and was granted independence when the Crusaders seized Constantinople. Later, the Genoese gained control. Next to arrive, in 1309, were the Knights of St John, who ruled Rhodes for 213 years until being ousted by the Ottomans. They were in turn kicked out by the Italians nearly four centuries later. In 1947, after 35 years of Italian occupation, Rhodes finally became part of Greece, along with the other Dodecanese islands.

ℹ Getting There & Away

AIR

Olympic Air (✈ 22410 24571; www.olympicair. com; Ierou Lohou 9) connects Rhodes' Diagoras airport with Athens and destinations throughout Greece, including several Dodecanese islands. Flights to the nearby islands of Kassos, Karpathos and Kastellorizo are more frequent than the corresponding ferries and, with fares starting at less than €50, only slightly more expensive.

Minoan Air (www.minoanair.com) flies up to four days a week to Heraklion (Crete; €69, one hour) and once weekly to Santorini (€79,50 minutes).

BOAT

Rhodes is the main port in the Dodecanese. Two interisland ferry operators operate from the Commercial Harbour, immediately outside the walls of Rhodes Old Town. **Dodekanisos Seaways** (Map p480; ✈ 22410 70590; www.12ne.gr; Afstralias 3, Rhodes Town) runs daily high-speed catamarans north up the chain, while **Blue Star Ferries** (✈ 21089 19800; www.bluestarferries. com) provides slower and less frequent services to several of the same islands, continuing west to Astypalea and Piraeus. It also heads southwest to Karpathos, Kasos and Crete. Tickets are available at the dock and from travel agents in Rhodes Town.

The tiny port at Skala Kamirou, 45km southwest of Rhodes Town, has a daily ferry service to the island of Halki, operated by **Nissos Halki** (✈ 6973460968) and **Nikos Express**

(☑ 6946826905). There's an hour-long connecting bus service with Rhodes Old Town.

In addition, daily excursion boats head to Symi from Mandraki Harbour in summer (day trips only, €25). Check out the boats at the harbour before you decide which to take.

International

Catamarans connect Rhodes' Commercial Harbour with Marmaris, Turkey (50 minutes), with two daily services in summer and two weekly in winter. Tickets cost €27 each way, plus €13 Turkish port tax. Same-day returns cost €45, including tax, and longer-stay returns, €63. For schedules and bookings, visit www.rhodes. marmarisinfo.com.

Boat Services from Rhodes

DESTINATION	TIME	FARE	FREQUENCY
Agathonisi*	5hr	€46	1 weekly
Astypalea	9hr	€32	1 weekly
Halki	2hr	€9	3 weekly
Halki*	1¼hr	€16	2 weekly
Kalymnos	6hr	€19	3 weekly
Kalymnos*	3hr	€38	1 daily
Karpathos	5hr 40min	€20	3 weekly
Kasos	8hr	€24	3 weekly
Kastellorizo	4hr 40min	€22	2 weekly
Kastellorizo*	2hr 20min	€36	1 weekly
Kos	5hr	€23	3 weekly
Kos*	2½hr	€30	1 daily
Leros	8hr	€30	1 weekly
Leros*	3½hr	€41	5 weekly
Lipsi	9hr	€25	1 weekly
Lipsi*	5½hr	€45	5 weekly
Nisyros	4hr	€13	2 weekly
Nisyros*	2¾hr	€28	2 weekly
Patmos	10hr	€37	1 weekly
Patmos*	5hr	€46	4 weekly
Piraeus	18hr	€44	3 weekly
Samos	6hr 40min	€55	1 weekly
Sitia	11hr	€27	2 weekly
Symi	1hr 40min	€13	2 weekly
Symi*	50min	€17	1-4 daily
Tilos	2½hr	€14	2 weekly
Tilos*	2hr	€25	2 weekly

* high-speed services

All boats listed depart from the Commercial Harbour.

❶ Getting Around

TO/FROM THE AIRPORT

Diagoras airport is near Paradisi on the west coast, 16km southwest of Rhodes Town. Taxis charge a set fare of €22 to Rhodes Town, while buses connect the airport with Rhodes Town's Eastern Bus Terminal (€2.40, 25 minutes) between 6.30am and 11.15pm daily.

BICYCLE

Bicycles are available for rent from Margaritis in the New Town.

BOAT

The quay at Mandraki Harbour is lined with excursion boats offering day trips to east-coast towns and beaches, including Faliraki and Lindos, and also to the island of Symi.

Several islands can also be visited as day trips on Dodekanisos Seaways (p473) catamarans, departing from the Commercial Harbour. These include Symi and Kos (both daily), Halki and Tilos (twice weekly), and Kastellorizo (once weekly).

BUS

Two bus terminals, a block apart in Rhodes Town, serve half the island each. There is regular transport across the island all week, with fewer services on Saturday and only a few on Sunday. Pick up schedules from the kiosks at either terminal, or from the EOT (Greek National Tourist Organisation; p484) office.

The **Eastern Bus Terminal** (Map p476; ☑ 22410 27706; www.ktelrodou.gr) has frequent services to the airport (€2.40), Kalithea Thermi (€2.20), Salakos (€4.30), Ancient Kamiros (€5) and Monolithos (€6). From the **Western Bus Terminal** (Map p476; ☑ 22410 26300) there are services to Faliraki (€2.20), Tsambika Beach (€3.50), Stegna Beach (€4) and Lindos (€5).

CAR & MOTORCYCLE

All the major car-rental chains are represented at Rhodes airport, and plenty more car- and motorcycle-rental outlets are scattered throughout Rhodes Town and the resorts. Competition is fierce, so shop around. Several agencies will deliver vehicles to renters.

Drive Rent A Car (☑ 22410 68243, 22410 81011; www.driverentacar.gr; Diagoras Airport) Sturdier, newer scooters and cars.

Margaritis (☑ 22410 37420; I Kazouli St 17) Reliable cars, scooters and bicycles in the New Town.

TAXI

Rhodes Town's main taxi rank is east of Plateia Rimini, on the northern edge of the Old Town. There are two zones on the island for taxi meters: zone one is Rhodes Town and zone two (for which rates are slightly higher) is everywhere else. Rates double between midnight and

5am. Set taxi fares are posted at the rank and include the airport €22, Faliraki €17, Kalithea €9 and Lindos €55. You can also phone for a taxi (☑ 22410 69800 in Rhodes Town, ☑ 22410 69600 outside Rhodes Town) or disabled-accessible taxi (☑ 22410 77079). Note that taxis cannot access most locations in the largely pedestrianised Old Town; expect to be dropped at the gate nearest your destination.

Rhodes Town   Ρόδος

POP 86,000

Rhodes Town is really two distinct and very different towns. The Old Town lies within but utterly apart from the New Town, sealed like a medieval time capsule behind a double ring of high walls and a deep moat. Nowhere else in the Dodecanese can boast so many layers of architectural history, with ruins and relics of the classical, medieval, Ottoman and Italian eras entangled in a mind-boggling maze of twisting alleys. Strolling its hauntingly pretty cobbled lanes, especially at night, is an experience no traveller should miss. Half the fun is letting yourself get lost. The New Town, to the north, boasts upscale shops and waterfront bars servicing the package crowd, along with the city's best beach, while bistros and bars lurk in the backstreets behind.

Interisland ferries and catamarans use the **Commercial Harbour**, just outside the walls east of the Old Town. Excursion boats and private yachts are based at **Mandraki Harbour**, further north beside the New Town.

◉ Sights

◉ Old Town

A glorious mixture of Byzantine, Turkish and Italian architecture, erected atop far more ancient and largely unidentifiable remains, the Old Town is a world of its own. In theory, it consists of three separate sections, though casual visitors seldom notice the transition from one to the next. To the north, sturdy stone mansions line the arrow-straight streets of the **Knights' Quarter**, laid out by the medieval Knights of St John. South of that, the **Hora**, also known as the Turkish Quarter, is a tangle of cobbled alleyways that's now the main commercial hub, packed with restaurants and shops as well as derelict mosques and Muslim monuments. The **Jewish Quarter** in the southeast, which lost most of its inhabitants during World War II, is now a sleepy residential district.

Although there's no public access to the imposing 12m-thick ramparts that encircle the Old Town, you can descend at various points into the broad moat that separates the inner and outer walls. Now filled with lush gardens rather than water, the moat makes for a great stroll and is ideal for picnickers.

Of the nine *pyles* (gateways) to the Old Town, the busiest and most dramatic are the northernmost two, closest to the New Town. **Liberty Gate** (Map p480), the nearest to Mandraki Harbour and the taxi rank, leads to a small bridge and on towards the main tourist areas, while the atmospheric **D'Amboise Gate** (Map p480), further inland, crosses an especially attractive section of the moat en route to the Palace of the Grand Master.

★ **Archaeological Museum**   MUSEUM
(Map p480; ☑ 22410 65256; Plateia Mousiou; admission €6; ⊙ 8am-8pm) By far the best museum in the Dodecanese, spreading through the 15th-century Knights' Hospital and out into its beautiful and surprisingly wild gardens. Room after room holds magnificently preserved ancient treasures, excavated from all over the island and ranging over 7000 years. Highlights include an exquisite marble statue of Aphrodite from the 2nd century BC, a pavilion displaying wall-mounted mosaics, and a reconstructed burial site

THE COLOSSUS OF RHODES

A giant bronze statue of the sun god Helios, the Colossus of Rhodes was erected to celebrate the end of an unsuccessful siege of Rhodes. It took 12 years to build, was completed in 292 BC, and stood for less than a century, before being toppled by an earthquake in 227 BC.

The statue became remembered as one of the Seven Wonders of the Ancient World because, according to legend, its two legs straddled the entrance to what's now Mandraki Harbour – so tall that high-masted triremes were able to pass beneath. While historians argue that can't possibly have been true, it's known that the Colossus remained in ruins on the waterfront for almost 1000 years. It was broken into pieces and sold by invading Arabs to a Syrian Jew in 654 AD, who supposedly transported it abroad on the backs of 900 camels.

Rhodes Town

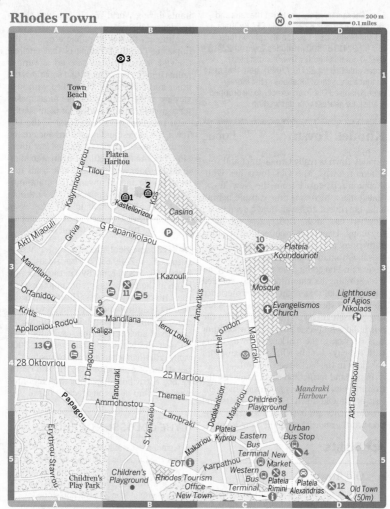

0 — 200 m
0 — 0.1 miles

Town Beach

Plateia Haritou

Tilou

Kalymnou-Lerou

Plateia Haritou

Kastellorizou

Kos

Casino

Akti Miaouli

Griva

G Papanikolaou

Mandilana

Orfanidou

Kritis

Apolloniou Rodou

I Kazouli

Mandilana

Kaliga

Ierou Lohou

Amerikis

Ethel ondon

Mosque

Evangelismos Church

Plateia Koundourioti

Lighthouse of Agios Nikolaos

13

6

28 Oktovriou

I Dragoum

Fanouraki

25 Martiou

Themeli

Ammohostou

S Venizelou

Lambraki

Makariou

Dodekanision

Makariou

Plateia Kyprou

Mandraki

Mandraki Harbour

Akti Boumbouli

Children's Playground

Urban Bus Stop

Papagou

Erythrou Stavrou

Children's Play Park

Children's Playground

EOT

Rhodes Tourism Office – New Town

Eastern Bus Terminal

Karpathou

Western Bus Terminal

New Market

Plateia Rimini

Plateia Alexandrias

Old Town (50m)

DODECANESE RHODES TOWN

from 1700 BC that held not only a helmeted warrior but also his horse.

Palace of the Grand Master HISTORIC BUILDING
(Map p480; ☎ 22410 65270; admission €6; ⊙ 8.30am-8pm) From the outside, the magnificent Palace of the Grand Master looks much as it did when erected by the Knights Hospitaller during the 14th century. During the 19th century, however, it was devastated by an explosion, so the interior as you see it today is an Italian reconstruction, completed in the '18th year of the Fascist Era' (1940). The dreary magisterial chambers upstairs hold haphazard looted artworks, so the most interesting section is the exhibit on ancient Rhodes downstairs.

Street of the Knights HISTORIC SITE
(Map p480; Ippoton) Austere and uncommercialised, the Street of the Knights (Ippoton, in Greek) was home from the 14th century to the Knights Hospitaller who ruled Rhodes. They were divided by birthplace into seven 'tongues', or languages – England, France, Germany, Italy, Aragon, Auvergne and Provence – each responsible for a specific section of the fortifications. As wall displays explain, the street holds an 'inn', or palace, for each tongue. Its modern appear-

ance, though, owes much to Italian restorations during the 1930s.

Jewish Synagogue Museum   MUSEUM
(Map p480; ☏22410 22364; www.rhodesjewish museum.org; Dosiadou; ◷10am-3pm Sun-Fri May-Oct) **FREE** In the 1920s, the Old Town's Jewish Quarter was home to a thriving Jewish community of around 4000 people. Tragically, 1673 Rhodian Jews were sent to Auschwitz in 1944 and it's now a time-forgotten neighbourhood of sleepy streets and dilapidated houses. Early 20th-century photos and intricately decorated documents in the museum, which adjoins Greece's oldest synagogue, the 1577 **Kahal Shalom Synagogue** (Polydorou 5), tell the whole story.

Muslim Library   LIBRARY
(Map p480; Sokratous; ◷9.30am-3pm Mon-Sat) **FREE** After the Ottomans captured Rhodes in 1522, the Old Town acquired a crop of Muslim monuments, with many churches being converted to mosques. Sadly, this peaceful little library, founded in 1794, is the only Muslim site currently open to visitors and, with just a handful of minimally captioned exhibits in its one room, there's little to see. It can only be hoped that the pink-domed **Mosque of Süleyman** opposite, and the **hammam** (Plateia Arionis) nearby, will reopen soon.

Museum of Decorative Arts   MUSEUM
(Map p480; ☏22410 65246; Plateia Argyrokastrou; admission €3) Home to an eclectic array of artefacts gathered from around the Dodecanese, this one-room museum is chock-a-block with instruments, pottery, carvings, clothing and spinning wheels, all of which provide a colourful view into the past. Closed for restoration at time of research, it was expected to reopen soon.

◎ New Town

The so-called New Town of Rhodes has existed for 500 years, since Ottoman conquerors drove the local Greek population to build new homes outside the city walls. Almost nothing in the area, north of the Old Town and centering on Mandraki Harbour and the casino, though, holds any historic interest. Instead the New Town is a busy modern resort area, alive with hotels and restaurants, from gleaming skyscrapers to tiny tavernas, along with banks, boutiques and all the businesses that keep Rhodes ticking along.

The town **beach**, starting north of Mandraki Harbour, stretches around the island's northernmost point and down the west side of the New Town. The best spots tend to be on the east side, where there's usually calmer water and more sand and facilities.

Modern Greek Art Museum   GALLERY
(Map p476; ☏22410 43780; www.mgamuseum. gr; Plateia Haritou; admisssion €3, covers all sites; ◷8am-8pm Tue-Sat) The main gallery of the Modern Greek Art Museum, near the New Town's northern tip, holds paintings, engravings and sculptures by Greek artists including Gaitis Giannis, Vasiliou Spiros and Katraki Vaso. Its three other sites are the **Nestoridi Building** (Map p476; Kos; ◷8am-2pm Tue-Sat), nearby in the New Town; the **Art Gallery** (Map p480; Plateia Symi; ◷8am-2pm Tue-Sat), the original Old Town side, which holds a reconstruction of its initial exhibition from 1964; and the **Centre of Modern Art** (Map p480; 179 Sokratous; admission €3; ◷8am-2pm Tue-Sat) in the Old Town.

Rhodes Aquarium   AQUARIUM
(Map p476; ☏22410 27308; www.rhodes-aquarium. hcmr.gr; Kos 1; adult/child €5.50/2.50; ◷9am-8.30pm Apr-Oct, to 4.30pm Nov-Mar) The New Town's modest aquarium is housed in an art deco building that was constructed by the Italians in the 1930s as a biological research station. While it doesn't have the large tanks you might expect, it's not bad for younger kids, with the interior imaginatively kitted out to resemble an underwater cave, and touch tanks where you can lay hands on rays, starfish and other squirming sea beasts.

GEORGE TSAFOS / GETTY IMAGES ©

3

IKOR / GETTY IMAGES ©

FREEARTIST / GETTY IMAGES ©

1. Rhodes Old Town (p475)
Byzantine, Turkish and Italian architecture can be found in a tangle of cobbled alleyways.

2. Olymbos (p495)
Go back in time and be stunned be the views in this once-isolated Karpathos village.

3. Nisyros (p508)
Calamari drying in the sun on the small, sleepy volcanic island of Nisyros.

4. Gialos (p501)
The stunning harbour greets visitors to the beautiful island of Symi.

Rhodes Old Town

Rhodes Old Town

Waterhoppers Diving Centre
DIVING

(Map p476; ☑ 22410 38146; www.waterhoppers. com; Mandraki Harbour) Operating out of Mandraki Harbour and several other bases on the island, Waterhoppers offers an 'experience scuba' one-day program (€85) and a range of diving courses, including two- and three-day PADI open-water certifications. Choose from night, wreck and cave dives if you're an advanced diver.

Sleeping

Even if you're only passing through to catch a morning ferry, it's definitely worth staying in the Old Town rather than the New Town. That's the only way to experience the full magic of one of Europe's best-preserved historic towns. Room rates are considerably higher in both parts of the city than elsewhere in the Dodecanese and it's essential to reserve ahead in summer. In winter most budget options close altogether. Be warned, too, that most Old Town hotels are not accessible by taxi, so you may well have to haul your own luggage along the narrow cobbled lanes. Arrange to be picked up if possible.

Old Town

★ Marco Polo Mansion
BOUTIQUE HOTEL €€

(Map p480; ☑ 22410 25562; www.marcopolomansion .gr; Agiou Fanouriou 40; d incl breakfast €80-180; ☉ Apr-Oct; ❄ ☎) In the 15th century, this irresistible garden-set mansion, tucked away on an ancient alleyway, was home to an Ottoman official. It's now a gloriously romantic B&B hotel, its cool, high-ceilinged rooms decorated with exquisite taste and old-world flair. Amazing buffet breakfasts are spread out in the flower-filled courtyard, which is open to all every evening as a fabulous restaurant.

Hotel Andreas
HOTEL €€

(Map p480; ☑ 22410 34156; www.hotelandreas. com; Omirou 28d; s/d incl breakfast €70/80; ☉ May-late Oct; ❄ @ ☎) A former Ottoman house, in a sleepy alley near the walls, where seven guest rooms offer varying levels of luxury. Our favourite, the penthouse at the top, has a raised captain's bed and a smart new bathroom. Two others share a balcony. Breakfast is served in the open-sided, bougainvillea-crowned bar, with sweeping views across the Old Town and out to sea.

Medieval Inn
B&B €€

(Map p480; ☑ 22410 74786; www.medievalinn.com; Timokida 9; s/d/tr €60/65/80; ☉ Apr-Oct; ☎) Simple, welcoming family-run inn, in a pretty

---

Acropolis of Rhodes
ARCHAEOLOGICAL SITE

(☉ unrestricted access) FREE The site of the ancient Hellenistic city of Rhodes, now known as the Acropolis of Rhodes, stretches up the slopes of Monte Smith, 2km southwest of the Old Town. Restored structures include a tree-lined stadium from the 2nd century AD and the adjacent theatre, originally used for lectures by the Rhodes School of Rhetoric. Steps climb from there to the Temple of Pythian Apollo. Get here on city bus 5, or on a stiff half-hour hike.

Activities

The quay along Mandraki Harbour, on the east side of the New Town, is lined with boats offering all sorts of excursions, including day trips to island beaches, the island of Symi, or Turkey. Exactly what's available changes from day to day; simply stroll along and you'll soon find out.

spot in the Old Town's quieter southern lanes. The 10 rooms are plainly furnished and some are small, but they're clean and bright. Good breakfasts available for €5 extra.

Mango Rooms
PENSION €€

(Map p480; ☑ 22410 24877; www.mango.gr; Plateia Dorieos 3; s/d/tr €50/60/72; 🕸 @ 🛜) Overlooking one of the Old Town's loveliest squares, these simple but spotless rooms have safety deposit boxes, fridges and nicely updated bathrooms, and are set above a friendly restaurant and cafe. Guests can also relax on a peaceful roof terrace.

Minos Pension
PENSION €€

(Map p480; ☑ 22410 31813; www.minospension. com; 5 Omirou St; r €50-80; 🕸 @ 🛜) Family-run Minos, perched attractively above a quiet lane on the south side of the Old Town, has well-appointed, if slightly old-fashioned, studio rooms with gleaming kitchenettes and fridge. The compelling attraction, though, is the fabulous rooftop cafe, a lovely spot offering superb Old Town views; breakfast is not included. Downstairs there's a cosy communal lounge and book exchange.

Hotel Cava d'Oro
B&B €€

(Map p480; ☑ 22410 36980; www.cavadoro.com; Kisthiniou 15; s/d/tr incl breakfast €75/90/140; 🅿 🕸 🛜) Originally a storage building dating from the era of the Knights of St John, this small family-run hotel offers rooms of varying sizes, with canopied beds, exposed-stone walls and high arching ceilings. Breakfast is served in a cool garden courtyard, and guests can even walk on the hotel's own short stretch of the Old Town walls.

Niki's Pension
PENSION €€

(Map p480; ☑ 22410 25115; www.nikishotel.gr; Sofokleous 39; s/d/tr €55/65/85) Friendly, fairly basic hotel in the southern half of the Old Town, showing its age in parts but still offering good value. The rooms vary considerably and not all are equipped with air-con; stay higher in the building for the best views. There's also a shared roof terrace.

★ Spirit of the Knights
BOUTIQUE HOTEL €€€

(Map p480; ☑ 22410 39765; www.rhodesluxuryhotel.com; Alexandridou 14; s/d incl breakfast €160/200; 🕸 🛜) Six sumptuous suites in a splendidly transformed old home, nestled close to the Old Town walls. Each has its own historical theme, evoked through lavish linens, hangings and furniture and details such as stained glass, while all share a library inside and a whirlpool spa outside. Linger over breakfast in the tranquil gardens.

Avalon Boutique Hotel
BOUTIQUE HOTEL €€€

(Map p480; ☑ 22410 31438; www.avalonrhodes. gr; Charitos 9; d incl breakfast €170-230; 🕸 @ 🛜) This old stone house has stood for 700 years, but its inventive owners have given it a stunning contemporary overhaul to create half a dozen dazzling suites that combine historical charm with modern style and comfort. The courtyard cafe makes a great venue for breakfast and a welcome all-day oasis for visitors to the nearby palace.

🛏 New Town

New Village Inn
PENSION €

(Map p476; ☑ 22410 34937, 6976475917; www. newvillageinn.gr; Konstantopedos 10; d €50; 🕸) Hidden on a back alleyway, a few steps from the bustle of the New Town, this well-kept little pension centres on an attractive, leafy courtyard ornamented with icons. Two of its four whitewashed en suite rooms have their own private balconies.

★ Hotel Anastasia
PENSION €€

(Map p476; ☑ 22410 28007; www.anastasia-hotel. com; 28 Oktovriou 46; s/tw/d/tr €47/55/65/75; 🕸 @ 🛜) The New Town's friendliest and most peaceful accommodation option, this handsome white-painted villa is set well back from the road and offers charming, ochre-coloured en suite rooms with wooden shutters, tiled floors and traditional furnishings. Some have private balconies and there's an inviting breakfast bar in the lush garden.

Florida Hotel
HOTEL €€

(Map p476; ☑ 22410 22111; www.florida-rhodes. com; Amarandou 5; s/d €43/63) Small, simple modern hotel in a quiet little pedestrian street towards the New Town's northern tip. It has crisp, clean, whitewashed rooms with kitchenettes and air-con, and each has its own flower-bedecked terrace or balcony.

Eating

🍴 Old Town

Old Town Corner Bakery
BAKERY €

(Map p480; ☑ 22410 38494; Omirou 88; snacks €1-5; ⏰ 8am-9pm) This welcome find, away from the crowds on the southern edge of the Old Town, is exactly what the name suggests – a neighbourhood bakery/cafe serving espresso and juices, plus freshly baked bread, pastries and muffins, along with sandwiches and filled pittas. Tables out on the cobbles are ideal for lingering over an inexpensive snack.

Fournariko
BAKERY €

(Map p480; ☑ 22410 43057; Platonos; mains €7-12; ☺ 7am-late) First and foremost, this is a large modern bakery, with trays of sweet and savoury pies and pastries around the central oven and plenty of outdoor seating where you can wash them down with coffee. The adjoining dining room, though, known as Il Forno, serves a full menu of tasty Italian dishes, including pizza straight from the oven.

★ Marco Polo Cafe
MEDITERRANEAN €€

(Map p480; ☑ 22410 25562; Agiou Fanouriou 40-42; mains €14-20; ☺ 7pm-midnight) ⏀ Magical, irresistibly romantic restaurant in a delightful garden courtyard. The passion and flair of the cuisine is astounding, while the service epitomises *filoxenia* (hospitality). Menus change nightly, with specials such as calamari and prawn balls in a couscous crust, tuna in sesame marinated with orange, or lamb souvlaki on a bed of risotto, plus inventive desserts like semifreddo of tahini.

★ Nireas
SEAFOOD €€

(Map p480; ☑ 22410 21703; Sofokleous 45-47; mains €8-16; ✴) Nireas' status as Rhodes' favourite seafood restaurant owes much to the sheer enthusiasm and verve of genial owner Theo, from Symi – that and the beautifully prepared food, served under a vine-shaded canopy outside, or in the candlelit, lemon-on-walled interior. Be sure to sample the Symi shrimp, salted mackerel and, if you're in the mood, the 'Viagra' salad of small shellfish.

Romios Restaurant
GREEK €€

(Map p480; ☑ 22410 25549; www.romios-rhodes.gr; Sofokleous 15; mains €8-20; ☺ 11am-midnight) Don't be misled by the enchanted-grotto setting of canopied couches, birdcage nooks and fairy lights. Romios (not to be confused with run-of-the-mill Romeo's, nearby) is actually very serious about its food, serving a classically Rhodian menu of local delicacies such as pork in chestnut sauce, veal with olives, and delicious octopus cooked with orange.

Petaladika
GREEK €€

(Map p480; ☑ 22410 27319; Menakleous 8; mains €8-15; ☺ noon-late) Petaladika might look like just another tourist trap, tucked into a corner just off the main drag, but it has quickly established itself as the finest newcomer on the Old Town dining scene. Locals swoon over highlights such as deep-fried baby squid, zucchini balls and freshly grilled fish.

Pizanias
TAVERNA €€

(Map p480; Sea Star; ☑ 22410 22117; Sofokleous 24; mains €8-15; ☺ noon-midnight Feb-Oct) This atmospheric little taverna, opening onto one of the Old Town's most attractive and peaceful squares, is famed for its fresh seafood – from squid stuffed with cheese to 'grooved sea squirt' – and flavoursome *fava*. Dine under the trees, with the night sky above.

✖ New Town

★ Koykos
GREEK €

(Map p476; ☑ 22410 73022; Mandilana 20-26; mains €3-8; ☺ breakfast, lunch & dinner; ✴ 🛜) This inviting complex, off a pedestrian shopping street, consists of several antique-filled rooms – a couple hold vintage jukeboxes – along with two bougainvillea-draped courtyards and a floral roof terrace. Best known for fabulous homemade pies, it also serves all the classic mezedhes, plus meat and fish dishes, or you can drop in for a coffee or sandwich.

Niohori
TAVERNA €

(Map p476; ☑ 22410 35116; I Kazouli 29; mains €6-10; ☺ noon-midnight) This simple, great-value taverna – the open courtyard is basically a garage – delivers with a meat-accented menu. The owner is a butcher, with a shop across the street, so he selects the best cuts. Tuck into veal liver with oil and oregano, *stifadho* (meat with onions in a tomato puree), steak and meatballs, seasoned with organ music from the nearby church.

Meltemi
TAVERNA €€

(Map p476; ☑ 22410 30480; Kountourioti 8; mains €9-21; ☺ noon-late; 🅿 ✴ 🐾) The most charming option along the New Town shoreline, this breezy beach taverna offers widescreen sea views from its terrace and a cosy, nautically themed interior. The menu is swimming in fishy delights, such as shrimps with cheese and saffron, but you can also get feisty salads, pork and lamb dishes and vegetarian alternatives such as grilled oyster mushrooms.

Indigo
CAFE €€

(Map p476; ☑ 6972663100; New Market 105-106; mains €8-15; ☺ 11am-11pm Mon-Sat; 🛜) Set beside an old watchmaker, facing the whitewashed dome in the inner courtyard of the bustling market (and festooned, for no obvious reason, with pink sun hats), this friendly bistro/cafe is a haven of blue calm. Sample specials such as pork with honey or octopus with fava beans, or standards like halloumi and Greek salad.

Drinking & Nightlife

Old Town

Rogmi Tou Chronou
BAR

(Map p480; ☑ 22410 25202; Plateia Arionos 4; ⊗ 6pm-5am; 🔊) Dark enough to please a goth and lively enough to keep you awake till dawn, this down-and-dirty drinking den puts on regular live rock. The name means 'crack in time' – hence the clock fragments everywhere. Enjoy an early-evening drink outside, though, and the only soundtrack comes from the birds in the trees.

Walk Inn
PUB

(Map p480; ☑ 22410 74293; Plateia Dorieos 1; ⊗ 10am-late) There's nothing glitzy about this indoor-outdoor backstreet bar, but with its lively beer garden, street tables and ultra-friendly staff, there's no better place for a late-night drinking session in the Old Town. It also serves a bar menu of salads and focaccia sandwiches to keep you going.

Rock & Roll
BAR

(Map p480; ☑ 22410 25202; Plateia Arionos 2; ⊗ 9am-late; 🔊📶) Cool diner-style haunt with tiled walls and '50s songs playing as you plant yourself at the bar, fix your quiff in the mirror and tuck into a burger. It doubles as a juice bar during the day. Great balls of fire!

New Town

While there's a very lively drinking scene in the New Town, concentrated along the bar-lined I Dragoum, there's no great reason to recommend any tourist-dominated hang-out over its identical neighbours.

Christos Garden
BAR

(Map p476; ☑ 22410 32144; Griva 102; ⊗ 10pm-late) With its grottolike bar and pebble-mosaic courtyard abloom with flowers, Christos offers New Town visitors an escape into tranquillity. During the day it doubles as an art gallery; after dark the fairy lights twinkle. Perfect for a romantic cocktail.

☆ Entertainment

Cafe Chantant
LIVE MUSIC

(Map p480; ☑ 22410 32277; Dimokratou 3; ⊗ 11pm-late Fri & Sat) Locals flock to sit at the long wooden tables and listen to live traditional Greek music while drinking ouzo or beer. It's dark inside and you won't find snacks or nibbles, but the atmosphere is warm-hearted and friendly and the band, always lively.

Shopping

The Old Town is very much the place to pick up artworks, gifts and souvenirs, with shops and stalls piled high with icons, classical busts, leather sandals and jewellery – release your inner magpie. The New Town is much more down to earth, with busy markets, groceries and general stores, but also holds a clutch of big-name fashion and style brands.

Byzantine Iconography
ARTS, CRAFTS

(Map p480; ☑ 22410 74127; www.sirimis.gr; Kisthiniou 42; ⊗ 9am-5pm Mon-Fri) Visit artisan Basilios Per Sirimis in his cramped studio, the walls shimmering with gold and the air thick with resin and paint. His main business is in commissions for churches, but he also sells paintings and icons for €210 to €2000.

Antique Gallery
ARTS, CRAFTS

(Map p480; ☑ 22414 00126; Omirou 45; ⊗ 9am-9pm) Best viewed by night, this Aladdin's cave of a shop, with its shiny brass lamps, ornate antique rings and Eastern mosaic lights glowing like clusters of fireflies, conjures up thoughts of the *Arabian Nights*.

ℹ️ Information

MEDICAL SERVICES

Emergencies & Ambulance (☑ 166)

Euromedica General Hospital (☑ 22410 45000; www.euromedica-rhodes.gr; Koskinou) The largest private health facility on the island, with English-speaking staff. It's 6km south of the Old Town, in Koskinou.

General Hospital (☑ 22410 80000; Andreas Papandreou) State-of-the-art hospital.

MONEY

You'll find plenty of ATMs throughout Rhodes Town, with useful ATM-equipped branches of Alpha Bank next door to the Old Town tourist office at the corner of Platonos and Ippoton, and on Plateia Kypriou in the New Town.

POLICE

Port police (☑ 22410 22220; Mandraki)

Tourist police (☑ 22410 27423; ⊗ 24hr) Next door to the EOT.

POST

Main post office (Map p476; ☑ 22410 35560) At Mandraki Harbour.

TOURIST INFORMATION

EOT (Greek Tourist Information Office; Map p476; ☑ 22410 44335; www.ando.gr/eot; cnr Makariou & Papagou; ⊗ 8am-2.45pm Mon-Fri) National tourism information, including brochures, maps and transport details.

Tourism Office – New Town (Map p476; ☑22410 35495; www.rhodes.gr; Plateia Rimini; ☺7.30am-3pm Mon-Fri) Conveniently poised between Mandraki Harbour and the Old Town.

Tourism Office – Old Town (Map p480; ☑22410 35945; www.rhodes.gr; cnr Platonos & Ippoton; ☺7am-3pm Mon-Fri) In an ancient building at the foot of the Street of the Knights, this helpful office supplies excellent street maps, leaflets and brochures.

TRAVEL AGENCIES

Rodos Sun Service (☑22410 26400; 14 New Market, New Town) Books flights and boat tickets.

Skevos Travel Agency (☑22410 22461; www.skevostravel.gr; 111 Amerikis) For help with airline and ferry tickets throughout Greece, speak to Charoula.

Triton Holidays (☑22410 21690; www.tritondmc.gr; Plastira 9, Mandraki; ☺9am-8pm) Air and sea travel, hire cars, accommodation and tours throughout the Dodecanese, as well as tickets to Turkey.

USEFUL WEBSITES

Rhodes guide (www.rhodesguide.com) What's on, where to stay and where to hang out.

ⓘ Getting Around

Local buses leave from the **urban bus stop** (Map p476; Mandraki) on Mandraki Harbour. Bus 11 makes a circuit around the coast, up past the aquarium and on to the Acropolis. Bus 2 goes to Analipsi, bus 3 to Rodini, bus 4 to Agios Dimitrios and bus 5 to the Acropolis. Buy tickets on board.

Northeastern Rhodes

Most of the sandiest beaches on Rhodes lie along the island's northeastern coast, between Rhodes Town and Lindos. As a result, this stretch is now punctuated by a long succession of resorts, filled with package holidaymakers in summer and holding endless strips of tourist bars. Frequent buses ply the main road, connecting the best-known beaches. If you're happy to hike, you can walk down to much emptier strands at several points along the way.

Ladiko Beach, 15km south of Rhodes Town, just beyond Faliraki, is touted locally as 'Anthony Quinn Beach'. Back in the 1960s, the star of *Zorba the Greek* actually bought the beach from the Greek government, but according to his family the authorities failed to honour the sale. It consists of two back-to-back coves, with a pebbly beach on the north side that's better for swimming, and volcanic rock platforms on the south.

Two fine beaches, **Kolymbia** and **Tsambika**, are located either side of the massive Tsambika promontory, 10km further south. Both are sandy but get crowded in summer. Not far beyond, the coast road curves inland, but a short detour seawards brings you to the low-key little resort of Stegna, arrayed along sandy, idyllic **Stegna Beach**.

The headland that marks the start of the final curve towards Lindos, 40km south of Rhodes Town, is topped by the ruins of the 15th-century **Castle of Faraklos**. Once a prison for recalcitrant knights, this was the last stronghold on the island to fall to the Turks and now offers fabulous views. A footpath climbs from the appealing little resort of **Haraki**, immediately south, where the neat horseshoe bay is lined by a pebbly beach.

⊙ Sights

Kalithea Thermi ARCHITECTURE
(☑22410 65691; www.kallitheasprings.gr; Kalithea; admission €3; ☺site 8am-8pm Apr-Oct, to 5pm Nov-Mar, cafe stays open later) Italian architect Pietro Lombardi constructed this opulent art deco spa, on the site of ancient thermal springs, in 1929. Its dazzling white-domed pavilions, pebble-mosaic courtyards and sweeping sea-view colonnades appeared in movies such as *Zorba the Greek* and *Guns of Navarone*, and have now been restored after years of neglect. In peak season, though, its small sandy bathing beach and cafe get impossibly crowded. Just 9km south of Rhodes Town, it can be accessed by driving directly along the coast.

Epta Piges SPRING
(Seven Springs; Kolymbia; ☺unrestricted access) Seven natural springs at this beauty spot, in the hills 4km inland from Kolymbia, feed a river that's channelled into a narrow tunnel, exactly the size of an adult. Thrill-seeking visitors can walk a few hundred metres in pitch darkness, ankle deep in fast-flowing water, to reach the shaded lake at the far end. There's also a taverna and the House of the Python gift shop, so called because it is indeed home to a colossal live snake.

Lindos Λίνδος
POP 3600

Your first glimpse of the ancient and unbelievably pretty town of Lindos is guaranteed to steal your breath away: the towering Acropolis radiant on the cypress-silvered hill, and the sugar-cube houses of the whitewashed town tumbling below it towards the aquamarine bay. Entering the town itself, you'll find yourself in a magical warren of hidden alleys, packed with the ornate houses of long-vanished sea captains that now hold appetising tavernas, effervescent bars and cool cafes. Pick your way past donkeys as you coax your calves up to the Acropolis and one of the finest views in Greece.

Lindos has been enjoying its wonderful setting for 4000 years, since the Dorians founded the first settlement at this excellent harbour and vantage point. Since then it has been successively overlaid with Byzantine, Frankish and Turkish structures, the remains of which can be glimpsed all around.

◉ Sights

★ Acropolis of Lindos   ARCHAEOLOGICAL SITE
(☑22440 31258; admission €6; ☻8am-8pm Apr-Oct, 8.30am-3pm Nov-Mar) A steep footpath climbs the 116m-high rock above Lindos to reach the beautifully preserved Acropolis. First walled in the 6th century BC, the cliff-top is now enclosed by battlements constructed by the Knights of St John. Once within, you're confronted by stunning ancient remains that include a **Temple to Athena Lindia** and a 20-columned **Hellenistic stoa**. Silhouetted against the deep blue sky, the stark white columns are dazzling, while the long-range coastal views are out of this world.

Be sure to pack a hat and some water, as there's no shade at the top, and take care to protect young kids from the many dangerous drop-offs. Donkey rides to the Acropolis from the village entrance only spare you around three minutes of exposed walking on the hillside, and you should note that animal-rights groups urge people to consider the treatment of the donkeys before deciding to take a ride.

Beaches

Two magnificent beaches line the crescent harbour that curves directly below the village. The larger, logically known as **Main Beach**, is a perfect swimming spot – sandy with shallow water – for kids. Follow a path north to the western tip of the bay to reach the smaller, taverna-fringed **Pallas Beach**. Don't swim near the jetty here, which is home to sea urchins, but if it gets too crowded you can swim from the rocks beyond.

Ten minutes' walk from town on the other, western, side of the Acropolis, sheltered **St Paul's Bay** is similarly caressed by turquoise waters.

🛏 Sleeping

Accommodation in Lindos is very limited, so be sure to book in advance. And check carefully, as most hotels that include 'Lindos' in their names and/or addresses are in fact located not in the town, but along the coast nearby.

Electra Studios   PENSION €
(☑22440 31266; www.electra-studios.gr; s/d/tr €40/50/60; ☻Apr-Oct; ✳) Simple family-run pension, where the plain, but very pleasant, whitewashed rooms have varnished wooden twin beds, fridges and air-con. Some have balconies and there's also a lovely communal roof terrace overlooking a lemon grove and the sea.

Anastasia Studios   APARTMENT €€
(☑22440 31751; www.lindos-studios.gr; d & tr €60; P✳🛜) Focused around a geranium-filled courtyard on Lindos' eastern side, these six split-level apartments enjoy soaring Acropolis views. Each has a tiled floor, sofa bed, well-equipped kitchen and separate bedroom, while room 6 has its own private balcony.

★ Melenos   BOUTIQUE HOTEL €€€
(☑22440 32222; www.melenoslindos.com; ste incl breakfast from €306; ✳@🛜) 🗲 Magical Moorish-style palace with bougainvillea walkways, pebble-mosaic floors, verandahs festooned in lanterns and bauble lights casting a glow on Ottoman furniture. Staff glide discreetly around as you soak up the stunning bay view. Rooms are lovingly re-created in traditional Lyndian style, with raised beds, wooden ceilings and private balconies, and there's a superb restaurant.

Filoxenia Cozy   BOUTIQUE HOTEL €€€
(☑22440 32080; www.lindos-filoxenia.com; d/ste incl breakfast €170/215; ✳@) Bursting with flowers, this enclosed courtyard accommodation holds six bright, stylish and beautifully finished rooms and family-sized suites. All have modern furniture, wood-beamed ceilings and traditional raised-platform beds, plus fridge and kitchenette. It's next to the police station, at the south end of town.

🍴 Eating & Drinking

Most tavernas serve their customers on roof terraces high above the tangle of streets. These give fabulous views up to the Acropolis and over the bay, but you can't always tell whether there's anyone in your chosen venue until you've committed to eat there.

Village Cafe BAKERY €
(☑ 22440 31559; www.lindostreasures.com; mains €8; ⏱ 8.30am-7pm; ✱ 🛜) Near the start of the path up to the Acropolis, this whitewashed bakery/cafe has an enticing vine-covered pebble-mosaic courtyard and comfortable couches in its cool interior. Drop in for hot or frozen coffee, juice or ice cream and a mouth-watering array of cheese cakes, cherry pies, salads, wraps and freshly prepared sandwiches. Don't miss the delectable *bougatsa* (vanilla custard pie).

Mare Mare CAFE €
(☑ 22440 31651; Pallas Beach; mains €9; ⏱ breakfast, lunch & dinner; 🛜 ☕) This chic beach bar, near the jetty on the smaller of the two beaches below Lindos, makes a wonderful place to relax at any time of day, with a menu that ranges from breakfasts and souvlakia to succulent steaks and calamari. To miss the crowds, come early, or in the late afternoon.

★**Kalypso** TAVERNA €€
(☑ 22440 32135; www.kalypsolindos.gr; mains €8-15; ⏱ lunch & dinner; ✱ 🛜) Dine in the high-ceilinged main room of this 17th-century sea captain's house, or simply admire the facade from the roof terrace. The menu ranges through seafood, meat and vegetarian delights, plus tasty Lyndian dishes, including 'Kalypso bread' with feta and tomato. Specialities like baked lamb or goat should be ordered in advance. Take the second right off the main drag.

Melenos MEDITERRANEAN €€€
(☑ 22440 32222; www.melenoslindos.com; mains €26; ⏱ 8am-midnight; 🛜) Gorgeous sea-view terrace restaurant that's the most romantic spot in Lindos. The rich, gourmet's-dream menu features salmon marinated in ouzo, steamed sea bass with mussels in asparagus sauce, and grilled beef fillet with mushrooms, wine and caramelised onions. Round things off with a sumptuous dessert.

❶ Information

The core of Lindos is entirely pedestrianised. Vehicles can go no further than Plateia Eleftherias, the square from which the main drag, Acropolis, begins. All coastal buses to and from Rhodes stop here. Cars have to park either further down towards the beach, or in large car parks higher up by the main road, served by frequent shuttle buses (€0.60). There are several ATMs in the town.

Island of the Sun Travel (☑ 22440 31264; Acropolis) Local excursions, rental cars and accommodation.

Lindos tourist office (Plateia Eleftherias; ⏱ 9am-3pm Mon-Sat, 10am-1pm Sun) Small info kiosk at the entrance to central Lindos.

Southeastern Rhodes

As you continue south of Lindos along the east coast, the island takes on a windswept appearance and sees less tourist traffic. Villages here seem to have a slower pace.

Just 2km south of Lindos, sandy **Pefki Beach** is deservedly popular. If it's too crowded, try **Glystra Beach**, just down the road and a great spot for swimming.

Gennadi Γεννάδι
POP 660

Sleepy one-street Gennadi consists of a few *kafeneia* (coffee houses), friendly locals and a cluster of whitewashed buildings set back a few hundred metres from the pebbled beach. You'll find a fruit market, bakery, supermarket and a couple of tavernas.

🛏 Sleeping

Effie's Dreams Apartments APARTMENT €
(☑ 22440 43110; www.effiesdreams.com; s/d €38/55; ✱ @ 🛜) Flanked by a 1000-year-old mulberry tree, these six simple, good-value studios, 10 minutes' walk up from the beach, have lovely sea views, and balconies from which to enjoy them. The freshly revamped cafe downstairs, Mouria, is utterly charming, with snacks, cocktails and some great vintage touches, and there's a welcoming garden courtyard where you can read and relax.

Gennadi to Prasonisi
Γεννάδι προς Πρασονήσι

An almost uninterrupted beach of pebbles and sand dunes extends down from Gennadi as far as **Plimmyri**, 11km south. Watch for a signposted turning to **Lahania**, 2km inland off the main highway, and head downhill into the centre to find an old village of winding alleyways and traditional buildings.

The coast road continues south past countless chapels to the village of **Kattavia**, a friendly place that doesn't see a lot of tourists. Beyond that, a windswept 10km road snakes south to remote **Cape Prasonisi**, the island's southernmost point. Joined to Rhodes by a tenuously narrow sandy isthmus in summer months, it's cut off completely when water levels rise in winter. The Aegean Sea meets the Mediterranean here, creating ideal wind and wave conditions for kitesurfers and windsurfers. Outfitters stand ready to help with everything from rental equipment and lessons to overnight accommodation in surfer-dude-style hostels, but it all closes down in winter.

🛏 Sleeping & Eating

★ Four Elements APARTMENT €€
(☑6939450014, 22440 46001; www.thefourelements.be; Lahania; apt €90-135; [P ❄ @ ☎ ⛱]) Four exceptionally homey and spacious apartments, perfect for taking a rural holiday in comfort. All have full kitchens, one is adapted for wheelchair users, and there's a divine pool, outdoor BBQ and garden. The friendly Belgian owners run an on-site cafe-bar named the Fifth Element (beer being the fifth element after earth, air, fire and water).

Taverna Platanos TAVERNA €
(☑6944199991; www.lachaniaplatanos.com; Lahania; mains €6-8) Classic village taverna, tucked behind the church in Lahania's tiny main square and famed throughout the island. With its traditional decor and flower-filled patio, it's a great place to take a break. Hearty lamb, beef or chicken stews cost well under €10, with salads and dips less than half that.

Western Rhodes & the Interior

Western Rhodes is redolent with the scent of pine, its hillsides shimmering with forests. More exposed than the east side, it's also windier – a boon for kite and windsurfers – so the sea tends to be rough and the beaches mostly pebbled. If you're cycling, or have a scooter or car, the hilly roads that cross the interior abound in wonderful scenery and are well worth exploring.

For sightseers, the most significant potential stopoffs are the ruined ancient cities of Ialysos and Kamiros. Otherwise, once past the airport, settlements are few and far between. **Skala Kamirou**, 45km southwest of Rhodes Town, is a small port with direct ferries to the nearby island of Halki. Although it does have a couple of tavernas, and a twice-daily bus service, it's so isolated that it's much more use for locals than independent travellers.

The ruins of 16th-century **Kritinia Castle** stand proudly on a headland immediately south of Skala Kamirou. Detour off the main road for awe-inspiring views along the coast and across to Halki, in a magical setting

where you half expect to encounter Romeo or Rapunzel. Continuing south, the road is sublimely scenic. Vast mountainous vistas open up as you approach **Siana**, a picturesque village below Mt Akramytis (825m), and the village of **Monolithos**, 5km beyond. The spectacularly sited 15th-century castle that's perched on a sheer 240m-high rock above Monolithos can be reached on a dirt track. To enter, climb through the hole in the wall.

👁 Sights

Ancient Ialysos ARCHAEOLOGICAL SITE
(☑22410 92202; admission €3; ⊙8.30am-8pm May-Oct, to 3pm Nov-Apr) Constructed in the 3rd century BC, atop what's now Filerimos Hill, 10km southwest of Rhodes Town, the Doric city of Ialysos was repeatedly conquered thereafter. The resultant hotchpotch of Doric, Byzantine and medieval remains is now barely intelligible to casual visitors. Stairs from the entrance lead to the ruined foundations of the Temple of Athena Ialysia and the peaceful restored 14th-century Chapel of Agios Georgios. Follow the path left from the entrance to reach another 12th-century chapel, filled with frescoes.

Ancient Kamiros ARCHAEOLOGICAL SITE
(☑22410 40037; admission €4; ⊙8am-8pm May-Oct, 8.30am-3pm Nov-Apr) The extensive remains of the Doric city of Kamiros stand above the coast, 34km southwest of Rhodes Town. Known for its figs, oil and wine, Kamiros was at its peak in the 7th century BC, but was swiftly superseded by Rhodes and devastated by earthquakes in 226 and 142 BC. Visible ruins include a Doric temple, with one column still standing, a temple to Athena and a 3rd-century great stoa. Come in the afternoon, when fewer visitors are around.

Petaloudes FOREST
(☑22410 82822; admission €3; ⊙9am-5pm) Petaloudes, 7km up from the coast, is better known as the Valley of the Butterflies. Visit in June, July or August, when these colourful insects mature, and you'll quickly see why. They're actually tiger moths (*Callimorpha quadripunctarea*) drawn to the gorge by the scent of the resin exuded by storax trees. In summer the whole place is choking with tour buses. Out of season, you'll likely have the gorgeous forest path, streams and pools to yourself – but no butterflies.

Emery Winery WINERY
(☑22460 41208; Embonas; ⊙9.30am-4.30pm Apr-Oct) [FREE] Perched on the flanks of Mt Attavy-

ros (1215m), the island's highest mountain, the village of Embonas is the wine capital of Rhodes. This cottage winery, on the town's eastern edge, offers tours of its facility and provides a good opportunity to taste and buy top-quality tipples such as the red Cava Emery or Zacosta and the white Villare.

✗ Eating

To Stolidi Tis Psinthoy   TAVERNA **€**
(☑ 22410 50009; Psinthos; mains €8-10; ☺ lunch & dinner) The pick of several appealing lunch spots in lively Psinthos, 10km southeast of Petaloudes, To Stolidi has a deeply rural feel with wooden beams, checked tablecloths and family photos on the walls. Try the spicy pork, grilled aubergine, dolmadhes and fresh-baked country bread.

Mylos   CAFE **€**
(☑ 6940641475; Kritinia; snacks €5-7; ☺ 9am-late) Set beside the main road, with tremendous views down to Kritinia Castle, this welcoming little cafe serves coffee, drinks and snacks such as salads, omelettes and sandwiches. Best of all, though, it has its own **folklore museum**, filled with local costumes and alarming farming implements.

HALKI   ΧΑΛΚΗ

POP 330

Thanks to the gorgeous Italianate mansions that surround its harbour, the former sponge-diving island of Halki makes an irresistible first impression. Stepping off the ferry, you enter a composite of all that's best about Greece: an old fisherman shelling prawns under a fig tree, an Orthodox priest flitting down a narrow alley, brightly painted boats bobbing along the quay. There's little to do except relax and indulge in the sleepy splendour, venturing out to tempting little beaches lapped by aquamarine waters and, in cooler seasons, hiking along the island's spectacular high-mountain spine.

ℹ Getting There & Away

The **Dodekanisos Express** (www.12ne.gr) catamaran stops at Halki on Tuesday and Thursday as it heads from Rhodes to Tilos, Nisyros, Kos and Kalymnos in the morning, and back to Rhodes in the evening. On those days, you can visit the island as a day trip from Rhodes. Blue Star Ferries (p473) connects Halki with Rhodes up to three times weekly, and with Karpathos, Kasos, Crete, Santorini and Piraeus twice weekly.

Two boats, **Nissos Halki** (☑ 6973460968) and **Nikos Express** (☑ 6946826905), link Halki daily with the tiny port of Skala Kamirou on the west coast of Rhodes; there's an hour-long connecting bus service with Rhodes Old Town. **Stelios Kazantzidis** (☑ 6944434429) runs an on-demand water-taxi service to Skala Kamirou.

BOAT SERVICES FROM HALKI (EMBORIOS)

DESTINATION	TIME	FARE	FREQUENCY
Kalymnos*	3hr	€35	2 weekly
Karpathos	4hr	€12	3 weekly
Kos*	2hr 20min	€26	2 weekly
Nisyros*	1½hr	€24	2 weekly
Piraeus	24hr	€41	2 weekly
Rhodes	2hr	€9	3 weekly
Rhodes*	1¼hr	€16	2 weekly
Rhodes (Skala Kamirou)	1¼hr	€10	1-2 daily
Santorini (Thira)	12hr	€26	1 weekly
Tilos*	40min	€24	2 weekly

*high-speed services

ℹ Getting Around

Most visitors get around Halki on foot. In summer, regular minibuses connect Emborios with Pondamos, Ftenagia and Kalia beaches (€1.50 each way), while on Friday evenings there's also a round trip to Moni Agiou Ioanni monastery (€5). A water taxi also serves the main beaches, while Zifos Travel (p490) can provide details of summer-only excursion boats, for example to the uninhabited island of Alimia (€30), with its fields of wild herbs.

Emborios   Εμπορειός

POP 300

Halki's one tiny town, Emborios, curves luxuriantly around a sheltered turquoise bay. The waterfront is a broad expanse of flagstones, almost entirely pedestrianised, populated by as many cats as humans and lined with enticing tavernas and cafes. Climbing in tiers up a low ridge, the cream, ochre, stone and rose-hued homes of 19th-century fishermen and sea captains form a magnificent backdrop. There's no town beach, but here and there ladders enable swimmers to enter the water.

◉ Sights

The neoclassical mansions of Emborios are a visual feast. A few have crumbled into complete ruination, but most have been restored to their original glory and many now serve as rental properties.

The impressive central **clock tower** was donated by the expat Halki community in Florida; the clock itself hasn't worked for over 20 years. Nearby, the **Church of Agios Nikolaos** has the tallest belfry in the Dodecanese, incorporating stones from an ancient temple of Apollo, and boasts a picturesque mosaic-pebbled courtyard.

Traditional House of Chalki HISTORIC BUILDING
(☑22460 45284; admission €3; ☺11am-3pm & 6-8pm) Perched on the hillside, not far up from the harbour (signed to the right off the road to Pondamos beach), the Traditional House of Chalki – an alternative transliteration of Halki – is a two-storey family home, built a century ago. It's now meticulously preserved as a museum, displaying authentic furniture, tableware and costumes, old photos – and even the owner's grandmother's underwear, neatly framed.

🛏 Sleeping

Halki holds little accommodation, so book ahead in summer. Most visitors stay in self-catering villas and apartments; contact Zifos Travel or **Nissia Holidays** (www.nissia-holidays.com) for details.

Captain's House PENSION €
(☑6932511762, 22460 45201; capt50@otenet.gr; d €40; ❄🛜) Attractive white-painted 19th-century house just up from the sea, near the church, featuring antique clocks and model schooners. Two lovely rooms have high ceilings, wood floors, air-con and good bathrooms, and the relaxing garden courtyard holds a sun terrace with great harbour views.

St Nicolas Boutique Hotel HOTEL €€
(☑22460 45208; www.stnicolas.com; d/ste incl breakfast €110/120; ❄🛜) Larger and less intimate than its 'boutique' name might suggest, Halki's only hotel holds 20 sizeable, white-walled modern rooms. Each has its own waterfront balcony or terrace and you can swim from the quay in front.

🍴 Eating

Around a dozen bars, cafes and tavernas line the harbour in Emborios.

Taverna Lefkosia TAVERNA €
(☑6946978151; mains €7-12; ☺lunch & dinner) Much-loved taverna, where the check-clothed tables and blue chairs spread out onto the quay and the menu abounds in homemade island specialities such as baked pasta. The fried cheese balls are a crispy, chewy delight, and fresh-caught fish comes in generous portions.

Black Sea TAVERNA €
(☑22460 45021; mains €7-14; ☺lunch & dinner; 🛜) 🍴 Sitting peacefully on the left side of the harbour, metres from bobbing boats, this brightly coloured haunt is run by a charming Georgian family. It's a great spot for fresh fish, from octopus and little shrimp to grilled bream, but the vegetable dishes, including fried mushrooms, are good too.

Dimitri's Bakery BAKERY €
(mains €2; ☺breakfast, lunch & dinner) Generations of residents and visitors have stocked up on Dimitri's delicious sweet and savoury pies and pastries, available from early morning. Cheese, spinach and apple pies, plus croissants and, in the evening, slices of pizza.

ℹ Information

Boats arrive in the centre of Emborios, with all services and accommodation within easy walking distance. The only ATM is often out of action, so bring plenty of spare cash.

Clinic (☑22460 70910; ☺9am-2pm & 6-8pm Mon-Fri) Doctor phone numbers are posted on the door of Zifos Travel.

Police and Port Police (☑22460 45220) On the harbour.

Post office (☺9am-1.30pm Mon-Fri) On the harbour, with an ATM.

Zifos Travel (☑22460 45028; www.zifostravel.gr; ☺10am-8pm) The best source of help with accommodation, boat tickets, excursions and currency exchange.

Around Halki

A broad concrete road crosses the low hill above Emborios harbour to reach **Pondamos Beach**, the most popular of Halki's handful of tiny shingle beaches, after 500m. Beyond that, it climbs to the abandoned village of **Horio**, 3km along, then continues west to the hill-top monastery of **Agiou Ioanni**. That's a total one-way hike of 8km, recommended in the cooler months only.

Two more pebble beaches, both equipped with decent tavernas and served by buses in summer, lie within walking distance of Emborios. **Ftenagia Beach** is beyond the headland 500m south of the harbour, while **Kania Beach** is an enjoyable but unshaded 2.5km hike north, signposted off the main road halfway to Pondamos.

Sights

Pondamos Beach   BEACH

Pretty little Pondamos Beach is lapped by the turquoise waters of a crescent bay 10 minutes' walk up and over the hill west of Emborios. The only way to get a comfortable shaded spot is to rent a €3 sunbed alongside **Nick's Taverna** (mains €6-15; ☺ breakfast, lunch & dinner), where separate sections serve good seafood meals or drinks and snacks.

Horio   ARCHAEOLOGICAL SITE

A stiff switchback climb along the road from Pondamos Beach leads up through Halki's fertile central valley to Horio. This picturesque ruin was originally the island's main village, hidden away to escape the eyes of roving pirates. A freshly cobbled footpath heads up to the battlements of the **Knights of St John Castle** that once protected it. Pass through its forbidding gateway to see a restored chapel and amazing long-range views.

KARPATHOS   ΚΑΡΠΑΘΟΣ

POP 6200

Celebrated for its wild mountains and petrol blue coves, this long craggy island is among the least commercialised in Greece. Legend has it Prometheus and his Titans were born here, and with its cloud-wrapped villages and rugged beauty, there's still something undeniably primal in the air. Homer, never a man to mince his words, called it 'Krapathos', but actually it's a lovely island.

Popular with adrenaline junkies, southern Karpathos is in the spotlight each summer when it hosts an international kitesurfing competition. Meanwhile, the fierce wind that lifts the spray from the turquoise waves blows its way to the mountainous north, battering pine trees and howling past sugar-cube houses. Karpathian women at this end of the island still wear traditional garb, especially in the time-forgotten village eyrie of Olymbos, perched atop a perilous mountain ridge.

Getting There & Away

The airport at the very southern tip of Karpathos is linked by **Olympic Air** (www.olympicair.com) two to four times daily with Athens (€92, one hour) and Rhodes (€45, 40 minutes), and once daily with Kasos (€40, 15 minutes) and Sitia (€63, one hour) in Crete.

The island's main port, Pigadia, is served by Blue Star Ferries (p473), with all sailings also calling at the northern village of Diafani either before Pigadia (when southbound) or after it (when northbound). Ferries head three times weekly to Halki and Rhodes, and three times weekly to Kasos, with two continuing to Crete and one to Santorini.

BOAT SERVICES FROM KARPATHOS

DESTINATION	TIME	FARE	FREQUENCY
Halki	4hr	€12	3 weekly
Kasos	1½hr	€8	3 weekly
Milos	16hr	€36	1 weekly
Piraeus	17hr	€41	2 weekly
Rhodes	5hr 40min	€20	3 weekly
Santorini (Thira)	8hr	€25	1 weekly
Sitia	4hr	€18	2 weekly

Getting Around

TO/FROM THE AIRPORT

The airport is 14km south of Pigadia. There's no airport bus, and a taxi will cost €22, so it makes sense to rent a car.

BOAT

Day trips head from Pigadia up to Diafani, where they connect with buses to Olymbos, or continue north to remote beaches.

BUS

KTEL (www.karpathosbus.wordpress.com) runs buses all over the island from the bus station on Mattheou in Pigadia, just up from the harbour. Only two a week go all the way north to Olymbos.

CAR & MOTORCYCLE

All major car-rental chains have outlets at the airport, and there are local agencies all over the island. Recommended operators include **Europcar** (☑ 22450 23238; www.europcar.com) and **Lefkos Rent A Car** (☑ 22450 71487; www.lefkosrentacar.com).

TAXI

Taxi prices are posted at Pigadia's central **taxi rank** (☑ 22450 22705; Dimokratias). Fares are prohibitively high, with trips to Lefkos costing €50 and Olymbos, €75.

Pigadia   Πηγάδια

POP 1690

Karpathos' capital and main ferry port, Pigadia, sprawls beside a long bay on the southeast shore of the island. Decent beaches stretch away to the north, but the town itself lacks the photogenic good looks and geometrically pleasing whitewashed houses of other islands. Give it a little time, though, wandering its harbour and among waterfront bars and backstreet bakeries, and the place may grow on you. Determinedly Greek, it barely looks up from its afternoon retsina to acknowledge your arrival. But isn't that what travellers sometimes long for?

Karpathos

0 ————— 5 km
0 ————— 2.5 miles

Karpathos Strait / Cape Paraspori
Saria
Excursion Boat
Tristomo
Cape Vroukounda
Vroukounda
Moni Agiou Ioanni
Vananda Beach
Avlona
Halki (50km); Rhodes (132km)
Moni Agiou Konstantinou
Mt Profitis Ilias (716m) / Diafani
Olymbos
Sea of Crete
Papa Mina Bay
Agios Minas
Spoa
Mesohori
Agios Nikolaos
Karpathos / Apella Beach
Roman Cistern / Excursion Boat
Lefkos Beach
Mertonas / Kyra Panagia Beach
Lefkos
Kali Limni (1215m)
Kato Lakos Beach
Volada / Aperi
Ahata Beach
Adia / Othos
Cape Proni / Pyles
Vrondi Bay
Flaskia Gorge
Pigadia
Basilica of Agia Sophia & Acropolis
Finiki / Menetes
Ammoöpi
Arkasa
Agios Nikolaos Beach
Cape Volakas
Cape Agios Theodoros
Afiartis Bay
Cape Akrotiri
Cape Lingi
Cape Kastello
Kasos (10km); Crete (80km)

🛏 Sleeping

Budget options are concentrated in the hillside streets that rise from central Pigadia, while newer and more luxurious options spread northwards around the bay.

Rose's Studios
APARTMENT €

(☎ 22450 22284; www.rosesstudios.com; r €35; ✳ 🖥) For good-value budget lodgings, it's well worth trudging 300m up from the port to reach these eight simple but fresh rooms. They have clean en suite bathrooms, large sea-view balconies and decent fittings, including minimal kitchenettes.

Atlantis Hotel
HOTEL €€

(☎ 22450 22777; www.atlantishotelkarpathos.gr; s/d incl breakfast €54/66; 🖥) A friendly, long-established, family-run hotel that's a real bargain for such a prime spot, across from the Italian-era town hall just above the west end of the harbour. The pleasant, no-frills rooms are nicely maintained – it's well worth paying a little extra for one with a balcony facing the sea rather than the (decent-sized) pool.

Oceanis Hotel
HOTEL €€

(☎ 22450 22975; www.oceanishotel.gr; r from €70; 🅿 ✳ 🖥) The mirrored lobby and gold-trim bar of this sizeable family-run hotel, five minutes' walk west of the harbour, fairly scream its '80s origins. There's no faulting the 50 rooms upstairs, though, with their neat blue-and-white trimmings, tasteful furniture and, especially, sea-facing balconies. Rates include a buffet breakfast spread, and the terrace is also great for sundowners.

Nereides Hotel
HOTEL €€

(☎ 22450 23347; www.nereideshotel.gr; Nereidon St; d incl breakfast €110; 🅿 ✳ 🖥 🍽) This charming little hotel has been open a few years, but everything, from the paintwork to its up-to-the-minute bathrooms, still gleams like new. Set on the hillside, five minutes' walk from the beach and 10 from the harbour, it offers 30 stylish rooms with sea-view balconies, plus a good pool. There's a snack bar but no restaurant.

🍴 Eating

Both the quay and the pedestrian streets behind it are lined with seafood tavernas, all-purpose brasseries, cafes and bars. Look out, too, for the two Italian *gelaterias* on Apodimon Karpathion, parallel to the harbour.

★ To Hellenikon
TAVERNA €

(☎ 22450 23932; Apodimon Karpathion; mains €7-17; ⊗ lunch & dinner; ✳ 🖥 🍽) This deeply traditional taverna, a block from the sea, offers seating on an open-sided footpath terrace as well as indoors, alongside a kitchen filled with bubbling pots and appetising aromas. The menu is enticing enough, but it's the inexpensive specials, like the squid stew, or local lamb stuffed with cheese and served with roast potatoes, that really catch the eye.

Orea
TAVERNA €

(22450 22501; harbour; mains €7-15; ⊙noon-midnight) Quayside taverna near the ferry jetty, serving authentic Karpathian specialities such as gnocchi-like *makarounes,* sprinkled with cheese and onions. Most meat mains cost under €10, and a whole grilled fish is more like €12 to €14. Groups can share a large mixed plate of hot starters for €18.

Pantheon Cafe
CAFE €

(22450 22502; Papathanassiou; snacks & breakfast €5-7) The pick of the best-of-both-worlds cafes along this pedestrian street, with a fine old wood-panelled interior and a balcony terrace at the back, perched high above the harbour with fabulous views. Come for a full English (€6) or Karpathian (€7, with cucumber, olives and local bread) breakfast, as well as fruit, yoghurts, juices and espresso.

Akropolis
BRASSERIE €€

(22450 23278; Apodimon Karpathion; mains €15-25; ⊙breakfast, lunch & dinner) This welcoming and supremely relaxing harbourfront cafe/restaurant is as suited to breakfast or a sunset cocktail as it is to a full dinner. Most are drawn here for steak rather than Greek food, with the menu ranging through cuts from entrecôte, T-bone, fillet, sirloin and rib-eye up to a delectable chateaubriand for two (€50).

🍷 Drinking & Nightlife

Pretty much any of the waterfront bars and cafes is ideal for a sunset drink or two.

Caffe Karpathos
CAFE

(21022 87383; www.cafekarpathos.com; Apodimon Karpathion; ⊙8am-late) Enjoying a morning coffee or evening glass of local wine in the wicker chairs outside this cosy little cafe, a few steps from the waterfront on a pedestrian street that climbs away near the jetty, you feel as though you're relaxing in the front room of a friend's house. The owners lived for years in Italy – hence the Italian touches.

ℹ Information

Pigadia's ferry quay juts out from the eastern end of the broad harbour. Walk east to reach the town centre within five minutes. Follow the main street, Apodimon Karpathion, which climbs from the waterfront then runs parallel to the sea, and in 500m you'll reach Plateia 5 Oktovriou, home to the Italian-era municipal buildings. The sandy beaches of Pigadia Bay begin not far beyond.

Both the National Bank of Greece on Apodimon Karpathion, and Alpha Bank, a block higher on Dimokratias, have ATMs.

Police (22450 22224) Near the hospital at the western end of town.

Possi Travel (22450 22235; ⊙8am-1pm & 5.30-8.30pm) The main travel agency for ferry and air tickets, excursions and accommodation. The helpful staff speak excellent English.

Post office (Ethnikis Andistasis) Near the hospital.

Tourist office (22450 23926; www.karpathos.org; ⊙Jul & Aug) Summer-only kiosk, in the middle of the seafront.

Southern Karpathos

Thanks to their sandy beaches, several appealing villages in the southern half of Karpathos have reinvented themselves as small-scale resorts. Yet-more-peaceful villages nestle amid the hills inland, an area that's also criss-crossed by scenic walking tracks.

Menetes
Μενετές

Buffeted by mountain gales, the tiny village of Menetes sits high in the cliffs above Pigadia. Climb to the church at its highest point and explore its narrow whitewashed streets.

👁 Sights

Folklore Museum
MUSEUM

(6985847672; donations welcome; ⊙9am-1pm & 5-8pm) **FREE** Spend a few minutes walking around Menetes, and you're sure to run into Irini, custodian of the keys to the ancient chapel that houses this two-room museum. Having unlocked it, she'll talk you through its haphazard treasures and point you towards the tunnels in the hillside nearby, used by German troops in WWII.

🍴 Eating

Dionysos Fiesta
TAVERNA €

(22450 81269; mains €6-9; ⊙breakfast, lunch & dinner) Set in a restored traditional house, in the twisting village lanes just up from the main road, this relaxed and welcoming taverna spreads onto a raised garden terrace. Local specialities to savour include goat stew, lemon chicken, artichoke omelettes and succulent Karpathian sausages.

Arkasa   Αρκάσα

Arkasa, on the southwest coast, 9km from Menetes, is one of the oldest settlements on Karpathos. The original village centre, just up from the water, is now complemented by a burgeoning beach resort below. A waterside track leads 500m to the remains of the 5th-century **Basilica of Agia Sophia**, where two chapels stand amid mosaic fragments and columns, and to an ancient **acropolis** on the headland. The best beach hereabouts, sandy Agios Nikolaos Beach, stretches south from the acropolis, but to reach it by road you have to turn left from the village itself.

🛏 Sleeping

★ Glaros Studios   APARTMENT €

(☑ 22450 61015; www.glarosstudios-karpathos.com; Agios Nikolaos Beach; studios €50-55; ℗ 🛜) This well-managed and ever-expanding garden-set complex pretty much has broad Agios Nikolaos Beach to itself. There are spotless white studios, decorated in traditional Karpathian style with raised platform beds and small kitchenettes, plus a relaxed and good-value adjoining restaurant.

Finiki   Φοινίκι

Arrayed along a neat little south-facing crescent bay, picturesque Finiki stands just 2km north of Arkasa. White-and-blue houses, interspersed with a peppering of tavernas, front its sleepy harbour and small grey-sand beach. The best local swimming is at **Agios Georgios Beach**, a short way south towards Arkasa.

🛏 Sleeping & Eating

Finiki View Hotel   HOTEL €€

(☑ 22450 61400; www.finikiview.gr; r/apt €85/100; 🛜🛜🏊) Smart little family-owned studio hotel, five minutes' walk up from the village on the main coast road, with dramatic views of the beach and harbour below. There's a fresh, homey feel to the place and all studios and apartments have kitchenettes, pine green furniture, white walls and sea views. Some have traditional raised beds.

Marina Taverna   TAVERNA €

(☑ 22450 61100; mains €6-16; ⊙ breakfast, lunch & dinner) Laid-back taverna with an expansive terrace surveying the gentle turquoise bay from within metres of the waterfront. Inexpensive breakfasts, snack lunches and an enjoyable seafood-accented evening menu featuring squid, crab and grilled meats.

Lefkos   Λευκός

The largest but also the prettiest of the low-key west-coast resorts, 20km north of Finiki and a 5km detour down from the main road. Lefkos is here for a very good reason – its curving sandy beach is absolutely delightful. This is the kind of place where two weeks can vanish in gentle wanderings between beach and brunch. While Lefkos is connected by bus with Pigadia, it's definitely worth renting a car or scooter through Lefkos Rent a Car (p491) while here.

🛏 Sleeping & Eating

Le Grand Bleu   HOTEL €€

(☑ 22450 71009; www.karpathos-legrandbleu.com; studio/apt €85/120; ℗ ✳ 🛜) Very nicely equipped studios and two-bedroom apartments beside the graceful main beach, kitted out with crisp fresh linen, tasteful art and sumptuous balconies with cushioned armchairs. The recommended on-site tavern closes at 10pm to let guests sleep.

Dramountana   TAVERNA €

(☑ 22450 71373; mains €6-15; ⊙ breakfast, lunch & dinner) Part of a cluster of four similar cafe/tavernas with waterside tables at the northern end of Lefkos harbour, this all-day cafe serves everything from fresh juices and coffee to fish soup, grilled squid, roast lamb and souvlaki. Its owners also run a new restaurant 50m away, and another in the mountain village of Mesohori, 10km north.

Northern Karpathos

Locals often describe Karpathos as being two distinct islands, with its rugged, mountainous and astonishingly beautiful northern half in stark contrast to the fertile, low-lying south. That said, the east-coast road starts to climb as soon as you head north from Pigadia and the scenery turns ever more spectacular. Only within the last decade has the route been sealed all the way to the far north, with the unfortunate effect that the once-isolated village of Olymbos has become swamped with day trippers in summer. Olymbos is still a magnificent place, though, most memorably reached by taking a boat to Diafani from Pigadia, then catching a connecting bus. And it's still worth spending a few nights here too, especially if you fancy some high-mountain hiking, or swimming at remote beaches.

Apella Beach Απέλλα

However determined you may be to reach Olymbos, allow time to take the precipitous spur road that drops seawards from the east-coast highway 17km north of Pigadia. Backed by a cascading hillside of wildflowers, with towering cliffs to both north and south, Apella Beach here is the finest beach in the Dodecanese. A broad and utterly unspoiled expanse of pure white sand, it's more like a Hawaiian beach than anything you'd expect to find in the Aegean. There's a good taverna at road's end, just above the beach.

Olymbos Όλυμπος

POP 330

Few moments can beat rounding a curve in the mountain road to receive your first glimpse of this mist-blown eyrie of pastel-coloured houses. Olymbos clings precariously to the summit of Mt Profitis Ilias (716m), as if flung there by a Titan's paw. Thread your way along its wind-tunnel alleys, passing old ladies in vividly coloured traditional dress, and you may feel as though you've strayed onto a film set. Many locals even speak with a dialect that still contains traces of ancient Dorian Greek.

So many day trippers make their way here that the main street is these days lined with shops selling soaps, rugs, embroidered linen and leather sandals, and tavernas sporting garish, laminated menus. The views, though, remain as jaw-dropping as ever, and if you can avoid the day trippers by arriving in the late afternoon or early morning, Olymbos continues to cast its timeless spell.

🛏 Sleeping & Eating

Hotel Aphrodite HOTEL €
(☑ 22450 51307; www.discoverolympos.com; d €35) A village hotel, just beyond the central square at the far end of Olymbos. It has two rooms with two single beds, and two rooms with three. All are bright, airy and attractively decorated, but above all – literally – they have astonishing west-facing sea views. The owners run the recommended Parthenon restaurant nearby, topped by a roof terrace.

Hotel Olymbos GUESTHOUSE €
(☑ 22450 51009; r incl breakfast €45) 🍴 Hidden away beneath the owners' excellent street-level restaurant, these three little en suite studios have raised beds and traditional furnishings. Tread carefully; the walls are festooned with delicate decorated plates. Ask to see the family's carefully preserved blacksmith shop alongside.

Edem Garden TAVERNA €
(mains €6-9) Village taverna with a broad mountain-view terrace, check-cloth tables and a menu featuring delicious rural specialities such as *makarounes* (homemade pasta cooked with cheese and onions), country sausage and local goat *stifadho*, along with pizzas and salads. And yes, maybe the name should really be 'Eden', but it isn't.

Diafani Διαφάνι

POP 250

Diafani is an intimate, wind-blasted huddle of white houses fronted by cobalt blue water, backdropped by a mountain. Bar the crash of the waves and old men playing backgammon, nothing else stirs. Most travellers pass through Diafani, so if you stay you'll likely have the beaches and trails to yourself.

🏃 Activities

Boat Trips

Boat excursions head north daily from Diafani to inaccessible beaches on Karpathos and the nearby island of Saria. Some boats originate in Pigadia and call at Diafani en route, while others set off from here. Expect to pay around €8 to be dropped off at a beach, or up to €20 for a day trip to Saria.

Hiking

Hiking trails from Diafani village are way-marked with red or blue markers or stone cairns. The most popular route heads inland, straight up the valley to Olymbos. That takes around two hours – though some prefer to catch a bus uphill and walk back down. Alternatively, a 50-minute track leads 4km north along the coast, through the pines, to **Vananda Beach**, which has a seasonal taverna.

A more strenuous three-hour walk takes you 11km northwest to the Hellenistic site of **Vroukounda**, passing the agricultural village of Avlona along the way. There are no facilities, so carry food and water with you. Anyone planning serious walking should get the 1:60,000 *Karpathos-Kasos* map, published by **Terrain** (www.terrainmaps.gr) and available in Pigadia. For advice on current conditions, call in at the Environment Management office (10am to 4pm Monday to Friday) on Diafani's seafront before you set off.

🛏 Sleeping & Eating

Balaskas Hotel   HOTEL €

(☑22450 51320; www.balaskashotel.com; s €30, d €35-45; ✳🛜) Very friendly hotel, a short walk inland from the beach but lacking sea views. The 19 fresh rooms have tiled floors and whitewashed walls; some have kitchenettes. The owners operate two excursion boats and offer a free beach trip for each guest.

Corali   TAVERNA €

(☑22450 51332; mains €6-11; ⊙breakfast, lunch & dinner) It may not be the most eye-catching taverna along Diafani's quay, but its peaceful shaded terrace is pleasant enough and, more importantly, it serves the best food in the village. Whether you're looking for grilled octopus (€10), hearty *stifadho* (€8), or just a homemade cake and a cup of coffee, this is the place to come.

ℹ Information

There's no bank, post office, petrol station or ATM, so bring cash and fuel. **Orfanos Travel** (☑6974990394; ⊙8am-1pm & 5.30-8.30pm) runs boat trips and sells ferry and air tickets.

ℹ Getting There & Away

Blue Star Ferries (p473) call in at Diafani's small jetty three times weekly heading for Halki and Rhodes, and three times weekly en route towards Pigadia and Kasos (two of which continue to Crete and one to Santorini). There are also day trips by boat to Pigadia in summer, as well as assorted excursions. Tourist coaches carry day trippers from the jetty up to Olympos. There are two scheduled buses on weekdays, one of which continues to Pigadia on Friday only, and one on weekends.

KASOS   ΚΑΣΟΣ

POP 1080

Kasos, the southernmost Dodecanese island, looks like the Greece that time forgot. Deceptively inviting in summer, it can feel very isolated in winter, when it's battered by severe winds and imprisoned by huge turquoise waves. Most of its visitors are rare seabirds; 90% of the human returnees are Kasiots on fleeting visits. Come here, though, and you may well succumb to its tumbledown charm.

In 1820, under Turkish rule, Kasos was home to 11,000 inhabitants. Tragically, Mohammad Ali, the Turkish governor of Egypt, saw its large merchant fleet as an impediment to his plan to establish a base in Crete. On 7 June 1824, therefore, his men landed on Kasos and killed around 7000 of its people. The island never really recovered, but each year Kasiots return from all over the world to commemorate the massacre.

Kasos

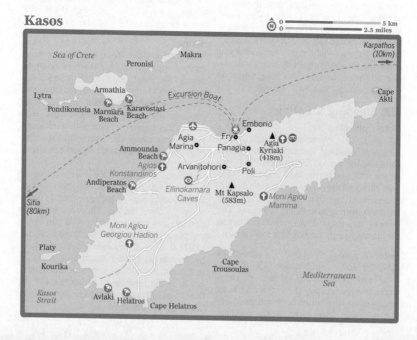

Getting There & Away

There are daily flights to Karpathos (€21, 10 minutes), Sitia (€38, 40 minutes) and Rhodes (€34, one hour) with **Olympic Air** (☑ 22450 41555; Kritis Airport). The only ferry service is with Blue Star Ferries (p473), en route between Rhodes and Karpathos, and Crete and Piraeus.

BOAT SERVICES FROM KASOS (FRY)

DESTINATION	TIME	FARE	FREQUENCY
Heraklion	6hr	€20	1 weekly
Karpathos	1½hr	€8	3 weekly
Piraeus	19hr	€41	2 weekly
Rhodes	8hr	€24	3 weekly
Santorini	9hr	€25	2 weekly
Sitia	2½hr	€11	2 weekly

Getting Around

The airport is 1km west of Fry. Either walk for 10 minutes along the coast road – yes, it's exposed, but you won't half feel pleased with yourself – or call a **taxi** (☑ 6973244371, 6977904632). In theory, a bus connects all the island's villages, but it hasn't been working for years. Cars and scooters can be hired from **Oasis Rent-a-Car** (☑ 22450 41746).

Fry   Φρυ

POP 350

The capital, Fry *(free)*, is on the north coast. The broad gentle valley behind it is the only fertile land on Kasos, so the only other villages are dotted across the surrounding hillside. Although Fry is more of a working port than a tourist destination, the tiny old harbour at its core, known as **Bouka**, is impossibly photogenic. Pretty white houses with navy blue trim line the quay, a few cafes sit waiting for customers, grizzled fishers patiently mend their nets, and the pastel blue church of Agios Spyridon surveys the scene. Even as late as June, though, Fry still has the feel of a ghost town. The nearest beach is 10 minutes' walk east along the shoreline, in the tiny satellite port of **Emborio**. There are patches of gravel amid the sand, but the sea is clear and sheltered, so it's a good place for a quick dip.

Sights & Activities

Archaeological Museum   MUSEUM

(☺ 9am-3pm, summer only) **FREE** Housed in a grand 19th-century villa above the harbour, this seasonal museum displays objects pulled from ancient shipwrecks, assorted Greek oil lamps and Hellenistic finds, including inscribed stone slabs.

Excursion Boat   BOAT TOUR

(☑ 22450 41047, 6977911209; trip €10) When they can round up 10 or more passengers, two boats, *Athina* and *Kasos Princess*, offer summer-afternoon excursions to the uninhabited islet of Armathia, which has superb sandy beaches. The *Kasos Princess* also runs full-day trips to Pigadia on Karpathos, on summer Wednesdays only.

Sleeping

Hotel Anagennissis   HOTEL €

(☑ 22450 41495; www.anagennisishotel.gr; s/d €41/54; ❄ ☎) An old-fashioned midrange hotel, close to the waterfront in the village centre, where the plain but perfectly adequate en suite rooms have comfy beds, fridges and sea-view balconies. Staff are seldom present in the hotel itself; the owners run Kasos Maritime & Travel Agency next door.

Angelica's   APARTMENT €€

(☑ 22450 41268; www.angelicas.gr; apt €65-95; ❄ ☎) Attractive, traditionally furnished apartments in a fine old village home with a pebble-mosaic courtyard, a five-minute walk up from the harbour. Two are on the ground floor, with private courtyards, and two upstairs, with sea-view verandahs. All have painted floors and stencils on their white walls. The largest sleeps up to five.

Eating & Drinking

⭐ **Taverna Emborios**   TAVERNA €

(☑ 22450 41586; Emborio Beach; mains €6-13; ☺ lunch & dinner) Crisp, beautifully neat beachfront restaurant, 10 minutes' walk from Fry, that's unquestionably the best place to eat on Kasos. The friendly owner, who lived in New York for many years, serves up wonderful local specialities, including delicious octopus, tiny home-grown olives and his own salty preserved fish.

Orea Bouka   TAVERNA €

(☑ 22450 41053; mains €6-9) There's no menu at this simple little taverna, which sets out tables on the sea wall on the west side of Bouka harbour. The owner just shows or tells you whatever she happens to be cooking. In summer, expect a choice of fresh fish, baked meats and vegetable stews. At quieter times, you simply get what you're given.

O Mylos   TAVERNA €

(☑ 22450 41825; Plateia Iroön Kasou; mains €7; ☺ lunch & dinner; ☎ ☑) Overlooking the

DODECANESE FRY

commercial port (as opposed to Bouka), this conspicuous taverna has unbroken sea views and serves a reliable menu of local favourites such as 'mountain grass roots' – village sausage and pot-roast rabbit – along with fresh fish. Almost everything costs less than €10.

ℹ Information

Both the Commercial Bank beside the harbour and Alpha on Plateia Iroön Kasou have ATMs.

Kasos Maritime & Travel Agency (☑ 22450 41495; www.kassos-island.gr; Plateia Iroön Kasou) For all travel tickets.

Police (☑ 22450 41222) On a narrow sealed street running south from Fry's main road.

Port police (☑ 22450 41288) Behind the Agios Spyridon church.

Post office (⊙ 7.30am-2pm Mon-Fri) Diagonally across from the police.

Around Kasos

None of the beaches on Kasos offer shade. The best is the isolated pebbled cove of **Helatros**, near Moni Agiou Georgiou Hadion, 11km southwest of Fry, but you'll need your own transport to reach it, and it has no facilities. There's another small but decent beach, **Avlaki**, in walking distance.

Agia Marina, 1km southwest of Fry, is a pretty village with a gleaming white-and-blue church that celebrates a festival on 17 July. Beyond it, the road continues to verdant **Arvanitohori**, with abundant fig and pomegranate trees. **Poli**, 3km southeast of Fry, is the former capital, built on the ancient acropolis.

KASTELLORIZO (MEGISTI)
ΚΑΣΤΕΛΛΟΡΙΖΟ (ΜΕΓΙΣΤΗ)

POP 280

So close to the Turkish coast – Kaş is just 2km away – that you can almost taste the East, the tiny, far-flung island of Kastellorizo is, above all else, insanely pretty. Its one village, also called Kastellorizo, consists of a spellbinding array of pastel-painted neoclassical houses, cradling a deeply indented horseshoe bay. The island enjoys an enviable 320 days of sunshine each year and the sheer quality of the light is stunning. While it may lack powder-fine beaches, the coast is still well worth exploring, with highlights including the fabulous Blue Cave.

Kastellorizo is not an easy place to reach, but anyone who makes the effort will be rewarded with beauty, tranquillity, warmth and a great choice of accommodation and food.

History

Home to the best harbour between Beirut and Piraeus, Kastellorizo was successively a prosperous trading port for the Dorians, Romans, Crusaders, Egyptians, Turks and Venetians. Under Ottoman control, from 1552 onwards, it had the largest merchant fleet in the Dodecanese. A 1913 revolt against the Turks briefly resulted in it becoming a French naval base, and it subsequently passed into the hands of the Italians. The island progressively lost all strategic and economic importance, especially after the 1923 Greece–Turkey population exchange. Many islanders emigrated to Australia, where around 30,000 continue to live.

After Kastellorizo suffered bombardment during WWII, English commanders ordered the few remaining inhabitants to abandon the island. Most fled to Cyprus, Palestine and Egypt and those that later returned found their houses in ruins. While the island has never regained its previous population levels – the village alone was once home to 10,000 people – more recent returnees have finally restored almost all the waterfront buildings, and Kastellorizo is looking better than it has for a century.

ℹ Getting There & Away

AIR

Olympic Air (www.olympicair.com) flies four times a week between Kastellorizo and Rhodes (€44, 40 minutes).

BOAT

Kastellorizo has a very limited ferry service. Blue Star Ferries (p473) call in twice a week to and from Piraeus (23 hours, €59) via Rhodes (4¾ hours, €22). On summer Saturdays, Dodekanisos Seaways (p473) sails from Rhodes (2¼ hours, €36) to Kastellorizo and back. Used as a day trip, it gives you four hours on the island.

ℹ Getting Around

Kastellorizo's tiny airport is up on the central plateau, 2.5km above the village. There's no bus, so you'll have to take the island **taxi** (☑ 6938739178) to and from the harbour (€5).

Kastellorizo Village
Καστελλόριζο

POP 250

Kastellorizo Village is the main settlement on the island. Pastel-painted three-storey mansions, each with a tiled roof and wrought-iron balcony, stand guard beside the turquoise water, while traditional life continues in the labyrinthine cobbled backstreets behind. An amazing 80% of the villagers are returned Aussie expats, which adds a definite upbeat energy to the community.

◉ Sights

The village holds two small museums. The **Megisti Museum** (admission $3; ⏱8.30am-3pm Tue-Sat), in a former mosque near the ferry jetty, devotes itself largely to display panels telling the island's story. Not far above it, the **Archaeological Museum** (⏱7am-2pm Tue-Sun) FREE holds an assortment of ancient finds, costumes and photos. At the top of the hill, a rickety stairway leads to the ruins of the **Knights of St John Castle**, which gave the island its name – thanks to the red cliff on which it stood, this was the 'Castello Rosso'. It offers splendid views of Turkey.

A coastal pathway around the headland below passes precarious steps that climb to a rock-hewn **Lycian tomb** from the 4th century BC, with an impressive Doric facade. There are several such tombs on Turkey's Anatolian coast, but they're very rare in Greece.

It's also possible to walk the 1km up to **Paleokastro**, the island's ancient capital. Follow the concrete steps that start just past a soldier's sentry box on the airport road. The old city's Hellenistic walls enclose a tower, a water cistern and three churches.

🏃 Activities

The main destinations for boat trips are Kaş in Turkey and the spectacular **Blue Cave** (Parasta), famous for its mirrorlike water, on the remote southeast shore. Look for the *Varvara* or the *Agios Georgios* (both ☎6977855756), moored on the quay between trips.

🛏 Sleeping

Damien & Monika's PENSION €€
(☎22460 49028, 6978066375; www.kastellorizo.de; Plateia Kastellorizou; r €60; ✻) These comfy central rooms are tastefully finished with traditional furnishings, fridge and lots of windows to let in that special Kastellorizo light. You'll also find a book exchange and heaps of local info. For wi-fi, you have to go to the owners' nearby Olive Garden restaurant. Considerable discounts outside peak season.

Mediterraneo PENSION €€
(☎22460 49007; www.mediterraneo-kastelorizo.com; s/d/ste €70/80/180; ⏱May-Oct; ☎) A mustard-hued waterfront villa, near the

western end of the harbour, offering simple fan-only rooms with white bedspreads, icon-dotted walls and shabby-chic touches. The cheapest face the garden, while the best is the sea-level suite, with loungers right on the water outside your door.

Megisti Hotel HOTEL €€
(☎22460 49220; www.megistihotel.gr; d/ste €140/220; ✻@☎) A smart white-painted hotel, facing the ferry jetty directly across the harbour, where you can lower yourself into the sea from the chequerboard waterfront terrace. Its four suites and 15 rooms are dazzlingly bright and modern, with rain showers, DVD players and crisp fresh linen.

Poseidon HOTEL €€
(☎6956617585, 22460 49212; www.kastelorizo-poseidon.gr; Plateia Australias; d/ste €110/150; ✻☎) Spreading through five beautifully restored village houses, a block from the waterfront on the west side of the harbour, Poseidon offers large rooms with private verandahs and big sea views. Some have traditional-style platform beds and the main hotel building has a lovely roof terrace.

🍴 Eating & Drinking

Tables spill out onto the narrow harbour, cats entwine themselves around diners' legs and, by night, the atmosphere is magical – just don't tip into the water!

★Alexandra's TAVERNA €
(☎22460 49019; mains €7-15; ⏱lunch & dinner) It's no coincidence that the friendliest and least pushy of Kastellorizo's many quayside restaurants also serves the island's best food. Everything from the fried chickpea patties to the squid-ink risotto is freshly prepared and beautifully cooked (by Alexandra herself), while the waterfront setting is especially irresistible at night.

Radio Cafe CAFE €
(☎22460 49029; breakfast €3-6; ⏱8am-late; ✻☎) This welcoming little wi-fi-equipped cafe, close to the jetty, offers Greek- and English-style breakfasts – from yoghurt with honey to fried eggs and bacon – until 1pm. The kitchen closes after that, but it carries on serving coffee, juices and light snacks, and it's a perfect spot for an evening cocktail, with sunset views thrown in for free.

Mediteraneo TAVERNA €
(Horafia; mains €7-12; ⏱breakfast, lunch & dinner Jun-Sep; ✻☎) Atop the hill east of the harbour, beside the church en route to

Mandraki bay, this spacious summer-only restaurant has a peaceful garden where you can enjoy local specialities such as octopus *stifadho* and cabbage-leaf dolmadhes. The ever-changing array of specials will keep your taste buds tingling.

Faros Bar BAR
(☑ 22460 49509; ⊘ 9am-late; 🛜) Occupying an enviable location in the former lighthouse, beyond the ferry jetty, this bar offers a wonderful opportunity to swim in turquoise shallows before taking breakfast and drinking in wide-screen views of Turkey. It even has its own quayside loungers. Salads and snacks all day, then tapas come 6pm.

ⓘ Information

Ferries arrive on the eastern side of the bay. The village only stretches one or two blocks back from the harbour. It takes 10 minutes to walk all the way round to the west – the main square, Plateia Ethelondon Kastellorizou, is halfway along, and you'll pass a National Bank ATM en route. There's another open square, Plateia Australias, at the southwest corner. Reach the hill-top settlement of Horafia, and Mandraki bay beyond, by climbing the broad steps east of the harbour.

Papoutsis Travel (☑ 22460 70630, 22460 49356) Ferry and air tickets, bike and scooter rental and yachting services.

Police station (☑ 22460 49333) On the bay's western side.

Port police (☑ 22460 49010) At the eastern tip of the bay.

Post office (⊘ 9am-2pm Mon-Fri) Next to the police station.

SYMI ΣΥΜΗ

POP 2610

Beautiful Symi is guaranteed to evoke oohs and aahs from ferry passengers before they even get off the boat. The first sight of the harbour of island capital Gialos, framed against an amphitheatre of biscuit- and wine-coloured houses rising on all sides, is unforgettable. It's all thanks to the Italians, who ruled the island almost a century ago and established the neoclassical architectural style that Symi has followed ever since.

Although Symi is far from small, it's mostly barren and the only settlements are Gialos, the old village of Horio, which sprawls over the hilly ridge behind, and Pedi, down in the valley beyond. One road runs all the way to the monastery at Panormitis, near Symi's southern tip. The rest of this spellbinding island is largely deserted, but it's surrounded by blue coves and beaches, aglitter with crystal-clear water so transparent that boats can look as if they're floating on thin air.

History

Symi has long traditions of both sponge diving and shipbuilding and is mentioned in the *Iliad* as sending three ships to assist Agamemnon's siege of Troy. During Ottoman times it was granted the right to fish for sponges in Turkish waters. In return, Symi supplied the sultan with first-class boat builders. This exchange enriched the island – gracious mansions were built and culture and education flourished. By the early 20th century, the population was 22,500 and Symi was launching around 500 ships a year. But the Italian occupation, the advent of the steamship and the decline of the sponge industry put an end to prosperity, obliging Symi to reinvent itself as a tourist destination.

ⓘ Getting There & Away

Dodekanisos Seaways (p473) runs catamarans to and from Rhodes at least once daily – four each week stop at Panormitis en route – and also offers frequent sailings northwest, to Kos and beyond. Blue Star Ferries (p473) calls in twice weekly heading towards Rhodes, and also en route for Tilos, Nisyros, Kos, Kalymnos, Astypalea and Piraeus. Symi fills up every morning with day trippers from Rhodes, with several Rhodes-based excursion boats complementing the high-speed catamaran.

Look out for summer day trips from Gialos to Datça in Turkey (€40, including Turkish port taxes).

BOAT SERVICES FROM SYMI (GIALOS)

DESTINATION	TIME	FARE	FREQUENCY
Kalymnos*	2hr 20min	€31	4 weekly
Kos	3hr	€14	2 weekly
Kos*	1½hr	€22	4 weekly
Leros*	3hr	€40	4 weekly
Lipsi*	3hr 10min	€41	4 weekly
Nisyros	3hr 20min	€10	1 weekly
Patmos*	4hr	€44	4 weekly
Piraeus	15hr	€51	2 weekly
Rhodes	1hr 40 min	€13	2 weekly
Rhodes*	50min	€17	1-4 daily
Rhodes*	1hr	€16	1 daily
Samos	5hr	€49	1 weekly
Tilos	2hr	€9	1 weekly

*high-speed services

Getting Around

BOAT

Water taxis lined up along the inner side of Gialos harbour run regular trips to the beaches. Most head north to Nimborios (€6) or south to Agia Marina, Agios Nikolaos, Nanou and Marathounda (€6 to €14). In high season there's at least one departure an hour, from 9am onwards, with the last boat back at 5pm or 6pm. Larger boats offer day trips to remote west-coast beaches, the monastery at Panormitis, or island-circuit tours (up to €40, including BBQ lunch).

BUS & TAXI

The island bus makes hourly runs between the south side of Gialos harbour and Pedi Beach, via Horio (flat fare €1.50). There's also service to Panormitis, two to three times daily (€1.50). Taxis depart from a rank 100m west of the bus stop, and cost €25 (each way) to Panormitis.

CAR

Glaros (☎ 22460 71926, 6948362079; www.glarosrentacar.gr), near the clock tower, rents cars and scooters.

Gialos   Γιαλός

POP 2200

Gialos is beyond words, a neoclassical gem that has to be the most stunning harbour in all Greece. Stay a week and you'll still be

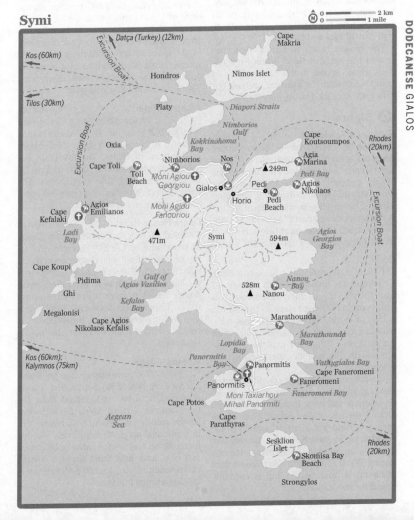

Symi

swooning at the glorious ensemble, with tier upon tier of magnificent mansions and tidy villas, each following the same simple, but obligatory, triangular-topped template and painted in a subtle and ever-varying palette of custard, ochre and pastel colours.

Along the quay, a basilica and clock tower punctuate rows of enticing cafes, bars and tavernas, while the harbour itself jostles with all manner of water craft, from colossal cruise ships to tiny water taxis. Wander away from the sea to find backstreets spilling with sponge stores and aromatic bakeries.

Head north along the seafront from the clock tower, away from the centre, and you're immediately in smaller **Harani Bay**. Traditionally a base for shipbuilding, it still holds assorted beached boats, along with its own crop of bars and tavernas.

The closest beach to Gialos, **Nos**, lies around the next headland, 500m from the clock tower. Access to this narrow strip of gravel is controlled by a taverna and bar, but it's a great spot for a swim, nonetheless.

◎ Sights

Nautical & Folklore Museum MUSEUM
(admission €2; ⊗ 9.30am-9pm) The two upper floors of a colourfully painted villa on Gialos' main square hold the separate halves of this freshly restored museum. Crammed with relics of Symi's sponge-diving era, including a pair of bulky helmets, the Nautical section at the top is more interesting than the rather haphazard Folklore part below, but both contain fascinating old photos of the island.

Horio VILLAGE
Climbing calf-crunching, knee-knobbling Kali Strata, the broad stair path that sets off from the alleyways behind the harbour, will bring you in 500-or-so steps to the hill-top village of Horio. En route you'll pass a bewitching succession of majestic villas built for long-gone Symi sea captains – some are utterly dilapidated, others restored to splendour.

Constructed to deter marauding pirates, Horio is an absolute warren of a place. All its tavernas and bars, though, are clustered around the top of Kali Strata. Most of the houses beyond are in ruins, and so is the **Knights of St John Kastro** at the very top, thanks to an explosion of German munitions during WWII. The island's **Archaeological Museum** is up here too, but is currently closed for restoration.

⏴ Sleeping

With demand high, accommodation on Symi tends to be more expensive than on other islands. Many visitors prefer to stay in rented neoclassical villas: both Kalodoukas Holidays (p504) and Symi Visitor (p504) offer wide selections. If you're staying up in Horio, arrange a pick-up or catch a taxi – don't even dream of walking up Kali Strata with your bags.

★**Hotel Fiona** HOTEL €€
(☑ 22460 72088; www.fionahotel.com; Horio; r/ste incl breakfast €60/70; ✲ 🅰) Offering Symi's best-value accommodation, this simple but charming family-run hotel perches on the edge of Horio (turn left at the top of Kali Strata). The views across the harbour are truly astonishing, both from the balconies of its spacious and attractively decorated rooms, kitted out with turquoise furniture, and from the breakfast area downstairs. There's also a peaceful courtyard.

Albatros Hotel HOTEL €€
(☑ 22460 71707; www.albatrosymi.gr; Gialos; r incl breakfast €62; ⊗ Apr-Nov; ✲ 🅰) A small hotel, a couple of blocks back from the harbour in the heart of Gialos. The five plain but spotless and tasteful air-con rooms have little balconies giving side-on sea views. The friendly French owner also rents out some larger houses and apartments.

Opera House Hotel APARTMENT €€
(☑ 22460 72034; www.symioperahouse.gr; Gialos; r & ste incl breakfast €70-150) This attractive array of freshly built island-style neoclassical villas stands well away from the sea, towards the back of town. Options range from small double rooms to large suites that sleep up to six. Upper-level apartments have balconies with mountain views. Breakfast in the central courtyard; there's a snack bar but no restaurant.

Iapetos Village APARTMENT €€
(☑ 22460 72777; www.iapetos-village.gr; Gialos; d & apt €135; ✲ @ 🅰 ☷) Set around a leafy courtyard, a short walk inland from the main square, Iapetos holds 28 high-class rooms, studios and apartments, newly built in traditional style. All have lovely wooden high ceilings and private patios or balconies, and most have fully fitted kitchens. There's also a beautiful pool, tucked under the arches, plus a sauna and bar.

Old Markets
BOUTIQUE HOTEL **€€€**

(☑ 22460 71440; www.theoldmarkets.com; Gialos; r/ste incl breakfast €220/395; ❉ 🛜) Very much the swishest place to stay on the island, this upscale B&B stands a few steps up Kali Strata. Housed in what was once a small marketplace, now opulently restored, holds three rooms and one sumptuous suite, which share use of a harbour-view roof terrace where daily champagne breakfasts are served. Spa treatments available.

✕ Eating

✕ Gialos

Meraklis
SEAFOOD **€**

(☑ 22460 71003; www.tavernaomeraklis.com; mains €8-10; ⊙10am-late; 🛜) Old-school backstreet taverna, its Santorini-blue walls decked out with vintage diving photos and antique mirrors. The menu is straight from the table of Poseidon. Souvlakia, meatballs and roast lamb are all tasty, but most diners come to feast on fresh octopus, sea bream, Symi shrimp and swordfish. Why not try the lot, with a mixed seafood plate (€30 for two)?

★Tholos
TAVERNA **€€**

(☑ 22460 72033; Harani; mains €8-14; ⊙lunch & dinner May-Oct) There's no more romantic restaurant in the Dodecanese than this lovely taverna, poised at the tip of Harani Bay, along the quay from central Gialos. The sunset views from its waterfront tables are stupendous, and so too is the food, which includes local meat and vegetables as well as fresh fish. Be sure to sample the succulent, bright-red Symi shrimp.

To Spitiko
TAVERNA **€€**

(☑ 22460 72452; Gialos; mains €8-18; ⊙breakfast, lunch & dinner) There's little to distinguish this small, very local harbourfront taverna from its neighbours – until you sit down to eat. Quite simply, Spitiko gets it right, with no-frills but top-quality home cooking. Everything from the country sausage to the grilled octopus in lemon sauce is recommended.

Muses
FUSION **€€**

(☑ 6958734503; www.muses-symi.com; mains €12-24; ⊙7pm-late May-Oct) Gourmet dinner-only option that's rapidly established itself as Symi's most exciting new restaurant. Its modern Mediterranean menu changes daily, combining signature dishes such as octopus with *fava* and orange, or pork with pears and retsina, with inventive desserts –

carrot granita, anyone? Seating is on a flowery terrace, beside the town square just back from the harbour.

✕ Horio

Olive Tree
CAFE **€**

(☑ 22460 72681; www.olivetreesymi.eu; light meals €3-8; ⊙8.30am-3.30pm; 🛜🖉📶)🖊 English-run cafe that's a favourite morning rendezvous for the island's expats. Sit yourself down on its vine-shaded terrace at the top of Kali Strata and tuck into a wide array of smoothies, juices, cakes, locally sourced salads and sandwiches.

★Syllogos
GREEK **€€**

(☑ 22460 72148; Plateia Syllogou; mains €8-17; ⊙7pm-late) The star attraction at the village's largest restaurant is its huge terrace, open to soothing evening breezes high above Pedi Bay. Its traditional Greek menu is excellent, though, with specials such as sesame-crusted feta, lamb with lemon potatoes, or chicken stewed with prunes delivered in large portions. Friendly service.

Taverna Giorgo & Maria
TAVERNA **€€**

(☑ 22460 71984; Horio; mains €8-12; ⊙lunch & dinner) This much-loved Horio fixture is deeply traditional, from its roofed but open-sided pebble-mosaic courtyard to its no-frills menu of Symi lamb, rabbit stew, dolmadhes and sea-urchin salad. Its raised terrace has great views down to the bay. Live music from 9pm on Friday and Saturday.

🍷 Drinking & Nightlife

The lively waterfront is peppered with bars and cafes staying open late into the night, and there are plenty more bars up in Horio for good measure.

★Tsati
BAR

(☑ 22460 72498; Harani, Gialos; ⊙11am-late) Ultra-welcoming quayside bar, 100m along Harani Bay beyond the clock tower. As well as tables on a tree-shaded terrace, it offers stone benches carved into the sea wall. Cushioned and whitewashed, they're perfect for a sunset cocktail, served with free snacks.

ℹ Information

Ferries and catamarans dock beside the clock tower on the north side of the harbour entrance. Excursion and taxi boats dock along the south side, near its inland end. All activity in Gialos focuses on the quay, while the Kali Strata stairway sets off up to Horio from the southeast corner.

Both the National Bank and Alpha Bank have ATM-equipped branches on the northern side of the harbour.

Kalodoukas Holidays (☑22460 71077; www.kalodoukas.gr) In the absence of an official tourist office, this helpful agency, at the foot of Kali Strata, is the next best thing. It also rents houses, sells tickets, organises excursions and offers yachting services.

Police (☑22460 71111) By the ferry quay.

Port police (☑22460 71205) By the ferry quay.

Post office By the ferry quay.

Symi Tours (☑22460 71307; www.symitours.com) This agency, just behind the southeast side of the harbour, organises excursions, including island bus tours and boat trips to Datça in Turkey, provides yachting services and sells ferry tickets.

Symi Visitor (☑22460 71785; www.symi-visitor.com) Very friendly agency, just off the southeast side of the quay, with a fine roster of rental properties and a full-service laundry.

Around Symi

Apart from the monastery at Panormitis, the only tourist destinations on Symi are the beaches scattered along its coastline.

Nimborios   Νιμπόρειος

Nimborios is a pebble beach 3km west of Gialos, reached by walking or driving all the way around the harbour and simply continuing along the exposed but utterly beautiful shore-front road beyond. It's a peaceful spot, with a good little taverna that allows its customers to spend the day on sunbeds beneath the tamarisk trees alongside.

Pedi   Πέδι

Once a village, now more of a yachting marina and low-key resort, Pedi stretches along the inner end of a large bay south of Gialos, immediately below Horio. The gentle valley behind it has always been the agricultural heartland of Symi.

Two beaches, to either side of the mouth of the bay, can be reached on foot from Pedi or by water taxi from Gialos; both have appealing tavernas. **Agia Marina** to the north is a lagoonlike little bay, facing a delightful chapel-topped islet across turquoise waters, which gets very crowded indeed in summer. **Agios Nikolaos**, on the south side, is broader and sandier, with decent tree cover and idyllic swimming.

Nanou & Marathounda   Νανού & Μαραθούντα

Two large bays south of Pedi, Nanou and Marathounda, hold large beaches and tavernas and make great destinations for water-taxi day trips. Goat-roamed Marathounda, backed by a lush valley and also accessible via a rough road, is especially recommended.

✕ Eating

★**Marathounda Taverna**   TAVERNA €€
(☑22460 71425; Marathounda; mains €8-12; ⊙breakfast, lunch & dinner) A quintessential beach taverna, where the owner's goats – responsible for the delicious homemade cheese and, whisper it, the goat stew, too – nuzzle up to the tables. Be sure to sample the Symi shrimp and grilled fish, along with herbs and vegetables from the organic gardens alongside. If you can't bear to leave, it also has plush beachfront rental studios (€125).

Panormitis   Πανορμίτης

Near Symi's southern tip, beyond the scented pine forests of the high interior, spectacular Panormitis Bay is home to the large **Moni Taxiarhou Mihail Panormiti** (☑22460 72414; ⊙dawn-sunset) **FREE**. Monasteries have stood here since the 5th century, but the present building dates from the 18th century. The principal church contains an intricately carved wooden iconostasis, frescoes and an icon of St Michael, protector of sailors and patron saint of Symi.

Pilgrims who ask the saint for a favour leave an offering; you'll see piles of these, plus prayers in bottles, that have been dropped off boats and found their own way here. The large complex comprises a Byzantine museum and folkloric museum, a bakery with excellent bread and a basic restaurant-cafe. Visitors should dress modestly. Buses come here from Gialos, and some ferries call in, too.

TILOS   ΤΗΛΟΣ

POP 550

If you're looking for a green adventure on a lost island, Tilos is the place for you, with its mountains turning russet gold in the afternoon and fishing boats bobbing in Livadia's pretty harbour. Unlike some of its barren neighbours, the island is abloom with wildflowers and home to a beguiling biodiversity, drawing birdwatchers and wildlife buffs from across the globe. Work up a sweat hiking through its meadows, mountains and valleys then flop onto one of many deserted beaches. Its azure waters play host to monk seals and sea turtles.

History

Amazingly, ancient Tilos is best known for its population of midget elephants. Full-sized elephants are thought to have found their way here six million years ago, when the island was still attached to Asia Minor. When cut off by the rising waters of the Mediterranean, the elephants were left with no natural predators, and a diminished food supply, and shrank in size. They became extinct around 4000 BC, possibly due to the arrival of the island's first human inhabitants. A large cache of their bones was discovered in 1974 in Harkadio Cave, just off the Livadia–Megalo Horio road, which is not open to visitors.

🛈 Getting There & Away

Tilos has no airport and only a minimal ferry service. The **Dodekanisos Express** (www.12ne.gr) catamaran stops at Tilos on Tuesday and Thursday, heading from Rhodes and Halki to Nisyros, Kos and Kalymnos in the morning, and back to Rhodes in the evening. On those days, you can visit the island as a day trip from Rhodes

or Halki. In addition, Blue Star Ferries (p473) sails twice each week to Piraeus via Nisyros, Kos and Kalymnos, and twice to Rhodes, one of which stops at Symi.

BOAT SERVICES FROM TILOS (LIVADIA)

DESTINATION	TIME	FARE	FREQUENCY
Halki*	40min	€13	2 weekly
Kalymnos	3hr 20min	€13	2 weekly
Kalymnos*	2¼hr	€29	2 weekly
Kos	3hr	€10	2 weekly
Kos*	1½hr	€22	2 weekly
Nisyros	1½hr	€7	2 weekly
Nisyros*	45min	€13	2 weekly
Piraeus	16hr	€51	2 weekly
Rhodes	2½hr	€14	2 weekly
Rhodes*	1½hr	€25	2 weekly
Symi	2hr	€9	1 weekly

*high-speed services

🛈 Getting Around

Five buses each day connect Livadia with Megalo Horio, Eristos Beach and Agios Antonios (€1.50). There is no taxi, but you can rent a car or scooter from **Drive Rent A Car** (☑ 22460 44173; www.drivetilos.gr) or Tilos Travel (p507).

DODECANESE TILOS

Tilos

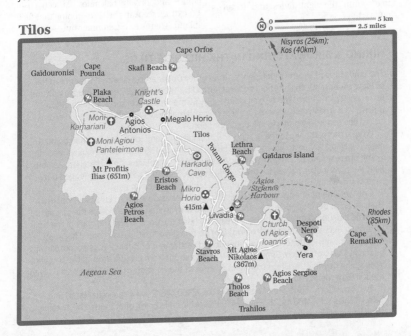

Livadia Λιβαδειά

POP 470

Whitewashed and inviting, Livadia, on Tilos' southeast shore, is sure to be the first thing you see of the island. Believe it or not, this deliciously low-key little port is the main centre for tourism. Almost all the island's accommodation options are arrayed along its 2km shingle-pebble beach lining large, sheltered Agios Stefanos bay, while its little central square is hugged by cafes, old-time tavernas and Italian-era municipal buildings.

Most visitors are content simply to relax on its beach, but Livadia also makes a great base from which to explore Leros (p530), either by hiring a car or scooter, or just hiking off into the hills.

Sights

Mikro Horio
ARCHAEOLOGICAL SITE

When pirates prowled the Dodecanese, the medieval settlement of Mikro Horio was Tilos' main population centre. Its last inhabitants only left around 50 years ago and it now stands empty, 45 minutes' walk up from Livadia. With its houses in various states of ruin – one opens as a music bar in summer – it's a fascinating place to wander around. Linger until the light fades and it turns downright eerie.

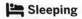 Sleeping

Apollo Studios
APARTMENT €

(22460 44379; www.apollostudios.gr; d/apt €50/80; ❄ ☎) Fresh, well-appointed studios, run by a pleasant couple and set a few streets back from the harbour, with spotless kitchenettes, modern en suites, private balconies and a great communal roof terrace. They also offer roomy apartments with tiled floors and sofa beds – ask for number 3.

★ Eleni Beach Hotel
HOTEL €€

(22460 44062; www.elenihoteltilos.gr; s/d incl breakfast €60/70) Very welcoming and beautifully maintained beachfront hotel in the middle of the bay, 10 minutes' walk along the promenade from the jetty. Almost all of its bright, well-equipped rooms have balconies facing directly out to sea. Rates include breakfast (served in the garden) as well as a sunbed right on the beach.

Ilidi Rock Hotel
HOTEL €€

(22460 44293; www.tilosholidays.gr; studio/apt €90/100, ste €120-160, incl breakfast; ❄ @ ☎ ☒) The first property you see from the ferry, this gleaming white hotel drops down the hillside just west of the harbour to reach two tiny beaches. Its dazzling studios and larger apartments have four-poster beds, self-catering facilities and private balconies. Air-con costs €6 extra, except in the three rooms that face inland. There's also a summer-only cafe/bar.

HIKING & BIRDWATCHING IN THE HILLS OF TILOS

The landscape of Tilos is much gentler than other Dodecanese islands. Rather than forbidding mountains, the interior is characterized by fertile valleys carved into agricultural terraces. It's criss-crossed by trails laid out by farmers that now serve as perfect footpaths. With small-scale ancient fortifications and medieval chapels scattered in profusion, Tilos makes a wonderful hiking destination.

What's more, thanks to the island's low population – and long-standing ban on hunting – it's also a favourite haunt for rare birds. More than 150 species have been recorded. Some are residential, some migratory. An estimated 46 species are threatened. As you hike, keep your eyes peeled for the Bonelli's eagle, Eleonora's falcon, long-legged buzzard, Sardinian warbler, Scops owl and Mediterranean black shag.

One well-maintained and very scenic 3km walk leads north from Livadia to **Lethra Beach**, an undeveloped pebble-and-sand cove with limited shade. Follow the tarmac behind the Ilidi Rock Hotel, at the northwestern end of the port, to find the start of the trail. Returning via the picturesque **Potami Gorge** brings you to the main island highway.

A longer walk leads to the small abandoned settlement of **Yera** and its accompanying beach at **Despoti Nero**. Simply follow the road south from Livadia around the bay and keep going beyond the Church of Agios Ioannis at the far eastern end. Allow half a day for the full 6km round trip.

Two operators, **Tilos Heritage Tours** (22460 44379; www.apollostudios.gr) and **Tilos Trails** (22460 44128, 6946054593; www.tilostrails.com), offer guided hikes tailored to all levels of difficulty.

🍴 Eating

★**Omonoia Cafe**   CAFE €
(☎22460 44287; breakfast €3-5, mains €8-11;
⊘8am-late; 🛜🍴) Shaded by a mature fig tree
on the main square, just up from the quay,
this much-loved all-day cafe is ideal for breakfast, light lunch or dinner. Its delightful elderly owners prepare everything from grilled
meats and seafood to simple juices and salads, but you'll probably lose your heart – and
your waistline – to their sponge cake.

To Mikro Kafé   CAFE €
(snacks €5-7, mains €5-12; ⊘6.30pm-late Mon-Fri,
4pm-late Sat & Sun; ❄🛜🍴🐾) Micro in size it
may be, but there's nothing diminutive about
this cosy nook's appeal. With its exposed
stone walls and nautical eclectica, Micro is
great for the kids, offering porthole windows,
board games and little corners to play in
while you nurse a sundowner on the beach-
view patio (there's also a roof terrace). Salads,
seafood, pies, mezedhes and sandwiches.

★**Armenon**   TAVERNA €€
(☎22460 44134; www.tilosarmenon.gr; mains €8-
18; ⊘breakfast, lunch & dinner) Open-fronted
taverna on the beach walkway, serving
top-quality seafood (the steamed mussels are
out of this world) and local favourites such
as lentil and anchovy salad. The charming
couple who run it are so committed to home-
grown ingredients they keep their own bees.
Customers get a free sunbed for the day.
Look for the blue and yellow parasols.

🍷 Drinking & Nightlife

Cafe Bar Georges   BAR
(☎22460 44257; ⊘7am-late) Venerable stone
bar on the square, where the old boys gather
to discuss the issues of the day. The interior
is refreshingly blue, with glass-topped tables, walls bedecked in pictures of long-gone
fishermen and coffee strong enough to wake
the dead.

Spitiko   CAFE
(⊘7am-late) Overlooking the square, this
cosy cafe is a popular stopoff for its great
coffee, cheese and/or spinach pies, baklava
and local sweets. The sign is in Greek, but
everybody knows the place.

ℹ️ Information

All ferries arrive at Livadia's small quay, at the
west end of the bay, just below the main square,
which holds the post office and an Alpha Bank
with ATM.

Clinic (☎22460 44219; ⊘noon-5pm) Behind
the church.
Police (☎22460 44222) In the white Italianate
building on the quay.
Port police (☎22460 44350) On the harbour.
Tilos Park Association (☎22460 70883;
⊘10am-12.30pm Mon-Fri) Tilos has no official
tourism office, but this beachfront centre,
aimed at promoting ecological conservation,
has displays and brochures on local wildlife
and trails.
Tilos Travel (☎22460 44310; www.tilos-travel.
com; ⊘9am-10pm) Helpful agency at the port,
also known as Stefanakis Travel, which sells
ferry tickets, rents out cars and motorbikes
and offers credit-card cash withdrawals.

Megalo Horio Μεγάλο Χωριό
POP 50
Megalo Horio, the tiny 'capital' of Tilos, is
a hillside village where the narrow streets
hold sun-blasted cubic houses and teem
with battle-scarred cats. Enthusiastic volunteers can tell you all about the island's
famous dwarf elephants at the one-room
museum (☎6984378079; ⊘9am-2pm, summer
only) FREE on the main street.

A taxing one-hour hike from the north
end of Megalo Horio climbs to the **Knight's
Castle**, passing the island's most ancient
settlement en route.

🛏️ Sleeping & Eating

Miliou Studios   APARTMENT €
(☎22460 44204, 6932086094; d €50; ❄) Comfortable, cosily furnished rooms and self-
catering studios just outside town as you
head to Eristos Beach, with a supermarket
conveniently close at hand. The balconies
boast sweeping long-range sea views.

Kastro Cafe   TAVERNA €
(☎22460 44232; mains €7-12; ⊘lunch & dinner)
The best taverna in the village, with a glorious hillside terrace commanding a fabulous panorama of the bay. Everything on the
menu is good, from the organic spit-roasted
goat and locally raised pork to the fresh little
dolmadhes and tiny red shrimp.

Northwest Tilos
The northwestern end of Tilos is home
to several attractive beaches. The best for
swimming is long, broad **Eristos Beach**,
lapped by sapphire-hued waters, 2.5km
south of Megalo Horio. Generally deserted

but for the odd local line-fishing, its greyish sands are fringed by tamarisk trees.

The quiet settlement of **Agios Antonios**, in the large bay 1.5km northwest of Megalo Horio, is a narrow strip of shingle with a taverna at either end. Much prettier **Plaka Beach**, in a cove another 3km west, is completely undeveloped. The water is slightly warmer, there's shade in the afternoon and, once you wade in a little, the rock shelves are good for snorkelling.

Beyond Plaka, the coast road climbs the sheer hillside, skirting 3km of alarming drop-offs to reach cliff-edge **Agiou Panteleimona** monastery.

🛏 Sleeping & Eating

Nitsa Apartments APARTMENT €
(☎ 22460 44093; www.nitsa-tilosapartments.com; Eristos Beach; r/ste incl breakfast €50/70) Smart, modern studio block, 100m inland from Eristos Beach and holding simple rooms plus one- or two-bedroom self-catering apartments. It's attached to the all-day En Plo taverna, which serves delicious squid *saganaki* (fried cheese traditionally served as a mezes) and goat in tomato sauce – lovely washed down with a glass of retsina.

Eristos Beach Hotel HOTEL €€
(☎ 22460 44025; www.eristosbeachhotel.gr; Eristos Beach; d/ste €60/90; 🅿 ❄ 🛜 🏊) Just off the beach, this large hotel is set in lush gardens crowded with hibiscus, orchids and lemon trees. Fresh rooms with tiled floors have balconies that look out to the sea beyond, while larger studios have kitchenettes and sleep four. There's also a lovely pool, plus a restaurant and a bar.

NISYROS ΝΙΣΥΡΟΣ

POP 950

Despite the spectacular volcanic crater that fills its interior, the small and very intimate island of Nisyros retains a low profile. Most of its visitors are day trippers from nearby Kos, so even the main settlement, Mandraki, is a sleepy little village that kicks off its shoes each evening and relaxes into mellow contemplation of the setting sun.

It's the volcano that's the main attraction here, responsible for the island's fertility and drawing botanists and gardeners to see its unique flora. Otherwise, in the absence of good beaches, Nisyros is more a place for exploring dazzling hill-top villages such as

Nikea and Emborios, hiking a little and sampling the local produce. Keep an eye out for *koukouzina,* a drink produced from grapes and figs.

ℹ Getting There & Away

Catamarans run by Dodekanisos Seaways (p473) call in at Nisyros on just Tuesday and Thursday, heading to and from Kos and Rhodes. Blue Star Ferries (p473) also stops twice in each direction, en route to either Kos, Kalymnos, Astypalea and Piraeus, or Tilos, Symi and Rhodes.

There are also daily links with Kos. The *Panagia Spyliani* sails to either Kos Town or Kardamena (€8), while the smaller *Agios Konstantinos* runs to and from Kardamena (€6).

BOAT SERVICES FROM NISYROS (MANDRAKI)

DESTINATION	TIME	FARE	FREQUENCY
Halki*	1½hr	€24	2 weekly
Kalymnos	2½hr	€10	2 weekly
Kalymnos*	1½hr	€21	2 weekly
Kos	1¼hr	€10	daily
Kos*	45min	€16	2 weekly
Piraeus	14hr	€51	2 weekly
Rhodes	5hr	€14	2 weekly
Rhodes*	2¾hr	€28	2 weekly
Tilos*	40min	€13	2 weekly

*high-speed services

ℹ Getting Around

BOAT
Summer-only excursion boats head for the pumice-stone islet of Giali (€8), where there's a sandy beach.

BUS
Up to 10 bus tours run to the volcano each day (€6), allowing around 40 minutes at the crater. Three daily buses run from the port to Nikea via Pali (free).

CAR, MOTORCYCLE & TAXI
Diakomihalis (p510) offers good-value car rental. A taxi from Mandraki to the volcano costs €20 return; call **Irini** (☎ 22420 31474).

Mandraki Μανδράκι

POP 660

This pretty whitewashed town stretches languidly along the northern shore of Nisyros. Unusually, it's not a port or harbour. Instead there's simply a long, straight sea wall, lapped by gentle waters and lined with cafes and tavernas.

◉ Sights

Mandraki is almost completely pedestrianised, so its maze of winding backstreets is tranquil and timeless, with a fertile valley sloping up towards the rim of the volcano behind. The major landmark is at the far western end, where the ruins of a 14th-century **Knights Castle** tower atop a cliff face. Its lower levels are occupied by an equally old monastery, **Moni Panagias Spilianis** (Virgin of the Cave; admission by donation; ⊙10.30am-3pm), accessed by climbing a short but steep stairway.

With Nisyros being very short on beaches, local kids are glad of tiny but sandy **Mandraki Beach**, at the eastern end of town. It's a popular swimming spot, despite being sometimes covered in seaweed. There's also an exposed black-stone beach to the west, **Hohlaki**, reached by following a dilapidated and precarious footpath around the headland below the monastery. Don't attempt this walk in bad weather.

Archaeological Museum　　MUSEUM
(☑22420 31588; admission €2; ⊙8.30am-3pm Tue-Sun) This showpiece modern museum, on Mandraki's main pedestrian street, displays a fascinating collection of Hellenistic and Roman pottery and sculpture, as well as earlier artefacts made of obsidian quarried on neighbouring Giali. One ancient Greek inscription records a then-recent influx of migrants from Syria and Palestine.

Paleokastro　　ARCHAEOLOGICAL SITE
(⊙24hr access) FREE Best reached by a lovely 20-minute hike through the fields, along a trail that starts southwest of the monastery, this astonishing Mycenaean-era acropolis was founded 3000 years ago. Its restored Cyclopean walls are a little newer, from the 4th century BC – what looks like modern graffiti is in fact ancient dedications. Pass through the forbidding gateway and you can climb atop the massive blocks of volcanic rock for breathtaking views. Good explanatory signs in English are scattered throughout.

⌷ Sleeping

Hotel Porfyris　　HOTEL €
(☑22420 31376; www.porfyrishotel.gr; s/d/tr incl breakfast €46/54/59; ☀❋☎) The only hotel in Mandraki town itself stands proudly on the hillside, set above a citrus orchard five minutes' walk from the sea. If you're arriving from the ferry, fork left at Piccolo Bar. Beyond the elegant marble lobby, expect simple, cosy en suite rooms with comfy beds and terrace or balcony. There's also a very welcome pool.

Nisyros

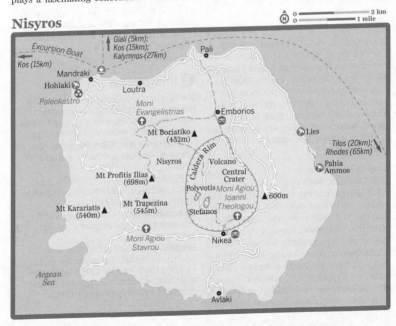

Hotel Romantzo
PENSION €

(☑ 22420 31340; www.nisyros-romantzo.gr; s/d/tr incl breakfast €35/45/55; ❄ 🛜) Handy for early ferry starts, this nicely spruced-up veteran is just up from the jetty and has simple but sunny and spotless rooms with fridges and marble floors. Best of all, there's a fabulous communal suntrap of a terrace up on the 2nd floor. The nearest restaurants, though, are in town, 10 minutes' walk away.

★ Ta Liotridia
B&B €€

(☑ 22420 31580; www.nisyros-taliotridia.com; r incl breakfast €140) Two large and very lovely B&B rooms at the heart of the waterfront, on the upper floor of a smart wood-panelled bar. Each is furnished in comfortable traditional style, without being at all cluttered, and has a double bed in an alcove, another box bed, polished floors, stone walls and a sea-view balcony. Look for off-season discounts.

✖ Eating

It's hard to choose between Mandraki's all-but-identical waterfront tavernas, all trying to tempt the daily influx of visitors from Kos with seafood specials. If views aren't important to you, you'll find better food in the backstreets. Ask for the local speciality, *pitties* (chickpea and onion patties), and wash them down with a refreshing *soumada*, a nonalcoholic beverage made from almond extract.

Irini
TAVERNA €

(☑ 22420 31365; Plateia Ilikiomenis; mains €8-12; ⊙ lunch & dinner; ❄ 🛜 🍴 🚶) The pick of the four no-nonsense tavernas whose tables fill this lively pebble-mosaic square, 100m from the waterfront. Sit beneath the spreading fig trees and enjoy the earthy menu of rich island favourites such as rabbit or goat with tomato sauce, stuffed peppers, or beautifully tender octopus. The salads are fresh and generous too.

Taverna Panorama
TAVERNA €

(☑ 22420 31185; mains €8-10; ⊙ lunch & dinner; 🍴) A hillside taverna between Plateia Ilikiomenis and Hotel Porfyris – look for the blue-checked tables on the lane outside with the namesake sea-view 'panorama'. The menu changes daily, but you can tell what's cooking from the appetising aromas that waft from the kitchen. Staples include *seftelies* (Cypriot-style herb-laced sausages), homemade meatballs, dolmadhes, *mousakas*, stuffed tomatoes and fresh fish.

To Kazanario
GREEK €

(☑ 6972240556; snacks €1.50-8; ⊙ noon-late) In-the-know locals escape the day trippers in this garden *ouzerie*, tucked off the pedestrian lane a block from the sea. A dark staircase drops from its inconspicuous doorway to a friendly old drinking den and garden beyond, where amazingly cheap snacks include souvlakia, sausages and a calzone-style pitta sandwich, bursting with feta, pepper and tomato.

Trattoria da Michele
ITALIAN €€

(☑ 22420 31054; mains €7-12; ⊙ lunch & dinner Mon-Sat, dinner Sun) Why would you eat Italian food on a Greek island? Because it tastes this good. Italian-trained chef Michele has established his simple seafood restaurant as a true Nisyros favourite thanks to his meticulously prepared pizzas, risottos, salads and desserts. Of course, having your tables perched right above the waves helps too.

🍷 Drinking

Mandraki's waterfront is lined with cafes and bars, with terraces perfectly aligned for watching the sun set over Kos.

Proveza
CAFE

(☑ 22420 31618; www.proveza.net; ⊙ 11am-late; 🛜) This welcoming seafront bar started life as an internet cafe and still has a few computers at the back. The wi-fi's as dependable as ever, but these days customers are more likely to linger over a morning coffee, an afternoon smoothie or a sunset cocktail, sitting out beside the sea wall.

ℹ Information

The ferry jetty is 500m northeast of Mandraki proper. Simply walk straight along the coast to reach the centre. Visit www.nisyros.gr for information on sights, history and local services.

Alpha Bank has an ATM at the harbour and a branch in Mandraki, and there's another ATM in town.

The island **police** (☑ 22420 31201), **port police** (☑ 22420 31222) and post office are all lined up facing the quay.

Diakomihalis (☑ 22420 31015; www.visit nisyros.gr) Ferry and air tickets, car rental and bus tours.

Enetikon Travel (☑ 22420 31180; www. enetikontravel.com) Run by the ever-helpful Michelle, 100m from the quay towards Mandraki, Enetikon runs boat trips and bus tours, dispenses free advice and sells tickets.

Around Nisyros

The Volcano   Το Ηφαίστειο

Nisyros sits on a volcanic fault line that curves around the southern Aegean. While 25,000 years have passed since the volcano that formed it last erupted, it's officially classified as dormant rather than extinct. Its summit originally stood around 850m tall, but three violent eruptions 30,000 to 40,000 years ago blew off the top 100m and caused the centre to collapse. White-and-orange pumice stones can still be seen on the northern, eastern and southern flanks of the island, while a large lava flow covers the entire southwest around Nikea.

The islanders call the volcano Polyvotis. Legend has it that during the battle between the gods and Titans, Poseidon ripped a chunk off Kos and used it to trap the giant Polyvotis deep beneath the rock of Nisyros. The roar of the volcano is his angered voice.

Visitors keen to experience the power of the volcano head by bus, car or on foot into the island's hollow caldera, a vast and otherworldly plain that was home to thousands of ancient farmers. Ruined agricultural terraces climb the walls, while cows graze amid sci-fi-set rocks. A fenced-off area at the southern end (€3, open 9am to 8pm) encloses several distinct craters. Get there before 11am and you may have the place to yourself. A path descends into the largest, **Stefanos**, where you can examine the multicoloured 100°C fumaroles, listen to their hissing and smell the sulphurous vapours. The surface is soft and hot, making sturdy footwear essential. Don't stray too far out, as the ground is unstable and can collapse.

An obvious track leads to the smaller and wilder crater of **Polyvotis** nearby. You can't enter the caldera itself, and the fumaroles are around the edge here, so take great care.

Emborios   Εμπορειός

The ravishing but largely ruined village of Emborios is perched high on the jagged northern rim of the caldera, 9km up from Mandraki. Tumbledown houses cling to the steep flanks of the rocky ridge. A few are freshly whitewashed, but most are in stark disarray and overgrown with crimson bougainvillea. Apart from yawning cats, almost no one lives here these days.

🍴 Eating

Balcony Restaurant   GREEK €
(☑ 22420 31607; mains €7; ⊙ 9am-10pm Mon-Sat) The streetside terrace, facing the church, may look inviting, but opt if you can for a table on the namesake balcony at the back for an unforgettable panorama of the vast hollow crater. The menu is meat heavy, with mouth-watering chops and steaks, but it also serves various vegetable fritters.

Apiria Taverna   TAVERNA €
(☑ 22420 31377; mains €6-12; ⊙ lunch & dinner; 🛜 🅿) Opening off a tiny alcove behind the

---

A HOT SPOT FOR HIKERS

Nisyros has become a major destination for hikers, especially in the cooler months of May and October. Trails are detailed on the superb 1:20,000 *Nisyros* Map by **Terrain** (www.terrainmaps.gr).

The volcano itself, of course, makes the obvious goal. You can walk to the heart of the caldera in around 2½ hours from Mandraki, either by hiking directly up the switchback footpath that crosses the rim beyond Evangelistrias monastery, or following the longer track that circles around to its shallower southern side.

Alternatively, you can hike down from Nikea. The trail drops to the right behind the volcano museum and takes 45 minutes to reach Stefanos crater. Take careful note of landmarks on your way down, as it's much harder to find the path on your way back up again.

If you'd rather not tackle the gruelling elevation changes, you can also hike from Nikea to Emborios. Simply keep going straight ahead when the steps and concrete footpath end just below Nikea, rather than turning left towards the crater floor, and follow the path, just below the rim, for around 1½ hours.

Bear in mind that you don't have to hike all the way back to Mandraki – arrange to meet a taxi or tour bus at the volcano, or catch a bus back from Nikea or Emborios.

Finally, for a quick taste of the joys of rural Nisyros, don't miss the exhilarating 20-minute jaunt up from Mandraki to the Paleokastro (p509).

church, this friendly taverna has tasteful burgundy-and-mustard walls and a few sheltered outdoor tables. Local specialities range through souvlakia, octopus, meatballs, stuffed peppers and wood-fired goat.

Nikea   Νικαία

Unlike Emborios, the village of Nikea, 4km south along the crater's edge, is still very much alive. No vehicles can penetrate this tight warren of dazzling white houses, so every visitor experiences the thrill of walking along the narrow lane from road's end to reach its tiny central square. Less a square than a circle actually, it's among the most jaw-droppingly beautiful spots in the Dodecanese, with geometric pebble-mosaic designs in the middle, whitewashed benches around the edges, and the village church standing above. Throughout Nikea, signposted overlooks command astonishing views of the volcano, laid out far below. The challenging trail down into the crater drops from behind the Volcanological Museum.

◉ Sights

Volcanological Museum   MUSEUM
(☎22420 31400; Plateia Nikolaou Hartofyli; admission €2; ☺11.30am-6.30pm Mon-Thu, 10.30am-2.30pm Fri & Sat May-Sep) Beside the end of the road, this modern museum does a good job of explaining the history and mythology of the volcano and its impact on the island. As it consists almost entirely of display panels, the experience is much like reading a book.

✗ Eating

Porta   CAFE €
(☎22420 31832; snacks €3-7; ☺8.30am-late) Two cafes share Nikea's divinely pretty central square, looking out towards the sea not the volcano. Like the neighbouring Nicola, Porta is a wonderfully relaxing place to enjoy a cool drink, toasted sandwich, juice or beer, but it only serves light snacks.

Pali   Πάλοι

This wind-buffeted seaside village is 5km east of Mandraki, just beyond the turn-off to the volcano. Primarily a yachting marina, it has a handful of tavernas among the sun-beaten buildings on the quay. The coast road continues another 5km to **Lies**, Nisyros' most usable beach. Walking 1km along a precarious track from here brings you to **Pahia Ammos**, a shadeless expanse of volcanic sand.

🛏 Sleeping & Eating

Mammis' Apartments   APARTMENT €
(☎22420 31824; www.mammis.com; d €40; ☺year-round; ❄☎) Set 100m up from the marina in gardens, this peaceful complex holds 12 simple but imaginatively decorated apartments with kitchenettes, separate sofa beds for kids and private balconies with sea views.

Captain's House   TAVERNA €
(☎22420 31016; mains €7-10; ☺8am-midnight) Festooned with yellow nets and so close to the water you can taste the salt, this tavern attracts yachties and wizened fishers alike with a menu that's packed to the gills with octopus, calamari, baby shark and cuttlefish.

KOS   ΚΩΣ
POP 33,300

Fringed by the finest beaches in the Dodecanese, dwarfed beneath mighty crags, cut through with lush valleys and everywhere displaying proud relics of its storied past, Kos is an island of endless surprises and varied treasures. Visitors soon become blasé at side-stepping millennia-old Corinthian columns that poke through the rampant wildflowers – even in Kos Town, the lively capital, ancient Greek ruins are scattered everywhere you turn, and a mighty medieval castle still watches over the harbour. One moment you can be dining in a rustic mountain tavern, the next you find yourself in a busy cosmopolitan cafe – there really is something for everyone.

History

So many people lived on this fertile island in Mycenaean times that Kos was rich enough to send 30 ships to the Trojan War. In 477 BC, after suffering an earthquake and subjugation to the Persians, it joined the Delian League and again flourished. Hippocrates (460–377 BC), the Greek physician known as the founder of medicine, was born and lived on the island. After his death, the Sanctuary of Asclepius and a medical school were built, which perpetuated his teachings and made Kos famous throughout the Greek world.

That Ptolemy II of Egypt was also born on Kos secured the island the protection of Egypt. It became a prosperous trading centre, but fell under Roman domination in 130 BC and was administered by Rhodes from the 1st century AD onwards. Kos has shared the same ups and downs of fortune ever since, including conquest and/or occupation by the Knights, the Ottomans and the Italians and, much like Rhodes, its economy is now heavily dependent on tourism.

🛈 Getting There & Away

AIR

From the only airport on Kos, in the middle of the island, **Olympic Air** (www.olympicair.com) offers up to four daily flights to Athens (from €50, 55 minutes) and three weekly to Rhodes (€61, 30 minutes), Kalymnos (€54, 20 minutes) Leros (€61, 55 minutes) and Astypalea (€68, one hour 40 minutes). **Minoan Air** (www.minoanair.com) flies once weekly in summer to Heraklion in Crete (€69, 50 minutes).

BOAT

From the island's main ferry port, in front of the castle in Kos Town, Dodekanisos Seaways (p473) runs catamarans up and down the archipelago, southeast to Rhodes via Nisyros, Tilos, Halki and Symi, and north to Samos, with stops including Kalymnos, Leros and Patmos. Blue Star Ferries (p473) also sails to Rhodes, as well as west to Astypalea and Piraeus.

The **Panagia Spiliani** (☑ 22420 31015), which runs day trips from Nisyros to Kos in summer, carries one-way passengers to Nisyros on sailings that leave from Kos Town at 2.30pm four days a week, and from Kardamena at 6.10pm on the other three days. Eight daily ferries also connect Mastihari with Kalymnos (€5, 50 minutes); see www.anekalymnou.gr and www.anemferries.gr.

Boat Services from Kos

DESTINATION	TIME	FARE	FREQUENCY
Astypalea	4hr	€18	1 weekly
Kalymnos	50min	€5	8 daily
Kalymnos	1hr 20min	€6	3 daily
Kalymnos*	40min	€15	1-2 daily
Leros	3¼hr	€14	1 weekly
Leros*	1½hr	€22	1-2 daily
Lipsi*	2hr	€29	1-2 daily
Nisyros*	55min	€16	2 weekly
Patmos*	3hr	€29	1-2 daily
Piraeus	11hr	€51	3 weekly
Rhodes	3hr	€24	1 daily
Rhodes*	2½hr	€30	1 daily
Samos	4hr	€42	4 weekly
Symi	3hr	€14	2 weekly
Symi*	1½hr	€22	5 weekly

*high-speed services
All depart from Kos Town except the Kalymnos ferry, which departs from Mastihari.

International

High-speed catamarans connect Kos Town with both Bodrum (two daily) and Turgutreis in Turkey (one daily). Both journeys take 20 minutes. Tickets cost €18 each way, with same-day returns €24 and longer-stay returns €32. For schedules and bookings, visit www.rhodes.marmarisinfo.com.

🛈 Getting Around

TO/FROM THE AIRPORT

The **airport** (KGS; ☑ 22420 51229) is 24km southwest of Kos Town and served by several daily buses to and from Kos Town's bus station (€3.20). A taxi to Kos Town costs around €30. Note that Kefalos-bound buses stop at the big roundabout near the airport entrance.

BICYCLE

Cycling is very popular, so you'll be tripping over bicycles for hire. Prices range from as little as €5 per day for a boneshaker, up to €20 for a decent mountain bike. In Kos Town, George's Bikes (p518) offers reasonable rates. **Kos Mountain-bike Activities** (☑ 6944150129; www.kosbike-activities.com; Psalidi) offers bike rentals and guided tours.

BOAT

Several boats moored in Kos Town offer excursions around Kos and to nearby islands. The 'three island' day trip to Kalymnos, Pserimos and Platy costs around €30, including lunch, while you can find day trips to Bodrum for as little as €10.

BUS

The main **bus station** (☑ 22420 22292; Kleopatras 7, Kos Town), well back from the waterfront in Kos Town, is the base for services to all parts of the island, including the airport and south-coast beaches, with **KTEL** (☑ 22420 22292; www.ktel-kos.gr).

CAR & MOTORCYCLE

Outlets all over Kos rent cars, motorcycles and scooters, and many hotels offer special deals. All the international chains have airport offices. The airport is so far from Kos Town that if you're planning to rent a car anyway, it's worth doing so when you first arrive. A recommended local operator is **Auto Bank Car Rental** (☑ 22420 23397; www.autobank-carrentalkos.com), with outlets at the airport, Kos Town and Mastihari.

Kos Town   Κως

POP 14,750

A handsome harbour community, fronted by a superb medieval castle and somehow squeezed amid a mind-blowing array of ancient ruins from the Greek, Roman and

Kos & Pserimos

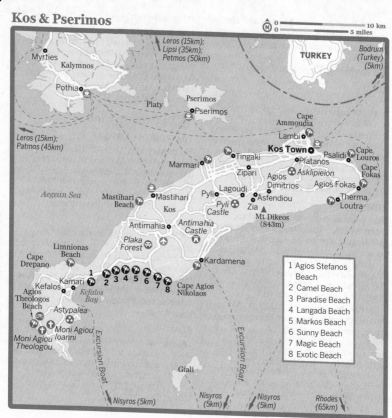

0   10 km
0   5 miles

Leros (15km);
Lipsi (35km);
Petmos (50km)

TURKEY

Bodrum
(Turkey)
(5km)

Myrties
Kalymnos

Pothia

Platy

Pserimos
Pserimos

Cape
Ammoudia

Lambi

Kos Town

Cape
Louros

Leros (15km);
Patmos (45km)

Tingaki
Marmari

Psalidi
Platanos

Cape
Fokas

Zipari

Agios
Dimitrios

Asklipieion

Agios Fokas

Aegean Sea

Mastihari
Beach

Mastihari

Pyli

Lagoudi

Asfendiou

Therma
Loutra

Kos

Pyli
Castle

Zia

Antimahia

Antimahia
Castle

Mt Dikeos
(843m)

Plaka
Forest

Limnionas
Beach

Kardamena

Cape
Drepano

Kamari

Kefalos
Bay

Cape Agios
Nikolaos

Kefalos

Agios
Theologos
Beach

Astypalea

1 2 3 4 5 6 7 8

Moni Agiou
Ioanni

Moni Agiou
Theologou

Excursion Boat

Giali

Excursion Boat

1	Agios Stefanos Beach
2	Camel Beach
3	Paradise Beach
4	Langada Beach
5	Markos Beach
6	Sunny Beach
7	Magic Beach
8	Exotic Beach

Nisyros (5km)

Nisyros
(5km)

Nisyros
(5km)

Rhodes
(65km)

DODECANESE KOS TOWN

Byzantine eras, Kos Town is the capital, main ferry port and only sizeable town on Kos. While some central streets tend to be overrun by partying tourists, most remain stylish and attractive. The port is the most appealing area of all, lined by cafes and tavernas and with an unbroken row of excursion boats, fishing vessels and fancy yachts bobbing and bristling against each other along the waterfront. You can buy fresh-caught fish from makeshift stalls on the quay.

Popular beaches stretch away in either direction from the harbour. Long sandy **Kritika Beach**, running northwest in easy walking distance of the town centre, is lined with hotels and restaurants, and tends to be dominated by their clients. Its counterpart southeast of the harbour, officially known as **Kos Town Beach**, offers a thin strip of sand that's polka-dotted with parasols in summer, and deep water for swimming. It too fills up with guests from adjacent hotels.

○ Sights & Activities

Castle of the Knights
CASTLE
(☎ 22420 27927; admission €4; ☉ 8am-8pm) Kos' magnificent 15th-century castle was constructed not on a hill top, but right beside the entrance to the harbour. Access it by the bridge from Plateia Platanou, crossing what was once a seawater-filled moat but is now a road. Visitors can stroll atop the intact outer walls, surveying all activity in the port and keeping a watchful eye on Turkey across the strait. The precinct within, however, is now largely overgrown, with cats stalking through a wilderness of wildflowers.

Plateia Platanou
SQUARE
The warm, graceful charm and sedate pace of Kos Town is experienced at its best in this lovely cobblestone square, immediately south of the castle. Sitting in a cafe here, you can pay your respects to the **Hippocrates Plane Tree**. Hippocrates himself is

said to have taught his pupils in its shade. The ancient sarcophagus beneath it was converted into a fountain by the Ottomans, while the 18th-century **Mosque of Gazi Hassan Pasha**, now sadly boarded up, stands opposite.

Ancient Agora ARCHAEOLOGICAL SITE

(⊙ dawn-dusk) **FREE** Exposed by a devastating earthquake in 1933, Kos's ancient centre, the *agora*, occupies a vast area south of the castle. Back in the 4th century BC, this was the first town ever laid out in blocks, and you can still discern the original town plan, even though it's very overgrown. Landmarks include a massive columned **stoa** and the ruins of a **Shrine of Aphrodite, Temple of Hercules** and Christian basilica.

The site is fenced, but usually open all day. Locals use it as a short cut.

Western Excavation Site ARCHAEOLOGICAL SITE

(⊙ dawn-dusk) **FREE** This open site, south of the centre, holds fascinating ancient ruins uncovered by the 1933 earthquake. Its real treasures are the mosaics of the **House of Europa**, dating from the 2nd century AD and protected by rudimentary shelters. In front of them, there's a section of the **Decumanus Maximus**, the Roman city's main thoroughfare, while the site also holds the **Nymphaeum**, the **Xysto** and the overgrown but evocative **Temple of Dionysos**. Across the street stands an impressive 2nd-century **Odeion** (theatre).

Archaeological Museum MUSEUM

(Plateia Eleftherias; admission €3; ⊙ closed for restoration) Housed in an Italian-era building in the central square, the small archaeological museum is currently closed for restoration. When it reopens, expect to see sculptures from the Hellenistic to late Roman eras, with a statue of Hippocrates and a 3rd-century-AD mosaic as the star attractions.

🛏 Sleeping

★ Hotel Afendoulis HOTEL €

(☎ 22420 25321; www.afendoulishotel.com; Evripilou 1; s/d €30/50; ⊙ Mar-Nov; ❋ @ 🛜) Peaceful Afendoulis has unfailingly friendly staff and sparkling rooms with white walls, small balconies and spotless bathrooms. Downstairs, the open breakfast room and flowery terrace have wrought-iron tables and chairs for enjoying the feast of homemade jams and marmalades. There may be more modern, plush hotels in Kos, but none with the special soul of this fine, family-run establishment.

Hotel Sonia HOTEL €€

(☎ 22420 28798; www.hotelsonia.gr; Irodotou 9; s/d/tr €45/60/75; ❋ 🛜) A block from the waterfront on a peaceful backstreet, this pension offers a dozen sparkling rooms with parquet floors, fridges, smart bathrooms and an extra bed if required. Room 4 has the best sea view. Breakfast is served on a relaxing communal verandah, there's a decent book exchange and it plans to open up the garden to visitors.

Kosta Palace HOTEL €€

(☎ 22420 22855; www.kosta-palace.com; cnr Akti Kountourioti & Averof; s/d/apt €65/85/110; ❋ @ 🛜 🏊) This swanky harbour-front edifice, facing the castle across the port, holds 160 rooms with kitchenettes and private balconies. Apartments have separate rooms. There are also pools for kids and adults and a snack bar on the roof. While it's clean and functional, it can be rather impersonal.

Kos Aktis Art Hotel HOTEL €€€

(☎ 22420 47200; www.kosaktis.gr; Vasileos Georgiou 7; s/d from €165/210; ❋ @ 🛜 🏊) What makes this an Art Hotel? Well, sky-high prices, obviously, but also lots of stylish minimalist touches, including floor-to-ceiling windows opening onto seafront balconies, and exclusive tinted-glass dining and drinking spaces. From its plush bedrooms – with granite floors and bathrooms too perfect to insult with your presence – you can see Bodrum lit up like a chandelier at night.

🍴 Eating

★ Pote Tin Kyriaki TAVERNA €

(☎ 22420 27872; Pisandrou 9; ⊙ 7pm-5am) Named for Melina Mercouri's Oscar-winning 1960 song, 'Never on Sunday', this is not the sort of place you expect to find in modern Kos – and it takes a lot of finding. This traditional *ouzerie* serves delicious specialities such as stuffed zucchini flowers, dolmadhes with lemongrass, and steamed mussels. It plans to open for breakfast and lunch too – just never on Sunday.

Aegli CAFE €

(☎ 22420 30016; www.aiglikos.gr; Plateia Eleftherias; snacks €3-5; ⊙ breakfast, lunch & dinner) Stretching from beneath the arches of a municipal building onto the main square, this bakery/cafe is run by a cooperative supporting low-income women and employs only female staff. The speciality is *marmarites* – translated as 'crumpets', but more like

Kos Town

sourdough flatbread – with sweet or savoury toppings, but it also serves pies, superjuices, coffee and gigantic breakfasts (€16 for two).

Pikoula
BAKERY €

(☎ 22420 26200; Kanari 8, at Salaminos; items €1-3; ☉ 7am-10pm) All three outlets of Kos Town's favourite bakery (the others are at Ethnikis Antistaseos 5 and Makrigianni 28) sell the same dizzying array of doughnuts, pies, cinnamon buns, baklava and chocolate cake, as well, of course, as bread. Drop by first thing in the morning and set yourself up for the day.

Elia
GREEK €€

(☎ 22420 22133; www.elia-kos.gr; Appelou Ifestou 27; mains €6-12; ☉ 12.30pm-late; ❄ 🕾 🎤 🐾) 🍴 Friendly restaurant with seating in the garden and venerable interior as well as on the lively pedestrian street. The menu draws on traditional dishes from all over Greece, with standouts including the chunky rustic sausage, bream baked with oregano and rosemary, and drunken pork (cooked in wine). Simple starters such as *fava* and fried onions are equally tasty.

🍷 Drinking & Nightlife

Kos Town has a very lively party scene. Aimed squarely at tourists bussed in from the coastal resorts, it centres a block south of the harbour and along the waterfront on Kritika Beach. Locals congregate on weekends to drink coffee and gossip in the cafes on Plateia Eleftherias (Freedom Sq).

Aenaos
CAFE

(☎22420 26044; Plateia Eleftherias; sweets €3.50; ⊙8am-late; 🛜) Tucked beneath an exquisite, still-active mosque, this lovely, well-shaded cafe makes a pleasant stop for an iced coffee or espresso. Treat yourself to its delectable spectrum of chocolate confections (the forest fruit and strawberry, say), cakes, brownies and juices.

Law Court Cafe
CAFE

(Plateia Platanou; ⊙7.30am-late) Despite being set on Kos Town's prettiest square, facing Hippocrates' Plane Tree, this timeless little cafe feels remote from the tourist scene. Instead, as the name suggests, it's where local lawyers and businesspeople meet to discuss the order of the day, while savouring their morning espressos.

Global Cafe
BAR

(☎22420 26003; Ifestou 1; ⊙8.30am-late; 🛜) The rendezvous of choice for Kos Town's see-and-be-seen young hipsters, who fuss with their phones when not playing backgammon at the streetside tables, or drift into the rear courtyard bar, with its stone walls, canvas-sail canopy and DJ soundtrack. Join them to read, work, drink a beer or a cocktail, or grab a sandwich.

🛍 Shopping

For high-street-style shops, head to the eastern end of Ioannidi and the pedestrian streets south of Ippokratous.

Dimotiki Agora
MARKET

(☎22420 22900; Plateia Eleftherias; ⊙8am-late) Kos Town's restored central market building, on the main square, houses a bijou bazaar where you can buy anything from herbs, fresh cherries, olive oil and indigenous honey to mythological curios and Kalymnian sponges.

News Stand
BOOKS

(☎22420 30110; Riga Fereou 2) Has foreign-language newspapers and publications, as well as guides to Kos.

Petrino Meze Restaurant
MEZEDHES €€

(☎22420 27251; www.petrino-kos.gr; Plateia Theologou 1; mains €9-28; ⊙lunch & dinner; 🌸🛜) Peaceful and balmy, this graceful restaurant has a leafy garden shaded by bougainvillea, overlooking Kos Town's western group of archeological ruins. Highlights on its upscale menu include hearty meat concoctions such as beef stuffed with blue cheese and pork with plums, but it also serves lighter dishes such as steamed swordfish or pasta, as well as mixed mezedhes platters.

Kos Town

⊙ Sights
1	Ancient Agora	D3
2	Archaeological Museum	C3
3	Castle of the Knights	C2
4	Decumanus Maximus	B5
5	House of Europa	B5
	Mosque of Gazi Hassan Pasha	(see 8)
6	Nymphaeum	A4
7	Odeion	A5
8	Plateia Platanou	D3
9	Temple of Dionysos	C5
10	Western Excavation SIte	A5
11	Xysto	A5

⊟ Sleeping
12	Hotel Afendoulis	F4
13	Hotel Sonia	A3
14	Kos Aktis Art Hotel	E3
15	Kosta Palace	B1

⊗ Eating
16	Aegli	C4
17	Elia	B4
18	Petrino Meze Restaurant	A4
19	Pikoula	B2
20	Pote Tin Kyriaki	B4

⊙ Drinking & Nightlife
21	Aenaos	C3
22	Global Cafe	C4
23	Law Court Cafe	D3

⊗ Entertainment
24	Orfeas	C3

⊟ Shopping
25	Dimotiki Agora	C4
26	News Stand	C3

ⓘ Information

Kos Town has several ATMs, including at the branches of Alpha Bank on El Venizelou and the National Bank of Greece on Riga Fereou. The useful official website is www.kos.gr.

Fanos Travel & Shipping (☏ 22420 20016; 11 Akti Koundourioti) Tickets for the hydrofoil service to Bodrum and other ferries, plus yachting services.

Kentrikon Travel (☏ 22420 28914; Akti Kountouriotou 7) The offical agents for Blue Star Ferries also sells all other ferry and air tickets.

Police (☏ 22420 25462; Eparhio Bldg, Akti Miaouli)

Post office (Vasileos Pavlou)

Port police (☏ 22420 26594; cnr Akti Koundourioti & Megalou Alexandrou)

Tourist police (☏ 22420 22444; Akti Miaouli)

ⓘ Getting Around

BICYCLE

Cycle lanes thread all through Kos Town, with the busiest route running along the waterfront to connect the town with Lambi to the north and Psalidi to the south. Many hotels have bikes for guests, or you can rent one from **George's Bikes** (☏ 22420 24157; Kanari 8).

BUS

Local buses, run by **DEAS** (☏ 22420 26276; flat fare €2), operate within Kos Town, but have little relevance to visitors. Buses to the rest of the island, including the airport, depart from the KTEL bus station (p513).

TAXI

Taxis (☏ 22420 23333, 22420 22777) congregate on the south side of the port.

TOURIST TRAIN

One way to get your bearings in summer is to take a 20-minute city tour on the **tourist train** (☏ 22420 26276; €5), which departs frequently from Akti Kountouriotou on the harbour front.

Around Kos

Visitors to Kos naturally tend to focus their attention on its beaches. In addition to the beaches around Kos Town, there are three main resort areas. Kardamena, on the south coast, is very much dominated by package tourism, but Mastihari, on the north coast, and Kamari, in the far southwest, are much more appealing. Away from the resorts, the island holds considerable wilderness, with the rugged Dikeos mountains soaring to almost 850m just a few kilometres west of Kos Town.

Beaches near Kos Town

The nearest beach to Kos Town, crowded **Lambi Beach**, begins just 2km northwest and has its own strip of hotels and restaurants. Further west along the coast, a long stretch of pale sand is fringed by two more resorts – **Tingaki**, 10km from Kos Town, and the slightly less crowded **Marmari Beach** beyond. Windsurfing is popular at all three beaches, while the island of Pserimos is only a few kilometres offshore and served by excursion boats from Marmari in summer.

Heading south from Kos Town along Vasileos Georgiou, on the other hand, brings you to the three busy beaches of **Psalidi**, (3km from Kos Town), **Agios Fokas** (8km), and finally **Therma Loutra** (12km), where hot mineral springs warm the sea.

Asklepieion   Ασκληπιείον

The island's most important ancient **site** (☑22420 28763; admission €4; ☉8am-8pm Tue-Sun) stands on a pine-covered hill 3km southwest of Kos Town, commanding lovely views across town towards Turkey. A religious sanctuary devoted to Asclepius, the god of healing, it was also a healing centre and a school of medicine. It was founded in the 3rd century BC, according to legend by Hippocrates himself, the Kos-born 'father' of modern medicine. He was already dead by then, though, and the training here simply followed his teachings.

Until the sanatorium was destroyed by an earthquake in AD 554, people came from far and wide for treatment.

The ruins occupy three levels, with the *propylaea* (approach to the main gate), Roman-era public baths and remains of guest rooms on the first level. The second holds an **altar of Kyparissios Apollo**, with the 1st-century-BC **Temple to Apollo** to the east and the first **Temple of Asclepius**, built in the 4th century BC, to the west. The remains of its successor, the once magnificent 2nd-century-BC **Temple of Asclepius**, are on the third level. Climb a little further, to the cool pine woods above, for the best views of all.

A modern museum on the path down preserves ancient inscriptions and shows films explaining the site.

The hourly bus 3 runs from Kos Town to the site. It's also a pleasant bike ride.

Mountain Villages

The villages scattered on the green northern slopes of the Dikeos mountains make ideal destinations for day trips.

ZIA   ΖΙΑ

Kos' prettiest mountain village – Zia, 14km west of Kos Town – is now essentially a one-street theme park. The views down to the sea are as wonderful as ever, but coachloads of tourists are deposited every few minutes to stroll along its gauntlet of souvenir shops and competing tavernas.

✖ Eating

Taverna Oromedon   GREEK €€
(☑22420 69983; www.oromedon.com; mains €9-15; ☉lunch & dinner) Zia's finest restaurant is justly acclaimed for its vine-laced sun terrace, unbroken sea views and traditional Greek menu of shrimp *saganaki*, dolmadhes and *stifadho*. Meat-eaters should be sure to spare some room for the chunky local sausages.

PYLI   ΠΥΛΙ

Continuing 6km west beyond Zia brings you to the less commercialised village of Pyli. Even better, just before the village, a left turn leads to the extensive remains of its medieval predecessor, **Old Pyli**, scattered amid the towering rocks and pine trees of a high and very magical hillside. The summit here is crowned by the stark ruins of **Pyli Castle** and the whole place is so wild you half expect Pan to pop up. A well-marked trail climbs from the roadside parking area, forking left to the castle and right to the old village, where the only building still in use is a tavern hidden in the woods.

The idyllic **Oria Taverna** (☑6981764991; Old Pyli; mains €7-10; ☉9am-9pm) is only accessible by hiking up the hillside facing the 1000-year-old Pyli Castle and enjoying what are certainly the best views on Kos...and quite possibly in the world. It's open all day for snacks and cooling drinks, but you can't beat a sunset dinner here, tucking into the seasonal, locally sourced menu of steaks, meatballs, zucchini and tzatziki.

Buses connect Kos Town with Pyli itself, but not Old Pyli (€2, two to three daily).

Mastihari   Μαστιχάρι

Hardly more than a village, this delightful little old-fashioned beach resort holds everything you need for a straightforward family holiday. There's a lovely broad strip of powder-fine sand scattered with tamarisk trees, a clutch of whitewashed rental studios and small hotels, and a row of appetising waterfront tavernas and bars. There's no historic core and nothing of any architectural interest, but as a place to spend a day or a week in the sun, Mastihari has it all.

Mastihari's tiny port is served by frequent **ANE Kalymnou** (www.anekalymnou.gr) and **ANEM** (www.anemferries.gr) ferries to Pothia on Kalymnos, as well as excursion boats to the islet of Pserimos in summer.

🛏 Sleeping

Athinas Studios
APARTMENT €

(☑6974180326; www.athinas-studios.gr; d/tr €40/50) Superfresh studio rooms with blue Aegean trim and spotless kitchenettes. They're a block back from the seafront, but upper-level rooms have private sea-view terraces and there's a roof garden. One room has bunk beds, double bed and a large balcony.

Studios Diana
APARTMENT €

(☑22420 59116; apt €40) Clean and basic studios, opening onto the sea, with private balconies and very tiny kitchens. Turning on the air-con costs €5 extra.

🍴 Eating

El Greco
TAVERNA €

(mains €7-10; ⊙breakfast, lunch & dinner) A beachside taverna – follow the blue-painted walkway up from the sand – that consistently pleases with its fresh salads, zucchini, souvlakia and lamb with rosemary, as well as grilled sardines, cod and octopus. Only the very fanciest fish dishes cost more than €10, and it also serves breakfast all day.

Kali Kardia
SEAFOOD €€

(☑22420 59289; mains €6-15; ⊙breakfast, lunch & dinner) Atmospheric taverna, right on the harbour, with tables out on the footpath and a wooden interior patronised by older folk staring out to sea. Piping aromas of squid, shrimp and souvlakia emerge from the kitchen, and large mixed platters cost €10 per person.

Kamari & Kefalos Bay
Καμάρι & Κέφαλος

Enormous Kefalos Bay, a 12km stretch of high-quality sand, lines the southwest shoreline of Kos. For most of its length, the beach itself is continuous, but the main road runs along a crest around 500m inland, so each separate section served by signposted tracks has its own name. Backed by scrubby green hills and lapped by warm water, these are the finest and emptiest beaches on the island. The most popular is **Paradise Beach**, while the least developed is **Exotic Beach**. **Langada Beach** (which you may also see referred to as Banana Beach) makes a good

compromise, but the best of the lot is **Agios Stefanos Beach**, at the far western end. A small beachfront promontory here is topped by a ruined 5th-century basilica, while the absurdly photogenic islet of **Kastri** stands within swimming distance immediately offshore.

Once past Agios Stefanos, you reach the burgeoning resort strip of Kamari, where the main road is lined by tacky tourist shops, restaurants and hotels. Kamari Beach ends at a small jetty, from where excursion boats offer day trips to Nisyros twice weekly in summer; contact **Asklipios Tours** (☑22420 72143) for schedules. Buses to and from Kos Town (€4.40, three to four daily) stop nearby.

The village of **Kefalos**, on the bluff above Kamari, is similarly dominated by tourism. If you're determined to escape the crowds, continue on to the island's southern peninsula beyond. Across the rugged hills, on the west coast, **Agios Theologos Beach** is backed by meadow bluffs carpeted in olive groves, and feels far removed from the resort bustle.

🛏 Sleeping & Eating

Albatross Apartments
APARTMENT €€

(☑22420 71981; albatross@hotmail.com; Kamari Beach; apt €70; P❄🛜🏊) Has 11 simple, spotless and identical kitchenette studios, so crisply maintained they might have been built yesterday. All have sea views, there's a good swimming pool and the beach is just across the road, with the jetty a short walk away. There's an on-site bar but no restaurant. Airport pick-up for stays of three nights or more.

Restaurant Agios Theologos
TAVERNA €€

(☑6974503556; Agios Theologos Beach; mains €7-15; ⊙lunch & dinner daily May-Oct, Sat & Sun only Nov-Apr) From its well-shaded terraces, dropping towards the sweeping beach, this much-loved seasonal taverna enjoys the best sunsets in Kos. Its zesty homemade cheese, courtesy of its flock of inquisitive goats, is at its most flavoursome fried, while a fresh grilled bream costs around €15. Fantastic mezedhes too – you'll miss out if you just order a burger or pizza.

ASTYPALEA
ΑΣΤΥΠΑΛΑΙΑ

POP 140

Swathed in silky aquamarine waters, far-flung, butterfly-shaped Astypalea is richly rewarding for walkers, campers and history buffs. For any island hunter, this is the ultimate escape – think mountainous meadows straight from the pages of Homer, and rugged beaches fringed in petrol-blue water. Chance of sighting a mermaid: fair.

The island's main settlement, hilltop Hora, is a tumble of bleached-white houses that cascade amphitheatrically down from a medieval fortress to the fishing port of Skala. Although boutique hotels have been sprouting in recent years, the tourist infrastructure – and ferry service – remains minimal, and 90% of visitors are Greek, with the rest largely French and Italian. Fed up with the package crowds and fish and chips? You've come to the right place.

ⓘ Getting There & Away

AIR

Olympic Air (www.olympicair.com) has three flights a week to Leros (€61, 25 minutes), Kalymnos (€57, one hour 40 minutes), and Kos (€68, one hour 40 minutes), and five per week to Athens (€122, one hour). Buy tickets online, or via Astypalea Tours (p523).

BOAT

Only two ferry operators serve Astypalea. Blue Star Ferries (p473) arrive, inconveniently, in the dead of night at the isolated little port of Agios Andreas, 6.5km north of Skala. A bus is scheduled to meet each boat, but don't bank on it. One ferry arrives four times weekly, having sailed from Piraeus via Paros, Naxos and Amorgos, and sets off back along the same route a couple of hours later. The other stops once in each direction en route between Piraeus and Rhodes, calling also at Kalymnos, Kos, Tilos and Nisyros.

In adition, the **Nisos Kalymnos** (www.anekalymnou.gr) connects Skala's small harbour once weekly with Kalymnos.

Boat Services from Astypalea

DESTINATION	TIME	FARE	FREQUENCY
Kalymnos	2½hr	€13	1 weekly
Kalymnos	3½hr	€11	1 weekly
Kos	4hr	€18	1 weekly
Naxos	4hr	€27	4 weekly
Paros	5½hr	€34	4 weekly
Piraeus	8½hr	€35	5 weekly
Rhodes	9hr	€32	1 weekly

ⓘ Getting Around

Astypalea's airport is on the flat, narrow 'neck' of the island, 8km northeast of Skala. Buses connect with flights in summer, while taking either of the island's two **taxis** (☑ 6975706365) to Skala costs around €10. Summer buses also link Skala with Hora and Livadi to the west, and Analipsi/Maltezana to the east, stopping at beaches en route (€2). Of the island's three vehicle-rental

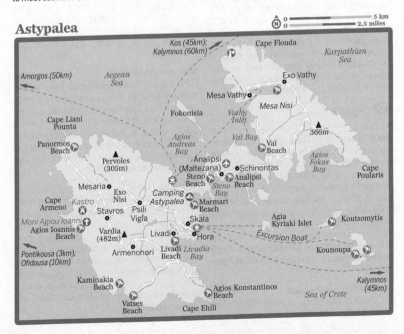

Astypalea

agencies, **Vergoulis** (☑22430 61351; www.rent-a-car-astypalaia.com; scooters per day €15, cars €30-60) is particularly recommended.

In July and August, boats head out for the day from Skala to the remote western beaches of Agios Ioannis, Kaminakia and Vatses, as well as to the islets of Koutsomytis (with ethereal, emerald-green water) and Kounoupa. They also make complete circuits around the island. Contact Astypalea Tours (p523) for details.

Skala & Hora

Σκάλα & Χώρα

Astypalea's main town, Skala, lies on the southern shore of the island's western half, curving around an attractive bay that's too shallow for large interisland ferries. Little more than a village, with aromatic odours drifting from its bakery, Skala holds a small sand-and-pebble beach that's popular with locals. Bars and tavernas punctuate the quay, which is the sole preserve of old sea dogs in low season, but surprisingly lively on summer evenings.

Modern visitors delight in the sheer beauty of the old settlement of Hora looming above, its white houses spilling down the hillside beneath its impressive *kastro* (castle). For the original inhabitants of Skala, however, the upward migration was prompted by the endless threat of marauding pirates. These days Hora is a delightful maze to explore, strolling around the hushed tangle of streets and climbing up to the fort. Suitably exhausted, you can then relax in the clutch of inviting *kafeneia* and tavernas alongside the restored Cycladic-style windmills that mark the village entrance.

◉ Sights

Kastro
CASTLE

(Hora; ⊙dawn-dusk) **FREE** Astypalea's imposing castle was built by the Venetian Quirini family early in the 15th century. For the next 300 years, up to 4000 people lived within this ever-expanding precinct, sheltered from pirate attacks. Its last inhabitants left in 1956, after an earthquake caused the stone houses integrated into its walls to collapse. The only entrance is through a gateway that burrows beneath the **Church of the Virgin of the Castle**; the magical **Church of Agios Georgios** lies beyond.

Archaeological Museum
MUSEUM

(☑22430 61500; Skala; admission €2; ⊙9am-1pm & 6-8.30pm Tue-Sun Jun-Sep) Skala's small archaeological museum, set back from the sea at the start of the road up to Hora, holds treasures found across the island, from earliest times up to the Middle Ages. Highlights include grave offerings from two Mycenaean chamber tombs and a little bronze Roman statue of Aphrodite.

🛏 Sleeping

Reservations are essential in July and August.

Hotel Paradissos
HOTEL €

(☑22430 61224; www.astypalea-paradissos.com; Skala; d/tr €55/65; ❄🐾) Stately and peaceful, and crisp and stylish following recent renovations, Paradissos is so close to the harbour you can taste salt on your lips. Its 18 dazzling-white sea-view rooms hold desks, en suite bathrooms and private balconies. There's also a great cafe and attached travel agency.

★ Studios Kilindra
BOUTIQUE HOTEL €€

(☑22430 61131; www.astipalea.com.gr; Hora; d/apt incl breakfast €125/150; ❄@🐾☀) 🐾 Just below the *kastro,* this enchanting boutique hotel has a swish pool with a terrace overlooking the mouthwash-green bay. The lobby is scattered with eclectic antiques as well as a grand piano, while studios and larger maisonettes fuse the contemporary with the traditional, featuring split-level floors, raised beds, sofas and kitchenettes. Massage, acupuncture and herbal treatments are also available.

Mariakis Studios
APARTMENT €€

(☑22430 62072; www.mariakis.gr; Hora; s/d incl breakfast €70/80) Four attractive, spotlessly white rental apartments, adjoining a family home just steps from the heart of Hora. Island-style touches include traditional furnishings and exposed stone walls, while the spacious terraces enjoy great sea views and the breakfasts are superb.

Thalassa Hotel
BOUTIQUE HOTEL €€

(☑22430 59840; www.stampalia.gr; Skala; r incl breakfast €120; ❄@🐾) Thalassa's 12 rooms are marble floored with four-poster beds, Caribbean blue fittings and floral bedspreads. Best of all, their spacious terraces boast incredible views across the harbour to the tumbling houses of Hora. Summer rates are a little on the high side, though, even if they do include excellent breakfasts and free airport transfers.

✗ Eating

Barbarossa
TAVERNA €

(☑ 22430 61577; Hora; mains €8-14; ☉ lunch & dinner; ❋ 🛜 🅿) 🍴 You can't miss this friendly taverna, serving food with soul along the main approach to Hora, with a buzzing terrace near the town hall. Inside are exposed stone walls covered with antique Greek poster girls, and there are amazing views to the rear. Menu highlights like pork fillet with prunes, mussels *saganaki* and grilled shrimps ensure you won't be disappointed.

Agoni Grammi
TAVERNA €

(☑ 22430 61988; Hora; mains €7-12; ☉ lunch & dinner) It's the outdoor terrace that first catches the eye here, close to Hora's landmark windmills, but the whitewashed interior is equally appealing at night, stippled by stone flags and lit with red pendant lights. As well as homemade pasta and pizza, this island favourite is renowned for its fish soup and traditional *kokoretsi* (kebab of lamb innards).

Maïstrali
TAVERNA €

(☑ 22430 61691; Skala; mains €8-12; ☉ 10am-late; ❋ 🛜 🅿) Tucked one street back from the harbour, near the stairway to heaven (well, Hora, anyway), this stylish restaurant dishes up everything from zucchini balls, lamb chops and eggplant salad to grilled shrimp *saganaki* and rabbit in tomato sauce.

🛍 Shopping

Koursaros
ACCESSORIES

(☑ 22430 59839; Skala; ☉ 5pm-1am) An eclectic cave of jewellery, hats, icons, pashminas, bags and Thai and Indian linen blouses, along with natural sponges. Look out for the sign depicting Jack Sparrow with a mermaid, just along the street from Hotel Paradissos.

ℹ Information

Astypalea Tours (☑ 22430 61571; www.astypaleatours.gr; Skala; ☉ 6-9pm) For air and ferry tickets and boat excursions.

Emporiki Bank (☑ 22430 59890; Skala) The island's only bank, with an ATM on the waterfront.

Municipal tourist office (☑ 22430 61412; www.astipalea.org; Hora; ☉ 6-9pm Jun-Sep) In a restored windmill.

Paradise Travel Agency (☑ 22430 61224; paradisostravel@yahoo.gr) Books ferry tickets.

Police (☑ 22430 61207; Skala) In an Italianate building on the waterfront.

Port police (☑ 22430 61208; Skala) Shares premises with the police.

Post office (☑ 22430 61223; Hora) At the top of the Skala–Hora road.

Livadi
Λειβάδι

Astypalea's most popular beach, Livadi Beach, stands at the mouth of a lush valley in the first bay south of Hora. An easy 20-minute walk down from the old town, it's also served by local buses. In summer it's effectively transformed into a buzzing little resort, with a string of funky restaurants and bars lining the waterfront.

🛏 Sleeping & Eating

Mouras Studios
APARTMENT €€

(☑ 22430 61127; www.mourastudios.gr; studios €77; ☉ May–mid-Oct) Radiating off a beachfront courtyard, these seven stunning whitewashed studios vary in size, but all have stylish dark-wood furniture, kitchenettes and private balconies. Full-on sea views cost a few euros extra.

Fildisi Hotel
BOUTIQUE HOTEL €€€

(☑ 22430 62060; www.fildisi.net; studios €140-260; ❋ 🛜 🏊) Split into terraces, this boutique dream has for its centerpiece an infinity pool accompanied by a juice bar and marvellous view of the sea. The breakfast/chill room is chic, while the 10 ubercool rooms, each named for a precious gem, enjoy private balconies, kitchenettes and sea views. Breakfast is disappointing, though.

Astropelos
GREEK €€

(☑ 22430 61473; mains €10-15; ☉ 8am-midnight; 🛜 🅿) First-class dining by the beach, on a decked veranda with chic white tables and a menu ranging through octopus salad, breaded crab pincers and lobster. Lounge tunes under the shade of tamarisk trees accompany the view of Hora on the hill-top horizon.

West of Skala

West of Skala, you swiftly hit the Astypalea outback – gnarled, bare rolling hills, perfect for a Cyclops. There's scarcely a sealed road to speak of, but it's just about drivable. Cross the western massif by heading directly inland from Hora, and from the point where the road finally peters out after 8km, where the **Kastro** ruins and **Moni Agiou Ioanni** stand proudly cheek by jowl above the shoreline, energetic walkers can hike down to **Agios Ioannis Beach**. Alternatively, follow the track that branches northwards shortly before road's end and you'll probably have **Panormos Beach** to yourself.

The rough track that winds along the southern coast west of Livadi, on the other hand, leads through mountainous meadows to several remote beaches. First along the way, reached on a brief detour, is the pretty, tree-shaded **Agios Konstantinos Beach** on the south side of Livadi Bay. This beach and **Kaminakia Beach** in the far west, where the track reaches its terminus, hold excellent seasonal tavernas. Bookended by granite boulders, Kaminakia is Astypalea's best altar to sun worshipping, boasting water so clear you can see the pebbles through the turquoise.

East of Skala

The slender isthmus that links Astypalea's two 'wings' holds some of the island's most popular beaches. Each of the three bays at **Marmari**, just 2km northeast of Skala, has its own pebble-and-sand beach, right beside the road. **Steno Beach**, another 2km along, is sandy, shady and conveniently shallow for kids. The name means 'narrow', with the isthmus being a mere 100m wide near this spot.

The only resort area away from Skala, **Analipsi**, is a pleasantly laid-back place that spreads through a fertile valley alongside the airport, 8km northeast of Skala. Also known as Maltezana, having once been the lair of Maltese pirates, it's grown recently thanks to long **Analipsi Beach** to the southeast, which offers sand, pebbles, shade and clean, shallow water. Nearby the remains of the Tallaras Roman baths still hold some mosaics.

Almost no one lives on Astypalea's eastern half. The only settlement is the remote hamlet of **Mesa Vathy**, tucked into the shelter of an enormous bottleneck bay and home to barely half a dozen families. A summer yacht harbour, it doesn't have a decent beach.

🛏 Sleeping & Eating

Camping Astypalea   CAMPGROUND €
(☑22430 61900; www.astypalaiacamping.gr; Marmari; camp sites per adult/tent €7/2; ☉Jun–early Sep) Shaded by tamarisk trees and shielded by bamboo groves, this summer-only camping ground is next to Marmari beach, which means it's also right beside the road. A lively scene in peak season, it has 24-hour hot water, a kitchen, cafe and mini-market.

Hotel Maltezana Beach   APARTMENT €€
(☑22430 61558; www.maltezanabeach.gr; Analipsi; s/d incl breakfast €75/90; P❋�)Ideal for families, this welcoming hotel stands amid manicured gardens a few metres from the beach. There are fresh, spacious rooms, with balconies, in white-cubed blocks set around a fine pool, plus good home cooking in the restaurant. Sea-view rooms cost €15 extra.

Analipsi Taverna   GREEK €
(☑22430 61466; Analipsi; mains €8-12; ☉11am–9pm) This simple quayside taverna stays open year-round to keep local fishers suitably fed and watered. In summer, though, its traditional island meat and seafood staples go down a treat with visitors.

KALYMNOS ΚΑΛΥΜΝΟΣ

POP 16,000

The wild and wonderful island of Kalymnos is characterised above all by its dramatic mountains, which draw hardy climbers from all over the world. Along its western flank in particular, the scenery is utterly spectacular, with the coastal highway lined with pink oleanders and forming a slender strip between steepling crags above and dazzling blue waters below. Kalymnos is also greener than most of its neighbours, cradling fertile valleys and verdant enclaves. Add the enticing, car-free islet of Telendos, immediately offshore, and you have a compelling destination. To do it justice, you'll need to allow at least three days, and ideally rent your own transport.

While its sponge-fishing heyday is long past, Kalymnos remains inextricably entwined with the sea. Its turquoise bays hold some delightful beaches, albeit largely pebble rather than sand, while gastronomic treats include octopus in ouzo, and *spinialo* (devilfish and urchins in seawater). The island's nautical heritage is at its most conspicuous in its capital and main ferry port, Pothia, where you'll still find stalls piled high with unearthly looking sponges, and a statue of Poseidon surveying the harbour. Pothia is essentially a working town, however, so it's more fun to stay in the smaller west-coast settlements such as Emborios and Myrties, or over on Telendos.

ⓘ Getting There & Away

AIR

Kalymnos' airport, 6km northwest of Pothia, is served by daily **Olympic Air** (www.olympicair. com) flights to and from Athens (€90, one hour), Leros (€54, 15 minutes) and Kos (€54, 20 minutes). Connecting buses meet flights in summer.

BOAT

Kalymnos' main ferry port, Pothia, is linked by daily Dodekanisos Seaways (p473) catamarans with Kos, Rhodes, Leros, Patmos and other nearby islands. **Blue Star Ferries** (☎22430 26000) connects Pothia with Piraeus, Kos and Rhodes three times weekly, and with Astypalea and Symi once or twice weekly.

Nisos Kalymnos (www.anekalymnou.gr) runs three to four times weekly to and from Leros, Lipsi, Patmos and the islets to the north, and also connects Kalymnos once weekly with Skala on Astypalea.

The **Kalymnos Star** and **Kalymnos Dolphin** (www.anekalymnou.gr) run several times daily between Pothia and Mastihari on the north shore of Kos, as does **ANEM** (www.anemferries.gr). Several excursion boats offer day trips from Kos Town to Pothia.

The little resort of Myrties on Kalymnos' west coast is connected three times weekly with Lipsi and Agia Marina on Leros by **Anna Express** (www.annaexpress.eu), and five times weekly with either Xirokambos (€10) or Pandeli (€15) on Leros by **Captain Yiannis** (☎6944819073).

Boat Services from Kalymnos

DESTINATION	TIME	FARE	FREQUENCY
Astypalea	2hr 40min	€12	2 weekly
Kos	1hr 20min	€6	3 daily
Kos*	35min	€15	1-2 daily
Leros	35min	€10-15	18 weekly
Leros	1½hr	€9	4 weekly
Leros*	45min	€20	1-2 daily
Lipsi	1¼hr	€20	3 weekly
Lipsi*	1hr 5min	€20	1 daily
Patmos	4hr	€12	4 weekly
Patmos*	1hr 40min	€29	6 weekly
Piraeus	11hr	€38	3 weekly
Rhodes	6hr	€19	3 weekly
Rhodes*	3hr	€38	1-2 daily
Samos*	3¾hr	€38	5 weekly

*high-speed services

DODECANESE KALYMNOS

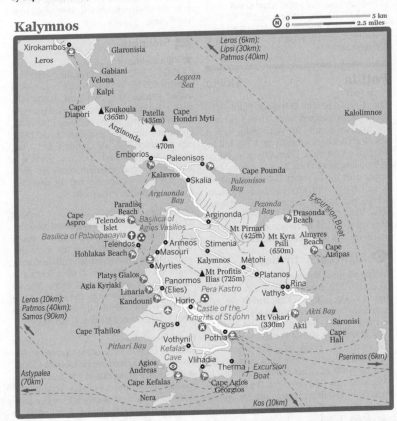

Kalymnos

ℹ Getting Around

BOAT

In summer, excursion boats run from Pothia to destinations including Kefalas Cave (€20), where an impressive 103m corridor is filled with stalactites and stalagmites; and the island of Pserimos, with its big, sandy beach and tavernas. Frequent boats also connect Myrties with Telendos islet year-round.

BUS

Buses from Pothia harbour serve Myrties, Masouri and Armeos (€1.50, seven daily), Emporio (€2, two daily) and Vathys (€2, three daily). Check timetables at www.kalymnos-isl.gr.

CAR & MOTORCYCLE

Vehicle-hire companies along the harbour in Pothia include the friendly, good-value **Auto Market** (☑ 6927834628, 22430 24202; www.kalymnoscars.gr) and **Rent-a-Bike** (☑ 6937980591; www.kalymnosrent.com). Expect to pay €20 to €40 per day for a car, or €12 to €15 for a scooter.

TAXI

Shared taxis, based at Pothia's **taxi stand** (☑ 22430 50300; Plateia Kyprou), cost little more than buses. Private taxis cost around €9 to Myrties, €10 to the airport, €15 to Vathys and €30 to Emborios.

Pothia

Πόθια

POP 12,300

The principal port on Kalymnos, Pothia is by far the island's largest town. As well as curving for 2km around its south-facing bay, it also stretches back up and over a low hill towards the west coast. Framed by a backdrop of brooding mountains, it's a functional harbour rather than a resort, but the waterfront is garlanded with tavernas and *kafeneia*, where nut brown fishers nurse retsinas, while the intricate labyrinth of whitewashed alleyways behind holds some splendid old mansions and an excellent museum.

⊙ Sights & Activities

Archaeological Museum MUSEUM
(☑ 22430 23113; admission €3; ⊙ 8am-3pm Tue-Sun Jul & Aug, 8.30am-2.30pm Wed-Fri Sep-Jun) Kalymnos' modern Archaeological Museum is hard to find, hidden in the backstreets behind the right end of Pothia's waterfront. It's worth the effort to enjoy beautifully displayed ancient artefacts dating as far back as 5300 BC. There's some remarkable glassware and gold jewellery, but the highlight is an exquisite, larger-than-life bronze statue of a woman from the 2nd century

BC. Swathed in a chiton, she was discovered underwater off Kalymnos in 1994.

Nautical & Folklore Museum MUSEUM
(☑ 22430 51361; admission €3; ⊙ 9am-5pm daily mid-Jun–mid-Sep) The two parts of the Nautical and Folklore Museum, on the central waterfront, are not always open simultaneously. The folklore section holds costumes and furniture, while the nautical museum focuses on sponge fishing, displaying mighty stone weights used by ancient divers and haunting photos of their 20th-century counterparts wearing early model diving suits. Many suffered terrible injuries before the bends were understood.

Kalymnos Scuba Diving Club DIVING
(☑ 22430 47253, 6974646413; www.kalymnosdiving.com; 1-day dive €50, 3-day open-water PADI €350) One-day dives to wrecks, underwater volcanoes, reefs and caves. Owner Dimitris also runs boat trips explaining the history of sponge diving and can demonstrate the ancient art of *skandalopetra* (stone and rope free-diving).

🛏 Sleeping

⭐**Villa Melina** BOUTIQUE HOTEL €
(☑ 22430 22682; www.villa-melina.com; r incl breakfast €55-65; 🕸🛜🏊) Set in a colourful walled garden, this rose pink 1930s villa exudes old-world charm, its wood-panelled rooms featuring stucco ceilings, lilac walls, mahogany armoires and huge beds. Don't expect luxury – it's all slightly faded – but owner Antonios and his cats provide a homely welcome, the bathrooms are spotless, the library extensive and the sparkling swimming pool is irresistible.

Archontiko Hotel PENSION €
(☑ 6942838524; www.apxontiko-hotel.com; s/d €30/45; 🕸) Overlooking the harbour just five minutes' walk from the ferry, this custard-hued neoclassical gem offers simple, bright sea-view rooms with tiled floors and balconies. Air-con costs €5 extra. There's bags of atmosphere from the moment you step through its original stone archways and meet helpful owner Henrik. Great value.

Hotel Panorama HOTEL €
(☑ 22430 23138; www.panorama-kalymnos.gr; Ammoudara neighbourhood; s/d incl breakfast €30/40; 🕸🛜) Named in honour of the breathtaking rooftop views from its hill-top eyrie (a stiff climb from the ferry dock – ask for free pickup), this friendly, family-run hotel offers 13

rooms with private balconies, contemporary furniture and a communal sun terrace where the basic breakfast is served.

Evanik Hotel
HOTEL €€

(✆22430 22057; www.evanik-hotel.gr; s/d/tr incl breakfast €40/60/75; ❄🅿) Beyond its smart lobby, this modern hotel, a few blocks up from the harbour and lacking views, holds 28 plush rooms of varying size, with tiled floors, Ikea-style furniture, reading lamps and immaculate en suite bathrooms. Downstairs there's a pleasant breakfast area. Ask for a quieter room at the back.

✖ Eating

Dozens of bars, cafes, restaurants and tavernas, as well as food shops and appetising local bakeries, line the quay in Pothia. Just keep walking and you're sure to find whatever you're looking for.

Pantelis Restaurant
GREEK €

(✆22430 51508; mains €7-14; ⊗noon-midnight; 🅿🍴) Homey taverna, set slightly back off a corner of the harbour near the ferry dock, where island specialities include goat in red-wine sauce and homemade dolmadhes. Be sure to try the 'Ancient Greek' salad with apple and walnuts, and the fresh fish of the day. There's a good wine selection, too.

Stukas Taverna
GREEK €

(✆6970802346; mains €6-12; ⊗lunch & dinner) Great-value local restaurant, towards the far end of the harbour as you head away from the ferry dock, with quayside tables and very friendly English-speaking staff. Three-course set menus cost €9 for vegetarians and €10 for fish- or meat-eaters, or you can get the Kalymnian versions of *mousakas* or *stifadho* for even less.

Barba Yiannis
GREEK €

(mains €8-12; ⊗9am-midnight) Smart, mercifully breezy and enjoying fine harbour views from its pretty decked terrace, Yiannis is a great spot to head for traditional Greek dishes such as *stifadho* and souvlakia, and offers a daily two-course lunch for €8.

🍷 Drinking & Nightlife

Neon Center
CAFE

(✆22430 59120; ⊗8am-1am; 🛜) Backstreet cafe, handy for its free wi-fi, with outdoor garden seating. It's especially popular with local youngsters for its pool tables and online gaming – and there's even a four-lane, full-sized bowling alley!

❶ Information

Pothia's ferry dock is at the southern, left-hand end of the port. The entire quay is commercialised, but the real centre of activity is around the Italian-era municipal buildings in the middle, 600m from the ferry dock. Several banks close to the waterfront hereabouts offer ATMs. Stay alert; traffic can be hectic on the narrow, footpathless roads.

Magos Travel (✆22430 28777; www.magos-tours.gr) The island's main travel agency, near the ferry dock, sells ferry and catamaran tickets and has a 24-hour ticket machine outside. It also offers round-island bus tours, and boat excursions in summer.

Main post office A 10-minute walk inland, northwest of the centre.

Municipal Tourist Information (✆22430 29299; www.kalymnos-isl.gr; ⊗7.30am-3pm Mon-Fri) An excellent, well-organised source of info for buses and ferries, climbing and diving, festivals and general island practicalities. At the entrance to the ferry dock.

Police (✆22430 29301; Venizelou)

Port police (✆22430 24444; 25 Martiou)

Around Pothia

The former capital of Kalymnos, **Horio**, stands atop the brow of the low ridge behind Pothia, around 4km up from the sea. A steep, stony and unshaded old stairway that's a little hard to find climbs up from its eastern edge to the pirate-proof village of **Pera Kastro**, which was inhabited until the 18th century. Beyond its forbidding walls and stern gateway, it now lies almost entirely in ruins and overgrown with wildflowers, but amid the wreckage it's well worth seeking out nine tiny 15th-century churches that still hold stunning frescoes.

A tree-lined road drops for 2km beyond Horio to reach the pretty village of **Panormos**. Two neighbouring beaches are within walking distance: **Linaria** and the more attractive cove of **Kandouni**, surrounded by mountains and holding a small beach where cafes, bars and hotels overlook the water.

Myrties, Masouri & Armeos
Μυρτιές, Μασούρι & Αρμεός

Three lively and nominally distinct little resorts line the west coast of Kalymnos, facing Telendos islet across 800m of generally placid sea. Both Myrties and Masouri have attractive beaches, with the strand at

Masouri being larger and sandier. Beyond the Telendos ferry quay in Myrties, the west-coast road is a one-way loop. To continue any further north, you have to double back and follow a largely empty stretch higher up the hillside. Only if you're heading south do you see the main commercial strip that connects the two resorts in a seamless row of restaurants, rental studios, bars, souvenir shops and mini-markets, one block up from sea level.

North of Masouri, the road becomes two-way once more and swiftly leads into Armeos, perched above the coast without a beach. Smarter and newer than its neighbours, it consists almost entirely of larger hotels and apartment complexes targeted at climbers.

🛏 Sleeping

Hotel Atlantis
HOTEL €

(☑ 22430 47497; www.atlantis-kalymnos.gr; Myrties; d/tr €35/40; ☺ Apr-Oct; ❇) A family-run hotel, perched above the main road a block up from the sea, with amazing views, a trellised terrace and a lobby decked in myth-ological reliefs. The 18 simple, pleasant studios have great balconies, comfy beds and kitchenettes.

Hotel Philoxenia
HOTEL €

(☑ 22430 59310; www.philoxenia-kalymnos.com; Armeos; s/d €40/50; ❇) This small but spa-cious modern hotel, below some enticing crags at Armeos, makes an ideal base for climbers. Each of its plain tile-floored rooms has its own sea-view blacony and there's a decent pool with snack bar.

Myrties Boutique Apartments
APARTMENT €€

(☑ 6986285888; www.myrtiesboutiqueapart-ments.gr; Myrties; apt €106) Two delightful, dazzling rental studios, a couple of min-utes' walk up from the beach, each with two rooms, sleeping up to five guests and equipped with kitchenette and broad sea-view patio. They're cleaned daily and linen includes robes and beach towels.

🍴 Eating

★ Smuggler's Restaurant
TAVERNA €

(☑ 22430 48508; Myrties; mains €7-12; ☺ 8am-late; ❇ 🌿) This lovely seafront taverna, close to the jetty at the south end of Myr-ties, is built to resemble an old fishing boat caressed by the waves. The perfect spot, then, to enjoy fresh tuna steaks, mussels or shrimps in garlic and other deep-sea treas-ures, all at very reasonable prices.

CLIMBING & HIKING IN PARADISE

Steep crags, stark cliffs and daredevil overhangs have turned Kalymnos into Greece's pre-mier destination for rock climbers. It now boasts more than 80 designated climbing sites, holding almost 2500 bolted routes. Most are located above the island's west-coast road, especially around and north of Armeos – white roadside markers identify the precise spots – though several of the finest ascend the flanks of Telendos islet, just across the water.

Climbing season runs from March to mid-November, with the busiest period from mid-September until the end of October. An annual climbing festival takes place during the first 10 days of October.

The man largely responsible for the boom is Aris Theodoropolous, who, along with Katie Rousseau writes the astonishingly detailed and comprehensive *Kalymnos Rock Climbing Guidebook* and maintains the useful www.climbkalymnos.com website, which includes a climbers' forum.

Kalymnos is also increasingly popular with hikers. Established routes are detailed on the excellent 1:25,000 *Kalymnos* map published by **Terrain** (www.terrainmaps.gr). Seri-ous hikers may want to undertake all or part of the highly demanding, multi-day **Kalym-nos Trail**, a 100km route that circles the island and also goes around Telendos for good measure. Carl Dawson published a useful guide to that and other island trails in 2015; see www.thekalymnostrail.co.uk.

The welcoming roadside **Kalymnos Adventure Center & Climbing Shop** (☑ 6984933327, 22480 48160; www.kalymnos-adventure.com; Masouri; ☺ 9am-noon & 4-8pm Mar-Nov) sells and rents climbing equipment, along with maps and guidebooks, and also arranges a wide program of activities. As well as half-day beginners and leaders climbing courses, starting at €60 per person, it offers weeklong courses, along with diving, hiking and horse riding – and yoga and massage for the after-effects!

★**Fatolitis Snack Bar**   CAFE €
(☑22430 47615; Masouri; snacks €4-7) The plump pop-art cushions at this cosy roadside cafe, opposite Kalymnos Adventure Center, make the ideal place to relax before or after a day's climbing – no wonder it's also known as 'Climber's Station'. Swap your stories over breakfast, coffee, ice cream, all-day snacks or an evening beer.

Telendos Islet
Νήσος Τέλενδος

The bewitching islet of Telendos looms from the Aegean just off the west coast of Kalymnos. Crowned by a mountainous ridge that soars 450m high, it's thought to have been set adrift from the rest of Kalymnos by an earthquake in AD 554. It now makes a wonderful, vehicle-free destination for a day trip or longer stay, easily reached on a 10-minute boat ride from Myrties (€2, departing every half-hour from 8am to midnight).

Daily life on Telendos focuses on the short line of tavernas, cafes and whitewashed guesthouses that stretches along the pretty waterfront to either side of the jetty. Head right to reach the ruins of the early Christian basilica of **Agios Vasilios** and a footpath that climbs to the similarly dilapidated basilica of **Palaiopanayia**. Head left, on the other hand, and you can either cross a slender ridge, rich in colourful oleander, to access windswept, fine-pebbled **Hohlakas Beach**, or explore the islet's low-lying southern promontory, which holds some tiny early-Christian tombs now inhabited by goats and a gloriously tranquil little swimming cove.

The cliffs along the northern flanks of Telendos hold several hugely popular **rock-climbing routes**, which can be accessed either by walking for an hour or so along a rough, exposed footpath, or, more enjoyably, by the **Theofilis** (☑6974329670; from €5 per person) taxi boat, usually found moored to Telendos' main quay.

🛏 Sleeping & Eating

★**On The Rocks**   PENSION €
(☑22430 48260, 6932978142; www.otr.telendos. com; s/d/tr €40/50/60; 🕸@🛜) Behind its seafront garden restaurant, open bar and terrace strung with nautical eclectica, 200m right from the jetty, this welcoming complex is a haven for active climbers and indolent beach bunnies alike. The spacious studios have kitchenettes, private balconies, foot massage and washing machines. Airport transfers available.

To Kafouli   TAVERNA €
(☑22430 47363; mains €7-12; ☉ lunch & dinner) Sitting at the waterfront tables of this impossibly picturesque little taverna, you can watch fishers cleaning fish on the quay, straight from their own jaunty little boats, then dine on the freshest meat or seafood, scrutinised by a posse of purring pussycats.

Zorba's   TAVERNA €
(☑22430 48660; www.telendos.net; mains €6-12; 🕸🛜) A traditional cafe, a short walk left from the jetty, with great sea views. The owner fishes for the seafood himself (guests can go with him), bringing up squid, octopus, tuna and swordfish. It also has three small but pleasant pink-walled en suite rooms (€30).

Emborios
Εμπορειός

North of Armeos, Kalymnos' west-coast road leaves civilisation behind. Its final stretch, skirting the deep inlet that cradles tiny Arginonda, is utterly magnificent, cut into the flanks of mighty cliffs and bordered with flowering oleander. It comes to an end 20km from Pothia at sleepy little Emborios, where sugar white houses cluster around a long, narrow pebble beach.

This is the best place to swim on the island, with its crystal-clear waters sheltered by the tiny island of Kalavros just offshore and the mountains on Telendos and above Armeos dominating the horizon. Two daily buses connect Emborios with Pothia, and in summer excursion boats come here for the day from Myrties – they have no fixed schedule.

🛏 Sleeping & Eating

Five similar tavernas line the seafront at Emborios, with tables on terraces or on the beach itself. All offer free, all-day sunbeds to customers and they're generous with free snacks to accompany sunset drinks.

★**Harry's Paradise**   APARTMENT €
(☑22430 40062; www.harrys-paradise.gr; d/f apt €48/90; 🕸@) A true island favourite, set in its own garden of Eden, bursting with jasmine, roses, hibiscus and aromatic herbs. Fantastic-value accommodation incorporates charming shabby-chic elements, rocking chairs, kitchenettes and large balconies – if possible, opt for the garden-facing

studios rather than the separate sea-view block – while the divine home cooking gives locally sourced, quintessentially Kalymnian ingredients a modern twist.

★ **To Kyma**   TAVERNA €

(☑ 22430 40012; www.tokyma-kalymnos.gr; mains €5-10; ⊙ breakfast, lunch & dinner) Despite its humdrum laminated menu board, this extremely friendly beach taverna serves truly exceptional food, including a delicious barley-bread salad, salted mackerel and swordfish souvlakia. Its name, 'The Wave', refers to the swell whipped up by late summer's *meltemi* wind.

Vathys & Rina Βαθύς & Ρίνα

Follow the barren coast road northeast from Pothia, instead of heading straight over to the west coast, and, after winding for 13km along the cliffs, it enters a long, lush, east-facing valley that was historically the agricultural heartland of Kalymnos. Narrow roads here thread between citrus orchards, bordered by high stone walls known as *koumoula*.

The valley takes its name from the inland settlement of Vathys, but the attraction for visitors is the little harbour of Rina. From the sea, it's accessed by a slender twisting inlet that's more like a fjord than anything you'd expect to find on a Greek island. Large excursion boats bring troupes of day trippers from Kos for lunch here in summer, keeping a clutch of competitive quayside tavernas busy, but it's a lovely spot at quieter times. Easy walks lead to 1500-year-old chapels on the hillside to either side of the bay.

Inland, beyond Vathys, a windswept road switchbacks up and over the mountains to reach the island's northwest coast, providing a speedier way to reach Emborios from Pothia than the built-up route through Myrties and Masouri.

✗ Eating

Galini Taverna   TAVERNA €

(☑ 22430 31241; Rina; mains €8-14; ⊙ breakfast, lunch & dinner; P✻⊛) With its checked tablecloths, friendly manager, bougainvillea ceiling and fine view of the harbour, Galini makes a pleasant place to enjoy salads, seafood, flavourful dolmadhes and grilled meat. The attached hotel holds simple en suite rooms (€30).

LEROS   ΛΕΡΟΣ

POP 8210

Leros is said to have been the original home of Artemis the Huntress. There's certainly something alluringly untamed and beautiful about the island, which is scattered with stunning Orthodox churches, dazzling blue coves and whitewashed villages. The capital, Platanos, with its stark windmills and ancient fortress towering above, makes a striking centrepiece, while down below, the busy little harbour of Agia Marina pulses with enterprise. Leros is less about chasing activities and more about worshipping Helios, seeking out your favourite beach and allowing the magic of the place to slowly unfold.

❶ Getting There & Away

AIR

Olympic Air (www.olympicair.com) has daily flights to Athens (€76, one hour) and thrice-weekly flights to Rhodes (€68, 1¾ hours), Kalymnos (€54, 15 minutes), Kos (€61, 55 minutes) and Astypalea (€61, 25 minutes).

BOAT

High-speed catamarans operated by Dodekanisos Seaways (p473) call in at Leros between two and four times daily as they ply their way to and from Kos, Kalymnos, Patmos, Samos, Rhodes and other nearby islands. Confusingly, though, some stop at Agia Marina on the island's east coast, and some at Lakki on the west coast – what's worse, they may change which port they use according to each day's weather. Always check the relevant port when you buy tickets, double-check on the day you're due to depart and be prepared for a last-minute taxi dash across the island if the weather's in doubt.

Blue Star Ferries (☑ 22470 26000; Lakki) makes late-night stops at Lakki twice each week, heading once towards Rhodes via Kos and Kalymnos, and once towards Piraeus via Patmos and Lipsi.

Patmos Star (www.patmos-star.com) sails between Agia Marina and the islands of Lipsi and Patmos with varying frequency, increasing to daily in peak season.

The **Nisos Kalymnos** (www.anekalymnou.gr) connects Lakki with Kalymnos to the south, and Lipsi, Patmos and assorted islets to the north, three to four times weekly.

Anna Express (www.annaexpress.eu) connects Agia Marina three times weekly with Lipsi and with Myrties on the west coast of Kalymnos, while **Captain Yiannis** (☑ 6944819073) sails five times weekly from either Xirokambos (€10) or Pandeli (€15) on Leros to Myrties.

Boat Services from Leros

Dodekanese Seaways catamarans may dock at either Agia Marina or Lakki.

DESTINATION	TIME	FARE	FREQUENCY
Agathonisi*	1hr 50min	€16	1 weekly
Kalymnos	2hr	€9	4-5 weekly
Kalymnos*	50min	€20	1-2 daily
Kos	3¼hr	€14	1 weekly
Kos*	1hr	€22	1 weekly
Lipsi	1hr	€9	3-4 weekly
Lipsi*	20min	€14	1 daily
Patmos	2hr	€10	3-4 weekly
Patmos*	45min	€16	daily
Piraeus	10hr	€39	1 weekly
Rhodes	8hr	€30	1 weekly
Rhodes*	3½hr	€41	3 weekly
Samos*	2hr 50min	€16	5 weekly

*high-speed services

Getting Around

Leros' airport is at the northern end of the island. A **taxi** (☑6972014531, 6974316421) to Agia Marina, 6km to the south, will cost around €10.

Green-and-beige-striped buses travel the full length of Leros between three and six times daily, calling at the airport as well as Alinda, Agia Marina, Platanos, Pandeli, Lakki and Xirokambos (€4 flat fare). They'll usually stop anywhere if you flag them down.

Outlets in all resort areas rent cars, scooters and bikes; **Motoland** (☑22470 24103, 22470 24584; www.motoland.gr) in Alinda and Pandeli is recommended.

The **Agios Georgios** (☑22470 23060) and **Barbarossa** (☑6978048715) excursion boats make assorted day trips in summer, around the island and north to islets such as Arki and Marathi, typically costing €20 to €25.

DODECANESE LEROS

Leros

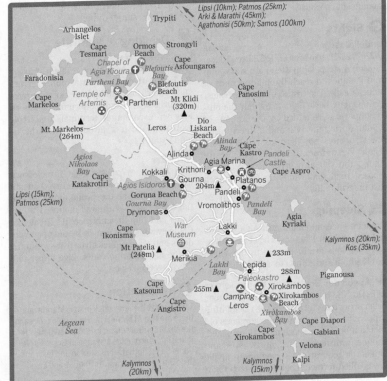

Agia Marina & Platanos

Αγια Μαρίνα & Πλάτανος

POP 3000

If you're arriving by catamaran or local ferry, the charming little port of Agia Marina (ay*i*-a ma-*ri*-na) may well provide your first glimpse of Leros. While it's not a resort, and holds no hotels, it's a very pleasant, low-key place to while away a couple of hours. Bars, cafes and bakeries line the quay, while attractive ochre- and wine-coloured Italian-era buildings, along with a handful of quirky little shops, stretch along its single waterfront street.

Heading to the right from the ferry quay, following the shoreline, will bring you to Krithoni and Alinda. Leros' main settlement, though, the whitewashed town of **Platanos**, lies straight ahead, a gentle 10-minute walk up the hillside facing the dock. Parts have become somewhat rundown, but stately mansions still pepper the slopes and the row of renovated **windmills** that marches up towards its imposing cliff-top castle makes a magnificent spectacle.

◉ Sights

Pandeli Castle   CASTLE
(✆22470 23211; admission €1; ⊙8.30am-12.30pm & 4-8pm) A steep, stony step-path zigzags up from Platanos to reach the hill-top ruins of Pandeli Castle. The castle's oldest, innermost sections date back 1000 years, but the outer ramparts were added by the Knights of St John during the 14th and 15th centuries. Few structures now survive, but the 360-degree views from the walls are breathtaking. You can also drive here, along an exposed road that winds up from Pandeli past the windmills.

⊟ Sleeping

There's no accommodation in Agia Marina, and very little in Platanos. The closest alternative options are in Pandeli to the south, and Krithoni and Alinda to the north.

★Maison des Couleurs   BOUTIQUE HOTEL €€
(✆22470 23341; www.maisondescouleurs.com; Platanos; r inc breakfast €100-150; ❀) Delightfully peaceful little hotel, set in a gorgeous old villa that holds five spacious, high-ceilinged, antique-furnished rooms. Breakfast – and dinner, on request – is served on an idyllic flower-filled terrace. Look for a steep flight of steps just west of the bus stop and taxi rank in Platanos.

✕ Eating

Smoked mackerel and thyme honey are specialities of Leros.

★To Paradosiakon   BAKERY €
(Agia Marina; snacks €2-5; ⊙7am-11.30pm; ❀❀) ❂ Set in a handsome Italianate building, with colour-coordinated pastel-blue and green tables that spread onto the quay, this bakery-cafe is prized for its baklava, cheesecakes, strawberry tarts, croissants, spinach pies and locally made ice cream.

★Taverna Mylos   SEAFOOD €€
(✆22470 24894; www.mylosexperience.gr; Agia Marina; mains €9-16; ⊙1pm-late; ❀❀❀❀) ❂ Lapped by turquoise waves, beside an old windmill at the far end of the pebbled beach that curves north from the ferry dock, Mylos infuses classic recipes with a modern twist. Go for the octopus carpaccio, the peppery basil squid or the fabulous mixed-seafood spaghetti. The waterfront terrace is perfect for romantic sunset dinners.

❦ Drinking & Nightlife

Enallaktiko Cafe   CAFE
(✆22470 25746; Agia Marina; ⊙10am-midnight; ❀) Facing the quay, with a roomy terrace and waterfront tables, the port's largest bar turns stylish and modern once indoors. Free wi-fi, computer terminals and table football make it a favourite with the island's youth.

Faros Bar   BAR
(Agia Marina; ⊙7pm-late; ❀) Tumbledown haunt, partly hollowed into a cave beneath the lighthouse at the promontory beyond the ferry dock. With wall-mounted accordions and dim-lit ambience, it's great fun. Come evening, you can sit by the open windows and watch quicksilver fish swimming in the aquamarine water. Live music and DJs at weekends.

❶ Information

Taxis wait at the ferry dock in Agia Marina, and there are two ATMs nearby. Head uphill to reach the small central square in Platanos, Plateia N Roussou, which holds a branch of Greece's National Bank. Both the bus station and taxi rank are 50m downhill, towards Pandeli and Lakki.

For information about local history and facilities, visit www.leros.org.uk or www.leros island.com.

Kastis Travel (☑ 22470 22140) Useful agency, facing the quay in Agia Marina, which sells ferry tickets and organises boat trips to nearby beaches and islets.

Leros Active (☑ 22470 24590; www.leros active.com; Agia Marina) Agency and tour operator specialising in alternative tourism. It arranges activities including diving and hiking, as well as tours of wartime sites, and can provide information about accommodation.

Police (☑ 22470 22221) In Agia Marina.

Post office Right of the quay in Agia Marina.

Pandeli   Παντελή

The picture-postcard village of Pandeli, arrayed around a crescent bay 800m south of Platanos, has become a popular resort in recent years. White houses tumble down the valley that slopes towards the sea, the sand-and-shingle beach is flanked by white windmills, and yachts moor along a modern marina.

🛏 Sleeping & Eating

Studios Happiness   APARTMENT €
(☑ 22470 23498; www.studios-happiness-leros. com; d/studio/apt €45/55/70; ❋) Very friendly family-run place, perched in colourful gardens beside the road down into Pandeli, 50m up from the beach. Its vibrant white-and-blue studios have kitchenettes, twin beds and private balconies with great sea views. The rooms vary in size and are spotless throughout.

Panteli Beach Hotel   APARTMENT €€
(☑ 22470 26400; www.panteli-beach.gr; studio/apt €100/140) Pretty, very comfortable complex, arrayed around an open courtyard right in front of the beach. All 14 studios have fresh white walls, nice duvets and sparkling kitchenettes, and the attached Sorokos beach bar offers all-day sunbeds.

El Greco   SEAFOOD €
(☑ 22470 25066; www.elgrecoleros.gr; mains €6-12; ⊙ lunch & dinner) Offering tables right on the beach or on a thatch-roofed terraces, this stylish taverna prepares up-to-the-minute versions of traditional seafood cuisine. Be sure to sample the king-crab croquettes and the lip-smacking salted mackerel, served on buttered toast.

Vromolithos   Βρωμόλιθος

Accessible only by walking or driving over the headland immediately south of Pandeli (there's no coastal footpath), Vromolithos consists of a long, narrow beach caressed by waters of a perfect shade of Aegean blue, scattered with turquoise.

🍴 Eating & Drinking

Dimitris O Karaflas   GREEK €
(☑ 22470 25626; Marcopoulo St; mezedhes €4-8; ⊙ noon-4pm & 6pm-late) The sign may say 'O Karaflas', but everyone knows this hill-top eyrie as 'Bald Dimitri's'. Bouzouki music washes over its pretty terrace, where diners feast on a wonderful array of dishes such as sea-urchin salad, hearty island sausages, octopus carpaccio, steamed mussels and substantial helpings of calamari.

Cafe Del Mar   BAR
(☑ 22470 24766; snacks €3-8; ⊙ 9am-late) An irresistibly languorous hillside lounge bar, nestling just above the north end of the beach with paradisiacal sea views. There are chill-some pine-shaded patios, comfy sofas and deckchairs, plus cool tunes and DJs spinning the decks by night. Call in any time for coffee and juice, as well as sandwiches, salads and pasta dishes, and don't miss a sunset mojito or two.

Lakki   Λακκί
POP 2000

Between 1912 and 1948, when the west-coast port of Lakki was a significant Italian naval base, the town was transformed beyond recognition by the construction of grandiose administrative and military buildings. The prevalent architectural style, now classified as streamline moderne, started out resembling art deco and ended up distinctly more fascist. Lakki these days is an extraordinary-looking place, its broad streets scattered with bizarre behemoths but lacking much sign of life, or even traffic. Larger ferries and some catamarans dock at its jetty, a long walk from the centre of town, but there's no reason to linger.

◉ Sights

War Museum   MUSEUM
(☑ 22470 22109; Merikia; admission €3; ⊙ 9.30am-1.30pm) Who remembers now that a major WWII battle was fought on this remote

little island? After British troops forced the Italians to surrender in September 1943, a massive German air onslaught recaptured the island in the Battle of Leros. A network of tunnels dug by the Italians beneath the woods west of Lakki now serve as a museum, housing countless relics of the conflict.

Xirokambos   Ξηρόκαμπος

At the southern end of Leros, Xirokambos Bay holds a pebble-and-sand beach with some good spots for snorkelling. As well as a few village houses, it's home to a good beach taverna and is served by small excursion boats from Kalymnos. Up the hill, 1km inland towards Lakki, a signposted path climbs to the ruined **Paleokastro** fortress, which offers tremendous views.

🛏 Sleeping & Eating

Camping Leros   CAMPGROUND €
(☑ 22470 23372, 6944238430; www.campingleros.com; camp sites adult/tent €8/4; ☺ Jun-Sep) Set 500m up from the beach, and 3km south of Lakki, the island's camping ground stands in a 400-year-old olive grove and holds a welcoming cafe that puts on evening BBQs. It's also a centre for scuba diving, offering introductory dives and week-long courses.

To Aloni   TAVERNA €
(☑ 22470 26048; mains €9-12; ☺ lunch & dinner) You can't miss this prominent beachfront taverna. With tables beside the water and a perfectly prepared panoply of traditional Greek snacks and mains, from seafood to meat, it's the perfect place to escape the heat of the day.

Krithoni & Alinda
Κριθώνι & Αλιντα

Starting just beyond the first headland north of Agia Marina, the twin resorts of Krithoni and Alinda sit next to each other on Alinda Bay, running parallel to the beach and bordered by *kafeneia* and restaurants. Leros' longest beach is at Alinda – although narrow, it's shaded and sandy with clean, shallow water. Set just back from the sea, a poignant war cemetery holds British casualties from the 1943 Battle of Leros.

For the best sun worshipping in these parts, continue through Krithoni and Alinda to **Dio Liskaria Beach** (a few minutes'

scooter ride). Bookended by rocks and backdropped by a taverna, it's lapped by aquamarine waves.

◎ Sights

Historic & Folklore Museum   MUSEUM
(☑ 22470 24775; Alinda; admission €3; ☺ 9am-1pm & 6-8pm Tue-Sun) Housed in an incongruous castellated villa on the seafront, the Historic and Folklore Museum covers several aspects of local history. The upstairs rooms are given over largely to weapons, helmets and photos relating to WWII. Downstairs you'll find displays of traditional costumes and an emotive gallery devoted to artworks created by political prisoners incarcerated on the island during the colonels' dictatorship of the 1960s and 1970s.

🛏 Sleeping

★ To Archontiko Angelou   HOTEL €€
(☑ 6944908182, 22470 22749; www.hotel-angelou-leros.com; Alinda; r incl breakfast €85-170; 🅿 ☀ ☎) 🏊 Spilling with oleander and jacaranda, this incurably romantic, 19th-century rose-coloured villa, five minutes' walk from the beach, is like stepping into a vintage Italian film. Think wood floors, Viennese frescoes, antique beds and old-world-style rooms. Breakfast on the sun-dappled terrace is an event, the owner producing mouthwatering homemade bread, jams and marmalades. One of the finest hotels in the Dodecanese.

Nefeli Hotel   APARTMENT €€
(☑ 22470 24611; www.nefelihotels.com; Krithonia; studio €90, apt €110-170, incl breakfast; 🅿 ☀ ☎) Vividly coloured in lavender and pink, these sugar white apartments, 10 minutes' walk beyond the northern edge of Agia Marina, are beautifully finished with stone floors, gleaming kitchens, moulded-stone couches and swallow-you-up beds. All have private balconies and there's a tempting cafe in the herb-fragrant courtyard.

Hotel Alinda   HOTEL €€
(☑ 22470 23266; www.alindahotel-leros.gr; Alinda; s/d €45/60; ☀ ☎) The very pleasant rooms in this beachfront hotel have private balconies that look out across the leafy garden and the coast road to the bay. They vary in size, but all are spotless with comfy beds, armoire and desk. The charming owner also runs an excellent on-site Greek restaurant.

Eating

The waterfront in Alinda is lined with stylish cafes and restaurants.

O Lampros TAVERNA €

(☑ 22470 24154; Alinda; mains €8-12; ⊘ breakfast, lunch & dinner) With a clientele that consists in large part of gnarled elderly gents flicking beads, O Lampros is a very traditional taverna offering breakfast, snacks and traditional cuisine such as tzatziki, mezedhes, Greek salads, swordfish and octopus. Treat yourself to shrimp *saganaki*.

Fanari GREEK €

(☑ 6984135216; Alinda; mains €8-10; ✳ ☎) At shabby-chic Fanari you can eat on the patio or by the waves. The menu ranges from breakfast, mezedhes and lamb *stifadho* to pasta dishes. But you can also try combo dishes for two (€20), which give you meatballs, halloumi, tzatziki and green peppers.

Northern Leros

The north of Leros is dotted with small fishing communities, beehives and rugged terrain. Just west of the airport, the **Temple of Artemis** (the island's ancient patroness) dates from the 4th century BC, but has yet to be excavated. East of here, **Blefoutis Beach** is a narrow stretch of sand and pebble on a pretty enclosed bay.

PATMOS ΠΑΤΜΟΣ

POP 3040

Little seems to have changed in Patmos during the 2000 years since St John experienced his awesome Revelation here. His hillside cave is now a monastery, and an even larger monastery now bristles atop the island's highest hill. There are no sizeable towns, though, just the picturesque little harbour community of Skala and the labyrinthine whitewashed village of Hora, and Patmos still abounds in barely disturbed bays lined with sand and pebble beaches, lulled by limpid waters and overlooked by pine-clad and heather-coated hillsides. Even the cruise ships seem to come and go without troubling the essential, timeless mystery of an island that remains palpably steeped in history.

History

St John the Divine was banished to Patmos by the pagan Roman Emperor Domitian in AD 95. Living as a hermit in a cave above what's now Skala, St John heard the voice of God issuing from a cleft in the rock and transcribed his terrifying visions as the Book of Revelation. Around 1000 years later, in 1088, the Byzantine Emperor Alexis I Komninos gave the Blessed Christodoulos permission to erect a monastery in John's memory. Pirate raids necessitated powerful fortifications, so the monastery took the form of a mighty hill-top castle.

In the centuries that followed, Patmos became a semiautonomous monastic state and achieved such wealth and influence that it was able to resist Turkish oppression.

ⓘ Getting There & Away

All Patmos ferries dock in Skala. Dodekanisos Seaways (p473) catamarans connect Patmos with Lipsi, Leros, Kalymnos, Kos, Rhodes and other islands to the south, and also with Arki, Agathonisi, Ikaria, Fourni and Samos to the north.

Blue Star Ferries (p473) calls in twice each week, once heading south through the Dodecanese chain towards Rhodes, and once towards Piraeus.

The **Nisos Kalymnos** (www.anekalymnou.gr) connects Patmos with Kalymnos, Lipsi and Leros to the south, and the islets to the north, three to four times weekly.

The **Patmos Star** (☑ 22470 32500; www.patmos-star.com) sails between Patmos and Lipsi and Leros, daily in peak season and less frequently otherwise.

BOAT SERVICES FROM PATMOS (SKALA)

DESTINATION	TIME	FARE	FREQUENCY
Agathonisi*	55min	€16	1 weekly
Kalymnos	4hr	€12	3-4 weekly
Kalymnos*	1hr 40min	€26	1-2 daily
Kos*	3hr	€29	1-2 daily
Leros	2hr	€11	4-5 weekly
Leros*	40min	€16	1-2 daily
Lipsi	50min	€9	3-4 weekly
Lipsi*	25min	€13	6 weekly
Piraeus	7hr	€36	1 weekly
Rhodes	10hr	€37	1 weekly
Rhodes*	5hr	€46	4 weekly
Samos*	1hr	€30	5 weekly
Symi*	4¼hr	€44	4 weekly

*high-speed services

Patmos

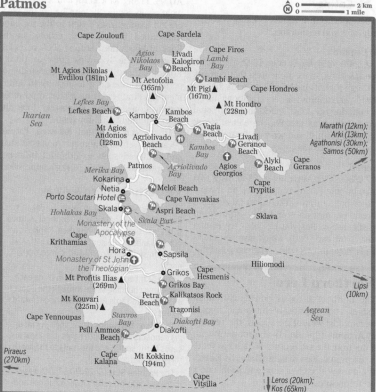

🛈 Getting Around

BOAT

Patmos Daily Cruises (☏ 22470 31425; www.patmosdailycruises.com) offers summer boat excursions to beaches around the island, including Psili Ammos, and also to nearby islets.

BUS

Buses (flat fare €1.50) connect Skala with Hora seven times daily, and with Grikos and Kambos four times daily, and more frequently in July and August.

CAR & MOTORCYCLE

The main seafront street in Skala holds several car- and motorcycle-hire outlets, including **T & G Automoto** (☏ 22470 33066) and **Avis** (☏ 22470 33025). Demand often exceeds supply in high season, so book ahead if possible. The best scooter shop, **Moto Rent Faros** (☏ 22470 34400; www.patmos-motorentfaros.com), is behind the harbour on the road to Hora, and has quick, regularly serviced bikes.

TAXI

You can catch a **taxi** (☏ 22470 31225) from Skala's taxi rank, opposite the police station.

Skala   Σκάλα

Skala, Patmos' photogenic ferry port, is set on a huge bay on the eastern shore of the island. Apart from those moments when mighty cruise ships suddenly obliterate the entire harbour, like a giant Monty Python foot, it's a laid-back little place. There's even a tiny patch of sandy beach – albeit covered with restaurant tables – within steps of the dock.

Skala's waterfront is an unbroken string of tavernas, cafes and fading Italian buildings from the 1930s, while whitewashed houses, along with plenty more shops and cafes, fill the maze of backstreets that stretch away inland. The island is barely 700m wide at this point, so a 10-minute walk will take you all the way to stony, windswept **Hohlakas Beach** on its western side.

Sights & Activities

Skala has a couple of religious sites, including the place where St John first baptised the locals in AD 96, just north of the beach. To find out more and to see religious objects from across the island, visit the Orthodox Culture & Information Centre (p538) in the harbourside church.

If you feel like a workout, climb to the remains of an ancient **acropolis** on the hillside to the west of town. The route is not well signposted – head for the prominent chapel then follow the dirt trail across the fields full of wildflowers and lizards. The views from the top are stunning.

Sleeping

Hotel and studio owners often meet boats at the port, but it's best to call ahead and arrange a pick-up.

★ Porto Scoutari Hotel   HOTEL €€
(☑ 22470 33123; www.portoscoutari.com; d incl breakfast €145-235; P ❄ @ ☎ ☲) Focused around a lavish swimming pool and spa centre, this elegant wedding-dress-white hotel complex surveys the Aegean from a rural spot 3km north of Skala. It has palace-sized rooms with nautical frescoes, sofas, spotless en suites, private balconies and antique beds plus, above all, stunning sea views. Check for amazing low-season rates.

Captain's House   HOTEL €€
(☑ 22470 31793; www.captains-house.gr; d/apt incl breakfast €70/80; ❄ ☎ ☲) Delightful wharfside digs, 100m walk left from the quay, holding high-spec rooms and apartments with en suite bathrooms and crisp white lines. Five have their own sea-facing balconies. There's also a lovely swimming pool out back with sun loungers, along with a great breakfast terrace. Perfect family option.

Delfini Hotel   HOTEL €€
(☑ 22470 32060; www.delfini-patmos.gr; s/d incl breakfast €50/60; ❄ ☎) Waterfront Delfini is a simple, good-value hotel with sea- and Hora-facing rooms with tiled floors, balconies and clean en suites. No extra charge for an additional kid's bed. The decent on-site restaurant spreads onto the tiny beach and serves all meals, including breakfast.

Kalderimi Apartments   BOUTIQUE HOTEL €€
(☑ 6972008757, 22470 33008; www.kalderimi. com; apt incl breakfast €120; ☉ late May-early Oct; ❄ ☎) Peaceful, whitewashed B&B inn, set well back from the sea at the start of the footpath up to Hora, with a shaded courtyard that's overflowing with palms, bougainvillea and Moorish lanterns. The five spacious apartments have a traditional feel, featuring wooden beams and stone walls, plus sparkling kitchens.

Eating

Tzivaeri   SEAFOOD €
(☑ 22470 31170; mains €9; ☉ 5pm-late) Skala's best option for a romantic feast, spreading over a balcony terrace at the north end of the harbour. With its walls covered in shells, sponges and black-and-white photos, and the air thick with bouzouki, it makes a memorable stop for Cretan-style sardines, shrimp or octopus, though you can also get a burger or kebab. Live music on Fridays.

Chiliomodi   TAVERNA €
(☑ 22470 34080; mains €5-9; ☉ lunch & dinner) Traditional *ouzerie* a few metres back from the sea, as the road sets off inland to Hora, with outdoor tables squeezed into a narrow alley. Great-value, no-nonsense island delicacies range from salted cod to succulent sausages, with nothing costing as much as €10.

Pantelis   TAVERNA €
(☑ 22470 31230; mains €6-15; ☉ lunch & dinner) Long-standing taverna, with locals and visitors alike packed onto tables on the narrow pedestrian street that runs parallel to the port. If you're not feeling adventurous enough to try the smoky sea-urchin salad or the *fouskes* 'sea figs' (definitely an acquired taste), you can always get staples such as meatballs and *mousakas* for around €7.

Drinking & Nightlife

★ Koukoumavla   CAFE
(☑ 22470 31321; ☉ 10am-late Tue-Sun; ☎) ✎ Imagine the love child of Tim Burton and Frida Kahlo opening a coffee house and you're getting close – interesting art spattered across green and orange walls, cool tunes, cocktails and excellent coffee. The 'owl' also sells crafts, books and toys and has a little garden terrace as well as tables on the alleyway, just back from the sea.

DODECANESE SKALA

★ Art Café
BAR

(☑ 22470 33092; ⊙ 7pm-late) Escape the harbour hubbub by climbing to a fabulous panoramic roof terrace then blissing out over sunset cocktails (€7 to €9) amid plump pillows and white-cushioned benches. The friendly German owner also serves great homemade hummus and there's often live music in the indoor lounge below.

Arion
BAR

(☑ 22470 31595; ⊙ 9am-late; 🛜) Over 100 years old, this venerable, high-raftered, wood-panelled bar, at the heart of the waterfront, is a major local landmark and rendezvous point for locals. Travellers generally prefer to sit outside, watching the world and the waves go by as they hook up to the wi-fi.

Meltemi
CAFE

(☑ 22470 31839; ⊙ 9am-late; 🛜) Irresistible beach bar at the far end of the harbour that curves 500m north from the ferry dock. Sit on the sand, savouring a cocktail as the sun sinks into the sea, or come earlier for breakfast (full breakfast €6) or a midday sandwich, fruit salad or milkshake under the shade of a tamarisk tree.

🛍 Shopping

Selene
ARTS, CRAFTS

(☑ 22470 31472; ⊙ 9am-1pm & 3-11pm) A real curiosity shop, right on the harbour and packed with everything from contemporary sculptures and puppets, to ceramics, icons and jewellery.

ℹ Information

All Patmos ferries dock in the heart of Skala. Taxis wait at the quay, and the bus terminal is close by, as are three ATM-equipped banks. From the roundabout straight ahead, a road climbs inland towards Hora. Skala itself stretches away to the right, with the road skirting first a narrow beach and then the yacht port as it heads north. There's another little sandy beach to the left as the coast road sets off south.

Both www.patmos-island.com and www.patmosweb.gr provide copious information.

Astoria Travel (☑ 22470 31205; www.astoriatravel.com) The best outlet for ferry tickets, along with all practical aspects of visiting Patmos, including accommodation.

Health centre (☑ 22473 60000) Located 2km along the road to Hora.

Orthodox Culture & Information Centre (☑ 22470 33316; ⊙ 9am-1pm & 6-9pm Mon, Tue, Thu & Fri, 9am-1pm Sat & Sun) There's no general-purpose visitor centre, but this quayside office provides details on the island's religious sites, including current opening hours.

Police (☑ 22470 31303) On the main waterfront.

Port police (☑ 22470 31231) Behind the quay's passenger-transit building.

Hora
Χώρα

Crowned by the battlements of the monastery of St John, hill-top Hora stands very much apart from the rest of Patmos. Yes, its twisting, tangled lanes and alleyways hold more than a few jarring juice bars and designer boutiques and become clogged with visitors at peak periods, but behind their high whitewashed walls, the village houses continue to guard their secrets, and after dark Hora still feels like an mysterious, ancient and holy place.

While Hora is easily reached by road, it's much more atmospheric and memorable to hike up through the woods. Following the Byzantine footpath, signposted off the road roughly 10 minutes up from Skala, takes a total of around 40 minutes. Allow extra time, though, to stop off at the Monastery of the Apocalypse en route.

◉ Sights

Monastery of St John the Theologian
MONASTERY

(☑ 22470 31223; admission €6; ⊙ 8am-1.30pm Sun, Mon, Wed & Fri, 8am-1.30pm & 4-6pm Tue, Thu & Sat) As this immense 11th-century monastery-cum-fortress remains active, only a small portion is open to visitors. The entrance courtyard leads to a sumptuously frescoed chapel, fronted by marble columns taken from an ancient temple. Don't expect to attend a service; daily worship is at 3am! The museum of church treasures upstairs displays the original edict establishing the monastery, signed by the Byzantine emperor in 1088.

Monastery of the Apocalypse
MONASTERY

(☑ 22470 31398; admission €2; ⊙ 8am-1.30pm Sun, Mon, Wed & Fri, 8am-1.30pm & 4-6pm Tue, Thu & Sat) Nestled amid the pines halfway to Hora, the Monastery of the Apocalypse focuses on the cave where St John lived as a hermit and received his Revelation. Pilgrims and less-than-devout cruise passengers alike stream into the chapel built over the recess, to see the rocky pillow where the saint rested his head, the handhold with which he'd haul himself up from his prayers and the stone slab that served as his writing desk.

Holy Monastery of Zoodohos Pigi CONVENT
(22470 31991; ⊘9am-1pm & 5-8pm Mon-Sat, 9am-1pm Sun) FREE The Orthodox convent known as the Holy Monastery of Zoodohos Pigi is tucked away in the back alleys of Hora. You can't go beyond its pretty little courtyard, where a small church holds remarkable 17th-century frescoes. One of the 40 resident nuns will cheerfully point out Jesus on Judgement Day dispatching assorted bishops and clerics down a river of fire that flows into the maw of the beast.

🛏 Sleeping & Eating

★ Archontariki B&B €€€
(22470 29368; www.archontariki-patmos.gr; ste incl breakfast €200; ⊘Easter-Oct; 🕸🐾) One of the loveliest B&Bs in the entire Dodecanese, hidden in a little alley near the Zoodohos Pigi monastery. There are four gorgeous suites in a 400-year-old village home, equipped with every convenience, traditional furnishings and plenty of plush touches. Relaxing under the fruit trees in the cool, quiet garden courtyard, you'll never want to leave.

Jimmy's Balcony GREEK €
(22470 32115; mains €6-12; ⊘10am-11pm; 🐾📵) Perched above the road, on the principal lane through the village to the monastery, the shaded terrace of this welcoming all-day cafe/restaurant commands regal views across Skala to the islands to the north. Drop in for a cooling drink, or to enjoy its delicious salads, breakfast, *mousakas* and vegie dishes.

Vaggelis TAVERNA €€
(22470 31967; mains €10-15; ⊘lunch & dinner) A long-standing taverna in Hora's central square, given a contemporary twist by new owners in 2015. Now the octopus comes with 'foamy cream' and there's a seafood *mousaka* too, but it still serves impeccably prepared traditional dishes such as baked Patmos goat. Sit in the square itself, or under the carob tree out back, for jaw-dropping views.

Loza GREEK €€
(22470 32405; mains €10-20; ⊘breakfast, lunch & dinner) With its sumptuous tiled terrace gazing far across the Aegean, this upscale taverna at the village entrance is the obvious spot to relax before or after visiting Hora. The menu ranges from tasty traditional mezedhes to anything-goes fusion concoctions such as *mousaka* crepes, and good but pricey grilled steaks.

🛍 Shopping

Patmos Gallery ARTS
(6988024890; ⊘no fixed hours) Byzantine icon artist Andreas Kalatzis lives and works in a 1740s traditional home just east of the St John monastery. As and when the urge takes him, he opens it as a gallery, selling an eclectic mix of abstract and figurative paintings, jewellery and illuminated sculptures, created by himself and other local artists.

North of Skala

The most popular and readily accessible beach in northern Patmos is wide, sandy **Kambos Beach**, which lies 5km northeast of Skala, just downhill from the village of

---

ST JOHN THE DIVINE & THE APOCALYPSE

A great deal of confusion and uncertainty surrounds the Book of Revelation. But don't worry – it's not the end of the world. Well, maybe some of it is – the bits about the Four Horsemen of the Apocalypse, the Battle of Armageddon and the final defeat of Satan, say – but biblical scholars broadly agree that Revelation should in fact be read as a denunciation of the era in which its author lived.

St John experienced his Revelation on Patmos at the end of the 1st century AD, making it too late for him to have been either John the Evangelist, the author of the Gospel according to St John, or John the Apostle, or John the Baptist. Instead he was simply a wandering Jewish/Christian prophet of whom very little is known, though in afterlife he acquired the titles of John the Divine, John the Revelator, John the Theologian and, most simply of all, John of Patmos. His actual Revelation took the form of a letter to seven Christian churches in Asia Minor, condemning the Roman subjugation under which they then suffered and predicting an imminent apocalypse in which the Roman Empire would be swept away.

Kambos. Crowded with local families in summer, it's a perfect spot for kids, with safe swimming and plenty of activities.

Remoter and, with luck, quieter beaches can be reached by driving a little further. Fork inland, left, immediately after Kambos Beach and you'll soon find yourself winding down green slopes to **Lambi Beach**, an impressive expanse of multicoloured pebbles on the north shore. Stick to the coast road east of Kambos Beach, on the other hand, to come to **Vagia Beach**, a sheltered little cove that offers good snorkelling, and beyond it the turquoise-watered, tamarisk-shaded **Livadi Geranou Beach**, where a tiny white-washed chapel beckons from the islet just offshore.

🏃 Activities

Kambos Beach Watersports
WATER SPORTS

(📱 6972123541; www.patmoswatersports.com; Kambos Beach) Based on Kambos Beach itself, this outfit can take you wakeboarding and waterskiing, set you loose you on a pedalo or, for the less athletically inclined, simply rent you a sunbed and leave you in peace.

🍴 Eating

George's Place
CAFE €

(📱 22470 31881; Kambos Beach; snacks €5-8; ⊗ breakfast, lunch & dinner; 🅿 ❄ 🛜 👪) 🧡 Super-chilled beach bar, accessed straight off the sand, with an enticingly shaded, sun-dappled terrace facing the peacock-blue bay. Easy tunes, wi-fi, toilets that can double as changing rooms, and a simple menu of salads, homemade pies, chocolate cake, milkshakes and pastries keep the customers happy.

Lambi Fish Tavern
TAVERNA €

(📱 22470 31490; Lambi Beach; mains €8-15; ⊗ 10am-late; 🅿 ❄ 👪) Idyllic beach taverna with tree-shaded tables propped up amid the pebbles and the soothing sound of the waves nearby. The no-frills local menu includes salted mackerel, stuffed vine leaves, souvlakia and octopus cooked in wine.

Livadi Geranou Taverna
TAVERNA €

(📱 22470 32046; Livadi Geranou Beach; mains €9-12; ⊗ 10am-late) With its flower-bedecked terrace perched on the heather-clad hillside at road's end, a few metres above the beach, this hugely popular taverna benefits from heavenly sea views. Feast on a seafood spread of whitebait and octopus, or opt for a simple platter of meatballs or souvlakia.

South of Skala

The southern half of Patmos is scattered with small, tree-filled valleys and picturesque beaches. The first settlement south of Skala is tiny, peaceful **Sapsila**. **Grikos**, 1km further along over the hill, has a long, sandy beach that holds a handful of tavernas and is dominated by a plush resort hotel. St John is believed to have baptised islanders here during the 1st century AD, at a spot now marked by the chapel of **Agios Ioannis Theologos**.

South again, **Petra Beach** is peaceful and has plenty of shade, while a spit leads out to the startling **Kalikatsos Rock**. Both a rough coastal track from the beach and a longer paved road from Hora continue as far as **Diakofti**, the island's southernmost community. From there, a demanding half-hour hiking trail scrambles over the rocky hillside to reach the fine, tree-shaded stretch of sand known as **Psili Ammos Beach**, which holds a seasonal taverna.

🍴 Eating

Benetos
GREEK €€

(📱 22470 33089; www.benetosrestaurant.com; Sapsila; mains €10-27; ⊗ 7.30pm-late Tue-Sun Jun-Sep; 🅿) 🧡 Dropping down to the sea from the coast road, a couple of kilometers south of Skala, this boutique, dinner-only restaurant centres on a working farm. The menu draws its inspiration from all over the Mediterranean, adding fusion (at times Asian) twists to dishes such as seared, herb-crusted tuna and zucchini blossoms stuffed with mushrooms and cheese.

LIPSI
ΛΕΙΨΟΙ

POP 700

Lipsi might be small, at just 8km in length, but what a powerful impact it has on the traveller, with its low-slung harbour bunched with crayon yellow nets and the whitewashed, church-crowned village of Lipsi climbing the hill behind. If rugged hills, serene blue coves and deserted beaches are what you seek, you may have just found heaven. In the *Odyssey*, Lipsi was where the nymph Calypso waylaid Odysseus for several years. Abandon yourself to sun worshipping and wandering the backstreets, and you may fare the same.

Check too the local speciality, *mzithra* cheese, made from goat's milk and seawater, and pick up a jar of distinctive thyme honey.

❶ Getting There & Away

Lipsi has frequent connections with its neighbours. **Dodecanese Seaways** (www.12ne.gr) catamarans head north to Arki, Agathonisi and Samos, and south to Patmos, Leros, Kos and other islands. The **Nisos Kalymnos** (www.anekalymnou.gr) runs to Patmos, Leros and the islets to the north three to four times weekly, while the **Patmos Star** (www.patmos-star.gr) sails to both Patmos and Leros, daily in summer. The Lipsi-based **Anna Express** (www.annaexpress.eu) sails three times weekly to Leros and Myrties on western Kalymnos.

A small **office** (☑22470 41290; ⊙30min prior to departures) on the ferry jetty sells all boat tickets.

BOAT SERVICES FROM LIPSI

DESTINATION	TIME	FARE	FREQUENCY
Agathonisi	3hr	€7	4 weekly
Agathonisi*	1½hr	€12.50	1 weekly
Kalymnos	3hr	€9	4 weekly
Kalymnos*	1½hr	€20	1 daily
Kos*	4½hr	€29	1 daily
Leros	50min	€6.50	1 daily
Leros*	20min	€13	6 weekly
Patmos	1hr	€9	1 daily
Patmos*	25min	€13	6 weekly
Piraeus	10hr	€38	1 weekly
Rhodes*	5½hr	€45	1 daily
Samos*	1½hr	€32	2 weekly

*high-speed services

❶ Getting Around

Frequent buses connect Lipsi Village with the main island beaches in summer (€1.50). There are also two **taxis** (☑6942409679, 6942409677). Hire scooters and bicycles in Lipsi Village from **Maria and Marcos** (☑22479 41358), next to Poseidon Apartments.

Lipsi Village   Λειψοί

POP 600

Hugging the deep harbour, Lipsi Village – the island's only settlement – is a cosy, intimate affair, with an atmospheric old town of blue-shuttered houses radiating up the hill in a tangle of alleyways. The harbour is the

hub of the action, and there's everything you need here, from an ATM and a great bakery, to delectable seafood restaurants.

◎ Sights & Activities

Be sure to visit the beautiful blue-domed church of **Panagia tou Harou**, with its panoramic harbour-view terrace.

The closest beach to the village, **Liendou Beach**, is a couple of minutes' walk north of the ferry port over a small headland. It's a narrow strip of sand, washed by calm, shallow water.

Two boats, *Rena* (€20) and *Margarita* (€15), offer summer excursions from Lipsi's smaller jetty, heading to islets such as exquisite Aspronisia and Makronisi (with their sapphire waters and weird rock formations) for a picnic and swim.

✯ Festivals & Events

Panagia tou Harou   RELIGIOUS
On 22 August each year, visitors flock to pay homage to a famous icon of the Virgin in the village church and see the lilies inside its glass cabinet, which, despite being rootless and unwatered, burst miraculously into bloom. A procession is followed by all-night revelry in the lower square.

Wine Festival   FOOD
(⊙Aug) This Dionysian festival takes place for three days with dancing and free wine. Check locally for precise dates.

🛏 Sleeping

★**Nefeli Hotel**   APARTMENT €€
(☑22470 41120; www.lipsinefelihotel.com; r €100, apt €150-180, incl breakfast; ⓟ❄🤖) Stylish, welcoming boutique hotel in splendid isolation above lovely Kambos Beach, 10 minutes' walk north of the village. The apartments are spacious, with comfy beds, kitchenettes, sofa beds and private sea-view patios. Prepare to be lulled to sleep by the call of owls. There's also an opulent bar, lounge and dining area, bedecked in lavender and purples.

★**Rizos Studios**   APARTMENT €€
(☑6976244125; www.lipsi-annaexpress.com; d €70; ❄🤖) Superior rooms with interior flair – think lavender blue fittings, private balconies with harbour views, stone-flag floors and kitchenettes stocked with cooking utensils. It's 10 minutes' walk up from the dock; call ahead to be picked up.

Lipsi

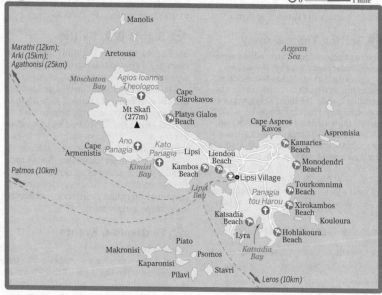

Aphroditi Hotel HOTEL €€

(☎22470 41000; www.hotel-aphroditi.com; s/d/apt incl breakfast €60/70/110; ✱) Spearmint-fresh Aphroditi, facing Liendou Beach and fronted by its own blue-and-white windmill, holds 28 studios (sleeping up to three) and apartments (sleeping four) with tiled floors, kitchenettes, balconies and a jazzy contemporary feel. A swish cafe serves breakfast then snacks until early evening.

Poseidon Studios APARTMENT €€

(☎6975368647, 22470 41130; www.lipsiposeidon.com; d €65; ✱) On the low ridge to your left as you walk from the ferry towards the village, these simple rooms are spacious and cool with tiled floors, private sea-view balconies and kitchenettes. Family-sized apartments have additional sofa beds, washing machines and a larger kitchen.

✗ Eating

★**Theologos Fish Tavern** SEAFOOD €

(☎6978647354; mains €7-10; ⊙lunch & dinner) Set on the waterfront near the ferry dock, with some of its blue-and-white tables right on the quay, this friendly, no-nonsense place delivers exactly what it promises: ultra-fresh, beautifully prepared fish, ranging from huge prawns to 'tope fish' – that's a

kind of shark – souvlakia. With chips. What more could you want?

Yiannis TAVERNA €

(☎22470 41395; mains €7-12; ⊙lunch & dinner May-Oct) Deservedly popular taverna, close to the ferry jetty, with seating on a raised harbour-view terrace and its own impossibly jaunty little boat moored below. The most dependable all-rounder in the village, it's equally recommended for its stewed goat in red sauce as for its salads and thin-sliced swordfish carpaccio.

Manolis Tastes TAVERNA €

(☎22470 41065; www.manolistastes.com; mains €8-10; ⊙noon-4pm & 5.30pm-late; ☜) ✐ Chef Manolis only cooks with food whose origin he can trace. Tucked into a twisting alleyway up near the church, this village favourite keeps regulars happy with creations such as goat cheese with muesli and honey, chef's sausage, mushrooms stuffed with bacon, chicken in lemon sauce with rosemary and olives, and very moreish *pannacotta*.

Cafe du Moulin CAFE €

(☎22470 41316; mains €4-8; ⊙8am-late) This colourful cafe/taverna, in the peaceful, whitewashed square behind the village church, is handy for breakfast as well as traditional Greek dishes such as lamb souvlakia, calamari and shrimp.

Bakery Shop BAKERY €
(☎ 22470 41050; sweets €1-3; ❄ 🛜 ♿) 🖉 This lively bakery-cum-gelateria-cum-cafe, at sea level beside the steps up to the village centre, is the social hub of the island – it even stays open all night. It's a veritable treasure trove of fresh-baked cookies, croissants, sausage rolls, pies, sandwiches, baklava, alcohol and some very fancy cakes, presided over by its charming and gregarious owner.

ℹ️ Information

The main ferry jetty is at the northern, left-hand end of the port; there's an Alpha Bank with ATM nearby. Following the quay towards the village centre, up on the hill ahead, you'll pass the smaller excursion-boat jetty, while the *Anna Express* docks immediately below the church. The post office is up in the old town.

Lipsi Bookings (☎ 22470 41130; www.lipsi-bookings.com) Very helpful agency alongside Poseidon Studios by the port, selling tickets for all ferries and organising activities including camping, hiking, horse riding, sailing, snorkelling and visits to a winery and ecofarm.
Police (☎ 22470 41222) At the port.
Port police (☎ 22470 41133) At the port.

Around Lipsi

Lipsi is remarkably green for a Greek island. Walking to its further-flung beaches leads you through countryside dotted with olive groves, cypress trees and endless views. A minibus also services the main beaches.

Just 1km north of Lipsi Village, around the headland beyond Liendou, **Kambos Beach** is narrower but sandier than its neighbour and somewhat shaded by tamarisk trees. The water is also deeper and rockier underfoot.

Fork inland at Kambos and a delightful 2.5km hike over the low-lying spine of the island will lead you to the shallow and child-friendly **Platys Gialos Beach**. Ringing with goat bells and shelving gently into crystal-clear water, it's home to an excellent summer-only taverna, which closes at 6pm.

Just 2km south of Lipsi Village, sandy **Katsadia Beach** is wilder, especially if it's windy. There's a certain amount of shade and another good summer-only taverna, which stays open late as a bar.

The beaches at Lipsi's eastern end are harder to reach, with the roads being too rough for taxis or buses.

ARKI & MARATHI
ΑΡΚΟΙ & ΜΑΡΑΘΙ

Arki and Marathi, just north of Patmos and Lipsi, are the most peaceful islets in the Dodecanese chain. The former is home to only 50 inhabitants, who make a living from farming, goat breeding and fishing. The turquoise-ometer of the water? Off the scale! Expect an eclectic mix of yachties, artists and the occasional backpacker. There are neither cars nor motorbikes – just calmness. Pack your books, bathers and headphones and leave chaos behind.

ℹ️ Getting There & Away

Three ferry companies stop off at Arki, but not Marathi, as they sail up and down the island chain. All call at Patmos, Leros, Lipsi and Agathonisi. Weekly Dodekanisos Seaways (p473) catamarans run south as far as Kos and north to Samos. **Anna Express** (www.annaexpress. eu) also goes to Samos (two weekly), and **Nisos Kalymnos** (www.anekalymnou.gr) starts from Kalymnos (three to four weekly).

In summer, Lipsi-based excursion boats and Patmos-based caïques offer frequent day trips (€20) to Arki and Marathi. A local caïque runs between Marathi and Arki.

BOAT SERVICES FROM ARKI & MARATHI

DESTI-NATION	PORT	TIME	FARE	FREQUENCY
Arki	Marathi	1¼hr	€7	1 daily
Kos	Arki	3hr	€31	1 weekly
Lipsi	Arki	45min	€13.50	6-7 weekly
Patmos	Arki	1hr	€14	6-7 weekly
Samos	Arki	1hr	€20	6-7 weekly

Arki Αρκοί
POP 50

Only 5km north of Lipsi, tiny Arki has rolling hills and secluded, sandy beaches. Away from its only settlement – a little west-coast port also called Arki – the peace and stillness verges on the mystical.

There is no post office or police. The **Church of Metamorfosis** stands on a hill behind the settlement, while several sandy coves can be reached along a path skirting the north side of the bay.

Tiganakia Bay, on the southeast coast, has a good sandy beach. To walk there from Arki village, follow the road heading south and then the various goat tracks down to the water. Keep an eye out for dolphins.

🛏 Sleeping & Eating

Arki holds a handful of tavernas with comfortable, well-maintained rooms. Bookings are essential in July and August.

O Trypas Taverna & Rooms   PENSION €
(☑ 22470 32230; www.arki-island.com; d €40; 🖥) Just to the right of the quay, at the island's main 'road junction' (!), this popular taverna offers five attractive, simply furnished rooms with outdoor space and serves excellent local specialities (mains €6 to €9) such as *fasolia mavromatika* (black-eyed beans) and *pastos tou Trypa* (salted fish). It also puts on live local music.

Taverna Nikolaos   PENSION €
(☑ 22470 32477; d €45; ❄) Simple central taverna where the spacious, white-walled, twin-bedded rooms have sunset views. As well as whatever seafood the boats have brought in, the kitchen (mains €8 to €10) dishes up potatoes au gratin, stuffed peppers with cheese, and the local goat cheese called *sfina*, resembling a mild form of feta.

Marathi   Μαράθι

Marathi, the largest of Arki's satellite islets, has a superb sandy beach. The old settlement, with an immaculate little church, stands on a hill above the harbour. While just three people remain on Marathi year-round, local families return each summer to reopen its seasonal tavernas.

🛏 Sleeping & Eating

Pantelis Taverna   PENSION €
(☑ 22470 32609; www.marathi-island.gr; d €50; ❄🖥) The closest Marathi comes to having a fully fledged beach resort, at the northern end of the sands. As well as spacious and attractively furnished rooms in a white-painted studio block, it also rents a larger maisonette. The taverna itself serves a fine menu of home cooking (mains €8 to €12), from octopus croquettes to goat stew.

AGATHONISI   ΑΓΑΘΟΝΗΣΙ

POP 160

Arriving in Agathonisi's harbour – enclosed by a fjord-like formation and holding so few buildings you could count them in a breath – is pure magic. So far off the tourist radar its neighbours barely acknowledge it, Agathonisi is quiet enough to hear a distant Cyclops break wind. There's little to do here but read, swim and explore the caves where islanders once hid from pirates...and then do it again.

Keep an eye out too for the *klidonas* ritual of jumping through fire to cleanse your spirit.

ℹ Information

From Agios Georgios, where the boats dock, roads ascend right to Megalo Horio and left to Mikro Horio. There is no tourist office, but you'll find an ATM at the post office in Megalo Horio.

ℹ Getting There & Away

Three ferry companies connect Agathonisi with Patmos, Lipsi and points south. Both Dodekanisos Seaways (p473) catamarans (weekly) and **Anna Express** (www.annaexpress.eu, two weekly) continue north to Samos; **Nisos Kalymnos** (www.anekalymnou.gr) only goes as far north as Pythagoreios (three to four weekly).

BOAT SERVICES FROM AGATHONISI

DESTINATION	TIME	FARE	FREQUENCY
Arki	45min	€8	6-7 weekly
Kalymnos*	2hr	€26	1 weekly
Kos*	3¼hr	€29	1 weekly
Lipsi	1hr	€7	6-7 weekly
Patmos	2hr	€8	6-7 weekly
Samos	1hr	€7.50	6-7 weekly

*high-speed services

Agios Georgios   Αγιος Γεώργιος

The port village of Agios Georgios (*agh*-ios ye-*or*yi-os), the island's primary settlement, holds a few tavernas and simple sugar-cube pensions. The high point of a day is sitting on the harbour beach pondering the turquoise and watching the fishers roll in with their catches. **Spilia Beach**, 900m southwest beyond the headland, along a track around the far side of the bay, is quieter and better for swimming. A further 1km walk will bring you to **Gaïdouravlakos**, a small bay and beach where water from one of the island's few springs meets the sea.

🛏 Sleeping & Eating

Mary's Rooms   PENSION €
(📞 6979201537, 22470 29003; www.maryroomsagathonisi.com; s/d €35/45) Very simple but house-proud rooms in the middle of the waterfront, offering kitchenettes, fridges and tiny balconies with sea views. There's also a flower-filled courtyard.

Glaros Restaurant   TAVERNA €
(📞 22470 29062; mains €9-12; ⊘ lunch & dinner; 📶📶) Of the few harbourside tavernas, the bougainvillea-draped terrace of the 'Seagull' is probably the best place to dine. Owners Voula and Giannis are very engaging and serve *markakia* (feta cheese fingers in vine leaves with a special sauce), along with standard oven-cooked meals, grills and fish dishes, all made from predominantly organic produce.

Megalo Horio

The tiny hamlet of Megalo Horio is a steep and sweaty 1.5km trek uphill from the harbour, but the effort is rewarded by the stupendous views from the cliff. The village barely stirs until June, and the ideal times to come are for the festivals of **Agiou Panteleimonos** (26 July), **Sotiros** (6 August) and **Panagias** (22 August), when Megalo Horio celebrates with abundant food, music and dancing.

A series of accessible beaches lie within easy walking distance to the east: **Tsangari Beach**, **Tholos Beach**, **Poros Beach** – the only sandy option – and **Tholos (Agios Nikolaos) Beach**, close to the eponymous church.

🛏 Sleeping & Eating

Studios Ageliki   APARTMENT €
(📞 22470 29085; s/d €35/45; ❄) If you prefer an even quieter stay than at the port, these four basic but quite comfortable studios will serve you very well. All have stunning views over a small vineyard and down to the port, and come equipped with kitchenette, fridge and bathroom.

Restaurant I Irini   GREEK €
(📞 22470 29054; mains €7; ⊘ lunch & dinner) Welcoming taverna on Megalo Horio's central square, renowned for its rich lamb stew and meaty *stifadho*.

Northeastern Aegean Islands

Best Places to Eat

➡ Hotzas Taverna (p571)

➡ Thea's Restaurant & Rooms (p555)

➡ Taverna Angelos (p585)

➡ Taverna Artemis (p561)

➡ Mandouvala (p556)

➡ Soulatso (p588)

Best Places to Stay

➡ Rooms Dionysos (p553)

➡ Archipelagos Hotel (p557)

➡ Kouitou Hotel (p588)

➡ Ino Village Hotel & Restaurant (p561)

➡ Aldebran Pension (p603)

➡ Alkaios Rooms (p581)

Why Go?

The northeastern Aegean Islands (τα νησιά του Βορειοανατολικού Αιγαίου) are notable (like the Dodecanese) for their proximity to the Turkish mainland. Influences from Asia Minor abound in old-fashioned island cuisines, traditional village culture, dramatic celebrations and even the language.

Eccentric Ikaria is marked by jagged landscapes, pristine beaches and a famously long-lived, left-leaning population. Nearby Chios provides fertile ground for the planet's only gum-producing mastic trees. Other islands range from rambling Lesvos, producer of half the world's ouzo, to midsize islands such as semitropical Samos and workaday Limnos, and bright specks in the sea such as Inousses and Psara. Samothraki is home to the ancient Sanctuary of the Great Gods, while well-watered Thasos seems an extension of the mainland. Lesvos, Chios and Samos offer easy connections to Turkey's coastal resorts and historically Hellenic sites.

When to Go
Vathy (Samos)

Apr & May Wild red poppies adorn the back roads and Greek Easter livens up every village.

Jul & Aug Succulent apricots are in season, perfect for a picnic at the beach.

Oct & Nov Summer crowds evaporate, and hearty soups return to the tavernas.

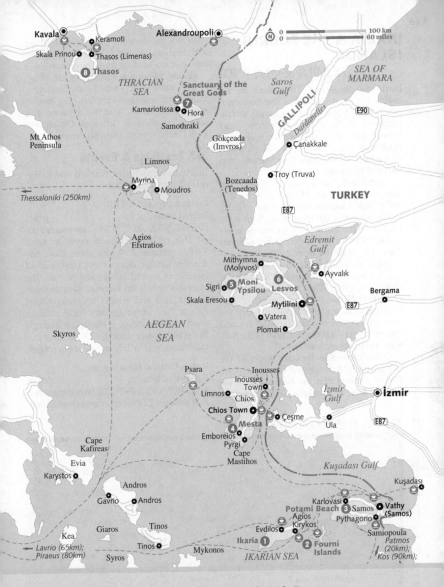

Northeastern Aegean Islands Highlights

❶ Challenging your brain cells at **Ikaria's** annual international chess tournament (p548).

❷ Enjoying sunset and the Aegean's best lobster on the **Fourni Islands** (p556).

❸ Wading through the river to wooded waterfalls near **Potami Beach** (p567).

❹ Wandering the winding medieval alleyways of **Mesta** (p574) on Chios.

❺ Savouring hill-top views and medieval manuscripts at **Moni Ypsilou** (p587).

❻ Getting up close to 20-million-year-old trees at the petrified forest (p587) in **Lesvos**.

❼ Contemplating the mysteries of the 10th-century-BC **Sanctuary of the Great Gods** (p598) on Samothraki.

❽ Cycling through lush old-growth forests at **Thasos'** annual international mountain-biking race (p603).

IKARIA & THE FOURNI ISLANDS

ΙΚΑΡΙΑ & ΦΟΥΡΝΟΙ

Ikaria and the Fourni archipelago are arguably the most magical of the northeastern Aegean Islands. Ikaria's varied terrain comprises dramatic forested gorges, rocky moonscapes and hidden beaches with aquamarine waters, while the bare, sloping hills of Fourni's islets graze the horizon, surrounded by a lobster-rich sea.

Fourni, a former refuge for pirates and bandits, was a source of frustration for Byzantine and Ottoman rulers. More recently, Ikaria became a dumping ground for communist sympathisers during Greece's 1946–49 Civil War and again during the infamous 'time of the colonels' from 1967 to 1974.

Ikaria is named for Icarus, son of Daedalus, the legendary architect of King Minos' Cretan labyrinth. When the two tried to escape from Minos' prison on wings of wax, Icarus ignored his father's warning, flew too close to the sun, crashed into the sea and created Ikaria – a rocky reminder of the dangers of overweening ambition.

Greek myth also honours Ikaria as the birthplace of Dionysos, god of wine. Indeed, Homer attested that the Ikarians were the world's first winemakers. Today travellers can enjoy the signature local red here, along with fresh and authentic local dishes in a serene environment far from the crowds.

Hiking, swimming and cycling are all excellent, while Ikaria's light-hearted summertime *panigyria* (religious festivals) involve much food, drink, traditional dance and song – combining Orthodox Christianity with Ikaria's deeper Dionysian roots.

🎎 Festivals & Events

In late July and August, Ikaria is host to several islandwide festivals.

Ikaria International Chess Tournament

SPORTS

(☑6947829772, 6977730286; www.ikaroschess. gr) This traditional annual event in Agios Kyrikos, organised by local chess aficionado Kosmas Kefalos, draws chess players of all types from around Europe and beyond. The tournament will celebrate its 40th anniversary in 2017 and retains a distinctly local flavour (one event features local children enacting chess moves at the square during a live grand-master match). This battle of wits takes place in mid-July, lasting about a week.

Icarus Festival for Dialogue Between Cultures

CULTURAL

(☑22940 76745, 6979783201; www.icarusfestival. com; per event €10; ☉ performances from 9.30pm)

Ikaria & the Fourni Islands

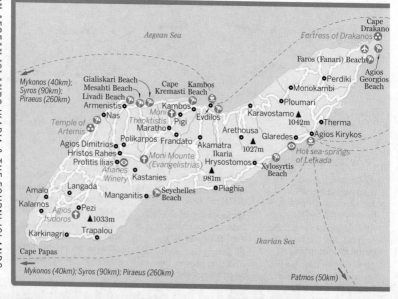

This summer-long (June to August), island-wide series of concerts, new cinema, dramatic works and music workshops pulls in prominent Greek and international artists. Events are scattered around the island, with shuttle buses for festivalgoers.

Frikaria Music Festival   MUSIC
The hip Frikaria Music Festival attracts music freaks and free spirits alike to various locations. The three-day event, held in late July or early August, features Greek rock bands and DJ sets. Programs are available from cafes in Evdilos (try Rififi, p552) and Agios Kyrikos.

Dionysos Theatre Festival   THEATRE
(📞 22750 71390/1; www.aegean-exodus.gr; events €10; ⊗ Aug) This islandwide festival stages classical Greek plays, complete with masks and traditional costumes, in open-air theatres at Akamatra, Karavostamo and other villages. Contact George Paroikos at Hotel Daidalos (p554) in Armenistis.

ℹ Getting There & Away

AIR
Ikaria is served by **Olympic Air** (📞 22750 22214; www.olympicair.com), Aegean Air and Astra Air. Tickets available at agencies in Agios Kirykos and Evdilos, and at the airport.

Domestic Flights from Ikaria

DESTINATION	TIME	FARE	FREQUENCY
Athens	35min	€73	1-2 daily
Limnos	45min	€44	2 weekly
Thessaloniki	1½hr	€74	6 weekly

BOAT
Get tickets in Agios Kirykos (where most departures are from) at Ikariada Travel (p551) or Dolihi Tours Travel Agency (p551). In Evdilos, try **Amfitriti Travel** (📞 6940430526, 22750 32757; www.amfitrititravel.gr; Evdilos), or the Hellenic Seaways agent, **Roustas Travel** (📞 22750 23441, 22750 32931), both on the waterfront. In addition to regular ferries, there are also weekly day-trip excursion boats between Agios Kirykos and Patmos (€32, 55 minutes, one to two per week), 20km south.

Boat Services from Ikaria

DESTINATION	TIME	FARE	FREQUENCY
Chios	5½hr	€17	1 weekly
Fourni	1hr	€6.50	3 weekly
Fourni*	20min	€14	2-3 weekly
Kalymnos	2hr 50min	€32	1 weekly
Kavala	18hr	€45	1 weekly
Lesvos (Mytilini town)	9½hr	€22	1 weekly
Limnos	14hr	€32	1 weekly
Mykonos	3hr	€19	4-5 weekly
Naxos	2hr	€19	1 daily
Patmos	1½hr	€12	3 weekly
Patmos*	1hr	€22	1 weekly
Piraeus	9½hr	€29	3 weekly
Piraeus**	8½hr	€29	3 weekly
Samos (Karlovasi)**	1½hr	€10	4 weekly
Samos (Pythagorio)*	50min	€25	2 weekly
Samos (Vathy)	3hr	€11.50	4 weekly

* hydrofoil service
** from Evdilos port

ℹ Getting Around

BOAT
In summer a daily caïque (water taxi) goes from Agios Kirykos to Therma (€3). Another boat on Ikaria's south coast links Manganitis with the idyllic Seychelles Beach, 2.5km away, for swimming and sunbathing. Weekly day-trip excursion boats to Fourni depart from Agios Kirykos (€25).

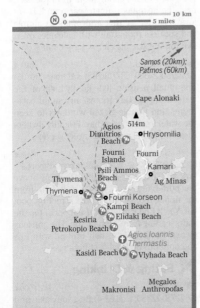

BUS & TAXI

A daily bus makes the winding route from Agios Kirykos to Hrisos Rahes (€9), via Evdilos (€6) and Armenistis (€9). A local bus makes the 10-minute trip to Therma every half-hour (€1). A taxi between Agios Kirykos and Evdilos costs around €55.

CAR & MOTORCYCLE

It's a good idea to hire a car or scooter for travel beyond the main towns (though hitchhiking is very common and considered safe by locals). For cars, try Dolihi Tours Travel Agency or Ikariada Travel in Agios Kirykos, **Mav Cars** (☑ 6932908944, 22750 31036; mav-cars@hol. gr) in Evdilos, and **Aventura** (☑ 6972284054, 22750 31140; aventura@otenet.gr) in Evdilos and Armenistis. Most car-hire offices can arrange for airport pick-up or drop-off, too. You can also rent good motorbikes from **Pamfilis Bikes** (☑ 6979757539; Agios Kirykos), up the steps from Alpha Bank in Agios Kirykos.

Agios Kirykos
Άγιος Κήρυκος
POP 1880

Ikaria's capital is an easygoing and dependable Greek port, with clustered old streets, tasty restaurants, hotels and domatia, along with a lively waterfront cafe scene. Xylosyrtis Beach (4km southwest) is the best of several nearby pebble beaches, and the renowned radioactive hot springs attract aching bodies from around Europe.

◉ Sights & Activities

Archaeological Museum   MUSEUM
(☉8am-3pm Tue-Sun) FREE Refurbished and handsome museum highlighting Neolithic to Byzantine periods, including a mother-and-child marble figure and urns recovered from shipwrecks. Set back 100m from the port.

Asklipios Bathhouse   HEALTH & FITNESS
(☑22750 50400; admission €5; ☉8am-1pm & 5-8pm Jun-Oct) There are a few radioactive

ⓘ BUSSING IT

Taking a bus on Ikaria is to be part of a travelling village. Passengers call the driver by first name and chat as friends and neighbours get on and off. If you're travelling between Agios Kirykos and Evdilos, you'll get a friendly introduction to the island. If you need a car in Evdilos, or even Amenistis, you can generally return it to the airport at no extra charge.

saltwater springs in and around Agios Kirykos. They're famed for their beneficial effects on health issues such as arthritis and rheumatism and you can sample their salutary effects in town at this simple bathhouse, named for the mythical Greek god of healing.

Hot water is piped in from a spring in the sea, and an average bath takes about 30 minutes, by which time you should be able to melt back into the landscape. In terms of safety, the waters, which contain minute levels of radiation, are carefully monitored and supervised by health authorities.

Other radioactive springs are at Therma, and the outdoor sea spring at Lefkada.

🛏 Sleeping

★**Hotel Akti**   HOTEL €
(☑22750 23905; www.pensionakti.gr; s/d from €35/50; ❄☀☎) A fine budget choice in a prime spot, Akti has cosy and attractive modern rooms with fridge, TV, overhead fans and mosquito netting, plus friendly, English-speaking owners. A modern and locally popular cafe-bar overlooks the sea and port below. Follow the steps just right of Alpha Bank.

Hotel Maria-Elena   HOTEL €
(☑22750 22835; www.mariaelena.gr; s/d €35/50; ❄@☎) Charming, welcoming and quiet, the Maria-Elena, about 500m from the port, near the hospital, is open year-round. It enjoys a garden setting and offers 21 simple and spotless rooms, all with balconies overlooking the sea, plus a few larger suites.

Isabella Hotel   HOTEL €
(☑22750 22839, 6977196515; s/d from €30/35) This small, pension-style family hotel on the waterfront has tidy rooms, airy sunlit bathrooms and double-glazed windows to keep the waterfront buzz at bay. Friendly owners Alex and Isabella provide sweet service.

Hotel Kastro   HOTEL €
(☑22750 23480; www.ikariakastro.com; d from €40; ❄☎❄) This well-appointed lodging above the port offers great views, especially from the upper rooms, along with a rooftop pool bar. You'll find it 30m to the left once atop the stairs leading from Alpha Bank. The gracious owner, Dimitris, is usually around with tips and opinions on local destinations.

✕ Eating & Drinking

★**Tzivaeri**   FAST FOOD €
(☑22750 22850; food €2-4) Best souvlakia and *gyros* (meat slithers cooked on a vertical

rotisserie; usually eaten with pitta bread) at the port. Look for the umbrellas, next to Taverna Klimataria.

Taverna Klimataria   TAVERNA €
(mains €6-10) An inviting backstreet taverna, behind the national bank, with a lovely shaded courtyard. It's strong on grilled meats and *pastitsio* (layers of buttery macaroni and seasoned minced lamb), with generous salads.

Restaurant Tsouris   TAVERNA €
(mains €7-10) On the waterfront facing the square, this busy and traditional eatery serves tasty grills and several very good *mayirefta* (ready-cooked meals) and fresh fish (fairly priced by the kilo). Open year-round.

Kazino Cafe   CAFE
(✆22750 23290; ⊙8am-midnight) One of several decent waterfront cafes, Kazino occupies an 1850-era building and serves coffee and fresh juices, made-to-order chocolate milkshakes and fresh *tyropita* (cheese pie), all managed by the philosophical Makis.

ⓘ Information

Banks with ATMs are at the *plateia* (square). The post office is on the street above it.
Dolihi Tours Travel Agency (✆22750 23230; dolichi@otenet.gr) Full-service agency, next to Alpha Bank.
Hospital (✆22753 50200)
Ikariada Travel (✆22750 23322; www.ikariada.gr) Full-service waterfront travel agency next to Diagonios souvlaki shop.
Island Ikaria (www.island-ikaria.com)
Police (✆22750 22222) Above Alpha Bank.
Port police (✆22750 22207)

Around Agios Kirykos

The hot sea-springs of **Lefkada**, 2km west of Agios Kirykos, are free, therapeutic and relaxing. This is a designated radioactive saltwater spring, but in truth, it's just a beautiful spot on the beach, identifiable by an irregular circle of rocks. You'll know you're in the right spot when you feel the now-it's-hot-now-it's-not intermingling of spring and seawater. To find the springs, look for a small red-and-white sign (saying 'hot springs') next to a path leading to the rocky beach below.

Ikaria's eastern tip boasts the 2km-long **Faros (Fanari) Beach**, 10km north along the coast road, and the 4th-century-BC **Fortress of Drakanos** (⊙8.30am-3pm Tue-Sat), which sponsored religious rites dedicated to Eilythia, a fertility deity. A 13m-high lookout tower anchors the site, which features informative signboards and two helpful English-speaking volunteers. A path from a small chapel here leads to tiny **Agios Georgios Beach**.

In the village of **Therma**, just east of Agios Kyrikos, time seems to have stopped. In addition to the traditional **Therma Hot Springs** (Apollon Spa; ✆22750 22665, 22750 24049; Therma; €4.50-8; ⊙8-11am), you'll find an enjoyable cave-like natural sauna, **Spilio Baths** (To Spilio; ✆22750 24048; €3-4.50; ⊙daily to dusk).

🛏 Sleeping & Eating

★**Evon's Rooms**   APARTMENT €
(✆22750 32580, 6977139208; www.evonsrooms.com; Faros; studio/ste from €30-90; P❋@☎)
Less than 100m from Faros Beach, friendly

RELIGIOUS REVELRY ON THE ISLAND OF WINE

Pagan god Dionysos may no longer reign over Ikaria's vineyards, but his legacy lives on in Christianised form in the summertime *panigyria* (all-night festival celebrations held on saints' days across the island). There's no better way to dive head-first into Greek island culture than drinking, dancing and feasting while honouring a village's patron saint. Bring your wallet, however: *panigyria* are important fundraisers for the local community. Use this fact to explain away any overindulgences as well-intended philanthropy.

Panigyria occur across the island on the following dates:

Kambos 5 May	**Arethoussa** 17 July
Armenistis 40 days after Orthodox Easter	**Agios Panteleinonas** (Fidos) 27 July
Agios Isidoros (Pezi) 24 June	**Hristos Rahes & Dafne** 6 August
Agios Giannis (Raches) 24 June	**Akamatra** 15 August
Platani 29 June	**Evdilos** 15–20 August
Karavostamo 1 July	**Agios Sofia & Monokambi** 17 September
Agios Kirykos & **Ikarian Independence Day** 17 July	

Greek-Australian Evon Plakidas rents out high-quality suites, some with spiral stairs, all with kitchenettes. The studios hold up to six people. The adjoining cafe serves breakfast, delicious crepes, sweet *loukoumadhes* (ball-shaped doughnuts served with honey and cinnamon) and fresh juices and salads.

★ Agriolykos Pension
PENSION €

(✆6944907023, 22750 22433; www.agriolykos.gr; s/d/tr incl breakfast from €40/50/60) This exceedingly charming lodging is the work of Mrs Voula Manolarou, who oversees every detail of the budget jewel on its own perch, with stairs to the small bay it overlooks.

Taverna Arodou
TAVERNA €

(✆22750 22700; mains under €10) An excellent traditional seaside eatery overlooking the sea, 5km southwest of Agios Kirykos.

Evdilos
Εύδηλος

POP 460

Evdilos, Ikaria's second port, is 41km northwest of Agios Kirykos; they're connected by Ikaria's two main roads. The memorable trip takes in high mountain ridges, striking sea views and slate-roof villages. Evdilos itself skirts a small semicircular bay and rises in tiers up a hillside. It features stately old houses on winding streets and a relaxed and appealing waterfront with a small free car park to one side.

🛏 Sleeping

Hotel Atheras
HOTEL €

(✆22750 31434; www.atheras-kerame.gr; s/d/tr from €30/45/55; P❄🖥🌊) The friendly and modern Atheras has an almost Cycladic feel due to its bright-white decor contrasting with the blue Aegean beyond. There's an outdoor bar by the pool and the hotel is in the backstreets, 200m from the port. Open year-round, with breakfast available (€7).

Room-for-Rent
PENSION €

(✆22750 31518; s/d €40/50) Otherwise known as 'Anna's place', these five simple and spotless rooms above Alpha Bank overlook the port and have overhead fans.

Kerame Studios
APARTMENT €€

(✆22750 31434; www.atheras-kerame.gr; studio/apt/ste from €40/70/90; P❄🖥🌊) These studio apartments (1km before Evdilos) are the sister establishment of Hotel Atheras. Prices are as variable as the quarters, which feature kitchens and spacious decks with views. A breakfast cafe is built into a windmill.

🍴 Eating & Drinking

Restaurant Koralli
TAVERNA €

(Plateia Evdilou; mains €4-9) A local favourite among the waterfront tavernas, specialising in fresh fish and chips, excellent meat grills, veg salads and oven-ready *mayirefta*.

Xalara
FAST FOOD €

(pitta snacks €1.50-4; ⊙lunch & dinner) Xalara means 'relaxed' in Greek, which is kind of a motto in laid-back Evdilos. On the other hand, this snappy eatery keeps it moving with great *gyros* and souvlakia.

Tsakonitis Cafe
CAFE €

(Plateia Evdilou; mezedhes €4-7) This *ouzerie* (place that serves ouzo and light snacks) on the waterfront is known for traditional meat and seafood mezedhes (to accompany the local *tsipouro* firewater), along with homemade Greek yoghurt, pasta and rice pudding. Look for the stone edifice.

★ Café-Bar Rififi
CAFE

(✆22750 33060; Plateia Evdilou) This snappy portside bar with great pitta snacks, draught beer and good coffee owes its name to the bank next door, with which it shares an interior wall. Rififi in Greek is a nickname for 'bank robber', and the servers are happy to point out where the serious money is stashed.

MOUNTAIN WALKS & MONKS' SKULLS

With its solitude and rugged natural beauty, Ikaria's perfect for mountain walks. One that's invigorating, but not too hard on the bones, is the one-day circular walk along dirt roads from **Kambos** south through **Dafni**, the remains of the 10th-century Byzantine **Castle of Koskinas** and picturesque **Frandato** and **Maratho** villages.

When you reach **Pigi**, look for the Frandato sign; continue past it for the unusual little Byzantine **Chapel of Theoskepasti**, tucked into overhanging granite. You must clamber up to get to it, and duck to get inside. The rows of old monks' skulls have been retired, but the chapel makes for an unusual visit, along with nearby **Moni Theoktistis**, with frescoes dating from 1686. The adjacent *kafeneio* (coffee house) is good for a coffee or juice with Maria, the kindly owner.

Cafe Kymmata
CAFE

(☑ 22750 31262) A rambling and cheerful cafe on the waterfront with Greek coffee, ice cream, ouzo, beer, bakery goodies and small plates from morning till night.

ℹ Information

The waterfront has two ATMs and the ticket agency for **Hellenic Seaways** (☑ 22750 32931). **Medical Center** (☑ 22750 33030, 22750 32922) Around 2km east of Evdilos, with an English-speaking doctor and staff. **Police** (☑ 22750 31222)

West of Evdilos

Kambos
Κάμπος

POP 250

Kambos, 3km west of Evdilos, was once mighty Oinoe (derived from the Greek word for wine), Ikaria's capital. Traces of this ancient glory remain, compliments of a ruined Byzantine palace, Ikaria's oldest church and a small museum. Kambos' other main attractions are its sand-and-pebble beach and scenic hill walks.

◉ Sights

Entering Kambos from Evdilos, you'll pass the modest ruins of a **Byzantine palace**, which also served as a parliament/theatre during Hellenistic times. To find it, take the short path leading from Agia Irini Church.

Agia Irini Church
CHURCH

Built on the site of a 4th-century basilica, this 12th-century church contains some columns from this original. Alas, many of Agia Irini's frescoes remain covered with protective whitewash because funds are scarce to pay for its removal.

Archaeological Museum
MUSEUM

(☑ 22750 32935; ◷ 8.30am-3pm Wed) FREE Kambos' small museum displays neolithic tools, geometric vases, classical sculpture fragments, figurines and ivory trinkets. If it's closed, ask Vasilis Kambouris (at Rooms Dionysos) to open it.

🛏 Sleeping & Eating

★ **Rooms Dionysos**
PENSION €

(☑ 22750 31688, 6944153437; www.ikaria-dionysos rooms.com; d/tr/q from €25/35/45; 🅿 🛜) The many happy guests who return every year attest to the magical atmosphere of this pension run by the charismatic Vasilis 'Dionysos'

Kambouris, his Australian-born wife Demetra and Italian-speaking brother Yiannis. Rooms are simple, with private bathrooms, while the rooftop beds are a summer steal at €10. There's a communal kitchen, book exchange and great tips on exploring Ikaria.

Breakfast (€5) is served on a shaded patio overlooking nearby Kambos Beach and guests can enjoy the relaxed atmosphere over an evening glass of local wine.

★ **Ikaros**
GREEK €

(mains €3.50-7; ◷ 11am-late) Ikaros is a classic village *ovelistirio*, or grill house, referring to the upright grill for making *gyros*. Excellent food, lively atmosphere, snappy service. Opposite the pharmacy.

Partheni
TAVERNA €

(mains €6-8) On Kambos Beach, the Partheni serves tasty Greek standards, including great *kalamari* (fried squid), and is a relaxing place to eat after a swim at the 'virgins' beach' – Partheni means 'virgin' and the beach was once reserved for young women in long swimming dresses.

Popi's
TAVERNA €

(Fytema Beach; mains €5-8.50; ◷ dinner) Very traditional setting on the road halfway between Kambos and Evdilos. Excellent taverna fare, cooked and happily served by Popi.

Sourta-Ferta
CAFE €

(☑ 22750 31651; snacks €1.50-4) Tiny roadside cafe with good coffee and small plates through the day. Sourta-Ferta means 'back and forth' in Greek.

Kambos to the Southwest Coast

From Kambos, two roads head west: the main road, which hugs the northern coast until Armenistis and then becomes a secondary road continuing down the northwestern coast; and another secondary road, half of which is a good dirt track, that winds its way southwest through stunning moonscapes to remote Karkinagri on the southern coast.

The road through central Ikaria accesses **Moni Theoktistis** and the tiny **Chapel of Theoskepasti**, just northwest of Pigi. From Pigi, continue south to Maratho, then southwest for the impressive **Moni Mounte**, also called Moni Evangelistrias. Around 500m beyond it lies a tiny dam with goldfish, croaking frogs and a canteen open in summer.

Another fork leads to popular **Hristos Rahes**, an eclectic hillside village and good hiking base, known for its late-night shopping and cafe scene. Stop in at the Women's Cooperative for local jams, herbs and sweet treats. Along with various traditional products, there's a useful walking map, *The Round of Rahes on Foot* (€4), sold at most shops; proceeds go to maintaining the trails.

Just above Hristos Rahes, the excellent **Afianes Winery** (☑22750 40008, 6977893731; www.afianeswines.gr; ⊙noon-8pm Thu-Tue) **FREE** offers tours and free tastings. An exhibition room features vintage equipment and 19th-century wedding dresses.

After Hristos Rahes, the road south finds rustic **Profitis Ilias** and then the signposted village of **Pezi**. The landscape now becomes even more rugged and extreme, with windwhipped thick green trees clinging to bleak boulders, and wild goats a common sight. The road finally reaches tiny **Karkinagri**, which has a few tavernas, rooms and a nearby beach.

The southwest coast is also home to **Manganitis** village, with the star attraction being nearby **Seychelles Beach**, a secluded stretch of white pebbles and azure waters, tucked in a protected cove. In summer a boat makes daily trips between village and beach. To reach it from the coastal road connecting Manganitis with Evdilos and Agios Kirykos, look for an unmarked parking area on the right-hand side, 125m after the tunnel. From here, clamber down the path (10 to 15 minutes) to the beach.

🛏 Sleeping & Eating

Fakaros Rooms
PENSION €
(☑22750 41269; Hristos Rahes; s/d €20/30) Modest and immaculate domatia, a few metres from the *plateia* at Hristos Rahes. It's attractive, clean and comfortable, and managed by the English-speaking Fakaros family.

★Taverna Platanos
TAVERNA €
(☑22750 42395; Agios Dimitrios; mains €5-9.50; ⊙lunch & dinner) Nestled under the shade of a rambling plane tree, a 500m stroll from Hristos Raches, Platanos offers authentic Ikarian dishes, including *soufiko,* a summer favourite of stewed vegies, generally featuring whatever was picked fresh that morning. Great grills, hearty salads and local wine round out the table. Owner-cook-server Maria speaks English, Italian and French.

Women's Cooperative
MARKET €
(☑22750 41076; Hristos Raches) Wonderful market-deli-bakery in the heart of Hristos Raches, selling jams, herbs and sweet treats made on the premises.

Sta Perix
GREEK €€
(☑22750 31056; Akamatra; mains €5-11; ⊙lunch & dinner) Classy eatery in Akamatra, 6km south of Evdilos, and well regarded for traditional Ikarian recipes, a variety of local cheeses, even its own wine.

Armenistis to Nas
Αρμενιστής Προς Να

Armenistis, 15km west of Evdilos, is Ikaria's humble version of a resort. It boasts two long, sandy beaches separated by a narrow headland, a fishing harbour and a web of hilly streets to explore on foot. Cafes and tavernas line the beach. Moderate nightlife livens up Armenistis in summer with a mix of locals and Greek and foreign tourists.

◉ Sights & Activities

Livadi Beach
BEACH
Just 500m east of Armenistis is Livadi Beach, where currents are strong enough to warrant a lifeguard service and waves are sometimes big enough for surfing. Beyond Livadi are two other popular beaches, **Mesahti** and **Gialiskari**.

Nas Beach
BEACH
Westward 3.5km from Armenistis lies the pebbled beach of Nas, below the road and tavernas. Nudist-friendly, it has an impressive location at the mouth of a forested river, behind the trace ruins of an ancient **Temple of Artemis**, easily viewed from Taverna O Nas.

🛏 Sleeping

Armenistis has its share of package pensions. Try these exceptions for a change of pace.

★Pension Astaxi
PENSION €
(☑6982446227, 22750 71318; www.island-ikaria. com/hotels/PensionAstaxi.asp; Armenistis; d/ tr incl breakfast from €35/50; 🅿@🗑) This excellent and attractive budget gem is tucked back 30m from the main road, just above the Carte Postal cafe and Baido Taverna. The gracious owner, Maria, has created a relaxing and welcoming lodging, with a dozen brightly outfitted rooms with fans and balcony views to the sea.

Hotel Daidalos
HOTEL €
(☑22750 71390; www.daidaloshotel.gr; Armenistis; s/d incl breakfast from €40/50; ⊙May-Oct; 🅿❄🗑) You can't miss the traditional blue-and-white island colour scheme at this attractive and well-managed midsized hotel (25 rooms). Rooms are large and cheerful, most with sea views. There's a small bar off

the lobby as well. It's 200m west of the small bridge entering Armenistis.

Armenistis View
HOTEL €

(☑6977621806, 22750 71529; www.armenistis. eu; d/apt from €40/60) You could easily miss these five friendly and well-managed studio apartments below the road, about 30m before the bridge, with kitchenettes and roomy sea-view verandahs.

Atsachas Rooms
HOTEL €€

(☑22750 71226; www.atsachas.gr; Livadi Beach; d from €60) Right on Livadi Beach, the Atsachas has clean, well-furnished rooms, some with fully equipped kitchens. Most have breezy, sea-view balconies. The cafe spills over to a flowery garden, where a stairway descends to a nice stretch of beach.

✖ Eating & Drinking

★ Thea's Restaurant & Rooms
TAVERNA €

(☑6932154296, 22750 71491; www.theasinn.com; Nas; mains €5-9; ⊙lunch & dinner) There are a few fine tavernas in Nas, but Thea's excels, serving up outstanding mezedhes, meat grills and a perfect vegie *mousakas*. Good barrel wine and local *tsipouro* firewater complete the deal. An outdoor patio overlooks the sea. Thea (aka Dorothy) also has five bright and cosy rooms (€35) above the restaurant, with breakfast.

★ Taverna Baido
TAVERNA €

(☑6982331539; Armenistis; mains €4.50-8) Past the bridge towards Nas, this interesting taverna is the work of Marianthi, who serves well-priced dishes using local products, fresh fish and Ikarian wine. Exceptional *soutzoukakia* (Turkish meatballs) and *taramasalata* (a thick pink or white purée of fish roe, potato, oil and lemon juice).

Pashalia Taverna
TAVERNA €

(☑22750 71302, 6975562415; Armenistis; mains from €5; ⊙lunch & dinner) Meat dishes such as *katsikaki* (kid goat) or veal in a clay pot are specialities at this, the first taverna along the Armenistis harbour road. Great mezedhes and fresh fish are popular. Father-and-son owners, Haris and Vasilis, have apartments (single/double €35/45) above the taverna.

Taverna Symposio
TAVERNA €

(☑6972264046; appetisers & mains €3-8.50) A small taverna in tiny Gialiskari, next to Armenistis, overlooking the marina and popular for good mezedhes and *mayirefta*.

Kelaris Taverna
SEAFOOD €

(☑22750 71227; Gialiskari; mains €6-11; ⊙lunch & dinner) Kelaris serves its own fresh-caught fish, cooked over coals, along with midday *mayirefta* from the oven. Look for the landmark church on the point, 1.5km east of Armenistis.

Carte Postale
CAFE, BAR

(☑6981719567, 22750 71031; ⊙10am-2am) Hip cafe-bar, 100m west of Armenistis' church, high over the bay. Snacks range from small pizzas and salads to breakfast omelettes and evening risotto, all managed by the welcoming Myrto; her father makes the olives. There's a mellow ambience and an eclectic music mix, from world beat to Greek fusion.

Mythos
BAR

(⊙10am-late) Cosy, atmospheric bar managed by Dimitiros and Mariza, who deliver good drinks, fresh juices and live music now and then in the summer.

Karnayo
CAFE, BAR

(☑22750 71240; Gialiskari) Cool bar with an eclectic music mix, midway among several good *ouzeries* strung together above the beach at Gialiskari.

Ammos
BAR

(☑22750 71250; Livadi Beach) Chilled beach bar at Livadi Beach, equal parts sand, palm fronds, pizza, drinks and juices.

🛍 Shopping

Kedroi Ceramics
CERAMICS

(☑6984733455; Armenistis) On the road out of Armenistis toward Nas, this attractive shop and studio is named for the *kedroi* (cedar tree). Lots of handmade ceramics, fired on the premises by Stavros and Kristina.

❶ Information

Aventura (☑22750 71117; aventura@otenet. gr; Armenistis) Full-service travel agency by the patisserie just before the bridge. Offers car and motorbike rentals, and is one of the few places that hires out mountain bikes. Also does airport pick-up and drop-off.

Dolihi Tours & Lemy Rent-a-Car (☑22750 71122, 6983418878; lemy@otenet.gr; Armenistis) Efficient travel agency next to the village market. Rents cars and organises walking tours and 4WD safaris.

East of Evdilos

Karavostamo   Καραβόσταμο
POP 550

One of Ikaria's largest and most beautiful coastal villages is Karavostamo, 6km east of Evdilos. From the main road, the village cascades down winding paths scattered with flowering gardens, village churches, vegie patches, chickens and goats, finally reaching a cosy *plateia* and small fishing harbour. Here, you'll find nothing more than a bakery, small general store, a few domatia, tavernas and *kafeneia* where the villagers congregate each evening to chat, argue, eat, play backgammon, drink and tell stories. To reach the *plateia,* take the signed road off the main road. Arethousa, 3km above Karavostamo, is the serene village home of the Ikarian Centre (6979024066, 22750 61140; www.greek ingreece.gr), a Greek-language school which runs intensive short-term residential courses.

Sleeping & Eating

Despina Rooms   PENSION €
(6973050505, 21066 14371; r €40-60; P✿🖥) Well-appointed two-floor studios in the heart of the village, with kitchen and laundry, about 200m from the sea and village square.

★ Xylakias   GREEK €
(22750 61181; mains €3-7; ☺lunch & dinner) Snappy bistro atmosphere at this excellent village grill house, with excellent *gyros,* souvlakia, fried fresh potatoes and plenty of house wine or beer. The name is a pun, meaning 'stick man', a reference to the skewered *kalamaki* on hand.

To Steki   MEZEDHES €
(☺lunch & dinner) Join the regulars for good grills and salads, fresh chips, beer or

A VILLAGE BAKERY

In Karavostomo, everything you need to know about island values can probably be found at the village bakery, where Stephanos Kranas bakes long loaves of bread in his wood oven, along with crunchy *paximadia* (rusks) and sweet *koulouria* (fresh pretzel-style bread).

The bakery makes deliveries each morning by motorbike to village homes. But villagers can also drop by, grab a loaf from the wicker basket on the counter and, if no one's around, leave money in a counter cup. If the bakery seems closed, they might just go upstairs and knock on the owner's door to enquire if there's any bread. The system has worked for years, another reason perhaps why Ikarians don't get too excited about fluctuations in the global price of oil. Olive oil, maybe.

tsipouro at this small and unpretentious *mezedhopoleio* (place serving mezedhes) on the square. Summer evenings find half the village at the outdoor tables.

Taverna I Plaka   TAVERNA €
(6972512551; Arethousa; mains €4.50-8.50; ☺lunch & dinner) Excellent traditional taverna in Arethousa, serving traditional Greek dishes from a terrace overlooking the sea.

★ Mandouvala   GREEK €€
(22750 61204; mains €7-12; ☺lunch & dinner) Karavostamo's most upscale eatery is at the end of the small waterfront, along a narrow cobbled lane 50m from the square. Excellent fish, grills, top wines and service add to the breezy seaside ambience.

Fourni Islands
Οι Φούρνοι

POP 1500

The Fourni archipelago is one of Greece's great unknown island gems. Its low-lying vegetation clings to gracefully rounded hills that overlap, forming intricate bays of sandy beaches and little ports. This former pirates' lair is especially beautiful at dusk, when the setting sun turns the terrain shades of pink, violet and black.

A clue to the area's swashbuckling past can be found in the name of the archipelago's capital, Fourni Korseon. The Corsairs were French privateers with a reputation for audacity, and their name became applied generically to all pirates and rogues then roaming the eastern Aegean.

Nowadays, Fourni Korseon offers most of the accommodation and services, plus several beaches. Other settlements include little Hrysomilia and Kamari to the north, plus another fishing hamlet on the islet of Thymena. In the south of the main island, the monastery of Agios Ioannis Prodromos stands serene over the far horizon.

Sights & Activities

The island's rolling hills are ideal for hiking, and trails inevitably find a beach. The nearest to Fourni Korseon, Psili Ammos Beach, waits 600m north on the coast road, with umbrellas and a beach bar that hums all night. Along the coast road heading south, Kampi Beach is excellent. A further 2km along, Elidaki Beach has a gentle sandy bottom, followed by the small-pebbled Petrokopio Beach.

Near Fourni's southernmost tip, near the **Monastery of Agios Ioannis Thermastis**, the fine, sandy **Vlyhada Beach** lies before the more secluded **Kasidi Beach**. The other main settlements, **Hrysomilia** and **Kamari**, are 17km and 10km from Fourni Korseon respectively (approximately a 30-minute drive on winding roads). Both are tranquil fishing settlements with beaches, but limited services. The trip from Fourni Korseon to these villages is spectacular, opening onto myriad views of sloping hills and hidden coves.

🛏 Sleeping

Most accommodation is in Fourni Korseon, though sleeping in the smaller settlements is possible, as is free beach camping.

★ Archipelagos Hotel   HOTEL €
(☑6973494967, 22750 51250; www.archipelagos hotel.gr; Fourni Korseon; s/d/tr incl breakfast from €35/45/50; ⓟ🌀🌐) This elegant and welcoming small hotel on the harbour's northern edge comprises Fourni's most sophisticated lodgings. From the patio restaurant, set under stone arches bursting with geraniums and roses, to the well-appointed rooms and cafe-bar, the Archipelagos combines traditional architecture with modern luxuries.

Studios Nektaria   APARTMENT €
(☑6973097365, 22750 25134; studiosnektaria@ya hoo.gr; Fourni Korseon; d/tr €35/45; 🌀🌐) On the harbour's far side is this Fourni bargain with small, clean rooms, three of which have shaded balconies overlooking the small beach that skirts the southern end of the bay.

Toula Studios   PENSION €
(☑22750 51332, 6976537948; info@fournitoula studio.gr; s/d from €25/35; 🌀🌐) Look for the Aegean blue balconies at this friendly seafront standby near shops and tavernas. It has clean and simple self-catering rooms, 10 with sea views, surrounding a large courtyard, along with overhead fans.

Nikos Kondilas Rooms & Studios   ACCOMMODATION SERVICES €
(☑6979732579, 22750 51364; Fourni Korseon; d/tr €35/45; 🌀🌐) Contact the helpful and resourceful owner, Nikos, for several good sleeping options around the island, including in Kampi.

🍴 Eating & Drinking

Fourni is famous for seafood, especially *as-takomakaronadha* (lobster with pasta).

Psarotaverna O Miltos   SEAFOOD €
(☑22750 51407; Fourni Korseon; mains €7-10) Fourni lobster and fresh fish are expertly prepared at this iconic waterfront taverna. Excellent mezedhes and traditional salads. Fish and lobster fairly priced by the kilo.

Taverna Kali Kardia   TAVERNA €
(Fourni Korseon; mains €5-8) Hearty Kali Kardia, on the *plateia* at the end of the cobbled main street, is the place to go for excellent grilled and spit-roasted meats, and is enlivened by animated old locals around the shady square. With luck, you may find *ameletita,* a rare speciality of which only a male lamb can provide two of.

Taverna Kotaras   TAVERNA €
(☑22750 32797; Thymina; mains €4.50-8) When Fourni folk need to get away from it all, they take a water taxi over to Thymina for dinner at this excellent *psarotaverna* (fish taverna). If you miss the boat back, fear not as the owners maintain three spotless rooms (single/double €30/35) above.

Taverna Almyra   TAVERNA €
(Kamari; mains €5-9) Up in the little village of Kamari, 9km from the harbour, this relaxing waterfront taverna has subtle charm and plenty of fresh fish and lobster.

🛍 Shopping

Melanthi Shop   FOOD
(☑22750 51037) Inviting shop on the main street with nicely packaged fresh herbs (thyme, lavender, oregano and the unique *throubi),* along with honey, cheese, oils, balms and salves, all from Fourni.

ℹ Information

Perpendicular to the central waterfront, the main street of Fourni Korseon runs inland to the *plateia*. This nameless thoroughfare hosts the National Bank with ATM, travel agency, post office and village **pharmacy** (☑22750 51188).
Health Centre (☑22750 51202)
Karla Irini Travel (☑22750 51481, 6978373416; Fourni Korseon) Helpful hole-in-the-wall agency opposite the port for ferry bookings and accommodation.
Port police (☑22750 51207)

ℹ Getting There & Away

Fourni is connected to Ikaria (Agios Kyrikos) and Samos by ferry and hydrofoil services. Karla Irini Travel provides information and sells tickets.

BOAT SERVICES FROM FOURNI

DESTINATION	TIME	FARE	FREQUENCY
Ikaria (Agios Kirykos)	1hr	€7	4-5 weekly
Patmos	1½hr	€25	2 weekly
Piraeus	8hr	€35	3 weekly
Samos (Karlovasi)	1½hr	€5	3 weekly
Samos (Pythagorio)	1hr	€20	2 weekly

ⓘ Getting Around

Weekly caïques serve Hrysomilia, while another two to three go daily to Thymena.

Gleaming new sealed roads, all 20km of them, connect Fourni Korseon with Hrysomilia and Kamari. Everyone seems to walk everywhere in Fourni, and then walk some more. Rental cars are a recent addition to the Fourni transport scene. Hire a small car or scooter at **Escape Car & Bike Rental** (☑22750 51514; www.fourni-rentals.com; Fourni Korseon) on the waterfront.

Hitching is common and considered quite safe, and there's also the island's lone **taxi** (☑6970879102), commandeered by the ebullient Georgos.

SAMOS ΣΑΜΟΣ

POP 32,820

Lying just off the Turkish coast, Samos is one of the northeastern Aegean Islands' best-known destinations, yet beyond the low-key resorts and the lively capital, Vathy, there are numerous off-the-beaten-track beaches and quiet spots in the cool, forested inland mountains, where traditional life continues.

Famous for its sweet local wine, Samos is also historically significant. It was the legendary birthplace of Hera, and the sprawling ruins of her ancient sanctuary, the Heraion, are impressive. Both the great mathematician Pythagoras and the hedonistic father of atomic theory, 4th-century-BC philosopher Epicurus, were born here. Samos' scientific genius is also affirmed by the astonishing 524 BC Evpalinos Tunnel, a spectacular feat of ancient engineering that stretches for 1034m deep underground.

ⓘ Getting There & Away

AIR

Samos' airport is 4km west of Pythagorio. **Aegean Airlines** (☑801 112 0000; www.aegeanair.com), **Astra Airlines** (☑23104 89392; www.astra-airlines.gr), **Olympic Air** (www.olympicair.com) and **Sky Express** (☑28102 23835; www.skyexpress.gr) all serve Samos and have offices at the airport. Charters serve Chios from Holland, Oslo and Vienna. The following are domestic flights from Samos.

DESTINATION	TIME	FARE	FREQUENCY
Athens	45min	€80	2-3 daily
Chios	35min	€56	2 weekly
Lesvos	2hr	€66	2 weekly
Limnos	2hr	€66	2 weekly
Rhodes	45min	€66	1-2 weekly
Thessaloniki	55min	€50	1 daily

BOAT

Samos is home to three ports – Vathy (aka Samos), Pythagorio and Karlovasi. The new ferry terminal in Vathy, for ferries to domestic destinations only, is at the harbour's southeast end, 1.7km from the old ferry terminal, which is only for boats to Turkey. A taxi between the terminals is €5.

ITSA Travel (☑22730 23605; www.itsa-travelsamos.gr; Themistokleous Sofouli; ◷8am-8pm), directly opposite Vathy's old ferry terminal, provides detailed information, offers free luggage storage and sells tickets, including to Turkey. The helpful staff will also pick you up at the new terminal for free. Tickets to Turkey also available next door from **By Ship Travel** (☑22730 27337; www.byshiptravel.gr).

A MATTER OF MEASUREMENTS

While the obsession with the 'proper pint' may seem modern, the ancient Greeks also fixated on measuring their alcohol. Pythagoras, that great Samian mathematician (and, presumably, drinker), created an invention that ensured party hosts and publicans could not be deceived by guests aspiring to inebriation. His creation was dubbed the *Dikiakoupa tou Pythagora* (Just Cup of Pythagoras). This mysterious, multiholed drinking vessel holds its contents perfectly, unless filled past the engraved line, at which point the glass drains completely from the bottom, punishing the glutton!

Today faithful reproductions, made of colourful, glazed ceramic, are sold in Samos gift shops, tangible reminders of the Apollan Mean: 'Everything in moderation.'

TURKISH CONNECTIONS

Visiting Turkey's Aegean coastal resorts and historical sites from Samos, Chios and Lesvos is easy. Visas aren't usually necessary for day trips. While boat itineraries, prices and even companies change often, the following explains how things generally work.

Samos

Boats leave daily from Vathy for the 80-minute trip to **Kuşadası**, a coastal resort near **ancient Ephesus** (Efes). The Greek *Samos Star* usually leaves at 8.30am (€25/30, one way/return) and the Turkish-flagged *Kudasi Express* departs at 5pm. From Pythagorio, a boat connects with Kuşadası once or twice a week. Tickets cost €35/45 one way/ open return, plus €10 for Turkish port taxes (pay upon arrival). Daily excursions run from May through October, with the option to also visit Ephesus (€25 extra). For tickets and information in Vathy, contact ITSA Travel, opposite the old ferry terminal for boats to Turkey, or adjoining By Ship Travel. In Pythagorio, contact By Ship Travel (p566) at the main junction entering town. Additionally, as of 2015, the *Samos Star* connects from Karlovasi in northern Samos to **Sığacık** (one way/return €20/30, five weekly) in Turkey (between Kuşadası and the airport at Izmir).

Chios

There are daily departures year-round from Chios Town for **Çeşme**, a port near bustling **İzmir**, though they're most frequent in summer. Boats depart around 8am for the 40-minute journey (one way/return €15/25), returning by 6pm to Chios Town. Sunday ferries usually return by 5pm. A popular package day tour to Izmir costs €35, which includes lunch and the one-hour bus trip each way between Çeşme and Izmir. These Izmir excursions run six days a week in summer, and twice weekly in winter. Get information and tickets from Hatzelenis Tours (p573) or Sunrise Tours (p577).

Lesvos

Boats leave Mytilini town for **Ayvalik**. Two Turkish companies, Turyol and Jale, leave Mytilini town at 9am daily from May through October, returning at 6pm (€10 return, one hour 20 minutes each way). Another Turkish operator, Jalem Tours, runs a faster catarmaran (hydrofoil) that takes 40 minutes each way (€15 return). Thursday boats are popular for market day in Ayvalik. During high season, there is usually a twice-weekly option to include a day tour of **ancient Pergamon** (Bergama) for €45, including lunch and the one-hour bus ride there and back to Ayvalik. Most Mytilini town travel agencies sell Turkish tours; try Olive Groove Travel (p584), Mitilene Tours (p584), or Tsolos Travel (p584).

In Pythagorio, check ferry/hydrofoil schedules with the tourist office (p566), the **port police** (☎22730 61225), or By Ship Travel (p566).

Boat Services from Samos

DESTINATION	TIME	FARE	FREQUENCY, PORT
Chios	3-4hr	€13-16.50	2-3 weekly, V/K
Fourni	1hr	€20	2 weekly, P
Fourni	2½hr	€6	4 weekly, V
Ikaria (Agios Kirykos)**	2-3½hr	€8-11.50	4 weekly, V/K
Ikaria (Evdilos)**	4hr	€12.50	3 weekly, V
Kavala	15hr	€45	2 weekly, V/K
Lesvos (Mytilini)	6hr	€21	3 weekly, V/K
Limnos	12hr	€34	2 weekly, V/K
Mykonos	3½-5½hr	€37-41	2-3 weekly, V/K
Naxos	4½hr	€37	2-3 weekly, P
Patmos	2hr	€30	4 weekly, P
Piraeus	12hr	€32	3 weekly, V
Rhodes	5½hr	€55	1 weekly, P

V/K - Vathy or Karlovasi, V - Vathy, P - Pythagorio
** via Fourni

ⓘ Getting Around

TO/FROM THE AIRPORT

Buses run to and from the airport three to four times daily (€2). Taxis from the airport cost €25 to Vathy or €6 to Pythagorio, from where there are local buses to Vathy.

Samos

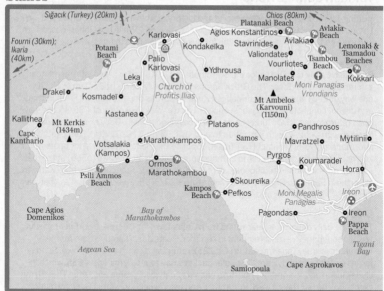

BOAT

Summer excursion boats travel twice daily (except Saturday) from Pythagorio to Patmos (return €30), leaving at 8am. Daily excursion boats go from Pythagorio to Samiopoula islet (including lunch, €20).

BUS

From Vathy **bus station** (☑ 22730 27262; www.samospublicusses.gr; Themistokli Sofouli) frequent daily buses serve Kokkari (€1.50, 20 minutes), Pythagorio (€1.70, 25 minutes), Agios Konstantinos (€2.30, 40 minutes), Karlovasi (€4, one hour), the Ireon (€2.30, 25 minutes), Mytilinii (€1.60, 20 minutes) and Portrokali (€1.90, 20 minutes).

From Pythagorio, five daily buses reach the Ireon (€1.60, 15 minutes), while four serve Mytilinii (€1.90, 20 minutes) and Marathokambos (€5.60, one hour). Buy tickets on the buses. Services are reduced on weekends.

CAR & MOTORCYCLE

Opposite the port entrance in Vathy, **Manos Moto-Auto Rental** (☑ 6974392157, 22730 23309; www.manos-rentals.gr; Grammou & Kounturioti) runs an efficient service. Another good option is **Pegasus Rent-a-Car** (☑ 22730 24470, 6972017092; www.samos-car-rental.com; Themistoklis Sofouli 5, Vathy), with good rates on car, 4WD and motorcycle hire.

In Pythagorio, try **John's Rentals** (☑ 6972338103, 22730 61405; www.johns-rent-a-car.gr; Likourgou Logetheti) on the main road near the waterfront.

TAXI

The **taxi rank** (☑ 22730 28404) in Vathy is by the National Bank of Greece. To the airport, the fare is €25, to Pythagorio €10. In Pythagorio the **taxi rank** (☑ 22730 61450) is by the waterfront at the bottom of Lykourgou Logetheti.

Vathy (Samos) Βαθύ (Σάμος)

POP 2025

Vathy (also called Samos) is the island's capital and enjoys a striking setting within the fold of a deep bay, creating a curving waterfront lined with bars, cafes and restaurants. The historic quarter, filled with steep, narrow streets and red-tiled 19th-century hillside houses, brims with atmosphere.

⊙ Sights & Activities

Vathy's attractions include the Ano Vathy old quarter (inland 1km via Sofouli), relaxing municipal gardens and Roditzes and Gagos Beaches, as well as a first-rate archaeological museum and the splendid church of **Agios Spyridonas** (Plateia Dimarheiou; ⊙ 8-11am & 6.30-7.30pm). About 15km east of Vathy is one of the island's best and least crowded beaches, at the fishing hamlet of **Agia Paraskevi**.

iently include free tasting, with several reasonably priced wines for sale.

🛏 Sleeping & Eating

Pythagoras Hotel   HOTEL €
(☎22730 28422; www.pythagoras-hotel.com; Kallistratou 12; s/d/tr incl breakfast from €20/30/35; ☺Feb-Nov; ❄@☎) This budget gem, 500m up from the old port, owes its efficient charm to the hospitality of manager Stelios Mihalakis. Many rooms have breezy, sea-facing balconies and all have large fans. A pebbled beach lies below the shaded breakfast patio. Ring ahead for free pick-up from the ferry or bus station.

Pension Dreams   PENSION €
(☎6944518690, 22730 28422; Areos 9; r with/without balcony €35/25; P❄☎) This small, quiet and central pension, 100m up from the waterfront, claims a hill-top view of the harbour. All seven rooms are bright and very well kept, some with large balconies and garden views, and all feature screened bathroom windows. The owner also speaks English and French.

Hotel Medousa   HOTEL €
(☎22730 23501, 6976559972; Themisokleous Sofouli 25; s/d €25/35) A clean, friendly and appealing budget choice, especially for the six sea-view rooms with quieter glazed windows overlooking the waterfront, not to mention the handy ice-cream parlour downstairs.

★ Ino Village Hotel & Restaurant   HOTEL €€
(☎22730 23241; www.inovillagehotel.com; Kalami; d incl breakfast €70-145; P❄☎☒) With its courtyard pool flanked by ivy-clad, balconied white buildings, Ino Village, just 500m above Vathy, feels remote and elegant. While this mini-resort is sometimes booked by small tour groups, walk-in travellers can expect reasonable rates and a welcoming atmosphere. The hotel also boasts the popular Elea restaurant and cocktail bar, which serves fine Samian wines.

★ Taverna Artemis   TAVERNA €
(Kefalopoulou 4; mains €5-9; ☺noon-late) The Vathy Greek crowd relies on Artemis for fresh fish and well-prepared mezedhes and *mayirefta*, though it is perhaps best known for *sardeles pandremenos*. In Greek *pandremenos* means 'married', and the sardines are served open-faced, in pairs, like a couple. It's open year-round, about 20m up from the port authority at the northwest end of the port.

Archaeological Museum   MUSEUM
(☎22730 27469; adult/child €3/free, Sun Nov-Mar free; ☺8am-3pm Tue-Sun) One of the best museums in the islands, and housed in two adjacent buildings, this handsome complex contains finds starting from the rule of Polycrates (6th century BC). The most famous item is the imposing *kouros* (male statue of the Archaic period), plucked from the Heraion (Sanctuary of Hera) near Pythagorio. At a height of 5.5m, it's the largest-known standing *kouros*. A shaded museum cafe awaits outside. Many other statues, most also from the Heraion, as well as bronze sculptures, stelae and pottery, round out the collection.

Ecclesiastical (Byzantine) Museum   MUSEUM
(28 Oktovriou; adult/student €3/2, Sun free; ☺8.30am-3pm Tue-Sun) Houses rare manuscripts, liturgical objects of silver and gold and striking icons dating from the 13th century. Samos owes some of this holy loot to its status as a bishopric (administering also Ikaria and Fourni).

★ Museum of Samos Wines   WINERY
(☎22730 87551; ☺8am-8pm Mon-Sat) **FREE** Look for this handsome stone building opposite the new ferry quay to find one of Samos' best vintners. Winery tours usually take place when you show up and conven-

1. Lesvos Petrified Forest (p587)
This 20-million-year-old forest is a Protected National Monument on the island of Lesvos.

2. Pyrgi (p574)
The pretty central square in the largest village of the Mastihohoria region of Chios.

3. Kokkari (p567)
Once a fishing village, Kokkari is one of many captivating beach resorts along the coast of Samos.

4. Sanctuary of the Great Gods (p598)
Initiation ceremonies and rituals took place here, at one of Greece's most mysterious archaeological sites, on the island of Samothraki.

Vathy (Samos)

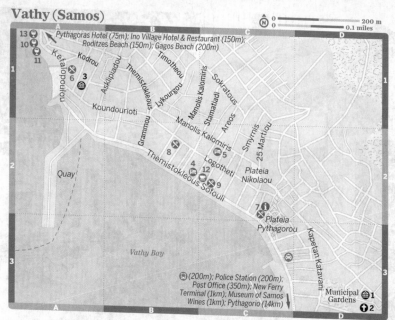

Telion

GREEK €

(☑ 22730 27526; gyros & small plates €1.50-3.50; ☺ lunch & dinner) Outstanding grill house on the waterfront near the main square, with snappy service and a good choice of pork, chicken and lamb *gyros*, pitta souvlaki, plus dinner specials, deliveries included.

Zen Restaurant

SEAFOOD €

(☑ 22730 80983; Themisokleous Sofouli; mains €6-9; ☺ lunch & dinner) Among several *etsi-ketsi* (so-so) seafront eateries, Zen stands out for well-prepared fresh fish, salads and mezedhes, along with surprises such as schnitzel to go along with good grills and draught wine.

To Steki

TAVERNA €

(Aogotheti 61; mains €4.50-7.50; ☺ lunch & dinner) An unpretentious and welcoming back-alley eatery with generous grills, *gavros* (marinated small fish), salads and homemade soups.

Drinking & Nightlife

Among the plentiful waterfront cafes, the best for quality and service is **Joy** (☑ 22730 89770; ☺ 8am-midnight), open morning till late. The nightlife in Vathy is more Hellenic than it is in Pythagorio, where the bars tend to be frequented by northern Europeans. While most cafes and bars cling to the waterfront, the coolest ones, such as **Escape** (☑ 22730 28345; Kefalopoulou 9; ☺ 10pm-6am), **Ble** (Ke-

falopoulou 7; ☺ 11am-4am) and **Mezza Volta** (Kefalopoulou), hang over the water along Kefalopoulou 100m beyond the quay. Music and dancing is usually in full swing by midnight.

ⓘ Information

Banks with ATMs line Plateia Pythagora and the waterfront. There is free wi-fi at Plateia Pythagora and all along the waterfront.

Port police (☑ 22730 27890)

Post office (Plateia Nikolaou; ☺ 7.30am-2pm)

Samos General Hospital (☑ 22730 27407) Efficient regional hospital for surrounding islands; opposite Pythagoras Hotel, north of the port.

Pythagorio Πυθαγόρειο

POP 1330

On the southeastern coast, opposite Turkey, pretty Pythagorio has a yacht-lined harbour and Samos' main archaeological finds. All boats departing south from Samos leave from Pythagorio, including day trips to Samiopoula islet. A 1.5km walk west of Pythagorio brings you to a pristinely clean beach with umbrellas, toilets and decent swimming.

◎ Sights

Evpalinos Tunnel

ARCHAEOLOGICAL SITE

(☑ 22730 61400; adult/child €4/free; ☺ 8am-3pm Tue-Sun) In 524 BC, when Pythagorio (then

Vathy (Samos)

called Samos) was the island's capital and a bustling metropolis of 80,000, securing sources of drinking water became crucial. To solve the problem, ruler Polycrates put his dictatorial whims to good use, ordering labourers to dig into a mountainside according to the exacting plan of his ingenious engineer, Evpalinos. Many workers died during the dangerous dig, but the result was the 1034m-long Evpalinos Tunnel. In medieval times, locals used it to hide from pirates.

The Evpalinos Tunnel is actually two tunnels: a service tunnel and a lower water conduit visible from the walkway. You enter the tunnel on narrow stairs, and it's single file from there. Not much more than 100m of tunnel is accessible, but it's enough to be impressed by this golden-age engineering feat.

Castle of Lykourgos Logothetis　CASTLE
(☉9am-dusk Tue-Sun) Samians took the lead locally in the 1821 War of Independence and this castle, built in 1824 by resistance leader Logothetis, is the major relic of that turbulent time. It's situated on a hill at the southern end of Metamorfosis Sotiros, near

---

ℹ **BUY ONE, GET TWO**

If you want to visit both the intriguing Evpalinos Tunnel, just north of Pythagorio, and the Heraion, the outdoor temple honouring Hera, heart-throb of Zeus, located just west of the airport, you can save by asking for a combination ticket (€6) to both.

---

the car park. The **city walls** once extended from here to the Evpalinos Tunnel.

**Archaeological Museum
of Pythagorio**　MUSEUM
(☎22730 62811; Polykratous; admission €4; ☉9am-3pm Tue-Sun) This sparkling and renovated museum contains well-displayed finds from Pythagorio and also from the 6th-century-BC Heraion, less than 5km away, along with striking pottery pieces spanning 9th century BC through Greece's golden age. Museum labels are in Greek, English and German.

Moni Panagias Spilianis　MONASTERY
(Monastery of the Virgin of the Grotto; ☎22730 61361; ☉9am-8pm) FREE About 1.5km northwest of Pythagorio, the road forks right past traces of an ancient theatre, before reaching this grotto monastery. The walk meanders up through old olive groves and, despite tourist kiosks, is a welcome respite from the summer heat, with views to the nearby Turkish coast.

🏃 Activities

Along with swimming and sunbathing, try scuba diving with **Samos Dive Center** (☎6972997645; samosdiving@gmail.com; Konstantinou Kanari 1) or **Aegean Scuba** (☎6936565707, 22730 23006; Agios Nikolaou 8). Professional instructors lead dives in search of moray eels, sea stars, octopuses, lobsters and other critters lurking in the sponge-covered crevices around Pythagorio. A two-dive half-day for beginners costs around €35; a full-day dive, including open-water options, starts around €80. Snorkelling (€20) is also offered.

🛏 Sleeping

⭐ **Pension Despina**　PENSION €
(☎6938120399, 22730 61677; www.samosrooms.gr/despina/more.html; A Nikolaou; r/studio €35/40; ❄ 🛜) An impeccably well-kept and quiet pension on the small and central Plateia Irinis, the Despina offers attractive rooms and studios with overhead fans, balconies (some kitchenettes), plus a relaxing back garden, along with very friendly owner Athina.

Philoxenia Pension　PENSION €
(☎6973768371, 22730 61055; www.pensionphiloxeniasamos.blogspot.com; r/studio from €30/35; ❄ @ 🛜) Opposite the archaeological museum, look for the small courtyard bursting with flowers. Rooms are spotless and comfortable, with overhead fans and balcony views of the hills, along with common kitchen and laundry facilities. The owner's family lives in an adjacent apartment, so help is never far off.

Polyxeni Hotel   HOTEL €
(☑ 22730 61590; www.polyxenihotel.com; s/d/tr incl breakfast from €40/50/65; ✻ ☎) In the middle of the port, turn left from the main road to find this well-managed seafront lodging with several balcony harbour-view rooms (with overhead fans and double-glazed windows), a popular lobby cocktail bar, adjacent gift shop and cheerful staff.

🍴 Eating & Drinking

★ Kafeneio To Mouragio   CAFE €
(☑ 22730 62390; mezedhes €3-6; ⊙ 8am-midnight; ☎) The warm ambience and predominantly Greek clientele hint at the fact that this place delivers the goods with snacks such as chickpea croquettes and assorted mezedhes. Coffee in the morning, and later iced ouzo, wine and beer. Customers are welcome to leave their luggage for free.

Faros   TAVERNA €
(☑ 22730 62464; mezedhes €4-6, mains €6.50-10; ⊙ 11am-midnight; ☎) This eastern harbour eatery, beyond Elia Taverna, sits on the bay. A tad pricey, Faros is a minimalist, contemporary Mediterranean bistro serving excellent versions of *mesklo* cheese, dolmadhes or grilled octopus for mezedhes and *exohiko* (stuffed lamb) and ever-popular *barbounia* (red mullet) for mains.

To Tigani tis Platias   TAVERNA €
(☑ 6971673770; Plateia Irinis; mains €5-9; ☑) Beautiful Greek standards, served just opposite Pension Despina. Popular with both locals and visitors, especially for great veg choices such as baked feta, *gigantes* (white beans) and zucchini balls, all a cut above. Meat grills also superb, along with shady setting, cheerful service and good wine.

Robinson   FAST FOOD €
(pitta gyros €2-4; ⊙ 11am-11pm) Excellent pit stop for juicy pitta souvlaki and *gyros*. At the main junction of Pythagorio, a few doors towards the port.

Elia Taverna   GREEK €
(☑ 22730 61436; mains €5.50-9; ⊙ lunch & dinner; ☎) At the far northeast corner of the port, Elia (Olive) serves excellent *mayirefta* such as *yemista* (stuffed tomatoes) and *kleftiko* (slow oven-baked lamb) in a shaded outdoor setting, a relaxing distance from the harbour buzz.

Taverna Maritsa   TAVERNA €€
(☑ 22730 61957; mains €5-11; ⊙ lunch & dinner) Relax away from the waterfront at this side-street *psarotaverna,* near the car park for Pythagorio. Fresh fish by the kilo and hearty soups and salads, with draught wine.

Notos   BAR
(☑ 22730 62351; Tarsanas Beach; ⊙ noon-late; ☎) From the main road, turn right (south) at the port to find this popular late-night music bar and taverna, opposite a public car park. Live music most Tuesdays and Saturdays.

ℹ Information

There are several ATMs along the main streets. Most cafes and restaurants offer free wi-fi. Taxis gather on Egeou Pelagous, next to the harbour.

By Ship Travel (☑ 22730 62285; www.byship travel.gr) Helpful full-service travel agency, offering car hire, accommodation, and air and ferry tickets. At the junction entering town.

Post office (Lykourgou Logotheti; ⊙ 7.30am-2pm)

Tourist office (☑ 22730 61389; deap5@otenet. gr; Lykourgou Logotheti; ⊙ 8am-9.30pm)

Tourist police (☑ 22730 61100; Lykourgou Logotheti)

Around Pythagorio

The Heraion   Το Ηραίον

Ireon, the resort village beyond the archaeological site, is smaller and lower key than Pythagorio. It has a variety of nightlife and bathing options and is popular for moonrise watching.

◉ Sights

Heraion   ARCHAEOLOGICAL SITE
(adult/child €4/free; ⊙ 8.30am-3pm Tue-Sun) From the scattered ruins of the Heraion, one can't imagine the former magnificence of this ancient sanctuary of the goddess Hera, 4km west of Pythagorio. The 'Sacred Way' was once flanked by thousands of marble statues, and led from the city to this World Heritage–listed site, built at Hera's legendary birthplace. However, enough survives to provide a glimpse of a sanctuary that was four times larger than the Parthenon.

Built in the 6th century BC, the Heraion was constructed over an earlier Mycenaean temple. Plundering and earthquakes have left only one column standing, though extensive foundations remain. Other remains include a stoa, a 5th-century Christian basilica and the headless, and unsettling, statues of a family, the Geneleos Group. Archaeologists continue to unearth treasures.

🛏 Sleeping & Eating

★**Hotel Restaurant Cohyli**   HOTEL €
(☑ 6977809389, 22730 95282; www.hotel-cohyli.com; Ireon; s/d/tr incl breakfast from €35/45/55; P❄🤶) You'll sleep and eat well at this welcoming hotel-taverna gem. Rooms are cosy and clean, with fridges and fans. When you're hungry, just relocate to the shaded courtyard next door to sample excellent mezedhes, *saganaki* (fried cheese), fresh fish and breakfast with 'sunshine eggs'. A small beach is across the road, and there's live acoustic music many summer evenings.

AegeioTaverna   SEAFOOD €
(Ireon; mains €4.50-8.50; ⊙lunch & dinner) This popular waterfront taverna fills up on Sundays in particular, when Greeks come from Pythagorio and environs to eat fresh seafood.

Restaurant Glaros   SEAFOOD €
(☑ 22730 95457; Ireon; mains €4-7.50) This no-frills Ireon original serves traditional fish soup and finger-wrapped dolmadhes, enjoyable from the vine-covered verandah facing a topaz blue sea.

Psili Ammos   Ψιλή Άμμος

Sandy Psili Ammos, 11km east of Pythagorio, is the best of the southeastern beaches. A lovely cove facing Turkey, it's bordered by shady trees and has shallow, kid-friendly waters. Several good fish tavernas compete for the best bay view. Sleep the sea and sardines off at the classy **Apartments Elena** (☑ 6974029932, 22730 23645; www.elenaapartments.gr; Psili Ammos; s/d from €30/40; P❄🤶), where the rooms are spacious and comfy.

Pythagorio to Drakeï
Πυθαγόριο προς Δρακαίους

The drive west from Pythagorio traverses spectacular mountain scenery with stunning views of the south coast. This route also features many little signposted huts, where beekeepers sell superlative but inexpensive Samian honey.

Along the way, around the village of **Pyrgos**, you'll be treated to magnificent views of mountain, sky and sea before reaching **Ormos Marathokambou**. Another 4km west is **Votsalakia** (often called Kambos), with its long, sandy beach. To escape the midsummer mob, however, head 3km further west to more tranquil **Psili Ammos Beach**, stay the night in domatia here and sample the fresh fish at the beach tavernas.

Hikers keen on exploring the flanks of **Mt Kerkis**, or even reaching its peak (1434m), should enquire in Votsalakia for the trailhead, which passes the **convent of Evangelistrias** on the way. Past Kambos, the rugged western route, undeveloped and tranquil, skirts Mt Kerkis until reaching the villages of **Kallithea** and Drakeï, where the road abruptly ends. A walking trail is the only link between this point and Potami on the north coast.

Northern Samos

Vathy to Karlovasi
Βαθύ προς Καρλόβασι

From Vathy, the coast road west passes a number of beaches and resorts. **Kokkari** (10km from Vathy) was once a fishing village, but has become more of a small resort. Windsurfers test the waves from its long pebble beach in summer, and the nearby beaches of **Lemonaki**, **Tsamadou**, **Tsambou** and **Livadhaki** draw swimmers and sunbathers.

Continuing west, the landscape becomes more forested and mountainous. Take the left-hand turn-off after 5km to reach the lovely mountain village of **Vourliotes**. Its multicoloured, shuttered houses cluster around a *plateia*. Walkers can enjoy an 8km **loop trail** between Vourliotes and Kokkari through olive groves and lofty woodlands – one of those magical *monopati* (footpath) routes where you hardly realize you've been climbing at all. Find the free walking map in Vourliotes.

Back on the coast road, look for the signposted turn-off for another fragrant village, **Manolates**, 5km further up the lower slopes of Mt Ambelos (Karvouni; 1150m). Set amid thick pine and deciduous forests, and boasting gorgeous traditional houses, Manolates is nearly encircled by mountains and offers a cooler alternative to the sweltering coast.

The shops of both Vourliotes and Manolates sell handmade ceramic art and icons. Good tavernas are plentiful and, despite the more touristy patina of Manolates, both villages are worth visiting for a glimpse of old Samos.

Back on the coast heading west, the road continues through flowery **Agios Konstantinos** before coming to workaday Karlovasi, Samos' third port, home to several hotels, tavernas and **Rhenia Tours** (☑ 22730 62280) for ferry tickets and reliable information. The town's blue-collar history is on display at the **Karlovasi Tannery Museum** (⊙9am-

1pm Tue-Sun) `FREE` and the **Karlovasi Folk Art Museum** (☑ 22730 62286; ⊙ 9am-1pm Tue-Sun) `FREE`. The old village, Palio Karlovasi, above the port is well worth the short drive up the hill, though you can't go further than the small car park, from where a 500m walk brings you to the chapel of Agia Triada with panoramic views.

Just 3km beyond Karlovassi lies the sand-and-pebble **Potami Beach**, blessed with good swimming and a reggae beach bar. It's complemented by nearby **forest waterfalls**; head west 50m from the beach and they're signposted on the left. Entering the forest you'll first encounter the centuries-old **Metamorfosis Sotiros chapel**, where the devout light candles. Continuing about 1.5km through the wooded trail along the river brings you to a river channel where you must wade or swim before enjoying a splash under the 2m-high waterfalls.

🛏 Sleeping

⭐ Studios Angela
APARTMENT €

(☑ 22730 94478; www.studios-angela.gr; Manolates; d €35; ❄) A great budget choice, these five studios near the church in Manolates, built into a hillside overlooking the sea, are traditionally furnished with modern kitchenettes, views to the sea and the hospitality of owner Angela.

Kokkari Beach Hotel
HOTEL €€

(☑ 22730 92238; www.kokkaribeach.com; Kokkari; s/d/tr incl breakfast €50/60/75; P ❄ 🛜 🏊) This striking, upmarket establishment, 1km west of the bus stop, is set back from the road in a pastel-green-and-blue building, just opposite the beach. The airy and cool rooms are equally colourful.

🍴 Eating

⭐ Hippy's Restaurant Café
TAVERNA €

(☑ 6976770021, 22730 33796; Potami Beach; mains €2-7; ⊙ 9am-after sunset; P 🛜) This cool open-air cafe-bar is a family affair, combining Greek and South Seas decor with jazz, reggae, classical, trip hop and ambient sounds. There are good omelettes, pasta, grilled fresh fish and skewers, plus owner Apolstolis' naturally fermented wine and assorted drinks and juices. The place has a relaxing and rambling end-of-the-road feel to it, with hospitality and character to spare.

Taverna Bira
TAVERNA €

(☑ 22730 92350; Kokkari; mains €5-9; ⊙ lunch & dinner) Opposite the bus stop, Bira is an el-egant, old-fashioned taverna, offering local favourites such as *ladhera*, traditional olive-oil-rich vegie dishes that are the mainstay of religious fasting. *Horta* (wild greens) and *anthoi* (stuffed zucchini flowers) are among the tasty offerings.

Café Bar Cavos
CAFE €

(☑ 22730 92426; Kokkari; mains €6-12; ⊙ 9am-midnight; 🛜) Efficient and comfortable Kokkari harbour bar, with good breakfasts, afternoon snacks, fresh juices and evening cocktails. Decent prices, plus free wi-fi and satellite TV for big sport events. Ask about Uli's homemade cake of the day.

O Tarsanas Restaurant
TAVERNA €

(☑ 22730 92337; Kokkari; mains €6-12; ⊙ 5pm-midnight; 🛜) Named for Kokkari's old boat-building area, this authentic old-style Greek taverna – nothing more, nothing less – does great pizzas and *mousakas*. Welcoming owner Kyriakos rolls out luscious dolmadhes and pours his own homemade wine.

Galazio Pigadi
TAVERNA €

(Vourliotes; mains €5-8; ⊙ 9am-11pm) Just past the *plateia* in Vourliotes, this atmospheric old eatery has a variety of mezedhes, including *bourekakia* (crunchy cheese-in-filo pastries). Worthy local wine on hand.

Loukas Taverna
TAVERNA €

(Manolates; mains €5-8; ⊙ lunch & dinner) Upon entering Manolates, you'll see signs, one after the other, pointing the way to this traditional eatery above the village where proud owner Manolis serves up excellent and hearty taverna standards along with his own wines – red, white and sweet.

Taverna AAA
TAVERNA €

(☑ 22730 94472; Manolates; mains €5-10; ⊙ lunch & dinner) Step down into a cosy and flowery courtyard at 'Tria Alpha', an inviting taverna along the main walk through Manolates with traditional Greek-kitchen cuisine and cheery service.

ℹ Information

Find Terrain Editions' map of Samos for exploring the region, available from **Lexis Bookstore** (☑ 22730 92271; ⊙ 9.30am-10.30pm) in Kokkari, which also carries foreign books, magazines and newspapers.

EOT (Greek National Tourist Organisation; ☑ 22730 92217; Kokkari; ⊙ 9am-1pm Mon-Sat; 🛜)

CHIOS

ΧΙΟΣ

POP 53,820

Likeable Chios (*hee*-os) is one of Greece's bigger islands and, with its small neighbour Inousses, is significant in national history as the ancestral home of shipping barons. Its varied terrain ranges from lonesome mountain crags in the north, to the citrus-grove estates of Kampos, near the island's port capital in the centre, to the fertile Mastihohoria in the south – the only place in the world where mastic trees (p575) are commercially productive. Chians are a hospitable lot who take great pride in their history, traditions

Chios

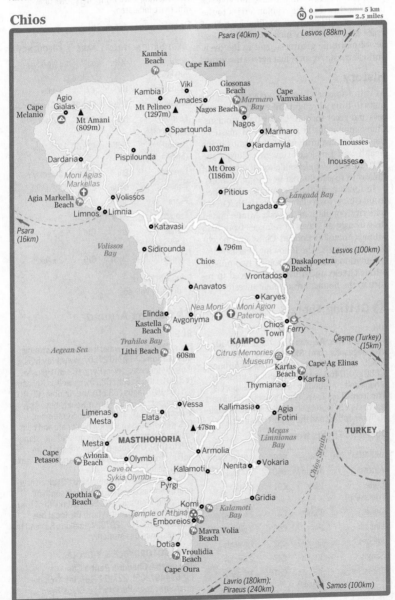

and livelihood. For the visitor, this translates into opportunities for interaction with Chian culture, ranging from art and cuisine to hiking and eco-activities.

Chios enjoys regular boat connections throughout the northeastern Aegean Islands, and has an airport. Between them, the ports of Chios Town in the east and Volissos in the northwest offer regular ferries to the intriguing, little-visited satellite islands of Psara and Inousses, which share Chios' legacy of maritime greatness, and to the lively Turkish coastal resorts just across the water.

History

As with Samos and Lesvos, geographic proximity to Turkey brought Chios both great success and great tragedy. Under the Ottomans, Chios' monopolistic production of mastic – the sultan's favourite gum – brought Chians wealth and privilege. However, during the 1821–29 War of Independence, thousands of Chians were slaughtered by Ottoman troops.

In 1922 a military campaign launched from Chios to reclaim lands with Greek-majority populations in Asia Minor ended disastrously, as waves of refugees from Asia Minor (Anatolia) flooded Chios and neighbouring islands. The following year saw the 'population exchange', in which two million ethnic Greeks and Turks were forced to return to the homelands of their ancestors.

🛈 Getting There & Away

AIR

During summer, **Aegean Air** (☑ 801 1120000; www.aegeanair.com), **Sky Express** (☑ 28102 23835; www.skyexpress.gr) and **Astra Airlines** (☑ 801 7007466; www.astra-airlines.gr) serve Athens and surrounding islands. The airport is 4km from Chios Town. There's no bus; an airport taxi costs €8. Tickets are available from Hatzelenis Tours (p573) and the airport counters.

Domestic Flights from Chios

DESTINATION	TIME	FARE	FREQUENCY
Athens	45min	€50-72	3-4 daily
Crete (Heraklion)	1¼hr	€91	2 weekly
Lesvos	35min	€47	2 weekly
Limnos	1¾hr	€56	2 weekly
Rhodes	1¾hr	€62	2 weekly
Samos	30min	€47	2 weekly
Thessaloniki	3hr (via Athens)	€81	1-2 daily

BOAT

Buy tickets from Hatzelenis Tours (p573) or Michalakis Travel (p573).

In addition to regular ferry service to nearby Inousses, daily **water taxis** (☑ 6945361281, 6944168104) go between Langada and Inousses (€65, shared between up to eight passengers). The following leave from Chios Town unless otherwise indicated.

Boat Services from Chios

DESTINATION	TIME	FARE	FREQUENCY
Ikaria (Agios Kirykos)	4½hr	€17	1 weekly
Inousses	1hr	€7	1 daily
Kavala	12hr	€31.50	2-3 weekly
Lavrio (via Psara)*	8hr	€26	1-2 weekly
Lesvos (Mytilini town)	2½hr	€19.50	2-3 daily
Limnos	8hr	€31	2 weekly
Piraeus	6-9hr	€38	1-2 daily
Psara	3hr	€7-14	1 daily
Psara**	1¼hr	€7-14	2 weekly
Samos (Karlovasi)	2hr	€14	1-2 weekly
Samos (Vathy)	2½hr	€16	2 weekly

* departs Mesta
** departs Volissos

🛈 Getting Around

BUS

From Chios Town's waterfront **long-distance bus station** (☑ 22710 27507; www.ktelchios.gr), daily green buses serve Pyrgi (€2.80), Mesta (€3.90), Lithi Beach (€2.70), as well as Kardamyla (€3.10), Nagos (€3.80) and Kambia (€5.40) via Langada (€1.80). Thrice-weekly buses serve Volissos (€4.50). From June to September, this well-organised station (with cafe and coin lockers) offers bus day tours around the island (€8 to €15). One tour takes in Volisso to the north, stopping at Agia Markela and then Limnis with time for a swim.

Blue city buses (on Vounakiou Sq) also serve nearby Karfas Beach (€1.50), just south of town, and Vrontados (€1.50), just north of town. Schedules are posted at both the **local bus station** (☑ 22710 22079; Vounakiou Sq) and the long-distance bus station.

CAR, MOTORCYCLE & BICYCLE

The reliable **Chandris Rent a Car** (☑ 6944972051, 22710 27194; info@chandrisrentacar.gr; Porfyra 5) is Chios Town's longest-running agency, and owner Kostas Chandris gladly provides island information and reasonable rates.

A new municipal service provides coin-op **bicycle rentals** (☑ 22713 06724; per hourr/day €3/8) by the hour or the day, at the northwest corner of the waterfront.

TAXI

Taxis are plentiful in Chios Town, and can also be hired by the hour (€25). Red taxis are for Chios Town, and grey taxis for the villages.

Chios Town   Χίος

POP 23,780

The main port and capital on the central east coast is home to almost half the island's inhabitants. Behind the long, busy waterfront lies a quieter, intriguing old quarter, where some lingering traditional Turkish houses stand around a Genoese castle and city walls. There's also a busy market area behind the waterfront, and spacious public gardens (Vounaki) where an open-air cinema operates on summer evenings. An old-fashioned *hammam* (Turkish baths) can be explored at the *kastro* (castle). The nearest decent beach is popular Karfas, 6km south.

⊙ Sights

Korais Library & Argentis Folkloric Museum   MUSEUM
(☑ 22710 44246; www.koraeslibrary.gr; Korai 3; entry €2; ⊙ 8am-3pm Mon-Fri, 5-8pm Tue & Fri, 9am-2pm Sat) On the upper floor of the remarkable Korais Library, the Filippos Argenti Folkloric Museum contains a 19th-century birthing chair, along with shepherds' tools, embroidery, traditional costumes and portraits of the wealthy Argentis family. Born in Marseilles in 1891, Argentis devoted his life to researching Chian history. The library holds medicinal texts from the 15th century.

Archaeological Museum   MUSEUM
(☑ 22710 44239; Mihalon 10; entry €2; ⊙ 8am-3pm Tue-Sun) Along with prehistoric and Archaic treasures from the excavations of the British School at Emporios, there are impressive Neolithic and classical finds (coins, sculptures, pottery) from Agios Galas and Fana.

Byzantine Museum   MUSEUM
(☑ 22710 26866; Plateia Vounaki; entry €2; ⊙ 8.30am-3.30pm Tue-Sun) The museum, in a 19th-century Ottoman mosque, the Medjitie Djami, contains relics from the Byzantine, post-Byzantine, Genoese and Islamic periods,

including old canons, fine icons and Jewish, Muslim and Armenian tombstones.

Giustiniani Palace Museum   MUSEUM
(☑ 22710 22819; entry €2; ⊙ 8am-3pm Tue-Sun) Near the main gate of the *kastro*, the tiny museum (or 'Palataki') still looks like the 15th-century fortress it once was. Of particular interest are 12 Byzantine frescoes of the prophets, dating from the 13th century, along with an 18th-century full-length icon of the Archangel Michael.

🛏 Sleeping

★**Chios Rooms**   PENSION €
(☑ 22710 20198; www.chiosrooms.gr; Aigaiou 110; s/d/tr from €25/30/40; 🛜) An eclectic, hostel-like neoclassical house on the waterfront, Chios Rooms is the inspiration of its owner, native New Zealander Don, who also provides fresh spring water for his guests. Marked by handsome vintage furnishings, traditional rugs and lofty ceilings, the place has character to spare. Most rooms have private bathrooms; other rooms share.

Rooms Alex   PENSION €
(☑ 6979535256; roomsalex@hotmail.gr; Livanou 29; s/d €30/45) Host and former sea captain Alex Stoupas' handmade model ships decorate each of the simple but clean rooms. The *kapetanios,* '100% helpful', as he'll happily tell you, picks guests up from the ferry and speaks English, French and Spanish.

Ionia Rooms   PENSION €
(☑ 22710 82979, 6932467821; www.ioniarooms. gr; s/d/tr incl breakfast from €25/35/45; ✱🛜) A short block from the busy waterfront brings you to this attractive, clean and efficient seven-room domatia, with minifridge and mosquito screens. Ask for a rear room if you're not fond of the sound of early-morning motorbikes.

Hotel Kyma   HOTEL €€
(☑ 22710 44500; www.hotelkyma.com; Evgenias Chandris 1; s/d/tr incl breakfast from €50/65/80; ✱🛜) Aside from the sea-view balconies and stately decor of this converted mansion, what makes the Kyma more than just another period hotel is its service – owner Theodoros Spordylis solves problems in English, Italian, Turkish and German.

🍴 Eating

★**Hotzas Taverna**   TAVERNA €
(☑ 22710 42787; Kondyli 3; mains €5.50-9; ⊙ dinner Mon-Sat) This comfortable and attractive

taverna above Chios Town serves fine Greek standards with a twist, such as lamb kebab with yoghurt and aragala, and white beans with tomato and mandarin, and dolmadhes (vine-wrapped rice parcels) with lemon. There is a variety of great vegie dishes, including risotto. Everything is *herisia* (handmade), from pasta to dessert.

★ Kechibari Ouzerie
MEZHEDES €

(6942425459; Agion Anargyron 7; mains €4-7; ⊙ lunch Jun-Sep) This cosy gem of an *ouzerie*, a 10-minute walk up from the waterfront, serves a variety of small plates in addition to excellent fish, mussels, baked potatoes and grilled meats. Snappy service and reasonable prices. Opposite the church.

Ixthioskala
SEAFOOD €

(22710 42114; mains €4.50-9; ⊙ lunch & dinner) Very good, very Greek *psarotaverna*, behind the north end of the port, towards the old Turkish baths. A favourite of fishers and other port regulars, a world away from the mostly so-so waterfront eateries.

Ouzeri Tzivaeri
TAVERNA €

(22710 43559; Neorion 13; mezedhes €3-8) Busy portside eatery that touts oil-drenched sun-dried tomatoes, grilled cod, traditional Chios sausages and fresh *gavros*.

Chios Town

🛍 Shopping

Mastihashop   BEAUTY
(📞 22710 81600; www.mastihashop.com; Aigaiou
36) Efficient and attractive shop with a
range of mastic-based products such as lotions, toothpaste, soaps and condiments.
Ask for a sample of pure mastic to chew.

Sarandis Tourist Shop   SOUVENIRS, BOOKS
(📞 22710 24224; www.saranti.gr; cnr Aigaiou &
Roïdi) Rambling Sarandis carries a bit of
everything, from cold drinks and wine to
mastic-style lotions and good island maps.

ℹ Information

Banks with ATMs can be found along the waterfront and in the *plateia*. Free wi-fi is common at
waterfront cafes.

Chios General Hospital (📞 22710 44302; El
Venizelou 7)

Chios Tourist Office (📞 22713 51726; www.
chios.gr; Kanari 18; ⏱ 7am-3pm & 6-10pm Jul
& Aug) Island transport and accommodation
info, plus useful free booklet, *Cultural Routes
of Chios*.

Hatzelenis Tours (📞 22710 20002; www.info-
chios.com; Aigaiou 2) Opposite the port, this
dependable full-service travel agency arranges
ferry and air tickets, excursions (including to
nearby Inousses), accommodation and reasonable car hire.

Michalakis Travel (📞 22710 40070; www.
michalakistravel.gr; Neorion)

Post office (📞 22710 44350; Plateia Vounaki;
⏱ 7.30am-2pm)

Tourist police (📞 22710 44427/9; Neorion)

Chios Town

◉ **Sights**
1 Archaeological Museum C5
2 Byzantine Museum..............................A2
3 Giustiniani Palace Museum................ A1
4 Korais Library & Argentis
    Folkloric Museum B4

🛏 **Sleeping**
5 Chios Rooms C4
6 Hotel Kyma D4
7 Ionia Rooms...B4
8 Rooms Alex...C4

🍽 **Eating**
9 Ouzeri Tzivaeri B1

🛍 **Shopping**
10 Mastihashop..B2
11 Sarandis Tourist Shop B2

Central Chios

North of Chios Town about 4km, **Vrontados**
is the site of Homer's legendary stone chair,
the **Daskalopetra** ('Teacher's Stone'), a rock
pinnacle close to the sea that's an obvious
choice for holding class.

Immediately south of Chios Town is
Kampos, a lush area with citrus trees where
wealthy Genoese and Greek merchant
families summered from the 14th century onwards. You can see elaborate gardens
and high-walled mansions, some restored,
others crumbling. The handsome **Citrus
Memories Museum** (📞 22710 31513; www.
citrus-chios.gr; Kampos; ⏱ 10am-9pm Jun-Sep, to
6pm Oct-Apr) FREE documents the agricultural base of this community with summer
concerts and art exhibits.

At the island's centre is **Nea Moni** (New
Monastery; ⏱ 9am-1pm & 4-7pm) FREE, a World
Heritage–listed 11th-century Byzantine monastery. Once one of Greece's richest monasteries, Nea Moni attracted preeminent
Byzantine artists to create the mosaics in its
katholikon (principal church). Disastrously,
during the Greek War of Independence, the
Turks torched the monastery and massacred
its monks. Another catastrophe occurred
with an 1881 earthquake that demolished the
katholikon dome. It is now a convent.

Another solemn site lies 10km northwest,
at the end of a silent road. **Anavatos**, filled
with abandoned grey-stone houses and
narrow stepped pathways, was built on a
precipitous cliff over which villagers hurled
themselves to avoid capture during Turkish
reprisals in 1822. Nowadays, it's referred to
as the 'ghost village'.

The nearby village of **Avgonyma**, in between Anavatos and Nea Moni, is a perfect
base to explore the area. **Pyrgos** (📞 22710
42175; www.chiospyrgosrooms.gr; Avgonyma;
mains €5-10; ⏱ breakfast, lunch & dinner) awaits,
along with the adjacent **To Asteri** (📞 22710
20577; Avgonyma; mains €4-7.50; ⏱ lunch & dinner), great for a drink or ice cream at sunset.

Of the quieter central-west-coast beaches,
picturesque **Lithi** is most popular, with several inviting tavernas next to the small bay.

🛏 Sleeping

Spiti Elaionas   APARTMENT €
(📞 22710 20002; mano2@otenet.gr; Kampos;
d from €40) Two traditional and tastefully
decorated stone houses, 300m from Karfas
Beach in a quiet hillside setting, with great
views across to the Turkish coast.

Perleas Mansion HISTORIC HOTEL **€€**

(☑ 22710 32217; www.perleas.gr; Vitiadou, Kampos; s/d/tr incl breakfast from €80/100/120; P ✳ 🛜) The restored Perleas Mansion offers seven elegant and well-appointed apartments. The relaxing estate, built in 1640, exemplifies high Genoese architecture. The restaurant serves traditional Greek cuisine.

Northern Chios

The craggy peaks of Mt Pelineo, Mt Oros and Mt Amani mark the drive north from Chios Town across the island's boulder-strewn lunar interior.

Near to Chios Town and the scattered settlements of Vrontados, Langada is the next village of note, a relaxed cove of pine trees, homes, domatia and tavernas and a launching point for water taxis to nearby Inousses. The most noise you're likely to hear might be a few caged birds entertaining the taverna tables where the octopus you see drying in the sun come evening time.

The main villages of Marmaro and Kardamyla follow, containing ancestral homes of many wealthy shipowning families. At Nagos, the road continues northwest, skirting Mt Pelineo (1297m), then winding and twisting its way through Kambia, high on a ridge overlooking the sea. In the northwest, wild camping is allowed around Agia Galas, also home to a popular cave.

The central road will lead you south via Fita and Diefha to Volissos, Homer's legendary birthplace, with its impressive Genoese fort. Around 5km beyond Volissos' working port of Limnia (for departures to Psara Island), you will reach Moni Agias Markellas, named for Chios' patron saint. From Volissos the coastal road continues south until Elinda, then returns eastward. Worth the trip to Volissos by itself is the excellent restaurant (and domatia), Taverna Fabrika (☑ 22740 22045, 6976255829; fabrika_chios@yahoo.com; Volissos; mains €6-8.50; ⊙ lunch & dinner).

Southern Chios

Unique southern Chios is arguably the island's best destination. Though it grows elsewhere in the Aegean, the gum-producing mastic tree of Chios has for centuries been the sole commercial producer of mastic gum. The tree thrives in a fertile, reddish territory known as the Mastihohoria (Mastic villages). This region of rolling hills, criss-crossed with elaborate stone walls

running through olive and mastic groves, is highly atmospheric.

The Ottoman rulers' penchant for mastic made the Mastihohoria wealthy for centuries. Some architectural wonders remain in the villages of Pyrgi and Mesta. The former features houses decorated in unusual colourful patterns, while the latter is a car-free, walled fortress settlement built by the Genoese in the 14th century.

Pyrgi Πυργί

POP 1040

Located 24km southwest of Chios Town, Pyrgi (peer-*ghi*), the Mastihohoria's largest village, juxtaposes traditional and modern architecture, with facades decorated in intricate grey-and-white patterns, some geometric and others based on flowers, leaves and animals. The technique, called *xysta,* uses equal amounts of cement, volcanic sand and lime as well as bent forks and a fine eye.

Pyrgi's central square is flanked by tavernas, shops and the little 12th-century Church of Agios Apostolos (⊙ 10am-1pm Tue-Thu & Sat). East of the square, note the house with a plaque attesting to its former occupant – one Christopher Columbus, also a fan of mastic gum, though he apparently preferred it as a sealant in boat construction.

Six kilometres southeast of Pyrgi, Emboreios was the Mastihohoria's port back when the mastic producers were high rollers. Today it's much quieter, though it does boast Mavra Volia Beach, named for its black volcanic pebbles. Domatia and tavernas are available, and the archaeological ruins of an early Bronze Age temple to Athina are signed nearby.

Mesta Μεστά

Mesta (mest-*aah*) is a truly memorable village and one of Greece's most unusual. Here, appealing stone alleyways, intertwined with flowers and intricate balconies, are completely enclosed by thick defensive walls – the work of Chios' former Genoese rulers, who built this fortress town in the 14th century to keep pirates and would-be invaders out.

Mesta is an ingenious example of medieval defensive architecture, featuring a double set of walls, four gates and a pentagonal structure. Since the rooftops are interconnected, with the right guide you can actually walk across the entire town. In medieval times, mastic was a hot commodity, prized for its medicinal powers, meaning Mesta had to be especially well fortified.

As a car-free village, it's a relaxing, romantic place where children can run around safely. Mesta also makes a good base for hill walking, exploring southern beaches and caves, and participating in cultural and ecotourism activities.

Village life converges on the central square with its small cafes and restaurants and, nearby, the enormous Church of the Taxiarhes. Along the tranquil, secluded lanes, rooms for rent are almost indistinguishable from the attached residences.

Sights & Activities

Churches of the Taxiarhes CHURCH
(⊙9am-1pm Tue-Sat) There are two Churches of the Taxiarhes (Archangels). The older and smaller one dates from Byzantine times and features a magnificent 17th-century iconostasis. The larger, 19th-century church was built entirely from the townspeople's donations and labour.

★Masticulture Ecotourism Activities ECOTOUR
(☑22710 76084, 6976113007; www.masticulture.com; tours from €18) To get your hands dirty and participate in traditional cultural activities like Chian farming, contact Vassilis and Roula, who provide unique ecotourism opportunities that introduce visitors to the local community, its history and culture. Activities include mastic cultivation tours, stargazing and bicycle and sea-kayak outings. They can help find area accommodation and offer tips for visiting nearby Psara island.

Tortuga Diving Center WATER SPORTS
(Chios Underwater; ☑6906062901; www.medi-sea.blogspot.com) Provides certified scuba diving and offers sea kayaking and snorkeling, along with coffee, snacks, great views and a chilled-out ambience at Apothika Beach.

Sleeping & Eating

Masticulture Ecotourism Activities can help arrange rooms in Mesta, Pyrgi and even less-visited Olymbi.

Dhimitris Pipidhis Rooms PENSION €
(☑22710 76029, 6937829450; www.pippidisrooms.gr; house €60-70; ☀) Friendly, English-speaking Dhimitris and Koula Pipidhis (aka Popi) rent two traditional houses in Mesta. Each is well appointed, with two bedrooms, a *pounti* (Mesta-styled atrium), kitchen and washing machine. Excellent value; book ahead in summer.

Lida Mary Rooms & Suites HISTORIC HOTEL €
(☑22710 76217, 6976629668; www.lidamary.gr; r from €45; ☀☎) A lovely and well-managed option in the village, run by the hospitable and helpful Tasos. A few rooms overlook the *plateia*.

Despina Karabela Traditional Apartments APARTMENT €
(☑22710 76065; www.taste-mesta.gr; s/d €40/50; ☀☎) A short walk from the square (outside the walled village), these lovely apartments are cosy and tastefully decorated. Exposed stone highlights the interior, while the loft 'bedroom' is a raised platform. Despina also promotes the local food scene; ask for a wander to the nearby family fields.

Anna Floradis Rooms PENSION €
(☑6972490707, 22710 76455; www.floradirooms.gr; s/d €40/50; ☀☎) Friendly and welcoming Anna Floradis speaks French and some English and maintains handsome rooms, studios and kitchenette suites throughout Mesta village.

Medieval Castle Suites HOTEL €€
(☑22710 76025; www.medievalcastlesuites.com; d/tr/f from from €60/80/110) The Castle Suites are a collection of 20 rooms spread throughout the village, all with traditional stone touches, modern bathrooms and a few with fireplaces and even computers. Rooms vary considerably in size and proximity to the *plateia*.

★Meseonas TAVERNA €
(☑22710 76050; Plateia Taxiarhon; mains €5-10) With tables spread across Plateia Taxiarhon, this relaxed and reliable eatery appeals to locals and tourists alike and serves hearty

portions of *mayirefta,* beef *keftedhes* (rissoles) and grills. Everything is local, right down to the friendly host family's *souma* (mastic-flavoured firewater).

Shopping

Ceramic Art Studio   ARTS
(Nikos Balatsos; ☑ 22710 76257) Artist and master ceramicist Nikos Balatsos runs this rambling and delightful studio on the road just outside the main wall of the village.

Getting There & Away

From Mesta there are regular buses to Chios Town. English-speaking **Dimitris Kokkinos** (☑ 6972543543) provides a taxi service – sample fares from Mesta include Limenas Mesta €7, Olymbi €5, Pyrgi €20 and Chios Town €45.

Around Mesta

Mesta's west-coast port of **Limenas Mesta** (also called Limenas) is home to a couple of decent port tavernas and is a short drive from Mesta. For swimming, head to **Apothia Beach** (7km south of Olymbi), a curving, sandy cove where the water is a stunning turquoise, backed by two *almiriki* (tamarisk) shade trees and a canteen in summer.

Around 3km southeast of Mesta is **Olymbi** – like Mesta and Pyrgi, a mastic-producing village characterised by its defensive architecture. A well-maintained 3km **trail** connects Oympi and Mesta.

A popular side trip takes you 5km south to the splendid **Cave of Sykia Olymbi** (☑ 22710 93364; entry €5; ◷ 9am-3pm Tue-Sun), signposted as 'Olympi Cave', a 150-million-year-old cavern discovered accidentally in 1985. The cave is 57m deep and is filled with multicoloured stalactites and other rock formations with whimsical names such as the Pipe Organ, Cacti and Jellyfish. It's lit with floodlights, and a series of platforms and staircases with handrails connects it all – be prepared for some climbing. The cave maintains a steady temperature of 18°C and humidity is a moist 95%. Guided tours are mandatory and run every 30 minutes.

INOUSSES   ΟΙΝΟΥΣΣΕΣ

POP 400

Just northeast of Chios Town, serene Inousses is the ancestral home of nearly a third of Greece's shipping barons (the *arhontes*), whose wealthy descendants return here annually for summer vacations from their homes in London, Paris or New York. Inousses was settled in 1750 by shipowning families from Kardamyla in northeastern Chios and some amassed huge fortunes during the 19th and early 20th centuries. Traces of this history linger in Inousses' grand mansions and ornate family mausoleums high above the sea.

Although Inousses is little visited, it does get lively come summer, with an open-air cinema, very friendly residents and a buzzing night-time waterfront. The island's port attests to its seafaring identity. Arriving by ferry, you'll see a small, green sculpted mermaid watching over the harbour – this is the **Mitera Inoussiotissa** (Mother of Inoussa), protector of mariners. Inousses also boasts a merchant marine academy.

Sights & Activities

Inousses has numerous hill-walking opportunities and pristine beaches. Just a 10-minute walk from the port, you'll find pretty and swimmable **Kakopetria Beach**. Another five to 10 minutes will bring you to **Bilali Beach**, set on a tranquil bay with a not-quite-tranquil beach cantina that buzzes all night in summer. Orthodox pilgrims visit the **Evangelismou Theotokou Monastery** at the western end of the island.

Nautical Museum of Inousses   MUSEUM
(☑6973412474, 22710 55182; Stefanou Tsouri 20; admission €1.50; ◷9am-2pm) Created in 1965, this handsome museum showcases the collection of local shipping magnate Antonis Lemos. Many of the models on display (some intentionally half-completed then set flush against a mirror so that you 'see' the whole vessel) were made by French prisoners of war during the Napoleonic Wars. There's also a swashbuckling collection of 18th-century muskets and sabres, a WWII-era US Navy diving helmet, a hand-crank from a 19th-century lighthouse and paintings of Nazi submarines attacking Greek sailing vessels.

NAUTICAL DILEMMA

The Nautical Museum of Inousses and ferry schedules don't mix well. For one-night visitors, the ferry arrives after the museum's daily 3pm closing and departs before it opens the following morning at 9am. But worry not, as the gracious manager-curator, Eleni Achlipta, promises to open up for anyone who calls ahead.

Mausoleum of Inousses
CEMETERY

In the leafy courtyard of the Church of Agia Paraskevi stands the Nekrotafion Inousson (Mausoleum of Inousses), where the island's shipowning dynasties have endowed the tombs of their greats with huge chambers, marble sculptures and miniature churches. It's a melancholy, moving place and speaks volumes about the worldly achievements and self-perception of the extraordinary natives of these tiny islands.

Perhaps more touching is the elegant **Platia tis Naftosynis** (Seamanship Sq) near the port, with nothing more than a proud statue, backed by a commemorative panel with the names of sailors who have died at sea, with room still for more.

🛌 Sleeping

Rooms Bilali
APARTMENT €

(☑ 6944677882; d €45-70; ❄) Contact Kostas at Bilali Beach Bar for information on well-appointed one- and two-bedroom apartments in the upper village.

Rooms Tsouri
ACCOMMODATION SERVICES €€

(☑ 6946286791; oinoussesstudios@ymail.com; d incl breakfast from €60; ❄ 🗢) For help in finding attractive rooms, contact the resourceful Despina Tsouri, in the upper village.

🍴 Eating & Drinking

Palio Teloneío
TAVERNA €

(Old Customs; mains €5-9) Excellent new eatery on the waterfront, with a bit of everything Greek, but proudest of its daily fresh catch of of *barbounia* (red mullet) and crispy *gavros*.

To Pateroniso
TAVERNA, CAFE €

(mains €5-8) Reliable taverna near the *plateia* with good grills and seafood, including the Inousses/Chios speciality of *atherinopita*, a scrumptious heads-and-all pan-fry of onions and fresh anchovies.

Tsoumpari
TAVERNA €

(mains €3.50-8) Try Tsoumpari in the upper village, 40m before the church, for a change of pace and a taste of local cooking.

Naftikos Omilos Inousson
BAR

(Yacht Club; ☑ 22720 55596; ⊙ 9am-3am; 🗢) Towards the end of the waterfront, the Inousses Yacht Club's long bar and outdoor patio are filled mostly with young Greeks and their vacationing diaspora relatives, and not a few day trippers from Chios.

Bilali Beach Bar
BAR

Cool spot on the small and shallow swimming bay at Bilali Beach, with shady tables, thumping music, good drinks, juices, smoothies and snacks. Very popular summer hang-out, from morning till wee hours.

☆ Entertainment

There's a summertime **open-air cinema** (tickets €3; ⊙ 9.30pm) near the central waterfront.

ℹ Information

The bank (with ATM) and post office are next to the nautical museum. Wi-fi is available in waterfront cafes.

Dimarhio (Town Hall; ☑ 6973412474 (after hours), 22713 51314; ⊙ 8am-3pm) Free brochures and accommodation help, opposite the ferry dock. Ask for Kostas Lignos.

Doctor (☑ 22710 55300)
Police (☑ 22710 55222)

ℹ Getting There & Away

The little *Oinoussai III* (€5 one way, one hour, daily) leaves from Chios in the afternoon and returns the next morning, warranting overnight stays. Purchase tickets on board or from **Sunrise Tours** (☑ 22710 41390; www.sunrisetours.gr; Kanari 28) in Chios Town. There are weekend summertime excursions (€20).

Daily **water taxis** (☑ 22710 55329, 6938370129, 6944168104) travel to/from Langada (20 minutes), 15km north of Chios Town. The one-way fare is a hefty €60, but split among up to eight passengers.

ℹ Getting Around

Inousses has neither buses nor car hire; ask at the port for its one semitaxi. You can also bring a bicycle or scooter on the ferry from Chios.

PSARA
ΨΑΡΑ

POP 420

Celebrated Psara (psah-*rah*) is one of maritime Greece's true oddities. A tiny speck in the sea 16km northwest of Chios, this island of scrub vegetation, wandering goats and weird red-rock formations has one settlement (also called Psara), a remote monastery and pristine beaches.

Psara looms inordinately large in modern lore. The Psariot clans became wealthy through shipping, and their participation in the 1821–29 War of Independence is etched into modern Greek history, particularly the daring exploits of Konstantine Kanaris (1793–1877), whose heroic stature propelled him, six times, to the position of prime minister.

Kanaris' most famous operation occurred on the night of 6 June 1822. In revenge for

Turkish massacres on Chios, the Psariots destroyed the Turkish admiral's flagship while the unsuspecting enemy was holding a post-massacre celebration. Kanaris' forces detonated the ship's powder keg, blowing up 2000 sailors and the admiral himself. However, as on Chios, their involvement sparked a brutal Ottoman reprisal, with help from Egyptian and French mercenaries, that decimated the island in 1824.

Over the next century, many Psariots resettled in America and other foreign lands. Their descendants still return every summer, so don't be surprised if the first Greek you meet speaks English with a New York accent.

⊙ Sights & Activities

Psara village is tucked within a long bay on the island's southwest. When you disembark from the ferry, you can't miss the jagged Mavri Rachi ('Black Shoulder'), the rock from which thousands of Psariots are said to have hurled themselves during the 1824 Ottoman assault.

Psara's main cultural attraction, the **Monastery of Kimisis Theotokou** (Dormition of the Virgin), 12km north of town, is a small chapel surrounded by protective walls, containing rare hieratic scripts from Mt Athos and a sacred icon that is paraded through the village on the night of 4 August. There are 67 chapels across the island, each cared for by a local family. In the centre of Psara village is the **Konstantinos Kanaris Monument**, where Greeks honour their national hero, who is actually buried in Athens while his heart is kept in the Naval Museum in Piraeus.

LOCAL KNOWLEDGE

FLAG: SEEING RED

Throughout Psara village, you will notice the island's memorable red-and-white flag waving proudly in the breeze. Emblazoned with the revolutionary slogan 'Eleftheria i Thanatos' (Freedom or Death), it features a red cross at its centre, with an upturned spear jutting from one side, while on the other is an anchor impaling a green snake. As if the reference to the Islamic rule of the Turks wasn't apparent enough, there's an upside-down crescent moon and star under these items for good measure. The yellow dove of freedom flutters patiently to one side.

Hiking

Visitors should take the splendid introductory walk along the **Black Shoulder** (aka Black Rock) to the little chapel of **Agios Ioannis** and the **lookout memorial**. The views are impressive from up top, especially at sunset. A further three relatively short and documented hiking trails can also be tackled. The first one takes you to the **cannon emplacements** at the northwestern tip of Psara (2km each way); the second takes you to remote **Limnonaria Beach** (900m each way) on the south coast; and the third is a circular route (3km) taking in **Adami** and **Kanalos Bays**. All three hikes are detailed on the Terrain (www.terrainmaps.gr) map of Psara.

Beaches

There are a number of clean pebble-and-sand beaches stretched along Psara's jagged edges. The closest are the village beaches of **Kato Gialos** and **Katsouni**. The former is on the west side of the headland and is pebbled, while the latter is a short walk north of the harbour and is sandy with shallow water, ideal for kids. Both have tavernas. Further afield, just over 1km northeast, are the twin beaches of **Lazareta** and **Megali Ammos**, consisting of fine pebbles. **Lakka Beach**, 2.5km up the west coast, is the next option, followed by **Agios Dimitrios**, 3.5km from Psara.

🛏 Sleeping

Village accommodation consists primarily of rooms and studios. Contact Psara Travel, Michalakis Travel (p573) or Masticulture Ecotourism Activities (p575) on Chios to book ahead for rooms.

Kato Gialos Apartments APARTMENT €
(☑22740 61178, 6945755321; studios from €40; ❄) Spyros Giannakos rents out clean, bright rooms and kitchenette apartments overlooking Kato Gialos Beach. Ask at Psara Travel.

Studios Psara ROOMS €
(☑22740 61386; studios from €40; ❄🐱) At the edge of the village, in a palm-tree garden, are these clean and airy rooms with kitchenettes, plus a popular *kafeneion* attached.

🍴 Eating & Drinking

To Iliovasilema TAVERNA €
(☑22740 61121; Kato Gialos Beach; mains €4.50-9) Sit under the outdoor canopy at the village's newest fish taverna and *ouzerie*.

Spitalia TAVERNA €
(Katsounis Beach; mains €5-8; ☺11am-1am) Formerly a seaside Ottoman quarantine station,

this excellent eatery is great for a lazy beachside lunch or dinner, with stuffed goat the signature dish.

Kaza
TAVERNA €

(mains €2.50-7) At the beach, near the *plateia*, this *ovelistirio* (grill house) is where you'll find the rotating grill for making *gyros*.

Idrahoos
CAFE, BAR

(⊙10am-midnight) Snappy waterfront cafe, open all day, with all variety of drinks, plus grilled cheese sandwiches.

ⓘ Information

An ATM is on the waterfront square, where wi-fi works well. A doctor and **police** (☑22740 61222) are available for emergencies.

For tourist information, Diana Katakouzinou of **Psara Travel** (☑6932528489, 22740 61351) is ever-helpful and conducts a morning €6 tour of Psara. There's also a summer tourist kiosk at the port, open 9am to 11pm.

ⓘ Getting There & Away

In Chios Town, buy tickets to Psara from Hatzelenis Tours (p573) or Michalakis Travel (p573). In Volissos, contact **Michalakis Travel** (☑22710 25848; www.michalakistravel.gr; Limnia, port of Volissos). Ferries reach Psara from Chios Town (€12 return, three hours, Monday to Friday), Volissos (€7, 1½ hours, weekends only) and Piraeus (€36, five hours, weekly).

ⓘ Getting Around

Neither car nor motorbike hire is available on Psara, and there's no taxi, so consider ferrying a rental car or motorbike from Chios. Hitchhiking is common on the island.

LESVOS (MYTILINI)
ΛΕΣΒΟΣ (ΜΥΤΙΛΗΝΗ)

POP 95,330

Greece's third-largest island, after Crete and Evia, Lesvos is marked by long sweeps of rugged, desert-like western plains that give way to sandy beaches and salt marshes in the centre. Further east are thickly forested mountains and dense olive groves (around 11 million olive trees are cultivated here).

The island's port and capital, Mytilini town, is a lively place year-round, filled with exemplary *ouzeries* and good accommodation, while the north-coast town of Molyvos (aka Mythimna) is an aesthetic treat, with old stone houses clustered on winding lanes overlooking the sea.

Along with hiking and cycling, Lesvos is a mecca for birdwatching, with more than 279 species, ranging from raptors to waders, are often sighted. The island boasts therapeutic hot springs that gush with some of the warmest mineral waters in Europe.

Despite its undeniable tourist appeal, hard-working Lesvos makes its livelihood chiefly from agriculture. Its olive oil is highly regarded, as is its ouzo – the island's farmers produce around half of the aniseed-flavoured firewater sold worldwide.

Lesvos' great cultural legacy stretches from the 7th-century-BC musical composer Terpander to 20th-century figures such as Nobel Prize–winning poet Odysseus Elytis and primitive painter Theophilos. The ancient philosophers Aristotle and Epicurus also led a philosophical academy here. Most famous, however, is Sappho, one of ancient Greece's greatest poets. Her sensuous, passionate poetry has fuelled a modern-day following and draws lesbians from around the world to the village of Skala Eresou, where she was born (c 630 BC).

ⓘ Getting There & Away

AIR
The airport is 8km south of Mytilini town. A taxi to town costs €10 and a bus, €1.60.

Aegean Air (☑22510 61120; www.aegeanair. com), **Olympic Air** (☑22510 61590; www. olympicair.com), **Sky Express** (☑28102 23500; www.skyexpress.gr), **Astra Airlines** (☑80170 07466; www.astra-airlines.gr), and **Air Minoan** (☑28103 22771; www.minoanair.com/en) have offices at the airport. Mytilini town travel agents sell tickets, too.

Domestic Flights from Lesvos (Mytilini)

DESTINATION	TIME	FARE	FREQUENCY
Athens	40min	€50	3-4 daily
Chios	30min	€47	2 weekly
Crete (Iraklio)	50min	€96	5-6 weekly
Limnos	30min	€56	5 weekly
Rhodes	1hr 10min	€75	4-5 weekly
Samos	40min	€56	2 weekly
Thessaloniki	55min	€69	2-3 daily

BOAT
In Mytilini town, buy ferry tickets from Mitilene Tours (p584), Olive Groove Travel (p584), and Tsolos Travel (p584).

Boat Services from Lesvos (Mytilini)

DESTINATION	TIME	FARE	FREQUENCY
Chios	3hr	€19.50	1-2 daily
Kavala	8hr	€34	2 weekly
Limnos	6hr	€24	2 weekly
Piraeus	11-12hr	€42	1 daily
Samos (Karlovasi)	7½hr	€22	1 weekly
Samos (Vathy)	8hr	€22	2 weekly

ⓘ Getting Around

BUS

From Mytilini's **long-distance bus station** (KTEL; ☑22510 28873; El Venizelou), near Agias Irinis Park, one to two daily buses serve Skala Eresou (€11.20, 2½ hours) via Eresos; two to three serve Molyvos (Mithymna, €7.50, 1½ hours) via Petra; and one reaches Sigri (€10.70, 2½ hours). Three daily buses serve Plomari (€5, 1¼ hours), three serve Agiasos

(€3.20, 45 minutes) and three end at Vatera (€6.80, 1½ hours), the latter via Polyhnitos. Travelling between these smaller places often requires changing in Kalloni, which receives three to four daily buses from Mytilini (€4.90, 45 minutes). Three to four daily buses also go north from Mytilini town to Moni Taxiarhon (€4.50, one hour).

Mytilini's **local bus station** (KTEL; ☑22510 46436; Pavlou Kountourioti), near Plateia Sapphou, serves in-town destinations and nearby Loutra, Skala Loutron and Tahiarhis.

CAR & MOTORCYCLE

Two local companies, **Discover Rent-a-Car** (☑22510 20391, 6936057676; www.discover1. gr; Aristarchou 1) and **Billy's Rentals** (☑22510 20006, 6944759716; www.billys-rentacar.com; waterfront, 87 Kountouriotou; ☺7.30am-10pm), have newish cars and flexible service. Billy's also has motorbikes, as do others along Pavlou Kountourioti. In Molyvos, you can hire a vehicle from **Kosmos Rent-a-Car** (☑22530 71710; www. lesvosrentals.com).

Lesvos (Mytilini)

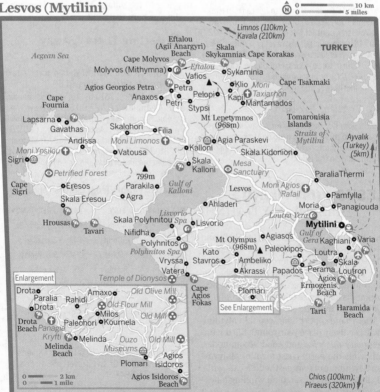

Mytilini Town   Μυτιλήνη

POP 29,650

Lesvos' port and major town, Mytilini, is a lively student town with great eating and drinking options, plus eclectic churches and grand 19th-century mansions and museums. The remarkable Teriade Museum boasts paintings by Picasso, Chagall and Matisse, along with home-grown Theophilos. In fact, the island is known in equal parts for its poets and painters as for its olive oil and ouzo.

Ferries dock at the northeastern end of the curving waterfront thoroughfare, Pavlou Kountourioti, where most of the action is centred. Handmade ceramics, jewellery and traditional products are sold on and around the main shopping street, Ermou, and there are many fine *ouzeries* and student-fuelled bars.

◉ Sights & Activities

Fortress   FORTRESS
(Kastro; adult/child €2/free; ⊘ 8.30am-2.30pm Tue-Sun) Mytilini's imposing early Byzantine fortress was renovated in the 14th century by Genoese overlord Francisco Gatelouzo, and then the Turks enlarged it again. Flanked by pine trees, it's popular for a stroll, with great views included.

Teriade Museum   MUSEUM
(📞 22510 23372; http://museumteriade.gr; Varia) Varia, 4km south of Mytilini, is the unlikely home of the Teriade Museum with its astonishing collection of paintings by artists such as Picasso, Chagall, Miro, Le Corbusier and Matisse. The museum honours the Lesvos-born artist and critic Stratis Eleftheriadis, who brought the work of primitive painter and Lesvos native Theophilos to international attention.

Theophilos Museum   MUSEUM
(📞 22510 41644; Varia; adult/child €2/free; ⊘ 10am-2pm Mon-Fri) This humble structure contains 86 paintings by the primitive painter Theophilos, who remains a folk hero among Greek literati. He barely scratched out an existence, moving frequently and painting coffee-house walls for his daily bread, depicting the people he met at work and at play. A year after his death in 1934, his work was exhibited at the Louvre.

Archaeological Museum   MUSEUM
(📞22510 40223; 8 Noemvriou; adult/child €3/2; ⊘8.30am-3pm Tue-Sun) This handsome refurbished museum, about 500m above the eastern quay (and the closed Old Archaeological Museum), portrays island life from the 2nd century BC to the 3rd century AD, including striking floor mosaics with a walking 'trail' across the protective glass surface.

Church of Agios Therapon   CHURCH
(Arionos; ⊘ 9am-1pm) The bulbous dome of this church crowns Mytilini's skyline. Its ornate interior boasts a huge chandelier, an intricately carved iconostasis, a priest's throne and a frescoed dome. Within the church courtyard, you'll find the icon-rich **Byzantine Museum** (📞 22510 28916; www.immyt.net/museum; adult/student €2/1).

Yeni Tzami   MOSQUE
This early-19th-century Turkish mosque, with crumbling atmosphere to spare, is near the end of Ermou, where a Turkish market used to thrive.

🛏 Sleeping

★Alkaios Rooms   PENSION €
(📞 6981314154, 22510 47737; www.alkaiosrooms.gr; Alkaiou 16; s/d/tr incl breakfast €35/45/55; ✱ 🛜) This collection of 30 spotless and well-kept rooms nestled discreetly in two renovated traditional buildings is Mytilini's most attractive budget option. It's a two-minute walk up from the west side of the waterfront (and Kitchen 19 cafe). The reception is in a restored mansion, where breakfast is served in a flowery courtyard.

Iren Rooms   PENSION €
(📞 22510 22787; cnr Komninaki & Imvrou; s/d/tr €35/45/55; ✱ 🛜) Welcoming Iren has reasonably priced and spotless rooms, up the stairs from a small, inviting lobby. It's the sister establishment of Alkaios Rooms, though a closer walk if coming from the ferry dock, and next to an internet cafe.

Porto Lesvos Hotel   HOTEL €
(📞 22510 41771; www.portolesvos.gr; Komninaki 21; s/d incl breakfast from €35/50; ✱ 🛜) Behind the far end of the waterfront, this efficient and friendly lodging is good value, with a decent breakfast buffet. Rooms are a tad snug, but clean and comfortable. Upper rooms overlook the sea or the old castle.

Hotel Lesvion   HOTEL €€
(📞 22510 28177; www.lesvion.gr; harbour; s/d/tr incl breakfast from €45/60/70; ✱ 🛜) The modern and well-positioned Lesvion, smack on the harbour, has friendly service and attractive and spacious rooms, some with excellent port-view balconies. A breakfast bar overlooks the harbour.

Theofilos Paradise Boutique Hotel

BOUTIQUE HOTEL €€

(☎22510 43300; www.theofilosparadise.gr; Skra 7; s/d/q/ste incl breakfast from €65/90/110/140; P ❄ @ ⬧ ⬚) This smartly restored 100-year-old mansion is elegant, cheerful and good value, with modern amenities along with a traditional *hammam*. The 22 swanky rooms (plus two luxe suites) are spread among three adjacent buildings around an inviting courtyard.

✗ Eating

Polytechnos

FAST FOOD €

(☎22510 44128; waterfront; mains €2-5.50; ⏱lunch & dinner) Hands-down favourite for excellent *gyros*, pitta souvlaki and snappy service. Great for carry-out picnic lunches, too. Find it at the south end of the harbour.

Ouranos

TAVERNA €

(☎22510 47844; N Ellis 15; mezedhes €3-6) You'll catch good views of Turkey from this patio on the old northern port. Tempting mezedhes include *kolokythoanthi* (fried pumpkin flowers stuffed with rice) and hefty servings of *kalamari*. Go inside to choose among at least a dozen local ouzos.

Taverna Kalderimi

TAVERNA €

(☎22510 46577; cnr Ermou & Thasou; mains €5-10; ⏱lunch & dinner Mon-Sat) This reliable alley-

Mytilini Town

0 200 m
0 0.1 miles

Ouranos (100m)

Kornarou
Lesvonaktos
Romanou Melodou
Ermou
Adramytiou
Mikras Asias
Tsertseti
8 Noemvriou
Path to Fortress

Kyparision
Pittakou
Ermou
Mitropoleos
Vernardaki
Mitrelia

Sapfous
Alkaiou
Local Bus Station
Plateia Sapphou
Komninaki
Skra
Argiri Eftalioti
EOT

Paviou Kountourioti
Southern Harbour
Municipal Tourist Office
Quay

Plomari (42km);
Molyvos (62km)
Bostaneio General Hospital (1km)
Agias Irinis Park
Fanari
Long-distance bus station
Ferries to Piraeus, Chios, Limnos
Teriade Musuem;
Theofilos Museum (4km)

way cafe is between Ermou and the waterfront, with everything from *gavros* and grilled pork chops to *mayirefta* and seasonal salads. A mezedhes plate that serves four is a reasonable €15.

O Ermis
TAVERNA €

(cnr Kornarou & Ermou; mezedhes €5-9) This no-frills taverna began life in 1800 as a cafe in the Turkish quarter, as the traditional decor within reveals in faded bits and pieces. Good Macedonian and Limnos wines are offered, with generous plates of Greek standbys.

Cafe P
CAFE €

(mains €2-7; ⊘11am-3am) This hip back-alley bistro draws a mostly university crowd for its unusual and well-priced small plates, small menu, eclectic music mix and all-round chill atmosphere. Oven-cooked pork with leeks or baked feta in a fig balsamic, plus a draught beer, is €6. About 50m in from Plateia Sappho. Look for the single Greek letter, 'Π'.

Averoff Restaurant
TAVERNA €

(☑22510 22180; Kountourioti; mains €6-10; ⊘10am-10pm) No-frills old-fashioned eatery with waiters in ties, specialising in generous *mayirefta* such as chicken and potatoes, stuffed tomatoes and *briam* (mixed vegies). On the central waterfront.

🍷 Drinking & Nightlife

Mytilini's loud waterfront cafes are inevitably busy, though the best watering holes are found in the backstreets.

★Mousiko Kafenio
CAFE

(cnr Mitropoleos & Vernardaki; ⊘7.30am-2am) This hip student favourite is filled with eclectic paintings, old mirrors and well-worn wooden fixtures, giving it a relaxed, arty vibe. Mix in the great music and it's one of the most fun places in town. It offers great drinks, fresh juices and coffee and even homemade iced tea on hot summer days.

Hotspot
BAR

(waterfront; ⊘10am-3am) Along the far end of the waterfront where the big bars dominate, little Hotspot stands up for itself with its cosy interior and great mix of sounds.

Briki
CAFE, BAR

(⊘11am-2am) Briki is the name of the little brass pot you see everywhere in Greece for making Greek and Turkish coffee, but this friendly hole-in-the-wall place serves a bit of everything.

🛍 Shopping

Book & Art
BOOKS.

(☑22510 37961; Komninaki 5) Unusual and inviting side-street bookshop, gallery and toy store near Mousiko Kafenio.

Gaia Ceramics
ARTS

(☑6973279147; Ermou 219) Intimate hole-in-the-wall spot with unusual ceramic jewellery made by local artisans who run the shop. Near the Yeni Tzami (p581) mosque.

ℹ Information

The long-distance bus station is beside Irinis Park, near the domed church. The local bus station is opposite Plateia Sapphou. The airport is 8km south along the coast. ATMs line the southern waterfront. Free wi-fi is in most cafe-bars.

Bostaneio General Hospital (☑22510 57700; E Vostani 48)

EOT (☑22510 42512; Aristarhou 6; ⊘9am-2pm Mon-Fri)

Mytilini Town

Mitilene Tours (☑22510 54261; www.mitilene tours.gr; Kountourioti 87) Full-service agency on the east side of the port. Helps with accommodation, car rentals and trips and tours to Turkey.

Olive Groove Travel (☑22510 37533; www. olive-groove.gr; 11 Pavlou Kountourioti; ⊘7.30am-10pm) All-purpose travel agency on the central waterfront, selling tickets, including to Turkey, and helpful with local info.

Port police (☑22510 28827; waterfront)

Post office (Vournasson; ⊘7.30am-2pm)

Tsolos Travel (☑22510 25346; www.flytsolos. com; Fanari St) Full-service agency on the south side of the port. Sells ferry tickets to Turkey.

South of Mytilini

The small, olive-groved peninsula south of Mytilini has several unique attractions. Following the coast road 7km south, opposite the airport, you'll find the long, pebbled **Neapoli Beach** hosting a few chilled-out beach bars, popular with swimsuited students and usually pulsating with reggae and Greek sounds.

In Skala Loutron, the **Museum of the Memorial of the Refugees of 1922** (☑22510 23901, 22510 91086; Skala Loutron; ⊘5-8pm & by request) FREE honours Anatolia's lost Greek culture, abruptly ended after 2000 years by the Greek-Turkish population exchanges of 1923. By 1922 most ethnic Greeks had fled the Anatolia region of Asia Minor, a fact made official in 1923 at the Convention Concerning the Exchange of Greek and Turkish Populations, signed in Lausanne. Interestingly, it was neither ethnicity nor language that put people on the mandatory time-to-go list, but religion. Even native-speaking Greek Muslims, and native-speaking Turkish Orthodox, were required to switch countries, like it or not.

Around 9km south, the peninsula wraps around to the popular sand-and-pebble **Agios Ermogenis Beach** and **Haramida Beach**, which has toilets and showers under pine trees on the bluff above the beach.

Northern Lesvos

With rolling hills covered in pine and olive trees, peaceful beaches and the aesthetically harmonious town of Molyvos (also called Mithymna), northern Lesvos offers both solitude and low-key resort action. Traditional seaside hot springs and intriguing Byzantine monasteries round out the region's offerings.

Mantamados   Μανταμάδος

Around 36km north of Mytilini town, near Mantamados village, is one of Lesvos' most important pilgrimage sites. An axis of Orthodoxy, myth and militarism, the grand 17th-century monastery **Moni Taxiarhon** (⊘8am-dusk) FREE is pretty full-on – note the fighter plane parked out front, reminding the faithful that the Archangel Michael is the patron saint of the Hellenic Air Force. While here, visit the shop of the **Agricultural Co-op of Mandamados** (☑22530 61096), which sells numerous natural products from local farmers, such as the unique hard cheese, *ladotyri,* made from sheep's milk.

Molyvos (Mithymna)   Μόλυμβος (Μήθυμνα)

POP 1500

Molyvos, also known as Mithymna, is a well-preserved Ottoman-era town of narrow cobbled lanes and stone houses with wooden balconies wreathed in flowers, overlooking a pebble beach below. Its grand 14th-century Byzantine castle, good nearby beaches and north-central island location combine to make Molyvos a good spot to explore Lesvos.

◉ Sights & Activities

Beach lovers can take an excursion boat at 10.30am daily for Skala Sykamnias village (10km) and nearby Eftalou (from €20). It's also possible to hike one way and catch the excursion boat back to Molyvos. Sunset cruises are also available. Enquire with Dimitris at the portside **Faonas Travel Agency** (☑22530 71630; tekes@otenet.gr), inside the Sea Horse Hotel, or **Lesvorama** (☑22530 72291; www. lesvorama.gr; ⊘9am-10pm) on the main road.

Additionally, a popular **yoga retreat** (www.angela-victor.com/work.html) is organised by Angela Farmer at the Yoga Hall. Workshop dates vary through the year.

Byzantine-Genoese Castle   CASTLE
(admission €2; ⊘8am-3pm Tue-Sun) This handsome 14th-century castle stands guard above Molyvos. The steep climb is repaid by sweeping views over the town, sea and even to Turkey shimmering on the horizon. In summer the castle hosts several **festivals**. Enquire at the municipal tourist office (p586).

🛏 Sleeping

More than 50 registered, good-quality domatia are available in Molyvos. Ask at the municipal tourist office or Molyvos Tourism Association (p586) on upper Agora.

★ Nassos Guest House
GUESTHOUSE €

(✆ 6942046279, 22530 71432; www.nassosguest-house.com; d/tr without bathroom €20/35; ⓦ) Head up to the old town's only blue house to reach this former Turkish mansion with a small enclosed garden and homey atmosphere throughout. There are seven rooms and two communal kitchens, along with two full bathrooms, one on each floor. Friendly Dutch manager Tom provides local information. Check ahead for availability.

★ Lela's Studios
APARTMENT €

(✆ 22530 71285, 6942928224; www.eftalou-olivegrove.com/lelas_studios.htm; studio from €40; ❄ⓦ) This handsome addition to the Molyvos sleep scene is a bargain. There are just two studios set in a courtyard of roses and geraniums, each with a fully outfitted kitchen and a sunset sea view from the relaxing stone verandah.

Marina's House
PENSION €

(✆ 22530 71470; waterfront; s/d from €35/40; ❄ⓦ) Look for geraniums climbing the steps of this well-managed pension, 50m from the port. Rooms are spotless, bright and have small sea-facing balconies over the main road. Marina's husband, Kostas, paints icons for village shops.

Sea Horse Hotel
HOTEL €€

(✆ 22530 71630; www.seahorse-hotel.com; harbour; s/d/tr incl breakfast from €55/65/75; Ⓟ❄ⓦ) In the heart of the port area you'll find modern and comfortable rooms (all with balconies overlooking the harbour), along with the family's restaurant and travel agency. Three family-friendly studios have kitchenettes with partial sea views.

Amfitriti Hotel
HOTEL €€

(✆ 22530 71741; www.amfitriti-hotel.com; s/d/apt incl breakfast from €50/70/90; Ⓟ❄ⓦⓢ) Just 50m from the beach, this well-managed traditional stone hotel has modern, tiled rooms and a large garden pool. Staff are friendly and helpful and the hotel's quiet location is a plus.

Molyvos I Hotel
HOTEL €€

(✆ 22530 71496; www.molyvos-hotels.com; waterfront; d incl breakfast from €65; ❄ⓦ) Although it's a package-tour favourite, this handsome waterfront hotel is also a good choice for independent travellers, with well-kept rooms opposite a narrow tree-shaded beach, friendly service and a good breakfast spread.

✖ Eating & Drinking

★ Taverna Angelos
GREEK €

(mains €4-8.50; ⊘ lunch & dinner) Look for the yellow awning, just past the National Bank, for this exceptional no-frills taverna serving great salads, vegie *briam* and *stifado* (meat, game or seafood cooked with onions and tomato). *Mayirefta* such as *yemista* and fresh fish are excellent, prices are reasonable, portions generous and service charming.

★ Betty's
TAVERNA €

(✆ 22530 71421; 17 Noemvriou; mains €3-10; ⊘ 8.30am-11pm) This restored Turkish pasha's residence on the upper street, overlooking the harbour below, offers a tasty variety of excellent *mayirefta* such as *mousakas* (meat or vegie), baked fish, lamb souvlaki and *kotiropitakia* (small cheese pies), plus tasty breakfast specials. Betty also has two spacious and well-appointed studio apartments occupying a quiet and shady corner near the restaurant.

To Hani
TAVERNA €

(✆ 22530 71618; agora; mains €5.50-9; ⊘ lunch & dinner) Snappy family taverna on the busy

---

ALL ABOUT OLIVES

With nearly 12 million olive trees on Lesvos, it's no wonder two museums are devoted to the endeavour.

Museum of Industrial Olive Oil Production (✆ 22530 32300; www.piop.gr; Agia Paraskevi; admission €3; ⊘ 10am-6pm Wed-Mon Mar-Oct) South of Molyvos, this museum is a handsomely restored oil mill, full of polished equipment and well-signed displays. The original 'people's machine' was a communal innovation in its time.

Vrana Olive-Press Museum (✆ 22510 82007; Papados; admission €1; ⊘ 9am-7pm Tue-Sun) Tucked away in the village of Papados, between Mytilini and south-coast Ploumari, the little Vrana Olive-Press Museum showcases 19th-century steam-powered presses and vintage paintings of a bygone era. It also occupies a bit of Greek literary history – it was built by Nicholas Vranas, grandfather of Greek Nobel Prize–winning poet Odysseas Elytis.

BIRDER TIPS

The wetlands around Skala Kallonis host more than 130 species of bird. If you can't tell the difference between a blue-eyed hawker dragonfly and a crested grebe, pick up Steve Dudley's *A Bird-watching Guide to Lesvos*. Steve leads birdwatching tours around the island. There are also 50 species of butterfly and dragonfly flitting about, as well as myriad marsh frogs filling the air with croaky crooning.

Agora (market) above the waterfront. Great for well-priced fresh fish, grills and stellar views of the sea.

Alonia TAVERNA €
(mains €4.50-7; ⊙lunch & dinner) Locals swear by this unpretentious spot just outside of town, on the road to Eftalou Beach. Convivial atmosphere and fresh fish, Greek salads and local wine.

Friends FAST FOOD €
(☑22530 71567; mains €1.60-2.50; ⊙10am-midnight) Between the National Bank and the town parking, this quick-stop eatery serves tasty pitta souvlaki, pork and chicken kebabs, whole and half chickens and small veg plates and salads. Free delivery another plus.

★ **Molly's Bar** BAR
(☑22530 71772; harbour; ⊙6pm-late; �) With its painted blue stars, beaded curtains and bottled Guinness, this whimsical British-run bar on the waterfront's far eastern side is always in ship-shape condition. Molly's caters to a lively local, international and expat crowd. A small balcony is perfect at sunset.

Sunset CAFE, BAR
(⊙8am-1am) On the waterfront, close to the Molyvos Hotel, this friendly all-day cafe has a great selection of coffees along with decent drinks come evening time.

❶ Information

There's a reliable ATM at the National Bank. Wi-fi widely available.
Com.travel (☑22530 71900; www.comtravel.gr) Efficient full-service agency in a converted olive oil factory on the main road.
Medical Centre (☑22530 71333)
Molyvos Tourism Association (☑22510 71990; Agora; ⊙8am-3pm) Tourist office on upper Agora, near the pharmacy.

Municipal Tourist Office (☑22530 71347; ⊙hr vary) Next to the National Bank, offering help with accommodation, maps and excursions.
Post office (Kastrou; ⊙7.30am-2pm)

Petra Πέτρα

This well-known destination is mostly a crowded beach village 5km south of Molyvos. Petra's one cultural site, situated above the giant overhanging rock for which the village was named, is the 18th-century **Panagia Glykofilousa** (Church of the Sweet-Kissing Virgin), accessible on foot up 114 rock-hewn steps. While Petra has accommodation, it lacks the character of Molyvos or nearby Eftalou Beach. The village itself is barely a strip of souvenir shops and restaurants, though its small *plateia* can be relaxing.

Eftalou Beach Παραλία Εφταλού

The place for solitude seekers, Eftalou Beach (also called Agii Anargyri Beach) is 2km northeast of Petra.

Backed by a cliff, the narrow, pebbled and serene Eftalou Beach has pristine waters and also boasts the charming **Mineral Baths of Eftalou** (☑22530 72200; old common/new private bathhouse €4/5; ⊙old bathhouse 6am-9pm), with clear, cathartic 46.5°C water. Nearby, the hot mineral water filters into the cool sea. A vintage bathhouse has a pebbled floor; the new, and comparatively sterile, bathhouse offers private bathtubs. The springs are said to treat various ailments from arthritis to hypertension. Professional **massage** is offered by Elefteria Vamvoukou and there are Greek dance evenings as well.

Beyond the baths, the beachfront **Hrysi Akti** (☑22530 71879; s/d €35/45) offers simple rooms with bathrooms in an idyllic pebbled cove, complete with the friendly owners' small **restaurant** (☑22530 71947; mains from €4.50) overlooking the sea.

Western Lesvos

Western Lesvos was formed by massive, primeval volcanic eruptions that fossilised trees and all other living things, making it an intriguing site for prehistoric-treasure hunters. The striking, bare landscape, broken only by craggy boulders and the occasional olive tree, is dramatically different to that in the rest of Lesvos.

Further to the southwest, however, a grassier landscape emerges, leading to the coastal village of Skala Eresou, birthplace of one of Greece's most famous lyric poets, Sappho, dubbed the 10th muse by Plato.

Skala Kallonis to Sigri
Σκάλα Καλλονής προς Σιγρί

Just south of agricultural Kalloni, coastal Skala Kallonis turns from sleepy fishing village to birding mecca every spring and autumn. During the spring migration, unrivalled across Europe, Lesvos' wetland reserves become home to thousands of birds, from flamingos and raptors to woodpeckers and marsh sandpipers. It's a spectacular show that has grabbed the attention of European birders, who flock to the island during the peak viewing season of mid-April to mid-May, and also mid-September to October. Skala Kallonis shares the enthusiasm, with the **Pasiphae Hotel** (☑22530 23212; www.pasiphaehotel.com; Skala Kollonis; s/d/tr incl breakfast from €45/55/75; P ❄ @ 🤖 🐾) serving as an unofficial centre, where birders gather to compare notes (or brag) at the lobby bar. Bring your binoculars.

After driving 34km west from Skala Kallonis, stop for a coffee or lunch break in **Andissa**, a jovial, rustic village of narrow streets kept cool by the two enormous plane trees that stand over its *plateia*. Listen to the crickets and the banter of old-timers over a Greek coffee or frappé.

About 9km west of Andissa, the Byzantine **Moni Ypsilou** (Monastery of Ypsilou; ⊘ dawn-dusk) **FREE** stands atop a solitary peak surrounded by volcanic plains. Founded in the 8th century, this storied place includes a flowering arched courtyard and a small but spectacular museum with antique icons and Byzantine manuscripts. From the top of the monastery walls, you can gaze out over the desolate ochre plains stretched out against the sea.

Sleepy Sigri is a fishing port with a sometimes-operational ferry port. The village has beautiful sea views, especially at sunset, and there are idyllic, little-visited beaches just southwest.

Skala Eresou   Σκάλα Ερεσού
POP 1560

Skala Eresou is part traditional fishing village, part laid-back bohemian beach town and part lesbian mecca, especially during September when a lively two-week festival honours the great lyrical poet Sappho, born here in 630 BC. The small seaside community has an easygoing, end-of-the-road ambience, with small cafes and tavernas hugging the shore and wispy *almariki* trees swaying in the breeze.

Near the town market, the remains of the early Christian **Basilica of Agios Andreas** include partially intact 5th-century mosaics.

PETRIFIED: 20 MILLION YEARS BEHIND GLASS

Heading west toward Sigri, a stark and ancient landscape awaits, home to the scattered remains of a petrified forest.

Lesvos Petrified Forest (www.petrifiedforest.gr; admission €2; ⊘8am-4pm) About 4km beyond the Moni Ypsilou monastery, a signposted left-hand road leads to this fascinating and rare monument of geological heritage. Its creation 20 million years ago is connected with the intense volcanic activity in the northern Aegean during the Miocene period. In 1985 the forest was declared a Protected Natural Monument and in 2004 it joined Unesco's Global Geopark Network.

Natural History Museum of the Lesvos Petrified Forest (☑22530 54434; www.lesvosmuseum.gr; Sigri; admission €5; ⊘9am-6pm Jul-Sep, 8.30am-4.30pm Oct-Jun; P ♿) Well-signed exhibits in this state-of-the-art museum in Sigri, a coastal village northwest of Skala Eresou, transport visitors to the moment when violent volcanic explosions discharged rapid flows of extremely hot ash and rock, which moved east to west, almost instantaneously covering western Lesvos' dense forest – trees, branches, root systems, leaves, fruits. What followed – hot fluids rich in pyrite, rising from molten magma – perfectly fossilised plant fibers. This process involved the molecule-by-molecule replacement of organic plant matter with inorganic matter.

Today's petrified forest reveals structural characteristics of plants, root systems and tree trunks, exactly as they existed 20 million years ago. Among star attractions are the giant trunks of petrified sequoia trees and tiny fossils of pistachio nuts and olive leaves. There's a gift shop and small cafe, and the museum staff often give impromptu tours for free.

INTERNATIONAL ERESSOS WOMEN'S FESTIVAL

The **International Eressos Women's Festival** (☑ 22530 52130; www.womensfestival. eu; ticket €50; ⊙ Sep) is an international event with a local feel. It rambles on in Skala Eressou for two weeks of partying and activities ranging from live music and open-air cinema to Greek dancing and beach volleyball. There are water sports, yoga, poetry and meditation, all in a gay-friendly atmosphere under the sun and stars.

Highlights include a LGBTQ film festival, live Greek, Turkish and Mediterranean folk music, 4WD safaris, an alternative fashion show (featuring festival participants), photography workshops and tattooing demonstrations. Live performances range from comedy and spoken word to burlesque and rock and roll.

The crystal waters offer swimming near cocktail bars or, for those who prefer clothing optional, a beach further on. For avid walkers and hikers, the area is threaded with inland and coastal routes. Nearby there are also thermal spas, archaeological remains, water sports, boat trips, birdwatching excursions and mountain biking.

🛌 Sleeping

Skala Eresou has reasonable domatia options, as well as (fairly pricey) hotels. Most former women-only places have gone unisex.

★ Kouitou Hotel
HOTEL €

(☑ 22530 53311; kouitou.hotel@gmail.com; s/d €25/45; ⓟ@🛜) Managed by the energetic Vaso and Alex, the Kouitou is a delightful and rambling lodging of clean and quirky rooms, each with different hand-painted decor, plus a fan. It's a five-minute walk to the seaside, visible from the shaded roof bar. Vaso offers a home-cooked meal each day, always with all-natural local ingredients, and carrot cake if you're lucky.

Heliotopos
APARTMENT €

(☑ 6977146229; www.heliotoposeressos.com; apt €45-70; ⓟ🌼🛜) A leisurely 15-minute walk from the village, this flowery garden lodging features five studios and three two-bedroom apartments, all with full kitchens. The hospitable owners, Debby and Patrick, like to have fresh fruit and vegies on hand and also lead nearby birdwatching excursions. Free bikes are available for pedalling around.

Hotel Gallini
HOTEL €

(☑ 22530 53138; www.hotel-galinos.gr; Alkaiou St; s/d incl breakfast from €30/45; ⓟ🌼🛜) This budget gem, about 80m back from the waterfront, has tile floors and small balconies overlooking the hillside. Breakfast, with homemade jams and cheeses, is served on the flowery verandah.

Aumkara Apartments
APARTMENT €

(☑ 6948131032, 22530 53190; www.aumkara.eu; s/d/q from €25/35/50; ⓟ🌼🛜) Smart and spotless apartments near the centre of the village, managed by the welcoming Maria

and crew. Self-caterers will like the handy kitchenettes, and rooms range from small studios to two-bedroom apartments. About 50m from the beach.

Sappho the Eresia
HOTEL €

(Sappho Hotel; ☑ 22530 53233; www.sappho-hotel .com; waterfront; s & d €35-50; ⓟ🌼🛜) The friendly 18-room Sappho is what passes for a big hotel. Its modest position on the quieter west end of the beach is appealing, along with overhead fans and an easygoing cafebar. The best rooms overlook the sea and the island of Psara.

🍴 Eating

Skala Eresou's restaurants and bars line the beach, as do *amariki* (salt trees). Fresh fish is a speciality. Look for the hanging squid and octopus. On clear days Chios emerges on the horizon.

★ Soulatso
SEAFOOD €

(boardwalk; fish €6-13; ⊙ lunch & dinner) This busy beachfront *ouzerie*-taverna, with large outdoor patio, specialises in fresh fish, reasonably priced by the kilo, and is also known for its excellent mezedhes. Good service, ample portions and worthy wines.

Aigaio
TAVERNA €

(boardwalk; mains €3.50-8.50; ⊙ lunch & dinner) Owner Theodoris spends most mornings fishing to provide the evening's fresh fish. There are also very good *mayirefta*, good grills and traditional Greek music in the background.

Taverna Karavogiannos
TAVERNA €

(boardwalk; mains €5-9) A fine seaside taverna overlooking the beach, with fresh fish, grills, several vegie dishes (such as *horta*) and a variety of salads.

Obelix   GREEK €

(mains €2-5.50; ☺lunch & dinner) Quick and tasty backstreet grill house near the supermarket, with great pork *gyros,* kebabs, mixed grills and salads.

Sam's Café-Restaurant   TAVERNA €

(Eresos; mains €4-8) Don't let the five-minute drive from Skala Eresos up to little Eresos keep you from trying this excellent Lebanese-Greek patio taverna for a taste of Sam and Niki's excellent Greek and Lebanese home cooking.

🍷 Drinking & Nightlife

Skala Eresou's low-key nightlife consists of a contiguous series of small cafe-bars strung along the eastern end of the short waterfront.

★Parasol   BAR

(☑22530 52050) With its orange lanterns and super-eclectic music mix, little Parasol does cocktails that match its South Seas decor. As the day rolls on, Christos and Anastasia's made-to-order breakfasts and cappucinos give way to lunch specials, fresh juice, noodles and handmade pizza.

★Portokali   CAFE, BAR

Tiny and convivial cafe-bar 3km up the hill in Eresos, and the village favourite for coffee and conversation, sweets and *tsipouro.*

Flamingo Beach Bar   BAR

(☑22530 52010) Colourful doesn't begin to describe this cheerful hang-out that anchors the far west end of the beach. Good drinks, snacks and a welcoming atmosphere.

Notia Jazz Bar   BAR

(plateia) Come for the drinks, stay for the jazz at this hip music bar. Live jazz on summer weekends. Good cocktails, Greek wine, draught beer, plus Miles and Monk.

Margaritari   CAFE, BAR

(waterfront) By day, an inviting cafe with tasty homemade sweets and cakes, and by night a cool bar scene with mellow music and clientele.

🛍 Shopping

Thalassaki   ARTS, CRAFTS

(☑6973525421; waterfront; ☺11am-11pm) Despina Iossifelli makes both the handmade ceramics and jewellery at this bright and inviting waterfront gift shop.

Polytechneio   ARTS

(☑6976045298) A bright spot along the waterfront, with well-displayed handmade jewellery, small paintings and constructions.

Leather Workshop   ACCESSORIES

Check out the old sewing machines at this friendly little leather and accessories shop. In his spare time, owner Kiriakos teaches kung fu to the village kids.

ℹ Information

The central square of Plateia Anthis faces the waterfront, where most cafes offer free wi-fi. Further west along Gyrinnis are two markets, an ATM and **pharmacy** (☑22530 53844).

Full-service **Sappho Travel** (☑22530 52130; www.sapphotravel.com) does car hire, accommodation and provides information about the International Eressos Women's Festival.

Southern Lesvos

Agiasos to Melinda
Αγιάσος προς Μελίντα

Interspersed groves of olive and pine trees mark southern Lesvos, from the flanks of Mt Olympus (968m), the area's highest peak, right down to the sea, where the best beaches lie. This is a hot, intensely agricultural place where the vital olive-oil, wine and ouzo industries overshadow tourism.

Just south of the Mytilini–Polyhtinos road, Agiasos is the first point of interest. On the northern side of Mt Olympus, it's a quirky, well-kept traditional hamlet of narrow cobbled streets where fishers sell their morning catch from the back of old pick-up trucks, village elders sip Greek coffees in the local *kafeneia,* and cheesemakers and ceramic artisans hawk their wares. It's a relaxing, leafy place and boasts the exceptional **Church of the Panagia Vrefokratousa**.

SAPPHO: ANCIENT POET, MODERN VOICE

The classical Greek poet Sappho is renowned for her lyrical verse. Her words speak of passion and love for both sexes, but her emotion is balanced by clarity of language and a simple style. Though only fragments of her work remain, we do know that she married, had a daughter and was exiled for a period to Sicily, most likely for her political affiliation. Her surviving poems and love songs seem to have been addressed to an inner circle of female devotees. She was certainly an early advocate for women's voices, and hers continues to resonate.

The road south along the western shore of the Gulf of Gera reaches **Plomari**, the centre of Lesvos' ouzo industry. It's an attractive, if busy, seaside village with a large, palm-lined *plateia* and waterfront tavernas. It also has the **Varvagianni Ouzo Museum** (☑22520 32741; Plomari; ◷9am-4pm Mon-Fri, by appointment Sat & Sun) **FREE** where the family has made ouzo for five generations. Adjacent to it is another well-regarded ouzo maker, Ouzo Plomariou. Both do free tours and you're invited to compare different ouzo tastes.

The popular beach settlement of **Agios Isidoros**, 3km east, absorbs most of Plomari's summertime guests. But **Tarti**, a bit further east, is less crowded. West of Plomari, Melinda is a tranquil fishing village with beach, tavernas and domatia.

Sleeping

Hotel Agia Sion
HOTEL **€**

(Agiasos Hotel; ☑6941569107; Agiasos; s/d/tr €20/25/30) Agiasos' only hotel (aside from a few domatia) is adjacent to the Church of Panagia and surrounds a leafy courtyard. Don't look for a sign; there isn't one! Call ahead to manager Stamatoula, enquire at the church info booth, or ask for English-speaking Sophia at the nearby pharmacy.

Drinking

Ouzerie To Stavri
CAFE

(☑6978226936; Agiasos) To Stavri, otherwise known as Vasilli's place, is an institution at the top end of Agiasos. It's worth a peek just for the vintage photos and old tools that compete for wall space with the new flat-screen TV, perhaps the only reminder of the current, or even previous, century.

Melinda to Vatera
Μελίντα προς Βατερά

From Melinda, the road less taken to the beach resort of Vatera passes through tranquil mountain villages, richly forested hills and steep gorges.

Driving north, you'll pass picturesque villages **Paleohori**, **Akrassi** and **Ambeliko**, from where a signposted, rental-car-friendly dirt road descends through serene olive and pine forests with great views to the coast. The total driving time from Melinda to Vatera is about an hour.

Hikers here can enjoy southern Lesvos' **olive trails**, which comprise paths and old local roads threading inland from Plomari and Melinda. The **Melinda–Paleohori trail**

(1.2km, 30 minutes) follows the Selandas River for 200m before ascending to Paleohori, passing a spring with potable water along the way. The trail ends at the village's olive press.

Another appealing trail leads to **Panagia Kryfti**, a cave church near a **hot spring** (built for two) and the nearby **Drota Beach**; or take the **Paleohori–Rahidi trail** (1km, 30 minutes), which is paved with white stone and passes springs and vineyards. Rahidi, which was only connected to electricity in 2001, has charming old houses and a *kafeneio*.

Other, more complicated hiking trails can get you directly from Melinda to Vatera; consult the EOT (p583) or the **tourist office** (EOT; ☑22510 43255; Gate B, port; ◷9am-3pm Mon-Sat), both in Mytilini town.

Vatera & Polyhnitos
Βατερά προς Πολυχνίτος

Despite its 10km-long sandy beach, Vatera (vah-ter-*ah*) remains a low-key getaway destination, with only a few small hotels and domatia operating, and even fewer bars.

On its western edge, at Cape Agios Fokas, the sparse ruins of an ancient **Temple of Dionysos** occupy a headland overlooking the sea. In the cove between the beach and the cape, evidence indicates an ancient military encampment. Indeed, some historians believe this is the place Homer was referring to in the *Iliad* as the resting point for Greek armies besieging Troy.

Vatera's ancient history includes fossils dating back 5.5 million years, including remains of a tortoise as big as a Volkswagen Beetle, though possibly faster, and fossils of a gigantic horse and gazelle. The inviting **Vrisa Natural History Museum** (☑22520 61890; Vryssa; admission €1; ◷9am-9pm Jun-Sep, 9.30am-3.30pm Wed-Sun Oct-May), in Vryssa's old schoolhouse, displays these and other significant remains.

Agricultural **Polyhnitos**, 10km north of Vatera on the road back to Mytilini town, is known for its two nearby **hot springs**, among the hottest in Europe. The more popular of the two, the **Hot Springs of Polyhnitos** (Polyhnitos Spa; ☑6977592991, 22510 41229; www.hotsprings.gr; adult/child €4/3, private bath €5.50; ◷noon-8pm Mon-Sat, 10am-8pm Sun), awaits just 1.5km east of the village, set in a pretty, renovated Byzantine building, with some of Europe's warmest bath temperatures at 40°C (104°F). Rheumatism, arthritis, skin diseases and gynaecological problems are treated here, along with the chance to simply enjoy a relaxing soak. Professional massage is available, and there's a small cafe on the grounds for drinks, lunch and dinner. A nearby, smaller hot spring, **Lisvorio Spa** (☑22530 71245; admission €4; ☺9am-7pm), 5km north of Polyhnitos, is popular for baths and massage.

About 5km northwest of Polyhnitos, the fishing port of **Skala Polyhnitou** lies on the Gulf of Kalloni, where caïques bob at the docks and fishers untangle their nets. It's great for low-key seafood dinners at sunset. If you want lower-key yet, head 6km west to seaside village of Nifidha.

🛏 Sleeping & Eating

★**Hotel Vatera Beach**   HOTEL €
(☑22520 61212; www.vaterabeach.com; Vatera Beach; s/d incl breakfast from €35/50; P ❋ @ ⸜) This peaceful beachfront hotel regards its guests, many of whom return annually, as old friends. The congenial brother-and-sister team of Takis and Jeannie Ballis provide great service and comfortable rooms, just opposite the beach. The hotel's excellent restaurant uses mostly local and organic ingredients to supply the small daily menu.

LIMNOS   ΛΗΜΝΟΣ

POP 16,990

Isolated Limnos, alone in the northeastern Aegean, save for neighbouring Agios Efstratios, appeals to those looking for Greek island life relatively unaffected by modern tourism. Its capital, Myrina, has retained its classic Greek-fishing-harbour feel, while a grand Genoese castle provides a dramatic backdrop.

The island's eastern lakes are visited by spectacular flocks of flamingos and the central plain is filled with spring wildflowers. Superb sandy beaches lie near the capital and in more distant corners of the island.

Limnos is perhaps best known as being the central command post of the Hellenic Air Force – a strategic decision, as Limnos is in an ideal position for monitoring the Straits of the Dardanelles leading into İstanbul. For this very reason the island was used as the operational base for the failed Gallipoli campaign in WWI – a moving military cemetery for fallen ANZAC (Australian and New Zealand Army Corps) soldiers remains near Moudros, where the Allied ships were based. A small town in Victoria, Australia, bears the name Lemnos to this day.

ℹ Getting There & Away

AIR

The airport is 22km east of Myrina, with offices for **Aegean Air** (☑801 1120000, 22540 92700; www.aegeanair.com), **Sky Express** (☑28102 23800; www.skyexpress.gr) and **Astra Airlines** (☑80170 07466; www.astra-airlines.gr). Taxis cost about €25.

Domestic Flights from Limnos

DESTINATION	TIME	FARE	FREQUENCY
Athens	50min	€59	1 daily
Chios	1½hr	€56	2 weekly
Ikaria	45min	€50	6 weekly
Lesvos	40min	€56	5 weekly
Rhodes	3hr	€82	5 weekly
Samos	2hr	€56	2 weekly
Thessaloniki	45min	€65	5 weekly

BOAT

Buy ferry tickets at Atzamis Travel (p594), Petrides Travel (p594), or **Aegean Travel** (☑22540 25936; www.aegeantravel.eu; waterfront).

Boat Services from Limnos

DESTINATION	TIME	FARE	FREQUENCY
Agios Efstratios	1½hr	€7	5-6 weekly
Chios	8hr	€23	2 weekly
Ikaria (Agios Kirykos)	13hr	€31	2 weekly
Kavala	4½hr	€16	5 weekly
Lavrio	9hr	€30	4 weekly
Lesvos (Mytilini)	6hr	€23	2 weekly
Piraeus	20hr	€56	1-2 weekly
Samos (Karlovasi)	10½hr	€28	1-2 weekly
Samos (Vathy)	11hr	€29	1 weekly

ℹ Getting Around

BUS

Limnos' bus service has one diabolical purpose: to bring villagers to town for their morning shopping and to get them home by lunch. Going and returning by bus in the same day is only possible to four destinations – by no means the most interesting ones, either. For example, buses serve Plaka, Skandali, Katalako and Kontias, but only return the next day.

From Myrina, five daily buses serve Moudros, via the airport (€3, 30 minutes), with the last

Limnos

return bus leaving at 12.15pm. However, the buses do not coordinate with flight departures.

Myrina's **bus station** (☑22540 22464; Plateia Eleftheriou Venizelou) displays schedules.

CAR & MOTORCYCLE

Petrides Travel Agency (☑22540 22039; www. petridestravel.gr) and **Aegean Travel** (☑22540 23280), both near the waterfront, hire cars from €30 per day. Motorcycle-hire outlets are on Kyda-Karatza.

TAXI

A **taxi rank** (☑22540 23820) is on Myrina's central square. It's €25 to the airport.

Myrina
Μύρινα
POP 5110

Backed by volcanic rock and a craggy Genoese castle, Limnos' capital is strikingly old-fashioned. Here you'll see fishers sipping Greek coffee while unfolding their nets, and colourful caïques dotting the harbour.

In summer Myrina comes to life, with shops selling traditional foods, handicrafts and more in its bustling *agora.* Its white-washed stone houses, old-fashioned barber shops and *kafeneia,* sitting amid weather-worn neoclassical mansions, create a relaxed old-world charm.

The town (and Limnos in general) is mostly frequented by Greek tourists, lending a distinct Hellenic flavour to its waterfront nightlife. Above the town, on the overgrown slopes of the castle, it's a different story. Here, shy, fleet-footed deer dart after dark, even venturing down to the *agora* on winter nights.

◉ Sights & Activities

Castle of Myrina   CASTLE

FREE Myrina's lonely hill-top *kastro* dates from the 13th century and occupies a headland that divides the town from its popular beach. The ruins of the Venetian-built fortress are imposing, but deserted, except for the deer that roam freely. It's worth the 20- to 25-minute walk up the hill for the sea views alone, which extend to Mt Athos and, come evening, the twinkling cafe lights below.

Archaeological Museum   MUSEUM

(☑22540 22990; admission €2; ◷8.30am-3pm Tue-Sun) Myrina's fine neoclassical mansion museum overlooks Romeïkos Gialos Beach and contains 8th- and 7th-century-BC finds from Limnos' three major sites of Poliohni, the Sanctuary of the Kabeiroi and Hephaistia. Worth seeing are the earthenware lamp-statuettes of sirens, along with details of the mandated Greek-Turkish population exchange of 1923.

Boat & Bus Tours TOUR

From June to September, a few travel agencies organise round-the-island boat (half/full day €20/25) and bus (full day €20) sight-seeing tours. Boat tours stop for lunch and swimming and take in the archaeological sites, usually ending at sunset. Bus tours can also visit the military cemeteries at Mourdros and Portianos. Contact Petrides Travel (p594) or Atzamis Travel (p594).

Beaches

The town's beaches include the wide and sandy **Rea Maditos**, and the superior **Romeïkos Gialos**, beyond the harbour; further on, it becomes **Riha Nera** (Shallow Water), named for its gently shelving sea floor. Waterfront cafes and restaurants stay open late through summer.

Five minutes south, on the road towards Thanos Beach, **Platy Beach** is a shallow, sandy crescent with cantinas, tavernas and a few lodgings.

🛏 Sleeping

Apollo Pavillion HOTEL €

(☑22540 23712; www.apollopavilion.gr; Garoufalidhou; s/d/tr incl breakfast from €40/50/55; P❉🛜) Tucked behind the port in a neoclassical house with charm to spare and large high-ceilinged rooms, each with kitchenette and balcony. Near the police station, 150m above the port.

Vicky Studios APARTMENT €

(☑22540 22137; www.vickystudios.com; Maroulas 5; studio/apt from €35/45; P❉🛜) This immaculate and friendly budget gem is a five-minute walk from shops and the beach at Riha Nera. Rooms face a lovely garden and feature kitchenettes, desk and fridge. Also in Platy.

Hotel Lemnos HOTEL €

(☑22540 22153; s/d/tr from €30/40/50; ❉🛜) The middle-of-the-waterfront Lemnos, under new management, is a decent budget choice with friendly staff and modern, if smallish, rooms, plus balconies overlooking the harbour or castle.

To Arhontiko BOUTIQUE HOTEL €€

(☑22540 29800; www.arxontikohotel.gr; cnr Sahtouri & Filellinon; s/d/tr incl breakfast from €45/65/75; P❉🛜) This restored mansion (and Myrina's first hotel) dating from 1851 impresses with swanky boutique rooms, fireplaces, helpful staff, cosy bar, classic charm throughout and a classic Greek breakfast to last the day. On a quiet alleyway near the *plateia* of Romeikos Gialos.

🍴 Eating

★ Ouzeri To 11 SEAFOOD €

(Plateia KTEL; seafood mezedhes €4.50-9.50) This unassuming little *ouzerie* by the bus depot is the local favourite for seafood. From *kydonia* (mussels with garlic and Venus clams) to sea urchins, crayfish and more, 'To *En*-dheka' (as it's pronounced) serves all the strange stuff, along with plenty of ouzo to help you forget what you're eating.

O Platanos Restaurant TAVERNA €

(Kyda-Karatza; mains €5-8) Homemade pasta, good Limni wine and excellent *mayirefta*, with an emphasis on meat, are served at this iconic place under two majestic plane trees, halfway along the main street of the agora.

To Steki tis Yefsis GREEK €

(☑6987930068; port; mains €2-6) Excellent eatery opposite the port – the best for quick *gyros*, pitta souvlaki, or a generous platter with pork or sausage. Snappy, cheerful service, sit down or take away.

To Limanaki TAVERNA €

(waterfront; mains €6-9.50) Near the end of the waterfront, with well-priced fresh seafood and cheery service, along with late-night meat grills and good Limnos wine.

O Sozos TAVERNA €

(Platy; mains €5-8) In Platy, 2km east of Myrina, O Sozos excels in traditional Greek fare. Specialities include *kokkaras flomaria* (rooster served with pasta), lamb and dolmadhes.

🍷 Drinking & Nightlife

Myrina's summer nightlife is mostly centred around the bars above Romeïkos Gialos beach.

Karagiozis BAR

(Romeïkos Gialos beach; ⏲9am-5am) On a leafy terrace near the sea, Karagiozis morphs from snazzy frappé-cafe by day to a drink-till-you-drop bar under the stars. Sturdy, fair-priced drinks.

Manos Bar BAR

(☑6932411134; Argonafton 20) Lively open-air beach bar at Riha Nera, open all day and most of the night, with decent drinks and all-ages clientele.

Alexandros BAR
(☑6977273187; old port) At the old port opposite the waterfront, this place has a mellow scene that draws a late-night crowd of regulars.

❶ Information

There are three ATMs around Myrina's central square, Plateia Eleftheriou Venizelou, which sits midway along the main thoroughfare of Kyda-Karatza (aka the *agora*). Another ATM is on the quay. Most waterfront cafes have free wi-fi.

Atzamis Travel (☑22540 25690; atzamisk@otenet.gr; waterfront) Arranges ferry and air tickets, accommodation, excursions and bicycle rentals. Also can arrange visits to the wetlands on Limnos' east coast.

Karaiskaki Travel (☑22540 22460, 22540 22900; hrissa5a@otenet.gr; waterfront) Specialises in trips to Agios Efstatios island. Formerly known as Myrina Travel.

Petrides Travel (☑22540 22039; www.petridestravel.gr; Kyda-Karatza 116) Helpful and informed staff arrange island sightseeing tours, boat trips, car hire, transfers and accommodation.

Police station (☑22540 22201; Nikolaou Garoufallidou)

Port police (☑22540 22225)

Post office (Nikolaou Garoufallidou; ☺7.30am-2pm)

Pravlis Travel (☑22540 24617; www.pravlis.gr) Efficient and helpful full-service agency at the port.

Western Limnos

North of Myrina, the road left after **Kaspakas** village accesses the appealing **Agios Ioannis Beach**, with a few tavernas and beach houses set nicely beneath an overhanging volcanic slab.

From Kaspakas continue east 2km to the junction for Kornos and Therma. The swanky, state-of-the-art **Therma Spa** (☑22540 62062; www.thermaspa.gr; Therma), a lavishly restored Ottoman-era bath, is 1km south of the junction. About 6km north of Therma, the popular **Mantella Taverna** (☑22540 61349; Sardes; mains €5-9.50) draws residents and travellers from Myrina and beyond.

Further east, the road turns south at **Livadohori**, passing barren, tawny hills and modest farmland until reaching charming **Kontias**, with traditional stone houses and vintage windmills. It then swings southwest

back to Myrina, on the way passing the exceptional and popular **Agios Pavlos Beach** and **Thanos Beach**, only a 10-minute drive from Myrina.

Central Limnos

Central Limnos' flat plateaus are dotted with wheat fields, small vineyards and sheep – plus the Greek Air Force's central command (large parts are thus off limits to tourists). Limnos' second-largest town, **Moudros**, occupies the eastern side of muddy Moudros Bay, famous for its role as the principal base for the ill-fated Gallipoli campaign in 1915, and home to Winston Churchill's secret wartime headquarters.

The **East Moudros Allied Military Cemetery**, with the graves of Commonwealth soldiers from the Gallipoli campaign, is 1km east of Moudros on the Roussopouli road. Here you can read a short history of the Gallipoli campaign. A second Commonwealth cemetery, **Portianos Military Cemetery** (6km south of Livadohori, on the road to Thanos Beach and Myrina) is the area's other sombre attraction. Conact Atzamis Travel or Petrides Travel in Myrina for tours.

Eastern Limnos

Historical remnants and remote beaches draw visitors to eastern Limnos. Its three archaeological sites include Poliohni, the Sanctuary of the Kaberioi and Hephaistia, all open from 8am to dusk. Contact Myrina's Petrides Travel for tour information.

Poliohni – on the southeast coast, considered the first prehistoric settlement in the Aegean – has the remains of four ancient settlements, the most significant being a pre-Mycenaean city that predated Troy VI (1800–1275 BC). The site, with a tiny and free museum (open 8am to 3pm), is fascinating, but remains are few.

The **Sanctuary of the Kabeiroi** (Ta Kaviria) lies at the northern tip of remote Tigani Bay. The worship of the Kabeiroi gods here actually predates that which took place on nearby Samothraki. The major attraction is a **Hellenistic sanctuary** with 11 partial columns. Nearby, the legendary **Cave of Philoctetes** is supposedly where that Trojan War hero was abandoned while his gangrenous, snake-bitten leg healed. A marked path from the site leads to the sea cave.

Once Limnos' main city, **Hephaistia** (Ta Ifestia) is where Hephaestus, god of fire and metallurgy, was hurled down from Mt Olympus by Zeus. Little remains, however, other than low walls and a partially excavated theatre.

Limnos' northeastern region has some rustic, little-visited villages, plus remote **Keros Beach**, popular with windsurfers. Flocks of flamingos sometimes strut on the coastal salt lagoon, **Lake Alyki**, and the nearby salt marsh, **Lake Hortarolimni**. From Cape Plaka, at Limnos' northeastern tip, Samothraki and Imvros (Gökçeada in Turkish) are visible. The three islands were historically considered as forming a strategic triangle for the defence of the Dardanelles, and thus İstanbul (Constantinople). This was Turkey's case for clinging to Imvros in 1923, even after Greece had won back most of its other islands a decade earlier.

AGIOS EFSTRATIOS
ΑΓΙΟΣ ΕΥΣΤΡΑΤΙΟΣ

POP 370

Little-visited Agios Efstratios lies isolated in the Aegean, 18km south of Limnos. Abbreviated by locals as 'Aï-Stratis', it attracts visitors for its isolation, remote beaches and quiet beauty. However, it hasn't always been serene – in 1968 a magnitude-7.1 earthquake, centered near the island, wreaked havoc throughout the Aegean and destroyed most of the port village's classic buildings, a bad situation made worse by Greece's military junta, which mismanaged the reconstruction.

Nevertheless, much of Agios Efstratios' charm has returned and the sparsely populated island has domatia, good seafood tavernas, relaxing hill walks and fine beaches. The main village, also Agios Efstratios, is often just called 'the village'.

History

Archaeological evidence from the island's northeast, opposite Limnos, points to early Bronze Age (2800–1900 BC) settlements. Later civilisations recognized the island as a strategic central point in the Aegean, and it was colonised frequently, first by the Mycenaeans, then in succession by the Athenians, Romans and, during the Middle Ages, by the Byzantine Empire, which was based in Constantinople (modern-day İstanbul).

The island is named for a St Efstratios from that period, who arrived here in AD 813 as a political exile.

Like the island's namesake saint, political prisoners were exiled here for decades in the early 20th century, especially by the divisive and dictatorial Metaxas regime of the 1930s, and again during the 'time of the colonels', as Greeks refer to the military junta that ruled from 1967–74. Many dissidents and suspected communists were banished to the island, including renowned composer Mikis Theodorakis and poets Kostas Varnalis and Giannis Ritsos.

◉ Sights & Activities

Sights are few but striking. The old village ruins, following the 1968 earthquake, include the standing **Maraslios School**. A single Byzantine monument has survived: **Agios Vassilios church**, dating from 1727, with a domed basilica.

Just south of the village are the sea caves of **Trypia Spilia**. Agios Efstratios' pristine beaches include the **village beach**, which has dark volcanic sand and warm waters, Agios Dimitrios beach (5km south) and Ftelio beach (8km south). The latter pair are best reached by local boat, 4WD or motorbike. Enquire with Mr Aris at Taverna Artemonas, near Agios Nikolas church.

Well-worn paths and trails criss-cross the island's meadows, which are covered with daffodils, fennel, thistles, amaranth, blackberries, poplars and willows. On the island's northeast corner, a 2.2km trail explores the hills of Avlakia, passing through a dense **oak forest**. On the east coast, you'll find graceful **sand dunes** at Alonitsi Beach.

On any walk, you're sure to see goats, sheep, cows and horses, which all tend to roam freely on the small island, along with migratory and resident birds, including herons, owls and kingfishers.

⌂ Sleeping & Eating

Most travellers book rooms for Agios Efstratios when they purchase ferry tickets. In Limnos, contact Karaiskaki Travel. A favourite lodging is **Rooms Kakali** (Rooms-to-Let; ☏ 6973061585; kakali1K1maria@yahoo.gr; s/d €30/35). Though popular in summer, the island's 50-odd rooms seldom fill up at once. The island's single *kafeneio* and two tavernas, including **Taverna Artemonas** (☏ 22540 93333; ⊙ 9am-midnight), offer inexpensive and fresh seafood.

❶ Getting There & Away

A small ferry, the *Aeolis*, runs between Limnos and Agios Efstratios five times a week (€8, 1½ hours, Monday to Friday). Buy tickets at Karaiskaki Travel (p594) in Myrina on Limnos. The ferry leaves Limnos at about 4.30pm, and returns from Agios Efstratios at 6am, so unless you're going for dinner, plan on staying at least two nights. However, weekend day trips (€20) are available in the summer; contact Petrides Travel (p594) in Myrina.

There are also four ferries a week from both mainland Lavrio (€25, eight hours) and Kavala (€23, seven hours).

SAMOTHRAKI
ΣΑΜΟΘΡΑΚΗ

POP 2860

Samothraki sits alone in the northeastern Aegean, halfway between the mainland port of Alexandroupoli and Limnos. This lush, forested island boasts one of the most important archaeological sites in Greece: the ancient Thracian Sanctuary of the Great Gods. Also here stands the Aegean's loftiest peak, Mt Fengari (1611m), from where Homer recounts that Poseidon, god of the sea, watched the Trojan War unfold.

Samothraki's mountainous interior, filled with massive gnarled oak and plane trees, is ideal for hiking and mountain biking, and the island's waterfalls, plunging into deep, glassy pools, provide cool relief on hot summer days. Remote southeastern beaches are pristine, while the north offers hot baths at Loutra (Therma). Inland from the main fishing port of sleepy Kamariotissa lies the former capital,

Hora, bursting with flowers and handsome homes, all overlooking the distant sea.

The island's remoteness means that it's often forgotten by island hoppers, but devotees of ancient archaeology, unique cuisine and superb hiking will find it worth the effort to get here. (Hikers should look for Terrain Maps' *Samothrace* map and Anavasi Maps' booklet *Canyoning in Samothraki*.)

✦ Activities

With its beaches, craggy peaks, lush jungle rivers and waterfalls, Samothraki is ideal for outdoor-adventure activities. However, paths are poorly marked and rushing mountain waters can turn torrential, making a good guide essential. Samothraki Travel (p598) offers guided **trekking** (€15) on hard-to-find mountain trails, as well as **canyoning** (from €40) along 10 spectacular routes. Both are guided by experienced Georgos Andreas, usually in August and September. The same agency offers **diving** trips that include equipment (€50 for two).

❶ Getting There & Away

SAOS Lines (p729) ferries connect Samothraki with Alexandroupoli twice daily in summer, less frequently out of season (€9.60 to €14.50, two hours). Purchase tickets from Niki Tours (p598) in Kamariotissa or at the port kiosk.

❶ Getting Around

BOAT

In summer the tour boat **Theodora** (☑694539 2089, 6974062054; €25) embarks on circular day trips of the island, departing from Therma at noon and returning by 6pm. The boat passes the Byzantine Tower of Fonias, the Panias rock formations and Kremasto Waterfall, stopping midway at Vatos Beach for swimming. Snacks are available on board and (sometimes) a beach BBQ is offered. To participate call the boat operator, or inquire at Kamariotissa's Samothraki Travel (p598).

BUS

In summer daily buses run from Kamariotissa **bus station** (☑25513 41533) to Hora and Palaeopolis (€1.50); and to Therma, the camping grounds and Profitis Ilias (each €2.20), the last via Alonia and Lakkoma.

CAR & MOTORCYCLE

Kyrkos Rent-a-Car (☑6972839231, 25510 41620) rents cars and small Jeeps, while motorcycles and scooters are offered by **Rent-a-Motor-Bike** (☑25510 41057). Both are opposite the ferry quay in Kamariotissa.

AUGUST FULL-MOON HIKE

The August full-moon hike to the summit of Mt Fengari (1611m), the highest peak on the island, organised by the Hellenic Trekking Association, is a beloved annual event that sees scores of enthusiastic young hikers climb to an open field at 1200m on the day of the full moon, drink in the sight of the peak during a night-time party, sleep on the mountain and continue to the summit the next morning for sunrise. Stragglers are welcome. Enquire at Niki Tours (p598) or Samothraki Travel (p598) in Kamariotissa, or Kafeseio Ta Therma (p600) in Loutra (Therma).

Samothraki

TAXI

The friendly **Evdohia Brahiolia Taxi** (📞 6976991270, 6976991271) serves most destinations from Kamariotissa, including Hora (€6), Profitis Ilias (€11), Sanctuary of the Great Gods (€7), Loutra (Therma; €14), Fonias River (€12) and Kipos Beach (€17).

Kamariotissa Καμαριώτισσα

POP 960

Samothraki's port, largest town and transport hub, Kamariotissa has the island's main services and a nearby pebble beach with bars and decent swimming. While most visitors don't linger, it's a likeable and attractive port filled with flowers and fish tavernas.

🛏 Sleeping

Most domatia and hotels are out of town and, unlike many Greek isles, you won't find locals hawking rooms to arriving ferry passengers.

Niki Beach Hotel
HOTEL €€

(📞 25510 41545; www.nikibeach.gr; s/d incl breakfast from €40/65; ❄️🛜🏊) This handsome and well-managed hotel with large, modern rooms is just opposite the town beach. Balconies face the sea, while flowers and poplar trees fill an interior garden. Owners Elena and Vasillis manage to give it a boutique feel, despite the 37 rooms.

Hotel Aeolos
HOTEL €€

(📞 25510 41595; s/d incl breakfast from €40/60; ❄️🛜🏊) Up behind Niki Beach Hotel, the comfortable Aeolos stands on a hill overlooking the sea. Front rooms face a swimming pool and garden, while back rooms overlook Mt Fengari.

🍴 Eating & Drinking

⭐ I Synantisi
TAVERNA €

(📞 25510 41308; fish €6-10) Excellent fresh fish and *gavros* (the owner is a spear diver), as well as fine meat dishes such as roasted goat and rice pilaf. The place is cosy and welcoming, with a small open kitchen, and often serves up *chaslamas,* a Turkish-named dessert unique to Samothraki.

Klimataria Restaurant
TAVERNA €

(mains €6-9) Highly regarded waterfront eatery serving the unusual *gianiotiko,* an oven-baked dish of diced pork, potatoes and egg, along with excellent *mousakas* and other *mayirefta* standbys.

Fournello
ITALIAN €

(mains €4.50-9.50) Close to Niki Beach Hotel, Fournello makes for a nice change of pace, with good pizza and spaghetti. One of the few places where you can dine by the sea.

Stasi
FAST FOOD €

(port; mains €2-4) Outstanding and cheery kitchen-on-wheels, across the car park just before the water. Best for tasty, clean, cheap pitta souvlaki.

Kafeneio Panagiotis Makris
CAFE

Voted one of the most traditional coffee shops in Greece. Step into little Panagiotis for a sip of *tsipouro* with saffron, with mezedhes of course. No wi-fi now or ever.

ℹ Information

Exiting the ferry, turn left 50m for the tourist kiosk and bus station. Nearby are the village cafes, restaurants, travel and rent-a-car agencies, an ATM and supermarket. Kamariotissa's small beach is 100m further east.

Niki Tours (☑ 25510 41465; niki_tours@ hotmail.com; waterfront) For tickets, tours and accommodation. Opposite the buses on the port road.

Port police (☑ 25510 41305)

Samothraki Travel (☑ 25510 89444, 6984908254; www.samothrakitravel.gr) Excellent tour and travel operation, offering information on lodging and outdoor adventures, from boating, diving and horseback riding to trekking and canyoning.

Tourist information kiosk (☑ 25510 89242; ☺ Jul & Aug)

Hora (Samothraki)
Χώρα (Σαμοθράκη)

Set within a natural fortress of two sheer cliffs, and with a commanding view of the sea, Hora (also called Samothraki) was the obvious choice for the island's capital. In the 10th century the Byzantines built a castle on its northwestern peak, though today's substantial remains mostly date from the 15th-century Genoese rule.

Marked by twisting and colourful cobbled streets wreathed in flowers, and vintage traditional houses with terracotta roofs, Hora is perfect for enjoying a leisurely lunch or coffee, and on summer evenings there's easygoing nightlife in the small lanes and rooftop bars. The pyrgos (tower) is a 10-minute walk from Hora centre and contains a display of medieval artifacts.

🛏 Sleeping

Hotel Axieros HOTEL €
(☑ 25510 41294, 6972415611; www.axieros.gr; s/d from €25/30; ❋ ☞) Hora has several domatia, and this one, in the heart of the village, is the best value. The handsomely furnished traditional rooms feature well-equipped kitchenettes and views of the village. Staff are friendly and welcoming.

🍴 Eating & Drinking

Cafes and tavernas are found high on the street, where there's a small fountain with mountain-spring water.

★ O Lefkos Pyrgos SWEETS €
(desserts €4-6; ☺ 9am-late Jul-Aug) The summer-only Lefkos Pyrgos is an excellent, inventive and all-natural sweets shop run by master confectioners Georgios and Dafni. Try lemonade with honey and cinnamon, or Greek

yoghurt with bitter almond, along with exotic teas, coffees and mixed drinks.

Café-Ouzeri 1900 TAVERNA €
(mains €3.50-9; ☺ breakfast, lunch & dinner) Start your day at this flower-filled taverna with yoghurt and honey, or sample the house *tzigerosarmades* (goat with onion, dill and spearmint). The large, colourful menu, printed to look like a newspaper, is a take-home memento.

★ Meltemi CAFE, BAR
(☑ 25510 41071; ☺ 8am-late) Opposite the fountain, discover this cool bar managed by the gracious Paniyioti, with great views from a rooftop garden that's popular from morning till late.

ℹ Information

Buses and taxis stop in the square, below the village. Walk up the main street to find the post office and **police station** (☑ 25510 41203).

Sanctuary of the Great Gods
Το Ιερό των Μεγάλων Θεών

About 6km northeast of Kamariotissa, the Sanctuary of the Great Gods (☑ 25510 41474; combination site & museum adult/student €3/2; ☺ 9am-4pm Tue-Sun summer, 8.30am-3pm Tue-Sun winter) is one of Greece's most mysterious archaeological sites. Thracians built this temple to their fertility deities around 1000 BC. By the 5th century BC, the secret rites and sacrifices associated with the cult had attracted famous pilgrims, including Egyptian Queen Arsinou, Philip II of Macedon (father of Alexander the Great) and Greek historian Herodotus. Remarkably, the sanctuary operated until paganism was forbidden in the 4th century AD.

The principal deity, the fertility goddess Alceros Cybele (Great Mother), was later merged with the Olympian female deities Demeter, Aphrodite and Hecate. Other deities worshipped here were the Great Mother's consort, the virile young Kadmilos (god of the phallus), later integrated with the Olympian god Hermes; and the demonic Kabeiroi twins, Dardanos and Aeton, the sons of Zeus and Leda. Samothraki's great gods were venerated for their immense power – in comparison, the bickering Olympian gods were considered frivolous.

Little is known about what actually transpired here, though archaeological evidence points to two initiations, a lower and a higher. In the first, the great gods were invoked to grant the initiate a spiritual rebirth; in the second, the candidate was absolved of transgressions. This second confessional rite took place at the sacred Hieron, the remaining columns of which are easily the most photographed ruin of the sanctuary.

We do know that the rituals at the sanctuary were open to all – men, women, citizens, servants and slaves – and since death was the penalty for revealing the secrets of the sanctuary, the main requirements seem to have been showing up and keeping quiet.

◉ Sights

The **Archaeological Museum** (✆ 25510 41474; free with site ticket; ☺ 8.30am-3pm Tue-Sun) at the Sanctuary of the Great Gods provides a helpful overview of the entire site. Pick up the free museum map before exploring the area. Museum exhibits include a striking marble frieze of dancing women, terracotta figurines and amphora, jewellery and clay lamps indicative of the nocturnal nature of the rituals. A plaster cast stands in for the celebrated **Winged Victory of Samothrace** (now in the Louvre), looted in 1863 by French diplomat and amateur archaeologist Champoiseau.

About 75m south of the museum stands the **Arisinoeion** (rotunda), a gift from Queen Arisinou of Egypt. The sanctuary's original rock altar was discovered nearby. Adjacent are the rectangular **Anaktoron**, where lower initiations took place; the **Temenos**, a hall where a celebratory feast was held; and the **Hieron**, site of higher initiations.

Opposite the Hieron stand remnants of a **theatre**. Nearby, a path ascends to the **Nike monument**, where once stood the magnificent Winged Victory of Samothrace (*nike* means 'victory' in Greek), which faced northward overlooking the sea – appropriate since it was likely dedicated to the gods following a victorious naval battle.

Loutra (Therma)
Λουτρά (Θερμά)

Loutra (also called Therma), 14km east of Kamariotissa near the coast, is Samothraki's most popular place to stay. This relaxing village of plane and horse-chestnut trees, dense greenery and gurgling creeks comes to life at night when people of all ages gather in its outdoor cafes.

◉ Sights & Activities

Paradeisos Waterfalls　　　WATERFALL
About 500m past Kafeneion Ta Therma, a lush wooded path (100m) leads to a series of rock pools and waterfalls, the most impressive being 30m in height. This is gorgeous, *Lord of the Rings*–like terrain, where gnarled, 600-year-old plane trees covered in moss loom out of fog over a forest floor of giant ferns and brackish boulders. Get ready for an ice-cold dip on a hot summer day.

Thermal Baths　　　HOT SPRING, BATHHOUSE
(✆ 25513 50800; admission €4-6; ☺ 7-10am & 5-8pm Jun-Sep) The village's name, Therma, refers to its warm, therapeutic, mineral-rich springs, reportedly curing everything from skin problems to infertility. The prominent white building by the bus stop houses the official bath, though there is **free bathing** at two small outdoor baths 75m up the hill.

Ghria Vathra Canyon　　　HIKING
Running roughly parallel with the Paradeisos Waterfalls, but further east along the coast road, this lush canyon is known for its shimmering series of rock pools and waterfalls, and is an easy and enjoyable hike-and-splash if going inland from the waterfront road.

🛏 Sleeping

★**Mariva Bungalows**　　　BUNGALOW €
(✆ 25510 98230; www.mariva.gr; d incl breakfast from €40; P ❋ 🛜) The secluded vine-covered stone bungalows, with breezy modern rooms, sit on a lush hillside near a waterfall. To reach them, turn from the coast road inland towards Loutra and follow the signs.

Municipal Camping　　　CAMPGROUND
(✆ 25513 50800) FREE Free, attractive shaded municipal camping ground behind the beach, with basic facilities.

Studios Ktima Holoway　　　APARTMENT €
(✆ 25510 98335, 6945947182; www.ktimaholoway. com; Fonias; d/tr €40/50; P ❋ 🛜) Located 5km east of Loutra, near the trail to Fonias Falls, this relaxing getaway has modern one- and two-room self-catering studios 50m from the beach, with a mini playground for kids. Friendly owner Elias also offers free port pick-up and drop-off.

Hotel Orfeas　　　HOTEL €
(✆ 6979330107, 25510 98233; christos1400@ yahoo.com; d/tr incl breakfast from €35/45; ❋ 🛜) Just across a leafy lane from the local stream, the Orfeas is simple, comfortable

and friendly. The best rooms have balconies overlooking the stream, and the gracious owner, Christos, can offer tips on exploring the shady hills around Loutra.

★ **Hotel Samothraki Village**　HOTEL €€
(☑6982303396, 25510 42300; www.samothraki village.gr; Paleopolis; s/d/tr/ste €50/60/70/110; ❄ 🛜 ≋) Located 4km east of Kamariotissa on the coast road, and 1km before the Sanctuary of the Great Gods, this excellent lodging consists of spacious modern rooms with sea-view balconies. There are two outdoor pools (and a mini-playground for kids), plus a fitness centre and *hammam*. Book ahead for free port pick-up.

✖ Eating

Loutra has decent and quick *gyros* and souvlaki spots.

★ **Kafeneio Ta Therma**　CAFE €
(☑6984994856; ⊙8am-2am; ❄) Run by the jovial Iordanis Iordaninis for more than 20 years, this is the centre of the action in Loutra, with live music, impromptu vendors, artists and dancers in the open areas around, plus coffee, beer and sweets. It's near the baths and several trails.

Taverna O Paradisos　TAVERNA €
(☑25510 98271; mains €4-8.50; ⊙lunch & dinner) Excellent fish and a popular summer-evening meeting place under a huge plane tree. Ask Andreas to see the day's catch.

Fonias River　Ποτάμι Φονιάς

After Loutra on the northeast coast is the Fonias River and the famous **Fonias rock pools** (€1). The walk starts at the bridge 4.7km east of Loutra, by the (summer-only) ticket booths. The first 40 minutes are along an easy, well-marked track leading to a large and swimmable rock pool fed by a dramatic 12m-high waterfall. The river is known as the 'Murderer', and in winter rain can transform the waters into a raging torrent. The real danger, however, is getting lost – though there are six waterfalls, marked paths are few. For hiking here and near Mt Fengari, consult Samothraki Travel (p598).

South Samothraki

The small villages of **Profitis Ilias**, **Lakkoma** and **Xiropotamos** in the southwest are all serene and seldom visited, though they're easily accessible.

The 800m-long **Pahia Ammos Beach** is a superb sandy beach along an 8km winding road from Lakkoma. In summer, caïques from Kamariotissa visit. The *Theodora* (p596) boat tour from Loutra stops around the southern headland at the equally superb, nudist-friendly **Vatos Beach**. Pretty and pebbled **Kipos Beach**, 15km from Loutra, marks the end of the southeast coastal road, from where the Turkish island of Imvros (Gökçeada) is sometimes visible.

The hillside Profitis Ilias has several tavernas, including **Vrahos** (☑25510 95264; mains €4.50-9) and **Paradisos** (☑6972441889; mains €5-9), both renowned for their roast goat. Seaside **Taverna Akrogiali** (☑25510 95123; Lakkoma Beach; mains €5-9) is noted for fresh fish.

THASOS　ΘΑΣΟΣ

POP 14,900

One of Greece's greenest and most gentle islands, Thasos lies 10km from mainland Kavala. Its climate and vegetation give the feeling that the island is an extension of northern Greece, yet it boasts enviable sandy beaches and a forested mountain interior. Quite inexpensive by Greek-island standards, it's popular with families and students from Bulgaria and the ex-Yugoslav republics. Frequent ferries from the mainland allow independent travellers to get here quickly, and the excellent bus network makes getting around easy.

Over its long history, Thasos has benefitted from its natural wealth. The Parians, who founded the ancient city of Thasos (Limenas) in 700 BC, struck gold at Mt Pangaion, creating an export trade lucrative enough to subsidise a naval fleet. While the gold is long gone, Thasos' white Parian marble is still being exploited, though scarring a mountainside in the process.

For visitors today, the island's main sources of wealth are its natural beauty, beaches, inland villages and historic attractions. The excellent archaeological museum in the capital, Thasos, is complemented by the Byzantine Moni Arhangelou, with its stunning cliff-top setting, and the ancient Greek temple at Alyki on the serene southeast coast.

ⓘ Getting There & Away

Thasos is only accessible from the mainland ports of Keramoti and Kavala. There are hourly

Thasos

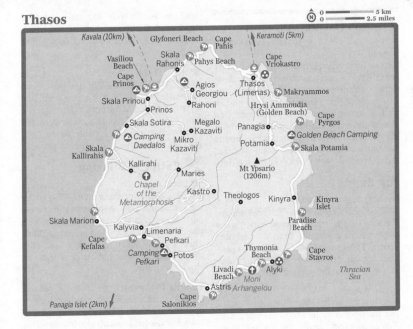

ferries between Keramoti and Thasos (€3, 40 minutes). There are two to three a day between Kavala and Skala Prinou (€4.70, 1¼ hours).

Get ferry schedules at the **ticket booths** (☑ 25930 22318) in Thasos (Limenas) and from the port police (p602) at Skala Prinou.

ℹ Getting Around

BICYCLE

Basic bikes can be hired in Thasos (Limenas), but top-of-the-line models and detailed route information are available in Potos on the southwest coast from Velo Bike Rental (p603).

BOAT

The **Victoria** (☑ 6977336114; day trip €27; ☉ Jul & Aug) excursion boat makes full-day trips around Thasos, with stops for swimming and lunch. The boat departs the old harbour in Thalos (Limenas) at 10am. Water taxis run regularly to Hrysi Ammoudia (Golden Beach) and Makryammos Beach from the old harbour. Excursion boats of varying sizes and alcohol content also set sail regularly from the coastal resorts. Enquire at Visit North Greece (p602) or Billias Travel Service (p602) in Thalos (Limenas).

BUS

Frequent buses serve the entire island coast and inland villages too. Buses meet arriving ferries at Skala Prinou and Thasos (Limenas), the island's transport hub. The two port towns are connected by eight daily buses (€2, 20 minutes).

Daily buses run throughout the day from Thasos (Limenas) to west-coast villages such as Skala Marion (€3), Limenaria (€4.50), Potos (€4.70) and Theologos (€5.90). Buses from Thalos (Limenas) also reach the east-coast destinations of Hrysi Ammoudia (€2), Skala Potamia (€1.70) via Panagia (€1.50) and Potamia (€1.60), Paradise Beach (€2.90) and Alyki and nearby Moni Arhangelou (€6.10).

A full circular tour (about 100km) runs six to eight times daily (€10.60, 3½ hours) – three clockwise and three anticlockwise. This round-the-island ticket is valid all day, so you can jump on and off without paying extra. The **bus station** (☑ 25930 22162) on the Thasos (Limenas) waterfront provides timetables.

CAR & MOTORCYCLE

Potos Car Rentals (☑ 25930 52071) is reliable and reasonable. **Avis Rent-a-Car** (☑ 25930 22535) is in Thasos, Potamia, and Skala Prinou.

Mike's Bikes (☑ 25930 71820), 1km from the old harbour in Thasos (Limenas), and **Crazy Rollers** (☑ 6978937536; crazyrollers@gmail.com), above the port, rent motorbikes and bicycles.

TAXI

The Thasos (Limenas) **taxi rank** (☑ 25930 22394, 6944170373) is on the waterfront, next to the main bus stop (Skala Prinos €20, Panagia €12, Skala Potamia €20, Alyki €40, Potos €50). In Potos, a taxi rank with listed prices is beside the main road's bus stop.

Thasos (Limenas)
Θάσος (Λιμένας)

POP 2610

Thasos (also called Limenas) has the island's main services and year-round activity, along with a picturesque fishing harbour, sandy beach, shopping, a few ancient ruins and an archaeological museum. If you're exploring the eastern side of town, note the signpost for historical sites, beginning a five-minute walk up a shaded trail to the lovely chapel of Agioi Apostoli, with views over the seafront.

◉ Sights

Archaeological Museum   MUSEUM
(☑ 25930 22180; admission €2; ⊙ 8.30am-3pm Tue-Sun) Thasos' archaeological museum displays neolithic utensils from a mysterious central Thasos tomb, along with an impressive 5m-tall 6th-century-BC *kouros* (male statue of the Archaic period) carrying a ram.

Ancient Agora   RUIN
Next to the archaeological museum stand the foundation ruins of the ancient *agora,* the commercial centre in ancient times. About 100m east of the *agora,* the ancient theatre stages performances of ancient dramas and comedies during the Philippi Thasos Festival. The theatre is signposted from the harbour. A path connects the *agora* to the acropolis, where substantial remains of a medieval fortress stand, with commanding views of the coast. Carved rock steps descend to the foundations of the ancient town.

✸✸ Festivals & Events

Philippi Thasos Festival   CULTURAL
(www.philippifestival.gr) In late July and August, this lively festival takes place in both mainland Kavala and Thasos. Classical drama, painting exhibitions and contemporary Greek music are featured. Programs are available at hotels, cafes and tourist agencies. Kavala **tourist information centre** (☑ 25102 31011; www.kavalagreece.gr; Eleftherias Sq, Kavala), the Thasos tourist police and the Visit North Greece travel agency have ticket information.

🛏 Sleeping

Hotel Possidon   HOTEL €
(☑ 25930 22739; www.thassos-possidon.com; old harbour; s/d from €40/50; P ❋ 🛜) This friendly waterfront hotel's rambling lobby bar straddles the harbour and main shopping street of 18 Oktovriou. Smallish rooms are modern, many with comfortable sea-view balconies.

★ Hotel Galini   HOTEL €€
(☑ 6945443322, 25930 22195; Theageneou; s/d incl breakfast €50/60; P ❋ 🛜) This small and smartly updated hotel, next to Euro Bank, a short block inland from the waterfront, has 16 attractive and comfortable rooms (four with sea views) and a flowery back garden.

✕ Eating & Drinking

★ Simi   TAVERNA €
(☑ 25930 22517; old harbour; mains €6-9) Locals agree that this year-round eatery at the old port serves Limenas' best fish, along with fine fish soup, *stifado* and grilled sardines. There's a kids' menu, good wine and spicy mezedhes, including hot peppers that can change your life.

Taverna To Karanti   TAVERNA €
(Miaouli; mains €5-9.50) An outdoor *ouzerie* opposite the fishing boats on the old harbour, frequented by locals and tourists alike, with traditional music and tasty mezedhes.

Island Beach Bar   CAFE, BAR
(Miaouli; 🛜) This swanky outdoor bar has free wi-fi, good breakfasts, decent drinks and a mix of music into the night.

ⓘ Information

ATMs can be found near the central square.
Billias Travel Service (☑ 25930 24003; Gallikis Arheologikis Scholis 2) Full-service travel agency.
Port police (☑ 25930 22106)
Tourist police (☑ 25930 23111)
Visit North Greece (☑ 25106 20566, 6942524337; www.visitnorthgreece.com; Pavlou Mela 17) Well-managed and unique tour operator offering hiking, walking and cycling excursions, along with 4WD safaris and sailing trips. The helpful owners, Chrisoula and Stelios, also can handle transfers and suggest accommodation.

West Coast

Thasos' west coast has been assailed by package tours for years, though there are still a few idyllic spots and quiet sandy beaches. Better still, the inland mountain villages preserve a traditional pace of life and fine stone architecture.

Following the coast west from Thasos, two sandy beaches emerge: decent **Glyfoneri** and the superior **Pahys Beach**.

Continuing west, the port of **Skala Prinou** has ferries to Kavala, though little else to warrant a stop. But 6km inland, past the town of Prinos, the hillside villages of **Mikro Kazaviti** and **Megalo Kazaviti** (aka the Prinou villages) offer a lush break from the touristed coast, with undeniable character and a few places to stay and eat, including **Menir Luxury Apartments** (☑25930 58270; www.menir-thassos.gr; Mikros Kazaviti; s/d incl breakfast from €50/80). An easy-to-follow trail network branches off from the pretty *plateia* in Megalo Kazaviti, with a sign marking the routes.

The next real point of interest, the whimsical fishing port of **Skala Marion**, lies further south. Its few canopied tavernas overlooking the sea are faithfully populated by village elders shuffling backgammon chips while children scamper about. The village has a few domatia and a bakery on the northern jetty. On the village's feast day (24 June), church services are followed by folk dancing around the square.

The coast road south passes more beaches until reaching **Limenaria**, Thasos' second-largest town, followed quickly by **Pefkari** and **Potos**, two fishing villages turned package resorts, both with long sandy beaches lined with cafes and tavernas. Limenaria is also home to a unique and rambling **sculpture garden** (☑6973080081; www.reocities.com/birou/index.html) and studio.

From the Theologos-Potos corner of the main road, head southeast round the coast for views of stunning bays. The last southwestern settlement, **Astris**, has a good beach with tavernas and the **Astris Sun Hotel** (☑25930 51281; www.astrissunhotel.gr; Astris; r incl breakfast from €40).

🏃 Activities

Despite its touristy feel, Thasos' west coast offers worthwhile outdoor activities such as scuba diving, mountain biking, birdwatching and walking trails above the coast.

★ Velo Bike Rental
CYCLING
(☑25930 52459, 6946955704; www.velobikerental.com; regular/used/new mountain bikes per day €10/15/20) Hires out bikes year-round in Potos, and also runs guided biking and hiking tours to Mt Ypsilariou.

DAY TRIP: EXPLORING HIGHLAND VILLAGES

Two interior villages warrant a day trip inland. About 6km from Skala Marion, forested **Maries** rewards visitors with cool highland air and a handsome monastery, Agios Taxiarchis. Thasos' medieval and Ottoman capital, **Theologos**, is only accessible from Potos, where the road leads inland to the forested hamlet of 400 souls, notable for its whitewashed slate-roofed houses. Find the 1803 Church of Agios Dimitrios, distinguished by its grand slate roof and white-plastered clock tower. Relax at one of the local cafes or tavernas to soak it all in.

Inspired owner Yiannis Raizis also organises a popular amateur **international mountain-biking race** (www.mtb-thassos.com, entry €15) on the last Sunday in April that draws more than 200 contestants to Potos. They race across the island's wooded interior, scaling Mt Ypsario (1206m) and returning through scenic Kastro village.

Panagia Islet
BIRDWATCHING, BOATING
(☑6973209576; www.gothassos.com; trip €25) The rocky, uninhabited Panagia Islet, southwest of Potos, is home to Greece's largest shag colony (www.yrefail.net/Thasos/habitats.htm). Local environmentalist Yiannis Markianos at Aldebran Pension arranges birdwatching boat trips, weather permitting.

Diving Club Vasiliadis
DIVING
(☑6944542974; www.scuba-vas.gr; Potos) Diving for beginners and open-water divers is offered in Potos by Vasilis Vasiliadis, including to Alyki's submerged ancient marble quarry.

🛏 Sleeping

★ Aldebran Pension
PENSION €
(☑25930 52494, 6973209576; www.gothassos.com; Potos; d from €40; ❊🐾) Well-informed and attentive owners Elke and Yiannis make Aldebran the best value in southern Thasos. Along with a leafy courtyard and table tennis, it boasts modern bathrooms, well-equipped communal kitchen and all-day coffee and tea. Resident ornithologist Giannis offers spring-to-autumn birdwatching tours for guests, plus info on local hiking trails and more.

OFF THE BEATEN TRACK

POETRY TRAIL

One of Thasos' inland delights is a short steep path at Kallarahi, dubbed the Poetry Trail, an 800m-long path starting at the eastern edge of the village and ending at the Chapel of the Metamorphosis. Along the way, the poetry and writings of Herman Hesse, Rainer Maria Rilke and Goethe, along with the riddle of the Sphinx, among others, are inscribed on marble slabs. From the chapel, a circular hike of 11km, known as the Kallirahi Circuit, ascends to the one of the best viewpoints on Thasos.

Domatia Filaktaki PENSION €
(☑ 25930 52634, 6977413789; Skala Marion; r from €30; ❄️🍴) These simple air-conditioned rooms are situated above the home of kind Maria Filaktaki and family in Skala Marion. It's the first place you'll reach when descending to the serene waterfront.

Camping Pefkari CAMPGROUND €
(☑ 25930 51190; www.camping-pefkari.gr; camp sites per adult/tent €5/5; ⊙Jun-Sep) Wooded spot above Pefkari Beach that's popular with families and features spotless bathrooms, laundry and cooking facilities.

Camping Daedalos CAMPGROUND €
(☑ 25930 58251; tseltha@otenet.gr; camp sites per adult/tent €6/4) Clean beachfront camping ground, 1km north of Skala Sotira. Includes a mini-market and restaurant, with water sports available.

✕ Eating

★**Armeno** TAVERNA €
(Skala Marion; mains €5-9) A well-regarded waterfront taverna in offbeat Skala Marion where you can have a look at the day's fish catch. The organic produce is from the gardens of the friendly Filaktaki family, who also rent rooms and can help with local information.

Piatsa Michalis TAVERNA €
(Potos; mains €6-10) Potos' 50-year-old beachfront taverna started working well before mass tourism came to town, and sticks to the recipe with specialities such as stewed rabbit and octopus in red-wine sauce, plus a full menu of taverna fare.

O Georgios TAVERNA €
(Potos; mains €4.50-7) This traditional Greek grill house, set in a pebbled rose garden, is a local favourite away from Potos' more touristy main road, offering friendly service and generous portions.

Kafeneio Tsiknas CAFE €
(Theologos) At the beginning of Theologos, just before the church, this charming cafe has balcony seating, coffee and snacks.

❶ Information

There are ATMs in Skala Prinou, Limenaria and Potos.

East Coast

Thasos' east-coast beaches are beautiful in summer and less crowded than the more developed west coast. The dramatic coastal landscape features thick forests that run from mountains to the sea. There are fewer organised activities here and the warm, shallow waters are excellent for families. Tiny Alyki may be the most overlooked spot on the southeast coast, with a village great for unwinding, a few shops, domatia and taverna and two fine sandy beach coves, separated by a small olive grove dotted with ancient ruins comprising the archaeological site of Alyki.

◉ Sights & Activities

★**Archaeological Site of Alyki** ARCHAEOLOGICAL SITE
FREE This well-signed site is not to be missed. It lies alluringly and accessibly above the southeastern beach and includes the considerable, and photogenic, remains of an ancient temple where the gods were once invoked to protect sailors. A partially submerged nearby marble quarry operated from the 7th century BC to the 6th century AD. Follow the marked path to its striking location at the west harbour.

Panagia VILLAGE
This inland village, just south of Thasos, is nothing if not photogenic. Its characteristic architecture includes its stone-and-slate rooftops and the elegant blue-and-white domed and icon-rich **Church of the Kimisis tou Theotokou** (Church of the Dormition of the Virgin). To reach this peaceful quarter, follow the sound of rushing spring water upwards along a stone path heading inland.

Moni Arhangelou
MONASTERY

(⊙9am-2pm & 5pm-sunset) FREE West from Alyki, past Thymonia Beach, is the cliff-top Moni Arhangelou, an Athonite dependency and working convent, notable for its 400-year-old church (with some ungainly modern touches) and stellar sea views. Those improperly attired will get shawled up for entry by the friendly nuns.

Mt Ypsario
HIKING

Potamia makes a good jumping-off point for climbing Thasos' highest peak, Mt Ypsario (1206m). A tractor trail west from Potamia continues to the valley's end, after which arrows and cairns point the way up a steep path. The three-hour Ypsario hike is classified as moderately difficult. You can sleep at the Ypsario Mountain Shelter by contacting Leftheris of the **Thasos Mountaineering Club** (☑6972198032) to book and get the key. The shelter has fireplaces and spring water.

Beaches

Panagia and Potamia are 4km west of the east coast's most popular beaches: sand-duned **Hrysi Ammoudia (Golden Beach)**, tucked inside a long, curving bay; and gentle **Skala Potamia**, on its southern end. A bus between the two (€1.30) runs every couple of hours. Both have accommodation, restaurants and a bit of nightlife.

Further south from Skala Potamia is the deservedly popular and nudist-friendly **Paradise Beach**, 2km after tiny Kinyra village.

About 1.5km west of Moni Arhangelou, a small dirt road heads 1km to **Livadi Beach**, one of Thasos' most beautiful, with aquamarine waters ringed by cliffs and forests and just a few umbrellas set in the sand.

🛏 Sleeping & Eating

There's some accommodation at Kinyra, Alyki and Paradise Beach, but more at Hrysi Ammoudia and Skala Potamia.

Studios Vaso
APARTMENT €

(☑25102 33507, 6946524706; www.vaso-studios.gr; Alyki; r incl breakfast €50; P❄) Just east of Alyki's bus stop on the main road, look for the big burst of flowers and a sign pointing up the drive to this charming set of nine self-catering domatia, run by welcoming Vaso Gemetzi and daughter Aleka. There's a leafy courtyard, and kids stay free.

Thassos Inn
HOTEL €

(☑25930 61612; www.thassosinn.gr; Panagia; s/d from €35/50) Just follow the sound of rushing spring water to this rambling hotel by the church, with great views of Panagia's slate-roofed houses. The welcoming owners, Toula and Tasos, can also advise hikers who want to be close to the trailhead to Mt Ypsario.

Golden Beach Camping
CAMPGROUND €

(☑25930 61472; www.camping-goldenbeach.gr; Hrysi Ammoudia; camp sites per adult/tent €5/4; P) Golden Beach Camping is seldom dull, with mini-market, bar, beach volleyball and visitors from around Greece, Serbia, Bulgaria and Turkey.

★Hotel Kamelia
HOTEL €€

(☑698898767, 25930 61463; www.hotel-kamelia.gr; Skala Potamia; s/d/studios incl breakfast from €40/60/75; P❄🌐) This beachfront gem is the best in town – understated, with cool jazz in the garden bar and friendly service throughout. The gracious owners, Eleni and Stavros and family, serve a fine Greek breakfast overlooking the sea and provide plenty of tips about the area. It's 500m north of the busier main beach, over a very small bridge.

★Souvlaki Special
GREEK €

(Skala Potamia; mains €2-5; ⊙lunch & dinner) Prepare to stand in line at this modest souvlaki spot next to Supermarket Enira, where the main road meets the beach. The sign is in Greek, the owner is Thanasis, the food is great. Look for the red-and-black digital clock. Worth the wait.

Arhontissa Alyki
GREEK €

(☑25930 31552; Alyki; mains €5-10; ⊙lunch & dinner) The friendly Anastasios Kuzis and family run this tranquil taverna with great sea views, east of the village car park and signposted up a steep drive. It serves excellent fare, with fresh fish and mezedhes among the star offerings.

Taverna Grill Elena
TAVERNA €

(☑25930 61709; Panagia; mains €6-10; ⊙10am-midnight) This classic taverna under a shady patio off the square, run by Georgios and Elena, specialises in spit-roasted lamb and goat. For appetisers, before you get to the *kokoretsi* on the spit, sample the *bougloundi* (baked feta with tomatoes and chilli).

Taverna Krambousa
SEAFOOD €

(mains €4.50-10; ⊙lunch & dinner) Relaxing, popular and well-priced fish taverna on the beach, just before Hotel Kamelia.

Evia & the Sporades

Best Places to Eat

➡ Dina's Amfilirion Restaurant (p611)

➡ Taverna-Ouzerie Kabourelia (p616)

➡ To Perivoli Restaurant (p621)

➡ Hayiati (p626)

➡ Stefanos Taverna (p630)

Best Places to Stay

➡ Hotel Nefeli (p629)

➡ Atrium Hotel (p618)

➡ Pension Sotos (p619)

➡ Liadromia Hotel (p625)

➡ Perigiali Hotel & Studios (p630)

Why Go?

Evia (Εύβοια) and the four Sporades islands (Οι Σποράδες) remain largely off the beaten path. Although Evia is Greece's second-largest island, it seems hidden in plain view, only separated from the mainland by the narrow Evripos Channel at busy Halkida. Away from this commercial hub, the pace slows as the landscape stretches out, dotted by hilltop monasteries, small farms, vineyards, hidden bays and curious goats.

The Sporades ('scattered ones') seem like extensions of the forested Pelion Peninsula, and, in fact, they were joined in prehistoric times. Skiathos, easily the most developed of the group, claims the sandiest beaches in the Aegean. Low-key Skopelos kicks back with a postcard-worthy harbour and forest meadows. Remote Alonnisos anchors the National Marine Park of the Northern Sporades. Skyros, the southernmost of the chain, is known for its culinary and artistic traditions that date from Byzantine times when these islands were home to rogues and pirates.

When to Go
Skiathos Town

°C/°F Temp
40/104 —
30/86 —
20/68 —
10/50 —
0/32 —

Rainfall inches/mm
— 0.79/20
— 0.39/15
— 0.2/5
— 0

J F M A M J J A S O N D

Feb & Mar Carnival season keeps things warm with plenty of merrymaking.

Apr & May Spring is in the air and Easter festivities linger long into the night.

Jun & Sep Perfect temperatures and clear skies – ideal hiking and swimming conditions.

Evia & the Sporades Highlights

1 Swimming year-round in the thermal-fed bay at **Loutra Edipsou** (p610) on Evia.

2 Hiking the lush 10km **Dimosari Gorge** (p613) in south Evia, then cooling off in the sea near trail's end.

3 Watching for dolphins and cliff-dwelling falcons while sailing around Greece's only national marine park at **Alonnisos** (p623).

4 Finding crimson poppies and majestic butterflies while hiking the inland meadows of **Skopelos** (p622).

5 Nuzzling up with one of the gentle and rare Skyrian horses on **Skyros** (p631).

6 Hearing bouzouki music above the *kastro* overlooking **Skopelos Town** (p621).

7 Dancing with masked revellers at the carnival in **Skyros** (p627).

8 Sampling the monks' wine at Moni Evangelistrias (p617) on **Skiathos**.

EVIA   EYBOIA

Evia (*eh*-vih-ah), Greece's second-largest island after Crete, offers glorious mountain roads, challenging treks, major archaeological finds and many uncrowded beaches. A north–south mountainous spine divides the island's eastern cliffs from the gentler and resort-friendly west coast. Ferries link the island to the mainland, along with two bridges at Halkida. One of these bridges is a sliding drawbridge (the original span dates from 410 BC) over the narrow Evripos Channel and reverses direction about seven times daily, an event whose full explanation has eluded observers since Aristotle, and was dreaded by ancient mariners.

❶ Getting There & Away

There are regular buses between Halkida and Athens (€7.50, 1¼ hours, half-hourly), Ioannina (€43, seven hours, one to two daily) and Thessaloniki (€43, 6¼ hours, one to two daily).

There is also a regular train service between Halkida and Athens (€5.50, 1½ hours, 11 daily) and an express service between Halkida and Thessaloniki (€44, 5½ hours, six daily).

Five ports on Evia serve the mainland; one serves the island of Skyros; and another serves Skopelos and Skiathos.

Central Evia

Beyond the mainland bridge entry to Evia at Halkida, the road veers south, following the coastline to Eretria, a bustling resort and archaeological site. Further on, a string of hamlets and fishing villages dot the route until the junction at Lepoura, where the road forks north towards Kymi, and south towards Karystos. A rough dirt road winds west from Kymi to the long beach at Paralia Hiliadou.

Halkida   Χαλκίδα
POP 69,900

Mentioned in *The Iliad,* powerful Halkida (aka Halkis or Chalkis) spawned several colonies around the Mediterranean. The name derives from the bronze that was manufactured here in antiquity ('halkos' means bronze in Greek). Today, it's a lively commercial centre, and gateway to Evia. As evening approaches, the waterfront promenade by the Old Bridge comes to life.

⦿ Sights

To glimpse Halkida's diverse religious history, head up Kotsou towards the *kastro* (castle) to find a striking 15th-century **mosque** and 19th-century **synagogue**, adjacent to Plateia Tzami. About 150m south is the **Byzantine church** of Agia Paraskevi, and a striking Venetian **aqueduct**.

Archaeological Museum   MUSEUM
(☑ 22210 15131; Leoforos Venizelou 13; admission €2; ⊙ 8.30am-3pm Tue-Sun) Houses 7th-century-BC artefacts from both Halkida and nearby Eretria, including a headless torso of Apollo. Other remarkable finds include a Hellenistic-era beak-mouthed jug and two golden wreaths.

Kokkino Spiti (Red House)   ARCHITECTURE
(Mallias Mansion; cnr Tziarntini & Dimitrou Karaoli; admission €2; ⊙ 9am-4pm Tue-Sun) Halkida's 19th-century grandeur endures at waterfront Kokkino Spiti (Red House). Carved into the rock, it became headquarters for the occupying Germans in WWII.

🛏 Sleeping & Eating

Hotel Paliria   BUSINESS HOTEL €€
(☑ 22210 28001; www.paliria-hotel.gr; Eleftheriou Venizelou 2; s/d incl breakfast €60/80; P ✴ @ 🛜) The Paliria bears more than a passing re-

---

BOAT SERVICES FROM EVIA

DESTINATION	PORT	COST	TIME	FREQUENCY
Agia Marina	Nea Styra	€3.50	45min	6-9 daily
Alonnisos	Paralia Kymis	€24	3½hr	3 weekly
Arkitsa	Loutra Edipsou	€3.70	40min	8-14 daily
Glyfa	Agiokambos	€2.30	20min	5-7 daily
Rafina	Marmari	€8	1hr	3-4 daily
Skala Oropou	Eretria	€2	25min	half-hourly
Skopelos (Glossa)	Mantoudi	€18	1½hr	3 weekly
Skyros	Paralia Kymis	€10	1¾hr	1-2 daily

semblance to a modern seven-storey cruise ship, and occupies a prime seaside spot near the Old Bridge, with spacious carpeted rooms and amenities to spare.

Pantheon 1900 TAPAS €

(Voudouri; €3-7; ☺lunch & dinner) Nestled in a handsome waterfront neoclassical building, this smart tapas bar features Greek wines, tasty small plates and snappy service.

ⓘ Information

Several ATMs cluster at the waterfront near the corner of Venizelou and Voudouri.

Hospital (☑22210 21902; cnr Gazepi & Hatzopoulou)

Pharmacy (☑22210 25424; Isaiou 6)

Post office (cnr Karamourtzouni & Kriezotou; ☺8am-2pm Mon-Fri)

Tourist police (☑22210 77777)

ⓘ Getting There & Away

From Halkida, buses serve Athens (€7.50, 1¼ hours, half-hourly), Ioannina (€39, seven hours, four to six daily) and Thessaloniki (€40, 6¼ hours, eight to 10 daily). Regular trains also connect Halkida with Athens, and an express service runs to Thessaloniki.

From **Halkida KTEL bus station** (☑22210 20400; cnr Styron & Arethousis), 3km east of the Old Bridge, buses also connect to the following destinations on Evia:

DESTINATION	FARE	TIME	FREQUENCY
Eretria	€2	25min	hourly
Karystos	€14	3hr	3 daily
Kymi Town & Paralia Kymis	€9.50	2hr	hourly
Limni	€7.90	2hr	3 daily
Loutra Edipsou	€14	3½hr	2 daily
Mantoudi	€8	2hr	3 daily
Steni	€3.50	50min	3 daily

Eretria Ερέτρια

POP 3220

Southeast about 20km from Halkida, the first place of interest on Evia for travellers coming from the mainland is Eretria, with a small fishing harbour and touristy boardwalk of lively tavernas, open-air cafes and beach bars.

⊙ Sights

West of the **ancient acropolis** are the remains of a theatre with a subterranean passage used by actors to reach the stage.

Archaeological Museum of Eretria MUSEUM

(☑22290 62206; www.gtp.gr/archaeologicalmuseumoferetria; Archaiou Theatrou & Isidos; admission €2; ☺9am-4pm Tue-Sun) The Archaeological Museum of Eretria includes the fascinating House of Mosaics, dating from the 4th century BC. Its signature exhibit features a terracotta depiction of the mythical Medusa, whose tresses were turned into live serpents by the goddess Athena as revenge for Medusa's dalliance with Poseidon in Athena's temple, giving mythic meaning to the term 'bad hair day'.

🍽 Sleeping & Eating

Milos Camping CAMPGROUND €

(☑22290 60420; www.camping-in-evia.gr; camp sites per adult/tent €6/4) This well-managed and shaded campground 1km northwest of Eretria has a small restaurant, bar and 200m-long pebble beach.

Diamanto Rooms PENSION €

(☑6946836529, 22290 62214; www.diamantorooms.gr; Varvaki 2, cnr Theatre; s/d €25/35; P✴@🖙) Ten sparkling domatia with balconies, cheerful service and a common kitchen.

Villa Belmar Apartments APARTMENT €€

(☑6971588424; www.villabelmar.gr; s/d/f incl breakfast from €45/65/90; P✴@🖙) Southwest of the port, these stylish apartments with a private waterfront deck are managed by welcoming sisters Lina and Renia.

Romeo Taverna TAVERNA €€

(waterfront; mains €5-17; ☺lunch & dinner) Snappy service and tasty seafood dishes single out this waterfront taverna. The €25 fixed menu features fresh fish and salads, more than enough for two.

ⓘ Getting There & Away

Ferries travel daily between Eretria and Skala Oropou (€2, 25 minutes, half-hourly). Purchase tickets from the dock kiosks.

Steni Στενή

POP 1080

From Halkida, it's 31km to the picturesque mountain village of Steni, with its gurgling springs, and shady plane and chestnut trees. Steni is also the starting point for hikers tackling Mt Dirfys. A twisting road continues from Steni to **Paralia Hiliadou** on the north coast, where a grove of maple and chestnut trees borders a fine pebble-and-sand beach, along with a few domatia and tavernas.

🏃 Activities

Steni is the starting point for hiking up **Mt Dirfys** (1743m), Evia's highest mountain. The **Dirfys Refuge** (☑6974057517, 22210 85760, 22210 25230; www.eoschalkidas.gr; per person €12), at 1120m, can be reached along a 9km dirt road. From there, it's a steep 7km to the summit. Experienced hikers should allow about six hours from Steni to the summit. For refuge lodging information (and key), as well as current hiking conditions, contact **Minas Patsourakis** (☑22210 85760, 6974057517; www.facebook.com/groups/eoschalkidas) and the EOS-affiliated **Halkida Alpine Club** (☑25930 23412, 22210 25230; www.eoschalkidas.gr; Angeli Gouviou 22, Halkida; ⊙9am-5pm Mon-Sat). See Anavasi's detailed topo map, *Mt Dirfys*.

🛏 Sleeping & Eating

Hotel Dirfys   HOTEL €
(☑6972319451, 22280 51270; dirfis@otenet.gr; Steni village; s/d incl breakfast €35/45; P 🐾) This is the most appealing of Steni's three hotels. All rooms have balcony views of the surrounding forest, sparkling bathrooms, and the hotel taverna draws locals come evening.

O Neromylos   TAVERNA €
(Agia Kyriaki, Kampia; mains €5-10; ⊙lunch & dinner) The 'watermill' shares the lush landscape of nearby Agia Kyriaki, signposted 3km southeast of Steni. Kitchen favourites include roast mushrooms and homemade sausages.

Kymi & Paralia Kymis
Κύμη & Παραλία Κύμης
POP 3040

Workaday Kymi perks up at dusk when the town square comes to life. Kymi is a prosperous agricultural centre surrounded by vineyards and fruit orchards. The port of Paralia Kymis, 4km downhill, is the departure point for ferries to Skyros, Alonnisos and Skopelos.

⊙ Sights

Folklore Museum   MUSEUM
(☑22220 22011; Kymi; admission €1.50; ⊙10.30am-1.30pm & 6-8pm daily Jul & Aug, 10.30am-2pm Wed, Sat & Sun Sep-Jun) The Folklore Museum, 30m downhill from the main square of Kymi, includes a display honouring Kymi-born Dr George Papanikolaou, inventor of the Pap smear test.

Figs of Kymi   CO-OP
(☑22220 31722; figkimi@otenet.gr; Platana; ⊙9am-9pm Sep-Nov & by appointment) FREE

Platana, 3km south of Paralia Kymis, is home to Figs of Kymi, a lively agricultural co-op supporting local fig farmers and sustainable production. Preservative-free figs and jams are on sale.

🛏 Sleeping & Eating

In Paralia Kymis, a string of tavernas lines the waterfront. Just 3km south in tiny Platana, check out the exceptional fish taverna **Koutelos** (☑22220 71272; Platana; mains €7-11; ⊙lunch & dinner).

Hotel Beis   HOTEL €
(☑22220 22604; Paralia Kymis; s/d/tr incl breakfast €40/55/65; P ❋ 🐾) Reliable, basic and clean 30-room hotel just opposite the port for the ferry to Skyros.

Thea Rooms   HOTEL €
(☑6945880113; cafetheahotel@gmail.com; Paralia Kymis; s/d incl breakfast from €35/40; P ❋ 🐾) A cosy, friendly budget option 200m from the ferry port, where all six rooms face the sea.

Taverna Spanos   TAVERNA €
(☑22220 22641; Paralia Kymis; mains €4.50-9.50; ⊙lunch & dinner) Rambling seaside taverna with a bit of everything, from fresh fish to big salads and meaty grills in the evening.

Northern Evia

From Halkida a road threads north, reaching the beautiful village of **Prokopi**, whose inhabitants are descended from refugees who came from Prokopion in Turkey's Cappadocia region in 1923. They established the pilgrimage church of **St John the Russian**, named for the saint who remains central to the town's identity and livelihood to this day, and is celebrated by a festival on 27 May.

Loutra Edipsou   Λουτρά Αιδηψού
POP 3600

The sedate spa resort of Loutra Edipsou is the most visited spot in northern Evia. Its therapeutic sulphur waters have been celebrated since antiquity, and continue to draw a stream of medical tourists. Famous skinny dippers have included Aristotle, Strabo, Plutarch, Plinius and Sylla.

Today, the town has Greece's most up-to-date hydrotherapy and physiotherapy centres, and several hotels have their own modern facilities. The town beach (Paralia Loutron) heats up year-round thanks to the thermal waters that spill into the bay.

🏃 Activities

Most hotels offer various spa treatments, from simple hot baths (€5) to four-hand massages (€160).

EOT Hydrotherapy-Physiotherapy Centre   SPA
(☑ 22260 23501; 25 March St 37; ⊙ 7am-1pm & 5-7pm Jun-Oct) The more affordable of the resort's two big spas, the welcoming EOT Hydrotherapy-Physiotherapy Centre is speckled with palm trees and has a large outdoor pool that mixes mineral and sea water. Hydromassage bath treatments start at a modest €8.

Thermae Sylla Hotel & Spa   SPA
(☑ 22260 60100; www.thermaesylla.gr; Posidonos 2; ⊙ 9am-8pm) An ultraposh spa, with a late-Roman ambience befitting its name, offering assorted health and beauty treatments, from thermal mud baths to seaweed body wraps.

🛏️ Sleeping & Eating

Three snappy waterfront eateries worth a taste are **Ouzerie Ta Kohilia** (☑ 22260 23478; 28 October; mains €4-7; ⊙ lunch & dinner) for mezedhes, **Alli Yefsi** (☑ 6984460759; mains €2-4; ⊙ lunch & dinner) for skewered grills and **Captain Cook Self-Service** (mains €3-7; ⊙ lunch & dinner) for everything else.

⭐ Hotel Kentrikon   HOTEL €
(☑ 22260 22302; www.kentrikonhotel.com; 25 Martiou 14; s/d/tr incl breakfast €40/50/60; ❄ @ 🛜 ⚡ 🏊) Managed by Greek-Irish Konstantinos and Una, the Kentrikon is equal parts kitsch and old-world charm, with modern rooms and balcony views. A free thermal pool awaits, along with professional massage therapist **Vicky Kavartziki** (☑ 6945146374).

Hotel Istiaia   HOTEL €
(☑ 22260 22309; www.istiaiahotel.com; 28 Octovriou 2; s/d/tr incl breakfast from €35/45/65; ❄ @ 🛜) The vintage Istiaia comes with an old-world feel, high-ceilinged rooms and a grand staircase that looks to be out of a 1950s Cecil B DeMille Hollywood movie. A handsome cafe-wine bar faces the sea, should you need a drink before your close-up.

Thermae Sylla Hotel & Spa   HOTEL €€€
(☑ 22260 60100; www.thermaesylla.gr; Posidonos 2; s/d/ste incl breakfast from €100/160/250; 🅿 ❄ @ 🛜 ⚡ 🏊) This posh, in-your-mud-masked-face seaside resort offers elegant luxury accommodation as well as countless beauty treatments. Day visitors can sample the outdoor thermal pool (€30).

⭐ Dina's Amfilirion Restaurant   GREEK €
(28 Octovriou 26; mains €7-10; ⊙ lunch & dinner) Daily specials, *sans* menu, await at this simple eatery 20m north of the ferry dock. A tasty grilled cod with oven potatoes, tomato cucumber salad and wine runs to €12 per person. Look for the small wooden sign with green letters.

ℹ️ Information

Free wi-fi is available on the waterfront. For medical needs, contact English-speaking **Dr Symeonides** (☑ 22260 23220; Omirou 17).

ℹ️ Getting There & Away

BOAT
Regular ferries run between Loutra Edipsou and mainland Arkitsa (€3.70, 40 minutes), and also between nearby Agiokambos and mainland Glyfa (€2.30, 20 minutes). Purchase tickets at the dock kiosks.

BUS
From the **KTEL bus station** (☑ 22260 22250; Thermopotamou), 200m from the port, buses run to Halkida (€14, 3½ hours, twice daily), Athens (€14, three hours, three to four daily via Arkitsa) and Thessaloniki (€27, four hours, daily via Glyfa).

Limni   Λίμνη
POP 2120

Picturesque Limni's maze of whitewashed houses and narrow lanes spill onto a cosy harbourside speckled with cafes and tavernas.

◉ Sights

Museum of History & Folk Art   MUSEUM
(☑ 22270 31335; www.gtp.gr/historicalandfolklore museumoflimni; Anagnosti Goviou 7; admission €2; ⊙ 9am-1pm Mon-Sat, 10.30am-2pm Sun) The town's quaint folk museum, 50m from the waterfront, houses handsome village costumes.

Convent of Galataki   CONVENT
(☑ 22270 31489; ⊙ 9am-noon & 5-8pm) The 16th-century Convent of Galataki, 9km southeast of Limni at the end of a narrow road that hugs a picturesque shoreline, is home to a coterie of six nuns and a fine fresco in its *katholikon* (principal church), the *Entry of the Righteous into Paradise*.

✨ Festivals & Events

Skyllias Swimming Marathon SPORTS
(https://sites.google.com/site/skylliaslimni) Limni's mid-summer Elimnia Festival kicks off with the 14.5km marathon between mainland Theologos and Limni. It's named for the long-distance swimmer who, in 480 BC, warned the Greeks of the approaching Persian fleet.

🛏 Sleeping & Eating

Zaniakos Domatia PENSION €
(☑ 6973667200, 22270 32445; www.zaniakos.gr; r €35; 🅿 ❄) English may be in short supply at this tidy domatia 200m above the waterfront, but the welcoming owners go out of their way to be helpful.

Home Graegos APARTMENT €
(☑ 22270 31117; www.graegos.com; apt from €55; 🅿 ❄ 🛜) The handsome Graegos has four apartments with modern kitchenettes and sweeping verandah sea views.

Rovies Camping CAMPGROUND €
(☑ 22270 71120; www.campingevia.com; camp sites per adult/tent €6.50/6; 🅿 🛜) Attractive, well-managed Rovies borders a pebble beach and a grove of olive and pine trees, 12km northwest of Limni. A restaurant and mini-market are open all day.

Southern Evia

East of Eretria, the road branches south at Lepoura as the north's rich vegetation gives way to sparse, rugged mountains. A turn-off leads to Lake Dhistos, a shallow lake bed favoured by migrating egrets. You'll pass high-tech windmills and views of both coasts as the island narrows before reaching Karystos,

---

WORTH A TRIP

WHISTLING VILLAGE OF ANTIA

East of Karystos, the 'whistling village' of Antia is famous for its linguistically talented villagers who speak a whistling language, devised during Byzantine times to warn of danger and invasion from pirates. Today, it's mostly the old-timers who still put their lips together and blow, though perhaps not as well as when many of them had all their teeth. The good news involves a resurgence of interest in the whistling among the kids of Antia. Stay tuned.

---

where friendly locals enjoy life at a pace that makes you forget how close you are to Athens.

Karystos Κάρυστος
POP 5130

Set on wide Karystos Bay below Mt Ohi (1398m), and flanked by two sandy beaches, this low-key coastal resort is the starting point for treks to Mt Ohi and Dimosari Gorge. Karystos' lively Plateia Amalias faces the harbour, which glitters come evening with lights and bobbing boats.

◉ Sights

**Archaeological Museum
of Karystos** MUSEUM
(☑ 22240 29218, 22240 25661; admission €2; ☺ 8.30am-3pm Tue-Sun) Karystos, mentioned in Homer's *Iliad,* was a powerful city-state during the Peloponnesian Wars. The displays at the museum range from tiny neolithic clay lamps to an exhibit of the 6th-century-BC *drakospita* (dragon houses) of Mt Ohi and Styra.

Bourtzi CASTLE
🆓 This is Karystos' striking 14th-century Venetian castle.

👉 Tours

South Evia Tours (☑ 22240 26200; www.evia travel.gr; Plateia Amalias), on the main square, can help with accommodation, ferry tickets and hiking excursions to Mt Ohi's and Styra's *drakospita* dragon houses, as well as bicycle and kayak rentals, and cruises around the Petali Islands (€35). Owner Nikos and staff also arrange transport for hikes to the summit of Mt Ohi and back, and four-hour guided walks through Dimosari Gorge (€25).

✨ Festivals & Events

Wine & Cultural Festival CULTURAL
(☑ 22240 22246; ☺ Aug & Sep) This lively festival includes theatre performances, traditional dancing to the tune of local musicians, and exhibits by local artists, as well as local wines, free for the tasting.

🛏 Sleeping & Eating

★ Hotel Karystion HOTEL €
(☑ 22240 22391; www.karystion.gr; Kriezotou 3; s/d incl breakfast from €40/50; 🅿 ❄ 🛜) The handsome Karystion sits above the beach just beyond Bourtzi castle, and features modern, well-appointed rooms, a filling breakfast and a helpful multilingual staff. A

stairway leads to a sandy beach that's great for swimming.

★**Cavo d'Oro** TAVERNA €

(mains €5-8; ⊙lunch & dinner) 🍴 Join the locals in this cheery alleyway restaurant off the main square for well-prepared Greek mainstays and country salads featuring local produce and olive oil. The genial owner, Kyriakos, is a regular at the summer wine festival, bouzouki in hand.

🍷 Drinking & Nightlife

Aeriko BAR

(☎22240 22365; ⊙8am-late; 🛜) Aeriko is the pick of the harbour beach bars: live music on summer weekends, sun beds, decent drinks and a copacetic all-ages clientele.

ℹ️ Information

Alpha Bank and Piraeus Bank ATMs are on the main square.

ℹ️ Getting There & Away

BOAT

There is a regular ferry service from Marmari (10km west of Karystos) to Rafina (€8, one hour), and from Nea Styra (35km north of Karystos) to Agia Marina (€3.50, 45 minutes).

Purchase tickets from either the dock kiosk or from South Evia Tours in Karystos.

BUS & TAXI

From the **Karystos KTEL bus station** (☎22240 26303) opposite Agios Nikolaos church, buses run to Halkida (€11.70, three hours), Athens (€18.60, three hours) and Marmari (€1.50, 20 minutes). A taxi to Marmari costs €18.

Around Karystos

The ruins of **Castello Rosso** (Red Castle), a 13th-century Frankish fortress, are a short walk from **Myli**, a well-watered village 4km inland from Karystos. The aqueduct behind the castle once carried water from the mountain springs to the Bourtzi in Karystos. A 3km walk from Myli brings you to a 2nd-century-AD **Roman quarry** (Kylindroi, meaning 'cylinder') strewn with massive columns of Karystian *cipollino* marble, abandoned during the time of Caesar.

With your own transport you can explore the pristine **Cavo d'Oro** villages nestling in the southern foothills of Mt Ohi. Highlights include **Platanistos**, **Potami** and the walled ruins of an ancient settlement at **Helleniko**.

HERA & ZEUS: MYTH ON THE MOUNTAIN

Once upon a time, or so the myth goes, Hera and Zeus, rulers of the heavens, hooked up on the slopes of Mt Ohi. But to get close to the shy goddess, Zeus disguised himself as a cuckoo, Hera's favourite bird, and only revealed himself when she held the cuckoo to her breast. Before rocking the mountain, she made Zeus promise to marry her. The well-known king of heaven and one-night stands readily agreed. The word 'Ohi' in Greek comes from the ancient Greek word 'ohevo', meaning to ride.

👁️ Sights & Activities

In addition to Dimosari Gorge and Mt Ohi, worthy day hikes above Karystos include ambles through the natural springs of **Agios Dimitrios Gorge**, where a branch trail ascends to scenic **Boublia Peak** (1127m). From tiny **Thymi**, a narrow dirt track reaches beautiful **Archampoli Beach**, about an hour's walk.

Mt Ohi MOUNTAIN

From Myli, it's a four-hour hike up Mt Ohi (1398m) for magnificent Aegean views. It's possible to stay overnight at a refuge at 1000m, then hike up to catch sunrise. The summit (Profitis Ilias peak) is home to the ancient and mysterious *drakospita* (dragon houses), Stonehenge-like dwellings or temples dating from the 7th century BC, hewn from rocks weighing several tonnes and joined without mortar.

The dragon houses' commanding position near marble quarries suggest that they were guard posts; another theory holds that they honoured mythological deities that roamed the Mt Ohi, in particular the goddess Hera. Another dragon house near the road to Styra (30km north of Karystos) is equally fascinating.

★**Dimosari Gorge** HIKING

The Dimosari Gorge offers day hikers a beautiful and well-maintained 10km trail that can be covered in four hours (including time for a swim). The path begins in the village of Petrokanalo at 950m, descending through the village of Lenosei to the sea. Much of this stunning trek follows a cobbled path, splashing through shady creeks, ponds, giant ferns and forest before ending at the sand-and-pebble beach of Kallianos.

★ **BikeGreece**   MOUNTAIN BIKING
(☑6944618565; www.bikegreece.com) Find out what mountain bikes are really for with BikeGreece. Week-long bicycle tours of the wild south Evian landscape explore the slopes of Mt Ohi, the Dimosari Gorge, and include beach bonfires and an occasional village wine tasting. Rates cover vehicle support, food and lodging. Semi-expat James Brown organises the show with a deep appreciation of the local landscape and culture.

THE SPORADES

The Sporades are home to four unique islands. Skiathos and its 60-odd beaches draws the most visitors by far, while handsome Skopelos strikes a cooler pose with its hidden bays and inland trails. Easternmost Alonnisos, with one bus, four taxis and 27 churches, is the most remote and pristine of this northern group, while southeasterly Skyros is home to wild horses and a lively arts scene.

Skiathos   Σκιάθος
POP 6110

Skiathos is blessed with some of the Aegean's most beautiful beaches, so it's little wonder that in July and August the island can fill up with sun-starved northern Europeans, as prices soar and rooms dwindle. Skiathos Town, the island's major settlement and port, is on the southeast coast. The rest of the south coast is interspersed with walled-in holiday villas and pine-fringed sandy beaches.

ⓘ Getting There & Away

AIR

During summer there are one to two flights daily to/from Athens (€88), in addition to numerous charter flights from northern Europe. **Aegean Air** (☑ 24270 29100; www.aegeanair.ccom) has an office at the airport.

BOAT

Skiathos' main port is Skiathos Town, which has links to Volos and Agios Konstantinos on the mainland, and island-destinations Skopelos and Alonnisos. Tickets can be purchased from **Hellenic Seaways** (☑ 24270 22209; www.skiathosoe.com; cnr Papadiamantis, waterfront).

ⓘ Getting Around

BOAT

Water taxis depart hourly from the old port for Achladies Bay (€2.50, 15 minutes), Kanapitsa (€3, 20 minutes) and Koukounaries (€5, 30 minutes).

BUS

Buses leave Skiathos Town for Koukounaries Beach (€2, 30 minutes, half-hourly) between 7.30am and 11pm. The buses stop at 26 numbered beach access points along the south coast.

CAR & MOTORCYCLE

Reliable motorbike and car-hire outlets in Skiathos Town include **Europcar/Creator Tours** (☑ 6932382332, 24270 22385; www.creatortours.com), which also rents bicycles, and **Heliotropio Tourism & Travel** (☑ 24270 22430; www.heliotropio.gr). Both are located at the new port.

TAXI

Taxis (☑ 24270 21460) leave from the stand opposite the ferry dock. A taxi to/from the air-

BOAT SERVICES FROM SKIATHOS

DESTINATION	COST	TIME	FREQUENCY
Agios Konstantinos	€30	2½hr	1 daily
Agios Konstantinos*	€37	1½hr	1-2 daily
Alonnisos	€11	2hr	1 daily
Alonnisos*	€17	1½hr	2 daily
Skopelos (Glossa)	€6	30min	1 daily
Skopelos (Glossa)*	€10	20min	2 daily
Skopelos (Skopelos Town)	€10	1hr	1 daily
Skopelos (Skopelos Town)*	€17	55min	2 daily
Volos	€23	2½hr	1-2 daily
Volos*	€37	1½hr	1-2 daily

*hydrofoil services

Skiathos

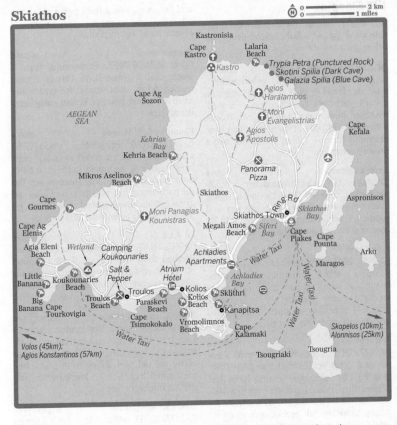

port costs €7, to Koukounaries €17 and to Moni Evangelistrias €8.

Skiathos Town   Σκιάθος

The town is a major tourist centre, with hotels, souvenir shops, galleries, travel agents, tavernas and bars spread along the waterfront and the cobbled pedestrian thoroughfare Papadiamanti. Opposite the waterfront via a 15m causeway lies shady and inviting **Bourtzi Islet**.

◎ Sights

Papadiamanti House Museum   MUSEUM
(☑24270 22240; Plateia Papadiamanti; admission €1; ☺9.30am-1.30pm & 5-8.30pm Tue-Sun) Skiathos was the birthplace of the famous 19th-century Greek novelist and short-story writer Alexandros Papadiamanti, whose writings draw upon the hard lives of the islanders he grew up with. His hum-

ble 1860 house is now a charming museum with books, paintings and vintage photos.

☞ Tours

Excursion boats make half- and full-day trips around the island (from €15 to €25), and usually visit Cape Kastro, Lalaria Beach, Trypia Petra (Punctured Rock) and the two *spilies* (caves) of Skotini (Dark Cave) and Galazia (Blue Cave). Other boats (€12) visit the nearby islets of Tsougria and Tsougriaki for swimming and snorkelling; you can take one boat over and return on another. Check out the signboards in front of each boat at the old port.

For a splendid **sailing tour** of the island waters between Skiathos and Alonnisos, climb aboard the **Argo III** (☑6932325167; www.argosailing.com; per person €65), managed by husband-and-wife team George and Dina.

🛏 Sleeping

In July and August, there's a helpful quayside **kiosk** (☎24270 23172; harbour dock) with prices, pictures and pitches.

★ Gisela's House-in-Town   PENSION €
(☎24270 21370, 6945686542; gisbaunach@hotmail.com; r from €45; ❄📶) Cosy and quiet on a back street off Papadiamanti, this well-managed budget gem has just two rooms, with two twin beds in each, overhead fans, mosquito screens, tables, tea kettles and a flowery verandah.

Lena's Rooms   PENSION €
(☎24270 22009; ts1otr4s@gmail.com; Bouboulinas; r from €35; ❄📶) These six double rooms over the owner's flower shop are airy and spotless, each with mini-fridge, balcony, common kitchen and a shady verandah.

Hotel Meltemi   HOTEL €
(☎24270 22493; www.meltemiskiathos.com; s/d/f €45/55/80; ❄@📶) You could easily miss the friendly Meltemi, set back in a shady courtyard at the new port, but its old-fashioned charm is appealing, from its antique-filled hallways to super-tidy rooms.

Hotel Mouria   HOTEL €
(☎24270 21193; www.mouriahotel.com; Papadiamanti; d/tr/f incl breakfast from €40/60/80; ❄@📶) The handsome Mouria hides just behind the national bank, set back in a flowery courtyard. There's a common kitchen for guests, though a full breakfast awaits, plus bright rooms and vintage photos all around.

Hotel Bourtzi   BOUTIQUE HOTEL €€
(☎24270 21304; www.hotelbourtzi.gr; Moraitou 8, cnr Papadiamanti; s/d/f incl breakfast from €80/130/180; P❄📶🏊) On upper Papadiamanti, the swanky Bourtzi features austere modern rooms, attentive staff and an inviting garden and pool.

🍴 Eating

Skiathos has its share of overpriced touristy eateries with *etsi-ketsi* (so-so) food. Explore the narrow lanes around the old port to find exceptions.

★ Taverna-Ouzerie Kabourelia   TAVERNA €
(☎24270 21112; Old Harbour; mains €4-9; ⊙noon-midnight; 📶) Poke your nose into the open kitchen to glimpse the day's catch at this popular year-round eatery at the old port. Perfect fish grills and house wine are served at moderate prices. Grilled octopus

and *taramasalata* (a thick purée of fish roe, potato, oil and lemon juice) are just two of several stand-out mezedhes.

Foodie   SNACKS €
(Igloo; ☎24270 24076; Papadiamanti; drinks & snacks €1.50-3; ⊙6am-11pm) This is a great quick stop for cold drinks, ice cream and fresh breakfast goodies before early ferry departures.

Fasoulas Grill House   GREEK €
(☎24270 22080; Evangelistrias; snacks €2.50, mains €6.50; ⊙lunch & dinner) Fasoulas translates roughly as 'beanpole' in Greek, a bit of humour from the proudly short owner. But the portions are big, with great souvlakia and *gyros* (meat slithers cooked on a vertical rotisserie; usually eaten with pitta bread).

Lo & La   MEDITERRANEAN €
(☎6972408465; mains €7-12; ⊙lunch & dinner) Perched above the old port, Lo & La shows off an Italian-Greek couple's kitchen favourites. Pastas are handmade, and the risotto with local mushrooms excels.

★ La Cucina di Maria   RISTORANTE €€
(☎6977466732; Plateia Trion Ierarhon; ⊙dinner) Excellent thin-crust pizza twirled in the air is just the beginning at this popular spot above the old port. Enjoy fresh pasta, fine meat and fish grills in a colourful setting under the mulberry tree.

Bakaliko Restaurant   RESTAURANT €€
(☎24270 22669; mains €5-11; ⊙lunch & dinner) This seaside eatery, 300m east of the new port, serves up great standards and appetisers suc as grilled feta, *kritamos* (rock samphire salad), lamb *kleftiko* (slow oven-baked meat) and *taramasalata*. A vintage radio collection adds to the ambience.

Marmita   MEDITERRANEAN €€
(☎24270 21701; 30 Evangelistrias; mains €8-14; ⊙dinner) Elegant eatery on upper Papadiamanti combines traditional Greek and Mediterranean flavours, from baked feta and wild greens to veal ragout and seafood pasta. There's also a solid Greek wine list on hand.

🍷 Drinking & Nightlife

The drink-till-you-drop scene heats up after midnight on the club strip past the new harbour. For clubbing, the best DJs are at **Club Pure** (☎6979773854) and **Kahlua** (☎6978011870; www.kahluaclub.com), open till dawn.

Kentavros
BAR

(☑24270 22980; ☺10am-late) Handsome Kentavros, opposite Plateia Papadiamanti, promises rock, jazz and blues, and gets the thumbs-up from locals and expats for its mellow ambience, artwork and sturdy drinks.

Main Street
BAR

(Papadiamanti; ☺8.30am-late) Convivial cafe-bar on mid-Papadiamanti.

Rock & Roll Bar
BAR

(☑24270 22944; Old Port; ☺7pm-late) This lively bar on the steps by the old port is a late-night standby. Solid drinks, fair prices.

☆ Entertainment

Cinema Attikon
CINEMA

(☑24720 22352, 6972706305; tickets €7) Catch current English-language movies at this open-air cinema. Sip a beer and practise speed-reading your Greek subtitles.

🔒 Shopping

Loupos & His Dolphins
ANTIQUES

(☑24270 23777; Plateia Papadiamanti; ☺10am-1.30pm & 6-11.30pm) Delicate hand-painted icons, handsome ceramics and silver jewellery at this quality low-key gallery shop in the courtyard by Papadiamanti Museum.

Galerie Varsakis
ANTIQUES

(☑24270 22255; www.varsakis.com; Plateia Trion Ierarhon; ☺10am-2pm & 6-11pm) Browse for unusual antiques such as 19th-century spinning sticks made by grooms for their intended brides. The collection rivals the best Greek folklore museums.

ℹ Information

The bus terminus is at the northern end of the new harbour. You'll find free wi-fi all along the port and in most cafes on Papadiamanti. Numerous ATMs are on Papadiamanti and the waterfront.

Health Centre Hospital (☑24270 22222; above Old Port)

Port Police (☑24270 22017; New Harbour)

Tourist Police (☑24270 23172; Ring Rd; ☺8am-9pm)

Around Skiathos

🏊 Beaches

With 65 beaches to choose from, beach-hopping on Skiathos can become a full-time occupation. Buses ply the south coast, stopping at 26 numbered beach access points. The first long stretch of sand worth hopping off for is the pine-fringed **Vromolimnos Beach**. The road then continues to the white sands of **Koukounaries Beach**, which is backed by pine trees and a small wetland. Come the busy midsummer period, it's best viewed at a distance, from where the 1200m long sweep of pale gold sand does indeed sparkle.

West of Koukounaries, **Big Banana Beach**, known for its curving shape, soft sand and beach-bar buzz, lies across a narrow headland. Skinny-dippers prefer to hang at equally frenetic **Little Banana Beach** (also popular with gay and lesbian sunbathers) around the rocky corner. About 400m north, elegant **Agia Eleni Beach** is a favourite with windsurfers. Sandy **Mandraki Beach**, a 1.5km walk along a pine-shaded path, is distant enough to keep it clear of the masses, while sporting a good taverna. From Troulos, it's 4km to **Megalos Aselinos Beach**, a long and lovely stretch of sand, with tiny **Mikros Aselinos** and secluded **Kehria Beach** a few kilometres further.

Northwest coast beaches are less crowded but are subject to summer *meltemi* (northeasterly winds). **Lalaria Beach** is a tranquil strand of pale grey, egg-shaped pebbles on the northern coast, but can only be reached by excursion boat from Skiathos Town.

◉ Sights

Kastro
RUIN

Perched dramatically on a rocky headland above the north coast, Kastro was the fortified pirate-proof capital of the island from 1540 to 1829. An old cannon remains at the northern end, along with four restored churches, including Christos, home to several fine frescoes. Excursion boats come from the old port in Skiathos Town to the beach below Kastro, from where it's an easy clamber up to the ruins.

Moni Evangelistrias
MONASTERY

(☑24270 22012; museum admission €2; ☺10am-dusk) This famously historic monastery was a hilltop refuge for freedom fighters during the War of Independence, and the Greek flag was first raised here in 1807. Today, two monks do the chores, which include winemaking. You can sample the tasty results in the museum shop. An adjacent shed of vintage olive and wine presses recalls an earlier era, before the satellite dish appeared above the courtyard.

Moni Panagias Kounistras
MONASTERY

(☺morning-dusk) From Troulos, a road heads 4km north to the serene 17th-century Moni

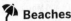

EVIA & THE SPORADES SKIATHOS

Panagias Kounistras, worth a visit for the fine frescoes adorning its *katholikon*.

Activities

Diving

The small islets off the south shore of Skiathos make for great diving and snorkeling. The dive-instructor team of Theofanis and Eva of **Octopus Diving Centre** (☑ 24270 24549, 6944168958; www.odc-skiathos.com; New Harbour; half-day dives €45-55) leads dives around Tsougria and Tsougriaki islets for beginners and experts alike. Enquire at their boat on the new harbour in Skiathos Town.

Hiking

A 6km-long hiking route begins at Moni Evangelistrias and eventually reaches **Cape Kastro** before circling back through **Agios Apostolis**. Kastro is a spring mecca for **birdwatchers**, who may spot long-necked Mediterranean shags or blue rock thrushes skimming the waves.

🛏 Sleeping & Eating

Achladies Apartments APARTMENT €
(☑ 24270 22486; www.achladiesapartments.com; Achladies Bay; d/tr/f incl breakfast €45/60/75; P 🐾) This welcoming gem, 5km south of Skiathos Town, features comfortable kitchenette rooms with ceiling fans, plus an eco-friendly tortoise sanctuary and a rambling succulent garden winding down to a sandy beach. From here, water taxis connect to Skiathos Town and Koukounaries Beach.

Camping Koukounaries CAMPGROUND €
(☑ 24270 49250; Koukounaries Beach; camp sites per adult/tent €11/free; P 🐾) Shaded by fig and mulberry trees opposite Koukounaries Beach, with spotless bathroom and cooking facilities, a mini-market and a taverna.

★ **Atrium Hotel** HOTEL €€
(☑ 24270 49345; www.atriumhotel.gr; Paraskevi Beach; s/d/ste incl breakfast from €105/130/170; P ❄ @ 🐾 ⛱) Traditional architecture and modern touches make this hillside perch the best in its class. Elegant rooms feature basin sinks and private balconies overlooking the sea. Amenities include a sauna, a children's pool, billiards, ping-pong and a lavish breakfast buffet to start the day.

Panorama Pizza PIZZA €
(pizzas €7-10; ⊙ noon-4pm & 7pm-late; 🐾) Hilltop retreat off the Ring Rd for brick-oven pizza and perfect views.

Taverna Sklithri TAVERNA €€
(☑ 6946932869; Sklithri; mains €7-14; ⊙ lunch & dinner) Excellent seafood restaurant on the beach at Sklithri, with hospitality and wine to spare. It's about 4km southwest of Skiathos Town, near bus stop 11.

Skopelos Σκόπελος

POP 5400

Skopelos is a handsome island of pine forests, vineyards, olive groves and orchards of plums and almonds, which find their way into many local dishes. Like neighbouring island Skiathos, the high cliffs of the northwest coast are exposed, while the sheltered southeast coast harbours several sand-and-pebble beaches. There are two settlements: the main port of Skopelos Town on the east coast and the northwest village of Glossa, 2km north of Loutraki, the island's second port.

❶ Getting There & Away

BOAT

Skopelos has two ports, Skopelos Town and Glossa (aka Loutraki). Both link to Volos and Agios Konstantinos on the mainland, and the islands of Skiathos, Alonnisos and Skyros.

Tickets are available from **Hellenic Seaways** (☑ 24240 22767; fax 24240 23608) in Skopelos Town and the port of Glossa; and from Madro Travel (p621), and **Lemonis Travel** (☑ 6944582365, 24240 22363), both on the waterfront.

❶ Getting Around

BOAT

A water taxi departs Skopelos Town late morning for Glysteri Beach (€5 each way).

BUS

In summer there are four to six buses per day from Skopelos Town to Glossa/Loutraki (€5.30, 55 minutes) and Neo Klima (Elios; €3.80, 45 minutes); and three more that go to Panormos (€2.90, 25 minutes), Milia (€3.60, 35 minutes), Agnontas (€1.60, 15 minutes) and Stafylos (€1.50, 15 minutes).

CAR & MOTORCYCLE

Car- and motorcycle-hire outlets line the eastern end of the Skopelos Town waterfront near the Ring Rd. These include **Magic Cars** (☑ 6973790936, 24240 23250) and **Motor Tours** (☑ 24240 22986; fax 24240 22602).

TAXI

Taxis wait by the bus stop in Skopelos Town. A taxi to Stafylos is €7, to Limnonari €13 and to Glossa €32.

Skopelos Town   Σκόπελος

Skopelos Town skirts a semicircular bay and rises in tiers up a hillside of dazzling white houses with bright shutters and flower-adorned balconies, ending at an old fortress and a cluster of four churches. The town's waterfront is flanked by two quays. The old quay wraps around the western end of the harbour; the new quay at the eastern end is used by all ferries and hydrofoils.

⊙ Sights & Activities

Strolling around town and sitting at the waterside cafes might be your chief occupations in Skopelos, but there are also two small museums.

Folklore Museum   MUSEUM
(☑24240 23494; Hatzistamati; admission €3; ⊙10am-2pm & 7-10pm Mon-Fri) This handsome museum features a Skopelean wedding room, complete with traditional costumes and bridal bed. It's a block west of Agios Nikolaou Church.

Bakratsa Mansion Museum   MUSEUM
(☑24240 23494; admission €3; ⊙10am-2pm & 6-9pm) Housed in a doctor's 18th-century mansion, 100m inland from Ploumisti Shop, this museum displays medical instruments of the era and clothing for married and unmarried men and women.

Skopelos Cycling   CYCLING
(☑24240 22398, 6947023145; skopeloscycling@yahoo.gr; per 24hr €8-18) High-quality trekking and mountain bikes, and bike tours, are available from Panos Provias at Skopelos Cycling. You'll find it next to the post office.

⚲ Courses

SkopArt   COURSE
(Skopelos Foundation for the Arts; ☑24240 24143; www.skopartfoundation.org) Perched high above Skopelos Town, SkopArt offers popular residential classes, ranging from painting and drawing to ceramics and paper-making.

☞ Tours

Day-long **cruise boats** (€20-40) depart from the waterfront by 10am and usually take in the National Marine Park of Alonnisos, pausing en route for lunch and a swim. There's a decent chance of spotting dolphins along the way. For bookings, contact Madro Travel (p621), Thalpos Holidays (p621) or **Dolphin Tours** (☑6977468190, 24240 29191; www.dolphinofskopelos.com; town beach) on the waterfront.

⌸ Sleeping

★**Pension Sotos**   PENSION €
(☑24240 22549; www.skopelos.net/sotos; s/d from €30/45; ❋☞) The pine-floored rooms at this charming waterfront pension are

BOAT SERVICES FROM SKOPELOS

DESTINATION	PORT	TIME	FARE	FREQUENCY
Agios Konstantinos	Skopelos Town	4hr	€38	1 daily
Agios Konstantinos**	Skopelos Town	2½hr	€50	1 daily
Agios Konstantinos**	Glossa	2½hr	€43	1 daily
Alonnisos	Glossa	1hr	€14	1 daily
Alonnisos*	Skopelos Town	30min	€6	2-3 daily
Alonnisos**	Skopelos Town	20min	€9	2 daily
Skiathos (via Glossa)	Skopelos Town	1½hr	€10	2-3 daily
Skiathos*	Skopelos Town	45min	€17	2 daily
Skiathos**	Glossa	30min	€10	2 daily
Evia (Mantoudi)	Glossa	1¾	€18	3 weekly
Evia (Paralia Kymis)	Skopelos Town	4hr	€24	4-6 weekly
Volos	Skopelos Town	3¾hr	€28	2 daily
Volos**	Glossa	2½hr	€40	1 daily
Volos*	Skopelos Town	3hr	€48	2-3 daily

*fast-ferry services
**hydrofoil services

Skopelos

each a bit different; an old brick oven serves as a handy shelf in one. There's a relaxing interior courtyard, a flowery terrace and a communal kitchen, all managed by the welcoming and resourceful Alexandra.

Hotel Agnanti
HOTEL €

(☏24240 22722, 6978713252; www.skopelos.net/agnanti; s/d/tr from €35/40/60; P✳@🛜) Theo and Eleni run the show at this rustic 12-room oasis on the old (and quieter) quay. Features include ceiling fans, period furniture, ceramic decorations and a paperback lending library.

Hotel Dionyssos
HOTEL €€

(☏24240 23210; www.dionyssoshotel.com; s/d/tr incl breakfast €65/75/90; P✳@🛜⛱) The low-key Dionyssos, sited between the Ring Rd and the waterfront, attracts the occasional group, but rooms have a homey feel with wooden floors and woven rugs. Nights liven up by the small pool bar.

✗ Eating

Just 100m up from the dock, Plateia Platanos (aka Souvlaki Sq) is perfect for a quick bite of *gyros* or souvlakia.

★ Nastas Ouzerie
GREEK €

(mezedhes €2.50-5, mains €6-10; ☺lunch & dinner) At the Ring Rd junction, Nastas serves excellent mezedhes, meat grills and fresh fish entrees and, of course, *tsipouro* (distilled spirit similar to to ouzo). A favourite among loyal locals for both quality and price.

Taverna Klimataria
TAVERNA €

(mains €5.50-10; ☺lunch & dinner) One of a cluster of fine tavernas near the end of the quay, Klimataria is excellent for point-and-eat *mayirefta* dishes, fish soup and good grills come evening time.

O Michalis
CAFE €

(8am-late; snacks €3-5) The red door gives away this snappy hole-in-the-wall serving superb *tyropita* (cheese pie). At night the place morphs into a mellow wine bar. It's mid waterfront, a block inland from Pension Sotos.

To Rodi   GREEK €
(☑ 24240 24601; mains €4.50-10; ⊙ 7pm-midnight) Classy and comfortable courtyard eatery a short block in from the waterfront, opposite Kromata Ceramics.

★ **To Perivoli Restaurant**   GREEK €€
(☑ 24240 23758; mains €7-14; ⊙ 7.30pm-midnight) Perivoli delivers excellent Greek cuisine in an elegant and secluded courtyard setting just above Plateia Platanos. Specialities include rolled pork with *koromila* (local plums) in wine sauce, plus fine Greek wines.

🍷 Drinking & Nightlife

Molon Lave   CAFE
(☑ 24247 70757; ⊙ 7am-2pm & 4-9pm) Efficient mid-waterfront morning hole-in-the-wall for coffee and handmade cheese pies. Its ancient Greek name roughly translates as 'come and get it', the defiant reply of Spartan general Leonides to the Persian Xerxes' request for the Greeks to surrender their arms prior to the battle at Thermapolae in 480 BC.

Bardon   BAR
(☑ 24240 24494; ⊙ 7pm-late) Comfortable courtyard bar scene in a renovated olive factory, with live music most summer weekends. It's 75m inland from the town parking lot.

Hidden Door   BAR
(☑ 6978252848; ⊙ 7pm-late) Mellow bar on a quieter lane behind the waterfront, in a converted 100-year-old house where a side, or hidden, door once led to the kitchen. Three blocks inland from Agios Nikolaos Church.

Pablo's Bar   COCKTAIL BAR
(☑ 24240 24804; Old Port; ⊙ 6pm-3am) Owner bartender Christos serves up mellow jazz and mellower cocktails; there's a breezy roof terrace above it all. Far southeast end of the waterfront, above Taverna Ta Kymata.

☆ Entertainment

Ouzerie Anatoli   TRADITIONAL MUSIC
(⊙ 8pm-2am summer) Wait till at least 11pm, then head to this breezy outdoor *ouzerie* (place that serves ouzo and light snacks), high above the *kastro* near the southeast corner of the waterfront, to hear traditional *rembetika* (blues songs) sung by Georgos Xindaris, Skopelos' own exponent of the Greek blues and a bouzouki master.

🛍 Shopping

Waterfront standbys include **Ploumisti Shop** (☑ 24240 22059; waterfront; ⊙ 10am-9pm) and **Archipelagos Shop** (☑ 24240 23127; ⊙ 10am-9pm) for quality ceramics, small paintings, icons and handmade jewellery.

Chromata Skopelou   CERAMICS
(☑ 6940 269636; ⊙ 10am-2pm & 8-11pm) This unique ceramics workshop displays the delicate touch of English potter Elizabeth McGhie. It's opposite Rodi Taverna, one street in from the waterfront.

❶ Information

There are four ATMs along the waterfront, which is also set up for free wi-fi access.

Health Centre (☑ 24240 22222; Ring Rd, opposite fire station)

Madro Travel (☑ 24240 22300; www.madro travel.com; waterfront) At the end of the old port, family-run Madro does accommodation and ticketing, arranges walking trips, marinepark excursions, cooking lessons and even marriages (partners extra).

Police (☑ 24240 22235; New Quay) Above National Bank.

Port police (☑ 24240 22180; Old Quay) Next to the ferry dock.

Post office (⊙ 7.30am-2pm) Opposite Panagia Church.

Thalpos Holidays (☑ 24240 29036; www.holi dayislands.com; waterfront) The friendly staff at this full-service waterfront agency can help with apartment and villa accommodation, boat hire, hiking, island excursions and weddings.

Glossa & Loutraki
Γλώσσα & Λουτράκι

Glossa, Skopelos' second settlement, is a whitewashed cluster of shops and eateries. A 2km road winds down from the small square to the laid-back port of Loutraki ('Glossa' in ferry timetables). A shorter *kalderimi* (cobblestoned path) connects both villages as well. Fans of the 2008 movie *Mamma Mia!* can start their pilgrimage in Glossa to reach the film's little church, **Agios Ioannis Kastri** (St John of the Castle).

Loutraki means 'small bath' and you can see the remains of ancient **Roman baths** at the archaeological kiosk on the port.

🛏 Sleeping & Eating

Pansion Platana   PENSION €
(☑ 6973646702, 24240 33188; pansionplatana@hot mail.com; Glossa; r from €35; P ❋ ☎) This cosy

and welcoming domatia has overhead fans, kitchenettes and views overlooking the port of Loutraki. Welcoming Greek-Australian owner Eleni provides tea and tips. About 30m past the Shell petrol station on the left.

★ **Flisvos Taverna** TAVERNA €
(☎24240 33856; Loutraki; mains €4-7.50; ⓧlunch & dinner) Simple Greek fare at its best, friendly Flisvos offers fresh fish at reasonable prices, along with traditional standards *mousakas* (baked layers of eggplant or zucchini, minced meat and potatoes topped with cheese sauce) and *stifadho* (meat, game or seafood cooked with onions in a tomato purée). Appetisers such as tzatziki and *taramasalata* excel.

Agnanti Taverna & Bar GREEK FUSION €€
(☎24240 33076; Glossa; mains €8-14; ⓧlunch & dinner) Enjoy views of Evia from swank Agnanti's rooftop terrace while grazing on superb Greek fusion dishes such as grilled sardines with sea fennel, and garlic feta with red peppers.

Around Skopelos

Skopelos visitors can see several monasteries via a scenic drive or day-long trek above Skopelos Town. Begin by following Monastery Rd, which skirts the bay and then climbs inland to 18th-century convent **Moni Evangelistrias**, home to a solitary nun. The monastery's prize, aside from superb views, is a gilded *iconostasis* containing an 11th-century icon of the Virgin Mary.

Further on, 16th-century **Moni Metamorfosis Sotiros** is the island's oldest monastery. From there a narrow road continues to 17th-century **Moni Varvaras** overlooking the bay below, and 18th-century convent **Moni Prodromou**, 8km from Skopelos Town.

🐾 Beaches

Most of Skopelos' best beaches are on the sheltered southwest and west coasts. The first beach you come to is sand-and-pebble **Stafylos Beach**, 4km southeast of Skopelos Town. From its eastern end, a path leads over a small headland to the quieter **Velanio Beach**, the island's official nudist beach and coincidentally a great snorkelling spot. Lovely **Agnontas**, 3km west of Stafylos, has a pebble-and-sand beach from where caïques depart to sheltered and sandier **Limnonari Beach**. From Agnontas the road cuts inland through pine forests before re-emerging at pretty **Panormos Beach**, which has tavernas and domatia. The next two bays, **Milia** and **Kastani**, are excellent for swimming. On

the island's northeast coast, serene **Perivoliou Beach** is a 25-minute drive from Glossa.

🚌 Tours

Heather Parsons' Guided Walks WALKING TOUR
(☎6945249328; www.skopelos-walks.com; tours €15-20) If you can't tell a twin-tailed pascha butterfly from a leopard orchid, join one of island resident Heather's guided walks. Her four-hour Panormos walk follows a centuries-old path across the island, ending at a beach taverna, with wonderful views to Alonnisos and Evia. Her book *Skopelos Trails* contains graded trail descriptions.Heather and a loyal band of volunteers continue to clear, signpost and GPS trails across the island. She also offers *Mamma Mia!* jeep tours to most of the movie's filming locations.

🛏 Sleeping & Eating

There are small hotels, domatia, tavernas and beach canteens at Stafylos, Agnontas, Limnonari, Panormos, Andrines and Milia.

Limnonari Rooms & Taverna APARTMENT €
(☎6946464515, 24240 23046; www.skopelos. net/limnonarirooms; Limnonari Beach; d/tr/ste from €35/60/80; ⓟ❋🛜) This cluster of 10 well-equipped apartments faces beautiful Limnonari Bay. The family's garden taverna serves vegetarian *mousakas,* fish and meat grills, and homemade olives and feta.

Guesthouse Mando Beachfront APARTMENT €€
(☎6936131316, 24240 23917; mando_skopelos @yahoo.gr; Stafylos; d/tr/f incl breakfast from €70/80/110; ⓟ❋🛜) Behind a cove on Stafylos Bay, this well-managed, family-oriented lodging offers modest rooms alongside luxe villas, plus an outdoor communal kitchen and a solid platform over the rocks from which to enter the sea for swimming and snorkelling.

★ **Taverna Pavlos** TAVERNA €€
(☎24240 22409; Agnondas; mains €8-14; ⓧlunch & dinner) Locals think nothing of driving over to Agnontas for beautifully prepared fresh fish and excellent mezedhes at this shaded taverna just steps from the bay. Octopus *stifadho* and fava dip are just two of the star offerings.

Alonnisos Αλόννησος

POP 2700

Alonnisos rises from the sea in a mountain of greenery, with thick stands of aleppo pine and kermes oak, mastic and arbutus bushes, vineyards, olive and fruit trees, all threaded with perfumy patches of wild oregano, sage and

BOAT SERVICES FROM ALONNISOS

DESTINATION	TIME	FARE	FREQUENCY
Agios Konstantinos*	2½hr	€50	4 weekly
Agios Konstantinos**	4hr	€38	1 daily
Evia (Paralia Kymis)	2½hr	€24	2-3 weekly
Skiathos	2hr	€11	4 weekly
Skiathos*	1½hr	€17	4-5 daily
Skopelos	40min	€6	1 daily
Skopelos*	20min	€9.50	2-3 daily
Skopelos (Glossa)*	45min	€14	3-4 daily
Volos*	2½hr	€42	1-2 daily
Volos**	3½hr	€28	1-2 daily

*hydrofoil services
**fast-ferry services

thyme. The west and north coasts are steep and rocky, but the east coast is speckled with small bays and pebble-and-sand beaches.

Alonnisos has had its share of bad luck. In 1952 a thriving cottage wine industry collapsed when vines imported from California were infested with phylloxera insects. Robbed of their livelihood, many moved away. Then, in 1965, an earthquake destroyed the hilltop capital of Old Alonnisos. The inhabitants were rehoused at Patitiri, which has since evolved into a quaint island port.

🏃 Activities

Hiking opportunities abound on Alonnisos and more than a dozen trails have been way-marked. Popular trails are highlighted on the Terrain and Anavasi maps of Alonnisos. Albedo Travel (p623) in Patitiri can help arrange guided walks.

❶ Getting There & Away

Alonnisos' main port of Patitiri has links to mainland Volos and Agios Konstantinos; to Paralia Kymis on Evia; and to nearby Skopelos and Skiathos. Tickets can be purchased from **Alkyon Travel** (☑ 24240 65220; ☺ 9am-10pm), **Albedo Travel** (☑ 24240 65804; www.alonis sosholidays.com; ☺ 9am-10pm) or **Alonnisos Travel** (☑ 24240 65188; www.alonnisostravel. gr; ☺ 9am-10pm) in Patitiri.

❶ Getting Around

BUS

A bus plies the route between Patitiri and Old Alonnisos (€1.60), and then heads to Steni Vala (€1.70). Additionally, a summer **beach bus** (☑ 6973805610; €5) leaves Patitiri around 10.30am for points to the north and returns after 4pm.

CAR & MOTORCYCLE

Several motorcycle-hire outlets cluster near the waterfront in Patitiri, including reliable **I'm Bike** (☑ 24240 65010). For cars, try Albedo Travel or Alonnisos Travel, also in Patitiri.

TAXI

The four taxis on the island (driven by Georgos, Periklis, Theodoros and Spyros) congregate opposite the quay in Patitiri. It's €6 to Old Alonnisos, €10 to Leftos Gialos and €13 to Steni Vala.

Patitiri   Πατητήρι

Patitiri ('wine press') sits between two sandstone cliffs at the southern end of the east coast. The quay is in the centre of the waterfront, from where two roads lead inland.

◉ Sights

★ Folklore Museum of the Northern Sporades   MUSEUM
(☑ 24240 66250; www.alonissosmuseum.com; adult/child €4/free; ☺ 11am-6pm May & Sep, to 8pm Jun-Aug) This exceptional museum includes extensive and well-signed displays of pirates' weapons, blacksmith tools and antique nautical maps. A small cafe overlooking the harbour exhibits the work of local artists, and a gift shop is open to the public. It's at the west end of the harbour.

National Marine Park of Alonnisos Northern Sporades   NATIONAL PARK
(www.alonissos-park.gr) In a country not noted for its ecological foresight, the National Marine Park of Alonnisos (the largest marine

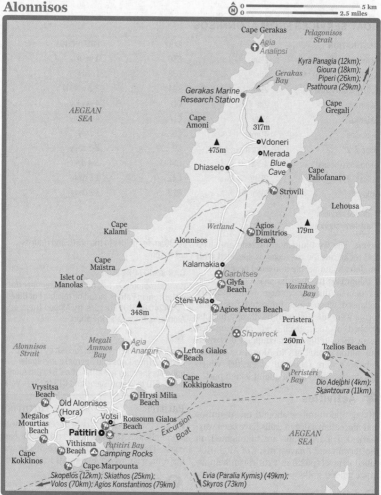

EVIA & THE SPORADES ALONNISOS

park in Europe) is a welcome innovation. Created in 1992 its prime aim has been the protection of the endangered Mediterranean monk seal and several rare seabirds. In summer, licensed boats from Alonnisos and Skopelos conduct excursions through the pristine park. Though it's unlikely you'll find the shy monk seal, your chances of spotting dolphins are fairly good. Excursion tickets are available from all waterfront agencies. The marine park is divided into two zones, A and B. Alonnisos lies within Zone B, along with the islets of Peristera and Dio Adelphi. Access to Zone A is more restricted, with boats allowed no closer than 400m to most islets.

Piperi Islet is protected by a 5km radius due to its importance for monk seal reproduction.

MOM Information Centre   MUSEUM

(☑24240 66350; www.mom.gr; waterfront; ⊙10am-10pm Jun-Sep) **FREE** Excellent waterfront info centre all about the protected Mediterranean monk seal. Great displays, videos in English and helpful multilingual staff on hand.

🏃 Activities

A cobbled 2km *kalderimi* (cobblestoned) path winds up through shrubbery and orchards to Old Alonnisos. Albedo Travel (p623) can help arrange guided walks.

Kayaking & Boat Trips

Sea kayaking excursions around Alonnisos, from half-day to overnight cove camping, are arranged by Albedo Travel (p623). Both Alonnisos Travel (p623) and Albedo Travel hire out four-person 18HP to 25HP motorboats (from €48 to €60 per day).

Diving

A few ancient sailing vessels have been discovered at the bottom of the shallow sea around Alonnisos. Efforts are under way to open these sites to guided dives. Contact **Alonissos Blue Dive Center** (☑24240 65804; www.alonissosdiving.com) at Albedo Travel in Patitiri, or **Ikion Diving** (☑24240 65158, 6984181598; www.ikiondiving.gr) in Steni Vala.

☞ Tours

Two full-service agencies on the waterfront, Albedo Travel and Alonnisos Travel (p623) provide maps, run marine-park trips and organise snorkelling and swimming excursions to Skantzoura and nearby islands.

Popular round-the-island excursions (€40) aboard the classic *Gorgona,* captained by charming island native **Pakis Athanasiou** (☑6978386588), visit the **Blue Cave** on the northeast coast and the islets of **Kyra Panagia** and **Peristera** in the marine park, with lunch and swimming breaks along the way.

🛏 Sleeping

★**Liadromia Hotel**　　　　　　　HOTEL €
(☑24240 65521; www.liadromia.gr; d/tr/ste incl breakfast from €40/60/75; ᴘ🌀@🌐) This wel-

coming and impeccably maintained hotel overlooking the harbour was Patitiri's first. All rooms have character to spare, from hand-embroidered curtains to period furnishings. The gracious owner, Maria, takes obvious delight in making it all work.

Ilias Studios　　　　　　　　　　HOTEL €
(☑24240 65451; www.ilias-studios.gr; Pelasgon 27; r from €30) Just 100m from the port, owners Ilias and Magdalini provide a genuine welcome. Rooms are spotless, airy and light, and a common kitchen awaits self-caterers.

Camping Rocks　　　　　CAMPGROUND €
(☑24240 65410, 6973230977; rocks.camping@gmail.com; Marpounta; camp sites per adult/tent €7.50/3) Follow the signposts 800m south of the port to this clean and shaded coastal spot with cafe.

★**Paradise Hotel**　　　　　　　HOTEL €€
(☑24240 65160; www.paradise-hotel.gr; s/d incl breakfast from €60/75; ᴘ🌀🌐🏊) Wood ceilings and stone-tiled floors give a rustic feel to these quiet, comfortable rooms, along with modern bathrooms and shuttered balconies that overlook the bay. Beyond the pool bar, a stairway leads to a small cove for swimming.

🍴 Eating & Drinking

★**Ouzerie Archipelagos**　　　　　GREEK €
(mains €4-8; ⊙lunch & dinner) To get the feel of this very Greek establishment, opposite the ferry dock, pick a table towards the back where locals gather to order round after round of fine mezedhes, always-fresh grilled fish and local firewater favourite *tsipouro.*

Cafe Bistro Helios　　　　　　　BISTRO €
(☑24240 65667; snacks €3-7; ⊙6pm-midnight) Snappy bistro hidden in plain view, up the steps from the National Bank. Well-priced small plates, harbour view plus an international twist.

Pi & Fi　　　　　　　　　　　　　KEBAB €
(snacks €2-4; ⊙lunch & dinner) Pi & Fi roughly means 'quick and easy', like its grab-and-go kebabs and pitta souvlakia. Opposite the police station on the main road.

Drunk Seal　　　　　　　　　　　　BAR
(⊙10am-late) One of several cheery dives serving unique cocktails at the port, tilting in the direction of the Folklore Museum.

ℹ Information

National Bank of Greece ATM (main road, near taxi rank)

THE MONK SEAL

Once populating hundreds of colonies in the Black Sea, the Mediterranean Sea and along Africa's Atlantic coast, the Mediterranean monk seal has been reduced to about 600. Half of these live in the seas around Greece. One of the earth's rarest mammals, the monk seal is now one of the 20 most endangered species worldwide. Major threats include decreasing food supply and destruction of habitat. Thankfully, the once-common killings by fishers – who saw the seal as a pest that tore holes in nets and robbed their catch – have diminished with the recognition that protecting the seal also promotes recovery of fish stocks. For more information about monk seals, visit **MOM Information Centre** .

Police (☎ 24240 65205; main road)
Port police (☎ 24240 65595; quay)
Post office (main road; ⊙7.30am-2pm)

Old Alonnisos   Παλιά Αλόννησος

Old Alonnisos (aka Palia Alonnisos and Hora) is an enchanting place with panoramic views and winding stepped alleys. From the main road just outside the village, an old 1km donkey path leads down to Megalos Mourtias Beach. At the bus stop you'll find a blue noticeboard that details several area walks.

🎓 Courses

Kali Thea   YOGA
(☎ 24240 65513, 6975930108; www.kalithea.org; ⊙May-Oct) Hatha yoga and massage, courtesy of Bibi and Lee, on the outskirts of Old Alonnisos.

🛏 Sleeping

Pension Chiliadromia   PENSION €
(☎ 24240 65814; chiliadromia@alonissos.com; Plateia Hristou; r/studio from €35/50; ❄️📶) Tucked into the heart of the old village, this homey pension is a budget gem, with small balconies, comfortable beds, well-equipped kitchens and traditional decorations. There's a morning cafe downstairs.

Elma's Houses   APARTMENT €
(☎ 24240 66108, 6945466776; www.elmashouses.com; studio/apt from €45/75; ❄️📶) Families will appreciate either of Elma's two roomy stone houses, each traditionally decorated and with full kitchen, comfy beds and great views from the courtyard. It's near the old school in the village.

★ Konstantina Studios   APARTMENT €€
(☎24240 66165, 6932271540; www.konstantinastudios.gr; s/d incl breakfast from €50/85; 🅿️❄️📶) Among the nicest accommodation on Alonnisos, these handsome and quiet studios with fully equipped kitchens come with balcony views of the southwest coast. The resourceful owner, Konstantina, fetches her guests from the dock and serves homemade breakfasts.

🍴 Eating & Drinking

★ Hayiati   SNACKS €
(☎24240 66244; Old Alonnisos; snacks €2-4; ⊙9am-2am) A *glykopoleio* (sweets shop) by day and a piano bar by night, with sweeping views round the clock. Morning fare includes made-to-order cheese *tyropita*. Later, you'll find homemade pastas along with the gracious hospitality of owner-cooks Meni and Angela. It's just above the village square.

Astrofengia   GREEK €€
(mains €7-15; ⊙dinner) Choose from the well-prepared Greek standards, rare veggie *mousakas*, mixed seafood souvlakia and good house wines. Or go straight for the *galaktoboureko* custard dessert. It's opposite the small car park at the village entrance.

Aerides Cafe-Bar   BAR
(⊙9am-5pm & 7pm-2am) Maria and Yiannis make the drinks, pick the music and scoop the ice cream at this hip hole-in-the-wall on the village square.

Piperi   CAFE, BAR
(☎24240 66384; ⊙9am-midnight) Sparkling cafe on the village square great for morning coffee or evening drinks.

Around Alonnisos

From Patitiri, Alonnisos' main road reaches 19km to the northern tip of the island at Gerakas, home to an EU-funded marine research station. North of Patitiri, roads descend to small fishing bays and secluded beaches.

Along the east coast, the first bay from Patitiri is tiny **Rousoum Gialos**. Next is **Votsi**, home to **Maria's Votsi Pension** (☎24240 65510; www.pension-votsi.gr; Votsi; d/tr from €40/50; 🅿️❄️@📶), with immaculate rooms and hospitality to spare. Two kilometres on, **Cape Kokkinokastro** is the site of the ancient and submerged city of Ikos. Continuing north, the road reaches **Leftos Gialos**, which is home to a pebble beach and the superb **Taverna Eleonas** (☎69450 81006; Leftos Gialos; mains €5-11; ⊙lunch & dinner).

Steni Vala, a small fishing village and deep-water yacht port, has 50-odd rooms in domatia. Try friendly **Ikaros Cafe & Market** (☎24240 65390) for reliable lodging information. Four tavernas overlook the small marina; **Tassia's Cooking** (☎24240 65545; Steni Vala; mains €4.50-9; ⊙lunch & dinner) is a favourite. Small and sandy **Agios Petros Beach**, just 500m south of the village, is home to **Lithea Studios** (☎24240 66435, 6932586001; www.lithea.gr; Agios Petros; studios/villas from €60/90; 🅿️❄️📶), an inviting stone lodge.

Kalamakia, 2km further north and the last village of note, has a few domatia and three fine dockside fish tavernas, including **Korali** (Steni Vala; mains €5-11; ⊙lunch & dinner), where the morning catch seems to jump from boat to plate.

Islets Around Alonnisos

Alonnisos is surrounded by eight uninhabited islets, all rich in flora and fauna. **Piperi**, the furthest island northeast of Alonnisos, is a refuge for the monk seal and is strictly off limits. **Gioura**, also off limits, is home to an unusual species of wild goat known for the crucifix-shaped marking on its spine. Excursion boats visit an old monastery and olive press on **Kyra Panagia**. The most remote of the group, **Psathoura**, boasts the submerged remains of an ancient city and the brightest lighthouse in the Aegean. **Peristera**, just off Alonnisos' east coast, has sandy beaches and the remains of a castle. Nearby **Lehousa** is known for its stalactite-filled sea caves. **Skantzoura**, to the southeast of Alonnisos, is the habitat of the Eleonora's falcon and the rare Audouin's seagull. The island situated between Peristera and Skantzoura is known as **Dio Adelphi** (Two Brothers). Each 'brother' is actually a small island.

Skyros   Σκύρος

POP 2890

Skyros, the largest of the Sporades group, can seem like two separate islands: the north has small bays, rolling farmland and pine forests while the south features arid hills and a rocky shoreline. In Greek mythology, Skyros was the hiding place of the young Achilles. It was also the last port of call for the English poet Rupert Brooke (1887–1915), who died of septicaemia on a French hospital ship off the coast of Skyros en route to the Battle of Gallipoli.

ℹ Getting There & Away

AIR

In addition to domestic flights, Skyros airport has occasional charter flights from Oslo, Amsterdam and destinations in France. For tickets, contact **Sky Express** (22220 91876, 28102 23500; www.skyexpress.gr; airport), **Aegean Airlines** (22220 91684; www.aegeanair.com; Skyros airport) or visit Skyros Travel Agency (p629) in Skyros Town. Domestic flights from Skyros head to Athens (€28, 25 minutes) and Thessaloniki (€50, 45 minutes) three times a week.

BOAT

Skyros' main port is Linaria. Ferries link to Evia (Paralia Kymis; €9, 1¾ hours, one to two daily), and Alonnisos and Skopelos in summer (€24, 4½ to five hours, three weekly). Purchase tickets from Skyros Travel (p629) in Skyros Town or from the ticket kiosk at the dock in Linaria or in Paralia Kymis (Evia).

ℹ Getting Around

BUS & TAXI

A bus runs from Linaria to Skyros Town, Magazia and Molos (€1.60); and from Skyros Town to the airport (€2.50). A **taxi** (6972894088) from Skyros Town to Linaria is €15; to the airport, €25.

CAR & MOTORCYCLE

Cars, motorbikes and bicycles can all be hired in Skyros Town from **Martina's Rentals** (6974752380, 22220 92022), near the Feel InGreece tour office; and from **Vayos Motorbikes** (22220 92957) – also for bikes – and **Angelis Cars** (22220 91888), both near the bus station.

Skyros Town   Σκύρος

Skyros' capital is draped over a high rocky bluff. It's topped by a 13th-century Venetian fortress, and is laced with labyrinthine, smooth cobblestone streets that invite wandering, but were designed to keep out the elements, and also pirates.

Agoras, the main thoroughfare, is lively jumble of tavernas, bars and shops flanked by winding alleyways. About 100m past the

---

SKYROS CARNIVAL

In this wild pre-Lenten festival, in the last four weekends before Lent and Orthodox Easter, young men portray their elders' vigour as they don goat masks, hairy jackets and dozens of copper goat bells. They then proceed to clank and dance through Skyros Town, each with a male partner dressed up as a Skyrian bride but also wearing a goat mask. The overtly pagan revelries include much singing and dancing, and equal parts drinking and feasting.

The transvestism evident in the carnival derives from the cult of Achilles, associated in Greek mythology with Skyros as the childhood hiding place for Achilles. His mother feared a prophecy requiring her son's skills in the Trojan War. He was given to the care of King Lykomides, who disguised him as one of his daughters. Achilles was outwitted, however, by Odysseus, who arrived with jewels and finery for the girls, along with a sword and shield. When Achilles alone showed interest in the weapons, Odysseus persuaded him to go to Troy.

The festival draws more than 2000 visitors for the final weekend, so book early.

plateia, the main drag of Agoras forks left and zigzags to two small museums adjacent to Plateia Rupert Brooke, from where the steps descend 1km to Magazia Beach.

Sights & Activities

★ Manos Faltaïts Folk Museum MUSEUM

(☑22220 91232; www.faltaits.gr/english/museum .htm; Plateia Rupert Brooke; admission €2, incl tour €5; ☉10am-2pm & 6-9pm) This not-to-be-missed gem details the mythology and folklore of Skyros. The 19th-century mansion is a multilevel labyrinth of Skyrian costumes, embroidery, antique furniture, ceramics, daggers, cooking pots and vintage photographs. There's also a small gift shop and terrace overlooking the sea. In mid-July a **rembetika music festival** (☑22220 91232; www.rebetiko seminar.com/index.php) is hosted here.

Archaeological Museum MUSEUM

(☑22220 91327; Plateia Rupert Brooke; admission €2; ☉8.30am-3pm Tue-Sun) Along with Mycenaean pottery found near Magazia and artefacts from the ongoing Bronze Age excavation at Palamari, this museum features a traditional Skyrian house interior, transported in its entirety from the benefactor's home.

Tours

★ Feel Ingreece CULTURAL TOUR

(☑22220 93100; www.feelingreece.gr; off upper Agoras; from €20) Local owner Chrysanthi Zygogianni is dedicated to helping sustain the best of Skyrian culture. The focus is on local arts and the island's natural environment, in co-operation with the EU-supported Skyros Life Project. The office arranges hiking excursions to glimpse wild Skyrian horses; birdwatching trips; pottery, woodcarving, Skyrian cooking and Greek dance lessons; and boat trips.

Niko Sikkes GUIDED TOURS

(☑69769 83712, 22220 92707; nikonisi@hotmail. com) Contact the well-informed and resourceful Niko Sikkes for his impromptu

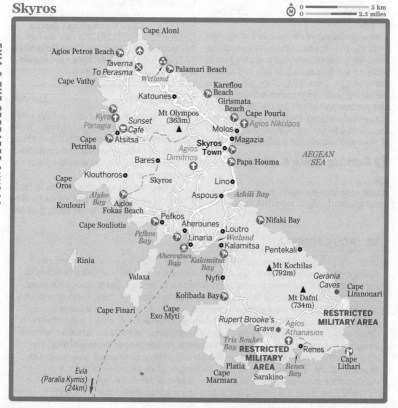

Skyros

tours of the island, the town and the remarkable Manos Faltaïts Folk Museum.

🛏 Sleeping

Pension Nikolas   PENSION €
(☎22220 91778; s/d/tr €35/45/55; P❄🐕) Set back on a quiet road on the edge of town, this friendly pension and budget gem is a five-minute walk to busy Agoras. Upper rooms have air-con and balconies; lower rooms have fans and open onto a shady garden.

★Hotel Nefeli &
Skyrian Studios   BOUTIQUE HOTEL €€
(☎22220 91964; www.skyros-nefeli.gr; Skyros Town; d/studio/ste incl breakfast from €70/90/240; P❄@🐕🏊) This smart and welcoming hotel on the edge of town has an easy minimalist-meets-Skyrian feel to it, with handsome furnishings and swanky bathrooms. The hotel and adjacent studios share a saltwater swimming pool and outdoor bar. Breakfast includes savoury and sweet Greek favourites.

🍴 Eating

Skyros welcomes a steady number of visiting Athenians, with the result that island cooks cater for Greek rather than tourist tastes.

★O Pappous Kai Ego   TAVERNA €
(Agoras; mains €6-9; ⊙lunch & dinner) The name of this small taverna means 'my grandfather and me' and it's easy to see how one generation of family recipes followed another. It's well known for the Skyrian dolmadhes made with a touch of goat milk.

Maryetis Restaurant   GREEK €
(☎22220 91311; Agoras; mains €6-9; ⊙lunch & dinner) The local favourite in town for grilled fish and octopus *stifadho*, great grills and mezedhes such as black-eyed beans and fava dip. Wines and service are excellent.

Amaltheia   GREEK €
(mains €5-10; ⊙lunch & dinner) Opposite Nefeli Hotel as you enter town, this popular eatery is known for traditonal Greek dishes and generous portions. Order for one; eat for two.

🍸 Drinking & Nightlife

Nightlife in Skyros Town centres mostly around the bars on Agoras; the further north you go from the *plateia,* the more mellow the sounds.

Kalypso   BAR
(Agoras; ⊙noon-late; 🐕) Classy Kalypso plays lots of jazz and blues, and owner bartender Hristos serves beer on tap and makes a

---

ARTISTS & PIRATES

Skyros has a flourishing community of working artists, from potters and painters to sculptors and weavers. In Byzantine times passing pirates collaborated with rogue residents, whose houses became virtual galleries for stolen booty looted from merchant ships: hand-carved furniture, ceramic plates and copper ornaments from Europe, the Middle East and Asia Minor. Today, similar items adorn almost every Skyrian house.

To see the legacy of this particularly Skyrian tradition, check out these favourite artists: sculptor and painter **George Lambrou** (☎22220 91334; Magazia; ⊙11am-1pm & 7-9pm); ceramicist **Stamatis Ftoulis** (☎22220 91559, 22220 92220; Magazia); embroiderers and woodcarvers **Olga Zacharaiki** (☎6974666113; Agoras, Skyros Town), **Andreou Stamatiou** (☎22220 92827; Agoras, Skyros Town) and **Amersa Panagiotou** (☎22220 92827; Agoras, Skyros Town); and potter **Stathis Katsarelias** (☎22220 92918, 6971889647; Magazia).

To find these artists at work, contact Chrysanthi at **Feel Ingreece** (left). Several of them display their work between the Plateia and upper Agoras.

---

fine straight-up margarita along with homemade sangria.

Rodon   BAR
(Agoras; ⊙8am-late; 🐕) Smart late-night hang-out at which to end the evening, with tasty small plates, sturdy drinks and mellow music; return in the morning for breakfast.

Agora Cafe-Bar   BAR
(Plateia; 🐕) This cosy bar next to the post office is open early till late and escapes the thump of the main drag.

ℹ Information

National Bank of Greece ATM (Agoras)
Police (☎22220 91274; Agoras)
Post Office (⊙7.30am-2pm; Plateia) On the main square.
Skyros Travel Agency (☎6944884588, 22220 91600; www.skyrostravel.com; Agoras; ⊙9.30am-1.30pm & 6.30-9.30pm) Helpful full-service agency that arranges accommodation; transfers and onward travel; car and motorbike hire; and jeep and boat excursions around Skyros.

Magazia & Molos
Μαγαζιά & Μώλος

The resort of Magazia is a compact, colourful maze of winding alleys that skirts the southern end of a long, sandy beach beneath Skyros Town. 'Magazia' comes from the Greek word for shop; the original buildings were storehouses for olive oil, produce and dry goods. Near the northern end of the beach, once-sleepy Molos now has its own share of tavernas, bars and rooms. Its landmark windmill and adjacent rock-hewn church of **Agios Nikolaos** are easy to spot. Skinny-dippers can leave it all behind at nude-friendly **Papa Houma** near the southern end of Magazia.

🛏 Sleeping

⭐ **Perigiali Hotel & Studios**   HOTEL €
(☑ 22220 92075; www.perigiali.com; Magazia; d/tr/apt incl breakfast from €55/80/115; P ✳ @ 🛜 ✹) Leafy Perigiali feels secluded despite being only 60m from Magazia beach. The Skyrian-style rooms overlook a garden with pear and apricot trees, while an upscale wing sports a pool with luxe apartments. Owner Amalia is full of ideas for travellers.

Antigoni Studios   APARTMENT €
(☑ 6945100230, 22220 91310; www.antigonistudios.com; d/f from €50/80; P ✳ 🛜) Outstanding addition to Magazia's sleep scene. Large studios, each with handsome furnishings, kitchens, modern bathrooms, and just a three-minute walk to the beach. Managed by the hospitable Katarina. On the right side entering Magazia.

Georgia's House   PENSION €
(☑ 22220 91357, 6973819787; www.georgiashouse.com; Magazia; r from €30; ✳ 🛜) You can't get much closer to the sea than at these well-managed, geranium-adorned domatia 20m from the beach, opposite a car park and cafe.

Ammos Hotel   HOTEL €€
(☑ 6974354181, 22220 91234; www.skyrosammoshotel.com; Magazia; d/f incl breakfast from €65/100; P ✳ ✳ 🛜 ✹) This strikingly well-designed lodging is low-key and inviting, with handsome bathrooms, overhead fans and made-to-order Skyrian breakfasts to start the day, plus a rooftop terrace to catch the sunset.

🍴 Eating & Drinking

⭐ **Stefanos Taverna**   TAVERNA €
(☑ 6974350372; Magazia; mains €5.50-9.50; ☺ breakfast, lunch & dinner) Sit on the terrace overlooking Magazia beach and choose from a range of baked dishes such as *yemista*

(stuffed tomatoes), juicy grills and locally made sausage, wild greens and fresh fish. Breakfast omelettes start at €3.

Apostolis   CAFE, TAVERNA €
(Magazia; mains €5-9; ☺ dinner) At this easy-to-miss cafe-taverna, owner Apostolis offers a simple Greek menu including fresh fish, and when the mood strikes, a respectable Spanish *paella*. Look for steps by a small signpost for Perigiali upon entering Magazia.

Oi Istories Tou Barba   TAVERNA €
(☑ 22220 91453; Molos; mains €4-10; ☺ lunch & dinner) Look for the light-blue railing above the beach in Molos to find this excellent cafe-*tsipouradhiko* (a northern *ouzerie*).

Juicy Beach Bar   BAR
(☑ 22220 93337; Magazia; snacks €2-5; ☺ 9am-midnight) Escape the midday sun or chill under the stars at busy beach bar Juicy, which serves all-day breakfasts.

Ammoudia   BAR
(☑ 6949207460; Magazia; ☺ 10am-late) Cool and sandy, with a long bar, fresh snacks and sturdy drinks, this is one of the newer additions to the beach.

Linaria   Λιναριά

Linaria, the port of Skyros, is tucked into a small bay filled with fishing boats and a few tavernas and *ouzeries*. Things perk up briefly whenever the *Achileas* ferry comes in, its surreal arrival announced with the sound of Strauss' *Also Sprach Zarathustra* booming from hillside speakers above the port.

Just opposite the ferry dock, look for **King Lykomides Rooms** (☑ 6972694434, 22220 93249; soula@skyrosnet.gr; r incl breakfast from €40-60; P ✳ @ 🛜), an efficient domatio managed by the hospitable Soula Pappas, with spotless rooms and balconies.

Join the regulars under the big plane tree at the friendly **Taverna Psariotis** (☺ lunch & dinner) for reasonably priced fish and lobster. Next to the dock, **Taverna Ivilai** (mains €4-9; ☺ lunch & dinner) is popular for mezedhes and grills. **Kavos Bar** (drinks & snacks €2-5; ☺ 9am-midnight), overlooking the port, pulls in Skyrians for sunset drinks.

Kalamitsa   Καλαμίτσα

This low wetland area, the largest on Skyros, takes its name from the Greek *'kalamia'* or reed. It's an important Aegean stopover for migrating egrets, herons and falcons. In ancient times, young Achilles set off for Troy from nearby Achili Bay.

Taverna Mouries (☑22220 93555; Kalamitsa; ⊘lunch & dinner) serves traditional Greek fare that's generous and tasty. 'Mouries' means mulberry, and several rambling old trees, planted by owner Manolis' grandfather, provide welcome shade in summer. Lamb and goat grills are specialities.

Atsitsa   Ατσίτσα

The picturesque port village of Atsitsa on the west coast occupies a woody shoreline setting. The snappy all-organic **Sunset Cafe** (drinks & snacks €1.50-4; ⊘breakfast-sunset) overlooking the bay offers Greek coffee and wine, fresh juices, ice cream, delicate cakes and salads, all compliments of Mariana and family. Two kilometres north, find the excellent roadside taverna Cook-Nara.

Northwest Coast

On the northwest coast, near **Agios Petros Beach**, find the outstanding **Taverna Agios Petros** (☑6972842116; mains €5-8), set among a grove of pines and featuring its own produce, meat and cheese. At azure-blue **Cape Petritsa**, 1.5km south of Atsitsa, the coastal road turns inland, finding the sea again at sandy **Agios Fokas Bay**, with a taverna and great swimming. A beautiful horseshoe-shaped beach graces **Pefkos Bay**, 10km southeast of Atsitsa. Nearby, the beach at **Aherounes** has a gentle kid-friendly sandy bottom, along with two tavernas and domatia.

Tris Boukes Bay
Τρεις Μπούκες Όρμος

The southernmost corner of the island is a windswept landscape partly restricted by a Greek naval station. Many come here to visit English poet **Rupert Brooke's grave**. The marble grave is in a quiet olive grove just inland from the bay; it's marked with a wooden sign in Greek on the roadside. The gravestone is inscribed with Brooke's most famous sonnet, 'The Soldier'. The inscription on the original cross (now in England) said: 'Here lies the servant of God, sub-lieutenant in the English Navy, who died for the deliverance of Constantinople from the Turks'.

A nearby rough dirt road (4WD recommended) leads to **Renes Bay**, from where a 5km hiking trail skirts a coastal plateau, ending at the lighthouse at **Cape Lithari**. Wild Skyrian horses are often glimpsed here, along with Eleonora's falcons that nest in the steep cliffs nearby from April to October.

Palamari   Παλαμάρι

At the northeast of the island, uncrowded Palamari occupies a graceful stretch of sandy beach, and is the site of a fascinating **archaeological excavation** (http://geomorphol ogie.revues.org/668; Palamari; ⊘8am-2pm) FREE of a Bronze Age town dating from 2500 BC. Work began in 1981, uncovering artefacts, stone walls, even drainpipes and paved walkways. The ongoing excavation continues to provide, and display, evidence of a powerfully fortified prehistoric coastal settlement near the heart of early Mediterranean trade routes. A small well-organised **visitor centre** opened in 2014, and more findings from Palamari are on display at the Archaeological Museum (p628) in Skyros Town. An adjacent **wetland** is the remnant of an ancient alluvial lagoon that supported this fishing and hunting community. Today it remains a birdwatching mecca, especially for long-legged waders like herons and ibises.

EVIA & THE SPORADES SKYROS

THE ENDANGERED SKYRIAN HORSE

The small-bodied Skyrian horse (Equus cabalus skyriano) is valued for its intelligence, beauty and gentleness. Common in Greece in ancient times, today there are fewer than 300, with a small minority living on the southern slopes of Mt Kochilas on Skyros.

Several Skyrians are working to conserve the species. In 2006 Amanda Simpson and Stathis Katsarelias started **Friends of the Skyrian Horse** (☑6986051678; http://sky rosislandhorsetrust.com; Skyros Town) with just three horses. Their facilities have expanded to accommodate around 40 horses as they seek to re-establish a herd of wild, pure-bred Skyrian horses. Visitors are welcome at the small ranch near Skyros Town. Check out their Facebook page at 'Friends of the Skyrian Horse, Katsarelia-Simpson-Project'.

Each summer in late June, the free three-day **Skyrian Horse Festival** features parades, music and traditional dance. Children can ride the horses safely at **Mouries Farm** (☑6947465900; www.facebook.com/skyrianhorses), opposite Taverna Mouries in Kalamitsa.

For information, visit the **Skyrian Horse Society** (☑6974694023, 22220 92345; www. skyrianhorsesociety.gr) at the Skyros Life Project office near the bus station in Skyros Town.

Ionian Islands

Best Places to Eat

➡ Arriva Fish Restaurant (p649)

➡ Arhontiko (p658)

➡ Klimataria (p644)

➡ Irida (p662)

➡ Il Vesuvio (p640)

Best Places to Stay

➡ Hotel Perantzada (p664)

➡ Petani Bay Hotel (p660)

➡ Siorra Vittoria (p639)

➡ Levant Hotel (p646)

➡ Torri E Merli (p649)

Why Go?

With their cooler climate, abundant olive and cypress trees and forested mountains, the Ionians (Τα Ιόνια Νησιά) are a lighter, greener version of Greece. The Venetians, French and British have all in their own way shaped the architecture, culture, (excellent) cuisine – and the unique feel of Ionian life.

Though the islands appear linked in a chain down the west coast of mainland Greece, each has a distinct landscape and cultural history. Corfu Town has Parisian-style arcades, Venetian alleyways and Italian-inspired delicacies. Kefallonia boasts soaring mountains and vineyards; Paxi's Italianate harbour villages are impossibly pretty; and soulful Ithaki preserves wild terrain and a sense of history. Zakynthos has sea caves and waters teeming with turtles. Lastly, Lefkada has some of the best turquoise-lapped beaches in Greece, while Kythira feels off-the-beaten-path and mysterious. The Ionians offer something for adventure seekers, food lovers, culture vultures and beach bums alike.

When to Go
Corfu Town

May Life is still quiet and the wildflowers are abloom everywhere.

Jul Escape the heat in the rest of Greece and head to its coolest islands.

Sep Leaves change colour, and the Robola grapes are being harvested in Kefallonia.

Ionian Islands Highlights

1 Exploring world-class museums, fortresses, restaurants and Venetian, French and British architecture in **Corfu Town** (p637).

2 Hopping from one gorgeous harbour to another in pastoral **Paxi** (p646).

3 Treating yourself to top restaurants in Kefallonia's charming **Fiskardo** (p661) and striking **Assos** (p661).

4 Learning to windsurf at **Vasiliki** (p652; Lefkada) or diving, kayaking and caving in **Kefallonia** (p655).

5 Ranking your favourite beaches, from the busiest on Corfu or Zakynthos to the quieter joys of Paxi or **Lefkada's west coast** (p653).

6 Walking the paths of Homer in **Ithaki** (p662).

7 Discovering the tiny villages, waterfalls and remote coves of **Kythira** (p669).

History

The origin of the name 'Ionian' is obscure, but it's thought to derive from the goddess Io. One of Zeus' paramours, Io fled the wrath of a jealous Hera, passing through what's now known as the Ionian Sea. According to Homer, the islands were important in Mycenaean times, though only tombs (no villages or palaces) have been unearthed. By the 8th century BC, the islands were in the hands of city-state Corinth. A century later, Corfu staged a successful revolt. The Peloponnesian Wars (431–404 BC) left Corfu as little more than a staging post for whoever happened to be controlling Greece.

By the end of the 3rd century BC, the Romans ruled the Ionian region. Following the decline of the empire, the islands suffered waves of invaders: the Byzantine Empire (until the fall of Constantinople), Venice, Napoleon (in 1797), Russia (from 1799 to 1807), Napoleon again. In 1815, after Napoleon's downfall, the Ionians became a British protectorate. The British constructed roads, bridges, schools and hospitals, established trade links, and developed agriculture and industry. But their rule was oppressive, nationalists wanted independence, and by 1864 Britain relinquished the islands to Greece.

WWII was rough on the Ionians and the islands saw mass emigration, and again following devastating earthquakes in 1948 and 1953. By the 1960s foreign holidaymakers were visiting in increasing numbers, and the tourist trade flourished.

ℹ Useful Websites

Corfu www.corfu.gr, www.allcorfu.com, www.corfuland.gr (in Greek)

Ionian Islands www.greeka.com/ionian

Ithaki www.ithacagreece.com

Kefallonia www.kefalonia.net.gr

Lefkada www.lefkada.gr, www.lefkas.net

Paxi www.paxos-greece.com, www.paxos.tk

Zakynthos www.zakynthos-net.gr, www.zanteweb.gr

CORFU   ΚΕΡΚΥΡΑ

POP 102,071

At the end of his travails, Odysseus was shipwrecked on the island of the Phaecans, who patiently heard his tale before setting him on a boat home to Ithaki. This island is Corfu and you can expect the same level of kindness from this cosmopolitan jewel.

Ever since it was first settled by the Corcyrans in the 8th century, Corfu, or Kerkyra (*ker*-kih-rah) in Greek, has been an object of desire for its untamed beauty and strategic position in the Mediterranean. It was a seat of European learning in the early days of modern Greece, with cultural institutions such as libraries and academic centres. To this day, Corfiots remain fiercely proud of their intellectual and artistic roots, a legacy visible from its fine museums and cultural life.

There are pockets of overdeveloped resorts, particularly north of Corfu Town and in the far north, but the island is large enough to easily escape the crowds – venture up its woody mountains studded with spear-sharp cypress trees and explore vertiginous villages, coves fringed by cobalt-blue water, and the fertile interior ashimmer with olive groves.

ℹ Getting There & Away

AIR

Corfu's **airport** (CFU; ☑ 26610 89600; www.corfu-airport.com) is about 2km southwest of the town centre.

Domestic

Aegean Airlines (☑ 26610 27100; www.aegeanair.com) Direct flights to Thessaloniki.

Astra Airlines (A2; ☑ 2310 489 392; www.astra-airlines.gr) Thessaloniki-based airline.

Olympic Air (☑ 801 801 0101; www.olympicair.com) At the airport.

Sky Express (☑ 2810 223500; www.skyexpress.gr) Operates a thrice-weekly route to Preveza, Kefallonia, Zakynthos and Kythira, making multiple stops, and (from June to September) to Iraklio, Crete.

DESTINATION	TIME	FARE	FREQUENCY
Athens	1hr	€105	3 daily
Iraklio	1¾hr	€142	3 weekly, high season
Kefallonia	1hr 5min	€55	3 weekly
Kythira	3¼hr	€80	1 weekly
Preveza	30min	€55	3 weekly
Thessaloniki	55min	€90	3 weekly
Zakynthos	2hr	€68	3 weekly

International

EasyJet (www.easyjet.com) has daily direct flights between the UK and Corfu (May to October) and high-season flights to Milan, Rome and Paris, while **British Airways** (BA; ☑ 210 890 6666; www.britishairways.com) now flies from the UK to Corfu. Air Berlin (p649) serves Germany. From May to September, many charter flights come from northern Europe and the UK.

BOAT

Neo Limani (New Port), with all ferry departures, lies west of hulking Neo Frourio (New Fortress).

Domestic

Ticket agencies in Corfu Town are near the new port, along Xenofondos Stratigou and Ethnikis Antistaseos.

Ilida (☑ Corfu 26610 49800, Paxi 26620 32401) hydrofoil goes between Corfu New Port and Paxi from mid-March to mid-October. The boat *Despina* serves Corfu New Port, Lefkimmi, Igoumenitsa and Paxi. Book ahead with Kamelia Lines (p647); places fill quickly.

Some international ferries from Corfu also call in at Igoumenitsa and Kefallonia. For schedules see www.openseas.gr or the **ferry information office** (☑ 26650 26280) in Igoumenitsa. Note that it is currently not possible to sail directly to Zakynthos; you'll have to catch the Sky Express (p634) plane instead. If you're heading to Patra, catch the ferry to Igoumenitsa first.

Boat Services from Corfu

ROUTE	TIME	FARE	FREQUENCY
Igoumenitsa-Corfu	1¼hr	€10	hourly
Igoumenitsa-Lefkimmi	70min	€7	6 daily
Paxi-Corfu*	55min	€25	1-3 daily

*high-speed service

Corfu

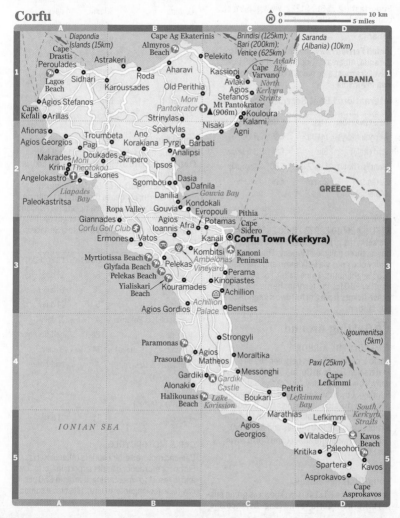

Italy

Corfu has regular connections with Brindisi, Bari and Ancona, operated by a handful of companies sailing between Italy and Igoumenitsa and/or Patra. It's only possible to go to direct to Venice in July and August. Check with the domestic shipping agents or online. You can also sail between Italy and Igoumenitsa or Patra, then transfer to a local ferry.

ANEK Lines (☑ 210 419 7420; www.anek.gr) Crete-based long-haul ferries. Its Igoumenitsa–Patra route is now jointly operated with Superfast Ferries.

Endeavor Lines (☑ 210 940 5222, Corfu 26610 25000; www.endeavor-lines.com; Ethnikis Antistaseos 2, Sea Pilot Travel)

Superfast (☑ 26610 81222; www.superfast. com; Ethnikis Antistaseos 18)

Albania

Ionian Ferries (www.ionianferries.gr) sail to Saranda, Albania. In addition to the €19 ticket, travellers must also pay €10 for a temporary visa to Albania.

International Boat Services from Corfu

DESTINATION	TIME	FARE	FREQUENCY
Ancona (Italy)	14½hr	€85	2 weekly
Bari (Italy)	8hr	€85	3 weekly
Brindisi (Italy)	5½–6¼hr	€80	4 weekly
Saranda (Albania)	25min	€19	1 daily

BUS

KTEL (☑ 26610 28927, 26610 28898; www. ktelkerkyras.gr) services go to Athens (€45, 8½ hours, three daily; on Monday, Thursday and Friday one goes via Lefkimmi) and Thessaloniki (€35, eight hours, twice daily). For both, budget another €10 for the ferry to the mainland. Purchase tickets from Corfu Town's long-distance bus station.

🛈 Getting Around

TO/FROM THE AIRPORT

Corfu local bus 15 goes between the airport and Plateia San Rocco in Corfu Town (€1.50, seven daily Monday to Friday, four or five Saturday and Sunday); buy tickets on board. The schedule is posted at the stop. If you miss bus 15, buses 6 and 10 stop on the main road 800m from the airport (en route to Benitses and Achillion).

Taxis between the airport and Corfu Town cost €10.

BUS

Long-Distance Buses

Long-distance KTEL buses (known as green buses) travel from Corfu Town's **long-distance bus station** (☑ 26610 28927; www.ktelkerkyras.gr; Ioannou Theotoki, Corfu Town), between Plateia San Rocco and the new port.

Fares cost €1.60 to €4.10. Timetables are at the ticket kiosk or online. Saturday services are reduced; on Sunday and holidays they're reduced considerably, or nonexistent.

DESTINATION	TIME	FREQUENCY
Agios Gordios	45min	5 daily
Agios Stefanos	1½hr	4 daily
Aharavi (via Roda)	1¼hr	6 daily
Arillas (via Afionas)	1¼hr	2 daily
Barbati	45min	7 daily
Ermones	30min	6 daily
Glyfada	30min	4 daily
Kassiopi	45min	6 daily
Kavos	1½hr	8 daily
Messonghi	45min	8 daily
Paleokastritsa	45min	8 daily
Pyrgi	30min	5 daily
Sidhari	1¼hr	7 daily
Spartera	45min	2 daily

Local Buses

Local blue buses depart from the **local bus station** (☑ 26610 31595; Plateia San Rocco) in Corfu Old Town.

Tickets are €1.10 or €1.50 depending on journey length; purchase them at the booth on Plateia San Rocco (although tickets for Achillion, Benitses and Kouramades are bought on the bus). All trips are under 30 minutes. Service is reduced on weekends.

DESTINATION	BUS NO	FREQUENCY
Agios Ioannis (via Afra)	8	13 daily
Achillion	10	6 daily
Benitses	6	14 daily
Evropouli (via Potamas)	4	11 daily
Kanoni	2a	half-hourly
Kombitsi (via Kanalia)	14	3 daily
Kondokali & Dasia (via Gouvia)	7	half-hourly
Kouramades (via Kinopiastes)	5	16 daily
Pelekas	11	11 daily

CAR & MOTORCYCLE

Car- and motorbike-hire outlets (Alamo, Hertz, Europcar etc) abound at the airport, in Corfu Town and in resort towns, starting at around €50 per day (less for longer-term hire). Most local companies have offices on the northern waterfront.

Budget (☑ 26610 22062; www.budgetrentacar.gr; Eleftheriou Venizelou 50, Corfu Town)

Sunrise (☑ 26610 26511, 26610 44325; www.corfusunrise.com; Ethnikis Antistaseos 6, Corfu Town)

Top Cars (☑ 26610 35237; www.carrental-corfu.com; Donzelot 25, Corfu Town)

❶ CORFU TOWN SIGHTS PASS

A joint sightseeing pass (adult/concession €8/4) is good for the Palaio Frourio (Old Fortress), Antivouniotissa Museum, the Archaeological Museum and the Museum of Asian Art. Get it at any of the included sights.

Corfu Town   Κέρκυρα

POP 35,000

Elegant Corfu Town (also known as Kerkyra) leaves you spellbound from the moment you wander its cobbled streets aglow with evil eyes and redolent with sandalwood, past old ladies bedecked in widow-black robes measuring their afternoons with worry beads, and washing strung from balconies. Corfu means 'twin peaks' – the town is bookended by two hills, on which two massive fortresses were built to repel the aggression of five successive Ottoman sieges. Besides some fascinating museums, there are plenty of upscale shops and some of the region's top restaurants to savour.

◉ Sights & Activities

The grand seaside esplanade, known as the **Spianada**, is lined by an arcaded promenade, the **Liston**. Built by the French as a precursor to Paris' Rue de Rivoli, the Liston, with its swath of packed cafes, is today the town's social hub. At the Spianada's northern end stands the grand neoclassical Palace of St Michael and St George. Inland, marble-paved streets lined with shops lead to the bustling modern town, centred on busy **Plateia San Rocco** (G Theotoki Sq).

At the time of writing, Corfu's **Archaeological Museum** was closed for extended renovations.

There is a striking **memorial to Corfu's Jews** in Plateia Solomou, near the Old Port in the area still known as **Evraiki**, the Jewish Quarter. People **swim** off the point just north of the Palaio Frourio.

★ Palace of St Michael & St George   PALACE

Originally the residence of a succession of British high commissioners, this palace now houses the world-class **Museum of Asian Art** (☑ 26610 30443; www.matk.gr; adult/child incl audioguide €3/free, incl Antivouniotissa Museum & Old Fortress €8; ☉ 8.30am-3.30pm Tue-Sun), founded in 1929. Expertly curated with extensive, informative English-language placards, the collection's approximately 10,000 artefacts, collected from all over Asia, include priceless prehistoric bronzes, ceramics, jade figurines, coins and works of art in onyx, ivory and enamel. Additionally, the palace's **throne room** and **rotunda** are impressively adorned in period furnishings and art.

Behind the eastern side of the palace, the **Municipal Art Gallery** (admission €2; ☉ 9am-5pm Tue-Sun) houses a fine collection featuring the work of leading Corfiot painters, a collection of splendid icons, rotating exhibitions, and a lovely seafront **cafe**.

★ Palaio Frourio   FORTRESS

(Old Fortress; ☑ 26610 48310; adult/concession €4/2; ☉ 8am-8pm Apr-Oct, 8.30am-3pm Nov-Mar) Constructed by the Venetians in the 15th century on the remains of a Byzantine castle (and further altered by the British), this spectacular landmark offers respite from the crowds and superb views of the region. Climb to the summit of the inner outcrop, which is crowned by a lighthouse, for a 360-degree panorama. The gatehouse contains a Byzantine **museum**.

★ Church of Agios Spyridon   CHURCH

(Agios Spyridonos; ☉ 7am-8pm) **FREE** The sacred relic of Corfu's beloved patron saint, St Spyridon, lies in an elaborate silver casket in the 16th-century basilica.

Antivouniotissa Museum   MUSEUM

(☑ 26610 38313; www.antivouniotissamuseum.gr; off Arseniou; adult/child €2/1; ☉ 9am-3.30pm Tue-Sun) The exquisite, timber-roofed, 15th-century **Church of Our Lady of Antivouniotissa** holds an outstanding collection of Byzantine and post-Byzantine icons and artefacts dating from the 13th to the 17th centuries.

Neo Frourio   FORTRESS

(New Fortress; ☉ 9am-5pm May-Oct) **FREE** A steep climb leads to this austere example of Venetian military architecture, added to extensively by the British. The interior is an eerie mass of tunnels, rooms and staircases, while the exterior has fine views.

Corfu Old Town

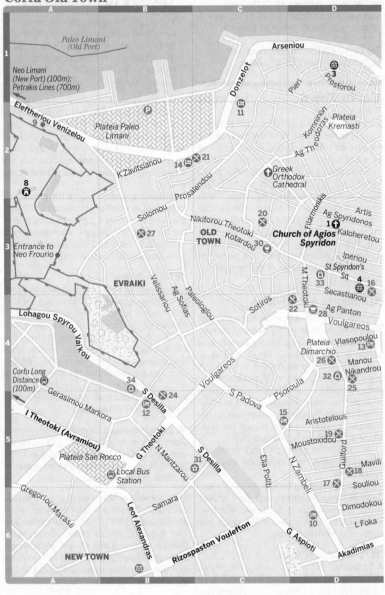

Mon Repos Estate PARK
(Kanoni Peninsula; ☺8am-7pm May-Oct, to 5pm Nov-Apr) **FREE** On the Kanoni Peninsula on the southern outskirts of town, an extensive, wooded parkland estate surrounds an elegant neoclassical villa. It houses the **Muse-** um **of Palaeopolis** (☎26610 41369; www.cor fu.gr; adult/concession €3/2; ☺8am-7pm Tue-Sun May-Oct), with entertaining archaeological displays and exhibits on the history of Corfu Town. Paths lead through lush grounds to the ruins of two Doric temples; the first

is truly a ruin, but the southerly **Temple of Artemis** is serenely impressive.

Take a picnic and plenty of water, as there are no nearby shops. Bus 2a goes to Kanoni from the Spianada (€1.70, every 20 minutes).

Corfu Philharmonic Society MUSEUM
(📞26610 39289; www.fek.gr; N Theotoki 10; ⏲9.30am-1.30pm Mon-Sat) FREE Founded in 1840 by Nikolaos Mantzaros, the forward-thinking composer of the Greek national anthem, the society funds free music programs and hosts a **museum** dedicated to the vibrant musical history of the island.

Corfu Reading Society HISTORIC BUILDING
(☑26610 39528; www.anagnostikicorfu.com; Kapodistriou 120; ◷9.30am-1.30pm Mon-Sat) FREE Founded in 1836, the oldest cultural institution in modern Greece houses 30,000 volumes. The art-filled mansion's upstairs map room has the first map of Corfu (from the 15th century). Also hosts concerts and lectures.

Vidos Island ISLAND
Boats from the old port (€5) go to Vidos Island, off the coast – great for **beaches** or a ramble through **fortresses** and a WWI Serbian **cemetery**.

☞ Tours

Sarris Cruises BOAT TOUR
(☑ 26610 25317; Eleftheriou Venizelou 13) Organises day trips from Corfu Town, including an excursion to the Butrinti World Heritage–listed ancient ruins in Albania (€59; passports required) and a boat trip taking in Paxi, the Blue Caves and Antipaxi (€40; go an a calm day). Transfers included.

⌂ Sleeping

Corfu tends towards the pricey: even in low season you'll find it more costly than many other islands. Book ahead in high season.

★ **Bella Venezia** BOUTIQUE HOTEL €€
(☑26610 46500; www.bellaveneziahotel.com; N Zambeli 4; s/d incl breakfast from €120/125; ❀✿🗟) From the instant you enter this neoclassical former girls' school – with its elegant lobby decked in candelabras, velvet chairs and grand piano – the place will charm you with its pure old-world charm. The Venezia has plush, high-ceilinged rooms with fine city views (some with balcony). Conscientious staff welcome you, and the gazebo breakfast room in the garden is delightful.

★ **Siorra Vittoria** BOUTIQUE HOTEL €€
(☑26610 36300; www.siorravittoria.com; Stefanou Padova 36; s/d incl breakfast from €99/135, ste €193; P❀🗟) Expect luxury and style at this quiet 19th-century mansion where painstakingly restored traditional architecture meets modern amenities; marble bathrooms, crisp linens and genteel service make for a relaxed stay. Breakfast in the garden beneath an ancient magnolia tree. The Vittoria suite encompasses the atelier and has sea views.

Arion Hotel HOTEL €€
(☑26610 37950; www.arioncorfu.gr; Sxerias 6 Mon Repo Anemomylos; s/d/tr €60/65/75; ❀🗟) Set

15 minutes' walk south of Corfu Town down waterfront Dimokratias Street, this large hotel has pleasant rooms with small balconies and clean bathrooms. Avoid cheaper corner rooms and those facing the road, and plump for one with a sea view. There's a handsome lobby, pool, great bar, and a terrific breakfast smorgasbord. Good value and tranquil.

Hermes Hotel HOTEL €€
(☑26610 39268; www.hermes-hotel.gr; Markora 12; s/d/tr from €55/65/75; ❀🗟) Peaceful Hermes has cool, lime-hued rooms in a central location (though mercifully the windows are double glazed), with old-fashioned bathrooms, laminate floors and a classy breakfast area. Rooms have a TV, fridge and CD player. Find it up a stairway, overlooking the market.

Hotel Konstantinoupolis PENSION €€
(☑26610 48716; www.konstantinoupolis.gr; K Zavitsianou 11; s/d/tr incl breakfast €67/74/100; ❀🗟) Climb into the antique lift and rattle up to the homely reception and breakfast area. Rooms, even those facing the sea, suffer road noise and a lack of flair, but are comfortable enough. Expect a fridge, bathroom and comfy beds.

City Marina Hotel HOTEL €€
(☑26610 39505; www.citymarina.gr; Donzelot 15; r with/without sea view incl breakfast €100/80; ❀🗟) The sea-facing Marina has an imposing lobby and pleasantly airy en suite rooms with shabby-chic fittings, orange bedspreads and choice art on the walls. More expensive sea views are wondrous but cheaper city views are also a delight. There's also a lift here.

Hotel Arcadion HOTEL €€
(☑26610 37670; www.arcadionhotel.com; Vlasopoulou 2; s/d/tr incl breakfast €90/150/180; ❀🗟) Straightforward, cool-tiled rooms, some with four-posters, are not the enticement here – it's the location. Right on the Liston's busiest corner, balconies overlook the hubbub and the old fort. A little noisy.

✖ Eating

Corfiot cuisine has been deliciously influenced by many cultures, particularly Italian. A horde of good options cluster on Guilford.

★ **Il Vesuvio** GREEK €
(☑26610 21284; Guilford; mains €10; ◷noon-late) The Neapolitan owner of this classy Italian restaurant, which has premises on both sides of the street, won the 'Best Italian

Restaurant in Greece' award for his moreish homemade gnocchi, tortellini and ravioli. Eat on the street or inside but don't neglect a taste of their silky-smooth panna cotta – so fresh it will make your taste buds sing.

★**To Tavernaki tis Marinas**   TAVERNA €

(📋 69816 56001; 4th Parados, Agias Sofias 1; mains €6-16; ⊙ noon-midnight) Restored stone walls, hardwood floors and cheerful staff lift the ambience of this taverna. Check daily specials or choose anything from *mousakas* (baked layers of eggplant or zucchini, minced meat and potatoes topped with cheese sauce) or grilled sardines to steak. Accompany it all with a dram of ouzo or *tsipouro* (a spirit similar to ouzo).

Corfu Sailing Club   GREEK €

(Old Fortress, Mandraki; mains €9; 🕿) Head to this charming harbourfront restaurant for a sundowner and to soak up the atmosphere in the skirts of the old fortress; feast on a menu rich in squid, sea bream and bass, as well as liver and bacon and pork medallion. Incurably romantic and a world away from the hubbub. To reach it pass through the security gate and wait for the free bus (or else walk from this point, around five minutes).

Chrisomalis   TAVERNA €

(📋 26610 30342; N Theotoki 6; mains €8-12; ⊙ noon-midnight) Going strong for 150 years, this taverna was formerly patronised by the Durrells and Anthony Quinn. The sign outside is in Greek, so just follow your nose to the traditional grill for souvlaki, pork chops and swordfish. Warm service and tables outside make this an excellent spot for people-watching.

Rouvas   TAVERNA €

(📋 26610 31182; S Desilla 13; mains €9; ⊙ 9am-5pm) As authentically Greek as it gets, this earthy gourmand's delight is a Corfiot institution. Look out for dishes like beef stew in tomato sauce and roast salmon with potatoes, as well as plenty of veggie dishes. Even celebrity chef Rick Stein was impressed.

Starenio   BAKERY €

(📋 26610 47370; Guilford 59) Magical Starenio is loved by Corfiots for its sweet-toothed homemade delicacies: baklava, cookies and pain au chocolat, plus fresh coffee to get you going. Grab a chair and eat outside.

Markas Grill   GREEK €

(Zavitsianou 5; mains €13; ⊙ 8am-late; ❄🕿) Sea-facing Markas has blue-topped tables and a wind-protected terrace favoured by lo-

cals. Its menu features squid, shrimp, mussels, swordfish and charcoal-cooked meat. A good breezy lunch option.

Panetteria   BAKERY €

(📋 26610 22654; Vrahlioti 3; sweets from €3) This super *boulangerie* has pastries, fresh bread and divine brownies.

★**La Cucina**   ITALIAN €€

(📋 26610 45029; Guilford 17; mains €13-25; ⊙ 7-11pm; ❄🕿) A long-established favourite, well-run La Cucina shines for its creative cuisine, with hand-rolled pasta dishes to the fore. The original Guilford location has cosy, warm tones and murals, while the **Moustoxidou** (📋 26610 45799; cnr Guilford & Moustoxidou; ⊙ 7-11pm) annexe (with identical menu) is chic in glass and grey.

La Famiglia   ITALIAN €€

(📋 26610 30270; Maniarizi-Arlioti 26; mains €13; ⊙ lunch & dinner) Tucked away in a back street, with its chequered cloth tables and peach interior, this cosy restaurant delights with antipasti, quiche, linguini, and carpaccio with smoked salmon.

Rex   MEDITERRANEAN €€

(📋 26610 39649; www.rexrestaurant.gr; Kapodistriou 66; mains €12-18; ⊙ lunch & dinner) On majestic Liston is this elegant, olive-hued grand dame, with a Mediterranean-leaning menu of pasta, salads and specialities such as veal *sofrito* (veal cooked in wine and garlic) and Corfiot rooster (chicken cooked in tomato sauce). Add to this warm service, chandelier-lit ambience and a range of microbrews, and you can see why it's always busy.

To Dimarchio   ITALIAN €€€

(📋 26610 39031; www.todimarchio.com; Plateia Dimarchio; mains €9-25; ⊙ noon-midnight) Overlooking a beautiful neoclassical square, this sky-blue restaurant has a flower-filled terrace and Italian-accented menu that excels with pasta, risotto and nicely executed seafood dishes. You may feel as if you've just been airlifted to Venice. Pure class.

🍷 Drinking & Nightlife

By night the best place to head for is the stylish Liston arcade, where Corfiots go to see and be seen; or head up to the rooftop bar of the Hotel Cavalieri for a pre-dinner drink and romantic views of the Spianada park.

For dance venues, after 11pm head to Corfu's disco strip, 2km northwest of the new port, along Ethnikis Antistaseos; take a taxi, as it's a busy, unlit road without walkways. A €10 admission fee usually includes one drink.

Café Bristol   CAFE
(Voulgareos 40, cnr M Theotoki; ⊙9am-late; 🛜) With its mint-green walls, wood ceiling hung with myriad lightbulbs and dimly lit ambience, this easy-tunes haunt packed with good looking Corfiots may remind you of a Parisian cafe.

Mikro Café   BAR
(☑26610 31009; www.mikrocafe.com; N Theotoki 42, cnr Kotardou) Laid-back locals gather at this convivial cafe-bar with occasional live entertainment. Forget the smoky interior and head for a drink outside on their delightful, vine-shaded terrace.

Cavalieri Hotel   BAR
(Kapodistriou 4) Have some mellow pre-dinner drinks, with excellent views from the rooftop garden bar.

Edem Beach Nightclub   CLUB
(☑26610 93013; www.edemclub.com; Dasia; ⊙11am-5am) Voted one of the top 10 beach bars in Greece. Head here for a sunset chill-out before the party starts at around 11pm. Located in Dasia Beach; take bus 7 (€1.70, 30 minutes) from Plateia San Rocco.

☆ Entertainment

Corfu Town has a lively cultural life of concerts, readings and the like. Check www.corfuland.gr (in Greek) for current listings.

Municipal Theatre   PERFORMING ARTS
(☑26610 33598; G Theotoki 68, cnr Mantzarou) Corfu's cultural powerhouse stages classical music, opera, dance and drama here and at the theatre next to Mon Repos.

🔒 Shopping

Corfu Town is crammed with goodies. Head to Filarmonikis street for everything from upscale pashminas and fine jewellery to cheap 'evil eye' amulets and sandalwood carvings.

Icon Boutique Gallery   CRAFTS
(www.iconcraft.gr; Guilford 52; ⊙10am-10.30pm; 🛜) True to its name, this tasteful hole-in-the-wall boutique sells stunning icons, handmade by an artists' co-op, as well as fine heraldic art and antiques.

Papagiorgis   FOOD & DRINK
(N Theotoki 32; ⊙8am-late) Offering 40 different flavours of ice cream, as well as homemade tarts, honey and biscuits, this old-fashioned shop is a sweet-tooth's dream.

Public Market   MARKET
(⊙morning Mon-Sat) North of Plateia San Rocco; sells fresh fruit, vegetables and fish.

❶ Information

Get *The Corfiot* (€2), an English-language monthly newspaper with listings, at kiosks.

Bits & Bytes (☑26610 36812; cnr Mantzarou & Rizospaston Voulefton; internet per hr €3; ⊙24hr; 🛜)

Corfu General Hospital (☑26613 60400; Kontokali) About 8km west of the town centre.

Municipal tourist kiosk (Palaio Frourio; ⊙9am-4pm Mon-Sat Jun-Sep) Offers helpful information for things to do around Corfu, accommodation and transport timetables.

Pachis Travel (☑26610 28298; Guilford 7; ⊙9am-2.30pm & 5.30pm-9pm, closed Sun) This helpful travel agency can assist with ferry and plane tickets, and hotels. They also organise charter boats and excursions to Paxi.

Tourist police (☑26610 29168; 3rd fl, Samartzi 4) Off Plateia San Rocco.

North & Northwest of Corfu Town

To explore fully all regions of the island outside Corfu Town, your own transport is best. Much of the coast just north of Corfu Town is overwhelmed by beach resorts such as **Gouvia**, **Dasia** and the linked resorts of **Ipsos** and **Pyrgi** – all with close-quarters humanity and narrow beaches, but with everything for a family holiday.

Beyond Pyrgi the tawny slopes of **Mt Pantokrator** (906m), the island's highest peak, spill down to the sea and reclaim the coast at some lovely scenic stretches along a winding road. Just beyond Pyrgi, the road corkscrews upwards and eventually passes through the picturesque villages **Spartylas** and **Strinylas**, then climbs through stark terrain – transformed by wildflowers in spring – to the mountain's summit and

---

THE DURRELLS

The writers Lawrence and Gerald Durrell, prominently associated with Corfu, lived in Kalami for many years prior to WWII. Lawrence's nonfiction *Prospero's Cell* is a lyrical evocation of Corfu; his brother Gerald's equally excellent *My Family and Other Animals* was based on the Durrell family's eccentric and idyllic life on the island during the 1930s.

ISLAND ACTIVITIES

Corfu brims with great outdoor action. Dinghy **sailing** and **windsurfing** buffs should find **Greek Sailing Holidays** (☑26630 81877; www.corfu-sailing-events.com) at Avlaki. For charters try **Corfu Sea School** (☑26610 97628; www.corfuseaschool.com) or **Sailing Holidays Ltd** (www.sailingholidays.com), both at Gouvia marina.

For **diving** in crystal-clear waters you'll find operators at Kassiopi, Agios Gordios, Agios Georgios, Ipsos, Gouvia and Paleokastritsa.

Corfu has excellent **walking**. The **Corfu Trail** (www.thecorfutrail.com) traverses the island north to south and takes between eight and 12 days to complete. For help with accommodation along the trail, contact **Aperghi Travel** (☑26610 48713; www.travelling.gr/aperghi). The book *In the Footsteps of Lawrence Durrell and Gerald Durrell in Corfu* (Hilary Whitton Paipeti, 1999) is an excellent buy.

For **mountain-biking**, especially off-road, the **Corfu Mountainbike Shop** (☑26610 93344; www.mountainbikecorfu.gr; Dasia) rents bikes and organises day trips and cycling holidays. Go **horse riding** through olive groves and on quiet trails through **Trailriders** (☑26630 23090; www.trailriderscorfu.com; Ano Korakiana), in Ano Korakiana. **Corfu Golf Club** (☑26610 94220; www.corfugolfclub.com) is near Ermones, on Corfu's west coast.

the monastery, **Moni Pantokrator**, which is now dominated by a massive telecommunications tower. Superb all-round views stretch as far as the mountains of Albania and the Greek mainland.

Hugging the coast north from Pyrgi, the first decent spot is **Barbati**, with its shingle beach and water-sports centre. The bayside village of **Kalami** is famous for the former home of Lawrence and Nancy Durrell, called **White House** (☑26630 91040; www.corfu-kalami.gr; Kalami) and now a rental villa.

North again is **Agios Stefanos**, another attractive fishing village and resort nestled in a sheltered bay with a shingle beach.

Gorgeous little **Avlaki** lies beyond a wooded headland north of Agios Stefanos and has a substantial beach with very little development and only a couple of tavernas. It is popular for windsurfing.

Kassiopi is now crammed with shops, tavernas and bars, but its strategic headland saw Roman and Venetian settlement. Nero is said to have holidayed outrageously here; nowadays British politicians visit the Rothschild estate nearby. Kassiopi is noted for its fine **embroidery**, sold in several shops. In the main street, opposite the church of the Blessed Virgin, steps climb to the ruins of the **Venetian castle**. Walks over the headland bring you to nearby **Battaria** and **Kanoni** beaches. Drive the winding road inland to magnificent **Old Perithia** to see a carefully restored Venetian village.

Beyond Kassiopi, the main road heads west along Corfu's north coast past the hugely popular resorts of **Aharavi**, **Roda** and **Sidhari**, all served by a succession of crowded beaches. **St George's Bay Country Club** (☑26630 63203; www.stgeorgesbay.com), in Aharavi, makes for a deluxe pool or spa outing, and has a seaside restaurant, and studios. It's possible to visit the nearby **Diapondia Islands**, 40 minutes away by ferry from Sidhari's little harbour.

Corfu's other **Agios Stefanos**, on the island's northwest coast, has a large sandy beach. From the nearby fishing harbour regular excursion boats head for the **Diapondia Islands**, a cluster of little-known satellite islands; contact **San Stefano Travel** (☑26630 51910; www.san-stefano.gr).

🛏 Sleeping

Dionysus Camping Village　　CAMPGROUND €

(☑26610 91417; www.dionysuscamping.gr; Dafnila Bay; camp sites per adult/car/tent €6.50/4/4.50, huts per person €12; 🛜🞉) About 9km from Corfu Town and close to Dasia Beach, sites are in a shaded, tiered 400-year-old olive grove. There are also rondavel huts and a pool.

★**Manessis Apartments**　　APARTMENT €€

(☑26610 34990; www.manessiskassiopi.com; Kassiopi; 4-person apt €70-100; 🞉🛜) The friendly Greek-Irish owner has flower-filled gardens and bougainvillea-draped two-bedroom apartments (some with waterfront balconies). The location, at the end of Kassiopi's picturesque harbour, makes a lovely base.

Casa Lucia　　APARTMENT, BUNGALOW €€

(☑26610 91419; www.casa-lucia-corfu.com; Sgombou; studios & cottages €70-120; 🞉Apr-Oct; 🅿🞉) A garden complex of lovely studios and cottages, Casa Lucia has a strong artistic and community ethos. There are yoga, t'ai chi and Pilates sessions and cultural events. It's on the road to Paleokastritsa.

Rou Estate   RESORT €€€
(☑(44) 020 8392 5854; www.rouestate.co.uk; ❋⒡☲) Restored by a British architect in 2005, the village of Rou, with its 200-year-old houses, radiates Corfiot authenticity combined with super luxe accommodation in two- to five-bedroom villas. There's also a restaurant, health spa, gym, yoga room, swimming pool and beautiful ornamental garden.

✕ Eating

Little Italy   ITALIAN €
(☑26630 81749; Kassiopi; mains €10; ☉lunch & dinner) Inside a cosy, stone-floored interior, yellow chequer-cloth tables and old B&W photos on the walls, a feast of carpaccio, crêpes, risotto, pasta and pizza variations awaits you in this Kassiopi favourite.

Taverna Galini   GREEK €€
(☑26630 81492; www.galinitaverna.gr; Agios Stefanos; mains €15-18; ☉lunch & dinner) Lit by hurricane lamps, this olive-and-cream gem is romantically shaded by vines, with a semi-alfresco terrace by the sea. Enjoy *stifadho, kleftiko,* souvlaki and fresh local fish.

Cavo Barbaro   SEAFOOD €€
(☑26630 81905; Avlaki; mains €11-15; ☉lunch & dinner) With widescreen views of the beach, this pretty, peaceful garden restaurant picks up the breeze as you tuck into octopus, calamari, *saganaki, mousakas* and swordfish.

Piedra del Mar   MEDITERRANEAN €€
(☑26630 91566; www.piedradelmar.gr; Barbati; mains €7-22; ☉lunch & dinner Jul-Aug or Sep) Dust off your best togs for a dose of the good life. Beachfront chic melds perfectly with terrific Mediterranean cuisine here.

South of Corfu Town

The coast road south from Corfu Town leads to well-signposted Achillion Palace near the village of Gastouri. South of the Achillion, sleepy resort **Benitses** is enhanced by its pleasant old village, from where tracks and paths lead into the steep, wooded slopes above.

Further south again are the popular beach resorts of **Moraïtika** and **Messonghi**, from where the winding coastal road follows at sea level through twisty sun-dappled woods to more appealing, and endlessly tranquil, **Boukari** with its little harbour. It's incredibly low-key.

Lefkimmi, in the southern part of the island, is one of Corfu's most down-to-earth towns, where the locals just get on with everyday life. Fascinating churches dot the older section; it's divided by a rather quaint (though sometimes odorous) canal.

◉ Sights

Achillion Palace   HISTORIC BUILDING
(☑26610 56210; www.achillion-corfu.gr; Gastouri; adult/child €7/2, audio guide €3; ☉8am-8pm Apr-Oct, 8.45am-4pm Nov-Mar) In the 1890s the Achillon Place was the summer palace of Austria's Empress Elizabeth (King Otho of Greece was her uncle). Be sure to climb the stairs to the right of the villa to the marbled terrace for a view of the fresco depicting Achilles, to whom she dedicated the villa. The beautifully landscaped garden is guarded by elaborate statues of mythological heroes. Kaiser Wilhelm II bought the palace in 1907, and added a ferocious statue of Achilles Triumphant. Arrive early to beat the crowds and journey through neoclassicism, fabulous furnishings and bold statuary (high style or low kitsch?).

🛏 Sleeping & Eating

Golden Sunset Hotel   HOTEL €
(☑26620 51853; www.goldensunsetcorfu.gr; Boukari; s/d incl breakfast €45/60; ❋) Offers stunning views from its simple 16 rooms. There's also a terraced **restaurant**.

Spiros Karidis   SEAFOOD €
(☑26620 51205; Boukari; fish per kg €35-50; ☉lunch & dinner) Eat in the shade of giant eucalyptus trees by the shoreline while lobster swim in the restaurant's aquarium. The mullet, bass, grouper and octopus, to name a few, are all caught in local waters. Rick Stein stopped here to learn a few tips from the excellent owner.

★Klimataria   TAVERNA €€
(☑26610 71201; www.klimataria-restaurant.gr; Benitses; mains €8-14; ☉7pm-midnight Feb-Nov) This tiny, humble taverna in Benitses is worth a pilgrimage in its own right – every item on the menu is absolutely delicious. From the olive oil and specially sourced feta to the tender octopus or range of mezedhes, the owners will not serve anything that they cannot find fresh. Call for reservations in summer.

O Paxinos   TAVERNA €€
(☑26610 72339; Benitses; mains €12; ☉lunch & dinner) This traditional restaurant, in the heart of the village, has a wine-red facade

and spooky Russian dolls on parade – as well as terrific meatballs, octopus, mousakas, squid and anchovies.

West Coast

Some of Corfu's prettiest countryside, villages and beaches line the west coast. The scenic and popular resort area **Paleokastritsa**, 26km from Corfu Town, rambles for nearly 3km down a valley to a series of small, picturesque coves between tall cliffs. Craggy mountains swathed in cypresses and olive trees tower above. Venture to nearby grottoes or one of the dozen or so local beaches by small **boat** (per person €8.50; ☺30min) or partake in a range of water sports.

Perched on the rocky promontory at the end of Paleokastritsa is the icon-filled **Moni Theotokou** (☺9am-1pm & 3-8pm) [FREE], a monastery founded in the 13th century (although the present building dates from the 18th century). Just off the monastery's lovely garden, a small **museum** (☺Apr-Oct) [FREE] and olive-mill exhibition have a shop selling olive oils and herbs. The kids will enjoy a trip on the **Yellow Submarine** (☎697409246; www.yellowsubmarine.gr; Harbour, Paleokastritsa; €5; ☺10am-6pm, night cruises 9pm), a glass-bottomed boat experience.

From Paleokastritsa a path ascends 5km inland to the unspoilt village of **Lakones**, which is fantastic for coastal views.

Quaint **Doukades** has a historic square and atmospheric tavernas. The 6km road north from Paleokastritsa to **Krini** and **Makrades** climbs steeply to spectacular views. A left turn towards the coast leads through Krini's tiny town square and down to **Angelokastro**, the ruins of a Byzantine castle and the western-most bastion on Corfu.

Further north, via the village of **Pagi**, the pleasant beach resorts of **Agios Georgios** and **Arillas** straddle the knuckly headland of **Cape Arillas**, with the little village of **Afionas** straggling up its spine. South of Paleokastritsa, the pebbly beach at **Ermones** is dominated by heavy development.

Hilltop **Pelekas**, 4km south, is a confection of biscuit-cream-hued buildings perched above wooded cliffs; the place has a gentle buzz about it and makes for a decent spot to catch your breath after you've lost it admiring the mountain view. Push on a little further to the summit, where the **Kaiser's Throne** marks the spot to which Kaiser Wilhelm rode his horse to get 360-degree island views. In the village itself head to **Kalimera Bakery** (Pelekas; pastries from €2; ☺7am-late) for fresh pastries. Almost opposite is the frog-green **Witch House** (☎6974525376; Pelekas; ☺10am-10pm), perfect for offbeat gifts.

The delightful old vineyard estate at **Ambelonas** (☎6932158888; mezedhes €8-12, prix fixe incl wine €16-27; ☺from 6.30pm Wed-Fri, otherwise by appointment), 6km from Corfu Town on the Pelekas road near Karoubatika, produces enticing local products, from vinegars to olives and sweets. Tour the olive-oil mill and winery, and sample the wares, including Corfiot mezedhes and wines from local grapes such as Kakotrygis.

Near Pelekas village are two sandy beaches, **Glyfada** and **Kontogialos** (also called **Pelekas**), a resort with water sports and sun beds galore. These quite-developed beaches are backed by large hotels and other accommodation. A free shuttle runs to them from Pelekas village. Further north is the breathtaking, but dwindling (due to erosion) **Myrtiotissa Beach**. It's a long slog down a steep, partly surfaced road (drivers, use the parking area on the hilltop). **Elia**, a taverna and bar partway down, makes a welcome break.

Agios Gordios is a popular resort south of Glyfada, where a long sandy beach accommodates the crowds.

Just along the turn-off from the main road to **Halikounas Beach** is the Byzantine **Gardiki Castle**; though it has a picturesque entranceway, it's a ruin inside. Just south of the castle is the vast **Lake Korission**, separated from the sea by a narrow spit fronted by a long sandy beach, where you can usually escape from the crowds.

🛏 Sleeping

Paleokastritsa and Pelekas are loaded with accommodation.

Yialiskari Beach Studios   APARTMENT €
(☎26610 54901; Yialiskari Beach; studios €60; ❄❔; ☺late May-Sep) Studios with great views are perfect for those who want seclusion away from neighbouring Pelekas Beach.

Rolling Stone   PENSION €
(☎26610 94942; www.pelekasbeach.com; Pelekas Beach; r/apt €60/88; @❔) Close to the beach, this funky traveller's oasis has new two-bedroom family apartments, with fresh rooms, bathroom and kitchenette. The original apartments are also spotless and encircle a shaded terrace where people gather to chat. Laid-back and friendly.

Pink Palace
HOSTEL €

(☑ 26610 53103; www.thepinkpalace.com; Agios Gordios Beach; dm incl breakfast & dinner €22, r €29-32; ❄ @) Painted bright pink and a party place par excellence, Pink Palace offers a range of utilitarian rooms, quad bikes, activities galore...and loads of backpackers.

Jimmy's Restaurant & Rooms
PENSION €

(☑ 26610 94284; www.jimmyspelekas.com; Pelekas Village; s/d/tr €30/40/50; ☺Apr-Oct; ❄) Decent rooms with rooftop views sit above a popular restaurant (mains €6 to €12).

Sunrock
HOSTEL €

(☑ 26610 94637; www.sunrockhostel.com; Pelekas Beach; dm/r incl breakfast & dinner €18/28; @ ☎) ✎ Run by the charming Magdalena, this complex, 30m from the sea, has dorms and doubles. Faded on the outside, perhaps, but inside it's fresh and friendly. There's a great balcony for soaking up the sun, a large bar full of travellers and a lunchtime menu of pasta and sandwiches, as well as food produced on the farm.

Paleokastritsa Camping
CAMPGROUND €

(☑ 26630 41204; www.paleokastritsa-bliss.com; Paleokastritsa; camp sites per adult/car/tent €5/3.10/3.50; ☺late-May–mid-Oct; P ❄) On the right of the main road to town, this shady and well-organised campground set in historic olive terraces also has pool access.

★Hotel Zefiros
HOTEL €€

(☑ 26630 41244; www.hotel-zefiros.gr; Paleokastritsa; d/tr/q incl breakfast €64/80/130; ❄ ☎) Wine-coloured Zefiros, just 20m from the pretty beach, has a shabby-chic cafe with a tasty menu of mezedhes and snacks, plus beautiful rooms with modern flourishes and balconies. Room 107 has the best view.

★Levant Hotel
HOTEL €€

(☑ 26610 94230; www.levantcorfu.com; Pelekas Village; s/d incl breakfast €70/90; ☺May–mid-Oct; P ❄ ☎) Up in the gods close to the Kaiser's Throne, this grand hotel exudes romance with pastel-blue rooms, wood floors, belle époque-style lights and balconies. Rooms also have fridges and marble-accented bathrooms. Add to this a refined restaurant serving shrimp, risotto and *stifadho* on a terrace overlooking the island of Corfu. Tempted?

Kallisto Resort
APARTMENT €€€

(☑ 6977443555; www.corfuresorts.gr; Pelekas Beach; apt €160, villa €240-450; P ❄) From its vaunted spot on the hill, these lush, terraced gardens are host to tasteful apartments and two sparkling pools. The well-appointed villas sleep two to 12, and cascade down the hillside overlooking the north end of Pelekas Beach.

✕ Eating & Drinking

★Alonaki Bay Taverna
TAVERNA €

(☑ 26610 75872; Alonaki; mains €8-10; ☺lunch & dinner) Ride the dirt roads out to the point north of Lake Korission for this simple, family-run taverna, which serves a small menu of home-cooked meat and *mayirefta* (ready-cooked meals). Clean rooms (€35) and apartments (€45) overlook a garden and dramatic cliffs.

To Stavrodromi
TAVERNA €

(☑ 26610 94274; Pelekas; mains €7-11; ☺dinner) Located at the crossroads of the Pelekas and Corfu Town roads, this homey joint turns out delicious local specialities. It's known for the best *kontosouvli* (pork on a spit covered in paprika and onions) on the island, as well as rabbit *stifadho* and pepper steak.

Nereids
TAVERNA €€

(☑ 26630 41013; Paleokastritsa; mains €12-15; ☺lunch & dinner) Halfway down the winding road to Paleokastritsa beach – and best experienced at night, when its terrace of rockpools and urns is softly lit – this is a romantic spot for dinner. Try dolmadhes, meatballs in tomato sauce, *kleftiko* and *stifadho*.

Limani
TAVERNA €€

(☑ 26630 42080; Paleokastritsa; mains €9-17; ☺lunch & dinner) Swordfish, lamb *kleftiko* and grilled prawns are all accompanied by good service at this nautical-themed taverna by the harbour.

La Grotta
CAFE

(www.lagrottabar.com; Paleokastritsa) Secluded in a rocky cove lapped by peacock-green water, this decked terrace with sun beds and diving board is an ideal escape from the buzz of the beach. Located down steep steps opposite the Hotel Paleokastritsa driveway.

Corfu Beer
BREWERY

(www.corfubeer.com; Arillas) This local microbrewery brews a delicious range of ales. Free tours offered every Saturday 11am to 1pm.

PAXI
ΠΑΞΟΙ

POP 2300

From the instant you arrive at this tiny Ionian gem (only 13km long), sailing into the bottle-green fjord toward Gaïos, Paxi will have you in her thrall. Poseidon is said to have crafted the island by placing his trident into the sea, and with its blue bays, centuries-old olive groves and diminutive pink-and-cream harbour villages – Gaïos, Loggos and Lakka – there is something truly special about her.

Spend a few days snorkelling in the crystalline water, eat locally caught seafood at a clutch of refined restaurants, or just sit in one of the harbours and people-watch while soaking up the calm.

Unspoilt coves can be reached by motorboat, if not by car or on foot. On the less accessible west coast, sheer limestone cliffs punctuated by caves and grottoes plunge hundreds of metres into the azure sea. Old mule trails are a walker's delight. Find *Bleasdale Walking Map of Paxos* (€12) at travel agencies.

ℹ Getting There & Away

BOAT

Ferries dock at Gaïos' new port, 1km east of the central square. Excursion boats dock along the waterfront.

Two busy passenger-only hydrofoils link Corfu and Paxi (€23, 55 minutes, one to three daily, May to mid-October) and, occasionally, Igoumenitsa. **Bouas Tours** (📋 26620 32401; www.bouastours.gr; Gaïos) and **Zefi** (📋 26620 32114; Gaïos) handles *Ilida*, while tickets for the boat *Despina* (€17, 90 minutes, daily in high season) are sold by **Kamelia Lines** (www.kamelialines.gr; near Gaïos bus station; €17).

Two daily car ferries (€8.50) link Paxi and Igoumenitsa from the end of June to the start of September. For schedules try the ferry information office (p635) in Igoumenitsa.

Fast sea taxis are priced by boat. Corfu to Paxi costs €300; try **Nikos** (📋 6932232072, 26620 32444; www.paxosseataxi.com; Gaïos).

A caïque to Antipaxi (return €10) can be caught from Gaïos from June onward through summer.

BUS

Twice-weekly direct buses go between Athens and Paxi (€55, plus €8.50 for the ferry between Paxi and Igoumenitsa, seven hours) in high season. On Paxi, get tickets from Bouas Tours.

ℹ Getting Around

A bus links Gaïos and Lakka via Loggos up to four times daily (€2.50). Taxis between Gaïos and Lakka or Loggos cost around €12; the taxi rank in Gaïos is by the inland car park and bus stop. Many travel agencies rent out small boats (€40 to €90, depending on engine capacity) – great for accessing coves.

Daily car hire starts at €38 in high season. Try **Alfa Hire** (📋 26620 32505; Gaïos).

Arvanitakis Travel (📋 26620 32007; Gaïos) is a helpful travel agency.

Gaïos Γαϊος
POP 498

Rosé- and biscuit-hued neoclassical houses form a necklace around the crecent-shaped harbour of Gaïos, insulated by the nearby wooded islet of Agios Nikolaos and lapped by beautiful teal water. Kids line-fish from the dockside, yachties polish decks and wine glasses clink at harbourside tavernas as handsome old sailors ponder the open seas.

🛏 Sleeping & Eating

San Giorgio Apartments   PENSION €€
(📋 26620 32223; studios €70; ❄) Just 100m before you arrive in Gaïos and up a set of steps, these homely studios are spotless with kitchenette, bathroom, toasty bedspreads and an outdoor sun-trap patio. Rooms 1 and 2 have balconies over the channel.

Theklis Studios   PENSION €€
(Clara Studios; 📋 697292838, 26620 32313; www.theklis-studios.com; studios €90; ❄) Lovely Theklis, who is also a freediver with her own boat, has a handsome house with beautiful shabby-chic rooms commanding serene

Paxi & Antipaxi

N 0 ———— 2 km
   0 ———— 1 mile

Corfu (10km)
Igoumenitsa (25km)

Harami Beach
Lakka
Monodendri Beach
Kastanitha Cave
Loggos
South Kerkyra Straits
Paxi
Levrecchio Beach
Ermitis Bay
Magazia
Fontana
Achai Bay
Bogdanatika
Panagia Islet
Agios Nikolaos Islet
Avlaki
Gaïos
Agrilas Bay
Vellianitatika
Ozias
Mongonisi
Excursion Boat
Agrapidia Bay
Vrika Beach
Voutoumi Beach
Vigla
Antipaxi
Ionian Sea

views of the sea. Nicely finished with touches like candelabra and fine art, they also have a well-equipped kitchenette and bathroom. Head past the museum and turn right up the hill. Theklis can pick you up from the port. There are only four rooms and they book up fast, so call ahead.

Paxos Beach Hotel HOTEL €€€
(☑26620 32211; www.paxosbeachhotel.gr; d incl breakfast €120-190, ste €225-265; ❄🛜🏊) Sitting on a tiny cove with private beach, jetty, swimming pool, tennis court and restaurant, 1.5km south of Gaïos, Paxos Beach has a family-run feel and is fragrant with jasmine and flowers at every turn. Its new 'superior' rooms are very nicely finished, with more space. Port transfers available, and boats for hire (€50).

Karkaletzos TAVERNA €
(☑26620 32129; mains €9; ⊙7.45-11pm) Worth the walk out of town, this rustic taverna redolent with the aromas of souvlaki and lamb chops fired up on the grill will have you licking your lips in anticipation. The meatballs in tomato sauce are also bursting with flavour.

Capriccio Creperie CAFE €
(crêpes €3-6; ⊙9am-3am) Toward the end of the harbour headed south, this arty gem perches on the waterfront with a glass arbour and a scattering of antiques. The waffles and crêpes are super-fresh, while their delicious homemade ice cream is a tonic for the soul.

Carnayo MEDITERRANEAN €€
(☑26620 32376; www.carnayopaxos.gr; mains €12; ⊙lunch & dinner) Elegantly executed cuisine in a peaceful courtyard setting, 1km behind town. Flavoursome dishes include mussels in garlic broth, lamb *kleftiko*, *stifadho* and freshly caught fish.

Dal Pescatore GREEK €€
(mains €13; ⊙lunch & dinner) Festooned in nets at the corner of the square nearest the water, this dinky restaurant with turquoise tables out front excels with lovely service and tasty mezedhes, calamari and pasta dishes.

ℹ️ Information

The main street (Panagioti Kanga) runs inland from the square towards the back of town, where you'll find the bus stop, taxi rank and car park. Banks and ATMs are near the square. There's no tourist office, but travel agencies, such as **Paxos Magic Holidays** (☑26620 32269; www.paxos-magic.com), organise excursions, book tickets and arrange accommodation.

Loggos Λόγγος

Bookended by white cliffs and the remains of an oil factory, with pretty Venetian houses huddled around a tiny bay of crystal-clear water, Loggos willl steal your breath with its good looks. Bars and restaurants overlook the sea and wooded slopes climb steeply above.

🍴 Sleeping & Eating

Arthur House APARTMENT €€
(☑26620 31330; http://paxos-arthur.blogspot.gr; 1-/2-bedroom apt €80/120; 🅿) A 50m walk inland from the waterfront and set in a pleasant garden, these are simple apartments with plenty of space, equipped with kitchenettes, washing machines and balconies. Very clean.

O Gios TAVERNA €
(☑26620 31735; mains €15-20; ⊙lunch & dinner) Looking onto the water where the boats look like they're floating, this stone-interior taverna excels with home-cooked, good-value seafood and grill dishes.

Vasilis MEDITERRANEAN €€
(☑26620 31587; mains €9-16; ⊙lunch & dinner) Terracotta-coloured Vasilis dishes up pan-fried cuttlefish, risotto, sea urchin and octopus in red-wine sauce, just yards from the sea, with an emphasis on locally sourced organic ingredients. Reserve ahead in summer.

ℹ️ Information

The village and **Café Bar Four Seasons** (☑26620 31829; 🛜) have wi-fi. Hire boats (€50 to €70) and scooters (€20) from Julia's Boat & Bike at Arthur House.

Magazia Μαγαζιά

Barely more than a crossroads several kilometres southwest of Loggos, on the western side of the island, Magazia makes a great pit stop for a couple of cafe-bars.

Erimitis Bar MEDITERRANEAN €€
(☑6977753499; www.erimitis.com; mains €13-16; ⊙noon-10pm May-Oct) This spectacular spot overlooks cliffs plunging straight into the bluest of seas. It's well worth the journey down dirt roads to reach it, if you have your own wheels.

Lakka Λάκκα

So languid it's almost slipping into the yacht-dotted bay, Lakka will both make you smile and slow your pulse. There are a few choice restaurants piping bouzouki music and tempting aromas, plus a few guest-houses. Small beaches like **Harami Beach** lie round the bay's headland, while pleasant walks crisscross the area.

🛏 Sleeping & Eating

Yorgos Studios   APARTMENT €€
(📱26620 31807; www.routsis-holidays.com; d €75; ❄️🛜) Immaculate and comfy, it's next door to and run by Routsis Holidays, which represents many area studios and apartments.

★ Torri E Merli   BOUTIQUE HOTEL €€€
(📱26212 34123; www.torriemerli.com; ste from €390; ☺May-Oct; P❄️🛜🏊) Built in 1750 by a wealthy Paxiot, its towers constructed specially to repel pirates, this beautiful boutique accommodation sits in olive groves and successfully combines the building's Venetian elements with contemporary style to create the best hotel on the island (if not in the Ionians). White-wood floors, mushroom-grey walls; all rooms are suites and redefine cool. The kidney-shaped pool? Perfection.

Not surprisingly this oasis is popular with Hollywood A-List celebrities looking for peace. It's 800m south of Lakka.

★ Arriva Fish Restaurant   GREEK €€
(📱26620 33041; mains €10-15; ☺lunch & dinner) With sublime views of the turquoise fjord this peaceful taverna boasts 25 different mezedhes. Freshly caught fish and seafood, from lobster to red mullet, is packed in ice for your inspection, while stand-out dishes like octopus in red-wine sauce are delectable.

ℹ Information

Helpful **Routsis Holidays** (📱26620 31807; www.routsis-holidays.com) books well-appointed apartments and villas for all budgets and arranges transport and excursions.

Paxos Blue Waves (📱26620 31162; www.paxos-studios.gr) rents out boats (€35 to €65) and scooters (€20); harbourside **Sun & Sea** (www.paxossunandsea.com; ☺8.30am-2.30pm & 5.30pm-11pm) rents out boats and cars (€40).

ANTIPAXI   ΑΝΤΙΠΑΞΟΙ

POP 25

The stunning and diminutive island of Antipaxi, 2km south of Paxi, is covered with vineyards and olive groves with the occasional hamlet here and there. Caïques and tourist boats run daily, in high season, from Gaïos

and Lakka, and go to two beach coves – the small, sandy **Vrika Beach** and the pebbly **Voutoumi Beach**. Floating in the water here, with its dazzling clarity, is a sensational experience. An inland path links the two beaches (a 30-minute walk). The very energetic can walk up to the village of **Vigla**, or as far as the lighthouse at the island's southernmost tip; take plenty of water and allow at least 1½ hours each way.

Voutoumi and Vrika each have two restaurants (mains €7 to €15). Accommodation is available through tavernas.

ℹ Getting There & Away

Boats to Antipaxi (return €7, high season only) leave Gaïos at 10am and return around 4.30pm (with more services in July and August).

LEFKADA   ΛΕΥΚΑΔΑ

POP 22,652

Lefkada (or Lefkas) is ringed by electric-blue water, and shimmers with wild olive groves and the spear-shaped forms of cypress trees. Despite being connected to the mainland by a narrow causeway, it feels in places distinctly untamed by tourism – developed enclaves tend to be on the east coast.

In the wild centre of the island you'll find wandering old women in traditional dress and shepherds benignly tending sheep; on the western side are a couple of the best beaches in the world. A strong wind assaults Lefkada and has made the island hugely popular with kitesurfers and windsurfers, and a major fixture on the professional circuit.

Lefkada is less insular than most islands; once attached to the mainland by a narrow isthmus, occupying Corinthians breached it with a canal in the 8th century BC.

ℹ Getting There & Away

AIR

The closest airport is 20km north of Lefkada, near Preveza (Aktion; PVK) on the mainland. **Sky Express** (📱28102 23500; www.skyexpress.gr) connects Preveza to Corfu (€53, 25 minutes), Kefallonia (€49, 20 minutes), Zakynthos (€55, one hour), Kythira (€60, 2½ hours) and Sitia (Crete; €99, two hours, June to September only). Olympic Air (p115) also flies from Preveza to Athens, Thessaloniki, Karpathos, Corfu, Heraklion, Rhodes and Chania. **Air Berlin** (AB; 📱210 353 5264; www.airberlin.com) has occasional flights. May to September charter flights from northern Europe and the UK serve Preveza.

Lefkada & Its Satellites

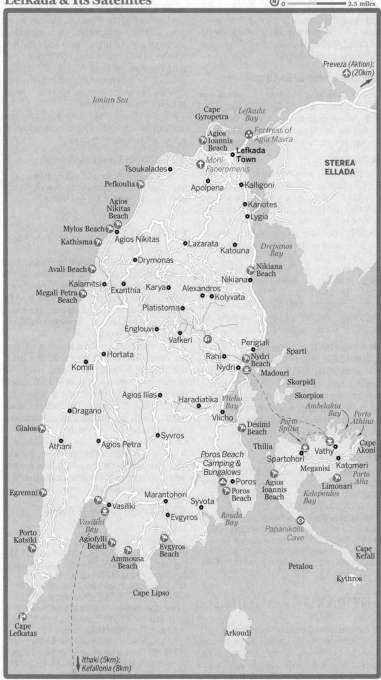

BOAT

West Ferry (☑ 26450 31520; www.westferry.gr) runs daily boats on an ever-changing schedule from Vasiliki to Kefallonia and Ithaki. In high season (July and August) daily ferries run from Lefkada to Ithaki and Kefallonia. Some months, the ferry **Ionian Pelagos** (☑ 26450 31520) goes from Vasiliki via Piso Aetos in Ithaki to Fitzcardo and Sami in Kefallonia. For information and booking use **Samba Tours** (☑ 26450 31520; www.sambatours.gr; Vasiliki).

DESTINATION	TIME	FARE	FREQUENCY
Fiskardo (Kefallonia)	1hr	€10	2 daily
Frikes (Ithaki)	2hr	€10	5 weekly
Piso Aetos (Ithaki)	1hr	€10	2 weekly
Sami (Kefallonia)	1¾hr	€10	1 daily

BUS

Lefkada Town's **KTEL bus station** (☑ 26450 22364; www.ktel-lefkadas.gr; Ant Tzeveleki), 1km from the centre and opposite the new marina, serves Athens (€33.80, 5½ hours, four daily), Patra (€16, three hours, two weekly), Thessaloniki (€35, eight hours, three weekly), Preveza (€2.70, 30 minutes, six daily) and Igoumenitsa (€12.20, two hours, daily).

❶ Getting Around

There's no bus between Lefkada and Preveza's Aktion airport. Taxis cost €40 to Lefkada Town, €60 to Nydri. From the airport it's cheaper to take a taxi to Preveza and then a bus to Lefkada.

BUS

From Lefkada Town, frequent buses ply the east coast in high season; Sunday and low-season services are greatly reduced. Services go to Agios Nikitas (€1.60, 30 minutes, three daily), Karya (€1.60, 30 minutes, four daily), Nydri (€1.60, 30 minutes, 20 daily), Vasiliki (€3.40, one hour, four daily) and Vlicho (€1.80, 40 minutes, 11 daily).

CAR

Rentals start at €40 per day; there are countless car- and bike-hire companies in Nydri and several in Vasiliki. It's possible to arrange for hire-car delivery at Preveza's Aktion Airport and then a return in Vasiliki if you are catching a ferry south (or vice versa).

Europcar (☑ 26450 23581; www.lefkaseuropcar.gr; Panagou 16, Lefkada Town)

Santas (☑ 26450 25250; www.ilovesantas.gr; Lefkada Town) Hires out bikes and scooters, from €16 per day. Next to Ionian Star Hotel.

Lefkada Town   Λευκάδα

POP 8673

The island's bustling main town has a relaxed, happy feel. It is built on a promontory at the southeastern corner of a salty lagoon where earthquakes are a constant threat. The town was devastated by one in 1948, only to be rebuilt in a distinctively quake-proof and attractive style, with the upper-storey facades of some buildings in brightly painted corrugated tin. Stroll the vibrant main pedestrian thoroughfare, Dorpfeld, and through lively Plateia Agiou Spyridonos, or visit the handsome churches.

◉ Sights

Archaeological Museum   MUSEUM
(☑ 26450 21635; adult/child €3/2; ◷ 8am-3pm Tue-Sun) In the cultural centre at the west end of Agelou Sikelianou, with island artefacts spanning the Palaeolithic to late Roman periods. The prize exhibit is a 6th-century BC terracotta figurine of a flute player with nymphs.

Collection of Post-Byzantine Icons   MUSEUM
(☑ 26450 22502; Rontogianni; ◷ 8.30am-3.30pm Tue-Sat plus 6-8.15pm Tue & Thu) FREE Works by icon painters from the Ionian school and Russia dating back to 1500 are displayed in an impressive building off Ioannou Mela.

Fortress of Agia Mavra   FORTRESS
(◷ 9am-1pm) FREE This 14th-century Venetian fortress squats immediately across the causeway. It was first established by Crusaders, but the remains date mainly from the Venetian and Turkish occupations.

Moni Faneromenis   MONASTERY
(☑ 26450 21305; ◷ museum 9am-1pm Mon-Sat) FREE Founded in 1634, the monastery, on a hilltop 3km west of town, was destroyed by fire in 1886 and later rebuilt. Views of the lagoon and town are worth the ascent, as is the monastery's **museum** of ecclesiastical art.

⌂ Sleeping

★**Boschetto Hotel**   BOUTIQUE HOTEL €€
(☑ 26450 20244; www.boschettohotel.com; Dorpfeld 1; d incl breakfast from €100; ❄@◈) This exquisite building (c 1900) has four tasteful, capacious rooms with wood floors, flat-screen TVs, fine linen, marble bathrooms and balconies overlooking the bright blue sea and the hubbub of the cafe scene.

Hotel Santa Maura   HOTEL €€
(☑ 26450 21308; Sp Vlanti 2; s/d/tr incl breakfast €55/70/80; ❄◈) This flamingo-pink

dame is decked in flowers and green shutters; 18 fresh rooms offer flat-screen TVs, balconies and clean bathrooms. Plenty of late-19th-century flourishes remain.

Pension Pirofani HOTEL €€
(☑6936873735, 26450 25844; Dorpfeld 10; r €110-120; ❀❀❀) From plush lobby to boutique-flavoured rooms decked in occasionally overpowering oranges and purples, modern lights and furniture, Pirofani is stylish and immaculate. Sparkling bathrooms add to the luxe feel.

✗ Eating & Drinking

Bars and cafes line the western waterfront and Plateia Agiou Spyridonos.

Ciao ICE CREAM €
(Mitropoleos 8) Scoop up fresh-made ice cream, just off Dorpfeld, with flavours from *mastiha* (a sweet liquor from Chios) to chocolate.

Frini Sto Molo TAVERNA €
(☑26450 24879; Golemi; mains €8; ☺lunch & dinner) This restaurant has a homely interior, plenty of light on its wind-free terrace and a seafood-leaning menu featuring octopus, squid, shrimp and fresh fish.

Ey Zhn INTERNATIONAL €€
(☑6974641160; Filarmonikis 8; mains €9-12; ☺dinner Jan-Oct) Think 'roadhouse meets artist's loft' at this ambience-rich restaurant with excellent, eclectic food. Exposed wood floors, soft lighting and jamming music complement dishes from mushroom risotto to tender tandoori chicken.

Burano GREEK €€
(☑26450 26025; Golemi; mains €8-16; ☺lunch & dinner) Sizzles with atmosphere, with a wide menu spanning dishes like lamb *kleftiko*, sea bass, grilled octopus, and shrimp pasta.

East Coast

Lefkada's east coast has seen heavy tourist development over the years, with the main focus at **Nydri**, once a gorgeously placed fishing village but now a crowded strip of kiss-me-quick tourist shops without much of a beach. Escape inland, however, to another world of scattered villages, small tavernas and pretty walks. Amblers enjoy the lovely walk to the **waterfalls** 3km out of Nydri.

From Nydri itself, you can escape seaward to the islets of **Madouri**, **Sparti**, **Skorpidi** and **Skorpios**, plus **Meganisi**. Excursions go to Meganisi and stop for a swim near Sko-rpios (€15 to €25), and some visit Ithaki and Kefallonia as well (€20). **Borsalino Travel** (☑26450 92528; www.borsalinotravel.gr; internet per 20min €1) on Nydri's main street organises just about everything. Fishing boats bob alongside yachts in the relaxed harbour of **Syvota**, 15km south of Nydri (best reached with your own transport).

🛏 Sleeping & Eating

Galini Sivota Apartments PENSION €
(☑26450 31347; Syvota; studios €45, 4-person apt €70; ❀) Fifteen metres up from the harbour, these simple, whitewashed rooms overlook a lemon grove, and feature kitchenette, TV, balcony and spotless bathroom. Conveniently near the supermarket.

Poros Beach Camping & Bungalows CAMPGROUND €
(☑26450 95452; www.porosbeach.com.gr; Poros Beach; camp site per adult/car/tent €9/5/5, studios from €80; P❀@❀❀) Sitting on the shores of perfect Poros beach, this well-equipped, organised campsite has a great pool, olive-grove tent sites, a nice bar and expansive cafe restaurant with a huge veranda. There are also some attractive new studio rooms with flat-screen TVs, bathroom and balcony.

Sivota Bakery BAKERY €
(Syvota; crêpes €6; ☺8am-late) Its harbourfront walls hung with antique bikes and carriage lamps, this is a cool arbour to stop for juices, homemade pies, fresh croissants, crêpes and ice cream. No extra charge for the company of swallows whistling around the ceiling.

★ Minas Taverna TAVERNA €€
(☑26450 71480; www.minas-restaurant.gr; Nikiana; mains €8-15; ☺dinner nightly, lunch Sat & Sun, reduced hours in low season) Find this top-notch taverna 5km north of Nydri, just south of Nikiana. It's known island-wide for excellent everything – from pasta to grilled meat and seafood. Tables fill the restored stone building and terrace on the inland side of the road overlooking the sea.

Stavros TAVERNA €€
(☑26450 31181; Syvota; mains €9-13; ☺breakfast, lunch & dinner Easter-Oct) Shaded by a giant rubber plant, this taverna sits on the harbour and is bursting at the gills with lobster, snapper, grouper and oodles of atmosphere.

Vasiliki Βασιλική

More than just a handy transport hub for Kefallonia and Ithaki, this friendly harbour village, replete with stony beach, is one of the top places to learn windsurfing in Greece, graced as the bay is by Aeolus' gusts. Aside of a tasty clutch of eucalyptus-shaded tavernas on the waterside, there are fine crafts and dress shops here, opened by many Athenians who have returned to their roots since the financial crisis. By night the main street is a pretty garland of fine boutiques.

🏃 Activities

Caïques take visitors to the island's better beaches and coves, including **Agiofylli Beach**, south of Vasiliki. Helpful Samba Tours (p651) organises car and bike hire, sells boat tickets and answers queries.

Along the beach, water-sports outfits stake their claims with flags, equipment and their own hotels for their clients.

Club Vass   WATER SPORTS
(☑ 26450 31588; www.clubvass.com) One of the best clubs in Europe for learning how to windsurf, Vass has 25 years' experience. There's windsurf hire (per hour/day €40/65), private lessons (€50) and even a one-week program (€250).

Nautilus Diving Club   DIVING, KAYAKING
(☑ 6936181775; www.underwater.gr) Options include snorkelling trips (€10 including lunch), single dive (€45), PADI open-water course (€410) and sea-kayak hire (per hour single/double €15/20).

🛏 Sleeping & Eating

Pension Holidays   PENSION €
(☑ 26450 31426; www.pensionholidays.gr; s/d incl breakfast €55/60; ❀ 🛜) Friendly Spiros and family offer Greek hospitality, breakfast on the balcony and excellent views of the bay and harbour. Find these simply furnished but kitchen-equipped rooms conveniently close to the ferry dock.

Vasiliki Bay Hotel   HOTEL €€
(www.hotelvassilikibay.gr; s/d €40/80; ❄ ❀ 🛜 ❀) Set a street back from the harbour and main street, this excellent hotel represents terrific value for your money. Find large, nicely furnished rooms with fresh walls and modern bathroom, air-con and balcony. There's a lift and a lovely breakfast area to enjoy the buffet. The staff are a delight.

Delfini   TAVERNA €
(☑ 26450 31430; mains €6; ⊘ breakfast, lunch & dinner) Traditional old taverna on the harbour packing in a local crowd with its aromatic grilled seafood and souvlaki.

Taverna Vagelaras   GREEK €€
(mains €7-15; ⊘ 8am-late; 🛜) Vagelaras sits at the end of the harbour and serves great salads, mezedhes, pasta dishes and fresh seafood. The best of the bunch on the waterfront.

🍷 Drinking

155   BAR
(www.155cocktailbar.com; ⊘ May-Oct) Imbibe top cocktails (€8) on the harbourfront at this friendly watering hole.

West Coast

Serious beach bums should head straight for Lefkada's west coast, where the sea lives up to every cliché: it's an incredible turquoise colour, with beaches ranging from arcs of cliff and white stone to broad expanses of uninterrupted sand. The long stretches of white-pebbled **Pefkoulia** and **Kathisma** in the north are lovely (the latter is becoming more developed and has a few studios for rent), as is **Megali Petra**, south of Kalamitsi.

Undrenched in accommodation, the tiny village of **Agios Nikitas** cascades down a central street of inviting tavernas to a pebbled beach lapped by aquamarine water. Drink up the view and grab a bite to eat before heaing further down the west coast to discover your own stretch of isolated sand. **Mylos Beach** is just around the headland. To walk, take the path by Taverna Poseidon; it's about 15 minutes up and over the peninsula, or take a water taxi (€3) from tiny Agios Nikitas Beach.

Remote **Egremni Beach** is a sure contender for having the most achingly turquoise water in Greece. To reach it follow the winding, and at times unpaved, road that terminates in a makeshift car park; from here it's 720 steps down to the beach. For silence and solitude this is where locals in the know come for their quota of paradise. Passing the village of Athani, past local stalls selling olive oil, honey and wine, you will eventually wind your way to breathtaking **Porto Katsiki** in the extreme south. Imagine white cliffs turned gold in the afternoon glow, beneath which sits a beach of soft pebbles lapped by water airbrushed by the gods. Not surprisingly it is considered one of the world's top beaches. For lunch head up to handy **Bilvi** (www.bilvi.gr; Porto Katsiki; snacks €6; ⊘ 9am-late; ❀ 🍴) on the hill.

🛏 Sleeping

Aloni Studios   APARTMENT €
(☑ 26450 33604; www.alonistudios-lefkada. com; Athani; studio/5-person apt €50/60; 🅿 ❀)

Choking on flowers, lime-green Aloni has stunning views of the sea below. Clean, fresh apartments with kitchenette, fridge and communal terrace.

Olive Tree Hotel HOTEL €
(26450 97453; www.olivetreehotel.gr; Agios Nikitas; s/d/studio from €50/60/75; ⊙May-Sep; ❋🖧) Modest rooms run by friendly Greek-Canadians.

★ **Mira Resort** APARTMENT €€
(6977075881, 26450 24967; www.miraresort.com; Tsoukalades; maisonette incl breakfast from €80; ⊙May-Oct; P❋🖧🏊) Perfectly positioned on the mountain with astonishing panoramic views of the glittering sea, Mira has a large pool and cafe-bar. Its maisonettes are immaculate and cosy. Find it 6km southwest of Lefkada Town.

Hotel Agios Nikitas HOTEL €€
(26450 97460; www.agiosnikitas.gr; Agios Nikitas; d incl breakfast €70; ⊙May-Sep; ❋🖧) Set at elevation from the beach in this stunning hotel, these 30-odd rooms are tasteful with baby-blue walls, striped bedspreads, modern bathroom, balcony and TV. There's also a snack bar and an indoor cafe.

Hotel Agatha HOTEL €€
(6948620615; www.agatha-hotel.com; Agios Nikitas; studio/apt €70/90; ❋🖧) Ringing with birdsong, welcoming Agatha is just a few minutes' walk from the beach. Lovely studios and two-room apartments are flooded with sunlight and fresh yellow walls, and have a kitchenette and cool tile floor. Number 1 is our favourite.

✗ Eating & Drinking

★ **Lefkatas** TAVERNA €
(26450 33149; www.lefkatas.gr; Athani; mains €7-12; ⊙lunch & dinner May-Sep; 🖧) ✦ An inspiring view of the olive-skinned mountain and sea beyond are just the beginning at this delightful terrace restaurant with cream-coloured tables and the shade of a cedar tree. Enjoy breakfast, salad, seafood and burgers, and look out for daily specials like hornbeam fish with garlic and tomato. It's in the middle of the village; you can't miss it.

T'Agnantio TAVERNA €
(26450 97383; www.tagnantio.gr; Agios Nikitas; mains €7-10; ⊙lunch & dinner Easter-Oct) The vine-shaded terrace of Agios Nikitas' best taverna sits up on the south side of the beach, with marvellous views to feast on between mouthfuls of local cheese, souvlaki, meatballs, swordfish and octopus.

Kambos Taverna TAVERNA €
(26450 97278; Tsoukalades; mains €7; ⊙lunch & dinner mid-May–Sep) Follow the small lane from the main road just south of the Tsoukalades church to find this tiny, family-run taverna tucked among vineyards and olive groves. Try authentic cuisine like *kleftiko* and zucchini – basically whatever the cook is dreaming up that day.

Central Lefkada

The spectacular central spine of Lefkada – with its traditional farming villages, lush green peaks, fragrant pine trees, olive groves and vineyards, plus fleeting views of the islets – is well worth exploring if you have time and transport.

The small village of **Karya** is the most touristy, but has a pretty square with plane trees and tavernas and is famous for its **embroidery**, introduced in the 19th century by a remarkable one-handed local woman, Maria Koutsochero, and commemorated by a **museum** in a traditional house. For rooms, ask Brit Brenda Sherry at **Café Pierros** (6938605898).

The island's highest village, **Englouvi**, a few kilometres south of Karya, is renowned for its honey and lentil production. Book ahead for a guided **herbal walk** (6934287446; www.lefkas.cc) or a workshop near quaint **Alexandros**.

Kolyvata Taverna (26450 41228, 6984056686; mains €5-8; ⊙Apr-Oct) offers a rural, culinary dream for the truly intrepid. Gregarious Kiria Maria opens the front terrace of her home to guests (reserve ahead to be sure she's there), and serves up fresh, perfectly cooked treats – whatever's ready in her garden. The *koutsoupia* (Judas) tree blooms purple in springtime, and the views of the nearby hills are idyllic. Find the tiny stone hamlet of **Kolyvata**, signposted off the road between Alexandros and Nikiana.

MEGANISI ΜΕΓΑΝΗΣΙ

POP 1040

Meganisi, with its verdant landscape and turquoise bays fringed by pebbled beaches, is the easiest escape from overloaded Nydri. It can fit into a day visit or a longer, more relaxed stay. The narrow lanes and bougainvillea-bedecked houses of **Spartohori** perch on a plateau above Porto Spilia (where the ferry docks; follow the steep road or steps behind). Pretty **Vathy** is the island's second harbour, 800m behind which sits the village of Katomeri. With time to spare, visit remote beaches such as Limonari.

Asteria Holidays (☑26450 51107; www. asteria.gr), at Porto Spilia, can help with everything related to the island. Hotel Meganisi (☑26450 51240; www.hotelmeganisi.gr; Katomeri; d incl breakfast €60; ❄️ 🛜 🌊) has simple rooms with some sea views. The undisputed favourite fish taverna Porto Vathy (☑26450 51125; Vathy; mains €6-14; ⏱️lunch & dinner) is cast out on a small quay in Vathy.

ℹ️ Getting There & Around

The ferry runs between Nydri and Meganisi (per person/car €2/14, 25 to 40 minutes, five daily) to Porto Spilia and Vathy. A local bus runs five to seven times daily between Spartohori and Vathy (via Katomeri), but it's worth bringing your own transport on the ferry.

KEFALLONIA ΚΕΦΑΛΛΟΝΙΑ

POP 35,801

The largest of the Ionian Islands, Kefallonia is a place where it's easy to lose yourself, surrounded by air thick with oleander and the bells of wandering goats. Lush, mountainous and blessed with wild meadows, vineyards and secret coves lapped by water bluer than a supermodel's iris, Kefallonia has it all. Despite the seismic earthquake of '53 that razed much of the original architecture, a few villages with Italianate good looks still survive, namely Fiskardo and Assos. Underexplored areas like the Paliki Peninsula, excellent unique cuisine and great wines round out a spectacular island.

ℹ️ Getting There & Away

AIR

The airport (EFL; ☑26710 41511) is 9km south of Argostoli.

Air Berlin has high season flights. From May to September, many charter flights come from northern Europe and the UK.

Olympic Air (☑26710 41511; www.olympicair. com) Serves Athens.
Sky Express (☑28102 23500; www.skyex press.gr) Serves Corfu, Preveza and Zakynthos.

DESTINATION	TIME	FARE	FREQUENCY
Athens	55min	€118	2 daily
Corfu	1hr	€55	3 weekly
Kythira	1¾hr	€56	3 weekly
Preveza	20min	€55	3 weekly
Zakynthos	25min	€55	3 weekly

BOAT

Port Authority (☑26710 22224)

Domestic

Frequent Ionian Ferries (www.ionianferries. gr) connect Poros to Kyllini in the Peloponnese. The ferry Ionian Pelagos (☑in Sami, Kefallonia 26740 23405, in Vasiliki, Lefkada 26450 31520) links Sami with Astakos in the Peloponnese, Piso Aetos in Ithaki, and Vasiliki in Lefkada. Some months, ferries (☑26450 31520) go directly from Sami to Vasiliki.

West Ferry (www.westferry.gr) goes from Fiskardo, and sometimes Sami, to Vasiliki (Lefkada). They sometimes serve Frikes (Ithaki), usually from Vasiliki, but occasionally from Fiskardo. Get information and tickets at Nautilus Travel (☑26740 41440; Fiskardo).

May to September, two daily ferries (☑26710 91280) connect the remote port of Pesada in the south to Agios Nikolaos on the northern tip of Zakynthos. Buses to the ports are rare, so an easier, cheaper alternative is to sail from Poros to Kyllini in mainland Peloponnese, and from there to Zakynthos Town.

Some Italy ferries stop in Sami on their way to/ from Corfu or Igoumenitsa.

International

Sami–Patra ferries have now stopped running due to the recent closure of Endeavour Lines; Ventouris (p729) still connects Sami to Bari, Italy. Red Star Ferries (☑26710 27301) go to Brindisi from Sami once a week on Mondays in high season (seat from €87, bunk from €115, 16 hours).

BOAT SERVICES FROM KEFALLONIA

DESTINATION	DEPARTS	TIME	FARE	FREQUENCY
Agios Nikolaos (Zakynthos)	Pesada	1½hr	€8	2 daily (May-Sep)
Astakos (mainland)	Sami	3hr	€11	1-2 daily
Kyllini	Poros	1½hr	€9	5-6 daily
Piso Aetos (Ithaki)	Sami	30min	€3	2 weekly
Vasiliki (Lefkada)	Fiskardo	1hr	€7	2-3 daily
Vasiliki	Sami	1¾hr	€9	2 weekly (seasonal)

Kefallonia & Ithaki

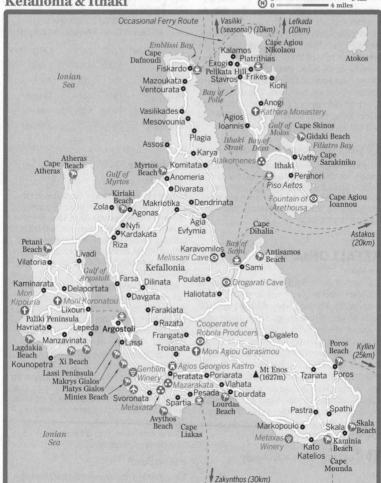

Blue Sea Travel (☑ 26740 23007; www.samistar.com; Sami) On Sami's waterfront.

Vassilatos Shipping (☑ 26710 22618; Antoni Tritsi 54, Argostoli) Opposite Argostoli port authority.

BUS

Three daily buses connect Argostoli with Athens via Poros (€38, seven hours, three daily) using the ferry, Poros (€35, four hours, one daily) and Lixouri (€42, seven hours, one daily).

KTEL Bus Station Argostoli (☑ 26710 22276; www.ktelkefallonias.gr; Antoni Tritsi 5) On Argostoli's southern waterfront. Excellent printed schedule.

ⓘ Getting Around

There's no airport bus; taxis cost around €20.

BOAT

Car ferries connect Argostoli and Lixouri, on the island's western Paliki Peninsula (per person/car €3.50/4.50, 30 minutes, hourly from 7.30am to 10.30pm, plus half-hourly and to midnight July and August).

BUS

KTEL Buses serve Lassi Peninsula (€1.50, seven daily), Sami (€4, four daily), Poros (€4.50, two daily), Skala (€4.50, two daily) and Fiskardo (€6, one daily). Once-daily east-coast service links

KEFALLONIA'S GREAT OUTDOORS

While the EOT occasionally stocks excellent leaflets with walking routes around the island, it's well worth enlisting an experienced local to guide you off the beaten path.

Sea Kayaking Kefalonia (☑6934010400; www.seakayakingkefalonia-greece.com) Full range of day-long kayak tours with lunch and snorkelling gear (€60), multiday excursions and certified courses.

Bavarian Horse Riding (☑6977533203; www.kephalonia.com; Koulourata; per 1hr/4hr €20/€80) Ride upon sturdy Bavarian horses on short trips through the Kefallonian countryside. Longer 4-hour treks take you over Ainosa mountain to the sea on the island's other side, where you can take the horses for a swim.

Elements (☑6979987611; www.kefalonia-elements.com) All manner of trips, from hiking (from €50) and caving (from €80) to canyoning (€60), kayaking (€60) and jeep safaris (€65).

Donkey Trekking (☑6980059630; www.donkeytrekkingkefalonia.com; €20) Slow donkey treks around Sami exploring evergreen valleys and ruined villages. Bring sturdy footwear.

Panbike (☑26710 27118; www.panbike.gr; Lithostroto 72, Argostoli) Bicycles cost from €6 per day. Owner Pandelis, the bike champion, can deliver for a fee, or arrange tours.

Katelios with Skala, Poros, Sami, Agia Evfymia and Fiskardo. No buses run Sunday.

CAR & MOTORCYCLE

Car- and bike-hire companies fill major resorts.

Europcar (☑26710 42020) At the airport.

Hertz (☑26710 42142) At the airport.

Kefalonia2Ride (☑6944437045; www.kefalonia2ride.rentals; waterfront, Sami; per day €23; ☺9.30am-9pm) This excellent outfit has brand new scooters with built-in cell phone chargers and GPS systems.

Karavomilos (☑26740 22779; Sami) Offers delivery.

Argostoli   Αργοστόλι

POP 9748

Thanks to being laid flat during the 1953 earthquake, Argostoli's rebuilt streets feel very new. And though it might like lack architectural gravitas it has a lively buzz about it, with **Lithostroto**, a long pedestrianised street, running past stylish shops. The main focus of activity is charming **Plateia Valianou**, where locals come to chat and eat at the many restaurants. In summer, *kantadoroi* amble the streets singing *kantades,* traditional songs accompanied by guitar and mandolin.

◎ Sights

Pick up the events booklet from the EOT (p659) to see what's on.

Korgialenio History & Folklore Museum   MUSEUM
(☑26710 28835; www.corgialenios.gr; Ilia Zervou 12; admission €3; ☺9am-2pm Mon-Sat) Dedicat-

ed to preserving Kefallonian art and culture, this fine museum houses icons and pre-earthquake furniture, clothes and artwork from the homes of gentry and farmworkers.

Focas-Kosmetatos Foundation   MUSEUM
(☑26710 26595; Valianou; adult/child €3/free; ☺10am-1pm Mon-Fri, by appointment in low season) See displays on Kefallonia's cultural and political history in a pre-earthquake building. The **Cephalonia Botanica** (☺8.30am-2.30pm Mon-Fri) **FREE**, a lovely botanical garden, is about 2km from Argostoli centre.

Archaeological Museum   MUSEUM
(☑26710 28300; Rokou Vergoti; admission €3; ☺8am-3pm Tue-Sun) A collection of island relics, including Mycenaean finds.

Makrys Gialos   BEACH
Often rammed to the gills, Makrys Gialos is popular with holidaying Brits. It has lovely turquoise water.

Platys Gialos   BEACH
Has plenty of shade, very clear water and a few places to eat.

Lourdas Beach   BEACH
Set 16km from Argostoli on the Argostoli–Poros road. Has an attractive expansive beach set against a mountainous green backdrop.

⛏ Sleeping

★Vivian Villa   PENSION €
(☑26710 23396; www.kefalonia-vivianvilla.gr; Deladetsima 11; d/studio €45/55; ❉🖱) Everything runs like clockwork in these lovely studios

Argostoli

Camping Argostoli (2km);
Katavothres (2km)

Ferries to
Lixouri

i EOT

Argostoli Bay

Plateia
Valianou

Children's
Park

Lavraga

Napier
Gardens

Church of
Agios Spiridon

Minoos

Panbike (350m);
KTEL Argostoli (450m);
Makrys Gialos (5km);
Platys Gialos (5km)

Cephalonia
Botanica (1km);
Lourdata (16km)

and apartments on a quiet street. Think cosy rooms with tasteful decor, separate bedroom for the kids, well-stocked kitchenettes, balconies, and a plant-filled garden fragrant with thyme and basil. The loft apartment is stunning and can sleep five. There's also a lift.

Camping Argostoli
CAMPGROUND €

(☑26710 23487; www.campingargostoli.gr; camp sites per adult/car/tent €6.50/3/5; ⊗Jun-Oct; P🛜) Pleasant, quiet spot near the lighthouse on the northernmost point of the peninsula.

Hotel Ionian Plaza
HOTEL €€

(☑26710 25581; www.ionianplaza.gr; Plateia Valianou; d/tr/q incl breakfast from €95/110/130; P❄@🛜) Argostoli's smartest hotel has played host to Tinseltown actors Nicolas Cage and Penelope Cruz, and has a stylish, marble-decorated lobby and small but lavish rooms with flat-screen TV and balcony. Top-floor rooms have the best views of the square.

Mirabel Hotel
HOTEL €€

(☑26710 25381; www.mirabelhotel.com; Plateia Valianou; s/d/tr incl breakfast €60/76/102; ❄@🛜) Clean, functional rooms – veering toward bland – at this business traveller's choice on the corner of the square. Flat-screen TV and desk.

✗ Eating

Ladokolla
SOUVLAKI €

(☑26710 25522; Xarokopou 13; dishes €2-8; ⊗12.30pm-2am) Piping-hot chicken, pork or lamb kebabs and pittas are delivered without plates onto table-top covers.

★ Arhontiko
KEFALLONIAN €€

(☑26710 27213; Risospaston 5; mains €7-17; ⊗breakfast, lunch & dinner) This friendly, wood-ceilinged and stone-walled traditional restaurant offers delights of the local waters such as squid, grilled shrimp and octopus, plus carnivorous favourites like Kefallonian meat pie or *exohiko* (pork stuffed with tomatoes,

Argostoli

onions, peppers and feta). Good house wines, relaxed, helpful service and a cosy atmosphere – no wonder it's always busy.

Casa Grec   MEDITERRANEAN €€
(☎26710 24091; S Metaxa 12; mains €12-22; ⊙dinner nightly, reduced hours in low season) A terracotta courtyard rich in plants, flickering candles and a fountain is the romantic setting for this culinary escape. Chicken in thyme, pasta dressed with nuanced sauces, succulent steaks, delicious desserts and a varied wine list are the reasons you should visit.

🍷 Drinking & Nightlife

Cafes line Plateia Valianou and Lithostroto and bounce by late evening. **Bass Club** (www.bassclub.gr; cnr S Metaxa & Vergoti) draws the younger set. Popular club-restaurant **Katavothres** (☎26710 22221; waterfront) contains unusual geological formations, top-name DJs and a mixed crowd. Beach bar **Stavento**, in Makrys Gialos (p657), hops in summer.

ℹ Information

The main ferry quay is at the northern end of the waterfront and the bus station is at its southern end. Banks with ATMs line the northern waterfront and Lithostroto.

EOT (☎26710 22248; ⊙7am-2.30pm Mon-Fri) Helpful tourist bureau on the northern waterfront beside the port police.

Around Argostoli

You can make a gorgeous loop connecting Agios Georgios Kastro, Moni Agiou Gerasimou, Robola vineyards and the sea coast, or walks in **Mt Enos**.

⊙ Sights

Agios Georgios Kastro   RUIN
(Castle of St George; ⊙8.30am-3pm Tue-Sun) **FREE** This Venetian *kastro* (castle) from the 1500s sits atop a hill southeast of Argostoli; it was the capital of Kefallonia for about two hundred years. Well worth a visit for its stellar views, the castle is also surrounded by a small village with Byzantine churches and restaurants (also with stunning vistas). **Palatino** (☎26710 68490; mains €7-10; ⊙lunch & dinner May-Oct) creates home-cooked Kefallonian specialities. **Astraios** (☎26710 69152; ⊙9pm-late) is a bar with live Greek music owned by venerated musician Dionysos Frangopoulos.

Moni Agiou Gerasimou   MONASTERY
(adult/child €7/4; ⊙9am-1pm & 3.30-8pm) Dedicated to Kefallonia's patron saint, this monastery (16km east of Argostoli) is cared for by nuns. Inside the chapel lies the famous cave where Gerasimos escaped from the rigours of monastic life to even greater self-abnegation. Descend via a steep metal ladder into a small chamber 6m below.

IONIAN ON THE VINE

The Ionian Islands would not be the same without wine, and Kefallonia especially has outstanding vintages, most notably from the unique Robola grape (VQRPD). Other varieties like Mavrodaphne (AOC) and Muscat (AOC) enhance the viniculture.

High in the mountains southeast of Argostoli, at the heart of verdant Omala Valley, lies the fascinating winery of the **Cooperative of Robola Producers of Kefallonia** (☎26710 86301; www.robola.gr; Omala; ⊙9am-8pm May-Sep, to 3pm Mon-Fri Oct-Apr) **FREE**. Here, grapes from about 300 independent growers are transformed into the yellow-green Robola, a dry white wine of subtle yet lively flavours. The grape is said to have been introduced by the Venetians. Smaller yet distinguished **Gentilini** (☎26710 41618; Minies), 2km south of Argostoli on the airport road, has a charming setting with a range of superb wines, including the scintillating Classico.

Paliki Peninsula
Χερσόνησος Παλική

Anchored by the bustling gulf-side town of **Lixouri**, the Paliki Peninsula is an under-explored region of spectral white, cream and red clay cliffs; verdant farmland and vineyards; and hilltop villages. White-sand **Petani Beach** in the north will melt your heart with water so clear it could entice a jaded mermaid. Red-sand **Xi Beach** is also charming but gets packed in summer. **Moni Kipouria**, a monastery built by a lone monk, overlooks stark cliffs, azure seas and robust vineyards, and is worth the trip to the far west of the peninsula.

Lixouri's central square sits waterside and throngs with life. The easiest way to access the peninsula from Argostoli is by the car ferry (per person/car €3.50/4.50, 30 minutes, hourly September to June, half-hourly July and August), and makes a fun half-day trip even if you don't have your own wheels. **Perdikis Travel** (☑ 26710 91097; tvrperdi@hol.gr), on Lixouri's southern seafront, helps with accommodation and arrangements.

🛏 Sleeping & Eating

Xi Village
PENSION €€

(☑ 26710 93830; www.xi-village.gr; Xi; d/tr/q €60/70/80; P ✳ 🛜 🛋) Overlooking Xi Beach, with a pool and basic, wood-accented, white-walled apartments with balcony and kitchenette, Xi Village is a good choice.

Niforos
APARTMENT €€

(☑ 26710 97350; Petani; studios €85; ☺ May-Oct; P ✳ 🛜 🛋) Spacious, immaculate studios above Petani Beach have balconies overlooking the open sea. Friendly owners, large pool and on-site restaurant add to the charm.

★ Petani Bay Hotel
HOTEL €€€

(☑26710 97701; www.petanibayhotel.gr; Petani; d incl breakfast €220-300; P ✳ 🛜 🛋) Boasting one of the best infinity pools in Greece, this lovely boutique eyrie overlooks the cobalt-blue bay far below and has 13 romantic suites with marble floor, wood-blade fan, kitchenette and mushroom-grey walls. It's all about peace here, the only sound being the bleating of goats and tinkle of your chilled wineglass.

Erasmia
TAVERNA €

(☑ 26710 97372; Petani Beach; mains €6-9; ☺ lunch & dinner May-Sep) Buzzing beachside taverna ever-popular for its no-nonsense seafood menu. Imagine a perfect, fiery sunset enjoyed over freshly grilled bass.

Apolafsi
SEAFOOD €

(☑ 26710 91691; www.apolafsi.gr; Lepeda; mains €8-10; ☺ lunch & dinner; P ✳ 🛜) Fresh seafood and grilled meats, as well as a convenient hotel. Rooms (doubles including breakfast €45 to €55) have kitchen and bathroom. It's 2km south of Lixouri.

Mavroeidis
BAKERY €

(baked goods from €1.50) Perfect pit stop on the main square in Lixouri for the best *amygdalopita* (sweet almond cake) on the island.

Oi Nisoi Vardianoi
TAVERNA €€

(☑ 6986948528; Xi; mains €7.50-15; ☺ 1.30pm-late) With widescreen views of the beach from its breezy terrace and a menu spilling over with seafood and fish dishes, this is a choice spot for lunch.

Sami & Around
Σάμη
POP 1025

Sami, 25km northeast of Argostoli and the main port of Kefallonia, has a waterside strip loaded with tourist-oriented cafes – but beyond this it's an attractive town, nestled in a bright bay and flanked by steep hills. There are several monasteries, ancient castle ruins, walks and nearby beaches (such as **Antisamos Beach**) that are worth a trip, though **Agia Evfymia** on the north side of the bay makes for a quieter alternative. Nearby caves **Melissani** and **Drogarati** are rather overrated.

🏃 Activities

The tourist office offers brochures outlining **walks** through the area; one covers Sami and Antisamos, another the trail from Agia Evfymia to Myrtos.

🛏 Sleeping & Eating

Karavomilos Beach Camping
CAMPGROUND €

(☑ 26740 22480; www.camping-karavomilos.gr; Sami–Karavomilos Rd; camp sites per adult/car/tent €8.50/3.50/6; ☺ May-Sep; @ 🛜 🛋) This is a large, award-winning campground in a great beachfront location, with fantastic bathrooms and loads of facilities.

Gerasimos Dendrinos
APARTMENT €

(☑ 26740 61455; Agia Evfymia; s/d €50/60; ✳) Expect super whitewashed studios with sofa, TV and bathroom in a lovely old house and garden abloom with flowers on the north side of the village. The upper rooms have balconies. Better still, it's next to Paradise Beach (p661) restaurant.

Hotel Athina
HOTEL €€

(✍ 26740 22779; www.athinahotel.gr; Karavomilos; studios €60, d incl breakfast from €80-95; ☺May-Oct; ❄ @) Painted in cool greys, this simple resort hotel has studios overlooking the bay. Guests use the pool next door at swank **Ionian Emerald Resort** (✍ 26740 22708; www.io-nianemerald.gr; d incl breakfast from €220), which has the same owner.

Melissani Hotel
HOTEL €€

(✍ 26740 22464; Dihalion 23, Sami; d/tr €60/75; ☺May-Oct; ❄) Retro quirks like orange 1970s phones and old-fashioned showers are many at this welcoming place two blocks up from the waterfront. It's basic but has terrific sunset views from its balconies.

★ Paradise Beach
KEFALLONIAN €

(Dendrinos; ✍ 26740 61392; Agia Evfymia; mains €6-13; ☺lunch & dinner mid-May–mid-Oct) At the northern end of Agia Evfymia harbourfront, this pretty taverna has a vine-shaded terrace overlooking the Bay of Sami. Favoured by the talent of *Captain Corelli's Mandolin* and everyone else who catches wind of its aromas: locally reared meat (exceptionally tender lamb chops), dolmadhes, Kefallonian meat pie, or braised rabbit. You'll be coming back, believe us!

❶ Information

All facilities, including post office and banks, are in Sami. Buses for Argostoli usually meet ferries. Hire cars through Karavomilos (p657).

Port Authority (✍ 26740 22031; Sami)

Assos
Άσσος

POP 88

Too photogenic for words, pint-sized Assos is a confection of Italianate cream- and ochre-coloured houses hugging a pretty cove protected by a wooded peninsula. The **fortress** up top makes for a great hike, and the bay is eminently swimmable. A few tasty tavernas plus a pace so slow you can palpably feel your pulse dropping are your reasons for visiting.

🛏 Sleeping & Eating

Apartment Linardos
APARTMENT €€

(✍ 26740 51563; www.linardosapartments.gr; d/qu €75/85; ☺May-Sep; ❄) Tastefully finished studios with postcard-perfect views of the fortress, a stone's throw from the beach. With TV, kitchenette, balcony and fridge. Let the waves lull you to sleep.

Molos
GREEK €

(✍ 26740 51220; mains €7-10; ☺9.30am-late) At the far end of the bay this custard-hued harbourside taverna catches the late afternoon 'golden hour' upon its blue-chequered tablecloths. Salads, grilled veal, pork tenderloin, octopus, red mullet. Flavoursome.

Platanos
TAVERNA €

(mains €6-15; ☺breakfast, lunch & dinner Easter-Oct; ❄) Admired island-wide for locally sourced, fresh ingredients, Platanos fills part of an attractive shady plaza near the waterfront. Strong on meat dishes, there are also fish and vegetarian options such as veg *mousakas*.

Fiskardo
Φισκάρδο

POP 189

Intimately positioned beside coral-blue water, this tiny village packs a heady punch with its romantically-coloured Venetian buildings – Fiskardo was mercifully spared the worst of the '53 earthquake – with a clutch of upmarket restaurants and very choice accommodation. Choking on yachties in the summer, it exudes a cosmopolitan buzz unmatched by the rest of the island.

🛏 Sleeping

Rooms are deeply discounted in low season.

Villa Romantza
PENSION €

(✍ 26740 41322; www.villa-romantza.gr; r/studio/apt €50/70/85; ❄) An excellent budget choice with simple, spacious clean rooms and studios.

Regina's Rooms
PENSION €

(✍ 26740 41125; www.regina-studios-boats.gr; d/tr €50/70; ❄ 🛜) Regina's sits above the waterfront and has great-value rooms with waffled

---

SECRETS OF THE DEEP

Fiskardo Divers (✍6970206172; www.fiskardo-divers.com; 3hr beginner course €50, open-water 4-day PADI course €400), behind the waterfront, has established a great new dive centre. Exhibits include the skeletons of monk seals, loggerhead turtles, Cuvier's beaked whales and sharks. Run by marine biologist Cedric, this excellent outfit runs dives to caves, wrecks, reefs and a Bristol Beaufort bomber shot down in WWII. The waters around Fiskardo, with visibility of 40m, make it a perfect place to learn to dive.

quilts, kitchenette, balcony and TV. The owner also rents out **boats** at preferential rates for residents.

Kiki Apartments
APARTMENT €€

(www.kiki-apartments.gr; ste €120-130; ❄️🌐) Six new apartments with a chic Provençal feel; think wood-top tables, green and cream colour schemes, gleaming kitchenette, sofa, private balcony and stunning bedrooms. There's also a pool. The property sits beside a beach.

Archontiko
PENSION €€

(☎26740 41342; www.archontiko-fiskardo.gr; d without/with sea view €80/90, apt €100; ❄️) Stately rooms in an old stone mansion, with four-poster beds, tasteful linen and balconies with sea views; there's also a roomy top floor apartment with kitchenette that sleep five.

Stella Apartments
APARTMENT €€

(☎26740 41211; www.stella-apartments.gr; studio/apt from 100/125; ❄️@🌐) On Fiskardo's quiet southern outskirts, these welcoming rooms are cosily finished, with fridge and satellite TV, and have large balconies to drink up the view of the nearby sea and distant lighthouse. There's also a lift.

Emelisse Hotel
RESORT €€€

(☎26740 41200; www.arthotel.gr; Emblissi Bay; d/ste from €352/378, 4-person apt from €893; ⏰mid-Apr–mid-Oct; 🅿️❄️@🌐🏊) Situated in a superb position 1km west of Fiskardo overlooking Emblissi Bay, this luxurious hotel has beautifully appointed rooms in immaculately cultivated terraces leading down to the crowning glory: a lavish swimming pool and restaurant with fantastic sea views to Lefkada, Ithaki and beyond. Breakfast is included.

✖️ Eating & Drinking

Fiskardo has some seriously top-level restaurants. Bars and cafes dot the dollhouse waterfront – great for people-watching.

⭐ Irida
GREEK €

(www.irida-fiscardo.com; mains €8-13; ⏰9am-late) Eclectically hung with an antique diving helmet and objets d'art, it's not only the shadowy boho interior of this 200-year-old salt store that tempts – you can feast on calamari, meatballs and lamb cutlets, or try the stuffed fillet of sole with prawns and champagne sauce.

Tassia
MEDITERRANEAN €€

(☎26740 41205; mains €13; ⏰lunch & dinner May-Oct) To the west of the waterfront, with its lavender chairs and linen-topped tables, Tassia delights with homemade pies, mezedhes and zucchini croquettes. Try the 'fisherman's pasta', incorporating finely chopped squid, octopus, mussels and prawns in a magic combination with a dash of cognac. Meat dishes are equally splendid.

Café Tselenti
ITALIAN €€

(☎26740 41344; mains €15; ⏰lunch & dinner May-Oct) Owned by the Tselenti family since 1893, this noted restaurant has a romantic outdoor terrace at the heart of the village. Outstanding cuisine includes aubergine rolls and terrific linguine with prawns, mussels and crayfish, as well as lamb shank, beef *stifadho*, and swordfish with calvados sauce.

Vasso's
SEAFOOD €€€

(☎26740 41276; mains €10-40; ⏰lunch & dinner May-Oct) Lapped by the nearby sea, Vasso's is *the* place to head for exceptional seafood, such as honeyed octopus with mashed fava, mussels *saganaki* and *sofigado* (veal in tomato sauce).

ℹ️ Information

Nautilus Travel (p655) and **Pama Travel** (☎26740 41033; www.pamatravel.com; Fiskardo) arrange everything. Both have internet access (€2 per 30 minutes). Visit www.fiscardo.com for town info.

ITHAKI
ΙΘΑΚΗ

POP 3231

Sleepy, underpopulated and with a Circean charm that enchains you to its mythical soul, Ithaki is something special. With its ancient ruins, tiny harbours and rugged coast fringed in petrol-blue water, this island between the mainland and Kefallonia stays in your memory long after others have melted away.

Ithaki is celebrated as the mythical home of Homer's Odysseus, where his loyal wife Penelope waited patiently for his much-delayed homecoming. The butterfly-shaped island is made up of two large bodies of land joined by a narrow isthmus. Sheer cliffs, occasional olive groves and precipitous, arid mountains gild this Ionian jewel, while monasteries and churches offer Byzantine delights and splendid views.

ℹ️ Getting There & Away

BOAT

The ferry **Ionian Pelagos** (☎26740 32104; www.ionionpelagos.com) runs daily (sometimes twice a day) in high season between Piso Aetos, Sami (Kefallonia) and Astakos (on the mainland).

BOAT SERVICES FROM ITHAKI

DESTINATION	DEPARTS	TIME	FARE	FREQUENCY
Astakos (mainland)	Piso Aetos	2hr 20min	€10	1-2 daily
Sami (Kefallonia)	Piso Aetos	30min	€3	2 daily
Nidri (Lefkada)	Frikes	1hr	€8	2 daily
Vasiliki	Piso Aetos	1¼hr	€8	2 weekly, seasonal

West Ferry (☑ in Kefallonia 26740 41440, in Lefkada 26450 93182; www.westferry.gr) runs an ever-changing schedule from Frikes to Vasiliki (Lefkada). Sometimes they go from Frikes to Fiskardo (Kefallonia), but usually you have to go via Vasiliki. **Kefallonia Lines** (☑ 21095 15100; www.kefalonianlines.com) runs a ferry from Vathy on Friday and Saturday to Kyllini in the Peloponnese (€13.60, 2½ hours)

You can get information and tickets from Vathy's two travel agencies (p664); they each serve different ferry companies.

Port Authority (☑ 26740 32909)

BUS

You can buy a bus ticket to Athens (€38 includes the ferry ticket, one daily), which requires boarding the ferry in Vathy; then when the boat arrives at Sami in Kefallonia, the Athens-bound bus loads on and you must find it.

❶ Getting Around

Piso Aetos, on Ithaki's west coast, has no settlement; taxis often meet boats, as does the municipal bus (in high season only).

The island's one bus runs twice daily (weekdays only, more often in high season) between Kioni and Vathy via Stavros and Frikes (€3.90). Its limited schedule is not suited to day-trippers.

To travel around the island your best bet is to hire a scooter or car (high season from €35), or motorboat. Companies will make deliveries for a fee (€10 to €15).

AGS (☑ 26740 32702; Vathy) Western harbourfront.

Alpha Bike & Car Hire (☑ 26740 33243; www.alphacarsgreece.com; Vathy) Behind Alpha Bank. Great new scooters.

Sea Taxi (☑ 26740 33581, 6972142374)

Taxis (☑ 6944790943, 6944686504, 6945700214) Taxis are relatively expensive (about €30 for the Vathy–Frikes trip).

Vathy Βαθύ

POP 1820

Pretty Vathy, with its neoclassical sky-blue and ochre mansions, sits around a sheltered, horseshoe-shaped harbour, backdropped by mountains. The central square, Plateia Efstathiou Drakouli is ornamented by a fabulous verdigris statue of Odysseus and buzzes with seafront traffic and cafes, while narrow lanes wriggle inland from the quay. Vathy is the only place on the island with nightclubs, banks, travel agencies and the like.

Ithaki's compact nature ensures dramatic scenery changes over short distances on **walks** (ranging from 5km to 13km) that can reveal 360-degree views of the sea and surrounding islands. Several marked trails exist (see www.ithacagreece.com for information on walking tracks); go on a guided walk to explore little-seen parts of the island.

🏃 Activities

★**Island Walks** WALKING TOUR
(www.islandwalks.com; walks €15-18) Run by Ester, walks vary in length. The best-known route is the **Homer Walk**, which takes in the museum in Stavros, then winds up the nearby hillside to the ruins where the real Odysseus may have lived 2800 years ago. This walk takes around three hours; bring sensible footwear, a hat and water.

Mersini Massage & Reiki HEALTH & FITNESS
(☑ 6980961691; full-body/hot-stone massage per hr €40/35, reiki per hr €35) Ease those tired calves after your efforts on the Homer's Walk with a gentle massage at this peaceful studio close to the waterfront (behind the square).

Boat Trips

Albatross (☑ 6976901643) and **Mana Korina** (☑ 6976654351) sail from Vathy in high season around Ithaki and in various combinations to Fiskardo (Kefallonia), Lefkada and 'unknown islands', including Atokos and Kalamos (charter for a maximum of 10 persons €400). They also make runs to **Gidaki Beach** (€10). (To access Gidaki on foot, follow the walking track from **Skinos Beach**.)

🛏 Sleeping

Grivas Gerasimos Rooms PENSION €
(☑ 26740 33328; d/tr €45/55) Great-value, lemon-walled, spacious rooms with wooden beds topped in turquoise quilts. TV, fridge, desk and small terrace overlooking the

harbour. Ask for the upstairs room with the larger balcony. To get here, turn right at the Century Club on the waterfront, then take the first left at the road parallel to the sea and continue another 50m.

Odyssey Apartments APARTMENT €€
(✆ 26740 33400; www.odysseyapartments.gr; studio €100, 1-/2-bedroom apt €130/160; P ✳ ☜) Perched on a hill 500m out of town, these spotless studios and apartments (some for five people) have balconies with magical views of the harbour and beyond. It's signposted at the eastern end of the waterfront.

Hotel Familia BOUTIQUE HOTEL €€
(✆ 26740 33366; www.hotel-familia.com; Odysseos 60; s/d incl breakfast from €110/120; ✳ ☜) This former olive press has been turned into a swanky boutique hotel. Chic slate is juxtaposed with soft tapestries and gentle lighting to create a 'wow' effect. Family-run and family-friendly – but only one room has a courtyard, and there are no sea views.

Hotel Mentor HOTEL €€
(✆ 26740 32433; www.hotelmentor.gr; s/d/tr/q incl breakfast €70/85/105/135; ✳ ☜) Simple, stylish rooms with TV, desk, armoire and balcony, plus an inviting contemporary breakfast room. Right on the waterfront.

★**Hotel Perantzada** BOUTIQUE HOTEL €€€
(✆ 26740 33496; www.arthotel.gr/perantzada; Odyssea Androutsou; d/tr/q incl breakfast from €265/415/490; ☉ Easter–mid-Oct; ✳ @ ☜ ☜) Low-lit Perantzada hovers by the harbour with an infinity pool and large balconied rooms as minimal as white clouds – with iPod player and flat-screen TV, granite-and-wood bathrooms and baths large enough to free-dive in. The breakfast buffet is pure decadence, and the main lobby so bookworm-cosy you may just spend your holiday there.

✖ **Eating**

Trehantiri TAVERNA €
(✆ 26740 33444; mains €5-9; ☉ lunch & dinner) Every day there is something different cooking up in the kitchen, from goat stew to stuffed tomatoes, *saganaki* to *kleftiko*. It's just behind the square, with blue tables and the siren's song of a pet canary.

Karamela Cafe CAFE €
(mains €5; ☉ 6.30am-late; ✳ ☜) Perfect for breakfast in its shaded garden or within its cool interior. Snacks, pizza and salads. At the waterfront.

🛈 **Information**

Ithaki has no tourist office. **Polyctor Tours** (✆ 26740 33120; www.ithakiholidays.com) is on the main square, while **Delas Tours** (✆ 26740 32104; http://delastours.blogspot.gr) is on the waterfront; both can help with information and boat tickets.

The main square has the island's only banks (with ATMs) and post office.

Around Ithaki

Ithaki reaches back into the mythical past to claim several sites associated with Homer's *Odyssey,* though finding them can be an epic journey of its own: signage is scant. The **Fountain of Arethousa**, in the island's south, is where Odysseus' swineherd, Eumaeus, is believed to have brought his pigs to drink. The exposed and isolated hike, through unspoilt landscape with great sea views, takes 1½ to two hours (return) from the turn-off; this excludes the hilly 5km trudge up the road to the sign itself.

The location of Odysseus' palace has been much disputed and archaeologists have been unable to find conclusive evidence; some present-day archaeologists speculate it was on **Pelikata Hill** near Stavros, while German archaeologist Heinrich Schliemann believed it to be at **Alalkomenes**, near Piso Aetos.

Take a break from Homeric myth and head north from Vathy along a fabulously scenic mountain road to sleepy **Anogi**, the old capital. Its restored church of **Agia Panagia** (claimed to be from the 12th century) has incredible Byzantine frescoes and a Venetian bell tower; to visit get keys from the neighbouring *kafeneio.* About 200m uphill, the small but evocative ruins of **Old Anogi** fill a rock-studded landscape.

Further north again, the inland village of **Stavros**, above the Bay of Polis, is also reachable via the west-coast road, and has the only ATM outside of Vathy. Visit its small but interesting **archaeological museum** (✆ 26740 31305; ☉ 8.30am-3pm Tue-Sun) FREE, with local artefacts dating from 3000 BC to the Roman period.

Driving north, make your way to the top of **Exogi** for panoramic views; on the way you'll pass the **House of Homer** archaeological dig, down a dirt road signposted on the right.

Heading northeast from Stavros takes you to tiny seafront **Frikes**, the ferry departure point for Lefkada. Clasped between windswept cliffs, it has a swath of waterfront restaurants and busy bars.

From Frikes a serpentine road hugs the beautiful coastline past twisting cliffs to end at lovely **Kioni**, a hamlet of Venetian houses tumbling down to the bijou harbour. Kioni will almost certainly melt your heart with its clutch of tasty tavernas and view of three disused windmills across the bay. Grab a chilled drink and wait for sunset.

🛏 Sleeping

Ourania Apartments APARTMENT €
(☑26740 31027; www.ithacagreece.com/ourania/ourania.htm; Stavros; studio/apt €40/65; P ✿) Two minutes' walk up the hill from Stavros, this romantic, shuttered villa is swimming in flowers and has amazing views across olive groves down to the sea. Studios are homely, with kitchenette and balcony. There is also a larger apartment that sleeps four. The owners are warmth itself.

Captain's Apartments APARTMENT €€
(☑26740 31481; www.captains-apartments.gr; Kioni; 2-/4-person apt €65/85; ✿ 🛜) Basic yet tidy studios with TV, pine fittings and well-stocked kitchenette. Look out for the turn just before you reach the harbour on the winding road down the hill.

Kioni Apartments APARTMENT €€
(☑26740 31144; www.ithacagreece.eu; Kioni; apt €100; ⊙May-Oct; ✿) In the corner of the harbour and choked with bougainvillea, this handsome Italianate building has welcoming apartments with wood ceilings and large balcony. Stylish but homely, central but quiet. In a word: perfect.

🍴 Eating & Drinking

En Plo GREEK €
(Kioni; mains €6-8; ⊙8am-midnight; ✿ 🛜) The upstairs terrace is a lovely spot for watching the sun set and the lights switch on in the distant windmills across the bay. Cocktails, salads, ice cream, breakfast and crêpes. Chic.

Mythos TAVERNA €
(☑26740 31122; Kioni; mains €8.50; ⊙lunch & dinner) In Kioni, Mythos sits by the waves and has excellent *pastitsio,* veal *stifadho,* homemade chicken pie and prawns *saganaki.*

Rementzo TAVERNA €
(☑26740 31719; Frikes; mains €6-12; ⊙lunch & dinner) Right on the harbour in Frikes, this is a great place for trad cuisine like *stifadho,* fresh bream and dried apricots, as well as local speciality *savoro* (fish with vinegar, currants and garlic).

Sunset CAFE €
(Stavros; mains €5; ⊙breakfast, lunch & dinner) Perfectly located at the side of the mountain just shy of Stavros' centre, Sunset earns its moniker with sublime sunset views of the bay. Treasures like baklava, cheesecake, panna cotta and crêpes sweeten the experience.

★Yefuri TAVERNA €€
(☑26740 31131; Platrithias; mains €7-16; ⊙dinner Tue-Sun, reduced hours in low season) Perhaps the best restaurant outside of Vathy is Yefuri, with its fresh produce and rotating menu. It's on the road between Stavros and Platrithias.

Ithaki Restaurant TAVERNA €€
(☑26740 31080; Stavros; mains €8-14; ⊙lunch & dinner) This chic taverna on the corner of the square has a terrace with a beautiful view. Charcoal-fired veal, pork and lamb souvlaki.

Polyphemus TAVERNA €€
(☑26740 31794; Stavros; mains €10-17; ⊙lunch & dinner) Lit by tealights, its romantic garden restaurant is popular for its grilled squid, sundried grilled octopus and steamed mussels.

Cafe Spavento CAFE
(☑26740 31427; Kioni; 🛜) Great for breakfast. Has wi-fi.

To Kentro CAFE
(Stavros; ⊙9am-late) At the side of the square, this *kafeneio* is popular with local pensioners. Sip an afternoon glass of retsina to the quiet *thrup* of worry beads and enjoy the feeling of time slowing down.

ZAKYNTHOS ΖΑΚΥΝΘΟΣ
POP 40,759

Zakynthos, also known by its Italian name, Zante, battles against heavy package tourism along its eastern and southeast coasts. Beneath this it's a beautiful island – you just have to make a determined beeline to western and central regions of forested mountains dropping off to unreal turquoise waters to leave them behind. The northern and southern capes are verdant and also less exploited. Full of restaurants and cherry-red bougainvillea, Zakynthos Town adds a bit of sparkle to the overrun east, where the loggerhead turtle population struggles in the face of development.

ℹ Getting There & Away
AIR
Zakynthos Airport (ZTH) is 6km southwest of Zakynthos Town. For flights to/from Thessaloniki, try Astra Airlines (p634).

Zakynthos

Olympic Air (☐ 801 801 0101, 26950 42617; ☺ 8am-10pm Mon-Fri) Flies to Athens.

Sky Express (☐ 28102 23500; www.skyexpress.gr) Flies to Corfu via Kefallonia and Preveza, and to Kythira.

May to September, charter flights come from northern Europe and the UK.

Air Berlin (www.airberlin.com) Flies to Germany.

EasyJet (www.easyjet.com) Flies to London (Gatwick), Rome and Milan in high season.

BOAT

Port Authority (☐ 26950 42556)

Ionian Ferries (☐ 26950 22083; www.ionianferries.gr; Lomvardou 40 & 72, Zakynthos Town) runs between four and eight ferries daily, depending on the season, between Zakynthos Town and Kyllini in the Peloponnese. Occasional international ferries call in on their way to/from Igoumenitsa, Sami (Kefallonia), and Bari and Brindisi, Italy.

Ionian Ferries also sells tickets for high-season services to Brindisi, Italy via Igoumenitsa and

Corfu on Minoan Lines (p729), Superfast (p729) and Blue Star Ferries (p729). Ventouris (p729) goes to Bari.

From the northern port of Agios Nikolaos a ferry serves Pesada in southern Kefallonia twice daily from May to October; **Chionis Tours** (☐ 26950 48996; Lomvardou 8, Zakynthos Town) sells tickets. There are barely any buses to these two ports though, so unless you have wheels or a ride, it's far easier and cheaper to cross to mainland Kyllini from Zakynthos Town and catch another ferry to Kefallonia.

BUS

KTEL Bus Station (☐ 26950 22255; www.ktel-zakynthos.gr; Zakynthos Town) On the bypass to the west of Zakynthos Town. A bus runs from St Denis church at the harbour to the station. Services include Athens (€26.10, six hours, three daily), Corinth (€18.80, four daily), Patra (€8, 3½ hours, three daily) and Thessaloniki (€49.60, 10 hours, two weekly). Budget an additional €8 for the ferry to Kyllini.

BOAT SERVICES FROM ZAKYNTHOS

DESTINATION	DEPARTS	TIME	FARE	FREQUENCY
Kyllini (Peloponnese)	Zakynthos Town	1hr	€7.50	10 daily
Pesada (Kefallonia)	Agios Nikolaos	1½hr	€8	2 daily, seasonal

❶ Getting Around

There's no bus between Zakynthos Town and the airport; a taxi costs around €12.

Frequent buses go from Zakynthos Town's KTEL bus station to the developed resorts of Alikes, Tsilivi, Argasi, Laganas and Kalamaki (all €1.60). Several useful local buses take the upper or lower main roads to Katastari (€3) and Volimes (€3.40). Bus services to other villages are infrequent.

Rent cars (from €40 in high season) and motorcycles at the airport or in larger resorts.

Auto Moto Sakis (☑26950 23928; www.automotosakis.gr; Dessila 4, Zakynthos Town; car/scooter per day €40/20; ☺8am-4pm & 6pm-9pm) This reliable outfit rents cars and scooters. Run by Mr Sakis.

Europcar (☑26950 43313; www.europcar-greece.com; Zakynthos Town) At the airport.

Hertz (☑26950 45706; www.hertz.gr; Lomvardou 38, Zakynthos Town; ☺8am-2pm & 5.30pm-9.30pm) Locations in town and at the airport.

Zakynthos Town Ζάκυνθος

POP 9772

Wrapped around an enormous blue bay and peppered with lively restaurants, Zakynthos Town is the pulsing capital and port of the island. The town was devastated by the 1953 earthquake, but was reconstructed with arcaded streets, imposing squares and gracious neoclassical public buildings. A Venetian fortress looks down from a hill on the hubbub of town life.

❍ Sights & Activities

Plateia Agiou Markou, ordinarily the heartbeat of town life, is currently a victim of the ongoing financial crisis, and is closed until further notice as it awaits reconstruction.

★ **Byzantine Museum**   MUSEUM
(☑26950 42714; Plateia Solomou; admission €3; ☺8.30am-3pm Tue-Sun) Two levels of fabulous ecclesiastical art, rescued from churches razed by the earthquake. The beautiful building overlooks the main plaza. Inside, the 16th-century St Andreas Monastery has been artfully replicated to house its restored frescoes.

Museum of Solomos   MUSEUM
(☑26950 48982; Plateia Agiou Markou 15; adult/child €4/free; ☺9am-2pm) The museum houses the memorabilia and archives of Dionysios Solomos (1798–1857), who was born on Zakynthos and is regarded as the father of modern Greek poetry. His *Hymn to Liberty* became the Greek national anthem.

Church of Dionysios   CHURCH
This church for the patron saint of the island, in Zakynthos Town's south, holds amazing giltwork and frescoes. Its **ecclesiastical museum** (admission €2; ☺9am-1pm & 5-9pm) contains intriguing icons from the Monastery of Strofades (home to Dionysios for several years), plus scrolls from the 13th and 14th centuries. Every 24 August the curiously preserved 400-year-old body of St Dionysios is paraded in the streets.

Kastro   RUIN
(☑26950 48099; admission €3; ☺8am-3pm Tue-Sun) This peaceful, shady and pine tree–filled ruined Venetian fortress sits high above Zakynthos Town. It's 2.5km from town; use the car park in Bochali and walk 300m.

Big Game Fishing   FISHING
(☑26950 52521, 6977357590; www.biggamefishingzante.com; boat charter (up to 6 people) per hr €120) Captain Yiannis can take you deep-sea fishing for swordfish, tuna and spearfish. All game caught is released back into the water. Find his harbourside mooring roughly opposite Hotel Strada Marina (p668).

🛌 Sleeping

Hotel Alba   PENSION €
(☑26950 26641; www.albahotel.gr; L Ziva 38; s/d €44/55; ✼@🖥) Alba ticks the budget boxes with clean, smallish, marble-accented rooms with old-fashioned bathroom, plus balcony, TV and fridge. Nice management and centrally located.

Hotel Palatino   HOTEL €€
(☑26950 27780; www.palatinohotel.gr; Kolokotroni 10; d/tr from €75/95; ✼@🖥) Slick and central, Palatino has a palatial lobby and 70 stylish rooms with minibar, TV, thick carpets, large bathroom and fresh powder-blue walls. A few have sea-view balconies.

Hotel Strada Marina   HOTEL €€

(📞26950 42761; www.stradamarina.gr; Lombardou 14; s/d/q incl breakfast from €50/75/90; ✳🛜🖳) Smack on the main harbourfront, this recently revived early-1900s giant was the first luxe hotel in town; it retains an elegant appeal with international-standard rooms boasting wide views of the marina. There's a lovely rooftop terrace **restaurant** and a pool commanding the best 360-degree views in town.

Hotel Diana   HOTEL €€

(📞26950 28547; www.dianahotels.gr; Plateia Agiou Markou; s/d/q incl breakfast €55/70/85; ✳@🛜) Salubrious and businesslike, these wood-floored rooms have a balcony, satellite TV, swish bathroom and fridge. There's also a two-bedroom family suite, plus a roof garden.

Plaza Hotel   HOTEL €€

(📞26950 45733; www.plazante.gr; Kolokotronis 2; s/d €75/85) Plaza feels new, with marble floors and plush rooms with sea-view balconies, modern bathroom, fridge, TV and safety deposit box. There's a lift.

🍴 Eating & Drinking

⭐**Malanos**   TAVERNA €

(📞26950 45936; www.malanos.gr; Agiou Athanasiou, Kiri; mains €7-12; ⏰noon-4pm & 8pm-late) Popular for Zakynthos specialities, this family-run taverna with simple tables and a covered porch serves up hits like rooster, rabbit and wild boar. On the south edge of town, in the countryside (ask a local for directions).

Mesathes   MEDITERRANEAN €

(📞26950 49315; Ethnikis Antistaseos; mains €8.50; ⏰lunch & dinner) On a side street behind the Byzantine Museum, Mesathes has a rose-hued interior and a few tables outside. The owner plays a mean tune on the guitar to accompany beautifully presented dishes like rabbit *stifadho,* grilled shrimp and panna cotta that melts on your tongue.

Base   BAR

(www.basecafe.gr) Base commands the flow through Plateia Agiou Markou, dispensing coffee, drinks and music to a people-watching local crowd.

Around Zakynthos

Transport of your own is really necessary to unlock the charms of Zakynthos.

⊙ Sights

Amid all of the southern sprawl, **Vasilikos Peninsula**, bordering the Bay of Laganas, remains the most forested and serene. Nevertheless, development has started – **Banana Beach**, for example, is a long, narrow strip of golden sand on the peninsula's northern side full of crowds, water sports and umbrellas. **Kaminia** is a decent option. Zakynthos' best beach, long, sandy **Gerakas**, is on the other side of the peninsula, facing into Laganas Bay. Note, however, that this is one of the island's main turtle-nesting beaches, so access is forbidden between dusk and dawn from May to October; follow conservation recommendations, available at the booth near the beach access path.

With transport, you can reach the raw terrain of the far southwest of the island. Beyond the traditional village of **Keri**, a tiny road leads – past a taverna claiming the biggest Greek flag in the country – to **Cape Keri** and its lighthouse above sheer cliffs, just beyond which you'll find a coastal viewpoint with benches and a kiosk selling snacks.

Scenic and sometimes happily confusing roads lead north from here through beautiful wooded hill country, where locals sell honey and other seasonal products. The route leads to the few land-accessible west-coast coves such as **Limnionas** or **Kambi**, and to inland gems like **Kiliomeno**, whose **Church of St Nikolaos** features an unusual roofless campanile. The bell tower of the church in **Agios Leon** was formerly a windmill. Lovely **Louha** tumbles down a valley surrounded by woodlands and pastures. **Exo Hora** has a collection of dry wells and what is reputed to be the oldest olive tree on the island. **Volimes** is the unabashed sales centre for traditional products such as olive oil, honey, tablecloths and rugs.

The east coast north of Zakynthos Town is filled with resorts, but the further north you go the more charming the island becomes. The road narrows at the ferry village **Agios Nikolaos**, where development is slight. Carry on to reach pastoral, breezy **Cape Skinari**.

Boats leave from Agios Nikolaos and Cape Skinari for the **Blue Caves**, sea-level caverns that pierce the limestone coastal cliffs. Boats enter the caves, where the water turns a translucent blue from 9am to 2pm when sunlight shines in.

The boats also go to famous **Shipwreck Beach**, magnificent photos of which grace every tourist brochure about Zakynthos; it's in **Navagio Bay**, about 3km west of Volimes at the northwest tip of the island. In low season it is indeed gorgeous, but in high season some say it feels like a D-Day beach landing at Normandy, so crowded are the waters – go early in the day. From land, a precariously perched **lookout platform** (signposted between Anafonitria and Volimes) gives great views. **Potamitis Trips** (📞26950 31132; www.potamitisbros.gr; Cape Skinari) and **Karidis** (📞6974492193; Agios Nikolaos) run boat trips to just the Blue Caves (€7.50), or a combo trip that includes Shipwreck Beach (€15).

🛏 Sleeping

Book villas through **Aresti Club** (📞26950 26151; www.aresti.com.gr), and houses around the Vasilikos Peninsula through **Ionian Eco Villagers** (📞in the UK 0871 711 5065; www.relaxing-holidays.com).

Panorama Studios APARTMENT €
(📞26950 31013; www.panorama-studios.gr; Agios Nikolaos; studios €40; P❄🤙) The English-speaking hosts offer excellent studios with sea views on the main road 600m uphill from Agios Nikolaos, set in a lovely garden.

★**Villa Christina** APARTMENT €€
(📞26950 49208; www.villachristina.gr; Limni Keriou; studio €55, apt €65-80, 5-person maisonette €150; ☺May-Oct; P❄@❄) In an Edenic olive grove, these clay-coloured studios sit in flowering gardens teeming with birdsong. Apartments are clean, pine-accented affairs with balcony and kitchenette. There's a library/TV room, small shop, barbecue areas and a sparkling pool. Found between Limni Keriou and the Laganas road.

Windmill PENSION €€
(📞26950 31132; www.potamitisbros.gr; d €130; ❄) This converted windmill and old stone house enjoy a fantastic cliff-top location in Cape Skinari. Rooms have cool tiled floors, exposed stone interiors and many boutique flourishes. Steps lead to a lovely swimming area. There are cooking facilities and a cafe-bar.

🍴 Eating

Restaurants around Zakynthos are pretty bland. Keri, Limnionas and Kambi have good basic tavernas in high season only.

Louha's Coffee Shop CAFE €
(📞26950 48426; Louha; mains €4-7; ☺May-Oct) Eat or drink under a vine-shaded terrace opposite the Church of St John the Theologian. Good local wine accompanies one daily special, salads and soothing views of cypress-dotted hills.

★**Alitzerinoi** TAVERNA €€
(📞26950 48552; www.alitzerinoi.gr; Kiliomeno; mains €8-14; ☺9am-late, dinner only Fri-Sun in winter) Locals make the trek to the mountain hamlet of Kiliomeno for great island cooking at Alitzerinoi, which uses local produce and cheeses. Eat inside their cosy, 18th-century stone house for live music come evening, or out on the terraced courtyard that spills down the hillside.

KYTHIRA ΚΥΘΗΡΑ

POP 4041
The island of Kythira (*kee-thih-rah*) dangles 12km off the tip of the Peloponnese's Lakonian peninsula, between the Aegean and Ionian Seas. It's so quiet even the cats are yawning. Often veiled in sea mists like sudden shrouds across its rugged terrain, Kythira is for much of the year really a ghost land, an unspoilt wilderness of lush valleys, canyons and cliffs falling abruptly into the vivid blue sea. Despite its proximity to the Peloponnese, it is considered a part of the Ionian Island group, and while the stands of cypress trees help remind you, there is something time-trapped about this isolated isle, as if it simply forgot to join the 21st century. The island's population is spread among more than 40 rural villages, which with their sugar-cube design style have a distinctly Cycladic feel, punctuated by neo-classical manors and old-style *kafeneia*.

Tourism remains very low-key – except in July and August, when the island goes mad. Descending visitors include the Kythiran diaspora returning from abroad (especially Australia). For the rest of the year, Kythira and its fine beaches are wonderfully peaceful.

ℹ Getting There & Away

AIR
Kythira Airport (KIT), 10km southeast of Potamos, has **Olympic Air** (📞801 801 0101; www.olympicair.com) flights to Athens (€63, 50 minutes, two daily). Sky Express (p115) operates

> ## ℹ KYTHIRA RESOURCES
> For more detail on Kythira, visit www.kythira.gr, www.kithera.gr, www.kythira.info or www.visitkythera.gr. The informative English-language newspaper *Kythera* is available in some travel agencies, hotels and shops. Walkers should find *Kythira on Foot: 32 Carefully Selected Walking Routes* (€10) by Frank van Weerde (for sale around Hora and Potamos), or check www.kytherahiking.com for self-guided walks.

Kythira & Antikythira

IONIAN ISLANDS

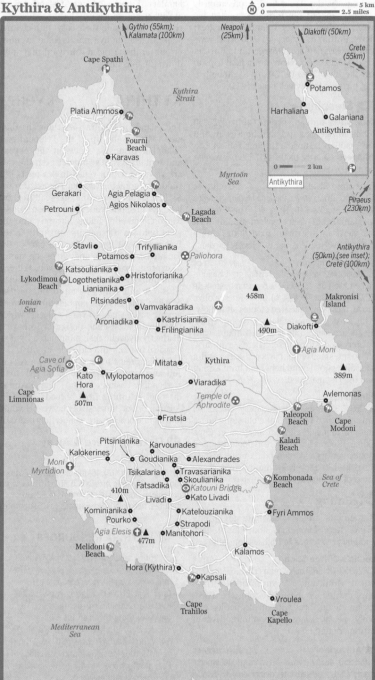

0 ——————— 5 km
0 ——————— 2.5 miles

Gythio (55km);
Kalamata (100km)

Neapoli
(25km)

Diakofti (50km)

Crete
(55km)

Cape Spathi

Kythira
Strait

Potamos

Harhaliana

Galaniana

Platia Ammos

Antikythira

Fourni
Beach

Karavas

Myrtoön
Sea

0 ——— 2 km

Antikythira

Gerakari

Agia Pelagia

Agios Nikolaos

Lagada
Beach

Piraeus
(230km)

Petrouni

Stavli

Trifyllianika

Paliohora

Antikythira
(50km) (see inset);
Crete (100km)

Potamos

Katsoulianika

Hristoforianika

Lykodimou
Beach

Logothetianika

Lianianika

458m

Makronisi
Island

Pitsinades

Vamvakaradika

Ionian
Sea

Aroniadika

Kastrisianika

Frilingianika

490m

Diakofti

Cave of
Agia Sofia

Mitata

Kythira

Agia Moni

Kato
Hora

Mylopotamos

Viaradika

389m

Cape
Limnionas

507m

Temple of
Aphrodite

Avlemonas

Fratsia

Paleopoli
Beach

Cape
Modoni

Kaladi
Beach

Pitsinianika

Karvounades

Kalokerines

Goudianika

Alexandrades

Moni
Myrtidion

Tsikalaria

Travasarianika

Kombonada
Beach

Sea of
Crete

Fatsadika

Skoulianika

Katouni Bridge

410m

Livadi

Kato Livadi

Kominianika

Katelouzianika

Fyri Ammos

Pourko

Strapodi

Agia Elesis

Manitohori

Melidoni
Beach

477m

Kalamos

Hora (Kythira)

Kapsali

Cape
Trahilos

Vroulea

Cape
Kapello

Mediterranean
Sea

a route to Zakynthos, Kefallonia, Preveza and Corfu (from June to September).

BOAT

The main connection is between Diakofti and Neapoli in the Peloponnese. Get tickets at the port just before departure, or at Kithira Travel (p672).

LANE Lines (p729) calls at Diakofti on its weekly routes between Piraeus, Kythira, Antikythira, Kissamos-Kastelli (Crete) and Kalamata and Gythio (Peloponnese). Get info and tickets from **Porfyra Travel** (☑ 27360 31888; www.kythira.info; Livadi) in Livadi.

DESTINATION	TIME	FARE	FREQUENCY
Gythio	2½hr	€10	1 weekly
Kalamata	5hr	€20	1 weekly
Kissamos-Kastelli	2½-4hr	€20	4 weekly (2 via Antikythira, €9)
Neapoli	1¼hr	€11	1 daily
Piraeus	6½hr	€25	2 weekly

Getting Around

Occasional buses operate in August. **Taxis** (☑ 6944305433) are pricey and charge around €25 between Hora and the airport. Given that the island is large it's better to hire your own wheels at the airport on arrival. Alternatively, car-hire companies can drop off a car at your hotel.

Panayotis Rent A Car (☑ 6944263757, 27360 31004; www.panayotis-rent-a-car.gr; car/scooter per day from €45/15) Panayotis has a fleet of 120 cars – including 4x4s, small cars, motorbikes and scooters – as well as an airport branch and numerous offices across the island.

Drakakis Tours (☑ 27360 31160; www.drakakistours.gr; Livadi) Cars, vans and 4WD.

Hora (Kythira)
Χώρα (Κύθηρα)

POP 281

Hilltop Hora (or Kythira), the island's capital, is smartly attired in Cycladic white-and-blue trim, and perches on a long, slender ridge that stretches north from an impressive 13th-century Venetian *kastro* overlooking the sea. Most of the action is based around the town square, while the shops that line the road to the *kastro* are particularly tasteful, ranging from fine antiques to bespoke jewellery.

Sights & Activities

★**Kastro**   CASTLE
(⊙8am-3pm) **FREE** Hora's beautiful Venetian *kastro* was built in the 13th century and is one of Kythira's highlights. At its southern extremity, past the **Church of Panagia**, you come to a sheer cliff with a stunning view of Kapsali and, on a clear day, Antikythira.

Pyrgos House   TOUR
(☑6989863140; www.pyrgoshouse.com; Plateia Potamos) Offers a range of outdoor pursuits, from abseiling (€25 per person, minimum group of three, Thursday 4pm) to guided walks around Hora's *kastro* (€15 per person, minimum group of four, Wednesday morning 10am) and churches.

Sleeping & Eating

Castello Rooms   PENSION €
(☑27360 31069; www.kythera-castelloapts.gr; Spyridonos Staï; studios from €40; ❈ ☎) Eminently cosy studios with white walls, kitchenette and balcony in a garden of flowers and fruit trees set back from the main street. The owners are super friendly. You'll find it down the bottom of the street that runs to the *kastro*.

Hotel Margarita   PENSION €€
(☑27360 31711; www.hotel-margarita.com; off Spyridonos Staï; s/d/tr €60/90/110; ⊙Easter-Oct; ❈ @) White-walled, blue-shuttered, immaculate and charming, this hotel offers 12 atmospheric rooms (all with TV and telephone) in a renovated 19th-century mansion, featuring B&W marble floors and a quirky old spiral staircase. The terrace affords fantastic *kastro* and sea views.

Corte O Suites   APARTMENT €€
(☑27360 39139; www.corteo.gr; studio/2-bedroom apt incl breakfast €100/190; ⊙Apr-Oct; ❈ @ ☎) Modern, minimal decor in these three beautiful, kitchen-equipped, two-bedroomed apartments (and single studio), which have private terraces and sea or valley views. The setting is in a late-18th-century house a spit away from the *kastro*.

★**Zorba's**   TAVERNA €
(☑27360 31655; mains €9; ⊙dinner Tue-Sun) The interior might look simple at first

THE BIRTH OF APHRODITE

Mythology suggests that Aphrodite, goddess of love, desire and beauty, was born offshore of Kythira, near Avlemonas. She rose resplendent from the foam upon a giant scallop (famously painted by Botticelli), where Cronos threw Uranus' sex organs after castrating him. The goddess of love then re-emerged near Pafos in Cyprus, so both islands haggle over her exact birthplace.

glance but don't be fooled: freshly displayed meat in the refrigerator is seasoned with local herbs and spices and fired on the open grill. Superbly succulent lamb chops and huge salads. Recommended.

Drinking

Fos Fanari CAFE
(📞27360 31644; ⏰8am-late; 🛜) This spacious cafe sells fresh croissants, juices and homemade ice cream, and has a well-stocked bar and views of the sea and mountains.

Shopping

Aquarium JEWELLERY
(📞6977287741; www.aquarium.com; ⏰10am-9pm) On the street leading down the hill to the main square of Hora, Aquarium is tucked between souvenir shops and not always open, but persevere: within is the eponymous tank of fish radiating light onto exquisite one-off pieces of bespoke jewellery.

ℹ️ Information

Banks with ATMs and the post office are on the central square.

Kithira Travel (📞in Hora 27360 31390, in Potamos 27360 31848; www.kithiratravel.gr; ⏰9am-2pm & 6pm-8pm Mon-Sat) For flights and boat tickets. Helpful staff.

Police station (📞27360 31206) Near the *kastro*.

Kapsali Καψάλι

POP 34

Set 2km south of Hora, photogenic Kapsali sits by two peaceful bays with tavernas and accommodation strung around it. The protected harbour served as Hora's port in Venetian times, and the ochre beach has sheltered swimming. Kapsali's curving bays look dazzling when viewed from Hora's *kastro*. There are some chic cafes opening up here.

The rocky island offshore is known as **Itra** ('cooking pot') because when clouds gather above it locals say it looks like a steaming pot.

Panayotis Rent a Car (p671) on the waterfront rents canoes, pedal boats, cars, mopeds and bicycles. **Kaptain Spiros** (📞6974022079) takes daily cruises on his glass-bottomed boat (from €12 per person), including to Itra, where you can swim. **Kapsali Diving School** (📞27360 37400; www.kytheradive.gr) has recently set up at the harbour here; they run PADI open-water courses (€380) and can take you to various reef and cave dives (€40).

🛏️ Sleeping

Spitia Vassili PENSION €
(📞27360 31125; www.kythirabungalowsvasili.gr; d/tr incl breakfast from €45/55; 🅿️❄️🛜) This tree-lined complex overlooks Kapsali Beach. Rooms are light and welcoming, with wood ceilings and floors, shabby-chic furniture and wrought-iron beds. The more expensive larger rooms feature bay views.

Aphrodite Apartments APARTMENT €
(📞27360 31328; www.hotel-aphrodite.gr; d/tr/q from €55/70/75; ❄️🛜) Run by Irene and Yiannis, roadside Aphrodite dishes out the love with cosy, spacious rooms and apartments with kitchenette and balcony; you're barely a minute from the sea. Rooms are cleaned daily. The top floor has the best views.

DON'T MISS

MYLOPOTAMOS ΜΥΛΟΠΟΤΑΜΟΣ

Do not miss quaint Mylopotamos, nestled in a small valley 13km north of Hora. Its central square is flanked by a charming church and bell tower, and by authentically traditional **Kafeneio O Platanos** (📞27360 33397; mains €6-8), which in summer becomes an outdoor restaurant. Staff can help with accommodation. Close by, **O Delis** (📞27360 33813; www.odelis.gr; mains €8-12; ⏰8am-late) serves up excellent Greek dishes in the shade of a plane tree by a peaceful stream.

The **Neraïda waterfall** ('water nymph'), with luxuriant greenery along the path and an aquamarine pool, feels like pure poetry as it changes colour in shifting light. Take the right-hand fork in the road after the church and follow the signs. A portal leads into Mylopotamos' cool, crumbling **kastro**, a warren of well-preserved (locked) little churches along a spectacular promontory that has views down a gorge and to the sea. To reach it, take the left-hand fork in the road after the church and follow the signs to Kato Hora.

Other fabulous walks start in Mylopotamos; refer to *Kythira on Foot: 32 Carefully Selected Walking Routes* (€10) by Frank van Weerde. The most picturesque and challenging walk heads along a gorge with ruins of former flour mills; you'll pass waterfalls and swimming holes along the way.

★**El Sol Hotel** HOTEL €€
(☎27360 31766; www.elsolhotels.gr; d €120-140, 5-person apt €170-180, both incl breakfast; 🅿🌐🐕🛜🏊) These striking white-cube apartments have Olympian views of the sea and the dramatic backdrop of the *kastro*. Immaculate, minimalist rooms have balcony, modern bathroom and coffee-making facilities; there's a terrific pool, plenty of loungers and a breakfast room packed with board games for rainy days (don't hold your breath!). Signposted off the Hora–Kapsali road.

✖ Eating & Drinking

★**Filio** TAVERNA €
(☎27360 31549; Kalamos; mains €7; ⏱lunch & dinner Jun-Sep) Though 5km outside of Kapsali (signposted near Kalamos), Filio is worth the orienteering it takes to find it. In the shade of fig trees and glow of blooming roses, feast on old faves like braised rabbit in tomato sauce, eggplant stuffed with meat, and Kytherian sausages.

Goldfish Waffle House FUSION €
(☎6988766716; mains €6; ⏱breakfast, lunch & dinner; 🛜) More than just a waffle house, this is the coolest joint on the strip, with orange chairs and baby-blue tables right by the waterfront. Fusion food with noodles, omelettes and, of course, waffles soaked in ice cream.

Hytra TAVERNA €
(☎27360 37200; mains €7-9; ⏱lunch & dinner; 🛜) Slap-bang in the middle of the waterfront, this traditional joint with the green awning dishes up casseroles, tasty spinach pies, fire-grilled lamb chops, veal steak and plenty of fresh seafood.

Fox Anglais BAR
(🛜) With its wood ceiling and cosy bar there's a nautical feel to this friendly haunt on the waterfront.

Potamos Ποταμός
POP 476

Pretty, hillside Potamos is full of cafes and restaurants, and has a bank and a travel agent. The busiest place on the island, its Sunday-morning **flea market** attracts locals, while its flower-filled central square is great for people-watching any day of the week.

✖ Eating & Drinking

Taverna Panaretos TAVERNA €€
(☎27360 34290; mains €7-12; ⏱lunch & dinner daily Mar-Oct, Thu-Sun Nov-Feb) On the main square with alfresco dining at cream-coloured tables and chairs, Panaretos sits in the fragrant shade of pine trees and excels with dishes using home-grown produce, such as wild goat with olive oil and oregano sauce, pork fillet with thyme, and various *mezedhes*.

Kafe Astikon CAFE
(☎27360 33141; ⏱7am-late; 🛜) Bags of atmosphere await you in this high-ceilinged shadowy music bar opposite the main square: coral-green walls, leather 'egg' chairs, an illuminated penny-farthing and a stage set and ready for impromptu jam sessions. Also serves pizza, pasta and breakfast.

Agia Pelagia Αγία Πελαγία
POP 419

Kythira's northern port of Agia Pelagia is a simple waterfront village set amid stunning cliffs and wooded inland valleys. Its sand-and-pebble beaches have vibrant azure waters, but better still are the magnificent volcanic beaches south of the headland, ending at **Lagada Beach**. The red, pink and tawny beaches are backed by cliffs, and also make for a good walk.

🛌 Sleeping & Eating

Hotel Pelagia Aphrodite HOTEL €€
(☎27360 33926; www.pelagia-aphrodite.com; s/d/tr incl breakfast €80/90/125; ⏱Easter-Oct; 🅿🌐🛜) Right on the beach and run by returning Aussie Kythirans, this lovely hotel has 13 terrific new rooms with wood ceilings and huge, sea-facing balconies. The original rooms are even closer to the waves; whitewashed and simple, with balcony, TV and bathroom. Downstairs is a welcoming breakfast room. Find it at the southern end of town.

Maneas Beach Hotel HOTEL €€
(☎27360 33503; www.maneashotel.com; d with/without sea view incl breakfast €120/90; 🅿🌐🛜) This upscale beach hotel has a contemporary feel, with rooms boasting modern units, fridge, flat-screen TV and large balcony affording awesome views of the sea.

★**Kaleris** GREEK €
(☎27360 33461; mains €9; ⏱lunch & dinner Easter-Oct) Kaleris sits in the cool shade of tamarisk trees and is renowned for its creative cuisine: think dishes like yoghurt salad with smoked aubergine, homemade filo pastry parcels with feta drizzled with local thyme-infused honey, beef *stifadho* and *vrechtoladea* (traditional rusks) and homemade beef tortellini. The place has been here since 1954. Owner Yiannis is a charismatic host.

Akrogiali SEAFOOD €

(mains €7; ⊙11am-late) A great waterfront spot for seafood; keep an eye out for the awning sign with the mermaid riding a dolphin. Red mullet, mackerel, bream, mussels and shrimp are but a few dishes on offer.

Around Kythira

Get your own transport to explore beautiful back roads: hills, cliffs, hidden beaches, stands of cypress and olive groves. The monasteries of **Agia Moni** and (especially) **Agia Elesis** are mountain refuges with superb views; beautiful **Moni Myrtidion** stands on peaceful grounds on a plateau above the sea.

North of Hora, in **Kato Livadi**, find a small but excellent collection of artwork in the **Museum of Byzantine and Post-Byzantine Art on Kythira** (☑27360 31731; adult/child €2/free; ⊙8.30am-2.30pm Tue-Sun). Just north of Kato Livadi make a detour to see iconic **Katouni Bridge**. The largest stone bridge in Greece, it was built by the British in the 19th century, when Kythira was part of the British Protectorate.

Continue northeast through **Paleopoli**, with its wide, pebbled beach; and to the pretty fishing village, **Avlemonas** – sugar-white and huddled around an emerald cove. Archaeologists spent years searching for evidence of a temple near Avlemonas, known as **Aphrodite's birthplace**. See if you can spot the **kofinidia** (two small rock protrusions): the sex organs of Uranus that Cronos tossed into the sea foam. Top beaches include nearby **Kaladi**, with its grey-brown stones. It takes a spectacular drive down twisty roads to reach the mauve-grey stone beach **Fyri Ammos**. **Kombonada Beach** is another good bet.

The island's port, **Diakofti**, is picturesque to zip through, especially with its offshore shipwreck, but there's no need to linger.

In the northeast, the spectacularly situated ruins of the Byzantine capital of **Paliohora** are amazing to explore – they sit atop an isolated promontory surrounded by gorges.

Further north, the verdant, attractive village of **Karavas** is near the broad grey beach at **Platia Ammos**.

🛏 Sleeping & Eating

Maryianni APARTMENT €€

(☑27360 33316; www.maryianni.gr; Avlemonas; 3-person studio €110, apt €120-130; P❄) Cycladic-style white-and-blue studios stack above the Avlemonas seaside. Rooms are far above average, with boutique flourishes like wrought-iron beds, classical art and choice furniture. They have kitchens and terraces with amazing sea views. The apartments are superior still, with added luxuries like marble tables and more space. Free use of kids' and adults' bikes.

Skandia TAVERNA €

(☑27360 33700; Paleopoli; mains €6-11; ⊙lunch & dinner daily Apr-Oct, Fri-Sun Nov-Mar) This delightful taverna offers authentic Greek fare and freshly sourced food, ranging from grilled fish and fish soup to roasted eggplant. Relax under the spreading elm trees, away from the madding crowds.

Psarotaverna O Manolis SEAFOOD €

(☑27360 33748; Diakofti; mains €6-9; ⊙lunch & dinner; 🐾) Locals head here for the excellent fresh fish and to watch the boat pull in from Piraeus under moonlight.

Pierros TAVERNA €

(☑27360 31014; www.pieros.gr; Livadi; mains €6-8; ⊙lunch & dinner) Since 1933 this family-run favourite has served up no-nonsense Greek staples.

Sotiris SEAFOOD €

(☑27360 33722; Avlemonas; fish per kg €30-75; ⊙lunch & dinner, reduced hours low season) A popular spot for seafood and fish soup.

Varkoula TAVERNA €

(☑27360 34224; Platia Ammos; mains €6-12; ⊙hours vary) Sup on freshly cooked fish accompanied by the tunes of the bouzouki-strumming owner. Ring ahead to confirm erratic hours.

ANTIKYTHIRA
ΑΝΤΙΚΥΘΗΡΑ

Given that the tourist infrastructure in tiny 9.5km by 3km Antikythera is nonapparent, very few visit this sun-blasted rock. Located 38km southeast of Kythira and laying claim to a permanent population of just 40-odd people, it is arguably the remotest island in Greece, and has only one settlement, **Potamos**. Here you'll find a doctor, police officer, telephone, *kafeneio*-cum-taverna and a monastery. (Oh, and a heliport.) It has no post office or bank. Rooms for rent open in summer only. Check www.antikythira.gr for details. Lane Lines (p729) calls at Antikythira on its route between Kythira (€9, 1¾ hours, three weekly) and Kissamos-Kastelli in Crete (€10, two hours, one weekly). Some boats stop at Monemvasia and Gythio in the Peloponnese, or Piraeus (€24, 10½ hours). Contact Porfyra Travel (p671) in Livadi (Kythira).

Understand
Greece

Greece Today

Greek resilience has been stretched thin, leaving many disillusioned and apprehensive of a future that no longer necessarily includes them in the eurozone. The continued deterioration of the Greek economy is taking its toll on virtually every aspect of society. Few have been unaffected by savage wage and pension cuts, new taxes, record joblessness and thousands of shops and businesses closing. Meanwhile, the government threatens to capsize due to its drastic attempts to keep the country afloat.

Best in Print

The Odyssey (Homer; 8th century BC) Plagued by Poseidon, Odysseus struggles to return home to Ithaca.

Zorba the Greek (Nikos Kazantzakis; 1946) A spiritual bible to many; one man's unquenchable lust for life.

The Magus (John Fowles; 1966) Creepy mind games set on fictional island Phraxos.

Falling For Icarus: A Journey among the Cretans (Rory MacLean; 2004) A writer fulfills his ambition to build his own plane in the land of Icarus.

Colossus of Maroussi (Henry Miller; 1941) A travelogue of prewar Greece and heralded as Miller's best work.

Best on Film

300 (2007) Testosterone-fuelled retelling of the Spartans' epic stand against the might of the Persian army.

Mamma Mia (2008) Skopelos shines to the soundtrack of ABBA.

Guns of Navarone (1961) Allied soldiers enter Nazi-occupied Greece in this compelling boy's-own thriller.

Shirley Valentine (1989) Classic Greek island romance on Mykonos.

Captain Corelli's Mandolin (2001) Lavish retelling of Louis de Bernières' novel, set in occupied Greece.

Before Midnight (2013) The third in a trilogy following the relationship of a French-American couple, filmed in the Peloponnese.

Austerity Measures

The multi-billion-euro bailouts loaned to Greece by its European Union and International Monetary Fund creditors in 2009, and again in 2010, 2011 and 2015, have come with strong strings attached. To secure them, the Greek government was forced to implement austerity measures that saw severe wage cuts, while living costs soared at an unpalatable rate. At the same time, the rising unemployment rate has reached around 26%. The start of 2015 saw approximately 59 business close per day with the economic growth predicted for 2014 nowhere to be seen.

The austerity measures and declining living standards have also widened Greece's stark economic and social disparities – the hedonistic lifestyles of Athenians taking weekend jaunts to Mykonos bear no resemblance to struggling pensioners or workers in rural Greece. Homelessness, suicides and once-rare violent crime are on the rise. Growing anger and social unrest has sparked mass demonstrations and violent clashes with police. Disillusioned young Greeks are bearing the brunt of years of economic mismanagement – the country's most educated generation face bleak prospects as youth unemployment tips 60%. There is a feeling of despair that is decidedly un-Greek.

The Rize of Syriza & Grexit Crisis

In January 2015, Alexis Tsipras took the helm as prime minister, wooing voters with an anti-austerity platform. It was the first ever election win for radical left-wing Syriza, which ousted the ruling conservative New Democrats. To reach a majority, Syriza established a coalition with right-wing Independent Greeks (ANEL), unlikely bedfellows united by their mutual condemnation of the bailout program. Initially, Tsipras stuck to his guns and June 2015 saw Greece become the first first-world nation to go into arrears with the EU and IMF. Attempts to negotiate a new bailout and avoid default were unsuccessful as Tsipras took the offer back to Greece and held a referendum. Over 61% of voters were not willing to accept the bailout conditions.

The week that followed was one of turmoil. Greek banks closed and began running out of cash, and markets around the world fell as the EU produced a detailed plan for a possible Grexit – Greece's removal from the EU. At the eleventh hour, Tsipras secured an €86 billion bailout loan – but the austerity measures attached were even more rigorous than those proposed before the referendum and many felt that, with Greek banks on the brink of collapse, Tsipras had been bullied into accepting the terms. Further tax hikes, pension reforms, and privatisation of €50 billion worth of public companies have left many viewing Greece as a financial ward of Europe.

Dissent within Syriza and ANEL, brought on by hardliners opposed to the bailout, led Tsipras to resign in August 2015 and return to the polls in September. This was Greece's fourth election in just over three years. The outcome was an unexpectedly large victory for Tsipras, just six seats short of an absolute majority. Nevertheless, voter turnout was 57%, the lowest recorded in Greece. For many Greeks, choosing between the austerity measures and Grexit has become akin to rearranging deck chairs on the Titanic.

Immigration & Asylum

The primary entry point for immigrants to Europe, Greece is seeing unprecedented numbers of illegal migrants from Afghanistan, Iraq, Syria and Africa via the porous Turkish border and Greece's outlying islands. With over 1000 immigrants arriving in Greece daily in 2015, islands like Lesvos, Chios and Kos are feeling huge pressure on their resources. The United Nations High Commission for Refugees (UNHCR) has declared it an emergency situation, while international criticism for Greece's immigrant policies, and the conditions in which immigrants are held, remains strong.

Economic decline has fuelled xenophobia within Greece, sparking anti-immigrant rallies and growing hostility, yet deep-rooted Greek hospitality has reared its noble head, particularly on the islands. Despite their own financial struggles, many Greeks independently offer food and clothing to immigrants while local doctors volunteer to care for them.

Brain Drain

The country's once-shrinking villages are welcoming a new wave of nouveau poor Greeks. Families of out-of-work professionals and tradesmen, along with unemployed university graduates, are returning to ancestral homes on the islands to help with family businesses, often in tourism or farming. An increase in agricultural employment is one of the by-products of the times, going back to Greece's traditional strength and way of life. An increasing number of educated under-30s are also migrating to other parts of Europe, America and Australia in hopes of finding employment.

GDP: **€218 BILLION (US$238 BILLION)**

PER CAPITA INCOME: **€16,842 (US$18,377)**

INFLATION: **-2.2%**

UNEMPLOYMENT: **25.6%**

EXTERNAL DEBT: **€329 BILLION (US$359 BILLION)**

if Greece were 100 people

92 would be Greek
8 would be other

belief systems
(% of population)

98
Greek Orthodox

1.3
Muslim

0.7
Other

population per sq km

GREECE   USA   UK

= 30 people

History

A doorstep between Asia Minor and Europe, through ancient and modern times Greece has been tied to the rising and waning fortunes of its neighbours. In the 5th century BC Greece was almost devoured by the unstoppable spread of the Persian Empire, reversed only by Alexander. Later still the Roman Empire overwhelmed old Hellas, but the nation revived once more under Byzantine rule. However, the Greeks' genius was their ability to adapt elements of other cultures' architecture and craft, taking it to new heights of their own.

Early Days

Homer's classic work, the 'Iliad', written in the 8th century BC, relates in poetic epithet a mythical episode of the Trojan War. Its sequel, the 'Odyssey', recounts the epic adventures of Odysseus and his companions in their journey home from the Trojan War.

The discovery of a Neanderthal skull in a cave on the Halkidiki peninsula of Macedonia confirmed the presence of humans in Greece 700,000 years ago. People from the Palaeolithic times (around 6500 BC) left bones and tools in the Pindos Mountains, while pastoral communities emerged during neolithic times (7000–3000 BC), primarily in the fertile region that is now Thessaly. Agriculturally sophisticated, they grew crops, bred sheep and goats, and used clay to produce pots, vases and stylised representations of idols as figures of worship.

Artistic & Cultural Legacies

Ancient Civilisations

By 3000 BC, settlements had developed into streets, squares and mud-brick houses. Indo-European migrants introduced the processing of bronze into Greece and from there began three remarkable civilisations: Cycladic, Minoan and Mycenaean.

The Cycladic civilisation was a cluster of fishing and farming island communities with a sophisticated artistic temperament. The most striking legacy is the carving of statuettes from Parian marble – the famous Cycladic figurines. Cycladic sculptors are also renowned for their impressive, life-sized *kouroi* (marble statues).

The Minoans were Europe's first advanced civilisation, named after King Minos, the mythical ruler of Crete (and stepfather of the Minotaur). Around 1900 BC, the splendid complex of Knossos was first built with its frescoes, ventilation shafts and sewerage systems marking an abrupt ac-

TIMELINE	7000–3000 BC	3000–1100 BC	2000 BC
	For 4000 years, inhabitants of the Greek peninsula live a simple agrarian life, growing crops and herding animals. Communities with housing and planned streets appear around 3000 BC.	The discovery of blending copper and tin into a strong alloy heralds the Bronze Age. Trade gains traction; increased prosperity births the Cycladic, Minoan and Mycenaean civilisations.	Minoan civilisation reaches its peak in Crete: architectural advances lead to the first palaces in Knossos, Phaestos, Malia and Zakros, while pottery-making improves and Crete's first script emerges.

celeration from neolithic life. Using bronze, the Minoans built great sea vessels and their reach extended across Asia Minor and North Africa.

The jury is out on what triggered the demise of this great civilisation. Was it the tsunami and ash fallout caused by the volcanic eruption in Thira, Santorini, in 1500 BC? Or perhaps the invading force of Mycenae?

The decline of the Minoan civilisation coincided with the rise of Mycenae (1600–1100 BC), which reached its peak between 1500 and 1200 BC with mainland city-states like Corinth, Tiryns and Mycenae. Warrior kings, who measured their wealth in weapons, now ruled from heavily fortified palaces. Commercial transactions were documented on tablets in Linear B (a form of Greek language 500 years older than the Ionic Greek used by Homer). The Mycenaean's most impressive legacy is their magnificent gold masks, refined jewellery and metal ornaments, the best of which are in the National Archaeological Museum in Athens.

Geometric & Archaic Ages

The Dorians were an ancient Hellenic people who settled in the Peloponnese by the 8th century BC. In the 11th or 12th century BC these warrior-like people fanned out to occupy much of the mainland, seizing control of the Mycenaean kingdoms and enslaving the inhabitants. The following 400-year period is often referred to as Greece's dark age; however, the Dorians introduced iron and developed a new intricate style of pottery, decorated with striking geometric designs. Significantly they were to introduce the practice of *polytheism* (the worship of many gods), paving the foundations for Zeus and his pantheon of 12 principal deities.

During the Archaic period, about 1000–800 BC, Greek culture developed rapidly, with advancements in literature, sculpture, theatre, architecture and intellectual endeavour. This revival overlapped with the Classical age (the two eras are often called the Hellenic period). Advances included the Greek alphabet, the verses of Homer (the 'Odyssey' was possibly the world's first epic work of literature), the founding of the Olympic Games, and the creation of central sanctuaries such as Delphi. These common bonds gave Greeks a sense of national identity and intellectual vigour.

By about 800 BC, Greece had been divided into a series of independent city-states, the most powerful being Argos, Athens, Corinth, Elis, Sparta and Thiva (Thebes). Most abolished monarchic rule and aristocratic monopoly, establishing a set of laws that redistributed wealth and allowed the city's citizens to regain control over their lands.

Classical Age

Greece's Golden Age, from the 6th to 4th centuries BC, saw a renaissance in cultural creativity. Literature and drama blossomed as many city-states enjoyed increased economic reform, political prosperity and a surge in mental agility, led by the noble works of Aeschylus, Euripides and Sophocles

1700–1550 BC	1500–1200 BC	1200–800 BC	1100 BC
Santorini erupts with a cataclysmic volcanic explosion, causing a Mediterranean-wide tsunami that scholars suggest contributed to the destruction of Minoan civilisation.	The authoritarian Mycenaean culture from the Peloponnese usurps much of the Cretan and Cycladic cultures. Goldsmithing is a predominant feature of Mycenaean life.	The Dorians herald 400 years of obscurity in terms of international trade, but excel in the use of iron weaponry and ironwork in architecture, and develop striking geometric designs on pottery.	The Dorians overrun the Mycenaean cities in Crete. They reorganise the political system, dividing society into classes. A rudimentary democracy replaces monarchical government.

who contributed dramatic tragedies, and Aristophanes who inspired political satire with his comedies. Today the potency of this fertile era still resonates – many ideas discussed today were debated by these great minds. And that's not forgetting the journalistic blogs of historians Herodotus – widely regarded as the father of history – and Thucydides.

Athens reached its zenith after the monumental defeat of the Persians at the Battle of Marathon in 490 BC, founding the Delian League, an alliance formed to liberate city-states still occupied by Persia. Many Aegean and Ionian city-states swore an allegiance to Athens, making an annual contribution to the treasury of ships, bringing it fantastic wealth unrivalled by its poor neighbour, Sparta, and also turning it into something of an empire.

When Pericles became leader of Athens in 461 BC, he moved the treasury from Delos to the Acropolis, reappropriating funds to construct grander temples upon it, including the majestic Parthenon, and elsewhere, including the Temple of Zeus at Olympia. It was also during this Classical period that sculptors developed a more naturalistic, aesthetic style for marble pieces and bronze casts, such as the enduring marble friezes of the Parthenon and the sculpture of the city's patroness, Athena.

With the Aegean Sea safely under its wing, Athens began to look westwards for further expansion, bringing it into conflict with the Sparta-dominated Peloponnesian League. A series of skirmishes and provocations subsequently led to the Peloponnesian Wars.

The Histories, written by Herodotus in the 5th century BC, chronicles the conflicts between the Ancient Greek city-states and Persia. The work is considered to be the first narrative of historical events ever written.

War & Conquest

The Persian Wars

Athens' rapid growth as a major city-state also meant heavy reliance on food imports from the Black Sea; and Persia's imperial expansion westward threatened coastal trade routes across Asia Minor. Athens' support for a rebellion in the Persian colonies of Asia Minor sparked the Persian drive to destroy the city. Persian Emperor Darius spent five years suppressing the revolt and remained determined to succeed. A 25,000-strong Per-

---

DEMOCRACY

The seafaring city-state of Athens was still in the hands of aristocrats when Athens' greatest reformist, Solon, was appointed chief magistrate in 594 BC. His mandate was to defuse the mounting tensions between the haves and have-nots by cancelling all debts and liberating those who'd become enslaved because of them. Declaring all free Athenians equal by law, Solon abolished inherited privileges and restructured political power, establishing four classes based on wealth. Although only the first two classes were eligible for office, all four could elect magistrates and vote on legislation. Solon's reforms have become regarded as a blueprint of the ideological democratic system.

---

sian army reached Attica in 490 BC, but was defeated when an Athenian force of 10,000 outmanoeuvred it at the Battle of Marathon.

When Darius died in 485 BC, his son Xerxes resumed the quest to conquer Greece with a massive land and sea invasion in 480 BC. Some 30 city-states met in Corinth to devise a defence, forming the Hellenic League with an army and navy under Spartan command. The army held at Thermopylae, near present-day Lamia, the main passage into central Greece from the north. Despite the Greeks being greatly outnumbered, this bottleneck was easy to defend until a traitor showed the Persians another way over the mountains, from where they attacked the Greeks who retreated.

The Greeks fell back on their second line of defence, an earthen wall across the Isthmus of Corinth, while the Persians advanced upon Athens and razed it to the ground. The Persian naval campaign, however, was not successful. By skilful manoeuvring, the smaller, more agile Greek warships trapped the larger Persian ships in the narrow waters of Salamis. Xerxes returned to Persia in disgust, leaving his general Mardonius to subdue Greece. The result was quite the reverse: a year later, the Greeks obliterated the Persian army at the Battle of Plataea.

The Peloponnesian Wars

The Peloponnesian League was a military coalition governed by the iron hand of Sparta, who maintained political dominance over the Peloponnesian region. Athens' growing imperialism threatened Spartan hegemony; the ensuing power struggle was to last almost 30 years.

Athens support for Corcyra (present-day Corfu) against Sparta's powerful ally Corinth sparked the first Peloponnesian War (431–421 BC). Athens knew it couldn't defeat the Spartans on land, so withdrew behind its mighty walls and blockaded the Peloponnese with its navy. Athens suffered badly during the siege; plague broke out killing a third of the population but the defences held firm. The blockade of the Peloponnese eventually began to hurt and the two cities negotiated an uneasy truce.

The truce lasted until 413 BC, when the Spartans went to the aid of the Sicilian city of Syracuse, which the Athenians had been besieging for three years. The Spartans ended the siege, destroying the Athenian fleet and army. Athens fought on for a further nine years before it surrendered to Sparta in 404 BC. Corinth urged the total destruction of Athens, but the Spartans felt honour-bound to spare the city that had saved Greece from the Persians. Instead, they crippled it by confiscating its fleet, abolishing the Delian League and tearing down the walls between the city and Piraeus.

The Rise of Macedon & Alexander the Great

By the late 4th century BC the Greeks were engineering their own decline. Sparta began a doomed campaign to reclaim the cities of Asia Minor from

The Trial of Socrates by IF Stone frames in a contemporary investigative light Plato's version of events surrounding the philosopher Socrates' life and death.

HISTORY WAR & CONQUEST

480 BC	477 BC	461–32 BC	413–404 BC
Darius' son Xerxes seeks revenge for the Marathon defeat and sacks Athens. The Greeks retaliate by smashing the Persian army at the decisive Battle of Plataea. The Persian Wars are over.	Seeking security while building a de facto empire, the Athenians establish a political and military alliance called the Delian League. Many city-states and islands join the new club.	New Athenian leader Pericles shifts power from Delos to Athens and uses the treasury wealth of the Delian League to fund massive works, including the construction of the magnificent Parthenon, an enduring legacy.	A second war between Sparta and Athens breaks out over the distant colony of Sicily, ending an eight-year truce. The Spartans break the Athenian siege and Sparta assumes total dominance.

Persian rule, bringing the Persians back into Greek affairs where they found willing allies in Athens and an increasingly powerful Thebes (Thiva). The rivalry between Sparta and Thebes culminated in the decisive Battle of Leuctra in 371 BC, where Thebes inflicted Sparta's first defeat. Spartan influence collapsed and Thebes filled the vacuum. In a surprise about-turn, Athens now allied itself with Sparta, and their combined forces battled the Theban army in the Peloponnese in 362 BC. Thebes won the battle, but their leader was killed and Theban power soon crumbled.

The political influence of the major city-states had by now been significantly eroded and they were unable to combat the new power in the north, Macedon (modern Macedonia), which was gathering strength under its aggressive monarch, Philip II. In 338 BC, Philip II marched into Greece and defeated a combined army of Athenians and Thebans at the Battle of Chaeronea. Philip persuaded all the city-states (except Sparta) to swear allegiance to Macedonia by promising to campaign against Persia. Before the campaign began, Philip was assassinated and his 20-year-old son, Alexander, became king in 336 BC.Philip II's death sparked rebellions throughout the empire, but Alexander quickly crush them, making an example of Thebes by razing it to the ground. Upon his black stallion he was always the first into battle ahead of his men, and was renowned for his valour, cunning and recklessness. After restoring order in Thebes, he turned his attention to the Persian Empire and marched his seasoned army of 40,000 men into Asia Minor in 334 BC. After a few bloody battles with the Persians, Alexander succeeded in conquering Syria, Palestine and Egypt – where he was proclaimed pharaoh and founded the city of Alexandria. To minimise future resistance from his new subjects, he interbred them with his soldiers. Alexander continued his reign east into what is now Uzbekistan, Balkh in Afghanistan and northern India. His

THE HELLENISTIC AGE

The Greeks perceived themselves as part of a larger empire, and this concept characterised Hellenistic society. Arts, drama, sculpture and philosophy reflected growing awareness of a new definition of Greek identity. Alexander the Great was obsessed with carrying the ideal of Hellenism to as far as his genius and his horse, Bucephalus, would take him.

Hellenism would continue to prosper even under Roman rule. As the Roman province of Achaea, Greece experienced an unprecedented period of peace for almost 300 years, known as the Pax Romana. The Romans had always venerated Greek art, literature and philosophy, and aristocratic Romans sent their offspring to school in Athens. The Romans adopted most aspects of Hellenistic culture, from its dress to its gods, spreading its unifying traditions throughout their empire. The Romans were also the first to refer to the Hellenes as Greeks, derived from the word *graikos* – the name of a prehistoric tribe.

399 BC	359 BC	334–23 BC	86 BC–AD 224
Socrates stands trial, accused of corrupting the young with pedagogical speeches. A jury condemns him to death. Rather than appealing for voluntary exile, Socrates defiantly accepts a cup of hemlock.	In Macedonian, King Philip II seizes power. He seeks alliances with Sparta and Athens on a promise to wage war again on Persia. Following Phillip's untimely murder, his son Alexander assumes leadership.	Alexander the Great sets out to conquer the known world. Thebes (Thiva) is the first victim, followed by the Persians, the Egyptians and finally the peoples of today's central Asia. He dies in 323 BC.	Roman expansion includes Greek territory. First defeating Macedonia at Pydna in 168 BC, the Romans ultimately overtake the mainland and establish the Pax Romana. It lasts 300 years.

ambition was to conquer the world, which he believed ended at the sea beyond India, but his now aged soldiers grew weary and in 324 BC forced him to return to Mesopotamia, where he settled in Babylon. The following year, at the age of 33, he fell ill suddenly and died. His generals swooped like vultures on the empire and, when the dust settled, Alexander's empire was carved up into fractious, independent kingdoms. Macedonia lost control of the Greek city-states to the south, which banded together into the Aetolian League, centred on Delphi, and the Achaean League, based in the Peloponnese. Athens and Sparta joined neither.

Foreign Rule

Roman Era

While Alexander the Great was forging his vast empire in the east, the Romans had been expanding theirs to the west, and now they were keen to start making inroads into Greece. After several inconclusive clashes, they defeated Macedon in 168 BC at the Battle of Pydna.

The Achaean League was defeated in 146 BC and the Roman consul Mummius made an example of the rebellious Corinthians by destroying their city. In 86 BC Athens joined an ill-fated rebellion against the Romans in Asia Minor staged by the king of the Black Sea region, Mithridates VI. In retribution, the Roman statesman Sulla invaded Athens and took off with its most valuable sculptures. Greece now became the Graeco-Roman province of Achaea. Although officially under the auspices of Rome, some major Greek cities were given the freedom to self-govern to some extent. As the Romans revered Greek culture, Athens retained its status as a centre of learning. During a succession of Roman emperors, namely Augustus, Nero and Hadrian, Greece experienced a period of relative peace, the Pax Romana, which was to last until the middle of the 3rd century AD.

The Byzantine Empire & the Crusades

The Pax Romana began to crumble in AD 250 when the Goths invaded Greece, the first of a succession of invaders spurred on by the 'great migrations' of the Visigoths and then the Ostrogoths from the middle Balkans.

In AD 324, in an effort to resolve the conflict in the region, Roman Emperor Constantine I transferred the capital of the empire from Rome to Byzantium, on the western shore of the Bosphorus, which was renamed Constantinople (present-day İstanbul). While Rome went into decline, the eastern capital began to grow in wealth and strength as a Christian state. In the ensuing centuries, Byzantine Greece faced continued pressure from the Persians and Arabs, but managed to retain its stronghold over the region.

It is ironic that the demise of the Byzantine Empire was accelerated by fellow Christians from the west – the Frankish Crusaders. The stated mission of the Crusades was to liberate the Holy Land from the Muslims,

Alexander the Great is considered to be one of the best military leaders of all time. He was never beaten in battle and by the age of 30 reigned over one of the largest ancient empires stretching from Greece to the Himalayas.

AD 63	250	324	394
Christianity emerges after St Paul visits Crete and leaves his disciple, Titus, to convert the island. St Titus becomes Crete's first bishop.	The first Christian martyrs, the so-called Agii Deka (Ten Saints) are killed in the Cretan village of the same name, as Roman officials begin major Christian persecutions.	The AD 250 invasion of Greece by the Goths signals the decline of the Pax Romana and in 324 the capital of the Roman Empire is moved to Byzantium (later renamed Constantinople). Christianity gains traction.	Christianity is declared the official religion of Byzantium. All pagan worship of Greek and Roman gods is outlawed. Christian theology supplants classical philosophy.

but in reality they were driven as much by greed as by religious zeal. The first three Crusades passed by without affecting the area, but the leaders of the Fourth Crusade (in the early part of the 13th century) decided that Constantinople presented richer pickings than Jerusalem and struck a deal with Venice, which had helped prop up the Crusades.

Constantinople was sacked in 1204 and much of the Byzantine Empire was partitioned into fiefdoms ruled by self-styled 'Latin' (mostly Frankish or western-Germanic) princes. The Venetians, meanwhile, had also secured a foothold in Greece. Over the next few centuries they acquired all the key Greek ports, including Methoni, Koroni and Monemvasia in the Peloponnese (then known as the Morea), and the island of Crete, and became the wealthiest and most powerful traders in the Mediterranean.

Despite this state of affairs, Byzantium was not yet dead. In 1259 the Byzantine Emperor Michael VIII Palaeologos recaptured the Peloponnese and made the city of Mystras his headquarters. Many eminent artists, architects, intellectuals and philosophers converged on the city for a final burst of Byzantine creativity. Michael VIII managed to reclaim Constantinople in 1261, but by this time Byzantium was a shadow of its former self.

Ottoman Rule

Constantinople was soon facing a much greater threat from the east. The Seljuk Turks, a tribe from central Asia, had first appeared on the eastern fringes of the empire in the middle of the 11th century. The Ottomans (the followers of Osman, who ruled from 1289 to 1326) supplanted the Seljuks as the dominant Turkish tribe. The Muslim Ottomans began to rapidly expand the areas under their control and by the mid-15th century were harassing the Byzantine Empire on all sides.

On 29 May 1453, Constantinople fell under Turkish Ottoman rule (referred to by Greeks as *turkokratia*). Once more Greece became a battleground, this time fought over by the Turks and Venetians. Eventually, with the exception of the Ionian Islands (where the Venetians retained control), Greece became part of the Ottoman Empire.

Ottoman power reached its zenith under Sultan Süleyman the Magnificent, who ruled between 1520 and 1566. His successor, Selim the Sot, added Cyprus to their dominions in 1570, but his death in 1574 marked an end to serious territorial expansion. Although they captured Crete in 1669 after a 25-year campaign, the ineffectual sultans that followed in the late 16th and 17th centuries saw the empire go into steady decline.

Venice expelled the Turks from the Peloponnese in a three-year campaign (1685–87) that saw Venetian troops advance as far as Athens. During this campaign, Venetian artillery struck gunpowder stored inside the ruins of the Acropolis and badly damaged the Parthenon.

The Ottomans restored rule in 1715, but never regained their former authority. By the end of the 18th century, pockets of Turkish officials and

The Green Line separating Greece and Turkey in modern-day Cyprus is a ghost town, a desert of silence where the clock stopped in 1974. Greeks still peer through the barb-wire partition to the place they were born and banished from, and are unlikely to return to.

529	1204	1453	1460
Athens' cultural influence is dealt a fatal blow when Emperor Justinian outlaws the teaching of classical philosophy in favour of Christian theology, by now regarded as the ultimate form of intellectual endeavour.	Marauding Frankish Crusaders sack Constantinople. Trading religious fervour for self-interest, the Crusaders strike a blow that sets Constantinople on the road to a slow demise.	Greece becomes a dominion of the Ottoman Turks after they seize control of Constantinople, sounding the death knell for the Byzantine Empire.	By 1460, the Venetian stronghold of Morea (Peloponnese) falls to the Turks and centuries of power struggles between the Turks and Venetians follow.

aristocrats had emerged throughout Greece as self-governing cliques that made cursory gestures of obligation to the sultan in Constantinople. Also, some Greeks had gained influence under the sultan's lax leadership or enjoyed privileged administrative status; they were influential church clerics, wealthy merchants, landowners or governors, ruling over the provincial Greek peasants. But there also existed an ever-increasing group of Greeks, including many intellectual expatriates, who aspired to emancipation.

Russia campaigned to liberate its fellow Christians in the south, and sent Russian agents to foment rebellion, first in the Peloponnese in 1770 and then in Epiros in 1786. Both insurrections were crushed ruthlessly.

Independence

In 1814, businessmen Athanasios Tsakalof, Emmanuel Xanthos and Nikolaos Skoufas founded the first Greek independence party, the Filiki Eteria (Friendly Society). The underground organisation's message spread quickly. Supporters believed armed force was the only effective means of liberation, and made generous financial contributions to the Greek fighters.

On 25 March 1821, the Greeks launched the War of Independence. Uprisings broke out almost simultaneously across most of Greece and the occupied islands. The fighting was savage and atrocities were committed on both sides; in the Peloponnese 12,000 Turkish inhabitants were killed after the capture of the city of Tripolitsa (present-day Tripoli), while the Turks retaliated with massacres in Asia Minor, most notoriously on the island of Chios. The campaign escalated, and within a year the Greeks had captured the fortresses of Monemvasia, Navarino (modern Pylos) and Nafplio in the Peloponnese, and Messolongi, Athens and Thebes. The Greeks proclaimed independence on 13 January 1822 at Epidavros.

Regional differences over national governance escalated into civil war in 1824 and 1825. The Ottomans took advantage and by 1827 the Turks (with Egyptian reinforcements) had recaptured most of the Peloponnese, as well as Messolongi and Athens. Western powers intervened and a Russian, French and British naval fleet sunk the Turkish-Egyptian fleet in the Battle of Navarino in October 1827. Sultan Mahmud II proclaimed a holy war, prompting Russia to send troops into the Balkans to engage the Ottoman army. Fighting continued until 1829 when, with Russian troops at the gates of Constantinople, the sultan accepted Greek independence with the Treaty of Adrianople. Independence was formally recognised in 1830.

The Modern Greek Nation

The Greeks had been busy organising the independent state they had proclaimed several years earlier. In April 1827 they elected Ioannis Kapodistrias, a Corfiot and former diplomat of Russian Tsar Alexander I, as the first president of the republic. Nafplio, in the Peloponnese, was chosen as the capital. There was, however, much dissent within Greek ranks. Kapodistrias

Greece is home to the oldest mosque in Europe. The Bayezit's Mosque at Didymotiho was built by Ottoman Sultan Bayezit I in the late 14th century.

The best-seller *Eleni*, written by Nicholas Gage, tells the gripping personal account of his family's life in the village of Lia, and the events leading to the execution of Gage's mother by communist guerrillas during the Greek Civil War.

1541	1684–87	1770s & 80s	1814
Dominikos Theotokopoulos, later known as 'El Greco', is born in Candia; his subsequent creations in Italy and Spain are marked by both Cretan School influence and bold personal innovation.	The Venetians expel the Turks from the Peloponnese in a campaign that sees Venetian troops advance as far as Athens.	Catherine the Great of Russia dislodges the Turks from the Black Sea coast and assigns several towns with Ancient Greek names. She offers Greeks financial incentives and free land to settle the region.	The underground Hellenic Independence organisation known as the Filiki Eteria (Friendly Society) is established in the town of Odessa on the Black Sea coast. Its influence spreads throughout Greece.

was assassinated in 1831 after he had ordered the imprisonment of a Maniot chieftain, part of a response to undermine rising rebellion among the many parties whose authority had been weakened by the new state.

Amid the ensuing anarchy, Britain, France and Russia declared Greece a monarchy. They set on the throne a non-Greek, 17-year-old Bavarian Prince Otto. The new kingdom (established by the London Convention of 1832) consisted of the Peloponnese, Sterea Ellada, the Cyclades and the Sporades. After moving the capital to Athens in 1834, King Otto proved to be an abrasive ruler who had alienated the independence veterans by giving the most prestigious official posts to his Bavarian court. By the end of the 1850s, most of the stalwarts of the War of Independence had been replaced by a new breed of graduates from Athens University.

The Great Idea

Poet Lord Byron was one of a large group of philhellenic volunteers who played an active role in fanning the independence cause. Byron's war effort was cut short when he died in 1824.

Greece's foreign policy (dubbed the 'Great Idea') was to assert sovereignty over its dispersed Greek populations. Set against the background of the Crimean conflict, British and French interests were nervous at the prospect of a Greek alliance with Russia against the Ottomans, especially after 1862 when Otto was ousted in a bloodless coup.

British influence in the Ionian Islands had begun in 1815 (following a spell of political ping-pong between the Venetians, Russians and French). The British did improve the islands' infrastructure and many locals adopted British customs (such as afternoon tea and cricket). But Greek independence put pressure on Britain to give sovereignty to the Greek nation and, in 1864, the British left. Meanwhile, Britain simultaneously eased onto the Greek throne the young Danish Prince William, crowned King George I in 1863. His 50-year reign eventually brought some stability to the country, beginning with a new constitution in 1864 that established the power of democratically elected representatives.

In 1881 Greece acquired Thessaly and part of Epiros as a result of a Russo-Turkish war. But Greece failed miserably when, in 1897, it tried to attack Turkey in the north in an effort to reach *enosis* (union) with Crete (which had persistently agitated for liberation from the Ottomans). The bid drained much of the country's resources and timely diplomatic intervention by the great powers prevented the Turkish army from taking Athens.

Crete was placed under international administration, but the government of the island was gradually handed over to the Greeks. In 1905 the president of the Cretan assembly, Eleftherios Venizelos, announced Crete's union with Greece, recognised by international law in 1913. Venizelos went on to become prime minister of Greece in 1910.

WWI & Smyrna

In March 1913, King George was assassinated and his son Constantine became the monarch. King Constantine, who was married to the sister

1821	1822–29	1827–31	1833
On 25 March, Bishop Germanos of Patra (a member of the Filiki Eteria) signals the beginning of the War of Independence on the mainland. Greece celebrates this date as its national Independence Day.	Independence is declared at Epidavros on 13 January 1822, but fighting continues for another seven years. The Ottomans capitulate and accept the terms of the Treaty of Adrianople.	Ioannis Kapodistrias is appointed prime minister of a fledgling government with its capital in the Peloponnesian town of Nafplio. Discontent ensues and Kapodistrias is assassinated.	The powers of the Entente (Britain, France and Russia) decree that Greece should be a monarchy and dispatch Prince Otto of Bavaria to Greece to be the first appointed monarch in modern Greece.

of the German emperor, insisted that Greece remain neutral when WWI broke out in August 1914. As the war dragged on, the Allies (Britain, France and Russia) put increasing pressure on Greece to join forces with them against Germany and Turkey, promising concessions in Asia Minor in return. Prime Minister Venizelos favoured the Allied cause, placing him at loggerheads with the king. The king left Greece in June 1917, replaced by his second-born son, Alexander, who was more amenable to the Allies.

Greek troops served with distinction on the Allied side, but when the war ended in 1918 the promised land in Asia Minor was not forthcoming. Venizelos led a diplomatic campaign to further the case and, with Allied acquiescence, landed troops in Smyrna (present-day İzmir in Turkey) in May 1919, under the guise of protecting the half a million Greeks living in the city. With a seemingly viable hold in Asia Minor, Venizelos ordered his troops to march ahead, and by September 1921 they had advanced as far as Ankara. By this stage foreign support for Venizelos had ebbed and Turkish forces, commanded by Mustafa Kemal (later to become Atatürk), halted the offensive. The Greek army retreated but Smyrna fell in 1922, and tens of thousands of its Greek inhabitants were killed.

The outcome of these hostilities was the Treaty of Lausanne in July 1923, whereby Turkey recovered eastern Thrace and the islands of Imvros and Tenedos, while Italy kept the Dodecanese (which it had temporarily acquired in 1912 and would hold until 1947).

The treaty also called for a population exchange between Greece and Turkey to prevent future disputes. Almost 1.5 million Greeks left Turkey and almost 400,000 Turks left Greece. The exchange put a tremendous strain on the Greek economy and caused great bitterness and hardship. Many Greeks abandoned a privileged life in Asia Minor for one of extreme poverty in emerging urban shanty towns in Athens and Thessaloniki.

The Republic of 1924–35

The arrival of the Greek refugees from Turkey coincided with, and compounded, a period of political instability unprecedented even by Greek

Eugène Delacroix' oil canvas *The Massacre at Chios* (1824) was inspired by the events in Asia Minor during Greece's War of Independence in 1821. The painting hangs in the Louvre Museum in Paris.

HISTORY THE MODERN GREEK NATION

BALKAN WARS

Although the Ottoman Empire was in its death throes at the beginning of the 20th century, it had still retained Macedonia. This was a prize coveted by the newly formed Balkan countries of Serbia and Bulgaria, as well as by Greece, and led to the outbreak of the Balkan Wars (1912 and 1913). The outcome was the Treaty of Bucharest (August 1913), which greatly expanded Greek territory (and with it, its fertile agricultural resources). Its borders now took in the southern part of Macedonia, including Thessaloniki, the vital cultural centre strategically positioned on the Balkan trade routes; part of Thrace; another chunk of Epiros; and the northeastern Aegean Islands.

1862–63	1863–64	1883	1883
The monarchy takes a nosedive and King Otto is deposed in a bloodless coup. The British return the Ionian Islands (a British protectorate since 1815) to Greece in an effort to quell Greece's expansionist urges.	The British engineer the ascension to the Greek throne of Danish Prince William, later crowned King George I. His 50-year reign begins with a new constitution in 1864.	Greece completes construction of the Corinth Canal that cuts through the Isthmus of Corinth. The engineering feat opens a link between the Aegean and Ionian Seas.	Greece's most famous writer, Nikos Kazantzakis, is born in Iraklio. He becomes famous for works like *Zorba the Greek* and *The Last Temptation of Christ* in the mid-20th century.

standards. In 1920, King Alexander died from a monkey bite and his father Constantine was restored to the throne. But the ensuing political crisis deepened and Constantine abdicated (again) after the fall of Smyrna. He was replaced by his first son, George II, who was no match for the group of army officers who seized power after the war. A republic was proclaimed in March 1924 amid a series of coups and counter-coups.

A measure of stability was attained with Venizelos' return to power in 1928. He pursued a policy of economic and educational reform, but progress was inhibited by the Great Depression. His anti-royalist Liberal Party faced a growing challenge from the monarchist Popular Party, culminating in defeat at the polls in March 1933. The new government was preparing for the restoration of the monarchy when Venizelos and his supporters staged an unsuccessful coup in March 1935. Venizelos was exiled to Paris, where he died a year later. In November 1935 King George II reassumed the throne and installed the right-wing General Ioannis Metaxas as prime minister. Nine months later, Metaxas assumed dictatorial powers with the king's consent, under the pretext of preventing a communist-inspired republican coup.

On 25 November 1942, a coalition of Greek resistance groups, aided by the British, blew up the Gorgopotamos railway bridge near Lamia in Sterea Ellada, sabotaging for weeks German supply routes through the country.

WWII

Ioannis Metaxas' grandiose vision was to create a utopian Third Greek Civilisation, based on its glorious ancient and Byzantine past, but what he created was more like a Greek version of the Third Reich. He exiled or imprisoned opponents, banned trade unions and the recently established Kommounistiko Komma Elladas (KKE, the Greek Communist Party), imposed press censorship, and created a secret police force and fascist-style youth movement. But Metaxas is best known for his reply of *ohi* (no) to Mussolini's ultimatum to allow Italians passage through Greece at the beginning of WWII, thus maintaining Greece's policy of strict neutrality. The Italians invaded Greece, but the Greeks drove them back into Albania.

A prerequisite of Hitler's plan to invade the Soviet Union was a secure southern flank in the Balkans. The British, realising this, asked Metaxas if they could land troops in Greece. He gave the same reply as he had given the Italians, but then died suddenly in January 1941. The king replaced him with the more timid Alexandros Koryzis, who agreed to British forces landing in Greece. Koryzis committed suicide when German troops invaded Greece on 6 April 1941. The Nazis vastly outnumbered the defending Greek, British, Australian and New Zealand troops, and the whole country was under Nazi occupation within a few weeks. The civilian population suffered appallingly during the occupation, many dying of starvation. The Nazis rounded up more than half the Jewish population and transported them to death camps.

1896	1900	1912–13	1914
The staging of the first modern Olympic Games in Athens marks Greece's coming of age. Winners receive a silver medal and olive crown, and second and third places receive a bronze medal and a laurel branch, respectively.	Sir Arthur Evans begins excavations at Knossos, quickly unearthing the palace and stunning the archaeological world with the discovery of the advanced Minoan civilisation.	The Balkan Wars erupt when Greece and Serbia initially side with Bulgaria against Turkey over Macedonia. Then Greece and Serbia fight for the same territory against Bulgaria. Greece's territory expands.	The outbreak of WWI sees Greece initially neutral but eventually siding with the Western Allies against Germany and Turkey on the promise of land in Asia Minor.

Numerous resistance movements sprang up. The dominant three were Ellinikos Laïkos Apeleftherotikos Stratos (ELAS), the left-wing Ethnikon Apeleftherotikon Metopon (EAM) and the right-wing Ethnikos Dimokratikos Ellinikos Syndesmos (EDES). These groups fought one another with as much venom as they fought the Germans, often with devastating results for the civilian Greek population. The Germans began to retreat from Greece in October 1944, but the communist and monarchist resistance groups continued to fight one another.

Civil War

By late 1944 the royalists, republicans and communists were polarised by interparty division and locked in a serious battle for control. The British-backed provisional government was in an untenable position: the left was threatening revolt while the British were pushing to prevent the communists from further legitimising their hold over the administration and vying to reinstate the Greek monarchy.

On 3 December 1944, the police fired on a communist demonstration in Plateia Syntagmatos (Syntagma Sq) in Athens, killing 28 people. The ensuing six weeks of fighting between the left and the right, known as the Dekemvriana (events of December), marked the first round of the Greek Civil War. British troops intervened and prevented an ELAS-EAM coalition victory. In February 1945 formal negotiations for reconciliation between the government and the communists fell flat, and the friction continued. Many civilians on all political sides were subjected to bitter reprisals at the hands of leftist groups, the army or rogue right-wing vigilantes. The royalists won the March 1946 election (which the communists had unsuccessfully boycotted), and a plebiscite (widely reported as rigged) in September put George II back on the throne.

In October the left-wing Democratic Army of Greece (DSE) was formed to resume the fight against the monarchy and its British supporters. Under the leadership of Markos Vafiadis, the DSE swiftly occupied a large swath of land along Greece's northern border with Albania and Yugoslavia.

In 1947 the US intervened and the civil war developed into a setting for the new Cold War theatre. Communism was declared illegal and the government introduced its notorious Certificate of Political Reliability (remaining valid until 1962), which declared that the document bearer was not a left-wing sympathiser; without this certificate Greeks could not vote and found it almost impossible to get work. US aid did little to improve the situation on the ground. The DSE continued to be supplied from the north (by Yugoslavia, Bulgaria and indirectly by the Soviets through the Balkan states), and by the end of 1947, large chunks of the mainland were under its control as well as parts of the islands of Crete, Chios and Lesvos. The fighting dragged on until October 1949, when Yugoslavia fell out with the Soviet Union and cut the DSE's supply lines.

Inside Hitler's Greece: The Experience of Occupation, 1941–44, by Mark Mazower, is an intimate and comprehensive account of Greece under Nazi occupation and the rise of the resistance movement.

HISTORY THE MODERN GREEK NATION

1919–23	1924–34	1935	1940
Greece embarks on the 'Great Idea' to unite former Hellenic regions, including those in Asia Minor. It fails and leads to a population exchange between Greece and Turkey in 1923 (aka the Asia Minor catastrophe).	Greece is proclaimed a republic and King George II leaves Greece. The Great Depression counters the nation's return to stability. Monarchists and parliamentarians under Venizelos tussle for control.	The monarchy is restored and King George II is reappointed to the throne. Right-wing General Ioannis Metaxas adopts the role of prime minister while introducing dictatorial measures of governance.	On 28 October Metaxas famously rebuffs the Italian request to traverse Greece at the beginning of WWII. The Italians engage Greek forces and are driven back into Albania.

The civil war left Greece politically frayed and economically shattered. More Greeks had been killed in three years of bitter civil war than in WWII, and a quarter of a million people were homeless. The sense of despair became the trigger for a mass exodus. Almost a million Greeks headed off in search of a better life elsewhere, primarily to Australia, Canada and the US.

The 1963 political assassination of Grigoris Lambrakis is described in Vassilis Vassilikos' novel *Z*, which later became an award-winning film.

Reconstruction

After a series of unworkable coalitions, the electoral system was changed to majority voting in 1952 – which excluded the communists from future governments. The November 1952 election was a victory for the right-wing Ellinikos Synagermos (Greek Rally). The leader, General Alexander Papagos (a former civil-war field marshal), remained in power until his death in 1955, when he was replaced by Konstandinos Karamanlis.

Greece joined NATO in 1952, and in 1953 the US was granted the right to operate sovereign bases. Intent on maintaining support for the anti-communist government, the US gave generous economic and military aid.

In 1958, Georgios Papandreou founded the broadly based Centre Union (EK), but elections in 1961 returned the National Radical Union (ERE), Karamanlis' new name for Greek Rally, to power for the third time in succession. Papandreou accused the ERE of ballot rigging, and the political turmoil that followed culminated in the murder, in May

DIVIDED CYPRUS

Since the 1930s Greek Cypriots (four-fifths of the island's population) had desired union with Greece, while Turkey had maintained its claim to the island ever since it became a British protectorate in 1878 (it became a British crown colony in 1925). Greece was in favour of a union, a notion strongly opposed by Britain and the US on strategic grounds. In 1959, after extensive negotiations, Britain, Greece and Turkey agreed on a compromise solution whereby Cyprus would become an independent republic, with Greek Cypriot Archbishop Makarios as president and a Turk, Faisal Kükük, as vice-president. In reality this did little to appease either side: right-wing Greek Cypriots rallied against the British, while Turkish Cypriots clamoured for partition of the island.

In July 1974, Greece's newly self-appointed prime minister Ioannidis tried to impose unity with Cyprus by attempting to topple the Makarios government. However, Makarios got wind of an assassination attempt and escaped. Consequently, mainland Turkey sent in troops until they occupied northern Cyprus, partitioning the island and displacing almost 200,000 Greek Cypriots who fled their homes for the safety of the south (reportedly more than 1500 remain missing).

The UN-protected Green Line separating modern-day Cyprus is a ghost town, where the clock stopped in 1974. Decades on, negotiations have failed to resolve the issue. A divided Cyprus joined the European Union in 2004 after a failed referendum on unification, and international mediation continues.

1941–44	1944–49	1967–74	1974
Germany invades and occupies Greece. Monarchists, republicans and communists form resistance groups that, despite infighting, drive out the Germans after three years.	The end of WWII sees Greece descend into civil war, pitching monarchists against communists. The monarchists recover in 1946, but the civil war takes its toll and many Greeks emigrate in search of a better life.	Right- and left-wing factions continue to bicker, provoking in April 1967 a right-wing military coup d'état by army generals who establish a junta. They impose martial law and abolish many civil rights.	A botched plan to unite Cyprus with Greece prompts the invasion of Cyprus by Turkish troops and results in the fall of the military junta. This acts as a catalyst for the restoration of parliamentary democracy in Greece.

1963, of Grigoris Lambrakis, the deputy of the communist Union of the Democratic Left (EDA). All this proved too much for Karamanlis, who resigned and went to live in Paris. The EK finally came to power in February 1964 and Papandreou wasted no time in implementing a series of radical changes. He freed political prisoners and allowed exiles to come back to Greece, reduced income tax and the defence budget, and increased spending on social services and education.

Colonels, Monarchs & Democracy

The political right in Greece was rattled by Papandreou's tolerance of the left, and a group of army colonels, led by Georgios Papadopoulos and Stylianos Patakos, staged a coup on 21 April 1967. They established a military junta with Papadopoulos as prime minister. King Constantine tried an unsuccessful counter-coup in December, after which he fled to Rome, then London. The colonels declared martial law, banned political parties and trade unions, imposed censorship and imprisoned, tortured and exiled thousands of dissidents. In June 1972, Papadopoulos declared Greece a republic and appointed himself president.

On 17 November 1973, tanks stormed a building at the Athens Polytechnio (Technical University) to quell a student occupation calling for an uprising against the US-backed junta. While the number of casualties is still in dispute (more than 20 students were reportedly killed and hundreds injured), the act spelled the death knell for the junta.

The junta dictatorship collapsed. Karamanlis was summoned from Paris to take office and his New Democracy (ND) party won a large majority at the November elections in 1974, against the newly formed Panhellenic Socialist Union (PASOK), led by Andreas Papandreou (son of Georgios). A plebiscite voted 69% against the restoration of the monarchy and the ban on communist parties was lifted.

The 1980s & 1990s

When Greece became the 10th member of the EU in 1981, it was the smallest and poorest member. In October 1981, Papandreou's PASOK party was elected as Greece's first socialist government. PASOK ruled for almost two decades (minus 1990–93), and promised ambitious social reform, to close the US air bases and to withdraw from NATO. US military presence was reduced, but unemployment was high and reforms in education and welfare were limited. Women's issues fared better: the dowry system was abolished, abortion legalised, and civil marriage and divorce implemented.

Economic scandal, a series of general strikes and fundamental policy wrangling over the country's education system damaged PASOK, and in 1990 Konstandinos Mitsotakis led the ND back to office. Intent on redressing economic problems (high inflation and high government spending) the government imposed austerity measures, including a wage freeze for

Prince Philip, the Duke of Edinburgh, was part of the Greek royal family – born on Corfu as Prince Philip of Greece and Denmark in 1921. Former king of Greece, Constantine, is Prince William's godfather and Prince Charles' third cousin. Constantine and his family remained exiled in London for 46 years and only returned to live in Athens in 2013.

1981	1981–90	1999	2001
Greece joins the EU, effectively removing protective trade barriers and opening up the Greek economy to the wider world for the first time. The economy grows smartly.	Greece acquires its first elected socialist government (PASOK) under the leadership of Andreas Papandreou. The honeymoon lasts nine years. The conservatives ultimately reassume power.	Turkey and Greece experience powerful earthquakes within weeks of each other that result in hundreds of deaths. By pledging mutual aid and support, the two nations initiate a warming of diplomatic relations.	Greece adopts the Euro, joining the first wave of European countries to introduce the new currency on 1 January 2002.

civil servants and steep increases in public-utility costs and basic services. By late 1992, corruption allegations were being levelled against the government. By mid-1993 Mitsotakis supporters had abandoned the ND for the new Political Spring party; the ND lost its parliamentary majority and an early election in October returned Andreas Papandreou's PASOK party.

Papandreou stepped down in early 1996 due to ill health and died on 26 June. His departure produced a dramatic change of direction for PASOK, with the party abandoning Papandreou's left-leaning politics and electing experienced economist and lawyer Costas Simitis as the new prime minister, who won a comfortable majority at the October 1996 polls.

The 21st Century

The new millennium saw Greece join the eurozone in 2001, amid rumblings from existing members that it was not economically ready – its public borrowing was too high, as was its inflation level. In hindsight, many look back on that year and bemoan the mis-callibration of the drachma against the euro, claiming Greece's currency was undervalued, and that, overnight, living became disproportionately more expensive. That said, billions of euros poured into large-scale infrastructure projects across Greece, including the redevelopment of Athens – spurred on largely by its hosting of the 2004 Olympic Games. However, rising unemployment, ballooning public debt, slowing inflation and the squeezing of consumer credit took their toll. Public opinion soured further in 2007 when the conservative government (who had come to power in 2004) was widely criticised for its handling of severe summer fires, responsible for widespread destruction throughout Greece. Nevertheless, snap elections held in September 2007 returned the conservatives, albeit with a diminished majority.

In the following years, a series of massive general strikes and blockades highlighted mounting electoral discontent. Hundreds of thousands of people protested against proposed radical labour and pension reforms and privatisation plans that analysts claimed would help curb public debt. The backlash against the government reached boiling point in December 2008, when urban rioting broke out across the country, led by youths outraged by the police shooting of a 15-year-old boy in Athens following an alleged exchange between police and a group of teenagers. Youths hurled stones and firebombs at riot police who responded with tear gas. Concern continued over political tangles in investigations regarding alleged corruption among state executives (on both sides of the political fence) in connection with the Siemens Hellas group. This followed another controversy that involved land-swap deals between a monastery and the government, which some commentators believe to have gone heavily in the monastery's favour, at the expense of taxpayers. A general election held in October 2009, midway through Karamanlis' term, saw PASOK (under Georgios Papandreou) take back the reins in a landslide win against the conservatives.

Greek is Europe's oldest written language, second only to Chinese in the world. It is traceable back to the Linear B script of the Minoans and Mycenaeans. For more on Linear B script, visit www.ancientscripts.com/linearb.html.

2004	2007	2008	2009
Greece successfully hosts the 28th Summer Olympic Games amid much muffled rumour that infrastructure would not be complete in time. Greece also wins the European football championship.	Vast forest fires devastate much of the western Peloponnese as well as parts of Evia and Epiros, causing Greece's worst ecological disaster in decades. Thousands lose their homes and 66 people perish.	Police shoot and kill a 15-year-old boy in Athens following an alleged exchange between police and youths. This sparks a series of urban riots nationwide.	Eurozone countries approve a €110 billion rescue package for the country's economic crisis, in exchange for tougher austerity laws.

Sink or Swim

In 2009 a lethal mix of high public spending and widespread tax evasion, combined with the credit crunch of global recession, threatened to cripple Greece's economy. In 2010 Greece's fellow eurozone countries agreed to a US$145 billion package (half of Greece's GDP) to get the country back on its feet, though with strict conditions – the ruling government, PASOK, still led by Georgios Papandreou, would have to impose austere measures of reform and reduce Greece's bloated deficit. Huge cuts followed, including 10% off public workers' salaries, but it was too little too late and foreign creditors continued to demand ever higher interest rates for their loans.

Greece was stuck between a real-life Scylla and Charybdis – to receive yet another bailout, which was absolutely essential to stop them toppling the euro as a credible currency, they had to effect reforms that penalised the average Greek even further, pushing formerly non-political citizens towards revolution. Some longed for a return to the drachma, however, many believed Greece would still be saddled with massive debt and a monetary system with absolutely no standing.

Georgios Papandreou asked the people for a referendum on the EU bailout, then failed to form a coalition government and stepped down from office. In November 2011, Lucas Papademos – a former vice president of the European Central Bank – became prime minister. Antonis Samaras, leader of the New Democracy party, succeeded him the following year and assembled a coalition with third-placed PASOK and smaller groups to pursue the austerity program. A second bailout of €130 billion brought further austerity requirements and Athens again saw major strikes aimed at the massive cuts – 22% off the minimum wage, 15% off pensions and the axing of 15,000 public sector jobs. Suicide rates in the capital were up by 40%. Also up was support for the far-right fascist organisation, the Golden Dawn, bringing with them a rising tide of racism aimed squarely at Greece's immigrant population.

In June 2013, the Hellenic Broadcasting Corp (ERT) was shut down after 70 years of operation, in the government's attempt to shave off 2500 workers as part of a cost-cutting drive demanded by Greece's international creditors. The closure prompted journalist unions to stage a 24-hour strike in solidarity, creating a nationwide news blackout. It was reopened six days later, following intervention by Greek's high court.

These were indeed brutal times for the average Greek, with wage cuts of around 30% and up to 17 'new' taxes crippling monthly income. While the EU and IMF initially predicted that Greece would return to growth in 2014, the inability for many Greeks to pay their taxes at the end of the year meant that growth was a mere 0.4%. In January 2015, the New Democrat party lost at the polls to left-wing Syriza. The new prime minister, 40-year-old Alexis Tsipras, won the election with an anti-austerity platform.

The web portal www.ancient greece.com is great for all things ancient and Greek.

HISTORY THE 21ST CENTURY

2011	2012	2013	2015
Protesters march on parliament to oppose government efforts to pass new austerity laws. Prime Minister Papandreou resigns and a coalition government is formed by Antonis Samaras of the New Democracy party.	Parliament passes a €13.5 billion austerity plan to secure a second €130 billion and IMF bailout. Cuts include 22% off minimum wage and 15% off pensions, plus the loss of 15,000 public sector jobs.	Unemployment rises to 26.8% – the highest rate in the EU. Youth unemployment climbs to almost 60%.	Greece defaults on its bailout loans and is threatened with Grexit: removal from the eurozone.

Ancient Greek Culture

When the Roman Empire assimilated Greece it did so with considerable respect and idealism. The Romans in many ways based themselves on the Ancient Greeks, absorbing their deities (and renaming them), along with literature, myths, philosophy, fine arts and architecture. So what made the Ancient Greeks so special?

The Golden Age

Marcel Camus' *Black Orpheus* (1959) won an Oscar for its reimagining of the Orpheus and Eurydice tale, set in a favela (slum) in 1950s Brazil to a bossa nova soundtrack. The lovers flee a hitman and Orfeu's vindictive fiancée.

In the 5th century BC, Athens had a cultural renaissance that has never been equalled – in fact, such was the diversity of its achievements that modern classical scholars refer to it as 'the miracle'. The era started with a vastly outnumbered Greek army defeating the Persian horde in the battles of Marathon and Salamis and ended with the beginning of the inevitable war between Athens and Sparta. It's often said that Athens' 'Golden Age' is the bedrock of Western civilisation, and had the Persians won, Europe today would have been a vastly different place. Like Paris in the 1930s, Athens was a hotbed of talent. Any artist or writer worth their salt left their hometown and travelled to the great city of wisdom to share their thoughts and hear the great minds of the day express themselves.

Drama

The great dramatists such as Aeschylus, Aristophanes, Euripides and Sophocles redefined theatre from religious ritual to become a compelling form of entertainment. They were to be found at the Theatre of Dionysos at the foot of the Acropolis, and their comedies and tragedies reveal a great deal about the psyche of the ancient Greeks.

Across the country large open-air theatres were built on the sides of hills, designed to accommodate plays with increasingly sophisticated backdrops and props, choruses and themes, and to maximise sound so that even the people in the back row might hear the actors on stage. The dominant genres of theatre were tragedy and comedy. The first known actor was a man called Thespis, from whose name we derive the word 'thespian'.

The World of the Ancient Greeks (2002), by archaeologists John Camp and Elizabeth Fisher, is a broad and indepth look at how the Greeks have left their imprint on politics, philosophy, theatre, art, medicine and architecture.

Philosophy

While the dramatists were cutting their thespian cloth, late 5th and early 4th century BC philosophers Aristotle, Plato and Socrates were introducing new trains of thought rooted in rationality, as the new Greek mind focused on logic and reason. Athens' greatest, most noble citizen, Socrates (469–399 BC), was forced to drink hemlock for allegedly corrupting the youth by asking probing, uncomfortable questions, but before he died he left behind a school of hypothetical reductionism that is still used today.

Plato (427-347 BC), his star student, was responsible for documenting his teacher's thoughts, and without his work in books such as the *Symposium,* they would have been lost to us. Considered an idealist, Plato wrote *The Republic* as a warning to the city-state of Athens that unless its people respected law, leadership and educated its youth sufficiently, it would be doomed.

Plato's student Aristotle (384–322 BC), at the end of the Golden Age, focused his gifts on astronomy, physics, zoology, ethics and politics. Aristotle was also the personal physician to Philip II, King of Macedon, and the tutor of Alexander the Great. The greatest gift of the Athenian philosophers to modern-day thought is their spirit of rational inquiry.

Sculpture

Classical sculpture began to gather pace in Greece in the 6th century BC with the renderings of nudes in marble. Most statues were created to revere a particular god or goddess and many were robed in grandiose garments. The statues of the preceding Archaic period, known as *kouroi*, had focused on symmetry and form, but in the early 5th century BC artists sought to create expression and animation. As temples demanded elaborate carvings, sculptors were called upon to create large reliefs upon them.

During the 5th century BC, the craft became yet more sophisticated, as sculptors were taught to successfully map a face and create a likeness of their subject in marble busts. Perhaps the most famous Greek sculptor was Pheidias, whose reliefs upon the Parthenon depicting the Greek and Persian Wars – now known as the Parthenon Marbles (formerly the Elgin Marbles)– are celebrated as among the finest of the Golden Age.

Two of Socrates' most famous quotes are: 'The only true wisdom consists of knowing that you know nothing' and 'The unexamined life is not worth living'.

The Heroes

Some of the greatest stories of all time – and some say the wellspring of story itself – are to be found in the Greek myths. For many of us, the fantastical stories of Heracles and Odysseus we heard as kids still linger in our imagination, and contemporary writers continue to reinterpret these stories and characters for books and films. Standing in the ancient ruins of an acropolis and peering across the watery horizon, it's not difficult to picture the Kraken (Poseidon's pet monster) rising from the Aegean, nor to imagine that fishing boat you see heading into the sunset as Jason's *Argo* en route to Colchis for the Golden Fleece.

The average Greek is fiercely proud of their myths and will love entertaining you with a list of the gods, but they'll love it even more if you know a few of them yourself.

Heracles (Hercules)

The most celebrated, endearing hero of ancient Greece, the son of Zeus and the mortal Alcmene, Heracles was set 12 labours by his enemy Eurystheus, King of Mycenae, as punishment for killing his family in a fit of madness induced by the jealous Hera. These labours were slaying the

---

ISLANDS IN MYTHOLOGY

Greece is steeped in mythology and its many islands provided dramatic settings for its many legends and interactions between gods and mortals.

Crete Zeus' mother allegedly gave birth to him in a cave to prevent him from being eaten by his father, Cronos. It was also home of the dreaded minotaur.

Delos This island rose up from the waves when the goddess Leto was looking for a place to give birth to Apollo and Artemis.

Kythira Aphrodite is said to have been born out of the waves surrounding Kythira.

Lesvos When Orpheus was killed and dismembered by the Maenads, the waves brought his head here and it was buried near Antissa.

Mykonos Zeus and the Titans battled on this island and Hercules slew the Giants here.

Myrina, Lemnos Believed to have been founded by Myrina, queen of the Amazons.

Rhodes The island given to Helios the sun god after Zeus' victory over the Giants.

Nemean Lion and the Lernian Hydra; capturing the Ceryneian Hind and the Erymanthian Boar; cleaning the Augean Stables in one day; slaying the arrow-feathered Stymphalian Birds; capturing the Cretan Bull; stealing the man-eating Mares of Diomedes; obtaining the Girdle of Hippolyta and the oxen of Geryon; stealing the Apples of the Hesperides; and capturing Cerberus.

From the Greek stories of Oedipus and the castration of Uranus by Cronos, Sigmund Freud drew the conclusion that myths often reflect strong, taboo desires that are otherwise unable to be expressed in society.

Theseus

The Athenian hero volunteered himself as one of seven men and maidens in the annual sacrifice to the Minotaur, the crazed half-bull, half-man offspring of King Minos of Crete. Once inside its forbidding labyrinth (from which none had returned), Theseus, aided by Princess Ariadne (who had a crush on him induced by Aphrodite's dart), loosened a spool of thread to find his way out once he'd killed the monster.

Icarus

Along with Daedalus (his father), Icarus flew off the cliffs of Crete pursued by King Minos and his troops. Using wings made of feathers and wax, his father instructed him to fly away from the midday sun. Icarus became carried away with the exhilaration of flying...wax melts, feathers separate and the bird-boy falls to his death.

Perseus

Perseus' impossible task was to kill the gorgon, Medusa. With a head of snakes Medusa could turn a man to stone with a single glance. Armed with an invisibility cap and a pair of flying sandals from Hermes, Perseus used his reflective shield to avoid Medusa's stare. Having cut off her head and secreted it in a bag, it was shortly unsheathed to save Andromeda, a princess bound to a rock and about to be sacrificed to a sea monster. Medusa's head turned the sea monster to stone and Perseus got the girl.

Oedipus

Oedipus was the ancient Greeks' gift to the Freudian school of psychology. Having been abandoned at birth, Oedipus learned from the Delphic oracle that he would one day slay his father and marry his mother. On the journey back to his birthplace, Thiva (Thebes), he killed a rude stranger and then discovered the city was plagued by a murderous Sphinx (a winged lion with a woman's head). The creature gave unsuspecting travellers and citizens a riddle: if they couldn't answer it, they were dashed on the rocks. Oedipus succeeded in solving the riddle, felled the Sphinx and so gained the Queen of Thiva's hand in marriage. On

TOP FIVE MYTHICAL CREATURES

Of the grotesque and fantastic creatures whose stories are dear to Greek hearts, these five are the most notorious.

Cerberus The three-headed dog of hell, he guards the entrance to the underworld – under his watch no one gets in or out.

Cyclops A one-eyed giant. Odysseus and his crew were trapped in the cave of one such cyclops, Polyphemus.

Hydra Cut one of its nine heads off and another two will grow in its place. Heracles solved the problem by cauterising each stump with his burning brand.

Medusa The snake-headed one with the deadly glance is punished by the gods for her inflated vanity. Even dead, her blood is lethal.

Minotaur This half-man, half-bull mutant leads a life of existential angst in the abysmal labyrinth, tempered only by the occasional morsel of human flesh.

discovering the stranger he'd killed was his father and that his new wife was in fact his mother, Oedipus ripped out his eyes and exiled himself.

Mythology

Ancient Greece revolved around careful worship of 12 central gods and goddesses, all of which played a major role in the *mythos* (mythology), and none of whom can be commended for their behaviour. They frequently displayed pettiness, spitefulness, outright cruelty and low self-esteem that led to unworthy competitions with mortals that were always rigged in the gods' favour. Each city-state had its own patron god or goddess to appease and flatter, while on a personal level a farmer might make sacrifice to the goddess Demeter to bless his crops, or a fisherman to Poseidon to bring him fish and safe passage on the waves.

The Ancient Pantheon

Here's a quick guide to the 12 central gods and goddesses of Greek mythology – their Roman names are in brackets.

➡ **Zeus (Jupiter)** The fire-bolt-flinging king of the gods, ruler of Mt Olympus, lord of the skies and master of disguise in pursuit of mortal maidens. Wardrobe includes shower of gold, bull, eagle and swan.

➡ **Hera (Juno)** Protector of women and family, the queen of heaven is both the embattled wife and sister of Zeus. She was the prototype of the jealous, domineering wife who took revenge on Zeus's illegitimate children.

➡ **Poseidon (Neptune)** God of the seas, master of the mists and younger brother of Zeus. He dwelt in a glittering underwater palace.

➡ **Hades (Pluto)** God of death and also brother of Zeus, he ruled the underworld, bringing in the newly dead with the help of his skeletal ferryman, Charon. Serious offenders were sent for torture in Tartarus, while heroes enjoyed eternal R&R in the Elysian Fields.

➡ **Athena (Minerva)** Goddess of wisdom, war, science and Guardian of Athens, born in full armour out of Zeus' forehead. The antithesis of Ares, Athena was deliberate and, where possible, diplomatic in the art of war. Heracles, Jason (of Jason and the Argonauts fame) and Perseus all benefited from her patronage.

➡ **Aphrodite (Venus)** Goddess of love and beauty who was said to have been born of sea foam. When she wasn't cuckolding her husband, Hephaestus, she and her cherubic son Eros (Cupid) were enflaming hearts and causing trouble (cue the Trojan War).

➡ **Apollo** God of music, the arts and fortune-telling, Apollo was also the god of light and an expert shot with a bow and arrow. It was his steady hand that guided Paris' arrow towards Achilles' only weak spot – his heel – thus killing him.

➡ **Artemis (Diana)** The goddess of the hunt and twin sister of Apollo was, ironically, patron saint of wild animals. By turns spiteful and magnanimous, she was closely associated with the sinister Hecate, patroness of witchcraft.

➡ **Ares (Mars)** God of war, bloodthirsty and lacking control. Zeus' least favourite of his progeny. Not surprisingly, Ares was worshipped by the bellicose Spartans.

➡ **Hermes (Mercury)** Messenger of the gods, patron saint of travellers and the handsome one with a winged hat and sandals. He was always on hand to smooth over the affairs of Zeus, his father.

➡ **Hephaestus (Vulcan)** God of craftsmanship, metallurgy and fire, this deformed and oft derided son of Zeus made the world's first woman of clay, Pandora, as a punishment for man. Inside that box were the evils of mankind.

➡ **Hestia (Vesta)** Goddess of the hearth, she protected state fires in city halls from where citizens of Greece could light their brands. She remained unmarried, inviolate.

No original works by the celebrated classical sculptor Pheidias survive, though copies were made by Roman sculptors. Pheidias' colossal chryselephantine (gold and ivory) statue of Zeus was one of the Wonders of the Ancient World.

The Greek tragedy *Medea*, by Euripides, is about the sun god Helios' granddaughter who takes revenge on her husband by killing her children and finds new life in the dark. It was turned into a fatalistic namesake film (1988) by Lars von Trier.

The Greek Way of Life

What crisis? Visitors may be forgiven for wondering about the state of the nation when they see Athens' bustling cafes and what appears to be business as usual on the Greek islands. The Greek way of life took a major hit as austerity measures further sunk the country into recession, but it's not in the Greeks' nature to retreat into the gloom.

National Psyche

The word *xenos* means both stranger and guest, and Greeks see *filoxenia* (hospitality, welcome, shelter) almost as a duty and matter of personal pride and honour.

Greeks have always shared good and bad times in the company of family and friends; they've danced when sad or defiant and sought solace in their country's rich culture and simple pleasures. Someone will always buy an unemployed youth a coffee, or their *yiayia* (grandmother) will give them *hatziliki* (pocket money) from her shrunken pension.

Greek values and the national character have come under attack during the crisis – with Greeks universally characterised as lazy, leisure-loving, corrupt tax-evaders recklessly bringing Europe to the brink of economic collapse. The realities are far more complex – for every 'lazy' Greek there are hard-working people juggling two jobs to provide for their families.

Greeks pride themselves on their *filotimo,* a hard-to-translate Greek concept that underpins society's cultural norms. It encompasses personal and family honour, respect and loyalty to parents and grandparents, sacrifice and help for friends and strangers alike, pride in country and heritage, and gratitude and hospitality. Though some would argue it has been eroded, the concept remains an important part of Greek identity.

The Greeks also generously extend their *filoxenia* (hospitality). Despite the current fiscal problems, the average Greek will still lavish you with free drinks, fresh cake from their kitchen, and the warmth they have always been famous for. Curious by nature, as well as passionate, loyal and fiery, Greeks engage in animated personal and political discussions rather than polite small talk. Nothing is off limits for conversation, and you may find yourself quizzed as to why you haven't got children,

SPORTING PASSIONS

If the streets are quiet, you can't get a taxi or you hear a mighty roar coming from nearby cafes, chances are there's a football (soccer) game underway. Greece's most popular spectator sport inspires local passions and often unedifying fan hooliganism.

Football's first division is dominated by the big clubs: Olympiakos of Piraeus and arch-rivals Panathinaikos of Athens, along with AEK Athens and Thessaloniki's PAOK.

While the top clubs have won European championships, Greece has remained in the shadow of Europe's soccer heavyweights since its 2004 European Cup win.

Greece is also one of the powerhouses of European basketball. Panathinaikos has won six Euroleague championships, while Olypiakos claimed its third title in 2013. Nigerian-born Greek basketballer Giannis Antetokounmpo became the poster boy for Greece's immigrants in 2013 when he was picked for the Milwaukee Bucks in the NBA draft (having had his Greek citizenship fast-tracked).

THE NEW GREEKS

Greece has long been a magnet for foreigners seeking an idyllic island lifestyle and an escape from the rat race. Apart from those owning holiday houses, the small resident population of disparate *xenoi* (foreigners) has largely been somewhat eccentric or retired Europeans, ex-hippies and artists, or people married to locals. In recent years, there has also been a steady stream of Americans, Australians and others with Greek heritage returning to their ancestral islands.

But Greece has also become home to many of the economic migrants who have settled here since the 1990s, when the country suddenly changed from a nation of emigration to one of immigration. The surge in the number of illegal immigrants arriving from Afghanistan, Iraq and Africa has become a focal point for politicians and right-wing activists, while overwhelming many of the smaller, remote islands where the immigrants arrive and are detained.

why you're not married and how much you earn. They can be fervently patriotic, nationalistic and ethnocentric. Issues are debated with strong will. Greeks are unashamed about staring and blatantly observing (and commenting on) the comings and goings of people around them. They prefer spontaneity to making plans and are notoriously unpunctual (turning up on time is referred to as 'being English').

Today's Greeks cherish the achievements of their ancient forebears, and so they should. Without the Golden Age of Ancient Greece (about 500 BC to 300 BC) the world would arguably not have developed its classical sculpture, mathematics, geometry, philosophy, democracy, drama and politics – not to mention the rich tapestry that Greek myths brought to the well of story and imagination. Show just a little appreciation of this to the average Greek and they will love you for it.

Social & Family Life

Greek life has always taken place in the public sphere, whether it's men talking politics at the local *kafeneio* (coffee house) or the elderly gathering in neighbourhood squares while their grandchildren play into the evening. While entertainment spending has been seriously curtailed, the gregarious Greeks nonetheless enjoy a vibrant social and cultural life and infamously lively nightlife.

Rather than living to work, Greeks work to live. People of all ages take their afternoon *volta* (outing) along seafront promenades or town centres, dressed up and refreshed from a siesta (albeit a dying institution). On weekends they flock to the beach and seaside tavernas, and summer holidays are the highlight of the year – traditionally, the capital virtually shuts down mid-August as people take off for the islands, beach towns or their ancestral villages. A peculiarly Greek social talking point is how many swims you've had that summer.

Greek society remains dominated by the family, and while many men may appear soaked with machismo, the matriarchal domestic model is still very much commonplace, with women subtly pulling the strings in the background. These strong family ties and kinship are helping Greeks survive testing times. Greece's weak welfare system means Greeks rely on families and social groups for support. Most Greek businesses are small, family-run operations and parents strive to provide homes for their children when they get married. Greeks rarely move out of home before they marry, unless they go to university or work in another city. While this was changing among professionals and people marrying later, low wages and rising unemployment have forced many young people to stay – or return – home.

Debunking the myth of the lazy Greek, OECD research suggests Greeks actually work longer hours than their European and US counterparts, though they have lower productivity and labour participation rates. Greek wages are among Europe's lowest and living costs among the highest.

Greeks retain strong regional identities and ties to their ancestral villages. Even the country's most remote villages are bustling during holidays. Greece's large diaspora plays a significant role in the life of many islands and villages, returning each summer in droves.

The State

Personal freedom and the right to protest and protect their democratic rights are sacrosanct to Greeks. Trade-union activism, mass demonstrations and crippling general strikes are a routine part of life in Athens and other major cities, with police and property normally bearing the brunt of anti-establishment sentiment. This rebellious spirit came to the fore during anti-austerity protests, as Greeks resisted economic reforms crucial to help curb Greece's soaring national debt.

The nation's capacity to overcome its economic woes has been stifled by systemic problems with Greece's political and civil life, aspects of society that Greeks have long criticised and perpetuated. A residual mistrust of the state and its institutions is a legacy of years of foreign occupation, while political instability fostered a weak civil society based on tax evasion, political patronage and nepotism, and a black market economy. Merit has long taken second place to political interests when allocating coveted public-sector jobs or EU funds. Making headway with Greece's bloated and inefficient bureaucracy required *meson* (the help of someone working in the system). The infamous *fakelaki* (envelope of cash) became a common way to cut red tape. At its worst, the system fed corruption and profiteering.

Aversion to the perceived over-regulated approach of Western nations is also part of the national psyche. An undercurrent of civil disobedience extends to lax attitudes to road rules or parking restrictions (you will see motorcyclists carrying their helmets as they chat on their mobile phones).

Faith & Identity

Families flock to church for lively Easter celebrations, weddings, baptisms and annual festivals, but it's largely women and the elderly who attend church services regularly. While most Greeks aren't devout, the Orthodox faith – the official religion of Greece – remains an important part of their identity and culture.

Religious rituals are part of daily life. You will notice taxi drivers, motorcyclists and people on public transport making the sign of the cross when they pass a church; compliments to babies and adults are followed by the *'ftou ftou'* (spitting) gesture to ward off the evil eye; and people light church candles in memory of loved ones. Hundreds of privately built small chapels dot the countryside, while the tiny roadside *iconostases* (chapels) are either shrines to road accidents victims or dedications to saints.

During consecutive foreign occupations the church was the principal upholder of Greek culture, language and traditions, and it still exerts significant social, political and economic influence, though recent scandals have taken their toll.

Showing solidarity in the face of austerity, enterprising locals in Volos have developed the TEM, an alternative currency unit to the euro, establishing a novel informal bartering system for goods and services, where participants exchange anything from olive oil to car repairs.

The Greek year revolves around saints' days and festivals of the Orthodox Church calendar. Easter is bigger than Christmas and name days (celebrating your namesake saint) are more important than birthdays. Most people are named after a saint, as are boats, suburbs and train stations.

The Arts

Greece is revered for its artistic and cultural legacy, and the arts remain a vibrant and evolving element of Greek culture, identity and self-expression. Despite, or because of, Greece's current economic woes, it has seen a palpable burst of artistic activity and creativity. While savage cuts in meagre state-arts funding have some sectors reeling, an alternative cultural scene is fighting back with low-budget films, artistic collectives, and small underground theatres and galleries popping up in the capital.

Modern Greek Art

Until the start of the 19th century, the primary art form in Greece was Byzantine religious painting. There was little artistic output under Ottoman rule, during which Greece essentially missed the Renaissance.

Byzantine church frescoes and icons depicted scenes from the life of Christ and figures of the saints. The 'Cretan school' of icon painting, influenced by the Italian Renaissance and artists fleeing to Crete after the fall of Constantinople, combined technical brilliance and dramatic richness. Cretan-born Renaissance painter El Greco ('The Greek' in Spanish), née Dominikos Theotokopoulos, got his grounding in the tradition of late-Byzantine fresco painting before moving to Spain in 1577.

Modern Greek art per se evolved after Independence, when painting became more secular, focusing on portraits, nautical themes and the War of Independence. Major 19th-century painters included Dionysios Tsokos, Theodoros Vryzakis, Nikiforos Lytras and Nicholas Gyzis, a leading artist of the Munich School (where many Greek artists of the day studied).

Early 20th-century artists such as Konstantinos Parthenis, Fotis Kontoglou, Konstantinos Kaleas and, later, the expressionist George Bouzianis, drew on their heritage and incorporated developments in modern art.

Leading 20th-century artists include cubist Nikos Hatzikyriakos-Ghikas, surrealist artist and poet Nikos Engonopoulos, Yiannis Tsarouhis, Panayiotis Tetsis, Yiannis Moralis, Dimitris Mytaras and pioneer of the Arte Provera movement, Yiannis Kounellis.

The National Art Gallery in Athens has the most extensive collection of Greek 20th-century art, with significant collections at the New Art Gallery in Rhodes and the Museum of Contemporary Art in Andros.

Modern and contemporary sculpture is shown at the National Sculpture Gallery in Athens. Greece's marble sculpture tradition endures on Tinos, birthplace of foremost modern sculptors Dimitrios Filippotis and Yannoulis Halepas, as well as Costas Tsoclis, whose work fills the island's new museum.

> Athens' metro stations feature an impressive showcase of Greek art from prominent artists including Yannis Gaitis (Larisa), Giorgos Zongolopoulos (Syntagma) and Alekos Fassianos (Metaxourgio), whose work fetches record prices for a living Greek artist.

Contemporary Greek Art Scene

Contemporary Greek art has been gaining exposure in Greece and abroad, with a growing number of Greek artists participating in international art events. The Greek arts scene has become more vibrant, less isolated and more experimental, and Athens street art is gaining recognition. Many Greek artists have studied and made their homes and

GREECE ON SCREEN

Greece's new generation filmmakers have been gaining attention for what some critics have dubbed the 'weird wave' of Greek cinema. The award-winning films of Yorgos Lanthimos *(Alps, Dogtooth)* and Athina Rachel Tsangari *(Attenburg)*, at the weirder end of the scale, represent a new style of independent films emerging from Greece.

While Ektoras Kygizos' extraordinary *Boy Eating Bird Food* is an allegory for Greece's current plight, other notable recent films are a product of it – small, creative collaborations largely produced in the absence of state or industry funding.

The focus on Greek film comes in the wake of the loss of Greece's most critically acclaimed filmmaker, Theo Angelopoulos, who was hit by a motorcycle during a film shoot in 2012. Angelopoulos was renowned for his epic, dreamlike cinematic style and long takes, as well as his melancholy symbolism and commentary on modern Greek history and society.

International festivals may be lauding art-house Greek films, but domestic audiences prefer comedies such as box-office hits *Nisos* (2009), *Sirens in the Aegean* (2005) and *What If* (2011), a film set with the country's economic crisis.

Few Greek films get commercial releases abroad. Exceptions include Tasos Boulmetis' *A Touch of Spice* (2003), Pantelis Voulgaris' *Brides* (2004) and Yannis Smaragdis' big-budget *El Greco* (2007). Greece's most internationally acclaimed film remains the classic 1964 Oscar winner *Zorba the Greek*.

reputations abroad, but a new wave is returning or staying put, contributing to a fresh artistic energy.

Greeks have had unprecedented exposure to global art through major international exhibitions held in impressive new art venues, small private galleries and artist-run initiatives such as the annual Hydra School Project. Since 2007, Biennials in Athens have put the capital on the international contemporary-arts circuit, while the National Museum of Contemporary Art was moved into its permanent home in a renovated brewery in 2015.

Modern Greek Literature

Quirky, Rebus-like Inspector Haritos, from Petros Markaris' popular crime series, provides an enjoyable insight into crime and corruption in Athens. *Che Committed Suicide* (2010), *The Late Night News* (2005) and *Zone Defence* (2007) have been translated into English.

Greek literature virtually ceased under Ottoman rule, and was then stifled by conflict over language – ancient Greek versus the vernacular Demotic or *katharevousa*, a compromise between the two (*dimotiki* won in 1976).

One of the most important works of early Greek literature is the 17th-century 10,000-line epic poem 'Erotokritos', by Crete's Vitsenzos Kornaros. Its 15-syllable rhyming verses are still recited in Crete's famous *mantinadhes* (rhyming couplets) and put to music.

Greece's most celebrated (and translated) 20th-century novelist is the controversial Nikos Kazantzakis, whose novels are full of drama and larger-than-life characters, such as the magnificent title character in *Alexis Zorbas* (Zorba the Greek). Another great novelist of the time, Stratis Myrivilis, wrote the classics *Vasilis Arvanitis* and *The Mermaid Madonna*.

Eminent 20th-century Greek poets include Egypt-born Constantine Cavafy and Nobel-prize laureates George Seferis and Odysseus Elytis, awarded in 1963 and 1979, respectively.

Greece's literary giants include Iakovos Kambanellis, Alexandros Papadiamantis, Kostis Palamas and poet-playwright Angelos Sikelianos. The plays of Yiorgos Skourtis and Pavlos Matessis have been translated and performed abroad.

Contemporary Writers

Greece has a prolific publishing industry but few works of fiction are translated into English.

Contemporary Greek writers have made small inroads into foreign markets, such as Apostolos Doxiadis with his international bestseller *Uncle Petros and Goldbach's Conjecture*, and award-winning children's writer Eugene Trivizas.

Greek publisher Kedros' modern literature translation series includes Dido Sotiriou's *Farewell Anatolia*, Maro Douka's *Fool's God* and Kostas Mourselas' bestselling *Red-Dyed Hair*, which was made into a popular TV series. Other prominent writers in translation include Ersi Sotiropoulou, Thanassis Valtinos, Rhea Galanaki, Ziranna Ziteli, Petros Markaris and Ioanna Karystiani.

Bypassing the translation issue, London-based Panos Karnezis (*The Maze*, *The Birthday Party* and *The Convent*) and Soti Triandafyllou (*Poor Margo*) write in English. Other notable contemporary authors available in translation include Alexis Stamatis (*Bar Flaubert, American Fugue*) and Vangelis Hatziyiannidis (*Four Walls* and *Stolen Time*).

Music

For most people, Greek music and dance evokes images of spirited, high-kicking laps around the dance floor to the tune of the bouzouki (a musical instrument in the lute family). Greece's strong and enduring music tradition, however, is a rich mosaic of musical influences and styles.

While many leading performers draw on traditional folk, *laïka* (popular urban folk) and *rembetika* (blues), Greece's vibrant music scene is also pumping out its share of pop, club dance music, jazz, rock and even hip-hop.

The memorable opening-credits track from the 1994 film *Pulp Fiction* was based on surf guitar legend Dirk Dale's 1960s version of 'Misirlou' – originally recorded by a Greek *rembetika* (blues) band around 1930.

Traditional Folk Music

Traditional folk music was shunned by the Greek bourgeoisie after Independence, when they looked to Europe – and classical music and opera – rather than their Eastern or 'peasant' roots.

Greece's regional folk music is generally divided into *nisiotika* (the lighter, upbeat music of the islands) and the more grounded *dimotika* of the mainland – where the *klarino* (clarinet) is prominent and lyrics refer to hard times, war and rural life. The spirited music of Crete, dominated by the Cretan *lyra* (a pear-shaped, three-string, bowed instrument) and lute, remains a dynamic musical tradition, with regular performances and recordings by new-generation exponents.

GREEK GIG GUIDE

In summer Greece's leading acts perform in outdoor concerts around the country. In winter they perform in clubs in Athens and large regional towns.

Authentic folk music is harder to find. The best bet is at regional *panigyria* (open-air festivals) during summer. Look for posters, often around telephone and power poles, or ask around.

Athens' live music scene includes intimate *rembetika* (blues) clubs and glitzy, expensive, cabaret-style venues known as *bouzoukia*. Second-rate *bouzoukia* clubs are referred to as *skyladhika* (doghouses) – apparently because the crooning singers resemble a whining dog. *Bouzoukia* are the venues for flower-throwing (plate-smashing is rare these days), wanton (and expensive) displays of exuberance, excess and *kefi* (good spirits or mojo). *Opa!*

Laïka & Entehna

Laïka (popular or urban folk music) is Greece's most popular music. A mainstream offshoot of *rembetika, laïka* emerged in the late 1950s and '60s, when clubs in Athens became bigger and glitzier, and the music more commercial. The bouzouki went electric and the sentimental tunes about love, loss, pain and emigration came to embody the nation's spirit. The late Stelios Kazantzidis was the big voice of this era, along with Grigoris Bithikotsis.

Classically trained composers Mikis Theodorakis and Manos Hatzidakis led a new style known as *entehni mousiki* ('artistic' music). They drew on *rembetika* and used instruments such as the bouzouki in more symphonic arrangements, and created popular hits from the poetry of Seferis, Elytis, Ritsos and Kavadias.

Composer Yiannis Markopoulos later introduced rural folk music and traditional instruments such as the *lyra, santouri,* violin and *kanonaki* into the mainstream, and brought folk performers such as Crete's legendary Nikos Xylouris to the fore.

During the junta years the music of Theodorakis and Markopoulos became a form of political expression (Theodorakis' music was banned and the composer jailed).

> The sound of the bouzouki, immortalised in Mikis Theodorakis' 1960s soundtrack to *Zorba the Greek,* has become synonymous with Greece. The long-necked lute-like instrument became central to *rembetika* and dominates *laïka.*

Contemporary & Pop Music

While few Greek performers have made it big internationally – 1970s genre-defying icons Nana Mouskouri and Demis Roussos remain the

---

REMBETIKA: THE GREEK BLUES

Known as the Greek 'blues', *rembetika* emerged in Greece's urban underground and has strongly influenced the sound of Greek popular music.

Two styles make up what is broadly known as *rembetika. Smyrneika* or Cafe Aman music emerged in the mid- to late-19th century in the thriving port cities of Smyrna and Constantinople, which had large Greek populations, and in Thessaloniki, Volos, Syros and Athens. With a rich vocal style, haunting *amanedhes* (vocal improvisations) and occasional Turkish lyrics, its sound had more Eastern influence. Predominant instruments were the violin, *outi* (oud), guitar, mandolin, *kanonaki* and *santouri* (a flat multistringed instrument). The second style, dominated by the six-stringed bouzouki, evolved in Piraeus.

After the influx of refugees from Asia Minor in Piraeus following the 1922 population exchange (many also went to America, where *rembetika* was recorded in the 1920s), the two styles somewhat overlapped and *rembetika* became the music of the ghettos. Infused with defiance, nostalgia and lament, the songs reflected life's bleaker themes and *manges* (streetwise outcasts) who sang and danced in the *tekedhes* (hash dens that inspired many songs).

In the mid-1930s, the Metaxas dictatorship tried to wipe out the subculture through censorship police harassment and raids on *tekedhes.* People were arrested for carrying a bouzouki. Many artists stopped performing and recording, though the music continued clandestinely. After WWII, a new wave of *rembetika* emerged that eliminated much of its seedy side.

Rembetika legends include Markos Vamvakaris, who became popular with the first bouzouki group in the early 1930s, composer Vasilis Tsitsanis, Apostolos Kaldaras, Yiannis Papaioannou, Giorgos Mitsakis and Apostolos Hatzihristou, and the songstresses Sotiria Bellou and Marika Ninou, whose life inspired Costas Ferris' 1983 film *Rebetiko.*

Interest in genuine *rembetika* was revived in the late 1970s to early 1980s – particularly among students and intellectuals – and it continues to be rediscovered by new generations.

Rembetika ensembles perform seated in a row and traditionally play acoustically. A characteristic feature is an improvised introduction called a *taxim.*

best known – Greece has a strong local music scene, from traditional and pop music to Greek rock, heavy metal, rap and electronic dance.

Some of the most interesting music emerging from Greece fuses elements of folk, *laïka* and *entehna* with Western influences. One of the most whimsical examples was Greece's tongue-in-cheek 2013 Eurovision contender, in which *rembetika* veteran Agathonas Iakovidis teamed up with the ska-Balkan rhythms of Thessaloniki's kilt-wearing Koza Mostra.

Big names in contemporary Greek music include Dionysis Savopoulos, dubbed the Bob Dylan of Greece, and veteran George Dalaras and Haris Alexiou.

Stand-out contemporary performers include Cypriot-born Alkinoos Ioannides, Eleftheria Arvanitakiis, Savina Yannatou, and ethnic jazz fusion artists Kristi Stasinopoulou, Mode Plagal and the Cretan-inspired Haïnides.

Mihalis Hatziyiannis is the current darling of the pop scene with a string of platinum records, while headline *laïka* performers include Yiannis Ploutarhos, Antonis Remos and Thanos Petrelis.

Classical Music & Opera

Despite classical music and opera appealing to an (albeit growing) minority of Greeks, this field is where Greece has made the most significant international contribution, most notably through composers Mikis Theodorakis and Manos Hatzidakis and opera diva Maria Callas.

Dimitris Mitropoulos led the New York Philharmonic in the 1950s, while distinguished composers include Stavros Xarhakos and the late Yannis Xenakis. Leading contemporary performers include pianist Dimitris Sgouros, tenor Mario Frangoulis and sopranos Elena Kelessidi and Irini Tsirakidou.

The country's concert halls and major cultural festivals such as the Hellenic Festival offer rich international programs, while opera buffs have the Greek National Opera and Syros' Apollo Theatre.

Greek Dance

Greeks have danced since the dawn of Hellenism. Some folk dances derive from the ritual dances performed in ancient temples – ancient vases depict a version of the well-known *syrtos* folk dance. Dancing was later part of military education; in times of occupation it became an act of defiance and a covert way to keep fit.

Regional dances, like musical styles, vary across Greece. The slow and dignified *tsamikos* reflects the often cold and insular nature of mountain life, while the brighter islands gave rise to light, springy dances such as the *ballos* and the *syrtos*. The Pontian Greeks' vigorous and warlike dances such as the *kotsari* reflect years of altercations with their Turkish neighbours. Crete has its graceful *syrtos*, the fast and triumphant *maleviziotiko* and the dynamic *pentozali*, with its agility-testing high kicks and leaps. The so-called 'Zorba dance', or *syrtaki*, is a stylised dance for two or three dancers with arms linked on each other's shoulders, though the modern variation is danced in a long circle with an ever-quickening beat. Women and men traditionally danced separately, and had their own dances, except in courtship dances such as the *sousta*.

Folk dance groups throughout Greece preserve regional traditions. The best place to see folk dancing is at regional festivals and the Dora Stratou Dance Theatre in Athens.

Contemporary dance is gaining prominence in Greece, with leading local troupes taking their place among the international line-up at the Athens International Dance Festival.

Byzantine music is mostly heard in Greek churches these days, though Byzantine choirs perform in concerts in Greece and abroad, and the music has influenced folk music.

Men dance the often spectacular solo *zeïmbekiko* (whirling, meditative improvisations with roots in *rembetika*). Women do the sensuous *tsifteteli*, a svelte, sinewy show of femininity evolved from the Middle Eastern belly dance.

THE ARTS GREEK DANCE

Architecture

Cast your eyes around most major Western cities and you'll find a reinterpretation of classical Greek architecture. The Renaissance was inspired by the ancient style, as was the neoclassical movement and the British Greek Revival. For those of you with an eye to the past, part of the allure of Greece is the sheer volume of its well-preserved temples. Stand in the ruins of the Parthenon and with a little imagination it's easy to transport yourself back to classical 5th-century Greece.

Minoan Magnificence

Most of our knowledge of Greek architecture proper begins at around 2000 BC with the Minoans, who were based in Crete but whose influence spread throughout the Aegean to include the Cyclades. Minoan architects are famous for having constructed technologically advanced, labyrinthine palace complexes. The famous site at Knossos is one of the largest. Usually characterised as 'palaces', these sites were in fact multi-functional settlements that were the primary residences of royalty and priests, but housed some plebs, too. Large Minoan villages, such as those of Gournia and Palekastro in Crete, also included internal networks of paved roads that extended throughout the countryside to link the settlements with the palaces. More Minoan palace–era sophistication exists at Phaestos, Malia and Ancient Zakros (also in Crete), and at the Minoan outpost of Ancient Akrotiri on the south of Santorini.

Several gigantic volcanic eruptions rocked the region in the mid-15th century BC, causing geological ripple-effects that at the very least caused big chunks of palace to fall to the ground. The Minoans resolutely rebuilt their palaces on an even grander scale, only to have more natural disas-

---

TOP FIVE PROVINCIAL ORIGINALS

Considering the historical mishmash of cultural influences peppered across Greece, alongside a varying landscape, it's hardly surprising to find unique variations in architectural design.

Pyrgi See the medieval, labyrinthine, vaulted island village of Pyrgi in Chios, for its unique Genoese designs of intricate, geometric, grey-and-white facades.

Zagorohoria Gaze at the slate mansions of the Zagorohoria: schist-slab roofs, stone-slab walls and fortified courtyards.

Vathia Watch out for the lovely Vathia in Mani, for its startling meercat-esque stone tower houses with round turrets as sentry posts.

Oia Squint at the volcanic rock–hewn clifftop village of Oia in Santorini, with its dazzlingly whitewashed island streetscapes and homes.

Lefkada Town Discover the strangely attractive wooden-framed houses of Lefkada Town: the lower floors are panelled in wood, while the upper floors are lined in painted sheet metal or corrugated iron.

THE COLUMNS OF ANCIENT GREECE

Columns are columns are columns, right? Recognising the differences between them is, in fact, the easiest way to differentiate between the three distinct architectural orders of Ancient Greece.

Doric The most simple of the three styles. The shaft (the main part of the column) is plain and has 20 sides, while the capital (the head) is formed in a simple circle. Also there's no base. An obvious example of this is the Parthenon.

Ionic Look out for the ridged flutes carved into the column from top to bottom. The capital is also distinctive for its scrolls, while the base looks like a stack of rings.

Corinthian The most decorative and popular of all three orders. The column is ridged; however, the distinctive feature is the capital's flowers and leaves, beneath a small scroll. The base is like that of the Ionic.

ters wipe them out again. The latter effected an architectural chasm that was filled by the emerging Mycenaean rivals on mainland Greece.

Grandeur of Knossos

According to myth, the man tasked with designing a maze to withhold the dreaded Minotaur was famous Athenian inventor Daedalus, father of Icarus. He also designed the Palace of Knossos for King Minos.

First discovered by a Cretan, Milos Kalokirinos, in 1878, it wasn't until 1900 that the ruins of Knossos were unearthed by an Englishman, Sir Arthur Evans. The elaborate palace complex at Knossos was originally formed largely as an administrative settlement surrounding the main palace, which comprised the main buildings arranged around a large central courtyard (1250 sq metres). Over time the entire settlement was rebuilt and extended. Long, raised causeways formed main corridors; narrow labyrinthine chambers flanked the palace walls (this meandering floor plan, together with the graphic ritual importance of bulls, inspired the myth of the labyrinth and the Minotaur). The compound featured strategically placed interior light wells, sophisticated ventilation systems, aqueducts, freshwater irrigation wells, and bathrooms with extensive plumbing and drainage systems. The ground levels consisted mostly of workshops, cylindrical grain silos and storage magazines.

Thanks to its restoration, today's Knossos is one of the easiest ruins for your imagination to take hold of.

Mycenaean Engineering

The Mycenaeans had a fierce reputation as builders of massive masonry. These war-mongering people roamed southern mainland Greece, picking off the choice vantage points for their austere palaces, fenced within formidable citadels. The citadels' fortified Cyclopean-stone walls were on average an unbreachable 3m (10ft) to 7m (25ft) thick. The immense royal beehive tomb of the Treasury of Atreus (aka Tomb of Agamemnon) at Mycenae was constructed using tapered limestone blocks weighing up to 120 tonnes. The palace at Tiryns has stupendous corbel-vaulted galleries and is riddled with secret passageways, and the incredibly well-preserved Nestor's Palace, near modern Pylos, also illustrates the Mycenaeans' structural expertise.

Classic Compositions

The classical age (5th to 4th centuries BC) is when most Greek architectural clichés converge. This is when temples became characterised by the famous orders of columns, particularly the Doric, Ionic and Corinthian.

The mother of all Doric structures is the 5th century BC Parthenon, the ultimate in architectural bling: a gleaming, solid marble crown. To this day, it's probably *the* most obsessively photographed jewel in all of Greece.

In the meantime, the Greek colonies of the Asia Minor coast were creating their own Ionic order, designing a column base in several tiers and adding more flutes. This more graceful order's capital (the head) received an ornamented necking, and Iktinos fused elements of its design in the Parthenon. This order is used on the Acropolis' Temple of Athena Nike and the Erechtheion, where the famous Caryatids regally stand.

Towards the tail end of the classical period, the Corinthian column was in limited vogue. Featuring a single or double row of ornate leafy scrolls (usually the very sculptural acanthus), the order was subsequently adopted by the Romans and used only on Corinthian temples in Athens. The Temple of Olympian Zeus, completed during Emperor Hadrian's reign, is a grand, imposing structure. Another temple design, the graceful, circular temple *tholos* (dome) style, was used for the great Sanctuary of Athena Pronea at Delphi.

The Greek theatre design is a hallmark of the classical period (an example is the 4th century BC theatre at Epidavros) and had a round stage, radiating a semicircle of steeply banked stone benches that seated many thousands. Cleverly engineered acoustics meant every spectator could monitor every syllable uttered on the stage below. Most ancient Greek theatres are still used for summer festivals, music concerts and plays.

BEST FUTURISTIC ATHENS

Despite its massive contribution to ancient architecture, Athens is not stuck in the past. Its modern architects are innovative and fearless.

Acropolis Museum (p73) This new space houses Greece's antiquities. Designed by Bernard Tschumi, the museum features an internal glass *cella* (inner room) mirroring the Parthenon with the same number of columns (clad in steel) and a glass floor overlooking excavated ruins in situ.

Stavros Niarchos Foundation's Cultural Center (SNFCC) The Pritzker Prize–winning architect Renzo Piano is designing the SNFCC. Plans include new venues for the National Library of Greece, the National Opera and the National Ballet School, to be set amid natural surroundings that will also feature an *agora* (market) and a canal that will link the park (at the old horse-racing tracks in Faliro) with the sea. Completion is due in 2016.

Planetarium (p89) This is one of the world's largest digital hemispherical dome, with a dome-diameter of 25m. It provides 360-degree 3D virtual rides through the galaxy in a space the size of 2.5 basketball courts.

Athens Olympic Complex (OAKA; 210 683 4777; www.oaka.com.gr; Marousi; mterolrini) Designed by well-known Spanish architect Santiago Calatrata to house the 2004 Olympics, this complex has a striking, ultramodern glass-and-steel roof, which is suspended by cables from large arches. The laminated glass, in the shape of two giant leaves, is capable of reflecting 90% of the sunlight.

National Museum of Contemporary Art (p75) The abandoned FIX brewery in central Athens has been hollowed out and renovated to create 20,000 sq metres of space to house the gallery. Built in the 1950s, the building retains much of its postwar industrial architecture including the horizontal feel achieved with lateral linear glass, while one side of the facade has been covered in stone reminiscent of the riverbed that was once here. Inside, it's all about glass and light with a sculpture garden on the roof.

THE CAPTAIN'S HOUSE

During the 17th century, Greek ship captains grew increasingly prosperous. Many of them poured their new-found wealth into building lofty homes that towered over the traditional village houses. These captains' houses are now dotted throughout the islands and many have been given a new lease on life as boutique hotels or restaurants.

While the size of the house often reflected the wealth of a captain, some of the smallest of these 400-year-old homes are the most grand. Captain's houses didn't need to be large as they spent so much time at sea. Whitewashed walls stretch upward the soaring resin ceiling, often intricately painted with elaborate, colourful patterns. The windows are up very high and sea-facing, often with wooden lofts to reach them. This was to let the heat out in summer and also so that the captain's wife could watch the sea for the arrival of her husband's ship. The traditional stone doorways, or *pyliones,* are hand-carved with symbolic pictures. Corn means good harvest, birds mean peace, the cross brings safety and the sunflowers sunlight. The number of ropes carved around the perimeter of the door shows how many ships the captain had.

Some of the finest examples of these houses are found in Lindos, on Rhodes.

Hellenistic Citizens

In the twilight years of the classical age (from about the late 4th century BC), cosmopolitan folks started to weary of temples, casting their gaze towards a more decadent urban style. The Hellenistic architect was in hot demand for private homes and palace makeovers as wealthy citizens, dignitaries and political heavyweights lavishly remodelled their abodes in marble, and striking mosaics were displayed as status symbols (read *more* bling). The best Hellenistic ancient home displays are the grand houses at Delos.

Byzantine Zeal

Church-building was particularly expressive during Byzantium in Greece (from around AD 700). The original Greek Byzantine model features a distinctive cross-shape; essentially a central dome supported by four arches on piers and flanked by vaults, with smaller domes at the four corners and three apses to the east. Theologian architects opted for spectacular devotional mosaics and frescoes instead of carvings for the stylistic religious interiors. In Athens, the very appealing 12th-century Church of Agios Eleftherios incorporates fragments of a classical frieze in Pentelic marble; and the charming 11th-century Church of Kapnikarea sits stranded, smack bang in the middle of downtown Athens – its interior flooring is of coloured marble and the external brickwork, which alternates with stone, is set in patterns. Thessaloniki's 8th-century Church of Agia Sofia, with its 30m-high dome, is a humble version of its namesake in İstanbul. There are numerous Byzantine chapels in Mystras, many of which were originally private chapels attached to enchanting 17th- and 18th-century *arhontika* (mansions once owned by *arhons,* wealthy bourgeoisie merchants).

Several Byzantine monastic sites have made it to the Unesco World Heritage register, including the *katholikon* (main churches) of Osios Loukas, significant for their late-Byzantine multidomed style, and the 11th-century Moni Dafniou, which stands on the site of an ancient Sanctuary of Apollo.

Frankish Keeps & Venetian Strongholds

After the sacking of Constantinople by the Crusaders in 1204, much of Greece became the fiefdoms of Western aristocrats. The Villehardouin family punctuated the Peloponnesian landscape with Frankish castles, such as at Kalamata and at Mystras, where they also built a palace that ended up a court of the Byzantine imperial family for two centuries. When the Venetians dropped by to seize a few coastal enclaves, they built the impenetrable 16th-century Koules fortress in Iraklio, the very sturdy fortress at Methoni, and the imposing 18th-century Palamidi fortress at Nafplio. The rambling defence at Acrocorinth is studded with imposing gateways, and the rock-nest protecting the enchanting Byzantine village at Monemvasia commands spectacular ocean views.

Ottoman Offerings

Interestingly, remarkably few monuments are left to catalogue after four centuries of Ottoman Turkish rule (16th to 19th centuries). Though many mosques and their minarets have sadly crumbled or are in serious disrepair, some terrific Ottoman-Turkish examples still survive. These include the prominent pink-domed Mosque of Süleyman in Rhodes' Old Town. The Fethiye Mosque and Turkish Baths are two of Athens' few surviving Ottoman reminders, and the architect for the 16th-century Koursoun Tzami in Trikala also designed the Blue Mosque in İstanbul. The Turkish quarter of Varousi in Trikala, and the streets of Thessaloniki and of Didymotiho, near the Turkish border, showcase superb Turkish-designed homes with stained-glass windows, wooden overhangs on buttresses, decorated plasterwork and painted woodwork.

The distinctive blue-and-white Cycladic-style architecture most associated with the Greek islands was pragmatic and functional. The cuboid flat-roofed houses, huddled together along labyrinthine alleys, were designed to guard against the elements: strong winds and pirates.

Neoclassical Splendour

Regarded by experts as the most beautiful neoclassical building worldwide, the 1885 Athens Academy reflects Greece's post-Independence yearnings for grand and geometric forms, and Hellenistic detail. Renowned Danish architect Theophile Hansen drew inspiration from the Erechtheion to design the Academy's Ionic-style column entrance (guarded over by Apollo and Athena); the great interior oblong hall is lined with marble seating, and Austrian painter Christian Griepenkerl was commissioned to decorate its elaborate ceiling and wall paintings. In a similar vein, the Doric columns of the Temple of Hephaestus influenced Theophile's solid marble National Library, while Christian Hansen (Theophile's brother) was responsible for the handsome but more sedate Athens University, with its clean lines.

Meticulously restored neoclassical mansions house notable museums such as the acclaimed Benaki Museum.

Many provincial towns also display beautiful domestic adaptations of neoclassicism. In Symi, the harbour at Gialos is flanked by colourful neoclassical facades (still striking even if a little derelict) and Nafplio is also embellished with neoclassical buildings.

Modern Ideas

Athens today is embracing a sophisticated look-both-ways architectural aesthetic by showcasing its vast collection of antiquities and archaeological heritage in evolutionary buildings, and by beautifying landscapes for pedestrian zones to improve the urban environment. Examples include the well-designed facelift of the historic centre, including its spectacular floodlighting (designed by the renowned Pierre Bideau) of the ancient promenade, and the cutting-edge spaces emerging from once-drab and derelict industrial zones, such as the Technopolis gasworks arts complex in Gazi.

Nature & Wildlife

While Greece is a perfect place to rub shoulders with ancient statues, it's equally ideal for getting up close to nature. Hike through wildflowers, come eye-to-eye with a logger-head turtle, or simply stretch out on a beach. Greece has something for everyone who wants to get out and explore.

Experiencing the Outdoors
Greek Geography

No matter where you go in Greece, it's impossible to be much more than 100km from the sea. Rugged mountains and seemingly innumer-able islands dominate the landscape, which was shaped by submerging seas, volcanic explosions and mineral-rich terrain. The mainland cov-ers 131,944 sq km, with an indented coastline stretching for 15,020km. Mountains rise over 2000m and occasionally tumble down into plains, particularly in Thessaly and Thrace. Meanwhile, the Aegean and Ionian Seas link together the country's 1400 islands, with just 169 of them in-habited. These islands fill 400,000 sq km of territorial waters.

During the Triassic, Jurassic, Cretaceous and even later geological peri-ods, Greece was a shallow, oxygen-rich sea. The continuous submerging of land created large tracts of limestone through the whole submarine land mass. Later, as the land emerged from the sea to form the backbone of the current topography, a distinctly eroded landscape with crystalline rocks and other minerals began to appear, marking the spine that links the north and south of the mainland today. Limestone caves are a major feature of this karst landscape, shaped by the dissolution of a soluble layer of bedrock.

Volcanic activity once regularly hit Greece with force – one of the world's largest volcanic explosions was on Santorini around 1650 BC. Today earthquakes continue to shake the country on a smaller scale, but with almost predictable frequency. In 1999, a 5.9-magnitude earthquake near Athens killed nearly 150 people and left thousands homeless. Since

> The Greek Ortho-dox Church is the second-largest landowner in Greece.

A BURNING ISSUE

Each year, forest fires rage across Greece, destroying many thousands of hectares, often in some of the country's most picturesque areas. Mt Parnitha and the Peloponnese are still recovering from fires in 2007 that changed the face of the landscape. In the summer of 2012, more than 170 fast-burning fires swept across the country, swallowing entire villages and leaving more than 50 dead. One of the worst-hit islands was Chios, where more than 64 sq km of forest and farmland were destroyed. As the fires reached the outskirts of Ath-ens, the government declared a state of emergency and asked for water-bombing aircraft from Spain and Italy. By early in the summer of 2013, fires again threatened the capital and, in 2014, Greece requested help from the EU in fighting blazes in central Greece.

The increasing scale of recent fires is blamed on rising Mediterranean temperatures and high winds. Many locals argue that the government is ill-prepared and that its at-tempts to address the annual fires are slow. Fearing they won't receive help, many locals refuse to leave areas being evacuated, preferring to take the risk and attempting to fight the flames themselves.

2006, the country has had six quakes ranging from 6.4 to 6.9 in magnitude. None caused major damage. To check out Greece's explosive past, visit the craters of Santorini, Nisyros and Polyvotis.

Greece is short on rivers, with none that are navigable, although they've become popular locations for white-water rafting. The largest rivers are the Aheloös, Aliakmonas, Aoös and Arahthos, all of which have their source in the Pindos Mountains of Epiros.

The long plains of the river valleys, and those between the mountains and the coast, form Greece's only lowlands. The mountainous terrain, dry climate and poor soil leave farmers at a loss, and less than 25% of the land is cultivated. Greece is, however, rich in minerals, with reserves of oil, manganese, bauxite and lignite.

> Greece is the most seismically active country in Europe, with more than half of the continent's volcanic activity.

Wildflowers & Herbs

Greece is endowed with a variety of flora unrivaled in Europe. The wildflowers are spectacular, with more than 6000 species, including more than 100 varieties of orchid. They continue to thrive because most of the land is inadequate for intensive agriculture and has therefore escaped the ravages of chemical fertilisers.

The regions with the most wildflowers are the Lefka Ori Mountains in Crete and the Mani area of the Peloponnese. Trees begin to blossom as early as the end of February in warmer areas and the wildflowers start to appear in March. During spring, hillsides are carpeted with flowers, which seem to sprout even from the rocks. By summer the flowers have disappeared from everywhere but the northern mountainous regions. Autumn brings a new period of blossoming.

Herbs grow wild throughout much of Greece and you'll see locals out picking fresh herbs for their kitchen. Locally grown herbs are also increasingly sold as souvenirs and are generally organic.

Forests

> *Herbs in Cooking* is an illustrative book by Maria and Nikos Psilakis that can be used as both an identification guide and a cookbook for Greek dishes seasoned with local herbs.

The lush forests that once covered ancient Greece are increasingly rare. Having been decimated by thousands of years of clearing for grazing, boat building and housing, they've more recently suffered from severe forest fires. Northern Greece is the only region that has retained significant areas of native forest – there are mountainsides covered with dense thickets of hop hornbeam *(Ostrya carpinifolia)*, noted for its lavish display of white-clustered flowers. Another common species is the Cyprus plane *(Platanus orientalis insularis)*, which thrives wherever there's ample water.

Watching for Wildlife

On The Ground

In areas widely inhabited by humans, you're unlikely to spot any wild animals other than the odd fox, weasel, hare or rabbit. The more remote mountains of northern Greece continue to support a wide range of wildlife, including wild dogs and shepherds' dogs, which often roam higher pastures on grazing mountains and should be given a wide berth.

The brown bear, Europe's largest land mammal, still manages to survive in very small numbers in the Pindos Mountains, the Peristeri Range that rises above the Prespa Lakes, and in the mountains along the Bulgarian border. It's estimated that around 200 survive; your best bet for seeing one is at the **Arcturos Bear Sanctuary** (www.arcturos.gr; Nymfeo) in Macedonia.

The protected grey wolf is officially classified as stable with an estimated 200 to 300 in the wild. It's believed up to 100 are killed annually by farmers' (illegal) use of poison baits in retaliation for the occasional marauding of their flocks. The Greek government and insurance companies pay compensation for lost livestock but it doesn't appear to slow the killings. The surviving wolves live in the Pindos Mountains and the Dadia

Forest Reserve area. Head to the Arcturos Wolf Sanctuary in Agrapidia, near Florina, which houses nine wolves rescued from illegal captivity.

The golden jackal is a strong candidate for Greece's most misunderstood mammal. Although its diet is 50% vegetarian (and the other 50% is made up of carrion, reptiles and small mammals), it has traditionally shouldered much of the blame for attacks on stock and has been hunted by farmers as a preventative measure. Near the brink of extinction, it was declared a protected species in 1990 and now survives only in the Fokida district of central Greece and on the island of Samos.

Once roaming across all of mainland Greece, the graceful red deer is now restricted to the Sithonia peninsula, the Rhodope Mountain bordering Bulgaria and Mt Parnitha north of Athens.

Greece has an active snake population and in spring and summer you will inevitably spot them on roads and pathways around the country. Fortunately the majority are harmless, though the viper and the coral snake can cause fatalities. Lizards are in abundance too.

The **Hellenic Wildlife Hospital** (www.ekpazp.gr) is the oldest and largest wildlife rehabilitation centre in southern Europe.

In the Air

Birdwatchers have a field day in Greece as the country is on many north–south migratory paths. Lesvos (Mytilini) in particular draws a regular following of birders from all over Europe, who come to spot some of more than 279 recorded species that stop off at the island annually. Storks are more visible visitors, arriving in early spring from Africa and returning to the same nests year after year. These are built on electricity poles, chimney tops and church towers, and can weigh up to 50kg. Keep an eye out for them in northern Greece, especially in Thrace in Macedonia. Thrace has the richest colony of fish-eating birds in Europe, including species such as egrets, herons, cormorants and ibises, as well as the rare Dalmatian pelican. The wetlands at the mouth of the Evros

Nature Conservation

Pelicans and pygmy cormorants (www.spp.gr)

Birdlife (www. ornithologiki.gr)

Wildflowers (www. greekmountain flora.info)

Sea turtles (www. archelon.gr)

Going green (www. cleanupgreece. org.gr)

NATURE & WILDLIFE WATCHING FOR WILDLIFE

NATIONAL PARKS

National parks were first established in Greece in 1938 with the creation of Mt Olympus National Park. There are now 10 national parks and two marine parks, which aim to protect Greece's unique flora and fauna. Facilities for visitors are often basic, abundant walking trails are not always maintained and the clutch of refuges is very simple. To most, the facilities matter little when compared to nature's magnificent backdrop. It's well worth experiencing the wild side of Greece in one of these settings.

Cape Sounion (p125) A cape with panoramic views and home to the Temple of Poseidon.

Iti National Park (p204) Tranquil stretches of forest, meadows and pools; home to eagles, deer and boar.

Mt Olympus National Park (p256) Home to Greece's tallest mountain, rich flora and considered the home of the gods.

Mt Parnitha National Park (p126) Very popular wooded parkland north of Athens; home to the red deer.

National Marine Park of Alonnisos Northern Sporades (p623) Covers six islands and 22 islets in the Sporades and is home to monk seals, dolphins and rare birdlife.

National Marine Park of Zakynthos An Ionian refuge for loggerhead turtles.

Parnassos National Park (http://en.parnassosnp.gr) Towering limestone and scenic views down to Delphi.

Prespa Lakes (p262) One of Europe's oldest lakes, steeped in wildlife and tranquillity.

Samaria Gorge (p454) Spectacular gorge in Crete, a refuge for the kri-kri (Cretan goat).

Vikos-Aoös National Park Excellent hiking with caves, canyons and dense forest.

River, close to the border with Turkey, are home to two easily identifiable wading birds – the avocet, which has a long curving beak, and the black-winged stilt, which has extremely long pink legs.

Upstream on the Evros River in Thrace, the 72-sq-km Dadia Forest Reserve hosts Europe's largest range of birds of prey. Thirty-six of the 38 European species can be seen here, and it is a breeding ground for 23 of them. Permanent residents include the giant black vulture, whose wingspan reaches 3m, the griffon vulture and the golden eagle. Europe's last 15 pairs of royal eagle nest on the river delta. About 350 pairs of the rare Eleonora's falcon (60% of the world's population) nest on the island of Piperi in the Sporades and on Tilos, which is also home to the very rare Bonelli's eagle and the shy, cormorant-like Mediterranean shag.

Under the Sea

As Europe's most endangered marine mammal, the monk seal *(Monachus monachus)* ekes out an extremely precarious existence in Greece. Approximately 200 to 250 monk seals, about 50% of the world's population, are found in both the Ionian and Aegean Seas. Small colonies also live on the island of Alonnisos and there have been reported sightings on Tilos.

The waters around Zakynthos are home to the last large sea turtle colony in Europe, that of the endangered loggerhead turtle *(Caretta caretta)*. Loggerheads also nest in smaller numbers in the Peloponnese and on Kefallonia and Crete. Greece's turtles have many hazards to dodge – entanglement in fishing nets and boat propellers, consumption of floating rubbish, and the destruction of their nesting beaches by sun-loungers and beach umbrellas that threaten their eggs.

There is still the chance that you will spot dolphins from a ferry deck, though a number of the species are now considered vulnerable. The number of common dolphins *(Delphinus delphis)* has dropped from 150 to less than 20 in the past decade. The main threats to dolphins are a diminished food supply and entanglement in fishing nets.

Loggerhead turtle hatchlings use the journey from the nest to the sea to build up their strength. Helping the baby turtles to the sea can actually lower their chances of survival.

GREEN ISSUES

Environmental awareness is beginning to seep into the fabric of Greece society, leading to slow but positive change. Environmental education happens in schools, recycling is common in cities, and even in the smallest villages you may find organic restaurants and environmentally sustainable businesses. However, problems such as deforestation and soil erosion date back thousands of years. Live cultivation, goats, construction and industry have all taken their toll.

Illegal development of mainly coastal areas, and building in forested or protected areas, has gained momentum in Greece since the 1970s. Despite attempts at introducing laws, and protests by locals and environmental groups, corruption and the lack of an infrastructure to enforce the laws means little is done to abate the land-grab. The issue is complicated by population growth and increased urban sprawl. Developments often put a severe strain on water supplies and endangered wildlife. While a few developments have been torn down, in more cases illegal buildings are legalised as they offer much needed, affordable housing.

In 2014 NATO's plan to decommission 700 tonnes of Syria's chemical weapons off the southern coast of Crete was protested by over 10,000 islanders concerned for the environment and their livelihood. Scientists claimed seawater would neutralise the chemicals within 90 days, but after Albania, Thailand, Belgium, Germany and Norway all refused to have the process take place in their waters, the UN approved the international waters between Crete and Malta. Protesters claimed the effectiveness of hydrolysis was unclear and warned that there was no way of knowing the impact of the discharge into the Mediterranean, which could be devastating for the marine ecosystems and tourism. Sadly, only time will tell if they were right.

Survival Guide

Directory A–Z

Accommodation

There is a range of accommodation available in Greece to suit every taste and pocket. All places to stay are subject to strict price controls set by the tourist police. By law, a notice must be displayed in every room, stating the category of the room and the price charged in each season. It's difficult to generalise accommodation prices in Greece as rates depend entirely on the season and location. Don't expect to pay the same price for a double on one of the islands as you would in central Greece or Athens.

Other points to note when considering hotel prices:

➡ Prices include community tax and VAT (value-added tax).

➡ A 10% surcharge may be added for stays of fewer than three nights, but this is not mandatory.

➡ A mandatory charge of 20% is levied for an additional bed (although this is often waived if the bed is for a child).

➡ During July and August accommodation owners will charge the maximum price, which can be as much as double the low season price.

➡ In spring and autumn prices can drop by 20%.

➡ Rip-offs are rare; if you suspect that you have been exploited, make a report to the tourist or the regular police, and they will act swiftly.

Camping

Camping is a good option, especially in summer. There are almost 350 camping grounds in Greece, found on the majority of islands (with the notable exception of the Saronic Gulf Islands). Standard facilities include hot showers, kitchens, restaurants and mini-markets – and often a swimming pool.

Most camping grounds are open only between May and October although always check ahead; particularly in the north, some don't open until June. The **Panhellenic Camping Association** (www.panhellenic-camping-union.gr) website lists all of its camping grounds and relevant details.

If you're camping in the height of summer, bring a silver fly sheet to reflect the heat off your tent (dark tents become sweat lodges). Between May and mid-September the weather is warm enough to sleep out under the stars. Many camping grounds have covered areas where tourists who don't have tents can sleep in summer; you can get by with a lightweight sleeping bag. It's a good idea to have a foam pad to lie on, a waterproof cover for your sleeping bag and plenty of bug repellent.

Some other points:

➡ Camping fees are highest from mid-June through to the end of August.

➡ Camping grounds charge €5 to €7 per adult and €3 to €4 for children aged four to 12. There's no charge for children under four.

➡ Tent sites cost from €4 per night for small tents, and from €5 per night for large tents.

➡ You can often rent tents for around €5.

➡ Caravan sites start at around €6; car costs are typically €4 to €5.

Domatia

Domatia (literally 'rooms') are the Greek equivalent of the British B&B, minus the breakfast. Once upon a time, domatia were little more than

---

BOOK YOUR STAY ONLINE

For more accommodation reviews by Lonely Planet authors, check out http://lonelyplanet.com/greece/hotels. You'll find independent reviews, as well as recommendations on the best places to stay. Best of all, you can book online.

spare rooms in the family home; nowadays, many are purpose-built appendages with fully equipped kitchens. Standards of cleanliness are generally high.

Domatia remain a popular option for budget travellers. Expect to pay from €25 to €50 for a single, and €35 to €65 for a double, depending on whether bathrooms are shared or private, the season and how long you plan to stay. Domatia are found throughout the mainland (except in large cities) and on almost every island that has a permanent population. Many domatia are open only between April and October.

From June to September, domatia owners are out in force, touting for customers. They meet buses and boats, shouting 'room, room!' and often carrying photographs of their rooms. In peak season it can prove a mistake not to take up an offer – but be wary of owners who are vague about the location of their accommodation.

Hostels

Most youth hostels in Greece are run by the **Greek Youth Hostel Organisation** (www.athens-yhostel.com). There are affiliated hostels in Athens, Olympia, Patra and Thessaloniki on the mainland, and on the island of Crete.

Hostel rates vary from around €10 to €20 for a bed in a dorm and you don't have to be a member to stay in them. Few have curfews.

Hotels

Hotels in Greece are divided into six categories: deluxe, A, B, C, D and E. Hotels are categorised according to the size of the rooms, whether or not they have a bar, and the ratio of bathrooms to beds, rather than standards of cleanliness, comfort of beds and friendliness of staff – all elements that may be of greater relevance to guests.

➡ **A and B class** Full amenities, private bathrooms and constant hot water; prices range from €50 to €85 for a single and from €90 and up for double.

➡ **C class** A snack bar and rooms with private bathrooms, but not necessarily constant hot water; prices range from €35 to €60 for a single in high season and €45 to €80 for a double.

➡ **D class** Generally have shared bathrooms and they may have solar-heated water, meaning hot water is not guaranteed; prices range from €25 to €50 for a single, and €35 to €65 for a double.

➡ **E class** Shared bathrooms and hot water may cost extra; prices are around €25 for a single and €35 for a double.

Mountain Refuges

There are 55 mountain refuges dotted around the Greek mainland, Crete and Evia. They range from small huts with outdoor toilets and no cooking facilities to very comfortable modern lodges. They are run by the country's various mountaineering and skiing clubs. Prices start at around €10 per person, depending on the facilities. The **EOT** (Greek National Tourist Organisation; www.visitgreece. gr) publication *Greece: Mountain Refuges & Ski Centres* has details about each refuge; copies are available at all EOT branches.

Pensions

Pensions are indistinguishable from hotels. They are categorised as A, B or C class. An A-class pension is equivalent in amenities and price to a B-class hotel, a B-class pension is equivalent to a C-class hotel, and a C-class pension is equivalent to a D- or E-class hotel.

Rental Accommodation

A really practical way to save money and maximise comfort is to rent a furnished apartment or villa. Many are purpose-built for tourists while others – villas in particular – may be owners' homes that they are not using. Some owners may insist on a minimum stay of a week. A good site to spot prospective villas is www. greekislands.com. The booking site airbnb.com also has lots of rental properties listed in Greece and can be great way to hunt down reasonable accommodation if you're going to be staying in one location for more an a couple of nights.

Customs Regulations

There are no longer duty-free restrictions within the EU. Upon entering the country from outside the EU, customs inspection is usually cursory for foreign tourists and a verbal declaration is generally all that is required. Random searches are still occasionally made for drugs. Import regulations for medicines are strict; if you are taking medication, make sure you get a statement from your doctor before you leave home. It is illegal, for instance, to take codeine into Greece without an accompanying doctor's certificate.

It is strictly forbidden to export antiquities (anything more than 100 years old) without an export permit. This crime is second only to drug smuggling in the penalties imposed. It is an offence to remove even the smallest article from an archaeological site. The place to apply for an export permit is the Antique Dealers and Private Collections section of the **Athens Archaeological Service** (http://nam.culture. gr; Polygnotou 13, Plaka, Athens) website.

Vehicles

Cars can be brought into Greece for six months without a carnet; only a green card (international third-party insurance) is required. If arriving from Italy, your only proof of entry into the country may be your ferry-ticket stub, so don't lose it. From other countries, a passport stamp will be ample evidence.

Discount Cards

Camping Card International (CCI; www.campingcardinternational.com) Gives up to 25% savings in camping fees and third-party liability insurance while on the camping ground. Valid in over 2500 campsites across Europe.

European Youth Card (www. eyca.org) Available for anyone up to the age of 30 (you don't have to be a resident of Europe); provides discounts of up to 20% at sights, shops and for some transport. Available from the website or travel agencies in Athens and Thessaloniki for €10.

International Student Identity Card (ISIC; www.isic.org) Entitles the holder to half-price admission to museums and ancient sites, and discounts at some budget hotels and hostels. Available from travel agencies in Athens. Applicants require documents proving their student status, a passport photo and €10.

Seniors cards Card-carrying EU pensioners can claim a range of benefits such as reduced admission to ancient sites and museums, and discounts on bus and train fares.

GOVERNMENT TRAVEL ADVICE

The following government websites offer travel advisories and information on current hot spots.

➡ **Australian Department of Foreign Affairs** (www. smarttraveller.gov.au)

➡ **British Foreign Office** (www.fco.gov.uk)

➡ **Canadian Department of Foreign Affairs** (www. voyage.gc.ca)

➡ **US State Department** (http://travel.state.gov)

Electricity

220V/50Hz

220V/50Hz

Embassies & Consulates

All foreign embassies in Greece are in Athens and its suburbs, with a few consulates in Thessaloniki.

Albanian Embassy (☎210 687 6200; embassy.athens@ mfa.gov.al; Vekiareli 7, Athens)

Australian Embassy (☎210 870 4000; www.greece. embassy.gov.au; Ambelokipi, 6th fl, Thon Building, cnr Leoforos Alexandras & Leoforos Kifisias, Athens)

Bulgarian Embassy (☎210 674 8105; www.mfa.bg/embas sies/greece; Stratigou Kalari 33a, Psychiko, Athens)

Canadian Embassy (☎210 727 3400; www.greece.gc.ca; Ethnikis Antistaseos 48, Cha-landri, Athens)

Cypriot Embassy (☎210 723 7883; Irodotou 16, Athens)

French Embassy (☎210 361 1663; www.ambafrance-gr. org; Leoforos Vasilissis Sofias 7, Athens)

German Embassy (☎210 728 5111; www.athen.diplo.de; Dimitriou 3, cnr Karaoli, Kolo-naki, Athens)

Irish Embassy (☎210 723 2771; www.embassyofireland.gr; Leoforos Vasileos Konstantinou 5-7, Athens)

Italian Embassy (☎210 361 7260; www.ambatene.esteri.it; Sekeri 2, Athens)

Netherlands Embassy (☎210 725 4900; www.dutch embassy.gr; Leoforos Vasileos Konstantinou 5-7, Athens)

New Zealand Embassy (☎+39 06 853 7501; www. nzembassy.com/italy; Via Clitunno 44, Rome) Travellers from New Zealand should con-tact the embassy in Rome.

Turkish Embassy (☎210 726 3000; embassy.athens@ mfa.gov.tr; Vassileos Gheorgiou B'8) Has an additional branch in Athens (☎210 724 5915; turkbaskon@kom.forthnet.gr; Leoforos Vasileos Georgiou 8, Athens) and one in Thessaloniki (☎2310 248 452; turkbaskon@ kom.forthnet.gr; Agiou Dimi-triou 151).

UK Embassy (☎210 727 2600; www.ukingreece.fco.gov. uk; 1 Ploutarchou, Athens) Also has a branch at Thessa-loniki (☎2310 278 006; www. ukingreece.fco.gov.uk/en; Tsimiski 43).

US Embassy (☎210 721 2951; http://athens.usembassy. gov; 91 Vasilisis Sophias, Athens) Also has a branch at Thessaloniki (☎2310 242 905; http://athens.us embassy.gov; Tsimiski 43).

Gay & Lesbian Travellers

In a country where the church still plays a prominent role in shaping society's views on issues such as sexuality, it comes as no surprise that homosexuality is generally frowned upon by many locals – especially outside major cities. While there is no legislation against homosexual activity, it pays to be discreet.

Some areas of Greece are, however, extremely popular destinations for gay and les-bian travellers. Athens has a busy gay scene, but most gay and lesbian travellers head for the islands. Mykonos has long been famous for its bars, beaches and general hedon-ism, while Skiathos also has its share of gay hang-outs. The island of Lesvos (Myt-ilini), birthplace of the lesbian poet Sappho, has become something of a place of pil-grimage for lesbians.

The *Spartacus Interna-tional Gay Guide* (www.spart-acusworld.com), published by Bruno Gmünder (Berlin), is widely regarded as the lead-ing authority on the gay trav-el. The Greek section contains a wealth of information on gay venues everywhere from Alexandroupoli to Xanthi.

Health
Availability & Cost of Health Care

Although medical training is of a high standard in Greece, the public health service is badly underfunded. Hospi-tals can be overcrowded, hygiene is not always what it should be, and relatives are expected to bring in food for the patient – which can be a problem for a tourist. Conditions and treatment are much better in private hospitals, which are expen-sive. All this means that a good health-insurance policy is essential.

➡ If you need an ambulance in Greece call ☎166.

➡ There is at least one doctor on every island and larger islands have hospitals.

➡ Pharmacies can dispense medicines that are available only on prescription in most European countries.

➡ Consult a pharmacist for minor ailments.

Environmental Hazards

➡ Dangerous snakes include the adder and the less common viper and coral snakes. To minimise the possibilities of being bitten, always wear boots, socks and long trousers when walking through undergrowth where snakes may be present.

➡ Mosquitoes can be an annoying problem, though there is no danger of contracting malaria. The electric mosquito-repellent devices are usually sufficient to keep the insects at bay at night. Choose accommodation that has fly screen on the windows wherever possible. Some mosquitoes in northern Greece can provoke a severe reaction.

➡ The Asian tiger mosquito (*Aedes albopictus*) may be encountered in mountainous areas, can be a voracious daytime biter, and is known to carry several viruses, including Eastern equine encephalitis, which can affect the central nervous system and cause severe complications and death. Use protective sprays or lotion if you suspect you are being bitten during the day.

Insurance

If you're an EU citizen, a European Health Insurance Card (EHIC) covers you for most medical care but not emergency repatriation or non-emergencies. It is available from health centres and post offices in the UK. Citizens from other countries should find out if there is a reciprocal arrangement for free medical care between their country and Greece. If you do need health insurance, make sure you get a policy that covers you for the worst possible scenario, such as an accident requiring an emergency flight home. Find out in advance if your insurance plan will make payments directly to providers or reimburse you later for overseas health expenditures.

Worldwide travel insurance is available at www.lonelyplanet.com/bookings. You can buy, extend and claim online anytime – even if you're already on the road.

Water

Tap water is drinkable and safe in much of Greece but not always in small villages and on some of the islands. Always ask locally if the water is safe and, if in doubt, drink boiled or bought water. Even when water is safe, the substances and bacteria in it may be different from those you are used to and can cause vomiting or diarrhoea. Bottled water is widely available.

Internet Access

There has been a huge increase in the number of hotels and businesses using the internet, and free wi-fi is available in most cafes, restaurants and hotels. Some cities even have free wi-fi zones in shopping and eating areas. There are fewer and fewer internet cafes or computers for guests to use as people increasingly carry their own smartphone or tablet.

Legal Matters

Arrests

It is a good idea to have your passport with you at all times in case you are stopped by the police and questioned. This is particularly true if you are travelling in border areas. Greek citizens are presumed always to have identification on them; foreign visitors are similarly presumed to by the police. If you are arrested by police insist on an interpreter (*dierminéas; the-*lo dhi-ermi-nea) and/or a lawyer (*dik-igóros; the-*lo dhi-ki-go-ro).

Drugs

Greek drug laws are the strictest in Europe. Greek courts make no distinction between possession and pushing. Possession of even a small amount of marijuana is likely to land you in jail.

Maps

Unless you're going to hike or drive, the free maps given out by the EOT and larger hotels will probably suffice, although they're not 100% accurate.

Anavasi (www.mountains.gr). Athens-based company publishing maps with excellent coverage. Hikers should consider their *Topo* series, which have durable, waterproof paper and detailed walking trails for many of the Aegean islands.

Terrain (www.terrainmaps.gr) Maps published in Athens and offering equally good coverage. All maps can be bought online or at major bookstores in Greece.

Money

ATMs

ATMs are found in every town large enough to support a bank and in almost all the tourist areas. If you've got MasterCard or Visa, there are plenty of places to withdraw money. Cirrus and Maestro users can make withdrawals in all major towns and tourist areas. Be aware that many ATMs on the islands can lose their connection for a day or two at a time, making it impossible for anyone (locals included) to withdraw money. It's useful to have a backup source of money.

Automated foreign-exchange machines are common in major tourist areas. They take all the major European currencies, Australian and US dollars and Japanese yen, and are useful in an emergency, although they charge a hefty commission.

Be warned that many card companies can put an automatic block on your card after your first withdrawal abroad, as an antifraud mechanism. To avoid this happening, inform your bank of your travel plans.

Cash

Nothing beats cash for convenience – or for risk. If you lose cash, it's gone for good and very few travel insurers will come to your rescue. Those that will, normally limit the amount to approximately US$300. That said, in the current financial climate, many businesses are requesting cash only. It's best to carry no more cash than you need for the next few days. It's also a good idea to set aside a small amount of cash, say US$100, as an emergency stash.

Note that Greek shopkeepers and small-business owners have a perennial problem with having any small change. If buying small items it is better to tender coins or small-denomination notes.

Credit Cards

Credit cards are now an accepted part of the commercial scene in Greece, although they're often not accepted on many of the smaller islands or in small villages. In larger places, credit cards can be used at top-end hotels, restaurants and shops. Some C-class hotels will accept credit cards, but D- and E-class hotels very seldom do.

The main credit cards are MasterCard and Visa, both of which are widely accepted in Greece. They can also be used as cash cards to draw cash from the ATMs of affiliated Greek banks in the same way as at home. Daily withdrawal limits are set by the issuing bank and are given in local currency only.

Tipping

In restaurants a service charge is normally included in the bill, and while a tip is not expected (as it is in North America), it is always appreciated and should be left if the service has been good. Taxi drivers normally expect you to round up the fare, while bellhops who help you carry your luggage to your hotel room or stewards on ferries who take you to your cabin normally expect a small gratuity of between €1 and €3.

Travellers Cheques

The main reason to carry travellers cheques rather than cash is the protection they offer against theft. They are, however, losing popularity as more and more travellers opt to put their money in a bank at home and withdraw it at ATMs as they go. American Express, Visa and Thomas Cook cheques are available in euros and are all widely accepted and have efficient replacement policies.

Photography & Video

➡ Digital memory cards are readily available from camera stores.

➡ Never photograph a military installation; some are less than obvious and near to wildlife viewing areas.

➡ Flash photography is not allowed inside churches, and it's considered taboo to photograph the main altar.

➡ Greeks usually love having their photos taken, but always ask permission first.

PRACTICALITIES

Weights & Measures Greece uses the metric system.

Post To send post abroad, use the yellow post boxes labelled *exoteriko* (for overseas).

Newspapers Greek current affairs are covered in the daily English-language edition of Kathimerini within the International Herald Tribune.

DVDs Be aware that Greece is region code 2 when buying DVDs to watch back home.

➡ At archaeological sites you will be stopped from using a tripod as it marks you as a 'professional'.

Public Holidays

All banks and shops and most museums and ancient sites close on public holidays.

Many sites (including the ancient sites in Athens) offer free entry on the first Sunday of the month, with the exception of July and August. You may also gain free entry on other locally celebrated holidays, although this varies across the country.

National public holidays:

New Year's Day 1 January

Epiphany 6 January

First Sunday in Lent February

Greek Independence Day 25 March

Good Friday March/April

Orthodox Easter Sunday 1 May 2016, 16 April 2017, 8 April 2018, 28 April 2019

May Day (Protomagia) 1 May

Whit Monday (Agiou Pnevmatos) 50 days after Easter Sunday

Feast of the Assumption 15 August

Ohi Day 28 October

Christmas Day 25 December

St Stephen's Day 26 December

Safe Travel

Drinks

Adulterated drinks (known as *bombes*) are served in some bars and clubs in Athens and at resorts known for partying. These drinks are diluted with cheap illegal imports that leave you feeling worse for wear the next day.

At many party resorts catering to large budget-tour groups, spiked drinks are not uncommon; keep your hand over the top of your glass. More often than not, the perpetrators are foreign tourists rather than locals.

Tourist Police

The *touristikí astynomía* (tourist police) work in cooperation with the regular police and are found in cities and popular tourist destinations. Each office has at least one member of staff who speaks English. Hotels, restaurants, travel agencies, tourist shops, tourist guides, waiters, taxi drivers and bus drivers all come under the jurisdiction of the tourist police. If you have a complaint about any of these, report it to the tourist police and they will investigate. If you need to report a theft or loss of passport, go to the tourist police, and they will act as interpreters between you and the regular police.

Smoking

In July 2009 Greece brought in antismoking laws similar to those found throughout most of Europe. Smoking is now banned inside public places, with the penalty being fines placed on the business owners. Greece is home to some of the heaviest smokers in Europe, so it

OPENING HOURS

While opening hours can vary depending on the season, day or mood of the proprietor, it's possible to make some generalisations. It's worth noting that while the government establishes opening hours for major sites, these are not always consistently followed. Always try to double-check opening hours before visiting. In summer, many shops in major tourist destinations are also open Sunday.

Banks 8am-2.30pm Monday-Thursday, 8am-2pm Friday

Bars 8pm-late

Cafes 10am-midnight

Clubs 10pm-4am

Post offices 7.30am-2pm Monday-Friday (rural areas); 7.30am-8pm Monday-Friday, 7.30am-2pm Saturday (urban offices)

Restaurants 11am-3pm and 7pm-1am

Shops 8am-3pm Monday, Wednesday and Saturday; 8am-2.30pm and 5pm-8.30pm Tuesday, Thursday and Friday; in Crete, 9am-2pm Monday-Saturday, increased hours Tuesday, Thursday and Friday, open all day summer in resorts

is a challenge for these laws to be enforced and they are often imposed in only a nominal way in remote locations where proprietors fear they would lose business.

Telephone Services

The Greek telephone service is maintained by the public corporation known as OTE (pronounced o-*teh*; Organismos Tilepikoinonion Ellados). There are public telephones just about everywhere, including in some unbelievably isolated spots. The phones are easy to operate and can be used for local, long-distance and international calls. The 'i' at the top left of the push-button dialling panel brings up the operating instructions in English. Note that in Greece the area code must always be dialled when making a call (ie all Greek phone numbers are 10 digits).

Mobile Phones

There are several mobile service providers in Greece, among which Panafon, Cosmote, Vodafone and Wind are

the best known. Of these four, Cosmote tends to have the best coverage in remote areas. All offer 2G connectivity and pay-as-you-talk services for which you can buy a rechargeable SIM card and have your own Greek mobile number. If you're buying a package, be sure to triple-check the fine print. There are restrictions on deals such as 'free-minutes' only being available to phones using the same provider.

The use of a mobile phone while driving in Greece is prohibited, but the use of a Bluetooth headset is allowed.

Phonecards

All public phones use OTE phonecards, known as *telekarta*, not coins. These cards are widely available at *periptera* (street kiosks), corner shops and tourist shops. A local call costs around €0.30 for three minutes.

It's also possible to use payphones with the growing range of discount-card schemes. This involves dialling an access code and then punching in your card number. The OTE version of this

card is known as 'Hronokarta'. The cards come with instructions in Greek and English and the talk time is enormous compared to the standard phonecard rates.

Time

Greece maintains one time zone throughout the country. It is two hours ahead of GMT/UTC and three hours ahead on daylight-saving time – which begins on the last Sunday in March, when clocks are put forward one hour. Daylight saving ends on the last Sunday in October.

Toilets

➡ Most places in Greece have Western-style toilets, especially hotels and restaurants that cater for tourists. You'll occasionally come across Asian-style squat toilets in older houses, *kafeneia* (coffee houses) and public toilets.

➡ Public toilets are a rarity, except at airports and bus and train stations. Cafes are the best option if you get caught short, but you'll be expected to buy something for the privilege.

➡ The Greek plumbing system can't handle toilet paper; apparently the pipes are too narrow and anything larger than a postage stamp seems to cause a problem. Toilet paper etc should be placed in the small bin provided next to every toilet.

Tourist Information

Tourist information is handled by the Greek National Tourist Organisation, known by the initials GNTO abroad and EOT within Greece. The quality of service from office to office varies dramatically; in some you'll get information aplenty and in others you'll be hard pressed to find anyone behind the desk. EOT offices can be found in major tourist locations, though they are increasingly being supplemented or even replaced by local municipality tourist offices (such as in the Peloponnese).

The tourist police also fulfil the same functions as the EOT and municipal tourist offices, dispensing maps and brochures, and giving information on transport. If you're really stuck, the tourist police may be able to help to find accommodation.

Travellers with Disabilities

Access for travellers with disabilities has improved somewhat in recent years, though mostly in Athens where there are more accessible sights, hotels and restaurants. Much of the rest of Greece remains inaccessible to wheelchairs, and the abundance of stones, marble, slippery cobbles and stepped alleys creates a further challenge. People who have visual or hearing impairments are also rarely catered to.

Careful planning before you go can make a world of difference. The site www.greecetravel.com/handicapped) links to local articles, resorts and tour groups catering to tourists with physical disabilities.

Sailing Holidays (www.charter ayachtingreece.com/DRYachting/index.html) Two-day to two-week sailing trips around the Greek islands in fully accessible yachts.

Sirens Resort (www.hotelsof greece.com/central/loutraki/sirens-wheelchair-accessable-resort/index.html; Skaloma, Loutraki, Corinthia) Family-friendly resort with accessible apartments, tours and ramps into the sea.

Visas

The list of countries whose nationals can stay in Greece for up to three months without a visa includes Australia, Canada, all EU countries, Iceland, Israel, Japan, New Zealand, Norway, Switzerland and the USA. Other countries included are the European principalities of Monaco and San Marino and most South American countries. The list changes though – contact Greek embassies for the latest.

If you wish to stay in Greece for longer than three months within a six-month period, you require a visa from the Greek embassy in your country of residence. You are unable to apply for this in Greece. Unlike student and work visas, tourist visas are rarely granted for more than three months.

Volunteering

Earth Sea & Sky (www.earth seasky.org) Conservation and research based in the Ionian Islands.

Hellenic Society for the Study & Protection of the Monk Seal (Map p60;[☎]210 522 2888; www.mom.gr; Solomou 53, Exarhia, Athens) Volunteers assist with monitoring programs on the Ionian Islands.

Hellenic Wildlife Hospital (Elliniko Kentro Perithalpsis Agrion Zoön;[☎]22970 28367; www.ekpazp.gr; ⊙10am-7pm) Volunteers head (particularly during the winter months) to Aegina to this large wildlife rehabilitation centre.

Sea Turtle Protection Society of Greece (☎21052 31342; www.archelon.gr) Includes monitoring sea turtles in the Peloponnese.

WWOOF (World Wide Opportunities on Organic Farms; www.wwoofgreece.org) Offers opportunities for volunteers at one of around 57 farms in Greece.

Women Travellers

Many women travel alone in Greece. The crime rate remains relatively low and solo travel is probably safer than in most European countries. This does not mean that you should be lulled into complacency; bag snatching and sexual assault do occur, particularly at party resorts on the islands.

The biggest nuisance to foreign women travelling alone is the guys the Greeks have nicknamed *kamaki*. The word means 'fishing trident' and refers to the *kamaki's* favourite pastime: 'fishing' for foreign women. You'll find them wherever there are lots of tourists: young (for the most part), smooth-talking guys who aren't in the least bashful about approaching women in the street. They can be very persistent, but they are usually a hassle rather than a threat. The majority of Greek men treat foreign women with respect.

Working

EU nationals don't need a work permit, but they need a residency permit and a Greek tax file number if they intend to stay longer than three months. Nationals of other countries need a work permit.

English Tutoring

If you're looking for a permanent job, the most widely available option is to teach English. A TEFL (Teaching English as a Foreign Language) certificate or a university degree is an advantage but not essential. In the UK, look through the *Times* educational supplement or Tuesday's edition of the *Guardian* newspaper for opportunities; in other countries, contact the Greek embassy.

Another possibility is to find a job teaching English once you are in Greece. You will see language schools everywhere. Strictly speaking, you need a licence to teach in these schools, but many will employ teachers without one. The best time to look around for such a job is late summer.

The noticeboard at the Compendium in Athens sometimes has ads looking for private English lessons.

Transport

GETTING THERE & AWAY

Flights, cars and tours can be booked online at lonelyplanet.com/bookings.

Entering the Country

Visitors to Greece with EU passports are rarely given more than a cursory glance, but customs and police may be interested in what you are carrying. EU citizens may also enter Greece on a national identity card.

Visitors from outside the EU may require a visa. Be sure to check with consular authorities before you arrive.

Air

Airports

Greece has four main international airports that take chartered and scheduled flights.

Other international airports across the country include Santorini (Thira), Karpathos, Samos, Skiathos, Hrysoupoli, Aktion, Kefallonia and Zakynthos. These airports are most often used for charter flights to and from the UK, Germany and Scandinavia.

Eleftherios Venizelos International Airport (ATH; ☑210 353 0000; www.aia.gr) Athens' Eleftherios Venizelos International Airport lies near Spata, 27km east of Athens. It has all the modern conveniences, including 24-hour luggage storage in the arrivals hall and a children's playroom – even a small archaeological museum above the check-in hall for passing time.

Nikos Kazantzakis International Airport (HER; ☑general 28103 97800, info 28103 97136; www.heraklion-airport.info) About 5km east of Iraklio (Crete). Has a bank, ATM, duty-free shop and cafe-bar.

Diagoras Airport (RHO; ☑22410 88700; www.rhodes-airport.org) On the island of Rhodes.

Makedonia International Airport (SKG; ☑2310 985 000; www.thessalonikiairport.com) About 17km southeast of Thessaloniki. Served by local bus 78 (half-hourly); a taxi costs around €15 to €20.

Greek Airlines

Aegean Airlines (☑801 112 0000; www.aegeanair.com) and its subsidiary, **Olympic Air** (☑801 801 0101; www.olympicair.com), have flights between Athens and destinations throughout Europe, as well as to Cairo, İstanbul, Tel Aviv, New York and Toronto. They also operate flights throughout Greece, many of which transfer in Athens. Both airlines have exemplary safety records. The contact details for local Olympic and Aegean offices are listed throughout this book.

Tickets

If you're coming from outside Europe, consider a cheap

CLIMATE CHANGE & TRAVEL

Every form of transport that relies on carbon-based fuel generates CO_2, the main cause of human-induced climate change. Modern travel is dependent on aeroplanes, which might use less fuel per kilometre per person than most cars but travel much greater distances. The altitude at which aircraft emit gases (including CO_2) and particles also contributes to their climate change impact. Many websites offer 'carbon calculators' that allow people to estimate the carbon emissions generated by their journey and, for those who wish to do so, to offset the impact of the greenhouse gases emitted with contributions to portfolios of climate-friendly initiatives throughout the world. Lonely Planet offsets the carbon footprint of all staff and author travel.

OVERLAND FROM WESTERN EUROPE

If you're keen to travel without flying and enjoy the independence of a road trip, you can reach Greece by heading overland to an Italian port and hopping on a ferry. A high-speed ferry trip from Venice to Patra can be completed in around 26 hours. From Patra to Athens it's 3½ hours' drive.

Fancy a bit more convenience and speed than a bus or a car? Overland enthusiasts can reach Greece by rail through the Balkan peninsula, passing through Croatia, Serbia and the Former Yugoslav Republic of Macedonia. Or head to the western coast of Italy (there are connections throughout most of Europe) and then take a ferry to Greece. Not only will you be doing your bit for the planet, but you'll see some gorgeous scenery from your window.

A sample itinerary from London would see you catching the Eurostar to Paris and then an overnight sleeper train to Bologna in Italy. From there, a coastal train takes you to Bari, where there's an overnight boat to Patra on the Peloponnese. From Patra, it's a 4½-hour train journey to Athens. You'll be in Athens within two days of leaving London. See www. raileurope.com for more routes and tickets.

Greece is part of the Eurail network (www.eurail.com). Eurail passes can be bought only by residents of non-European countries; they should be purchased before arriving in Europe, but can be bought in Europe if your passport proves that you've been there for less than six months. Greece is also part of the Inter-Rail Pass system (www.interrailnet. eu), available to those who have resided in Europe for six months or more, and the Rail Plus Balkan Flexipass (www.raileurope.com), which offers unlimited travel for five, 10 or 15 days within a month. See the websites for full details of passes and prices.

flight to a European hub (eg London) and then an onward ticket with a charter airline such as **easyJet** (📞210 967 0000; www.easyjet.com), which offers some of the cheapest tickets between Greece and the rest of Europe. Some airlines also offer cheap deals to students. If you're planning to travel between June and September, it's wise to book ahead.

Land

Travelling by land you can really appreciate the landscape, as well as the many experiences that go along with train or bus travel. International train travel, in particular, has become much more feasible in recent years, with speedier trains and better connections. You can now travel from London to Athens by train and ferry in less than two days. By choosing to travel on the ground instead of the air, you'll also be reducing your carbon footprint.

Border Crossings

ALBANIA

The main crossing at Kakavia can have intensely slow queues.

Kakavia 60km northwest of Ioannina

Krystallopigi 14km west of Kotas on the Florina–Kastoria road

Mertziani 17km west of Konitsa

Sagiada 28km north of Igoumenitsa

BULGARIA

As Bulgaria is part of the EU, crossings are usually quick and hassle-free.

Exohi A new, 448m-tunnel border crossing 50km north of Drama

Ormenio 41km from Serres in northeastern Thrace

Promahonas 109km northeast of Thessaloniki

FORMER YUGOSLAV REPUBLIC OF MACEDONIA (FYROM)

Doïrani 31km north of Kilkis

Evzoni 68km north of Thessaloniki

Niki 16km north of Florina

TURKEY

Kipi is more convenient if you're heading for İstanbul. The route through Kastanies goes via Soufli and Didymotiho in Greece, and Edirne (ancient Adrianoupolis) in Turkey.

Kastanies 139km northeast of Alexandroupoli

Kipi 43km east of Alexandroupoli

Train

The Greek railways organisation **OSE** (Organismos Sidirodromon Ellados; www.trainose. gr) runs daily trains from Thessaloniki to Sofia and to Belgrade (via Skopje), with a weekly onward train to and from Budapest.

Sea

Ferries can get very crowded in summer. If you want to take a vehicle across it's wise to make a reservation

Ferry Routes

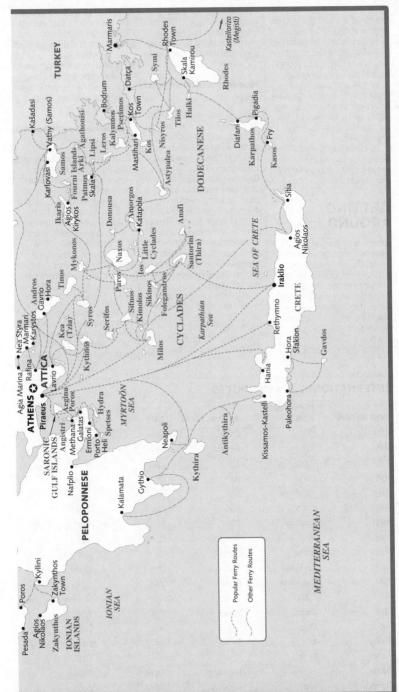

beforehand. The services indicated are for high season (July and August). Please note that tickets for all ferries to Turkey must be bought a day in advance – and you will almost certainly be asked to turn in your passport the night before the trip. It will be returned the next day before you board the boat. Port tax for departures to Turkey is around €15.

Another way to visit Greece by sea is to join one of the many cruises that ply the Aegean.

GETTING AROUND

Greece is an easy place to travel around thanks to a comprehensive public transport system. Buses are the mainstay of land transport, with a network that reaches out to the smallest villages. Trains are a good alternative, where available. If you're in a hurry, Greece also has an extensive domestic air network. To most visitors, though, travelling in Greece means island-hopping via the multitude of ferries that criss-cross the Adriatic and the Aegean.

Air

The vast majority of domestic mainland flights are handled by the country's national carrier **Aegean Airlines** (☎801 112 0000; www.aegean air.com) and its subsidiary, **Olympic Air** (☎801 801 0101; www.olympicair.com). You'll find offices wherever there are flights, as well as in other major towns. There are also a number of smaller Greek carriers, including the Crete-based airlines **Astra Airlines** (www.astra-airlines. gr) and **Sky Express** (www. skyexpress.gr).

The prices listed in this guide are for full-fare economy, and include domestic taxes and charges. There are discounts for return tickets for travel between Monday and Thursday, and bigger discounts for trips that include a Saturday night away. Find full details and timetables on airline websites.

The baggage allowance on domestic flights is 15kg, or 20kg if the domestic flight is part of an international journey.

Bicycle

Cycling is not popular among Greeks – but it's gaining kudos with tourists. You'll need strong leg muscles to tackle the mountains; or just stick to some of the flatter coastal routes. Bike lanes are rare to nonexistent; helmets are not compulsory. The island of Kos is about the most bicycle-friendly place in Greece, as is anywhere flat, such as the plains of Thessaly or Thrace.

➡ You can hire bicycles in most tourist places, but they are not as widely available as cars and motorcycles. Prices range from €5 to €12 per

INTERNATIONAL FERRY ROUTES

DESTINATION	DEPARTURE POINT	ARRIVAL POINT	TIME	FREQUENCY
Albania	Corfu	Saranda	25min	1 daily
Italy	Patra	Ancona	20hr	3 daily
Italy	Patra	Bari	14½hr	1 daily
Italy	Corfu	Bari	8hr	1 daily
Italy	Kefallonia	Bari	14hr	1 daily
Italy	Corfu	Bari	10hr	1 daily
Italy	Igoumenitsa	Bari	11½hr	1 daily
Italy	Patra	Brindisi	15hr	1 daily
Italy	Corfu	Brindisi	6hr	1 daily
Italy	Kefallonia	Brindisi	12hr	1 daily
Italy	Zakynthos	Brindisi	15hr	1 daily
Italy	Patra	Venice	30hr	12 weekly
Italy	Corfu	Venice	25hr	12 weekly
Turkey	Chios	Çeşme	1½hr	1 daily
Turkey	Kos	Bodrum	1hr	1 daily
Turkey	Lesvos	Ayvalik	1hr	1 daily
Turkey	Rhodes	Marmaris	50min	2 daily
Turkey	Samos	Kuşadası	1½hr	2 daily

day, depending on the type and age of the bike.

→ Bicycles are carried free on ferries. You can buy decent mountain or touring bikes in Greece's major towns, though you may have a problem finding a ready buyer if you wish to sell it on. Bike prices are much the same as across the rest of Europe: anywhere from €300 to €2000.

Boat

Greece has an extensive network of ferries – the only means of reaching many of the islands. Schedules are often subject to delays due to poor weather and industrial action, and prices fluctuate regularly. In summer, ferries run regular service between all but the most out-of-the-way destinations; however, services seriously slow down in winter (and in some cases stop completely).

Domestic Ferry Operators

Ferry companies have local offices on many of the islands.

Aegean Flying Dolphins (210 422 1766; www.aegean flyingdolphins.gr) Hydrofoils between Athens, Aegina and the Sporades.

Aegean Speed Lines (210 969 0950; www.aegean speedlines.gr) Super-speedy boats between Athens and the Cyclades.

Aegeon Pelagos (210 419 7470; www.anek.gr) A subsidiary of ANEK Lines.

ANEK Lines (210 419 7420; www.anek.gr) Crete-based long-haul ferries. Its Igoumenitsa–Patra route is now jointly operated with Superfast Ferries.

ANES (210 422 5625; www.anes.gr) Old-style ferries servicing Evia and the Sporades.

Anna Express (22470 41215; www.annaexpress.eu)

Small, fast ferry connecting the northern Dodecanese.

Blue Star Ferries (210 891 9800; www.bluestarferries.com) Long-haul, high-speed ferries and Seajet catamarans between the mainland, the Cyclades, the northeastern Aegean Islands, Crete and the Dodecanese.

Dodekanisos Seaways (22410 70590; www.12ne.gr) Runs large, high-speed catamarans in the Dodecanese.

Evoikos Lines (210 413 4483; www.ferriesglyfa.gr) Comfortable short-haul ferry services between Glyfa on the mainland and Agiokambos in northern Evia.

Fast Ferries (210 418 2005; www.fastferries.com.gr) Comfortable ferries from Rafina to the Cyclades islands of Andros, Tinos and Mykonos.

Hellenic Seaways (210 419 9000; www.hellenicseaways.gr) Conventional long-haul ferries and catamarans from the mainland to the Cyclades and between the Sporades and Saronic islands.

Ionian Ferries (210 324 9997; www.ionianferries.gr) Large ferries serving the Ionian Islands.

LANE Lines (210 427 4011; www.ferries.gr/lane) Long-haul ferries serving the Ionian Islands, Dodecanese and Crete.

Minoan Lines (210 414 5700; www.minoan.gr) High-speed luxury ferries between Piraeus and Iraklio, and Patra, Igoumenitsa and Corfu.

Patmos Star (22470 32500; www.patmos-star.com) Small, local ferry linking Patmos, Leros and Lipsi in the Dodecanese.

SAOS Lines (21062 50000; www.saos.gr) Big, slow boats calling in at many of the islands.

Sea Jets (210 412 1001; www.seajets.gr) Catamarans calling at Athens, Crete, Santorini (Thira), Paros and many islands in between.

Skyros Shipping Company (22220 921164; www.sne.gr) Slow boat between Skyros and Kymi on Evia.

Superfast Ferries (261 062 2500; www.superfast.com) As the name implies, speedy ferries from the mainland to Crete, Corfu and Patra. Its Igoumenitsa–Patra route is jointly operated with ANEK Lines.

Ventouris Ferries (210 411 4911; www.ventouris-sealines.gr) Big boats from the mainland to the Cyclades.

Zante Ferries (26950 49500, in Athens 210 410 0211; www.zanteferries.gr) Older ferries connecting the mainland with the western Cyclades.

Bus

The bus network is comprehensive. All long-distance buses, on the mainland and the islands, are operated by regional collectives known as **KTEL** (Koino Tamio Eispraxeon Leoforion; www.ktel.org). Details of interurban buses throughout Greece are available by dialling 14505. Bus fares are fixed by the government and bus travel is very reasonably priced. A journey costs approximately €5 per 100km.

Services

Every prefecture on the mainland has a KTEL, which operates local services within it and to the main towns of other prefectures. With the exception of towns in Thrace, which are serviced by Thessaloniki, all the major towns on the mainland have frequent connections to Athens. The islands of Corfu, Kefallonia and Zakynthos can also be reached directly from Athens by bus – the fares include the price of the ferry ticket.

Most villages have a daily bus service of some sort, although remote areas may have only one or two buses a week. They operate for the benefit of people going to town to shop, rather than for tourists, and consequently leave the villages very early in the morning and return early in the afternoon.

Practicalities

→ It is important to note that big cities like Athens, Iraklio, Patra and Thessaloniki may have more than one bus station, each serving different regions. Make sure you find the correct station for your destination. In small towns and villages the 'bus station' may be no more than a bus stop outside a *kafeneio* (coffee house) or taverna that doubles as a booking office.

→ In remote areas, the timetable may be in Greek only, but most booking offices have timetables in both Greek and Roman script and many bus stations are now posting them online.

→ It's best to turn up at least 20 minutes before departure to make sure you get a seat – buses have also been known to leave a few minutes before their scheduled departure.

→ When you buy a ticket you may be allotted a seat number, printed on the ticket. The seat number is indicated on the *back* of each seat of the bus, not on the back of the seat in front; this causes confusion among Greeks and tourists alike. Often, the seat numbers are simply ignored.

→ You can board a bus without a ticket and pay on board, but on a popular route or during high season, you may have to stand.

→ The KTEL buses are safe and modern, and these days most are air conditioned – at least on the major routes. In more remote, rural areas they tend to be older and less comfortable. Buses on less-frequented routes do not usually have toilets on board and stop about every three hours on long journeys.

→ Smoking is prohibited on all buses in Greece.

Car & Motorcycle

No one who has travelled on Greece's roads will be surprised to hear that the country's road fatality rate is one of the highest in Europe. More than a thousand people die on the roads every year, with ten times that number of people injured. Overtaking is listed as the greatest cause of accidents.

Heart-stopping moments aside, your own car is a great way to explore off the beaten track. The road network has improved enormously in recent years; many roads marked as dirt tracks on older maps have now been asphalted and many of the islands have very little traffic. There are regular (if costly) car-ferry services to almost all islands.

MOTORCYCLE WARNING

Greece is not the best place to initiate yourself into motorcycling. There are still a lot of gravel roads, particularly on the islands, and dozens of tourists have accidents every year. Scooters are particularly prone to sliding on gravelly bends. Try to hire a motorcycle with thinner-profile tyres. If you plan to use a motorcycle or moped, check that your travel insurance covers you: many insurance companies don't cover motorcycle accidents. Another option gaining popularity on the islands is to rent quad bikes – they're slightly more expensive but don't require a motorcycle licence.

Practicalities

AUTOMOBILE ASSOCIATION

Greece's domestic automobile association is **ELPA** (Elliniki Leschi Aftokinitou kai Periigiseon; ☎ 210 606 8800; www. elpa.gr; Leoforos Mesogion 395, Agia Paraskevi, Athens).

ENTRY

EU-registered vehicles enter free for up to six months without road taxes being due. A green card (international third-party insurance) is required, along with proof of date of entry (ferry ticket or your passport stamp). Non-EU-registered vehicles may be logged in your passport.

DRIVING LICENCE

EU driving licences are valid in Greece. Drivers from outside the EU may require International Driving Permits; while rental agencies will rarely ask for one, local authorities may if you're stopped. International Driving Permits can only be obtained in the country where your driving licence was issued.

FUEL

Available widely throughout the country, though service stations may be closed on weekends and public holidays. On the islands, there may be only one petrol station; check where it is before you head out. Self-service and credit-card pumps are not the norm in Greece. Petrol is cheaper here than in many European countries, but expensive by American or Australian standards.

Petrol types:

→ *Super* (leaded)

→ *amolyvdi* (unleaded)

→ *petreleo kinisis* (diesel)

Hire
CARS

→ All the big multinational companies are represented in Athens; most have branches in major towns and popular tourist destinations. The majority of islands have at least one outlet.

→ By Greek law, rental cars have to be replaced every six

ROAD DISTANCES (KM)

	Alexandroupoli	Athens	Corinth	Edessa	Florina	Igoumenitsa	Ioannina	Kalamata	Kastoria	Kavala	Lamia	Larisa	Monemvasia	Nafplio	Patra	Pyrgos	Sparta	Thessaloniki	Trikala	Tripoli
Athens	854																			
Corinth	884	84																		
Edessa	427	569	596																	
Florina	497	592	251	353																
Igoumenitsa	816	473	393	380	353															
Ioannina	702	447	364	298	320	96														
Kalamata	1055	284	175	767	763	501	467													
Kastoria	535	489	519	108	67	286	204	690												
Kavala	177	682	655	250	320	615	525	878	358											
Lamia	643	214	244	355	360	353	263	415	274	466										
Larisa	493	361	389	218	231	309	209	561	239	323	151									
Monemvasia	1156	350	266	869	855	613	579	156	756	976	505	655								
Nafplio	947	165	63	659	664	482	427	163	582	770	307	455	215							
Patra	828	220	138	567	513	281	247	220	483	664	193	341	332	201						
Pyrgos	924	320	234	636	643	367	347	119	542	747	284	432	275	208	96					
Sparta	1025	225	145	737	759	517	483	60	660	848	385	533	96	119	236	180				
Thessaloniki	349	513	544	89	159	452	362	715	220	169	303	154	807	610	488	584	711			
Trikala	554	330	356	227	233	247	148	520	159	377	115	62	597	419	310	400	501	216		
Tripoli	964	194	110	713	681	457	430	90	639	820	324	472	157	81	176	155	61	624	466	
Volos	556	326	355	278	293	371	271	518	301	383	115	62	620	417	308	408	524	214	124	435

years, so most vehicles you hire will be relatively new.

➡ The minimum driving age in Greece is 18 years, but most car-hire firms require you to be at least 21 (or 23 for larger vehicles).

➡ High-season weekly rates with unlimited mileage start at about €280 for the smallest models (eg a Fiat Seicento), dropping to about €200 per week in winter. These prices don't include local tax (known as VAT).

➡ You can often find great deals at local companies. Their advertised rates can be up to 50% cheaper than the multinationals and they are normally open to negotiation, especially if business is slow.

➡ On the islands, you can rent a car for the day for around €30 to €50, including all insurance and taxes.

➡ Always check what the insurance includes; there are often rough roads or dangerous routes that you can only tackle by renting a 4WD.

➡ If you want to take a hire car to another country or onto a ferry, you will need advance written authorisation from the hire company, as the insurance may not cover you.

➡ Unless you pay with a credit card, most hire companies will require a minimum deposit of €120 per day.

The major car-hire companies in Greece:

Avis (☎210 322 4951; www.avis.gr)

Budget (☎210 349 8800; www.budget.gr)

Europcar (☎210 960 2382; www.europcar.gr)

MOTORCYCLES

➡ Mopeds, motorcycles and scooters are available for hire wherever there are tourists to rent them. Most machines are newish and in good condition. Nonetheless, check the brakes at the earliest opportunity.

➡ You must produce a licence that shows proficiency to ride the category of bike you wish to rent; this applies to everything from 50cc up. British citizens must obtain a Category A licence from the **Driver & Vehicle Licensing Agency** (www.dft.gov.uk/dvla) in the UK (in most other EU countries separate licences are automatically issued).

➡ Rates start from about €15 per day for a moped or 50cc motorcycle, ranging to €30 per day for a 250cc motorcycle. Out of season these prices drop considerably, so use your bargaining skills.

➡ Most motorcycle hirers include third-party insurance in the price, but it's wise to check this. This insurance will not include medical expenses.

➡ Helmets are compulsory and rental agencies are obliged to offer one as part of the hire deal.

Road Conditions

➡ Main highways in Greece have been improving steadily over the years but many still don't offer smooth sailing.

➡ Some main roads retain the two-lane/hard-shoulder format of the 1960s, which can be confusing and even downright dangerous.

➡ Road works can take years and years in Greece – especially on the islands, where funding often only trickles in. In other cases, excellent new tarmac roads may have appeared that are not on any local maps.

Road Hazards

➡ Slow drivers – many of them unsure and hesitant tourists – can cause serious traffic events on Greece's roads.

➡ Road surfaces can change rapidly when a section of road has succumbed to subsidence or weathering. Snow and ice can be a serious challenge in winter, and drivers are advised to carry snow chains. In rural areas, keep a close eye out for animals wandering onto roads.

➡ Roads passing through mountainous areas are often littered with fallen rocks, which can cause extensive damage to a vehicle's underside or throw a motorbike rider.

Road Rules

➡ In Greece, as throughout Continental Europe, you drive on the right and overtake on the left.

➡ Outside built-up areas, traffic on a main road has right of way at intersections. In towns, vehicles coming from the right have right of way. This includes roundabouts – even if you're in the roundabout, you must give way to drivers coming onto the roundabout to your right.

➡ Seatbelts must be worn in front seats, and in back seats if the car is fitted with them.

➡ Children under 12 years of age are not allowed in the front seat.

➡ It is compulsory to carry a first-aid kit, fire extinguisher and warning triangle, and it is forbidden to carry cans of petrol.

➡ Helmets are compulsory for motorcyclists if the motorcycle is 50cc or more. Police will book you if you're caught without a helmet.

➡ Outside residential areas the speed limit is 120km/h on highways, 90km/h on other roads and 50km/h in built-up areas. The speed limit for motorcycles up to 100cc is 70km/h; for larger motorcycles, 90km/h. Drivers exceeding the limit by 20% are liable to receive a fine of €60; exceeding it by 40% costs €150.

➡ A blood-alcohol content of 0.05% can incur a fine of €150, while over 0.08% is a criminal offence.

➡ If you are involved in an accident and no one is hurt, the police will not be required to write a report, but it is advisable to go to a nearby police station and explain what happened. You may need a police report for insurance purposes. If an accident involves injury, a driver who does not stop and does not inform the police may face a prison sentence.

Hitching

Hitching is never entirely safe in any country in the world, and we don't recommend it. Travellers who decide to hitch should understand that they are taking a small but potentially serious risk. People who do choose to hitch will be safer if they travel in pairs; they should let someone know where they are planning to go. In particular, it is unwise for women to hitch alone; women are better off hitching with a male companion.

Some parts of Greece are much better for hitching than others. Getting out of major cities tends to be hard work and Athens is notoriously difficult. Hitching is much easier in remote areas and on islands with poor public transport. On country roads it is not unknown for someone to stop and ask if you want a lift, even if you haven't stuck a thumb out.

Local Transport

Bus

Most Greek towns are small enough to get around on foot. All the major towns have local buses, but the only places you're likely to need them are Athens, Patra, Kalamata and Thessaloniki.

Metro

Athens is the only city in Greece large enough to warrant the building of an underground system. Note that only Greek student cards are valid for a student ticket on the metro.

Taxi

Taxis are widely available in Greece, except on very small or remote islands. They are reasonably priced by European standards, especially if three or four people share costs. Many taxi drivers now have sat-nav systems in their cars, so finding a destination is a breeze as long as you have the exact address.

Yellow city cabs are metered, with rates doubling between midnight and 5am. Additional costs are charged for trips from an airport or a bus, port or train station, as well as for each piece of luggage over 10kg. Grey rural taxis do not have meters, so you should always settle on a price before you get in.

Some taxi drivers in Athens have been known to overcharge unwary travellers. If you have a complaint about a taxi driver, take the cab number and report your complaint to the tourist police. Taxi drivers in other towns in Greece are, on the whole, friendly, helpful and honest.

Tours

Tours are worth considering if your time is very limited or if you prefer someone else do the planning. In Athens, you'll find countless day tours, with some agencies offering two- or three-day trips to nearby sights. For something on a larger scale, try **Intrepid Travel** (www. intrepidtravel.com), with offices in Australia, the UK and the USA: it offers an eight-day tour from Athens to Santorini (€1300) and an eight-day sailing tour through the Cyclades (€1200), including everything except meals and flights. **Encounter Greece** (www.encountergreece.com) offers a plethora of tours; a 10-day tour across the country costs €1085 while

eight days on the mainland is €885. (Flights to Greece are not included.)

More adventurous tours include guided activities such as hiking, climbing, white-water rafting, kayaking, canoeing or canyoning.

The following options are also available:

Alpin Club (www.alpinclub. gr) For kayaking, rafting, canyoning and mountain biking – just to name a few. In Athens but operates out of Karitena in the Peloponnese.

Robinson Expeditions (www.robinson.gr) For hiking and mountain biking. Runs tours from the centre and north of Greece.

Train

Trains are operated by the Greek railways organisation **OSE** (Organismos Sidirodromon Ellados; www.trainose.gr). The Greek railway network is limited; its northern line is the most substantial. Standard-gauge services run from Athens to Dikea in the northeast via Thessaloniki and Alexandroupoli. There are also connections to Florina and the Pelion Peninsula. The Peloponnese network runs only as far as Klato, with bus services to Plata for ferry connections.

Due to financial instability, prices and schedules are very changeable. When you can, double-check on the OSE website. Information on departures from Athens or Thessaloniki can also be sought by calling ☎1440.

Classes

There are two types of service: regular (slow) trains that stop at all stations, and faster, modern intercity (IC) trains that link most major cities. The slow trains represent the country's cheapest form of public transport: 2nd-class fares are absurdly cheap, and even 1st class is cheaper than bus travel.

The IC trains that link the major Greek cities are an excellent way to travel. The services are not necessarily fast – Greece is far too mountainous for that – but the trains are modern and comfortable. There are 1st- and 2nd-class tickets and a cafe-bar on board. On some services, meals can be ordered and delivered to your seat. The night service between Athens and Thessaloniki also offers a choice of couchettes, two-bed compartments and single compartments.

Train Passes

➡ Eurail, Inter-Rail and Rail Plus Balkan Flexipass cards are valid in Greece, but they're generally not worth buying if Greece is the only place where you plan to use them. For IC and sleeper cars, a costly supplement is required.

➡ On presentation of ID or passports, passengers more than 60 years old are entitled to a 25% discount on all lines, except in July and August and over the Easter week.

➡ Whatever pass you have, you must have a reservation to board the train.

Language

The Greek language is believed to be one of the oldest European languages, with an oral tradition of 4000 years and a written tradition of approximately 3000 years. Due to its centuries of influence, Greek constitutes the origin of a large part of the vocabulary of many Indo-European languages (including English). It is the official language of Greece and co-official language of Cyprus (alongside Turkish), and is spoken by many migrant communities throughout the world.

The Greek alphabet is explained on the following page, but if you read the pronunciation guides given with each phrase in this chapter as if they were English, you'll be understood. Note that dh is pronounced as 'th' in 'there'; gh is a softer, slightly throaty version of 'g'; and kh is a throaty sound like the 'ch' in the Scottish 'loch'. All Greek words of two or more syllables have an acute accent ('), which indicates where the stress falls. In our pronunciation guides, stressed syllables are in italics.

In this chapter, masculine, feminine and neuter forms of words are included where necessary, separated with a slash and indicated with 'm', 'f' and 'n' respectively. Polite and informal options are indicated where relevant with 'pol' and 'inf'.

BASICS

Hello.	Γειά σας.	ya·sas (pol)
	Γειά σου.	ya·su (inf)
Goodbye.	Αντίο.	an·di·o
Yes./No.	Ναι./Όχι.	ne/o·hi

WANT MORE?

For in-depth language information and handy phrases, check out Lonely Planet's *Greek Phrasebook*. You'll find it at **shop.lonelyplanet.com**, or you can buy Lonely Planet's iPhone phrasebooks at the Apple App Store.

Please.	Παρακαλώ.	pa·ra·ka·lo
Thank you.	Ευχαριστώ.	ef·ha·ri·sto
You're welcome.	Παρακαλώ.	pa·ra·ka·lo
Excuse me.	Με συγχωρείτε.	me sing·kho·ri·te
Sorry.	Συγγνώμη.	sigh·no·mi

What's your name?

| Πώς σας λένε; | pos sas le·ne |

My name is ...

| Με λένε ... | me le·ne ... |

Do you speak English?

| Μιλάτε αγγλικά; | mi·la·te an·gli·ka |

I don't understand.

| Δεν καταλαβαίνω. | dhen ka·ta·la·ve·no |

ACCOMMODATION

campsite	χώρος για κάμπινγκ	kho·ros yia kam·ping
hotel	ξενοδοχείο	kse·no·dho·khi·o
youth hostel	γιουθ χόστελ	yuth kho·stel

a ... room	ένα ... δωμάτιο	e·na ... dho·ma·ti·o
single	μονόκλινο	mo·no·kli·no
double	δίκλινο	dhi·kli·no

How much is it ...?	Πόσο κάνει ...;	po·so ka·ni ...
per night	τη βραδυά	ti·vra·dhya
per person	το άτομο	to a·to·mo

air-con	έρκοντίσιον	er·kon·di·si·on
bathroom	μπάνιο	ba·nio
fan	ανεμιστήρας	a·ne·mi·sti·ras
window	παράθυρο	pa·ra·thi·ro

DIRECTIONS

Where is ...?
Πού είναι ...;   pu *i*·ne ...

What's the address?
Ποια είναι η διεύθυνση;   pia *i*·ne i dhi·*ef*·thin·si

Can you show me (on the map)?
Μπορείς να μου δείξεις   bo·*ris* na mu *dhik*·sis
(στο χάρτη);   (sto *khar*·ti)

Turn left.
Στρίψτε αριστερά.   *strips*·te a·ri·ste·*ra*

Turn right.
Στρίψτε δεξιά.   *strips*·te dhe·*ksia*

at the next corner
στην επόμενη γωνία   stin e·*po*·me·ni gho·*ni*·a

at the traffic lights
στα φώτα   sta *fo*·ta

behind	πίσω	*pi*·so
far	μακριά	ma·kri·*a*
in front of	μπροστά	bro·*sta*
near (to)	κοντά	kon·*da*
next to	δίπλα	*dhi*·pla
opposite	απέναντι	a·*pe*·nan·di
straight ahead	ολο ευθεία	o·lo ef·*thi*·a

EATING & DRINKING

a table for ...	Ένα τραπέζι γία ...	*e*·na tra·*pe*·zi ya ...
(eight) o'clock	στις (οχτώ)	stis (okh·*to*)
(two) people	(δύο) άτομα	(*dhi*·o) a·to·ma
I don't eat ...	Δεν τρώγω ...	dhen *tro*·gho ...
fish	ψάρι	*psa*·ri
(red) meat	(κόκκινο) κρέας	(*ko*·ki·no) *kre*·as
peanuts	φυστίκια	fi·*sti*·kia
poultry	πουλερικά	pu·le·ri·*ka*

What would you recommend?
Τι θα συνιστούσες;   ti tha si·ni·*stu*·ses

What's in that dish?
Τι περιέχει αυτό το   ti pe·ri·e·hi af·*to* to
φαγητό;   fa·ghi·*to*

Cheers!
Εις υγείαν!   is i·*yi*·an

That was delicious.
Ήταν νοστιμότατο!   *i*·tan no·sti·*mo*·ta·to

Please bring the bill.
Το λογαριασμό,   to lo·ghar·ya·*zmo*
παρακαλώ.   pa·ra·ka·*lo*

GREEK APLHABET

The Greek alphabet has 24 letters, shown below in their upper- and lower-case forms. Be aware that some letters look like English letters but are pronounced very differently, such as **B**, which is pronounced v; and **P**, pronounced r. As in English, how letters are pronounced is also influenced by the way they are combined, for example the **ου** combination is pronounced u as in 'put', and **οι** is pronounced ee as in 'feet'.

Α α	a	as in 'father'
Β β	v	as in 'vine'
Γ γ	gh	a softer, throaty 'g', or
	y	as in 'yes'
Δ δ	dh	as in 'there'
Ε ε	e	as in 'egg'
Ζ ζ	z	as in 'zoo'
Η η	i	as in 'feet'
Θ θ	th	as in 'throw'
Ι ι	i	as in 'feet'
Κ κ	k	as in 'kite'
Λ λ	l	as in 'leg'
Μ μ	m	as in 'man'
Ν ν	n	as in 'net'

Ξ ξ	x	as in 'ox'
Ο ο	o	as in 'hot'
Π π	p	as in 'pup'
Ρ ρ	r	as in 'road',
		slightly trilled
Σ σ, ς	s	as in 'sand'
Τ τ	t	as in 'tap'
Υ υ	i	as in 'feet'
Φ φ	f	as in 'find'
Χ χ	kh	as the 'ch' in the
		Scottish 'loch', or
	h	like a rough 'h'
Ψ ψ	ps	as in 'lapse'
Ω ω	o	as in 'hot'

Note that the letter **Σ** has two forms for the lower case – **σ** and **ς**. The second one is used at the end of words. The Greek question mark is represented with the English equivalent of a semicolon (;).

LANGUAGE EMERGENCIES

Key Words

appetisers	ορεκτικά	o·rek·ti·ka
bar	μπαρ	bar
beef	βοδινό	vo·dhi·no
beer	μπύρα	bi·ra
bottle	μπουκάλι	bu·ka·li
bowl	μπωλ	bol
bread	ψωμί	pso·mi
breakfast	πρόγευμα	pro·yev·ma
cafe	καφετέρια	ka·fe·te·ri·a
cheese	τυρί	ti·ri
chicken	κοτόπουλο	ko·to·pu·lo
coffee	καφές	ka·fes
cold	κρυωμένος	kri·o·me·nos
cream	κρέμα	kre·ma
delicatessen	ντελικατέσεν	de·li·ka·te·sen
desserts	επιδόρπια	e·pi·dhor·pi·a
dinner	δείπνο	dhip·no
egg	αυγό	av·gho
fish	ψάρι	psa·ri
food	φαγητό	fa·yi·to
fork	πιρούνι	pi·ru·ni
fruit	φρούτα	fru·ta
glass	ποτήρι	po·ti·ri
grocery store	οπωροπωλείο	o·po·ro·po·li·o
herb	βότανο	vo·ta·no
high chair	καρέκλα	ka·re·kla
	για μωρά	yia mo·ra
hot	ζεστός	ze·stos
juice	χυμός	hi·mos
knife	μαχαίρι	ma·he·ri
lamb	αρνί	ar·ni
lunch	μεσημεριανό	me·si·me·ria·no
	φαγητό	fa·yi·to
main courses	κύρια φαγητά	ki·ri·a fa·yi·ta
market	αγορά	a·gho·ra
menu	μενού	me·nu
milk	γάλα	gha·la
nut	καρύδι	ka·ri·dhi
oil	λάδι	la·dhi
pepper	πιπέρι	pi·pe·ri
plate	πιάτο	pia·to
pork	χοιρινό	hi·ri·no
red wine	κόκκινο κρασί	ko·ki·no kra·si
restaurant	εστιατόριο	e·sti·a·to·ri·o
salt	αλάτι	a·la·ti
soft drink	αναψυκτικό	a·nap·sik·ti·ko
spoon	κουτάλι	ku·ta·li
sugar	ζάχαρη	za·kha·ri
tea	τσάι	tsa·i
vegetable	λαχανικά	la·kha·ni·ka
vegetarian	χορτοφάγος	khor·to·fa·ghos
vinegar	ξύδι	ksi·dhi
water	νερό	ne·ro
white wine	άσπρο κρασί	a·spro kra·si
with/without	με/χωρίς	me/kho·ris

KEY PATTERNS

To get by in Greek, mix and match these simple patterns with words of your choice:

When's (the next bus)?
Πότε είναι (το επόμενο λεωφορείο); — po·te i·ne (to e·po·me·no le·o·fo·ri·o)

Where's (the station)?
Πού είναι (ο σταθμός); — pu i·ne (o stath·mos)

Do you have (a local map)?
Έχετε οδικό (τοπικό χάρτη); — e·he·te o·dhi·ko (to·pi·ko khar·ti)

Is there a (lift)?
Υπάρχει (ασανσέρ); — i·par·hi (a·san·ser)

Can I (try it on)?
Μπορώ να (το προβάρω); — bo·ro na (to pro·va·ro)

Could you (please help)?
Μπορείς να (βοηθήσεις, παρακαλώ); — bo·ris na (vo·i·thi·sis, pa·ra·ka·lo)

Do I need (to book)?
Χρειάζεται (να κλείσω θέση); — khri·a·ze·te (na kli·so the·si)

I need (assistance).
Χρειάζομαι (βοήθεια). — khri·a·zo·me (vo·i·thi·a)

I'd like (to hire a car).
Θα ήθελα (να ενοικιάσω ένα αυτοκίνητο). — tha i·the·la (na e·ni·ki·a·so e·na af·to·ki·ni·to)

How much is it (per night)?
Πόσο είναι (για κάθε νύχτα); — po·so i·ne (yia ka·the nikh·ta)

EMERGENCIES

Help!	Βοήθεια!	vo·i·thya
Go away!	Φύγε!	fi·ye
I'm lost.	Έχω χαθεί.	e·kho kha·thi
Where's the toilet?	Πού είναι η τουαλέτα;	pu i·ne i tu·a·le·ta

Signs

ΕΙΣΟΔΟΣ	Entry
ΕΞΟΔΟΣ	Exit
ΠΛΗΡΟΦΟΡΙΕΣ	Information
ΑΝΟΙΧΤΟ	Open
ΚΛΕΙΣΤΟ	Closed
ΑΠΑΓΟΡΕΥΕΤΑΙ	Prohibited
ΑΣΤΥΝΟΜΙΑ	Police
ΓΥΝΑΙΚΩΝ	Toilets (Women)
ΑΝΔΡΩΝ	Toilets (Men)

Call ...! Φωνάξτε ...! fo·*nak*·ste ...

a doctor ένα γιατρό e·na yi·a·*tro*

the police την tin
αστυνομία a·sti·no·*mi*·a

I'm ill.
Είμαι άρρωστος. i·me a·ro·stos

I'm allergic to (antibiotics).
Είμαι αλλεργικός/ i·me a·ler·yi·*kos*/
αλλεργική a·ler·yi·*ki* (m/f)
(στα αντιβιωτικά) (sta an·di·vi·o·ti·*ka*)

SHOPPING & SERVICES

I'd like to buy ...
Θέλω ν' αγοράσω ... *the*·lo na·gho·*ra*·so ...

I'm just looking.
Απλώς κοιτάζω. ap·*los* ki·*ta*·zo

Can I see it?
Μπορώ να το δω; bo·*ro* na to dho

I don't like it.
Δεν μου αρέσει. dhen mu a·*re*·si

How much is it?
Πόσο κάνει; *po*·so *ka*·ni

It's too expensive.
Είναι πολύ ακριβό. i·ne po·*li* a·*kri*·vo

Can you lower the price?
Μπορείς να κατεβάσεις bo·*ris* na ka·te·*va*·sis
την τιμή; tin ti·*mi*

ATM	αυτόματη	af·*to*·ma·ti
	μηχανή	mi·kha·*ni*
	χρημάτων	khri·*ma*·ton
bank	τράπεζα	*tra*·pe·za
credit card	πιστωτική	pi·sto·ti·*ki*
	κάρτα	*kar*·ta
internet cafe	καφενείο	ka·fe·*ni*·o
	διαδικτύου	dhi·a·dhik·*ti*·u
mobile phone	κινητό	ki·ni·*to*
post office	ταχυδρομείο	ta·hi·dhro·*mi*·o
tourist office	τουριστικό	tu·ri·sti·*ko*
	γραφείο	ghra·*fi*·o

TIME & DATES

What time is it?
Τι ώρα είναι; ti o·ra i·ne

It's (two) o'clock.
Είναι (δύο) η ώρα. i·ne (*dhi*·o) i o·ra

It's half past (10).
(Δέκα) και μισή. (*dhe*·ka) ke mi·*si*

morning	πρωί	pro·*i*
(this)	(αυτό το)	(af·*to* to)
afternoon	απόγευμα	a·*po*·yev·ma
evening	βράδυ	*vra*·dhi
yesterday	χθες	hthes
today	σήμερα	*si*·me·ra
tomorrow	αύριο	av·ri·o
Monday	Δευτέρα	dhef·*te*·ra
Tuesday	Τρίτη	*tri*·ti
Wednesday	Τετάρτη	te·*tar*·ti
Thursday	Πέμπτη	*pemp*·ti
Friday	Παρασκευή	pa·ras·ke·*vi*
Saturday	Σάββατο	*sa*·va·to
Sunday	Κυριακή	ky·ri·a·*ki*
January	Ιανουάριος	ia·nu·*ar*·i·os
February	Φεβρουάριος	fev·ru·ar·i·os
March	Μάρτιος	*mar*·ti·os
April	Απρίλιος	a·*pri*·li·os
May	Μάιος	*mai*·os
June	Ιούνιος	i·u·ni·os
July	Ιούλιος	i·u·li·os
August	Αύγουστος	av·ghus·tos
September	Σεπτέμβριος	sep·*tem*·vri·os
October	Οκτώβριος	ok·*to*·vri·os
November	Νοέμβριος	no·em·vri·os
December	Δεκέμβριος	dhe·*kem*·vri·os

Question Words

How?	Πώς;	pos
What?	Τι;	ti
When?	Πότε;	*po*·te
Where?	Πού;	pu
Who?	Ποιος;	pi·os (m)
	Ποια;	pi·a (f)
	Ποιω;	pi·o (n)
Why?	Γιατί;	yi·a·*ti*

TRANSPORT

Public Transport

boat	πλοίο	pli·o
city bus	αστικό	a·sti·ko
intercity bus	λεωφορείο	le·o·fo·ri·o
plane	αεροπλάνο	ae·ro·pla·no
train	τραίνο	tre·no

Where do I buy a ticket?
Πού αγοράζω εισιτήριο;   pu a·gho·ra·zo i·si·ti·ri·o

I want to go to ...
Θέλω να πάω στο/στη ...   the·lo na pao sto/sti...

What time does it leave?
Τι ώρα φεύγει;   ti o·ra fev·yi

Does it stop at (Iraklio)?
Σταματάει στο   sta·ma·ta·i sto
(Ηράκλειο);   (i·ra·kli·o)

I'd like to get off at (Iraklio).
Θα ήθελα να κατεβώ   tha i·the·la na ka·te·vo
στο (Ηράκλειο).   sto (i·ra·kli·o)

I'd like (a) ...	Θα ήθελα (ένα) ...	tha i·the·la (e·na) ...
1st class	πρώτη θέση	pro·ti the·si
2nd class	δεύτερη θέση	def·te·ri the·si
one-way ticket	απλό εισιτήριο	a·plo i·si·ti·ri·o
return ticket	εισιτήριο με επιστροφή	i·si·ti·ri·o me e·pi·stro·fi

cancelled	ακυρώθηκε	a·ki·ro·thi·ke
delayed	καθυστέρησε	ka·thi·ste·ri·se
platform	πλατφόρμα	plat·for·ma
ticket office	εκδοτήριο εισιτηρίων	ek·dho·ti·ri·o i·si·ti·ri·on
timetable	δρομολόγιο	dhro·mo·lo·gio
train station	σταθμός τρένου	stath·mos tre·nu

Driving & Cycling

I'd like to hire a ...	Θα ήθελα να νοικιάσω ...	tha i·the·la na ni·ki·a·so ...
4WD	ένα τέσσερα επί τέσσερα	e·na tes·se·ra e·pi tes·se·ra
bicycle	ένα ποδήλατο	e·na po·dhi·la·to
car	ένα αυτοκίνητο	e·na af·ti·ki·ni·to
jeep	ένα τζιπ	e·na tzip
motorbike	μια μοτοσυκλέττα	mya mo·to·si·klet·ta

Numbers

1	ένας	e·nas (m)
	μία	mi·a (f)
	ένα	e·na (n)
2	δύο	dhi·o
3	τρεις	tris (m&f)
	τρία	tri·a (n)
4	τέσσερεις	te·se·ris (m&f)
	τέσσερα	te·se·ra (n)
5	πέντε	pen·de
6	έξη	e·xi
7	επτά	ep·ta
8	οχτώ	oh·to
9	εννέα	e·ne·a
10	δέκα	dhe·ka
20	είκοσι	ik·o·si
30	τριάντα	tri·an·da
40	σαράντα	sa·ran·da
50	πενήντα	pe·nin·da
60	εξήντα	ek·sin·da
70	εβδομήντα	ev·dho·min·da
80	ογδόντα	ogh·dhon·da
90	ενενήντα	e·ne·nin·da
100	εκατό	e·ka·to
1000	χίλιοι	hi·li·i (m)
	χίλιες	hi·li·ez (f)
	χίλια	hi·li·a (n)

Do I need a helmet?
Χρειάζομαι κράνος;   khri·a·zo·me kra·nos

Is this the road to ...?
Αυτός είναι ο   af·tos i·ne o
δρόμος για ... ;   dhro·mos ya ...

Where's a petrol station?
Πού είναι ένα πρατήριο   pu i·ne e·na pra·ti·ri·o
βενζίνας;   ven·zi·nas

(How long) Can I park here?
(Πόση ώρα) Μπορώ να   (po·si o·ra) bo·ro na
παρκάρω εδώ;   par·ka·ro e·dho

The car/motorbike has broken down (at ...).
Το αυτοκίνητο/   to af·to·ki·ni·to/
η μοτοσυκλέττα   i mo·to·si·klet·ta
χάλασε (στο ...).   kha·la·se (sto ...)

I need a mechanic.
Χρειάζομαι μηχανικό.   khri·a·zo·me mi·kha·ni·ko

I have a flat tyre.
Έπαθα λάστιχο.   e·pa·tha la·sti·cho

I've run out of petrol.
Έμεινα από βενζίνη.   e·mi·na a·po ven·zi·ni

Behind the Scenes

SEND US YOUR FEEDBACK

We love to hear from travellers – your comments keep us on our toes and help make our books better. Our well-travelled team reads every word on what you loved or loathed about this book. Although we cannot reply individually to your submissions, we always guarantee that your feedback goes straight to the appropriate authors, in time for the next edition. Each person who sends us information is thanked in the next edition – and the most useful submissions are rewarded with a selection of digital PDF chapters.

Visit **lonelyplanet.com/contact** to submit your updates and suggestions or to ask for help. Our award-winning website also features inspirational travel stories, news and discussions.

Note: We may edit, reproduce and incorporate your comments in Lonely Planet products such as guidebooks, websites and digital products, so let us know if you don't want your comments reproduced or your name acknowledged. For a copy of our privacy policy visit lonelyplanet.com/privacy.

OUR READERS

Many thanks to the travellers who used the last edition and wrote to us with helpful hints, useful advice and interesting anecdotes:

Abby Gershenzon, Alen & Andrea Lai, Alexandra Bliss, Allan Smith, Annette Stamatiadis, Cengiz Aksu, Christian Ulrich, Collado Marimar, Dirk van Norren, Francisco Buny, George Moss, Jenn Hicks, Jonathan Amies, Jordi Bibià, Joy Morrison, Judi Moriarty, Judy Ridge, Katherine Pezet, Kathleen Doherty, Laura van Eerten, Linde Barrera, Liz Killebrew, Lloyd Collyer, Matheus Ferreira, Mike Priaulx, Nadine Pilz, Pernille Sand, Rainer Feichter, Robert Burkill, Sarah Heretz, Sien Hasker, Simon Sy Lui

AUTHOR THANKS

Korina Miller

An enormous thank you to Kirk and my mum and dad for minding the fort while I was away and making it possible for me to take this project on. Thank you to my fabulous daughters, Monique and Simone, for letting me work and also encouraging me to take breaks. Thank you to Brana at LP for her support and to my co-authors for their insights and cameraderie. A warm *efharisto* to all of the people I met on the road – both locals and travellers – who shared their stories, knowledge and enthusi-asm for Greece and were unwaveringly hospitable despite such difficult times. And thanks to Bing the loyal coonhound for keeping me company while I burned the midnight oil.

Kate Armstrong

I am constantly humbled by the generosity of the Greek people in tough times. *Efharisto poli,* as always, to the Zotos family in Nafplion, to Yiannis at Alsos House for your knowledge and for sharing so much, to Alex Groth in Makrin-itsa for welcoming me regardless of time and distance, and to SB Barker for your Herculean friendship and driving skills. (I'll never catch up on the Omega intake.) Finally, to Brana – you're the best, as is the LP team and my fellow team of authors.

Alexis Averbuck

Boundless gratitude to Alexandra Stamopou-lou for her INSPIRATION. She travels with me everywhere. Ryan Ver Berkmoes was a peachy road companion and an aces navigator on unmarked Cretan tracks. Thanks to Ramona for an insider's take on Gavdos. Big cheer for Korina, Kate and Richard, who contributed so much to the Crete chapter. Applause for Brana: conscientious, informed and compassionate editor. Margarita, Kostas, Zisis, Anthy and Costas made Athens home. *Efharisto poli* to those who welcomed me so warmly around Crete, the Saronic Gulf and Athens.

Carolyn Bain

Efharisto poli to Brana Vladisavljevic for a wonderful gig, and to Team Greece for sterling work. Across the Cyclades, hundreds of kind, generous locals (and visitors) answered my questions, engaged in conversation, fed me (oh god, did they feed me!) and showed me the meaning of heartwarming Greek *filoxenia*. Sincere thanks to all of them. Thanks to old friends Fiona and William Reeve for fun on Santorini, and to my favourite co-traveller, Kelvin Adams, for three weeks of ace company and dedicated research of beaches and blue domes.

Michael Stamatios Clark

Ευχαριστω to all who made my ferry-hopping through the Greek islands a trip from the start. Special thanks to my splendiferous family, Janet, Melina and Alexandros, and to the editorial team of Brana Vladisavljevic and Korina Miller for cheerful support throughout. In the Sporades islands, many thanks to Chrysanthi, Amanda, Heather, Pakis, Alexandra, Georgos and Mahi, Makis, Bessie, Gisela; in the Aegean, thanks to Anastasia, Theofilos, the Fouskas family, Demetra and Vassilis, Naya and Petros, and Tasos, Margarita and Kostas.

Anita Isalska

Thank you to every shepherd who mimed driving directions, and every guesthouse owner who ushered me inside for *tsipouro*. Big thanks especially to the team at Arta's Archaeological Museum and Central Macedonia's tourism department, and Helen Tarbet for translations and insights. Thanks also to Richard Waters and Trent Holden for seasoned authorly advice. Bear hugs to Joe Revill, Jessica Crouch and Jane Atkin for cheering me on. Heartfelt thank yous to Normal Matt, for more than I can list.

Anna Kaminski

I would like to thank Brana for entrusting me with these chapters, my fellow scribes and everyone who enhanced my journey, particularly my mum for sharing two weeks on the road with me and being such an able research assistant; Mina of Antares; Byron in Monemvasia; Maria and Panos in Dimitsana; George in Kalavryta; Nikos in Kardamyli; Alexis and Ryan on Hydra; and Alexander in Nafplio.

Greg Ward

Thanks to the many wonderful people who make travelling in the Dodecanese such a pleasure, and thanks above all to my wife, Sam Cook, for sharing the fun.

Richard Waters

Special thanks to Michael in Corfu and Leonidas at Pachis travel. Also to Lily Alicabiotis. There are many Greek people who made my journey easy at what were difficult times for them, so my thanks to all. Thanks too to Korina Miller and Alexis Averbuck, my coordinating authors, for all their help and patience, and to Brana Vladisavljevic, my destination ed, for sending me out there.

ACKNOWLEDGMENTS

Climate map data adapted from Peel MC, Finlayson BL & McMahon TA (2007) 'Updated World Map of the Köppen-Geiger Climate Classification', *Hydrology and Earth System Sciences*, 11, 163344.

Illustrations pp64–5, pp428–9 by Javier Martinez Zarracina. Illustration pp190–1 by Michael Weldon.

Cover photograph: Parthenon, Athens; Alamy/Art Kowalsky

THIS BOOK

This 12th edition of Lonely Planet's *Greece* guidebook was researched and written by Korina Miller, Kate Armstrong, Alexis Averbuck, Carolyn Bain, Michael Stamatios Clark, Anita Isalska, Anna Kaminski, Greg Ward and Richard Waters. This guidebook was produced by the following:

Destination Editor
Brana Vladisavljevic
Product Editors
Kate James, Kate Mathews
Senior Cartographer
Valentina Kremenchutskaya
Book Designer Cam Ashley
Assisting Editors Andrew Bain, Pete Cruttenden, Melanie Dankel, Gabrielle Innes, Ali Lemer, Charlotte Orr, Susan Paterson
Cartographer Mick Garrett
Cover Researcher
Naomi Parker
Thanks to Claire Murphy, Kirsten Rawlings, Dianne Schallmeiner, Angela Tinson, Lauren Wellicome, Tony Wheeler, Amanda Williamson, Sofia Zournatzidi

Index

Map Legend

Sights

- Beach
- Bird Sanctuary
- Buddhist
- Castle/Palace
- Christian
- Confucian
- Hindu
- Islamic
- Jain
- Jewish
- Monument
- Museum/Gallery/Historic Building
- Ruin
- Shinto
- Sikh
- Taoist
- Winery/Vineyard
- Zoo/Wildlife Sanctuary
- Other Sight

Activities, Courses & Tours

- Bodysurfing
- Diving
- Canoeing/Kayaking
- Course/Tour
- Sento Hot Baths/Onsen
- Skiing
- Snorkelling
- Surfing
- Swimming/Pool
- Walking
- Windsurfing
- Other Activity

Sleeping

- Sleeping
- Camping

Eating

- Eating

Drinking & Nightlife

- Drinking & Nightlife
- Cafe

Entertainment

- Entertainment

Shopping

- Shopping

Information

- Bank
- Embassy/Consulate
- Hospital/Medical
- Internet
- Police
- Post Office
- Telephone
- Toilet
- Tourist Information
- Other Information

Geographic

- Beach
- Gate
- Hut/Shelter
- Lighthouse
- Lookout
- Mountain/Volcano
- Oasis
- Park
- Pass
- Picnic Area
- Waterfall

Population

- Capital (National)
- Capital (State/Province)
- City/Large Town
- Town/Village

Transport

- Airport
- Border crossing
- Bus
- Cable car/Funicular
- Cycling
- Ferry
- Metro station
- Monorail
- Parking
- Petrol station
- S-Bahn/S-train/Subway station
- Taxi
- T-bane/Tunnelbana station
- Train station/Railway
- Tram
- Tube station
- U-Bahn/Underground station
- Other Transport

Note: Not all symbols displayed above appear on the maps in this book

Routes

- Tollway
- Freeway
- Primary
- Secondary
- Tertiary
- Lane
- Unsealed road
- Road under construction
- Plaza/Mall
- Steps
- Tunnel
- Pedestrian overpass
- Walking Tour
- Walking Tour detour
- Path/Walking Trail

Boundaries

- International
- State/Province
- Disputed
- Regional/Suburb
- Marine Park
- Cliff
- Wall

Hydrography

- River, Creek
- Intermittent River
- Canal
- Water
- Dry/Salt/Intermittent Lake
- Reef

Areas

- Airport/Runway
- Beach/Desert
- Cemetery (Christian)
- Cemetery (Other)
- Glacier
- Mudflat
- Park/Forest
- Sight (Building)
- Sportsground
- Swamp/Mangrove